The Planning of Change

THE PLANNING OF CHANGE

Readings in the Applied Behavioral Sciences

Edited by

Warren G. Bennis MASSACHUSETTS
INSTITUTE OF TECHNOLOGY

Kenneth D. Benne BOSTON UNIVERSITY

Robert Chin BOSTON UNIVERSITY

HOLT, RINEHART AND WINSTON, New York

To our fathers

July, 1962

Copyright © 1961 by Holt, Rinehart and Winston, Inc.
All rights reserved
Library of Congress Catalog Card Number 61-14602
20893-0111
Printed in the United States of America

Preface

The task of merging the arts of social practice and the sciences of behavior presents both a practical and an intellectual challenge. Living in an age whose single constant is radical change, all men are in urgent need of whatever resources may be available as they seek to understand and manage their environment, to understand and solve the unprecedented social problems confronting them.

The intellectual challenge comes from the necessity of developing an adequate theory of the application process—of applying and adapting theories of social and personal change to the special and important case of *planned* change. It is only when this challenge is recognized and defined that the serious study and research which application deserves can begin.

In this volume—a product of the editors' concern with this dual challenge—we have tried, within the limits of the space available to us, to bring together some of the best current conceptualizations of different aspects of application and change process, and to tie these contributions together with extensive critical and theoretical introductions. The varied sources and practical relevance of these readings, coupled with their unifying general theme, lead us to hope that the book will prove useful both in courses in the behavioral sciences and in various professions of social practice. Some of the materials have been tested and used successfully in our own campus teaching and in numerous in-service education projects for trainers, consultants, administrators, and managers in different institutional settings.

This hope for the usefulness of *The Planning of Change* springs also from the reception given to its predecessor, *Human Relations in Curriculum Change,* edited by Kenneth D. Benne and Bozidar Muntyan and published in 1950. Although it was prepared primarily for educational administrators and teachers, it was used in courses in social psychology, sociology, religion, social work, adult education, agricultural extension, nursing, and business management, as well as

v

in education. It proved useful also to many individual practitioners in their own self-education. The interest in application and change processes is a pervasive one today, and it was this focus of attention in the earlier book that widened its usefulness beyond the audience for which it was originally prepared.

Preparation of the present book was originally undertaken as a revision and enlargement of the Benne-Muntyan volume. Although we have retained the original book's choice of planned social and personal change as the appropriate context for effective application of the behavioral sciences, we have prepared a new book rather than a revision. The present volume has been written with the problems of various professions of social practice, not merely those of teachers, centrally in mind. It has retained some emphasis upon "applied group dynamics" —a central preoccupation of the earlier book—but has included much relevant material from several other social disciplines as well. Most of the material included has been published since 1950. In addition, the extensive introductions, prepared by the editors, provide a theoretical framework and continuity largely missing from the earlier work. We hope that this book will, for these reasons, prove even more valuable to the many audiences who found its forerunner useful to them.

It is hard to know where to begin and where to end in acknowledging the contributions of the many people who have helped us, directly or indirectly, in preparing this book. Our most direct debt is to those contributors whose work we have reprinted. Specific acknowledgment of our obligation to each of them and to their publishers is made at the beginning of each selection.

The index shows many names in addition to those of our contributors. In a number of cases, these writers have published work that we wished to include. Space limitations made its inclusion impossible. We are nevertheless grateful for their very real help to us in maturing our own thinking.

The influence of Kurt Lewin's pioneering studies of planned social change is evident throughout this volume. All three authors have been associated with the National Training Laboratories, which built its laboratory approach to change upon Lewin's work. These associations have proved of inestimable value to us in developing our point of view. We gladly acknowledge a particular debt to Leland Bradford and Ronald Lippitt.

Special mention should be made here regarding M.I.T.'s School of Industrial Management in making this volume possible. Not only has it been a source of ideas, it has also provided a free and liberating environment where scholars from a wide range of disciplines have managed to work together in order to create more socially desirable ends. To Dean Howard Johnson we owe a special word of thanks not alone for encouraging the preparation of this book, but also for making a generous portion of the time of Warren Bennis available during one semester for work on it.

Many of the ideas in this volume have been developed and seasoned by work in the Boston University Human Relations Center during the eight years of its existence. Its chief concern throughout has been with the human aspects of social change, planned and unplanned. More particularly, we are grateful for our experiences in the Center's two graduate seminars and its annual Summer Laboratory in the Improvement of Human Relations. Contributions by both staff members and student participants in these seminars and laboratories have been deeply important to us in achieving our orientation.

Criticisms of our outline and initial manuscript by Amitai Etzioni, Alvin Gouldner, Murray Horwitz, Matthew Miles, and Morris Zelditch helped greatly in the later stages of our work.

Barbara Josephson and Ai-li Chin gave valuable editorial and bibliographical assistance. Janet S. Shepard and Jane S. Isherwood helped faithfully with secretarial work on the volume.

W.G.B.
K.D.B.
R.C.

BOSTON, MASSACHUSETTS
September 1961

Contents

PART TWO: CONCEPTUAL TOOLS FOR THE CHANGE-AGENT: SOCIAL SYSTEMS AND CHANGE MODELS   187

PART FOUR: PROGRAMS AND TECH-
NOLOGIES OF PLANNED CHANGE 617

The Planning of Change

Introduction

"In an important sense this world of ours is a new
world, in which the unity of knowledge, the nature of
human communities, the order of society, the order of
ideas, the very notions of society and culture have
changed and will not return to what they have been
in the past. What is new is new not because it has
never been there before, but because it has changed in
quality. One thing that is new is the prevalence of newness, the changing scale and scope of change itself, so
that the world alters as we walk in it, so that the years
of man's life measure not some small growth or rear-
rangement or moderation of what he learned in childhood, but a great upheaval . . . To assail the changes
that have unmoored us from the past is futile, and in
a deep sense, I think, it is wicked. We need to recognize
the change and learn what resources we have."

Robert Oppenheimer [1]

THE PROBLEM

Richard Weaver has remarked recently that the ultimate term in contemporary
rhetoric, the "god term," is "progress" or "change": [2] the world, as Oppenheimer
remarks, alters as we walk in it. It would appear, then, that we are beyond debating
the inevitability of change; most students of our society agree that the one major
invariant is the tendency toward movement, growth, development, process:
change. The contemporary debate has swung from change vs. no-change to the

[1] Robert Oppenheimer, "Prospects in the Arts and Sciences," *Perspectives USA, 11*:10–11,
Spring, 1955.
[2] Richard Weaver, "Ultimate Terms in Contemporary Rhetoric," *Perspectives USA, 11*:123,
Spring, 1955.

methods employed in controlling and directing forces in change. Dewey has re-marked that ". . . history in being a process of change generates change not only in details but also in the *method of directing social change.*" [3] The predica-ment we confront, then, concerns method; methods that maximize freedom and limit as little as possible the potentialities of growth; methods that will realize man's dignity as well as bring into fruition desirable social goals.

Concerning the methods of change, we can observe two idea-systems in the contemporary scene that are directly counterposed: the law of nonintervention and the law of radical intervention. The former stems from the "natural-law" and "invisible-hand" ideology of the laissez-faire doctrine—part economic analysis and part ideology. Tampering and social tinkering with man's natural and social universe interferes with the homeostatic forces, which if left unfettered, will bring about the perfectly maximized "good life." Keynsian and welfare economics, as well as the monopolistic structure of contemporary society, have all exposed the weaknesses in the natural-equilibrium position. (Keynes once remarked that classi-cal economic doctrines may well work in the long run; but, he poignantly added, in the long run, we'll all be dead.)

Marxian analysis, with its emphasis on conflict, inevitable class struggle, and radical intervention—occasionally at the price of human freedom—represents the other extreme. While Marxian theory developed as an indispensable antidote to the elegant rationalizations of the "laissez-faire" doctrine, it also suffers an obsolescence wrought by the accelerating changes of the world.

Planned change, as we view it, emerges as the only feasible alternative to these methods; that is, a method which employs social technology to help solve the problems of society. One may approve or deplore the concept of planned change —or look on it with scientific detachment. But no one will deny its importance. And this book was designed to bring about greater understanding of its methods, the social processes bearing on it, its potentialities, consequences, both ethical and pragmatic, as well as its limitations.

NATURE OF THIS BOOK

There is an old parable that has made the rounds about the grasshopper who decided to consult the hoary consultant of the animal kingdom, the owl, about a personal problem. The problem concerned the fact that the grasshopper suffered each winter from severe pains due to the savage temperature. After a number of these painful winters, in which all of the grasshopper's known remedies were of no avail, he presented his case to the venerable and wise owl. The owl, after patiently listening to the grasshopper's misery, so the story goes, prescribed a

[3] John Dewey, *Liberalism and Social Action*, New York: G. P. Putnam's Sons, 1935, p. 83 (our italics).

simple solution. "Simply turn yourself into a cricket and hibernate during the winter." The grasshopper jumped joyously away, profusely thanking the owl for his wise advice. Later, however, after discovering that this important knowledge could not be transformed into action, the grasshopper returned to the owl and asked him how he could perform this metamorphosis. The owl replied rather curtly, "Look, I gave you the principle. It's up to you to work out the details!"

All parables, supposedly, contain a moral, and the moral here provides one of the main cornerstones of this volume: How can the man of knowledge utilize his hard-won knowledge to help clients and lay personnel? And conversely, how can the lay public provide information and insight that will aid the man of knowledge, the "expert," in his role as helper as well as theory-builder?

These are not very simple questions, and unfortunately ways of answering them are not easily arrived at or even certainly known. And the condition of the world today—with the oft-noted "communication gap" between practitioners and scientists, clients and professional helpers—and the ever-increasing technocracy of science, tends to exacerbate the problem. In another part of the essay quoted above Oppenheimer states eloquently what can be taken as the basic leitmotif of this book of readings and text:

> The specialization of science is an inevitable accompaniment of progress; yet it is full of dangers, and it is cruelly wasteful, since so much that is beautiful and enlightening is cut off from most of the world. Thus it is proper to the role of the scientist that he not merely find new truth and communicate it to his fellows, but that he teach, that he try to bring the most honest and intelligible account of new knowledge to all who will try to learn . . . It is here in teaching of men who by profession must themselves be both teachers and taught, that the narrowness of scientific life can best be moderated, and that the analogies, insights, and harmonies of scientific discovery can find their way into the wider life of man.[4]

Putting the problem a little differently, we can say that the major foundation of this book is the *application of systematic and appropriate knowledge to human affairs for the purpose of creating intelligent action and change.* Thus, this is a book that focuses on *planned change:* a conscious, deliberate, and collaborative effort to improve the operations of a system, whether it be self-system, social system, or cultural system, through the utilization of scientific knowledge.[5]

Let us review briefly some of the organizing features of this volume. First, what

[4] Oppenheimer, *op. cit.*, p. 9.
[5] See Ronald Lippitt *et al., Dynamics of Planned Change,* New York: Harcourt, Brace, & World, Inc., 1958. This book would undoubtedly serve as an excellent companion text to this volume. Any book of readings, by definition, suffers from a lack of systematic integration of its contents; Lippitt's book may provide a welcome format for readers of this text. On the other hand, *Dynamics* represents a more constricted view of change than the present volume.

is meant by "systematic and appropriate knowledge"? The parable, of course, burlesques just this point. Yet we find that a substantial body of social science literature suffers this same deficiency. Whitehead, commenting pungently on this matter, said: "In this modern world the celibacy of the medieval learned class has been replaced by a celibacy of the intellect which is divorced from the concrete contemplation of complete facts." [6]

The relationship between theory and practice must constantly be kept within the same field of vision in order for both to cope with the exigencies of reality. We have developed a substantial body of theory and certainly a rich body of practice, but somehow our failure has been to provide the transformations and bridging between the two. Kurt Lewin, one of the intellectual forebears of this volume, was preoccupied with this issue of the relationship between the abstract and concrete. He once compared this task to the building of a bridge across the gorge separating theory from the full reality. "The research worker can achieve this only if, as a result of a constant intense tension, he can keep both theory and reality fully within his field of vision." [7] We seem, quite often, to become lost at the crossroads of a false dichotomy; the purity and virginity of theory on the one hand and the "knowledge for what" adherents on the other. This division oversimplifies the issue. The issue is far more complicated; it concerns the transformations and developmental conceptualizing that have to be undertaken before "theory becomes practical." [8]

Once these intellectual linkages between theory and practice are effectively established we have to be concerned with the social processes that bear on the infusion of knowledge into action and policy decisions. These two foci—"practical theory" and the social dynamics of utilizing knowledge in effecting change—make up two of the most dominant themes in this volume.

One other meaning that has implications for the organization of this book can be drawn from our parable. Reflect on the "relationship" between the owl and the grasshopper. The grasshopper, suppliant, comes to the expert owl for help. The owl listens to the problem, prescribes a remedy, and terminates the relationship. The owl did not discuss implementation or consequences of his therapy, nor did he seem to understand the "dependence" of the client, nor did he recognize the "transference" in the relationship. The owl simply proffered a rational "solution." The meaning, then, that now emerges from our parable has

[6] Alfred North Whitehead, *Science and the Modern World*, New York: Mentor Books.

[7] Remark attributed to Lewin by his wife, Getrud Weiss Lewin, in the introduction to *Resolving Social Conflicts*. New York: Harper & Brothers, 1948.

[8] Harold Guetzkow writes about the conversion barriers in using the social sciences. "Little attention has been given," he says, "to the way the very structure of knowledge affects its conversion for application. In the social sciences the role of scientist, engineer, technician, practitioner, and policy maker has not been well differentiated. It may be useful to sketch how the knowledge that the scientist develops may be converted by others for use and then to examine the impact of certain characteristics of basic knowledge upon the application process." This conversion process is one of the main concerns of this volume. See "Conversion Barriers in Using the Social Sciences," *Administrative Science Quarterly*, 4:68–81, 1959.

to do with the nature of the relationship between the man of knowledge, the expert, and his client. Our conviction, which is reflected in a number of articles in this volume, is that the extent to which knowledge can be effectively utilized by practitioners and clients—especially knowledge provided for social change— depends to a great extent on the nature of the relationship between the client and change-agent.[9] In other words, we do not view science in and of itself as the panacea. This naive technocratic viewpoint does not take into account the importance of the existential relationship between the man of knowledge (change-agent) and the client-system. Dewey once said that "Mankind now has in its possession a new method, that of cooperative and experimental science which expresses the method of intelligence." [10] In this book on the theory and practice of planned change we aim to stress the cooperative and collaborative aspects of the various relationships implicated in change—change-agent to client, among clients, and among change-agents—*as well as* the scientific findings related to change. (Too often social scientists neglect as legitimate inquiry the collaborative process and new interpersonal and methodological norms and rules required for an action-science.)

We are now in a better position to discuss the nature of this book. Perhaps our greatest emphasis is on the processes of planned change, on how change is created, implemented, evaluated, maintained, and resisted. The processes of change take us, given its enormous scope, into many fields. It fans out into the various dimensions of change processes (from "brainwashing" to introducing change in a factory), into the social and psychological consequences of change, into the antecedent conditions for effectively planned change, into strategic leverage points for effecting change. Included, also, under this heading are some of the major instruments in creating and maintaining change: *training, consulting, and applied research.*

Focusing on the processes and instruments of change, however, does not provide an adequate picture of the complications of change and changing. We have to illuminate the "targets" or systems to which the change is directed. In this book we make a strong effort to keep in mind four types (or levels) of systems: self, role, interpersonal or group, and larger systems such as formal organizations, communities, and in some cases, cultural systems. "The educational task," Dewey

[9] These terms have been developed in conjunction with the National Training Laboratories and used by Lippitt *et al.* in *Dynamics of Planned Change* (New York: Harcourt, Brace & World, Inc., 1958). "Client" refers to the person or group being helped, thus "client-system" whether it be person, group, organization, community, culture, family, club, or whatever. "Change-agent" refers to the helper, the person or group who is attempting to effect change. These are fairly clumsy terms but we cannot think of ready substitutes and they are coming into wider usage.

We might point out now that Lippitt *et al.* restrict the role of the change-agent by defining him as exogenous to the client-system, a person "from the outside" who attempts to effect change. We believe this is too narrow a view and we have encompassed in our definition the idea that the change-agent may be either in or outside the client-system.

[10] Dewey, *op. cit.*, p. 83.

once said, "cannot be accomplished merely by working on men's minds without action that effects actual changes in institutions." [11] We cannot overemphasize the importance of keeping the fact in mind that human behavior is like a centipede, standing on many legs. Nothing that we do has a single determinant. We emphasize this now because we believe there is a danger in focusing too narrowly on personality factors; elements in addition to the *personal* equipment of the client must be considered.

In addition to the change processes and the various client-systems we will present material, touched on earlier, relevant to the nature of the *collaborative* processes in planned change programs. Moreover, some attention will be given to the strategy and methodology of planned change, its complexities, vicissitudes, and outcomes (as well as evaluation procedures).

No discussion of planned change would be complete without some attention to the perplexing philosophical issues—both valuational and ethical—that this subject generates. In these times of "hidden persuaders," "brainwashing," payola, conformity, manipulation, and so on, lay and intellectual publics alike are exceedingly wary lest social and psychological knowledge bring about the specter of predictable—and thereby helpless—man. We share this concern also, as a number of articles in this volume attest; but we also join Spinoza in saying that our job as men of knowledge is not to weep or laugh, but to understand. One of our problems here is that our value-ethical positions are intimately related to our pragmatic positions. For example, when we postulate that collaboration is a *sine qua non* of effective planned change, we are insisting on an ethical imperative as well as on a scientific objective. The value issues tincture almost every statement in the book. The best we can hope to do is make our own values as explicit as we can. Throughout the course of the book we have attempted to do this.

This, in a very general way, depicts the nature of this volume. We think that the reader will recognize the editors' dilemma in constructing a book of readings and text that is of so enormous a range and that draws from all the major disciplines of the behavioral sciences, from philosophy of science, from ethical and moral theory, and from theories of application. However, that is, as we see it, the scope of the topic, and hence this book of readings.

[11] *Ibid.,* p. 4.

PART ONE

The Roots of Planned Change

P olicy makers, social scientists and social practition-
ers in America are not more agreed about the proper direction and management
of social change in 1960 than they were at the turn of the present century. But
the focus of the controversy has shifted. In 1900—in America at least—the issue
was typically stated in sweeping ideological terms. Should or should not men
seek, through deliberate and collaborative forethought in the present, to mold the
shape of their collective future? Or should confidence rather be placed in a principle of automatic adjustment, operating within the processes of history to re-
equilibrate, without human forethought yet in the interest of progress and human welfare, the inescapable human upsets and dislocations of changing society?

This issue raised a corollary issue concerning the proper relations of the emerging social sciences of the time, and of social scientists, to the guidance and management of practical affairs. In general, the "planners" saw an important place
for social science in informing policies and in rendering social practice more intelligent and reality-oriented. Proponents of "automatic adjustment" tended to
relegate social scientists to an observer role and to deny them participation or
leadership in influencing the direction or the form of practical affairs. This conception of "nonintervening" social science fitted the main-line traditions of the
natural sciences and of the older social studies—history, economics, and political
theory. This view of the proper relationships between social science and social

7

action was further reenforced by aspirations of the younger and more behavior-oriented sciences—psychology and sociology—to achieve and maintain their autonomy and "purity" within the academic world in which they were parvenus. The issue concerning "science" and "practice" has been raised anew as "applied social science" has been encouraged and supported by many policy-makers and social practitioners, and actively promoted by some social scientists. But intervening events have given to it, as to the more general issue of "planning," a new form and focus within discussions among students of human affairs.

Lester F. Ward was one of the earliest social scientists in America to proclaim that modern men must extend scientific approaches into the planning of changes in the patterns of their behaviors and relationships. He was well aware that men were already utilizing their accumulating collective and scientific intelligence deliberately to induce changes in their nonhuman environment. And he saw a major role for the emerging sciences of man in extending a similar planning approach into the management of human affairs.

> Man's destiny is in his own hands. Any law that he can comprehend he can control. He cannot increase or diminish the powers of nature, but he can direct them . . . His power over nature is unlimited. He can make it his servant and appropriate to his own use all the mighty forces of the universe . . . Human institutions are not exempt from this all-pervading spirit of improvement. They, too, are artificial, conceived in the ingenious brain and wrought with mental skill born of inventive genius. The passion for their improvement is of a piece with the impulse to improve the plow or the steam engine . . . Intelligence, heretofore a growth, is destined to become a manufacture . . . The origination and distribution of knowledge can no longer be left to chance or to nature. They are to be systematized and erected into true arts.[1]

Ward's proclamation seemed foolish boasting, if not downright sacrilege, to many among his contemporaries. William Graham Sumner was one of the leaders in sociology who emphasized both the folly and sacrilege of prophecies like Ward's.

> If we can acquire a science of society based on observation of phenomena and study of forces, we may hope to gain some ground slowly toward the elimination of old errors and the re-establishment of a sound and natural social order. Whatever we gain that way will be by growth, never in the world by any reconstruction of society on the plan of some enthusiastic social architect. The latter is only repeating the old error over again, and postponing all our chances of real improvement. Society needs first of all to be free from these meddlers—that is,

[1] Quoted in Henry Commager, *The American Mind*, New Haven: Yale University Press, 1950, pp. 208, 210, 213–214.

> to be let alone. Here we are, then, once more back at
> the old doctrine *laissez faire*. Let us translate it into
> blunt English, and it will read—Mind your own business.
> It is nothing but the doctrine of liberty. Let every man
> be happy in his own way.[2]

It may be fortunate or unfortunate that American controversies today over
the direction and management of social change seldom take the form of sweeping
societal prescriptions and counter-prescriptions or ideological debates—a form
which Ward and Sumner, along with their contemporaries, gave to them. In any
event, the form of the controversies has shifted. In large measure subsequent events
have foreclosed the factual basis for Sumner's argument. *Laissez faire* has been
widely abandoned in practice as a principle of social management, whatever
ghostly existence it yet enjoys in political platforms and pronunciamentos. Human interventions designed to shape and modify the institutionalized behaviors of
men are now familiar features of our social landscape. "Helping professions" have
proliferated since Ward's and Sumner's day. Professions of industrial and public
management have taken shape. The reasons for being of all of these is deliberately
to induce and coach changes in the future behaviors and relationships of their
various "client" populations. This is most apparent in "new" professions such as
psychiatry, social work, nursing, counseling, management, and consultation in
its manifold forms. But older professions too, such as medicine, law, teaching, and
the clergy, have been pressed increasingly to become agencies of social change
rather than of social conservation. Resistances to assuming the new role have, of
course, developed along with the situational pressures to enact it.

Behavioral scientists, neo-Sumnerians among others, have been drawn, with
varying degrees of eagerness and resistance, into activities of "changing," such as
consultation and applied research. "Helping professionals," "managers," and
"policy-makers" in various fields of practice increasingly seek and employ the
services of behavioral scientists to anticipate more accurately the consequences
of prospective social changes and to inform more validly the processes of planning designed to control these consequences.

We are widely seeking to plan social changes in the sixties. And both the products
and the methods of social research are being more and more widely utilized in the
processes of such planning. Sumner's ideological advice has been widely rejected
in practice.

But it is equally true that Ward's millennial hope seems far—indeed very far—
from realization today. Attempts to apply social knowledge in planning and controlling changes tend to be fragmented by the division of contemporary agents of
change into specialized and largely noncommunicating professions. These attempts are thwarted too by noncommunication and noncollaboration among
policy-makers and action planners in the various institutional settings where
planning has become familiar practice—industry, government, welfare, health,

[2] Quoted, *op. cit.*, pp. 201–202.

and education. Advocates and students of planned change have become more cautious in their claims, less millennial in their hopes than Ward tended to be. The modal question has shifted from "should we seek to plan change?" to "how plan particular changes in particular people in particular settings and situations?" Where the wider societal view has not been entirely lost the question is raised—"how interrelate the various forms which the planning of change has taken in conventionally isolated but actually interdependent settings of social action and practice?"

Men today have thus widely come to believe that they have no actual choice as to whether somebody will seek to plan continuing changes in the patterns of their lives. Men must try to plan their changing futures and this necessity is seen to be determined by cultural conditions, not primarily by the ideology men happen to hold. "Democratic," "communistic," and "fascist" peoples must alike try to plan social changes. This helps to account for the shift of many questions about planned change from an "ideological" to a "technical" form. This does not mean, as some who would reduce all questions of planning to purely technical form might believe, that questions about the values which should guide planners can or should disappear from discussions about planning or from the processes of planning. It means rather that these questions too have taken new forms.

Both Ward and Sumner worked within a framework of common assumptions about the actuality and desirability, if not the inevitability, of Progress. Their ideological differences centered on varying ways of achieving the Progress which both generally assumed to be, in some way, America's destiny, and by patriotic extension, human destiny as well. (The pessimism of Sumner grown old came more from despair over the course of events about him than from relinquishment of this ideal.) Differing means of achieving progress, of course, if carefully analyzed, meant different meanings of Progress as well. But the values of "rationality," "freedom," and the "extension through science of human control over the natural environment" were, in general, values acceptable to "planners" and "anti-planners" as well. Both sought to settle value issues by an appeal to living traditions of "liberalism" and "democracy," traditions not clearly distinguished one from the other.

Today this living tradition can no longer be assumed. Intellectually and practically, the core values of "liberalism" and "democracy" have been challenged and eroded, both in America and outside it. The actuality as well as the desirability of Progress, as defined and revered within this tradition, have been questioned and challenged. "Liberal" theology has been attacked by religious neo-orthodoxies of various types. "Liberal" politics has been denounced as unrealistic by nationalists and communists alike. "Progressive" education is inveighed against by conservative critics as negligent of "fundamentals" in knowledge and morality. Neoconservative attacks against "liberalism" in its various forms are thus alike in seeking a reaffirmation of "sound" traditions. ("Liberalism" is denounced just as roundly by Marxist "planners," though out of a different set of assumptions about man and society.) But different neoconservatives appeal to different "sound" traditions and betray in the very variety of the "authoritative" traditions to which they appeal the fragmentation and disruption of the community of values that once characterized American life. It is this fragmentation of traditional bases of community that forces the value-dilemmas of American planners of the sixties to a new and deeper level as compared with the planners of 1900.

As planners of change face conflicts about the proper direction of change among various segments of our population today, they encounter of necessity the question of the basis or bases upon which one value-orientation can be judged better than another. Indeed, they must face the deeper question, which various philosophers and depth psychologists have raised widely and vigorously in our time —can value and ideological differences be settled rationally at all? Is there an irreducible surd of irrationality that dogs all of the choices of men? More specifically, do "scientific methods" extend to the evaluation of the competing ends of human action or only to the evaluation of alternative means for reaching ends chosen on arbitrary and rationally "inarbitrable" grounds? [3]

Chapter 3 poses a few of the basic problems of value-orientation and judgment that efforts to plan changes in the lives of people inevitably raise for contemporary agents of change who are thoughtful about the normative grounds of their decisions and actions. One challenge that "planned change" brings to social scientists and social practitioners alike is thus to become more philosophic and self-critical about the normative bases of the enterprise in which they are engaged.

If "planned change" is to be lifted out of the specialist auspices and isolated institutional settings in which it has come, in some large part, to be practiced today, it must be conceptualized in terms that are not the exclusive property of any one helping profession or slanted toward the idiosyncracies of change problems in any one institutional setting. Yet the more general formulation must be applicable to change problems in various particular settings. A pioneering contribution to such conceptualization has been made by Lippitt, Watson, and Westley in their recent book, *The Dynamics of Planned Change*.[4]

It was largely in their terms that we broached our very general definition of "planned change" in the introduction to this book. We identified "planned change" there as *a deliberate and collaborative process* involving *change-agent* and *client-systems*. These systems are brought together to solve a problem or, more generally, to plan and attain an improved state of functioning in the client-system by utilizing and applying *valid knowledge*.

This definition is, of course, highly abstract. Its meaning may be thickened in

[3] See, for example, the argument on this point between Herbert Feigl and George Geiger in Benne and Swanson (ed), "Values and the Social Scientist," *Journal of Social Issues*, Volume VI, No. 4, 1950.
[4] Ronald Lippitt, Jeanne Watson, and Bruce Westley, *The Dynamics of Planned Change*, New York: Harcourt, Brace & World, Inc., 1958.

a number of ways. One way is to contrast and compare "planned change" with other forms of social change. This we will attempt to do in Chapter 4. Another way is to suggest some of the complexities that surround each of the key elements of our definition.

1. A deliberate collaborative process. One of the distinguishing features of planned change is the *collaborative* element that exists between change-agent and client.[5] The outcome of any planned change-attempt hinges, we believe, to a great extent on the relationship that becomes established between the giver and the receiver of help—how well it is understood by each, its control and dependency aspect, how open it is for examination and reconstruction by both parties, and so on.

A number of features distinguish the deliberate and collaborative relationship: (*a*) a joint effort that involves mutual determination of goals; (*b*) a "spirit of inquiry"—a reliance on determinations based on data publicly shared; (*c*) an existential relationship growing out of the "here-and-now" situation; [6] (*d*) a voluntary relationship between change-agent and client with either party free to terminate the relationship after joint consultation; (*e*) a power distribution in which the client and change-agent have equal or almost equal opportunities to influence the other; [7] and (*f*) an emphasis on methodological rather than content learnings. (See the introduction to Part III.)

Why this stress on collaboration in relationship? Obviously, there are important ethical connotations involved that the authors find desirable. But equally to the point, as far as we are concerned, is the pragmatic value of collaboration. The only way a change-agent can really help a client is by providing enough positive support so that the opposing forces in the client's situation can be re-equilibrated on a new and desirable level. This can come about only by facilitating the client's communication with himself—or, in more general terms, by making the client (as well as the change-agent) aware of the relevant data necessary to diagnose the situation. The source of much of this data is in the client-system itself, if only the client can make it publicly available. Without *trust,* generated in and by collaboration, the change-agent and client must work with limited and distorted data as children in the dark.

Field researchers studying natural organizations or cultures have long acknowledged their reliance on "trust" to counter the strong resistances on the subjects' parts to yielding important data. The rules and techniques of "establishing rapport" found in methodology textbooks also testify to this need. Clients are no different from research subjects in this respect. Though, in most cases, they

---

[5] For an example of this aspect of planned change within a hierarchical context, see Douglas McGregor, *The Human Side of Enterprise,* McGraw-Hill Book Co., Inc., 1960.

[6] See Rollo May (ed.), *Existence,* New York: Basic Books, Inc., 1958 (especially p. 82).

[7] See R. R. Blake, "Typical Laboratory Procedures and Experiments," in *An Action Research Program for Organization Improvement* (Ann Arbor, Mich.: Foundation for Research on Human Behavior, 1960, pp. 7–30) for an example of an experiment based on the effects of a collaborative relationship.

sincerely and seriously want help (want to change), powerful forces exist that tend to work against change.[8]

Accordingly we view collaboration as a necessary ingredient of the planned change concept. It is necessary not only because it generates the necessary trust that facilitates the collection and interpretation of meaningful data, but also because the positive aspects of the relationship *qua* relationship are vitally necessary in order to overcome some of the strong fears of and resistance to change in the client-system.

One last point should be made about collaboration. The process of developing a collaborative relationship between client and change-agent may in itself provide a crucible for understanding the problems the client faces in his or its ordinary work and life environments. To this extent the collaborative relationship provides a cognitive support *as well as* an affective prop. Many consultants and change-agents utilize problems in the developing relationships between themselves and their clients as existential exemplars of the other relationship problems the client confronts. To this extent, the collaborative relationship represents a microcosm of all other relationships and as such can, if generalized, augment the help the client requires.

Actually, in "real" life we rarely observe a purely collaborative relationship; the best we can hope for often is a commitment on the part of both the change-agent and client-system to work toward building such a relationship. Moreover, ambiguities in the elements of a collaborative relationship become evident when we consider specific examples.

Example: A client coming for help to a consultant cannot truly collaborate in a joint determination of his goals. Much of the time he may not know them and certainly he will have difficulty in formulating them. A patient may think he has a stomach ache when the doctor tells him it is hepatitis.

Example: A relationship between a change-agent and client cannot truly be "permissive," "totally democratic," and so on. A kind of coercion is present, a coercion hopefully in the service of liberation but nevertheless a coercion that the client, for good or bad reasons, can always reject. The patient in psychoanalysis is told the "fundamental rule," free association. He is continually rebuked for abrogating this rule; in effect, he is forced to verbalize whatever comes to his mind in whatever order. Methodological coercion is qualitatively different from content coercion. It is the difference between forcing someone to believe x and forcing someone to develop ways of discovery, which include, among the things to be discovered, belief in x. Nevertheless, an element of coercion operates in installing an unfamiliar methodology.

Example: A relationship cannot be wholly "voluntary." People are "driven" to various forms of change-agents, by their boss who insists they attend a training

[8] Psychoanalysts have a difficult time—as do organizational consultants—with clients when they are eager and change-desiring; enthusiasm for the "secondary gains" may provide strong forces against fundamental change.

course or by a family urging one of its members to consult a psychiatrist, or by the individual himself, who is internally driven for any number of reasons to ask for help.

Example: An equal power distribution may be unrealistic, particularly at first. The change-agent has real "power," a power based on his *expertise* and autistically augmented by the distortions of the client, who feels, at times, desperately dependent. After all, it is the client, not the change-agent, who requires the help. Yet this critical unequal power distribution will (or should) over time move toward a more even distribution. This comes about because of the same processes that activated the earlier inequality. The client learns to view the change-agent with much less ambivalent distortion, and the client, in fact, gains some of the change-agent's *expertise*.

Ambiguities multiply if we start to consider the interpersonal and intersystem dynamics between change-agent and client-system; questions of motives, dependencies, counter-transference, and the like are only vaguely understood at this stage of our knowledge. Yet some form of commitment to collaboration must be made, we insist, for any case of the influence process to be considered planned change.

2. *Valid knowledge.* What is meant by valid knowledge? It is both fascinating and sobering to observe the confusions surrounding discussions of the social uses of knowledge, on the part of both social scientists and social practitioners.

When Henry Adams returned to Boston after a long absence, he reported surprise at finding that the Unitarians, who dominated the Boston culture of that day, appeared to believe they had solved every great philosophical conundrum that had ever convulsed the human spirit.[9] At times, we fear, the social scientist labors, unwittingly or not, under the burden of a similar false omniscience. It should be noted that it is only relatively recently that the behavioral scientist (the new term for social scientist and used interchangeably here) has had a willing lay clientele, and that the newness of this relationship may produce utopian hopes on the part of clients—professional practitioners or harried policy-makers—who believe that by receiving some magical amulet, such as the memorization of non-understandable social-science jargon, all their day-to-day organizational headaches and heartaches will vanish. On the other hand, the social scientists on their part—with their zealous faith in the fruits of scientific method—can over-tout their wares and set up unfulfillable expectations. The danger here, of course, is that both parties may get trapped in false dreams.

With surprisingly few exceptions, social scientists themselves have tended to adhere to a rather narrow view of research, a tendency that has heightened the "knowledge-action" tension.[10] Even the name "pure research" implies that somehow its polar term "applied research" is "impure." And, as Gouldner has cogently pointed out, applied social science has generally been held to be "nothing but"

---

[9] Cited by Lawrence Kubie, "Is Preventive Psychiatry Possible?" *Daedalus*, 88:647, 1959.
[10] See C. Wright Mills, *The Sociological Imagination*, New York: Oxford University Press, 1959, for a recent polemic on this issue.

the application of generalizations developed by "pure" theorizing and research to concrete and practical cases. Though much reiterated, this conception of applied social science is misleading and inaccurate. For whatever complex of reasons, applied research has taken on in some social-science circles an opprobrious and/or menial connotation, detached from academic respectability and regarded by many as "not real research."

What is desperately needed is a new vision of applied social research. And it is to this vision that we and our authors address ourselves, realizing our own inadequacies and recognizing how much intellectual and experimental work remains to be done in formulating this vision.

There have been some promising signs of closing this breach, through the developments of a viable conceptual model of applied research. Louis Wirth, writing in 1936, put the issue this way.

> The literature of social science amply demonstrates that there are large and very definite spheres of social existence in which it is possible to obtain scientific knowledge which is not only reliable but which has significant bearings on social policy and action.[11]

Writing twenty-four years later, Richard Rovere, in an article proving Wirth's prescience, made the following observation.

> One of the most notable developments of recent years has been the letting of contracts for information and advice on matters of government policy to institutions [universities and learned societies] . . . [The Federal Government] has been purchasing ideas, analyses, and specialized knowledge pretty much as they might buy office furniture, typewriters, or food for the department cafeteria.[12]

But heartening as this reputed trend may be, it has bootlegged in its own cargo of serious problems. One clue is revealed in Rovere's enthusiastic quote: ". . . purchasing ideas . . . pretty much as they might buy office furniture. . . ." A similar situation has been commented on by Gouldner: the consulting "engineer" has conceived and completed his assignment largely in terms formulated by his client. The consultant has failed to ask himself just why it was that the company management requested this survey in the first place; what kinds of problems produced a felt need for such a research among the company people; and whether these problems will persist even after the proposed survey is successfully completed according to management's prescriptions. Without asking some of these questions, the consultant faces the risk of having his report "interred in that great graveyard of creativity, the filing room."

[11] Karl Mannheim, *Ideology and Utopia*, New York: Harvest Books, Harcourt, Brace & World, Inc., 1946. Introduction by Louis Wirth.
[12] *New Yorker*, February 27, 1960, "Letter from Washington."

The intellectual task of developing a valid framework for an applied social science is only beginning to be accepted by behavioral scientists and social practitioners, and we can take only the first step or two of the task here. But, given the conditions and problems spelled out by the various authors quoted and included in this volume, we can sketch out—at least in broad outline—the desiderata of what we here call *valid* knowledge.

a. An interdisciplinary applied social science that takes into consideration the behavior of persons operating within their specific institutional environments.

b. An applied social science capable of accounting for the interrelated levels (person or self, role, group, and large organization) within the social-change context.

c. An applied social science that includes variables the practitioner can understand, manipulate, and evaluate.

d. An applied social science that in specific situations can select from among variables those most appropriate to a specific local situation in terms of its values, ethics, and moralities.

e. An applied social science that is pluralistically "real"; accepting the premise that groups and organizations as units are as amenable to empirical and analytical treatment as the individual.

f. An applied social science that can take into account "external" social processes of change as well as the interpersonal aspects of the collaborative process.

g. An applied social science that includes propositions susceptible to empirical test, focusing on the dynamics of change.

These are only some of the elements required in a vigorous and viable—a valid —applied social science. The horizon is distant but visible.

3. The change-agent and the client-system. As already noted, Lippitt, Watson, and Westley have proposed a definition of planned change akin to the one presented here with one very important exception. As they see it, the change-agent is a "free" agent from *outside* the client-system; a person or team brought into the system to help. Empirically speaking, this definition has validity for many cases of planned change. More often than not consultants, applied researchers, psychotherapists, and trainers *are* imported from outside the client-system. Yet this is a narrower view than the one we subscribe to. We say this for three reasons. For one thing, client-systems contain the potential resources for creating their own planned change programs under certain conditions; they have inside resources, staff persons, applied researchers, and administrators who can act and do act as successful change-agents.[13] For another thing, we contend that a client-system must build into its own structures a vigorous change-agent function, in order for it to adapt to a continually changing environment.

[13] See Douglas McGregor, *op. cit.*, for some examples of administrators as agents of change. Recent work in Esso also testifies to this. See R. R. Blake, *op. cit.*

Finally, Lippitt and his colleagues seem to us to neglect the socia
involvements of "change-agents" in their own back-home social sy
change-agent in their view seems more free, flexible, and autonom
god-like, than even "outside" consultants ordinarily are. If, for exam
sultant comes from a university school or department to consult with
he is bound in his consultant relationships, in some degree, by the n
orientations of his home social systems—his school, his university, hi
profession. Much of the value of his work for the hospital comes from l
ing a novel and significant linkage of several social systems previousl
quately connected—in this case, university, learned profession, and hos
brief, we prefer intersystem models for explaining planned change. Robe
clarifies other bases of this preference in his paper *The Utility of System*
and Developmental Models for Practitioners (see Chapter 5).

And so, for our purposes, we view the "change-agent" as any agent used
client-system to help bring about improved performance. By client-syste
simply refer to the party who asks for help and desires some change in per
ance. Obviously, either could be a person, group, role, or larger collectivit
is also obvious that some clients require "help" in recognizing or articulatin
admitting their "problems." Sometimes the major help of a change-agent is
rected toward this recognition stage.

Thus our initial, abstract definition of planned change moves toward mea
ingful elaboration. We have preferred to point to complexities rather than
precise simplicities—not so much out of a professional preference for complexit
as out of a respect for the knotty contemporary state of practice and theory with
respect to "planned change." Our "definition" is designed to lead to a program
of action and study to reduce existing complexities, not to provide a specious
description of an accomplishment not yet in being.

CHAPTER 1 The Bases of Planned Change in the Conditions of Contemporary Culture

A planning approach to social change, we have argued, has become a necessity, under conditions of contemporary culture, rather than a live option. The live options to be faced by change-agents today are ancillary to this approach and center upon questions of how change should be planned and how the direction and ends of change processes may be validly determined. This generalization will be questioned by many. Some burden of proof, therefore, rests with us to identify the aspects of contemporary culture which have dictated the change in the meaningful questions about planning for men and women of today.

In the first place, the inexorable march of scientific and technological change has accelerated. The "artifactual" character of more and more conditions of our lives are now plain for all men, not just for the Wards, to see—from "natural" energies in production, human and animal, to nuclear energies; from craftsmanship to automation; from horseback to missiles. In *The Impact of Technological Change,* Counts traces the human consequences, good and bad, personal and social, of this continuing revolution. In large part, these consequences have not been adequately anticipated. Nor have human ill-effects been minimized or good effects maximized in any planned way. Our helping professions have tended to focus upon melioration of the accumulating personal and social disruptions that unplanned or segmentally planned changes have introduced into the social fabric. However, as professions shift from a "therapeutic" toward a "preventive" point of view—as they are now widely attempting to do—the planning of social change must come to be seen as a regular and necessary adjunct of continuing scientific and technological change.

The progression of historic events has tended to undermine rational confidence in the principle of automatic adjustment as adequate to accomplish just, equitable, and desirable re-equilibrations in persons, groups, and societies continually upset by accomplished or prospective technological changes. It was this

19 ✧ *The Bases of Planned Change*

assumed benevolent principle to which Sumner and the Sumnerians appealed in trying to protect social changes from the ministrations of various meddlers. Stanley, in *The Collapse of Automatic Adjustment,* argues the contemporary untenability of this principle of automatic adjustment. If it has become untenable, some sort of planful intervention in processes of change becomes the only valid alternative in our attitude toward change.

In *From Trial and Error to Planning,* Mannheim discusses the interrelations between the forms of social organization and the mentalities, the modes of thinking, required by men to fulfill their life functions in a particular social organization. He argues that "chance discovery" through "trial and error" yielded in modern history to "invention" as a way of introducing changes into the practices of society. The mode of thinking characteristic of the latter is now yielding progressively to a "planning" mentality as our society depends less upon "Edisons" and "Wrights" and more upon "Manhattan projects" and "research and development departments" as ways of "manufacturing" innovations in significant areas of social practice. As "planning" thus makes its way in crucial areas of social experience, less adaptive mentalities must yield precedence to "planning" mentalities in other, interdependent areas of human life, though these mentalities need not and probably will not lose all place in the new society.

Increasing interdependence among men in the contemporary world presses people in various segments of society toward closer and fuller collaboration in forming and implementing workable social policies to guide their lives. At the same time, traditional normative and institutional bases of "natural" community have been eroded, through the bureaucratization and urbanization of life and work. Full communication and collaboration among members of separately organized segments of society have become increasingly difficult, even as they have become increasingly necessary. Stein describes this fragmentation of community life and its effects on personal stability and maturity in *The Eclipse of Community.*[1] "Community" can no longer be assumed as a basis of joint decision and action. Planning of social change must extend beyond the effective and humane management of accelerating technological change to the building and rebuilding of valid bases for "community" life. This means, of necessity, helping people to build and rebuild their value orientations as well.

---

[1] The studies to which Stein refers in documenting the eclipse of community are:
Robert E. Park, *Human Communities,* New York: The Free Press of Glencoe, Inc., 1952.
W. Lloyd Warner and Paul S. Lunt, *The Social Life of a Modern Community,* New Haven, Conn.: Yale University Press, 1941.
Caroline C. Ware, *Greenwich Village,* Boston: Houghton Mifflin Co., 1935.
Robert Lynd and Helen Lynd, *Middletown,* New York: Harcourt, Brace & World, Inc., 1929.
Robert Lynd and Helen Lynd, *Middletown in Transition,* New York: Harcourt, Brace & World, Inc., 1937.
William Foote Whyte, *Street Corner Society,* Chicago, Ill.: The University of Chicago Press, second edition, 1955.
John R. Seeley, R. Alexander Sim, and Elizabeth Loosley, *Crestwood Heights,* New York: Basic Books, Inc., 1956.

Fragmentation of orientations has become a difficulty not only in the life of contemporary action but also in the practices of the helping professionals and behavioral scientists. Members of different professions are educated separately and relatively little cross-professional communication goes into the planning of their various educational policies and programs. Yet teachers, social workers, pediatricians, public health workers, recreationists, clergymen among others are trying to "help" the same people—the same persons, the same families, the same agencies, the same neighborhoods—to plan ways of meeting the changing demands, perils, and opportunities of life. It is small wonder that the voices of differing professions speaking to a problem such as juvenile delinquency, sound like "conversations" in the Tower of Babel. Frank analyzes this condition in *Fragmentation in the Helping Professions.*

❖❖❖❖❖❖❖❖❖❖❖❖❖❖❖❖❖❖❖ THE IMPACT OF TECHNOLOGICAL CHANGE *George S. Counts*

THE peoples of the world today are leaving behind the material forms and agencies of a civilization which in its broad outlines endured for many centuries. This civilization was based on agriculture, animal breeding, handicraft, simple trade, and human energy —a civilization that in its many variants dates practically from the beginning of recorded history. The civilization which our fathers and mothers brought to this continent in the first half of the seventeenth century and molded into a special pattern during the succeeding two hundred years was one of those variants.

We can see clearly that during the last several generations this early civilization of ours has been undergoing a process of profound change and transformation. Today its material foundations are only a memory. Gone are the simple tools with which the versatile farmer tilled his soil, harvested his crops, prepared his food, fashioned his garments, made his utensils, and erected his houses and barns. Gone are the great distances, the dirt roads and trails, the rude carts and sledges, the rafts, flatboats, and sailing ships. Gone are the self-contained rural households and closely knit neighborhoods. Gone also in relative measure are the oxen, horses, and waterwheels, the long years of unrelieved human toil. Gone too in like measure are the local markets, the little stores and shops with their limited wares and services. Gone for most of us is the intimate relation with the elements—with soil, stream, and forest, with wind, rain, and snow, with sun, moon, and stars. So swiftly have these material features of our old agrarian civilization passed away that Lincoln, Grant, and even Cleveland would feel bewildered in the America of today. In-

From George S. Counts, Education and American Civilization, *New York: Bureau of Publications, Teachers College, Columbia University, 1952, pp. 381–387. Abridged and used by permission.*

deed many members of the older generation now living experience a sense of bewilderment. And for the most part those of younger years who may feel at home in this new world really do not realize what kind of a world it is. They have experienced no other.

The uneven advance of industrial civilization, the swift transformation of the material foundations of life and the lag in institutional, ideological, and moral adjustment, have generated the terrifying crises, the wars and depressions, the revolutions and counterrevolutions, of our time. Our world, in both its domestic and its international aspects, is out-of-joint. Our practical inventiveness, in the words of Stanley Casson, has far outrun our "moral consciousness and social organization." We have one foot in a civilization that is passing away, the other in a civilization that is only beginning to take form. Or to phrase the dilemma more aptly perhaps, as our feet tread the earth of a new world our heads continue to dwell in a world that is gone.

Industrial Civilization Releases Science and Technology

Science has rightly been called, as we have noted, the most powerful force moving in the modern world. As a method of inquiry, it is man's most reliable source of knowledge about both his environment and himself. Experimental in temper and scornful alike of both sacred tradition and temporal authority, it has moved triumphantly during the past four and a half centuries from conquest to conquest. Beginning its revolutionary career in the sphere of astronomy, it has left its mark on every field of thought. It has penetrated to some degree, though by no means equally, all departments of life and overthrown countless ideas and customs hallowed by time.

The most distinctive and profound characteristic of industrial civilization is its attitude toward science. Although there is no place in the world today where the advance of science in certain fields is not blocked by fear or vested rights, our contemporary civilization is the first in history to promote scientific inquiry on a large scale and make eager use of many of its findings. In its turn, of course, science has reacted upon civilization and molded with great power man's way of life and his outlook upon the world. It has pushed its inquiries into the farthermost limits of the universe and the innermost structure of the atom, into the origins of the earth and the succession of geological ages, into the evolution of living forms and the closely guarded mysteries of the cell, into the emergence of man, the rise and fall of social systems, the growth and decay of civilizations, and the nature of mind.

In its practical aspects, in its application to the technics of living and making a living, to the modes of livelihood, the forms of communication, the ways of waging war, the control of the life process, science is coming to be called technology. To the ordinary citizen it is this practical aspect of science that is the most striking feature of the age. Indeed, during recent generations a veritable technological revolution has swept over a large part of the world— a revolution that has brought to the astonished gaze of mankind one wonder after another and again and again made truth far stranger than fiction. So enraptured by technological advance have we become that we have tended to conceive human progress largely in its terms. We are learning today, to our sorrow, that this advance, when not accompanied by equally profound reconstruction in the realms of understanding and value, of customs and institutions, of attitudes and loyalties, can bring trouble and disaster.

The technological revolution is revealed in its most obvious and spectacular form in the march of mechanical invention. Beginning with the invention of the reciprocating steam engine by James Watt in 1765 and the invention of the cotton gin by Eli Whitney in 1793, the devising of new machines and processes gradually established itself as a cultural pattern. By the close of the nineteenth century it had assumed the proportions of a great and rising flood. This story is told in the unsentimental language of statistics by the United States Patent Office. The total number of patents issued increased from 2425 for the five-year period ending in 1845 to 180,984 for the similar period closing just one hundred years later. And the end is not yet.

Technology Has Brought the Power-Driven Machine

It has displaced the simple hand tool of early America by mechanical giants which dwarf the physical powers of men. So overwhelming and impressive has been this trend that our age has commonly been called the machine age; and Clark Wissler has included the machine among the three distinctive characteristics of our culture. If we should suddenly lose our capacity to make and use power-driven machines, our entire civilization would collapse and millions would be consigned to starvation.

The changes which were destined to transform man's modes of livelihood throughout the world began in England in the middle of the eighteenth century in the iron, textile, and pottery industries. Here the power of steam was released and harnessed to machines with revolutionary consequences. It made England the first industrial nation and contributed mightily to the creation of the greatest empire of all times. This little island became the workshop of the world. But despite efforts to hold the new modes of production in their original home, they migrated swiftly to America and of course to other countries. Also they moved from one branch of the economy to another until all industry was brought under their sway. As the decades passed, iron gave way to steel and other metals, steam was supplemented by gasoline and electricity, and machines ever more complicated, precise, and powerful were contrived. Today we stand on the threshold of the age of atomic energy and automatic factories.

For the most part this entire transformation went forward under a regime of private enterprise. To be sure, government, through tariffs, subsidies, and concessions, through guarantees of property rights and enforcement of contractual obligations, made an indispensable contribution. But it was the class of businessmen emerging from the Middle Ages as artisans, merchants, tradesmen, and bankers that played the central and active role. Motivated by the desire for private gain, these men organized production, as well as exchange, and assembled resources for the launching of the machine on its spectacular career and for the perfecting of its operations. Whatever their faults and whatever their future, they provided the initiative, the daring, and the leadership for the most profound modification of the modes of livelihood in history. They supplied the necessary energizing principle for the advance of technology.

Technology Has Profoundly Changed the Role of Human Labor in the Process of Production

The power-driven machine obviously alters the function and the responsibility of the workman. No longer does he act directly on raw materials and, proceeding at his own tempo, shape them into a finished product stamped with his own personality. Rather, following the pace set by the total productive process, he becomes a tender of machines, a stoker of furnaces, an oiler of wheels, a manipulator of levers, a presser of buttons, a feeder of materials, a coordinator of operations, and a receiver of finished products. Though the operation as a whole is an expression of the creative genius of the engineer, the ordinary workman tends to become an ever more highly specialized automaton—one of many coordinated human appendages of the machine.

But as technology advances and the miraculous resources of electronics and electrochemistry are brought into the service of the economy, the role of human labor is reduced more and more and man is pushed further and further toward the periphery of operations. First, a single machine becomes automatic, then a machine is designed to control a series or group of machines, and finally the entire process from raw material to finished product is made automatic in an automatic factory. This trend of course is still in its infancy,

but it would seem that eventually any operation or series of operations susceptible of expression in mathematical formulas will be handed over to the machine. The perspectives now opening before *homo faber* leave the student of the history of human toil breathless.

The advance of the machine has been attended by a steady and rapid increase in the productivity of labor. Although this increase was particularly striking in the early stages of industrialization, it has continued with unabated strength down to the present time. According to J. Frederic Dewhurst, during the ninety-year period from 1850 to 1940 the estimated productivity per man-hour of labor for the entire gainfully employed population in terms of 1940 prices rose from 17.3 to 79.3 cents. This means that the "average rate of increase over the entire period" was "18.2 per cent per decade, or about 1.7 per cent per year compounded." [1] These figures probably record the most impressive sustained economic advance in the history of nations.

The increase in the productivity of labor has been accompanied by a revolutionary reduction in the hours of work. What these hours were in the self-sustaining rural household of 1800 we can only conjecture, but they were probably between eighty and ninety per week. On the basis of available data, Dewhurst concludes that in 1850, for agricultural and nonagricultural occupations combined, the figure was 70.6. In the decades that followed, the 12-hour day gave way to the 10-hour

[1] J. Frederic Dewhurst and Associates, *America's Needs and Resources* (New York, 1947), p. 23.

day, which in turn was superseded by the 8-hour day. By 1940 the average work-week was 43 hours.

Technology Has Brought Mass Production and Enlarged the Scale of Operations

The idea of mass production appears early in the history of American industry. In 1799 Eli Whitney contracted with the federal government to deliver within two years ten thousand muskets. Although he required ten years to fill the order and thus failed to meet the conditions of his contract, he introduced into industry the revolutionary principle of "interchangeable parts" and the revolutionary ideal of "absolute accuracy." This achievement, combined with the invention of the assembly line which apparently came later, laid the foundations of mass production and material abundance. But before this mode of industrial operation could be applied to the commodities of popular use, the market had to be greatly extended, the scale of operations enlarged, and mass purchasing power created. In time, with the steady and radical improvement of the means of communication and transportation, all of these conditions emerged.

The enlargement of the scale of operations was accompanied by a profound transformation in the conduct of the economy. It brought together in a single plant tens, scores, hundreds, and even thousands of workmen, each of whom performs a highly specialized function without knowing much about the total process. Indeed, the individual becomes a kind of interchangeable human part which with other parts compose the whole. While all of these developments have resulted in greatly increased efficiency, they have introduced into the economy a high degree of discipline and regimentation. The workman is required not only to begin and end his day by the clock; he is also expected to adjust all of his actions to the actions of his fellows and to the demands of the machine. The transformation of the independent and manysided farmer into an operative in a mass-production plant is one of the most revolutionary changes in our history. Jefferson's glorified tillers of the soil would doubtless have regarded this entire process as profoundly contrary to the "American way of life," as it assuredly was in their day. The problem thus created of giving to the common man, the workingman, a sense of social status and dignity is one of the major problems of our democracy. It goes to the root of much of the popular unrest of our time.

Large-scale operations have brought together, not only the labor power of many persons, but also the financial resources of many investors. As a consequence, the corporation, which scarcely existed at the time of the founding of the Republic, has come to dominate the economy of the nation. It is difficult to realize that "up to 1830 apparently only two industrial corporations in the United States had received charters authorizing a capital subscription of as much as a million dollars."[2] Moreover, motivated by the desire for profits, the corporation has striven within the sphere of its interest to achieve a condition of monopoly. The degree to which the forces of competition have been circumvented is clearly revealed in an exhaustive study by a Congressional committee. "The major

[2] George W. Stocking and Myron W. Watkins, *Monopoly and Free Enterprise* (New York, 1951), p. 18.

categories of business activity," says a report of this committee, "may be divided roughly into two groups. The first of these groups includes agriculture, wholesale and retail distribution, personal service, building construction, and a miscellany of smaller trades. The second includes transportation, public utilities, manufacturing, mining, and finance. In the first group business enterprises are numerous, the typical enterprise is small, the degree of concentration is low, and prices are relatively flexible. In the second, enterprises are less numerous, the typical enterprise is larger, the degree of concentration is higher, and prices are relatively rigid. Among the industries in the first group, it is probable that competition is more usual than monopoly. Among those in the second, it is possible that monopoly is as usual as competition." [3] Our giant corporations, our great monopolies and quasi-monopolies, because they represent concentrated power, have a disproportionate influence in the economy.

Mass production and large-scale enterprise have favored and even compelled the development of a new science and a new profession—the science and profession of management. The complex and far-flung undertakings of our economy, with their highly technical and intricate operations and their hundreds and thousands of personnel, do not run themselves.

We are bound together by the indissoluble ties of economic forces. No family, no neighborhood, no state, no region can live by itself. As the workmen of a great factory pursue their

many specialties, all of which are necessary to make the finished product, so the different parts of the country contribute their special talents and resources to achieve the welfare of the whole. Technology has written for our people a declaration of economic interdependence that neither laws nor force can successfully subvert. As manufacture is dependent on agriculture, so agriculture is dependent on manufacture; as the West is dependent on the East, so the East is dependent on the West. The thread of a common interest runs through all the industries and regions of the country. And millions of us earn our living by providing the communication services that make us all of one family. So complete and pervasive is our interdependence that either fortune or misfortune arising in one sector of the economy sends its reverberations swiftly throughout the entire structure.

Technology Has Created a Social Fabric of Surpassing Sweep, Complexity, and Dynamism

In its patterns of organization industrial society is coming to resemble one of its own great machines, with its thousands of separate parts each performing an essential function and articulating with the others in closest harmony. To perceive all of the relationships between workman and workman, labor and management, farm and factory, region and region, industry and commerce, production and distribution, economy and government, work and play, is beyond the powers of a single mind. Even to follow the system of communication through all of its ramifications from the great centers of finance and power down to field and forest and stream, to mine

[3] Temporary National Economic Committee, Monograph No. 21, *Competition and Monopoly in American Industry* (Washington, 1940), pp. 307–308.

and lathe and fishing boat, and back again, exhausts the imagination. When we add the interplay of social forces, of the hopes and fears and plans of people, of the designs and struggles of organized groups, of corporations, employers, farmers, labor unions, and co-operatives, we confront a condition that would have astonished and frightened the simple farmers and tradesmen of a few generations ago.

This vast system of relationships seems to be extremely sensitive and unstable. Unlike our old agrarian society, with its independent and quasi-independent neighborhoods, industrial society constitutes a single social fabric and is vulnerable as a whole. If it fails to function in any one of many of its innumerable parts, if the outlay for capital goods falls below the danger point, if speculation upsets the delicate financial balance, if purchasing power is insufficient to absorb the goods and services available, it may pass into a condition of general paralysis or crisis —loans are called, shops close their doors, wheels of production stop turning, millions of workmen are thrown on the streets, members of the middle classes consume their savings, farmers endeavor to resurrect the self-contained household of their ancestors, young men and women hesitate to marry and assume the responsibilities of parenthood, and all elements of the population become frightened and seek scapegoats for their troubles. This seems to be what happens when a great economic depression sweeps over the land.

A New Cultural Element Changes the Character of Both a Civilization and a People

The introduction of such an element is a serious business. It does not mean merely an addition to elements already present. A culture is much more than an aggregation of distinguishable elements. It is essentially a system of functional relationships in which the diverse constituents are bound together into a kind of organic unity. A new element therefore will affect eventually, according to its strength, the entire system of relationships. And this means that it will change the character of the people nurtured by the given culture or civilization. Horace Bushnell saw all this clearly in the middle of the last century. "This transition from mother and daughter power to water and steam-power is a great one," he wrote, "greater by far than many have as yet begun to conceive—one that is to carry with it a complete revolution of domestic life and social manners." [4]

A new element may merely enrich or perfect a civilization without modifying its configuration or shifting its tendencies. But it may, depending on its nature, give a new direction to cultural evolution or even profoundly disrupt the most basic institutions of a society. The coming of agriculture to a nomadic people changes in the course of time the whole way of life, undermines certain cultural traits, and compels the growth of others. The introduction of the horse among the Indians of the great plains of North America altered the modes of livelihood, the methods of warfare, and the character of the dwellings. The invention of firearms assisted in the destruction of the feudal social structure of Europe and gave the people of the West an overwhelming advantage in their struggle to occupy the earth. The compass made possible the discovery

4 Horace Bushnell, "The Age of Homespun," in *Work and Play* (New York, 1864), p. 376.

and settlement of the New World and placed England, previously on the borders of European civilization, in a strategic and favored position. The airplane changes the relations of nations and may convert certain regions, such as the Hudson Bay littoral and northern Russia, now remote from the highways of commerce, into centers of traffic between East and West. The prohibition of ceremonial head-hunting among peoples of the South Seas, according to one investigator, weakened their interest in life and led to rapid depopulation. And if slaves once get the idea of freedom, they will never be the same again.

Technology Is Changing the Character of Both Our Civilization and Ourselves

Most obviously technology transforms the material aspects of our civilization—our dwellings, our tools of production, our weapons of warfare, our instruments of communication, and even our landscape. But it must never be forgotten that the people who live in the new physical setting and use the new physical agencies are themselves changed. The new conditions call forth new habits, new powers, and new attitudes, new values, new conceptions of life, new hopes and fears. The man with the tractor is not the man with the hoe, even though developed from the same germ cells. The people of the Tennessee Valley today are not the people of fifteen years ago, even though we were to assume neither births nor deaths, neither immigration nor emigration. The little man with the revolver is not the same as the little man with the club. A nation or a world with the jet plane or the atomic bomb is something new under the sun. And a people possessing technology with all of its revolutionary possibilities opens a new epoch in the history of mankind.

These changes which technology has brought in the realm of physical means and agencies give rise to tensions between the new and the old elements of the civilization. Thus the power-driven machine changes the status of the workman, takes the woman out of the home, encourages the growth of the factory, and modifies the system of property relations. The building of a highway or the invention of the automobile stimulates exchange, widens the scope of the market, loosens family and neighborhood ties, and weakens age-old forces of social control. The development of the machine gun, the tank, and the airplane removes military power from the hands of the people, makes impossible popular revolutions on the eighteenth century model, and places democracies everywhere under the peril of dictatorship. The point to be emphasized is that changes in such a humble sphere as the tools for producing goods will affect sooner or later the entire civilization from bottom to top and from center to circumference. Until adjustments are achieved in economic institutions, social structure, education, government, and even religion and morals, the civilization will be in a state of disharmony and crisis.

We Enter the Atomic Age with Minds Formed Largely in the Day of the Hoe, the Horse, the Spinning Wheel, and the Sailing Ship

The fact must be emphasized repeatedly that the strange industrial civilization which has burst upon mankind so suddenly and which is sweeping across the world so swiftly is still in its early stages, even in America. In certain of its phases it is far more advanced than in others. Our functional ideas, moral conceptions, and social organization lag seriously behind our modes of livelihood, forms of communication, use of mechanical energy, and scientific knowledge. This lag is doubtless responsible for many of the troubles and conflicts of the time. It is certainly the underlying source of the more powerful and disrupting tensions to be observed both within our American society and among the nations of the world. Today a great gulf stands between many of the stubborn realities of our industrial civilization and our customs, loyalties, understandings, and outlooks—between our closely integrated economy and our competitive spirit, between our shrunken world and our tradition of isolation, between our knowledge in almost every field and our ways of life. The task of bringing our minds and our practices into harmony with the physical conditions of the new age is a gigantic and urgent educational undertaking. Indeed, we shall not know peace and serenity until this is accomplished.

✧✧✧✧✧✧✧✧✧✧✧✧✧✧✧✧✧✧ THE COLLAPSE OF AUTOMATIC ADJUSTMENT   *William O. Stanley*

Throughout its development in modern times the democratic tradition has been closely associated with another great tradition, usually referred to as classical liberalism but perhaps more accurately denoted by the term social atomism. Many, indeed, have asserted that the tenets of social atomism define the essential meaning of the democratic tradition; and it must be admitted that sincere democrats, including Thomas Jefferson himself, frequently employed the doctrines of social atomism in their formulation of the democratic faith. Nevertheless, competent historical scholarship on both sides of the Atlantic warrants the statement that democracy and social atomism are not identical— a conclusion which is confirmed by the fact that a large number of distinguished social atomists from the eighteenth century until the present day have sharply repudiated the equalitarian premises of democracy.

Fundamentally, social atomism rests upon four cardinal postulates. *First,* that the natural individual is a solitary rather than a social being; that he is, apart from and prior to his membership in the social group, fully possessed of the essential attributes of human personality and endowed by natural law with certain absolute rights, not created by society and not subject to social review or control; and, hence, that all social relationships are external, secondary, and contractual affairs in no way necessary to or constitutive of the self. *Second,* that governments were established, under the terms of the social

From William O. Stanley, Educational and Social Integration, *New York: Bureau of Publications, Teachers College, Columbia University, 1953. pp. 192–206. Abridged and used by permission.*

contract, for the sole purpose of protecting each individual in the peaceful enjoyment of his natural rights; and that their just powers are, therefore, strictly limited to those measures necessary for the preservation of property and person against private force or fraud, the enforcement of contracts, and the maintenance of civil order. *Third,* that outside the narrow orbit properly assigned to the state all social relationships and all associated activity, where any degree of formal control is involved, must be regulated in accordance with the provisions of voluntary covenants which, by virtue of the unanimous and free assent of the contracting parties, are transformed into a species of law, privately enacted but publicly enforceable, and binding upon all of the legally competent persons willingly entering into the associations and transactions specified by the agreement. And, *fourth,* that where, within the bounds of civil order, each individual is left free to think and act for himself, human affairs are so governed by the automatic operation of immutable natural laws, ordained and established by a beneficent Providence, that the complex multitude of discrete and frequently selfish individual acts are woven into a harmonious pattern which not only results, at any given time, in the maximum possible attainment of the public good but also constantly tends in the direction of a progressive and orderly advancement of human welfare. Thus, with complete assurance, Frédéric Bastiat proclaimed in 1850:

I undertake to demonstrate the Harmony of those laws of Providence which govern human society. What makes these laws harmonious and not discordant is, that all principles, all motives, all springs of action, all interests cooperate towards a grand final result. . . . I believe that He

who has arranged the material universe has not withheld His regard from the arrangements of the social world. I believe that He has combined and caused to move in harmony free agents as well as inert molecules. . . . I believe that the invincible social tendency is a constant approximation of men towards a common moral, intellectual and physical level, with, at the same time, a progressive and indefinite elevation of that level. I believe that all that is necessary to the gradual and peaceful development of humanity is that its tendencies should not be disturbed, nor have the liberty of their movements destroyed.

Logically, aside from the sharply circumscribed function of a police power state, the acceptance of social atomism entails the substitution of automatic adjustment for any form of deliberate social control. In practice, of course, Western civilization has never espoused either social atomism or automatic adjustment in a pure and complete form. It is significant that even in England the first of the factory acts preceded by more than a decade the repeal of the Corn Laws. Nevertheless, despite numerous violations of its tenets and despite the enormous moral authority of the democratic tradition, social atomism has been until very recently the dominant social philosophy in the Western world since 1800, in some respects, since 1690. In the United States, for example, in spite of its tariffs and its railway subsidies and in spite of a substantial degree of social and economic planning during the early national period, social atomism penetrated so deeply into American social and political thought that after the Civil War its doctrines were usually regarded by the courts as a part of the fundamental law of the land. Carl Becker, in fact, goes so far as to say that "in no country was the theory [of social atomism] more commonly accepted or more fully applied than in the United States."

The central role of the principle of automatic adjustment in the economic theory of the Western world since Adam Smith has been generally recognized. The heart of classical economics is patently the regulation of economic affairs through the free play of natural economic forces in the market place. The significance of this fact for European and American life as a whole, however, has not been so clearly perceived. The importance of the economic basis of life in molding the contours of society, of course, is a commonplace of historical interpretation. But economic relationships are particularly crucial in a social atomistic society. Classical economic theory represented a sustained attempt to transform the economic realm into a self-contained and self-regulative unit, free from all political, moral, or social interferences. Yet, in concrete reality, economic activity cannot be isolated from the rest of life since, in its capacity of means, material wealth is an essential ingredient in the achievement of almost all human ends. The effect of the relative independence thus secured for economic enterprise, therefore, has been to render the cardinal factors operative in the economic realm decisive for practically every other aspect of human life. Human nature has been conceived primarily in terms of the "economic man" with his calculating, pecuniary selfishness: the social status of individual men and women, their access to the esthetic, cultural and other goods of society, and even the extent of their effective liberties has been determined largely by the degree of success which they, or their families, have obtained in the market place. Consequently, economic considerations,

both as ends and as means, have assumed an importance in Western civilization far exceeding that which they have occupied in other societies. Accordingly, the central role of the principle of automatic regulation in the economic system has secured for it a commanding position among the constitutive principles of Western society.

Further, the idea of automatic adjustment did not arise in economics, nor has its impact on modern society been limited to the ramifications— great as they have been—of its place in the economic system. Automatic adjustment is the heart of social atomism, inherent in the very idea of the discrete, wholly autonomous individual bound only by contractual relationships. Hence, with the victory of social atomism, the theory of automatic adjustment permeated, in one way or another, nearly every aspect of society— from the confident expectation that a stable and peaceful world order would inevitably emerge out of the spontaneous interaction of independent and sovereign national states to the belief that social status and reward should depend upon individual achievement and success in a frankly competitive and acquisitive society.

Finally, the role of automatic adjustment has been almost as fundamental in the intellectual and moral sphere as it has been in the economic and social realm. Western civilization during the last few centuries has been definitely hostile to the claims of human authority in almost every aspect of life.* The

* Nevertheless social atomism was not devoid of its own peculiar form of institutional authority, although for the most part that authority was concealed behind the façade of freedom. Under the theory of social atomism economic institutions provided the constituent principle of society. But according to this

separation of church and state; the loosening of the bonds of authority in the family; the revolt against Mrs. Grundy; the rejection of indoctrination; the insistence on the neutrality of the teacher; and the emergence of elective courses in education: all these, in one way or another, are a reflection of this orientation. Historically, of course, such manifestations are in part a reaction against the outworn and arbitrary authoritarianism of the past. But they are more than that; as they have developed in Western society they are tantamount to an assertion that the only viable alternative to authoritarianism is the repudiation of all human authority. And the practical consequence of the abjuration of deliberate human authority—a consequence often explicitly recognized and espoused— is an enthronement of the processes of automatic adjustment. Intellectual and moral truth, in theory at least, like economic and social status was to be established by competition in the market place, with each individual free to accept that which seemed good to his natural reason. If the forum were kept free, right and truth, it was asserted, would automatically emerge victorious from the contest, just as competition on the free market would automatically assign each individual to his proper place and function in the social and economic life of society. In this vein, John Milton asked "who ever knew truth put to the worse in a free and open encounter?" and in this vein, too, Thomas Jefferson proclaimed that "it is error alone that

theory economic institutions are grounded in rigid and unchangeable natural laws. Hence, economic institutions were not recognized as a form of social or institutional authority. As Professor Benne remarks: "One does not obey the lightning. He adjusts to it if he is intelligent enough to recognize the natural necessity in it."

needs the support of government. Truth can stand by itself." Secure in this conviction, democrats and social atomists alike, since they had put their trust in the spontaneous operation of natural reason, saw no need for a disciplined method for the regulation and guidance of public discussion.

A powerful case probably can be made for the thesis that in the last few decades the theory of automatic control embodied in social atomism has broken down in practically every sphere of human life. The intellectual and moral postulates of social atomism have become increasingly untenable in the light of modern knowledge and of modern social conditions. Man has been shown to be a social being, nourished and shaped by the culture of the society in which he lives. Far from being endowed by nature, apart from society, with intelligence, personality, and inalienable rights, he is, without the benefit of a culture built by the cooperative efforts of countless generations of men, little more than a mere brute, devoid alike of language, reason, conscious selfhood, or any sense of moral right. Nor can men readily maintain either their emotional stability or their mental health except through their identification with the social group. In sober fact, man's *human* nature—all of the fundamental modes of behavior that elevate him above the sheer biological level—are the product of his participation in the associated life of his society. Amply sustained by the accumulative results of anthropological, sociological, and psychological investigations, these conclusions have thoroughly undercut not only the conception of the solitary individual prior to and independent of society but also the dogma of a fixed and unvarying human nature. Once it is established that, within the broad limits set by biological nature, personality and character are socially built, it is clear that human nature will vary with changes in ways of living. Further, since such laws must operate through human conduct, the rejection of the idea of a fixed and unvarying human nature entails the relinquishment of the doctrine that society is governed by rigid and eternal natural laws. With the collapse of this doctrine, the thesis that where men are left free to follow their natural inclinations the dross of private selfishness is inevitably transmuted by the silent operations of the hidden hand into the gold of the public welfare has lost its rational foundation. In the words of one of the most distinguished scholars of our time, Alfred North Whitehead, "The self-sufficing, independent man, with his peculiar property which concerns no one else, is a concept without any validity for modern civilization."

Equally important, the verdict of modern scholarship has been reinforced by the course of events. In less than a century the swift march of technological progress has created a vast, interdependent, and highly impersonal economic and social order which has apparently destroyed the institutional foundations of the social atomistic theory of automatic adjustment. With the growth of industrialization, specialization, and mass production, powerful organized interest groups have replaced, in large measure, both the individual and the local community as the effective unit of economic, political, and social action.

Internationally, the breakdown is complete; nowhere do men speak with confidence of the natural order of peace and prosperity founded on the spontaneous interaction of independent and sovereign nations. Global conquest or withdrawal into the doubtful security of the garrison state are the only alternatives to effective world organization which are now seriously proposed by any considerable or responsible voice.

Fundamental changes in the conduct of economic enterprise, including the emergence on a large scale of these organized groups, have progressively undermined the free market until today, in every great industrial country on earth, the economy is governed either by a system of national economic planning or by a medley of governmental, organized group, and market controls which, whatever else it may be, is certainly not the automatic regulation of natural economic laws contemplated by social atomism.

The central concern of this section, however, is with the breakdown of automatic adjustment in the intellectual and moral realm. Unfortunately, the facts show beyond any reasonable doubt that in contemporary society freedom of thought and expression, under the jurisdiction of the principle of automatic adjustment, has not been able to prevent, or to cope with, confusion and chaos in basic human evaluations. Indeed, the failure of automatic adjustment has been so pronounced that it has seriously weakened, where it has not destroyed, all faith in human reason, with the inevitable result that the last few decades have witnessed a remarkable resurgence of authoritarianism. In its most virulent form, of course, this trend has been represented by the emergence of totalitarianism on the left as well as on the right. But the resurgence of authoritarian principles has not been limited to the rise of totalitarian doctrines and parties. On the contrary, the modern world has been deluged with a wide variety of intellectual and moral absolutisms. Allegiance to authoritarian frames of reference, of course, has never died out completely in the Western world. The vast majority of men, in fact, have probably always retained a considerable tincture of authoritarianism in their personal and intellectual structure. But ever since the Renaissance, the trend in Western Europe and America, until very recently, has been constantly in the direction of freedom of thought and of reliance on human reason as the final arbiter of opinion and belief. Today, if only for the moment, the trend has been unmistakably checked and reversed.

However these emergent and renascent authoritarianisms are to be appraised, it is important to note that, severally and collectively, they represent significant attempts to deal with the intellectual, moral, and social confusions of our time. As such, they must be taken seriously. Men can and frequently will endure hardship and deprivation where the necessity for such evils can be rationally comprehended. But they cannot and will not long endure social and intellectual chaos. Unless individual judgment and freedom of thought can be reconciled with a reasonable degree of security in the basic intellectual and moral postulates of an ordered society, men will at some point sacrifice freedom for order.

Consequently, the collapse of the theory of automatic adjustment in the intellectual and moral realm has created an exceedingly difficult problem for the adherents of democracy. If, as the advocates of various brands of authoritarianism confidently assert, this collapse conclusively demonstrates the fatal deficiency of human reason as the primary method of social control, the democratic faith is itself untenable. The eighteenth-century architects of social atomism and of democracy undoubtedly overlooked the extent to which human thought and conduct are shaped by nonrational influences; and they were quite mistaken in the assumption that under all circumstances, given an educated population, right and truth would automatically emerge victorious from the anvil of public debate. Nevertheless, it is possible to doubt that discussion and reason as methods of social control are indissolubly dependent upon the principle of automatic adjustment.

Under these circumstances, from a democratic point of view, the problem is clear. If the intellectual and moral vacuum created by the collapse of the principle of automatic adjustment in the field of human evaluations is not to be filled by some form of authoritarianism, then it must be replaced by deliberate controls which, without destroying freedom of thought and speech, will enable public deliberation to discharge its essential office in the present period. Obviously, these specifications will not be easily satisfied. But it may be said, with considerable assurance, that any successful attempt to fulfill them will entail two distinct, if mutually dependent, types of control. The first has to do with the establishment of the conditions under which rationality in our society may prevail. The second involves the discovery of a disciplined method for the control and guidance of public deliberation.

A basic—if not, indeed, the basic—error of social atomism was its assumption that freedom is the antithesis of authority. There is no doubt that some forms of authority are inimical to freedom. But the opposite of authority is not freedom but anarchy. And in the domain of the fundamental human evaluations which define the meaning of the public welfare, anarchy is simply the prelude to an intellectual and moral chaos ultimately destructive to both individual and social sanity. Until quite recently this cardinal fact was obscured by the direct and spontaneous quality of the authority exercised by the closely knit local community in pre-industrial societies. In the great society, as the preceding discussion has shown, a more formal and deliberate type of discipline is necessary. The choice in the contemporary world, therefore, is not between authority and the absence of authority. It is, rather, a choice between a democratic principle of authority and some form of authoritarianism in which freedom of thought and discussion, in the realm of public policy, will have no important or secure place.

Consequently, in the absence of an uncoerced community of persuasion, intellectual and moral authority in a democratic society can be vested only in a competent methodology of group delib-

eration, controlled and directed by disciplined procedures organically united with freedom of thought and expression. Given the current clash of doctrines and interests, it may well prove difficult, or even impossible, to formulate and establish methodological standards capable of achieving this vital union. But is is important to note that continued failure at this point will mean the end of the democratic processes of free speech and discussion. And, it is important to note, also, that the establishment of a disciplined methodology which unites within itself both genuine freedom of thought and effective intellectual and moral authority is not inherently impossible. For in the domain of the natural sciences, once almost as confused and as controversial as the realm of human evaluations today, scientific method has already achieved an organic and fruitful union of individual freedom and disciplined authority.

✦✦✦✦✦✦✦✦✦✦✦✦✦✦✦✦✦✦✦✦ FROM TRIAL AND ERROR
TO PLANNING   *Karl Mannheim*

In the following paragraphs we want to show in detail how changes in the nature of thought are intimately and directly bound up with changes in the nature of the conduct and action of which it is really a part. As soon as a new type of conduct emerges in history a corresponding type of thought necessarily follows to accompany it. What even pragmatists do not, however, realize as a rule is that there are very different types of action, and that as long

as they are not carefully distinguished, the basic transformations in thought cannot adequately be described.

We shall distinguish here between radius of action and radius of foresight. By *radius of action* we understand the extent of the causal sequences directly brought about by our initial activity and remaining more or less under our control. By *radius of foresight* we understand the length of the causal chain which can be more or

From Man and Society in an Age of Reconstruction *by Karl Mannheim, 1941, pp. 140–155 and 163. Reprinted by permission of Harcourt, Brace & World, Inc.*

less accurately forecast in a given situation as regards this initial activity. Normally, every action sets up unlimited causal sequences and man is usually only able to foresee and control the more immediate consequences of his action. Thus, the greater the degree of technical and institutional control in a given society, the greater the radius of both action and foresight.

If, for instance, I sow seeds in spring, at a certain level of technical and social development I can predict with reasonable accuracy that a considerable proportion will later come up as corn. There are, however, a large number of incalculable elements, both social and natural. I cannot know, for instance, whether or not my crops will be spoiled by drought or flood. I cannot know, either, that the warriors of some neighbouring tribe will not march across my unripe fields. But as soon as I introduce new institutions—for instance, irrigation, to counteract drought, or a body of armed guards to watch over my fields— then the radius of my action grows in so far as more and more links in the causal chain come directly under my control, and correspondingly my range of foresight becomes both larger and more reliable.

Before we can attempt to examine how the needs of a changed social order create a corresponding new type of thought, we must be clear as to the nature of the following three fundamental stages in the history of thought, which may provide a frame of reference for such an investigation.

The first traces of thinking, which still betray the relationship between animal behaviour and primitive forms of human thought are, as far as we can see to-day, characterized by the fact of chance discovery preceded by trial and error. Both the animal's adjustment to nature and the behaviour of the primitive group which is ruled by custom and tradition are based on chance discovery (Finden). In a world in which man carries on his struggle with nature directly, and in which natural selection regulates every process, some individual or group discovers accidentally, among a very large number of possibilities, the kinds of reaction which fit a given situation. The achievement of thought then lies in remembering the correct solution which has been discovered. Natural selection henceforth works through this achievement in the sense that those groups which cannot retain and transmit the right way of doing things, inevitably die out. In order to preserve this find, there is no need for a precise, reflecting knowledge of the environment which brought about the successful adaptation. All that is necessary is that the positive prescriptions and taboos which the tribal ancestors had worked out on the basis of such a discovery, should be faithfully kept. If the surroundings or the social order change considerably, so that a new kind of collective behaviour is required, the older form of group organization must either be broken or limited in scope, so that better adjustments may again be discovered by the more or less conscious "trial and error" experiments of the individual. These in their turn become traditional by the same method of imitation and taboo and are preserved so long as one can adapt oneself socially to these conventions and the social order can be made to work. The primitive stage of food gatherers and hunters is an example of this type of social life, which is now commonly recognized as the original form of social and economic organization. Even to-day we react to many situations with a type of thought and conduct which is still at the level of "chance discovery".

Great progress was made beyond this "chance discovery" type of reasoning when single tools and institutions were consciously modified and then directed towards particular goals. This phase in the history of thought may be called the stage of *inventing* (Erfinden). At this level man had to imagine a definite goal and then think out in advance how to distribute his activities in a given way over a certain period of time with this goal in view. He did not in such cases have to think beyond the task immediately at hand. But he had at least to be able to imagine how the object of his thought fitted into the immediate environment. He had also to be able to foresee the most probable consequences of an event. The entire development of technology from the simplest tools and instruments through the use of the plough and the taming of domestic animals up to the use of steam and electricity and all inventions which, to achieve a given goal, deliberately combine ways of thought and action which we shall describe more exactly later, work within the framework of this type of thinking. In the same sense one can "invent" or establish an association or organize an administrative staff, with a definite goal in view, and give it a place in an existing society.

Once these objects, methods, and institutions have been invented within the framework of an only partially regulated society, a process of selection working behind the backs of the individuals concerned decides whether they will survive or die out. Historical events at this "inventing" stage of development are a peculiar mixture of the results of natural selection and of institutions which have been consciously formed and thought out. This means above all that this type of thinking, with its limited goals, is itself the product of natural events. What a man succeeds in perceiving in society and what he fails to see, what immediate tasks he sets as his goal, and the ends for which he organizes himself and society, depend on natural selection. He rationalizes and suppresses not in terms of his own whims, but rather according to adaptations and necessities, individual and collective, which in their turn are not created by the people involved. Social processes, controlled by the understanding on the one hand and intellectual achievements, regulated by social processes on the other, exist side by side. At one moment man has the upper hand, and at another human understanding bows to the actual social situation.

To-day we are in the main still lingering at this stage. But the tensions which underlie our conscious goals within the larger field of the forces of natural selection, are gradually compelling us to pass on to another stage. We will speak of *planning* and *planned thinking* (Planen) when man and society advance from the deliberate invention of single objects or institutions to the deliberate regulation and intelligent mastery of the relationships between these objects. Formerly these relationships were simply governed by the random working of cause and effect, and regulated by conflict, competition, and the selection they bring in their train. The most decisive change occurs when man awakes to the necessity of regulating these gaps between existing relationships and when, in response to this, new patterns of thought arise. First, the pattern of thought is a linear one; possible chains of causal sequences are foreseen of which only the first phases are initiated by the acting and thinking subject, the rest being left to take their own course according to their own laws. The linear pattern of thought takes the form of a circular flow where the first elements in the causal chain are in our new model of thought supplemented by further elements, the movement of which tends towards an equilibrium, and in which all the factors act upon each other simultaneously instead of in an endless succession.

The circular flow works automatically and it is quite unnecessary to interfere with it. This closed circle of mutual relationships is still on the level of inventive thinking, for it is one-dimensional, as can be seen most clearly in the case of classical economics. This one-dimensional pattern is turned into a multi-dimensional one when at the highest stage of development the separate spheres such as politics, economics, etc., which were formerly thought to be closed circles, are seen to interact upon each other and lead to a multi-dimensional structure. This structure is not considered as a static one, as it is continuously subject to change; and from now on the changes in its parts will only be felt to have been adequately interpreted if understood in terms of the changing whole.

This new way of thinking is balanced by a new way of acting. For planning not only changes individual links in the causal chain and adds new ones but also tries to grasp the whole complex of events from the *key position* which exists in every situation. The mechanism of the cycle of events can be mastered and guided only if the appropriate key positions are found and dealt with by a new method. Conduct directed from the centre of the cycle of events is far more effective, for by using a key position, a number of links in the causal chain can be either initiated, or controlled, or even circumvented. Instead of a too limited power over immediate goals, there now emerges at various points the possibility of direct control of the whole, and of the more indirect type of control in individual cases. As soon as it is possible to plan the whole and the key positions become clear, the single links in the causal chain are no longer regarded as immutable and complete in themselves.

The most essential element in the planned approach is, then, that it not only thinks out individual aims and limited goals, but also realizes what effects these individual aims will in the long run have on wider goals. The planned approach does not confine itself only to making a machine or organizing an army but seeks at the same time to imagine the most important changes which both can bring about in the whole social process.

It is of course clear that the line which divides inventive thinking, which is rationally striving to realize immediate goals, from planned thinking, is not a hard and fast one. No one can say for certain at what degree of foresight and at what point in the widening radius of conscious regulation the transition from inventive to planned thinking takes place. This transition is just as vague as the previous one between chance discovery and invention. The most primitive form of discovery is probably that in which two almost blindly interacting natural factors collide with one another: when the infinite variety of situations confronts the finite number of possible responses. Out of these the right sort of behaviour is crystallized and stabilized through unconscious adaptation and selection. We may ask, therefore, whether a discovery which is based on the conscious search for a more favourable situation is already an invention or whether invention emerges only when factors are spontaneously combined in a new way. It would be idle to pursue the problem of determining the transition point any further, for the fact that there are in reality indeterminate transitions does not abolish the fundamental differences between these two types of thinking. "Planning" as a new stage of the development of thought and action is realized in so far as the previously vast arena of competition and the consequent process of selection are increasingly narrowed by regulatory intervention and the forces at work are consciously controlled.

Discovery and invention by no means lose their function on the emergence of planning. But problems in thinking which can be solved only by planning, cannot be left to discovery just as, on the other hand, planning always must build upon the stages of discovery and invention. In the same way, thinking in terms of interdependence (which is one aspect of planning) does not supersede abstraction with its separation of spheres. But one must know precisely how each stage of thought is related to the others and how they supplement one another.

❖❖❖❖❖❖❖❖❖❖❖❖❖❖❖❖❖❖ THE ECLIPSE OF COMMUNITY

Maurice Stein

THE cities of the twenties were extremely heterogeneous entities composed of more or less culturally distinct, spatially segregated sub-communities. One's perspective on the city was that of one's sub-community and even the mobile were able to maintain some contact with their original sub-culture by congregating in the area of second settlement. But the commitment to subcultural values was already being weakened by the prospect of "Americanization." Even in towns as small as Newburyport, ethnic participation in and absorption into the American social system was beginning to weaken ethnic institutions and identities. The drift was toward standardization in the direction indicated by mass media stereotypes of middle-class America. Park's concern with the need for impersonal controls to prevent disruptive deviation becomes less cogent, until by the fifties these impersonal controls threaten to destroy the very diversity that once made city life attractive.

A step in the diminution of urban diversity is the disappearance of Bohemias. Caroline Ware provided a glimpse of the moment in the life of Greenwich Village when its transformation from a genuine to a false Bohemia was imminent. Here we can identify the mechanisms through which the very amorphousness and quest for marketable novelty dominating Ameri-

From Maurice Stein, The Eclipse of Community, *Princeton, N.J.: Princeton University Press, 1960, pp. 279–289. Used by permission. This selection is a condensed version of the extended discussion of suburbia in the book from which it is taken. Interested readers may want to look at Chapters 9 and 12 of the original volume for full treatment of these themes.*

can life rendered the consolidation of distinctive Bohemian patterns difficult if not impossible. The experimental family was taken over along with experimental art, though its meaning in the suburban context was quite different from that in Bohemia.

Park's students familiarized us with slum life in the twenties. Whyte helped to correct certain impressions about "disorganization" by exposing the distinctive social organization arising in ethnic lower-class neighborhoods. There are still a good many Americans living in neighborhoods properly classified, though often not by their residents, as "slums." Research in such sub-communities is often dominated by middle-class images, and it is here that the structural models of studies in earlier periods can themselves become blinders. Whyte has shown this to be true of Park's conception of slum structure and he provided a detailed picture of the institutional realities of slum life along with their human meanings to various categories of slum dwellers. Whyte shows that slum life styles and life plans are shaped by forces related to those found in Muncie and Newburyport.

Industrialization, spreading around the turn of the century, revolutionized the work process by requiring degrees of specialization that eliminated most vestiges of coherence or craft satisfactions from the work process. In addition, as Lynd has shown, it ripped apart the fabric of communal life by putting a premium on the superior strength and speed of the youngsters while devaluing the laboriously acquired craft skills of their parents. Meaning and purpose had to be sought outside the factory, but the more personal sources —religion and the family—were also in the throes of change. The teachings of the church became more and more remote from the activities of life while new economic necessities and opportunities overthrew established family patterns. Lynd indicates that dedication to an ever-rising "standard of living" was the only way to justify industrial work roles, though the commitment of the older generation was always tinged with nostalgia for a craft way of life. The younger generation, those now between forty and fifty, knew this other pre-industrial round of life only tangentially if at all. They were prepared to renounce "intrinsic" work satisfactions and, for that matter, practically any other kind of intrinsic satisfactions, so long as they could gather the emblems of economic success.

The people of Newburyport also climbed onto the mobility ladder. Their transition from a traditional, old-family-dominated New England town to an absentee-owned class-divided community brought with it the crucial experiences of the Middletowners, but heightened by simultaneous disintegration of a traditional system of social organization that had satisfied important needs. As Warner shows, prior to bureaucratization there was a community consciousness in Newburyport that allowed the old families to provide leadership that symbolized the aspirations of the whole community in a fashion rarely approximated in American life.

The American sense of remoteness from power centers was greatly accentuated by experiences during the depression when it became all too clear that national and international forces well beyond the purview of the local community determined life chances to an important degree. In Middletown, the people were forced to turn to the federal government for help and this established a pattern that has since persisted. The Lynds' most striking observation about the effects of the depression—that it actually heightened affiliation with the success formula—is certainly borne out by the present behavior of men who were young adults during that period. One cannot but wonder if some of the underlying anxiety and refusal to recognize the past is not a result of the traumatic circumstances suffered by persons committed to mobility during the depression. Certainly it must have contributed to their foreshortened time perspective.

World War II brought another set of difficulties. Most people were mobilized either in the army or in civilian war jobs so that pursuit of careers was seriously interrupted. At the same time, the Army itself provided experience with an authoritarian bureaucratic caste system that aroused almost as much resentment and anxiety as the war hazards themselves. Commitment to the military program, which could have been the occasion for arousing deep national sentiments, seems to have evoked mainly individualized responses. The war period became but another in the succession of upheavals and interruptions in the all-important upward climb.

In this historical context, neglect of the past by present day adolescents and repudiation of the past by their parents becomes intelligible. More so than ever before, energies have been thrust into creating a worldly paradise based on material acquisition. This version of the American Dream is embodied with greatest clarity in the prosperous suburb and can therefore be studied most conveniently in that setting. *Throughout the following discussion, the point of reference will always be the suburb unless a larger context is specifically indicated.* Many of the observations about suburbia can be extended to other sub-communities with only slight modifications. As the suburban style increases its hold on the dreams and the lives of Americans, the usefulness of this sub-community as a social laboratory increases correspondingly.

The social structure of the prosperous suburb is strangely paradoxical. On the one hand it arranges matters so that the daily life of the individual, no matter what his age or sex, is divided into many compelling tasks that leave little or no time for freely chosen activity. Like modern industrial employment, which it fundamentally resembles, the suburb is frantically devoted to the rhythm of keeping busy. Even the playtime of the children is routinized and many families find that the separate schedules of the various members leave no time for intimate moments with one another. On the other hand, while people are so desperately busy, they do not know or have forgotten how to perform some of the most elemental human tasks. The most glaring evidence for this is the genuine crisis in the American suburb over child rearing. Anxious mothers, uncertain how to raise their children, turn to scientific experts to find out if their children are normal or, even more important, what the standard of normality might be.

We face a curious and probably unprecedented situation here: a society of material comfort and apparent security in which the most fundamental of human relationships—that between mother and child—has become at the very least problematical. No one is surprised to discover that businessmen treat each other in impersonal and manipulative terms; but surely it should be cause for some dismay to find it habitual, as the authors of *Crestwood Heights* report, that mothers regard suburban children as "cases" the moment they lag behind the highly formalized routine accomplishments of their peers or, still worse, show signs of distinctive individuality. The paradox between busyness and helplessness, between outer bustle and inner chaos, may now become easier to explain: "Keeping on the go" is the prime way for the suburbanite to avoid facing the vacuum in which he lives. Hence, the peculiarly painful fact that in suburbanite society, for all that it is so conspicuously child-centered and for all that parents habitually make sacrifices in order to get "the best things" for their children, it is an unusual mother who really knows her own child.

For that matter, no one in the suburb really has to know anyone else as long as appearances are kept up. Housewives, taught to desire careers, are trapped in the home. Husbands, trapped in careers which drain their best energies, must look forward to a fate that has become as dreaded as death —that of retirement and free time. Looking ahead to their own prospective life cycles, the children soon learn to submerge the specter of a life that lacks rooted values and creative meanings by throwing themselves into the struggle for status. All of the vital roles wherein the human drama used to be played out—mother-son, father-daughter, worker-player, adult-child, male-female—now tend to be leveled. Their specific contents which had previously made them into channels for realizing a particular set of human possibilities have been bartered for an ephemeral and empty sense of status. Not to perform these roles is to lose one's place but, sadly enough, performing them can never give one a place.

Now it is true that all societies use status, the systematic allocation of prestige and esteem, as a way of motivating people to fill social roles. Those performing valued activities in a competent manner receive the awards of respect and approval. This presumes, however, that there *are* some stable roles which receive acclaim. Crestwood Heights, however, is distinguished by the absence of this kind of consensus. For not only does the suburbanite have to keep up with the Joneses; he also has to spend a tremendous amount of time and energy trying to find out which status models the Joneses are themselves currently keeping up with. Since no other activities are finally valued in and of themselves apart from this quest for status, it soon becomes obsessive. *Status becomes an autonomous motive and mode of life.* Human relationships are valued only as sources of status when status ceases to be the reward for having successfully become a valued kind of human being. We have reached here the result of that process within bourgeois society which, call it alienation with Marx or *anomie* with Durkheim, transforms the human being into an object —and this strikingly enough, at the very moment when human beings in the suburb believe they have triumphantly won the battle to gain control over objects.

From a social psychiatric perspective, the suburb presents many interesting problems. It appears that the character types and mechanisms considered most prominent in contemporary American life are often actually best exemplified in suburbs. There, if anywhere, would be found Erich Fromm's "marketing orientation," David Riesman's "other-direction," Harry Stack Sullivan's "exaggerated security operations," Erik Erikson's "identity diffusion," and even possibly the thoroughly unsavory "authoritarian personality." There are broad convergences among these various concepts deriving at least in part from the fact that the personality configuration described by all of them emerges from what can conveniently be called "mass" society. And the suburb is a better place in which to study this human type than most other city neighborhoods, even though all of them contain some form of the species.

All social psychiatric descriptions of personality types finding their natural habitat in suburbia emphasize the central role played by anxiety. This anxiety is rarely recognized as such but it need not be recognized in order to govern effectively the suburbanite's self-marketing operations. The children become wary of its sting when they discover that they are part of the status equipage of their parents and must comport themselves accordingly. They are loved for what they do rather than what they are, and this becomes especially bewildering and devastating because their parents constantly insist that the opposite is the case.

At this point, we can clearly see the most grievous human loss that life in the suburb entails. Dedication to a status-dominated life style forces individuals into a rigid mold from within which they can see only limited aspects of human reality. Other people become threats or objects to be used. Emotional growth stops at Sullivan's "juvenile" phase. The identity struggles of adolescence are resolved through stereotypes that simplify reality rather than through fresh perceptions that provide a basis for expanding contact with personal and interpersonal realities.

Yet it would be a mistake to assume that the typical suburbanite's anxious preoccupation with status as well as his anxious avoidance of genuine experience insulate him completely from life's conflicts. He may be able to postpone the conscious facing of some conflicts but he cannot permanently escape from their consequences. Women usually suffer from social contradictions more than men because they are confronted squarely and inescapably with at least one role conflict. Whether they choose housekeeping, careers, or a combination of both, they must sacrifice something important. Their busy schedules prevent them from finding too much time on their hands in which to reflect on their situation but those who do can always turn for help to one or another of the ubiquitous psychological experts who play an increasingly important role in Crestwood Heights. These experts begin to look like modern shamans exorcising the tribal ghosts so that the routines of living can be kept up without interference. But these shamans cannot touch the underlying causes of the anxiety they temporarily allay.

It is important, however, to recognize that the "human material"—just because it is human—does not completely adapt to the pressures. Continual distractions provided by busy schedules and supplemented by heavy doses of mass entertainment may turn attention from the real problems of life, but the half-dreaded, half-desired moments of unavoidable reverie cannot be entirely suppressed. These realities can break in symptomatically as with psychosomatic conditions or they can manifest themselves interpersonally in terms of "problem" children or "problem" marriages. Even more devastating, at least for the male, is the much-dreaded work "block" which can threaten careers. And there are more conventional disorders—people can't sleep or sleep too much; they can't eat or eat too much. In these seemingly minor matters, the malaise takes serious toll.

There is no reason to assume that the problems of identity diffusion and foreclosure described above stop at the boundary of the suburb. Few people reared in modern America manage to escape the pressures toward espousal of stereotyped self identities as a means of gaining a temporary resting place in the unending status struggles, even though the price may well be emotional and intellectual stagnation. The role conflicts of suburbanites in which elemental human identities and prob-

lems are distorted by the quest for status are by no means their exclusive prerogative. Establishing satisfactory masculine identities at each phase of the life cycle is as precarious among workers as among managers, while the wives of both groups struggle with the problems of femininity. Unfortunately, it is always easier to settle for the stereotyped juvenile patterns promulgated by the mass media, encouraged by an inner monitor, the self-system, and reinforced by the demands of modern social life. Still, growth does take place. People do occasionally find their way through the banalities of mass society and it is important to study with great care the conditions under which this occurs. Before individual progress can be made, identity must first be seen as problematic and the growth anxieties as real.

✦✦✦✦✦✦✦✦✦✦✦✦✦✦✦✦✦✦✦✦ FRAGMENTATION IN THE HELPING PROFESSIONS   *Lawrence K. Frank*

Rarely in human history has a social order undergone such far-reaching, all-embracing disturbances at one time. Changes have ordinarily come slowly and bit by bit; people apparently have been able to accommodate themselves to new ways of living, not always easily or peacefully, but with at least something to cling to, something to rely upon as a secure, stable core while they changed their tools and techniques of making a living, reformulated their ancient rituals and amended their codes, a little at a time. But we are both privileged and burdened to live in a

world that is undergoing a major upheaval everywhere, as immemorial customs and long-established ways of living have been violently overthrown or summarily rejected or become progressively anachronistic. As members of a changing social order we have been compelled to encompass in our own individual lives a range of incongruities, discrepancies and conflicts that are testing our human capacity to survive as personalities. How much ambiguity, contingency, ambivalence, confusion and conflict can we endure without being individually destroyed or with-

From Lawrence K. Frank, "The Interdisciplinary Frontiers in Human Relations Studies," Journal of Human Relations, *Fall 1954, pp. 9–23. Abridged and used by permission.*

out destroying our social order is a very pressing question today. What can we do, if self-consciously aware and courageously prepared, we undertake to renew our disintegrating culture and to reorient our confused social order guided by our enduring goal values, accepting this immense task as our share in the never-ending search to make living more orderly, more significant and fulfilling of human dignity? This, I take it, is the basic problem we face when we approach this interdisciplinary frontier in human relations study where we wish to invoke the knowledge, the skills, the understanding of all disciplines and professions to deal more adequately with this multidimensional problem, with which no one discipline or profession can cope alone and unaided.

Thus an identifiable individual person will alternately, if not simultaneously, utilize economic, political, legal, social and other patterns, including deviant modes, according to the time, place, the strategy and tactics of his life career, the ever shifting coalition and conflicts in his varied relations, etc. Are we justified in invoking a different explanation when a person seeks his objectives through various economic practices and symbols, then tries the political, then a variety of other practices of human relations, including mass actions by joining his individual endeavors to others?

The *same* individual human person, we must remember, engages in these varied social institutional practices and transactions, appears in all the statistical compilations of political, economic, social, legal and other studies when using these institutionalized, symbolic rituals we call prices, wages, rents, profits, votes and legislation, marriages, births, divorces, crimes, mental dis-

orders, litigation, etc. Man might well be called the data-creating animal. It is this identifiable individual who, in concert with others, makes up what we call "forces" which, obviously, are not mechanical or superhuman. Rather these "forces," if we must use that metaphor, are the aggregate of the human strivings and, let it be noted, of the various human relations we are here concerned with. Moreover, it is the same identifiable person who seeks or is dealt with by the various professions as I wish to point out later.

Every discipline, therefore, is concerned with these varied human relations when it studies its professional problems but may not be aware of these human relations because it is preoccupied with these symbolic, ritual performances.

Until recently we accepted these diverse and unreconciled theories of the social sciences and the humanities. But today the emerging new climate compels us to recognize that our long-accepted ideas and customary assumptions must be revised and even drastically replaced. Let me remind you of what is happening today.

Let us recognize here the current confusions and conflicts in the training and practices of the various professional groups today. Thus, in a single university we may observe graduate and professional students being prepared in the several professional schools with widely different and sometimes strongly contrasting assumptions about human nature and personality development, and conflicting approaches to human relations. Thus students in medical school, nursing, social work, law, education, divinity, journalism, business, engineering, architecture, public administration and the graduate departments of the social sciences and humanities are being inculcated each with a different conception of human nature, of human conduct, with different beliefs, assumptions, expectations about people, what and how they act and carry on their human relations. All of these students are going out to practice in our communities, with what Veblen once called the "trained incapacity" of specialists, unable to communicate or collaborate in their practice or even to recognize what other specialists see and do. Indeed, we often find bitter rivalry and open conflicts arising not entirely from professional competition but from these very different beliefs and expectations, these specialized conceptions of how people act or should act and how they should be treated, guided and helped when in need.

Thus, for example, a family may in its varied contacts receive professional care, advice and services from a physician, a nurse, a social worker, a nutritionist, a home economist, a probation officer, a lawyer or judge, a clergyman, a psychologist, a teacher, a guidance counsellor, an industrial relations advisor, a banker, a group worker, etc., etc.; each of whom may give that family irreconcilable advice and treatment, guidance in how to live, keep healthy, maintain a home and family, care for and rear children, resolve family discord, and all other aspects of living, especially human relations. The family is expected to resolve these professional conflicts, to reconcile these incongruities and often mutually contradictory advices into a coherent, consistent pattern of living, a reconciliation which the professionals will not or cannot attain. Is it wholly unwarranted to say that the American family is being demoralized and often torn asunder by the various agencies and professions upon which they are dependent for service?

We are perplexed and baffled today by the frequency of what we call delinquency among children and youth. In most of our communities, we may observe a wide variety of programs arising from different beliefs and conceptions as, for example, the legal view of crime and punishment for degrees of crime according to the traditional doctrine of intent, motive and guilt; the psychiatric conception of delinquency as a symptom of stunted or warped personalities to be diagnosed and treated; the sociological and group work approaches and the various theological and religious approaches. Each assumes a different kind of human nature, interprets human conduct according to its own beliefs and practices so that it is difficult, if not impossible to develop any coherent program to reduce this tragic human wastage.

Medicine only recently has recognized that various illnesses and dysfunctions may arise not only from infections, injuries and physiological deprivations, but also from repressed emotional reactions or chronic affective disorders, localized in one or more organ systems and functional processes. These so-called "psychomatic" disorders are enlarging the physician's concern to include the patient's varied relations in his work, play, his home, marriage and family living, his political and social activities, as relevant, indeed essential, to an understanding of his difficulties and their treatment.

Here we find another frontier to be crossed if more fruitful and much needed orchestration of professional knowledge and services is to be achieved. Beyond this frontier awaiting a genuine concerted multiprofessional endeavor we find the exigent problems of human relations, not as objective tasks for isolated, fragmented scientific research, but as acute problems exhibited by confused, perplexed, distracted living personalities anxiously seeking helpful guidance in all their varied human relations in this very confused and disorderly social life. The wastage of human lives today, with all of the resources now available for human conservation, is indeed appalling. It can be reduced only insofar as professional workers of every kind will accept this urgent need for joint explorations and concerted efforts to develop a more acceptable common understanding for all their specialized work. This will call for as high an order as any scientific investigation and offer possibilities for advancing human welfare of incalculable promise. I personally believe that each discipline and profession needs the awareness, the insight, the understanding of all the others so that it will recognize in each patient, client and situation what the other disciplines and professions can help to reveal and deal with.

At present we see economists, political scientists, sociologists, social psychologists, psychiatrists and other specialists making studies, giving advice and preparing directives to public officials and legislators, to business and industry relying upon one kind of data and one theory—economic, political, social, psychological, etc., for formulating broad social policies and enactments. Each specialist, confident of his own knowledge and techniques, tends to ignore the far-reaching implications of his findings and recommendations for our whole social life which only the other specialists can adequately assess and try to meet. Surely we cannot expect to cope with our many social conflicts and confusions, the perplexities

we face, until we accept a multidimensional conception of social order and focus the various disciplines and professions upon these vital issues.

Thus we must try to develop a common conception of human nature which all the disciplines and professions can use to replace the variety of beliefs and assumptions held by economists, political scientists, sociologists, lawyers, anthropologists, biologists, psychologists, psychiatrists, etc. Surely we must some time agree upon an acceptable theory or common assumption about human conduct and how it is produced if our scientific studies are to prosper and our hopes for multidisciplinary studies are to be realized. This does not imply that the various disciplines are to give up their chosen fields and problems, but rather that they construct some acceptable conceptual framework and some shared assumptions which each can use on whatever problems it may study in its field or profession.

Recent studies are showing with increasingly convincing evidence that the human personality strives to maintain his individuality, to keep stable and to defend his life-space, private world. Each personality exhibits in all the different aspects of living and in all his relationships a more or less consistent pattern of action with persistent emotional reactions or affective responses, often disguised or concealed. His early formal pattern of relations with his parents will appear in his relations with his teachers or his supervisor, or boss, in his relations with his wife and children, and with all others he must deal with. Moreover, if he is unhappy, burdened with chronic anxiety, guilt or resentment, having an image of himself he cannot accept, he may release his chronic feelings upon others when they are inappropriate and unjustified. He exhibits that unhappy image of self in all his intercourse with others. He will warp, distort or exploit others, utilizing our institutions and symbolic practices and rituals (economic, political, legal, social), for whatever purposes he seeks to achieve as his self-defeating objective. Thus, many of the confusions, the conflicts and clashes we find occurring between persons of different races and ethnic-cultural groups are expressions of their individual personality patterns, often provoked and aggravated by the frustrations and humiliations people experience in their daily living. We should, in the light of these recent studies, interpret intergroup and interracial conflicts in terms of both the individual personalitites involved and also the social-culture "field" in which they occur—the disorderly neighborhood, for example. Whatever is *intrapersonal,* operating within the personality, is also operating *interpersonally,* in his relations with others. But this calls for an understanding of personality development and expression which we find difficult to accept because of our many traditional beliefs about human nature and our long-accepted expectations.

Human relations is not a new disease or social epidemic. From the beginning of human living, man has faced the persistent problems of creating and maintaining a social order in and through which he could live with some peace and security relying upon the approved patterns of human relations for shared living and the division of labor. Social order is not a superhuman, supernatural system, but a human invention based upon the conception of the inviolability of things (private property of some kind) and of the person (integrity of the individual and his

human dignity). The patterns of human conduct and relations which our predecessors painfully established have served, with greater or less costs and sacrifices, to maintain social order. These are now becoming obsolete and self-defeating, giving rise to increasing disorder and conflict. They are no longer responsive to the new ways of living we are seeking as we create a technological civilization, no longer expressive of our enduring goal values as we are now reformulating them.

For generations, with only a few dissents or protests usually ignored or suppressed, many have been sacrificed, exploited, humiliated and sometimes destroyed by the operation of our established laws, institutions and relations. We have explained and justified these practices by a variety of social, economic, legal, political and theological beliefs and sanctions. These beliefs have been accepted, with little or no protest, by those who have been thus misused and exploited, until recently. Now those who formerly accepted their unhappy lot in life as inevitable, are becoming restless, sometimes resentful and increasingly are protesting against their inferior status and mistreatment. But this protest comes, may I say, as they begin to develop a new image of themselves, a sense of their own worth and dignity, a belief in themselves as personalities who should not be so mistreated. This new aspiration of people who have long accepted inferiority and offered submissive obedience to those who dominated them is of immense significance for our democratic aspiration toward a free social order.

Thus we can say that no matter how insignificant or unimportant he may seem to be, no one may be unnecessarily deprived, frustrated, humiliated or otherwise neglected and mistreated because those who are so ill-used will be unable to participate in a free society and incapable of developing the kind of human relations required for a democratic social order.

This, I take it, is the basic issue in our concern for human relations, our earnest desire to orchestrate the different disciplines and professions to cope with the many problems, scientific, professional, operational, and especially personal, in this interdisciplinary, this interprofessional, area of human relations. Perhaps we have to face the task of re-establishing again some kind of status, as basic to human dignity, as essential to all the varied human relations.

But thus far we have not been able to invent a technique of social change which will enable us to relinquish our now anachronistic beliefs and replace them with new assumptions and patterns consonant with our responsibilities, our new awareness of the meaning of human dignity so long ignored or ruthlessly denied by those who could dominate and exploit others. The great conflict facing the world today is between those who believe change must be imposed by force and coercion—the authoritarian program—and those who believe that a free social order can change through education and persuasion, exhibiting the capacity for self-repair and self-regulation which is the basic conviction of a democratic society.

CHAPTER 2

The Social Sciences and the Planning of Change

STRATEGY PROBLEMS IN CONTEMPORARY SOCIAL SCIENCE

Just how valuable and just how vulnerable are the social sciences in American society today? We have examined some of the pressures driving the American people toward a planning approach in determining changes in their ways of life—in their basic orientations and relationships as well as in more superficial areas of information and overt behavior. Where are the American people to find the knowledges required to make such planning informed and intelligent? Lester F. Ward's unequivocal answer to this question, as we have seen, was "from the sciences and scientists of society." It was also mentioned earlier that many students of human affairs are uncertain today about the validity of Ward's answer. The ideologically tinged objections that Sumner urged against Ward's faith in science now seem outmoded to most students of human affairs. What form then do current controversies about the practical value and disvalue of the social sciences take?

The flavor of current controversies about this question is revealed by comparing a recent article by Raymond Bauer, "The Social Sciences: Our Greatest Asset," [1] with a book review by Arthur Schlesinger, Jr., entitled "The Statistical Soldier." [2] Three basic questions emerge from this comparison.

1. Have the social sciences since Ward's day fulfilled the promise of furnishing valid and usable knowledge (and methodologies) for informing practical social policies and programs? Bauer argues that in some measure they have done so and that continued and expanded support of social-science research and of the practical utilization of its results is in the national interest. Schlesinger seems to

[1] Raymond Bauer, "The Social Sciences: Our Greatest Asset," *Harvard Business Review,* 36:125–136, 1958.
[2] Arthur Schlesinger, Jr., "The Statistical Soldier," *Partisan Review,* 16:852–856, 1949.

believe, on the contrary, that the claims of "social scientists" concerning the social value of their work have been largely unfulfilled, and that their claims are in some part grandiose boastings designed to justify the continuation of their largely unmerited economic support from government, industry, foundations, and universities.

2. Do the social sciences threaten to undermine the central traditional values of our liberal-democratic heritage? Many Americans—even as they have moved toward a planning approach to solving social problems—have become uneasy, and rightly so, about the weakening or loss of liberal-democratic values in the process. The comparative success of the Soviet Union in planning technological changes has increased the anxieties of Americans both about the adequacy of American planning and about the tenability of our traditional values if we are to compete successfully with the U.S.S.R. Students of contemporary affairs who are deeply committed to the maintenance and extension of our liberal-democratic heritage, as Schlesinger certainly is, sometimes identify the methodologies of "total manipulation" which they see as central in Russian planning with "social scientific" researches on human motivation, group conformity, and ways of changing human behavior. Schlesinger takes comfort for his anxiety about the sovietization of American life through the influence of the social sciences in practical affairs from his low opinion of their accomplishments—"we have a considerable distance to go before resigning ourselves to a regime of total manipulation." Bauer, on the other hand, points out that the Soviet Union has conspicuously failed to support the researches or utilize the findings of the social sciences in its planning to the extent that the U.S.A. has done. In his more optimistic estimate, the accomplishments and potentialities of its social sciences is one of America's chief advantages in its current competition with the U.S.S.R. and in its efforts to plan democratically. He does not deny that the findings of social research can be used manipulatively by a few. He argues, however, that generally shared knowledge of the determinants of human motivation and of behavioral controls is necessary precisely to defend against "total manipulation." (More will be said about the relations of planning to our traditional values of freedom and individuality in Chapter 3.)

3. Do social science findings challenge and correct "common-sense" predictions about human behavior or do they merely reassert these predictions in mysterious and tortured technical jargon? Schlesinger takes the latter position concerning behavioral researches on the American soldier in World War II. Bauer counters with a quote from Paul Lazarsfeld showing that these studies did challenge and reverse many "common-sense" predictions about the behavior of American soldiers. Bauer does not attempt to show how the technical languages of social scientists, which Schlesinger chooses to regard primarily as evidence of a penchant for mystification or of a clumsy prose style, have helped to make challenges to and revisions of "common sense" possible by finding a precise way of talking about human events, alternative to "common-sense" ways of discussing them. We believe that he might well have made such an attempt.

This comparison does reveal the flavor of at least some current debates concerning the value and utility of the social sciences in practical affairs. It need hardly be said that the authors of this book tend generally to side with Bauer's orientation rather than with Schlesinger's. Yet if we look behind Schlesinger's stance of "total rejection" of "social science," valid bases for self-criticism of current social sciences are suggested by the questions he raises. Do some social scientists oversell their craft and their product? Are some social scientists insufficiently aware of and responsible for the value orientations that guide their and others' attempts to apply their knowledge? Is some social science unwittingly bound by the shackles of unexamined and uncriticized "common-sense" assumptions held by leaders in the bureaucracies they serve in applied research and planning? And does elaborate technical language sometimes conceal intellectual poverty and limited imagination? We believe that the answer to all of these questions is yes. The need for self-criticism of social science along these lines becomes most crucial when social scientists choose to intervene in practical affairs in order to coach the plans and actions of social practitioners and men of affairs.

While the debates rage in academic circles, the fact is that the services of social scientists are being enlisted more and more in policy-oriented researches and consultations, principally under the sponsorship of business and government bureaucracies. And this fact raises serious questions, not alone about the aptness and adequacy of votaries of contemporary social science to inform social policy validly but also about the effects, good and bad, of these alliances upon the future of basic social research and theorizing. Thus the self-criticism demanded of social science, if it is to be valid, must look two ways. A notable example of such self-criticism in which the issues underlying the controversies already noted are clarified, logically and sociologically, is the first reading in this chapter, *Social Scientists and Research Policy,* by Merton and Lerner.

The fragmented condition of contemporary scientific knowledge of human behavior becomes apparent when solutions to problems demand knowledge from several isolated and independently institutionalized and specialized disciplines—psychology, sociology, and anthropology, for example. However, problems in the world of practical affairs are seldom if ever purely "psychological" or purely "sociological" or purely "anthropological." Planners of solutions to these problems require knowledges from various disciplines.

Various approaches to this condition of fragmentation have been attempted. Teams of researchers from various academic disciplines may work with social practitioners in diagnosing problem areas and projecting plans for solution. Provisional mergers of knowledges and of research methodologies may be broached under various new names—"human relations," "social relations," "human development," "administrative science," and so on. New disciplines emerge—"social psychology," "social anthropology," "social psychiatry." It is not surprising that conflicts break out among various brands of "interdisciplinarians" and between them and the "purists" in traditional disciplines, with charges of "benightedness," "irrelevance," and "stodginess," on the one hand, vying with charges of "impurity," "methodological unsoundness," and "opportunism," on the other.

If we are right in our analysis of today's cultural compulsions toward more practically relevant organization of knowledges of human behavior so that they may be applied intelligently, various confederations and federations of men of knowledge will continue to emerge and offer their services to the policy-makers and men of action. Clarification of the possible and desirable relations between these practically oriented mergers of knowledges and methodologies and the "traditional" disciplines of social research and theorizing is, therefore, highly desirable. Chin attempts such a clarification in his *Human Relations: A "New" Discipline or an Integrative Force?*

SOCIAL SCIENCE AND SOCIAL TECHNOLOGY

The separate organization of research disciplines in the behavioral sciences has been noted, along with some of the problems of communication, conflict, and collaboration which this separation has created. The professional disciplines of social practice took shape with a certain degree of isolation and estrangement from these research disciplines. Until recently, borrowings from the behavioral sciences by the practice professions have been sporadic and unsystematic. Also until recently, direct collaboration between social scientists and social practitioners in research upon problems of practice or in the planning of solutions of such problems has been relatively meager. Under the pressures toward a "preventive" as well as a "therapeutic" approach to the solution of human problems, practitioners in various professions have moved toward revision of their guiding theories and toward the installation of applied behavioral research as a central part of their professional task. This movement has brought along with it varied attempts at rapprochement between behavioral scientists and social practitioners.

Successful collaboration requires understanding and acceptance of differences as well as of similarities among the parties to the collaboration. What are the general differences between the disciplines of social science and social practice? In *The Practice of Science and the Science of Practice,* a university professor of social work formulates these differences for social work. His distinctions seem to us applicable also to other fields of social practice.

Philosophical and methodological analysis of the requirements that the disciplines of social science place upon their votaries have for the most part focused on the model of "pure research" or "basic knowledge building." Social scientists have in general been trained to the discipline of meeting these requirements. As they have increasingly assumed responsibilities for applied researches, they have necessarily faced requirements for which their training and traditions did not prepare them. It is under the pressure of such felt discrepancies that the construction and analysis of models of "applied research" have come recently to be seen as constituting an important theoretical problem in its own right. Gouldner, in *Theoretical Requirements of the Applied Social Sciences,* presents his own pioneering conceptualization of the processes and requirements of applied social research.

◇◇◇◇◇◇◇◇◇◇◇◇◇◇◇◇◇◇◇◇◇◇ SOCIAL SCIENTISTS AND RESEARCH POLICY

Robert K. Merton and Daniel Lerner

WORLD War II produced the most recent surge of social scientists into government. Here again, as is inevitable during crises, the initial emphasis was upon immediate needs, pressing problems, and *ad hoc* solutions. This emphasis remained predominant throughout the war. However, little by little, social scientists began to appear in quieter sectors of the war effort, in places where the day's problems were important but did not have to be solved on a now-or-never basis. Particularly the social psychologists and social anthropologists tended to move into positions where practical problems could be stated (and sometimes solved) within a context of systematic social theory. As their reports now appear in published form, it becomes increasingly clear that theirs was a significant contribution to delineating a new relationship between government and intellectuals—i.e., a new conception of the policy scientist's role.

The direction taken by these social scientists was, in some measure, an expression of dissatisfaction with the scientific value of results obtained by working under the pressure of conditions and problems decided by the "practical" policy-maker. The frustrations of this procedure have been articulated in methodological terms by Edward Shils:

Much of the acceptance and appreciation of the utility of social science in the circles with the power to finance it and use it, extends largely to just those aspects of social science research which are almost exclusively descriptive, or in which the task of explanation is disposed of by correlations of indices of ambiguous analytical meaning or by *ad hoc* common sense interpretations. The fact that the correlation among indices of ambiguous analytical meaning is often high and that the possibilities of successful practical manipulation are thus enhanced constitutes a barrier to our perception of the need for theory.[1]

[1] Edward A. Shils, Foreword to his edition of Max Weber's *Methodology of the Social Sciences* (1949), p. vii.

From a selection by Robert K. Merton and Daniel Lerner in The Policy Sciences: Recent Developments in Scope and Method, *edited by Daniel Lerner and Harold D. Lasswell, pp. 292–307. Reprinted with permission of the publishers, Stanford University Press. Copyright 1951 by the Board of Trustees of the Leland Stanford Junior University. Some footnotes omitted.*

Here we come upon a central problem confronting the policy-oriented social scientist today, as he faces the choice of affiliations with the academic, business, or government communities. If he is to play an effective role in putting his knowledge to work, it is increasingly necessary that he affiliate with a bureaucratic power-structure in business or government. This, however, often requires him to abdicate the academic privilege of exploring policy possibilities which he regards as significant. If, on the other hand, he remains unaffiliated to a power-structure in order to preserve fuller freedom of choice, he usually loses the resources to carry through his investigations on an appropriate scale and the opportunities of getting his findings accepted by policy-makers as a basis for action.

The bureaucratic intellectual who must now permit the policy-maker to define the scope and objective of his research problem thus functions only nominally as "policy adviser." His function becomes the accumulation of information needed either to convert a policy into a definite program of action or to assess its effectiveness once activated. He thus becomes less a policy adviser than a policy server, less a scientist than a technician; and his knowledge is applied only to the preservation of existing institutional arrangements. The unaffiliated intellectual has fewer opportunities to affect directly the prevailing policies. But he can devote his skills to producing knowledge which presumably would serve to modify current arrangements in the direction of goals he considers desirable—were his findings to reach an appropriate audience. Thus the social scientist makes his most significant decision in selecting his clientele, and

thereby the type of problem with which he shall be concerned.

We may take advantage of a trite but useful distinction to observe that the dilemma here presented is not logical, but sociological. That is, it is not inevitable that the policy-maker should formulate the problems with which the bureaucratic intellectual must deal, but in practice he habitually does so. The bureaucratic intellectual, in consequence, and often unaware of the consequences, tends by compliance to become routinized in the role of bureaucratic technician. Since the social science of a time and place can never be more than the regular practices and working habits of social scientists,[2] the choice of their social affiliations thus becomes crucial to the developing future of the social scientists in America. Will the recent trend toward government and business service continue, with the consequent loss to systematic theory upon which social science *qua* science depends? Will they withdraw from the bureaucratic power-structures, thereby forfeiting their opportunities to apply their knowledge directly to current issues and problems? Will they be able, once the need is clear, to modify existing relations between policy-makers and intellectuals so that they can function as genuine "policy scientists"?

Predictions would be rash, and none will be attempted here. We shall simply review some of the conditions which seem likely to affect the outcome. Among these conditions, as we said at the start, is the distribution of rewards which American society will provide its social scientists as policy scientists. It

[2] This view is elaborated in R. S. Lynd, *Knowledge for What? The Place of Social Science in American Culture* (1939).

is unlikely that any number of sermons, however well preached, will keep the social scientist righteous unless the preachments point to emoluments in prestige, as well as power and wealth. The caliber of teaching in American universities, to take a relevant example, has declined despite notably persuasive, and even brilliant, homilies. The diffusion of knowledge on the higher levels has become an unrewarding profession, and the function seems gradually to be passing over to the mass media. The heaviest blows which doomed university instruction were dealt by the increasingly higher rewards to research. In research, rather than teaching, the American man of knowledge came to find increased income, power, and prestige. Against these rewards, moral reminders were unavailing. A committee of the American Association of University Professors put the matter plainly: "It is idle to profess any special solicitude for the good teacher when existing conditions are such that a man's success in research is everywhere rewarded as a matter of course, while success in teaching is not." [3]

Thus the intellectual's function of *diffusing* knowledge on the higher levels was impaired, in an acquisitive society, by the rewards distributed for *acquiring* new knowledge. Today, the confidently acquisitive society having developed fears of the future in the course of a great depression and two world wars, the conflict is between the function of *advancing* knowledge and the need for *applying* as much of it as we have. The controversialists have taken sides under the slogans of "basic (or pure) research" versus "operational (or

[3] Quoted from Logan Wilson, *The Academic Man* (1942), p. 191.

applied) research." The conflicting symbolisms have not yet been elaborated in detail, for on both sides the prestige of scientific advance is still high while the need for social application is plain. The conflicting motivations, however, are profound. As the tension increases, rival symbolisms will be developed to suit. Rewards will determine the contest.

The reward which most clearly remains variable, subject to contingencies (e.g., depression, war) as well as planned manipulation, is the prestige of the policy scientist of the future. The rewards of income and power now tend clearly in favor of the bureaucratized intellectual as against the academic scientist, and it is unlikely that the private universities can reverse this tendency. Should the power-structures of business and government be able to match or exceed the prestige rewards which still are lodged mainly in the academic community, the issue probably would be settled in their favor. The paradox would seem to be that, in order to do this, business and government may have to elevate their affiliated social scientists from technicians to the status of policy scientists.

The physical scientists have shown the way. Aided by historians and philosophers of science, they have done a splendid public relations job of convincing their strategic publics that pure research is the source from which flow the "highly visible technologies" of applied research. It is safe to say that no responsible government executive now believes that every experiment in nuclear physics should yield a bigger atomic bomb. Neither, it is clear from their grants-in-aid to pure research, do the top captains of industry believe that any chemical experiment is useful only if it produces a better grade of nylon or a cheaper form of plastic.

The social scientists have not yet demonstrated the analogue to their strategic publics. As compared with the physical sciences, their receipts for pure research—from private foundations as well as from business and government—are small and pitifully inadequate to their needs. The needs are great, for the construction of a basic, coherent, and useful theory of the social sciences is still in its beginning. As a result, applied social research more often than not has proceeded, as Dr. Shils puts it, "by correlations of indices of ambiguous analytical meaning or by *ad hoc* common sense interpretations." Research of this order is not likely to produce high prestige, on any long-term basis, for social science. On the other hand, without an increase of prestige, social science is not likely to command the resources needed to improve the basic theory (i.e., perspectives derived from the combination, de-combination, and re-combination of variables through empirical research) upon which its applied research ultimately must depend. The situation appears to be viciously circular. Whether or not it turns out to be so in fact will depend, in large measure, upon the developing skills and persevering public relations of policy-oriented social scientists and upon the enlightened self-interest of their strategic publics. We turn, then, to an examination of some key problems which must be confronted and solved, by those interested in the future of policy science.

The Application of Social Science to Policy Formation

Although the application of social science to practical problems of policy and action is still in its early stages, a large body of experience has been accumulated. Social science has been applied in diverse spheres and with diverse results. The experience is there, but it has not been systematically reviewed and codified. Consequently, no one knows the present status of applied social science or, more importantly, its potentialities.

Quite apart from the direct intellectual merits of the problem, the most varied groups have a stake in an analysis of the present and potential roles of applied social science in American society. Most prominently, social scientists themselves stand to gain by such inquiry. Perhaps owing to the absence of any systematic appraisal of their role, social scientists are sometimes beset with exaggerated doubts and harassed by exaggerated claims concerning their contributions to solutions for the problems of our day. The actual workaday relations between basic and applied social science must for them be largely matters of opinion, sometimes well founded, at other times not, simply because these relations have not been made the object of systematic investigation.

Foundations and other philanthropic agencies engaged in endowing social science research have their stake in the inquiry as well. For until the *actual*, not the *supposed* or *ideal*, relations between basic and applied research are clarified, policies governing a program of endowed research must be based on rule-of-thumb experience. Yet it would seem the most elementary rule of intelligent administration to examine from time to time the consequences of diverse decisions. Are there types of applied research in social science which fructify basic theory? Do other types of applied research deflect scientific talent from fundamental inquiries into theory and methodology? Under which conditions does there occur a fruitful reciprocity between applied and basic research? A preliminary inventory may not succeed in providing circumstantial answers to these questions, but it can scarcely fail to lighten the fog of ignorance which, one must admit, now settles about the role of applied social science.

This inventory promises much the same returns for the maker of policy in government, business, and industry. To a large and growing but precisely unknown extent, applied social science does find a place in the world of practical decision. Much experience therefore exists, but this experience has not been codified. What are the obstacles to the effective utilization of applied social science? For which types of practical problems is the introduction of applied social science pointless at present and for which is it prerequisite to the formation of intelligent policy? Are there circumstances in which men of affairs have a direct stake in endowing basic research rather than calling for immediate applications of pre-existing knowledge? After all, the decision to utilize or to forego applied social science is itself a matter of policy, and it would seem useful to have this policy based on available, though as yet uncoordinated, information.

It is long since time for the intelligent layman who does not himself directly utilize applied social science to learn something of this current in contemporary life. His preconceptions of social science may range from unshakable scepticism to equally ill-founded fetishism. In either case, how is he to arrive at an appropriate opinion? He is subjected to varied propagandas. One day he is told by seemingly unimpeach-

able authority that social science is merely gobbledygook. The next day he hears from other authorities that science alone, including its social divisions, can build the road to salvation. His choices are thereby limited. He may remain in a state of suspended judgment, which, in the present instance, may be only a euphemism for a state of confusion. Or he may cast his vote for one or another conflicting authority and emerge with clear and erroneous images of the present-day role of applied social science.

As we have seen, the repute of applied social science, as of any other intellectual resource, is in part a product of its accomplishments. The cultural context of evaluation therefore has a basic place in any analysis of the utilization of applied social science. And here we find ourselves limited by an impressive gap in available data. What are the prevailing evaluations of social science? How do they differ among various groups and strata in the population? And how have they been changing in the course of time? Manifestly, we do not know. No systematic inquiries into the cultural evaluations of social science have been made.

In the absence of the facts, we must speculate on the prevailing public images of applied social science and on the determinants of these images. All this is premised on the view that these prevailing images in part determine the extent to which policy-oriented research in social science is sought, by whom it is sought, and the purposes for which it is sought.

Of the numerous dimensions which may be found in public images of social science, only a few can be itemized and fewer still briefly discussed. Experience suggests at least the following dimensions of these images:

objectivity—ranging from the view that social science is merely private opinion masquerading as science to the faith in its rigorously objective quality;

adequacy—ranging from belief in its unmitigated futility to belief in social science as the means of social salvation;

political relevance—ranging from belief in its inherently "subversive" nature to belief that democracy can function adequately only if social science data are at hand; and

"costs"—ranging from the naïve view that scientific results can be obtained with little expense (of time and funds) to the view that usable results are so costly as to be "uneconomic."

Other possible aspects of prevailing images will readily come to mind, but these suffice to set the problem. Of these, the first two are presented in brief outline.

THE DIMENSION OF OBJECTIVITY

We do not know the frequency of these images ranging from the view that social researches can be (and have been) "used to prove almost anything," to the view that they are wholly objective, uncontaminated by the researcher's predilections.

The fact that clients often, perhaps typically, publicize the findings of applied social science only when these are in accord with their own interests probably helps spread belief in the unobjective nature of this research. Thus, the *New York Times* has seized upon the curious coincidence between the interests of clients and social science find-

ings to conclude, in effect, that the wind of social science bloweth where it listeth. When an applied economist files a research report for the C.I.O. which differs basically in its findings from a comparable report filed by experts of the N.A.M., the *Times* not only stresses the discrepancies, but notes that, oddly enough, the disparate findings coincide with the rival economic positions of the sponsors. Competing interest-groups attack and counterattack with their own social science researches. This is not merely a problem of "who shall decide when doctors disagree?" Since they are ostensibly based on research, the disagreements may activate a disbelief in the objectivity of applied social research *in general*. The specific instance may be generalized with consequent deterioration of the status of the disciplines involved.

The difficulty of distinguishing between "genuine" and "spurious" social science research further supports this scepticism of objectivity. The layman (often including the administrator and potential client for research) cannot always discriminate between the genuinely disciplined investigation and the "research" which has all the outward trappings of rigorous investigation (sampling, design, controls) but which is defective in basic respects. The outward appearance is mistaken for the reality: "all social researchers look alike" to many laymen.

Since careless, undisciplined, irresponsible "research" may promise larger returns at less expense, there may be a tendency for "bad research to drive out good research." And when these spurious investigations are tested in the crucible of experience, the resulting disappointment may lead to a repudiation of social science in general.

THE DIMENSION OF ADEQUACY

There are apparently some enthusiasts who would seek in social science knowledge the *vade mecum* to a scientifically planned and altogether desirable world. There are others who view applied social science as only an elaboration of the obvious, and who therefore consider it entirely dispensable as a basis for policy and action. Still others hold that social research is adequate when it deals with picayune problems and inadequate when it deals with "significant" problems. Here again, more information on the diverse images of adequacy and the comparative frequency of those images would be of value in helping to shape the future of applied social research.

Obviously, existing social science knowledge may be sufficient to deal with certain types of practical problems and wholly inadequate to deal with others. Thus, specific types of market researches may quite typically satisfy the needs of clients, whereas researches on, say, propaganda may prove typically unsatisfactory. The demands now made of applied social scientists may far outrun the *present* capacity and equipment of social science knowledge. As long as there is no roughly established inventory of our present knowledge such that laymen and scientists alike may have some approximate idea of which applied researches are and which are not promising for policy-decisions, this lack will continue to provide a flow of disappointment and a consequent devaluation of the adequacy of applied social research in general. It is unwise to permit exaggerated public images of the immediately attainable achievements of applied social science to go unchecked.

Reacting against underestimates of the potentialities of applied social science, social scientists themselves may inadvertently supply exaggerated conceptions of what is now possible. Such propaganda for applied social science may boomerang and produce the excessive expectations which lead to subsequent disillusionment and popular reaction against the use of social science to any degree.

The preceding examples only touch upon the probably rich array of public images of applied social science. There is plainly a need for an "applied social research on applied social research" to ferret out the public images of social science, particularly among makers of policy in government, labor, and business.

The problems of utilizing applied social science research in policy formation probably differ according to the social position of both the research agency and the client (or sponsor). Each type of research agency may have diverse types of clients and each type of client may utilize diverse types of agencies.

To obtain a systematic picture of the various structures of social relations between researcher and clientele, we have only to cross-classify the two variables of research agency and of clients. Starting with some such classification, it should be possible to determine, through comparative analysis, the distinctive problems, procedures, and effects upon research of these several structures of social relations between researchers and clients. Do these structures characteristically differ, for example, with respect to the role of the researcher in defining the problem, in the types of research problem at the focus of attention, in the type of interaction between researcher and client, in the relevance of the research for policy and action, in the degree to which the research findings are utilized for policy purposes, and in the methodological and theoretical by-products of the research?

There appears to be no literature which collates the types of situations leading to the decision to conduct a research in applied social science. Which occasions call applied research into being? And how do these different types of situations affect the nature of the research and its utilization? The conventional picture of how this comes to pass is clear enough: a "problem" arises, and the research worker, as a professional solver of problems, is asked to discover a solution. But who originally perceives the problem? Is it invariably the practical man of affairs, or at times the social scientist himself? And which types of "problems" are subjected to applied research and which are characteristically met without recourse to research? What are the functions of the research as conceived by the sponsor? And how does all this relate to the utilization and development of applied social science?

No systematic inventory of situational contexts is attempted here, but at least several can be identified. We can first consider the situations in which the need for an applied research is initially perceived by policy-makers or by social scientists.

FUNCTIONS OF RESEARCH ORIGINATED BY POLICY-MAKERS

1. Individuals or organizations confront the problem of "influencing" or "persuading" others to a given course of action. They seek "objective data" to aid in persuasion. For example, an advertising agency has a research conducted in the hope of convincing a client of the greater effectiveness of its advertising program over alternatives proposed by rival agencies; a pressure group sponsors an applied research to obtain data in support of proposed legislation; a corporation vice-president solicits a research in defense of his policies as against those advocated by another vice-president; or a group of public-spirited citizens advocates a research on racial segregation to demonstrate the dangers of segregation to the general public. Since the chief function of these researches is persuasion, they are perhaps more subject to the tendency to have the research findings exploited for propagandistic aims. In these instances, the research findings are not likely to be subjected to the test of experience. They serve primarily to lend support to predetermined courses of action.

2. Individuals or organizations confront problems requiring action by them, and find that they do not have sufficient information for "intelligent" action. For example, an industrial plant is repeatedly strike-bound; it tries a variety of expedients which are unsuccessful, and then turns to research to suggest new alternatives. Under which conditions is social science research sought? How does the pattern of action-oriented research differ from the pattern of persuasion-oriented research?

3. Individuals or organizations wish to delay action to the point where the pressure for action from others is eliminated. In such contexts, the applied research is intended not to lead to action, but to preclude it. The function of the research is to allay criticism of inaction. Public officials not infrequently authorize a "thorough study" of a prob-

lem on which they do not wish to take action.

In different situations, then, the policy-maker may utilize applied research for quite different functions. We have mentioned three broad functions—persuasion, action, inaction. It is, of course important to learn how each of these affects the nature of the research.

FUNCTIONS OF RESEARCH ORIGINATED BY SOCIAL SCIENTISTS

1. Social scientists may seek to sensitize policy-makers to new types of achievable goals. Some applied research has its origins in the work of the academic social scientist. He may detect what he considers a "practical problem" which has not yet been so identified by the maker of policy. In these instances, it is the first task of the research worker to *create* a practical problem for the policy-maker.

What is a "practical problem"? It represents a gap between aspiration and achievement, and holds out a challenge for closing this gap. If a policy-maker has certain aspirations which are moderately well met, he of course perceives no "practical problem." But the social scientist may at times detect the possibility of at once heightening or extending these aspirations and of realizing new goals. This requires him to serve as a gadfly, stinging contented policy-makers into a state of discontent by widening their horizons, by introducing new criteria of the achievable and by orienting applied research toward ways of reaching these new goals. Thus, the manager of a housing community may feel that it is running smoothly and well. He experiences no acute "problem." Rents are paid promptly, tenant turnover is low, few complaints reach him. An inquiring social scientist may

find that there is little organized community life in the housing development and that the level of residents' satisfaction is less than it could be if specific provision were made for community organization. In effect, the researches of the social scientist are here aimed at introducing new and more demanding criteria of a "satisfactory state of affairs," of extending the goals of the housing manager. A major function of research emanating from social science circles, then, may be to establish new goals and bench marks of the attainable.

2. Social scientists may seek to sensitize policy-makers to more effective means of reaching established goals. In much the same fashion, administrators may assume that their organization is operating at a satisfactory level of effectiveness. The social scientist may discover more effective instrumentalities for approximating present goals. The task here is one of modifying criteria of effectiveness of ways and means. Thus, output in an industrial plant may be judged satisfactory by the policy-maker. Further inquiry may show that this is at the expense of a rigorous regimen which puts considerable strain upon the working force. Alternative methods may produce the same high level of output without exacting this price of workers. It is altogether likely, as these casual instances suggest, that the modification of criteria of effectiveness of ways and means will characteristically involve a modification of goals as well. The pattern is the same in both types of instances: sensitizing policy-makers to a wider range of realizable potentialities.

Practical problems are many-faceted. They can be examined from the perspectives of several different disciplines. Increasingly, policy-makers have been weaned from the naïve view that a practical problem is invariably in the orbit of one specialized body of science. High labor turnover, for example, is no longer automatically assumed to be in the province of "applied economics." Psychology and sociology may find partial determinants of rates of labor turnover in the human relations and social organization of the plant, or in the inadequacies of the local community from which the working force is drawn. On what grounds, then, does the policy-maker select certain disciplines rather than others as most appropriate for studying the problems at hand?

This question introduces several considerations which can only be mentioned here. It points to the fact that for many if not most practical problems demanding applied research, collaboration among several disciplines is required. It suggests the role of the specialized research worker himself in acquainting the policy-maker with the need for such collaboration. It points to the major organizational and scientific problems of providing for collaboration between the several applied social scientists. (The experience of the Tennessee Valley Authority should be especially instructive in this connection.) And, anticipating a later section of this discussion, it suggests that a major function of applied research is to provide occasions and pressures for inter-disciplinary investigations and for the development of a theoretic system of "basic social science," rather than discrete bodies of unco-ordinated specialized theory.

DEFINING THE PRACTICAL PROBLEMS AND THE RESEARCH PROBLEMS

Experience suggests that the policy-maker seldom formulates his practical problem in terms sufficiently precise to permit the researcher to design an appropriate investigation. Characteristically, the problem is so stated as to result in the possibility of the researcher being seriously misled as to the "basic" aspects of the problem which gives rise to a contemplated research. This initial clarification of the practical problem therefore, is the first crucial step in applied social science.

Two types of unwitting misstatement of the practical problem by the client can be itemized here. Further inquiry will undoubtedly disclose others.

1. *Overspecification of the problem.* The policy-maker often assumes that he has precisely identified his particular problem and comes to the researcher with a specific request for research. But this may be premature specification. The researcher has the task of ascertaining the central pragmatic problem rather than passively accepting its initial specifications by the policy-maker. Thus, a Jewish "defense agency" requests a research to determine which of alternative types of mass propaganda will probably be most effective in curbing anti-Semitism. This does not represent the *prime* objective, which is "reduction of anti-Semitism." The policy-maker has prematurely included in his statement of the problem a specification of *means* as well as the end. The expert redefines the practical problem. On the basis of previous researches, he indicates that deep-seated prejudices are not markedly vulnerable to propaganda campaigns. The problem becomes reformulated: it is no longer an inquiry into efficiencies of alternative propaganda, but the comparative efficiency of a given propaganda campaign and of interreligious voluntary organizations.

2. *Overgeneralization of the problem.* The maker of policy may instead

assume that he has sufficiently stated his problem when he indicates his general objective. He may seek fuller participation of the rank and file in a labor union or reduction of race tensions or increase of college attendance. But each of these general objectives may be approached through very different types of procedures, requiring different types of research.

When the policy-maker overspecifies his practical problem, the expert must clarify by searching out the prime objective, thus often redefining the problem. When the policy-maker overgeneralizes his practical problem, the expert must clarify by searching out the various alternative instrumentalities, and determine the consequences of each of these.

THE FRAMEWORK OF VALUES IN DEFINITION OF PROBLEMS

We assume that the policy-maker always has a set of values, tacit or explicit, which places limits upon the scope and nature of the applied research directed toward his problem. These "value constants" circumscribe the alternative lines of action to be investigated. It is the task of the researcher to search out these values in order to know in advance the limits set upon the investigation by the policy-maker's values. (This is not only an ethical task but also a technical task. If it is true that the policy-maker always assumes certain features of his problem situation as *given,* as *constant,* as items which he would not under any circumstances consider modifying, this at once limits the range and type of research which will be done with his support, thus affecting the social scientist's decision to undertake the research.) Thus, for example, policy-oriented research is requested on ways and means of improving morale of Negro workers

in an industrial plant. The constant assumed by the policy-maker is continued segregation of jobs, sanitary facilities, and the like. Or policy-oriented research is requested on means for increasing sales of a product. The constant assumed by the policy-maker is that there will be no change in the product itself.

These value-constants are probably of limited types. Two major types are noted here:

1. Objective factors of the situation shall remain unchanged, while attitudes toward the situation are modified (e.g., not changing objective fact of segregation but modifying Negro workers' morale; not changing product, but increasing sales; research may show that the proportion of Negroes and whites in an interracial housing project must be administratively stabilized if it is not to become an all-Negro project, but the policy-maker rejects this research conclusion since it implies a "quota system" which offends his values; etc.).

2. Objective factors in the situation shall be changed, but no arrangements are to be made to modify attitudes (e.g., eliminating racial segregation in a housing community but not providing for means of local acceptance of this change).

The research worker also has his values, tacit or explicit, which affect his definition of the problem, the lines of investigation which seem to him most fruitful, and the alternative policies to be explored. These values can be detected by determining the researcher's self image of his role.

As a technician, he will accept alternative proposals for policy as a basis for research, provided only that these alternatives be technically amenable to research. For example, since it is feasible to test symbolic (psychological) measures for improving the morale of

Negro workers without eliminating segregation, the technician finds this definition of the problem adequate and confines himself accordingly. In another typical situation, the researcher is asked to determine how a given radio program can reach a larger audience. Since this is a feasible problem, he searches out strategic listening periods, and is content to accept the policy-maker's constant of increasing audience without exploring effects upon audience size of changing the program content.

As a "socially oriented" scientist, he will explore only those policy alternatives which do not violate his own values. He not only includes in his study symbolic means of improving worker morale (e.g., symbolic awards for performance, and recreation groups) but also "realistic" changes in situation (e.g., modified wage-policies).

Study of the actual role played by the values of policy-maker and researcher in the formulation of the research should help to carry this question from the exclusively ethical context to that of the impact of values upon the relevance, scope, and utility of the research itself.

THE ECONOMIC FRAMEWORK OF THE RESEARCH

Whether "applied" or "pure," empirical research in social science is costly in time and money. But the economics of empirical research may affect the patterns of applied research and of basic research in quite different fashions. To be sure, the applied and the basic research alike may have a fixed budget and a definite deadline. But this is not to say that the degree to which and the ways in which these affect the research are alike in the two instances.

The tempo of policy-decisions and action is often much more rapid than the tempo of applied research. Since action cannot always wait upon the completion of a research, varying degrees of urgency in decision affect research in various ways. When there is great pressure for almost immediate decision, the *research* expert comes to be converted into the expert *adviser*. The policy-maker draws upon the cumulative knowledge of the expert and foregoes an actual research. At this extreme, urgency is lethal for research, though not necessarily for other social utilities.

When there is need for decision at a definite but more distant occasion a research may be designed to supply appropriate information. But since the "key" problems cannot be adequately investigated within this limited period, the research is necessarily confined to "practicable" though secondary problems. Furthermore, it becomes evident that data other than those needed for the immediate problem in hand may be expeditiously collected at the same time. But since this would prolong the period of field work, these collateral materials are not included. The potential theoretic usefulness of the research is thus further circumscribed. As the research proceeds, fresh implications, not closely related to the present practical problem, are sensed by the research worker. These provocative clues, barely crystallized and wholly unformulated, are lost to view as the researcher bends to his immediate task of meeting the unalterable deadline. How often does the researcher return to the materials, after the deadline has been met (or not met), in an effort to recapture the fresh perceptions experienced during the research?

Just as the pressure for immediate decision tends to eliminate research in favor of the considered judgments of expert advisers, so does the pressure to reduce costs. The comparative expensiveness of certain investigations leads to the substitution of advice for research. It would be useful to determine the grounds for opinions on the amount of money which can be justifiably expended for research on a given problem. How often is a given appropriation made first and the research tailored to fit this budget? How often does the researcher plan the seemingly most appropriate research, and then have the estimated budget accepted? How does this differ as between researches in applied and basic social science? Since there exists no social bookkeeping for determining the "economic value" of basic research, the criteria for allocating funds to basic social science cannot be narrowly "economic" in character. But what of applied researches? Are the economic returns of specific applied researches typically estimated by sponsors or clients? And do these economic calculations determine their appropriations for research? Is there a tendency for applied researches to be diverted to peripheral problems when it is clear that research on the central problems in hand would be "too costly"? And since costs are inevitably increased by following up purely scientific leads developed in the research—leads which can have no value for the immediate practical problem—does this practice not limit the "nonpractical" by-products of applied research?

SCIENTIFIC GAPS BETWEEN RESEARCH AND POLICY

To assess the current and potential role of applied social science, it is necessary to note the scope and scale of the practical problems with which it

has dealt. These might range from broad, generic problems (such as generalized means of reducing crime or race hostilities) to highly circumscribed problems in a specific setting (for example, the comparative effectiveness of two propaganda campaigns). It may develop that the extremes represent the least promising sectors of applied social science research. With the excessively large problem, only failure can presently be reported; and with the excessively limited problem, the results are often trivial. It would be important to identify the strategic, intermediate range of problems, namely, those which have generalized theoretical and practical significance, but which are not too large in scope to be subjected to disciplined research.

Several of the circumstances which seemingly make for applied researches not affecting policy have been considered. The values of the policy-maker, questions of time and cost, and inadequacies in the formulation of the problem conduce to discrepancies between research-based recommendations and actual policies. As suggested previously, these gaps are of two interrelated types—the "scientific" and the "organizational and interpersonal." We may consider briefly some of the scientific gaps.

1. *The research is not adequately focused on the practical problem*. When the research worker inadvertently accepts the "overspecified" or "overgeneralized" statement of his problem by the policy-maker, the resulting research will ultimately be found partly irrelevant to the actual problems of decision by the client. Alternative lines of action which have not been explored by the research may come to the later attention of the policy-maker and he will conclude that the choice between the explored alternatives is spurious.

2. *Concrete forecasts are contingent upon uncontrolled conditions.* Many, if not most, applied researches involve forecasts. These concrete forecasts in applied science differ significantly from abstract predictions in basic science.

Basic research typically deals with "abstract predictions"—predictions in which a larger number of "other factors" are, conveniently enough, assumed to remain constant. The prediction will of course include a statement of the conditions under which the predicted consequences will probably occur. *Ceteris paribus* is an indispensable concept in basic research.

In applied research, *ceteris paribus* is often an embarrassing obstacle—for what if the "other factors" do not remain constant? As a matter of well-known fact, the research worker in applied research is not permitted the luxury of the *supposition* that other pertinent factors will remain equal. If action is to be based on his findings, he must indicate whether relevant "other factors" *will* remain constant. And since they typically will not, he has the further large task of assessing the changes in these factors and their effect upon contemplated action.

In short, applied research requires the greatly complicated study of the interaction of many interrelated factors comprising the concrete situation. The research cannot be confined entirely to the interplay of a severely limited number of variables under severely limited conditions.

This requirement of applied research has several consequences: (*a*) Every applied research must include some speculative inquiry into the role of diverse factors which can only be roughly assessed, not meticulously studied. (*b*) The validity of the concrete forecast depends upon the degree of (noncompensated) error in any phase of the total inquiry. The weakest links in the chain of applied research may typically consist of the estimates of contingent conditions under which the investigated variables will in fact operate. (*c*) To this degree, the recommendations for policy do not flow directly and exclusively from the research. Recommendations are the product of the research *and* the estimates of contingent conditions, these estimates not being of the same order of probability or precision as the more abstract interrelations examined in the research itself. (*d*) Such contingencies make for indeterminacy of the recommendations derived from the research and thus create a gap between research and policy.

The foregoing account is far from exhaustive. It does, however, suggest leads for determining how and why applied research does or does not provide a direct mandate for policy and does or does not eventuate in policy formation. A key set of problems centers in the determinants of this leap from research to practice.

THEORY AND APPLIED SOCIAL SCIENCE

Everyone who has read a textbook on scientific method knows the ideally constructed relations between scientific theory and applied research. Basic theory embraces key concepts (variables and constants), postulates, theorems, and laws. Applied science consists simply in ascertaining the variables relevant to the problem in hand and the values of the variables, and, in accordance with previous knowledge, setting forth the uniform relationships between these variables.

It will be instructive to discover how often this ideal pattern actually occurs in the application of social science. We anticipate finding that it is the exceptional rather than the typical pattern. In one sense, a major objective of our proposed inquiry is to account for the discrepancies and coincidences between the "ideal pattern" and the "actual pattern" of relations between basic and applied social science. In passing, we merely note two major relations between applied research and theory.

1. Applied research tests the assumptions underlying theory. As noted earlier, basic research includes certain assumptions (e.g., *ceteris paribus*) in its abstract formulation of a problem. Since applied research is conceived as a basis for action, and since action must always occur in a concrete situation and not under abstractly envisaged conditions, the applied researcher is continuously engaged, *nolens volens,* in testing the assumptions contained in basic theory. This is perhaps a key function of applied research.

2. Immediate pragmatic success postpones theoretic analysis. Not infrequently research leads to an empirical finding which may be at once successfully applied, although the finding itself is not "understood" (i.e., located) in theoretical terms. Thus, it may be found that provision for several rest periods in an industrial plant reduces labor turnover and raises employee morale. The plant manager who finds that this program "works" may see no occasion for further research. If the research worker is not theoretically sensitized, he too may be content with this "successful" application of an empirical finding. The fact remains that he has not yet identified the critical variable in this result: Was it that rest periods reduced fatigue? Or was it possible that the degree of managerial concern with employees' problems, as symbolized by the rest pauses, was the decisive variable? Or, again, was it the part played by employee representatives in arriving at the decision regarding rest periods—in short, the manner in which this policy was introduced—that proved basic? Unless the crucial theoretical variable in the concrete practice of rest periods can be identified, there is no basis for assuming that the same results will be obtained on other occasions. It will be of interest to learn whether such practical successes tend to vitiate the continuance of inquiry until the theoretically significant findings have been extracted from the empirical results. It is at least possible that specific practical successes may invite theoretical failures.

The Prospect Before Us

The social scientist in America, like the intellectual everywhere, has been shaped largely by the socio-cultural environment in which he operates. Within the particular American environment, he has developed a tradition which emphasizes empirical focus, reliable techniques, and precise data. This contrasts strongly with the European tradition, for example, which values theoretical outlook, speculative methods, and approximate insights. Such comparisons make it clear that the theoretical and empirical emphases work better in a reciprocal relationship (which provides theory with opportunities to direct the techniques of research and provides empirical observation with opportunities to verify and enrich basic theory) than either of them does in isolation. This fructifying interrelationship of theory and technique not only should be, but can be, achieved.

One way of advancing the matter is

through systematic analysis of the process whereby certified knowledge improves policy-making. It is often the case that social scientists called in as advisers to decision-makers are dissatisfied with what they can contribute. They can advise as any other wise and informed citizen might. But, as Hilgard and Lerner point out, this often is frustrating to social scientists, who wish to draw upon their sciences for answers to the questions put to them by policy-makers. We often have the methods by which answers might be found, but we have not developed standard procedures for appraising the applicability of our methods to current issues and for applying them. To develop such procedures will take thought, trial, and time.

This must be brought home both to the social scientist and to the policy-maker. The American social scientist now increasingly finds himself called upon to "solve" practical problems. But often the problem is stated for him by an executive whose acquaintance with the uses and limits of social science is not intimate. The scientist is called upon to contribute information useful to implement a given policy, but the policy itself is "given," not open to question. This often throws the scientist off the right track, for the data may indicate the need to devise a policy other than that which is "given." Acceptance of such conditions of research may become a threat to the function of scientist *qua* scientist. So long as the social scientist continues to accept a role in which he does not question policies, state problems, and formulate alternatives, the more does he become routinized in the role of bureaucratic technician.

But the American social scientist has seen too many examples in recent history of the intellectual committing moral suicide by allowing himself to be routinized in the service of the directive-giving state. In a world where the threat of the "garrison-prison state" hangs heavy in the political atmosphere, he cannot slip comfortably into the role of bureaucratic technician. It has become apparent that the first condition which social scientists must observe, if they are to make a contribution toward the attainment of a world commonwealth of human dignity, is to retain their own freedom of choice—among goals and values, among policies and decisions, among ways and means. If the social scientist is to contribute significantly to human welfare, he must be ready, willing, and able to ask and seek answers for such questions as: Can we get human welfare without the "welfare state"? If so, how? If not, how can we get the welfare state without the total state?

These are large questions, and there is no intention here of suggesting that American social science has convincing answers to them. They are the sorts of questions, however, toward the solutions of which applied social research seems capable of supplying relevant data. We shall not know just how much of a contribution applied social research can make until we have tried. And we probably shall not make very rewarding efforts until we have subjected the past achievements and failures of applied social research to rigorous self-evaluation. With the surer knowledge of present capabilities and limitations gained from such self-scrutiny, social scientists will better be able to plan the future of their science, by deciding who their clients shall be and how to serve them.

While it is by no means certain that the decisions made by social scientists will determine the future, even of their own science, the making of such decisions will put them further along the path of the developing policy sciences of democracy. And this path, we venture to suggest, may well be the most promising alternative to involuntary suicide.

HUMAN RELATIONS: A "NEW" DISCIPLINE OR INTEGRATIVE FORCE? *Robert Chin*

THE purposes of this paper are (a) to describe some current usages of the term "human relations," including our specific working definition; (b) to analyze the forces, societal and otherwise, that require this slant; and (c) to examine the meaning of "disciplinary," "interdisciplinary" and "multidisciplinary" efforts in human relations.

Usages of the Term "Human Relations"

1. *Interdisciplinary:* A probably typical instance of this use of the term occurs with the Institute of Human Relations at Yale University. This seminal group has conducted various cross-disciplinary researches and studies and has been influential in defining a pattern of inclusion of member disciplines: psychoanalysis, behaviorist psychology, and anthropology.

2. *Industrial:* As management people and social scientists collaborated in efforts to study and improve industrial organizations, there grew up a definition of "human relations" that is still current. Elton Mayo and his collaborators "discovered" the influence of human-social factors upon production in work settings and set off studies in industrial sociology, usually called "human relations in industry." This use of "human relations," then, specifies an approach to the study of organizations: a focus on the social system involved when a group of people work together and the effects of that social system on performance and attitude.

3. *General Education:* A relatively popular use of the term occurs in colleges and universities, where "general education,"—cross-disciplinary courses usually introductory in psychology, sociology, and anthropology are labeled "human relations." These courses vary from homogenized knowledge that wipes out boundary lines of disciplines to various levels of sophistication in relating the disciplines of social and behavioral sciences to each other.

4. *Intergroup Relations and Advice on Interpersonal Problems:* Two usages on the practice side should be noted. The field of intergroup relations and its practitioner agencies have often defined their efforts as "human relations." Problems of prejudice, discrimination, and community relations are thus denoted as problems of human relations, and agencies concerned with these are called human relations agencies. A second practice use of the term

Prepared for the Pro-Seminar in Human Relations, Boston University Human Relations Center, Research Papers and Technical Notes, No. 5. Used by permission.

occurs at the journalistic level: "human relations" is advice-giving to help solve personal and relational problems. Both of these usages imply the presence of conflict or the inadequate realization of some goals and values, and the role of a helper to the person, group, or community in "trouble."

5. *Planned Change, Science and Practice:* Human relations is defined as the study and practice of planned social change. This is the orientation we shall follow. In a sense, this approach incorporates three trends: interdisciplinary efforts in the social sciences; interprofessional efforts in the fields of practice; and cross-disciplinary and cross-professional efforts joining theory and practice. It coordinates available resources, intellectual, technological, and ethical, so as to formulate and test strategies of change. It builds upon a theory of change some required modifications so as to formulate a theory for changing, theory from the change-agent's, not the observer's, viewpoint.

Integrative Forces behind Human Relations

The forces lying behind the push towards interdisciplinary and interprofessional work lie in several areas. We shall attempt to state these in terms applicable to both social scientist and social practitioner. First and foremost have been the confronting problems—a situation where real and novel social-cultural questions and alternatives are forcibly brought to the focus of decision. As our society has increased in complexity, specialization brought about the development of multiple disciplines—many tongues—and many helping professions. The parson and the barber of olden times have become the social worker, counselor, recrea-

tionist, educator, health educator, religious educator, and minister, doctor, surgeon, physical therapist, nurse, along with a whole host of related disciplines of knowledge. We agree wholeheartedly that development of knowledge depends upon the process of abstraction, and of "finding out more and more about less and less." But such fragmentation and specialization affect the esthetic, philosophical, and scholarly stances of the mind demanding integration, not to mention the stance of doubting young minds, our students, who ask for some reassurance that orderliness in the world does exist. We accept the necessity of "spending our intellectual lives trying to put together what we have conceptually put asunder." On the practitioner side, the increased specialization has brought about "team concepts"—in the church, the health fields, education, and the community. The "case" requiring action will not stand still, nor allow itself to be neatly compartmentalized into the "pure" conceptual framework of any one man of knowledge.

Second, a violent jolt has shaken us recently in the area of personal and group values. Challenges to our personal, group, and cultural values of democracy, of progress, of optimism have occurred in various minor ways before, as from the muckrakers of the 1900's or the protest literature of Jack London. But the tremendous impact of the great depression, the rise of totalitarianism, two convulsive World Wars, the amorality of increasingly powerful technical aspects of life, the discomfort of the individual in handling his ambivalences about interdependency—manifested as battles between "conformity" and "individualism"—the perceived failure of moral and religious preachments in recent years, has led to a host of jeremiads about the "crisis of our times." We have been searching for a way out, for an acceptance of the tragedy of action, for a mode of decompartmentalizing the self and professional roles, for a personal and group value system. The physicist starts to examine the limitations of his concept of the role of scientist in nuclear energy, the psychologist examines values in relationship to mental health and "control" over people, the planner studies the democratic, cooperative work process as an alternative to the totalitarian efficiency of "crash programs"; all move parallel to the practitioner's concern with a justification for his value assumptions in his work, as an executive, a nurse, a social worker, a minister, an educator, a community organizer, etc. These value challenges have been met with a partial recognition of the role of other fields in assisting and supporting one's redefinitions. Perhaps getting together with other fields can illuminate my problems, or at least provide supportive strength for my gropings, goes the thought.

A third source of disturbance has been the inherent frustration of application of knowledge and of technique. Why don't we get more success? Are we patching holes while new ones develop? Do our applications make a difference? Business is good—practitioners have lots of clients—but we wonder if other procedures are not just as useful? And the social scientist, when called on to act or to advise policy makers on programs of action, finds his own amateurishness disturbing. He finds himself in deep waters. Look at the historians who in advising the government on foreign policy may suddenly find themselves held accountable when failure occurs.

These forces give rise to motivations for reorganizing our knowledge about processes of change and for refocusing professional role involvements and values.

Discipline, Interdiscipline, and Multidiscipline Approaches

Let us return to one of the major trends as a reaction to these forces: the development of a potential discipline of "human relations" and/or a new profession of "change-agents." Those who think of a "new" profession point to the special problems involved in the operations of a consultant who is helping with change from outside the boundaries of a social system undergoing planned change. In looking for a professional "home," such practitioners may join together and establish a homeland for themselves, since the present professions do not meet their needs. Change-agents, perforce, are multidisciplinary. For example, the intergroup-relations officials in communities are working at community organization (social work), information and attitude change (education), community analysis (sociology, anthropology, etc.), and political action (law, political science). The adult educator takes on many functions as he works with training programs in schools, colleges, in the community, in industry, in foreign countries under technical assistance programs. The training directors, the applied researchers, are potential participants since they are to some major degree "alienated" or "anomic" in their present professional bases. But granted potential members, it seems to me that a profession cannot be established by fiat. It needs more than a name and an association. I suggest that a profession needs a unique conceptual approach and a unique set of goals for it to earn the right to its title. Thus, the building of a new discipline of knowledge must accompany any attempt to organize a profession.

Let us look at a morphology of so-called integrative or interdisciplinary work. First, there is one kind of imperialistic effort that erects a new conceptual framework which "takes over" the others. A new conceptual framework, the hallmark of any discipline, may become so productive that in subsuming traditional statements of problems the new interstitial discipline becomes a major approach and separate discipline. Such a claim may occur as the heightened morale and enthusiasm of its participants lead them to see their field as the "queen" discipline subsuming others. Disciplines, whether theology, sociology, philosophy, psychology, anthropology or psychoanalysis, have claimed overarching significance for their fields at various times in history. For example, Parsons works out a framework for institutional behavior called a "Theory of Action," which he claims can fit any of the behavioral sciences.

Second, another approach builds a framework that bridges two or more disciplines and becomes another discipline through competitive merit. For example, social psychology dwells upon the psychological dynamics of the individual in his social and group settings and is elbowing its way into a busy and sprawling field.

A third approach to interdisciplinary collaboration is the "import brokerage" activities—the borrowing of a useful concept, idea, etc., to import into one's own framework of analysis. For example, political science imported public opinion research into its field.

A fourth approach defines its problem in limited size, chooses a limited size theory, a middle-range theory, as its focus. For example, a communication theory may integrate relevant ideas from sociology, psychology, engineering, electronics, and so on. Or child-care theory may interrelate psychology of socialization, cross-cultural materials, sociology of family, health and pediatrics, and religious beliefs. Another illustration is provided by Lewin's concept of quasi-stationary equilibrium as a diagnostic tool in understanding change.

Finally, a fifth approach locates the common philosophy of the science issues, meta-conceptual assumptions, or methodology and procedures of several disciplines or fields. Suzanne Langer, for example, sees the process of symbolization and abstraction in a variety of fields such as art, anthropology, and language. Whitehead interrelates a variety of physical sciences under the concept of "organism." Or the general systems theorists see common conceptual modes of analysis or models of thought in psychology, sociology, economics and political science by generalizing the idea of "system."

The development of a theory for changing is to some degree proceeding on all these fronts of interdisciplinary or integrative efforts. We do not have an overarching conceptual framework proclaiming itself to be the "queen discipline," although some might say that any attempt at a common conceptual orientation for planned change is *ipso facto* an imperialistic venture that denies the uniqueness of social work, education, therapy, management, and so forth. The second approach may be a real possibility in the future development of a conceptual discipline which bridges the separate disciplines and fields of practice. Borrowing ideas, concepts, and methodology and incorporating them into an existing discipline or field of practice is proceeding rapidly, as shown by representatives of the social sciences located in professional schools of business, education, social work, and so forth. Or a psychologist may import anthropological concepts and data, a psychoanalyst bring in sociological concepts. The fourth approach is illustrated by a theory of influence, or attitude change, or notions such as "social contract" between change-agent and client or "conflict resolution" between people, groups, and nations. In these we find limited aspects of a theory for changing, studies that cross disciplinary lines and various institutional situations of practice. The last approach to integration is seen in the analysis of the common models of system and development in social science and social practice, or in the similar value choices

confronting the practitioner of science and of action.

In examining these integrative efforts, we are not saying that these are the only approaches to the common task of studying planned change. We might reformulate our original problem and look instead for theories of changing in many disciplines. A multidisciplinary orientation allows for autonomy of each discipline and field, for formulating its approach to changing. In so doing it does not bring about premature marriages of not yet potent partners or arouse unrealistic fears about the futility or the fertility of interdisciplinary integrations.

"Human relations" as a field of inquiry and practice will probably develop along the lines of a "new" discipline, an "integrative" discipline, and along the parallel paths of "multidisciplinary" efforts, simultaneously. Whether its major course of development will be along one or another line is hard to say. Hence the question mark in the title.

✧✧✧✧✧✧✧✧✧✧✧✧✧✧✧✧✧✧✧ THE PRACTICE OF SCIENCE AND THE SCIENCE OF PRACTICE

Ernest Greenwood

Introduction

I WILL discuss the characteristics of two sets of activities in society, viz., science and technology, and their relationship to each other, as these are

manifested in the social sciences and in the practices, more specifically in sociology and in social work. The complex of activities to which we refer as science and technology, respectively, have been institutionalized in the sense

From Ernest Greenwood, "The Practice of Science and the Science of Practice." Presented as a University Lecture at Brandeis University in October 1959, and published as one of the Brandeis University Papers in Social Welfare by The Florence Heller Graduate School for Advanced Studies in Social Welfare, 1960. Abridged and used by permission.

that scientists and technologists behave similarly wherever science and technology exist. A cluster of role behaviors has developed around each of these activities, which possesses sufficient stability to render it describable. In describing these clusters my plan of presentation will be as follows. First, I shall define the distinguishing difference between science and technology, so that we might be clear about our subject matter. Then I shall describe the primary activities of scientists and technologists; in the case of science this being theory-building, in the case of technology, problem-solving. Lastly, I will attempt to throw a bridge between science and technology by mapping out a border area where scientists and technologists might collaborate to mutual advantage.

Science versus Technology

FUNCTION OF SCIENCE

The purpose of scientific activity is the description and explanation of nature in all its manifestations. The social sciences differ from the physical and biological sciences in their attempts to describe the highest organization of nature, viz., the characteristics and products of human behavior in the context of culture. While the object of study of every social science is the same, each approaches it from a separate frame of reference. This artificial partialization of the social reality is justified on the grounds of efficiency. The social world is much too complex to be properly observed *in toto* by any one discipline, so that a division of labor is needed. The result is more knowledge than otherwise would be possible. However, the increase in knowledge is purchased at a cost, viz.,

its great fragmentation and the consequent difficulty of achieving an integrated understanding of the social world as a whole. In summary, the primary aim of science is an understanding of nature better than common sense can yield us.

FUNCTION OF TECHNOLOGY

The term technology refers to all disciplines designed to achieve controlled changes in natural relationships by means of procedures that are scientifically based. Convention makes a sharp distinction between those technologists who work with material objects and those who handle human beings. The former are referred to as engineers; the latter, as practitioners. Thus, physicians and dentists are called practitioners and not engineers. Some types of practitioners are, however, called human engineers. Social work is one variety of the species practice within the genus technology. Technologists are characterized by their skill in the application of knowledge to the solution of the problems that occur to human beings. This highlights the contrast between the social sciences and the practices. The scientist's prime aim is the description of the social world; the practitioner's prime aim is the control of that world.

Henceforth in this paper I shall employ the term practice instead of the term technology.

The Theory Construction Function of Science

SCIENCE AS THEORY BUILDING

Having defined science, let me describe in more specific language the nature of the scientific activity. The end product of the collective efforts of scientists within a given discipline is a system of internally consistent propositions which describe and explain the phenomena that constitute the subject matter of that discipline. This system is called a body of *theory*. The function of all science is to construct theories about the what, the how, and the why of the natural world. There is some current misunderstanding regarding this function of science, many laymen believing that only philosophers theorize and that scientists "stick close to facts". I wish to dwell a bit on the theory-construction focus of science. In this connection it will prove clarifying if I were to distinguish between two levels of knowledge with which scientists are concerned. On the first level are first-order facts called *empirical generalizations;* on the second and higher level are the explanations or interpretations of these facts called *theory*. These constitute two orders of abstraction.

NATURE OF EMPIRICAL GENERALIZATIONS

To make clear the distinction between these two orders of abstraction, let me present you with a few examples of an empirical generalization. Thus:

a. In Western societies Jews commit fewer suicides than Gentiles, and Catholics commit fewer suicides than Protestants.

b. American middle-class wives participate in communal health and welfare activities more than their husbands.

c. In cities key commercial facilities concentrate at points of convergence of transportation lines.

d. Juvenile delinquency rates are higher in urban census tracts with lower median monthly rentals.

An empirical generalization may be defined as a proposition about a class of units which describes the uniform recurrence of two or more factors among them. As the term empirical implies, such generalizations are derived inductively by actual observation of the class members. The procedures pursued in their derivation can be operationalized and textbooks on research method are written to describe them; these involve scaling, sampling, controlled observation, data manipulation, application of statistical tests, et cetera. Given time and patience, there is no limit to the number of hitherto unsuspected empirical generalizations, or first-order facts, that one could discover about the social world. The body of knowledge of a science, however, consists of more than empirical generalizations.

DESCRIPTION VERSUS EXPLANATION

That shrewd critic of the sociological scene, Robert Bierstedt, in a brilliant article, entitled "A Critique of Empiricism in Sociology," puts the matter in the following form.[1] Surveys, he states, have amassed an assortment of facts about bread consumption in the United States. Thus: Americans are consuming decreasing amounts of homemade and increasing amounts of factory-made bread. Most Americans prefer white to dark bread. Men consume more bread than women. Adolescents consume more bread than other age groups. Negroes consume more bread than Whites. Rural dwellers consume more bread than urban dwellers. Low income families consume more bread than high income families. This factual list might be extended without

[1] Robert Bierstedt, "A Critique of Empiricism in Sociology," *American Sociological Review*, Vol. 14, October 1949, pp. 584–592.

adding significantly to our comprehension of the American bread consumption phenomenon. To achieve the latter requires a formulation that will tie together these discrete generalizations and will explain their interrelationships. Such a formulation would constitute a theory of American bread consumption.

The function of social scientists is to develop theories which will explain such social phenomena as bread consumption, alcoholism, class conflict, crime, drug addiction, juvenile delinquency, marital discord, population migration, suicide, technological change, urban growth, et cetera. In constructing theory, the scientist uses empirical generalizations as building blocks.

AN EXAMPLE OF THEORY BUILDING

I would like to present an idealized description of theory construction taken from Durkheim's work on the social aetiology of suicide. Although now over a half century old, it still remains an impeccable model of theory construction.[2] I have deliberately selected an example at a relatively simple level of theory, thereby ignoring so-called grand and all-embracing theories.

Durkheim begins his search for the societal cause of suicide by casting his net far and wide, garnering all the available facts about the problem. The data yield him a series of empirical generalizations. Careful scrutiny of Durkheim's volume reveals over three

dozen such generalizations which assume a wide variety. Let me present some of them:

a. Countries predominantly Protestant in population have higher suicide rates than countries predominantly Catholic.

b. Christians have higher suicide rates than Jews.

c. Countries with high literacy rates have higher suicide rates than countries with low literacy.

d. The liberal professions as a group have a higher suicide rate than the manual occupations.

e. The unmarried have a higher suicide rate than the married.

f. The divorced have a higher suicide rate than the married.

g. The childless married have a higher suicide rate than the married with children.

h. Average size of family is inversely related to the suicide rate.

Having extracted these empirical generalizations from the data, Durkheim next, in essence, asks the question: What common thread runs through these generalizations? What do Protestants, high literacy countries, liberal professions, the unmarried, the divorced, the childless, have in common that should make for higher suicide rates among them than in their opposite classes? At this point Durkheim begins to speculate, and his speculation bears recapitulation.

If Protestants are more prone to suicides than Catholics, religious differences must be held accountable. Protestantism permits individualism and free inquiry, while Catholicism brooks no scrutiny by the faithful. The more binding the creed, the more unified the religious group and the more attached is the individual to the group. The atmosphere permitted by Protestantism weakens the traditional beliefs that

---

[2] Emile Durkheim, *Suicide. A Study in Sociology* (New York: The Free Press of Glencoe, 1951). Translation by John A. Spaulding and George Simpson. Durkheim's theory of suicide presented in this paper is a highly abstracted version of the original, necessitated by space requirements. Any distortions in the theory are the responsibility of this writer.

solidify the religious group. That group discipline exerts a preservative influence is borne out by the case of the Jews, a cohesive minority living in compact communities, with a low suicide rate. Attachment to a group must be a potent factor in the suicide phenomenon as indicated by the marital correlates of suicide. Note how the unmarried state encourages suicide and how the disruption of marriage by divorce and death increases its chances. Close examination of the facts reveals that even more preservative than the conjugal relationship between the spouses is the familial relationship between parents and children. In fact, the more children the better. The common thread that runs through these empirical generalizations is clear. A well-integrated group holds its members by strong bonds, preventing them from evading their social obligations by self-elimination, at the same time providing them the support to enable them to perform their obligations in the face of otherwise disabling personal stress. Where group solidarity is weak, the individual feels detached from the group and is thrown on his own feeble resources to sustain him in his personal frustrations.

This, highly condensed, is Durkheim's theory of the social cause of suicide. The theory may now be summarized into a single proposition, i.e., a law of suicide: *Suicide is a function of the degree of group integration which provides the psychic support to group members for handling acute stress.*

NATURE OF THEORY BUILDING

Durkheim's method epitomizes the scientific process. From a host of apparently disconnected first-order facts he theorizes to a law. He moves from the facts to an abstract proposition which interprets the interrelationship among them. Note the difference in levels of abstraction between the law and the empirical generalizations. Note how much more abstract is the proposition with which he terminates the theorizing process from the propositions with which he initiates it. Theory may thus be defined as a systematic interpretation in abstract terms of a generalizable trend that prevails within a set of varied facts, explaining the interrelationship among them. Law is the summarization of the theory in causal terms.

As indicated earlier, the derivation of empirical generalizations can be operationalized, but I have yet to find a textbook that will operationalize the theorizing process. The interpretive process, the development of a formulation which will account for a series of facts, is essentially a free-wheeling, speculative one. It is an inferential process whereby the inquiring mind churns the available information over and over, employing all the logical devices and bringing to bear upon it any and all kinds of relevant knowledge. The process allows for a considerable play of the imagination, and the final formulation bears the personal imprint of its formulator.

VALIDATION OF THEORY

What is there to prevent this theorizing process from degenerating into unbridled speculation and its product from becoming phantasy with little link to reality? It must not be forgotten that the spring-board from which the theorizing takes off consists of hard facts, viz., empirical generalizations derived from observations. Then too, the canons of science require that after the theory has been formulated, it must be subjected to empirical validation. This consists of making an extrapolation from the theory in the form of a prediction and testing by observation its correctness. Predictability is the scientist's criterion of validity. If our theoretical formulations of what causes suicides, snow storms, droughts, crime waves, and economic depressions, are correct, we should be able to predict where and when instances of these phenomena will occur, and the number of correct predictions should deviate decidedly from chance. Thus, if Durkheim's theory of suicide is true, then were we to locate highly and poorly integrated groups, other than those he observed, we should find the suicide rate to be lower in the former than in the latter. The proposition expressing this prediction is a *hypothesis* amenable to empirical research. To test it, we would have to locate social groups, apply an integration scale to them to separate the well-integrated from the poorly-integrated ones, and, assuming reliable suicide statistics, note whether the former groups have lower suicide rates than the latter. Therefore, a research hypothesis in science is a deduction from a theory, and its verification is a validation of the theory from which it sprang.

PURE RESEARCH

In his efforts to develop theory, the social scientist need not be concerned with its practical utility. His motivations are not practical, but intellectual and aesthetic. On the intellectual side he is curious to know nature and to picture it accurately. On the aesthetic side he seeks to develop formulations that have a certain elegance, completeness, and internal consistency, and

are efficient in the sense of accounting for a maximum variety of facts with a minimum number of concepts. Scientific investigation, the object of which is knowledge for its own sake, is referred to as pure or basic research.

The Problem-Solving Function of Practice

CONTROL FUNCTION OF PRACTICE

We may now turn to an examination of the nature of practice and of the manner in which practitioners work. The aim of practice is control. Every practice eventually develops a body of knowledge which serves as a guide to the practitioner. This knowledge is also abstract and generalized so that we can refer to it as a body of theory. To distinguish it from scientific theory, we will call it practice theory. However, there is a difference; scientific theory is descriptive, practice theory is prescriptive. Scientific theory consists of laws describing and explaining nature; practice theory consists of principles prescribing ways of controlling nature. The proposition that every organized group eventually develops a subculture of its own, is a scientific law. The proposition that every therapeutic plan must consider the subculture of the client is a principle of practice.

The problem that confronts a practitioner is customarily a state of disequilibrium that requires rectification. The practitioner examines the problem situation, on the basis of which he prescribes a solution, that, hopefully, reestablishes the equilibrium, thereby solving the problem. This process is customarily referred to as diagnosis and treatment.

NATURE OF PRACTICE THEORY

Let us examine the implications of the terms diagnosis and treatment. To diagnose a problem implies that, on the basis of certain factors observed in it, it is placed within a typology, or a classification scheme, in which each type represents a constellation of factors. A practice develops a refined diagnostic typology that embraces the gamut of problems confronted by the discipline. There has been formulated for each diagnostic or problem type a description of its properties, behavior, aetiology, and life-cycle, and a prescription of the steps needed to ascertain whether a specific problem is classifiable within the type. These propositions make up the diagnostic principles. In the diagnostic process the practitioner employs the principles of diagnosis to uncover factor after factor in a specific problem situation until the compound of factors which emerges begins to match one of the types in the typology.

A practice also develops a typology of treatment procedures. Here, too, a series of generalizing propositions, or principles of treatment, has been formulated, which describe operationally the stages in the treatment, indicating when the treatment is appropriate and specifiying the criteria whereby success or failure of the treatment may be determined. The diagnostic and treatment typologies are employed together. Each type description of the diagnostic typology contains implications for a certain type of treatment. The practitioner uses treatment as the empirical test of his diagnosis, success corroborating the diagnosis, failure negating it and thus requiring rediagnosis. The principles of diagnosis and of treatment constitute the principles of practice, i.e., with their elaborations and implications constitute practice theory.

BEHAVIOR CHARACTERISTICS OF PRACTITIONERS

The control function of a practice is bound to exert effects upon the ways of thinking and of behaving of the practitioner. In the limited time available to me I shall briefly describe four behavior characteristics of practitioners. These relate to the action and the individual focus, and the artistic and the intuitive components that typify their approach to their tasks.

Action focus. A practice is action-oriented. A social worker's function is to bring to bear upon a problem situation the accumulated knowledge about human behavior and social institutions, in order thereby to initiate certain social psychological processes in that situation, the end product of which is a resolution of the problem. This function stands in sharp contrast to that of the scientist. A scientist achieves success in his discipline by producing some new knowledge. The goal of the practitioner is not the expansion of knowledge, but its practical application for control. The practitioner can achieve success in his practice by superior industry in mastering what is already known and by superior skill in applying what he has thus mastered. Even in the most scientifically oriented of the practices, viz., medicine, the typical practitioner is not a producer, but a consumer of scientific knowledge.

Individual focus. The practitioner is individual focused; at any one moment he is engrossed in a particular case. As a physician he is treating a specific patient; as a social worker he is helping a specific client. When a scientist formulates a generalization describing a class of events or of individuals, he must, in large measure, ignore idiosyncracies and deviants—these he calls "erratic events". The practitioner, however, ignores individual peculiarities at his own peril. Any therapeutic plan which is indifferent to the peculiar vulnerabilities of the patient is an invitation to failure. True, the practitioner looks for characteristics that a case has in common with others, in order to be able to classify it within a diagnostic type. This will suggest the treatment principle that he might apply to the situation at hand. But he must also be attuned to characteristics that make this situation unique. Therefore, the practitioner must modify the treatment principles to fit the needs of the individual.

Artistic component. Every practice possesses a heavy ingredient of the artistic. This derives from the fact that successful practice requires, in addition to the intellectual mastery of the practice theory, the skill in applying and concretizing the abstract theory. This skill is personal, through which the practitioner expresses his individuality. It thus differs from the body of practice theory of the discipline which is shared and commonly held. Art injects the creative factor into practice; a practitioner rarely approaches a problem situation as though he were about to conduct a rigidly structured laboratory experiment. Hence the practices are often referred to as the practical or the scientific arts.

Intuitive component. Every practice involves a component of intuition, which may be defined as understanding reached without conscious reasoning. A practitioner is often confronted with a problem for which there are no guides in practice theory. He cannot afford the luxury of withholding action because of the insufficiency of validated knowledge. It is a universal fact of every practice, including the most scientifically oriented practice of medicine, that clients want immediate action even if it be on the basis of less than ideal knowledge. Every seasoned practitioner carries with him a fund of knowledge acquired through lengthy experience, which he has never systematized and verbalized. This knowledge, often uncommunicable, is his personal property, and he falls back upon it when systematic guides are lacking. In such instances he is operating intuitively. Resort to intuition is inevitable in a practice, because the growth of practice theory cannot keep pace with the novelty of the problems created by the dynamics of social life.

It should be apparent from the foregoing description that in their modes of operation practitioners and scientists are at polar ends of the behavior continuum.

A Suggested Science-Practice Relationship

In the time remaining to me I will attempt to map out a middle ground between science and practice where scientists and practitioners can meet to their mutual advantage.

THE HYBRIDS

My descriptions of the scientist and of the practitioner might have conveyed a picture of internal homogeneity greater than warranted by the facts. Thus, while the predominant preoccupation of scientists is with pure research, there is a minority among them which is more enticed by applied research. These scientists are called into industrial, commercial, military, educational, health, and welfare organizations to apply scientific theory toward the solution of new problems arising in these settings. Similarly, while the predominant preoccupation of practitioners is with action and control, there is a minority among them which is more enticed by theory construction. These practitioners are the ones who are willing to divert their time and energy from practice to research that results in the expansion of practice theory. These two breeds, the applied-oriented scientist and the theory-oriented practitioner, tread a common ground in the middle region of the behavior continuum; they can join forces to their mutual advantage.

I will illustrate my contention with the case of social science and social work; my thesis is that from the viewpoint of each of these disciplines there is much to be gained by collaboration along this middle region.

FROM THE VIEWPOINT OF SOCIAL SCIENCE

When a social scientist is called in by the administrator for assistance in developing a solution for a new problem type, he first relates the problem type to some large class of phenomena that has already been described and explained by his discipline. Let us suppose that the schools of social work seek more effective methods for indoctrinating students with the social work philosophy and for developing in them the professional self. The social scientist will see this problem as falling within the more general concept of acculturation, and he will bring to bear upon it all the theory on acculturation that his discipline has developed. He

will then try to derive possible solutions to the problem in the form of extrapolations from the theory, which will take the following logical form: If the theory of acculturation is correct, then if we apply such and such action to this indoctrination problem, such and such results should follow.

Note that in the process of applying social science theory the scientist tests its validity. For if a theory is a true representation of the reality that it purports to explain, then it should yield an extrapolation that will be a correct explanation of the problem and a reliable guide to its solution. A theory that cannot be applied is a questionable theory. If the proposed solution does actually work, the theory that yielded it has been to that extent corroborated; if it fails, the failure suggests the need for revising the theory. Therefore, while the immediate purpose of applied social science research is utilitarian, the ultimate result is to validate and refine social science theory. In the process social science laws become converted into principles of practice. The practice setting thus offers to the scientist a laboratory with live situations and potentials for experimentation. It opens up to him new sources of data contributing toward the corroboration and extension of scientific theory.

FROM THE VIEWPOINT OF SOCIAL WORK

Social work practice theory has to date been built in a trial-and-error, crudely empirical, and highly pragmatic manner. It was developed by practitioners, untutored in the rules of research, who relied solely upon the richness of their insights and upon the wisdom derived from day-to-day experiences on the job. The trend must now be altered. It is axiomatic that effective control must be grounded in thorough understanding. Understanding, in turn, consists of description and explanation, which is the function of science. Therefore, practice theory ultimately must rest on scientific theory. In other words, practice principles must be linked to and fashioned out of social science laws by means of research.

The problems that the social worker subjects to diagnosis and the treatment procedures that he applies to them are basically species of social phenomena and social processes which, as genera, the social sciences have long been describing and explaining. Every problem type in social work is ultimately classifiable under some large class of phenomena already studied by social scientists. The problem of rehabilitating a delinquent gang is a species of the general phenomenon of altering group motivation that has been examined by social psychologists; and the problem of the pauperization of public assistance recipients is a species of the general phenomenon of dependence-independence that has been examined by psychologists. There is scarcely a problem type in social work practice around which there has not developed some social science theory, meagre though at times it may be, and to which social scientists cannot contribute some clarification. But the link between the practice problem and the scientific theory must be sought for systematically, because the conversion of social science laws into principles of social work practice can only be achieved via research.

It should be apparent from what I have said that collaborative effort between the applied-oriented social scientist and the theory-oriented social work practitioner can produce benefits to their respective disciplines. The notion of such collaboration is not original with me. It has already been institutionalized in medicine. Medical research is conducted by teams consisting of two kinds of personnel. First, there are the physicians who prefer to devote all or most of their time to research rather than to the direct treatment of patients. Secondly, there are the physical and biological scientists who prefer to devote all or most of their time to applied rather than pure research. This is the model that I propose for social science and social work.

NEED FOR INSTITUTIONAL READJUSTMENTS

To bring about this collaborative effort on a scale sufficiently large to produce substantial benefits to both social science and social work, will require some institutional readjustments, a discussion of which probably does not belong in a paper on the logic of the science-practice relationship, as this purports to be. Such a treatment falls within the sociology of the science-practice relationship. In this connection I will make one concluding point. If we are convinced of the potential benefits of the science-practice collaboration, then we must create the social structure with its built-in rewards to foster and promote it. We cannot rely on isolated applied-oriented scientists and theory-oriented practitioners to collaborate on a voluntary, individual, and informal basis. Without societal supports to reinforce personal motivation such individual efforts will be spasmodic, haphazard, and abortive. We must, therefore, experiment with new forms of social organization and new social roles.

❖❖❖❖❖❖❖❖❖❖❖❖❖❖❖❖❖❖❖❖ THEORETICAL REQUIREMENTS OF
THE APPLIED SOCIAL SCIENCES

Alvin W. Gouldner

Iᴛ seems reasonable to assume that the applied social sciences develop more rapidly under some conditions than others. The aim of this paper is to take this simple assumption seriously, and to identify the theoretic and conceptual tools most conducive to the maturation of the applied social sciences. The ultimate objective is to codify these, so that they can constitute a paradigm useful for the systematic inspection of the different applied fields. Such a paradigm could provide a working model of what is "par" for the course. At the same time, it could also indicate those areas in pure social science where further work might bridge the gap between it and applied efforts.

Applied social science has distinctive intellectual requirements largely because it is exposed to special exigencies and tensions. Its theories and concepts not only have to pass inspection before the bar of science, but they must also prove serviceable in coping with this specific set of social tensions. It is not enough, therefore, to examine the intellectual tools of applied social science in terms of their manifest scientific functions as technical instruments. They must also be considered in the light of their latent social functions for the peculiar system of human relations in which they are implicated. In this way,

it may be seen that certain of the devices of applied social science, which sometimes seem scientifically senseless, are at least sociologically sensible.

Attention is directed to two historically different planes of work in applied social science. One of these is the ongoing work in such areas as race relations, housing, industrial sociology, criminology, or mass communications research. The second plane involves inspection of the work of such classic contributors to the applied social sciences as Karl Marx, Emile Durkheim, and Sigmund Freud.

The Model Outlined

Unlike pure science, the applied social sciences are not oriented solely to values intrinsic to science—such as increased information, objectivity, prediction, parsimony, replication, and the like. Applied social science is characterized by an orientation to the values of laymen, as well as of scientists. These lay values, extrinsic to science as such, are regarded by the applied social scientist as legitimate points of orientation for his professional and scientific work.

There seem to be four such value-foci on which the work of applied social scientists centers:

From Alvin W. Gouldner, "Theoretical Requirements of the Applied Social Sciences,"
American Sociological Review, Vol. 22, No. 1, February 1957, pp. 92–102. Some footnotes
omitted. Abridged and used by permission.

1. The reduction of various forms of social deviancy, as exemplified in efforts to rehabilitate criminals or juvenile delinquents

2. Improvement of the efficiency or effectiveness with which diverse lay goals are pursued, as exemplified in the work of some industrial sociologists or applied anthropologists

3. The reduction of tensions or conflicts, such as the work of some race relations specialists

4. The reduction of tensions that a group experiences in relation to its "environment," such as those found in personnel testing, market research, and public relations surveys.

Applied social scientists are more likely to use laymen as a reference group in organizing their professional work, and their work is more likely to occur in the context of, and be influenced by, their relationship with laymen.[1] For these reasons the applied social scientist is constrained to include among his dependent variables certain lay "social problems." As part of his work the applied social scientist is ultimately concerned with identifying those independent variables which can not only account for, but which can remedy, these "social problems." Preliminary though the model is at this point, it may yet be sufficient to permit discussion of why Marx, Durkheim, and Freud have been characterized as applied social scientists.

[1] It should be emphasized that the focus in this paper is on those characteristics common to various efforts at applied social science. There is no intention to suggest that there is but one kind of applied social science, or only one model of its social system. In a companion piece ["Explorations in Applied Social Science," *Social Problems,* 3 (January, 1956), pp. 169–181] attention was directed to variations in applied social science, and an effort was made to delineate two sub-models of its social system, the "clinical" and the "engineering."

Freud, Marx, and Durkheim

It is easy to accept Freud as an applied scientist, and, indeed he is widely regarded as the twentieth century's master clinician. However, in viewing Marx as an applied social scientist the stance needed is that of a Machiavellian operationalism. The objective is neither to bury nor to praise him. The assumption is simply that he is better understood for being understood as an applied sociologist. This is in part the clear implication of Marx's *Theses on Feurbach,* which culminate in the resounding 11th thesis: "The philosophers have only interpreted the world in different ways; the point, however, is to change it." This would seem to be the tacit creed of applied scientists everywhere.

Marx is no Faustian, concerned solely with understanding society, but a Promethean who sought to understand it well enough to influence and to change it. He was centrally concerned with the social problems of a lay group, the proletariat, and there can be little doubt that his work is motivated by an effort to reduce their suffering, as he saw it. His diagnosis was that their increasing misery and alienation engendered endemic class struggle; his prognosis claimed that this would culminate in revolution; his therapeutic prescription was class consciousness and active struggle.

Here, as in assessing Durkheim or Freud, the issue is not in whether this analysis is empirically correct or scientifically adequate. Furthermore, whether or not this formulation seems to eviscerate Marx's revolutionary core, as critics on the left may charge, or whether the formulation provides Marx with a new veneer of academic respectability, as critics on the right may allege, is entirely irrelevant from the present standpoint. Insofar as Marx's or any other social scientist's work conforms to a generalized model of applied social science, insofar as it is professionally oriented to the values and social problems of laymen in his society, he may be treated as an applied social scientist.

Despite Durkheim's intellectualistic proclivities and rationalistic pathos, he was too much the product of European turbulence to turn his back on the travail of his culture. "Why strive for knowledge of reality, if this knowledge cannot aid us in life," he asked. "Social science," he said, "can provide us with rules of action for the future." [2] Durkheim, like Marx, conceived of science as an agency of social action, and like him was professionally oriented to the values and problem of laymen in his society. Unless one sees that Durkheim was in some part an applied social scientist, it is impossible to understand why he concludes his monumental study of *Suicide* with a chapter on "Practical Consequences," and why, in the *Division of Labor,* he proposes a specific remedy for anomie.

Durkheim is today widely regarded as a model of theoretic and methodologic sophistication, and is thus usually seen only in his capacity as a pure social scientist. Surely this is an incomplete view of the man who regarded the *practical* effectiveness of a science as its principal justification. To be more fully understood, Durkheim also needs to be seen as an applied sociologist. His interest in religious beliefs and organization, in crime and penology, in educational methods and organization, in suicide and anomie, are not casually chosen problem areas. Nor did he select them only because they provided occasions for the development of his theoretical orientation. These areas were in his time, as they are today problems of indigenous interest to applied sociologists in Western society, precisely because of their practical significance.

Whatever their many differences, Marx, Durkheim, and Freud share the applied social scientist's concern with bringing social science to bear on the problems and values of laymen with a view to remedying their disturbances. In characterizing them as applied social scientists, reference is made to only one of many roles they played. An applied social scientist is a role, and the person playing this role can and does play others, and he may, therefore, also be a pure social scientist as well.

It is in such role-playing terms that these men are regarded as applied social scientists. It is to be expected that their work will bear the impress of the problems and needs of applied social science and may also contain some clues concerning the ways in which these needs can be variously satisfied, even by the applied social sciences today.

Laymen's Hypotheses

In dealing with lay "social problems," the applied social scientist is confronting questions for which laymen often believe they have answers. Laymen usually have some explanation or favored hypotheses concerning the source of their problems. However inadequate the applied social scientist may judge these to be, he cannot blithely ignore them. He must take some of the laymen's favored hypoth-

[2] Emile Durkheim, *The Rules of Sociological Method,* Chicago: University of Chicago Press, 1938, pp. 47 and xxxix.

eses into account if he is to establish or maintain a relationship with them. Thus Marx had to consider whether "love" or Christian Ethics could be regarded as an adequate lever of social change. Durkheim had to consider whether economic poverty could account for suicide, and Freud had to examine whether the prevailing biologistic explanations of mental disturbance were adequate. All of these men had to consider lay hypotheses, even if only to discredit them.

All social scientists, pure or applied, are of course obliged to test competing hypotheses in analyzing a problem. Applied social science, however, necessarily draws some of its competing hypotheses from a distinctive source, namely laymen. The applied social scientist may systematically examine a hypothesis, even if he puts little credence in it, because the resultant research may cement his rapport with a lay group.

The Western Electric studies thus began with experiments testing the effects of improved illumination or rest periods on industrial productivity, for these involved hypotheses then favored by industrial personnel.[3] Recent studies of jury behavior have sought to test hypotheses, favored by the legal profession, which had assumed that "hung juries" could be eliminated by relaxing the unanimity rule. The manifest function of testing independent variables favored by laymen is to provide compliances with lay expectations that strengthen the acceptance of social scientists. The latent function of such tests, however, is to document the in-

adequacy and breakdown of lay hypotheses, thus enlarging the area of intellectual discretion allowable to applied social scientists, and easing their introduction of independent variables that are novel to laymen.

Pure and Applied Science

If the applied social scientist is to find the theories of pure social science useful to him, there need to be in the pure theory some conceptual elements that can be reconceptualized into lay concepts, or vice versa. Unfortunately, however, this is not always the case.

An example may be found in the kind of phenomenon disaster specialists have been studying. Some of the difficulties encountered in the development of disaster research may occur because present pure theory in sociology does not allow for ready reconceptualization of the layman's notion of disaster. What after all is the common meaning of disaster? Webster defines it as "an unforeseen and ruinous mischance or misadventure which happens, often suddenly, either through culpable lack of foresight or through adverse external agency." Among other things, it commonly involves a sudden destruction of the material props of human action—homes, means of transportation, stores, furniture, food supplies, clothing—often, though not always, by the intrusion of sudden changes in the natural environment, such as floods, fires, blizzards, tornadoes, hurricanes, etc.

There are at least three counts on which pure sociological theory today fails to aid in the analysis of this problem: (1) It has very little to say about, and does not systematically deal with, the role of material props. Even the

---

[3] These are referred to as the "customary" statement of the human problems of management in F. J. Roethlisberger and W. J. Dickson, *Management and the Workers*, Cambridge: Harvard University Press, 1939, p. 590.

concept of "culture," which at one time involved reference to material traits, is increasingly defined in terms of normative elements alone. The theoretical location of material props, therefore, becomes steadily obscured as it gets thrust into a residual limbo. (2) Present pure sociological theory has given little thought to the relationship between social or cultural systems, and the so-called natural environment. Anthropologists like Meggers and Steward continue to confront this problem, but sociologists apparently find little of interest in it.[4] (3) A disaster involves not only a change, but usually a fairly sudden one. Pure sociological theory, however, has only begun to develop models adequate to cope with the analysis of change, and is even more removed from the analysis of change tempo involving questions of sudden transition. The problem of change tempo is important to almost all applied social scientists, as the controversy over "gradualistic" desegregation in the South presently dramatizes.[5]

Unless applied social scientists can find existent pure theories containing concepts that can be reconceptualized into independent and dependent variables significant to laymen, they are under pressure to design their own formal theories, into which they can build the necessary bridging concepts. Perhaps the best example of this is Freud's work, which deliberately in-

corporated such lay concepts as "sexuality" in its formal theory, in a sense at least partially convergent with the manner in which it is used in everyday thinking.

The applied social scientist not only focuses on social problems perceivable to laymen but also requires knowledge to remedy them. Applied social science, therefore, is greatly concerned with facilitating the prediction and production of social and cultural change. Regardless of whether the applied social scientist wishes to make workers more efficient, or to transform alcoholics into mild mannered tea-drinkers, or to reshape ethnic bigots into tolerant democratic citizens, he requires knowledge, theories, and concepts, which bear upon the processes of *change,* to help him analyze and facilitate it.

The applied sociologist seeks knowledge that will shed light upon the problems of men in his society and will facilitate their solution. Unlike the pure scientist, who delights in maximizing knowledge either for its own sake or to test hypotheses and extend theories, the applied social scientist will sometimes forgo sources of knowledge, however rich in data they may be, if he fears their use will impede the intended change. For example, psychoanalysts might better verify and extend data derived from their patients by enlisting the aid of the patient's family and friends, but they ordinarily and voluntarily forgo use of such channels. One finds a similar refusal to maximize sources of information in the work of the Tavistock group, the staff of which discourages respondents from communicating information in confidence.[6] The impulse toward change

---

[4] See Betty J. Meggers, "Environmental Limitations on the Development of Culture," *American Anthropologist*, 56 (October, 1954), pp. 801–824; and the collection of essays by Julian H. Steward, *Theory of Culture Change,* Urbana: University of Illinois Press, 1955.

[5] The problem of change tempo and desegregation is cogently examined in Kenneth Clark, "Desegregation: An Appraisal of the Evidence," *Journal of Social Issues,* 9 (1953), pp. 1–76.

[6] Elliott Jaques, *The Changing Culture of a Factory,* New York: Holt, Rinehart and Winston, 1952, p. 3.

dominates and may be at variance with the impulse to know.[7]

Criteria for Concept Selection

If it is to be useful for change purposes, the applied social scientist's knowledge must have certain characteristics, which distinguish it from that of the pure social scientist's. The latter, for example, aims at identifying variables with predictive power, and the more powerful and reliable the prediction, the better. The applied social scientist's criteria for assessing the adequacy of an independent variable include predictive potency but go beyond this, adding certain standards not relevant to the pure scientist. For one, the applied social scientist inspects his independent variables to determine the extent to which they are accessible to control. Since his ultimate objective involves the furtherance of some kind of change, not all independent variables are equally suitable for this purpose, nor is the one with the highest correlation coefficient always the best.

For example, no matter how high an inverse correlation is found between the rate of urbanization and the birth rate, the applied demographer can do little to reduce the birth rate by manipulating the degree of urbanization. Demographers can, however, focus on an item, namely contraceptive materials and information, which they can control, at least in greater measure. Even if urbanization and industrialization are much more highly correlated

with the birth rate than is the degree of available contraceptive material and information, the latter assumes strategic significance because of its controllability. Thus the applied social scientist is concerned not merely with identifying predictively potent independent variables, but also with discovering some that are accessible to control.

There are a number of circumstances in which even a predictively potent independent variable will be of little use to the applied social scientist. One such is where there exists no technology by means of which it can be managed. Therefore, for instance, Huntington's sunspot theory of economic cycles had little appeal to New Deal statesmen. Contrariwise, because Keynesian theory identified a controllable element, the state, which could be used to restore economic equilibrium, it became the dominant economic theory of New Deal liberals. As one writer puts it:

The system of economic thought which has become regnant in the last generation is the Keynesian. . . . Keynesian ideas have been accepted not because they explained more than others but because they provided a set of causal laws whose independent variables were accessible to action in the immediate present.[8]

For similar reasons, students of social disorganization have long been drawn to the hypothesis that there is a "casual linkage between 'bad' housing and social disorganization." This is so, not because they have regarded this hypothesis as possessing a shred of theoretical elegance, but rather because its independent variable was controllable and accessible. In this connection

[7] This classic tension was early recognized by Freud who commented, "It is indeed one of the distinctions of psychoanalysis that research and treatment proceed hand in hand, but still the technique required for the one begins, at a certain point, to diverge from that of the other." Sigmund Freud, *Collected Papers*, Vol. II, London: Hogarth Press, 1949, p. 326.

[8] Lewis S. Feuer, "Causality in the Social Sciences," *Journal of Philosophy*, 51 (November, 1954), pp. 683–684.

one might well inspect Loring's recent research, which appears to have found a correlation between certain indices of social disorganization and the amount of space occupied by a family, or a density factor. Loring's paper convincingly demonstrates that there is no inherent incompatibility between theoretical sophistication and a concern for controllable variables.[9]

Notice that the last two illustrations from demography and housing both invoke the forgotten man of sociological research, elements of so-called "material culture." It may be briefly indicated here that one meaning of Marx's materialism may be reappraised in this light. For while Marx was no crude materialist, there is a substantial sense in which he was impressed with the material props of human action, and stressed their importance. This, it may be guessed, was due as much to his commitment to an applied sociology as to his polemic against Hegel's idealism. For the material props of action are distinguished by their relative accessibility to control. Indeed, in one of its expressions "materialism" might almost be defined as an assertion, not of the ontological importance of "hard" matter, but of the strategic significance of any accessible variable, tangible or not. So-called material factors such as housing space, machines, or contraceptives are of interest to applied sociologists because they are open to control. It is likely that such concepts will continue to be required and highly regarded by applied sociologists.

In race relations research similar concerns with controllable variables are discernible. For reasons similar to those involved in Keynesian econom-

ics, the role of the state and of legal institutions continues to be given great stress by those seeking to modify patterns of ethnic discrimination. This despite the fact that, since Sumner's time, pure sociological theory has given scant analysis to legal institutions. The initial emphasis on the role of "stereotypes" involved a focus on the cognitive aspects of the prejudiced person's orientation to an ethnic minority, in part because these were regarded as the most controllable elements in his orientation. It was assumed that the beliefs bigots held about minorities could be more readily managed than could their affective feeling states, by directing accurate information at those holding the stereotypes. Even an excellent and recent volume on prejudice opens its section on methods of opposing prejudice with a discussion of ways of "eliminating false beliefs."[10] It is likely that the emergence of the concept of "stereotype," conceived of as a learned and not as a biologically given orientation to the minority group, and thus as relatively controllable, did much to foster modern race relations work.

There is a second circumstance in which even a predictively potent independent variable will provide little help to the applied social scientist. This involves situations in which, from the standpoint of the participating laymen, the instrumental management of a variable would violate their values. For example, even though contraceptives are technologically controllable, they are not instrumentally manageable from the value standpoint of a believing Catholic population. Similarly, even though changes in informal or-

[9] William C. Loring, "Housing and Social Disorganization," *Social Problems*, 3 (January, 1956), pp. 160–168.

[10] Gerhart Saenger, *The Social Psychology of Prejudice,* New York: Harper & Brothers, 1953, p. 159.

ganization are technologically feasible, they may violate values that stress that human beings should not be treated as means to an end, thus giving rise to charges of "manipulation." One reason that legal institutions and material props have played such a large part in the work of applied social scientists is that, in a culture such as our own, they are both instrumentally manageable and technologically controllable.

A third circumstance which may limit the value of an independent variable to an applied social scientist is the question of its cost. Utilization of a variable as a change agent always depends, in some measure, on whether or not there is some other variable available that can accomplish the same results with less cost. There is always a question of just how much change one is securing for a given expenditure of scarce resources. These are the kinds of problems that students of mass communication media frequently have to assess. Earlier, they sought to appraise whether it was most economical to use either the newspapers or the radio to communicate a given message. Presently, they may seek to assess how many minutes of radio time are worth a minute of television time. In like manner, Dodd's "Project Revere" seeks to determine the effectiveness of given amounts of a single type of communication stimulus, particularly leaflets, attempting to determine the proportion of a community that will be reached by varying amounts of leaflets.

Finally, it might be added that much of the interest in leadership in the applied social sciences functions to identify presumably efficient loci of intervention for purposes of group or mass persuasion. In Dean and Rosen's cogent *Manual of Intergroup Relations* for example, about a fourth of their 27 propositions, specifying ways and means of reducing discrimination, deal rather directly with the role of leadership.[11]

System Analysis

The applied social scientist's concern with the controllability and relative efficiency of different variables in producing given changes also has implications for the larger kinds of theoretical models he requires and utilizes. These distinctive contingencies dispose the applied social scientist to use models of system analysis, for several reasons: (1) System models forewarn the applied social scientist of the possibility that a change in one part of the system may yield unforeseen and undesirable consequences in another part of the system, due to the interdependence of its elements. (2) System models indicate that changes may be secured in one element, not only by a frontal attack upon it but also by a circumspect and indirect manipulation of more distantly removed variables. These, because of system interdependence, may ultimately produce the desired changes in the target variable.[12] (3) For this reason as well as others, system analysis therefore directs attention to the multiple possibilities of intervention with respect to a single problem.

Yet, insofar as such a model focuses

[11] John P. Dean and Alex Rosen, *A Manual of Intergroup Relations*, Chicago: University of Chicago Press, 1955. Similar implications of the studies of "opinion leaders" are found in Elihu Katz and Paul F. Lazarsfeld, *Personal Influence*, New York: Free Press of Glencoe, 1955.

[12] Robin Williams, *The Reduction of Intergroup Tensions*, New York: The Social Science Research Council, 1947, has by far the most sophisticated discussion of these problems in the context of race relations analysis.

only on the interdependence of elements within a system, it provides no clue, by itself, concerning preferential points of entry into that system. It fails to establish any generalized basis in terms of which the scarce resources available for change may be economically allocated among the diverse components of the system. It fails, in short, to satisfy the applied social scientist's interest in the comparative costs and efficiency of different variables.

Because the resources available for change-efforts are scarce, the applied social scientist requires some basis for assigning weights to different compo nents in the systems with which he deals. He needs some basis for assessing their differential influence in determining various outcomes. If this need occurs in the absence of determinate methods of mathematical resolution, there is a tendency for the system model to break down in monistic, single-factor directions. Thus in both Marx and Freud's work there is, on the one hand, a focus on *systems* of social relations and personality, respectively. On the other hand, however, there is also a tendency monistically to focus on certain factors, such as economic or production relations in Marx's case, or on sexual etiology in Freud's. Such monistic tendencies may be regarded as efforts to adapt to the economic exigencies of applied social science, and not merely as absolute expressions of theoretical preference. Tendencies toward monistic breakdown in the models of applied social science probably also derive, in some measure, from the scientist's relationship with a lay group who may find single-factor analysis more intelligible than system models.

A monistic resolution of the economic exigencies of applied social sci-ence seems to be manifested even in the analyses of a resolute system theorist such as Parsons. In his effort to develop a strategy for changing conquered Germany after World War II, Parsons identifies the economic-occupational structure as "much the most promising as a lever of institutional change . . . [because] it is a highly strategic point in the total structure . . . [and] through its close structural interdependence with kinship and the class structure, change there would have major repercussions in these neighboring areas." [13] Parson's stress here on the economic-occupational structure is surprisingly reminiscent of a Marxian analysis. If such a convergence between Parsons and Marx exists, it is certainly not because Parsons is a Marxist. Parsons converges with Marx because he confronts himself with a problem essentially similar to that to which Marx had persistently committed himself, namely, the introduction of planned change in a society. This necessarily involves questions of the economic allocation of scarce resources and thus requires the choice of efficient points of entry into a system of interdependent variables.

The Theory of Unanticipated Consequences

Still another expression of the applied social scientist's interest in the identification of controllable variables, is to be found in his persistent use of a theory of unanticipated consequences. It is noteworthy that Marx, Durkheim, and Freud, all, developed some version of a theory of unanticipated consequences.

[13] Talcott Parsons, *Essays in Sociological Theory, Pure and Applied,* New York: Free Press of Glencoe, 1949, p. 334.

Marx noted that the events that occur in a society governed by market institutions, and with only casually integrated economic enterprises, could not be predicted on the basis of knowing the actors' individual motives. For the things that happen, said Marx, are often sought by no man. Entrepreneurs seek profit and orient their production to this anticipation, yet their very actions have the unanticipated consequence of generating market gluts and economic depressions.

Durkheim's most prominent use of the theory of unanticipated consequences is in his analysis of suicide. Here he showed that events, which were seemingly understandable as acts of deliberate intention, could be understood as the unforeseen consequences of adherence to certain values. The higher suicide rate of Protestants, for example, is not regarded by Durkheim as due to their deliberate conformity with any cultural prescription concerning suicide, but as the unanticipated consequence of conformity to other values that have no explicit implication for suicide.

Similarly, Freud was interested in the play of unanticipated consequences on a third level, the psychological. In his analysis of *The Psychopathology of Everyday Life,* he sought to show how language lapses and dreams derived from conflicts in individual motivation. Freud observed that human behavior was replete with unanticipated consequences because human personality contained unconscious motivations, which conflicted with the aims of which people were aware.

This convergence of Marx, Durkheim, and Freud in the identification and analysis of unanticipated consequences would seem to stem in part from their common participation in a system of applied social science, which exerts pressure to focus on the problematic concerns of laymen. The lay vocabulary is filled with terms indicating an interest in discriminating between foreseen and unforeseen occurrences. In the lay vocabulary, moreover, the unexpected is almost equivalent to the undesirable. Thus synonyms (in Roget's) for unexpected are: bolt from the blue, bewilderment, disappointment, disillusionment, miscalculation, to be caught unawares or off one's guard, stunned, staggered, and the like.

Unforeseen consequences are not, of course, always undesirable to the layman, as indicated by a term such as a "pleasant surprise." Nevertheless, other things equal, that is, given two identical events, one foreseen and the other unexpected, the former is usually preferential from the actor's standpoint. One may have had to prepare even for *desired* events, but could not do so if they occurred unexpectedly. It is probably for this reason that the antonyms of unexpected, in lay terminology (again according to Roget), include words such as: preparation, provision, precaution, rehearsal, manufacture, arrange, and so forth. If not to the scientist, then to the layman, *prévoir* literally means *pouvoir*. The applied social scientist's interest in unforeseen events is, in important part, a focus on events that laymen find threatening. Stated differently, it is an interest in events over which laymen have lost control and for which, therefore, their need for assistance in regaining it has become manifest. A concern with unanticipated consequences by the applied social scientist, therefore, locks onto the motivations and engages the profoundest interests of laymen.

The theory of unanticipated consequences has its closest links with the needs of both laymen and applied social scientists alike when it implicates the layman himself in the very difficulties of which he complains. Insofar as a theory of unanticipated consequences implies, as in Marx's case that the layman's own profit-seeking activities produce economic depressions, that his adherence to certain values elicits suicide as in the Durkheimian case, or that his difficulties stem from his own unconscious motivations as in the Freudian analysis, then the problems have been defined as having more directly controllable roots. For if it is the layman's own behavior that produces his own problems, at least in part, then a change in his own behavior can aid in remedying the problem. Thus the theory of unanticipated consequences is particularly suitable to the needs of applied social science, because it identifies independent variables more directly accessible to control.

Selznick's important contribution to the theory of unanticipated consequences is of interest precisely on this count, for it directly stresses the degree to which unanticipated consequences derive from the controllable actions of those who suffer from them.[14] Selznick conceives of the action from which unanticipated consequences stem as "commitments." In so doing he focuses on the ways in which these actions contain voluntaristic components of decision and therefore of choice.

By stressing that there are elements of decision and choice even in constraining situations, the notion of commitment identifies areas of intervention and control in them. The concept of commitment also indicates the ways

in which present constraints are outcomes of earlier decisions and choices on the actors' part. This implies that the earlier choices were in some sense freer and possessed a greater variety of functional alternatives than did later ones. Different phases in the decision-making process are thus demarcated, distinguishing those phases having a greater area of controllability.

It is in part for these reasons that the work of present applied social scientists is replete with analyses of unanticipated consequences. In mass communications research, for example, an orientation to unanticipated consequences has been standardized in the notion of the "boomerang effect."[15] This concept directs the researcher to ascertain whether a given message has produced an audience response in conformity with the sender's intention, or whether it has yielded unforeseen consequences directly contrary to those intended. It has thus been discovered by students of race relations that certain communications intended to reduce ethnic intolerance have, in some measure, strengthened it, or have led the audience to an unexpected identification with the prejudiced person rather than the victim of prejudice. In criminology students of juvenile delinquency have indicated that arresting and booking juvenile delinquents may have the unforeseen consequence of crystallizing a criminal self-image.

In these and many other examples that can be drawn from current efforts in applied sociology, the problems of which laymen complain are analyzed as the unanticipated consequences of

---

[14] Philip Selznick, *TVA and the Grass Roots*, Berkeley and Los Angeles: University of California Press, 1949, esp. pp. 253–259.

[15] See, for example: Paul F. Lazarsfeld and Robert K. Merton, "Studies in Radio and Film Propaganda," *Transactions of the New York Academy of Sciences*, Series II, 6, pp. 58–79.

their own policies, actions, and commitments. Thus a theory of unanticipated consequences systematically directs the attention of laymen and applied social scientist alike to problem-generating forces most directly accessible to their control.

The theory of unanticipated consequences also has another, this time a rhetoric function, for the social system of applied social science. It systematically directs attention to factors most likely to be overlooked by laymen, that is, their own behavior and the ways in which it contributes to their own problems. This is not likely to be regarded as common-sensical by laymen. On the contrary, it is frequently an important source of sudden "insight" that contributes so powerfully to the layman's validation of the applied social scientist's status.

One of the needs of applied social science, therefore, is for the full development of a generalized theory of unanticipated consequences. Consistent though not identical with this, is a need for a diversity of concepts, varying with the field of application, which direct laymen's attention to patterns of behavior and belief of which he was unaware. In short, an applied social science greatly needs a multiplicity of middle range concepts of both latent functions and latent structures.

The modern era in industrial sociology, for example, hinges on the introduction of a concept of latent structure, namely, "informal organization," in the Western Electric studies. This concept identified new areas of social organization that were utilizable for the realization of organizational objectives. It has been used precisely in this way, not only in factories, but in schools and mental hospitals as well, where it has literally brought into focus hitherto neglected social resources.

In this connection it is instructive to recall Merton's rationale for introducing the concept of latent functions.[16] He observes that there is an unfortunate tendency for some social scientists to confine themselves to the study of manifest functions, thus allowing the focus of their studies to be set by the interests of practical men of affairs. Pressures in the direction noted by Merton arise most compellingly when a social scientist has implicated himself in the social system of applied science. In effect, then, it may be said that Merton sees the concept of latent functions serving as a corrective for the applied proclivities of social scientists, facilitating their pursuit of the theoretic issues of pure science. The point here, however, is that not even the needs of applied social science are well served by dealing solely with manifest functions. The concepts of latent function and latent structure are equally useful to the applied social sciences.

Conclusion

An effort has been made to indicate some of the theoretical and conceptual needs of applied social sciences. It should be clear that some of these needs are not well met by the present development of pure theory. There is no intention, however, to suggest that the program of pure or basic theory ought to be organized, either in whole or part, around the discernible needs of the applied fields. It is likely, however, that even the most inveterate of pure theorists will profit from examining the hiatuses between the needs of applied fields and the accomplish-

[16] Robert K. Merton, *Social Theory and Social Structure*, New York: Free Press of Glencoe, 1949, esp. pp. 64 *et seq.*

ments of the basic ones. For it may be that these gaps signalize, not only a handicap of the applied scientist, but also an unnecessary defect in pure theory itself.

If this paper has seemed to contain a curious juxtaposition of classical theorists and current empiricists, the implication is twofold. It is a mild suggestion to those presently involved in applied efforts that, even today, they may gain much from recognizing the continuity between their own efforts and those of the major and earlier sociologists. Current applied social scientists may see deeper significance in their work if they recognize that it is neither peripheral nor new foliage but that, on the contrary, it emerges from the deepest taproots of their disciplines and has the most venerable tradition. Finally, it is implied that the true office of the theorist is best performed when he exposes old theories to the current empirical tasks of his discipline.

CHAPTER 3

Goal and Value Dilemmas in the Planning of Change

Men and women do not today approach their task of planning improvements in their lives with confident and clear common notions of the meaning of "improvement." Changes we have come to expect. And we seek, through planning, to convert changes into "improvements." But which "changes" are "improvements"? To answer this question, men must agree upon some normative standards, some value criteria, by which changes can be judged good or bad, desirable or undesirable. Ready-made agreement on norms we can no longer assume. The processes of "engineering" valid and acceptable agreements on what "changes" are "improvements" must become more self-conscious and self-critical than in the past. Mannheim makes clear the social roots of the deep-cutting disruption of consensus in the value orientations of contemporary men in *Roots of the Crisis in Evaluation*.

Men have traditionally tended to regard the valid ends of human life, and, as a consequence, the valid directions for particular changes in persons and societies, as fixed and final. Men today confront at every turn discrepancies and conflicts among ends of human life, assumed and alleged by various individuals and groups to be absolutely valid. Such discrepancies occur between men in parts of our own national society—among men of various religions or of various social classes, for example. And the necessity of our living and working together on the world stage with peoples of other national cultures, once but no longer isolated from us, confronts us with even more apparent discrepancies and conflicts as to the valid ends of living. Those who would plan changes cannot, without unwarranted provincialism or imperialism, ignore the question of which directions of change are valid. But where are they to look for valid direction for change in the presence of discrepant and conflicting goal orientations?

Even more fundamentally, by what methods can men in conflict about values judge the validity of the values in such conflicts? And how build a community of acceptance for values as a basis for social and personal planning of action? To answer these questions, if they are to be answered validly, processes of choice, personal and collective, must be studied and analyzed both descriptively and normatively. And, since "science" is of integral importance in the planning of change, the interrelations of "choice" and the "methods of science" must be carefully analyzed and assessed, if any clarity concerning the direction of "good" change is to be attained. Geiger offers such an analysis and assessment in *Values and Social Science*.

Western men are today widely reviewing the tenability (often to the point of wholesale rejection) of the values of their liberal-democratic heritage. No values of that heritage are more basic to confidence in man's ability to plan for his future than the values related to "rationality." Scientific achievements do support confidence in men's growing ability rationally to assess alternative means for the achievement of an end of action, once the end is given. But can man rationally select from among alternative ends of action the better end? There is no doubt about the fact of deep cutting conflicts over alternative ends of action among various men and groups of men. This condition is part of our crisis in valuation. And this crisis is today more or less widely recognized, if usually oversimply explained. Doubts come rather as to whether men's rationality extends to choices among conflicting ends. In part these doubts stem from recent explorations of the irrational bases of many of men's normative orientations, once assumed to be rationally sourced and grounded. Lerner, in *The Discovery of the Irrational: Personal and Collective,* explores the "Copernican Revolution" that both psychological and historical-sociological explorations of "the irrational" determinants of human behavior have brought to human studies in the twentieth century.

Doubts about the efficacy of "reason" to validate social ideals and ends of action have been re-enforced from quarters other than depth psychology and sociology of knowledge. There have been neo-orthodox theologians seeking to lure liberal man back to reliance upon some favored "Faith"; political "realists," conservative or radical, seeking to short-circuit the "inefficiency and slowness" of democratic rationality in accomplishing the ends they wish to achieve, through an appeal to some allegedly necessary absolutism or another; logical empiricists, "philosophers of science," who, having identified "rationality" with "scientific method," find social ideals "nonrational" because they cannot be scientifically validated or invalidated; and no doubt others as well. Murphy, in *The Efficacy of Reason,* shows that the practice of rationality, properly interpreted, eludes the bombardments of these various detractors and incorporates, moreover, a social ideal capable of rational self-correction.

Another cluster of values in our liberal democratic heritage which is seen by many as doomed by the planning of change centers in "freedom" and "individuality." There is evident empirical justification in recent history for fear in this area. "Fascist" and "Nazi" planning explicitly sought to constrict and destroy these values, and "Soviet" planning radically subordinates them to other values. Planning efforts in the United States have not always or perhaps typically placed "freedom" and "individuality," as compared to "productivity," "health," "orderliness," or "efficiency," high in the hierarchy of values to be enhanced through planning. There is thus a genuine problem to be reckoned with in the relationships between "planning" on the one hand and "freedom" and "individuality" on the other. It is important that the relationship be seen as presenting a "practical" and "strategic" problem rather than an inherent and necessary contradiction. Mannheim, in *Freedom under Planning,* points to the relativity of "freedom" to particular modes and forms of social organization, defines the nature of the concrete freedoms possible under planning, and emphasizes that "freedom" in mass society can be secure *only* if it is planned for. There is thus no necessary contradiction between "planning" and "freedom." The practical problem is to build and maintain the value of "freedom" high in the hierarchy of values of those responsible for planning.

If men, planning for change, must find, construct, and validate common directions of action in the midst of the conflicts that divide them, what values are to guide them in these processes of discovery, construction, and validation? Geiger reminded us of the values inherent in the methodologies that men in a "community" use in settling differences and solving problems that divide their members. When faced with doubt or conflict, it is commitment to the values inherent in their ways of thinking and communicating together that maintains the community while its conflicts over substantive goals are being worked through and resolved. The values assumed in a methodology of planning need to be made much more explicit than they ordinarily are. Benne, in *Democratic Ethics and Human Engineering,* has formulated the normative principles of "democracy," seen basically as a methodology for dealing with conflicts among ends in a process of planning for change.

Science as a human enterprise also has a morality inherent in the methodologies it employs in seeking and building valid knowledge. And this inherent morality, often unarticulated by operating scientists and unrealized by most people who enjoy and suffer the practical consequences of scientific discoveries, is by no means inconsistent with the principles of a democratic morality. William Gruen suggests the broad outlines of the normative orientation internal to the "scientific community" in *The Moral Dimension of Science.*

Our hope is that all men, disciplined in democratic and scientific methodologies and commonly committed to the values inherent in these methodologies, can seek and find common and valid bases for cooperative planning without destroying the substantive differences in individual and group normative orientations that contemporary society incorporates. Pluralism, thus disciplined, can be a source of strength rather than of weakness in a changing society. Without such discipline in commonly accepted methods, however, pluralism breeds chaos and flabby eclecticism. Under the thrust of inexorable change, such eclecticism invites the despairing appeal to an authoritarian order that is akin to death.

◇◇◇◇◇◇◇◇◇◇◇◇◇◇◇◇◇◇◇◇ ROOTS OF THE CRISIS
IN EVALUATION   *Karl Mannheim*

Conflicting Philosophies of Life

AT first only a few people were aware of the approaching chaos and the crisis in our system of valuations. They noticed that the religious and moral unity which integrated mediaeval society was vanishing. Still, the disintegration was not yet quite apparent because the Philosophy of Enlightenment seemed to offer a new approach to life with a unified purpose, out of which developed the secularized systems of Liberalism and Socialism. No sooner had we made up our mind that the future would resolve itself into a struggle for supremacy between these two points of view than a new system of valuation emerged, that of universal Fascism. The basic attitude of the new outlook is so different from that of the previous systems that their internal differences seem almost to vanish.

Thus, in the very same social environment we now have the most contradictory philosophies of life. First, there is the religion of love and universal brotherhood, mainly inspired by Christian tradition, as a measuring-rod for our activities. Then there is the philosophy of Enlightenment and Liberalism, with its emphasis on freedom and personality, and its appreciation of wealth, security, happiness, tolerance and philanthropy as the means of achieving them. Then we have the challenge of the Socialists, who rate equality, social justice, basic security and a planned social order as the chief desiderata of the age. But beyond all this we have, as I said before, the most recent philosophy, with the demoniac image of man emphasizing fertility, race, power, and the tribal and military virtues of conquest, discipline and blind obedience.

We are not only divided against each other in our evaluation of the big issues, such as the principles of the Good Life and those of the best social organization, but we have no settled views, especially in our democratic societies, concerning the right patterns of human behaviour and conduct. One set of educational influences is preparing the new generation to practise and defend their rational self-interest in a competitive world, while another lays the emphasis on unselfishness, social service and subordination to common ends. One set of social influences is guided by the ideal of asceticism and repression, the other by the wish to encourage self-expression.

We have no accepted theory and practice concerning the nature of freedom and discipline. Some think that, owing to the self-regulating powers inherent in group life, discipline would spontaneously emerge if only full freedom were given and the pressure of external authority removed. In contrast to this anarchist theory, others hold that if strict regulation is applied

Excerpts from Karl Mannheim, Diagnosis of Our Time: Wartime Essays of a Sociologist, *England: Routledge & Kegan Paul Ltd, 1943, pp. 15–30. Abridged and used by permission.*

to those spheres of life where it is necessary, the scope for real freedom is not suppressed but rather created. To such thinkers discipline is the pre-condition of freedom. Since we have no settled views on freedom and discipline, it is not surprising that we have no clear-cut criteria for the treatment of criminals, and do not know whether punishment should be retributive and deterrent or a kind of readjustment and re-education for life in society. We hesitate whether to treat the law-breaker as a sinner or as a patient, and cannot decide whether he or society is at fault.

But the crisis in valuations does not only come to the fore in marginal cases of maladjustment such as crime; we have no agreed educational policy for our normal citizens, since the further we progress the less we know what we are educating for. On the primary levels of education we are undecided whether to aim at creating millions of rationalists who discard custom and tradition and judge each case on its merits, or whether the chief aim of education should be the handing on of that social and national inheritance which is focussed in religion. On the higher levels of education we do not know whether to educate for specialization, which is urgently needed in an industrialized society with a strict division of labour, or whether we should cater for all-round personalities with a philosophical background.

Again, it is not only in the world of education that we are hazy; we are equally vague concerning the meaning and value of work and leisure. The system of working primarily for profit and monetary reward is in process of disintegration. The masses are craving for a stable standard of living, but over and above that, they want to feel that they are useful and important members of the community, with a right to understand the meaning of their work and of the society in which they live. While this awakening is going on amongst the masses, there is a split in the ranks of the wealthy and educated few. To some their high position and accumulated wealth means primarily the enjoyment of limitless power; to others, an opportunity for applying their knowledge or skill, giving guidance, shouldering responsibility. The first group represent the potential leaders of Fascism, the latter are those who are willing to assist in building up a new social order under competent leadership.

As I have said it is not only work but also leisure that is subjected to entirely different interpretations and valuations. The puritan sense of guilt in connection with leisure and recreation is still at war with the emerging hedonistic cult of vitality and health. The idea of privacy and contemplation, and of their value, is at war with that of mass enjoyment and mass ecstasy. The same division of opinion appears in regard to our sex habits. Some still condemn sex altogether, trying to place it under a taboo, while others see a remedy for most of our psychological maladjustments in the removal of mystery and repression from that sphere of life. Our concepts and ideals of femininity and masculinity vary according to the different groups, and the lack of agreement creates conflicts which permeate not only philosophical discussions but also the day-to-day relations of men and women.

Thus there is nothing in our lives, not even on the level of basic habits such as food, manners, behaviour, about which our views are not at variance. We do not even agree as to whether this great variety of opinions is good or bad, whether the greater conformity of the past or the modern emphasis on choice is to be preferred.

There is, however, one last issue about which we are clear. It is definitely not good to live in a society whose norms are unsettled and develop in an unsteady way. We realize this even more now that we are at war, when we must act quickly and without hesitation and fight an enemy whose value system is deliberately simplified in order to achieve quick decisions. In peace-time it might have been stimulating for the historian and the individual thinker to study the great variety of possible responses to the same stimulus and the prevailing struggle between different standards and differences in outlook. But, even in peace-time, this variety in valuations tended to become unbearable, especially in marginal situations where a simple 'yes' or 'no' was required. In such situations, many a man faced with the slowness of democracies in making their decisions came to share the view of a well-known Fascist political scientist who said that a bad decision is better than no decision. This is true to the extent that the indecision of the laissez-faire system represents a drifting which automatically prepares the ground for the coming dictator. Thus, long before the outbreak of war a few far-sighted thinkers became aware of the dangers inherent in the crisis in valuations, and tried to find the deeper causes of that crisis.

Controversy about the Causes of our Spiritual Crisis

The two chief antagonists in the controversy about the causes of our spiritual crisis are the Idealists and the Marxists. To religious thinkers and philosophical idealists it seemed clear from the outset that the crisis in valuations was not the effect but rather the cause of the crisis of our civilization. To them all the struggles of history were due to the clash between different forms of allegiance to authority or to changing valuations. The abandonment of Christian and then of humanitarian valuations by modern man is the final cause of our crisis, and unless we restore spiritual unity our civilization is bound to perish. To the Marxist the exact opposite is true. What is happening in the world at present is nothing but a transition from one economic system to another and the crisis in values is, as it were, the noise made by the clash of these systems.

If you are a Liberal, your advice is to free the economic order from State interference with markets and let things of the spirit take care of themselves. If you are a Marxist, you see ideologies and valuations as a part of the social process, but in your strategy you too often focus your attack alone upon the economic aspects of society and hope that after the establishment of the right economic order a world of harmony will automatically emerge by the very action of dialectical interdependence. As the source of all our discord is to be sought in the antagonisms inherent in the Capitalist system, it is only natural that its removal will put everything right.

I think it was the great merit of the Marxist approach, as compared with the purely idealistic one, that it realized once for all that the life of culture and the sphere of valuations within it depend on the existence of certain social conditions, among which the nature of the economic order and of the corresponding class structure is of primary importance. This opened up a field of investigation which we call the sociology of culture. On the other hand, the exclusive emphasis on the economic foundations limited from the outset the outlook of the emerging sociology of culture. In my view, there are many other social factors and conditions upon which the life of culture depends, and the vocabulary of a sociology which approaches the crisis of culture with categories of 'class' only is far too limited, as is the view that economic and class factors alone are responsible for the crisis in our valuations.

The difference in outlook will become explicit when we consider the remedy which follows from the two sociological approaches, the Marxist and that which I am to expound. According to the Marxist, you have only to put your economic house in order and the present chaos in valuation will disappear. In my view, no remedy of the chaos is possible without a sound economic order, but this is by no means enough, as there are a great many other social conditions which influence the process of value creation and dissemination, each of which has to be considered on its own merits.

In my sociological approach, as in the Marxist's, it is futile to discuss values in the abstract; their study must be linked up with the social process. To us values express themselves first in terms of choices made by individuals: by preferring this to that I evaluate things. But values do not only exist in the subjective setting, as choices made by individuals; they occur also as objective norms, i.e. as advice: do this rather than that. In that case they are mostly set up by society to serve as traffic lights in the regulation of human behaviour and conduct. The main function of these objective norms is to make the members of a society act and behave in a way which somehow fits into the pattern of an existing order. Owing to this dual origin, valuations are partly the expression of subjective strivings, partly the fulfillment of objective social functions. Thus there is a continuous adjustment at work between what individuals would like to do if their choices were directed by their personal wishes only, and what society wants them to do.

As long as the structure of society is simple and static, established valuations will last for a very long time, but if society changes this will immediately be reflected in the changing valuations. Re-valuations and re-definitions of the situation will necessarily accompany the changed structure of society. A new social order cannot exist without these re-valuations and re-definitions, as it is through them alone that individuals will act in a new way and respond to new stimuli. Thus the valuation process is not simply an epiphenomenon superstructure, an addition to the economic order, but an aspect of social change in all its provinces where changed behaviour is wanted. But if valuations in their most important functions act as social controls, like traffic lights, it is obvious that we cannot bring order and harmony into the chaos of these controls unless we know a little more of the social processes which make these controls work, and about those social conditions which may upset the working of that signal system.

There is definitely a coherent system of social and psychological activities which constitute the process of valuation; among them value creation, value dissemination, value reconciliation, value standardization, value assimilation are the most important, and there are definite social conditions which favour or upset the smooth working of the process of valuation.

And this is exactly my contention. There has been a complete displacement of the social factors on which the smooth working of the process of valuation depended. But we have been so society-blind that we could not even properly distinguish these factors, let alone put right what went wrong. What I am going to do, therefore, is to try to enumerate some of those changed social conditions which upset the traditional functioning of the main factors in the process of valuations.

Some Sociological Factors upsetting the Process of Valuation in Modern Society

1. The first set of disturbances in the sphere of valuations arises from the simple fact of the uncontrolled and rapid growth of society. We pass from a stage where the so-called primary groups, family, neighbourhood, form the background to one where the larger contact groups prevail. As the American sociologist C. H. Cooley has pointed out, there is a corresponding transition from primary attitudes and virtues to derivative group ideals. The primary virtues of love, mutual help, brotherhood are deeply emotional and personal, and it is quite impossible to apply them without adjustment to the setting of larger contact groups. It is possible to love your neighbour whom you know personally, but it is an impossible demand to love people of a wider area whom you do not even know. In Cooley's view it is the paradox of Christianity that it tried to apply the virtues of a society based upon neighbourly relationships to the world at large. It did not only ask you to love the members of your tribe (a demand by no means peculiar to Christianity), but also to love the whole of mankind. The solution to the paradox is that the commandment 'Love your neighbour' should not be taken literally but should be translated according to the conditions of a great society. This consists in setting up institutions embodying some abstract principle which corresponds to the primary virtue of sympathy and brotherliness. The equal political rights of citizens in a democracy are abstract equivalents of the concrete primary virtues of sympathy and brotherliness.

In this case it is the method of translation which makes the value system function once more. But only social workers could tell us how often people fail in life because they never have been taught how to translate the virtues in which they have been trained in their homes into the conditions of society at large. To educate for family life and neighbourhood functions is different from educating for national and world citizenship. Our whole educational tradition and value system is still adapted to the needs of a parochial world, and yet we wonder that people fail when they are expected to act on a broader plane.

2. Whereas in this case the method of translation helped to give meaning to primary virtues in a world of widening contacts, in other cases values of the neighbourly world will only function adequately under modern conditions if they are linked up with complete reform. Take, for example, the whole system of valuations which is linked up with the idea of private property. This was a creative and just device in a society of small peasants or small independent craftsmen, for, as Professor Tawney has pointed out, in this case the law of property only meant

the protection of the tools of the man who did socially useful work. The meaning of the norm completely changes in a world of large-scale industrial techniques. Here the very same principle of the private ownership of the means of production implies the right to the exploitation of the many by the few.

This example shows from another aspect how, through the transition from simpler conditions to more complex ones, the very same rule, i.e. that of private property, may change its meaning completely, and may grow from an instrument of social justice into one of oppression. It is not enough to give a conscious reinterpretation of the value system organized around the idea of property; a complete reform is needed if the original intention, that the value of social justice should prevail, is to be put into practice again.

3. The transition from a pre-industrial world where handicrafts and agriculture prevailed is not only reflected in the changing meaning of the valuations, which are focussed in the property concept, but also in a changing set of aesthetic valuations and of values regulating our habits of work and leisure. It would not be at all difficult to demonstrate how in our appreciation of art the real struggle lies between the attitudes which are rooted in good craftsmanship and values which emanate from machine-made goods.

But the antagonism of values exists even more conspicuously in valuations which are linked up with the labour process. The working incentives and rewards of the pre-industrial age are different from those of our age. The prestige of the various occupations in a society of hand-made goods is different from the forms of prestige which emerge in the hierarchy of the factory and the business organization. New forms of

individual and collective responsibility emerge, but very often the lack of opportunity for taking responsibility depresses those who still strive for self-respect through the skill invested in their work. It has rightly been said that our society has not yet assimilated the machine. We have successfully developed a new type of 'taylorized' efficiency which makes man part of the mechanical process and moulds his habits in the interests of the machine. But we have not yet succeeded in creating those human conditions and social relationships in the factory which would satisfy the value aspirations of modern man and contribute to the formation of his personality.

The same applies to our machine-made leisure. The wireless, the gramophone and the cinema are now tools for producing and distributing new patterns of leisure. They are democratic in nature and bring new stimuli into the life of the humblest, but few of them have yet developed those genuine values which would humanize and spiritualize the time spent outside the workshop, factory and office.

Thus the machine age has either been incapable of producing adequate new values which would shape the process of work and leisure, or else is incapable of reconciling two different sets of competing ideals, both of which in their antagonism tend to disintegrate human character instead of integrating it. The same effect is visible in most of modern man's activities, as whatever he does in one compartment of his life remains unrelated to the others.

4. Confusion in the sphere of valuation arises not only out of the transition from the conditions of the past to those of the present, but also through the growing number of contacts be-

tween groups. Through the growth in the means of communication and through social mobility such as migration or the rise and fall in the social scale, values of different areas are dropped into the same melting-pot. Formerly one could refer to different value areas: habits, customs and valuations of one county differed from those of another, or the scale of valuations in the members of the aristocracy differed from that of the burghers. If groups made contact or even fused, there was time for assimilating one another's values; a kind of incorporation took place, and differences did not remain unreconciled nor survive as antagonistic stimuli. To-day we embody the most heterogeneous influences in our value system, and there is no technique for mediation between antagonistic valuations nor time for real assimilation. Against this background it becomes clear that in the past there were slow and unconscious processes at work, which carried out the most important functions of value mediation, value assimilation and value standardization. These processes are now either displaced or find neither time nor opportunity to do their work properly. This in itself reduces the value experience to insignificance. If a dynamic society is to work at all it needs a variety of responses to the changing environment, but if the variety of accepted patterns becomes too great it leads to nervous irritation, uncertainty and fear. It becomes gradually more and more difficult for the individual to live in a shapeless society in which even in the simplest situations he has to choose between various patterns of action and valuations without sanction; and he has never been taught how to choose or to stand on his own feet.

To counteract the ill-effects of this variety one would have to find some method of a gradual standardization of basic valuations in order to regain balanced attitudes and judgments. As this is lacking in our mass society, it is to be feared that out of the uncertainty there will emerge the cry for distorted values.

5. Another source of displacement and disturbance in our value system is due to the entirely new forms of authority and sanctions which have emerged, and to the new methods of justifying existing authority and sanctions. When society was more homogeneous the religious and political authorities coincided at many points, or else there was a violent conflict to define the spheres of the religious and political authorities. But now we are faced with a variety of religious denominations and the disagreement between various political philosophies which, as all of them act at the same time, only succeed in neutralizing each other's influence upon the minds of the people.

Added to this we have the different methods of justifying authority. At one time there were only two ways of justifying the authority of social regulations: either they were a part of tradition ('as our forefathers have done it') or they expressed the will of God. Against this, the new method of value justification grew up, which acknowledged as its one source of acceptance that which could be deduced from eternal rational law, supposedly common to the human race. When this belief in enlightenment by the Universal Ratio as lawgiving power disintegrated, the door was thrown open to value justification of the most various kinds. The Utilitarian justification of values by their usefulness or the belief in the uncontrollable inspiration of the Leader became as plausible as the belief in the law of the strongest. Whether the latter finds expression in the theory of an eternal struggle between races, classes or élites is not of primary importance. In all these cases there is no end to the process of mutual extinction, as the justification is such as to admit endless arbitrary claims: why should not my leader have the vision, my race or class the vocation, to rule the world?

Another difficulty of the same order is that of focussing responsibility on some visible social agent. Where there is no acknowledged value system authority is dispersed, methods of justification become arbitrary and nobody is responsible. The focussing of authority and the allotment of different grades of responsibility to different functionaries are pre-conditions of the functioning of social life. But this focussing becomes more difficult as different classes, with their varying historical origins and mental make-up, adhere to different standards and as no attempt is made to reconcile their differences.

6. An even worse predicament of our age is caused by the fact that whereas the most important values governing a society based upon the rule of custom were blindly accepted, the creation of the specifically new values and their acceptance are to a large extent based upon conscious and rational value appreciation. Whether one should love one's neighbour and hate one's enemy is based, as we have seen, upon the belief that this is either a demand of God or a part of our ancient traditions, but whether the democratic organization is preferable to the dictatorial one, or whether our educational system should pay more attention to the study of classics or to further specialization, these are decisions which have to be argued. Even if we agree that finally

the preference might rest upon some irrational decision, persuasion has to go through the stage of conscious deliberation, and new techniques of conscious value appreciation are continually in the making.

Although this process leading to greater consciousness and deliberation is in itself a great advance, yet when it is brought into the existing social context it completely upsets the balance between conscious and unconscious forces operating in our society. The change to conscious value appreciation and acceptance is a Copernicus-like change on the social plane and in man's history, and it can only lead to improvements if it is really assimilated by society at large. To bear the burden of a greater amount of consciousness is only possible if many other things (among them education) are changed at the same time. The origins of this upsetting novelty are to be found in those days when man for the first time realized that through the conscious direction of law he could somehow influence a changing society. He thereby realized that it was possible to link up value creation and value guidance with conscious deliberation, to foresee and to some extent influence social effects. What is happening now is that what is already a matter of course in the legal sphere is being transferred to other spheres. In the spheres of education, pastoral work and social work, values of a moral rather than a legal nature are being linked up with rational deliberation and appreciation. Thus value creation, value dissemination, value acceptance and assimilation become more and more the concern of the conscious ego.

7. This change is formidable, as in order to create a law-abiding citizen whose obedience is not solely based

upon blind acceptance and habit, we ought to re-educate the whole man. People who are conditioned to accept values blindly either through obedience, imitation or emotional suggestion will hardly be able to cope with those values that appeal to reason and whose underlying principles can and must be argued. We have hardly realized yet, to its full extent, what a tremendous reform of education would be necessary to make a democratic society, based upon conscious value appreciation, function. There is one thing every reformer and educationist ought to bear in mind, and that is, that every new system of social controls requires the re-education of the self. In a society where the value controls were traffic lights directly appealing either to conditioned responses or to the emotions and the unconscious mind, one could bring about social action without strengthening the intellectual powers of the ego. But in a society in which the main changes are to be brought about through collective deliberation, and in which re-valuations should be based upon intellectual insight and consent, a completely new system of education would be necessary, one which would focus its main energies on the development of our intellectual powers and bring about a frame of mind which can bear the burden of scepticism and which does not panic when many of the thought habits are doomed to vanish.

8. We have seen some of the social causes making for crisis in our laissez-faire societies. We have seen how the transition from primary groups to great society, the transition from handicrafts to large-scale industrial techniques, the contacts between formerly separated value areas, caused disturbances in the process of valuation. We have seen how the new forms of authority and sanctions, the new methods of justifying authority, the lack in the focussing of responsibility and the failure to educate for conscious value appreciation, each by itself and all of them together contribute to the present crisis in valuations. We have finally seen how all the mechanisms which used to regulate automatically the process of valuation have gradually been weakened or eliminated without being replaced by anything else. It is no wonder, therefore, that our society lacks that healthy background of commonly accepted values and everything that lends spiritual consistency to a social system. If there is any truth in the Aristotelian statement that political stability depends on the adaptation of education to the form of government, if at least we agree with those who realize that a society can only function when there is a certain harmony of prevailing valuations, institutions and education,—then our laissez-faire system is bound sooner or later to disintegrate.

In a society where disintegration has proceeded too far, the paradoxical situation arises that education, social work and propaganda, notwithstanding highly improved techniques, become less and less efficient because all the values that could guide them tend to evaporate. What is the use of developing exceedingly skilful methods of propaganda and suggestion, new techniques of learning and habit-making, of conditioning, de-conditioning and re-conditioning, if we do not know what they are for? What is the good of developing child guidance, psychiatric social work and psychotherapy if the one who is to guide is left without standards? Sooner or later everyone becomes neurotic, as it gradually becomes impossible to make a reasonable choice in the chaos of competing and unreconciled valuations. Only those who have seen the result of complete non-interference with valuations and deliberate avoidance of any discussion of common aims in our neutralized democracies, such as Republican Germany, will understand that this absolute neglect leads to drifting and prepares the ground for submission and dictatorship. Nobody can expect a human being to live in complete uncertainty and with unlimited choice. Neither the human body nor the human mind can bear endless variety. There must be a sphere where basic conformity and continuity prevail.

Of course, if we complain that our liberal and democratic system is left without a focus, we certainly do not want a regimented culture and an authoritarian education in the spirit of the totalitarian systems. But there must be something, a third way, between totalitarian regimentation on the one hand and the complete disintegration of the value system at the stage of laissez-faire on the other. The third way is what I call the democratic pattern of planning or planning for freedom. It consists essentially in the reverse of a dictatorial imposition of external controls. Its method is either to find new ways to free the genuine and spontaneous social controls from the disintegrating effects of mass society, or else to invent new techniques which perform the function of democratic self-regulation on a higher plane of awareness and purposeful organization.

By now it must have become obvious why I dwelt so long on the analysis of the main changes that have effected the working of the various factors in the process of valuations. One will also understand why I tried to enumerate some of the remedies, the techniques of readjustment in the process of valuations as, for instance, translation of values, creation of new values, complete reform, value assimilation, value standardization, value reconciliation, focussing of authority and responsibility, training in conscious value appreciation, etc. As the democratic planning of the value system will not consist in the inculcation of values, the careful study of the factors which make the spontaneous value process work in all its aspects in everyday life becomes an urgent task.

If we agree that real planning is democratic planning, then it follows that the problem is not whether we should plan or no, but to find the real difference between dictatorial and democratic planning.

❖❖❖❖❖❖❖❖❖❖❖❖❖❖❖❖❖❖❖ VALUES AND SOCIAL SCIENCE

George Geiger

Mᴏʀᴇ than anyone else, the social scientist should be sensitive to the phenomenon of cultural lag. As a matter of fact, the critical analysis of ceremonialisms and "pseudomorphs" does enlist a considerable share of his energies.

From George Geiger, "Values and Social Science," Journal of Social Issues, Vol. 6, No. 4, 1950, pp. 8–16. Some footnotes omitted. Abridged and used by permission.

It is a little surprising, then, that one of the most conspicuous (and mischievous) cultural hang-overs still plagues social science, just as it haunts natural science and philosophy. I refer to the antique dualism between fact and value. To be sure, the insulation is now being worn a little thin as "Atom" and "Hydrogen" begin to exert their pressure, and as presidents of learned societies and public figures deplore daily the unequal race between technology and morals; but, despite the spate of testimonials, even of confessions, the institutionalized separation of descriptive inquiry from normative inquiry continues to be respectable, academic, and stultifying.

One basic assumption, therefore, needs to be made clear at the start, and that is that the alleged fact-value dualism has already been pierced by contemporary events. These first five years of the Atom-Hydrogen Age have already made anachronistic the traditional compartmentalizing of human experience into what we do and what we ought to do. Not that something essentially novel has been introduced by the drama of released nuclear energy: the problem of the differential lag between knowledge and action has been a burning one since at least the days of the Hebrew prophets. But now it has been given an incandescence which can escape neither journalist nor philosopher, scientist nor layman.

Another assumption can be added, one which will direct the course of the entire argument: that in this question of a scientific approach to value the whole burden of proof has been misplaced. The characteristic assumption, in much of both science and philosophy, has been that human evaluations are automatically outside the ambit of scientific method, and that the burden

of proof rested on those who saw ethics as a candidate for scientific consideration. I suggest that this burden can and must be shifted. This suggestion involves the opening reference to cultural lag, for the contention here is that the reason for separating values from intelligent inquiry has been social and institutional, not theoretical. That is to say, there is nothing intrinsic in the nature of value which puts it forever beyond the pale. Indeed, the very question as to the commerce between ethics and science should never have been raised, not, at least, in that familiar and threatening form which has proved such a bogey to conscientious men.

These statements are being made abruptly and will have to be justified presently. Before that, it would appear that any philosophic analysis of a problem like this should start not only with assumptions but with definitions. After all, what is meant by "value," and what by "scientific method"?

It may seem plausible to start with definitions, but it is only a fake plausibility. For one thing, the definer has an unholy advantage in giving arbitrary meaning to his subject-matter at the outset. Particularly in a discussion such as this, where terms are controversial and supposedly "subjective," the danger of "the fallacy of initial predication" is enormous. The very definition of value or of scientific method can decide automatically the issue between them (one way or the other) without necessity for subsequent argument. Another evidence of misleading plausibility is found in the realization that definitions illustrate but do not institute a point of view. They are ordinarily after-the-fact rationalizations of a pattern of thinking. For example, even when values are "defined" as indefinable or as primitive and unanalyzable, this, too, is indicative of a whole school of logic, itself completely sophisticated and unprimitive. Yet, these qualifications being noted, it still seems necessary to indicate, first, what one has in mind by the term "value."

Values are being looked upon here as second-order phenomena, not as immediate. That is, values are the outcomes of human choices, of choices among competing human interests. (The word "interest" is a very wide one, standing for all the dynamic human urges whatever they be called—impulse, drive, instinct, appetite, and so on. Nor does "interest" discriminate between native or conditioned factors.) If there is anything "immediate," it would be the interests themselves—but "immediate" does *not* signify being impervious to historical and genetic analysis, at least. All values, thus, are interests but not all interests are values. Some "judgment"—not necessarily rational or even conscious—needs to be made before any interest in competition with another interest emerges as a value: a process of evaluation is required. As a most elementary illustration, the taste for, say, x becomes a value after it has been chosen over taste y. The taste x by itself is a candidate for the class of values; it is not automatically a member of the class. In ethics, the choices known as values are characteristically long-time preferences, involving those human interests regarded as unusually precious and intimate, yet capable, in general, of public expression and appreciation. But this does not seem to be an essential part of the definition of value. Nor does the question whether the choices are "good" or "bad." This is a third-order phenomenon of spectacular significance,

but it does not introduce an essentially new element into the process of interest-plus-choice. It steps up that process into one of choice between values but it does not break the circuit.

No one needs to be told that this kind of definition, if not arbitrary, is in any event a loaded one and aimed in a certain direction. What it is designed to point up is the contrast between an approach which regards values as unique, unmodifiable bias-facts, immune to ordinary intelligent investigation, and one which sees them as amenable to "outside" factors such as those handled by psychology, anthropology, and cultural history. In more technical language, the first attitude believes the discussion of values in terms of "outside" factors to be an illustration of the naturalistic fallacy, which is the illicit attempt to make values derivative and "reducible" to some other dimension. The second attitude is inclined to view the alleged fallacy as a kind of myth, traceable, in part, to man's ceremonial reverence for certain words (like "ought," "moral," "duty," *et al.*) and to the institutionalized and invidious split between philosophy and science. The definition of value in the preceding paragraph is, of course, a frank expression of the second attitude; and such expression seems to be a prime function of definition. Before this definition can be employed, what about the term "scientific method?"

To introduce this phrase must prove embarrassing, since we all know what scientific method is! Almost anything that can be said will be accepted—and rejected. Certainly in the broadest sense, scientific inquiry is not cut off from the common sense activities of man in the solving of problems. The familiar five-step analysis by Dewey of an act of reflective thinking makes clear the easy transition from lay intelligence to scientific. In making that transition, however, different items can be emphasized, the emphasis itself disclosing pretty clearly an implicit philosophy of science. For example, the problem situation itself can be underscored and a considerable share of attention devoted to increasing the sensitivity to unsuspected deformations and challenges in man's environment. Again, inadequacies in the formulation of problems may be seen as focal, the result being an increased interest in sharpening the tools of diagnosis. Or, predictability can be made the core of method around which the entire scientific enterprise can be built. Here the stress can be on any one of the three factors of exact science as outlined, for example, by Margeneau: postulation of general principles, deduction of theorems, empirical verification. In other words, the "if-then" character of science can be made crucial. This, in turn, may mean concentration on technical experimental operations or it may mean the celebration of the attitude and behavior of the scientific man.

This is not a contention that there is anything necessarily divisive in these different interpretations. They complement one another and are all aspects of the general procedure by which man increases his grasp of any given set of phenomena. To emphasize any single aspect as *the* definition of science is important chiefly as an illustration of a point of view and a philosophy. This would be the case even if the broadest features of science were singled out, features like attitude of mind, on the one hand, or technological operations on the other. Elevation of the one cannot depress the other.

These two large interpretations of

scientific method need to be carried a little further. The first interpretation —science as a temper of approach, a general way of handling problems—is, of course, extremely congenial to a philosophy that seeks to extend the orbit of science and to free it from the dominance of any solitary technique. Here scientific method is more than the routine of a laboratory, however essential that routine may be. Nothing less than a whole complex of human behavior and adjustment is what is indicated. This complex would include many elements. Perhaps the most significant would be the hypothetical spirit. The feeling for tentativeness and caution and the respect for probable error may indeed be the unique contribution scientific method can offer to human culture; it certainly is the only prophylactic against the authoritarian mystique so symptomatic of modern nerve failure. Scientists as men can, of course, resist the prophylaxis: we know of dogmatic and totalitarian "scientists." But they achieve that status only by sacrificing what, in their calling, is precious and irreplaceable.

Another obvious ingredient of the scientific spirit is experimentalism, the willingness to expose ideas to procedures and operations. When these are absent, ideas become meaningless and hypotheses barren. But operationalism is not simply a kind of gadgetry applicable only to physical or laboratory routine; it connotes a general attitude or methodological standard, to the effect that hypotheses of any nature in any field—even that of value—must carry with them the means for their clarification as well as for their justification or rejection. The experimental temper is a prime corrective of an imagination that otherwise might decline to what could be regarded as "merely speculative or philosophical." Equally corrective is the spirit of criticism. This, rather than the more familiar "objectivity," would seem a constituent of the scientific approach. For to be critical means more than to take nothing for granted, more than to be sceptical and impatient to be shown. It is not a synonym for indifference or neutrality. To be critical means to make decisions, to choose between alternatives, to say yes here and no there. And to choose signifies to establish a set of values. Scientific objectivity cannot be amoral in the sense of not giving a damn. Which does not mean that, *per contra,* the scientist is expected to load his dice or prefer alkalis to acids because he doesn't want his litmus paper to turn red. Caricatures like these cannot distort the functional connection between criticism and selectivity; even the pure physicist knows what he is after and what data are relevant before he enters his study or laboratory. Critical objectivity interpreted as the discounting of personal prejudice is elementary and unexceptionable: to take it as given should not, however, reduce it to triviality. And objectivity becomes trivial when it becomes neuter.

Attitude of mind, as was suggested above, is one of two broad descriptions of scientific method. The other is technological. What needs to be noticed here is that scientific operations are not all alike, nor are they the monopoly of physics and chemistry. Every field of experience demands its own peculiar tools. There may be a common pool of instruments, such as those of measurement and counting, but no science needs to be "reduced" to inappropriate mathematical operations nor does it have to become "physicalistic" to become respectable. The travesty of insisting, because men and nations cannot be crammed into test-tubes or be stained and cross-sectioned for the microscope, that, therefore, the sciences of psychology or sociology are misnomers is an evasion of this whole point. Operations can be as unlike those of physics as carrying on a fight against delinquency through the use of playgrounds and club-houses, or changing a nation's entertainment habits from those of listening to those of seeing, or even working on a political committee during a crucial election. What *is* generally negotiable in science-as-technique is the operational spirit mentioned in the preceding paragraph. Non-physical experiments may be incredibly long-range; they may seem, at times, like desperate fumbling and uninspired improvisation. But when hypotheses are referred to operations, remote as they may seem to the physicist, the way is open for the self-correcting devices of science to exert their enormous power. The "if-then" form of scientific statement becomes now more than a bow to tentativeness or a tolerant testimony to sweetness and light: it is a prosperous sign that the spirit and technique of science are being significantly fused.

Is there anything inherent in science —either as a way of approach or as a set of operations—which necessarily eliminates it from any given area of experience? Is it on *a priori* grounds, on *theoretical* grounds, that scientific method has for so long been almost automatically excluded from fields such as ethics and values? Or is the exclusion cultural and institutional, an item of history rather than one of logic? These, of course, are largely rhetorical questions, for the above descriptions of values and of scientific method have already indicated the direction the present answers would take. But that direction may be made a little more explicit.

The last question refers back to an opening contention that the whole problem of the relation of science to values involves a cultural dualism which has become almost a hallmark of Western civilization (not that it is absent from other civilizations). To account for the character of Greek metaphysics or of early Christian theology and for their dominating roles in the ideological drama of the Western world is hardly on the present agenda. But what must be noted is that perhaps the prime concept contributed by ancient thought to modern is the schizoid notion of a metaphysical and epistemological split between appearance and reality. There has been an almost linear development of the idea of an absolute and precious realm of essences, on the one hand, immaculate and unchangeable; and, on the other, of an aberrant dimension of private sensation, subjective, relative, and untrustworthy. Philosophy deals honorifically with one, science vulgarly with the other. Ideals are in the first, human failings in the second. Social institutions themselves are judged sacred or secular as they fit themselves into these amazingly neat and contrived categories, categories which have hypnotized even great scientists such as Galileo and Newton as much as they have the layman worrying about his body and his soul, this world and that, his hopes and his practices.

The compensatory character of this kind of dualism is so apt that it is startling. Genuine reality, the real Mc-Coy, is the place where man's wishes are fulfilled, where frustrations are resolved, the happy hunting-ground. The world of *mere* appearance remains then as testimony to his failures; here,

the animal did not always fall in the hunt, the thunder could not be controlled, the rains came and so did drought, and famine and disease and death. *Here,* the fumbling hand of experience unfortunately had to be relied upon. There, myth, magic, and metaphysics (if Dewey's analysis is correct) allowed man to escape a suffocating feeling of helplessness. The very word "reality" becomes a symbol not for existence but for value, and should really be followed by "loud cheers." This is an admittedly brusque statement of what has been recited at length many times. But it cannot be recited too often. The contemporary resurrection of absolutes in almost every field should demonstrate that.

What we are saying is that the dualism between philosophy (values) and science (facts) has been bequeathed to us, just as has the dichotomy between reality and appearances. It is not some hereditary dislocation. After all, it must not be forgotten that at one time the ambit of science did not include the stars, or disease and insanity, or even the drifting of the clouds or the working of a pump. These were precious and impervious. So, latterly, are human values. Institutionalized resistance to the Scientific Revolution could contract but it could not easily disappear.

But is the resistance only traditional? Is there not an intrinsic opaqueness to human decisions about taste, right and wrong, or even about the price market which must forever resist scientific handling? Consider, however, the suggestions already made about both values and scientific method. If values indeed derive from human choices and if scientific method relates to certain attitudes of approach plus a general commitment to instrumentalism of an "if-then" character, the gap between the two does not appear unbridgeable. Surely, objective, critical, and operational reports can be made about human decisions, and those reports, in turn, can themselves enter into the fabric of future decisions. The act of choosing can become a matter for investigation. So can the degree of approval or disapproval choices provoke, as well as the variety of choices and the possibility of discovering common elements between them. These empirical phenomena are not simply matters of casual introspection: they furnish the ground for much of social psychology, anthropology, and history. Nor is there anything which *automatically* prohibits human choices from accommodating themselves to tentativeness and provisionalism or even to the use of probable error. The compulsion which has deflected values from the realm of hypothesis to that of the absolute and unconditioned (and so to an area outside the province of intelligent inquiry) is but mere symptom of a compensatory hankering for prescientific certainties. And it would seem to be conditioned rather than native. Values do not oscillate between the extremes of absolutism and of bare emotional improvisation because of some inner organic magnetism but (at least so it is being argued here) because of a cultural dualism which is itself amenable to historical and scientific analysis.

All this, it may be said, misses the real question at issue. For these allegedly "scientific" manipulations are only descriptive. They never reach the nerve of the problem. Reports and analyses of choices are irrelevant to normative decisions. They cannot tell us how to choose between our choices. What are good and bad choices? What *ought* we choose?

These august terms are expected to have a paralyzing effect and they are almost deliberately designed to arrest discussion. Yet these are words only and should be capable of a linguistic analysis which might remove some of their inhibiting influence. George Lundberg is but one of many who have made fruitful suggestions along this line. He feels, for example, that the word "ought" is a predictive term and reducible to the familiar "if-then" form of any hypothetical statement. "We ought to avoid another war" is an elliptical phrasing of the proposition (or, rather, the propositional function) "if we want to avoid all the undesirable consequences involved in another war (*and we do*), then . . ." No element here, continues Professor Lundberg, including the usually suppressed "and we do," is exempt from the routine hypothesis-verification techniques of scientific method.

I believe an appeal like this is sound and I am convinced that semantic and symbolic analysis is vital as a necessary and preparatory step in relating values to science. But, as was suggested earlier in this paper, such analysis, even if necessary, is hardly sufficient either to convince the antinaturalist or to overcome a culture barrier as high as that now separating fact from value. What more is needed to insure sufficiency is not to be found in an essay, or a book, or in the work of any single philosopher or scientist, even one as dominating as John Dewey. It is to be found (if it ever is to be found) in the cooperative activities of research workers and creative thinkers in all the areas where the very data for investigation are human choices. What is needed is the cross-fertilization already beginning to be employed in the most seminal branches of social science. The expanding new sciences of man are even now calling for the wholesale reconstruction of basic concepts: among those concepts are those of "fact" and "value."

Such a direction, however, is not being indicated simply as an easy way of avoiding some of the responsibilities imposed by the present symposium. Even though it is sincerely believed that no exercise in logic or in polemics can replace the dogged, long-time energies required to bring values and scientific method together, some suggestions about value (bald and thin as they must be at this time) should be forthcoming; otherwise the point of the present controversy has not been faced. That point, to repeat it, is whether there is a way of choosing among values, whether there is some electric "good" which we "ought" to acknowledge. The following items are almost impertinently brief (and they have appeared before), but perhaps they may stimulate reaction.

The locus for any evaluation of human choices has been clearly indicated in the foregoing pages: it is the process of free inquiry itself, the continuum of scientific decision. Such an emphasis assumes, of course, the functioning of other continuities, *e.g.,* the biological and the social. That is, concentration on the places of intelligence is a refinement of, not a substitute for, the techniques of survival. This recognition would constitute one of a cluster of assumptions or postulates, a cluster all the parts of which are intimately related. (The laying down of assumptions may be the quickest way of presenting a position.) Basic in such a set would be the possibly primitive notion that the resolution of conflict, the solving of problems, is "good." Perhaps equally primitive would be the assumption that a social group or in-

dividual organism be judged by its ability to grow as well as to survive. Less foundational would be the proposition that growth is determined by the degree to which men understand their surroundings—surroundings (or environment) *being interpreted in the broadest possible sense as a culture matrix involving biological and psychic facts as well as social and physical.* Understanding or knowledge (to continue) is a matter of doing, of control and change, not simply of contemplation. Conversely, among man's potent tools are his conceptual tools. To this can be added: the scientific enterprise is the symbol of this line of technological growth. (Terms like "technology" and "continuum" are used, despite some possible misinterpretation, because the first calls attention to the significance of tools and technics—conceptual as well as motor—in man's expanding comprehension and control of his surroundings; while the second notes the steady cultural development, even "progress," to be found in the history of human tools and therefore—of human control. There is a cumulative and Promethean power here which can neither be ignored nor put outside the dimension of human choice and its determiners.)

Here, then, is a naked list. It may suggest a clue to an "intrinsic" standard of value—"intrinsic" signifying that the standard is part of a culture and not imposed from without. It may also suggest that scientific method is not "merely" a means to some extramural end, but that it contains within itself a dynamic and self-correcting purpose for which no ethical apologies need be made.

There is nothing facile in any attempted reconciliation of values and science. This is so obvious that it really needs no saying, but, for the record, it should be said so as to indicate that a possible charge of glibness has not been overlooked. Generations, if not centuries, of exploration in the new sciences of man may be required for a dualism so deeply rooted in Western Culture to yield. It may never yield and the race between our present versions of technology and morals may end in any one of the several catastrophic finishes we are asked to foresee almost every day. Not the facility but the necessity for engineering a change is what must be made clear. For what are the alternatives? What are the substitutes for scientific inquiry in the handling of human values? These questions must point up whatever may be important in these pages.

And they are not simply rhetorical questions. The answers can be found almost anywhere: in brute power or in mystical illumination, in retreat to The Church (whichever one) or in esoteric obscurantism, in Moscow or Rome, in Nirvana or on the Left Bank —the choices are generous ones. Are men driven to these—to absolutes, anarchy, or escape—because something called science has been tried and has failed? If there is any grosser libel than this it would be hard to find. Knowledge about man is barely beginning to be won; new disciplines are less than a generation old; methods of procedure are only now being devised. To propose that "Science" has had its chance—and look at the result! is, when honest, intellectual surrender of the most indefensible kind. The contrary is the case: the very methods of intelligent inquiry have been excluded from prosperous contact with whole segments of human experience, those of human decision, excluded not because of demonstrated failure but because of institutional blocks. Behind those blocks flourish now what have always flourished there—despair and absolutism. It is logically risky to employ strong disjunctions, but that values belong to science or to nonscience seems evident. The crucial choice would seem to lie here.

◆◆◆◆◆◆◆◆◆◆◆◆◆◆◆◆◆◆◆◆ THE DISCOVERY OF THE "IRRATIONAL": PERSONAL AND COLLECTIVE   *Max Lerner*

Aᴍᴏɴɢ the intellectual exiles from Germany after Hitler's capture of power in 1933 was a keen political and legal theorist, Professor Hermann Kantorowicz. I sat in a seminar with him for a short time at the University in Exile, one of the many brilliant achievements in Alvin Johnson's crowded life.

"You would not understand this perhaps," he said to us, "because you have not experienced it as we have in Germany. There is an important distinction between thoughts and ideas. Men possess thoughts but ideas possess men."

I shall not easily forget the impact of his remark and the illumination it

Excerpts from Max Lerner, Ideas are Weapons, *copyrighted by Max Lerner, reprinted by permission of The Viking Press, Inc., 1939, pp. 3–12.*

carried. It was not that the distinction between the words "thoughts" and "ideas" meant much to me in itself. Let us rephrase the statement. Let us say we are dealing with the whole realm of what, for lack of a better term, we shall call ideas—the whole intellectual realm. One phase of it is the rational: and here men are in possession of the ideas, using them to clarify their world and subject it to order. The other phase is the irrational: and here the ideas—big sweeping ideas like racism, individualism, Nazism, communism, democracy—are in possession of men. They possess us as evil spirits were once said to have entered into witches and possessed them and made them do their bidding. Under the spell of these ideas a madness seems to sweep over a people, like an engulfing sea that sweeps away the dikes that rationality has painfully and prayerfully built against it over the centuries.

It is the recognition and exploitation of this possessive power of ideas that makes the genius of our age. The great intellectual revolution of the seventeenth century was the discovery of scientific method and its possibilities. That of the eighteenth century was the charting of the map of reason and the subjecting of social institutions to the test of rationality. That of the nineteenth century was the discovery of the world as process rather than as structure, with ascertainable laws of development both in the biological realm (Darwinism) and in the historical and social realm (Marxism). The intellectual revolution of the twentieth century is likely to prove the charting of the *terra incognita* of the irrational and the extraction of its implications for every area of human thought.

If ever the story of this exploration of the irrational is written, it will be one of the exciting adventures in the history of ideas. Such forerunners as Stendhal, Dostoyevsky, and Nietzsche, who searched out the hidden fastnesses of the mind as only men of a tortured imagination can do, belong in the story. Freud is its dominating figure: as our century grows older the serious discussion of his work will be separated from the faddist wranglings over it, and we shall see more clearly his massive influence in exploring the "psychology of the depths" and setting our intellectual task for decades to come. The unfortunate things are that Freud is still regarded primarily as a creative figure in individual psychology, and that to the social sciences he is a pariah. Politics as an art has begun to build upon some of his insights, but politics as a science scorns to. We shall have to place Bergson in the story as well: his *élan vital* is a Gallic version of Nietzsche's *der dunkle Drang*—a life force that sweeps away logical constructions and is the matrix for revolutionary impulse. Sorel will be part of it, with his theory of the social myth and his emphasis of the desire of men to be part of the winning movements of history. Pareto will be part of it— the Pareto who wanders learnedly over the centuries, showing by brilliant illustration how men have built intellectual systems to rationalize their basic drives toward conformity or change. And Hitler will be part of it: for Hitler, whatever his ignorance of the academic lore of psychology, has shown that he has the intuitions of a genius in propaganda—and by intuitions I mean here simply the capacity to translate remembered experience into new and effective action.

This is not the place for an extended discussion either of the new age of propaganda or of the discovery of the irrational. For the present purpose, both must be taken as givens. What I want to emphasize here is how radically this has affected our intellectual orientation. It involves nothing short of a Copernican revolution in ideas. Many of us do not yet know it, because there is always a lag between intellectual change and our awareness of it; but it is nevertheless a fact that the rational right-thinking man has as surely ceased to be regarded the center of our intellectual system as the earth has ceased to be regarded the center of our planetary system.

This is bound to play havoc with intellectual history as it has been traditionally written. There have been two principal traditions in intellectual history. One has been the history of ideas, viewed narrowly in a genteel Matthew Arnold sense as the best that has been thought and said by accredited spokesmen in the proper quarters, and written, after the manner of Deuteronomy, as a genealogical succession of schools of thought. The second has been the history of states of social consciousness, or what Whitehead and after him Carl Becker have called "climates of opinion."

To these must be added now a third approach—that of seeing the history of ideas as the expression of broad social and class forces. Here we may place Taine in France in his studies of English literary history; Franz Mehring in his studies of German literature and especially in his *Lessing-Legende;* Harold Laski in England in his studies of the history of European political thought; and, in America, Charles Beard and Vernon Parrington in their approach to American intellectual history. Some of these are Marxian in their emphasis, the others only loosely

related to the class interpretation. They have in common what Karl Mannheim, in his *Ideology and Utopia,* has called the "unmasking" of ideologies. They view the history of thought as a succession of defensive and aggressive movements directed toward class and group interests and power relations. Their assumption is that both the intellectual apologies for a social order and the intellectual attacks upon it need to be recognized as such before we can lay bare the social impulses behind the work of individual thinkers.

The great merit of this approach is that it goes beyond the rhetoric of ideas. It is not content to consider them at their face-value, or to deal with them as in a pecuniary culture we deal with coins—so many counters of standardized value that have become ends in themselves. It deals with ideas as symbol-formations, half revealing and half concealing the real purposes beneath. It sees that the idea has meaning only in a dynamic context of a struggle over power and values.

But even after one has spelled out these merits, the approach still suffers from overrationalism. It concentrates on the thinker and the idea, and on the conscious or unconscious but none the less rational interests behind both. We shall have to shift our emphasis so as to include not only the conditions of the creation of ideas but also the conditions of their reception, not only the impulses behind the ideas but also the uses to which they are put, not only the thinkers but also the popularizers, the propagandists, the opinion skill-groups, the final audience that believes or disbelieves and acts accordingly. This is, in a sense, a naturalistic approach. It follows through to the actual shapes the idea assumes in its various uses and transformations. And this takes us out of the realm of the rational and of validity into the realm of the irrational and of belief.

For whatever may have been the personal intent or the biographical dilemmas of a thinker (an Adam Smith, an Emerson, a Nietzsche, a Lenin, a Spengler), we do not see his idea as a whole until we see the things that time and men have done to it. Ideas have not only origins and internal consistency; they have also direction and consequence. That Adam Smith would be used to impede economic progress by breaking the government restraints on the concentration of economic power, that Emerson would end up in the homilies of Elbert Hubbard and in editorials against labor legislation, that Nietzsche would be used to exalt a nationalism he despised, that Lenin would become an excuse for an equally mechanical extreme leftism and extreme opportunism, that Spengler would serve to bolster the crudest sort of racism—these may seem only deliciously ironic commentaries on the human comedy, or atoms in the senseless whirl of history. Neither explanation seems valid to me. Nor would I agree that these are merely instances of the distortion of ideas, and therefore irrelevant. For in the history of ideas even their distortions are part of their meaning—the unfolding of a line of direction inherent in the ideas themselves.

The Copernican revolution in intellectual history will not have borne fruit until we adopt a completely naturalistic approach to them. The meaning of an idea must be seen as the focus of four principal converging strains: the man and his biography; the intellectual tradition; the social context, or the age and its biography; the

historical consequences of the idea, or the successive audiences that receive it. When we have grasped this we shall have grasped also the force of the irrational in the history of ideas, the role of propaganda as well as of individual creativeness, the role of immaturity and fear as well as of class and national interest, the role of instinctual drives as well as of logical formulations. We shall, in short, be viewing the idea not wishfully but with our eye on what happens to it.

But does this mean a surrender on our part to the force of the irrational? By no means. There is an enormous difference between the recognition of the role of the irrational and the glorification of it. It is our failure to make this distinction that has largely prevented us from making use of the new insights into the irrational. Liberals and democrats alike have striven hard to keep their skirts clean of any contamination from the irrational—lest by recognizing it they strengthen it and thus play into the fascists' hands. The result is that the term "ideologies," in the sense of systems of belief that serve to energize a culture and make it cohesive and give it a fighting strength, has come to have a meaning restricted to the fascist and communist countries.

If we had more clearly recognized the distinction I speak of, we might have made greater strides than we have made thus far to the problem of reconciling Freud and Marx. The work of Freud himself is from this point of view revealing. Unlike Nietzsche, Sorel, and D. H. Lawrence, who not only recognize the force of the irrational but glory in it, and who seek to get at it through intuition and rhapsody—i.e., by the use of the irrational—Freud approaches it by rigidly scientific and rational procedures of study. Another example is Thomas Mann, whose novels, such as *The Magic Mountain* and the *Joseph* series, are profound explorations of depth-psychology, yet organize these perceptions of the daemonic in the human psyche into a framework of values that looks to the life of reason. We have here the foreshadowing of the task of political science in our time—in fact, of the principal task of our age: that of finding a resolution between the necessary role of the irrational and the demands of social rationality.

It is in some such terms that we shall have to approach the problem and fact of race. The fascists have used it so fantastically and unscrupulously that the rest of us feel as if we ought not to come even within hailing distance of the concept. Yet this is to adopt almost as untenable a position as that of some of the scholars who have been so frightened at the Marxist implications of the class-concept that they refuse to admit the existence of classes. Racial strains and racial differences do exist: for us to deny it is to play into the hands of the fascists by seeking to throw a veil of silence over a patent fact. But we must approach the race-concept scientifically. And thus far what science—both in biology and in anthropology—tells us is that racial strains are not clearly defined even physically and that their psychological and cultural by-products (if any exist) have not proved amenable to scientific study. But to say this is not to deny the role of something approximating a racial factor in history, nor to give up the task of studying its secondary products.

I have little doubt that, more than anything else, what will ultimately defeat fascism is its anti-scientific bias.

The shape that ideas take is relative to the culture and era in which they develop and are used; yet there are internal standards of validity in ideas themselves. The sum of those internal standards is what, for lack of a better term, we call "science," although the philosophers may prefer to call it "truth." The notions we have about science and the methods we use for it will also vary, but the existence of scientific standards cannot be brushed aside either by skepticism or by state fiat. And a culture that sets itself against science by expelling its physicists and biologists and chemists, its doctors and its engineers, is not a culture that will survive. Not only will its armaments be defective, and its synthetic products ultimately unusable; more important, that regard for fact and its validity upon which survival depends will inevitably wither away.

Is there then no real difference between the totalitarianisms and the democracies in their attitude toward the use of ideas? Thus far the difference has not been clear. But it can be made clear and it does exist.

It does not lie, as many would have us believe, in the assumption that a totalitarian state uses ideas for its purposes whereas a democracy does not. Ideas do not exist in the void, separated from the purposes and survival of the culture. In every culture they are weapons. They were used in the making of the Russian Revolution and they have been used in the consolidation of the Soviet power. They played their role in the Nazi revolution, and they have been conscripted for its entrenchment and extension. If we are to be successful in retaining democratic institutions and expanding their meaning, we must be clear about the meaning of democratic ideas, we must make those ideas persuasive, and we must above everything make them an integral part of our daily lives.

The important difference is the difference between the *instrumental* approach to ideas and the *manipulative* approach. The instrumental approach recognizes that ideas are used in behalf of a way of life and in the struggles for its achievement. But it is also humanist. It understands that, if democracy is to mean anything, it must have respect for the common man and not use him cynically as a pawn in the political game. The manipulative approach sees the common people only as so much material to be used. It has no more respect for that material than it would have for counters in any game. If you view ideas instrumentally, your primary regard is for their validity and for the creative action they will evoke through that validity, and for the social cohesion that will result. If you view them manipulatively, your only regard is for the use you can make of them. They become instruments not for creativeness but for contrivance.

The discoveries we have made in the realm of the irrational are important in the struggle for democracy because they pose the task and condition its achievement. Democratic ideas will have validity not because of any moral perfection in themselves but because they fulfill men's needs for security, for stature, for participation in a cultural experience. This means economic change, and of a drastic nature. It means a change in educational procedures which will place the full force of our educational agencies—the school, the press, the radio, the movies—behind the achievement of a socialized democracy. It means the enrollment of new skill-groups, especially those of economic, legal, engineering, and labor technicians, in the government of industry. It means an affirmativeness in our pursuit of cultural goals which will convert our old democratic stereotypes into ideas winged with fire, to touch the imaginations of the young.

The assumption of the fascist thinkers is that only the underlying masses are irrational, and that the ruling élite is a caste endowed with a divine rationality. They are men like gods, equipped to understand and exploit the weaknesses of the common herd but themselves untouched by the same weaknesses. This has unfortunately been the assumption of our liberal élites as well, insofar as they have recognized the problem of the irrational. But the assumption of a democratic culture must be at once more modest and more realistic. Granted individual differences, we are all—élite and mass—of the same basic human material. There can be no ruling caste that is not subject to the same irrationalisms as the people ruled. And there can be no noble and enduring democratic culture unless those who are leaders, while showing the way, do so with an understanding both of their own limitations and the creativeness of the mass.

I suspect that fascism will die in the end not only because of military adventurism and economic collapse, but also because it will have overreached itself in the realm of ideas. To pursue *Machtpolitik* as Hitler has been pursuing it means to be cynical of idea-systems and contemptuous of the minds you are manipulating. This cynicism and contempt may seem for a time to go unpunished. But all the time they are destroying the only principle of cohesiveness a culture can have—belief on the part of the common people in a way of life. When that crumbles the culture crumbles. War and economic collapse will simply remove the outward props, and reveal the inner principle of disintegration.

Hermann Rauschning has spoken of the lack of principle on the part of the Nazi élite as nihilism. He is right. But the ironic thing about his book is the note of hurt and disillusion in it, as if his original trust in the Nazi ideology had been betrayed. What he does not see is that the fear of the masses which first led him to join the Nazi movement is exactly the essence of the nihilism that developed out the movement.

What is cynical about Hitler, as about every adventurist leader, is not his lack of fixed principle. It is his basic contempt for people. And that means ultimately his hatred of life.

Ideas are necessarily weapons. But they will be effective as weapons only if the uses to which they are put are life-affirming. If the craftsmen in ideas have a belief in the possibilities of human society and a sense of the dignity of ordinary people, that will be the best safeguard of those ultimate standards of validity that we call science and truth.

◆◆◆◆◆◆◆◆◆◆◆◆◆◆◆◆◆◆◆◆ THE EFFICACY OF REASON

Arthur E. Murphy

We are now in a position to deal affirmatively with the issue whose mishandling has led to so much confusion. In what sense are social ideals true? How do they or ought they to correspond to facts, "realities," "the actual direction of events," and the "imperatives" of history? And what bearing has such correspondence or the lack of it on their validity as ideals and on the claims their protagonists make for our support? In outline, the answer has already been given. A valid ideal is a genuine and attainable good proposed as a goal for action and capable of uniting and directing the activity of the group to which it is addressed in the just and effective pursuit of the good it represents. That is what it ought to be, if its acceptance is to be reasonably justified, and that is what, when it proves reasonably justifiable, it is. Questions of factual truth are inseparably bound up with the assessment of the validity of ideals, and the determination of truth must here be made, as elsewhere, without appeals to any special insight, or authority or metaphysical illumination that transcends the pedestrian methods of fact-finding appropriate to the discovery of what is happening, has happened and is likely to happen in the world in which our bodies and their perceptually observable environment are palpably involved. But since questions of what has happened, is happening or will probably happen are here considered in their bearing on what is desirable as a goal for action, and since what is desirable, on the human level,

Excerpted from Arthur E. Murphy, The Uses of Reason, *New York: The Macmillan Company, 1943, pp. 251–280. Abridged and used by permission.*

is a question not only of what is actual and possible but also of what is good, the factual question is not the only one at issue. Information about matters of fact thus determined is necessary but not sufficient to the adequate validation of ideal claims. If this is what those have meant who tell us that an ideology cannot, from its very nature, claim "scientific" truth, but that it must none the less correspond to the conditions of actuality, then so far their pronouncement has been correct, though most unhappily stated. The manner of this correspondence, however, is what has been most radically misconceived. A valid ideal is itself neither a report nor the expression of an attitude or wish, but an estimate, based on reports, of the good worth pursuing under actual conditions in which a variety of wishes and attitudes in themselves incoherent and full of potential conflicts can attain a reasonable satisfaction. To call it irrational or mythical because it represents a good not now actual or capable of "verification" as a report of an existing state of affairs, is to apply an impertinent and wholly misleading criterion. In the context of social action, which is that of its relevant use, an ideal would be irrational, because inadequate to its essential intent, if it did *not* represent a good not now actual. For anyone who could suppose that the continuance of the existing state of affairs represented the best goal attainable for cooperative human action would be almost incredibly unwise. To call such ideals "myths" is misleading. "Myths" are, in common usage, ideas that have been found to lack a kind of validity which those who seriously accepted them supposed them to have, while a valid social ideal need not lack anything whatever that is required for

a reasonable acceptance of its claims. The suggestion, bound up with the use of the terms "myth," and "stereotype," that those who take social ideals seriously as standards for conduct are fooling themselves and are as deluded as those who thought to see Jupiter emerge from the heavens or Venus from the waves, is thoroughly unwarranted. The cynicism it engenders is less the fruit of uncommon penetration than of the uncritical use of an uncommonly careless terminology.

We can also reject as mistaken the view that the determination of what is good, as an ideal for cooperative social action, is a merely arbitrary affair. This view proceeds on the assumption that no other rational discipline is attainable than that which restricts its activity to the collection and reporting of facts and that this would, in the circumstances, be inadequate to justify the choice of an ideal. It gains its plausibility in part from the quite arbitrary classification on which it is based, everything not scientifically verifiable being relegated to the limbo of sentimental fantasy and the like. But it survives, also, through the ignorance, which a triumphant scientific specialism has fostered, of that rational discipline in which the facts of the sciences are organized for purposes of constructive and comprehensive wisdom in the direction of policy. We must try, therefore, to make clear the nature of this discipline and the way that reason can work, and does work, in the context of social action.

Social Science and Social Ideals

The proximate area of such activity, now, alas, a battleground for contending sects rather than a well developed field of inquiry, is that in which social scientists and their followers dispute about the social meaning and use of their findings. Should investigators in the fields of politics, economics and psychology maintain the "impartial objectivity" elsewhere associated with scholarly research, or is it rather their business to direct their activity to the promotion of causes whose merits they, more than other men, are in a position accurately to assess? The academic tradition still reveres what Mr. Lancelot Hogben calls the "idol of purity" in research, but an increasing number of practical minded researchers, Mr. Hogben among them, preach the duty of carrying through the implications of scientific findings to controversial and tendencious applications. And they practice what they preach. Mr. Robert Lynd, in a provocatively entitled volume *Knowledge for What?* has stated the case for the "tendencious" sect very ably, and I shall make use of his analysis in what follows.

It might be supposed that since the issue, basically, is that of the propriety of the social scientist sponsoring the use of his findings as guides for social policy, some careful attention would normally be given to the question of the bearing of these findings on issues of social action, and the kind of contribution a scientist can best make to their adjudication. It is just here, however, that the confusion has been greatest, with the result—not usual in such cases—that each side in the controversy maintains with fervor a half truth which it, and its antagonists, are unable to keep distinct from a whole error. Each, therefore, in defending his own morsel of insight against his opponent's error, commits an error of his own which that opponent is justified in exposing, and the exposure of which he takes as the sufficient justification

for the complementary error he has mistakenly espoused. This sort of thing can go on indefinitely, and does.

The defenders of "objective impartiality" in the social sciences stand initially on firm ground. The first, most basic, and most indispensable contribution that the social sciences can make to the adjudication of social issues is to supply reliable information on relevant matters of fact. This will be information about what happens, or would probably happen, under determinable conditions, and nothing is more painfully clear than that many well intentioned social policies have failed for lack of just such information. Under these conditions what matters is that the information should be accurate, and that its relevance to the probable success or failure of a proposed course of action should be clearly made out. The information may well be of a disappointingly unideal character. It may be such as to warrant the rejection of ideals which appeal to the best in human nature and which we should all like to subscribe to if we could. But if it is information that accurately portrays the situation within which our ideal activities must be carried on, it is the responsibility of reasonable men to take account of it and refuse to be deceived by false hopes.

Now, what the defenders of objectivity rightly affirm is that in the gathering and reporting of such factual information the researcher's first duty is to see things as they are or can be, not as he would like them to be, and that he must, in the pursuit of truth, rigidly repress his own desires and preferences and social enthusiasms. If he feels called upon to justify conclusions antecedently determined by the interests of the class or race or religious sect to which he belongs, and to accommodate his findings to such interests, he is selling his scientific birthright for a mess of pottage. Nothing that the scientist can contribute as seer, or sectarian propagandist, or lay preacher, can compare in value with what he contributes as purveyor of reliable—though sometimes discouraging—information about the nature of the world. It is, therefore, of the utmost importance that, as a researcher, he respect the canons of "purity," or of logical and factual accuracy which, here as elsewhere, are our best available means for distinguishing what in fact occurs from mistaken, though frequently attractive, beliefs and opinions about it. "The facts" apart from an evaluation of their social significance may be of little use; but the social significance of "facts" which are not facts at all is hardly an improvement on them. What is of supreme value is an adequate interpretation of facts which are genuinely what they purport to be. But for that we must first of all have the facts, and a zeal for social significance which gets in the way of their accurate determination is no help at all either to science or to society.

It might seem that this would go without saying—that no one worth considering would seriously question it. And there are indeed few, in this country at least, who would care to challenge it explicitly. There are plenty, however, who are prepared to deny its implications when they prove inconvenient. Nor is their procedure wanting in a kind of specious plausibility. For *mere* facts are quite surely not sufficient to provide a just basis for the criticism of a social ideal, and the disciples of "the facts, and nothing but the facts" have often supposed that they were sufficient. Hence, the reaf-

firmation of "spiritual" values, against the ostensible denial of "meanings" that "transcend" the facts can easily be made the basis for a resurgent idealism that will not stop until it has made its own deeper desires the measure of what is "ultimately" or "really" the case. Such enthusiasts need not call themselves idealists—they may be aggressively materialistic in their philosophy and still proclaim a doctrine of "the unity of theory and practice" which means in practice that no theory is to be accepted as true which is not subservient to the doctrines and policies they consider essential to the success of their cause. Or they may be racists who find in the deeper promptings of their "blood" a truth for which the abstractions of the sciences are but a feeble substitute. Against these forms of obscurantism, and others like them, it therefore remains pertinent to affirm that where a claim to factual knowledge is in question there is nothing so "ultimate" or worthy of credence as the evidence which bears on the factual truth or accuracy of statements made, and that the proper standard for the estimation of this evidence is not practical but theoretical. For this is a question of what is in fact the case, whether we like it or not, and however much or little the knowledge of it may contribute to the peace of the soul, the progress of the class struggle, or the meaning of life. And this, as we have seen, is not without bearing on the determination of social policy. For it is a primary obligation of a good society to keep open the channels of free inquiry and responsible research, without which the relevant facts cannot be found out and made available for the enlightened direction of action. So much has been already established, and its pertinence to the issue of "objectivity" in the social sciences is obvious. A science that refuses to be "practical"—in the sense that it refuses subservience, direct or indirect, to any other interest than the discovery and publication of the truth, within the area of its factual investigation—is one of the most practical—i.e., useful and valuable—factors in a civilized society. It should be valued and respected as such.

The question of the bearing of the findings of scientific research on social policy none the less remains. The interpretation must not be allowed to prejudice the facts, but the facts are of little use without the interpretation. What the more judicious advocates of a tendencious social science mean to say, I think, is that the scientist has not completed his work until he has shown what action the facts warrant and lent his active support to such action. "If one is not simply observing the inner orderliness of nature, the essence of science is to analyze, to draw inferences, *and then to implement action.*" [1] Action to what end? Is the scientist also to tell us that? Mr. Lynd thinks that he is. It is the sort of task once left to ethics, which was supposed to criticize ends, where the sciences gave information only concerning means. This distinction, Lynd believes, is no longer defensible. "The old, aloof ethics has evaporated, and ethics is today but a component in the cravings of persons going about the daily round of living with each other. And the science of human behavior in culture as the science charged with appraising man's optional futures in the light of himself and of present favoring and limiting conditions, can no more escape dealing with man's deep values

and the potential futures they suggest than it can avoid dealing with the expressions, overlayings, and distortions of man's cravings which appear in the institutions of a particular culture." [2]

There is little point in arguing whether it is "the scientist" or "the philosopher" who is licensed to perform a particular job. Anyone who can do it well ought by all means to do it, whatever his academic designation. But what are the requirements for doing this job well? That is an important question, and I do not think that even Mr. Lynd, who does much better at it than most of his colleagues, has given a satisfactory answer. How are we to "deal with" man's deepest cravings when our problem is to determine which social policies are desirable and which are not? We can, of course, catalogue them, and report on the way in which they manifest themselves in a variety of social conditions, but what we want to know is how they ought to be manifest in a social organization judged to be worth attaining. That such an organization ought to be such as to satisfy all our "deepest" cravings is a sound moral judgment—but it *is* a moral judgment and not a report of things as they are nor a prediction as to what in fact they will become. It involves an estimate of what they could become, under favorable conditions, but many other eventualities are just as possible, and some of them much more probable, unless a concern for what is felt to be right and good acts as a considerable motivating force in human behavior. Nor is the manner of this organization an affair merely of adjusting "cravings" to each other, so that all will continue to function without overt conflict. It is a matter of adjusting them all to the demands of re-

[1] Robert Lynd, *Knowledge for What?* p. 166. Italics in text.

[2] *Ibid.,* p. 191.

sponsible persons who act at times for ends they judge to be right and reasonable. If it is less than this, it is, as we have seen, a misrepresentation of the requirements for reasonable social action.

The trouble is that scientists, in their professional capacity have been very chary of using terms like "justice" in an evaluative sense, or of making judgments about what ought to be. Hence, when they feel called upon to pass judgment on the ends of reasonable action they are tempted to govern their estimate of this total situation by those factors which they have found pertinent and reliable in a more limited field of inquiry. "Cravings" are factual enough—everybody can identify them. What these cravings "demand" can perhaps be listed, and might even be measured, if we were just a little further advanced in these matters. But the question that has to be settled is not what these cravings or drives demand but what practical wisdom demands when drives are harmonized and disciplined with reference to a represented good which justifies and lends meaning to their inarticulate urgency. Again, it may be possible to estimate what our present technological equipment "demands" for its maximum efficient use, and there are bright young men who write as though the "demands" of technology stood as unconditional imperatives to which the rest of human life must accommodate itself on such terms as it can make. There are also "imperatives" of history, of geography, and even of thermo-dynamics [3] which are invoked to tell us scientifically what men and nations require and what, in

[3] Cf. L. Hogben, *The Retreat from Reason*, p. 7off. The page references are to the British edition.

consequence, they ought to have and to be. In the context of reasonable social action, however, all these are hypothetical imperatives—they are addressed not to partially embodied abstractions which reflect the limits of professional specialization, but to men whose business it is to decide how, in the kind of world the sciences describe to them, they want to live, and to what end. There is, however, one categorical imperative for men of good will, and that is that they consider their fellows as ends—as responsible moral agents —not merely as means to the ends set by considerations of economics, or geopolitics, or the adjustment of "drives" on a level at which a rat will do as well as a man or, in some cases, even better.

When, therefore, we express considerable doubt concerning the crusading social scientist as an arbiter of social policy, the reason is clear. The social scientist is also a man, and he may be a wise and conscientious one. If he is wise, his judgment on issues of social policy will be most valuable, and if he is conscientious he will want to bear his full share in supporting good causes. Let him by all means be as practical in both these ways as he can. But if he insists on guiding his practical decisions by the abstractions which have proved their use in his theoretical inquiry, and if he assumes in his support of practical causes the right to exclude from human concern everything that would be out of place in his scientific calculations, he will, at best, be wasting his time and ours. "The union of theory and practice" is a fine thing, if it means that plans for action are to have the benefit of reliable information, obtained by the soundest of theoretical methods, and that the results of theory are in this way to be put to practical use. But the confusion of theory and practice is a very bad thing and, at present, a very pervasive one. Those who suborn the pursuit of truth for "practical" purposes, and those who distort sound practical judgment by restricting its subject-matter to the abstractions with which their scientific inquiry has been professionally concerned, are more nearly related than either party would care to admit. They both have failed to distinguish the respective contexts of theoretical inquiry and practical judgment, and to observe in each the rational discipline proper to its effective exercise.

Should the social scientist deal with "values"? By all means. If he is "dealing with" them descriptively, in terms of the occurrence of valuations or their causes and effects, he can doubtless tell us a great deal that is both interesting on its own account and relevant to our further problems. The fact that he disapproves of some of these valuations, or wishes that they were more easily controlled by considerations of which he does approve should in no way influence the accuracy of his reporting. If it did, the report would be less genuinely "practical" than it ought to be —less reliable as information about what happens. If he is dealing with them evaluatively, from the standpoint of their worth as social ideals, he may again have something valuable to tell us. But it must be realized that he is here speaking from a different standpoint and that if he proposes to assume the authority of that standpoint, and in consequence to tell men categorically what their lives require and what they ought to value, he must accept its responsibilities. And here the requirements of reason are comprehensive wisdom and sound judgment in the determination of a good worth living for, not simplicity and accuracy in the description of selected aspects of behavior. If he is not called to this task or competent to perform it, he is under no obligation to undertake it. His scientific work is a sufficient and indispensable contribution to the good of the society in which he functions. But if he does undertake it he ought to do so responsibly and with an adequate knowledge of what he is about. Lacking this he gives us social cynicism in the guise of "objectivity" and insensitiveness to cultural values as "scientific humanism." We have had more than enough of both.

The Relativity of Principles and the "Taint of Ideology"

"But whence," we shall be asked, "are these lofty principles and impartial ideals supposed to be derived?" Men act, even at the best, from a partial and limited standpoint within the natural and social world, and their preferences will inevitably reflect the bias of that standpoint. The nations that fight for the freedom of mankind visualize freedom in the local terms with which they are familiar and have curious difficulty in focussing their moral insight on applications of the principle which would impair their own more mundane interests. "History relativizes all ideals," as Reinhold Niebuhr has remarked, and human beings and their ideas are creatures of time, circumstance and history.

This is true, and a clear understanding of it is indispensable to a just estimate of the rational cogency of social ideals. To quote Niebuhr again: "Man's ideas are conditioned not only by the means of production upon which he depends and the economic interests which he seeks to defend; they are also conditioned by racial history, geographic influences, family traditions, and every conceivable partial perspective of a mind embedded in a finite organism. Yet this creature of finitude touches the fringes of the infinite, and every awakened human mind reaches for the universally valid value and the unconditioned truth. [4]

So it is, and so, with any reasonably adequate grasp of the history of ideas, we should have expected it to be. Moreover, we use these very limited ideas as the means through which we reach for the values that are genuinely valid and the truths that are unconditionally true. And sometimes we reach our goal, though not quite in the manner that Mr. Niebuhr seems to suppose. If there is any mystery in this, and great mystery has been made of it for purposes of edification, there are two considerations about the functioning of human reason which can contribute substantially to its resolution. We have encountered them before, and can use them here, I believe, with some profit to the subject in hand.

The first is the observation that the conditions of the relativity of human ideals are also the conditions of their relevance to the needs and problems of the people who are to make use of them. Every claim to the recognition of a value is meaningfully addressed only "to whom it may concern," and it is the concerns of men who live at a point in time and a locality in space, with families, work to do, loyalties to acknowledge, and hopes that a reasonable ideal may redirect and clarify but cannot initially create, that form the stuff of purpose of which social action must be made. Nor is this a defect in their nature. If the Word is to become flesh and the Logos to achieve an his-

torical incarnation it must acquire a local habitation and genealogy in the process. Nor is this a mystery which achieves its idealizing effect once only, or in a single place. "The gods of the Ethiopians are black," said a cynical philosopher, and those who saw, and understood, Marc Connelly's *The Green Pastures* will add that it is well that it should be so. The content of valid human ideals is the content of human experience, organized, clarified and focussed on a represented good that can direct action that would otherwise be frustrated and incomplete to a fruitful and coherent issue. Those who, like Mr. T. S. Eliot, can find a good worth seeking only in dark adumbrations of an unspeakable revelation are indeed fastidious. They are also, in the context of social action, remarkably unperceptive. It is only a four dimensional ideal, of the earth, though not altogether earthy, and the people who live in it, that is good enough to find a place in the affairs of men. If we are still saddled with a view about practical reason which maintains its purity by divorcing itself from the context of its effective use, this might seem surprising enough. But we have seen good reasons for rejecting that view, and are, therefore, not inclined to be alarmed or intimidated when its unhappy implications parade as witnesses of a sinful bias in thinking that fails to conform to its arbitrary specifications.

For, and this is our second consideration, "bias" in any sense in which it is humanly or rationally objectionable, is not an affair of the origin of ideas, but of the way in which they are used in the situations in which they function. A limited ideal—and all ideals within the range of social action are limited— may be used narrowly and stupidly, to

[4] Reinhold Niebuhr, *Christianity and Power Politics*, p. 155.

blind those who accept it to possibilities of good which fall outside its scope. So far as this is the case it represents an interest which, relative to the good attainable in that situation, is partial and merely special. But if it is reasonably condemned it can only be in the light of a better ideal, one which also has its human origins and represents specific interests. If the latter interests define a more inclusive attainable good they are, *in that situation,* on the side of reason, which works through them to secure the best there attainable. To condemn an ideal as "biased" from the standpoint of a universal good which is not, in that situation, a real possibility, may be profound in some higher sense, but, in the context of social action, it is dangerously misleading and inept.

Mr. Niebuhr has seen this clearly and his insistence on it does much to compensate for the obscurities of his theology. Doubtless the spokesmen for freedom in this war have sinned as, indeed, from the standpoint of a wholly "unbiased" goodness, all men must. Nevertheless, the question that concerns us is whether the ideal they offer is a better goal for action than the alternative presented. On this point there can be no reasonable doubt, though when Niebuhr's book was written there was much doubt and contention among the theologians about it. For "it is sheer moral perversity to equate the inconsistencies of a democratic civilization with the brutalities which modern tyrannical states practice. If we cannot make a distinction here, there are no historical distinctions which have any value. *All the distinctions upon which the fate of civilization has turned in the history of mankind have been just such relative distinctions.*" [5] In so far,

[5] *Ibid.,* pp. 16–17, my italics.

then, as it is the function of reason in social action to help us to make just such decisions wisely, it is a relative good, which is also a genuine one, that we must expect to support. But not a "merely" relative and therefore arbitrary one. For the situation in which we act is one in which distinctions of better and worse are made from the standpoint of responsible moral action. The "justice" achieved will not be eternal nor its application independent of habits of thought about fair dealing which are local (like everything else that is capable of growth) in their origin, and limited in their scope. If it is, for all that, the means of achieving a measure of shared well-being not otherwise procurable, and if the effort to secure it favors, on the whole, the agencies and interests through which a further progress can later be made, it is right and reasonable and ought to be accepted by those responsible, in the given situation, for reaching a decision on its merits.

Because such ideals are limited and shaped to meet existing conditions, they may, of course, become impediments to further progress when conditions change and new needs and possibilities are to be dealt with. They have no inherent sanctity about them; their virtue is in their capacity to organize human purposes to an attainable good. The failure of traditional individualism to meet twentieth century needs is not proof that our ancestors were fooling themselves but that we should be fooling ourselves if we failed to apply to our problems as independent and discriminating a judgment about relevant ideals as they applied to theirs. The essential condition for the rational use of ideals is the capacity to refashion and readjust them to the requirements of changed conditions and, it is to be hoped, a broadening concern for human welfare. Those that can be so refashioned, that are in this way on the side of growth and humanity, are on the side of reason, and the interests which support them in this activity are, in their functioning, rational interests. Those that oppose them, though they speak with the authority of a good beyond space and time are, in this situation, anti-rational and their claim is an arbitrary and illegitimate one. For reason lives in its work, not in the monuments of its past success, and its work is in the world in which men discover what is true and use their knowledge to clarify and strengthen their common interests through cooperative activity that can complete itself in a common good. From the standpoint of this activity and no other is any social ideal properly judged as rational or irrational, "tainted" or pure.

Reason and the Future

There has been much said in the preceding chapters about foreseeing the future and acting under the guidance of ideals which present an anticipated good which functions, in the minds of reasonable men, in the organization of present conduct. But it needs only a little acquaintance with the history of ideas to convince us that our capacity to foresee the future, especially at the complicated level of social planning, is limited indeed, and that things rarely turn out as those who planned for them had anticipated.

One maxim at least we can affirm with some confidence. *There is no short cut to the future.* Forces we can now discern will indeed shape the "world of tomorrow," for it is through what now is that what is to be is made actual. But they will operate in conjunc-

tion with others we have barely been able to make out and they will, in the context of social action, function not as iron laws of destiny but as conditions and possibilities, setting problems for that future present to solve but by no means dictating in advance the inescapable terms of that solution. There is little use in transporting ourselves with our existing entanglement in the past and lack of adequate knowledge of the present, to a future peace conference, to lay down in advance the terms on which the nations of the world as they then will be are to live together. Not only is the world going then to be different, but we ourselves are going to be different, also. Effective decisions are made not in a now projected future but in the present in which that future becomes actual, and while we hope to have a hand in making those decisions, it doth not yet appear what we shall be.

Does this mean that there is no use in making plans, or in trying to see ahead? By no means. But it does have some bearing on the nature of our plans, and on the way in which we can reasonably use them. What we can determine, in *our* present, is not "the future" in its concrete complexity, with the decisions that will have to adjust themselves to that complexity if they are to be intelligent. It is rather the past, by which that future, when it becomes a present, will be conditioned. Nobody doubts that what we are and do today is tied down at every turn by what has gone before and cannot now be changed. We would change it if we could, but the time for that has gone by. But our present will be a part of the past by which the possibility of future good is, in its turn, determined. We cannot directly give our future selves a predetermined present, but we can give them a good past, and nothing will be more important or more valuable in the day when their decisions must be made. We cannot make those decisions now, but we can now help to make the selves who will make those decisions and the conditions under which the decisions can be wisely and perhaps even generously arrived at.

The future will be what it will be, and no man is wise enough to lay down in advance the rules to which wise future action must conform. But reasonable men, without any superhuman endowments, can often make out the rules according to which *present* action can be carried on in guaranteeing to that future resources and capacities which our own foresight has helped to prepare. It is in that spirit and with that end in view—a future end, like any other, toward which we try to work with the best knowledge available—that reasonable social action can fruitfully proceed.

Among these capacities, none has better proved its right to our continued confidence than the capacity to learn by experience—which is the capacity to make up one's mind on the basis of the best evidence available and to change one's mind when new evidence shows the wisdom of such change. And no-

where is the pertinence of what has just been said about the relation of present planning to future decision more obvious than here. It is to be expected that many of our present ideas about social policy will have to be altered, and ought to be altered, in the light of events that have not yet transpired. We cannot protect ourselves in advance against the necessity of having to change our minds, in the light of new knowledge, though some philosophers seem to think that there ought to be some epistemological or metaphysical device which would afford such protection— by supplying us in advance with certainties exempt from the vicissitudes of further inquiry. If such certainties anywhere exist, they are too empty, or too exalted, to be of serious use in the determination of social policy. But we can now develop the discipline which enables those who follow it to change their minds reasonably and thus to welcome and profit by new experience, not merely to ignore or be upset by it. And while our knowledge of the future is precarious and limited, there is good reason, based on four centuries of success in scientific inquiry, to believe that those who are prepared to learn in this way will find out much that is to their advantage.

◆◆◆◆◆◆◆◆◆◆◆◆◆◆◆◆◆◆◆◆◆◆ FREEDOM UNDER PLANNING

Karl Mannheim

Pₗₐₙₙᵢₙg raises the fundamental philosophical question: "Is not an ideally planned society a prison, a strait-jacket, even compared with the almost intolerable life led by many classes in an unplanned society? In the latter many

From Karl Mannheim, Man and Society in an Age of Reconstruction, *New York: Harcourt, Brace & World, Inc., 1941, pp. 364–381. Used by permission.*

people may be threatened with insecurity, but the individual is still (potentially at least) a free agent and can cope with his difficulties himself. Does not the continual development of social technique lead to the complete enslavement of the individual?" The question is only too justified, and if a human solution of our present problems is to be possible at all, an answer must be found.

It is all the more necessary to consider the possibility of freedom in an age of highly developed social technique, as a conception of freedom modelled on the preceding age is an obstacle to any real understanding of our problems and hinders the transition to a new type of action. Both the man in the street and the practical politician have vague conceptions of freedom, so that a historical and sociological explanation of the term is no barren speculation but the prelude to action.

We are gradually coming to realize that the contemporary forces which have led to the development of social technique express the desire of the human mind to control, not merely its environment but also, through the latter, itself. Half-hearted techniques lead to the enslavement of mankind; fully considered techniques to a higher level of freedom.

It is by no means an accident that the problem of freedom has been one of the most recurrent in the history of religion and the philosophy of man. In spite of all the efforts which have been made to solve it during the course of history, it seems to us that the problem of determinism and free will has always been couched in too abstract a form. The philosophies of the past in so far as they deal with the subjective aspects of the problem have penetrated into the deepest levels of the self. But the same cannot be said about the objective aspects. The question "Is man free?" in relation to the outside world can only become concrete if one does not think of the universe as a whole but becomes aware of the fact that the forms of freedom can only be formulated in reference to a given society and to the social techniques existing in it. The type of freedom whch is possible in one society cannot be reasonably demanded in another, which may have other forms of freedom at its command. In short the actual form depends to a large extent on the level of social technique and is also determined by the following factors:

1. The control which can be exercised over social affairs within the framework of the existing social structure.

2. The type of foresight which is possible in a given social pattern.

3. The strength of the desire for a science of government at the present stage of development; by which I mean the eagerness of the ruling élites to avail themselves of any existing or potential knowledge as to the fairest and most efficient methods of conducting social affairs.

To the abstract approach of a naïve mind which conceives of freedom in general terms without reference to the concrete historical situation, freedom corresponds to the strength of human initiative, the desire to influence social conditions which are as yet uncontrolled or uncontrollable. This definition is vague, so that the question how far and in which form initiative is possible in a given society, can receive many different answers according to the nature of the social structure. It is equally indeterminate with regard to another question: How far can a definite type of social environment be changed and where are the best points to intervene? The answer to these inquiries will again depend on the nature of the historical situation.

I should like to give two simple examples to prove that the possible types of freedom vary in different societies. In friendship I call myself free if I always have the opportunity of opposing my partner's wishes. If it were necessary to compromise I should still feel free, provided I agreed to this compromise of my own accord. But I should no longer feel free if my partner got his way by physical force or by psychological compulsion, for instance by hypnosis. Thus in a fairly simple social relationship such as friendship, freedom is expressed in the continual opportunity for resistance, in the continual possibility of taking the initiative, in the continual process of voluntary compromise with the wishes of one's partner. On the same level, coercion would correspond to permanent subjection, a permanent sacrifice of initiative.

The situation is quite different if we imagine a small organized group. It would be senseless to believe that its freedom consisted in all its members exerting their free will and demanding that every step which was taken by the group should always be an unstable compromise between different impulses. An organized group can only act collectively if, when organized action is necessary, individuals obey the prescribed rules. And yet one does not feel that in joining an organization a man necessarily renounces all initiative and free will, but rather that in spite of the sacrifice of unlimited individual freedom, the distinction between free and authoritarian organization can be seen in the methods of regulating collective action. In the former, freedom consists in a clear definition of the spheres where complete freedom of action is possible, and of democratic control over the rules governing the regulated spheres. But we should no longer call an organization free if it made continuous efforts to regulate every sphere of action, allowing individual members no say in the aim and organization of its activities, while its officials were not elected but dictatorially appointed from above. This example will suffice to show how senseless it is to translate one social relationship in terms of another, and to speak of lack of freedom in the abstract instead of thinking what form of freedom is possible in a given social setting.

In our next example we shall deal with another aspect of freedom. Here too we shall study the problem at different stages of group formation and in different social settings. But this time we shall understand by freedom, not so much freedom of action but the possibility of self-expression. We should scarcely call a friendship free, if the stronger partner would never allow the other to express his feelings spontaneously but forced him to act the hypocrite. We should say freedom of self-expression existed if there were a continual give and take of emotion, an emotional harmony based on a common outlook; the result of a spontaneous discussion of situations and events.

In an organization emotional freedom of this kind is out of the question. An organized group can only function if its members have become accustomed to certain institutional attitudes from the outset. Obedience to orders is not enough, emotions must be subject to control, at least in certain spheres. Instead of the complete freedom of self-expression to be found in the first example, education and training have produced certain permanent attitudes of mind, and therefore in some directions at any rate, have suppressed this freedom.

At the second stage social relationships have grown so complex that institutions are essential, though they can still be democratically controlled. But the same principle applies, and we can still decide whether an organization is wantonly depriving its members of their humanity and turning them into robots, and whether emotional control has been established by authority or by consent.

When character building has reached this stage, not every influence is regarded as a tyranny, but only those which are imposed by a minority without the consent of the group, or which interfere with self-expression to an unwarranted degree, considering the real needs of that particular environment. In any case freedom of self-expression cannot be measured by standards which are transferred from one social setting to another. Freedom in the family is one thing and freedom in the playground is another; the freedom of a religious sect differs from that of a political party, and the social guarantees of freedom must vary in conception accordingly.

But these sociological variations in the conception of freedom only become significant when we consider the problem, not merely in relation to the different groups and settings in any given society, but from the standpoint of the three stages in the development of social technique, which we have already discussed.

At the stage of chance discovery, of trial and error, freedom expresses itself in direct action on and reaction to the stimuli of the surroundings. Lack of freedom is felt if one is prevented from taking the necessary steps to satisfy one's wishes as they arise. At this stage, not unlike an animal which feels hampered when it is prevented from using its body as it wishes, man feels his freedom at stake when he is not allowed to handle things or people as he hoped to do. The immediateness with which freedom expresses itself at this stage is not essentially changed when man has learnt to use the simple tools. The difference is only that by identification with these tools he will feel frustrated when he is denied their use or possession just as though they were an extension of his body. Although the use of the simple tools does not surpass the stage of chance discovery, it marks an advance, for the process of adjustment is becoming more active. The equilibrium between man, his desires and his environment is now brought about by altering part of the surroundings instead of snatching at any pleasure which offers itself. Any obstacle to the occasional alteration of these surroundings is regarded as a threat to freedom.

In the process of this active adjustment to the surroundings we pass to the second stage—that of invention. Owing to an accumulated knowledge of tools and their combined uses we can set more and more intermediate ends and means between ourselves and some ultimate goal which might still be very vague. At the stage of invention we learn to make ourselves more and more independent of natural conditions as they happen to occur, so that this increased command over intermediate aims becomes the most vital expression of our freedom. An employer, a man of property, a bureaucrat and a general have greater freedom than their subordinates because they can determine both the aims of an enterprise and the methods of achieving them. Apart from freedom to decide one's own destiny and dispose of one's own property, freedom will depend on the influence one is able to exert in determining the aims which are to be realized by collective action.

Technique, while freeing us from the tyranny of nature, gives rise to two new forms of dependence. All progress in technique is bound up with additional social organization. If I use better weapons in a hunting expedition or irrigate the soil to make it more fertile, the necessary preliminaries such as the production of the weapons or the construction of canals can only be completed by means of a collective division of labour. Thus no sooner has technique made me independent of nature than it subjects me in the same measure to the inevitable social coercion which co-operation entails.

But there is another reason why technique is apt to produce a new form of determinism. It has an unintentional effect upon the choice of ends, and ultimately on the psychology of mankind. The first step towards the technical alteration of the surroundings, the first impulse which led a man for instance to collect leaves in order to make a comfortable bed, instead of going to sleep on the bare ground or in the nearest cave, had immediate reactions. Man has begun a series of actions which have made him more delicate and this process of civilization has changed him. When we consider the fact that every invention has helped to change mankind, it soon becomes clear that our own age is not the first in which man, in changing his environment, has changed himself. He has always done it quite unconsciously in the past. The more we consider the

history of this process the more obvious it becomes that the formation of character, even in the past, was in no way exclusively dependent on the inner development of the individual. The cumulative effect of civilization alters, not merely our relationship to nature, but our own character as well.

At the second stage (that of invention), a far more complicated "second nature" replaces the first. This "second nature" is technique—and the organized relationships which the mastery of technique demands. The more technique frees us from the arbitrary force of circumstance, the more we are entangled in the network of social relationships we have ourselves created. From the human point of view this "second nature" is no less chaotic and menacing than the first, as long as these relationships cannot be grasped in their totality and therefore controlled. It is immaterial whether man be destroyed by hunger and earthquake, or by social maladjustments leading to war and revolution; the effect is just the same, although the original calamity was due in the first case to natural, and in the second to social, causes. The course of events as a whole is unpredictable, just as natural events were unpredictable before they had been studied. We are free to produce and manipulate individual tools, or to devise certain organizations and then work them out in detail, but we are powerless at this stage both theoretically and practically to master the cumulative effects of mass psychology or of the trade cycle, or of maladjusted institutions.

In this context too it is clear that the meaning of freedom varies with the situation and that freedom in man's direct struggle with nature is something entirely different from freedom in his struggle with "second nature". At the level of the first man is free if he can adapt himself immediately to a given situation. He is in full possession of his freedom as long as he is confronted by absolutely chance conditions, but if anyone prevents him carrying out his own experiments with the situation he feels thwarted.

This direct sense of freedom, of not being thwarted in making one's adjustments, can still be maintained when further stages in the development of social technique produce new forms of determinism and also of freedom. This primary freedom will remain, in spite of a more complicated social structure, as long as men are bent on carrying out their immediate wishes and on finding spontaneous forms of self-expression. At the stage of invention the test of freedom is not mere spontaneity, but the desire to create conditions where social adjustment is possible instead of simply accepting things as they are. One feels free when one can make or choose one's own material or set up an organization with certain definite aims in view or at least take part in its administration; in short, when one is free to invent. For the sake of this freedom men are willing to forgo their primary liberty of action. They do not feel frustrated if they have to take the necessary mechanical steps to make an institution work or give up certain forms of self-expression, provided that they have a right to determine the aims in view or to have a voice in determining them. They allow educational and religious institutions to exercise a deliberate influence over the character and systematically to inculcate habits and ideals which are not the result either of trial and error or of a process of spontaneous growth. Of course there is nothing new in letting oneself be formed by institutions,

for mankind has always been moulded by customs and habits, but in the past this has been due to the irresponsible and invisible hand of history. The decisive factor at the present time is that isolated institutions such as schools and training colleges are deliberately established for a purpose. But the regulation of this vast interplay of institutions has never been attempted and at the second stage would be regarded as sheer audacity.

Although this unregulated mass of institutions is as impenetrable and as uncontrollable as nature itself (if on a different plane) men accept this determinism with the same resignation as they accepted the impossibility of controlling natural forces at an earlier stage. If men who had been moulded by the educational tendencies prevailing at the stage of invention had been told that by co-ordinating social institutions they could bring order out of chaos, they would have felt that this was not merely a foolhardy suggestion but an attack upon the freedom of mankind.

Although the blind play of social forces is destroying humanity they regard this destruction as part and parcel of their freedom, simply because it is anonymous and directed by the invisible hand of history. At an earlier date complete subjection to the caprices of nature was regarded as essential to individual freedom. Uncivilized man feels that his freedom is threatened when a doctor saves him from the blind forces of an epidemic by inoculation. It cost a tremendous effort to convince men at the stage of chance discovery that they could be free if they would make full use of technical devices to challenge the powers of nature; and it will require a thorough re-education to convince them that to combat the blindness of the social forces by the help of human regulation will make man freer than he has been before. The new forms of freedom will always be rejected until men have been spiritually prepared for them, and cease to think in terms of an earlier phase of social existence.

The new conception of freedom creates the desire to control the effects of the social surroundings as far as possible. This is no mere daydream, it is based on the fact that enormous advances in social technique allow us to influence the conduct of social affairs from the key positions, according to a definite plan. Once we have realized this, our outlook on life will change, and we shall feel that while this chaotic tangle of institutions continues we are no longer free. In order to clear up this confusion we must be willing to forgo our former liberties, just as we were in passing from the first stage to the second; provided that in doing so we gain control of the entire social environment. In many spheres we have abandoned those forms of freedom which allowed the individual to use his inventive powers as a means to his own ends, without considering the consequences for society as a whole. The sacrifice of this primary form of freedom will lead to our complete enslavement unless we are willing to accept the further implication of it and thus strive to regulate the entire social network: that is, to regulate all social relationships so as to secure the collective freedom of the group in accordance with a democratically recognized plan. From now on men will find a higher form of freedom in allowing many aspects of their individual lives to be determined by the social order laid down by the group, provided that it is an order which they themselves have chosen.

At the stage we have just reached, it seems to be greater slavery to be able to do as we like in an unjust or badly organized society, than to accept the claims of planning in a healthy society which we ourselves have chosen. The realization that fair and democratic planning does not involve the surrender of our freedom is the mainspring of those arguments which show that an unplanned capitalist society is not the basis of the highest form of liberty.

It has rightly been pointed out that the "liberties" of liberal capitalist society are often only available to the rich, and that the "have-nots" are forced to submit to the pressure of circumstances. The real representative of this society would be the free workman, who had the right to sell his labour in a "free" market, or if he preferred, to give up the struggle and starve. What is the use of freedom in teaching and learning to a poor man who has neither the time nor the means to acquire the necessary education? What use is the freedom to choose our own philosophy of life, to form our own opinions, if the sociological mechanisms of our society create insecurity, anxiety, neuroses, which prevent us from making sound and rational decisions?

Those who cling to the forms of freedom which were current at the stage of invention retort: "What use is the best social order if it is simply imposed on the individual and he cannot escape from it? What use are the wisest of institutions if I am not free to live my own life? I would rather work out my own solution, however inadequate, to a difficult state of affairs, than be forced into the mould of a situation, however skilfully designed."

This antagonism clearly shows that the question is only insoluble because the concept of freedom of the second stage has been applied to the third. It is just as impossible to want a rational and planned society without forgoing the luxury of arbitrary interference, as it was for the individual at the stage of invention to preserve his desire for an absolute spontaneity of adjustment.

The guarantees of freedom are entirely different at the three stages. At the first stage freedom is really equivalent to freedom to escape. The possibilities of fleeing from a tyrant, of taking one's head out of the noose, of escaping direct pressure, these are the most obvious marks of freedom. At the second stage where an increasing number of isolated institutions fill up the framework of society and where each is allowed, broadly speaking, to go its own way, the most vital guarantee of freedom consists in playing off these institutions against each other. This is reflected in the political theory of checks and balances. At this stage the balance of power seems to be guaranteed by the mutual supervision and control of individual institutions. Where there is no higher authority to which all lesser powers are subject, freedom can only be guaranteed by a balance of more or less subordinate authorities.

At the third stage, that of planning, freedom cannot consist in the mutual control of individual institutions, for this can never lead to planned co-operation. At the highest stage freedom can only exist when it is secured by planning. It cannot consist in restricting the powers of the planner, but in a conception of planning which guarantees the existence of essential forms of freedom through the plan itself. For every restriction imposed by limited authorities would destroy the unity of the plan, so that society would regress to the former stage of competition and mutual control. As we have said, at the stage of planning freedom can only be guaranteed if the planning authority incorporates it in the plan itself. Whether the sovereign authority be an individual or a group or a popular assembly, it must be compelled by democratic control to allow full scope for freedom in its plan. Once all the instruments of influencing human behaviour have been co-ordinated, planning for freedom is the only logical form of freedom which remains.

This must be carefully considered, for it would be easy to adopt the wrong tactics if we continued to think that freedom could be guaranteed by limiting the unity of the plan, instead of insisting that constitutional guarantees of freedom should be included in the plan itself, and that real political safeguards should be established for its maintenance. Where the key points of a society have already been determined, freedom can only be secured by strategic direction from the key points and not by their destruction.

As soon as the problem of freedom— as opposed to *laisser-faire*—is seen to consist in the creation of free zones within the planned structure, the whole question becomes more detailed. Instead of the unified and abstract conception, concrete issues arise. The various historical interpretations of freedom, freedom of movement, freedom of expression, freedom of opinion, freedom of association, freedom from caprice and tolerance are all special obligations which must be met by the new society. For naturally the advent of planned freedom does not mean that all earlier forms of freedom must be abolished. We saw in the former parts of the book that an advance to a higher social level does not exclude the preservation of former types of action, thought and freedom. On the contrary, the planned retention of ancient liberties is a guarantee against exaggerated dogmatism in planning. We have learnt to realize that even when society has passed to a new stage in many spheres of its existence, some of the old forms of adjustment could still continue. Wherever it is possible and the plan is not endangered every effort must be made to maintain the primary form of freedom—freedom for individual adjustment. This was legitimately retained at the stage of invention, and in spite of an increasing mechanization, it helped to preserve vitality and strengthen initiative. Thus one of the guarantees of freedom in a planned society will be the maintenance of the individual capacity for adjustment. In the same way the freedom achieved at the second stage of invention must be retained in a planned society wherever possible. Constitutional provision must be made for the creation of new institutions through the initiative of small groups, in order to supply the needs of local circles rather than those of the centralized bureaucracy. It is one of the greatest advantages of the Anglo-Saxon tradition that most public institutions, such as hospitals, schools, and universities, are not maintained by the state but are forced as a rule to be self-supporting in order to prove the necessity for their existence. This principle of corporate initiative, these conceptions of the responsibilities and risks which must be borne by small groups, are characteristic of the stage of invention and are genuinely sound. They may mitigate exaggerated tendencies towards centralization, for this technique is a safeguard against bureaucracy and helps to keep the planning authorities in touch with actual conditions. Of course once society has reached the stage of planning separatism and local

autonomy cannot be allowed to have the last word as at the stage of invention. Although even in the future corporations must take the initiative in suggesting new institutions, centralized control is essential, in order to criticize any tendencies which are likely to clash with the plan as a whole. This criticism might easily lead once more to an arbitrary bureaucracy, which under cover of objective criticism would oppose the natural growth of these institutions.

But this can only happen if there is no power greater than bureaucracy, for the problem of the democratic constitution of a planned society mainly consists in avoiding bureaucratic absolutism.

It all depends on whether we can find ways of transferring democratic, parliamentary control to a planned society. If this control is destroyed in the effort to establish a planned society, planning will be a disaster, not a cure. On the other hand, planning under communal control, incorporating safeguards of the new freedom, is the only solution possible at the present stage of social technique. The chances of achieving this new society, to be sure, are limited. It is not absolutely predetermined. But this is just where our new freedom begins. We have seen that the quality of freedom varies not only with the ages, but within the boundaries of a single society which gives different scopes to liberty of action. Our present society provides for one kind of freedom within the network of established relationships. But it offers us freedom of another degree outside them—in those spheres where our world is still in the making.

Within the framework of established relationships we can only gradually alter small details, burdened as we are by the pressure of that interdependent system which too often gives our acts only the scope of the mason replacing old bricks in a wall that is already built. But there is a space round the wall where new things have to be done, where new activity from key positions in required. There as much spontaneity is demanded of our actions as in the first stage where primary freedom reigned. Here is scope for the pioneer, for in face of future possibilities each of us must choose what he would strengthen, what he would overthrow. Thus human freedom is not extinguished when we reach the stage of mass society; on the contrary, this is where its genuine vigour is needed. If we are only willing to contemplate that sector of life in which it is required,

we shall see that the man of to-day has far more freedom in the determination of his destiny than the unsociological ethics of the past would have us believe. Why search the past with a romantic longing for a freedom that is lost, when that freedom is now ready to come into its own if we only have the courage to see what must be seen, to say what must be said, to do what must be done? Rightly understood, recent tendencies towards a mass society, and our ever increasing awareness of the determinism of sociological factors do not release us from responsibility for the future; responsibility increases with every advance in the course of history, and has never been greater than it is to-day.

✦✦✦✦✦✦✦✦✦✦✦✦✦✦✦✦✦✦✦ DEMOCRATIC ETHICS AND HUMAN ENGINEERING *Kenneth D. Benne*

THERE seems to be good reason for locating in the disequilibrated conditions of industrial society the requiredness of current social and educational change and of a planned, an engineering, approach to its control. These requirements do not stem primarily from undemocratic or anti-democratic ideologies. This insight helps to clear away any assumption of necessary incompatibility between a democratic system of values on the one hand and processes of social engineering which employ methods of collectively planned change on the other. This way of looking at contemporary change seems also to imply that democratic ideology will find effective application in shaping

contemporary culture only as it comes to operate in the processes by which planned social changes are formulated and effected and by which the necessary re-education of persons and groups to the behavior and relationships required by such planning is accomplished. *If this is accepted as a condition of effective service to democratic ideas and values at the present time, a translation of these values and ideas in terms of a methodology of social engineering would seem to be required.*

As this translation is attempted, it is important that the core convictions of democratic ideology be kept clearly in mind. In the first place, the unique person, because of his very uniqueness,

From Kenneth D. Benne, "Democratic Ethics in Social Engineering," Progressive Education, *Vol. 26, No. 7, May 1949. Used by permission.*

represents an irreplaceable and incomparable center of choice, deliberation and valuation. Persons are, therefore, to be taken as ends in the sense that all the ways of a society, its institutions, its practices and its faiths, are to be judged ultimately by their services to the development of each member-person. In the second place, a social policy is held to be poorer than it need be if it does not represent an induction from the unique insights and experiences of every person concerned with that policy. On both these bases, the principle of participation by all persons affected by a social policy, as equals, in the processes by which such policy is formulated and reconstructed has been approved as a (if not the) central norm of democratic operation.

Now it requires no great logical leap from this latter principle to an assertion that the central meaning of "democracy," in operational terms, is to be found in a methodology by which the ways, the policies, the norms of an institution, the school for example, are to be reconstructed when its traditional ways have fallen into dispute, when the society is confronted by alternative and conflicting views as to the proper direction of social effort, when the institution faces, defines and moves to solve its confronting problems. The democratic norms acquire operational meaning when they are interpreted as requirements of a methodology for resolving social and inter-personal conflicts in such a way that an adequate, mutually satisfactory, and socially wise resolution is effected. In a social setting where social conflicts tend to take a collective form, where change is inherent in the situation, where planning has become a social necessity, the norms of democracy will acquire directive power and clear meaning *only* as

they are seen to be required elements in a methodology of planned social change, of social engineering.

The Ethical Problem Restated

We can now restate with greater precision the problem raised earlier concerning the ethical responsibilities of the educator as social engineer in terms of democratic values. There is no inherent contradiction between a democratic ideology and the training of persons and groups committed to and skilled in the stimulation and development of planned change in social patterns and in human relationships. In fact, the effective maintenance and extension of democratic values in industrial society seem to require the services of such practitioners. Educators or other change agents must, however, be trained in ways of stimulating and guiding change which incorporate the democratic norms as basic elements of their operating methodology. The valid test of the democratic character of any engineering operation lies in the degree to which the methodology employed in them conforms to these norms. *It follows also that the best guarantee of the ethical operation of social engineers is that their basic training be focused in a methodology of planned change which unites the norms of democratic operation, relevant understandings of change processes and social structures, and skills in stimulating, inducing and stabilizing changes in persons and groups.*

Democratic Principles as Methodological Norms

Five basic democratic norms can be identified. All may be thought of as derivations from the basic principle of democratic participation stated above and from the analysis of the requirements which the current cultural situation puts upon processes of change. In presenting each, some clarification of its general meaning will be attempted. Some delimitation of the kind of skills which translation of each norm into social practice requires will also be indicated. It is in these skill requirements that the necessary fusion of social-psychological understandings with ethical norms of valid deliberation and decision is seen most clearly. It is not enough for an educational leader to accomplish this fusion in his own professional perspective. His training must also include development of skill in helping the persons, groups and organizations with whom he works to accomplish this fusion in planning and evaluating the changes for which they assume responsibility. Without such fusion, democratic values tend to remain verbalisms and skills for inducing change tend to be used without the direction and control which democratic values should provide.

DEMOCRATIC NORM 1

The engineering of change and the meeting of pressures on a group or organization toward change must be collaborative. This norm prescribes two general kinds of collaboration. In the first place, it emphasizes the need for collaboration across lines of divergent action interests in a given situation requiring change. Individuals and groups must be helped to see that the task is to discover and construct a common interest out of the conflicting interests which they bring to the interpretation of the situation and to the direction of changes in it. This requires a confidence that the common interest to

be built will be "better," will incorporate greater value for all concerned, than any partial interest initially brought to the deliberation concerning required changes. At the same time, the conflicting interests must be seen as the "raw materials" out of which the common interest is to be constructed.

The second kind of collaboration required is across lines of "theory" and "practice." A planned change in a school situation must be one which is based on the best available knowledge of relevant relationships and structures, of social forces and factors promoting and impeding various possible changes, of the consequences likely to result from alternative lines of action proposed and considered. This calls for knowledge from various social sciences. In addition, skills in creating those social-psychological conditions which will support a problem-solving approach in various phases of change must be available. It seems that planned educational change which is to be successful will require the collaboration of practitioners with social scientists and with engineering methodologists.

Neither of these modes of collaboration, between persons and groups with different interests in change and between "theorists" and "practitioners," comes "naturally" to people. "Departmental" barriers tend to divide various kinds of social scientists. "Institutional" barriers tend to divide scientists and action leaders. Yet both modes are required if change as planned is to be guided by the rational, informed consent of those concerned. The development of the skills of productive collaboration by practitioners, representatives of various "interests," and consulting social scientists sets a central goal for educational leadership which is devoted to the democratization of change processes.

DEMOCRATIC NORM 2

The engineering of change must be educational for the participants. Training for planned change cannot put the importance of other goals to be achieved through collaboration above the importance of developing the unique abilities of each person in and through the social change effected. Every change operation must, in this sense, be conceived as an educational enterprise. This is not dictated alone by the democratic conviction that each person is to be treated as an end and that social arrangements are to be judged by their effects on persons influenced by them. It is dictated equally by the conviction that planning is most intelligent when it accomplishes a maximum induction from the unique contributions of all individual participants.

Individuals need to learn the skills of contribution to collective thinking if these effects are to be achieved. Groups need to learn the skills of eliciting effective individual contributions to group thinking from all members. And organizations need to develop an atmosphere with permits individuals and sub-groups to mature and communicate effectively their unique contributions to organizational change and improvement.

It is important that this educational requirement of democratic engineering be interpreted dynamically instead of statically. It is not enough that persons grow in the skills, understandings and commitments appropriate to any given situation or to a plan for the effective management of that situation.

The more basic educational needs to be served in processes of planning for change are needs for the habits and skills required for further growth. The social engineer, if he is working democratically, must leave the persons and groups with whom he works better equipped to solve the particular problem which he has helped them to solve. But he must also leave them better equipped to solve subsequent problems of change, including the management of personal adjustments which change in social arrangements always requires.

DEMOCRATIC NORM 3

The engineering of change must be experimental. It has already been suggested that democratic ideology requires us to see all social arrangements as subject to modification and alteration when their effects upon the persons influenced by their operation can convincingly be called into question. This involves an "experimental" attitude toward *all* social arrangements. And *all* social arrangements include those formed and re-formed in processes of planning as well as those shaped and perpetuated by custom. Planned arrangements must be seen by those who make them as arrangements to be tested in use and to be modified in terms of their human effects when tried.

Now, if the planning of changes is to be collaborative along the dimensions already suggested, this means that all who collaborate must be trained toward an experimental attitude and a "research" approach toward social problems. It is not enough if only the "experts" involved are experimental and research minded. Accurate determination of the human effects of institutional arrangements requires research. Collaboration in such research becomes a prime requisite for intelligent sensitivity toward changes required prior to planning. Such research is of equal importance in the evaluation of arrangements instituted by planning. That all educational practitioners, children and laymen participating in educational change become experimental in their attitude toward relationship problems faced and "research-minded" in their search for and evaluation of solutions sets an impressive task for social engineering. But our democratic norms require us to set no lesser goal.

DEMOCRATIC NORM 4

The engineering of change must be task-oriented, that is, controlled by the requirements of the problem confronted and its effective solution, rather than oriented to the maintenance or extension of the prestige or power of those who originate contributions. In terms of social control, this means that democratic change must be anti-authoritarian. In methodological terms, this norm requires that contributions are to be judged by their relevance to the task or problem confronted, not by the prestige, position or power of those who originate them.

Persons adequate to implement this norm must be disciplined in recognizing continuously the social-psychological fact of emotional identification with ideas and proposals as both an asset and a liability. On the one hand, it is a source of effective motivation. On the other, it is a source of unintelligent resistance to counter-ideas of merit. Democratic persons must become skilled in inhibiting their tend-

encies to defend and promote ideas which are in need of objective evaluation and reformulation. It is important that persons achieve sensitivity in assessing the sources of influence upon themselves and to differentiate between dependence upon status figures and dependence upon fact-oriented and task-oriented influences.

Democratic groups need authority roles for effective coordination of their problem-solving activities. But groups need to learn to judge authority roles in terms of their contribution to such coordination and not in terms of the general prestige, respectability or status of certain members.

The task of training persons and groups to achieve effective communication across barriers of prestige and differential power is far from easy. This is nowhere more difficult than in educational change where the basic status differences between children and adults as well as the more usual status barriers between teachers (workers), supervisors and administrators must be taken into account. It is in creating conditions for releasing such productive communication that many of the most baffling social and psychological difficulties of training for democratic change are encountered. The task is complicated by a dogmatic attitude on the part of participants toward the viewpoints and ideas of their own groups. To the democratic planner "dogmas" are seen methodologically as "intellectual" attempts to save some privileged position from open collective criticism and modification. How to convert the perception of favored principles by those who hold them from dogmas to "hypotheses" remains a central problem for democratic social engineers.

DEMOCRATIC NORM 5

The engineering of change must be anti-individualistic, yet provide for the establishment of appropriate areas of privacy and for the development of persons as creative units of influence in our society. The "collective" character of our more pressing problems of change has been suggested and the necessity for "collective" solutions affirmed. We have also seen the affirmation of the central importance of persons as basic to the democratic ideology. The fact that these two requirements are often seen as antitheses stems from a confusion of the ideology of liberal individualism with that of democracy. No complete clarification of the former ideology can be attempted here. A few remarks may help to justify the statement that a democratic methodology must be anti-individualistic. In the liberal revolt against social restraints upon economic enterprise imposed by medieval culture and later against "mercantilist" restraints, a rationale for individual rights was sought in a conception of the "natural" as over against the "social" grounding of such rights. Individuals, naturally equipped with mind and conscience independent of social experience, were set over against a contractual and artificial system of social relationships and conventions. What was in fact an alternative social ideal was thus projected into a theory of the nature of human nature. Scientific studies of human nature have indicated that this rationalization of liberal ideology involved a false psychology and anthropology. Individual personalities are now seen to be products of social experience. Individuation and socialization, far from being capable of intelligible opposi-

tion, are generally regarded as alternative aspects of the same process of growth into the ways of a social culture. The norms and standards by which a person thinks and judges are learned in the processes by which he is enculturated. Human rights and duties are grounded in the institutions and ideologies of a culture, not in a nature independent of man's social relationships. If human rights are to be guaranteed, they must be guaranteed by appropriate social, political, and economic controls of human behavior, not by opposition to these.

The value of creative individuality which the liberal ideology as well as democratic ideology emphasized is valid as a value. But the conservation and extension of this value cannot be effected by reliance upon a false psychology and anthropology. If the realization of this value is blocked by certain social arrangements, as undoubtedly it often is today, the task is to change these social arrangements. And such change today requires collective planning and action, not reliance upon "providential" processes of natural or historical selection which have ceased to be providential under conditions of advancing industrialization or upon blind resistance to all collective action as inherently opposed to individuality.

Individualism today tends to threaten rather than to promote the values of individuality. We are brought back to processes of planned social change and to the formulation of an adequate methodology of social engineering as a necessary condition for the conservation and extension of democratic values.

The methodological correlate of individualism which democratic ideology leads us to oppose is the elevation of unchecked private, individual judgment as an ultimate arbiter in the control of human conduct. That a wise social policy will establish areas of privacy for persons and voluntary associations within the society is undoubtedly true. In such areas, private judgment may rule. But the determination of the proper boundaries of these areas must, in an interdependent society, be based on a collective judgment. The rights of private judgment can be defensibly defined and enforced on a democratic basis only by processes of collaborative planning. They cannot be guaranteed by dogmas concerning the nature of man.

The methodology of planned change which is consistent with democratic ideology must elevate informed and experimental collective judgment over unchecked private judgment. A methodology of training for participation in planned change must emphasize the development of skills necessary for creating common public judgments out of the disciplined conflict of "private" points of view. It must develop persons who see non-influenceability of private convictions in joint deliberations as a vice rather than a virtue. It is in this sense that democratic planning for change must be anti-individualistic.

It is equally important that groups and organizations be trained to develop standards of acceptance of individual differences and of expectation that out of such differences resources for group and institutional improvement can be developed. Groups and organizations should be helped to define and redefine those areas of life in which common values and standards are necessary and where efforts to build common out of contrasting beliefs and practices are required. In the same process, areas of life where divergence

in standard and belief is not alone to be tolerated but encouraged and supported need to be well-defined. To stress the essential character of certain universals in group life is in no way to contradict the need for special and unique developments where threats to common welfare are not involved. The democratic social engineer seeks to establish and support this essential distinction in the groups or organizations with whom he works. . . .

An attempt has been made to show that there is no incompatibility between an engineering approach to the solution of educational and social problems and the ethics of democracy. On the contrary, it has been urged that the effective maintenance and extension of democratic values in industrial culture requires such an approach. The necessity for planned changes in human relationships and institutional patterns stems from the conditions of industrial life today. And planned change requires leadership by persons equipped with the understandings, skills and techniques of the social engineer. Social engineering will serve democratic aims and observe democratic scruples and standards only if it is guided by a methodology which incorporates basic democratic values as procedural norms. The first task of believers in democratic ethics is, therefore, the theoretical job of translating democratic values into methodological norms for the control of processes of planned change. The second task is the practical one of devising ways, in training teachers or others as social engineers, to develop the skills and techniques for effective stimulation and induction of change in persons and groups and the social-psychological knowledge required for accurate diagnosis of change-situations *in integral relation* to developing commitments to the norms of democratic methodology. Knowledge or skills or techniques divorced from the ethical and methodological controls of democracy may be used for promoting undemocratic or anti-democratic ends. We must find ways for teaching the techniques of social engineering not as isolated "bags of tricks" but as the "hands and feet" which the ethical and methodological "heart and head" of democratic action require in today's world.

✧✧✧✧✧✧✧✧✧✧✧✧✧✧✧✧✧ THE MORAL DIMENSION OF SCIENCE

William Gruen

Science appears to most people as an esoteric profession whose methods of inquiry are of interest only to the professional scientists and to philosophers. Shall we be content to view science in the shape of its endless technological products, its machines, materials, and techniques? Scientific thought was not always so eclipsed by its services to the artisan and the engineer. For example, in ancient Greece, which in the eyes of many historians was the cradle of science, it was cultivated in almost complete separation from the crafts and the technical know-how of those times. Science was primarily a matter for intellectual enjoyment; it was an object of contemplation, withdrawn from the practical life of society.

Today, although there is an intimate association between science and technology we have achieved a new withdrawal of science from its social environment through its extreme professionalization. Our scientists are not amateurs, not individual investigators working in private studies and laboratories, as in former times. They are now professionals supported or employed by universities or large research organizations and the scientist would find it extremely difficult, if not impossible, to carry on his work without the aid of these institutions.

Besides, there has been a change in the meaning as well as in the social role of science. In the days of Franklin and Jefferson science was a pervasive intellectual attitude, an approach for every educated man to the problems of nature and society. Our culture on the whole has lost this attitude and, although we live in "an age of science," we have become estranged from nature as well. The order of nature, which was the wonder of former ages, moves us neither to wonder nor to reflection. The intellectual content of science has become less a matter of general human concern; we are likely to relegate it to the "institutions" of science and to regard science as an academic departmental responsibility.

This remoteness of science has tended

From William Gruen, "The Moral Dimension of Science," Pleasures in Learning, Notes and Essays No. 23 (a monthly publication for students of the Division of General Education and Extension Services, New York University, published by the Center for the Study of Liberal Education for Adults.) Used by permission.

to lessen its influence on prevailing ideologies and world views. It has also obscured certain human values implicit in scientific method, values which are independent of the many contributions that modern science has made toward our physical comfort, health, safety, and destructive power. Nevertheless, an adequate appreciation of the nature of scientific inquiry must take into account these underlying moral values. These values become explicit in the defense of science against social and moral authoritarianism.

During the twentieth century the attack on free inquiry in science has come not from its traditional antagonist, namely, institutionalized religion, but from organized communism and fascism. Outside of totalitarian countries there has been no significant attempt at the suppression of knowledge for the sake of perpetuating an orthodoxy, either political or religious. Usually the control exerted on science under democratic regimes has shown itself as a kind of influence, an indirect pressure on the scientific community. Industry through its own laboratories or through subsidized research in universities makes it difficult, if not impossible, for the individual scientist to ignore its scientific and technological needs. Governments too have a stake in scientific research and, by promoting inquiry into certain types of problems related to increased military or economic power, exert a directive pressure on trends in scientific research.

Do such incentives and influences amount to a limitation or restraint of inquiry in science? It is, of course, true that they create prevailing interests in certain problems to the neglect of others. But they do not prohibit inquiry outside these preferred channels and apply no restrictive sanctions against scientists who choose to pursue inquiries unrelated to current military or industrial needs.

Nevertheless, the *influence* exerted by economic or governmental forces has been regarded in some quarters as comparable to the controls exercised by totalitarian states. Some Marxists have in fact seen it as the class orientation of science in capitalist democracies. Such a view can arise only through a confusion of incentives with coercion, incentives that function within the tried methods of scientific inquiry, and coercion that substitutes authoritarian dogma in place of the warranted conclusions of science. If the prevailing climate of science interferes with a scientist's efforts to secure institutional support for some unpopular line of research, one might perhaps say that he is not "free" to carry on his inquiry. But the word has a very different meaning when we apply it to a scientist in a totalitarian country who is not *free* to affirm a conclusion to which he is led by the evidences of scientific inquiry.

The difference is fundamental, although we may lose sight of it if we consider only that in both cases an inquiry has been effectively stopped. The two cases may seem to be the same in effect. On the one hand, special interests in a democratic country divert available resources to the investigation of other problems, leaving the scientist without the means needed for the inquiry that those interests are trying to gag. On the other hand, a totalitarian state prohibits a certain inquiry, suppresses a warranted conclusion, or compels assent to doctrines not supported by scientific evidence. In both cases there is interference with the progress of inquiry as the scientist conceives it. But here the resemblance ends and the vital differences suggest that we are dealing here with two very different kinds of social phenomena. For in the first case there is no attack on either civil liberties or on scientific method. In the second case both are subverted. In the first case the scientist still retains the right to seek public support and to challenge any idea in the light of reflective inquiry. In the second case, however, we are dealing with a privation of fundamental rights and with a corruption of method, a surrender of scientific inquiry to coercive authority.

Suppose now that the scientist in the totalitarian country did not share our dismay and indignation over his condition. He sees himself as a tough-minded realist. "Your social philosophy," says he, "consists of grandiose clichés like 'fundamental rights' and 'scientific inquiry' and 'coercive authority.' All empty echoes of a bourgeois romanticism. First of all, why assume that the authority in this case was coercive? Perhaps I voluntarily withdrew my scientific findings. Second, if scientific method—as you call it—was surrendered it was only because it was properly subordinated to other values. Why should science be regarded as an absolute, ultimate end? Isn't it after all just a tool? As a means for achieving the desired ends of social action, science is merely an instrument in the service of social policy. Its role must be decided on the merits of each situation. And in some cases it must yield to more appropriate social instruments. There are occasions when ideas must be validated by political rather than by scientific considerations."

"But," we ask, "what about truth? Don't you feel an obligation to affirm only the truth as you see it?"

"Mere slogans and catchwords," says he. "When it comes to social action they are just archaic tokens of the Academy, relics of an age when science was an object of contemplation and not a tool of action. Today we speak of effective and ineffective ideas, not of the true and the false. Our science is practical. Its ideas serve to direct and influence behavior and to this end a so-called 'false' idea may be at times better than a 'true' one."

There is at least one important aspect of this argument with which it would be difficult to disagree, namely, that scientific inquiry is not an ultimate end. Most people recognize that inquiry in science as in any other cultural enterprise enjoys only a relative freedom; the range of its activities is circumscribed by the requirements of other social ideals. For example, we would not allow any inquiry in science that entails cruel or humiliating treatment of human beings. In principle it is acknowledged that some limitations of inquiry are justified. The essential question is whether such limitation of inquiry shall be imposed by arbitrary authority or by democratic policy based on a reflective examination of relative values and consequences.

And here we come upon the basic issues that separate the two social philosophies: one of authoritarian control, the other of relative democratic limitation of inquiry. These issues arise from conflicting views of the nature of science and the scope of scientific inquiry. The defense of authoritarian controls over science rejects the concept of a unified science that holds scientific method equally applicable to the natural and to the social sciences. Instead it is asserted that inquiry is limited to techniques and instrumentalities, while the choice of ends and values is guided by factors related to national, racial, or class loyalties. From this viewpoint science must be subordinated to dominant social and political aims. The resulting perversion of scientific inquiry not only invalidates it with regard to social and moral problems but also impugns its authority in the study of nature. The attack on free inquiry in the social sciences thus tends also to undermine the natural sciences.

It is significant to note that this dualism with regard to science is not confined to totalitarian states. It has gained support in democratic countries as well and has provided, if not a defense, then at least a friendly tolerance of authoritarian doctrines such as are fostered by Soviet Russia or other totalitarian states. Such tolerance is possible if we think of science merely in light of the esoteric abstractions of physical science and its intricate experimental apparatus. From this perspective science appears so removed from human relations and human values that it is easy to see it merely as technique. This is the more familiar conception of science since it is in this aspect that it has demonstrated its most conspicuous triumphs.

So long as science is esteemed only because of its serviceability, because of some obvious contribution to human comfort, pleasures, and security, its "freedom" will be a precarious and ambiguous thing. Too many people, like the totalitarian scientists in my earlier example, will be able to reconcile the technical uses of science with a failure to appreciate its role as an integral part of our culture. This failure derives from the idea of science as a body of conclusions and techniques. But science is also a cultural attitude embodied in the habitual will to employ certain methods of observation and re-

flection as the ground of belief. The cultivation of this attitude is a condition of enduring freedom in scientific inquiry and is in fact its cultural or moral dimension.

To see these moral aspects of scientific inquiry, it must be first disassociated from its more familiar subject matter, namely, the physical sciences and engineering. We will then see scientific inquiry, not as a technique restricted to special provinces of knowledge, but as an approach to any situation in which we are called upon to make dependable judgments. Conceived thus, scientific method entails two essential criteria that guide the formation of well-grounded beliefs. The first criterion is that the judgments we arrive at, as well as the grounds of evidence that support them, must be public, must be observable to all persons. Dependable judgment, in this sense, is communal. The second is that assent to any belief or evidence is voluntary; that is to say, every individual retains the right to dissent. But such dissent should not be arbitrary; it must also be guided by considerations that meet the first criterion of sharability.

These two criteria are in effect the affirmation of a community and a certain independence of all persons with respect to knowledge. The consensus of this community is never fixed, never closed. It is a community of method not of doctrine. It is an open community, a community of minds that are always open to the defense of new ideas or to criticism of old ones. Nothing is secure from this critical scrutiny, not even the most familiar or the most widespread or the most venerable of beliefs. Scientific method requires the social conditions of unrestrained communication and, while it recognizes that everything cannot be questioned at once, it affirms that nothing whatever is above question.

When Descartes resolved "to accept nothing as true which I did not clearly recognize to be so" he was affirming what was for his time a revolutionary program, a principle of skepticism toward those ideas whose only support is the endorsement by some authoritative person or tradition. A correlative of this skepticism is the right to independent judgment in the light of one's own reason. To deny this right is in effect to constrain belief. This constraint need not take the form of a reign of terror under which belief or at least public acquiescence is secured by intimidation and fear. Belief may be forced by denying to the individual all access to sources of critical and dissenting ideas, in other words, by indoctrination. Many people who would be quick to resent the propagation of beliefs by intimidation will placidly tolerate indoctrination.

The method of scientific inquiry is opposed to both forms of authoritarianism. It seeks to rest belief on grounds that are not peculiar to this or that culture or region or race even when it investigates matters of race or culture. It warrants only those beliefs that transcend cultural or religious barriers because scientific method addresses itself to the individual not as a member of his society or religion or country, but as *man* whose community with others is not affected by his ancestry, his color, his politics, his nation, nor any other restrictive association. For in respect to knowledge and belief, he is the equal of all other men, all of whom are equally independent members of that free community to which scientific method looks for warrant, namely, the universal community of man whose consensus, however precarious, is the only source of that unsteady glow and faltering excellence we call truth.

CHAPTER 4

The Concept of Planned Change

$\mathbf{I}$n the introduction to Part I, our abstract definition of "planned change" received a preliminary clarification and justification. The function of this chapter is to put more flesh on the bones of this definition and to offer similar but contrasting treatments of "planned change" out of three somewhat divergent theoretical orientations.

"Planned change" is only one species in the larger genus of "social change." The character of this particular species becomes clearer as it is compared and contrasted with other species of change. Warren Bennis undertakes such a comparison and contrast in *A Typology of Change Processes*.

We have mentioned the pioneering effort of Ronald Lippitt and his colleagues to conceptualize the processes of planned change. They have sought to abstract common elements in change efforts addressed to client-systems of various magnitudes—persons, groups, organizations, and communities. This conceptual scheme has thus brought into common focus the role dimensions of change-agents from various professions that superficially seem quite diverse—psychiatrists, counselors, group workers, trainers, organizational consultants, community consultants, and so forth. Lippitt presents a brief compendium of this work in *Dimensions of the Consultant's Job*.

"Therapy" is one form of planned change. Both Jaques and Pages stretch the term "therapy" beyond its traditional focus on change in individuals to include the treatment of larger social units as "patients." It is probably fair to say that the major theoretical influence in Lippitt's work comes from the social psychology of Lewin. Jaques' conceptual framework is derived from the Freudian tradition and Pages' analysis has been strongly influenced by the clinical approach of Carl Rogers as well as by Lewin's theories. These divergent outlooks lead to somewhat different pictures of change-agent functioning and of change process. But it is heartening to note convergence toward a common conceptualization of planned change in the three formulations.

❖❖❖❖❖❖❖❖❖❖❖❖❖❖❖❖❖❖❖❖ A TYPOLOGY OF CHANGE PROCESSES

Warren G. Bennis

ALL change is not "planned change." How is "planned change" to be distinguished from and interrelated to other forms of human change? A paradigm in which eight species of change may be identified may help to answer this question. Along the vertical axis of the paradigm we have shown two variables, dichotomized for convenience: mutual goal setting and deliberateness of change. Along the horizontal axis, power distribution among the parties to the change is shown; .5/.5 indicating a fairly equal distribution of power, 1/0 indicating a one-sided power situation. We have omitted the element of "valid knowledge" from the paradigm, since we are assuming that "valid knowledge" with respect to change is not possible where mutual goal setting is not undertaken.

a. Planned change entails mutual goal setting by one or both parties, an equal power-ratio, and deliberateness, eventually at least, on the part of both sides.

b. Indoctrination involves mutual goal setting and is deliberate, but involves an imbalanced power ratio. Many schools, prisons, and mental hospitals or other "total institutions" would fall into this category.

c. Coercive change is characterized by nonmutual goal setting (or goals set only by one side), an imbalanced power-ratio, and one-sided deliberateness. Coercive change, as we are using the term, may be exemplified by the thought-control and brainwashing practices of the Communists. Here there is little or no opportunity to engage in mutual goal setting. The deliberate-

PARADIGM FOR CHANGE PROCESSES

Power ratio	Mutual goal setting		Nonmutual goal setting (or goals set by one side)	
	Deliberate on the part of one or both sides of the relationship	*Nondeliberate on the part of both sides*	*Deliberate on the part of one side of the relationship*	*Nondeliberate on the part of both sides*
.5/.5	Planned change	Interactional change	Technocratic change	"Natural" change
1/0	Indoctrinational change	Socialization change	Coercive change	Emulative change

Prepared especially for this volume. Used by permission.

ness originates from one party, the change-agent.

The distinctions between "Indoctrination" and "Coercive change" are elusive and complex. Compare a patient in a "progressive" mental hospital (with an emphasis on psychoanalytic therapy as opposed to a custodial orientation) with a POW in a Red Chinese prison camp. A patient is legally committed: the administrator of the hospital has almost as much power as a POW commandant. The patient is forced to undergo some form of treatment—there is little choice for him. On the face of it, the similarities seem more important than the differences, at least from this example.

However, there are two differences which may possibly distinguish "Coercive change" from "Indoctrination." In the mental hospital example, the patient is allowed and even encouraged to express any form of antisocial feelings—up to the point of *acting* on them. Indeed, psychotherapeutic procedures encourage thoughts in exchange for action. It is doubtful, on the basis of what we know about Communist brainwashing, that the POW commandant would encourage—even on a verbal level—statements not in conformance with the accepted ideology, except where the prisoner was presumably "confessing."

Another difference is that the psychotherapists over time would attempt to develop a collaborative relationship; in fact, the early stages of psychotherapy are, wherever possible, devoted toward developing this type of relationship.

Still, when all is said and done, "Coercive change" as practiced by the Communists and "Indoctrination" as practiced by mental hospitals, for example, may in actuality share similar processes, and employ identical techniques. Our paradigm, like all paradigms, creates an "ideal" and abstract model to which actual empirical occurrences do not neatly conform.[1]

d. Technocratic change may be distinguished from planned change by the nature of the goal setting. The use of technocratic means to bring about change relies solely on collecting and interpreting data. Technocratic change follows primarily an "engineering model": the client defines his difficulties as deriving from inadequate knowledge, and assumes that his lack of knowledge is accidental or a matter of neglect —not something that is functionally a part of him. The technocrat colludes in this assumption and merely makes and reports his "findings."

e. Interactional change is characterized by mutual goal setting, a fairly equal power distribution, but no deliberateness on either side of the relationship. ("Unconsciously" either may be committed to changing the other in some direction.) Such changes can be observed among good friends "who help each other," married couples, and in various other nondeliberate transactions among people. Change occurs in such transactions, possibly with beneficial effects, but there is a lack of self-consciousness about it, thus a lack of any definite change-agent–client relationship.

f. Socialization change has a direct

[1] Edgar Schein's *Coercive Persuasion* (New York: Norton, 1961), deals with these problems in great detail. One of his main points is that there are many more similarities than would appear obvious between forms of "acceptable" social influences, such as, psychotherapy or teaching, and unacceptable modes of social influence, such as "brainwashing." We do not dispute this point as an empirical fact; we are, however, trying to sharpen some differences for purposes of conceptual analysis.

kinship with the interactional hierarchical control. Parent-child relationships would be the most obvious example, although counselor-camper, teacher-pupil relationships would also be applicable here. Greater deliberateness on the "adult" side of the relationship brings specific cases of socialization into the "Indoctrination" or "Planned Change" categories.

g. Emulative change is the sort of process we associate with formal organizations, where there is a clear-cut superior-subordinate relationship. To this extent it closely resembles Kelman's concept of influence through "identification." Change is brought about, possibly unconsciously, through a form of identification with and emulation of the "power figures" by the subordinates.

h. Natural change refers to changes

brought about with no apparent deliberateness and no goal setting on the part of those involved in it. Primarily, it is a residual category encompassing all "accidents," "quirks of fate," unanticipated consequences, and changes wrought in connection with cataclysms such as earthquakes, floods, etc. It may be that this category includes the operation of all those factors and causes which our limited knowledge cannot properly divine.

This typology is both too "crude" and too "pure" to provide ready linkages to empirical reality. The distinctions made in it are somewhat arbitrary and certainly not all-inclusive. However, we believe it does provide suggestions as to how "planned change" can be distinguished from other change processes.

✧✧✧✧✧✧✧✧✧✧✧✧✧✧✧✧✧ DIMENSIONS OF THE CONSULTANT'S JOB [1]   *Ronald Lippitt*

Consultation, like supervision, or love, is a general label for many variations of relationship. The general definition of consultation used in this paper assumes that—

1. The consultation relationship is a voluntary relationship between

2. a professional helper (consultant) and help-needing system (client)

3. in which the consultant is at-

tempting to give help to the client in the solving of some current or potential problem,

4. and the relationship is perceived as temporary by both parties.

5. Also, the consultant is an "outsider," i.e., is not a part of any hierarchical power system in which the client is located.

Some additional clarification of this condensed definition is needed. The client is conceived to be any functioning social unit, such as a family, industrial organization, individual, committee, staff, membership association, governmental department, delinquent

[1] Many of the ideas summarized in this paper are derived from my collaborations with Jeanne Watson and Bruce Westley as formulated in our joint publication *The Dynamics of Planned Change.*

Excerpts from Ronald Lippitt, "Dimensions of the Consultant's Job," Journal of Social Issues, *Vol. 15, No. 2, 1959, pp. 5–12. Abridged and used by permission.*

gang, or hospital staff. The consultant is usually a professional helper, such as a marriage counselor, management consultant, community organizer, minister, social worker, human relations trainer, psychiatrist, applied anthropologist, group therapist or social psychologist. The role of psychological "outsider" may sometimes be taken by a consultant located within the client system, such as a member of the personnel department.

One way of examining the role of the consultant is in terms of the series of questions or problems the consultant must pose for himself and work on during the course of a consulting relationship. Each of these questions can be viewed as a professional problem on which information is needed, about which theorizing must be done, action must be taken, and feedback must be sought by the consultant in order to get data about the consequences of the helping actions. The sequence of the questions formulated below does not represent any assumption that this is the orderly flow of questions and problems in the carrying through of a consultation relationship. Many of the questions are being worked on simultaneously at any one time, and the questions keep recurring as the process of consultation unfolds. But in order to formulate them as dimensions of a consultant's role we need to examine them one by one, rather than try to reproduce the multi-dimensional complexity of the consultant's job as he experiences it at any moment in time.

Question I: What seems to be the difficulty? Where does it come from? What's maintaining it?

Every consultant has a cluster of ideas, or a set of concepts, which guide his perception of "what exists" and "what is going on" when he comes in contact with a particular group or organization or other social unit. This cluster of ideas is his theory about the nature of groups and persons in groups and what makes them behave the way they do. For some consultants the theory may be largely inarticulate, and the concepts may not have much systematic refinement, or relationship to each other. Nevertheless the consultant must have some kind of theory in terms of which to select "what to see" and "how to understand it" when he views the complexities of group or organizational life. Other consultants approach their task with a relatively systematic framework of concepts such as psycho-analytic theory, structure-function theory, learning theory, social conflict theory, or role theory. Those without much theory have a harder time organizing and comprehending what they see. Those with a more systematic theory have a harder time noticing and interpreting important events which are not taken into account by the concepts of their theory.

In addition to having a systematic *descriptive-analytic theory*, the consultant must have a *diagnostic theory* which guides him in focusing on symptoms of pain or disruption in the system, on evidences that things are different from "normal" or "healthy." Usually a diagnostic theory includes both ideas about symptoms or clues that something is wrong, and conceptions about the basic causes of certain patterns of symptoms. In our study of a wide variety of consultants (Lippitt, Watson, and Westley, 1958) it seemed possible to delineate several typical diagnostic orientations such as:

1. An inappropriate distribution of power, too diffuse or too centralized.

2. Blockage and immobilization of productive energy.

3. Lack of communication between the subparts of the system.

4. A lack of correspondence between external reality and the situation as perceived by the client.

5. A lack of clarity or commitment to goals for action.

6. A lack of decision-making and action-taking skills.

These and other theories about "the source of trouble" provide the basis for selective probing to secure information from the client which will be used to interpret the nature of the difficulty and to make decisions about what type of helping should be tried. Also such a diagnostic theory helps to define the directions along which improvement is desired and expected, and therefore defines the symptoms of improvement which will be watched for in order to know whether there are desired consequences of the helping efforts.

Because these two frameworks of theory, systematic and diagnostic, play such a central role in the nature and quality of the performance of the consultant, it would seem particularly important for research to explore the use in practice of systematic theory, and the development of improved diagnostic theory. One of the most unexplored areas is that of the exact nature of the relationship between general systematic theory about groups and organizations and diagnostic theory about pathology of social systems.

Question II: What are my motives as a consultant for becoming involved in this helping relationship? What are the bases of my desire to promote change?

Being a *professional* helper implies responsibility for a high level of self-awareness about one's own values and needs as they may influence the helping relationship. Some critical observers of the American scene think we demon-strate the value that "any change is better than no change." Such a value would relieve both consultants and clients of a great deal of serious responsibility for goal setting, and would make it easy to label all resistance to change as bad. Clearly such a position is untenable. Another extreme position is sometimes taken which maintains that any planful efforts to stimulate change in others is *manipulative* and *undemocratic*. Very little significant work would get done in the world if this unrealistic conception prevailed. The observation of any meaningful social process indicates a picture of continuous efforts of people and groups to influence each other in the interest of various types of goals. The consultant must clarify for himself his own particular goals and motivations for influencing others.

Even in the field of individual psychotherapy a large proportion of the individuals in need of help do not, for various reasons, take the initiative to seek help. Much attention is being given currently to ways of stimulating self-referral and other ways of getting help-needing individuals into contact with consultant resources. It is even harder for groups or organizations as total systems to clarify a need for help and to take initiative to seek help. And if one individual, or subgroup, from the potential client approaches a consultant asking for help, can this be considered as a request for help from the total system?

This initiative problem means that consultants who work with groups must be prepared to take active initiative to stimulate and develop helping relationships. This requires a thoughtful job of clarifying values involved in such "intervention" into the ongoing life of a group. Various consultants have formulated different bases for "the right to intervene" with attempts to give help.

1. Some consultants feel that a group situation is "calling for help" when there is evidence that the social processes of the group are causing individual suffering, such as rejection, isolation, scapegoating. Individual discomfort and frustration of group members is taken as a valid basis for the value judgment that "something needs to be done."

2. Other consultants tend to take a "group welfare" orientation and perceive a basis for intervention when there are symptoms that the group is suffering because of inefficiencies and inadequacies of its efforts to move toward its goals, such as low productivity, or failure of group efforts.

3. Other consultants may take an "institutional welfare" orientation and evaluate a group situation as warranting intervention if efforts of a group are causing disruption or "pain" for the larger organization or for neighboring groups, such as breakdown in one department of an organization, or disruption of the neighborhood life by a delinquent gang.

Many consultants whose reports have been reviewed do not present any explicit rationale for making active influence attempts.

In addition to the "justification for intervention" there is the question of "what goals for change." On the basis of his diagnostic observations does the consultant formulate goals for change in the client, or does he work only in terms of goals formulated by the client?

Some consultants feel they are justified in acting only in terms of goals which have been collaboratively formulated and accepted by both the client and the consultant. Other consultants feel they have a right to certain methodological goals, such as using good procedures for problem solving, but have no right to take positions on the answers to the problems.

This aspect of the job of the group consultant has received very little critical exploration in the literature. There would seem to be need for active discussion and clarification of the various professional orientations.

Question III: What seem to be the present, or potential, motivations of the client toward change and against change?

The analysis of change forces and resistance forces is an important part of the initial assessment job for the consultant, and also a continuing challenge during all stages of the consulting relationship. A conceptual framework for analyzing these forces has been presented by Lewin (1947), by Coch and French (1948), and by Lippitt, Watson, and Westley (1958). Our comments here are limited to a few special aspects of the motivational situation in working with groups as clients.

In work with individuals feelings of pain and dissatisfaction with the present situation are most frequently the dominant driving forces for change, but in work with groups very often one of the most important motivations, or potential motivations, is a desire to improve group efficiency, to achieve some higher level of functioning, even though there may be no critical problems in the present situation. Therefore one of the consultant's jobs with groups is very frequently to help clarify "images of potentiality," rather than to focus on ways of alleviating present pain. Perhaps the most crucial aspect of motivational analysis in working with groups is the study of the nature and effects of the interdependence between the subparts (e.g., subgroups or departments) in the client system. An eagerness by one subgroup to change may not be a clue to readiness for change of other subgroups or of the total group or organization. Learning about the supporting and conflicting relationships between subgroups is a crucial task, and success in getting these facts will determine to a great degree whether the consultant is able to develop the necessary and appropriate relationship to the total group and to its various subparts. One of the most frequent forms of resistance to change in group clients is the perception by certain subgroups that the consultant is more closely related to other subgroups and is "on their side" in any conflict of interests.

Question IV: What are my resources, as a consultant, for giving the kind of help that seems to be needed now, or that may develop?

The requirements of time and skill needed to carry through a psychotherapeutic relationship with an individual have become fairly clear. Usually the situation is not so clear in working out a consultative relationship with a group or organization. Quite frequently a consultant relationship with a group is begun which will require much more time and a greater variety of helping skills than are available from the consultant. Two unfortunate things seem to happen more frequently in the consultation with social units than with individuals. Often the consultant offers diagnostic help and arrives at certain recommendations for improvement or change, but offers no continuity in the actual working through of the meaning of the diagnostic findings for changing procedures, practices, and interaction patterns. This dropping of the relationship with the client system at such an early stage in the process of changing

often results in disruption and demoralization because of the inadequacy of the client-group to cope with the implications for change without further technical help from a consultant. As in the field of medicine, very frequently in the area of group consultation the consultant who has the analytic skills for diagnosis does not have the training and therapeutic skills required for a working through of the implications of the diagnosis. A consultant team would seem to be the creative solution in many cases.

Question V: What preliminary steps of action are needed to explore and establish a consulting relationship?

As pointed out previously, groups as groups are much slower to develop and clarify an awareness of the need for help than are individuals. Therefore group consultants have a greater responsibility for developing techniques of helping the social system develop this awareness through appropriate communication procedures. This often requires taking an active initiative of a kind frowned on in the field of individual consultation. Examples of useful techniques are presented by Lippitt, Watson, and Westley (1958).

The defining of a "trial period" or pilot project as a basis for exploring a possible consulting relationship should also be emphasized. This provides an opportunity to establish relationships to all the different subgroups and to clarify expectations about a readiness to change and about the nature of the consultant's role.

The third problem which is typical at this stage is "getting trapped" into a special relationship with one of the subgroups which makes it difficult to move into a relationship with other subgroups and with the total client system. In initial contacts it is very difficult to know whether an administrator, for example, is speaking as a representative of the organization, as a representative of a small subgroup, or only for himself. The techniques of dual entry and multiple entry have been developed to meet this situation. Getting into contact with the whole client is one of the most challenging skill problems for the group consultant. In an organization or community this often means working closely with a group of representatives from all units to keep channels of communication open to all parts of the system.

Question VI: How do I as consultant guide, and adapt to, the different phases of the process of changing?

The consultant who works through the problems of changing with a group finds that there are several phases or stages to the process of working through, and that those phases require different levels of relationship and different kinds of helping skills. Starting from Lewin's (1947) three phase analysis, Lippitt, Watson, and Westley (1958) discovered in their comparative study of a population of consultants that seven phases could be identified with some degree of consistency. These were:

1. The development of a need for change.

2. The establishment of a consulting relationship.

3. The clarification of the client problem.

4. The examination of alternative solutions and goals.

5. The transformation of intentions into actual change efforts.

6. The generalization and stabilization of a new level of functioning or group structure.

7. Achieving a terminal relationship with the consultant and a continuity of change-ability.

These are very general labels for a great variety of activities, but do seem to help clarify some of the shifts of goal and changes of consulting activity that take place during the total cycle of a consulting relationship.

As the consultant works with a group on phase 4, the examination of alternative possibilities for improvement, it usually becomes clear that various types of special skill training will be needed to support the group's change efforts. This emphasizes the importance of Glidewell's distinction (in this issue) between the consultant and the consultant-trainer. It is our belief that most consulting relationships with groups require a consultant-trainer role to carry through an adequate job of problem solving. It is important for the consultant to clarify for himself the nature and the timing of this shift from the more non-directive role of helping a group develop and clarify its own goals for change to the more active directive role of helping the group learn the procedures and skills needed for them to move with efficiency and success toward the goals they have established. It is an unhappy picture to see a group floundering and unsuccessful in their change efforts because the consultant has not been able to shift from the consultant role appropriate to the earlier phases of consultation to the more active training role which is usually necessary for the successful carrying through of the later phases of consultation.

Question VII: How do I help promote a continuity of creative change-ability?

A successful process of consultation with an organization or a group ends with at least three kinds of learnings:

1. The organization has learned to cope more adequately with the prob-

lem or problems which initiated the consulting process.

2. The organization has learned how to function more adequately in clarifying future problems as they emerge and to make appropriate decisions about seeking for outside help when needed.

3. The organization has learned new procedures and new types of organization to help it maintain a healthy state of changeability in adapting to changing conditions and in utilizing potentialities for creative improvement in group functioning and productivity. Perhaps the most challenging task for the consultant in this regard is to discover ways of training the group to use procedures of data collection and analysis on a continuing basis which will permit the identification of new problems and possibilities. In small face to face groups this may mean helping the group to develop functions of group observation and feedback as a continuing part of the group practice, without continuing dependency on the consultant. In larger organizations it may mean helping in the setting up of new staff functions of data collection, feedback, and skill training which will keep the organization tooled up to a continuous process of creative adaptation and social invention.

This is a very incomplete itemization of the dimensions of the consult-

ant's job as explored in the several papers of this issue. We have tried to emphasize some of the dimensions which seem to represent a special challenge and need for exploration on the part of consultants working with organizations or groups as contrasted to those working with individuals as clients. Perhaps the greatest challenge is that of continuously exploring the relevance of systematic theory from the behavioral sciences, and finding opportunities for contributing to the body of theory through efforts to achieve a conceptual grasp of "what's going on" as we work at the job of giving help to groups in solving their problems of development and productivity. A basic integration of scientific theory and professional skills will be the continuing need as this field of social engineering develops.

References

Coch, Lester, & French, John R. P., Jr. Overcoming resistance to change. *Human Relations,* 1948, 1, 512–532.

Lewin, Kurt. Frontiers in group dynamics. *Human Relations,* 1947, 1, 5–41.

Lippitt, Ronald, Watson, Jeanne, & Westley, Bruce. *The Dynamics of Planned Change.* New York: Harcourt, Brace, & World, Inc., 1958.

✧✧✧✧✧✧✧✧✧✧✧✧✧✧✧✧✧✧✧✧ SOCIAL THERAPY: TECHNOCRACY OR COLLABORATION? *Elliott Jaques*

DURING the years of World War II there has been a widespread development and usage of social methods. Elab- orate techniques of personnel and leadership selection, social and anthropological surveys, propaganda studies and

From Elliott Jaques, "Social Therapy: Technocracy or Collaboration?" Journal of Social Issues, Vol. 3, No. 2, Spring 1947, pp. 59–66. Abridged and used by permission.

psychological warfare, the creation of transitional communities to facilitate the readjustment of repatriates, are examples of what has been done. Even such a list is long and the immensity of the job done is inspiring. In this common task teams of psychologists, sociologists, anthropologists, psychiatrists, social workers, economists, and political scientists have learned to work together and with administrators and executives who had to get a job done.

The civil community, harassed by the difficulties of the post-war world, is now looking for help, and certain sections of the community have already begun to turn to social science for assistance. The challenge of this demand is great. It forces on social science the necessity of developing a method of approach to the help-seeking community which will allow the expression and release of spontaneous adjustment mechanisms with consequent growth and maturation. Proper collaboration with the community in helping to straighten out its difficulties will in turn make possible the healthy maturation of social science itself.

The problem of collaboration, however, is complex. On the one hand, the community is somewhat uncertain about social science. This shows, for example, in misunderstandings of what social scientists can do. Thus, attitudes of submission to the omnipotence of mighty science occur on the one hand and feelings of anxiety, on the other. It is understandable that anxiety should arise in a group which finds itself unable to cope with a particular problem, but which reasonably enough resents the intrusion of the "expert" who is called in to help. On the other hand, there is the complex of attitudes of the social scientist himself, which range from feelings of power because of the special techniques which are available

to him and are unknown to the community, to feelings of anxiety and impotence because of being denied access by society to social problems with which he knows he could help.

In practise the problem usually boils down to the relationship between the "expert" and the administrator or executive responsible. We already know how difficult this relationship becomes even in the domain of the physical sciences and engineering; how much farmers, for example, often resent the intrusion of the government agricultural expert with his new and supposedly superior methods. How much more difficult does the problem of establishing a satisfactory relationship become, however, where not crops but the changing of human behaviour itself becomes the target of scientific endeavour. The very core of personality is touched and the deepest resistances are mobilized against the intruder. It is our belief that the study of how social scientists work with the community is one of the central problems of social science today.

Some Dangers of a Technocratic Approach

It is our conviction that the social scientist working in a collaborative role rather than a technocratic one will achieve the best results, and it is our goal to achieve such a role. One might roughly differentiate collaboration as doing things *with* people, as opposed to technocracy as doing things *to* people.

The very nature of the therapeutic role, however, often makes real collaboration difficult. The situation is often encountered where the social scientist is called in and given a complete mandate to "set things right" in his own way. These instructions commonly come in the form of requests to "tell us what to do", or even, "show us what we should do to set things right". Too frequently, such a mandate may represent an unconscious defeatist attitude on the part of the group concerned, with an underlying and understandable desire to evade, if possible, the responsibility for facing up to a complex and unpleasant situation. Because the solution of the problem may seem relatively simple there is a great temptation for the social scientist to jump in and take the responsibility "just for a short time". Having taken full responsibility on his own shoulders, however, he will to a greater or lesser degree have precluded the possibility of the group itself developing new roles which would allow them to cope with their own problems by themselves. Thus, although he may clear up the problem any thanks he receives may be given rather grudgingly, for he will presumably have exposed the inadequacies of the persons concerned without helping them towards new insights and self-reliance. Under these conditions further work is unlikely, and the project may suddenly come to a halt. On the other hand, he may fail with the task, in which case he will likely be left with the blame on his own shoulders for all the previous mistakes and results of mismanagement, the ill effects of which may be displaced and projected in his direction.

It is sometimes easier to do things to people than with them, easier to tell people what to do than to help them work through the emotional problems which stand in the way of their doing it for themselves. The results, however, are rarely as satisfactory. Continued dependence on the scientist without emancipation, understandable resentment against the social scientists and even against social science in general, or else confusion arising from advice

about what to do without instruction on how to do it, these are the most likely fruits of a technocratic approach. This is not just a theoretical point. One need only turn to the very strong antipathy of many workers towards the industrial psychologist, whom they regard as a person who comes into the factory with time-and-motion study apparatus in order to reorganize the work without the worker having any say. The administrator's dissatisfaction with the social science consultant is also well recognized in cases where, when called in to study the situation, the social scientist presents a diagnostic report, for which a fee is claimed, and then leaves the administrator with the report but with no real inkling of how it is to be used.

Some Features of a Collaborative Approach

It is the goal of collaboration in social therapy to enable the community to incorporate social science knowledge and techniques in order that it may cope more adequately with its own community problems. Collaboration is directed, therefore, towards the strengthening of positive recuperative tendencies and the elimination of factors which prevent adequate functioning. If this is to be achieved it will usually be found necessary to keep a number of points in mind.

In the first place, it is important to maintain a perfectly scientific approach, and not be caught up in the group emotion. To participate in a helpful way and yet observe objectively, that is the problem. It is not easy to do this in the atmosphere of group difficulties which one usually finds when called in to help with social problems without damaging one's own spontaneity. The emotion of the group is very potent, and an important part of the training for social therapy must include learning to participate actively in emotionally charged group situations while maintaining an objective and neutral attitude.

Secondly, from the very beginning the therapist must involve in the therapeutic process all individuals and groups who are likely to be affected by the final results. It is necessary *right from the start* to seek the assistance and cooperation of all groups concerned in the problem. If this is not done, then not only will the social scientist remain an object of suspicion to the non participant groups, but also inter-group tensions will be increased. Anxiety and suspicion are engendered in the nonparticipant groups just because they have been left out.

Thirdly, the therapist should be able to maintain an open mind towards all aspects of a social problem. Ordinarily, the aid of the therapist will be sought by one section of the group or community which has a problem. For example, the management of a factory, or the local government of a community may seek help. It must be clearly pointed out at the very beginning that it is the intention of the therapist to maintain a neutral attitude and to side with no special group. Where this is not agreed to, then the failure to agree can be interpreted to mean that the suspicion of the other groups has been transferred to the therapist. Resistance of this sort becomes the first problem in treatment since until it is successfully worked through, therapy cannot proceed.

Collaboration and Self-reliance

In order to achieve real collaboration which will eventually lead to weaning the group away from the social scientist, the adoption of the following general steps has been found useful either *in toto,* if possible, or with modifications to meet the requirements of a specific situation:

a. *The reconnaissance:* In this stage the therapist or team of therapists, comes in to survey the general situation. There is no commitment on either side, and the therapist assumes no responsibility other than to find out whether it is the sort of problem for which he is likely to be able to offer assistance. Such a survey may last from a day to a matter of months, depending on the complexities of the problem.

During this survey the therapist will immediately begin to involve all parties. He will set up a planning group to help in the task of the survey. Such a group should include representatives of all sections of the community under consideration. As a result of this survey, carried out in collaboration with those concerned in the problem, it may be that recommendations for further action can be made. Where this is the case, it should be pointed out that the recommendations are not made by the social scientist, but by the collaborating planning group, which includes the social scientist. In other words, the community begins to participate in its own therapy from the very beginning.

In the survey stage, it will frequently be found that the original complaint or request for help concerned problems which were really only superficial difficulties. A successful reconnaissance should go far towards relieving these presenting symptoms and thus make possible the uncovering of the more crucial problems.

b. *The pilot study:* On the basis of the findings of the survey stage, it will usually be possible to engage in a small pilot study, which is designed to investigate techniques for solving the larger problems, and to demonstrate the value of these techniques. This pilot experiment should be the responsibility of, and run by, those concerned with the problem, the social scientist acting merely in the role of technical adviser and collaborator. It will ordinarily be under the supervision and control of the original planning group involved in the survey. This pilot study, therefore, not only provides the opportunity for investigating the problem further, but allows the community itself to begin to familiarize itself with and incorporate for its own use, the techniques at the disposal of social science. The process of weaning the community or group away from the social scientist should already be well advanced by the end of this stage.

c. *The full project:* If the pilot run is a success, the community is then ready to proceed to the full utilization of the therapeutic techniques. By this time, however, there should be a sufficiently large number of persons involved in the pilot study, and intergroup tensions should have been sufficiently resolved, to allow those responsible for the solution of the problem to carry on the therapeutic process themselves. At this stage the social science adviser should be relegated to a fairly distant back seat. From this position he is available to advise and to assist in the clearing up of the special difficulties which may arise from time to time.

The development of War Office Selection Boards in the British Army during the war provides a useful example of this approach. The Army was faced with the problem of rapidly improving its techniques for selecting officer candidates. The Army psychiatrists were called in to help with the problem.

Their first step was an examination of the procedures already in use, and a tentative exploration of new methods. This was done in collaboration with the Presidents of the various selection boards then in operation. On the basis of this reconnaissance, a pilot selection board of a new kind was established. This pilot selection board was headed by one of the Colonels previously responsible for one of the old boards. In other words, the pilot selection board was run by regular Army personnel with the collaboration of a team of psychiatrists and psychologists. This pilot board was able to develop more successful selection techniques than had previously been used. As a result, it was visited by other Army officers, who saw a unit run, not by psychiatrists, but by regular Army personnel, and the functioning of the board was explained by fellow officers. The Army as a whole rapidly incorporated the new selection techniques, and within six months new type selection boards were in operation throughout the Army. The social scientists continued to collaborate as specialist technicians on these boards, but the continued operation of the boards remained an Army function. It is doubtful if this result could have been achieved had the social scientists concerned not taken such great precautions to remain in a collaborative role, leaving the main responsibility for the new developments in the hands of those previously concerned with officer selection.

The "Growing Pains" in Collaboration

The above example from army experience is in many ways an oversimplification. Various problems inevitably arise at different stages, and these problems are perhaps of major significance. They tend to arise out of ambivalent attitudes on the part of the community to the very process of solving its own problems. On the one hand, there is the desire for improvement, for resolution of tension, for the development of new techniques, and, on the other hand, there is the fear that treatment is likely to be more painful than the problem. Exposing the complexity of problems, with the inevitability of creating new roles for which the individuals concerned do not yet feel adequate, excites the desire to hang on to old modes of behaviour. Though the old modes are troublesome, until they are relinquished one can avoid facing up squarely to the fact that perhaps not all is as well as it might be. This ambivalence showed, for example, in criticism and attacks directed against the experimental selection board, and against psychiatry in particular, even though at the same time there was a general feeling that the new boards represented an advance.

This ambivalence towards treatment, an outstanding feature of individual psychotherapy, is likely to be found a constant feature of social therapy. And just as in individual therapy, the ambivalence tends to be directed against the therapist. This process, known as transference, is utilized by psychoanalysis as the basis of therapy, and it is our belief that it can similarly be used in social therapy.

Social treatment is made possible by the transference of positive feelings towards the social scientist and social science. These feelings reflect the desire for change and improvement, and can be interpreted as such. On the other hand, negative transference, or the transference to the social scientist of hostility and resentment arising out of anxieties about the changes which may occur, and out of inter-person and inter-group frictions in the social situation, will be reflected in resistances against going through with collaboration in treatment. The handling of these resistances is crucial. They show in many small and insignificant ways as pointed out by Wilson—in concealed hostility, in apparently innocent questions, in the continuous "testing out" of the good intentions of the therapist. Social change can be accomplished only as rapidly as resistances are overcome and removed. Lewin has pointed out that participation in group-decisions frequently overcomes individual resistances very rapidly. On the other hand, direct interpretation of the resistances, in terms of negative transference behaviour towards the therapist, has probably more deep rooted and lasting effects if properly worked through.

Take for example the previously mentioned case of the "expert" entering a group for the purpose of modifying its practises. He is commonly seen as a threat to security and as a usurper of the roles of members of the group. The result is the coming into play of various defense mechanisms, which are largely unconscious in their operation, and which have as their aim the manipulation of the intruder in order to render him "harmless". Crude refusal to cooperate is rarer than might be expected and these manipulations may take many subtle forms. They range from side-tracking the technician into an absorption in relatively unimportant details while the essentials of traditional methods remain as before, to disarming him by over-enthusiasm in order to dull his critical perception and undermine his independent status. It is also not uncommon for some important member of the group to become dependent on him and thus to absorb the bulk of his time and energy in dealing with what is really a personal problem. It is important to interpret these unconscious mechanisms to the group; that they be recognized as common reactions to all "experts", that they represent resistances to change and ingroup tensions played out in relation to the "expert". If this transference is successfully exposed, it should allow the members of the group to proceed to a consideration of the changes required and of their own roles in the new situation. Opportunity for such interpretations usually crops up in group or individual discussion, or in sociodramatic or other training sessions. The timing and dosage of interpretations are a matter of clinical judgment, and present one of the greatest problems of treatment. It is for this reason that the Institute sets a high value on psychoanalytic training. Such training is

the best guarantee that the technique of utilizing the transference situation in social therapy will never be taken lightly, and ensures that the therapist will maintain a continuous concern about working through tensions aroused by his own presence in the field.

By the interpretation of group resistance, the therapist can achieve a fully collaborative and neutral role. He participates in social change not as a manipulator, not as an engineer, but as a clarifier who helps the group to make manifest its own internal tensions so that such tensions can be better coped with by the group itself. Successfully worked through, social science collaboration of this type should be of benefit to the community. Eventually it may help society towards a greater awareness of some of the underlying and unconscious processes which contribute to difficulties of inter-person and inter-group adjustment.

◆◆◆◆◆◆◆◆◆◆◆◆◆◆◆◆◆◆ THE SOCIOTHERAPY OF THE
ENTERPRISE [1]   *Max Pages*

The Conditions of Psycho-social Change in Industrial Concerns and the Role of the Social Psychologist as an Agent of Social Change

TRANSLATED FROM THE FRENCH BY E. L. HERBERT

DﾁﾁﾁﾁREcTORS and managers of firms, trade-union officials, industrial consult-

[1] This paper was published in a special number of *Hommes et Techniques* entitled 'Psychosociologie industrielle', p. 215, 1959.

ants, and, more recently, social psychologists are daily faced with problems concerning the psycho-sociological functioning of their organizations. There are problems of coordination between

Excerpts from Max Pages, "The Sociotherapy of the Enterprise," Human Relations, Vol. 12, No. 4, 1959, pp. 317-334. ("Eléments d'une sociothérapie de l'entreprise," Hommes et Techniques, n. 169, 1959, pp. 158-170) Some footnotes omitted. Abridged and used by permission.

policy-making and executive departments, between headquarters and decentralized branches. Other problems are caused by lack of comprehension with regard to the policy of the firm or by divergent interpretations of it. Some members of the staff are unwilling to accept the new roles they are expected to assume. Some methods of leadership are ill-adapted to the social context. Methods of recruitment, training, promotion, or payment may be inadequate. All these problems regarding both personnel administration (such as employment, training, promotion, remuneration) and production (such as techniques, accountancy, and sales) affect the enterprise as a social organization, i.e. as a totality of social groups —work groups such as administrative departments and workshops, trade unions, friendly associations, employers' federations, clubs, and political parties. All these groups intersect, divide, and sometimes extend outside the firm itself. The psycho-sociological functioning of the enterprise represents the functioning of each of these groups and their connection with one another. In more precise though still very general terms, psycho-sociological functioning is the way in which the structures of these groups are bound together (their aims, roles, norms, sanctions), the mode of communication among the members of the group as well as the motivations and wishes of these members.

The psycho-sociological functioning is in constant need of adapting itself to the changing conditions of the environment. The conditions of work of all classes of personnel are profoundly affected not only by such factors as modernization of equipment or automatization but also by the greater concentration of firms, the increased division of administrative work resulting

in the multiplication of advisory services, and the increased influence of workmen's unions on the one hand and of professional associations on the other. From this point of view an important role of managers, trade unionists, and planners can be said to aim at facilitating the psycho-sociological adaptation of the enterprise to the changing conditions of its environment.

One of the main difficulties of this role is to achieve real changes in the organization, that is to say, changes that will affect the behaviour and attitudes of personnel in factual communication, in the actual aims pursued, in roles effectively assumed by the members of the firm. For every change successfully achieved, a large number of decisions and reforms are never implemented and a great many organizational reports remain in oblivion. Sometimes the blame can be put on the solutions adopted or on the quality of the diagnosis, but, on the other hand, there is often a strange disparity between the efficacy of the final result and the quality of the diagnosis.

In my opinion the main cause of this is that crucial problems that govern the psycho-sociological change of the firm, the strategy likely to bring about this change, and the role of the agents of social change have not been sufficiently studied. Indeed, they are often treated in the most empirical fashion by these agents themselves.

Thus diagnoses and solutions are often based upon the vaguest conceptions of psycho-sociological functioning. These conceptions are often coloured by social myths and stereotypes such as certain beliefs about the role of the chief executive. Most diagnoses and solutions often give pride of place to factors of structure and to formal decisions, whereas they disregard methods of communication and attitudes, which are the necessary condition of the establishment of any structure.

With regard to strategy the most current methods are either the mere communication of orders or 'solutions' or the presentation of a diagnosis followed by communication of a suggested solution, or again—and this is the most frequent case—the presentation of a diagnosis and the communication of a solution accompanied by persuasion and various techniques of social manipulation to 'get the solution through'. Such methods take no account of conclusions that might be drawn from the findings of the psycho-sociological sciences as to effective planning for social change.

In the course of this paper, I intend to submit the thesis that a scientific approach to problems of psycho-sociological change in industrial concerns is a possibility provided that it is based on the concepts and methods of the psycho-sociological sciences. The rapidly increasing contribution of these sciences is already considerable both with regard to the functioning of firms and other social organizations and to the more specific problem of social change.

It is true that the psycho-sociological sciences have not, up to the present, been much concerned with the application of their theories. Nevertheless, I should like to emphasize that the work of agents of social change in business organizations offers a field of scientific application whose relation to its basic sciences is comparable to the relation of the practical work of the engineer to the experimental work of physicists and chemists. In this case, there is a need to elaborate in the light of concepts, of methods of investigation, of

the results of psycho-sociological research, a theory of social change and a methodology of psycho-sociological action precise enough to be experimentally controlled. In this field practical workers can both profit by pure scientific research and bring new resources to it.

In what follows I shall outline the theories and methodology that have resulted from research carried out by a group of psycho-sociologists and from their practical application of this. Considerations of space will allow me to give only a brief outline without any description of examples. I shall limit myself to presenting the general theoretical and methodological framework that could guide the work of the social psychologist who intervenes in an enterprise in order to help it to solve its problems. I have elected to dwell more fully on the aspects specifically connected with the problem of change than on those of the psycho-sociological functioning of the firm. It must be made clear, however, that the two are inseparable.

The sciences that have been found most useful to fulfil our aim belong to two different fields, i.e. psychotherapy and social psychology. Indeed, psychotherapists are both scientists and practical agents of change, for they are concerned with bringing about a change in persons who are disturbed or mentally ill.

One is struck by the degree of agreement among psychotherapists upon the following fundamental conditions of change and this in spite of differences among the various schools of psychotherapy and the variety of their terminology.

1. The rejection of any pressure on the patient. Advice, persuasion, and

moral support are regarded as forms of pressure as much as are coercion and threats.

2. Communication to the patient and discussion of a diagnosis of his case such as might be obtained by means of tests can take place only as part of the general treatment and cannot be separated from it.

3. Free expression of feelings, opinions, and attitudes by the patient is encouraged to the maximum.

4. The aim of the therapeutic work therefore seems to consist in facilitating what one might call the patient's communication with himself, or, as it is sometimes expressed, communication between various layers or parts of his personality.

5. The therapist's action is a clinical one, a here-and-now response to the patient's free expression, aiming by various means—different schools use different methods—at facilitating the patient's communication with himself.

It is easy to see how helpful such hypotheses can be to the sociotherapist whose work it is to deal not with an individual but with a social organization. Indeed, some psychotherapists have themselves attempted to apply them to the treatment of business firms.

The experiment in counselling carried out at Western Electric is one of the best known. Other American firms regularly employ psychotherapists who have specialized in the application of psychotherapy to industrial work in counselling managers.

These two types of experiment are open to fairly obvious criticism. Individually centered as they are, they certainly tend to facilitate the adaptation of the individual to his group but they offer no guarantee that the adaptation of the group to individual needs receives sufficient attention. Moreover, since they are concerned with attitudes at a deep psychological level, they do not take enough account of total social behaviour in a definite context. For instance, in the case of a manager— the most useful for this kind of experiment—it is clear that the effect of his behaviour will not depend solely on his deep psychological attitudes. It will certainly depend, for instance, on the degree of his knowledge of the particular firm, on the communication network between himself and his associates, and on the particular techniques of communication he uses, as well as on all the same factors as they are found in his associates. Since the task we have set ourselves is the treatment of a social group, we cannot ignore any of these factors. Indeed, our work must take place at the focal point where the structure of the group, communication inside the group, and the attitudes of its members are found to converge.

A British social psychologist, Dr Elliott Jaques, has attempted in a London firm to apply a more thorough transposition of the psychotherapeutic approach to social treatment. He used a direct clinical approach with work groups, sometimes preceded by interviews with individual members of the firm, to deal with problems of group structure, communication, and attitudes. While the work of Jaques, who is a pioneer in this field, is of outstanding interest, it nevertheless lends itself to criticism on two counts. First, the treatment does not take sufficiently into account that a firm is a whole, with its own organization and hierarchy, in which the problems of one group can condition those of another group so that the process of change should be considered from the point of view of the total social organization. Failing this, although Jaques's method is different from and more thorough than that used by the counsellors of Western Electric, it is open to a similar objection, i.e. the use of means of partial adaptation and the disregard of overall phenomena which are of primary importance in the treatment of the total social organization.

Second, the treatment is exclusively based on the use of a single technique, the clinical approach to a group. It therefore tells us little about the process of change itself, which alone could justify the use of a particular technique or even the search for a different one.[2]

It would be extremely useful to find out whether the general hypotheses mentioned above on the process of change in psychotherapy remain valid when they are applied to a social organization instead of an individual. If so, how are they to be formulated so that they take account of the specific characteristics of a social organization?

As things are at present, it would seem that applications of psychotherapeutic techniques to social treatment have followed these techniques too closely. As a result, the transfer of therapeutic hypotheses to the social context at a deep level, a process which might have been so fruitful both in theory and practice, has not been thoroughly worked out.

If we turn to social psychology, one of the most interesting aspects of recent research is the possibility it opens of integrating concepts and fields of study hitherto separate, such as those of group structure, communications, and attitudes. Thus, for the first time in the history of the psycho-sociological science, it becomes possible to establish general hypotheses on the functioning of human organizations that take into account group as well as individual variables.

On the other hand, the work of the Lewinian school of social psychologists on the concept of change as a modification of a quasi-stationary equilibrium of forces and its bearing upon the strategy of change, which have been partly verified by experiment, offer a foundation for a theory of psycho-social change. Although these results have been attained by an independent approach they are in accord with the conclusions of psychotherapists.

Lastly, concrete experiments on change in a 'real' environment have been carried out by social psychologists. Such are the experiments of Lewin, and of Coch and French, showing the efficacy of group discussion and of participation in group decisions in the lowering of resistance to change. One of these studies bore on change in feeding habits and the other on the effect of adopting new methods of work and payment in industrial production. More recently the remarkable experiment carried out by Floyd Mann on 'feedback training' has shown that reporting back to the work groups concerned the results of research into attitudes towards authority and leadership behaviour within the group effectively brings about a change in these attitudes.

These experiments with change are invaluable to the social therapist for the light they throw upon certain aspects of social change. They can lead to the introduction of new techniques or make more accurate the

---

[2] We believe that Dr Jaques in his hitherto unpublished works has modified his theories in a way that renders these objections invalid. They refer, of course, to his first book.

mode of application of existing ones.

Nevertheless, it must not be denied that they provide but an incomplete answer to the problems facing the social therapist. These experiments are naturally influenced by the fact that they have originated in the laboratory. Since they are devised as a method of pure and not of applied research they are not directed primarily at solving industrial problems. Their aim is to show the correlations of a very limited number of variables artificially isolated. The research worker in the pursuit of his specific aim devises his techniques of change more or less independently of the problem in hand and of the motivations of his subjects. His method is one of 'guided change' not unlike that of 'social engineering', although in his case it is used for purely scientific ends.

None of these conditions applies to sociotherapy. The special task of the social therapist is to help the firm to solve its own most important problems. He is not entitled to make a choice dictated by other considerations than the solution of these problems. Lastly, he must concentrate upon facilitating the process of change inside the firm and not upon verifying particular scientific hypotheses. It follows that his planning must be entirely conditioned by this task and cannot be defined apart from the process of change inside the firm. Therefore, though the social therapist can learn from psycho-sociological experiments he cannot transfer them in their original form to his own field of work.

For all these reasons I consider that the theories and practical methods of the social therapist must fulfil the following conditions: (i) they must be based upon a 'unitary' conception of the firm as a total psycho-sociological field; (ii) it is incumbent upon social therapists to formulate general hypotheses about the process of change regarded as an intrinsic phenomenon within the firm: (iii) they must formulate hypotheses on the effects of different methods of planning change and of particular techniques upon the process of change inside the firm.

It is noteworthy that the various fields of socio-psychological research provide important though partial answers to these questions, but these answers have not been brought together from the special angle of sociotherapeutic treatment. As in the case of work based on psychotherapy, there appears to be a gap between the field of scientific study and specific experiments in social change. I feel convinced that there exists in these two fields a wealth of concepts and methods hitherto almost unexploited from the point of view of social treatment.

In the following brief attempt to answer these questions I shall consider, first, the general conditions of a process of psycho-social change in firms and the strategy of change; second, the evolution of this process; third, sociotherapeutic techniques favourable to its development.

General Conditions of a Socio-psychological Process of Change in the Enterprise

I propose to present below a series of hypotheses about the conditions of equilibrium of forces inside the enterprise and the modifications it undergoes. The terminology of Lewinian group dynamics will be used as the most apt to express such hypotheses. Indeed, these are nothing but a synthesis adapted to the present purpose of those usually advanced by workers on group dynamics and they are based on their extensive experimental work.

1. Each section of the structure of the enterprise and of its various component sub-groups corresponds to a system of opposing forces which determine its level. The opposing forces can be present within the same individual or in different individuals within the enterprise. A state of equilibrium appears when the opposing forces are almost equal. This equilibrium is quasi-stationary (Lewin).

Thus, the production objective is the result of forces tending towards raising the level of production, such as incentives of gain, of prestige attached to the work, of pleasure in working, etc., and of those forces tending towards the lowering of the level of production, such as fatigue, fear of reduction in the time allotted to the work, dislike of the chief executive or of colleagues, and so forth.

2. Within the same section of the structure and at the same level of functioning the systems of forces may show different states of tension determined by the respective dimensions of opposing forces.

It may happen, for instance, that two working groups reach the same level of production although in one of them powerful 'brakes', such as hostility towards management chief executives or colleagues, are compensated by equally powerful incentives, such as the stimulus of high wages or interest in the work, thus producing high tension; whereas in the other group both 'brakes' and incentives are weaker.

3. The higher the degree of tension, the smaller the fraction of total energy directly invested in the pursuit of objectives of groups or of those of the whole enterprise. In such cases the energy of the group is largely used for avoiding or solving conflicts. This state of affairs entails several consequences. It creates a high level of anxiety and there is present a tendency to form cliques and sub-groups in opposition to one another. It also leads to behaviour tending to total evasion of attempts at solving problems or to solutions based on the conflict of influences rather than on objective information. Lastly it results either in rigidity or, conversely, in absence of structural organization.

4. The change can be described as the passage from a quasi-stationary equilibrium to a different one. It occurs when the forces tending in one direction are stronger than the opposing forces. It ends when equilibrium is restored.

The change takes place with increased tension when it is due to the increase of forces working in one direction.

The change takes place with decreased tension when it is due to the decrease of forces working in one direction.

In the example mentioned above, where both changes result in a rise in the level of production, the increase of forces in the first case may be due to the stimulus of higher wages or of increased interest in the work. In the second case the decrease of forces may be the result of a reduction of fear, of hostility, or of the physical difficulties of the work.

5. External interventions in a group or an enterprise result in increased internal tension whenever they are aimed at modifying the group structure. This is because they correspond to an increase in one or the other sets of forces. These enter into conflict with the op-

posing forces, which in turn are increased according to the phenomenon of resistance to change.

Such interventions may produce no change. This situation occurs when the resistance of the opposing forces is sufficiently strong. Alternatively they may produce a change opposed to their intention. Or, lastly, they may produce the desired change. In the latter case the change takes place with increased tension and a less economic use of the group's total energy.

The aims of external interventions by increased pressure may bear on various points. They may be attempts to impose targets, to modify methods of work without consultation of the people concerned, to increase rewards or sanctions. Though they sometimes appear as threats, they may also take the form of persuasion, tactics, or emotional manipulation.

External interventions can also result in decreased tension in the group or in the enterprise if their immediate aim is not to modify the group structure but only to facilitate spontaneous communication inside the group.

6. Thus changes in tensions may appear spontaneously inside a group or an enterprise as the result of communication among the members of the group. For the tension of forces connected with group structure depends on each member's perception of it, while perception itself depends on the frequency or on the nature of communication established among the members of the group.

It may happen, for instance, that antagonism between heads of two different departments which tends to lower the level of cooperation is conditioned by mutual fears. These can be reduced by improved communication.

For example, awareness of these fears due to the attitude of one or other of the protagonists and the free expression of them may lead to their elimination. This may result in an increase in the level of cooperation and a decrease in tension. The energy thus liberated can be transferred to other fields; for instance, greater attention may be brought to bear on the task or on the closer supervision of subordinates. In this way changes in the level of communication can bring about changes in systems of forces leading to a higher or lower degree of tension. These in their turn influence other forces within the group.

It can therefore be said that the amount of energy available inside a group is constant as long as the environment remains unchanged. This energy can, however, be re-distributed into various combinations of forces leading to a higher or lower level of internal tension. The re-distribution depends on the nature of communication within the group.

7. In the case of groups or enterprises with a high level of internal tension two contradictory phenomena can be observed.

(a) On the one hand there is an urge to communicate on the part of the persons or groups representing the opposing forces;

(b) on the other hand there arise mechanisms of suppression tending to preserve the integrity of the system.

These two tendencies both grow in proportion to the degree of tension.

Suppression of communication may, for instance, be due to the establishment of rigid channels of communication tending to consolidate the existence of separate sub-groups; or to the existence of an implicit or explicit rule that certain topics are taboo or that certain things cannot be expressed in connection with certain topics. In such cases it is as if the group reacted to states of high tension by a tendency to break up communication into a series of groups, closed systems inside which the tension is lower.

Yet the urge to communicate persists. It may appear either through the breaking up of suppressive norms as in strikes, protests, incongruous or 'unsuitable' remarks; or in the emergence of parallel and semi-clandestine lines of communication—gossip, rumours, and so forth.

This twofold observation is of primary importance for our purpose, which is to formulate a concept of the strategy of change capable of determining the psychosociological development of the enterprise in a positive way, for it leads to the following consequences.

8. It is the very presence of opposing forces in the enterprise and its component sub-groups that creates conditions of communication leading to a reduction of tension. *In other words, there is present inside social groups a self-regulating mechanism tending to the reduction of tension.*

9. This self-regulation process comes into conflict with internal obstacles when tension is too high. In order to become effective it has to be *facilitated.* This process consists in arranging for spontaneous communication inside the enterprise and its component groups to have the fullest play so that messages can reach without distortion the person or group for whom they are intended. There is also a negative condition to be observed: no pressure (increase of force) must be exerted whether in the form of directives, advice, persuasion, or moral support.

In addition, many other positive con-

ditions, which will be described below, must be observed. Help must be given with *localizing* the spontaneous needs of communication, with collecting and conveying 'suppressed' messages and avoiding their being distorted, and with interpreting them.

The two key concepts that emerge from this examination of the sociopsychological process of change in the enterprise and of the strategy of change are (a) the self-regulation mechanism, and (b) the facilitation of communication.

There is a striking analogy between the concepts arrived at in connection with social treatment and the fundamental hypotheses of psychotherapists. The attempt to express them in a common terminology makes clear their affinity.

(a) The notions of conflict or tension and that of the reduction of tensions are central to both sets of concepts.

(b) The notions of suppression and distortion of communication correspond to those of censorship, repression, and displacement.

(c) The avoidance of any pressure (expressed by Rogers as the 'non-directive hypothesis' but also present in other therapeutic theories) is a fundamental characteristic of therapeutic action.

(d) The same is true of the facilitation of spontaneous communication—intra-personal in one case, interpersonal in the other—as a principle of therapeutic techniques. It could be shown that, in the case of psychotherapy, Freudian interpretations, Rogers's non-directive interviews, and in particular Moreno's psychodrama, can be regarded as various means of facilitation of the individual's communication with himself. On the other hand it will be seen that sociotherapeutic techniques represent various aspects of the facilitation of communication between groups and individuals.

The profound similarity between the basic hypotheses of psychotherapy and sociotherapy becomes obvious as soon as the same terminology is applied to both. No doubt it corresponds to the essential characteristics of human change. A systematic comparison of the concepts and results in each of these fields can be extremely fruitful.

Nevertheless, there is no evidence that the same resemblance can be found at the *technical* level. The conditions of facilitation in a social organization can be, and indeed are, different from those used in the case of an individual. To take an obvious example, the interview as a psychotherapeutic technique does not correspond to a sociotherapeutic research project, i.e. a series of sociotherapeutic interviews, but to an investigation *combined* with the communication of information to the people concerned.

Mention must also be made of the following objection to psycho-sociological methods directed to the reduction of tensions frequently raised in industrial circles. It is often said that the presence of tensions is a necessity in any group if it is to attain a satisfactory degree of productivity and an objective perception of reality. This objection is due to certain misunderstandings with regard to tension reduction.

(a) Reduction of tensions does not imply their suppression. On the contrary, as has just been shown, reduction of tensions implies the verbalization of conflicts.

(b) One must distinguish between latent tensions and those which are obvious or apparent. An apparently weak state of tension is not necessarily one of reduced tension for it can be accompanied by strong latent tensions.

(c) Reduction of tensions is a phenomenon that takes place over a certain length of time and follows a certain course.

(d) Lastly, one must distinguish between tensions within the group and those occurring between the group and its social or material environment.

The decrease of internal tensions, far from preventing the emergence of strong tensions between the group and its environment, would tend to increase them. These may vary from one member of the group to the other because of specific needs or actions. The emergence of internal tensions within a group is inevitable, whether as the result of different perceptions with regard to the pressure of the environment or through difficulties of communciation inside the group. A state of tension that remained constant and weak is a pure abstraction. The important factor is the form of the group's reaction to increased tension, whether it works towards an effective reduction of tension or, on the contrary, whether its functioning is so permanently affected by the increase of tensions that it runs the risk of eventually being destroyed. Thus it can be seen that insistence on the functional nature of group tensions is not incompatible with the theory that the reduction of tensions is necessary to the satisfactory functioning of a group. On the other hand, this theory is indeed incompatible with the deliberate keeping up of tensions (in the form of conflicting aims among the members of the group) as a means of increasing productivity.

That this practice has been proved wrong by experience has been shown in all research into competition.

The Unfolding of a Process of Change

The following remarks aim at giving a brief account of the unfolding of a process of change tending to the reduction of tensions inside a social group through the mechanism of self-regulation. They are the result of observations in enterprises in which the author's role was to facilitate the process of self-regulation according to the hypotheses described above, as well as from his observation of training groups of a particular kind (not unlike 'T' groups) based on the facilitation of the process of self-regulation. They are presented in a purely descriptive manner.

It seems possible on first analysis to distinguish the following three successive phases in a process of social change, i.e. (i) recognition; (ii) diagnosis; and (iii) action.

(i) *Recognition* consists in localizing and identifying social difficulties hitherto unperceived. At this stage they are only perceived in fragmentary fashion; they are not connected together. Sometimes they are placed in juxtaposition without any order, sometimes one of them is so emphasized that it obscures all the others. This kind of perception oscillates between juxtaposition and syncretism as happens in some stages of childhood. Another of its characteristics is that the difficulties are perceived in different ways by the different members of the social group and are not integrated into a common frame of reference.

Recognition appears in the first reactions of a group when, through the mechanism of self-regulation and the reappearance of spontaneous communication within the group, messages hitherto 'suppressed' suddenly find expression.

It is interesting to note that recognition is accompanied by an increase of overt tension in the group. This can be explained by the resumption of communication between sub-groups subject to tension that had remained isolated from one another. Thus the first stage of the process of tension reduction is seen as an increase in the apparent tensions.

Both 'carriers' and 'recipients' of messages adopt many defence reactions no doubt caused by anxiety and feelings of guilt. They take the forms of (a) the expression of a large number of value judgements; (b) aggressive remarks directed against others as well as against themselves; (c) explanations of difficulties largely based on individual personality factors; (d) rationalizations tending to deny or to minimize problems or to present them as unavoidable.

For all these reasons—perception through juxtaposition or syncretism, defence reactions—it is impossible to regard the material emerging at the recognition stage as truly explanatory, in spite of the fact that the remarks are often presented as an analysis of the *causes* of difficulties. In point of fact, the evidence they produce concerns *symptoms* rather than causes.

(ii) During the *diagnosis* stage the group tends to perceive the connecting links between various symptoms. It discovers the existence of a complex network of causes that affect the work of the group and its problems. It is a synthetic perception of a situation.

For instance the members of the group observe the links between various aspects of the group structure such as divergence in methods of work and divergence in aims. Similarly, they discover the connection between the group structure, its communication, and the attitudes of its members. The difficulties faced by the enterprise are no longer exclusively attributed to the personality of its chairman, to the nature of its professional activity, or to the absence of an organizational charter. Each of these causes is placed in its own context. Judgements expressed by members of the group become more differentiated. Value judgements and defense reactions are less frequent and the different members' perceptions of the same phenomena tend to become more homogeneous. Thus internal group tension is reduced.

The various characteristics of the 'diagnosis' stage are no doubt due, first, to the increase of relevant information that becomes available regarding the life of the group; second, to the effect of the explicit discussion of grievances. Both these factors bring about a decrease of tension—catharsis—and an increase in the mobility of perception.

(iii) The *action* stage follows on the preceding one. The network of causes discovered by the group constitutes a map of possible action capable of bringing about coordinated action of the group upon its environment. The members of the group become able once more to perceive the group as a means of influencing its environment instead of regarding it as an obstacle to external action. Naturally the first action will bear on the group itself and be intended to alter certain aspects of its structure and communication. In an enterprise certain functions may be given new objectives, improvements may be made in the organizational programme, and committees or liaison agencies may be established. Decisions may be taken as to new standards concerning the attitudes of the staffs of various departments towards one another. Not until such internal reforms are instituted can the group devote all its activities to the pursuit of an external task.

In terms of dynamics, during the *action* stage tensions between the group and the environment take precedence over internal group tensions.

As action develops, new tensions may appear inside the group until such time as self-regulating mechanisms set in motion a new process of tension reduction.

The above detailed description of a process of change shows how closely the phenomena of modification of tensions within a psycho-social field are linked with those of the re-organization of group perception—cognitive re-organization—achieved by communication between the various parts of the field. The heterogeneous nature of the field, i.e. the divergence between the perceptions of various individuals or groups, appears as an increase in internal tension. The latter tends to start communication between the heterogeneous parts resulting in greater homogeneity in the field. In the present case results show a lesser difference between the perceptions of individual members of the group.

The above account calls for three further remarks.

(a) The process described is clearly a *collective process* that implicates the whole of the particular social group or enterprise. Change can take place inside such a group only when the whole of the group recognizes its problems, succeeds in diagnosing them, and is able to plan a corrective form of action. Under no other condition can the existing tensions be dealt with or reduced.

This observation throws light upon the reasons why, as was stated earlier, any strategy of change is doomed to failure that is founded upon communication to the group of a diagnosis or of a plan of action not arrived at by the group itself. This kind of strategy is the result of the illusion that the process of change can be limited to certain elements of the group, e.g. management, trade-union officials, psychological counsellors, planners, and yet affect the totality of the group.

Naturally, certain members of the group may be ahead of the others in the development of the total group, either because they are in a better position to receive relevant information or are better equipped to deal with it. Nevertheless, this does not enable them to effect alone a change in the group capable of dispensing with its undergoing the process these members themselves have been through. For instance, it was found in enterprises that during the reporting sessions on some research project, each participating member had, as it were, to work through the research process in the light of his own experience before conclusions similar to those reported could be arrived at. Yet, in these cases, the research had concerned the very people present at the reporting session.

On the other hand, the 'advanced' members of the group may help to accelerate the development of the group and to make it more thorough if they make use of their advanced position to facilitate the process of change in the other members of the group. This takes us back to the fundamental condition of permissiveness in the strategy of change, i.e. absence of pressure and facilitation of communication—now ex-pressed as the facilitation of a process of cognitive re-organization.

(b) The division into three distinct phases can only be approximate, for on the one hand we are dealing with a continuous process without definite boundaries—the fact that, as was first shown, some members of the group may be more advanced than others is evidence of it—on the other hand and in a deeper sense the three phases overlap, since various levels of analysis are used. It is an interesting fact that during the stages of recognition and diagnosis, communication and attitudes inside the group are already in motion *in fact,* although no decision has been taken by the group on the subject. It often happens that changes that appear at this stage curiously foreshadow decisions to be taken by the group at a later stage.

Thus a Research Committee composed of members of two departments in an enterprise and specially appointed to investigate the relations between these two departments may eventually become one of the managing bodies in the enterprise. Reforms decided upon during the action stage often do no more than confer official sanction on procedure already accepted in fact.

(c) The process of change may fail or be disturbed in various ways.

If suppressed messages containing information necessary to the reform of the group are not carried, if anxiety is too high or defence mechanisms are too strong to be correctly detected, recognition may be incomplete, diagnosis superficial, partial, or completely lacking, and action may be undertaken that does not reduce tension or only does so partially. In such cases difficulties persist and the chances are that immediate progress will be stopped and a new process of change started.

The specific role of agents of social change such as general managers, planners, trade-union officials, and psycho-sociologists is to avoid these disturbances by facilitating the process of change.

Thorough and extensive research on the different phases of processes of change and their disturbances would be of the greatest value.

Sociotherapeutic Techniques Capable of Facilitating Change

The following are the various techniques used by sociotherapists to facilitate the process of change. I shall attempt to describe them and to examine the ways in which they influence it.

1. SURVEYS BY MEANS OF INTERVIEWS OR QUESTIONNAIRES

Surveys are a method of collecting and carrying messages generally suppressed inside a group. They may therefore be of greatest use at the beginning of a process of change when they serve to set the recognition phase in motion. Sociotherapeutic surveys must include all categories of persons concerned with the problem in question and not only some of them; e.g. workmen and management; headquarters and branch offices. Only in this way can two-way communication be re-established, the defence reactions of all concerned be reduced, and a concrete diagnosis based on the interaction of individuals and groups be arrived at.

Unfortunately the exact localization of surveys presents difficult problems in the case of large organizations. It is a question, for instance, whether in a large enterprise it is better to carry out a survey involving all grades of management, heads of departments, and personnel, or whether it is more advisable to carry out several smaller projects, each of which is analysed before the next one is started. In the latter the question arises as to the level at which the research should start.

In the present circumstances it seems necessary to examine each case on its own merits in order to estimate approximately for each one, (a) the need to receive certain messages in order to bring about positive change; and (b) the intensity of the likely defence reactions to the reception of the message.

Obviously the people who are to be interviewed are the best guides to the elucidation of these questions but more thoroughgoing research is needed on this point.

A sociotherapeutic survey must be followed by a report (feedback) to the people concerned. The mode of presentation of this report is of very great importance and should be carefully studied.

The selection of data to be communicated in the course of the feedback process is equally important. The following points have to be considered: should individual anonymity be observed? Should it apply to the carriers of messages and not to the recipients? Or again, should anonymity be observed even further so that no specific groups are named? Is it advisable, as in Floyd Mann's techniques, to communicate data at different times, moving from the general to the particular?

The same observations are valid with regard to these questions as in the case of localization of research.

Where the collection of messages is concerned Rogers's non-directive interview method seems particularly suitable from the point of view of a sociotherapeutic survey, since it favours the spontaneous communication of messages.

The giving of precise and extensive information about the aims and methods of the project to all groups directly or indirectly involved is an indispensable preliminary condition of its final success, for it reduces the anxiety attached to the communication of suppressed messages. Such information should preferably be given by those groups within the enterprise which are directly responsible for starting the project. Their approval of it gives sanction for the removal of certain barriers to communication. The role of the psycho-sociologists involved should be secondary in this respect. The information given should indicate at the outset what the mode of the report is to be, especially as regards anonymity.

2. RESEARCH INTO COMMUNICATION AND THE STRUCTURES OF THE ENTERPRISE

This kind of research differs from the survey in so far as it is directed not only to the discovery of symptoms but to the formulation of a coherent psycho-sociological diagnosis.

In order to achieve these aims it is indispensable: (a) that concepts and the testing of hypotheses should be elaborated with a high degree of precision; and (b) that methods of measurement and control should be used. In this case descriptive statistics are no longer sufficient, there must be planned research into the correlation of variables.

Such research can be useful at a more advanced stage of the psycho-sociological process of change in cases where the formulation of a sufficiently precise diagnosis proves difficult and must be verified.

The possible fields for, and the methods and techniques used in, projects are as numerous as those of psycho-socio-

logical research itself and it would be impossible to describe them fully in this paper.

The following are a few examples of projects carried out by the writer in the course of his sociotherapeutic work.

(a) Research into the differences of goal-perception inside interdependent work groups. This was carried out by means of specific questionnaires.

(b) Systematic study of obstacles to communication in a work circuit involving various operations leading to a single decision such as capital investment or the introduction of a new article into the stock of a shop.

(c) Study of communication networks and of obstacles to communication inside a group by means of a questionnaire.

(d) Study of sociometric choices within a group.

It should be noted that both pure sociotherapeutic research and surveys have a double characteristic. On the one hand they have a heuristic aspect directed towards pure research and the objective treatment of information; on the other a dynamic aspect bound up with their facilitation function. This dynamic aspect must never be overlooked by the sociotherapist, for all kinds of concrete decisions concerning the survey or the research will be affected by it. In the case of surveys it is connected with localization, with interviewing techniques, with the need for anonymity, the style of the report, and the form of preliminary information. In the case of research similar considerations will arise with regard to choice of topic, the groups involved, suitable timing, and preliminary description of the goals.

All these considerations may interfere with the purely disinterested quest for greater knowledge. The rule in case of conflict should be for the sociotherapist to give priority to dynamic criteria since these are the real goal of his work. This must be done, even at the risk of eventually having to reduce the depth and extent of his research without, however, his failing to maintain an objective position towards information.

3. THE ORGANIZATION OF COMMUNICATION

This is another important weapon in the sociotherapeutic armoury. The verbalization of symptoms and diagnoses can be efficacious in promoting change only as long as they are circulated within the enterprise and its component groups. Messages must reach the recipients under conditions favourable to the development of the stages of recognition, diagnosis, and action.

In practice, in the course of such a project these problems are raised by the organization of sessions in the course of which the results of the project or of a piece of research are to be discussed and decisions taken.

Several questions are raised by the constitution of these work groups. Are they to be mixed so as to bring together several hierarchical groups or departments or should they be homogeneous? Should they be based on the formal organization of the enterprise or be independent of it? Should there be separate sessions for subgroups? How long should the sessions last? What methods of work should be used? What should be the roles of the various members?

The sociotherapist may be in a position to help to answer these various questions by giving guidance to the people concerned in the analysis of the situation and in the consideration of the needs for communication and of obstacles to communication. He can eventually suggest specific communication techniques and provide the work groups with suitable methods of promoting a psycho-sociological examination of the enterprise.

On all these he must proceed with great care and avoid giving advice except on minor details. For the organization of communication itself even in groups assembled to discuss a project constitutes a form of pressure on the dynamics of the enterprise.

Because of this it has often been found useful, in the course of sociotherapeutic projects, to suggest the setting up of a study committee to include all the heads of departments concerned with the problem to be studied as well as the psycho-sociologist in charge of the project. Such a committee, if it is formally set up, makes it possible to define the responsibility of the psychologists *vis-à-vis* the total number of groups or persons involved and to avoid their being assimilated to one group or another. It provides an opportunity of dealing with certain problems of communication inside the management group. Lastly it may eventually foreshadow to a larger or smaller extent a model of collective management for the enterprise.

Another useful institution is the setting up of a mixed working team including the consultant psycho-sociologists and those members of the enterprise who could be regarded as technicians of social change such as planners, personnel managers, and psychologists. In the course of a project the latter gradually become the principal agents of social change as they learn with the help of the psychologists to apply psycho-sociological techniques for the facilitation of change. These may include the organization of communication, clinical interpretation, and even surveys and pure research. Moreover, they can thus be helped to examine their own needs as personnel managers, planners, and so on.

4. THE CLINICAL APPROACH THROUGH WORK GROUPS

Another important aspect of the sociotherapist's role consists in the immediate analysis of the difficulties encountered by a group in the course of its sessions.

The sociotherapist participates as an observer whose only function is to help the group to recognize problems and to diagnose or overcome obstacles that may obstruct its work.

The clinical approach presents in a concentrated form all the factors of facilitation of change:

(a) The collecting and conveying of forgotten messages in the form of significant phrases, gestures, or facial expression to which the leader draws the group's attention.

(b) Interpretation consists in the decoding of messages, i.e. making explicit the attitudes and goals implicitly contained in messages in order to improve their communication and thereby the chances of bringing greater homogeneity into the field of perception. Interpretation may be direct, a true translation of the same kind as Moreno's 'double'; or it may be given as an objective hypothesis of the same type as psycho-analytical interpretations.

(c) Diagnosis, which consists in bringing together symptoms connected with the structure, the communication, or the attitudes of the group

into a systematic explanation given to the group.

(d) Lastly, the organization of communication in various ways: through periods of analysis following on periods of work, the appointment of selected members to the role of observers, even through questions put to the group or to individuals by the sociotherapist.

The role of the sociotherapist in this case is identical with that of the leader of a 'T' group though the context is entirely different, since the group is a 'real' one whose aim is not the training of members. The development of the group may therefore be entirely different from that of a 'T' group, and the psychologist's work, though constantly based on the same criteria, may present a completely different picture. It could, for instance, be deeper and more active than in a 'T' group if the group seeks to solve old internal conflicts at a deep level. On the other hand, and this is the more usual case, it will be more unobtrusive and superficial if the group thinks it wiser to work at a fairly superficial level, having regard to the need to arrive at an agreement within a certain time, to continue living together outside group sessions, and to face certain unchanged external pressures.

The clinical approach may be used alone if there is no need to collect or transmit information from outside the group, for example in the case of a single small group or of a group whose main aim is to elucidate its own problems. Unfortunately, in such cases there is no means of comparing, at the present state of our knowledge, the effects of the exclusive use of the clinical approach with those of an inquiry eventually followed by clinical sessions.

Where there is need for an inquiry,

for research, or for discussion by groups on the results of research, clinical interpretation may be used in addition to these various techniques, either before the project or at the reporting stage. For such groups may find it difficult to become conscious of the results of the project or research or to make a diagnosis and decisions—in spite of all the relevant information contained in the report.

The advantage of the clinical approach is that it concerns the group in its here-and-now situation and that it takes place at the exact moment when the group is in a state of internal mobility. For those reasons it is a powerful instrument for the facilitation of change inside the group itself. It can make for a deeper level of assimilation by the group of a piece of research.

5. TRAINING AND IN-TRAINING FOR GROUP LEADERS

Specific training and in-training groups can be formed outside or inside the enterprise for the purpose of bringing about changes in attitudes and of acquiring techniques and knowledge connected with psycho-sociological functioning. This paper, however, is not concerned with such methods. All that needs to be pointed out here is that sociotherapists have to solve the strategic problem of the need of training sessions for certain individuals within the framework of a sociotherapeutic process inside the enterprise.

It might be said empirically that such training sessions could be advocated for the period immediately preceding a so-ciotherapeutic project consisting of the people likely to have to make decisions about its inception. They would thus have more concrete and deeper information about the problem. Similarly, at a more advanced stage of the project, training groups would be useful for those responsible for action provided that they clearly perceived and accepted its purpose. On the other hand it would seem inadvisable to use training groups in the intermediate period, for they might be perceived as exercising pressure upon the people concerned and their colleagues.

6. SOCIOTHERAPEUTIC TECHNIQUES

It follows from all this that sociotherapists dispose of various techniques. They can often resort to several of them either simultaneously or in succession. A sociotherapeutic project may sometimes be conducted by a team of sociotherapists in identical or differentiated roles.

The permanent background of these diverse techniques is the constant search for procedures needed to facilitate self-regulation in the enterprise and in the groups of which it consists.

The variety of possible roles for the sociotherapist is responsible in certain cases for the most difficult situations he has to face, since he must decide on the spot at what level—management, group, individual—and by what method he should intervene.

There is a need for much experience and for set experiments and research on these problems as well as on many others connected with sociotherapy.

Conceptual Tools for the Change-Agent: Social System and Change Models

PART TWO

The change-agent cannot afford to enjoy the intellectual luxury of the historian or archeologist who focuses upon understanding and delineating changes that are manifest only in the relics of completed events. Nor can he be satisfied with the stance of the detached observer who interprets changes, while they are going on, from some calculated vantage point of noninvolvement. Those who undertake the functions of a change-agent must not only diagnose the ongoing events in which they are involved but must also find ways to intervene in these events to maximize the valid human values implicit in the events. Ideally, the change-agent should combine in some measure the wisdom and sense of perspective of the historian and the penetrating acumen of the scientific observer, while putting into practice the skills and arts of appropriate and resolute action.

Can such paragons be produced among social scientists and social practitioners? The question cannot be fully answered before the event. But we consider it no less realistic to seek to fulfill hopes than to succumb to fears when both are realistically justified by an examination of the human situation. The answer to the question depends in part upon the type of "realism" men embrace in confronting their condition. We are voting here for the brand of "realism" that accepts the uncertainties and ambivalences of the contemporary situation, while trying to maximize the hopes inherent in it. The notion of "change-agent" seems to us consistent with this brand of realism. It points to a prospect and program, in only the early stages of achievement, not to a finished fact. In this sense it is "realistic." It calls for a reorientation and reorganization in the patterns of thought, practice, and association widely prevalent among social scientists and social practitioners.

Such a call for reorientation and reorganization is disturbing both to social scientists and to social practitioners. The disturbance arises in part from the "realistic" difficulties always involved in effecting changes of any magnitude in existing patterns of thought and relationship. But the sense of disturbance may also reflect valuatively and attitudinally tinged issues concerning the place of "science" in human affairs and certain "conceptions" of behavioral science that we consider to be misconceptions. What are some of these issues and misconceptions?

SCIENCE VERSUS ART IN PRACTICE

A practitioner who shapes and forms—or better, re-shapes and re-forms—materials of a certain sort must be something of an artist. He must have a "feel" for the materials with which he works. His knowledge of these materials must go beyond "knowledge about" them to "knowledge by acquaintance with" them. The latter knowledge does not come to him by detached observation and theorizing primarily or alone but by direct "handling" of his materials, by learning to appreciate their reluctances and readinesses, learning to guide his "handling" by the qualitative reactions of his materials to the "handling." Learning the arts of practice comes through a process of apprenticeship, preferably under the guidance of an experienced practitioner who has mastered the art, not through academic tutelage in theories and hypotheses "about" the materials handled by his craft.

This "art" dimension in practice is clearly evident in the functioning and the education of skilled artisans of various sorts. It is equally evident in the functioning and education of "helping professionals," whom we seek to characterize collectively as "change-agents." In seeking for conceptual tools to guide the functioning of change-agents, are we denying the "art" dimension in their work or selling it short? Are we, more pointedly, seeking to substitute scientific knowledge about people and their conduct in stability (structures) and change (processes), in sickness and in health, for knowledge by acquaintance with people as particular persons or kinds of persons, as particular groups, particular organizations, etc.

This is not what we are aiming to do, of course. What we are rather doing is to deny a logical gulf between the knowledge of the artist and the knowledge of the scientist, which, by assumption, frequently separates the functioning and education of social scientists and of social practitioners. This gulf, we believe, is widened by the conventions of traditionally institutionalized practice—conventions that masquerade as inherent logical contradictions in the thinking of many social practitioners and of many social scientists as well. The gulf has been institutionally bridged in some areas of practice more than in others. It is least bridged in the arts of practice where people are the "materials" practiced upon and best bridged in areas of practice where physical things and processes are the "materials" to be altered, re-shaped, and re-formed through practice.

What can we learn by analogy, from historical experience in the the latter areas of practice? Unfortunately, confidence in such analogies is undermined by a historical circumstance that probably reflects the unbridged gulf in thinking about "science" and "practice" previously mentioned. We have thriving scholarly disciplines in the history and philosophy of the "sciences" and in the history and philosophy of the "arts." Scholarly studies in the philosophy and history of "engineering" have been relatively neglected. Yet the growth of "engineering" disciplines has been the cultural response to the bridging of the gulf between the "physical sciences" on the one hand and the "practical arts" of altering, re-shaping, and re-forming physical things and processes on the other.

Despite the lack of adequate studies in the history and philosophy of engineering disciplines, two analogies between the place of "science" and "art" in "physical engineering" and the place of these in "human engineering" may be suggestive.

1. Engineering uses scientific knowledge of physical things and processes to exploit "new" possibilities and potentialities in the practices of handling and developing these things and processes. It continually passes beyond conventional views of "natural potentialities" in things and processes that are actually rationalizations of present techniques of practice. It is doubtful if artisans working with coal tar, for example, would or could ever have developed the flood of colors, old and new, locked up in coal tar, a substance so qualitatively different from the dyes that may be made to issue from it. Physiochemical knowledge derived from basic research about dyes and pigmentation and about the chemical composition of coal tar opened up for engineering diagnosis hitherto closed "natural potentialities" and led to the construction of "human artifacts" for actualizing these potentialities. In doing so, engineers transformed "nature" as conventionally seen by an addition to the arts of human culture. And "common sense" has generally absorbed this transformation of "nature," at least in cultures with a highly developed chemical technology. Newly invented concepts in basic research led to engineering concepts of practical utility.

Are the possibilities so different within the processes of human engineering? Are we limited in our current view of the possibilities and potentialities of human nature by our present arts of handling, managing, and developing human beings? Can basic scientific concepts and knowledge of processes of human conduct be introduced into practitioners' diagnoses of human potentialities and can the creation of social artifacts to elicit and stabilize hitherto unrealized possibilities in "human nature" be thus stimulated and facilitated? Can new arts of guiding human growth and development become a part of our culture through building bridges of "engineering" between our present arts of education, organization, and policy-making and the beginnings of basic scientific knowledge about human beings in their personal and collective behavior?

We see no logical reasons why analogous "engineering" developments in social practice are impossible. And we see the best hope of directing and managing processes of technological change toward humane ends in thus extending our conceptions of the possibilities of human nature and in building cultural and institutional artifacts to elicit and stabilize these new possibilities. One barrier to realizing this hope lies in the fear that "human nature," as we know it now, will be destroyed in deliberately devising new technologies for its renovation. Is this fear groundless?

2. This question brings us to a second analogue. Our fears about the dehumanizing effects of engineering practice stem from our experiences with past decisions about the uses of engineering competence that have involved neglect of or insensitivity to important moral and esthetic values. Competences in physical engineering have frequently been employed (or misemployed) by industrial and governmental bureaucracies to serve limited values, for example, maximization of economic advantages in the case of the former and maximization of "defense" advantages in the case of the latter. The effect has frequently been "selective inattention" by those with engineering competence to other human values at stake in the changes they have exercised their ingenuity to produce. Men fear that a similar "selective inattention" will work in the use of competences in social engineering as these develop. In fact, men can point to such "selective inattention" in "engineering" approaches to influence that have been widely publicized, for example, in manipulation of mass media by "hidden persuaders" or by votaries of "motivational research," and by the practitioners of "brainwashing."

The grounds for fear are evident enough. Where are the grounds for hope? We believe that they lie in the very fact that "values" have been served in the massing and utilization of engineering resources in the past. We need to unmask the pose of amorality that has, wittingly or unwittingly, been assumed by engineers, physical and social. A similar pose has been assumed widely by scientists and artists as well. Competitive economic advantage is a value and its disciplined pursuit a morality, albeit a limiting one. Similarly, competitive "defense" advantage in the cold war represents a value and its disciplined pursuit a morality, although again it is limited and constricting and probably eventually self-defeating, if exclusively employed in decisions about the development and utilization of engineering talent. No practitioner operates without the guidance of moral and/or esthetic norms, however unexamined, inarticulate, and uncriticized these may be. Our hope lies in this fact and in the possibility of stimulating examination, articulation, and criticism of the values that engineering competence does and should serve on the part of engineers themselves and those who employ their talents.

There is a morality inherent in the human enterprise of engineering itself (just as we have argued previously that there is a morality inherent in the human enterprise of science). Scholars like Veblen and Ayres have made this fact abundantly clear, however we may choose to criticize their particular articulations of its content.[1] As this inherent morality becomes clear to engineers and as they assume responsibility for extending and maintaining it in their work, it is doubtful to us that they will be able to collaborate wholeheartedly in inhumane utilizations of their talents. Since their role is increasingly necessary to the maintenance of both economic and political structures in "developed" countries, their moral voice will be heard. This is now true for engineers concerned with the development of things. It will become increasingly true of engineers concerned with the development of human beings as well. Meanwhile, for many, the articulation of their moral voice remains an unfinished task.

GENERALIZATIONS AND CASES

As we have seen (from Greenwood's article in Chapter 2), practitioners are certainly concerned with particular "cases," with their diagnosis and with planning treatments to effect improvements in them. Scientists, on the other hand, are concerned with particular "cases" primarily to verify or disprove generalizations about the relationships between variables that are somehow exemplified in the "cases." Claims for the utility of scientific findings for practitioners must take account of this important distinction between the two orientations. This valid distinction may be used to lend plausibility to the sharp conceptual cleavage between "knowledge about" and "knowledge by acquaintance with"—a cleavage already noted.

How do generalizations function in the thinking of practitioners about "cases" with which they are concerned? It is easy for practitioners who are focused on the "unique" character of case-situations to forget the "deductive" aspects of their diagnostic processes. Yet these "deductive" aspects are always present, however inarticulately. Previous experiences with other cases would have no meaning for this case if there were not some generalizations carried over from previous experiences and brought to bear upon the present one. An organizational consultant may have learned that some pattern of symptoms observed or revealed in the present instance connotes difficulties in communication upward in the hierarchy of the organization. Another pattern of symptoms may indicate unacknowledged competition between department heads. The practitioner thus develops "diagnostic orientations" in the course of his practice. And he deduces from these orientations meanings for observable symptoms and syndromes in the case he is diagnosing. Frequently these diagnostic orientations have not been well articulated by the

---

[1] Thorstein Veblen, *The Instinct of Workmanship, Engineers and the Price System* (New York: The Macmillan Company, 1914), and C. E. Ayres, *The Theory of Human Progress* (Chapel Hill: The University of North Carolina Press, 1944).

practitioners themselves. The process of deduction of meanings from them may operate implicitly and the end-product of diagnosis may emerge into his consciousness as an "insight" that illuminates the complexities of the confronting case with a meaning and a direction for intervention in treatment of the case. Insight and intuition are then opposed sharply to logical operations from preformed theories or hypotheses. The value of stressing the uniqueness of the case is to reduce the prevalence of mechanical or nonorganic diagnoses accomplished only by derivations from previous knowledge. The disvalue may lie in producing the same effect through failure to examine and articulate the diagnostic orientations that are actually at work, wittingly or not, in the processes of diagnosis.

It is at the point of formulating, criticizing, or revising diagnostic orientations toward the cases with which he works that the practitioner finds the most direct use for scientific generalizations. For these generalizations are designed to point to meaningful connections between variables *possibly* at work within any situation being analyzed. A perfect science of human behavior, if one were available to practitioners, would still point to structures of *possibility* within the cases with which he deals. It would not obviate the necessity for reconnaissance of particular situations to find which variables are at work there, for judgment of which variables are crucial in explaining the difficulty in the case, for measurement of the magnitudes of these variables as they combine to contribute to the difficulty. The arts of diagnosis are thus still necessary to the practitioner, but they can be validly informed by scientific generalizations that have been integrated into the diagnostic orientations he brings to the cases with which he deals.

CONCEPTS VERSUS FEELINGS IN PRACTICE

The gulf between the artist and the scientist divides them, often deeply, in their approaches to the emotions and feelings of men. First of all, there is an ideologically created distinction between concepts about knowledge, information, and other cognitive processes and those about emotions, feelings, and interpersonal relations. Philosophers and scientists long ago organized separately the terms and concepts for talking about and interpreting the cognitive and the affective aspects of man's behavior. Due to the process of abstracting, necessary for the creation of terms and concepts, a gulf between the two omnipresent aspects of man's behavior is made and widened. And we are then constrained to talk about separate and polarized entities: ideas versus emotions, rational versus nonrational, perceptions and cognitions as affected by emotions, rational task structures versus the structure of interpersonal relations in groups, and so on. What has been conceptually put asunder in the past by the use of separate terms has to be put back together again. The scientist takes his time in relating these polarized terms in his conceptual framework; the practitioner artist does it "on the fly" while working with a case. In so doing, the practitioner is led to another problem of his relationship to the scientist's concepts.

The gulf is widened when practitioners insist that the states of feelings or nonverbal emotional communications or the personal vocabularies of the emotions are destroyed or made trivial by the arid "scientific" concepts that are intended to capture, reflect, and analyze an emotional experience. The client's feelings, it is argued, can be understood primarily by the change-agent's apprehending the wholeness of the feelings, or some symbolic facsimile of them, and not through concepts intended to provide knowledge about the experiences of the client. It is as if the change-agent cannot know by conceptual and intellectual analysis, but can only comprehend by making use of his own feelings and reactions as a resonating instrument.

The impact of depth psychology upon man's view of man has both intensified and alleviated the struggle over the best way of apprehending man's feelings and emotions. Freud, on the one hand, stretched our horizons by redefining the range and explorable depths of the emotions, and thereby increased man's sense of awe and mystery about emotional manifestations and their role in man's behavior. In more recent times, Rogerian theory and therapy, existential psychology, and the widespread use of differentiated and complicated artistic mediums of emotional expression have strengthened assumptions about the fragile untranslatability of feelings and emotions into conceptual language. Further reinforcement for safeguarding the sanctity of the feelings and emotions comes from various defensive moves against the invasion of human affairs by "scientism" and from the poignant search of contemporary men for the wholeness and immediacy of experience that individual alienation and social fragmentation often deny him. Many seem to say "if you can talk about your feelings directly and conceptually, then they are not real, or have disappeared."

Yet, at the same time, Freud was using terms, concepts and constructions, metaphors and analogical language to provide a vehicle by which these very feelings and emotions could be organized and examined both by those who have them and by the analyst trained to recognize them and to make them accessible to scrutiny and analysis by the person with troubling or immobilizing feelings. By putting into concepts the very stuff of the irrational and nonrational feelings and emotions, he advanced immeasurably the use of concepts to describe and analyze the emotions and also to bring them under self-control.

This dilemma of the change-agent cannot be brushed away lightly. He must acknowledge the polarization of "feeling" and "rationality" that operates in many situations, he must recognize the limitations of present attempts to bridge the gulf between "knowledge" and "emotion," and he must supplement his diagnostic orientations with acknowledgement of the reality of his own personal feelings and those of others. In brief, the change-agent can and must learn to use his own feelings and emotional apparatus, along with his conceptual paraphernalia, to achieve the best understanding he can of his client's feelings and emotions.

Balancing these modes of understanding is part of the artistic skill required of the change-agent. Sharpening his conceptual tools is a necessary step in the controlled use of his own feelings and emotional reactions.

SELECTION OF CONCEPTUAL TOOLS

Contributing to the difficulty of the change-agent in making use of the knowledge of man contributed by social scientists is the sheer volume of clamorous and conflicting claims to primacy issuing from those in various scientific specializations. Shall he diagnose "role" difficulties? Or are personality mechanisms of the individuals concerned at the root of human difficulties? Or should the change-agent concentrate upon the power structure of the organization? How does the practitioner guide his selection from among the competing wares offered by various social sciences?

Two interrelated ideas are useful in sorting out and evaluating the conceptual tools that are of use to the change-agent. First, he needs to look at the functions and limitations of a "concept," "conceptual framework," or "model"; second, he must examine the size of human units and the level of analysis which are of central relevance to a particular change-agent.

Change-agents, accustomed to dealing with "facts," often find hard sledding in dealing with "theory." But, we reiterate, facts are always, in truth, observations made within some conceptual framework. Concepts are invented in order to fix a particular slant on reality and to guide the production of new facts. The preoccupation of behavioral scientists with new concepts unintelligible to present common sense is based on this supposition. The resistance by practitioners to "jargon" may be understandable but if pushed to the extreme would deny the cornerstone of the scientist's contributions to knowledge.

Change-agents themselves make use of concepts and conceptual schemas, even while they are most vociferously attacking unfamiliar concepts in the name of naive realism or common sense. Common sense itself is a loose collection of conceptual schemas, and is the end product of cultural accretions, of folk wisdom, habitual modes of thought and hidden assumptions about human nature, and the social arrangements of man. An explicit formulation of concepts into a conceptual schema to be used by the change-agent allows him to reveal, examine, and refine his "common-sense" diagnostic orientations. Conceding the fact that there are very many possible conceptual schemas, what underlying unity operates among all of them? Unity can be sought, and at the same time, valid groupings of particular conceptual schemas can be found by examining the thought model lying behind assorted conceptual schemas. The thought models of "system" and of "development" can, we believe, fulfill the function of sorting out and evaluating various concepts for use by change-agents.

But which is the correct model, the most useful conceptual schema, the most relevant and powerful concept for a particular change-agent? Again, as we have insisted in preceding sections, the artistic skills of the change-agent must be used in making such selective judgments. No cook book can tell him exactly what idea to use. He must select and combine from the available tools at hand and must create new tools when the existing stock is shown to be inadequate. He must in the last analysis create his own role and role relationships. But valid knowledge *will* be useful both in the process of creation and in evaluating its products.

Another assumption made by contemporary behavioral scientists is that when change-agents are dealing with an individual, a small group, an organization, or a community or nation, there are some similarities and some differences among these clients, regardless of size. All client-systems are assumed to be like all others in some ways, like some others in certain other ways, and like no others in still other ways. For example, an individual, a small group, an organization, or a community or nation all are analyzable in terms of the interdependent nature of a social system.

The discussion of *levels* of analysis may best be approached by an anecdotal illustration. A group of spectators sat watching a football game. They saw two groups of eleven men facing each other, heard a whistle blow, then suddenly action erupted, followed by another blast of the whistle, whereupon everyone stopped. One of the spectators said, "That was a good draw play, we gained eight yards." When questioned about his jargon, he said, "Well, the quarterback handed the ball to the fullback, who counted off several seconds, waiting for the opposition to be drawn in, and then crashed into the middle of the line and advanced eight yards before being tackled and stopped. That's what is called a 'draw play.'" Someone asked a second spectator, "What did you see?" "Well," he replied, "I saw the acting out in different degrees of the needs for aggression and achievement in the players and the effects of how each views himself in relation to the other twenty-one men." A third spectator said, "I saw eleven men on either side engage in a pattern of coordinated behavior with very well worked out expectations of action for each position in regard to other positions, until these patterns were disrupted by the other side." A fourth spectator said, "I also saw your role relationship and integrations. But additionally, I saw a leadership structure, which included a man in one position calling signals during the play and a captain exercising some limited authority. I saw a social system of eleven men opposing another social system, each of which was composed of many subsystems and structures like leadership, conflict, plus a coach attached to each system." A fifth spectator said,"I saw two kinds of traditions: the ritualistic and emotional meaning of a game of this sort and the heightened excitement and tension of this particular game due to the traditional rivalry between these two teams. Both traditions reflect the competitive and peer values of our young adult culture."

Here we have a football fan's description and analysis of his "jargon." He has learned the concepts and conceptual schemas of football, and finds that it is a useful shorthand for describing a set of events. Also, we find an analysis of motives and self by the second spectator (perhaps an individual psychologist); a role analysis of expectations in a small task group by the third spectator (perhaps a small-group man); a portrayal of social structures and social systems by the fourth (no doubt a sociologist); and a statement of how the traditions and values of the culture affect behavior by the fifth (a cultural anthropologist). The statements and analyses are pitched at different levels of analysis, each using a different set of concepts and terms. The point is that no one level of analysis is the "real" one. Each is applicable for pointing up a different aspect of the behavior being observed and analyzed. It is conceivable that a football coach or a football player might find interpretations from any of these levels of analysis useful, depending upon the difficulty his team is encountering and the goals of improvement that have been agreed upon by coach and team.

Change-agents may not, in relation to the confronting case, be able to select their conceptual tools of diagnosis at one level alone. They may be forced to become multidisciplinary. Furthermore, the change-agent must select his tools of analysis on the basis of his preferred intervention strategy, his diagnosis of what he has power to do, the degree of accessibility of various variables to his influence, and the nature of his influence on and relationship to various parts of the client-system.

PITFALLS FOR THE UNWARY

In any hasty rapprochement between behavioral science and the arts of practice, we find some pitfalls.

1. One of these we may call the "etiological" pitfall. A major concern of many behavioral scientists is to find out how a given state of affairs came about; they are interested in "causes." In his eagerness to use scientific knowledge, the practitioner of planned change frequently has been booby-trapped into using a theory of origins of the problem as a basis for his intervening in helping to solve the here-and-now problem. We consider this search for "basic causes" by practitioners as a pitfall because identification of the "causes" of a state of disorganization in a social system does not mean that the change-agent can or should work at undoing or remedying these original "causes." The strategic intervention to help restore an organization to effective functioning may well require an entirely different action from that of trying to affect the "basic causes" of the problem, which are frequently located earlier in its history. In short, etiology, the "science of causes," may uncover both states and, in Allport's term, the functional autonomy of the present. One way of avoiding this pitfall of extreme dependence upon "etiology" is for the change-agent to start with scientific formulations of a strategy of action and intervention and then test the relevance of the diagnosis of origins or causes against the proposed plan. The consequence of this procedure is that we limit the amount and kind of diagnosis performed to those diagnoses that reveal future consequences of presently alterable factors. A preventive program of action, compared to a corrective one, does frequently require more etiological knowledge.

2. Another issue revolves around predictability and control. The behavioral scientist seeks to unravel the complex causal connections in personal and social change processes, often under artificially controlled conditions, and to report his results as proven or disproven hypotheses. His example has sometimes lured the practitioner into thinking that a predictable specificity of consequences will follow if he but learns to act in the correct manner. But, as Merton and others have pointed out, unforeseen consequences are always built into any social action. A change-agent always encounters varying degrees of low predictability and lack of control. Therefore the despair of the change-agent over the limits of his ability to act "scientifically" must be converted to an acceptance of incomplete predictability as a condition of his work. We propose that a midpoint between unrealistic demands for predictability and control and defeatist acceptance of the all-too-true realities of unanticipatable consequences is the position for the change-agent to occupy. He must become a "probability expert." He should be a gambling man, who eschews "sure bets" and "long shots" simultaneously. But, like a professional gambler, he should seek the bets that give him a probability edge over pure chance. This is the best he can do in the immediately confronting problem, hoping in the long run he will come out ahead. The position suggested is actually in line with much current thinking in the natural and behavioral sciences; namely, to substitute probability calculations for oversimple cause and effect thinking.

3. Another issue of paramount concern is the approach of the scientist and of the practitioner to the working contexts of "comprehension" and "verification." Using a simplified procedure, we suggest examining these two contexts as if they were separate dimensions. "Comprehension" and "understanding" are concerned with the exploration, formulation, and grasp of some phenomenon. "Verification" attempts to prove or disprove the "truth" of some hypothesis. It involves the cautious skepticism that demands more explicitly stated bases of demonstrating whether or not some diagnosis is "actually" so. The methods of the scientist typically emphasize the latter context through more and more rigorous procedures of demonstrating whether or not something is so. On the other hand, "comprehension" uses more personal, less elaborately codified procedures. The immersion in their materials on the part of historians, anthropologists, and practitioners such as psychiatrists, social workers, and consultants is reminiscent of the German sociological term for understanding, *Verstehen*. The "proof" of their conclusions by verification is not so easily obtained, at least within the predominant value system of the scientist. The point of this

discussion is to suggest that we examine the issues surrounding our methods of diagnosing to assess the relative emphases to be placed on "understanding" and on "verification." Hopefully, we can maximize both; practically we may need to sacrifice some "comprehension" in achieving a high degree of "verification," and vice versa (and more typically), accept some lower degree of "verification" in order to achieve maximum "comprehension."

CHAPTER 5

Social Systems in Stability, Change, and Conflict

Since stability, change, and conflict have for a long time been major foci of attention in philosophy, the life sciences, and the social sciences, the voluminous literature on formal models of thought and their application in specific concepts and conceptual schemas has to be sampled judiciously.

In organizing this chapter the ideas of "system" and "development" are used as unifying themes because of their significance in the diagnostic orientations of practitioners. In general, we find "system" and its modifications useful to practitioners since it emphasizes the functional interrelations between the parts of a client, be the client a person, group, organization, or culture. Its use thus requires thinking about behavior in terms of multiple determinants and factors—a mode of thinking always required of intelligent practitioners in handling concrete situations. System models are weakest in clarifying and explaining development over time. "Developmental" models, therefore, have important utility for change-agents. Since "system" and "developmental" models have not been synthesized adequately, both are presented in this chapter. The reader must be warned that these ideas of "system" and "development" may be intertwined in a specific theory.

The paper on *The Utility of System Models and Developmental Models for Practitioners,* by Robert Chin, presents a review of the major conceptual approaches to system and developmental models. He points to the emergence of an intersystem model, which promises to have great utility for change-agents.

The Problem of the Theory of Change, by Talcott Parsons, is an excerpt from a larger work on social systems. It offers a useful distinction between the processes of change *within* a stable set of structures of a system (dynamics) and the processes of change *of* the structures of a system (change). As a leading theorist of "system," as applied to societies, he insists on the existence of many possible sources of change in a social system, and in his other writings traces through the complex interactions that ensue when change occurs, including problems of stability, equilibrium, control, and deviancy. His influence is seen in the papers by Moore and Loomis in this chapter.

Sociological Theory and Contemporary Politics, by Barrington Moore, Jr., analyzes the difficulties faced by the equilibrium (system) theorists in discussing change, arguing that the difficulty may lie in the concept of equilibrium itself. It should be pointed out that Moore does not differentiate the types of equilibrium in use in system models. In pointing out the uniqueness of the individual case in history, he presents the advantages of "process" theory (developmental model) and moves toward what Chin has called an intersystem model, in which interacting systems are analyzed simultaneously for their effects on each other.

Tentative Types of Directed Social Change Involving Systemic Linkage, by Charles P. Loomis, presents a synopsis of a conceptual schema originally developed for the study of planned change in communities. Loomis' approach is to view the relationship between change-agent and client-system as a systemic linkage. Chin's generalized statement of the intersystem model and its connectives borrows heavily from Loomis, who extends Parson's recent formulation of the similarities between socialization, therapy, and problem-solving to a general clarification of the role of the change-agent. In this way, Loomis provides an intriguing conceptual framework for analyzing the time phases of the change-agent's collaborative relationship with the client. Lippitt's view of the dimensions of the consultant's role (Chapter 4) should be reviewed at this point as closely allied to the position of Loomis.

Deliberate Changing as the Facilitation of Growth, by Kenneth D. Benne, uses system concepts of interdependence in advancing the thesis that client "growth" is the goal of the change-agent. The paper shows that consistency of the goal or end with the "methodology" of the change-agent is required. Facilitation of growth —defined as the increased ability of the client-system to face and solve problems— "requires" ways of working with the client-system that are consistent with this goal. The role of the change-agent thus has its logical requirements, given the goal of client growth.

The next three papers are based on Lewin's contributions. *Quasi-stationary Social Equilibria and the Problem of Permanent Change,* a classic paper in the field of planned change, offers a usable tool—force field analysis—for diagnosing situations for their changeability. *Force Field Analysis Applied to a School Situation,* by David Jenkins, is a direct and simplified application of Lewin's approach. Another useful notion of Lewin's for diagnosis is presented by George Levinger in *Kurt Lewin's Approach to Conflict and Its Resolution.*

The themes reflected in the selections in this chapter are carried through the other chapters of Part II.

THE UTILITY OF SYSTEM MODELS AND DEVELOPMENTAL MODELS FOR PRACTITIONERS *Robert Chin*

ALL practitioners have ways of thinking about and figuring out situations of change. These ways are embodied in the concepts with which they apprehend the dynamics of the client-system they are working with, their relationship to it, and their processes of helping with its change. For example, the change-agent encounters resistance, defense mechanisms, readiness to change, adaptation, adjustment, maladjustment, integration, disintegration, growth, development, and maturation as well as deterioration. He uses concepts such as these to sort out the processes and mechanisms at work. And necessarily so. No practitioner can carry on thought processes without such concepts; indeed, no observations or diagnoses are ever made on "raw facts," because facts are really observations made within a set of concepts. But lurking behind concepts such as the ones stated above are assumptions about how the parts of the client-system fit together and how they change. For instance, "Let things alone, and natural laws (of economics, politics, personality, etc.) will work things out in the long run." "It is only human nature to resist change." "Every organization is always trying to improve its ways of working." Or, in more technical forms, we have assumptions such as: "The adjustment of the personality to its inner forces as well as adaptation to its environment is the sign of a healthy personality." "The coordina-tion and integration of the departments of an organization is the task of the executive." "Conflict is an index of malintegration, or of change." "Inhibiting forces against growth must be removed."

It is clear that each of the above concepts conceals a different assumption about how events achieve stability and change, and how anyone can or cannot help change along. Can we make these assumptions explicit? Yes, we can and we must. The behavioral scientist does exactly this by constructing a simplified *model* of human events and of his tool concepts. By simplifying he can analyze his thoughts and concepts, and see in turn where the congruities and discrepancies occur between these and actual events. He becomes at once the observer, analyzer and modifier of the system [1] of concepts he is using.

The purpose of this paper is to present concepts relevant to, and the benefits to be gained from using, a "system" model and a "developmental" model in thinking about human events. These models provide "mind-holds" to the practitioner in his diagnosis. They are, therefore, of practical significance to him. This suggests one essential meaning of the oft-quoted and rarely explained phrase that "nothing is so practical as a good theory." We will try to show how the "systems" and "develop-

[1] "System" is used here as any organized and coherent body of knowledge. Later we shall use the term in a more specific meaning.

Prepared especially for this volume. Used by permission.

mental" approaches provide key tools for a diagnosis of persons, groups, organizations, and communities for purposes of change. In doing so, we shall state succinctly the central notions of each model, probably sacrificing some technical elegance and exactness in the process. We shall not overburden the reader with citations of the voluminous set of articles from which this paper is drawn.

We postulate that the same models can be used in diagnosing different sizes of the units of human interactions—the person, the group, the organization, and the community.

One further prefatory word. We need to keep in mind the difference between an "analytic" model and a model of concrete events or cases. For our purposes, *an analytic model* is a constructed simplification of some part of reality that retains only those features regarded as essential for relating similar processes whenever and wherever they occur. *A concrete model* is based on an analytic model, but uses more of the content of actual cases, though it is still a simplification designed to reveal the essential features of some range of cases. As Hagen[2] puts it: "An explicitly defined analytic model helps the theorist to recognize what factors are being taken into account and *what relationships among them are assumed* and hence to know the basis of his conclusions. The advantages are ones of both exclusion and inclusion. A model lessens the danger of overlooking the indirect effects of a change of a relationship" (our italics). We mention this distinction since we find a dual usage that has plagued behavioral scientists, for they themselves keep getting their feet entangled. We get mixed up in ana-

[2] E. Hagen, chapter on "Theory of Social Change," unpublished manuscript.

lyzing "the small group as a system" (analytic) and a school committee as a small group (concrete) or a national social system (analytic) and the American social system (concrete) or an organizational system (analytic) and the organization of a glue factory (concrete). In this paper, we will move back and forth between the analytic usage of "model" and the "model" of the concrete case, hopefully with awareness of when we are involved in a semantic shift.

The "System" Model

Psychologists, sociologists, anthropologists, economists, and political scientists have been "discovering" and using the system model. In so doing, they find intimations of an exhilarating "unity" of science, because the system models used by biological and physical scientists seem to be exactly similar. Thus, the system model is regarded by some system theorists as universally applicable to physical and social events, and to human relationships in small or large units.

The terms or concepts that are a part of the system model are "boundary," "stress or tension," "equilibrium," and "feedback." All these terms are related to "open system," "closed system," and "intersystem" models. We shall first define these concepts, illustrate their meaning, and then point out how they can be used by the change-agent as aids in observing, analyzing, or diagnosing—and perhaps intervening in—concrete situations.

THE MAJOR TERMS

System. Laymen sometimes say, "you can't beat the system" (economic or political), or "he is a product of the system" (juvenile delinquent or Soviet citizen). But readers of social science writings will find the term used in a rather more specific way. It is used as an abbreviated term for a longer phrase that the reader is asked to supply. The "economic system" might be read as: "we treat price indices, employment figures, etc., as if they were closely interdependent with each other and we temporarily leave out unusual or external events, such as the discovery of a new gold mine." Or in talking about juvenile delinquency in "system" terms, the sociologists choose to treat the lower-class values, lack of job opportunities, ragged parental images, as interrelated with each other, in back-and-forth cause-and-effect fashion, as determinants of delinquent behavior. Or the industrial sociologist may regard the factory as a "social system," as people working together in relative isolation from the outside, in order to examine what goes on in interactions and interdependencies of the people, their positions, and other variables. In our descriptions and analyses of a particular concrete system, we can recognize the shadowy figure of some such analytic model of "system."

The analytic model of system demands that we treat the phenomena and the concepts for organizing the phenomena as if there existed organization, interaction, interdependency, and integration of parts and elements. System analysis assumes structure and stability within some arbitrarily sliced and frozen time period.

It is helpful to visualize a system [3] by drawing a large circle. We place

[3] A useful visual aid for "system" can be constructed by using paper clips (elements) and rubber bands (tensions) mounted on a peg board. Shifting of the position of a clip demonstrates the interdependency of all the clips' positions, and their shifting relationships.

elements, parts, variables, inside the circle as the components, and draw lines among the components. The lines may be thought of as rubber bands or springs, which stretch or contract as the forces increase or decrease. Outside the circle is the environment, where we place all other factors which impinge upon the system.

Boundary. In order to specify what is inside or outside the system, we need to define its "boundary" line. The boundary of a system may exist physically: a tightly corked vacuum bottle, the skin of a person, the number of people in a group, etc. But, in addition, we may delimit the system in a less tangible way, by placing our boundary according to what variables are being focused upon. We can construct a system consisting of the multiple roles of a person, or a system composed of varied roles among members in a small work group, or a system interrelating roles in a family. The components or variables used are roles, acts, expectations, communications, influence and power relationships, and so forth, and not necessarily persons.

The operational definition of *boundary* is: the line forming a closed circle around selected variables, where there is less interchange of energy (or communication, etc.) *across* the line of the circle than *within* the delimiting circle. The multiple systems of a community may have boundaries that do or do not coincide. For example, treating the power relationships may require a boundary line different from that for the system of interpersonal likes or dislikes in a community. In small groups we tend to draw the same boundary line for the multiple systems of power, communications, leadership, and so on, a major advantage for purposes of study.

In diagnosing we tentatively assign a boundary, examine what is happening inside the system and then readjust the boundary, if necessary. We examine explicitly whether or not the "relevant" factors are accounted for within the system, an immensely practical way of deciding upon relevance. Also, we are free to limit ruthlessly, and neglect some factors temporarily, thus reducing the number of considerations necessary to be kept in mind at one time. The variables left outside the system, in the "environment" of the system, can be introduced one or more at a time to see the effects, if any, on the interrelationship of the variables within the system.

Tension, stress, strain, and conflict. Because the components within a system are different from each other, are not perfectly integrated, or are changing and reacting to change, or because outside disturbances occur, we need ways of dealing with these differences. The differences lead to varying degrees of tension within the system. *Examples:* males are not like females, foremen see things differently from workers and from executives, children in a family grow, a committee has to work with a new chairman, a change in the market condition requires a new sales response from a factory. To restate the above examples in conceptual terms: we find built-in differences, gaps of ignorance, misperceptions, or differential perceptions, internal changes in a component, reactive adjustments and defenses, and the requirements of system survival generating tensions. Tensions that are internal and arise out of the structural arrangements of the system may be called *stresses and strains* of the system. When tensions gang up and become more or less sharply op-posed along the lines of two or more components, we have *conflict.*

A word of warning. The presence of tensions, stresses or strains, and conflict within the system often are reacted to by people in the system as if they were shameful and must be done away with. Tension reduction, relief of stress and strain, and conflict resolution become the working goals of practitioners but sometimes at the price of overlooking the possibility of increasing tensions and conflict in order to facilitate creativity, innovation, and social change. System analysts have been accused of being conservative and even reactionary in assuming that a social system always tends to reduce tension, resist innovation, abhor deviancy and change. It is obvious, however, that tension and conflict are "in" any system, and that no living system exists without tension. Whether these facts of life in a system are to be abhorred or welcomed is determined by attitudes or value judgments not derivable from system theory as such.

The identification of and analysis of how tensions operate in a system are by all odds *the* major utility of system analysis for practitioners of change. The dynamics of a living system are exposed for observation through utilizing the concepts of tension, stress and strain, and conflict. These tensions lead to activities of two kinds: those which do not affect the structure of the system (dynamics), and those which directly alter the structure itself (system change).

Equilibrium and "steady state." A system is assumed to have a tendency to achieve a balance among the various forces operating within and upon it. Two terms have been used to denote two different ideas about balance. When the balance is thought of as a fixed point or level, it is called "equilibrium." "Steady state," on the other hand, is the term recently used to describe the balanced relationship of parts that is not dependent upon any fixed equilibrium point or level.

Our body temperature is the classic illustration of a fixed level (98.6° F.), while the functional relationship between work units in a factory, regardless of the level of production, represents a steady state. For the sake of simplicity, we shall henceforth stretch the term "equilibrium" to cover both types of balance, to include also the idea of "steady state."

There are many kinds of equilibria. A *stationary equilibrium* exists when there is a fixed point or level of balance to which the system returns after a disturbance. We rarely find such instances in human relationships. A *dynamic equilibrium* exists when the equilibrium shifts to a new position of balance after disturbance. Among examples of the latter, we can observe a *neutral* type of situation. *Example:* a ball on a flat plane. A small push moves it to a new position, and it again comes to rest. *Example:* a farming community. A new plow is introduced and is easily incorporated into its agricultural methods. A new level of agricultural production is placidly achieved. A *stable type of situation* exists where the forces that produced the initial equilibrium are so powerful that any new force must be extremely strong before any movement to a new position can be achieved. *Example:* a ball in the bottom of a goblet. *Example:* an organization encrusted with tradition or with clearly articulated and entrenched roles is not easily upset by minor events. An *unstable type of situation* is tense and precarious. A small disturbance produces large and rapid movements to a new position. *Example:* a ball balanced on the rims of two goblets placed side by side. *Example:* an organization with a precarious and tense balance between two modes of leadership style. A small disturbance can cause a large swing to one direction and a new position of equilibrium. *Example:* a community's balance of power between ethnic groups may be such that a "minor" disturbance can produce an upheaval and movement to a different balance of power.

A system in equilibrium reacts to outside impingements by: (*1*) resisting the influence of the disturbance, refusing to acknowledge its existence, or by building a protective wall against the intrusion, and by other defensive maneuvers. *Example:* A small group refuses to talk about a troublesome problem of unequal power distribution raised by a member. (*2*) By resisting the disturbance through bringing into operation the homeostatic forces that restore or re-create a balance. The small group talks about the troublesome problem of a member and convinces him that it is not "really" a problem. (*3*) By accommodating the disturbances through achieving a new equilibrium. Talking about the problem may result in a shift in power relationships among members of the group.

The concepts of equilibrium (and steady state) lead to some questions to guide a practitioner's diagnosis.

a. What are the conditions conducive to the achievement of an equilibrium in this case? Are there internal or external factors producing these forces? What is their quality and tempo?

b. Does the case of the client-system represent one of the typical situations of equilibrium? How does judgment on this point affect intervention strategy? If the practitioner feels the situation is tense and precarious, he should be more cautious in intervention than in a situation of stable type.

c. Can the practitioner identify the parts of the system that represent greatest readiness to change, and the greatest resistance to and defense against change? Can he understand the functions of any variable in relation to all other variables? Can he derive some sense of the direction in which the client system is moving, and separate those forces attempting to restore an old equilibrium and those pushing toward a new equilibrium state?

Feedback. Concrete systems are never closed off completely. They have inputs and outputs across the boundary; they are affected by and in turn affect the environment. While affecting the environment, a process we call output, systems gather information about how they are doing. Such information is then fed back into the system as input to guide and steer its operations. This process is called feedback. The "discovery" of feedback has led to radical inventions in the physical world in designing self-guiding and self-correcting instruments. It has also become a major concept in the behavioral sciences, and a central tool in the practitioner's social technology. *Example:* In reaching for a cigarette we pick up tactile and visual cues that are used to guide our arm and finger movements. *Example:* Our interpersonal communications are guided and corrected by our picking up of effect cues from the communicatees. *Example:* Improving the feedback process of a client system will allow for self-steering or corrective action to be taken by him or it. In fact, the single most important improvement the change-agent can help a client system to achieve is to increase its diagnostic sensitivity to the effects of its own actions upon others. Programs in sensitivity training attempt to increase or unblock the feedback processes of persons; a methodological skill with wider applicability and longer-lasting significance than solving the immediate problem at hand. In diagnosing a client system, the practitioner asks: What are its feedback procedures? How adequate are they? What blocks their effective use? Is it lack of skill in gathering data, or in coding and utilizing the information?

OPEN AND CLOSED SYSTEMS

All living systems are open systems —systems in contact with their environment, with input and output across system boundaries. What then is the use of talking about a closed system? What *is* a closed system? It means that the system is temporarily assumed to have a leak-tight boundary —there is relatively little, if any, commerce across the boundary. We know that no such system can be found in reality, but it is sometimes essential to analyze a system as if it were closed so as to examine the operations of the system as affected "only by the conditions previously established by the environment and not changing at the time of analysis, plus the relationships among the internal elements of the system." The analyst then opens the system to a new impact from the environment, again closes the system, and observes and thinks out what would happen. It is, therefore, fruitless to debate the point; both open and closed system models are useful in diagnosis. Diagnosing the client as a system of variables, we have a way then of managing the complexity of "everything depends upon everything else" in an orderly way. Use of system analysis has these possibilities: (*a*) diagnosticians can avoid the error of simple cause-and-effect thinking; (*b*) they can justify what is included in observation and interpretation and what is temporarily excluded; (*c*) they can predict what will happen if no new or outside force is applied; (*d*) they are guided in categorizing what is relatively enduring and stable, or changing, in the situation; (*e*) they can distinguish between what is basic and what is merely symptomatic; (*f*) they can predict what will happen if they leave the events undisturbed and if they intervene; and (*g*) they are guided in selecting points of intervention.

INTERSYSTEM MODEL

We propose an extension of system analysis that looks to us to be useful for the problems confronting the change-agent. We urge the adoption of an intersystem model.

An intersystem model involves two open systems connected to each other.[4] The term we need to add here is *connectives*. Connectives represent the lines of relationships of the two systems. Connectives tie together parts (mechanics) or imbed in a web of tissue the separate organs (biology); connectives in an industrial establishment are the defined lines of communication, or the leadership hierarchy and authority for the branch plants; or they represent the social contract en-

[4] A visualization of an intersystem model would be two systems side by side, with separately identified links. Two rubber band–paper clip representatives can be connected with rubber bands of a different color, representing the connectives.

tered into by a therapist and patient; or mutual role expectations of consultant and client; or the affective ties between family members. These are conjunctive connectives. But we also have conflicts between labor and management, teenage gang wars, race conflicts, and negative emotional responses to strangers. These are disjunctive connectives.

Why elaborate the system model into an intersystem model? Cannot we get the same effect by talking about "sub-systems" of a larger system? In part we can. Labor-management conflicts, or interpersonal relations, or change-agent and client relationships can each be treated as a new system with sub-systems. But we may lose the critical fact of the autonomy of the components, or the direct interactional or transactual consequences for the separate components when we treat the sub-systems as merely parts of a larger system. The intersystem model exaggerates the virtues of autonomy and the limited nature of interdependence of the interactions between the two connected systems.

What are some of the positive advantages of using intersystem analysis? First, the external change-agent, or the change-agent built into an organization, as a helper with planned change does not completely become a part of the client-system. He must remain separate to some extent; he must create and maintain some distance between himself and the client, thus standing apart "in another system" from which he re-relates. This new system might be a referent group of fellow professionals, or a body of rational knowledge. But create one he does and must. Intersystem analysis of the change-agent's role leads to fruitful analysis of the connectives—their nature in the beginning, how they shift, and how they are cut off. Intersystem analysis also poses squarely an unexplored issue, namely the internal system of the change-agent, whether a single person, consultant group, or a nation. Helpers of change are prone at times not to see that their own systems as change-agents have boundaries, tensions, stresses and strains, equilibria, and feedback mechanisms which may be just as much parts of the problem as are similar aspects of the client-systems. Thus, relational issues are more available for diagnosis when we use an intersystem model.

More importantly, the intersystem model is applicable to problems of leadership, power, communication, and conflict in organizations, intergroup relations, and international relations. *Example:* Leadership in a work group with its liaison, negotiation, and representation functions is dependent upon connectives to another group and not solely upon the internal relationships within the work group. Negotiators, representatives, and leaders are parts of separate systems each with its own interdependence, tensions, stresses, and feedback, whether we are thinking of foreign ministers, Negro-white leaders, or student-faculty councils.

In brief, the intersystem model leads us to examine the interdependent dynamics of interaction both within and between the units. We object to the premature and unnecessary assumption that the units always form a single system. We can be misled into an utopian analysis of conflict, change-agent relations to client, and family relations if we neglect system differences. But an intersystem model provides a tool for diagnosis that retains the virtues of system analysis, adds the advantage of clarity, and furthers our diagnosis of the influence of various connectives, conjunctive and disjunctive, on the two systems. For change-agents, the essence of collaborative planning is contained in an intersystem model.

Developmental Models

Practitioners have in general implicitly favored developmental models in thinking about human affairs, while social scientists have not paid as much attention to these as they have to system models. The "life sciences" of biology and pyschology have not crystallized nor refined their common analytic model of the development of the organism, despite the heroic breakthroughs of Darwin. Thus, we are forced to present only broad and rough categories of alternative positions in this paper.

Since there is no standard vocabulary for a developmental model, we shall present five categories of terms that we deem essential to such models: direction, states, forces, form of progression, and potentiality.

THE MAJOR TERMS

Developmental models. By developmental models, we mean those bodies of thought that center around growth and directional change. Developmental models assume change; they assume that there are noticeable differences between the states of a system at different times; that the succession of these states implies the system is heading somewhere; and that there are orderly processes which explain how the system gets from its present state to wherever it is going. In order to delimit the nature of change in developmental models we should perhaps add the idea of an increase in value accompanying the achievement of a new state. With this addition, developmental models focus on processes of growth and maturation. This addition might seem to rule out processes of decay, deterioration, and death from consideration. Logically, the developmental model should apply to either.

There are two kinds of "death" of concern to the practitioner. First, "death" or loss of some part or subvalue, as a constant concomitant of growth and development. Theories of life processes have used concepts such as katabolic (destructive) processes in biology, death instincts in Freud's psychology, or role loss upon promotion. On balance, the "loss" is made up by the "gains," and thus there is an increase in value. Second, "death" as planned change for a group or organization—the dissolution of a committee or community organization that has "outlived its purpose and function," and the termination of a helping relationship with deliberateness and collaboration of participants is properly included as part of a developmental model.

Direction. Developmental models postulate that the system under scrutiny —a person, a small group, interpersonal interactions, an organization, a community or a society—is going "somewhere"; that the changes have some direction. The direction may be defined by (*a*) some *goal* or end state (developed, mature); (*b*) the *process* of becoming (developing, maturing) or (*c*) the degree of achievement *toward* some goal or end state (increased development, increase in maturity).

Change-agents find it necessary to believe that there is direction in change. *Example:* self-actualization or fulfillment is a need of the client-system. When strong directional tendencies are present, we modify our diagnosis and intervention accordingly. A rough analogy may be helpful here. A change-agent using a developmental model may be thought of as a husbandman tending a plant, watching and helping it to grow in its own natural direction of producing flowers. He feeds, waters, and weeds. Though at times he may be ruthless in pinching off excess buds, or even in using "grafts," in general he encourages the plant to reach its "goal" of producing beautiful flowers.

Identifiable state. As the system develops over time, the different states may be identified and differentiated from one another. Terms such as "stages," "levels," "phases," or "periods" are applied to these states. *Example:* psychosexual definition of oral, and anal stages, levels of evolution of species, or phases of group development.

No uniformity exists in the definition and operational identification of such successive states. But since change-agents do have to label the past, present, and future, they need some terms to describe successive states and to identify the turning points, transition areas, or critical events that characterize change. Here, system analysis is helpful in defining how parts are put together, along with the tensions and directions of the equilibrating processes. We have two polar types of the shifts of states: (*a*) small, nondiscernible steps or increments leading to a qualitative jump. (*Example:* black hair gradually turning gray, or a student evolving into a scholar); (*b*) a cataclysmic or critical event leading to a sudden change. (*Example:* a sickness resulting in gray hair overnight, or an inspirational lecture by a professor.) While the latter type seems more frequently to be externally induced, internal factors of the system can have the same consequence. In other words, the internal disequilibration of a balance may lead to a step-jump of the system to a new level. Personality stages, group stages, and societal phases are evolved and precipitated from internal and from external relations.

Form of progression. Change-agents see in their models of development some form of progression or movement. Four such forms are typically assumed. First, it is often stated that once a stage is worked through, the client-system shows continued progression and normally never turns back. (Any recurrence of a previous state is viewed as an abnormality. Freudian stages are a good example: recurrence of a stage is viewed as regression, an abnormal event to be explained.) Teachers expect a steady growth of knowledge in students, either in a straight line (linear) or in an increasingly accelerating (curvilinear) form.

Second, it is assumed that change, growth, and development occur in a *spiral* form. *Example:* A small group might return to some previous "problem," such as its authority relations to the leader, but now might discuss the question at a "higher" level where irrational components are less dominant.

Third, another assumption more typically made is that the stages are really phases which occur and recur. There is an oscillation between various states, where no chronological priority is assigned to each state; there are cycles. *Example:* Phases of problem-solving or decision-making recur in different time periods as essential to progression. Cultures and societies go through phases of development in recurrent forms.

Fourth, still another assumption is that the form of progression is char-

acterized by a branching out into *differentiated* forms and processes, each part increasing in its specialization, and at the same time acquiring its own autonomy and significance. *Example:* biological forms are differentiated into separate species. Organizations become more and more differentiated into special task and control structures.

Forces. First, forces or causal factors producing development and growth are most frequently seen by practitioners as "natural," as part of human nature, suggesting the role of genetics and other in-born characteristics. At best, environmental factors act as "triggers" or "releases," where the presence of some stimulus sets off the system's inherent growth forces. For example, it is sometimes thought that the teacher's job is to trigger off the natural curiosity of the child, and that growth of knowledge will ensue. Or the leadership of an organization should act to release the self-actualizing and creative forces present in its members.

Second, a smaller number of practitioners and social scientists think that the response to new situations and environmental forces is a coping response which gives rise to growth and development. Third, at this point, it may be useful to remind ourselves of the earlier discussion of the internal tensions of the system, still another cause of change. When stresses and strains of a system become too great, a disruption occurs and a set of forces is released to create new structures and achieve a new equilibrium.

Potentiality. Developmental models vary in their assumptions about potentialities of the system for development, growth, and change. That is, they vary in assumptions about the capabilities, overt or latent, that are built into the original or present state so that the necessary conditions for development may be typically present. Does the "seed"—and its genetic characteristics—represent potentialities? And are the supporting conditions of its environment available? Is the intelligence or emotional capability or skill-potential sufficient for development and change in a social and human process?

Change-agents typically assume a high degree of potentiality in the impetus toward development, and in the surrounding conditions that effectuate the potential.

UTILITY TO PRACTITIONERS

The developmental model has tremendous advantages for the practitioner. It provides a set of expectations about the future of the client-system. By clarifying his thoughts and refining his observations about direction, states in the developmental process, forms of progression, and forces causing these events to occur over a period of time, the practitioner develops a time perspective which goes far beyond that of the more here-and-now analysis of a system-model, which is bounded by time. By using a developmental model, he has a directional focus for his analysis and action and a temporal frame of reference. In addition, he is confronted with a number of questions to ask of himself and of his observations of the case: Do I assume an inherent end of the development? Do I impose a desired (by me) direction? How did I establish a collaboratively planned direction? What states in the development process may be expected? What form of progression do I foresee? What

causes the development? His diagnoses and his interventions can become strategic rather than merely tactical.

The Change-Agent and Models

The primary concern of this paper has been to illustrate some of the major kinds of analytic models and conceptual schemas that have been devised by social scientists for the analysis of change and of changing human processes. But we need to keep in mind that the concern with diagnosis on the part of the social scientist is to achieve understanding, and to educe empirically researchable hypotheses amenable to his methods of study. The social scientist generally prefers not to change the system, but to study how it works and to predict what would happen if some new factor were introduced. So we find his attention focused on a "theory of change," of how the system achieves change. In contrast, the practitioner is concerned with diagnosis: how to achieve understanding in order to engage in change. The practitioner, therefore, has some additional interests; he wants to know how to change the system, he needs a "theory of changing" the system.

A theory of changing requires the selection, or the construction, by theoretically minded practitioners, of thought-models appropriate to their intended purpose. This has to be done according to explicit criteria. A change-agent may demand of any model answers to certain questions. The responses he receives may not be complete nor satisfactory since only piecemeal answers exist. At this period in the development of a theory of changing, we ask four questions as our guide lines for examining a conceptual model intended for the use of change-agents.

The first question is simply this: does the model account for the stability and continuity in the events studied at the same time that it accounts for changes in them? How do processes of change develop, given the interlocking factors in the situation that make for stability? Second, where does the model locate the "source" of change? What place among these sources do the deliberate and conscious efforts of the client-system and change-agent occupy? Third, what does the model assume about how goals and directions are determined? What or who sets the direction for movement of the processes of change? Fourth, does the model provide the change agent with levers or handles for affecting the direction, tempo, and quality of these processes of change?

A fifth question running through the other four is this: How does the model "place" the change-agent in the scheme of things? What is the shifting character of his relationship to the client-system, initially and at the termination of relationship, that affects his perceptions and actions? The questions of relationship of change-agent to others needs to be part and parcel of the model since the existential relationships of the change-agent engaged in processes of planned change become "part of the problem" to be investigated.

The application of these five questions to the models of systems and models of development crystallizes some of the formation of ingredients for a change-agent model for changing. We can now summarize each model as follows:

A "system" model emphasizes primarily the details of how stability is achieved, and only derivatively how change evolves out of the incompatibilities and conflicts in the system. A system model assumes that organization, interdependency, and integration exist among its parts and that change is a derived consequence of how well the parts of the system fit together, or how well the system fits in with other surrounding and interacting systems. The source of change lies primarily in the structural stress and strain externally induced or internally created. The process of change is a process of tension reduction. The goals and direction are emergent from the structures or from imposed sources. Goals are often analyzed as set by "vested interests" of one part of the system. The confronting symptom of some trouble is a reflection of difficulties of adaptability (reaction to environment) or of the ability for adjustment (internal equilibration). The levers or handles available for manipulation are in the "inputs" to the system, especially the feedback mechanisms, and in the forces tending to restore a balance in the system. The change-agent is treated as separate from the client-system, the "target system."

The developmental model assumes constant change and development, and growth and decay of a system over time. Any existing stability is a snapshot of a living process—a stage that will give way to another stage. The supposition seems to be that it is "natural" that change should occur because change is rooted in the very nature of living organisms. The laws of the developmental process are not necessarily fixed, but some effects of the environment are presumably necessary to the developmental process. The direction of change is toward some goal, the fulfillment of its destiny, granting that no major blockage gets in the way. "Trouble" occurs when there is a gap between the system and its goal. Intervention is viewed as the removal of blockage by the change-agent, who then gets out of the way of the growth forces. Developmental models are not very sharply analyzed by the pure theorist nor formally stated, usually, as an analytic model. In fact, very frequently the model is used for studying the unique case rather than for deriving "laws of growth"; it is for descriptive purposes.

The third model, a model for "changing," is a more recent creation. It incorporates some elements of anal-

ASSUMPTIONS AND APPROACHES OF THREE ANALYTIC MODELS

Models of change

ASSUMPTIONS AND APPROACHES TO:	SYSTEM MODEL	DEVELOPMENTAL MODEL	MODEL FOR CHANGING
1. *Content*			
Stability	Structural integration	Phases, stages	Unfreezing parts
Change	Derived from structure	Constant and unique	Induced, controlled
2. *Causation*			
Source of change	Structural stress	Nature of organisms	Self and change-agent
Causal force	Tension reduction		Rational choice
3. *Goals*			
Direction	Emergent	Ontological	Deliberate selection
Set by	"Vested interests"		Collaborative process
4. *Intervention*			
Confronting symptoms	Stresses, strains, and tensions	Discrepancy between actuality and potentiality	Perceived need
Goal of intervening	Adjustment, adaptation	Removal of blockages	Improvement
5. *Change-Agent*			
Place	Outside the "target" system	Outside	Part of situation
Role	External diagnoser and actor	External diagnoser and actor	Participant in here and now

yses from system models, along with some ideas from the developmental model, in a framework where direct attention is paid to the induced forces producing change. It studies stability in order to unfreeze and move some parts of the system. The direction to be taken is not fixed or "determined," but remains in large measure a matter of "choice" for the client-system. The change-agent is a specialist in the technical processes of facilitating change, a helper to the client-system. The models for changing are as yet incompletely conceptualized. The intersystem model may provide a way of examining how the change-agent's relationships, as part of the model, affect the processes of change.

We can summarize and contrast the three models with a chart (page 213). We have varying degrees of confidence in our categories, but, as the quip says, we construct these in order to achieve the laudable state of "paradigm lost." It is the readers' responsibility to help achieve this goal!

The Limitations

It is obvious that we are proposing the use of systematically constructed and examined models of thought for the change-agent. The advantages are manifold and—we hope—apparent in our preceding discussion. Yet we must now point out some limitations and disutility of models.

Models are abstractions from the concreteness of events. Because of the high degree of selectivity of observations and focus, the "fit" between the model and the actual thought and diagnostic processes of the change-agent is not close. Furthermore, the thought and diagnostic processes of the change-agent are not fixed and rigid. And even worse, the "fit" between the diagnostic processes of the change-agent and the changing processes of the "actual" case, is not close. Abstract as the nature of a model is, as applied to the change-agent, students of the change-agent role may find the concepts of use. But change-agents' practices in diagnosing are not immediately affected by models' analyses.

Furthermore, there are modes of diagnosing by intervening, which do not fall neatly into models. The change agent frequently tries out an activity in order to see what happens and to see what is involved in the change. If successful, he does not need to diagnose any further, but proceeds to engage in further actions with the client. If unsuccessful, however, he may need to examine what is going on in more detail.

The patch work required for a theory and model of changing requires the suspension of acceptance of such available models. For this paper has argued for some elements from both the system models and the developmental models to be included in the model for practitioners, with the use of a format of the intersystem model so as to include the change-agent and his relationships as part of the problem. But can the change agent wait for such a synthesis and emerging construction? Our personal feeling is that the planning of change cannot wait, but must proceed with the available diagnostic tools. Here is an intellectual challenge to the scientist-scholar of planned change that could affect the professions of practice.

◇◇◇◇◇◇◇◇◇◇◇◇◇◇◇◇◇◇◇◇ THE PROBLEM OF THE THEORY OF
CHANGE   *Talcott Parsons*

Before clarifying this statement further it is necessary to distinguish clearly between the processes *within* the system and processes of change *of* the system. It is very common to confuse these two things under the term "dynamic." For the purposes of our conceptual scheme the distinction derives from the concept of equilibrium and the way in which this has been used in the present work. Beyond the most general meaning of the concept of equilibrium, the meaning which is most directly applicable here is that applying to what we have called a "boundary-maintaining" system.

Seen from this point of view, the theory of motivational process *within* the system is built about the processes of maintenance of equilibrium. Besides the unproblematical continuance of interaction which was assumed to go on, this maintenance of equilibrium, as we have seen, revolves about two fundamental types of process. The first of these are the processes of socialization by which actors acquire the orientations necessary to the performance of their roles in the social system, when they have not previously possessed them; the second type are the processes involved in the balance between the generation of motivations to deviant behavior and the counterbalancing motivations to restoration of the stabilized interactive process which we have called the mechanisms of social control.

The special methodological significance of this approach to the analysis of motivational process, i.e., of "dynamics," lies in two interrelated sets of considerations. The first of these is the implication of the fact that we are dealing with the boundary-maintaining type of system. The definition of a system as boundary-maintaining is a way of saying that, *relative to its environment,* that is to fluctuations in the factors of the environment, it maintains certain constancies of pattern, whether this constancy be static or moving. These elements of the constancy of pattern must constitute a fundamental point of reference for the analysis of process in the system. From a certain point of view these processes are to be defined as the processes of maintenance of the constant patterns. But of course these are empirical constancies, so we do not assume any inherent reason why they have to be maintained. It is simply a fact that, as described in terms of a given frame of reference, these constancies are often found to exist, and theory can thus be

Excerpts from Talcott Parsons, "The Processes of Change of Social Systems," The Social System, New York: The Free Press of Glencoe, Inc., 1951, pp. 480–482 and pp. 493–494. This was published over ten years ago. Parsons' formulation of change has progressed quite a bit beyond this, viz. the Loomis article, included in this chapter, which makes use of one of his more recent analyses. Some footnotes omitted. Abridged and used by permission.

focused on the problems presented by their existence. They may cease to exist, by the dissolution of the distinctive boundary-maintaining system and its assimilation to the environment, or by transformation into other patterns. But the fact that they do exist, at given times and places, still serves as the theoretical focus for analysis.

The next main consideration is that on general grounds we are able to say that there are no one or two inherently primary sources of impetus to change in social systems. This is true both in general and with reference to particular types of social system. The "dominant factor" theories, which were so popular a generation ago, that is, with reference to the priority of economic factors, of the genetic constitution, of organisms or of "ideas," have no generalized basis in the theory of the social system.

The impetus to a process of change may perfectly well originate in the development of a cultural configuration, such as a development of science, or of religious ideas. It may also perfectly well originate in a change in the genetic constitution of the population, or a shift in the physical environment such as the exhaustion of a strategic resource. If a primary origin lies in the field of technological applications of scientific knowledge there is likely to be a development of science itself in the background, though certainly the process of invention is in important respects independent of that of science. Another very important possibility lies in the progressive increase of strains in one strategic area of the social structure which are finally resolved by a structural reorganization of the system. The conception of strain developed in this study is such that strain is not itself a "prime-mover," it is a

mode of the impingement of other factors on an interaction system. But a structured strain may well be the point at which the balance between forces tending toward re-equilibration of the previous structure and toward transition to a new structure may be most evident.

As our knowledge of the laws of social process develops we will be able to say more and more about the conditions under which certain types of states of affairs in various parts of social systems, and in the external variables impinging on them, tend to lead to various types of change. But the view that there is no simple intrinsic priority in the factors of the initiation of change is inherent in the conception of the social system which we have advanced here. The central methodological principle of our theory is that of the interdependence of a plurality of variables. At a variety of points empirical relationships between these variables can be demonstrated which, as in the case of the empirical clusterings we have reviewed, limit the range of logically possible variability. But these limitations must be empirically demonstrated. To lay down a general theory of the priority of factors in social change is, in the present state of knowledge, to beg the question of the empirical interdependences which have yet to be demonstrated. We, therefore, put forward what we may call the conception of the plurality of possible origins of change with the understanding that change may originate in any part of the social system described in structural terms or in terms of variables, and that restrictions on the generality of this statement may be introduced only as the outcome of empirical demonstration that relations of interdependence are such that certain parts cannot be independent sources of the impetus to change.

Probably considerably more important than the problems of the initiating factors of processes of social change, are those concerned with tracing the repercussions of a change once initiated throughout the social system, including the "backwash" of modification of the original direction of change. It is here above all that the conception of the social system as a *system* is crucial. The combination of our scheme for the analysis of the structure of the system with the paradigm of motivational process gives us a genuinely technical basis for tackling such a problem, for asserting some propositions about such repercussions and for locating the problems which cannot be solved without further empirical investigation.

✧✧✧✧✧✧✧✧✧✧✧✧✧✧✧✧✧✧✧ SOCIOLOGICAL THEORY AND CONTEMPORARY POLITICS

Barrington Moore, Jr.

WHAT theoretical tools does sociology now possess for a scientific study of unique social phenomena, especially of the major structural characteristics and trends of our own era?

In nineteenth- and twentieth-century theories one may distinguish two types of emphases. I shall designate one "equilibrium theory" and the other "process theory." They are by no means antithetical, but at the same time there are very significant differences in the type of research problems that each suggests.

In equilibrium theory the key assumption is that any social system tends toward a state of rest in which the conflicts and strains among its component parts are reduced to a minimum. In its recent elaboration by the structural functional school, the main line of questioning for empirical investigations concerns the determination of the functional imperatives, or prerequisites, of a society or part of a society. Were this social system to continue, what activities would have to be carried out, what forms of social organization would be necessary, and what limits are there on the ways in which these forms can be combined with one another? [1]

As Parsons makes quite explicit, the equilibrium assumption is not one about empirical facts. Instead it is a theoretical assumption that serves to order a larger body of theory into a consistent whole.[2] Those who work with structural functional theory are for the most part thoroughly aware

[1] Marion J. Levy, Jr., *The Structure of Society* (Princeton, N.J.: Princeton University Press, 1952), pp. 39, 211–226.
[2] Talcott Parsons, *The Social System* (New York: The Free Press of Glencoe, Inc., 1951), p. 481.

Excerpts from Barrington Moore, Jr., "Sociological Theory and Contemporary Politics," American Journal of Sociology, Vol. 61, No. 2, September 1955, pp. 111–115. Abridged and reprinted by permission of The University of Chicago Press.

that social systems do not continue without change. They see history as strewn with the wreckage of social systems that have failed to meet their functional imperatives. Nevertheless, by determining what is necessary for a system to continue, they argue, one may also discover the foci of strain and potential change. Therefore it is not true that structural functional theory is completely unable to cope with problems of social change, as its critics frequently assert.

Reading the literature of this school, one easily gains the impression that it is straining to create a form of process theory but is having great difficulty in so doing. Thus, in a chapter called "The Processes of Change of Social Systems," Parsons writes, in italics, that *"a general theory of the processes of change of social systems is not possible in the present state of knowledge."* [3] Elsewhere he speaks of a "moving equilibrium," which he defines in part as an "orderly process of change" in a society which nevertheless retains the "conditions of distinctiveness . . . within its boundaries over against its environment." [4]

No doubt there are several reasons for the difficulties faced by this school in treating historical change. However, a central obstacle may be the concept of equilibrium itself. Without doing violence to its principles, equilibrium theory cannot account for change except in one direction, that is, toward some point of ultimate stability. Hence it cannot cope effectively with some of the most important actual types of change. The elaboration of social institutions beyond the point of any visible utility, for example, finds no place in

the theory. [5] Likewise, the theory, at least in its present form, is inadequate for explaining how attempts to meet the functional requirements of a social system can lead to a modification in its structure. For example, in the judgment of some historians, the attempts made by later Roman emperors to strengthen the Empire contributed to the growth of feudalism or to the replacement of one social system by quite a different one. In modern times the New Deal may be plausibly regarded as an attempt to shore up American capitalism, that is, to meet its functional requirements. But this process in turn led to marked modification of American society. Precisely such large-scale movements, generated by internal as well as external conditions in a society, constitute the heart of the problem of understanding our epoch as well as others.

No doubt the structural functional school can find a place in its elaborate scheme of categories for the types of phenomena just mentioned. They might be described as unanticipated and dysfunctional consequences of behavior. However, that amounts to throwing the equilibrium assumption overboard. It says in effect that tendencies toward equilibrium are unexpectedly producing change, a contradiction in terms. Furthermore, this approach conceals causal relations that may exist over time as one social system generates its successor.

At this point it may be illuminating to contrast equilibrium theory with Marxism. As we have seen, under equilibrium theory it is very difficult and perhaps impossible to account for the vicious circle, so common in history, when a progressively deteriorating state of affairs leads to a revolu-

[3] *Ibid.*, p. 486.
[4] *Ibid.*, p. 36.
[5] As noted by Levy, *op. cit.*, p. 46.

tionary explosion. Marxism, among other forms of process theory, puts this situation at the center of its intellectual scheme. In this way time is brought in to reveal what is asserted to be a causal relationship. Where equilibrium theory produces correlations, Marxism tries to produce causal connections. For a Marxist it is almost as difficult to conceive of a situation returning to a state of maximum harmony as it is for an equilibrium theorist to conceive of a self-generating cycle of ever fiercer struggle culminating in destruction. Both equilibrium theory and Marxism, as well as other forms of process theory, if pursued with dogmatic vigor, give rise to elaborate intellectual structures that illuminate important segments of social reality and leave others obscure. Since equilibrium theory fails us at a crucial point, we must look further to process theory for help, aware that it, too, will have its limitations.

Among process theorists one may include, in addition to Marx, such diverse figures as Cooley, Durkheim, Keller, Sorokin, Ogburn, and many others. Within this diversified assembly of ideas it is possible to detect, nevertheless, a common proposition: Any given state of human affairs is likely to contain within it the seeds of its own transformation into a new and different state. This assumption of immanent and continuous change represents, I would suggest, the key assumption and distinguishing feature of process theory. At the same time we should be careful to note that the distinction between the two viewpoints is not watertight. Though fundamental differences appear, there is considerable overlapping.

Even theories emphasizing that every society harbors the seeds of its own destruction share with equilibrium theory the conception of some form of internal social order. Marx stresses the dependence of other social institutions on economic relationships. From a diametrically opposite standpoint Sorokin points out the significance of interrelated institutional forms that express a cultural system of meanings,[6] or what some anthropologists call the basic premises of a culture. Ogburn derives much of the institutional structure of a society from the state of technology. Thus, all theories express some view of the inherent compatibility or incompatibility of two or more social institutions, a fundamental tenet in equilibrium doctrine. The very notion of predictable change is impossible without some idea of the orderly relation of the parts in whatever is changing. Both a mechanical engine and a living organism display this orderly relation of parts whenever they are capable of movement. However, the difference between equilibrium and process theory lies in the latter's emphasis upon a kind of order that necessarily produces change.

In itself the assumption of ever present change is not particularly enlightening until it is coupled with some theory about the forces that produce change and the direction of the movement. Most comprehensive theories that have been put forth for this purpose have taken either an evolutionary or a cyclical form. It is fashionable just now to reject them as premature attempts at synthesis. Nevertheless, we may also be overhasty in jettisoning them in their entirety. As already noted, in the development of human thought it has often happened that ideas which were thought universally valid have

[6] See especially Pitirim Sorokin, *Social and Cultural Dynamics* (New York: American Book Co., 1941), IV, 31–40.

only a restricted field of application. They are valuable achievements nonetheless. Euclidean geometry is no longer the last work in its field. But its principles have been consciously or unconsciously used by house carpenters for thousands of years.

Cyclical theories are particularly close to equilibrium theory and are sometimes, as in Pareto, combined. They frequently assume, either explicitly or implicitly, that institutional change in a given direction sooner or later sets up counterforces that oppose or modify it. Toynbee's concept of the "nemesis of creativity" provides one of the more suggestive illustrations.[7] Any successful institutional device tends to persist beyond the point at which it is adaptive, becoming a danger to the society in which it has flourished. At the same time cyclical theories run into difficulty precisely because they assume a return to some original state, even though they differ from equilibrium theory by assuming that this original state also contains tensions which will renew the cycle. History simply does not repeat itself. There are massive and apparently irreversible changes, such as the industrial revolution, which cyclical theories cannot account for adequately.

Evolutionary theory puts such changes at the center of its scheme. Perhaps in partial combination with some theory of cycles, to give a spiral conception of change, this approach may some day provide the most satisfactory general synthesis. In the meantime it may be the better part of wisdom to avoid integrating theories that are dubious in themselves and to concentrate on finding ways to order smaller portions of reality into meaningful units.

For this purpose the evolutionary theory of stages provides suggestive clues and raises important problems. There is no doubt that the unilinear version of evolutionary theory contained serious mistakes. It posited an inevitable series of stages, in each of which all aspects of social structure (from economic organization to religion and the family) were similar and through which every society would sooner or later pass. Nevertheless, the theory of stages contains a residue of truth. Anthropologists now hold that in some areas, particularly technology, one may observe progressive and cumulative changes where the knowledge gained in one period provides the necessary foundation for further advance. One anthropologist suggests that an essential condition for cumulative change is the possibility of sharing a common core of knowledge and at the same time specializing within it. In the case of marriage, on the other hand, the fact that there are only two sexes limits the number of possible forms to four and precludes cumulative structural change. Since, however, culture changes as a whole, we find the impact of technological change on other parts, such as in the reduction of social functions performed by the modern family.[8] Thus the concept of stages, even of a more or less inevitable "next stage," has at least a limited range of applicability. This concept, however, need not be tied to a form of technological determinism: the dynamics of change may also be found in other parts of social structure.

However, the most interesting and

[7] Arnold J. Toynbee, *A Study of History* (New York: Oxford University Press, 1947), pp. 307–336.

[8] Harvey C. Moore, "Cumulation and Cultural Processes," *American Anthropologist*, LVI, No. 3 (June 1954), 347–357.

for our epoch the most significant problems occur in connection with the skipping of stages rather than with their orderly sequence. The transformation of Western liberal and rationalist ideas, together with the alterations in the structure of industrial society as this complex of doctrines and institutions spread eastward to Asia, constitutes perhaps the major example of contemporary stage-skipping. The results certainly cannot be expected to resemble very closely the so-called free capitalist institutions of Victorian England.

In such cases we are observing the interaction of two sets of processes that had been developing independently up to the time of coming in contact. The analysis of such a problem is a great difficulty. Using the illustration of the early impact of the West upon Japan, Sidney Hook argues that such a situation is inherently indeterminate.[9] Certainly one could not have foretold what would have happened solely through an analysis of the processes at work in Japanese society alone nor, for that matter, in the West alone.

One way to a partial solution may be the following: Contact between two or more autonomous processes frequently sets up another and larger process that in turn modifies the original set. The new process may be sufficiently orderly to permit prediction. For example, neither Soviet nor American policy during the second World War and the postwar years can be satisfactorily explained independently of one another. To some it appears that the United States was merely hypocritical in first trying to demilitarize Germany and Japan and then seeking to rearm them

as fast as possible. Others explain American behavior by referring to the larger process whereby a coalition, lately victorious against a common enemy, disintegrates when the common threat has disappeared. The next step, as is well known, is for the victors to become suspicious of one another, since the most serious danger now is from the victorious partner. There is therefore an ungraceful scramble for the assistance of former enemies. Soviet behavior conforms to the same pattern. Certain tendencies, though by no means all, toward the transformation of both societies into garrison states may also be traced to this general process.[10]

It is impossible, however, to reduce the clash of cultures and social systems to a single process. By no means everything, for example, can be explained by the growth and disintegration of international coalitions. Certain processes continue to develop within the state, even though profoundly modified by the latter's position in the international distribution of power. In China and other parts of Asia indigenous revolutionary forces were at work before extended contact with the West and continue down to the present day. Frequently, forces generated in the domestic and the foreign arena come into sharp conflict with one another, as now appears to be the case both in the United States and in France.

From a purely formal point of view there are three possible outcomes when processes that were developing separately come into contact with one an-

---

[9] See his "Determinism," *Encyclopedia of the Social Sciences* (New York: The Macmillan Company, 1937), V, 111.

[10] While from the first the Soviet system has displayed many traits of a garrison state, American society, now openly hostile to the Soviet system, has begun to show increasing signs of a totalitarian tendency. Politics may contain a process similar to that expressed by Gresham's law in economics, "the bad" driving out "the good."

other. New processes may be started; old ones may continue in modified form; and still others may persist independently as though nothing had happened. No ready formula exists, however, by which it would be possible to predict in every case where the dividing lines are to be found. The notion that technology, for example, will always spread more rapidly than other cultural traits is probably mistaken. New technology requires new psychological attitudes and new forms of social structure, just as variations in the existing social structure (e.g., in India and Japan) will affect receptivity to new technology.[11] Perhaps a general formula can no more be discovered in the interaction of processes than can a general theory of mixtures be given in chemistry without specifying the ingredients.

In general, sociological theory tends to be plagued with questions such as this, so broad as to have no specifiable meaning. We ask, for example, what is the role of ideas in social change? Instead, we ought to ask what is the role of certain types of ideas under specified circumstances? Much remains to be learned about the kinds of strain in industrial society that create increased demand for a return to some idealized version of the *status quo ante,* as in extreme right-wing movements here and in Nazi Germany. We should also know about corresponding movements in peasant countries now in the early stages of industrialization. Likwise we want to know about the sources and nature of movements aiming at a new and different type of society. In answering, we must comprehend the interaction of several processes taking place simultaneously.

Where the nature of the processes is properly understood, analysis can proceed toward outlining the range of possibilities for the future and the costs of alternative policies. We need not be deterred by the impossibility of precise prediction for relationships that are not completely determinate. The sociologist has added unnecessarily to his sense of professional inadequacy by feeling compelled to predict the inevitable outcome of any situation.

All that is necessary and all that is useful, in these large-scale instances of interaction among societies and cultures, is a reasonably accurate assessment of the limits and possibilities of effective human action. In turn, such an assessment makes sense only in terms of some prior set of values. Unless he is content to be a moral eunuch in the service of any bureaucracy that hires him, the student of society will do his best to bring disciplined intelligence to bear on these problems as well.

[11] For brief but illuminating comments on this point see Kingsley Davis, *The Population of India and Pakistan* (Princeton, N.J.: Princeton University Press, 1951), pp. 216–217.

◇◇◇◇◇◇◇◇◇◇◇◇◇◇◇◇◇◇◇ TENTATIVE TYPES OF DIRECTED
SOCIAL CHANGE INVOLVING
SYSTEMIC LINKAGE

Charles P. Loomis

IN a previous note[1] an attempt was made to demonstrate the utility of the concept, systemic linkage, in the analysis of social change in general. The present note will attempt to carry the demonstration further and propose hypothetical types of change involving systemic linkage.[2] Later to be intro-

duced will be social dimensions which appear to the author to be eminently adaptable to a theory of change; their introduction will be prefaced by some of the commonly known aspects of change which are here summarily stated in order to provide a background for that which follows.

Directed social change is consciously brought about by an actor or social system representative who for convenience may be designated as the *change agent.* The actor or social system he seeks to change may be designated as the *target system.* Social change has been traced in many dimensions; the oft-recurring *Gemeinschaft-Gesellschaft* continuum and similar polarities such as folk-urban, sacred-secular, primary-secondary, mechanical-organic solidarity, and many others.[3] Initiation, legitimation, and execution are terms by which it is convenient to designate stages of change. In terms of systemic

---

[1] Charles P. Loomis, "Systemic Linkage of El Cerrito," *Rural Sociology,* XXIV (1959), 54–57.

[2] "Systemic linkage may be defined as the process whereby the elements of at least two social systems come to be articulated so that in some ways they function as a unitary system" (*ibid.,* p. 55). For a more complete description of this process and the elements, processes, and patterns of social systems, see Charles P. Loomis, *Systemic Sociology: Essays on the Persistence and Change of Social Systems* (Princeton: Van Nostrand, in press). The elements of a social system as employed by the present author are the following: (1) belief (knowledge), (2) sentiment, (3) end or goal, (4) norms, (5) status-role, (6) power, (7) rank, (8) sanction, and (9) facility. These elements of social structure are articulated or made functional respectively by the following elemental processes: (1) cognitive mapping and validation, (2) communication of sentiment and tension management, (3) goal attaining and "latent" activity, (4) evaluation as a general process, (5) status-role performance, (6) decision making and its initiation into action, (7) evaluation of actors and allocation of status-roles, (8) application of sanctions, and (9) utilization of facilities. Structural-functional categories which encompass the "element-

process" pairs respectively are: (1) knowing, (2) feeling, (3) achieving, (4) standardizing and patterning, (5) dividing the functions and activities, (6) controlling, (7) ranking, (8) sanctioning, and (9) facilitating.

[3] Ferdinand Toennies, *Community and Society—Gemeinschaft und Gesellschaft,* tr. and ed. with introduction by Charles P. Loomis (East Lansing: Michigan State University Press, 1957). In the introduction to this translation various typologies are analyzed.

From Charles P. Loomis, "Tentative Types of Directed Social Change Involving Systemic Linkage," Rural Sociology, Vol. 24, No. 4, December 1959, pp. 383–390. Used by permission.

elements and processes as used by the present author the stage of initiation involves the process of decision making and initiation into action (articulating the element, power). Legitimation involves the processes of evaluation and communication of sentiment; other elements and processes may be perceived in the specifics of legitimizing procedures such as status-roles of prestigeful sponsors and the normative sentiments and beliefs expressed in ritual and prayer. In the stage of execution of change systemic linkage is achieved; the external pattern of the change agent's system unites with that of the target system. Among the elements which merge are end and power and their articulating processes.

In the analysis of systemic action and particularly in the analysis of change it is convenient to separate the internal and the external patterns somewhat along the line proposed by Homans.[4] It is also convenient to regard the two patterns as manifest in every social system but varying in the degree of primacy assigned to them by members of a given social system. In goal-attaining and adaptive activity the external pattern predominates. In terms of the systemic elements and processes used by the present author, the external pattern is marked principally by power, activated by decision making and its initiation into action and goal, activated by goal attaining activity. In integrative activity the internal pattern predominates and is marked principally by sentiment and the communication of sentiment as element and process respectively. As the activities of a social system proceed, goal-attaining and adaptive activity are usually marked

by periods of intense action in which the external pattern has primacy. Such periods are often followed by periods of activity in which the internal pattern has primacy in a sort of systolic-diastolic sequence not unlike the sequence of work and rest or sleep in the biological organism. These phases in social systems are *Gesellschaft*-like and *Gemeinschaft*-like sequences. This is recognized by Parsons, who writes that the integrative and instrumental norms of the system "very closely characterize what in much sociological literature have been thought of as polar types of institutional structure, the best known version of which perhaps has been the Gemeinschaft-Gesellschaft dichotomy of Toennies." [5]

Social change (constructed on Parsons' model of the socialization of the child or the therapy for the psychotic patient): In the socialization of the child and the therapy administered to the psychiatric patient Parsons recognizes four phases: the permissive phase, the phase of support, the phase of "denial of reciprocity," and the phase of "manipulation of rewards." These may be collapsed into two phases: the permissive and supportative, in which the internal pattern has primacy and where *Gemeinschaft*-like relations prevail; and the denying and withdrawal phase in which the external pattern has primacy and *Gesellschaft*-like relations prevail.

Applied to directed change, the change agent can be seen during the first phase to be developing what may be called "social capital." During this phase he wins the confidence of the members of the target system; he builds up his rank and power in the social system he intends to change so that

[4] George C. Homans, *The Human Group* (New York: Harcourt, Brace & World, Inc., 1950).

[5] Talcott Parsons *et al.*, *Working Papers* (New York: The Free Press of Glencoe, Inc., 1953), p. 208.

later he may apply the lever of denial of reciprocity and may manipulate the rewards to bring about the change. The change target "must be 'motivated' by depriving him [the change target] of accustomed gratifications if he continues to act in the old ways, and he must be presented with an opportunity, i.e., realistic facilities, which can be adapted to new ways of behaving." [6]

In this model of change it is to be emphasized that the change agent becomes a part of the target system by systemic linkage. Much of the strategy of change revolves about problems of deriving the benefits of favorable sentiment for the objectives of the change agent and his organization in the internal pattern of the target system. Professional fund raisers, for example, may merely advise target system leaders how to utilize the internal systems [7] since systemic linkage for the operation of fund raising is usually of short duration. It may not be necessary for the fund raiser to devote a great deal of attention to the objective of becoming a part of the internal pattern. However, Christian missionaries, Communist agents, and other change agents who in order to achieve their objectives must attain permanent systemic linkage must somehow devise means of becoming part of both the external and internal patterns. The strategy for systemic linkage of this type is particularly difficult and depends in large part upon the state of the institutionalized or normative structure of the change target. There is insufficient space to discuss this

[6] Talcott Parsons and Niel J. Smeltzer, *Economy and Society* (New York: The Free Press of Glencoe, Inc., 1956), pp. 257–258.

[7] Paul A. Miller, *Community Health Action —A Study of Community Contrast* (East Lansing: Michigan State University Press, 1953), ch. ix.

problem adequately but variation for strategy in two very different situations may be mentioned. In a community or other change target with low boundary maintenance and suffering from *anomie,* charismatic leaders and agents of various types may be able to enter the internal pattern with a minimum of effort if it has not disintegrated or if they create systems which meet needs unfulfilled by the existing order. On the other hand solidary systems with strong integration of external and internal patterns producing *Gemeinschaft-*like solidarity are not subject to such entree. The change agent must enter through the external pattern. His improved technology must be linked to the facilities of the existing order and the systemic linkage he derives will depend upon the process of evaluation carried on in the target system and upon many others factors. The facilities and services he provides to the external pattern must create "social capital" for him through their contribution to the external pattern. If this contribution is to become a part of the internal pattern, not only dollars or facilities but the personnel of the change agent system itself must have co-operated in the external pattern and thereby be linked in to the internal pattern.

Lessons learned about change from systemic analysis of disaster: Various studies of disaster reveal [8] that at a certain point after a social system has been stricken by such external forces as hurricanes, tornadoes, bombardment, and the like, the interaction which brings about recovery produces a high level of integration involving the members of the system in an internal interaction

[8] Charles P. Loomis, *Systemic Sociology,* essay 3, "Social Systems under Stress—Their Disruption and Persistence."

pattern in such a manner as to produce high solidarity and boundary maintenance. Immediately after the impact and during the rescue and early rehabilitation phase, the external pattern has primacy. This goal-attaining and adaptive effort on the part of many people who "come out of their shells" to become a part of a highly evaluated enterprise produces what is known as the halo effect manifest in the internal pattern. Once the intense co-operative effort of rescue and rehabilitation is under way, actors communicate sentiments which produce community and system morale and make the community an end to many for whom it was not before. As the urgency of the adaptive phase wanes and moments of relaxation become more frequent the internal pattern becomes dominant: the sentiment-laden moments are relived, emotion is communicated and shared, community-wide morale is high and boundary maintenance intense. Outside agencies such as the National Red Cross are treated as outsiders and subject to especially intense criticism while the ingroup enjoy the solidarity and integration of the halo effect. Outside agencies find it difficult to link their services to the community system which now exhibits a high degree of boundary maintenance. For a time there is a "therapeutic community," produced by the overlapping sequences of (1) the disaster, (2) the collaborative effort of the actors of the community to re-establish the equilibrium, (3) a cathartic halo effect and high morale, and (4) high boundary maintenance activity. Of course as the equilibrium of the original system in some form, changed or not, returns, subsystems and the old patterns tend to be re-established. The internal pattern of the community as a whole becomes less important rela-

tively, and the subsystems begin to absorb the activities of the actors.

It appears to the author that the social change analogy adapted from Parsons' socialization of the child and/or the therapy of the psychotic patient and the sequential march of events traced in most disasters leading to the community halo effect become germane to directed change in ways that can be perceived as the adopting of practices through peaceful involvement and persuasion is contrasted with that wrought by disruption. Keyed both to Parsons' analysis of socialization and therapy and to the above analysis of the halo effect in disaster, the following models are presented tentatively and hypothetically that their validity may be tested.

Systemic Linkage via Peaceful Involvement vs. Disruption and Violence

It is hypothesized that the sequence of events in directed change most common in the capitalistic western democracies is by type not unlike Parsons' stages in socialization and therapy, which, dichotomized, become (1) permissiveness and support followed by (2) denial of reciprocity and manipulation of rewards. By analogy the change agent handles the change targets of a community as a parent handles the child. First, involvements through actions create relationships which may be characterized as typical of the *Gemeinschaft*. If the target system is suffering from *anomie*, integrative, expressive, and consummatory action may be taken directly. If not, the change agent must prove the worth of his wares by demonstrated performance in the external or adaptive pattern. In either case the change agent's objective is that of achieving acceptance in the internal pattern. Affectivity and functional diffuseness of relationships between actors of the change agent and the change target must be developed. Once systemic linkage has been established in this manner and confidence developed, the "lever" or pressure toward change may be applied, preferably through the power figures of the target system itself.

The pressure for change may be applied by the change agent or, preferably, by "linked" power figures of the target system with whom he holds social capital. "We work *with* the people, not *for* them" [9] is the proud claim of successful change agencies, whose boast would be hollow had not goal-directed power-sustained activity been preceded by affective and diffuse involvements produced either directly by charismatic and other leaders in target systems suffering from *anomie* or through demonstration in the external pattern of integrated and solidary systems. The philosophy responsible for such change spurns paternalistic change only less than that brought about by disruption and violence.

It is hypothesized by the author that the changes wrought by Communist infiltrators must also follow roughly the stages of permissiveness and denial, of the internal pattern of interaction followed by the external or adaptive pattern. The change agent described in the paragraph above was a deviant in the target system only to the extent that he openly espoused a prescribed change, a change which was neither so extreme nor so radical from the point of view of members of the target system that its advocate was excluded as a deviant. The Communist infiltrator, by contrast

[9] Paraphrasing of Wilbert E. Moore, "Creation of a Common Culture," *Confluence,* IV (1955), 238.

is a deviant in the target system in a manner which usually is considered extreme, prescribed, and rigid and negatively evaluated by power figures in the target system. This change agent, therefore, is prevented by the normative evaluations of the members of the internal pattern of the target system from establishing effective, functionally diffuse relations on a very broad scale. Since fundamental changes require systemic linkage with the internal pattern involving affective, diffuse, supportive and permissive interaction in integrated target systems, before adaptive goal-directed action can begin the Communist change agent must find a setting in which his deviancy becomes relatively unimportant. Disaster provides such a setting; and the Communist change agent has been well trained in inducing disaster by disruption. The halo effect so frequent in disaster, when solidarity is high and all men are brothers, provides the opportunity to the Communist change agent for the development of the internal interaction pattern ordinarily denied him. Integration is so high and morale so solid that it is very easy for the members of the target system to remain in complete ignorance of the intentional and induced nature of the disaster. Clues concerning guilt may lead not to the change agent, who by this time is solidly inside the internal workings of the target system, but to his accomplices, who are locally unknown and against whom boundary maintenance is high. Thus far what has been hypothesized would establish the similarity of the process of change, whether accomplished through peace or through disruption, and would establish further that the halo effect of disaster is a required setting for those change agents whose proposed changes differ markedly from the expectations of those of the target system and are appraised negatively by them.

Systemic linkage has been achieved in some measure when the change agent is no longer an outsider. The postdisaster period is ordinarily marked by a gradual waning of the community-centered identity, the rise of the predisaster subsystems, and the eventual return to an equilibrium which closely resembles that which obtained in predisaster days. The systemic linkage achieved by the disaster-supported change agent will be of short duration if the old equilibrium is to be re-established. The change agent's next job is to prevent this. How he accomplishes this is not completely clear, but certainly among the methods in which the Communist agents are skilled are (1) the removal of figures who resist, (2) the leverage employed by the "linked" power figures of the target system, and (3) the organization from a formless and chaotic state into a disciplined and systematized state of the deviants and the potentially deviant—i.e., of the malcontents or those otherwise unfavorably disposed to the predisaster system. These and other techniques have been examined by various investigators.[10] It is not the purpose of this short note to investigate the individual techniques but to draw attention again to the basic similarity existing between this and the peace-attended change. Once the vital internal interaction pattern has been established, in normalcy or in disaster, the second stage (analogous to the denial of reciprocity and manipulation of rewards of Parsons' socialization and/or therapy) is executed by the peaceful change agent or by the change agent utilizing disaster. Denial of reciprocity,

[10] Philip Selznick, *The Organization Weapon* (New York: McGraw-Hill Book Co., 1952).

manipulation of rewards, and application of power are parts of the elaborate procedure for "leapfrog change." Probably in the nonviolent situation just as much as in the real or induced disaster, the design for change requires that the equilibrium of the change target be kept sufficiently off balance that the old alignments will not be re-established. A skillful juggling of the internally and externally patterned rank of the individual actors may well be one of the most potent preventives.[11]

Typologies of Systemic Linkage and Change [12]

Size of unit and sources of power. In terms of systemic linkage, directed change has many forms. Table 1 indicates two dimensions, or two axes that may be important. The change may require that the system give primacy to either the external or the internal pattern on the one hand, or on the other hand there may be an evaluation requiring that the size of the unit be changed, usually enlarged. The Communist countries emphasize the application of power on the community's external pattern and the regrouping of facilities, which results in collapsing former systems of various types includ-

[11] This is in line with findings of Zaleznik, Adams, Lenski, Landecker, Benoit-Smullyan, and others. See A. Zaleznik, *et al.*, *The Motivation, Productivity, and Satisfaction of Workers* (Boston: Harvard Business School, 1958), ch. ii; Stuart N. Adams, "Status Congruence as a Variable in Small Group Performance," *Social Forces*, XXXII (October 1953), 16–22; Gerhard E. Lenski, "Status Crystallization: A Non-vertical Dimension of Status," *American Sociological Review*, XIX (1954), 405–413.

[12] Charles P. Loomis, "Toward a Theory of Systemic Social Change," presented at the Interprofessional Conference on the Training of Personnel for Overseas Programs, Council on Social Work Education, Cornell University, June 21–26, 1959.

ing family and small-sized capitalistic and other localized units. Systems which inhibit the regrouping and resultant concentration of facilities are often liquidated. To accomplish this, coercion, often of a stark and cruel nature, may be applied in an effort within a few years to bring technology to that stage of development which exists in western countries after centuries of development. As indicated in Table 1,

as the revitalizing movements or other religious movements, emphasizing the internal pattern may likewise spread over large areas and result in the regrouping of units so far as the particular system involved is concerned.

Emphasis on retention of system boundaries and changes produced *by* the people and *for* the people, through skilled community development change agents such as extension workers and

TABLE I

FORMS OF SYSTEMIC LINKAGE—SIZE OF SYSTEM AND POWER EMPHASIS

Evaluative emphasis on size of unit	Source of power as applied on change target	
	EXTERNAL	INTERNAL
Enlargement through collapsing of subsystem boundaries and/or their incorporation	"Leapfrog" technological advance of "late-comer" systems: Communist collective farms, artels, etc.	Revitalizing movements: Indian ghost dance, ecumenical and Oxford movements
Conservation of system boundaries	ICA and other "democratic" community development	Sects, pietistic and localistic religious movements
	Extension Service, Point Four, Colombo, and similar plans	Bhoodan and Gramdan movements in India
	Communist communes, supervised farm family loans	
	Federal "matching fund" programs	

the "leapfrog technological change" for late-comer communistic nations results from the collapsing of subsystem boundaries and reorganizing with heavy emphasis upon the external system. As indicated by previous discussion, empirical knowledge of and skill in the employment of violence and disaster may be important in this form of systemic linkage. Various movements, such

others produces the changes listed in the lower left-hand cell of Table 1. The two approaches represented above and below the line at the left seem to be based on essentially different evaluations of facilities and the rights of individuals. In either case, systemic linkage is established.[13] In the Communist

[13] The types of change at the left of Table 1 assume that the change agent is an "action

approach opposition is liquidated; collaboration is fostered by sanctions and by a semireligious hope in the Marxist creed. Nondirected ideological movements may result as indicated in the column under internal systems.

———

agent." An action agent uses police power, power to tax, or the power of eminent domain, power derived from extended credit, from

grants-in-aid or subsidies, or from other forms. So-called "nonaction agencies" rely on education, demonstration, and extension. However, such agencies, like the religious sect to the extent that they attempt to control their environment, begin to use power. See Charles P. Loomis and J. Allan Beegle, *Rural Sociology —The Strategy of Change* (Englewood Cliffs, N.J.: Prentice-Hall, 1957), pp. 368 ff. See also Charles M. Hardin, *Freedom in Agricultural Education* (New York: The Free Press of Glencoe, Inc., 1955), p. 7.

———

✧✧✧✧✧✧✧✧✧✧✧✧✧✧✧✧✧✧✧✧ DELIBERATE CHANGING AS THE FACILITATION OF GROWTH

Kenneth D. Benne

THIS analysis is of the relationship between an agent of change (who may be one practitioner or a team of practitioners working simultaneously or in succession) and a social system, "larger" than a person and "smaller" than a "community," as client. (The analysis may also apply to work with persons as clients or with "total" cultures. The clinical experience of the author does not warrant such claims.) It is assumed further that the direction of change which the change-agent attempts to induce and/or to facilitate in the client is defined by the concept of "growth." "Growth" in turn is defined as increased ability on the part of the client to face and solve its problems, both those stemming from disequilibrations in the client's relations with its environment (adaptation) and those stemming from disequilibrations internal to its system (adjustment).

A key element in effective problem-solving by any social system is the meth-

odology of dealing with disequilibrations (guiding changes, solving problems) that has been institutionalized within the system. "Growth" may be defined in terms of progressive institutionalization by a social system of a methodology of problem-solving that is optimally adaptive and adjustive for that social system. A major goal of the agent of change is, therefore, facilitation of the institutionalization of appropriate methodology for adaptation and adjustment by the client-system.

The requirements of a methodology consonant with "growth" may be defined as norms of adaptive and adjustive behavior by the client-system, or as norms of optimum re-equilibration in the social system.[1] These norms may be stated as follows:

[1] Certain characteristics (*a*) of the general contemporary change situation and (*b*) of the process of social change are assumed rather than argued in this presentation.

a. Pressures toward continuing adaptation and adjustment of social systems are endemic

———

Prepared for the Pro-Seminar in Human Relations, Boston University Human Relations Center, 1956, Research Papers and Technical Notes. Used by permission.

1. Problem-solving should be *experimental*. Growth cannot be achieved by a social system that is stereotyped and inflexible in its modes of response to difficulties. An experimental norm re-

in contemporary society. The extension of rational control of its adaptive and adjustive processes is possible for any social system, within limits, wherever irrational and/or unconscious control now tends to prevail, except where demands for adjustment or adaptation are too strong for system survival. The limits of rationality are to be validly determined not a priori but by attempts to extend processes of rational control. Psychologically, "rationality" may be defined in terms of "reality orientation" or "task orientation" in processes of adaptation and adjustment. Sociologically, "rationality" may be defined in terms of effectiveness of "communication" among the parts of a social system and in terms of institutionalized mechanisms for relatively nondistorted feedback of internal and external information indicative of adjustment and adaptation needs and processes in the system. Methodologically, "rationality" may be defined in terms of the institutionalization of "scientific" and "collaborative" methods of meeting difficulties within the system.

b. The process of social change is essentially a process of "disequilibration–re-equilibration" within a social system. Pressures toward disequilibration may come from outside or inside the system. Pressures toward re-equilibration will be generated from within or from without the system. Planning of change is an attempt to evaluate these various pressures toward change, in terms of both their "realism" and their "desirability," and to alter and coordinate these pressures consistently with this evaluation. This view of change is generally consistent with the challenge-response concept of Toynbee, the quasi-stationary equilibrium notion of Lewin, the homeostatic model of Cannon and others, and the transactional model of Dewey and Bentley, whatever lesser differences there may be between these variously named models. Change tends to be cumulative where system–environment communication is maintained in the process of change. "Problem-solving" and "disequilibration–re-equilibration" may be used interchangeably where the "rational" (conscious, symbolic) elements of the latter are recognized.

quires the construction of a problem out of a difficulty, the consideration of alternative meanings for the situation that signify alternative responses, the massing of relevant evidence regarding the alternatives, the choice among these, and the building in of evaluation to check the success of the response in terms of hypothetical predictions, so that warranted and generalized learning follows from the experimentally chosen action.

In social-system terms, this requires sensitization to and institutionalization of feedback mechanisms regarding external impacts and internal functioning of parts, plus adequate coding and coordinating mechanisms to translate feedback information into appropriate responses. The image of the experimental social system is one of continuous collection and evaluation of relevant data regarding direction setting, means selection, and organizational effectiveness.

2. Problem-solving should be *collaborative*. All parts of the system ideally cooperate in identifying difficulties in operation, in increasing the internal and external meaning and validity of alternative adaptive and adjustive responses to the difficulty, in identifying and evaluating the results of the decision. This does not deny leadership functions within the system but orients these to the achievement of decisive collaboration, relevant to its analyzed environment, of all parts of the system.

3. Problem-solving should be *task (and "reality") oriented* rather than oriented to the maintenance of the prestige of some parts of the system over other parts. Growth requires optimum orientation to confronting realities and optimum release of human energies in creating and contriving effective and appropriate responses to the realities.

Channeling of energy toward the maintenance of nonfunctional prestige systems within the system detracts from availability of energy for creative responses. "Reality" orientation ideally makes for a distribution of power within the system that is optimally functional both in terms of adjustment (maintenance) and adaptation (organization for task achievement).

4. Problem-solving should be *educational and/or therapeutic* for individual participants involved in the change. The increasing maturity of the social system depends in some measure upon the increasing maturity of the persons who are members of the system. Changes in system functioning that result in disruption or repression for the personal systems of the participants tend to augment the difficulty of future problem-solving. Individuality of members is a merit, not a blemish, in growth-prone organizations.

5. Effective and efficient problem-solving requires *channels of communication* within the system that make available for public decision and choice, in undistorted form, all relevant data, including data concerning feelings and evaluations (negative and positive) from each and every sub-part of the system. This is actually a corollary of norm 2 above. It does emphasize, in addition to effective common motoric elements in group action, cognitive and symbolic elements that are necessary agencies of communication in processes of orientation, decision, and evaluation.

Barriers to Growth in Social Systems

A systematic pathology of social systems would identify barriers to growth (as defined in methodological and social-system terms above) as foci of treatment by the facilitating practitioner. The following identification of barriers is not systematic. It is based rather upon relatively unsystematized clinical experience in training and consultation. The barriers may be expressed as either methodological incapacities or as social-system characteristics inhibiting to growth.

1. Confusion of the ideological image of the system with the actual behaviors of the system. This indicates both limits in the capacity for objectivity in the system and defenses against increasing objectivity in self-observation and analysis. Tension between the "ideology" (as a map of desirable but unrealized potentialities in functioning) and the actuality of present functioning is healthy in a progressive social system. It is a confusion (identification) of actuality and potentiality that is inhibiting to reality orientation in a social system.

2. Lack of quality control over the feedback processes which provide information on which controlling decisions are based. Feedback mechanisms that feed back partial information, that rationalize away information contrary to the system self-image held by the controlling part of the system, that are insensitive to signs of trouble—such as increasing disarticulations between parts of the system or between system and environment—furnish an incomplete and/or inaccurate basis for deciding policy and action rationally and realistically.

A system may have well-developed liaison feedback regarding other social systems and environments in their relations to its own system and poorly developed feedback regarding internal functioning, or the opposite imbalance in feedback may prevail.

3. Suppression of dominant feelings

of some or all parts of the system in processes of decision-making. This may involve a denial of all feelings, as facts irrelevant to decision-making, or it may involve a denial of expression and consideration of the feelings of minority parts of the system. The two pathologies are often intertwined—a "scientistic" norm regarding suppression of feeling in decision and an "authoritarian" disregard of feeling-data from subordinate parts of the system. Occasionally, but perhaps less often, systems suffer the pathology of making decisions on the basis of internal feeling-data alone.

4. Narrow time-perspective within the decision-making processes—a lack of perception of long-range consequences of action as relevant to immediate decision—tends toward a pattern of living from crisis to crisis in the life of the system.

5. Inadequate and/or unbalanced role-differentiation in system functioning and in processes of decision-making. Some roles may be too abundant, judged by situational requirements, others may be missing. Coordination among differential roles may be lacking.

6. Inadequate and inaccurate interpretive processes for coding and weighting information received through feedback. This inadequacy may be in terms of inadequate concepts available commonly for use in interpretation, inadequate articulation of relevant values and criteria, inadequate skills of interpretation, standards against spending time in diagnosis and interpretation, and so on.

7. Inaccurate definition of limits and alternatives in decision-situations. Actual limitations of power and possibility may be ignored or denied. Available alternatives within the power of the system may not be seen or may be dis-

missed without explanation. This condition is closely related to inaccurate perception of the internal and external "power field" of the system and to prevailing attitudes of pessimism or optimism regarding change and improvement.

8. Lack of adequate mechanisms for mediation and adjustment of conflicts between parts of system and between the system and other systems in the environment.

Theory of Practitioner Functioning in Facilitating Growth in the Client-System

A complete system of practitioner theory would include two interrelated sets of formulations:

1. General formulations of ways of diagnosing the state of the client-system with respect to such barriers to growth (pathologies) as those identified above.

2. General formulations of ways of intervening in (treating) the system for any one pathology or combination of pathologies revealed by the diagnosis.

The first of these would involve developing a symptomatology for each pathology so that observations of the client-system and/or data collected through interviews with people in different parts of the system and/or other measures of system functioning could be related with a particular diagnosis of pathology.

For example, resistance to collection of data regarding actual functioning, consistent use of ideologically tinged language in describing the way the system works, rejection of data that indicate discrepancies between actual and ideal achievements, sharp dichotomization of the client-system from other systems in the environment in terms of discrepant ideologies, or massive evidence of control attempts within the system in terms of exhortation to maintain the ideology of the system, might indicate pathology *1* above.

On the other hand, willingness to accept scattered and subjective feedback as evidence of success or failure, implicit or explicit standards against members' raising questions concerning the quality of information about functioning on which policy decisions are based, refusal to budget time and/or money for the systematic collection of evaluation data, and little or no discrimination between data challenging existing evaluations on the basis of the parts of the system from which the challenges come, might indicate pathology *2*. Finally, if there is marked discrimination on the part of the controlling leadership between feedback data (particularly negative feeling data) coming from different parts of the system, one might expect some involvement in pathology *3* and look for further confirming evidence of this condition.

Social factors currently militating against the development of such a symptomatology are: resistance on the part of many practitioners toward conceptually articulating and formulating the assumed bases of their clinical insights so that these can be further tested, inadequate formulation of pathologies, lack of consensus upon "growth" as providing a major framework of values for the direction of change attempts, lack of interaction between various professions and practitioners, teachers, group workers, industrial consultants and trainers, etc.

The second set of general formulations to be sought for and tested rests upon the first in a logical sense. But, strategically, this may not be completely true. As practitioners enlist an entire client-system or representative parts of such a system in self-observation, fact-finding regarding functioning, experimentation with new ways and categories of fact interpretation, the client-system itself becomes a partner in the diagnostic process. It can develop *ad hoc* diagnoses of its distresses and can plan, try out, and evaluate provisional treatments of its ills, without access to or consideration of more fully and systematically developed theories of social change or of social practice. There is little doubt that more systematic general theories would increase the accuracy and power of practitioner efforts to facilitate growth in clients. And, perhaps, continued treatment efforts oriented to the need for more adequate theory can make a contribution to its development. It may be also that successful integration of research functions along with helping functions in a team approach to problems of social practice will accelerate this development.

✧✧✧✧✧✧✧✧✧✧✧✧✧✧✧✧✧✧ QUASI-STATIONARY SOCIAL
EQUILIBRIA AND THE PROBLEM
OF PERMANENT CHANGE

Kurt Lewin

1. *The objective of change.* The objective of social change might concern the nutritional standard of consumption, the economic standard of living, the type of group relation, the output of a factory, the productivity of an educational team. It is important that a social standard to be changed does not have the nature of a "thing" but of a "process." A certain standard of consumption, for instance, means that a certain action—such as making certain decisions, buying, preparing, and canning certain food in a family—occurs with a certain frequency within a given period. Similarly, a certain type of group relations means that within a given period certain friendly and hostile actions and reactions of a certain degree of severity occur between the members of two groups. Changing group relations or changing consumption means changing the level at which these multitude of events proceed. In other words, the "level" of consumption, of friendliness, or of productivity is to be characterized as the aspect of an ongoing social process.

Any planned social change will have to consider a multitude of factors characteristic for the particular case. The change may require a more or less unique combination of educational and organizational measures; it may depend upon quite different treatments or ideology, expectation and organization. Still, certain general formal principles always have to be considered.

2. *The conditions of a stable quasi-stationary equilibrium.* The study of the conditions for change begins appropriately with an analysis of the conditions for "no change," that is, for the state of equilibrium.

From what has been just discussed, it is clear that by a state of "no social change" we do not refer to a stationary but to a quasi-stationary equilibrium; that is, to a state comparable to that of a river which flows with a given velocity in a given direction during a certain time interval. A social change is comparable to a change in the velocity or direction of that river.

A number of statements can be made in regard to the conditions of quasi-stationary equilibrium. (These conditions are treated more elaborately elsewhere.[7])

(A) The strength of forces which tend to lower that standard of social life should be equal and opposite to

[7] K. Lewin, "Problems of Group Dynamics and the Integration of the Social Sciences: I Social Equilibria," *J. Hum. Relations* vol. 1, no. 1, 1947.

Excerpt from Kurt Lewin, "Group Decision and Social Change," in Readings in Social Psychology, *edited by Theodore M. Newcomb and Eugene L. Hartley, Holt, Rinehart and Winston, Inc., 1947, pp. 340–344. Used by permission.*

the strength of forces which tend to raise its level. The resultant of forces on the line of equilibrium should therefore be zero.

(B) Since we have to assume that the strength of social forces always shows variations, a quasi-stationary equilibrium presupposes that the forces against raising the standard increase with the amount of raising and that the forces against lowering increase (or remain constant) with the amount of lowering. This type of gradient which is characteristic for a "positive central force field" [8] has to hold at least in the neighborhood of the present level. . . .

(C) It is possible to change the strength of the opposing forces without changing the level of social conduct. In this case the tension (degree of conflict) increases.

3. *Two basic methods of changing levels of conduct.* For any type of social management, it is of great practical importance that levels of quasi-stationary equilibria can be changed in either of two ways: by adding forces in the desired direction, or by diminishing opposing forces. If a change from the level L_1 to L_2 [the present to a new level] brought about by increasing the forces toward L_2 [the new level] the secondary effects should be different from the case where the same change of level is brought about by diminishing the opposing forces.

In both cases the equilibrium might change to the same new level. The secondary effect should, however, be quite different. In the first case, the process on the new level would be accompanied by a state of relatively high tension; in the second case, by a state of relatively low tension. Since increase of tension above a certain degree is

[8] *Ibid.*

likely to be paralleled by higher aggressiveness, higher emotionality, and lower constructiveness, it is clear that as a rule the second method will be preferable to the high pressure method.

The group decision procedure which is used here attempts to avoid high pressure methods and is sensitive to resistance to change. In the experiment by Bavelas on changing production in factory work (as noted below), for instance, no attempt was made to set the new production goal by majority vote because a majority vote forces some group members to produce more than they consider appropriate. These individuals are likely to have some inner resistance. Instead a procedure was followed by which a goal was chosen on which everyone could agree fully.

It is possible that the success of group decision and particularly the permanency of the effect is, in part, due to the attempt to bring about a favorable decision by removing counterforces within the individuals rather than by applying outside pressure.

The surprising increase from the second to the fourth week in the number of mothers giving cod liver oil and orange juice to the baby can probably be explained by such a decrease of counterforces. Mothers are likely to handle their first baby during the first weeks of life somewhat cautiously and become more ready for action as the child grows stronger.

4. *Social habits and group standards.* Viewing a social stationary process as the result of a quasi-stationary equilibrium, one may expect that any added force will change the level of the process. The idea of "social habit" seems to imply that, in spite of the application of a force, the level of the social process will not change because of

some type of "inner resistance" to change. To overcome this inner resistance, an additional force seems to be required, a force sufficient to "break the habit," to "unfreeze" the custom.

Many social habits are anchored in the relation between the individuals and certain group standards. An individual P may differ in his personal level of conduct . . . from the level which represents group standards . . . by a certain amount. If the individual should try to diverge "too much" from group standards, he would find himself in increasing difficulties. He would be ridiculed, treated severely and finally ousted from the group. Most individuals, therefore, stay pretty close to the standard of the groups they belong to or wish to belong to. In other words, the group level itself acquires value. It becomes a positive valence corresponding to a central force field with the . . . [forces] keeping the individual in line with the standards of the group.

5. *Individual procedures and group procedures of changing social conduct.* If the resistance to change depends partly on the value which the group standard has for the individual, the resistance to change should diminish if one diminishes the strength of the value of the group standard or changes the level perceived by the individual as having social value.

This second point is one of the reasons for the effectiveness of "group carried" changes [9] resulting from procedures which approach the individuals as part of face-to-face groups. Perhaps one might expect single individuals to be more pliable than groups of like-minded individuals. However, experi-

ence in leadership training, in changing of food habits, work production, criminality, alcoholism, prejudices, all indicate that it is usually easier to change individuals formed into a group than to change any one of them separately.[10] As long as group standards are unchanged, the individual will resist changes more strongly the farther he is to depart from group standards. If the group standard itself is changed, the resistance which is due to the relation between individual and group standard is eliminated.

6. *Changing as a three-step procedure: unfreezing, moving, and freezing of a level.* A change toward a higher level of group performance is frequently short lived: after a "shot in the arm", group life soon returns to the previous level. This indicates that it does not suffice to define the objective of a planned change in group performance as the reaching of a different level. Permanency of the new level, or permanency for a desired period, should be included in the objective. A successful change includes therefore three aspects: unfreezing (if necessary) the present level . . . moving to the new level . . . and freezing group life on the new level. Since any level is determined by a force field, permanency implies that the new force field is made relatively secure against change.

The "unfreezing" of the present level may involve quite different problems in different cases. Allport [11] has described the "catharsis" which seems to be necessary before prejudices can be removed. To break open the shell of complacency and self-righteousness,

[9] N. R. F. Maier, *Psychology in Industry* (Boston: Houghton Mifflin Co., 1946).

[10] K. Lewin and P. Grabbe (eds.), *op. cit.*
[11] G. W. Allport, "Catharsis and the Reduction of Prejudice" in K. Lewin and P. Grabbe (eds.), *op. cit.*, 3-10.

it is sometimes necessary to bring about deliberately an emotional stir-up. . . .

The experiments on group decision reported here cover but a few of the necessary variations. Although in some cases the procedure is relatively easily executed, in others it requires skill and presupposes certain general conditions. Managers rushing into a factory to raise production by group decisions are likely to encounter failure. In social management as in medicine there are no patent medicines and each case demands careful diagnosis.

One reason why group decision facilitates change is illustrated by Wil-

lerman.[13] . . . [Willerman's study was concerned with] the degree of eagerness to have the members of a students' eating cooperative change from the consumption of white bread to whole wheat. When the change was simply requested the degree of eagerness varied greatly with the degree of personal preference for whole wheat. In case of group decision the eagerness seems to be relatively independent of personal preference; the individual seems to act mainly as a "group member."

[13] K. Lewin, "Forces behind Food Habits and Methods of Change", *Bull. Nat. Res. Coun.*, 1943, CVIII, 35–65.

◇◇◇◇◇◇◇◇◇◇◇◇◇◇◇◇◇◇◇ FORCE FIELD ANALYSIS APPLIED
TO A SCHOOL SITUATION

David H. Jenkins

. . . IN this article we would like to explore one approach toward problems of social engineering and to see how it might apply to the kinds of problems we find in the school setting. Suppose, for example, we feel that there is not enough teacher-pupil planning in the classrooms in our high school, and we want to see a change from the more teacher-centered methods of working with a class to methods using more pupil participation in planning. As a group of interested teachers, how can we begin to tackle a problem such as this?

Steps in Social Engineering

There seem to be four general steps which must be taken if the changes which are desired are to be effected: (1) Analyzing the present situation; (2) Determining the changes which are required; (3) Making the changes indicated by the analysis of the situation, and (4) Stabilizing the new situation so that it will be maintained. Let us look at these steps in detail to see what they may imply.

From David H. Jenkins, "Social Engineering in Educational Change: An Outline of Method," Progressive Education, Vol. 26, No. 7, May 1949, pp. 193–197. Used by permission.

Analyzing the Present Situation

Before effective plans for change can be made the present state of affairs must be defined as accurately as possible. This is the step familiar to most of us under various names such as "diagnosis" or "definition of the problem." The specific question that we might ask about our problem is, "Why don't we change our teaching methods, or *what are the forces which are keeping our methods in their present 'groove'?*" At first glance we often feel that the present condition exists because no one has the energy to make it any different—there is just too much "inertia." Yet, as we explore further it becomes clearer that there may be some very strong forces preventing substantial changes of any kind from occurring [as well as equal forces pressing toward change].

In our example, there might be several forces which point toward more teacher-pupil planning in the classroom: (a) a generally progressive philosophy of education may be accepted by a large number of teachers; (b) the teachers want to train students in the ways of living as citizens in a democracy; (c) the pupils desire some freedom in making decisions.

But there are also some forces which seem to be opposed to changes in that direction, such as: (a) many teachers lack training and skill in methods of planning cooperatively with pupils; (b) leaving the present methods and experimenting with the "unknown" makes us, like anyone else, feel insecure; (c) criticism may be directed against the school by the more conservative parents; (d) pupils have little skill in planning together. Forces like these which oppose each other determine the present level of methods which are used in the classroom.

Driving Forces and Restraining Forces

Forces such as those above seem to be of two kinds. *Driving forces* are those forces or factors affecting a situation which are "pushing" in a particular direction; they tend to initiate a change and keep it going. One's desire to be a more effective teacher is an example of a driving force; one is continually trying to improve regardless of his present skill.

Restraining forces may be likened to walls or barriers. They only prevent or retard movement toward them. . . . Any lack of skill we may have in using teacher-pupil planning methods in the classroom may be termed a restraining force against practicing this method.

As we see later, these two types of forces become particularly important when we attempt to stabilize a new condition to be sure it is continued.

The Force Field

A group of forces such as are shown in Figure 1 may be called a "force field." The top of the figure may be designated as teacher-pupil planning method, and the bottom of the figure as teacher-centered method. The arrows pointing downward represent the restraining forces which are keeping the methods from including more pupil participation and the driving forces toward more teacher-centered methods. The arrows pointing upward represent the restraining forces which are keeping the methods from becoming more teacher-centered and the driving forces toward more pupil participation. The length of each arrow represents the relative strength of the force at that particular point—the longer the arrow the stronger the force.

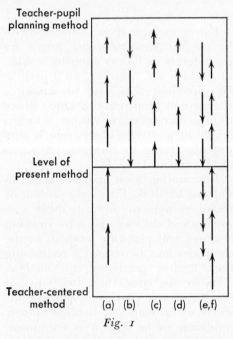

Fig. 1

As we see, the force field is made up of several forces of varying strengths which oppose each other. The strength of a particular force may itself vary at different levels (force (a) in Figure 1 is weak at levels near teacher-pupil planning but strong at levels near teacher-centered method). *The present condition (the present level of the method) is at that level where the sum of all the downward forces and the sum of all the upward forces are equal.*[1] It

[1] This type of analysis of the "equilibrium of change" was developed by the late Kurt Lewin in a pioneering article, "Frontiers in Group Dynamics: Concept, Method, and Reality in Social Science; Social Equilibria and Social Change," *Human Relations* Vol. I, No. 1, June, 1947, pp. 5-41.

is represented for our example by the line near the center marked "level of present methods." This means that all the forces which are affecting the methods being used in our school are such that our methods are being maintained at a level about half way between teacher-pupil planning and teacher-centered methods—we are probably doing some of each. If we analyze our situation and find that the opposing forces do not seem to be equal we may have overlooked some important factors.

Some Examples of Forces

Let us look briefly at some examples of the different kinds of forces we might find in our situation:

If the teachers in our group have a generally progressive philosophy of education it might be described by force (a) in Figure 1. This is a driving force having some effect throughout all levels of teaching method, but the more teacher-centered the current method (i.e., the lower the level of equilibrium) the greater pressure this force would exert toward increasing the amount of teacher-pupil planning.

If we lack skill in using pupil participation in planning, it might look like force (b). Here is a strong restraining force effective only at levels above our present level.

Force (c) represents our belief that as teachers increase the pupil participation in planning they will gain greater personal satisfactions from their teaching. These satisfactions will stimulate them to increase their use of this method. This force, one which acts as a driving force after some change has occurred, is described by the statement, "If I can only get them started, I know they will like it."

Sometimes we might find that the

administration in a school is hesitant to make changes because of the administrative procedures involved. However, once changes are decided upon, they may take a very active part in seeing that they are carried through. The hesitancy to make changes might be represented as a restraining force which reverses its direction when the change is decided upon and becomes a driving force when a change has been initiated. It would look something like force (d).

In our community there would be wide differences of opinion among the parents toward teacher-pupil planning. Some might feel that it was a valuable experience, others might feel that it was time wasted. Forces (e) and (f) together could represent these influences. As more parents come to feel that teacher-pupil planning is valuable, force (e) would be reduced, and force (f) would be increased.

These are some examples of a few of the different kinds of forces we might discover in any particular situation. They may be either driving or restraining forces in either direction, of varying strengths, and effective throughout the entire field or only a portion of the field. All of these characteristics help us do a thorough analysis of the present condition.

Planning for Change

Carrying through such an analysis as we have started, in terms of a specific situation, supplies the basis for planning change. When we have determined the nature of the forces which are affecting the present state of affairs we can think more clearly in selecting the forces or factors which should be modified if the conditions are to change in the direction we desire. *Changes will*

occur only as the forces are modified so that the level where the forces are equal is changed.

As we wish to change our teaching methods in the direction of increased use of teacher-pupil planning, our task then becomes either to increase the total strength of the driving forces in that direction (upward in Figure 1), or to decrease the total strength of forces opposing that direction (downward in Figure 1) or both.

Ways Forces Can Be Changed

The component forces can be modified in the following way: (1) *reducing or removing forces;* (2) *strengthening or adding forces;* (3) *changing the direction of the forces.*

In our example, one important force which almost necessarily requires reduction or removal is lack of skill in ways of using the methods of teacher-pupil planning. As we increase our skill in these methods we will, in effect, be reducing or removing a restraining force like (b) from being effective at the present level.

If we come to feel that these methods are essential if we are to put into effect our philosophy of education we have probably added a new driving force or strengthened one which was already present.

When it is possible, one of the most efficient ways to get change to occur is to change the direction of some of the forces. For instance, all teachers probably hold a common goal of training students to be good citizens in a democracy. However, there may be differences of opinion about the best way to do it. Many teachers may feel that an "efficient" classroom, directed by the teacher, will make the greatest contribution to good citizenship. For these teachers, the force representing their goal of good citizens would be in the downward direction in Figure 1. If these teachers come to believe, instead, that better citizens are trained through cooperative planning between teachers and pupils, this force toward citizenship training would be reversed in direction, now pointing upward toward teacher-pupil planning. A change in the direction of a driving force has something like a double effect—it acts as a removal of the force in one direction, and an addition of a force in the opposite direction.

Selection of the Forces to Be Modified

After we have analyzed a situation we are still faced with the problems of selecting which forces it will be possible and strategic to modify.

From the analysis, *the first step may be to determine what forces, if any, must be dealt with before a change can occur.* In our example it seems very likely that the restraining force representing lack of skill in actually using pupil participation in planning is one which must be removed before change can occur in that direction. We probably would find this force is of "infinite" strength and could not be overcome by adding strong driving forces. It must be reduced or removed.

When we have become aware of the forces which *must* be modified, we can then determine which of the remaining forces can most efficiently be modified to encourage a change in the level of present procedures.

Are there some forces whose direction can be reversed? How do we look at teacher-pupil planning? Do we see it as a means for training pupils for good

citizenship in a democracy? Do we see it as a way to encourage more creative development and ideas? How do the parents look at pupil participation in planning? If they question it as a worthwhile method can their questions be satisfied?

Which opposing forces can be reduced with the least effort? Does the administration encourage alterations in classroom procedures such as might be suggested by this method? Are there opportunities for getting increased experience and skill in using such methods in the classroom? How much of a job would it be to retrain the students to accept planning as a part of their responsibility in the classroom? How can we reduce our own insecurities which seem bound to arise whenever we try to do something a different way?

Which augmenting or upward forces can be increased? Do all of us feel that one of the legitimate tasks of the classroom is to help the class gain maturity in making decisions for itself? Do we feel, as teachers, that we have freedom to experiment with new methods in the classroom and to participate in decisions with the administration in establishing new procedures?

Questions like these represent the kinds of forces which will need to be considered when we make plans to initiate change in our classroom methods. They are the ones from which the forces to be modified in securing changes will be selected.

We might select, as a first step, for instance, getting parents interested in having more pupil participation in planning in the classroom. As a result there may be no immediate change in classroom methods but, as the parents become interested, we, as teachers, may feel encouraged toward increasing our skill in these methods. With increased skill and increased parent interest two important forces in the situation have been modified and the level of equilibrium of forces (the level of present method) should move upward toward more teacher-pupil planning.

The criteria in selecting forces to be modified, then, are: (1) what forces, if modified, will be most likely to result in changing the level of the present condition in the desired direction, and (2) what forces can be modified most easily or quickly? When we take action on a sound analysis of the forces in the situation we are most likely to move effectively toward the desired results. The ineffectiveness of many of our attempts at change which may be due to the "shotgun" approach is removed.

Modifying the Forces

When we are ready to modify a particular force we may find it necessary, of course, to analyze that particular force in the same manner as has been done for the more general problem. If we wish to train ourselves in the skills of securing pupil participation in planning we may find some specific forces which are directly related to the training program. Some of these might be a general resistance to being in a "training" situation, confusions of philosophy, and time limitations. Analysis of these problems, in turn, becomes the step required.

Clearly this process of analysis in planning change is a continuous one. We are able to make from our first analysis intelligent judgments for taking action. This action leads to the change in the situation and a change to the new level of equilibrium calls for renewed analysis.

Stabilizing the New Condition

Often, when changes in a situation have been achieved we "rest on our oars" and feel that the job has been completed. Later, upon examination, we may be surprised to find that the old situation has gradually returned and the changes need to be made all over again. *Whenever change is planned one must make sure that the new condition will be stable.* We need to develop in our analysis as clear a picture as possible of the forces which will exist when the new condition is achieved.

If we have secured a change by overcoming restraining forces, we can be assured that the new condition will continue. The restraining forces which have been overcome will not "push it back" to the old level. Such is not usually the case, however. More often the change has been made by overcoming some driving forces. In this instance there must be careful planning to make sure that the forces which support the new condition are stable, otherwise there will be a return to the old condition because of the opposing driving forces.

For example, we may become stimulated by a visiting teacher to try out some new methods. After she has left, however, we may run into difficulties, become discouraged, and return to our usual ways. If the change which has been initiated by this visiting teacher is to continue there will need to be some other force ready, when she leaves, to take the place of her stimulation. . . .

The method which we have discussed here is a general method which can be applied to any problem of changing human behavior. It supplies a framework for problem solving. We have used a problem of classroom technique to illustrate our discussion, but the method can be equally well applied to problems of changing the curriculum, changing pupil behavior in the classroom, school-community relations, administrative problems, etc. Clear analysis of any problem is the first step in problem solving.

❖❖❖❖❖❖❖❖❖❖❖❖❖❖❖❖❖❖❖❖ KURT LEWIN'S APPROACH TO CONFLICT AND ITS RESOLUTION

George Levinger

Three Basic Cases of Conflict Situations

THE conception that behavior is determined by forces or fields of forces lends itself readily to an analysis of conflict situations. Clearly, the constellation of forces which impinge on the life-space at any given moment finds many forces acting in opposition to one another. Strictly speaking, if conflict is defined as the collision of incompatible forces within the life-space, no person is ever free of conflict. If we consider that the person at any given moment has the possibility of locomoting in the direction of many different regions, then any particular action is the resultant of some implicit resolution of conflict.

In his discussion of this subject, Lewin defined psychological conflict as a situation where the forces acting on the person are *opposite in direction* and *about equal in strength*. It need not be specified as to whether the person is aware of the forces, whether the conflict is important to him, or whether there are many or few forces in opposition. The crucial point for the present paper is that, from the welter of many possible instances of conflict, we can *construct* dynamically different cases which have somewhat different implications for the person's behavior.

In several places (7, 8, 10) Lewin has outlined three dynamically different cases of psychological conflict, which we shall now discuss. We shall use the terms "plus," "positive valence," and "approach" in reference to the existence of forces directed *toward* a given region. Similarly, the term "minus," "negative valence," and "avoidance" will refer to forces *away from* some region.

THE CASE OF PLUS-PLUS CONFLICT

The first instance of psychological conflict is where the person stands midway between two positive valences. He has to choose one or the other of two equally attractive objects or activities. The classic example of Buridan's ass starving midway between two bales of hay is an illustration. Another illustration would be the choice confronting a man trying to decide between two television programs which he believes are equally enjoyable.

It can be demonstrated that the sim-

Excerpted from George Levinger, "Kurt Lewin's approach to Conflict and Its Resolution," Journal of Conflict Resolution, Vol. 1, No. 4, December 1957, pp. 331–335. Some footnotes omitted. Abridged and used by permission.

ple plus-plus situations depicted in Figure 1, *a,* will continue for only a short time before it is resolved. The equilibrium of the forces is unstable, since any slight change in the relative attractiveness of the two regions will drive the person off the exact center and toward one or the other of the goals. When this happens, the resultant force toward the nearer goal region increases progressively, and the person is induced to continue his locomotion in that direction. So, for example, the TV viewer who has selected Channel 2 over Channel 4 is unlikely to be driven back toward Channel 4 if the program lives up to his positive expectations. At the end of the program, a new constellation of forces may induce him to change his station or turn off the set.

Plus-plus conflict is a conceptual simplification of the usual situation where attaining either of the two goals also has its negative attributes—that is, attaining one goal entails sacrificing the other. Although neither TV program may be particularly noxious, tuning in one does mean missing the other. This more complex situation is pictured in Figure 1, *b.* Since almost any choice between attractive goals has a few negative features, we may subsume the plus-plus conflict under the more general case of "double plus-minus conflict."

If we restate Lewin's construction of this first case of conflict, it best represents a situation wherein the positive valences are predominant and the negative valences have the nature of costs or sacrifices rather than outright harmful or unpleasant events and, further, where resolution is relatively rapid.

THE CASE OF MINUS-MINUS CONFLICT

In this second case the person stands between two negative valences of about equal strength.[1] For example, if he is faced by the alternatives of either performing some extremely distasteful task or of suffering some punishment, the person is exposed to minus-minus conflict. His behavior resulting from such a conflict depends largely upon the other characteristics of the situation. That is, the stronger the barriers holding the person in the situation between

[1] Kenneth Boulding refers to this situation as "Buridan's ass between two skunks."

a   *b*

Fig. 1   *Situations of plus-plus conflict. a, Simple plus-plus conflict; b, complex plus-plus conflict, with recognition of the negative aspects of attaining each of the goals*

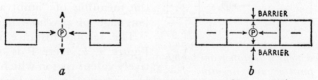

a   *b*

Fig. 2   *Situations of minus-minus conflict. a, Minus-minus conflict without barriers; b, minus-minus conflict with barriers*

the two negative valences, the more he will be forced to choose one of the unpleasant alternatives.

In Figure 2, *a*, *P* stands between two negative valences. However, there are no barriers preventing his exit from the situation. The resultant force governing his behavior will be in the direction of leaving the region between the two negative valences and presumably moving toward some other regions offering more positive attractions.

In Figure 2, *b*, *P* is propelled by the same resultant force. However, in this case his potential movement is blocked by impassable barriers. This is illustrated by the situation wherein a worker is faced with the alternative of performing an unpleasant task or of losing the respect of his fellows, where it is not possible for him to leave the job.

The conflict shown in Figure 2, *a*, is unstable, since the equilibrium of forces is readily dissolved if *P* moves out of the region where the negative driving forces are effective. Where barriers preventing such locomotion are present, on the other hand (see Fig. 2, *b*), the equilibrium is stable. In the plus-plus conflict situation, the increase in the forces upon *P*'s approach to the valent region leads to his further approach to that region and to the dissolution of the initial quandary. However, in the minus-minus situation, an approach to either of the regions leads to stronger forces driving *P* in the opposite direction. It

has been demonstrated empirically that minus-minus conflicts do indeed lead to less rapid resolution (1). It may be observed here that, if the negative valences in the minus-minus conflict situation are sufficiently strong, *P* will turn against the barriers in his attempts to escape.

THE CASE OF PLUS-MINUS CONFLICT

Whereas the previous cases involve the incompatibility of forces stemming from two different regions, the third case involves the incompatibility of forces stemming from the same region. As was seen in the plus-plus situation, it was relatively simple to resolve the conflict by moving toward one or the other of the two regions. Also in the minus-minus situation, *P* could leave the area of conflict by overcoming the barriers, and he was in little conflict concerning the desirability of heading for an exit. In the present case, however, the attractions of the goal region hold *P* nearby, whereas its unattractive aspects prevent him from attaining it.

We shall consider two kinds of plus-minus conflicts, as illustrated in Figure 3. The first involves an individual who is exposed to both positive and negative driving forces emanating from the same region. For example, the fellow who is attracted by the good looks of a certain co-ed may be equally repelled by her pungent and unwholesome breath. This situation comes closest to the meaning of "ambivalence" in the language of psychoanalysis.

The second instance is depicted in Figure 3, *b*. Here P is outside a positively valent region which is surrounded by negatively valent barriers. In order to reach his goal, *P* must undergo some unpleasant experience. For example, in

a   *b*

Fig. 3   Situations of plus-minus conflict. a, *Person located near a region from which emanate both positive and negative driving forces;* b, *person located near a region which produces positive driving forces, but he is blocked by restraining forces*

order to become an attorney, he must pass his bar exams.

The situation of plus-minus conflict is particularly interesting—and persisting—because of the differing steepness of the positive and negative force gradients. Lewin (7) has pointed out—and Miller and others (12) have confirmed experimentally—that, as *P* approaches the goal region, the strength of positive and negative forces increases and that the strength of the negative forces increases more rapidly than that of the positive ones. Thus, in this situation, *P* may approach rather near to the goal before its undesirable characteristics repel him and stop him. However, as soon as he goes in the opposite direction away from the goal, its desirable characteristics drive him back toward it.

In the typical plus-minus case, *P* vacillates around a point where the plus forces are strong enough to hold him but not strong enough to overcome the growing minus forces. We find here that reducing the negative character of the goal tends to be far more effective than increasing its positive aspects for resolving *P*'s conflict. If only the positive driving forces are increased, *P* approaches closer to the goal. This approach simultaneously arouses an increase in the negative forces impinging on him. Therefore, unless the approach forces are so strong that *P* is able to enter the goal region, his level of conflict increases, with an accompanying heightening of his psychological tension.

TENSION

Although the popular view may place a negative value on tension per se, Lewin treats tension states in a relatively value-free manner. Thus the person does not strive to eliminate tension: a tensionless life-space would be lifeless. Instead, there is a tendency toward the equalization of tensions in various neighboring regions of activity. Those regions where the greatest tensions exist are of the greatest concern until their tensions are reduced in relation to those of other regions.

Lewin is not very explicit concerning tensions with regard to conflict situations. Yet he does mention that conflicts deriving from strong opposing forces lead to heightened emotional tension. In turn, this results in "restless movements" and lowered efficiency for solving problems which require new insights. Furthermore, the tension is likely to persist until the equilibrium of opposing forces is altered.

A Brief Assessment

Lewin's approach has given us a basis for making some general observations about psychological conflict. By introducing such concepts as valence, barrier, direction and strength of force in the setting of *P*'s psychological environment, he has offered a point of view which furthers our understanding of the dynamics of conflict. Empirical studies by Barker (1) and by Meyers (11) have confirmed the validity of his observations. The fact that experimental psychologists of the Yale stimulus-response school have seen fit to refine his early insights and distinctions (cf. Hull, 6) bears added testimony to the fruitfulness of his views (e.g., Hull, 6; Miller, 12; Brown, 2).

On the other hand, Lewin's contribution is limited principally to the concepts and distinctions discussed above. There remain a number of "empty regions," which need to be explored to improve our understanding of conflict and its resolution. One of these areas of relative ignorance concerns the principles for predicting how conflicts will be restructured and in what direction future locomotion will occur. A second neglected area is the relation between the treatment of *intra*personal, or psychological, conflict and that of *inter*personal, or social, conflict. A third concerns the need for making quantitative predictions from these qualitative formulations.

Later we shall pay some conceptual attention to the former two areas. The last requires methodological work in the area of measuring the relevant psychological or social forces.

The Restructuring of Psychological Conflict

Can we look toward any rules by which the person's conflict is restructured or resolved? A few such rules seem implied by Lewin's essential position.

Let us consider *P,* who finds himself in a region of conflict. What alternatives are open to him for dealing with the conflict?

First, he may choose to tolerate it. It would seem that in situations of opposing forces, where the accompanying tension is low, *P* will find that tensions in other regions are higher, and he can tolerate their existence in this particular region.

Second, *P* may locomote in his actual behavior. He may go elsewhere physically. This will be likely in instances where the physical barriers are weak or non-existent.

Third, he may change his perception of the conflicting forces. He may locomote psychologically by saying to himself, for example, that one of the un-

pleasant alternatives in his conflict is really not so bad. This choice is most likely in situations where immediate behavioral resolution of the conflict is possible.

Fourth, either through choice or through circumstance, *P* may be relocated in a new behavior space, where the presently conflicting forces are overridden by a new force constellation. Thus the original conflict becomes either postponable or obsolete. For example, the man trying to decide between two TV programs is placed in a new situation if he receives a telephone call that an out-of-town friend is coming over to see him. Or an employee, in doubt whether to ask his boss for a raise, may learn that he has a good chance of obtaining a better job with another organization.

References

1. BARKER, R. "An Experimental Study of the Resolution of Conflict in Children." In A. McNEMAR and M. A. MERRILL (eds.), *Studies in Personality*. New York: McGraw-Hill Book Co., 1942.

2. BROWN, J. S. "Gradients of Approach and Responses and Their Relation to Level of Motivation," *J. Comp. Physiol. Psychol.,* XLI (1948), 450–465.

6. HULL, C. L. "The Goal-Gradient Hypothesis Applied to Some 'Field-Force' Problems in the Behavior of Young Children," *Psychol. Rev.,* XLV (1938), 271–299.

7. LEWIN, K. *Dynamic Theory of Personality*. New York: McGraw-Hill Book Co., 1935.

8. ——. "The Conceptual Representation and Measurement of Psychologi-

cal Forces," *Contr. Psychol. Theory,* Vol. I, No. 4 (1938).

10. ———. *Field Theory in Social Science.* Edited by D. CARTWRIGHT. New York: Harper, 1951.

11. MEYERS, C. E. "The Effect of Conflicting Authority on the Child."

Univ. Iowa Studies in Child Welfare, XX (1944), 31–98.

12. MILLER, N. E. "Experimental Studies of Conflict." In J. McV. HUNT (ed.), *Personality and the Behavior Disorders.* New York: Ronald Press, 1944.

CHAPTER 6

The Small Group in
Stability and Change

A new emphasis in empirical and experimental research on human behavior has elbowed its way into the disciplines of psychology and sociology during the last two decades. This new focus of interest has been variously named "small group" or "primary group" research, "group dynamics" or "microsociology." Whatever the name used, the "small group" has been established as a social system capable and worthy of study in its own right.

There can be no doubt of the rapid and accelerating spread of this new focus of research effort within the academic worlds of the United States and Western Europe. A bibliography of publications on "small group behavior" between 1900 and 1953 was published by Strodtbeck and Hare in 1954.[1] Nearly 1500 items were included. Most of these items were published in the 1940's and 1950's. The bibliography shows an accelerating annual rate of publications on "small groups" from 1940 on.

The reasons for this eruption of academic and professional interest in small group behavior are harder to state convincingly. A definitive history of the movement has still to be written.[2] But a glance at some aspects of this history may be useful in explaining why we have emphasized the small group literature in this book of readings.

"Small group" variables first forced themselves on the attention of researchers concerned with levels of human organization more familiar to those in the main line of psychological and sociological research and theorizing. Thus, Mayo, in his studies of formal organization in industry, was forced by his data to recognize the influence of primary group factors in explaining people's behavior in a bureaucracy, at a time when bureaucratic and management theories provided no

[1] F. L. Strodtbeck and A. P. Hare, "Bibliography of small group research (from 1900 through 1953), *Sociometry, 17*:107–178, 1954.
[2] See Edward Shils, "The Study of the Primary Group," Chapter 3 in Lerner and Lasswell (ed.) *The Policy Sciences.* Palo Alto: Stanford University Press, 1951, for a thoughtful overture to such a history.

or little place for such variables in their scheme of things. Primary groups were found to grow within the austere climate of *Gesellschaft* (society) as a result of continuing needs of workers for *Gemeinschaft* (community). These informal groups also served workers' needs to defend themselves against changes arbitrarily imposed upon them by "scientific" management. "Small groups" came thus to be seen as a "dynamic" element both in maintaining wholeness and stability of individuals within bureaucracy and in regulating imposed changes in patterns of organizational behavior. Later studies have shown that, under conditions of participation with management, the primary group organization in a bureaucracy can support and initiate rather than merely resist changes in its social organization.

Studies of personal development by Moreno and others found a need for "small group" variables in explaining how individuals develop. The "primary group" of the family came to be seen as a major influence in early socialization, and memberships in alternative "primary groups" as a major dynamic in a person's achieving freedom from early family identification. The *dynamics of personal change* came thus to be seen as powerfully affected by the *dynamics of primary group memberships*.

As the simple agrarian community yielded to a complex urban community, students of community organization and change were forced to recognize conflicts and collaborations between the various groupings within the community as important factors in community stability and/or change.

Thus it was in studies of the dynamics of other levels of human organization—bureaucracies, persons, communities—that the dynamics of small groups forced themselves upon the attention of psychological and sociological researchers. It remained for the social system of the "small group" to be isolated as an object of study by Lewin, Lippitt, and others in order to define a discipline of "group dynamics" in its own right. It is this newly defined discipline that has elbowed its way into the family of the behavioral sciences in recent years.

The important place the social system of the "small group" has been found to occupy in affecting stability and change in overlapping behavioral systems—persons, organizations, and communities—justifies special attention to it in this book on "planned change." (That the "small group" is, as a consequence, a major tool for all change-agents in achieving changes in people, whatever level of human organization their specialty may be, will be argued in Chapter 12.)

The enthusiasm engendered among its votaries for "group dynamics" as an important "new" field of behavioral studies led understandably to raised eyebrows and more active opposition on the part of some behavioral scientists ensconced in more familiar studies of other levels of human organization. Whether accidentally or not, a number of the leaders in establishing the research discipline of "group dynamics" were also concerned early in the game with studies of the application of social knowledge, with planned change, action research, etc. (Kurt Lewin's personal integration of these interests undoubtedly encouraged a similar combination of interests in some of those strongly influenced by him.) Some of the feelings of outrage which advocacy of the concept of "change-agentry" induces in academic men was, for this reason, displaced upon the "science" of "group dynamics" in the initial period of developing the field of study. There was no doubt a certain parochialism in some early efforts to define change-agent functions in terms primarily of "group dynamics" concepts, neglecting "personality," "economic," "political," and "social class" variables in the definition. And opposition, even from other academics similarly concerned with planned change, no doubt reinforced these tendencies toward parochialism. Of course, the notions of "planned change" and of "change-agent," properly construed, include much more than small group variables in their scope, as we trust this volume will help to show. "Group dynamics" has tended to become more respectable and connected within the family of the social sciences as new *avant-garde* siblings—"behavioral science," "conflict resolution," and so on—have appeared upon the academic stage.

The simultaneous appearance upon the intellectual landscape of "group dynamics research" and experimentation with "applied group dynamics" and their continued interaction led to confusion among academics and practitioners alike as to what sort of discipline "group dynamics" actually is. Is it "basic"? Is it "applied"? Is it "psychology"? Is it "sociology"? Is it a "science"? Is it a "cult"? This quandary was intensified by the fact that, even as the "new" discipline evoked opposition among some social scientists and social practitioners, it evoked enthusiastic, though often uncritical, support from others. Many practitioners, aware of the cultural pressures upon their role as "change-agents" and troubled by lack of definition of the nature of this new responsibility, found in applied group dynamics, which talked the language of "change-agentry," *the* answer to their quandaries. Uncritical advocacy of "group dynamics" as a technique of salvation by some harried and beleaguered practitioners who had found relief in "its teachings" reinforced the suspicions of its opponents that "group dynamicists" were much more members of a religious or therapeutic cult than scientists. It is hard to know how far these early attitudes and confusions persist in the minds of social scientists and social practitioners today. The careful study of the advent of "group dynamics" upon the academic and professional scene would itself provide a useful case for analyzing processes of innovation and change.

The first two readings in his chapter give the flavor of controversies about the nature of "group dynamics" already reviewed. Gunderson's *Group Dynamics— Hope or Hoax?* presents his honest, though not always well-informed, bewilderment over the character of the "new" discipline which some advocates within his own field of "speech" were pressing him to buy. His essay shows the confusion between "group dynamics" as a field of scientific research and as an applied study which the early close collaboration between "scientists" and "practitioners" in small group studies makes understandable. Kelman's rejoinder, *Group Dynamics*

—*Neither Hope nor Hoax,* attempts to make a distinction between the "research" and "applied" aspects of small group studies and to justify the place of research on small groups within the spectrum of social-psychological studies. The article by Cartwright and Lippitt provides an empirical basis, suggested by Kelman, that illuminates the impact of the group on the individual and the meaning of the group in society.

In *The Conceptual Status of Group Dynamics,* Horwitz presents a paradigm to clarify the place of small group studies within the range of studies directed to various levels of human organization. "Pure" studies of the relations between small group variables represent one emphasis in researches on group dynamics. But since the members of a group are personal systems as well as parts of a group, other studies may focus on the interrelations between small group variables and personality variables mediated in the group through its members. In other words, the personalities of group members represent "systems" that overlap the "social system" of the small group. These intersystem relationships may be examined. Similarly, the small group system overlaps the larger social systems of which it is in some sense a part. Therefore another range of intersystem studies, in which small group variables are related to "organizational," "community," and "culture" variables, is possible within small group research. In his review of selected small group researches, Horwitz identifies the principal "small group variables" that have been isolated in researches up to this time.

We have argued before that system models are useful to practitioners in holding together in relationship the various variables with which they must reckon in diagnosing and handling concrete situations. Jensen and Parsons, in *A Model for Analyzing Small Group Properties Pertinent to Planned Change,* have sought to demonstrate the usefulness of the "group system model" in conceptualizing behavioral phenomena in a classroom. Such conceptualization is useful both in suggesting problems for classroom research and in giving the practitioner (in this particular case, the teacher) "mindholds" for identifying and diagnosing problems in the human organization that he must negotiate and manage in carrying on his work.

One mark of social scientists, at least contemporary ones, is their concern with the latent or hidden dimensions of the phenomena they seek to explain. Phenomena do not explain themselves. In going beyond descriptions of manifest phenomena to explanations of patterns and regular recurrences in these, a latent world of forces and factors must be posited and explored. Under the surface of work and play as these evince themselves in the public life of groups, various interpersonal dramas are being played out. "Emotional" factors and forces are operating beneath the mask of explicit events. If the patterns of operation of such forces and factors can be detected, these patterns will help to explain behavioral events that seem inexplicable on the basis of observations of the manifest content of communications or of overt behavior alone. The intellectual purpose in charting the latent dimensions of group life is to achieve greater predictability in the behavioral events that are the overt aspects of member interactions of various sorts.

Greater predictability of behavioral events is as much a concern of practitioners as of scientists. The next two readings in this chapter explore ways in which the *terra incognita* of interpersonal relations in group settings has been mapped for research purposes and, hopefully also, for practitioner diagnoses as well. Bion's pioneer work on group emotionality,[3] in essentially Freudian terms, has been extended by Schutz in his *Interpersonal Underworld* to create a more elaborate scheme for study and explanation of the latent features of group structure and process. Leary, in *The Theory and Measurement Methodology of Interpersonal Communication,* builds more directly upon Harry Stack Sullivan's theorizing upon "interpersonal relations" as the proper subject matter of psychiatry (see Chapter 7). He has elaborated a somewhat different way of mapping the interpersonal underworld of small group operation.

The studies presented up to this point in Chapter 6 are oriented to examination and explanation of group phenomena occurring at any one time in a group's career. In this sense, these studies abstract from time as a major variable in explaining how groups work. An equally valid approach to the understanding of groups, and one which practitioners who work with groups cannot safely ignore, is to study the development (or growth) of groups through time. Developmental studies of groups have not been as plentiful as "time-slice" studies, partly because of the lack of adequate methodologies for managing such studies and partly because of the practical difficulties in making "long-lived" groups the object of the continuing "laboratory" observation that developmental studies require. Treatments of group development are, therefore, still somewhat speculative as compared with studies of the atemporal relationships between variables.

Three statements on group development are included in this chapter. Bennis and Shepard, in *A Theory of Group Development,* offer a plausible treatment of development in small groups in terms of the pivotal problems that the people in any group must face and solve in achieving a mature and stable organization of group effort. Thelen and Dickerman, in *The Growth of a Group,* approached their study through an analysis of the modal languages that characterize the discussions of a training group in various stages of its development through time. They found a succession of stereotypic vocabularies that suggest indices of accompanying changes in the interpersonal relations and social organization of the group.

Some Dimensions of Group Growth, by the staff of the National Training Laboratory in Group Development, provides two important reminders to those who would assess the "maturity" of a group. Group development is not a unitary process. There are several identifiable dimensions in the developing social system

[3] See W. R. Bion, "Experiences in Groups," published in seven installments in *Human Relations,* Vol. 1, 2, 3, and 4, 1948–1951.

of a small group. A group may, at any one time, have developed further along one of these dimensions than along some other. Further, the criteria of "group growth" are *normative* criteria, not exclusively or primarily *descriptive* categories. They suggest ways in which groups *should* develop, not invariant or necessary sequences of development. Of course, application of the criteria, if responsible, requires empirical studies of how a group actually is operating. This normative character of the criteria for judging group growth or maturity does not rule out their importance to practitioners who are working with groups to help them develop. But it does raise different questions about the bases on which such criteria can be validated than do nonevaluative hypotheses about structures and functions in small group operations.

◇◇◇◇◇◇◇◇◇◇◇◇◇◇◇◇◇◇◇◇◇ GROUP DYNAMICS—HOPE OR HOAX?

Robert Gray Gunderson

Aт the 1949 Convention of the Speech Association of America, Dr. Mayhew Derryberry, an official of the United States Department of Health, addressed the discussion section on 'the science of group dynamics.' Since Dr. Derryberry unhappily failed to define what he meant by *group dynamics,* one of his listeners was provoked to damn the term as nothing more than a ritualistic shibboleth. Less critical observers pointed out, however, that group dynamics is the theory held by a number of educationists, social psychologists, sociologists, and welfare workers who claim they have discovered a method for the application of 'science' to the process of human relations. Implicit in their use of the word *dynamics* is, of course, the analogy between physical laws of motion and the relation of forces within social groups. Exponents

hypothesize 'a psychical motion' in group discussion just as physicists postulate the motion of molecules in physical bodies. If their concept is somewhat mysterious, it must remain so temporarily—for, as two of the leaders have confessed, 'The science of group dynamics is so young that only a very meagre number of scientific facts and laws have been accumulated.' [1] . . .

The theory of group dynamics is but an outgrowth of Lewin's topological psychology. Taking issue with the early behaviorists, Lewin contended that human behavior must be related not only to physiological needs, but also to what he described as a *'much more complex . . . variable—the total situation as or-*

[1] Leland P. Bradford and John R. P. French, Jr., Conclusions, *The Journal of Social Issues,* 4 (Spring 1948), 71.

Excerpted from Robert Gray Gunderson, "Group Dynamics—Hope or Hoax?" The Quarterly Journal of Speech, Vol. 36, February 1950, pp. 34–38. Some footnotes omitted. Abridged and used by permission.

ganized or structured by the organism.' [2] In the case of hunger, for example, Lewin felt that behavior is not governed solely by the 'inner needs' of the individual. Instead, he maintained that food and intervening barriers to food contribute to the total and complex 'configuration.' In measuring such complexities, Lewin was hampered by the inadequacy of statistical methods which provide correlations between only a few variables in isolation from the total situation. Consequently, he turned to topological mathematics for tools which he might use in demonstrating the 'interrelations between *complex patterns of variables.'* [3] Thus, he utilized topological diagrams to demonstrate relationships which were too complicated for the usual statistical procedures. [4] Through the use of this new approach, Lewin expected to gather and explain, as he put it, 'reliable data on the structural properties of groups, on the relations between groups or sub-groups, and on the relation between a group and the life of its individual members.' [5] 'Only a man of Lewin's originality and courage,' said one sympathetic critic, 'could have [contributed] . . . the notion that actual experiments on groups could be carried out under precisely controlled conditions.' [6]

Current leaders in the dynamics movement come from several disciplines and delight in defying traditional academic boundaries. One of Lewin's students, Ronald Lippitt, performs the rituals of the order at the University of Michigan. Leland P. Bradford, Director of Adult Education for the National Education Association, and Kenneth Benne of the Education Department at the University of Illinois promote the cause among professional educators. Social workers hear of it from Gordon Hearn of the Department of Social Welfare at the University of California. Farmers have had dynamics translated for them by D. M. Hall of the Extension Service of the University of Illinois. [7] Labor unionists have been exposed to it through the writings of Clinton Golden. [8] Members of the speech profession hear it expounded by John Keltner of the University of Oklahoma.

While speech teachers have been slow to join the movement, they have not been unaware of the activities of Lewin and his followers. At the forthcoming Rocky Mountain Speech Conference, for example, Dr. P. Merville Larson announces that 'some of the newer principles of group dynamics' will be 'explored.' A joint committee of the NEA Department of Adult Education and the Speech Association of America has served as a meeting ground for speech teachers and exponents of dynamics. Magazines such as *The Jour*

[2] Robert W. Leeper, *Lewin's Topological and Vector Psychology: A Digest and a Critique* (Eugene, Oregon, 1943), 28.

[3] *Ibid.*, 33–34.

[4] See Kurt Lewin, *A Dynamic Theory of Personality,* trans. into English by Donald K. Adams and Karl E. Zener (New York, 1935); and Kurt Lewin, *Principles of Topological Psychology* (New York, 1936).

[5] Kurt Lewin, Frontiers in Group Dynamics: Concept, Method and Reality in Social Science; Social Equilibria and Social Change, *Human Relations,* 1 (1947), 8.

[6] Tolman, *Psychological Review,* 55 (1948), 4.

[7] See D. M. Hall, *The Dynamics of Group Discussion,* University of Illinois Extension Service, *Bulletin,* 1948.

[8] While Clinton Golden has been associated with the dynamics group, his book, written in collaboration with Harold J. Ruttenberg, *The Dynamics of Industrial Democracy* (New York, 1942), does not outline the usual doctrine.

nal of *Social Issues, Sociatry, Sociometry,* and *Human Relations* have publicized the work of the Research Center for Group Dynamics at the University of Michigan, the Sociometric Institute in New York City, and the Tavistock Institute of Human Relations in London.

Even better known, no doubt, is the work of the National Training Laboratory on Group Development which has met for the past three summers in Bethel, Maine. For three weeks each summer some 150 persons described as 'key education and action leaders' have gathered for a 'workshop' in group dynamics. Their objectives were (1) to provide research scientists an opportunity to communicate information to discussion leaders; (2) to give successful participation in democratic group processes; and (3) to offer an experimental laboratory for further research.[9] Delegates were subjected to a rigorous testing program which included the Vigotsky, the Rorschach, and the Runner-Seaver personality inventories. An anthropologist was appointed to 'secure anecdotal material on the cultural aspects of the laboratory community,' and two psychiatrists were assigned as councilors.[10]

A basic device of the Bethel laboratory was an adaptation of J. L. Moreno's psychodrama called *role playing*— which (according to Moreno's evaluation) is comparable only to the dramaturgical contributions of Aeschylus and Euripides:

Aeschylus is credited with having put the first actor upon . . . the stage. . . . Euripides credited with having put the second actor on the stage. . . . We may be credited to have put the psyche itself on the stage.[11]

To get 'the psyche itself on the stage' at Bethel, delegates gathered in 'Basic Skill Training Groups' of twelve to fourteen and 'spontaneously acted out human relations situations.'[12] 'BST Groups' would dramatize, for example, a crisis in a small town PTA. Various members would be assigned roles as the disgruntled parent, the harassed school principal, and the timid teacher. 'Behind the partial protection of the role,' it was noted, 'members became quite frank in expressing their perceptions. . . .'[13] After successfully mastering the problems of the hypothetical PTA, delegates felt competent to direct similar dramatizations before 'real-life' PTA's back home. As the Director, Leland Bradford, expressed it, 'The laboratory aimed to be an experiment in the training of trainers.'[14]

In a different use of the role-playing device, members would dramatize the various personality types in a poor discussion meeting. Delegates would portray the parts of 'the aggressor,' 'the blocker,' 'the recognition-seeker,' 'the special-interest pleader,' 'the scapegoat,' and 'the blamer.' Then, for con-

[9] National Training Laboratory on Group Development, *Preliminary Report*, Bethel, Maine, June 16 to July 4, 1947, iii. See also the *Report of the Second Summer Laboratory Session.*

[10] *School and Society*, 66 (December 20, 1947), 475–479.

[11] J. L. Moreno, Psychodrama and Group Psychotherapy, *Sociometry*, 9 (May–August, 1946), 253. For a more extended treatment of the Moreno doctrine, see his *Who Shall Survive? A New Approach to the Problem of Human Interrelations* (Washington, 1934).

[12] Leland P. Bradford, Human Relations Training, *The Group*, 10 (January, 1948), 9.

[13] Margaret E. Barron and Gilbert K. Krulee, Case Study of a Basic Skill Training Group, *The Journal of Social Issues*, 4 (Spring, 1948), 25.

[14] *Preliminary Report*, 4.

trast, a good discussion would be en-acted in which the various phases of effective leadership would be demon-strated. Members would play the roles of 'change-agent,' 'changee,' 'initiator,' 'encourager,' 'harmonizer,' 'facilitator,' 'orienter,' 'fact-seeker,' 'expediter,' 'com-promiser,' 'analyzer,' and so on through a long list of commendable attributes. This use of role playing is somehow reminiscent of the medieval morality plays which dramatized the seven dead-ly sins in contrast to the cardinal vir-tues.

While role playing is neither new nor the invention of the dynamics group, nevertheless, it may have limited use as a device for teaching relatively simple skills in speech and behavior. The adolescent male might well learn conventional courtesies by imperson-ating Beau Brummell. There may be even a bit of psychiatric benefit in having some shrew play the role of a timid school marm. But the inherent artificiality—if not actual mockery—involved in the process makes role playing absurd as a method for the dis-cussion and solution of serious public questions.

A second device used extensively at Bethel is known, rather inelegantly, as 'feedback.' 'Feedback,' says David H. Jenkins, 'is the procedure by which the group can become aware of its own difficulties, the reasons for those dif-ficulties, and the corrections which are necessary.' [15] In other circles, feedback is known as the process of evaluation. A 'group observer' was assigned to re-cord the content of the Bethel discus-sions; an 'interaction observer' classi-fied the relationship between members in twenty categories ranging from

praise to aggression; and an 'anecdotal observer' interpreted the dynamics of group and leader behavior. After each discussion these functionaries reported their observations, and members collab-orated by making critical suggestions. Published transcriptions of feedback sessions indicate that members occasion-ally pursued self-evaluation almost to the point of self-abasement.[16] Neverthe-less, delegates at Bethel have served to emphasize the importance of analyzing discussion procedures.

At Bethel, other techniques were used which are quite familiar to teach-ers of speech. An intensive testing pro-gram preceded formation of the dis-cussion groups. Once the groups were at work, observers prepared charts which indicated the distribution of member participation. After meetings, members were asked to fill out ques-tionnaires which research students later used as aids in evaluation. On the basis of this evidence, sociograms were con-structed which represented graphically the likes and dislikes members held for one another. While the use of such techniques would seem to be routine experimental procedure, the Bethelites apparently feel that they have hap-pened upon new ritual.

Whether or not group dynamics is a hope or a hoax may be determined by an analysis of its vocabulary. A group with pretensions of scientific objectiv-ity might be expected to develop a pre-cise terminology. Instead, one finds a conglomeration of loosely defined terms chosen from the sporting arena, the theatre and the fraternity lounge —as well as from the scientific labora-tory. Terms with popular connotations such as 'gate-keeper,' 'blocker,' 'role player,' and 'play boy,' are thus min-

---

[15] David H. Jenkins, Feedback and Group Self-Evaluation, *The Journal of Social Issues*, 4 (Spring, 1948), 51.

[16] Barron and Krulee, Case Study, *Ibid.* 25 ff.

gled with the vocabulary of topological and vector psychology. This conglomerate language leads not only to confusion in communication; it precludes scientific measurement.

Even if it were granted that the research expert in dynamics could define what he wished to measure, he still would lack measuring instruments worthy of the name. Personality inventories, interviewing techniques, and sociometric devices may be interesting experimental tools, but they hardly can be called accurate measuring devices. . . .

In spite of the skepticism of their colleagues in psychology, exponents of dynamics insist that there are 'structural properties in groups' which can be analyzed objectively and measured accurately.[17] While in no case have

[17] Kurt Lewin, *Human Relations*, 1 (1947), 8. The best comprehensive survey of Lewin's thinking is *Resolving Social Conflicts, Selected Papers on Group Dynamics*, ed. by Gertrud

they described clearly what the structural properties and relationships might be, nevertheless, they assiduously work at 'action research' in 'human relations.' The world community is their workshop, and Lewin's topological psychology exempts them from the rigors of the controlled laboratory situation. The observer crowds into the test tube with his experiment—but proximity to emotional flame cannot destroy his objectivity because of some magic inherent in 'the science of group dynamics.'

For those without the magic formula, there remain the difficult but prosaic methods of a psychology which demands controlled experimentation, carefully defined terminology, and an honest recognition of limitations. In the end, these virtues may contribute more to scientific progress than premature proclamations about 'the science of human relations.'

Weiss Lewin (New York, 1948). See particularly Chapter 5, 'Experiments in Social Space.'

❖❖❖❖❖❖❖❖❖❖❖❖❖❖❖❖❖❖❖ GROUP DYNAMICS—NEITHER HOPE NOR HOAX   *Herbert C. Kelman*

In the February issue of this journal, Professor Gunderson published an article entitled Group Dynamics—Hope or Hoax? I have to take exception to much of what he says. My purpose is not to make a point by point rebuttal, but to clarify certain basic distinctions which Gunderson's paper fails to make. I refer to the distinction between *group*

dynamics as an area of theoretical and experimental research, and *group dynamics* as an 'applied' approach to practical problems of group functioning. The article presents a confusing and one-sided picture of group dynamics because it shifts back and forth indiscriminately from theory to application; and because it underplays

Excerpted from Herbert C. Kelman, "Group Dynamics—Neither Hope Nor Hoax," The Quarterly Journal of Speech, Vol. 36, October 1950, pp. 371–377. Some footnotes omitted. Abridged and used by permission.

the theoretical and experimental contributions which have been made in this field.

Experimental work on group behavior had been done before the advent of group dynamics.[1] This work addressed itself to such questions as these: How does the product of an individual alone differ from his product in a group situation (e.g., in terms of efficiency and quality of performance on certain mental tasks)? How does the product of a group differ from the products of an equal number of individuals working in isolation? What effects do size of group, type of task, and other variables have on the group product? In short, most of this work dealt with the overall effects of the group situation, and not with the process of social interaction as such. One of the few people to bring the actual process of social interaction into the laboratory was Sherif.[2] His early studies are restricted, however, to special perceptual phenomena, and do not deal with functioning groups.

As far as I know, Kurt Lewin and his students were the first ones to make a large scale experimental attack on the process of interaction in the small group situation. During the 1930s, Lewin became increasingly aware of the importance of group phenomena as determinants of behavior, and wrote several theoretical papers along these lines.[3] The first experiments to be performed under his influence were Lippitt and White's studies on democratic and autocratic group atmosphere.[4] The next big landmark in the development of this research was the establishment, in 1945, of the Research Center for Group Dynamics at the Massachusetts Institute of Technology, under Lewin's direction.[5] With that the term *group dynamics* came into use.

Group dynamics is new and different only in the sense that it deals with a content area in which practically no experimental work has been done before. Of course, in order to deal with new content, it was necessary to find new theoretical approaches and new research tools; both of these are under-

[1] See J. F. Dashiell, Experimental Studies of the Influence of Social Situations on the Behavior of Individual Human Adults, in C. Murchison (ed.), *Handbook of Social Psychology* (Worcester, 1935), ch. 23; and G. Murphy, L. B. Murphy, and T. M. Newcomb, *Experimental Social Psychology* (New York, 1937), 686–739.

[2] M. Sherif, A Study of Some Social Factors in Perception, *Archives of Psychology*, no. 187 (1935); and M. Sherif, *The Psychology of Social Norms* (New York, 1936).

[3] K. Lewin, Psycho-Sociological Problems of a Minority Group, *Character and Personality*, 3 (1935), 175–187; K. Lewin, Some Social Psychological Differences Between the United States and Germany, *Character and Personality*, 4 (1936), 265–293; K. Lewin, Field Theory and Experiment in Social Psychology: Concepts and Methods, *American Journal of Sociology*, 44 (1939), 868–97.

[4] K. Lewin, R. Lippitt, and R. K. White, Patterns of Aggressive Behavior in Experimentally Created 'Social Climates,' *Journal of Social Psychology*, 10 (1939), 271–99; R. Lippitt, An Experimental Study of Authoritarian and Democratic Group Atmospheres, *Studies in Topological and Vector Psychology I, University of Iowa Studies in Child Welfare*, no. 16 (1940); R. Lippitt, Field Theory and Experiment in Social Psychology: Authoritarian and Democratic Group Atmospheres, *American Journal of Sociology*, 45 (1939), 26–49. For shorter summaries, see R. Lippitt and R. K. White, The 'Social Climate' of Children's Groups, in R. Barker, J. Kounin, and H. Wright, *Child Development and Behavior* (New York, 1943); and R. Lippitt and R. K. White, An Experimental Study of Leadership and Group Life, in T. M. Newcomb and E. L. Hartley (eds.), *Readings in Social Psychology* (New York, 1947).

[5] See K. Lewin, The Research Center for Group Dynamics at Massachusetts Institute of Technology, *Sociometry*, 2 (1945), 126–136.

going a continual process of change and development. On the theoretical side, the aim is to develop a conceptual framework which will be adequate for the explanation and prediction of group phenomena. On the methodological side, it is necessary to perfect techniques of observation, recording, and content analysis, which will yield information about social interaction. In all of this work only one assumption is added to the usual assumptions made in psychological experimentation: that the behavior of groups, and of individuals in groups, is predictable and measurable.

Thus, group dynamics deals with new content, and, of necessity, new theories and methods are being developed. This does not mean, however, as Professor Gunderson implies, that the research workers in the field feel that they have 'discovered' a new method for the application of science to the process of human relations; or that there is a magic formula in the 'science of group dynamics' which exempts it from the rigors of the controlled laboratory situation. There is nothing magic, nothing special or world-shaking in group dynamics. The contributions of this field have not depended on magic and novelty at all; on the contrary, the real value of group dynamics lies in the fact that the same old traditional scientific method is applied to problems to which it has not been before applied. Of course, the work is just beginning. A scientific approach to group behavior is not something that can be 'discovered,' but something that has to be worked at: techniques have to be invented and refined; theories have to be developed, and deductions from these theories tested in the experimental laboratory; field studies have to be undertaken in

order to verify experimental findings in real-life situations, and find new hypotheses. This is the spirit with which the workers in group dynamics approach their research.[6] To be sure, some of the early work is inadequate in certain respects; it represents, after all, the first efforts in an entirely new area. The more recent work is methodologically and theoretically quite sound. In all of this work, however, the objective is clearly one of developing scientific knowledge about groups.

In order to give the reader an idea about the kinds of studies that are done in this field, I shall give a brief description of an experiment by Alex Bavelas.[7] This experiment is a field experiment—i.e., it is conducted in a real-life situation, in this particular case in an industrial plant. Because of practical limitations, field experiments are not as well controlled, nor as theoretically oriented as laboratory experiments. Their main value lies in the fact that they are conducted in a naturalistic setting, and are therefore a good source of hypotheses for further investigation in the laboratory. I have chosen to describe this study rather than a laboratory experiment (of which a number of good examples are available), because it is simple and straight-

---

[6] For example, Lippitt writes: 'All these studies [on group functioning and productivity] are part of an exploration of the degree to which experimental methodology at various levels of refinement can be used to uncover the laws of behavior of groups, and individuals in groups. The problems, possibilities, and limitations of experimental manipulation of group life variables seem to us of crucial concern.' R. Lippitt, A Program of Experimentation on Group Functioning and Group Productivity, in W. Dennis, *Current Trends in Social Psychology* (Pittsburgh, 1948), 14.

[7] See *Ibid.*, 20–22; and N.R.F. Maier, *Psychology in Industry* (Boston, 1946), 264–266.

forward, and has direct practical applications.

Bavelas studied the effects of group decisions on workers' productivity. He had an experimental and a control group in an industry which used piece-rate methods of pay. In the experimental group, small work teams met with a skilled discussion leader for three weekly meetings. They discussed work problems, and finally decided on an increased production goal. In the control group, a similar procedure was followed: work teams met with the discussion leader, discussed their problems, and received the same kind of treatment as the experimental group. They differed only in that they made no group decision on production goals. Instead, the leader requested them to reach a certain level of productivity. The results show that the experimental group increased considerably in productivity, even though the workers in this group were already operating at top level for the plant. (Standard rate of production for the plant was *60 units* per hour; workers in the experimental group averaged *74 units,* but went up to an average of *87 units* after the group decision to set a higher production goal.) The control group showed no consistent increase in productivity as a result of the group meetings. Whatever changes did occur were only temporary, as compared to the experimental group which maintained its high level of productivity for at least several months. The experiment shows, then, that group decision about an increased production goal can lead to lasting changes in productivity. We do not know what the exact process is whereby these effects are achieved, but we do know that they are connected with the group decision, since all other factors are controlled in the experiment.

Bavelas' experiment is one of many studies done in group dynamics. [Dr. Kelman at this point illustrates field and laboratory experimental studies of eight aspects of group behavior.]

It is true that much of the work on which we would want to base our judgment of group dynamics is still unpublished. That may explain in part why Professor Gunderson mentions only three of the items which I have listed, and does not refer to a single experimental study; and why he concludes that 'Lewin's topological psychology exempts them from the rigors of the controlled laboratory situation.' I hope I have shown that in group dynamics there *is* experimental research, which follows the traditional lines of slow accumulation of knowledge, typical of all scientific endeavor; and which makes no claim to magic formulae and special dispensations from scientific rigor.

There is also an applied field of group dynamics, with which the readers of this journal are probably more familiar. It is characterized by a definite philosophy about group life, and a set of more or less specific techniques. I shall not review the principles in this field or the work that has been done in it (such as the Bethel laboratory to which Gunderson refers). But it should be clear that this represents an approach to practical problems, not a theory or science of group behavior.

Applied group dynamics has derived its inspirations from many sources. It has been influenced by recent developments in social group work, group psychotherapy, Moreno's sociodrama and psychodrama, progressive education, discussion techniques, industrial relations, personnel training. Theoretical and experimental work in group dynamics represents only one of a number of areas that have exerted an influence on practical applications.

Theoretical group dynamics has influenced the development of certain general principles of applied group dynamics, has helped practitioners to focus on certain problems, and has added to the over-all understanding of group process. It has not been used in a rigorous way in the development of techniques for group functioning, or in the use of such techniques in any specific situation. This kind of ideal relationship between theory and application, in which exact predictions about the effects of given actions are made in terms of theoretical laws, is impossible at the present stage of theoretical development. This does not, by any means, invalidate applied group dynamics, which is, after all, an approach to *practical* problems, and should be judged by different standards than a scientific system. The solution of practical problems cannot wait until a theory is fully developed. What is more, even if we had a complete theory, the evaluation of a practical approach is not only based on its conformity to this theory, but also entails references to practical experience and to ethical values. I feel, therefore, that we should not reject applied group dynamics just because it is not completely scientific. And *certainly* we should not reject the theoretical and experimental work in group dynamics—as Gunderson does —just because some of its applications are not completely scientific: we can draw no conclusions about the research in group dynamics by looking merely at its applications.

The confusion between theoretical and applied group dynamics has, at least in part, been fostered by Lewin and some of his students. Concerned about many pressing social problems, such as racial prejudice and the conduct of the war, Lewin tried to build theories which would be directly relevant to these problems, and to do action-oriented research. This tradition is carried on by Lippitt and other leaders of group dynamics. Their position is certainly valid and commendable. But, in their desire to integrate action and research, they have often overlooked and minimized the differences between the two. No matter how much we want to unite the two, their demands are different and not always compatible, and we should always know which is our primary interest in any given project. The failure to make this distinction is at least in part responsible for the confusion between theoretical and applied group dynamics, and for the difficulty in finding meaningful criteria by which to evaluate the field.

This confusion encourages the kind of practices that Gunderson justly deplores: the claim of scientific validity, the ritualism, the display of jargon. The responsible leaders of group dynamics know that their field is not a panacea, and agree that this kind of distortion is unhealthy. But, even though they are very well aware of the differences between scientific generalizations and value judgments, they do not always make that explicit. It is not surprising, therefore, that some of their followers are unable to discriminate between the scientific and the non-scientific in group dynamics. These followers give the stamp of science to every little technique that has been developed, and to every aspect of their ideology. Then they proceed to convert it into ritual and dogma without realizing that that is incompatible with the slow and cautious accumulation of knowledge which is the mark of science. Of course, the fact that such abuses occur on occasion does not invalidate the real scientific work that is done in the field, nor, for that matter, does it invalidate the applications.

I agree with Gunderson that this type of 'premature proclamations about the "science of human relations"' will not contribute anything. But, I believe that *premature criticisms* are at least equally harmful. In passing judgment on group dynamics, we must not only distinguish clearly between theory and application, and take account of the experimental literature, but also understand the problems involved in developing a scientific approach to group behavior. The aim of science is to arrive at general principles; precision of methods is only a means towards that end. In an area as complex and as new as group behavior, the scientific thing to do is to use the best methods available for the verification of general principles; and, of course, to work continually on methodological improvements. To reject methods because they are imperfect is to reject a scientific approach.

The research workers in group dynamics should be encouraged because they have chosen a difficult and a socially significant area of research. Their aim is to arrive at scientific laws of group behavior, by using scientific method. As scientists, they can promise no miracles, nor can they be accused of breaking such promises: group dynamics is neither a hope, nor a hoax.

✧✧✧✧✧✧✧✧✧✧✧✧✧✧✧✧✧✧✧✧✧✧ GROUP DYNAMICS AND THE INDIVIDUAL

Dorwin Cartwright and Ronald Lippitt

How should we think of the relation between individuals and groups? Few questions have stirred up so many issues of metaphysics, epistemology, and ethics. Do groups have the same reality as individuals? If so, what are the properties of groups? Can groups learn, have goals, be frustrated, develop, regress, begin and end? Or are these characteristics strictly attributable only to individuals? If groups exist, are they good or bad? How *should* an individual behave with respect to groups? How *should* groups treat their individual members? Such questions have puzzled man from the earliest days of recorded history.

In our present era of "behavioral science" we like to think that we can be "scientific" and proceed to study human behavior without having to take sides on these problems of speculative

From Dorwin Cartwright and Ronald Lippitt, "Group Dynamics and the Individual," International Journal of Psychotherapy, *Vol. 7, No. 1, January 1957, pp. 86–102. Used by permission.*

philosophy. Invariably, however, we are guided by certain assumptions, stated explicitly or not, about the reality or irreality of groups, about their observability, and about their good or bad value.

Usually these preconceptions are integral parts of one's personal and scientific philosophy, and it is often hard to tell how much they derive from emotionally toned personal experiences with other people and how much from coldly rational and "scientific" considerations. In view of the fervor with which they are usually defended, one might suspect that most have a small basis at least in personally significant experiences. These preconceptions, moreover, have a tendency to assume a homogeneous polarization—either positive or negative.

Consider first the completely negative view. It consists of two major assertions: first, groups don't really exist. They are a product of distorted thought processes (often called "abstractions"). In fact, social prejudice consists precisely in acting as if groups, rather than individuals, were real. Second, groups are bad. They demand blind loyalty, they make individuals regress, they reduce man to the lowest common denominator, and they produce what *Fortune* magazine has immortalized as "group-think."

In contrast to this completely negative conception of groups, there is the completely positive one. This syndrome, too, consists of two major assertions: first, groups really do exist. Their reality is demonstrated by the difference it makes to an individual whether he is accepted or rejected by a group and whether he is part of a healthy or sick group. Second, groups are good. They satisfy deep-seated needs of individuals for affiliation, affection, recognition, and self-esteem; they stimulate individuals to moral heights of altruism, loyalty, and self-sacrifice; they provide a means, through cooperative interaction, by which man can accomplish things unattainable through individual enterprise.

This completely positive preconception is the one attributed most commonly, it seems, to the so-called "group dynamics movement." Group dynamicists, it is said, have not only *reified* the group but also *idealized* it. They believe that everything should be done by and in groups—individual responsibility is bad, man-to-man supervision is bad, individual problem-solving is bad, and even individual therapy is bad. The only good things are committee meetings, group decisions, group problem-solving, and group therapy. "If you don't hold the group in such high affection," we were once asked, "why do you call your research organization the Research Center FOR Group Dynamics? And, if you are *for* groups and group dynamics, mustn't you therefore be *against* individuality, individual responsibility, and self-determination?"

Five Propositions About Groups

This assumption that individuals and groups must necessarily have incompatible interests is made so frequently in one guise or another that it requires closer examination. Toward this end we propose five related assertions about individuals, groups, and group dynamics, which are intended to challenge the belief that individuals and groups must necessarily have incompatible, or for that matter, compatible interests.

1. Groups do exist; they must be dealt with by any man of practical af-

fairs, or indeed by any child, and they must enter into any adequate account of human behavior. Most infants are born into a specific group. Little Johnny may be a welcome or unwelcome addition to the group. His presence may produce profound changes in the structure of the group and conseqently in the feelings, attitudes, and behavior of various group members. He may create a triangle where none existed before or he may break up one which has existed. His development and adjustment for years to come may be deeply influenced by the nature of the group he enters and by his particular position in it—whether, for example, he is a first or second child (a personal property which has no meaning apart from its reference to a specific group).

There is a wealth of research whose findings can be satisfactorily interpreted only by assuming the reality of groups. Recall the experiment of Lewin, Lippitt, and White (15) in which the level of aggression of an individual was shown to depend upon the social atmosphere and structure of the group he is in and not merely upon such personal traits as aggressiveness. By now there can be little question about the kinds of results reported from the Western Electric study (18) which make it clear that groups develop norms for the behavior of their members with the result that "good" group members adopt these norms as their *personal* values. Nor can one ignore the dramatic evidence of Lewin, Bavelas, and others (14) which shows that group decisions may produce changes in individual behavior much larger than those customarily found to result from attempts to modify the behavior of individuals *as* isolated individuals.

2. Groups are inevitable and ubiquitous. The biological nature of man, his capacity to use language, and the nature of his environment which has been built into its present form over thousands of years require that man exist in groups. This is not to say that groups must maintain the properties they now display, but we cannot conceive of a collection of human beings living in geographical proximity under conditions where it would be correct to assert that no groups exist and that there is no such thing as group membership.

3. Groups mobilize powerful forces which produce effects of the utmost importance to individuals. Consider two examples from rather different research settings. Seashore (22) has recently published an analysis of data from 5,871 employees of a large manufacturing company. An index of group cohesiveness, developed for each of 228 work groups, permitted a comparison of members working in high and in low cohesive groups. Here is one of his major findings: "Members of high cohesive groups exhibit less anxiety than members of low cohesive groups, using as measures of anxiety: (a) feeling 'jumpy' or 'nervous,' (b) feeling under pressure to achieve higher productivity (with actual productivity held constant), and (c) feeling a lack of support from the company" (p. 98). Seashore suggests two reasons for the relation between group cohesiveness and individual anxiety. "(1) that the cohesive group provides effective support for the individual in his encounters with anxiety-provoking aspects of his environment, thus allaying anxiety, and (2) that group membership offers direct satisfaction, and this satisfaction in membership has a generalized effect of anxiety-reduction" (p. 13).

Perhaps a more dramatic account of the powerful forces generated in groups can be derived from the publication by Stanton and Schwartz (24) of their studies of a mental hospital. They report, for example, how a patient may be thrown into an extreme state of excitement by disagreements between two staff members over the patient's care. Thus, two doctors may disagree about whether a female patient should be moved to another ward. As the disagreement progresses, the doctors may stop communicating relevant information to one another and start lining up allies in the medical and nursing staff. The patient, meanwhile, becomes increasingly restless until, at the height of the doctors' disagreement, she is in an acute state of excitement and must be secluded, put under sedation, and given special supervision. Presumably, successful efforts to improve the interpersonal relations and communications among members of the staff would improve the mental condition of such a patient.

In general, it is clear that events occurring in a group may have repercussions on members who are not directly involved in these events. A person's position in a group, moreover, may affect the way others behave toward him and such personal qualities as his levels of aspiration and self-esteem. Group membership itself may be a prized possession or an oppressive burden; tragedies of major proportions have resulted from the exclusion of individuals from groups, and equally profound consequences have stemmed from enforced membership in groups.

4. Groups may produce both good and bad consequences. The view that groups are completely good and the view that they are completely bad are both based on convincing evidence. *The only fault with either is its one-sidedness.* Research motivated by one or the other is likely to focus on different phenomena. As an antidote to such one-sidedness it is a good practice to ask research questions in pairs, one stressing positive aspects and one negative: What are the factors producing conformity? *and* what are the factors producing nonconformity? What brings about a breakdown in communication? *and* what stimulates or maintains effective communication? An exclusive focus on pathologies or upon positive criteria leads to a seriously incomplete picture.

5. A correct understanding of group dynamics permits the possibility that desirable consequences from groups can be deliberately enhanced. Through a knowledge of group dynamics, groups can be made to serve better ends, for knowledge gives power to modify human beings and human behavior. At the same time, recognition of this fact produces some of the deepest conflicts within the behavioral scientists, for it raises the whole problem of social manipulation. Society must not close its eyes to Orwell's horrible picture of life in 1984, but it cannot accept the alternative that in ignorance there is safety.

To recapitulate our argument: groups exist; they are inevitable and ubiquitous; they mobilize powerful forces having profound effects upon individuals; these effects may be good or bad; and through a knowledge of group dynamics there lies the possibility of maximizing their good value.

A Dilemma

Many thoughtful people today are alarmed over one feature of groups: the pressure toward conformity experienced by group members. Indeed, this single "bad" aspect is often taken as evidence that groups are bad in general. Let us examine the specific problem of conformity, then, in order to attain a better understanding of the general issue. Although contemporary concern is great, it is not new. More than one hundred years ago Alexis de Tocqueville wrote: "I know of no country in which there is so little independence of mind and real freedom of discussion as in America. . . . In America the majority raises formidable barriers around the liberty of opinion. . . . The master (majority) no longer says: 'You shall think as I do or you shall die'; but he says: 'You are free to think differently from me and to retain your life, your property, and all that you possess, but they will be useless to you, for you will never be chosen by your fellow citizens if you solicit their votes; and they will affect to scorn you if you ask for their esteem. You will remain among men, but you will be deprived of the rights of mankind. Your fellow creatures will shun you like an impure being; and even those who believe in your innocence will abandon you, lest they should be shunned in their turn'" (25, pp. 273–275).

Before too readily accepting such a view of groups as the whole story, let us invoke our dictum that research questions should be asked in pairs. Nearly everyone is convinced that individuals should not be blind conformers to group norms, that each group member should not be a carbon copy of every other member, but what is the other side of the coin? In considering why members of groups conform, perhaps we should also think of the consequences of the removal of individuals from group membership or the plight of the person who really does not belong to any group with clear-cut norms and values. The state

of anomie, described by Durkheim, is also common today. It seems as if people who have no effective participation in groups with clear and strong value systems either crack up (as in alcoholism or suicide) or they seek out groups which will demand conformity. In discussing this process, Talcott Parsons writes: "In such a situation it is not surprising that large numbers of people should . . . be attracted to movements which can offer them membership in a group with a vigorous esprit de corps with submission to some strong authority and rigid system of belief, the individual thus finding a measure of escape from painful perplexities or from a situation of anomie" (17, pp. 128–129).

The British anthropologist, Adam Curle, has stressed the same problem when he suggested that in our society we need not four, but five freedoms, the fifth being freedom from that neurotic anxiety which springs from a man's isolation from his fellows, and which, in turn, isolates him still further from them.

We seem, then, to face a dilemma: the individual needs social support for his values and social beliefs; he needs to be accepted as a valued member of some group which *he* values; failure to maintain such group membership produces anxiety and personal disorganization. But, on the other hand, group membership and group participation tend to cost the individual his individuality. If he is to receive support from others and, in turn, give support to others, he and they must hold in common some values and beliefs. Deviation from these undermines any possibility of group support and acceptance.

Is there an avenue of escape from this dilemma? Certainly, the issue is not as simple as we have described it. The need for social support for some values does not require conformity with respect to all values, beliefs, and behavior. Any individual is a member of several groups, and he may be a successful deviate in one while conforming to another (think of the visitor in a foreign country or of the psychologist at a convention of psychiatrists). Nor should the time dimension be ignored; a person may sustain his deviancy through a conviction that his fate is only temporary. These refinements of the issue are important and should be examined in great detail, but before we turn our attention to them, we must assert that we do *not* believe that the basic dilemma can be escaped. To avoid complete personal disorganization man must conform to at least a minimal set of values required for participation in the groups to which he belongs.

Pressures to Uniformity

Some better light may be cast on this problem if we refer to the findings of research on conformity. What do we know about the way it operates?

Cognitive processes. Modern psychological research on conformity reflects the many different currents of contemporary psychology, but the major direction has been largely determined by the classic experiment of Sherif (23) on the development of social norms in perceiving autokinetic movement and by the more recent study of Asch (1) of pressures to conformity in perceiving unambiguous visual stimuli.

What does this line of investigation tell us about conformity? What has it revealed, for instance, about the conditions that set up pressures to conformity? Answers to this question have taken several forms, but nearly all point out that social interaction would be impossible if some beliefs and perceptions were not commonly shared by the participants. Speaking of the origin of such cognitive pressures to uniformity among group members, Asch says: "The individual comes to experience a world that he shares with others. He perceives that the surroundings include him, as well as others, and that he is in the same relation to the surroundings as others. He notes that he, as well as others, is converging upon the same object and responding to its identical properties. Joint action and mutual understanding require this relation of intelligibility and structural simplicity. In these terms the 'pull' toward the group becomes understandable" (1, p. 484).

Consistent with this interpretation of the origin of pressures to uniformity in a perceptual or judgmental situation are the findings that the major variables influencing tendencies to uniformity are (a) the quality of the social evidence (particularly the degree of unanimity of announced perceptions and the subject's evaluation of the trustworthiness of the other's judgments), (b) the quality of the direct perceptual evidence (particularly the clarity or ambiguity of the stimuli), (c) the magnitude of the discrepancy between the social and the perceptual evidence, and (d) the individual's self-confidence in the situation (as indicated either by experimental manipulations designed to affect self-confidence or by personality measurements).

The research in this tradition has been productive, but it has emphasized the individual and his cognitive problems and has considered the individual apart from any concrete and meaningful group membership. Presumably any trustworthy people adequately equipped with eyes and ears could serve to generate pressures to conformity in the subject, regardless of his specific relations to them. The result of this emphasis has been to ignore certain essential aspects of the conformity problem. Let us document this assertion with two examples.

First, the origin of pressures to uniformity has been made to reside in the person whose conformity is being studied. Through eliminating experimentally any possibility that pressures might be exerted by others, it has been possible to study the conformity of people as if they existed in a world where they can see or hear others but not be reacted to by others. It is significant, indeed, that conformity does arise in the absence of direct attempts to bring it about. But this approach does not raise certain questions about the conditions which lead to *social* pressures to conformity. What makes some people try to get others to conform? What conditions lead to what forms of pressure on others to get them to conform? The concentration of attention on the conformer has diverted attention away from the others in the situation who may insist on conformity and make vigorous efforts to bring it about or who may not exert any pressure at all on deviates.

A second consequence of this emphasis has been to ignore the broader social meaning of conformity. Is the individual's personal need for a social validation of his beliefs the only reason for conforming? What does deviation do to a person's acceptance by others? What does it do to his ability to influence others? Or, from the group's point of view, are there reasons to insist on certain common values, beliefs, and behavior? These questions are not asked nor answered by an approach which limits itself to the cognitive problems of the individual.

Group processes. The group dynamics orientation toward conformity emphasizes a broader range of determinants. Not denying the importance of the cognitive situation, we want to look more closely at the nature of the individual's relation to particular groups with particular properties. In formulating hypotheses about the origin of pressures to uniformity, two basic sources have been stressed. These have been stated most clearly by Festinger and his co-workers (5), who propose that when differences of opinion arise within a group, pressures to uniformity will arise (a) if the validity or "reality" of the opinion depends upon agreement with the group (essentially the same point as Asch's), or (b) if locomotion toward a group goal will be facilitated by uniformity within the group.

This emphasis upon the group, rather than simply upon the individual, leads one to expect a broader set of consequences from pressures to uniformity. Pressures to uniformity are seen as establishing: (a) a tendency on the part of each group member to change his own opinion to conform to that of the other group members, (b) a tendency to try to change the opinions of others, and (c) a tendency to redefine the boundaries of the group so as to exclude those holding deviate opinions. The relative magnitudes of these tendencies will depend on other conditions which need to be specified.

This general conception of the nature of the processes that produce conformity emerged from two early field studies conducted at the Research Center for Group Dynamics. It was also influenced to a considerable extent by the previous work of Newcomb (16) in which he studied the formation and change of social attitudes in a college community. The first field study, reported by Festinger, Schachter, and Back (7), traced the formation of social groups in a new student housing project. As each group developed, it displayed its own standards for its members. The extent of conformity to the standards of a particular group was found to be related directly to the degree of cohesiveness of that group as measured by sociometric choices. Moreover, those individuals who deviated from their own group's norms received fewer sociometric choices than those who conformed. A process of rejection for nonconformity had apparently set in. The second field study, reported by Coch and French (3), observed similar processes. This study was conducted in a textile factory and was concerned with conformity to production standards set by groups of workers. Here an individual worker's reaction to new work methods was found to depend upon the standards of his group and, here too, rejection for deviation was observed.

The next phase of this research consisted of a series of experiments with groups created in the laboratory. It was hoped thereby to be able to disentangle the complexity of variables that might exist in any field setting in order to understand better the operation of each. These experiments have been reported in various publications by Festinger, Back, Gerard, Hymovitch, Kelley, Raven, Schachter, and Thibaut (2, 6, 8, 9, 11, 20). We shall not attempt to describe these studies in detail, but draw upon them and other research in an effort to summarize the major conclusions.

First, a great deal of evidence has been accumulated to support the hypothesis that pressures to uniformity will be greater the more members want to remain in the group. In more attractive or cohesive groups, members attempt more to influence others and are more willing to accept influence from others. Note that here pressures to conformity are high in the very conditions where satisfaction from group membership is also high.

Second, there is a close relation between attempts to change the deviate and tendencies to reject him. If persistent attempts to change the deviate fail to produce conformity, then communication appears to cease between the majority and the deviate, and rejection of the deviate sets in. These two processes, moreover, are more intense the more cohesive the group. One of the early studies which documented the process of rejection was conducted by Schachter (20) on college students. It has recently been replicated by Emerson (4) on high school students, who found essentially the some process at work, but he discovered that among his high school students efforts to influence others continued longer, there was a greater readiness on the part of the majority to change, and there was a lower level of rejection within a limited period of time. Yet another study, conducted in Holland, Sweden, France, Norway, Belgium, Germany, and England, found the same tendency to reject deviates in all of these countries. This study, reported by Schachter, et al. (21), is a landmark in cross-cultural research.

Third, there is the question of what determines whether or not pressures to uniformity will arise with respect to any particular opinion, attitude, and behavior. In most groups there are no pressures to uniformity concerning the color of necktie worn by the members. Differences of opinion about the age of the earth probably would not lead to rejection in a poker club, but they might do so in certain fundamentalist church groups. The concept of *relevance* seems to be required to account for such variations in pressures to uniformity. And, if we ask, "relevance for what?" we are forced again to look at the group and especially at the goals of the group.

Schachter (20) has demonstrated, for example, that deviation on a given issue will result much more readily in rejection when that issue is relevant to the group's goals than when it is irrelevant. And the principle of relevance seems to be necessary to account for the findings of a field study reported by Ross (19). Here attitudes of fraternity men toward restrictive admission policies were studied. Despite the fact that there was a consistent policy of exclusion in these fraternities, there was, surprisingly, little evidence for the existence of pressures toward uniformity of attitudes. When, however, a field experiment was conducted in which the distribution of actual opinions for each fraternity house was reported to a meeting of house members together with a discussion of the relevance of these opinions for fraternity policy, attitudes then tended to change to conform to the particular modal position of each house. Presumably the experimental treatment made uniformity of attitude instrumental to group locomotion where it had not been so before.

Sources of Heterogeneity

We have seen that pressures to uniformity are stronger the more cohesive the group. Shall we conclude from this that strong, need-satisfying, cohesive groups must always produce uniformity on matters that are important to the group? We believe not. We cannot, however, cite much convincing evidence since research has focused to date primarily upon the sources of pressures to uniformity and has ignored the conditions which produce heterogeneity. Without suggesting, then, that we can give final answers, let us indicate some of the possible sources of heterogeneity.

Group standards about uniformity. It is important, first, to make a distinction between conformity and uniformity. A group might have a value that everyone should be as different from everyone else as possible. Conformity to this value, then, would result not in uniformity of behavior but in non-uniformity. Such a situation often arises in therapy groups or training groups where it is possible to establish norms which place a high value upon "being different" and upon tolerating deviant behavior. Conformity to this value is presumably greater the more cohesive the group and the more it is seen as relevant to the group's objectives. Unfortunately, very little is known about the origin and operation of group standards about conformity itself. We doubt that the pressure to uniformity which arises from the need for "social reality" and for group locomotion can simply be obliterated by invoking a group standard of tolerance, but a closer look at such processes as those of group decision-making will be required before a deep understanding of this problem can be achieved.

Freedom to deviate. A rather different source of heterogeneity has been suggested by Kelley and Shapiro (12). They reason that the more an individual feels accepted by the other members of the group, the more ready he should be to deviate from the beliefs of the majority under conditions where objectively correct deviation would be in the group's best interest. They designed an experiment to test this hypothesis. The results, while not entirely clear because acceptance led to greater cohesiveness, tend to support this line of reasoning.

It has been suggested by some that those in positions of leadership are freer to deviate from group standards than are those of lesser status. Just the opposite conclusion has been drawn by others. Clearly, further research into group properties which generate freedom to deviate from majority pressures is needed.

Subgroup formation. Festinger and Thibaut (8) have shown that lower group-wide pressures to uniformity of opinion result when members of a group perceive that the group is composed of persons differing in interest and knowledge. Under these conditions subgroups may easily develop with a resulting heterogeneity within the group as a whole though with uniformity within each subgroup. This conclusion is consistent with Asch's (1) finding that the presence of a partner for a deviate greatly strengthens his tendency to be independent. One might suspect that such processes, though achieving temporarily a greater heterogeneity, would result in a schismatic subgroup conflict.

Positions and roles. A more integrative achievement of heterogeneity seems to arise through the process of role differentiation. Established groups are usually differentiated according to "positions" with special functions attached to each. The occupant of the position has certain behaviors prescribed for him by the others in the group. These role pescriptions differ, moreover, from one position to another, with the result that conformity to them produces heterogeneity within the group. A group function, which might otherwise be suppressed by pressures to uniformity, may be preserved by the establishment of a position whose responsibility is to perform the function.

Hall (10) has recently shown that social roles can be profitably conceived in the context of conformity to group pressures. He reasoned that pressures to uniformity of prescriptions concerning the behavior of the occupant of a position and pressures on the occupant to conform to these prescriptions should be greater the more cohesive the group. A study of the role of aircraft commander in bomber crews lends strong support to this conception.

In summary, it should be noted that in all but one of these suggested sources of heterogeneity we have assumed the process of conformity—to the norms of a subgroup, to a role, or to a group standard favoring heterogeneity. Even if the price of membership in a strong group be conformity, it need not follow that strong groups will suppress differences.

More Than One Group

Thus far our analysis has proceeded as though the individual were a member of only one group. Actually we recognize that he is, and has been, a member of many groups. In one of our current research projects we are finding that older adolescents can name from twenty to forty "important groups and persons that influence my opinions and behavior in decision situations." Indeed, some personality theorists hold that personality should be viewed as an "internal society" made up of representations of the diverse group relationships which the individual now has and has had. According to this view, each individual has a unique internal society and makes his own personal synthesis of the values and behavior preferences generated by these affiliations.

The various memberships of an individual may relate to one another in various ways and produce various consequences for the individual. A past group may exert internal pressures toward conformity which are in conflict with a present group. Two contemporaneous groups may have expectations for the person which are incompatible. Or an individual may hold a temporary membership (the situation of a foreign student, for example) and be faced with current conformity pressures which if accepted will make it difficult to readjust when returning to his more permanent memberships.

This constant source of influence from other memberships toward deviancy of every member of every group requires that each group take measures to preserve its integrity. It should be noted, however, that particular deviancy pressures associated with a given member may be creative or destructive when evaluated in terms of the integrity and productivity of the group, and conformity pressures from the group may be supportive or disruptive of the integrity of the individual.

Unfortunately there has been little systematic research on these aspects of multiple group membership. We can only indicate two sets of observations concerning (a) the intrapersonal processes resulting from multiple membership demands, and (b) the effects on group processes of the deviancy pressures which arise from the multiple membership status of individual members.

Marginal membership. Lewin (13), in his discussion of adolescence and of minority group membership, has analyzed some of the psychological effects on the person of being "between two groups" without a firm anchorage in either one. He says: "The transition from childhood to adulthood may be a rather sudden shift (for instance, in some of the primitive societies), or it may occur gradually in a setting where children and adults are not sharply separated groups. In the case of the so-called 'adolescent difficulties,' however, a third state of affairs is often prevalent: children and adults constitute two clearly defined groups; the adolescent does not wish any longer to belong to the children's group and, at the same time, knows that he is not really accepted in the adult group. He has a position similar to what is called in sociology the 'marginal man' . . . a person who stands on the boundary between two groups. He does not belong to either of them, or at least he is not sure of his belongingness in either of them" (p. 143). Lewin goes on to point out that there are characteristic maladjustive behavior patterns resulting from this unstable membership situation: high tension, shifts between extremes of behavior, high sensitivity, and rejection of low status members of both groups. This situation, rather than fostering strong individuality, makes belonging to closely knit, loyalty-demanding groups very attractive. Dependency and acceptance are a welcome relief. Probably most therapy groups have a number of members who are seeking relief from marginality.

Overlapping membership. There is quite a different type of situation where the person does have a firm anchorage in two or more groups but where the group standards are not fully compatible. Usually the actual conflict arises when the person is physically present in one group but realizes that he also belongs to other groups to which he will return in the near or distant future. In this sense, the child moves between his family group and his school group every day. The member of a therapy group has some sort of time perspective of "going back" to a variety of other groups between each meeting of the therapy group.

In their study of the adjustment of foreign students both in this country and after returning home, Watson and Lippitt (26) observed four different ways in which individuals cope with this problem of overlapping membership.

1. Some students solved the problem by "living in the present" at all times. When they were in the American culture all of their energy and attention was directed to being an acceptable member of this group. They avoided conflict within themselves by minimizing thought about and contact with the other group "back home." When they returned to the other group they used the same type of solution, quickly shifting behavior and ideas to fit back into the new present group. Their behavior appeared quite inconsistent, but it was a consistent approach to solving their problem of multiple membership.

2. Other individuals chose to keep their other membership the dominant one while in this country. They were defensive and rejective every time the present group seemed to promote values and to expect behavior which they felt might not be acceptable to the other group "back home." The strain of maintaining this orientation was relieved by turning every situation into a "black and white" comparison and adopting

a consistently rejective posture toward the present, inferior group. This way of adjusting required a considerable amount of distorting of present and past realities, but the return to the other group was relatively easy.

3. Others reacted in a sharply contrasting way by identifying wholeheartedly with the present group and by rejecting the standards of the other group as incorrect or inferior at the points of conflict. They were, of course, accepted by the present group, but when they returned home they met rejection or felt alienated from the standards of the group (even when they felt accepted).

4. Some few individuals seemed to achieve a more difficult but also more creative solution. They attempted to regard membership in both groups as desirable. In order to succeed in this effort, they had to be more realistic about perceiving the inconsistencies between the group expectations and to struggle to make balanced judgments about the strong and weak points of each group. Besides taking this more objective approach to evaluation, these persons worked on problems of how the strengths of one group might be interpreted and utilized by the other group. They were taking roles of creative deviancy in both groups, but attempting to make their contributions in such a way as to be accepted as loyal and productive members. They found ways of using each group membership as a resource for contributing to the welfare of the other group. Some members of each group were of course threatened by this readiness and ability to question the present modal ways of doing things in the group.

Thus it seems that the existence of multiple group memberships creates difficult problems both for the person and for the group. But there are also potentialities and supports for the development of creative individuality in this situation, and there are potentialities for group growth and achievement in the fact that the members of any group are also members of other groups with different standards.

Some Conclusions

Let us return now to the question raised at the beginning of this paper. How should we think of the relation between individuals and groups? If we accept the assumption that individuals and groups are both important social realities, we can then ask a pair of important questions. What kinds of effects do groups have on the emotional security and creative productivity of the individual? What kinds of effects do individuals have on the morale and creative productivity of the group? In answering these questions it is important to be alerted to both good and bad effects. Although the systematic evidence from research does not begin to provide full answers to these questions, we have found evidence which tends to support the following general statements.

Strong groups do exert strong influences on members toward conformity. These conformity pressures, however, may be directed toward uniformity of thinking and behavior, or they may foster heterogeneity.

Acceptance of these conformity pressures, toward uniformity or heterogeneity, may satisfy the emotional needs of some members and frustrate others. Similarly, it may support the potential creativity of some members and inhibit that of others.

From their experiences of multiple membership and their personal synthesis of these experiences, individuals do have opportunities to achieve significant bases of individuality.

Because each group is made up of members who are loyal members of other groups and who have unique individual interests, each group must continuously cope with deviancy tendencies of the members. These tendencies may represent a source of creative improvement in the life of the group or a source of destructive disruption.

The resolution of these conflicting interests does not seem to be the strengthening of individuals and the weakening of groups, or the strengthening of groups and the weakening of individuals, but rather a strengthening of both by qualitative improvements in the nature of interdependence between integrated individuals and cohesive groups.

Bibliography

1. Asch, S. E.: *Social Psychology*. New York: Prentice-Hall, 1952.
2. Back, K. W.: Influence Through Social Communication. *J. Abn. & Soc. Psychol.*, 46:9–23,1951.
3. Coch, L. and French, J. R. P.: Overcoming Resistance to Change. *Hum. Relat.*, 1:512–532, 1948.
4. Emerson, R. M.: Deviation and Rejection: An Experimental Replication. *Am. Sociol. Rev.*, 19:688–693, 1954.
5. Festinger, L.: Informal Social Communication. *Psychol. Rev.*, 57:271–292, 1950.
6. Festinger, L., Gerard, H. B., Hymovitch, B., Kelley, H. H., and Raven, B.: The Influence Process in the Presence of Extreme Deviates. *Hum. Relat.*, 5:327–346, 1952.
7. Festinger, L., Schachter, S., and Back, K.: *Social Pressures in Informal Groups*. New York: Harper, 1950.

8. FESTINGER, L., and THIBAUT, J.: Interpersonal Communication in Small Groups. *J. Abn. & Soc. Psychol., 46:* 92–99, 1951.

9. GERARD, H. B. The Effect of Different Dimensions of Disagreement on the Communication Process in Small Groups. *Hum. Relat., 6:*249–271, 1953.

10. HALL, R. L.: Social Influence on the Aircraft Commander's Role. *Am. Sociol. Rev., 20:*292–299, 1955.

11. KELLEY, H. H.: Communication in Experimentally Created Hierarchies. *Hum. Relat., 4:*39–56, 1951.

12. KELLEY, H. H. and SHAPIRO, M. M.: An Experiment on Conformity to Group Norms Where Conformity Is Detrimental to Group Achievement. *Am. Sociol. Rev., 19:*667–677, 1954.

13. LEWIN, K.: *Field Theory in Social Science.* New York: Harper, 1951.

14. LEWIN, K.: Studies in Group Decision. In: *Group Dynamics: Research and Theory,* ed. D. CARTWRIGHT and A. ZANDER. Evanston: Row, Peterson, 1953.

15. LEWIN, K., LIPPITT, R., and WHITE, R.: Patterns of Aggressive Behavior in Experimentally Created "Social Climates." *J. Soc. Psychol., 10:*271–299, 1939.

16. NEWCOMB, T. M.: *Personality and Social Change.* New York: Holt, Rinehart and Winston, 1943.

17. PARSONS, T.: *Essays in Sociological Theory.* (Rev. ed.) New York: Free Press of Glencoe, 1954.

18. ROETHLISBERGER, F. J. and DICKSON, W. J.: *Management and the Worker.* Cambridge: Harvard University Press, 1939.

19. ROSS, I.: Group Standards Concerning the Admission of Jews. *Soc. Prob., 2:*133–140, 1955.

20. SCHACHTER, S.: Deviation, Rejection, and Communication. *J. Abn. & Soc. Psychol., 46:*190–207, 1951.

21. SCHACHTER, S., et al.: Cross-cultural Experiments on Threat and Rejection. *Hum. Relat., 7:*403–439, 1954.

22. SEASHORE, S. E.: *Group Cohesiveness in the Industrial Group.* Ann Arbor: Institute for Social Research, 1954.

23. SHERIF, M.: *The Psychology of Social Norms.* New York: Harper, 1936.

24. STANTON, A. H. and SCHWARTZ, M. S.: *The Mental Hospital.* New York: Basic Books, 1954.

25. TOCQUEVILLE, A.: *Democracy in America,* Vol. 1. New York: Alfred A. Knopf, 1945 (original publication, 1835).

26. WATSON, J. and LIPPITT, R.: *Learning Across Cultures.* Ann Arbor: Institute for Social Research, 1955.

THE CONCEPTUAL STATUS OF GROUP DYNAMICS

Murray Horwitz

EXPERIMENTAL studies of behavior *in* face-to-face groups have a history dating back to the early 1920's and have been well summarized to 1935 in Dash-

Excerpted from Murray Horwitz, "The Conceptual Status of Group Dynamics," Review of Educational Research, Vol. 23, October 1953, pp. 309–328. Abridged and used by permission.

iell's review (31) in the *Handbook of Social Psychology*. A new and major development since the time of Dashiell's writing has been the experimental study of behavior *of* groups. Contributing greatly to this development has been the laying of the ghost of the "group mind" (1) and conceptual-methodological advances which have enabled workers to deal with properties of the group as a small social system (6, 21, 78).

Nonexperimental studies of groups under field conditions, especially by sociologically oriented researchers, have a longer history (131) and have also flourished during the present period (91, 128), but one may cite sociologists, such as Shils (115) and Swanson (123), in support of the view that the main impetus to increased rigor in theory construction and empirical testing has come from laboratory and field experimentation. For the interrelations among research methodologies used, see Miller (92).

These advances have forced into recognition a new class of variables, which greatly complicates the scientific task of understanding social behavior. Thus such earlier investigations as those by Shaw (113) and South (118) were concerned with comparing problem solving by individuals working alone and together. In more recent research, instead of asking how several people working together solve problems, investigators have tended first to specify such properties of the aggregate as its communication structure (10), degree of cohesiveness (45), power structure (83), and the like. The reformulated question then becomes one of how groups with given characteristics solve problems. A comprehensive review of the changed emphasis in research on group problem solving is given in an article by Kelley and Thibaut (68), to be included in the forthcoming *Hand-book of Social Psychology*, which is designed as a successor to the 1935 volume. Additionally, since the group comprises individuals with their own characteristics, a new set of problems has been raised concerning relations between group functioning and member characteristics. Finally, the group as a social system has been conceived as operating within a wider institutional or societal system (8, 57), and increasing consideration is being given to relations between the group and its external environment.

The complexities of those relationships among individual, group, and institutional systems are indicated by the nine cells of the matrix in Figure I. Community, societal, and cultural systems will be included here under the label "institutional," although it is clear that given institutions may be embedded within these wider systems. Since this article focuses on the face-to-face group, we bypass these distinctions to keep the matrix simple.

There are several features of this matrix which should be noted:

1. The three cells along the diagonal, A-A', B-B', C-C', represent the effects of variables within a given system on other variables within the *same* system and may thus be regarded as representing the internal dynamics of individual, group, or institutional systems, respectively.

2. When we consider how a larger system affects a smaller one, cells B-A' and C-B', the larger is to be regarded as the external environment within which the smaller is engaging in problem-solving activities. Cells B-A' and C-B' represent the effects of characteristics of the larger system in "steering" the goal-directed behavior of the smaller unit. Lewin's (77) topological geometry may be viewed as one attempt among others (130) to state the general conditions

FIGURE I

LEVELS AND INTERRELATIONS OF VARIABLES USED IN
EXPLAINING SOCIAL BEHAVIOR

		Effects of variables in the:		
Upon variables in the:		INDIVIDUAL SYSTEM	GROUP SYSTEM	INSTITUTIONAL SYSTEM
		A	B	C
Individual system	A′	*Variables* 1 2 • • • • • n	*Variables* 1 2 • • • • • n	*Variables* 1 2 • • • • • n
Group system	B′	*Variables* 1 2 • • • • • n	*Variables* 1 2 • • • • • n	*Variables* 1 2 • • • • • n
Institutional system	C′	*Variables* 1 2 • • • • • n	*Variables* 1 2 • • • • • n	*Variables* 1 2 • • • • • n

which must be taken into account when considering how the environment affects locomotion by a given system.

3. When we consider how a smaller system affects a larger one, cells A-B′ and B-C′, the smaller system is regarded as a part of the larger whole. Properties of the smaller system will affect the functioning of the larger unit, not as external environment, but by directly shaping the properties of the whole. Mathematical tools for systematically treating these part-whole relationships have yet to be developed, altho papers by Lewin (76) and Von Bertalanffy (127) may be noted as first steps in this direction.

Internal Dynamics of the Group (B-B′)

The types of concepts used in characterizing the group as a social system have been discussed by Cartwright and Zander (20), whose volume provides the only single overview of the field-theoretical approach to these problems. In this section, we describe some of these concepts and their empirical foundations. As successive concepts are discussed, we indicate interrelationships with preceding ones.

GROUP GOALS

If a group is engaged in problem solving, it may be conceived of as changing its situation, i.e., moving from one position in its environment to another (8, 112). A minimal definition of group goals appears to involve attributes similar to those ascribed to individual goals (77). A goal is a state of affairs in the external environment toward which activities may be directed, and which if reached terminates the sequence of activities (58). Just as with the individual, so group goals are dependent on possibilities existing in the environment and are influenced by environmental demands, e.g., institutional "imperatives" (34). The suggestion that, in addition, there exist internal processes in groups which influence selection of goals—in a fashion similar to the operation of need processes in individuals—is implicit in the notion of "hidden agenda," which has proved useful in work with therapy groups (15, 36) and training groups in human relations (17), and upon which Thelen and others (124) have begun quantitative research. The conception which seems to be involved is that certain disequilibria may occur in relationships among parts of a group, which then operate "homeostatically" to influence the selection of group goals. The question as to whether all groups have goals is implicit in Jennings' (64) broad distinction between psyche- and socio-groups, the latter being organized about group goals, the former about the satisfactions of associating with congenial people. It has been suggested that these are two ideal types defining a continuum (27). But it is difficult to see other than expository value in this typology, and why pure friendship groups, for example, are said to be without either implicit or explicit goals.

GROUP ACTIVITIES

In locomoting toward its goals, a group—more obviously than an individual—must provide for adequate working relationships or coordination among its subparts. Benne and Sheats (12) have analyzed functional roles which appear in discussion groups and have subsumed these under three broad functional categories pertaining to group locomotion, group maintenance, and personal goals of members. Heyns (55) has shown how functional roles tend to re-emerge in the group when a member who has performed a given role refrains from doing so by experimental prearrangement. Similar tendencies for members to "fill the breach" and perform apparently necessary, but neglected, functions were reported by Carter and Nixon (18), Gibb (48), and Kahn and Katz (65). Bales and Strodtbeck (7) found that experimental groups working on a standard problem go thru a regular sequence of activity phases, moving successively through functions which these investigators designated as orientation, evaluation, and control. Much research remains to be done, in which tasks and environmental conditions are systematically varied, before the interrelations between group goals (or task requirements) and group activities can be determined (33). The general point that group locomotion is adversely affected by failure of members to be steered by group goals is documented by Deutsch's study (32) of cooperative and competitive classroom groups, by Mintz's elicitation (94) of disorganization of group behavior under conditions of competition, and by the finding of Fouriezos, Hutt, and Guetzkow (44) that self-oriented behavior in conference groups is related to poor productivity.

GROUP STRUCTURES

Various types of structures can be identified for any given group. Among the most important of these are structures defined in terms of functional roles, communication, influence, and sociometric relationships, respectively.

Structure of functional roles. Where the type of task and environmental conditions are relatively enduring, one would expect a group to develop stability in functional roles as well. These roles may be regarded as positions which members can occupy in a group, and which given individuals come to occupy under the influence of expectations by others (98). Various suggestions have been made for the origin of expectations concerning roles. Barnard (8) discussed this in terms of a presumed recognition by members of the advantages of division of labor coupled with recognition of individual differences in abilities and temperament. Bales (6) suggested that common expectations develop in response to needs for individual security and, therefore, a predictable social environment.

Since much of the research dealing with the role structure of groups appears to have had its impetus in an interest in problems of "leadership," certain semantic unclarities in this term should be noted. In most current researches leadership is said to be exerted when individuals perform necessary group functions (83, 104, 119). This usage, according to which any or all members of a group are leaders when they are performing certain functional roles, is at variance with everyday usage, according to which we can designate a given person as *the* "leader" of the group. Following the former usage, Cattell (21) stated that leadership exists to the extent that properties of the group (syntality) are modified by the individual's presence. Krech and Crutchfield (70) asserted that the person is acting as a leader if he performs one or all of 14 group functions, ranging from planner to scapegoat. Redl (104), working in the psychoanalytic framework, listed a different set of leadership functions which center about group formation, maintenance, and disruption.

Due perhaps to the persisting effects of the popular meaning of leadership, many of the studies in this area appear to have been concerned with comparing group structures which concentrate important group functions in one person versus structures which distribute these functions more or less widely among various members. Bavelas (10) found that in five-person experimental groups, concentration of leadership functions produced greater group locomotion, but lower morale. Kahn and Katz (65) found with industrial work groups that supervisors of high-producing units tended to concentrate several key functions in their own hands, but to delegate certain other responsibilities and to encourage shared decisions. A number of studies conducted in other settings have found in general that a wide distribution of functions results in greater productivity (26, 74, 83). However, Maier and Solem (87), in studying what might be regarded as the limiting conditions of concentration versus dispersion, reported that led groups produce better solutions to complex problems than leaderless ones, apparently because the leaders in their experimental groups encouraged the consideration of minority opinions. Cartwright and Zander (20) suggested that rather than asking how much concentration is optimal, the question should be formulated in terms of the effects produced by combining functions in certain ways under specified circumstances. The study by Carter and others (19) is interesting in that it indicated that certain functions fell "naturally" to a person who was presented to a group as its designated "leader." Designated leaders tended to engage in the functions of "analyzing the situation" and "initiating action," as well as in certain other functions which, however, varied with the differential requirements of three different types of group tasks.

Communication structure. A necessary condition for the coordination of functions within a group is the existence of communication among subparts, and for reasons similar to those which lead to the development of stable roles, it is to be expected that groups will tend to develop relatively well-defined channels of communication (8). Festinger (38) suggested that besides forces to communicate which derive from the group, individuals require support for their beliefs in "social reality," and will therefore initiate communications either to ascertain what others believe, or to change others' beliefs in the direction of their own. An experiment by Festinger and Thibaut (41) showed that in line with this hypothesis, communications tend to be directed to individuals who are perceived as deviating from the group norm. Bavelas (11) constructed a mathematical model for dealing with communication structures, which enables one to compare groups in terms of the distances between positions in the structure and to compare positions within the same structure on the basis of "relative centrality." A number of laboratory experiments reported by Bavelas (10) attested to the fruitfulness of this approach. The influence of flow of information through different types of communication structures upon the effectiveness of group activities has been examined by Leavitt (72). In addition, Leavitt reported data which showed that position in the communication structure will affect the emergence of leadership, i.e., the types of role functions which will be performed. Reverse effects, which have indicated that position in the role structure will influence position in the communication network, have likewise been found (61).

Power structure. A further condition of coordination within a group is that some control system exists whereby members can influence each other's behavior. "Power" is used here to indicate the ability of members to influence the behavior of other members or of the group. Sociological uses of the term are considered by Bierstedt (14). Lippitt and others (85) showed that even without prior discussion of the matter, members of children's groups evidenced a high degree of agreement in their ratings of relative power of group members. This research distinguished two modes by which influence can be exerted, direct influence and behavioral contagion, and examined relationships between position in the power structure and members' initiation of, or response to, either mode of influence. A theory propounded many years ago by Simmel (116), to the effect that the stable power structure for three-person groups is a coalition of one pair arrayed against the third member, was experimentally confirmed by Mills (93). The greater the size of the group, the more likely it is that some members will be dissatisfied with the group goal. Since the attainment of greater power implies greater influence in setting group goals, one would expect that the larger the group, the greater the tendency for coalitions to form. Thus Hare (54) found that conflicting subgroups arose more frequently in groups of larger membership.

Among other complexities which made for difficulty in studying power is the fact that various positions within the power structure acquire differential valence for members, so that there tends to be some sort of overlap between one's power position and one's status or prestige position. Several investigations have been concerned with the effects of such "power-status" structures on the development of communication structures. Back and others (5) noted a tendency for rumors affecting the welfare of an organization to be transmitted upward in the power hierarchy. Kelley (66) found that low-status persons in experimental groups tend to communicate upward, which behavior he interpreted as a substitute for actual upward movement in the hierarchy. Hurwitz, Zander, and Hymovitch (61) found that tendencies to communicate up or down appear to be strongly influenced by whether the content of the message protects or threatens existing power relationships. Gardner (47) and Jaques (63) reported similar effects in industrial situations.

Sociometric structure. Attractions and repulsions among individual members seem to occur universally within groups. While Moreno (95) and Jennings (64) have equated the pattern of such positive and negative choices with the group's structure, it seems clear that the sociometric structure is but one of the various types of structures which a group may possess (115). A number of researches have explored relationships between sociometric structure and other group properties. Festinger, Schachter, and Back (42) showed how a communication structure which developed in a housing project under the influence of geographical location of neighbors influenced in turn the structure of friendship choices. Homans (57) proposed that liking among individuals is directly related to frequency of interaction, and Bovard (16) made a similar interpretation concerning sociometric choices in classroom groups. However, as Festinger and Kelley (40) have shown, liking was inversely related to frequency of interaction when the interaction was unpleasant. That sociometric structure may operate in turn to influence the communication structure was illustrated in the study by Festinger and others (43), in which it was shown that people tended to direct communication to those they liked. Whether the type of group goal involved members in relationships of competition or cooperation was an influence on the pattern of sociometric choices in the previously cited experiment by Deutsch (32). Bales and Strodtbeck (7) indicated that positive or negative reactions to others were influenced by the particular activity phase in which the group was engaged.

The sociometric technic has enjoyed great popularity partly because it is so easy to use, and partly because it offers a convenient way of approaching fuller diagnosis of structural and other properties of groups. In practice, many users of the technique have failed to explore the bases of attraction and repulsion, or their interrelations with other group properties, following Moreno in treating sociometric choices as primary variables from which other group properties may be derived. However, sociometric methods need not be confined to positive- and negative-liking choices. They have been extended, for example, to studies of communication linkages in formal organizations (121). As a measurement device, the sociometric test has stimulated valuable work on problems of validity, reliability, construction of scores, and tests of significance (30, 37, 86), all of which bear on the general problem of dealing with structural properties of groups. A review of the methods available for handling such data has been given by Proctor and Loomis (103).

Group standards. In discussing functional roles, we referred to the process whereby expectations influence member behavior. Besides expectations which apply differentially to functional roles —and, it might be added, which apply to positions in other structures of the group (9)—group members appear to develop expectations or standards which apply to the behavior, attitudes, and beliefs of all members, irrespective of their roles. While sociologists and cultural anthropologists have documented the existense of uniformities of behavior and belief within different societies or cultures, studies, such as those by Newcomb (97) of political attitudes in a college community, by Roethlisberger and Dickson (107) of work behavior in industrial settings, and by Lazarsfeld, Berelson, and Gaudet (71), of voting behavior in a national election, have suggested that face-to-face groups are the immediate bearers of pressures upon individuals to conform to these wider standards. Functional explanations of the origins of group standards have been proposed in such terms as minimizing factional splits

(6), and enabling the development of a common frame of reference for efficient communication about group activities (8). As was shown by Schachter (110), standards did, in fact, appear to be more strongly enforced the more relevant they were to the group's goals and activities. Enforcement may take place by the threat of expelling deviant members from the group, but Asch (3) and Sherif (114) found that conformity may arise from individual needs as well.

A number of studies may be cited to illustrate relationships between group standards and other aspects of groups. Thus, in the study by Lippitt and others (85) and in Whyte's study (129) of street gangs, members who were high in the power hierarchy tended to be perceived as enforcers of group standards. However, where group standards ("traditions") and powerful leaders were in opposition, Merei (90) found that in an experiment with nursery-school groups the influence of the standards was greater than that of the leaders. The previously cited study by Kelley (66) showed that high-status persons are subjected to less pressure to conform to standards. And the study by Festinger and Thibaut (41) indicated influence of standards upon communication structure. Bovard (16) and Preston and Heintz (102) varied the functional roles of appointed leaders and found that these, and perhaps other concomitant changes in group properties, affected the influence of group standards over members.

Group cohesiveness. Up to this point we have described certain concepts which seem to be required in treating a group as a problem-solving system. Lewin (80) suggested that from the standpoint of the individual member, however, the group can be conceived as a region of the person's life space which the person may desire to enter or to leave. Following this view, "group cohesiveness" has been defined in terms of the attractiveness of belonging to the group, specifically as the resultant of all the forces which tend to move members into or out of a group or to restrain such movement (42). Gross and Martin (52) criticized this definition on several grounds, one of which is that it makes cohesiveness rest on individual rather than on group properties. However, as with the attractiveness of any region of the life space, the valence of a group depends both on the needs of the person and the perceived suitability of the group for satisfying these needs. Thus, it would appear more accurate to say that "cohesiveness" as a concept applies to a *relationship* between group properties and individual needs. Back (4) attempted to alter cohesiveness experimentally by varying the desirability of other members as associates (the sociometric structure), the desirability of the group goal, and the status of the given group with respect to other groups in its environment. All of these, it is clear, involve variations in group properties. Back found that whichever variation was used to increase the attractiveness of the group, effectiveness of group standards likewise increased, although communication characteristics differed with different bases of attraction.

Festinger (38) proposed a general relationship between cohesiveness and standards such that the pressures which the group can exert toward conformity are only as great as the strength of attractiveness that the group holds for a given member. The more attractive the group, the more the person will fear being rejected, and in the experiment by Schachter (110) it was demonstrated

that cohesive groups apply this sanction more readily than noncohesive ones. Examples of conditions which may increase forces toward group membership are the member's position in the power structure (66) and the presence of group goals involving cooperative relationships (32). Conditions increasing forces away from a group include the group's performing poorly with respect to its goals (45), failure of other members to accept the group goals (44), and the existence of barriers to communication (106).

Utilization of Concepts in Change Programs

The matrix presented at the beginning of this article described three types of systems: the individual, the group, the institution. Each of these, it was suggested, can be regarded as a problem-solving unit. Some of the functions necessary for problem-solving behavior of groups were described under the heading of internal dynamics of the group. It is intriguing to speculate that certain functions are necessary for the behavior of any problem-solving system (68). Problems of control and coordination of parts, for example, would appear to exist in the case of any functioning unit, whether individuals, groups, or institutions.

One further property of the matrix should be noted, which is of especial importance to practitioners interested in introducing programs of change within groups. The variables within and among systems are all interdependent in the sense that variation within any cell may affect variables in the same or other cells. Indeed, a given change may result in chains of significant effects running through several cells of the matrix. This may be illustrated by a consideration of possible consequences of introducing "action research" procedures (75) into a group or institution. As these procedures have been developed in the case of training groups (96) and community self-surveys (111) they entail the introduction of at least three functional roles: fact finding, feedback, and evaluation. Such a change in functional roles may produce effects within the power structure of the group, since feedback of information, for example, can be employed to weaken the influence of some member or subgroup (88). If evaluation is shared by the group, it enables wider participation in decision making and will result, presumably, in greater motivation on the part of individual members (111). The practice of fact finding so far as it concerns other groups in the environment may engender hostility toward the fact-finding group (101) and create problems of intergroup conflict, with possible consequences, as we have seen above, for group cohesiveness and communication. In terms of the matrix, these examples illustrate that introducing the roles required for "action research" may involve processes in cell B-B', cell B-A', and in the chain consisting of cells B-C', C-B'. In principle, therefore, changes in any variable within a system should be considered in terms of effects upon other variables within the same system, and upon variables in related systems as well.

Bibliography *

1. ALLPORT, FLOYD H. *Social Psychology*. Boston: Houghton Mifflin Co., 1924. 453 p.

3. ASCH, SOLOMON E. "Effects of Group

* References not pertinent to the excerpt have been omitted.

Pressure upon the Modification and Distortion of Judgments." *Groups, Leadership, and Men*. Pittsburgh, Pa.: Carnegie Press, 1951. p. 177–91.

4. BACK, KURT W. "Influence Through Social Communication." *Journal of Abnormal and Social Psychology* 46:9–23; January 1951.

5. BACK, KURT W., and OTHERS. "The Methodology of Studying Rumor Transmission." *Human Relations* 3:307–13; August 1950.

6. BALES, ROBERT F. *Interaction Process Analysis*. Cambridge, Mass.: Addison-Wesley Press, 1950. 203 p.

7. BALES, ROBERT F., and STRODTBECK, FRED L. "Phases in Group Problem-Solving." *Journal of Abnormal and Social Psychology* 46:485–95; October 1951.

8. BARNARD, CHESTER I. *The Functions of the Executive*. Cambridge, Mass.: Harvard University Press, 1938. 334 p.

9. BARNARD, CHESTER I. "Functions and Pathology of Status Systems in Formal Organizations." *Industry and Society*. New York: McGraw-Hill Book Co., 1946. Chapter 4, p. 46–83.

10. BAVELAS, ALEX. "Communication Patterns in Task-Oriented Groups." *The Policy Sciences*. Stanford, Calif.: Stanford University Press, 1951. Chapter 10, p. 193–202.

11. BAVELAS, ALEX. "A Mathematical Model for Group Structures." *Applied Anthropology* 7:16–30; Summer 1948.

12. BENNE, KENNETH D., and SHEATS, PAUL. "Functional Roles of Group Members." *Journal of Social Issues* 4:41–49; Spring 1948.

14. BIERSTEDT, ROBERT. "An Analysis of Social Power." *American Sociological Review* 15:730–36; December 1950.

15. BION, WILFRED R. "Experience in

Groups, I-VI." *Human Relations* 1:314–20, 487–96, August 1948. 2:13–22, January; 295–303, October 1949. 3:3–14, February; 395–402, November 1950.

16. BOVARD, EVERETT W., JR. "Group Structure and Perception." *Journal of Abnormal and Social Psychology* 46:398–405; July 1951.

17. BRADFORD, LELAND P. "The Case of the Hidden Agenda." *Adult Leadership* 1:3–7; September 1952.

18. CARTER, LAUNOR F., and NIXON, MARY. "An Investigation of the Relationship Between Four Criteria of Leadership Ability for Three Different Tasks." *Journal of Psychology* 27:245–61; January 1949.

19. CARTER, LAUNOR F., and OTHERS. "The Behavior of Leaders and Other Group Members." *Journal of Abnormal and Social Psychology* 46:589–95; October 1951.

20. CARTWRIGHT, DORWIN, and ZANDER, ALVIN, editors. *Group Dynamics: Research and Theory*. Evanston, Ill.: Row, Peterson & Co., 1953. 642 p.

21. CATTELL, RAYMOND B. "New Concepts for Measuring Leadership, in Terms of Group Syntality." *Human Relations* 4:161–84; May 1951.

26. COCH, LESTER, and FRENCH, JOHN R. P., JR. "Overcoming Resistance to Change." *Human Relations* 1:512–33; August 1948.

27. COFFEY, HUBERT S. "Socio and Psyche Group Process: Integrative Concepts." *Journal of Social Issues* 8:65–74; No. 2, 1952.

30. CRISWELL, JOAN H. "Sociometric Concepts in Personnel Administration." *Sociometry* 12:287–300; November 1949.

31. DASHIELL, JOHN F. "Experimental Studies of the Influence of Social Situations on the Behavior of Individual Human Adults." *Handbook of Social Psychology*. Worcester, Mass.: Clark University Press, 1935. Chapter 23, p. 1097–1158.

32. DEUTSCH, MORTON. "The Effects of Cooperation and Competition upon Group Process." *Human Relations* 2:129–52, April, 199 231, July 1919

33. DEUTSCH, MORTON. "Task Structure and Group Process." (Abstract) *American Psychologist* 6:324–25; July 1951.

34. DUBIN, ROBERT, editor. *Human Relations in Administration*. New York: Prentice-Hall, 1951. 573 p.

36. EZRIEL, HENRY A. "A Psychoanalytic Approach to Group Treatment." *British Journal of Medical Psychology* 23:59–74; September 1950.

37. FESTINGER, LEON. "The Analysis of Sociograms Using Matrix Algebra." *Human Relations* 2:153–58; April 1949.

38. FESTINGER, LEON. "Informal Social Communication." *Psychological Review* 57:271–82; September 1950.

40. FESTINGER, LEON, and KELLEY, HAROLD H. *Changing Attitudes Through Social Contact*. Ann Arbor, Mich.: University of Michigan, Research Center for Group Dynamics, Institute for Social Research, 1951. 83 p.

41. FESTINGER, LEON, and THIBAUT, JOHN. "Interpersonal Communication in Small Groups." *Journal of Abnormal and Social Psychology* 46:92–99; January 1951.

42. FESTINGER, LEON; SCHACHTER, STANLEY; and BACK, KURT. *Social Pressures in Informal Groups*. New York: Harper and Brothers, 1950. 240 p.

43. FESTINGER, LEON, and OTHERS. "A Study of Rumor: Its Origin and Spread." *Human Relations* 1:464–86; August 1948.

44. FOURIEZOS, NICHOLAS T.; HUTT, MAX L.; and GUETZKOW, HAROLD. "Measurements of Self-Oriented

Needs in Discussion Groups." *Journal of Abnormal and Social Psychology* 45:682–90; October 1950.

45. FRENCH, JOHN R. P., JR. "The Disruption and Cohesion of Groups." *Journal of Abnormal and Social Psychology* 36:361–77; July 1941.

46. GAGE, NATHANIEL L., and SUCI, GEORGE. "Social Perception and Teacher-Pupil Relationships." *Journal of Educational Psychology* 42:144–52; March 1951.

47. GARDNER, BURLEIGH B. *Human Relations in Industry.* Chicago: Richard D. Irwin, 1945. 307 p.

48. GIBB, CECIL A. "The Principles and Traits of Leadership." *Journal of Abnormal and Social Psychology* 42:267–84; July 1947.

52. GROSS, NEAL, and MARTIN, WILLIAM E. "On Group Cohesiveness." *American Journal of Sociology* 57:546–53; May 1952.

54. HARE, A. PAUL. "Interaction and Consensus in Different Sized Groups." *American Sociological Review* 17:261–67; June 1952.

55. HEYNS, ROGER W. "Effects of Variation in Leadership on Participant Behavior in Discussion Groups." Ann Arbor: University of Michigan, 1940. 249 p. (Ph.D. thesis)

57. HOMANS, GEORGE C. *The Human Group.* New York: Harcourt, Brace & World, Inc., 1950. 484 p.

58. HORWITZ, MURRAY. "The Recall of Interrupted Group Tasks: An Experimental Study of Individual Motivation in Relation to Group Goals. *Group Dynamics: Research and Theory.* Evanston, Ill.: Row, Peterson & Co., 1953. Chapter 25, p. 361–86.

61. HURWITZ, JACOB I.; ZANDER, ALVIN F.; and HYMOVITCH, BERNARD. "Some Effects of Power on the Relations among Group Members." *Group Dynamics: Research and Theory.* Evanston, Ill.: Row, Peterson & Co., 1953. Chapter 32, p. 483–93.

63. JAQUES, ELLIOTT. *The Changing Culture of a Factory.* London: Tavistock Publications, 1951. 341 p.

64. JENNINGS, HELEN H. *Leadership and Isolation.* Second edition. New York: Longmans, Green & Co., Inc., 1950. 349 p.

65. KAHN, ROBERT L., and KATZ, DANIEL. "Leadership Practices in Relation to Productivity and Morale." *Group Dynamics: Research and Theory.* Evanston, Ill.: Row, Peterson & Co., 1953. Chapter 41, p. 612–28.

66. KELLEY, HAROLD H. "Communication in Experimentally Created Hierarchies." *Human Relations* 4:39–56; February 1951.

67. KELLEY, HAROLD H. "Two Functions of Reference Groups." *Readings in Social Psychology.* Revised edition. New York: Holt, Rinehart and Winston, Inc., 1952. p. 410–14.

68. KELLEY, HAROLD H., and THIBAUT, JOHN W. *Experimental Studies of Group Problem Solving and Process.* New Haven, Conn.: Yale University, Department of Psychology, 1952. 126 p. (Mimeo.)

70. KRECH, DAVID, and CRUTCHFIELD, RICHARD S. *Theory and Problems of Social Psychology.* New York: McGraw-Hill Book Co., 1948. 639 p.

71. LAZARSFELD, PAUL F.; BERELSON, BERNARD; and GAUDET, HELEN. *The People's Choice.* New York: Duell, Sloan & Pearce, Inc., 1944. 198 p.

72. LEAVITT, HAROLD J. "Some Effects of Certain Communication Patterns on Group Performance." *Journal of Abnormal and Social Psychology* 46:38–50; January 1951.

74. LEVINE, JACOB, and BUTLER, JOHN.

"Lecture vs. Group Decision in Changing Behavior." *Journal of Applied Psychology* 36:29–33; February 1952.

75. LEWIN, KURT. "Action Research and Minority Problems." *Journal of Social Issues* 2:34–46; November 1946.

76. LEWIN, KURT. *Analysis of the Concepts Whole, Differentiation, and Unity.* University of Iowa Studies in Child Welfare, Vol. 18, No. 1. Iowa City: University of Iowa Press, 1941. p. 226–61.

77. LEWIN, KURT. *The Conceptual Representation and Measurement of Psychological Forces.* Durham, N.C.: Duke University Press, 1938. 247 p.

78. LEWIN, KURT. "Frontiers in Group Dynamics, II." *Human Relations* 1:143–53; November 1947.

79. LEWIN, KURT. "Group Decision and Social Change." *Readings in Social Psychology.* Revised edition. New York: Holt, Rinehart and Winston, Inc., 1952. p. 459–73.

80. LEWIN, KURT. "Psycho-Sociological Problems of a Minority Group." *Character and Personality* 3:175–87; March 1935.

83. LIPPITT, RONALD. *An Experimental Study of Authoritarian and Democratic Group Atmospheres.* University of Iowa Studies in Child Welfare, Vol. 16, No. 3. Iowa City: University of Iowa Press, 1940. p. 43–195.

85. LIPPITT, RONALD, and OTHERS. "The Dynamics of Power." *Group Dynamics: Research and Theory.* Evanston, Ill.: Row, Peterson & Co., 1953. Chapter 31, p. 462–81.

86. LUCE, DUNCAN R. "Connectivity and Generalized Cliques in Sociometric Group Structure." *Psychometrika* 15:169–90; June 1950.

87. MAIER, NORMAN R. F., and SOLEM, ALLEN R. "The Contribution of a Discussion Leader to the Quality of Group Thinking: The Effective Use of Minority Opinions." *Human Relations* 5:277–88; August 1952.

88. MANN, FLOYD C. "Changing Superior-Subordinate Relationships." *Journal of Social Issues* 7:56–63; No. 3, 1951.

90. MEREI, FERENC. "Group Leadership and Institutionalization." *Human Relations* 2:23–39; January 1949.

91. MERTON, ROBERT K., and KITT, ALICE S. "Contributions to the Theory of Reference Group Behavior." *Continuities in Social Research.* New York: The Free Press of Glencoe, Inc., 1950. Chapter 2, p. 40–105.

92. MILLER, JAMES G., editor. *Experiments in Social Process.* New York: McGraw-Hill Book Co., 1950. 205 p.

93. MILLS, THEODORE M. "Power Relations in Three-Person Groups." *Group Dynamics: Research and Theory.* Evanston, Ill.: Row, Peterson & Co., 1953. Chapter 29, p. 428–42.

94. MINTZ, ALEXANDER. "Nonadaptive Group Behavior." *Journal of Abnormal and Social Psychology* 46:150–215; April 1951.

95. MORENO, JACOB L. *Who Shall Survive?* Washington: Nervous and Mental Disease Publishing Co., 1934. 440 p.

96. NATIONAL TRAINING LABORATORY IN GROUP DEVELOPMENT. *Exploration in Human Relations Training: An Assessment of Experiences—1947–1953.* Washington D.C.: National Training Laboratory in Group Development (1201 Sixteenth Street, N. W.), 1953. 87 p.

97. NEWCOMB, THEODORE M. *Personality and Social Change.* New York:

Holt, Rinehart and Winston, Inc., 1943. 225 p.

98. NEWCOMB, THEODORE M. *Social Psychology*. New York: Holt, Rinehart and Winston, Inc., 1950. 690 p.

101. POLANSKY, NORMAN, and OTHERS. "Problems of Interpersonal Relations in Research on Groups." *Human Relations* 2:281–91; July 1949.

102. PRESTON, MALCOLM G., and HEINTZ, ROY K. "Effects of Participatory vs. Supervisory Leadership on Group Judgment." *Journal of Abnormal and Social Psychology* 44:345–55; July 1949.

103. PROCTOR, CHARLES H., and LOOMIS, CHARLES P. "Analysis of Sociometric Data." *Research Methods in Social Relations*. Vol. 2. New York: Holt, Rinehart and Winston, Inc., 1951. Chapter 17, p. 561–85.

104. REDL, FRITZ. "Group Emotion and Leadership." *Psychiatry* 5:573–96; November 1942.

106. RIECKEN, HENRY W. "Some Problems of Consensus Development." *Rural Sociology* 17:245–52; September 1952.

107. ROETHLISBERGER, FRITZ I., and DICKSON, WILLIAM J. *Management and the Worker*. Cambridge, Mass.: Harvard University Press, 1939. 615 p.

110. SCHACHTER, STANLEY. "Deviation, Rejection, and Communication." *Journal of Abnormal and Social Psychology* 46:190–207; April 1951.

111. SELLTIZ, CLAIRE, and WORMSER, MARGOT H., issue editors. "Community Self-Surveys: An Approach to Social Change." *Journal of Social Issues* 5:1–65; Spring 1949.

112. SHARTLE, CARROLL L. "Leadership and Executive Performance." *Personnel* 25:370–80; March 1949.

113. SHAW, MARJORIE E. "A Comparison of Individuals and Small Groups in the Rational Solution of Complex Problems." *American Journal of Psychology* 44:491–504; July 1952.

114. SHERIF, MUZAFER. "A Study of Some Social Factors in Perception." *Archives of Psychology* 27:1–60; July 1935.

115. SHILS, EDWARD A. "The Study of the Primary Group." *The Policy Sciences*. Stanford: Stanford University Press, 1951. Chapter 3, p. 44–69.

116. SIMMEL, GEORG. *The Sociology of Georg Simmel*. Translated by Kurt H. Wolff. New York: The Free Press of Glencoe, Inc., 1950. 445 p.

118. SOUTH, EARL B. "Some Psychological Aspects of Committee Work." *Journal of Applied Psychology* 11:348–368; 1927.

119. STOGDILL, RALPH M. "Leadership, Membership and Organization." *Psychological Bulletin* 47:1–14; January 1950.

121. STOGDILL, RALPH M., and SHARTLE, CARROLL L. "Methods for Determining Patterns of Leadership Behavior in Relation to Organization Structure and Objectives." *Journal of Applied Psychology* 32: 286–91; June 1948.

123. SWANSON, GUY E. "Some Problems of Laboratory Experiments with Small Populations." *American Sociological Review* 16:349–58; June 1951.

124. THELEN, HERBERT A., and OTHERS. *Methods for the Study of Interaction in Groups*. Technical Report, ONR Project NR 170–176. Chicago: University of Chicago, Departments of Education and Psychology, Human Dynamics Laboratory. February 1953 (Mimeo.)

127. VON BERTALANFFY, LUDWIG. "An Outline of General System Theory." *British Journal of the Philosophy of Science* 1:134–65; August 1950.

128. WHYTE, WILLIAM F. "Observational Field-Work Methods." *Research Methods in Social Relations*. Vol. 2. New York: Holt, Rinehart and Winston, Inc., 1951. Chapter 14, p. 493–513.

129. WHYTE, WILLIAM F. *Street Corner Society*. Chicago: University of Chicago Press, 1943. 284 p.

130. WIENER, NORBERT. *Cybernetics*. Cambridge, Mass.: Technology Press, 1948. 194 p.

131. WILSON, LOGAN. "Sociology of Groups." *Twentieth Century Sociology*. New York: Philosophical Library Inc. 1945. Chapter 7. p. 180–71.

✧✧✧✧✧✧✧✧✧✧✧✧✧✧✧✧✧ **A MODEL FOR ANALYZING SMALL GROUP PROPERTIES PERTINENT TO PLANNED CHANGE**

Gale Jensen and Thomas Parsons

A REVIEWER's task involves examining many studies, selecting and classifying the important ones, and then reporting them tersely, often with the effect that whatever substance and value they contain remains a secret to everyone but himself. A notable departure was the ingenious system formulated by Horwitz in "The Conceptual Status of Group Dynamics." In an attempt to preserve Horwitz' advance and to reinforce, if possible, the conceptual gains resulting from group research completed during the interim, we present a conceptual model as a meaningful way to relate theory and research.

A Model for Conceptualizing Group Phenomena in the Classroom

In Figure I, variables representing group structural properties are designated "S"; variables representing dynamics of functional events in group life are designated "D"; variables derived from properties of the group-goal region and of members' needs are designated "G."

In Figure II, studies are classified according to the way they manipulate, control, or hypothesize relationships among variables in the S, D, or G categories. Most of the studies examined could be classified according to the locus of the independent and dependent variables in one or more of the possible combinations of these categories. Figure II shows the three-by-three matrix achieved by cross-classifying the independent and the dependent variables in terms of the S, D, and G categories; it also shows the resulting nine basic types of research, as well as several types derived from more complex combinations.[1]

[1] Horwitz' scheme is similar, but independent and dependent variables are classified ac-

Excerpted from Gale Jensen and Thomas Parsons, "The Structure and Dynamics of Classroom Groups and Educational Systems," Review of Educational Research, Vol. 29, No. 4, 1959, pp. 344 and Figures I and II. Abridged and published by permission of the American Educational Research Association.

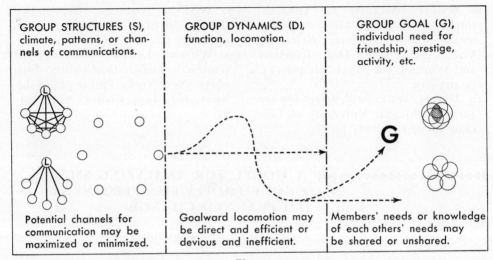

GROUP STRUCTURES (S), climate, patterns, or channels of communications.	GROUP DYNAMICS (D), function, locomotion.	GROUP GOAL (G), individual need for friendship, prestige, activity, etc.
Potential channels for communication may be maximized or minimized.	Goalward locomotion may be direct and efficient or devious and inefficient.	Members' needs or knowledge of each others' needs may be shared or unshared.

Fig 1

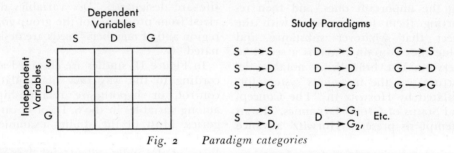

Fig. 2 *Paradigm categories*

cording to their level of complexity: A = individual variables, B = group variables, and C = institutional variables. His resulting nine-celled paradigm may readily be superimposed on the one proposed above, thus permitting the variables in any particular study to be identified not only in terms of their S, D, or G properties but also in terms of their level of complexity as well. Since all of the research reported here relates, in Horwitz' terminology, to the effects of the individual on the group (A-B'), the effects of the group on the individual (B-A'), or the effects of the institution on the group (C-B'), adding his designations would lead to undue complications, and they are not used in the body of this review.

✧✧✧✧✧✧✧✧✧✧✧✧✧✧✧✧✧✧✧ INTERPERSONAL UNDERWORLD

William C. Schutz

Aʟᴛʜᴏᴜɢʜ the businessman must spend a major part of his time dealing with other people, he has in the past had little help in overcoming the difficulties that inevitably arise when people get together. The terms which have been used to describe these problems—terms like "disciplinary problems," "human relations troubles," or the currently popular "communications difficulties"—have served only to hide the real difficulties, for they are descriptions of symptoms. The real causes must be sought at a deeper level; they lie in interpersonal relations.

In every meeting of two or more people two levels of interaction occur. One is the overt—the play that is apparently being played. The other is the covert—like a ballet going on in back of the performance on the interpersonal stage—a subtle struggle for attention and status, for control and influence, and for liking and warmth. This ballet influences the performance by pushing the overt players into unusual postures and making them say and do unusual things. Thus, the objective, hardheaded executive is overtly very resistant to a splendid idea suggested by the brash young fellow who

AUTHOR'S NOTE: For a fuller discussion of the points covered here, see my book, *FIRO: A Three-Dimensional Theory of Interpersonal Behavior*, New York: Holt, Rinehart and Winston, Inc., 1958.

may someday replace him. But this example is much too obvious. The ballet's effect on the actors is usually more subtle.

The importance of these covert factors can hardly be overestimated. The productivity of any particular group is profoundly influenced by them. One of the main functions of this article is to attempt to dispel the idea that strong interpersonal differences existing within a group setting can be effectively handled by ignoring them—as if by the magic of closing your eyes you could make problems go away. Rather, interpersonal problems must be understood and dealt with. If ignored, they are usually transformed so that they are not expressed directly as open hostility but find their expression through the task behavior of the group. Failure to allow these group processes to work in a direct fashion will decrease the group's productivity.

The types of behavior that result from interpersonal difficulties are various. In many cases it is difficult to recognize their connection with interpersonal relations in the work situation.

Behavioral Symptoms

Generally, interpersonal problems lead individuals to resist each other and each other's influence in various

Excerpted from William C. Schutz, "Interpersonal Underworld," Harvard Business Review, Vol. 36, No. 4, July–August 1958, pp. 123–135. Some footnotes omitted. Used by permission.

overt, but more often covert, ways. Each individual may oppose, delay, fail to support, or sabotage another. The mechanisms to be discussed here are largely covert, or unconscious; the individual does these things without being aware of his intention to resist or obstruct.

Common Issues

Certain problem situations that occur in group and interpersonal dealings with great frequency generate these symptoms. As an illustration of the nature of the problems and some of their vicissitudes, I shall now discuss three of them.

CONSENSUS FOR DECISION

In every group, sooner or later, a decision-making apparatus must be agreed on. Whether it be consensus, majority rule, unanimity, or any other method, there must be some *modus operandi* for the group to make decisions. By consensus I mean, here, that everyone in the group is agreed that a certain course of action is best for the group, regardless of whether or not he individually agrees with it. Ordinarily, if the group does not have consensus and a decision goes through, the group pays. For instance:

Let us suppose that a group, perhaps a committee, has gotten together with the task of deciding a particular issue. The issue has come to a vote, and the vote is fairly decisive, say six to two. The two people in the minority, however, do not really feel that they have had an opportunity to express their feelings about the issue. Although they are committed to go along with the decision, they have an inner reluctance to do so. This covert reluctance may manifest itself in any of the symptoms

already mentioned. Perhaps the most common symptom is a loss of interest, although this situation could be expected to give rise to any of them.

The question of consensus is central in decision making. In a deeper sense, consensus means that everyone in a group feels that the group understands his position and his feelings about it; and he feels, then, that the group should take a particular course of action even though he does not personally agree. If the individual is not allowed to voice his own feelings and reasons for voting against the particular issue, he will, at least unconsciously, resist the efficient functioning of the group from that point on. If consensus is not required, decisions can often be made more quickly (for example, by majority rule or by fiat), but delay will probably result, due to the unacknowledged members having various ways of resisting once the decision has been made and the action is undertaken.

The ability to detect a lack of consensus is, of course, a very important attribute for a group leader. A few rules of thumb might be of help here. The clue is that it is very difficult to find out whether there is a consensus unless each person is allowed to speak; for lack of disagreement does not necessarily indicate that the group has consensus. Frequently people simply are reluctant to raise their objections. However, if each member is asked separately whether or not he assents to the issue, the group leader can usually pick up objections:

He may be able to spot disagreement by noticing such things as changes in tone of voice. In one group the leader asked if everyone agreed on a suggested course of action. As he went around the room he got the following responses: *yes, yes, yes, yes, yes, okay.* This leader, being fairly astute, immediately began to question the man who had said *okay,* because this man apparently could not quite bring himself to be like the other members of the group with regard to this decision. This inability is usually a good indication of an objection. The individual is reluctant to object directly because of the weight of all the other members disagreeing with him.

After this man had been quizzed for a while, it became clear that he did have a strong objection. Once he was allowed to talk it out, he went along with the group and was quite willing to say *yes* and, in fact, to pitch in and work with the decision that was finally made.

Another good indicator of lack of consensus is any attempt by a member to postpone a decision by further discussion or by further action of some kind. Comments like, "What is it we are voting on?" or "Weren't we supposed to discuss something else first?" or "I have no objection to that, but . . ." all indicate that the individual is not yet ready to cast a positive vote for a given decision. He probably has an objection that ought to be brought out into the open and discussed.

Allowing the objector to raise his point for discussion is not just a hollow gesture. The objector will be more likely to go along with the final decision—or he may eventually carry the day because he reflects some objections that other people had but were not aware of. Whether the group actually changes its vote or not, it will be more likely to reach a correct decision. This opportunity for the group to discuss a previously covert factor is very important for its effectiveness.

AUTHORITY PROBLEM

Another group phenomenon that leads to reduced effectiveness concerns the relationship of the group members to the leader of the group. (The term *leader* will be used loosely to mean the person who is, in the eyes of the group members, supposed to head the group—usually a formal leader, a designated person who has a higher title.) It is the nature of such relationships that members of the group have ambivalent feelings toward the authority figure—both positive and negative feelings. The negative feelings can be particularly disturbing since it usually is hard for people to express such feelings directly, because their jobs may be in jeopardy or because they feel that they should not attack an authority figure.

Since the hostility must be expressed, however, they often transfer it to another member of the group. Some other member, usually one with characteristics similar to those disliked in the leader, will be attacked more than he realistically should be for his behavior in the group. He will be attacked not only for what he does, but also because the attack that the group would like to level toward the leader is displaced onto him. The term *scapegoat* is often used for this person. For example, if the group members are dissatisfied because the leader is not giving sufficient direction to the group, the dissatisfaction may be vented toward a silent or nonparticipating member, the member in the group who comes closest to having the characteristic of the leader which the group members do not like. For example:

In one marketing group the leader offered the group very little direction, far less than most members would have liked. Subsequently, everyone began to get very angry with one group member who did not say much and who occasionally missed meetings because of his other commitments. The group attacked him for his lack of interest and unwillingness to contribute to the group.

A key to what was really happening is found in the fact that he was actually quite interested and was contributing a great deal, thus making the attack somewhat undeserved; but significantly, the characteristics which angered the group members were precisely those that covertly irritated them about the leader. Apparently they displaced their aggression from the leader, whom they felt they could not attack directly, onto a group member who had similar attributes.

This same mechanism operates when the boss is too *authoritarian*. Somebody in the group who has similar tendencies will be severely attacked, again as a displacement of the attack they would like to level at the boss.

With regard to dealing with this phenomenon, perhaps the most useful thing to be said is that there are times when a leader, in order to allow a group to operate more effectively, must himself become the scapegoat. If he can absorb some of the hostility that is really meant for him or perhaps in some cases even absorb some of the hostility meant for other group members, he can be most useful in helping a group to function more effectively. Of course, in order to do this the leader must be aware that the hostility is not necessarily directed at him personally; it is just an inevitable consequence of group activity that hostility does arise. If he can absorb the hostility directly, it does not have to be deflected into the group where it is most destructive to the group and to the group's ability to fulfill its purposes. An important part of a leader's role is to be a scapegoat occasionally in order that the group may proceed and operate more effectively. This situation brings to mind an old saying, "A good king is one whose subjects prosper."

THE PROBLEM MEMBER

Another frequently occurring group difficulty is the presence of a problem member, one of the most difficult of all interpersonal problems for a group to deal with. Problem members are of two main types—the overactive member and the underactive member. Either can disrupt group functioning, and both are usually difficult to handle.

The overactive problem member dominates the group's attention far more than his abilities warrant. The difficulties arise partly because the apparent intensity of his feelings lead to a general reluctance of the group to hurt the individual while at the same time they cannot curtail his destructive activities. To illustrate what can happen in such a situation:

In one five-man group of military personnel working on a series of tactical problems, Mac immediately took over control of the group. Because he was reasonably competent and highly forceful, he went unchallenged for several meetings. The other group members were not very compatible, so they had a difficult time handling Mac. Gradually some members began losing interest in the group until one discussion of a very trivial topic, the postal rates from Washington to Chicago, came up in one of their rest periods. The exchange that followed was amazing in that Mac was attacked severely and at length by the other group members for his dogmatically stated opinion about postal rates. The group used this topic to vent their stored-up feelings toward Mac. By this time, however, the group had no resources to cope with these strong feelings, and it quickly disintegrated after the conflict.

The optimal solution to the problem represented by this member is to handle him in such a way that he can be retained in the group and his resources made use of and still not be allowed to obstruct the group's functioning:

Another group had this problem with Bob. But this group quickly deposed Bob and set up a leader of considerably less intellect but with superior coordinating abilities. For a short time after they had deposed Bob the group made sure he realized he was not going to run the group; then they gradually allowed him back into the group by paying more attention to his ideas. Finally, after about ten meetings, his ideas were highly influential and sought by the group, although he was not allowed to dominate. In this way the group took care of the problem presented by an overactive member and was still able to utilize his abilities. This is an ideal solution and the sign of a strong, compatible group.

Someone who will not become integrated into the group also poses a problem for the group. The lack of commitment of this member, perhaps even a lack of willingness to work, constitutes a serious group problem. One solution is to eject the member from the group. This is a solution only insofar as it removes the source of a difficulty; it does not allow the group to utilize the man's abilities. The problem member often serves a useful function by enabling other members to direct their hostility toward him, so that they do not have to deal with the real differences among themselves. Thus, it is not unusual that if a chronically negative member is absent, the group finds that it still has disagreements.

Framework for Behavior

Now that I have described examples of several interpersonal problem situations and various reactions to them, I shall present a brief outline of a theory of interpersonal behavior. In order to deal with interpersonal behavior it is necessary to have an understanding of the *general* principles of this behavior, since formulas for handling *specific* situations are of limited value at best. The following theory is by no means the only one extant in psychological literature, but it is offered as a possible framework for understanding phenomena of the type under discussion here.

INTERPERSONAL NEEDS

The basis for evolving this theory of interpersonal behavior is the individual's *fundamental interpersonal relations orientation* or, to abbreviate, FIRO. The basic assumption of this approach is that people need people. Every human being, because he lives in a society, must establish an equilibrium between himself and his human environment—just as he must establish an equilibrium between himself and the physical world. This social nature of man gives rise to certain interpersonal needs, which he must satisfy to some degree while avoiding threat to himself. Although each individual has different intensities of need and different mechanisms for handling them, people have three basic interpersonal needs in common:

The need for inclusion. This is the need to maintain a satisfactory relation between the self and other people with respect to interaction or belongingness. Some people like to be with other people all the time; they want to belong to organizations, to interact, to mingle. Other people seek much less contact; they prefer to be alone, to interact minimally, to stay out of groups, to maintain privacy.

If a continuum were to be drawn between these two extremes, every person could be placed at a point (or region) at which he feels most comfortable. Thus, to a certain degree each individual is trying to belong to a group, but he is also trying to maintain a certain amount of privacy. From the other point of view he wishes to some degree to have people initiate inter-action toward him through invitations and the like, and also wishes to some degree that people would leave him alone. For each dimension these two aspects may be distinguished: (1) the behavior he initiates toward others, his expressed behavior; and (2) the behavior he prefers others to ex-press toward him, his wanted behavior. This distinction will prove valuable in the discussion of compatibility.

The need for control. This is the need to maintain a satisfactory relation between oneself and other people with regard to power and influence. In other words, every individual has a need to control his situa-tion to some degree, so that his environ-ment can be predictable for him. Ordinarily this amounts to controlling other people, because other people are the main agents which threaten him and create an unpre-dictable and uncontrollable situation. This need for control varies from those who want to control their entire environment, including all the people around them, to those who want to control no one in any situation, no matter how appropriate con-trolling them would be.

Here, again, everyone varies as to the degree to which he wants to control others. In addition, everyone varies with respect to the degree to which he wants to be con-trolled by other people, from those who want to be completely controlled and are dependent on others for making decisions for them to those who want to be controlled under no conditions.

The need for affection. This is the need to maintain a satisfactory relation between the self and other people with regard to love and affection. In the business setting this need is seldom made overt. It takes the form of friendship. In essence, affection is a relationship between two people only, a dyadic relationship. At one extreme individuals like very close, personal relationships with each individ-ual they meet. At the other extreme are those who like their personal relationships to be quite impersonal and distant, perhaps friendly but not close and intimate.

Again, between these two extremes every-one has a level of intimacy which is most comfortable for him. From the other side, each individual prefers that others make overtures to him in a way that indicates a certain degree of closeness.

To clarify the various orientations in these three areas, EXHIBIT I presents the extreme positions taken on each of the dimensions. Everyone fits some-

EXTREME TYPES ON THE THREE INTERPERSONAL DIMENSIONS

Expressed behavior		*Dimension*	Wanted behavior	
EXTREME HIGH	EXTREME LOW		EXTREME HIGH	EXTREME LOW
OVERSOCIAL	UNDERSOCIAL	INCLUSION	SOCIAL-COMPLIANT	COUNTERSOCIAL
AUTOCRAT	ABDICRAT	CONTROL	SUBMISSIVE	REBELLIOUS
OVERPERSONAL	UNDERPERSONAL	AFFECTION	PERSONAL-COMPLIANT	COUNTERPERSONAL

Exhibit I

where between these two extremes, most of them in the middle.

Group Compatibility

This theory of interpersonal relations can be very useful to businessmen in determining the compatibility of the members of a group. If at the outset we can choose a group of people who can work together harmoniously, we shall go far toward avoiding situations where a group's efforts are wasted in interpersonal conflicts.

Our theoretical framework is designed to handle this problem. Suppose we consider in more detail the two aspects for each of the three interpersonal dimensions. One aspect is what we *do* with relation to other people;

everyone has some propensity, some preferred behavior, we can characterize each person by six scores: e^I, w^I, e^C, w^C, e^A, w^A.

In the course of my research I have developed a questionnaire, called FIRO-B (the "B" refers to *behavior*), comprising a check list of 54 statements designed to measure an individual's propensities in each of these six categories; a portion of it is shown in EXHIBIT III. The resulting scores for each need area can be plotted on a diagram, as in EXHIBIT IV.

TWO KINDS

Note that in EXHIBIT IV there are two diagonals, which may be used to

SCHEMA OF INTERPERSONAL BEHAVIORS

Expressed behavior	Dimension	Wanted behavior
I initiate interaction with people	INCLUSION	I want to be included
I control people	CONTROL	I want people to control me
I act close and personal toward people	AFFECTION	I want people to get close and personal to me

Exhibit II

let us call this "e" for *expressed* behavior. The second is what we *want* from other people, how we want them to act toward us; let us call this "w" for *wanted* behavior. Then we can use "e" and "w" to try to find out how people will relate to each other in the *inclusion* dimension ("I"), the *control* dimension ("C"), and the *affection* dimension ("A"), as shown schematically in EXHIBIT II.

If we make a ten-point scale, from zero to nine, and say that in each of the two aspects of the three dimensions

explain two different kinds of compatibility—"originator compatibility" (oK) and "interchange compatibility" (xK). Individuals can be located on these diagonals from their scores on FIRO-B.

In popular literature there are at least two well-known and apparently contradictory maxims relating to the bases of compatibility: "Opposites attract," and "Birds of a feather flock together." Considering the diagonals on EXHIBIT IV might aid us in coming to a sensible resolution of these maxims, since there seems to be some truth in each of them:

Originator diagonal. Let us take an example in the control dimension and consider the lower right to upper left line. The people who fall in the lower right quadrant are the ones who want to control others and do not want to be controlled themselves. These people can be called autocrat-rebels; they want to be the bosses and do not want anyone else to tell them what to do. In the upper left quadrant we have just the opposite. These are abdicrat-submissives; they want to be told what to do, and they do not want to control anyone else.

For smooth functioning it would appear that if we had one autocrat-rebel, we would not want another one, since they would both want to give orders and neither would want to take them. This is called *competitive* incompatibility. Also, if we had two abdicrat-submissives, a situation would be created wherein both people want someone to tell them what to do and neither wants to do the telling. This is called *apathetic* incompatibility. How-

---

NAME...

GROUP..

DATE...

MALE.............FEMALE.............

AGE...

FIRO-B

	I	C	A
e			
w			

Please place number of the answer that best applies to you in the box at the left of the statement. Please be as honest as you can.

1. I try to be with people.
   1. usually 2. often 3. sometimes 4. occasionally 5. rarely 6. never
2. I let other people decide what to do.
   1. usually 2. often 3. sometimes 4. occasionally 5. rarely 6. never
3. I join social groups.
   1. usually 2. often 3. sometimes 4. occasionally 5. rarely 6. never
4. I try to have close relationships with people.
   1. usually 2. often 3. sometimes 4. occasionally 5. rarely 6. never
5. I tend to join social organizations when I have an opportunity.
   1. usually 2. often 3. sometimes 4. occasionally 5. rarely 6. never

   other people strongly influence my actions.
   usually 2. often 3. sometimes 4. occasionally 5. rarely 6. never

   mal social activities.

23. I try to   3. sometimes 4. occasionally 5. rarely 6. never
    1. most   pe   th people.
    people   metimes
24. I let other people control my action   ionally 5. rarely 6. never
    1. most   2. many   3.
    people   people   peo
25. I act cool and distant with people.
    1. most   2. many   3. some   4. a few   5.   6. never
    people   people   people   people
26. I am easily led by people.
    1. most   2. many   3. some   4. a few   5. one or two 6. nobody
    people   people   people   people   people
27. I try to have close, personal relationships with people.
    1. most   2. many   3. some   4. a few   5. one or two 6. nobody
    people   people   people   people   people

© William C. Schutz 1957

Reproduction in whole or part permitted for any purpose of the United States Government

(See other side)

Exhibit III   Sample of questionnaire

ever, if we have one autocrat-rebel and one abdicrat-submissive, the relationship will probably be harmonious, since one person wants to give orders and the other wants to take them.

Interchange diagonal. Now, consider the other diagonal on the diagram. Let us take affection for an example this time. In the upper right quadrant are the people who express a lot of close personal behavior and want the same expressed to them. These are the people of "high interchange," and they can be called overpersonal-personal-compliants. They like an atmosphere in which there is a lot of affection; so, for instance, they would like a party better than a board of directors meeting. In the lower left quadrant are people of "low interchange," who like neither to give nor to receive affection. They can be called underpersonal-counterpersonals. They do not want anyone to get very close to them, nor do they want to get very close to anyone. They like their relations rather reserved, cool, and distant.

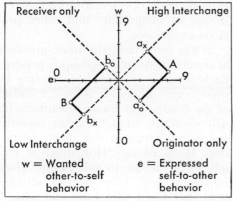

Exhibit IV   *Graphic representation of interpersonal dimensions*

Here the complementary idea of the originator diagonal—that opposites attract —does not apply; for, if one person likes to be very close and personal and the other person does not, they are going to threaten each other. One who likes to keep his relations reserved is not going to like

it when the other makes overtures; and, in the reverse direction, the one who wants very close relations is not going to be very happy if the other does not. So it seems reasonable that the situation would lead to harmony more readily if the people involved were close on this diagonal, unlike the situation on the originator diagonal.

In the inclusion dimension, again, it would be better if both interacting persons were very close to being either very high or very low on this diagonal so that one would not always want to be with people while the other wanted to stay home and read a book. Hence, on the interchange diagonal the "birds of a feather" maxim seems most appropriate; people should be similar in their values along this diagonal.

PREDICTABLE RELATIONS

To exemplify the working of the technique let us consider EXHIBIT IV for the control area:

From FIRO-B we learn that A has a score of 8 on e^C and 5 on w^C, while B has a score of 1 on e^C and 3 on w^C. These points are plotted on the diagram. Each score, for illustrative purposes, may be divided into two components, one on each diagonal. These components are represented by a_x and a_o and b_x and b_o on the diagram.

The measure of interchange compatibility (xK) of A and B is proportional to the distance between a_x and b_x. A smaller distance means a more similar orientation toward the amount of interchange of control that should exist in a relation. In the example, A believes that relations should involve a great deal of influence and control, while B's preference is for less structured, more laissez-faire relations. Their incompatibility in this regard is reflected in the relatively large distance between a_x and b_x.

Originator compatibility (oK) is proportional to the sum of a_o and b_o. Optimal originator compatibility occurs when one score is to the left of the midpoint of the diagonal and the other score is exactly the same distance to the right of the midpoint. In our example this is almost exactly true; thus A and B have high originator compatibility. A wishes to control others but not to be controlled, while B wishes to be controlled but not to control or influence others very much. Hence they complement each other.

Our conclusion then about this pair is the following: they disagree as to atmosphere they desire regarding mutual influence and control. A likes structured hierarchies while B prefers more permissive relations. However, when there is a situation of a certain structure, they are compatible with regard to the roles they will take in relation to each other. A will take the influential, responsible position, and B will take the subordinate role.

These psychological considerations can very easily be converted into formulas, and in research work and practical applications this is done. There have been several experiments performed which indicate the usefulness of this approach. These experiments demonstrate that groups of from two to eight can be composed—based on FIRO-B scores—in such a way that their productivity, and to some extent their interaction, is predictable. Much research is still to be done to improve the accuracy of these predictions, but the results are highly encouraging.

Group Development

Another major point in the theory is that every group, no matter what its function or composition, given enough time, goes through the three interpersonal phases of inclusion, control, and affection in the same sequence. To illustrate:

Recently I was interviewing a member of a group, which had just completed 30 meetings, to get an idea of her feeling about the experience. In response to the question, "How would you describe what happened in this group?" she replied, "Well, first you're concerned about the problem of where you fit in the group; then you're wondering about what you'll accomplish. Finally, after a while, you learn that people mean something. Your primary concern becomes how people feel about you and about each other."

IN OR OUT

First, *the inclusion phase centers around the question of "in or out."* It begins with the formation of the group. When people are confronted with each other, they must first find the place where they fit in. This involves being in or out of the group, establishing oneself as a specific individual, and seeing if one is going to be paid attention to and not be left behind or ignored. This anxiety area gives rise to individual-centered behavior such as overtalking, extreme withdrawal, exhibitionism, recitation of biographies and other previous experience.

At the same time the basic problem of commitment to the group is present. Each member is implicitly deciding to what degree he will become a member of the group, how much investment he will withdraw from his other commitments and invest in this new relationship. He is asking, "How much of myself will I devote to this group? How important will I be in this setting? Will they know who I am and what I can do, or will I be indistinguishable from many others?" This is, in short, the problem of identity. He is, in effect, deciding primarily on his preferred amount of inclusion interchange and his preferred amount of inclusion initiation with the other members—just how much actual contact, interaction, and communication he wishes to have.

Hence, the main concerns of the formative process are "boundary problems," problems that have to do with entering into the boundaries of a group and belonging to that group. These are problems of inclusion.

Characteristic of groups in this phase is the occurrence of what have been called "goblet issues." The term is taken from an analogy to a cocktail party where people sometimes pick up their cocktail glass, or goblet, and figuratively peer through it to size up the other people at the party. Hence, they are issues that in themselves are of minor importance to the group members but serve as vehicles for getting to know people, especially in relation to oneself.

Often a goblet issue is made of the first decision confronting a group. In some groups discussions leading to a decision about such an issue continue for an unbelievably long time and then never reach a conclusion. But there has been a great deal of learning in that the members have gained a fairly clear picture of each other. Each member knows who responds favorably to him, who sees things the way he does, how much he knows as compared to the others, how the leader responds to him, and what type of role he can expect to play in the group. Acquiring this knowledge is the unconscious purpose of the goblet issue.

The frustrating experience of having groups endlessly discuss topics of little real interest to anyone is very common. Every group finds its own goblet issues within the framework of its aim. "The weather" is fairly universal; "rules of procedure" is common in formal groups; "Do you know so-and-so?" often characterizes new acquaintances from the same location; relating incidents or telling stories has a goblet element for business gatherings; and "Where are you from?" often serves for military settings. Mark Twain apparently overlooked the fact that nobody really *wants* to "do anything about the weather"—they just want to use it as a topic for sizing up people. These discussions are inevitable, and, contrary to all outward appearances, they do serve an important function. Groups which are not permitted this type of testing out will search for some other method of obtaining the same personal information, perhaps using as a vehicle a decision of more importance to the work of the group.

TOP OR BOTTOM

After the problems of inclusion have been sufficiently resolved, control problems become prominent. *This phase centers around the problem of "top or bottom."* Once members are fairly well established as being together in a group, the issue of decision-making procedures arises. This involves problems of sharing responsibility and its necessary concomitant, distribution of power and control. Characteristic behavior at this stage includes leadership struggles; competition; and discussion of orientation to the task, structuring, rules of procedure, methods of decision making, and sharing the responsibility for the group's work. The primary anxieties at this phase revolve around having too much or too little responsibility and too much or too little influence. Each member is trying to establish himself in the group so that he has the most comfortable amount of interchange and the most comfortable degree of initiation with the other members with regard to control, influence, and responsibility.

NEAR OR FAR

Finally, following a satisfactory resolution of these phases, problems of affection become focal. *This phase centers on the issue of "near or far."* The individuals have come together to form a group; they have differentiated themselves with respect to responsibility and power. Now they must become emotionally integrated. At this stage it is characteristic to see such behavior expressed through positive feelings, direct personal hostility, jealousies, pairing behavior, and, in general, heightened emotional feeling between pairs of people.

The primary anxieties at this stage have to do with not being liked or close enough to people or with being too intimate. Each member is striving to obtain his most favorable amount of affectional interchange and most comfortable position regarding initiating and receiving affection—deciding, like Schopenhauer's porcupines, how to get close enough to receive warmth, yet avoid the pain of sharp quills.

TIGHTENING THE BOLTS

These are not distinct phases. The group development postulate asserts that these problem areas are *emphasized* at certain points in a group's growth, but all three problem areas are always present. Similarly, some people do not always go along with the central issue for the group. For certain individuals a particular problem area will be so personally potent that it will transcend the current group issue. The area of concern for any individual will result from his own problem areas and those of the group's current phase. Per-

haps a close approximation to the developmental phenomena is given by the tire-changing model:

When a person changes a tire and replaces the wheel, he first sets the wheel in place and secures it by tightening the bolts one after another just enough so the wheel is in place and the next step can be taken. Then the bolts are tightened further, usually in the same sequence, until the wheel is firmly in place. Finally each bolt is gone over separately to secure it.

In a similar way, the need areas are worked on until they are handled satisfactorily enough to continue with the work at hand. Later on they are returned to and worked over to a more satisfactory degree. If one need area has not been worked out well on the first sequence, it must receive more attention on the next cycle.

Applications of Theory

The next question is: What can we do about these problems so as to utilize this information practically? This is more difficult. The above analysis is derived largely from experience with experimental research on small groups selected for this purpose. Solutions for the problems observed are largely, though not entirely, speculative and can only be offered as suggestions which should be explored carefully in each individual case before being adopted.

More specifically, the interpretations presented here can be looked upon as suggestions for *diagnosis*. The more men in business can become aware of the basic factors underlying their interpersonal difficulties, the better they will be able to meet these difficulties. As in the practice of medicine, if the disease is properly diagnosed, the doctor has a better chance of curing it than if it is improperly or superficially diagnosed, even though a correct diagnosis by no means guarantees a cure.

CLEARING THE AIR

Serious interpersonal difficulties that are left covert only smolder and erupt at the expense of efficiency and productivity. The most effective way covert difficulties can be dealt with is by first making them overt. For example:

In one marketing group, the leader finally told one member that he did not like the way he was acting in the group and that he felt he should contribute more. After a brief but difficult and bitter exchange the two began to tell each other their feelings about the situation. They managed to clear the air, and the situation improved markedly.

When successful, overt discussion is like a cold shower: it is approached with apprehension, the initial impact is very uncomfortable, but the final result justifies the tribulations.

To summarize, "interpersonal problems" include difficulties such as members who are withdrawn from a group; personal hostilities between members; problem members who are either inactive and unintegrated or overactive and destructive; power struggles between group members; members battling for attention; dissatisfaction with the leadership in the group; dissatisfaction with the amount of acknowledgment that an individual's contributions are getting; or dissatisfaction with the amount of affection and warmth exhibited in the group.

If it becomes quite clear to the group members that their difficulties are so severe that their activity is being impaired, then bringing the issues out into the open and talking about them will help. It is somewhat difficult, however, to tell exactly when a problem is so severe that it is holding the group up. Perhaps some of the earlier discussion of symptoms will be useful for assessing the effect of interpersonal factors on the group.

It might be helpful to view groups (including anywhere from two to twenty people) on a continuum—from those that are completely compatible, that is, able to work well together, to those that are completely incompatible, that is, incapable of working together. Any particular group can be placed somewhere along this continuum. To illustrate:

The members of the group at the extreme compatible end of the continuum are able to work well together within a relatively short time with a minimum of difficulty and can operate effectively over a period of time on a wide variety of problems. They need no training or new awareness.

The group at the incompatible end, however, cannot work effectively. The interpersonal problems that cause the task difficulties are so deep-seated in the personalities of the individual members that no amount of outside assistance will be worthwhile. It would take so long before this group could operate effectively that, from a practical standpoint, any kind of training of the group members or any awareness of their problems would be unfruitful.

Between these two extreme types are groups that profit more or less by the kind of awareness which has been discussed. If a group is relatively near the compatible end, with a minimum of awareness and a minimum of discussion of its difficult problems, it will become a smoothly functioning group. If interpersonal problems in a group are very minor, they can usually be ignored without impairing the group seriously; or, if the problems exist between two members, they can often work out their difficulties by themselves outside the group.

With groups near the incompatible end much more intensive work has to be done to get through their problems so that they can function effectively. Such work should probably be guided by someone who is experienced with group process and can help group members to work out their difficulties.

Another advantage of this approach operates more through the individuals than the group. If the individual members can gain the kind of awareness of their own needs in situations as discussed in this article, then this in itself will help them to understand their reactions to other people and, perhaps, to operate more effectively. In addition, it is often helpful to point out to group members that other people have the same basic needs; for, if they understand what other people are trying to do, they may be more tolerant of other people's behavior. Since everyone has these needs, everyone tries to get the same thing from other people, even though each may use different adaptive patterns for achieving his ends. To illustrate such a mechanism:

It generally is felt that if an individual has an excessively strong negative reaction to another individual in the setting of a work group, the individual who is irritated fears deep down within himself that he is like the one who annoys him, that he himself has the trait that is so annoying. It is threatening for him to see it in some other individual, and he must immediately deny it and attack it, almost as if he were trying to deny to himself that he is like this.

Awareness of mechanisms of this type may help in understanding what is happening in the group and one's own reaction in the situation.

Conclusion

The time seems to have come for the businessman to make use of some of the social scientists' more recent findings on the unconscious, or covert, factors in human interaction. Since the businessman does deal so heavily in interpersonal relations, his skill and success are dependent on his ability to understand interpersonal relations and to deal effectively with them. Thus, it becomes important for him to gain a more basic understanding instead of simply trying out panaceas that aim only at the symptoms of the problems and not at the basic problems themselves. He must understand the vast interpersonal underworld that operates beneath the overt, observable behavior.

As I have already pointed out, current interest in what are called "communications problems" provides an example of the symptomatic approach, for these problems are symptoms of poor interpersonal relations rather than primary causes of operational difficulties. It is an error, therefore, to try to attack the problems of communication by building more effective physical lines of communication, when the trouble really lies in the relation between individuals. The way to attack the basic problem would seem to be to investigate what is going on among the individuals themselves and try to improve those relations.

If it is true that the unconscious factors are so all-important to understanding groups, then we ought to find out exactly how these factors do affect what the businessman is usually primarily interested in, namely effective operation. In this article I have tried to illustrate the inadequacy of attempting to operate by ignoring interpersonal difficulties and attending to the task only, since in reality the interpersonal factors somehow find their way into the task and directly affect the productivity of the group. No matter how much people try to keep interpersonal problems out by ignoring them, they will turn up in subtle forms such as loss of motivation, tiredness, or the group member's preoccupation with outside tasks; or they may get entangled directly with the solution of the task and have to be worked out in the body of the problem.

꘏꘏꘏꙰꙰꙰꙰꙰꙰꙰꙰꙰꙰꙰꙰꙰꙰꙰꙰꙰꙰ THE THEORY AND MEASUREMENT METHODOLOGY OF INTERPERSONAL COMMUNICATION * *Timothy Leary*

INTERPERSONAL communication, the subject of this paper, is the aspect of personality psychology which is concerned with the social impact that one human being has on another. In the following pages I shall describe some methods that the Kaiser Foundation has developed for isolating and defining human interactions and shall then discuss their implications for a theory of personality.

The phrase *interpersonal* relations has, in the past decade, won great popularity in psychiatry and personality psychology, and a wide variety of concepts and therapeutic techniques have been based upon this general idea. But considerable vagueness and conceptual looseness characterize many of the references to interpersonal concepts. The need is evident for, first, a systematic theory of interpersonal motivation and, second, an empirical methodology for measuring human interactions.

* The research upon which this article is based has been sponsored by grant no. 40-35 from the Kaiser Foundation and grant no. MH-331 from the United States Public Health Service. The Kaiser Foundation research in psychology is under the direction of D. Harvey Powelson. The associated USPHS project is co-directed by Saxton T. Pope and Hubert S. Coffey, of the University of California.

The present article is concerned with the measurement of interpersonal behavior—the overt, public, interpersonal expressions of the subject—and with some of the theoretical issues that are pertinent to this area of emotional expression.

Definitions and Illustrations

The basic unit involved here is the interpersonal motive as measured by its effect on others. The interpersonal motive of any behavior is determined by asking: "What is this person doing to the other? What kind of relationship is he attempting to establish through this particular behavior?" The answers to these questions define the interpersonal purpose; for example, "He is boasting and attempting to establish superiority," or "He is rejecting and refusing to help."

The concern at this level is with *what* one person communicates to another. A father, for example, may employ one or one thousand words to refuse his child's request. The mode, style, and content of the two rejecting expressions may be very different, but their interpersonal purpose is the same—rejection.

In studying the interpersonal motives

Excerpted from Timothy Leary, "The Theory and Measurement Methodology of Interpersonal Communication," Psychiatry, Vol. 18, No. 2, May 1955, pp. 147–161. Some footnotes omitted. Abridged and used by permission.

which underlie human behavior, the following hypothesis has developed: In a large percentage of interactions the basic motives are expressed in a reflex manner. They are so automatic that they are often unwitting and often at variance with the subject's own perception of them. The meaning of any interaction is therefore a difficult one to isolate and measure. It is frequently unverbalized and so subtle and reflex as to escape articulate description. Sometimes these interpersonal communications can be implicit in the content of the discussion: Grandfather talks incessantly about the lack of energy and initiative of modern youth in order to impress others with the fact that he is a successful self-made man. Grandmother talks incessantly about sickness, calamity, and death to remind others that the time may be short to repay her for the sacrifices she has made for her children. Grandfather never says openly, "I am better than you young people," and Grandmother never says, "You should feel guilty and devoted to me." Grandfather's remark may be concerned with the issue of the 40-hour week, and Grandmother may be quoting from the obituary column of the evening paper. But behind the superficial content of these expressions are the repetitive interpersonal purposes—superiority and reproach. Behind the superficial content of most social exchanges it is possible to determine the naked motive communications: I am wise; I am strong; I am friendly; I am contemptuous. The concomitant message is also there—you are less wise, less strong, less likeable, contemptible.

The following situation, in which a woman evokes the helpful attitude, exemplifies Level 1 purposive communications: A patient comes to a psychiatrist for an evaluation interview. She reports a long list of symptoms—insom-

nia, worry, depression—and an equally long list of unfortunate events—divorce, unsympathetic employer, and so on. She cries. Whether her expressions are scored separately and summarized or are judged on the over-all, a clear picture emerges of a dependent approach —"I am weak, unhappy, unlucky, in need of your help."

In response, the psychiatrist is under strong pressure to express sympathetic, nurturant communications. Helpless, trustful behavior tends to call forth assistance. Further, the patient-therapist situation is in essence one that lends itself easily to the "needs help—offers help" relationship. There is a tendency for the psychiatrist to express—either openly or, much more likely, by implication—that he knows how the patient can be assisted. This may be communicated, not in *what* he says, but in his bearing, attitude, his very quiet competence.

What makes it more complex is the fact that the verbal expression may be quite different from the actual developing relationship. The psychiatrist may interpret the dangers of dependence and the necessity for self-help. The patient may agree. If both of them tend to over-emphasize verbal symbols, there may be an illusion that a collaborative relationship exists. Actually the nurturant-interpreter—trustful-follower situation still exists, not in what the participants are *saying*, but in what they are *doing* to each other.

The Interpersonal System of Classification

A LISTING OF INTERPERSONAL REFLEXES

To make objective measurements of the reflex phenomena of Level 1, it was necessary to have a finite and defined list of interpersonal behaviors. Through extensive empirical research, a classificatory system for measuring human interaction has been constructed. This variable system is arranged in the form of a 16-point circular continuum which reflects the variety of interpersonal purposes expressed by human beings in their relationships with each other. Because the material dealt with at this level of personality is the communication process—what one person *does* to another—transitive verbs are used as the verbal descriptive terms for each of the 16 interpersonal variables. Fig. 1 presents the 16 generic interpersonal themes, together with a list of sample activities which illustrate the range of each point around the circle.

For each generic theme there is, of course, an inexhaustible list of verbs. The terms used here are most appropriate for verbal exchanges in therapeutic or diagnostic contexts. Thus, *to boast, to claim superiority, to establish autonomy and independence, to act self-confident* are all assumed to contain about the same proportion of dominance-hostility as indicated by the point B on the circle. This means that they all express the same qualitative purpose of narcissistic self-approval. The fact that they differ in amount, degree, or extremity of the purpose is handled by an intensity scale. The kind and not the amount of the purpose is what is concerned here. Other lists are necessary for categorizing nonverbal actions (frowns, gestures, voice tones) and preverbal situations (nursery school interactions, and the like).

INTERPERSONAL REFLEXES IN A
GROUP THERAPY SITUATION

The following passage, transcribed from a tape-recording of a group psychotherapy situation, illustrates this system of scoring social behavior. The exact words of the participants are given in regular type; and the interpersonal reflexes are scored in bold-faced type.[1] The scoring of each mechanism consists of three ratings, which are indicated in the following order: the verb considered most closely descriptive of the action, the code letter representing the location of the action along the circular continuum of interpersonal mechanisms, as shown in Fig. 1 and the numerical rating of the entensity of the mechanism along a four-point intensity scale.

In the illustrative situation used here, six male patients file into the therapist's office and seat themselves expectantly. Patient A glances at a Picasso print on the wall and begins the group therapy process by remarking upon it.

(1) *Patient A.* Is that supposed to be art on the wall, or is that something somebody drew in the hospital? **Ridicules (D-3).**

[1] Some mechanisms—for example, humor and play behavior—are, of course, much too complex to be captured in essence by a simple rating scheme. When humor and play occur, an attempt is made to score them as follows:

Humor: Most humor seems to have a mildly hostile loading. Some humor is wry, poking fun at self, and is scored H—Self-effacement. Some is mildly bitter, complaining at fate, and so on, and is scored F—Cynicism. Some is sarcastic, biting, poking fun at others; this is scored D—Hostility. Notice that all of these are on the left (hostile) side of the interpersonal circle.

Play: It might be conjectured that play can be a derivative of any basic interpersonal orientation, and that any of the 16 interpersonal variables can be expressed in a playful manner. For example, competition can be expressed in play by means of sports and the like, and is scored C. Hostility can be expressed in play—for instance, by teasing—and is scored E or D. Tenderness can be expressed in play and is scored N or O. Collaboration, love, or affiliation can be expressed in a playful way, and are scored L or M. Play seems to be a stylistic variable not necessarily tied to any one interpersonal motive or group of motives.

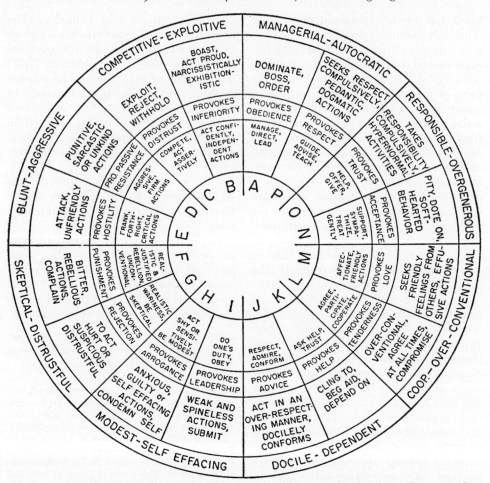

Fig. 1   Classification of interpersonal behavior into 16 mechanisms or reflexes. Each of the 16 interpersonal variables is illustrated by sample behaviors. The inner circle names adaptive reflexes, such as manage. *Proceeding outward, the next ring indicates the type of behavior that this interpersonal reflex tends to "pull" from the other one; thus the person who uses the reflex A tends to call up in others* obedience. *These findings involve two-way interpersonal phenomena—what the subject does and what the other does in return—and are therefore less reliable than the other interpersonal categories presented in the inner and outer rings. The next circle illustrates extreme or rigid reflexes, such as* dominates. *The perimeter of the circle is divided into eight general categories employed in interpersonal diagnosis. Each of these general categories has a moderate (adaptive) and an extreme (pathological) intensity, such as* managerial-autocratic.

(2) *Therapist.* Now, the purpose of our meeting in general is to help each of you to come to a better understanding of yourself, a deeper understanding of yourself. The meetings will last about an hour and a half, and we'll meet for at least four months, at least 15 or 16 times. [Therapist continues for several minutes to structure the situation.] **Teaches (P-2).**

(3) *Therapist.* . . . I'm going to throw

the burden of the conversation now to the group. I'd like to have you tell yourself and tell us, today and for the next few days, who you are, why you see yourself coming here, and what you might want to get from the group. **Directs (A-2).**

(4) *Patient A.* What if you don't know? What if you haven't the slightest idea what you want? **Passively resists (F-3).**

(5) *Therapist.* Well, that's a good place to start. You have already told us something interesting about yourself. **Supports (N-2).**

(6) *Patient A.* How can you talk about something you don't know anything about? **Passively resists (F-3).**

(7) *Patient B.* We could have a sympathizers' club here. **Ridicules self (H 1) and others (D-1).**

(8) *Patient C.* A friend of mine suggested that, as a matter of fact. **Agrees (L-1).**

(9) *Patient A.* Is that it? Are we supposed to cry on each other's shoulders? Is that the object of it? Crocodile tears and sympathetic ears, is that the idea? **Passively resists (F-3).**

(10) *Therapist.* [Smiles.] I hope we can help each other more than just by groaning together. **Ridicules (D-2).**

(11) *Patient B.* Mr. A has said—I felt that way too about knowing what I want, but I think that's more a problem of just —or you've just gotten so darn discouraged about things you just don't—well, there's a feeling, I know with myself—feeling that what a lot of people want just aren't worth a candle, that's all—it seems to take too much out of me in the way of effort and emotional drive or something. **Takes weak position (I-2).**

(12) *Therapist.* You don't just want the things that any other people want? **Summarizes (P-2).**

(13) *Patient B.* Yeah, I seem to have gotten into an attitude of what you might call emotional dumbness where I don't just seem to have the emotional level that some people have. **Condemns self (H-3).** Some people get enthused about going to a picnic, ball game, or this, that, and the other thing—I mean, speaking for myself, I'll say, "Ah, just let me alone." If somebody's go-

ing to a picnic, I don't give a damn whether they go to Milpitas, San Francisco, or what not. I don't expect to enjoy myself at a picnic. I'd rather stay home and sit on my butt and thumb through a magazine or something—keep comfortable and not bother with anything.

(14) *Patient D.* You're speaking generally now—not just about a picnic? About many things? Because I was going to say, there are a lot of people who take that attitude about certain things. You can never get them to work up enthusiasm, to get them to do anything, and yet they have other outlets, or are enthusiastic about—— **Explains (P-3).**

(15) *Patient B.* Yes, about a lot of things —like, for example, a good deal of my problems center about my work. **Depreciates self (H-3).** I kind of rationalize that by saying, "Oh, to hell with it! Most things people do aren't worth doing anyway." I repair air-conditioners for a living, for example. I have a very bad attitude about the sets. Firstly, I can't sympathize with my customers. I don't see why they want to keep the damn things going. [Laughs.] And they hound me to get the work. Of course, with my attitude, one could make a virtue of it. You could say that I have infinite patience. **Pulls for sympathy (J-3).** Frankly, I don't care. I'm not anxious to get paid, I'm not anxious to get started and I'm not anxious to finish. In fact, I feel a good deal of anxiety frequently about getting started and I think that's part of Mr. A's—that there's something there—a counterforce. It isn't that a person doesn't know what they want to do, really. I mean that there's some counterforce that makes anything that you want to do not worth the price. [He continues at length in this vein.]

(16) *Patient B.* . . . they feel that I don't have a damn bit of interest in their particular problems and even though my proposition is reasonable—in many cases I've gotten turned down. **Accuses others, describes self as exploited (G-3).** I had an example of that recently. By the way, am I taking up too much of the time? **Mildly criticizes self (H-1).**

(17) *Therapist.* Let's stop a minute be-

cause you have raised several interesting themes, the feeling of obligation, the feeling of being pressed in on by forces that —— **Directs (A-2). Summarizes (P-2).**

(18) *Patient B.* Like when I rest—like last night when my wife says, "Well, do you want to go out tonight?" I have already complained about being tired and I did feel tired. It was about eight-thirty that I started out. **Accuses others (G-3). Passively resists therapist's direction (F-3).**

(19) *Therapist.* Somewhat against your will, but you did go. **Reflects (O-2).**

(20) *Patient B.* That's right. **Participates (L-1).**

(21) *Therapist.* Now let's stop for a moment. **Directs (A-2).** Have these themes made anything click as you've listened to Mr. B describe them?

(22) *Patient A.* The idea of the annoyance of being pressed is common. That's common to everybody, isn't it? When you get somebody on your tail and you know that they are right and they have justification in their claims and that you can't satisfy them or—and then you feel a negative attitude—you would like to take their work and throw it out. **Gives opinion (P-2).**

(23) *Therapist.* What do you usually do when you feel that—do you throw their work out? **Therapeutic question (O-2).**

(24) *Patient A.* No, you just smile, and say, "Oh, that's too bad." **Depreciates self (H-2).**

(25) *Therapist.* Is that what you usually do? **Therapeutic question (O-2).**

(26) *Patient A.* Well, sometimes I sort of digress a little bit and I carry on a little campaign trying to impress people that there is a lot more to it—that they are expecting more—— **Mildly praises self (B-1).**

(27) *Therapist.* But you've never been in that position. **Summarizes (P-2).**

(28) *Patient A.* Never been in that position. Sometimes I've wanted things and the next day I got them and it seems as though when I got them it wasn't what I wanted after all. **Feels disappointed (G-2).**

(29) *Therapist.* What have your thoughts been as you have listened? **Focuses (A-2).**

(30) *Patient D.* Well, first of all, Mr. A's statement of enthusiasm, followed by a period of less enthusiasm or depression, according to my understanding is more or less normal to a certain degree; now if that goes to a greater degree, maybe that's not normal. All of us have periods where we work easily and enjoy our work. Now whether it is during that period you also suffer some of that anxiety, you said you worried about the periods that are coming —— **Pedantically teaches (P-3).**

(31) *Therapist.* How do you compare with Mr. A or Mr. B as they have presented their situation? **Therapeutic question (O-2).**

(32) *Patient D.* Well, it didn't quite fit in exactly. My work is a little different and I don't have to meet the public. **Denies problem (B-2).** I'm a physicist and as such I work under the directorship of the department head, the group leader, so that, while we have pressure on us at times to do work, it isn't the idea you're worrying about the business ahead or discouraging customers.

(33) *Patient E.* Do you worry about your work coming out right? Does that give you anxiety feelings? **Therapeutic question (O-2).**

(34) *Patient D.* I think scientific work is very frustrating in one respect and that is it seems like ninety percent of the time or greater your—what you do does not come out in a favorable manner. In other words you are only looking for a few successful experiments. That's what makes the money for the company. You have volumes and volumes of papers describing work you did that no one will ever look at again. **Describes frustration (G-2).**

(35) *Patient E.* Does that worry you— your relationship with your immediate superiors? Do you feel that maybe you haven't done things right or fast enough or careful enough? **Therapeutic question (O-2).**

(36) *Patient D.* Yes, you do have those feelings too, that's true. **Accepts (L-2).**

(37) *Patient B.* Well, I think there's a sort of tie-in, that basically it is simply probably you don't meet the general public so much as that your problems center

maybe on one or two individuals. **Gives opinion (P-2).**

(38) *Therapist.* Have you had this feeling of pressure that Mr. A or Mr. B have described? **Therapeutic question (O-2).**

(39) *Patient D.* No, not too much. No. **Denies problem (B-2).**

This passage nicely illustrates the development of interpersonal reflex patterns. The opening moments of a psychotherapy group are always most dramatic and important. Six strangers come together, meet for the first time, and begin automatically to train each other. The network of interaction, perception, and misperception begins to weave itself. Consider Patient A in the above passage. In the first five seconds, he has shot a critical and skeptical arrow. He challenges the therapist sarcastically, asking about a picture on the wall. It may be suspected that through these comments he is telling not just the therapist but the group in general, "I'm a negative, uncooperative person; you're going to have trouble with me." The record does not indicate what the five other patients were doing while Patient A was making his opening gambit. A motion picture record might have revealed that they were, in their own ways, beginning to develop their roles. Patient D, who later expresses himself verbally as a self-satisfied, executive person, might very well have been using nonverbal means to communicate his detached competence—crossing his legs briskly and shooting alert glances around the room. Patient B, who is soon to begin building a façade of self-critical weakness, may have been sending sheepish, apprehensive glances towards the others in these opening seconds.

In the subsequent moves of the grumpy Patient A, the same reflex pattern unfolds quite consistently. Inter-actions (6) and (9) continue to communicate the theme of uncooperative and passive resistance.

As Patient B enters the action, in remarks (11) and (13), a different set of reflexes appears. He begins a sequence of passive self-effacement. His self-deprecatory remarks are continued at length in (15), and by (16) it can be sensed that they have developed into a repetitive circle of pessimistic ruminations. He apologizes for monopolizing the discussion. Interactions (17) and (18) focus on a most interesting transaction. The therapist, in (17), attempts to check the flow of anxiety-driven words, but Patient B in (18) continues his reflex lamentations. In ignoring the therapist's intervention, Patient B provides a nice illustration of the involuntary nature of Level 1 communication. It is safe to guess that this patient did not deliberately or consciously interrupt and disregard the therapist. He has just expressed conscious anxiety about talking too much, but automatically goes on to provide a rather flagrant example of insensitive, anxiety-driven complaint.

At this point, Patient B has engaged in seven interactions—(7), (11), (13), (15), (16), (18), and (20). What impression has he made on his fellow group members? On the therapist? These seven communications provide the data for a small experiment in interpersonal relations in which the reader may participate. Glance back over Patient B's statements, imagining that you are a member of this therapy group. What feelings do you sense in response to his comments? Some readers have reported a feeling of sympathy, mixed with superiority and irritable impatience. To the extent that these feelings have been aroused, then to that extent Patient B has in seven easy steps taught or trained the reader to respond to him in a typical and consistent way. Patient B had an unusually rigid and inappropriate set of reflexes—apologetic, self-critical, and complaining. He trained the group members and the therapist just as he had trained everyone in his life to respond to him with tolerant and/or irritable superiority.

This set of reflex responses seemed to operate as a defensive maneuver. Occasionally he was able to show other responses. But the more anxious he became, the less able he was to respond appropriately and the more driven he was to continue his interpersonal defenses—as illustrated clearly in the sequence (17) and (18).

The Interpersonal Reflex

What did this patient do to get five strangers to agree on his social stimulus value? It seems that he trained them to react to him in a very specific way—with rejection and irritation. This question becomes more important —from the diagnostic viewpoint— when it is remembered that, as he reports, he has consistently tended to remain isolated and despised by others over the span of his life. How does he do this?

When his interpersonal actions are traced back to the original recorded protocols, a typical pattern of Level 1 interaction is discovered. The individual units of this behavior—the *interpersonal mechanisms or interpersonal reflexes*—are defined as functional, purposive units of face-to-face social behavior. These reflexes are automatic and usually involuntary responses to interpersonal situations, often independent of the content of the communication. They are spontaneous,

purposive methods of reacting to others.

The exact manner in which these Level 1 communications are expressed is a complex and unsolved problem. This much is clear: they are expressed partially in the content or verbal meaning of the communication and partially in the tone of voice, gesture, carriage, and external appearance. Although the specific method by which human beings express their purposive relationships to each other is unknown, the over-all, molar effect can be reliably rated. Raters—whether trained psychologists or untrained fellow patients —can agree with impressive reliability in rating what subjects do to each other in interpersonal situations. Preliminary research by Blanche Sweet suggests that more effective ratings can be arrived at by listening to recordings than by reading typed transcriptions. Sound movies would provide the optimal techniques for preserving the nuances involved in interpersonal reflexes. Future research may determine the specific way in which these spontaneous interpersonal meanings manifest themselves to others. The reflex manner in which human beings react to others and train others to respond to them in selective ways is, I believe, the most important single aspect of personality. The systematic estimates of a patient's repertoire of interpersonal reflexes is a key factor in functional diagnosis. Awareness of crippled reflexes and, if possible, modification of them should be a basic goal of psychotherapy. When more evidence as to the mode of expression—gesture, carriage, content of speech—is accumulated, some additions to therapeutic practice may develop.

Because of their automatic and involuntary nature, interpersonal reflexes are difficult to observe and measure.

For the same reason they are most resistant to therapeutic change. The more the members of the psychotherapy group tried to explain to the subject how and why he irritated them, the more he protested his feelings of injury. Later, intellectual insight and voluntary controlled changes to cooperative, self-confident behavior developed. These were, however, quite tentative and unnatural. During many months of treatment spontaneous reactivity brought a return of the original responses.

ROUTINE REFLEX PATTERNS

During any one day the average adult runs into a wide range of interpersonal stimuli. He is challenged, pleased, bossed, obeyed, helped, and ignored several times a day. Thus, the person whose entire range of interpersonal reflexes is functioning flexibly can be expected to demonstrate appropriately each of the 16 interpersonal reflexes many times in any day.

There are, however, many persons who do not react with consistent appropriateness or flexibility. One person might respond to the pleasant as well as the rude stranger with a disapproving frown. Another might smile in a friendly fashion at both of them. If an extended sample of a subject's interactions is studied, an interesting fact develops. Each person shows a consistent preference for certain interpersonal reflexes. Other reflexes are very difficult to elicit or are absent entirely. It is possible to predict in probability terms the preferred reflexes for most persons in a specific situation. A small percentage of persons get others to react to them in the widest range of possible behaviors and can utilize a wide range of appropriate reactions. But

most persons tend to train others to react to them within a narrower range of behaviors, and in turn show a restricted set of favored reflexes. Some persons show a very limited repertoire of two or three reflexes and reciprocally receive an increasingly narrow set of responses from others.

DEFINITION OF INTERPERSONAL ROLE

Almost everyone manifests certain role patterns which he automatically assumes in the presence of each significant other person in his life. These roles are probability tendencies to express certain interpersonal purposes with significantly higher frequency. The person may be quite unaware of these spontaneous tendencies—to complain to his wife, to be stern with his children, to boss his secretary, to depend on the office manager. It must be remembered that the terms used here are statistical probability terms. The subject may have thousands of interactive exchanges each day with each of his significant others, and these may range all over the interpersonal continuum. When evidence is obtained that he consistently and routinely tends to favor certain mechanisms with one person significantly more than can be explained by chance, and tends to pull certain responses from the other to a similar degree, then a role relationship can be said to exist.

This selective process of employing a narrowed range of reflexes with certain others works, as has been seen, in a double reinforcing manner. Most durable relationships tend to be symbiotic. Masochistic women tend to marry sadistic men; and the latter tend to marry women who tend to provoke hostility. Dependent men tend to seek nurturant superiors, who in turn are most secure when they have docile subordinates to protect.

The institutional role relationships —such as boss-secretary, prisoner-guard, student-teacher—tend to be more stereotyped and fixed. Even so, some room for role variability exists. Some secretaries do 'mother,' nag, or even boss their nominal superiors. In general, however, it can be surmised that personality factors do enter into the choice of occupation. Those people who are least anxious and most secure when they are submitting to and depending on strong authority tend to seek and hold subordinate jobs. The network of relationships even in the simplest office set-up can be bewildering in its multilevel complexity.

PATIENTS AS DIAGNOSTIC INSTRUMENTS

The instrument employed to measure interpersonal reflexes is another human being. Since interpersonal behavior is a functionally important dimension of personality, it is measured directly—in terms of the actual social impact that the subject has on others. Some interesting implications develop. By allowing the patient to react with others—say, in a group therapy situation—it is made possible for him to demonstrate directly and openly his repertoire of interpersonal reflexes. It is made possible for him to manifest in the group the pattern of social reactivity which characterizes his dealings with others. He tends to recreate to a mild extent in the group his neurotic adjustment. He accomplishes his own interpersonal diagnosis.

The therapeutic group thus serves as a small subsociety, a miniature world. Many patients tend to arouse in the other group members the reactions which they get from some of the significant others in their world. The members of a therapy group have a valuable diagnostic function. When they rate each other's interpersonal behavior —on a check list or sociometric blank, covering the range of the 16 generic variables—an estimate of what each patient has done to the others is obtained.

The Principle of Self-Determination

I have consistently employed in the preceding sections a rather cumbersome circumlocution to describe the interaction between the sample subjects and the others with whom they interact. Most statements describing what others did to the sample case have been worded so as to give responsibility to the subject. Thus I say, "He trained or provoked the group members to reject him," rather than "They rejected him." In the listing of illustrative interpersonal reflexes, it may have been noted that both active and passive phrases were used. Thus for the interpersonal reflex G both *acts rejected* and *provokes rejection* have been included. The subject is taken as the focus of attention and as the locus of responsibility.

I have tried to stress the surprising ease with which human beings can get others to respond in a uniform and repetitive way. Interpersonal reflexes operate with involuntary routine and amazing power and speed. Many subjects with maladaptive interpersonal patterns can provoke the expected response from a complete stranger in a matter of minutes. The defiant chip-on-the-shoulder attitude; the docile, fawning passivity; the timid, anxious withdrawal—these are some of the interpersonal techniques which can produce the reciprocal reaction from the other person with unfailing regularity. Severe neurotics—defined at this level as persons with limited ranges of reflexes —are incredibly and creatively skilled in drawing rejection, nurturance, and so on, from the people with whom they deal. In many cases the 'sicker' the patient is, the more likely he is to have abandoned all interpersonal techniques except one, which he can handle with magnificent finesse. Most clinicians who have dealt with the so-called catatonic negation will testify that this disorder involves a powerful interpersonal maneuver.

Assigning the causative factor in interpersonal relations to the subject is a standard procedure in dynamic psychiatry. The skillful therapist is usually not inclined to join the abused, unhappy, masochistic patient in lamentation. He is much more inclined to ask himself, and eventually the patient, "What do you do to people with consistent and consummate skill to get them to beat you up?" The principle involved here holds that interpersonal events just do not happen to human beings by accident or external design. The active and executive role is given to the subject.

The Principle of Reciprocal Interpersonal Relations

The principle of self-determination as it operates at Level 1 has several implications. The idea that people must take the credit or blame for their own life situations has had an obvious effect on clinical practice. It assigns to the patient the responsibility for developing and managing his own personality. This is a terrible power, and one which he is often not willing to accept. The key factors in personality seem to be the purposive messages that persons express to others in their Level 1 communications. For many patients these are signals of weakness and blame. "Others must help me; others are my undoing" are familiar and poignant themes expressed by many psychiatric patients. The idea of self-determination removes the protective devices of projection and externalization, giving in return a priceless, but often unwelcome, gift of personal power. If you made yourself and your world, then you can change yourself and your world. Since your own interpersonal communications have woven the unique tapestry of your life, then you are the only one who can create or change the pattern. The responsibility for the past and the endowment for the future are in your hands.

In my development of these themes, a rather curious imbalance may have been noted. For purposes of exposition I have concentrated on the viewpoint of the subject. At times this may have implied a paradoxical situation in which everyone goes around training others to respond to him in specified ways. This is, of course, rather puzzling. If everyone is actively creating his own interpersonal world, no one is left to be passively trained by others.

This dilemma is caused by the concentration on one side of the interpersonal exchange—the subject. Actually, interpersonal relationships can never be understood unless both sides of the interaction are studied. When only one side—the self or subject side—of interpersonal behavior is isolated and studied, there is a risk of distortion. When the various levels and areas are considered in turn, there is a danger of segmental overemphasis—one of the plagues of psychological theory. The principle of self-determination is a probability statement which has reference to the global organization of personality in general and to Level 1 in particular. The over-all counterbalance system of the total personality is, for all predictive purposes, the focal unit. It has special importance in shaping a strategy and tactic of psychotherapy. In the preceding section I have, for expository purposes, stressed the *self* response and understressed the *other,* or environmental factors. But in actuality both partners in any relationship share the responsibility for its development —a mutual determining operation is occurring. The mother does not create the child's personality. The child does not create the maternal reaction. Both mother and child are engaged in a most intricate reciprocal process to which both bring determinative motivations.

REINFORCEMENT OF THE ORIGINAL REFLEX THROUGH SOCIAL INTERACTION

In considering both sides of the interpersonal situation—the two-person commerce of communication—the first point worth comment is the reinforcing quality of social interaction. One's actions toward other people generally effect a mirror duplication or a countermeasure from the others. This in turn tends to strengthen one's original action. If you walk up and aggressively shove a stranger, the chances are good that he will shove you back. Of course, this rule does not work uniformly. One person out of a hundred might be that Christian soul who would tenderly embrace you. A few might slink away from you. A few might docilely attempt to placate you. But the largest percentage would mirror your aggression

—and probably shove back. Your counterresponse would then become the issue. You might apologize, you might retreat, but, assuming you are an aggressive shover to begin with, the statistically probable response would be to shove back, perhaps harder.

You have provoked a response which has reenforced your original action. This reenforcing process is called the principle of reciprocal interpersonal relations. This is a general probability principle which holds that: *Interpersonal reflexes tend (with a probability significantly greater than chance) to initiate or invite reciprocal interpersonal responses from the other person in the interaction that lead to a repetition of the original reflex.*

QUALIFICATIONS AND EXCEPTIONS

The reenforcing process I have described is not an all-inclusive principle. It is a probability function. It does not necessarily hold for the individual interaction. Aggression usually breeds counteraggression. Smiles usually win smiles. Tears usually arouse sympathy. In specific cases, however, these general rules break down. Aggression can win tolerant smiles. Tears can provoke curses.

When the thousands of interactions that make up each day of social existence are studied, this principle becomes increasingly useful. Many kinds of variation and inconsistency operate to lower perfect predictability of interpersonal behavior. The meaning of the cultural context, the personality of the other person, and oscillation tendencies in the subject are always complicating factors. Like any other principle which involves human emotions, the principle of reciprocal relations operates in probabilistic terms.

Reciprocal relations are more likely to develop with certain personalities than with others. The principle holds most uniformly with pairs of symbiotically 'sick' people. A phobic, dependent wife and a nurturant, strong husband would be such a pair. The more the husband takes care of her, the more the dependence repeats. The more the wife clings, the more pressure there is on the husband to be gentle and protective. Even in a symbiotic marriage of this sort, the reciprocity would tend to break down if other motives entered the behavior of either. If hostile reproach lies behind the wife's weakness, or if impatient superiority behind the husband's strength, then new chains of interaction may develop.

There is another aspect of this principle: the sicker a person is, the more power he has to determine his relationships with others. A maladjusted person with a crippled set of reflexes tends to overdevelop a narrow range of one or two interpersonal responses. These are expressed intensely and often, whether appropriate to the situation or not. Now a normal person has a fairly flexible range of reflexes. He can use any interpersonal response if the situation calls it out. He is less committed and, for that matter, less skillful in the use of any particular reflex. When the two interact, it is the 'sick' person who determines the relationship. The more extreme and rigid the person, the greater his interpersonal 'pull'—the stronger his ability to shape the relationships with others. The withdrawn catatonic, the irretrievable criminal, the compulsively flirtatious charmer can inevitably elicit the expected response from a more balanced other.

The flexible person can draw out a greater variety of responses from others —depending on his conscious or unconscious motives at the moment. He can get others to like him, take care of him, obey him, lead him, envy him, and so on. The 'sick' person has a very narrow range of interpersonal tactics, but these are generally quite powerful in their effect. I have seen compulsive, responsible group members after several months of treatment desperately trying to get the other group members to understand and commiserate with their inner feelings of weakness and despair. But they had trained the other members well to look up to them and respect them. Their own managerial reflexes kept firing even at the moment when they were verbally appealing for help and sympathy. Most of the patients seen in the clinic have protected themselves with automatic responses and train others much too easily to follow along the expected lines of interaction.

Another qualification of the principle of reciprocal relations must be emphasized—the effect of variations within the subject. In describing human behavior, the impression is often given that a consistent line of adjustment is exhibited. In most of the illustrations used in this article, the subject's role is made to appear fixed. Actually, inconsistency and changeability are the rule and not the exception in human emotions. The factors of change and stability have been treated elsewhere.[2] They are studied as a separate dimension of personality—the *variability dimension*. Included under this topic are all the measurable variations which affect human behavior—changes in cultural context, changes over time, changes due to conflict and variety among the levels of personality.

[2] See Leary and Coffey, "The Prediction of Interpersonal Behavior in Group Psychotherapy," reference footnote 1.

At this point it is sufficient to point out that no interpersonal role is absolutely pure or rigid. The most withdrawn catatonic sends out occasional tendrils of affect. The most hardened criminal occasionally has a moment of congeniality. The most autocratic five-star general occasionally admits he is wrong. Most people show considerable conflict or inconsistency in their actions from time to time. No matter how thick and effective the reflex defenses, underlying inconsistencies eventually manifest themselves.

When this happens, the principle of reciprocal relations tends to break down. The probable accuracy of the predictions drops. For instance, a flirtatious woman evokes seductive responses from a man. His approaches set off stronger flirtatious actions. The man becomes more seductive. But at some point in this process, underlying motives may step in to change the pattern. In some cases, a flirtatious façade may cover deeper feelings of competition or contempt toward men. The woman would then shift to rejecting behavior. The reciprocal pattern of entice versus seduce would shift. The man's reaction would then vary, depending on the nature of his multilevel pattern. He might continue to seduce, he might be hurt, he might become dependent.

The same process of circular interactions leading up to an intense breaking point often occurs between parent and child. Dependence evokes nurturance which evokes further dependence. In some cases the spiralling increase in intensity leads to a temporary crash. At some point the parent's underlying feelings of selfishness or self-protection lead to refusal. Father comes home one night tired and grumpy. Outside events may have set off underlying feelings of deprivation, or self-pity, or sadism. He

may snarl at the child. The child then whines. The whining may increase the father's irritation. A new series of reciprocal events may thus be initiated.

Alternations of behavior are, of course, not an unhealthy manifestation. Moods shift; feelings are carried over from one situation into another; past events may set off emotions which are quite irrelevant to the current reality situation. It is safe to suggest that everyone acts inappropriately many times each day. These inconsistencies can hardly be considered abnormal. The lines of interpersonal communication are constantly breaking down momentarily, but these breakdowns involve no permanent disasters. A healthy father-child relationship is not paralyzed because one of the two has a bad day or carries over inappropriate feelings.

On the other hand, very rigidly formed relationships can be upset badly by shifts in the pattern of reciprocal relations. Some institutional relationships are very inflexible and demand perfect reciprocity. The army officer expects to evoke consistent obedience. A rent in this kind of interpersonal fabric can be seen as unforgivable. Some kinds of symbiotic marriages are so rigid that deviation in reciprocal roles can cause intense anxiety. When a servile, docile husband shows a flash of rebellion against a dominating wife, the results can be explosive.

Thus many factors tend to qualify the principle of reciprocal relations. Among these I have considered variations in the cultural context, variations in the personality of the other person, and variations due to multilevel ambivalences in the subject's personality.

In this article, which is concerned with interpersonal communication, I have described a measurement methodology and a theoretical context for dealing with certain aspects of behavior. The empirical unit by which social interactions are categorized is called the interpersonal reflex—defined as the social impact which the subject's action has on the other person. In discussing this, I have tried to stress the automatic and often involuntary way in which human beings 'train' or provoke others to react in consistent ways.

One of the main theoretical implications of this approach is the *principle of self-determination,* which focuses on the process by which one tends to create or recreate one's interpersonal world along routinized channels. This assigns to the subject the causative responsibility for the interpersonal relations which he integrates with others. The other theoretical implication which I have stressed—the *principle of reciprocal interpersonal relations*—refers to the probability tendency for subjects to pull from others interpersonal responses which lead to a repetition of the subjects' own favored interpersonal security operations. Both of these principles are tentative and hypothetical concepts which can be tested by means of the measurement system developed by the Kaiser Foundation research group.

❖❖❖❖❖❖❖❖❖❖❖❖❖❖❖❖❖❖ A THEORY OF GROUP DEVELOPMENT [1]

Warren G. Bennis and Herbert A. Shepard

IF attention is focused on the organic properties of groups, criteria can be established by which phenomena of development, learning, or movement toward maturity can be identified. From this point of view, maturity for the group means something analogous to maturity for the person: a mature group knows very well what it is doing. The group can resolve its internal con-

[1] This theory is based for the most part on observations made over a 5-year period of teaching graduate students "group dynamics". The main function of the seminar as it was set forth by the instructors was to improve the internal communication system of the group, hence, a self-study group.

flicts, mobilize its resources, and take intelligent action only if it has means for consensually validating its experience. The person can resolve his internal conflicts, mobilize his resources, and take intelligent action only if anxiety does not interfere with his ability to profit from his experience, to analyse, discriminate, and foresee. Anxiety prevents the person's internal communication system from functioning appropriately, and improvements in his ability to profit from experience hinge upon overcoming anxiety as a source of distortion. Similarly, group development involves the overcoming of ob-

From Warren G. Bennis and Herbert A. Shepard, "A Theory of Group Development," Human Relations, Vol. 9, No. 4, 1956, pp. 415–457. Some footnotes omitted. Abridged and used by permission.

stacles to valid communication among the members, or the development of methods for achieving and testing consensus. Extrapolating from Sullivan's definition of personal maturity we can say a group has reached a state of valid communication when its members are armed with

". . . referential tools for analyzing interpersonal experience, so that its significant differences from, as well as its resemblances to, past experience, are discriminable, and the foresight of relatively near future events will be adequate and appropriate to maintaining one's security and securing one's satisfactions without useless or ultimately troublesome disturbance of self-esteem" (19, p. 111).

Relatively few investigations of the phenomena of group development have been undertaken. This paper outlines a theory of development in groups that have as their explicit goal improvement of their internal communication systems.

A group of strangers, meeting for the first time, has within it many obstacles to valid communication. The more heterogeneous the membership, the more accurately does the group become, for each member, a microcosm of the rest of his interpersonal experience. The problems of understanding, the relationships, that develop in any given group are from one aspect a unique product of the particular constellation of personalities assembled. But to construct a broadly useful theory of group development, it is necessary to identify major areas of internal uncertainty, or obstacles to valid communication, which are common to and important in all groups meeting under a given set of environmental conditions. These areas must be strategic in the sense that until the group has developed methods for reducing uncer-

tainty in them, it cannot reduce uncertainty in other areas, and in its external relations.

The Two Major Areas of Internal Uncertainty: Dependence (Authority Relations) and Interdependence (Personal Relations)

Two major areas of uncertainty can be identified by induction from common experience, at least within our own culture. The first of these is the area of group members' orientations toward authority, or more generally toward the handling and distribution of power in the group. The second is the area of members' orientations toward one another. These areas are not independent of each other: a particular set of inter-member orientations will be associated with a particular authority structure. But the two sets of orientations are as distinct from each other as are the concepts of power and love. A number of authorities have used them as a starting-point for the analysis of group behavior.

In his *Group Psychology and the Analysis of the Ego,* Freud noted that "each member is bound by libidinal ties on the one hand to the leader . . . and on the other hand to the other members of the group" (6, p. 45). Although he described both ties as libidinal, he was uncertain "how these two ties are related to each other, whether they are of the same kind and the same value, and how they are to be described psychologically." Without resolving this question, he noted that (for the Church and the Army) "one of these, the tie with the leader, seems . . . to be more of a ruling factor than the other, which holds between members of the group" (6, p. 52).

More recently, Schutz (17) has made

these two dimensions central to his theory of group compatibility. For him, the strategic determinant of compatibility is the particular blend of orientations toward authority and orientations toward personal intimacy. Bion (1, 2) conceptualizes the major dimensions of the group somewhat differently. His "dependency" and "pairing" modalities correspond to our "dependence" and "interdependence" areas; to them he adds a "fight-flight" modality. For him these modalities are simply alternative modes of behavior; for us, the fight-flight categorization has been useful for characterizing the means used by the group for maintaining a stereotyped orientation during a given subphase.

The core of the theory of group development is that the principal obstacles to the development of valid communication are to be found in the orientations toward authority and intimacy that members bring to the group. Rebelliousness, submissiveness, or withdrawal as the characteristic response to authority figures; destructive competitiveness, emotional exploitiveness, or withdrawal as the characteristic response to peers prevent consensual validation of experience. The behaviors determined by these orientations are directed toward enslavement of the other in the service of the self, enslavement of the self in the service of the other, or disintegration of the situation. Hence, they prevent the setting, clarification of, and movement toward group-shared goals.

In accord with Freud's observation, the orientations toward authority are regarded as being prior to, or partially determining of, orientations toward other members. In its development, the group moves from preoccupation with authority relations to preoccupation with personal relations. This movement defines the two major phases of group development. Within each phase are three subphases, determined by the ambivalence of orientations in each area. That is, during the authority ("dependence") phase, the group moves from preoccupation with submission to preoccupation with rebellion, to resolution of the dependence problem. Within the personal (or "interdependence") phase the group moves from a preoccupation with intermember identification to a preoccupation with individual identity to a resolution of the interdependence problem.

The Relevant Aspects of Personality in Group Development

The aspects of member personality most heavily involved in group development are called, following Schutz, the dependence and personal aspects.

The dependence aspect is comprised by the member's characteristic patterns related to a leader or to a structure of rules. Members who find comfort in rules of procedure, an agenda, an expert, etc. are called "dependent." Members who are discomfited by authoritative structures are called "counterdependent."

The personal aspect is comprised by the member's characteristic patterns with respect to interpersonal intimacy. Members who cannot rest until they have stabilized a relatively high degree of intimacy with all the others are called "overpersonal." Members who tend to avoid intimacy with any of the others are called "counterpersonal."

Psychodynamically, members who evidence some compulsiveness in the adoption of highly dependent, highly counterdependent, highly personal, or highly counterpersonal roles are regarded as "conflicted." Thus, the person who persists in being dependent upon any and all authorities thereby provides himself with ample evidence that authorities should not be so trustingly relied upon; yet he cannot profit from this experience in governing his future action. Hence, a deep, but unrecognized, distrust is likely to accompany the manifestly submissive behavior, and the highly dependent or highly counterdependent person is thus a person in conflict. The existence of the conflict accounts for the sometimes dramatic movement from extreme dependence to extreme rebelliousness. In this way counterdependence and dependence, while logically the extremes of a scale, are psychologically very close together.

The "unconflicted" person or "independent," who is better able to profit from his experience and assess the present situation more adequately, may of course act at times in rebellious or submissive ways. Psychodynamically, the difference between him and the conflicted is easy to understand. In terms of observable behavior, he lacks the compulsiveness and, significantly, does not create the communicative confusion so characteristic of, say, the conflicted dependent, who manifests submission in that part of his communication of which he is aware, and distrust or rebellion in that part of his communication of which he is unaware.

Persons who are unconflicted with respect to the dependence or personal aspect are considered to be responsible for the major movements of the group toward valid communication. That is, the actions of members unconflicted with respect to the problems of a given phase of group development move the group to the next phase. Such actions are called barometric events, and the initiators are called catalysts. This part of the theory of group development is based on Redl's thesis concerning the "infectiousness of the unconflicted on the conflicted personality constellation." The catalysts (Redl calls them "central persons") are the persons capable of reducing the uncertainty characterizing a given phase. "Leadership" from the standpoint of group development can be defined in terms of catalysts responsible for group movement from one phase to the next. This consideration provides a basis for determining what membership roles are needed for group development. For example, it is expected that a group will have great difficulty in resolving problems of power and authority if it lacks members who are unconflicted with respect to dependence.

Phase Movements

The foregoing summary has introduced the major propositions in the theory of group development. While it is not possible to reproduce the concrete group experience from which the theory is drawn, we can take a step in this direction by discussing in more detail what seem to us to be the dominant features of each phase. The description given below is highly interpretive, and we emphasize what seem to us to be the major themes of each phase, even though many minor themes are present. In the process of abstracting, stereotyping, and interpreting, certain obvious facts about group process are lost. For example, each group meeting is to some extent a recapitulation of its past and a forecast of its future. This means that behavior that is "regressive" or "advanced" often appears.

PHASE I: DEPENDENCE

Subphase 1: Dependence-flight. The first days of group life are filled with behavior whose remote, as well as immediate, aim is to ward off anxiety. Much of the discussion content consists of fruitless searching for a common goal. Some of the security-seeking behavior is group-shared—for example, members may reassure one another by providing interesting and harmless facts about themselves. Some is idiosyncratic—for example, doodling, yawning, intellectualizing.

The search for a common goal is aimed at reducing the cause of anxiety, thus going beyond the satisfaction of immediate security needs. But just as evidencing boredom in this situation is a method of warding off anxiety by denying its proximity, so group goal-seeking is not quite what it is claimed to be. It can best be understood as a dependence plea. The trainer, not the lack of a goal, is the cause of insecurity. This interpretation is likely to be vigorously contested by the group, but it is probably valid. The characteristic expectations of group members are that the trainer will establish rules of the game and distribute rewards. He is presumed to know what the goals are or ought to be. Hence his behavior is regarded as a "technique"; he is merely playing hard to get. The pretense of a fruitless search for goals is a plea for him to tell the group what to do, by simultaneously demonstrating its helplessness without him, and its willingness to work under his direction for his approval and protection.

We are here talking about the dominant theme in group life. Many minor themes are present, and even in connection with the major theme there are differences among members. For some, testing the power of the trainer to affect their futures is the major concern. In others, anxiety may be aroused through a sense of helplessness in a situation made threatening by the protector's desertion. These alternatives can be seen as the beginnings of the counterdependent and dependent adaptations. Those with a dependent orientation look vainly for cues from the trainer for procedure and direction, sometimes paradoxically they infer that the leader must want it that way. Those with a counterdependent orientation strive to detect in the trainer's action elements that would offer ground for rebellion, and may even paradoxically demand rules and leadership from him because he is failing to provide them.

The ambiguity of the situation at this stage quickly becomes intolerable for some, and a variety of ultimately unserviceable resolutions may be invented, many of them idiosyncratic. Alarm at the prospect of future meetings is likely to be group-shared, and at least a gesture may be made in the direction of formulating an agenda for subsequent meetings.

This phase is characterized by behavior that has gained approval from authorities in the past. Since the meetings are to be concerned with groups or with human relations, members offer information on these topics, to satisfy the presumed expectations of the trainer and to indicate expertise, interest, or achievement in these topics (ex-officers from the armed services, from fraternities, etc. have the floor). Topics such as business or political leadership, discrimination and desegregation, are likely to be discussed. During this phase the contributions made by members are designed to gain approval from the trainer, whose reaction to each comment is surreptitiously watched. If the trainer comments that this seems to be the case, or if he notes that the subject under discussion (say, discrimination) may be related to some concerns about membership in this group, he fails again to satisfy the needs of members. Not that the validity of this interpretation is held in much doubt. No one is misled by the "flight" behavior involved in discussing problems external to the group, least of all the group members. Discussion of these matters is filled with perilous uncertainties, however, and so the trainer's observation is politely ignored, as one would ignore a *faux-pas* at a tea-party. The attempts to gain approval based on implicit hypotheses about the potential power of the trainer for good and evil are continued until the active members have run through the repertoire of behaviors that have gained them favor in the past.

Subphase 2: Counterdependence-flight. As the trainer continues to fail miserably in satisfying the needs of the group, discussion takes on a different tone, and counterdependent expressions begin to replace overt dependency phase. In many ways this subphase is the most stressful and unpleasant in the life of the group. It is marked by a paradoxical development of the trainer's role into one of omnipotence and powerlessness, and by division of the group into two warring subgroups. In subphase 1, feelings of hostility were strongly defended; if a slip were made that suggested hostility, particularly toward the trainer, the group members were embarrassed. Now expressions of hostility are more frequent, and are more likely to be supported by other members, or to be met

with equally hostile responses. Power is much more overtly the concern of group members in this subphase. A topic such as leadership may again be discussed, but the undertones of the discussion are no longer dependence pleas. Discussion of leadership in subphase 2 is in part a vehicle for making explicit the trainer's failure as a leader. In part it is perceived by other members as a bid for leadership on the part of any member who participates in it.

The major themes of this subphase are as follows:

1. Two opposed subgroups emerge, together incorporating most of the group members. Characteristically, the subgroups are in disagreement about the group's need for leadership or "structure." One subgroup attempts to elect a chairman, nominate working committees, establish agenda, or otherwise "structure" the meetings; the other subgroup opposes all such efforts. At first this appears to be merely an intellectual disagreement concerning the future organization of group activity. But soon it becomes the basis for destroying any semblance of group unity. Fragmentation is expressed and brought about in many ways: voting is a favorite way of dramatizing the schism; suggestions that the group is too large and should be divided into subgroups for the meetings are frequent; a chairman may be elected and then ignored as a demonstration of the group's ineffectualness. Although control mechanisms are sorely needed and desired, no one is willing to relinquish the rights of leadership and control to anyone else. The trainer's abdication has created a power gap, but no one is allowed to fill it.

2. Disenthrallment with the trainer proceeds rapidly. Group members see him as at best ineffectual, at worst

damaging, to group progress. He is ignored and bullied almost simultaneously. His interventions are perceived by the counterdependents as an attempt to interrupt group progress; by the dependents, as weak and incorrect statements. His silences are regarded by the dependents as desertion; by the counterdependents as manipulation. Much of the group activity is to be understood as punishment of the trainer, for his failure to meet needs and expectations, for getting the group into an unpleasant situation, for being the worst kind of authority figure—a weak and incompetent one, or a manipulative, insincere one. Misunderstanding or ignoring his comments, implying that his observations are paranoid fantasies, demonstrations that the group is cracking up, references to him in the past tense as though he were no longer present—these are the punishments for his failure.

As, in the first subphase, the trainer's wisdom, power, and competence were overtly unquestioned, but secretly suspected; so, in the second subphase, the conviction that he is incompetent and helpless is clearly dramatized, but secretly doubted. Out of this secret doubt arises the belief in the trainer's omnipotence. None of the punishments meted out to the trainer are recognized as such by the group members; in fact, if the trainer suggests that the members feel a need to punish him, they are most likely to respond in injured tones or in tones of contempt that what is going on has nothing to do with him and that he had best stay out of it. The trainer is still too imposing and threatening to challenge directly. There is a secret hope that the chaos in the group is in fact part of the master plan, that he is really leading them in the direction they should be going. That he may really be helpless as they imply, or that the failure may be theirs rather than his, are frightening possibilities. For this reason subphase 2 differs very little in its fundamental dynamics from subphase 1. There is still the secret wish that the trainer will stop all the bedlam which has replaced polite uncertainty, by taking his proper role (so that dependent members can cooperate with him and counterdependent can rebel in the usual ways).

Subphase 2 thus brings the group to the brink of catastrophe. The trainer has consistently failed to meet the group's needs. Not daring to turn directly on him, the group members engage in mutually destructive behavior: in fact, the group threatens suicide as the most extreme expression of dependence. The need to punish the trainer is so strong, however, that his act of salvation would have to be magical indeed.

Subphase 3: Resolution-catharsis. No such magic is available to the trainer. Resolution of the group's difficulties at this point depends upon the presence in the group of other forces, which have until this time been inoperative, or ineffective. Only the degenerative aspects of the chain of events in subphases 1 and 2 have been presented up to this point and they are in fact the salient ones. But there has been a simultaneous, though less obvious, mobilization of constructive forces. First, within each of the warring subgroups bonds of mutual support have grown. The group member no longer feels helpless and isolated. Second, the trainer's role, seen as weak or manipulative in the dependence orientation, can also be perceived as permissive. Third, his interpretations, though openly ignored, have been secretly attended to. And, as the second and third points imply, some members of the group are less the prisoners of the dependence-counterdependence dilemma than others. These members, called the independents, have been relatively ineffective in the group for two reasons. First, they have not developed firm bonds with other members in either of the warring subgroups, because they have not identified with either cause. Typically, they have devoted their energies to an unsuccessful search for a compromise settlement of the disagreements in the group. Since their attitudes toward authority are less ambivalent than those of other members, they have accepted the alleged reason for disagreement in the group—for example, whether a chairman should be elected—at face value, and tried to mediate. Similarly, they have tended to accept the trainer's role and interpretations more nearly at face value. However, his interpretations have seemed inaccurate to them, since in fact the interpretations have applied much less to them than to the rest of the group.

Subphase 3 is the most crucial and fragile in group life up to this point. What occurs is a sudden shift in the whole basis of group action. It is truly a bridging phase; if it occurs at all, it is so rapid and mercurial that the end of subphase 2 appears to give way directly to the first subphase of Phase II. If it does not occur thus rapidly and dramatically, a halting and arduous process of vacillation between Phases I and II is likely to persist for a long period, the total group movement being very gradual.

To summarize the state of affairs at the beginning of subphase 3: 1. The group is polarized into two competing groups, each unable to gain or relinquish power. 2. Those group members who are uncommitted to either subgroup are ineffective in their attempts to resolve the conflict. 3. The trainer's contributions only serve to deepen the cleavage in the group.

As the group enters subphase 3, it is moving rapidly toward extinction: that is, splintering into two or three subgroups. The independents, who have until now been passive or ineffectual, become the only hope for survival, since they have thus far avoided polarization and stereotypic behavior. The imminence of dissolution forces them to recognize the fruitlessness of their attempts at mediation. For this reason, the trainer's hypothesis that fighting one another is off-target behavior is likely to be acted upon at this point. A group member may openly express the opinion that the trainer's presence and comments are holding the group back, suggest that "as an experiment" the trainer leaves the group "to see how things go without him". When the trainer is thus directly challenged, the whole atmosphere of the meeting changes. There is a sudden increase in alertness and tension. Previously, there had been much acting out of the wish that the trainer were absent, but at the same time a conviction that he was the *raison d'être* of the group's existence —that it would fall apart without him. Previously, absence of the trainer would have constituted desertion, or defeat, fulfilment of the members worst fears as to their own inadequacy or the trainer's. But now leaving the group can have a different meaning. General agreement that the trainer should leave is rarely achieved. However, after a little further discussion it becomes clear that he is at liberty to leave, with the understanding that he wishes to be a member of the group, and will return if and when the group is willing to accept him.

The principal function of the symbolic removal of the trainer is in its effect of freeing the group to bring into awareness the hitherto carefully ignored feelings toward him as an authority figure, and toward the group activity as an off-target dramatization of the ambivalence toward authority. The leadership provided by the independents (whom the group sees as having no vested interest in power) leads to a new orientation toward membership in the group. In the discussion that follows the exit of the trainer, the dependents' assertion that the trainer deserted and the counterdependents' assertion that he was kicked out are soon replaced by consideration of whether his behavior was "responsible" or "irresponsible." The power problem is resolved by being defined in terms of member responsibilities, and the terms of the trainer's return to the group are settled by the requirement that he behave as "just another member of the group". This phrase is then explained as meaning that he should take neither more nor less responsibility for what happens in the group than any other member.

The above description of the process does not do justice to the excitement and involvement characteristic of this period. How much transferable insight ambivalent members acquire from it is difficult to assess. At least within the life of the group, later activity is rarely perceived in terms of submission and rebellion.

An interesting parallel, which throws light on the order of events in group development, is given in Freud's discussion of the myth of the primal horde. In his version:

"These many individuals eventually banded themselves together, killed [the father], and cut him in pieces. . . . They then formed the totemistic community of brothers all with equal rights and united by the totem prohibitions which were to preserve and to expiate the memory of the murder" (6, p. 112).

The horde's act, according to Freud, was soon distorted into an heroic myth: instead of murder by the group, the myth held that the father had been overthrown single-handed by one person, usually the youngest son. In this attribution of the group act to one individual (the hero) Freud saw the "emergence of the individual from group psychology." His definition of a hero is ". . . a man who stands up manfully against his father and in the end victoriously overthrows him" (8, p. 9). (The heroic myth of Freud thus shares much in common with Sullivan's "delusion of unique individuality.")

In the training group, the member who initiates the events leading to the trainer's exit is sometimes referred to as a "hero" by the other members. Responsibility for the act is felt to be shared by the group, however, and out of their experience comes the first strong sense of group solidarity and involvement—a reversal of the original version, where the individual emerges from the group. This turn of events clarifies Freud's remark concerning the libidinal ties to the leader and to the other group members. Libidinal ties toward the other group members cannot be adequately developed until there is a resolution of the ties with the leader. In our terms, those components of group life having to do with intimacy and interdependence cannot be dealt with until those components having to do with authority and dependence have been resolved.

Other aspects of subphase 3 may be understood by investigating the dramatic significance of the revolt. The event is always marked in group history as "a turning-point", "the time we became a group", "when I first got involved", etc. The mounting tension, followed by sometimes uproarious euphoria, cannot be entirely explained by the surface events. It may be that the revolt represents a realization of important fantasies individuals hold in all organizations, that the emotions involved are undercurrents wherever rebellious and submissive tendencies toward existing authorities must be controlled. These are the themes of some of our great dramas—*Antigone, Billy Budd, Hamlet,* and our most recent folk-tale, *The Caine Mutiny.* But the event is more than the presentation of a drama, or an acting-out of fantasies. For it can be argued that the moments of stress and catharsis, when emotions are labile and intense, are the times in the group life when there is readiness for change. Leighton's analysis of a minor revolution at a Japanese relocation camp is worth quoting in full on this point:

"While this [cathartic] situation is fraught with danger because of trends which may make the stress become worse before it gets better, there is also an opportunity for administrative action that is not likely to be found in more secure times. It is fairly well recognized in psychology that at periods of great emotional stir the individual human being can undergo far-reaching and permanent changes in his personality. It is as if the bone structure of his systems of belief and of his habitual patterns of behavior becomes soft, is fused into new shapes and hardens there when the period of tension is over. . . . Possibly the same

can be true of whole groups of people, and there are historical examples of social changes and movements occurring when there was widespread emotional tension, usually some form of anxiety. The Crusades, parts of the Reformation, the French Revolution, the change in Zulu life in the reign of Chaca, the Meiji Restoration, the Mormon movement, the Russian Revolution, the rise of Fascism, and alterations in the social sentiments of the United States going on at present are all to some extent examples" (12, p. 360).

Observers of industrial relations have made similar observations. When strikes result from hostile labor-management relations (as contrasted to straight wage demands), there is a fluidity of relationships and a wide repertoire of structural changes during this period not available before the strike act.[2]

So it is, we believe, with the training group. But what are the new values and behavior patterns that emerge out of the emotional experience of Phase I? Principally, they are acceptance by each member of his full share of responsibility for what happens in the group. The outcome is autonomy for the group. After the events of subphase 3, there is no more attribution of magical powers to the trainer— either the dependent fantasy that he sees farther, knows better, is mysteriously guiding the group and protecting it from evil, or the very similar counterdependent fantasy that he is manipulating the group, exploiting it in his own interests, that the experience is one of "brain-washing." The criterion for evaluating a contribution is no longer who said it, but what is said. Thereafter, such power fantasies as the

[2] See A. Gouldner (10), W. F. Whyte, Jr. (22). Robert E. Park, writing in 1928, had considerable insight on some functions of revolution and change. See (14).

trainer himself may have present no different problem from the power fantasies of any other group member. At the same time, the illusion that there is a struggle for power in the group is suddenly dissipated, and the contributions of other members are evaluated in terms of their relevance to shared group goals.

SUMMARY OF PHASE I

The very word development implies not only movement through time, but also a definite order of progression. The group must traverse subphase 1 to reach subphase 2, and subphase 3 before it can move into Phase II. At the same time, lower levels of development coexist with more advanced levels. Blocking and regression occur frequently, and the group may be "stuck" at a certain phase of development. It would, of course, be difficult to imagine a group remaining long in subphase 3—the situation is too tense to be permanent. But the group may founder for some time in subphase 2 with little movement. In short, groups do not inevitably develop through the resolution of the dependence phase to Phase II. This movement may be retarded indefinitely. Obviously much depends upon the trainer's role. In fact, the whole dependence modality may be submerged by certain styles of trainer behavior. The trainer has a certain range of choice as to whether dependency as a source of communication distortion is to be highlighted and made the subject of special experiential and conceptual consideration. The personality and training philosophy of the trainer determine his interest in introducing or avoiding explicit consideration of dependency. There are other important forces in the group besides the trainer, and these may serve to facilitate or block the development that has been described as typical of Phase I. Occasionally there may be no strong independents capable of bringing about the barometric events that precipitate movement. Or the leaders of opposing subgroups may be the most assertive members of the group. In such cases the group may founder permanently in subphase 2. If a group has the misfortune to experience a "traumatic" event early in its existence—exceedingly schizoid behavior by some member during the first few meetings, for example—anxieties of other members may be aroused to such an extent that all culturally suspect behavior, particularly open expression of feelings, is strongly inhibited in subsequent meetings.

Table I summarizes the major events of Phase I, as it typically proceeds. This phase has dealt primarily with the resolution of dependence needs. It ends with acceptance of mutual responsibility for the fate of the group and a sense of solidarity, but the implications of shared responsibility have yet to be explored. This exploration is reserved for Phase II, which we have chosen to call the Interdependence Phase.

PHASE II: INTERDEPENDENCE

The resolution of dependence problems marks the transfer of group attention (and inattention) to the problems of shared responsibility.

Sullivan's description of the change from childhood to the juvenile era seems pertinent here:

"The juvenile era is marked off from childhood by the appearance of an urgent need for compeers with whom to have one's existence. By 'compeers' I mean peo-

TABLE I   PHASE I. DEPENDENCE—POWER RELATIONS *

	SUBPHASE 1 DEPENDENCE-SUBMISSION	SUBPHASE 2 COUNTERDEPENDENCE	SUBPHASE 3 RESOLUTION
1. Emotional Modality	Dependence—Flight	Counterdependence—Fight. Off-target fighting among members. Distrust of staff member. Ambivalence.	Pairing. Intense involvement in group task.
2. Content Themes	Discussion of interpersonal problems external to training groups.	Discussion of group organization; i.e. what degree of structuring devices is needed for "effective" group behavior?	Discussion and definition of trainer role.
3. Dominant Roles (Central Persons)	Assertive, aggressive members with rich previous organizational or social science experience.	Most assertive counterdependent and dependent members. Withdrawal of less assertive independents and dependents.	Assertive independents.
4. Group Structure	Organized mainly into multi-subgroups based on members' past experiences.	Two tight subcliques consisting of leaders and members, of counterdependents and dependents.	Group unifies in pursuit of goal and develops internal authority system.
5. Group Activity	Self-oriented behavior reminiscent of most new social gatherings.	Search for consensus mechanism: Voting, setting up chairmen, search for "valid" content subjects.	Group members take over leadership roles formerly perceived as held by trainer.
6. Group movement facilitated by:	Staff member abnegation of traditional role of structuring situation, setting up rules of fair play, regulation of participation.	Disenthrallment with staff member coupled with absorption of uncertainty by most assertive counterdependent and dependent individuals. Subgroups form to ward off anxiety.	Revolt by assertive independents (catalysts) who fuse subgroups into unity by initiating and engineering trainer exit (barometric event).
7. Main Defenses	Projection Denigration of authority		Group moves into Phase II

* Course terminates at the end of 17 weeks. It is not uncommon for groups to remain through-out the course in this phase.

ple who are on our level, and have generically similar attitudes toward authoritative figures, activities and the like. This marks the beginning of the juvenile era, the great developments in which are the talents for cooperation, competition and compromise" (20, pp. 17–18. Emphasis ours).

The remaining barriers to valid communication are those associated with orientations toward interdependence: i.e. intimacy, friendship, identification. While the distribution of power was the cardinal issue during Phase I, the distribution of affection occupies the group during Phase II.

Subphase 4: Enchantment-flight. At the outset of subphase 4, the group is happy, cohesive, relaxed. The atmosphere is one of "sweetness and light". Any slight increase in tension is instantly dissipated by joking and laughter. The fighting of Phase I is still fresh in the memory of the group, and the group's efforts are devoted to patching up differences, healing wounds, and maintaining a harmonious atmosphere. Typically, this is a time of merrymaking and group minstrelsy. Coffee and cake may be served at the meetings. Hours may be passed in organizing a group party. Poetry or songs commemorating the important events and persons in the group's history may be composed by individuals or, more commonly, as a group project. All decisions must be unanimous during this period, since everyone must be happy, but the issues on which decisions are made are mostly ones about which group members have no strong feelings. At first the cathartic, healing function of these activities is clear; there is much spontaneity, playfulness, and pleasure. Soon the pleasures begin to wear thin.

The myth of mutual acceptance and universal harmony must eventually be recognized for what it is. From the beginning of this phase there are frequent evidences of underlying hostilities, unresolved issues in the group. But they are quickly, nervously smoothed over by laughter or misinterpretation. Subphase 4 begins with catharsis, but that is followed by the development of a rigid norm to which all members are forced to conform: "Nothing must be allowed to disturb our harmony in the future; we must avoid the mistakes of the painful past." Not that members have forgotten that the painful past was a necessary preliminary to the autonomous and (it is said) delightful present, though that fact is carefully overlooked. Rather, there is a dim realization that all members must have an experience somewhat analogous to the trainer's in subphase 3, before a mutually understood, accepted, and realistic definition of their own roles in the group can be arrived at.

Resistance of members to the requirement that harmony be maintained at all costs appears in subtle ways. In open group discussion the requirement is imperative: either the member does not dare to endanger harmony with the group or to disturb the *status quo* by denying that all problems have been solved. Much as members may dislike the tedious work of maintaining the appearance of harmony, the alternative is worse. The house of cards would come tumbling down, and the painful and exacting work of building something more substantial would have to begin. The flight from these problems takes a number of forms. Group members may say, "We've had our fighting and are now a group. Thus, further self-study is unnecessary." Very commonly, the possibility of any change may be prevented by not coming together as a total group at all. Thus the members may subgroup through an entire meeting. Those who would disturb the friendly subgroups are accused of "rocking the boat."

The solidarity and harmony become more and more illusory, but the group still clings to the illusion. This perseveration is in a way a consequence of the deprivation that members have experienced in maintaining the atmosphere of harmony. Maintaining it forces members to behave in ways alien to their own feelings; to go still further in group involvement would mean a complete loss of self. The group is therefore torn by a new ambivalence, which might be verbalized as follows: 1. "We all love one another and therefore we must maintain the solidarity of the group and give up whatever is necessary of our selfish desires." 2. "The group demands that I sacrifice my identity as a person; but the group is an evil mechanism which satisfies no dominant needs." As this subphase comes to a close, the happiness that marked its beginning is maintained only as a mask. The "innocent" splitting of the group into subgroups has gone so far that members will even walk around the meeting table to join in the conversation of a subgroup rather than speak across the table at the risk of bringing the whole group together. There is a certain uneasiness about the group; there is a feeling that "we should work together but cannot". There may be a tendency to regress to the orientation of subphase 1: group members would like the trainer to take over.

To recapitulate: subphase 4 begins with a happy sense of group belongingness. Individual identity is eclipsed by a "the group is bigger than all of us" sentiment. But this integration is short

lived: it soon becomes perceived as a fake attempt to resolve interpersonal problems by denying their reality. In the later stages of this subphase, enchantment with the total group is replaced by enchantment with one's subgroup, and out of this breakdown of the group emerges a new organization based on the anxieties aroused out of this first, suffocating, involvement.

Subphase 5: Disenchantment-fight. This subphase is marked by a division into two subgroups—paralleling the experience of subphase 2—but this time based upon orientations toward the degree of intimacy required by group membership. Membership in the two subgroups is not necessarily the same as in subphase 2: for now the fragmentation occurs as a result of opposite and extreme attitudes toward the degree of intimacy desired in interpersonal relations. The counterpersonal members band together to resist further involvement. The overpersonal members band together in a demand for unconditional love. While these subgroups appear as divergent as possible, a common theme underlies them. For the one group, the only means seen for maintaining self-esteem is to avoid any real commitment to others; for the other group, the only way to maintain self-esteem is to obtain a commitment from others to forgive everything. The subgroups share in common the fear that intimacy breeds contempt.

This anxiety is reflected in many ways during subphase 6. For the first time openly disparaging remarks are made about the group. Invidious comparisons are made between it and other groups. Similarly, psychology and social science may be attacked. The inadequacy of the group as a basis for self-esteem is dramatized in many ways—from stating "I don't care what you think", to boredom, to absenteeism. The overpersonals insist that they are happy and comfortable, while the counterpersonals complain about the lack of group morale. Intellectualization by the overpersonals frequently takes on religious overtones concerning Christian love, consideration for others, etc. In explanations of member behavior, the counterpersonal members account for all in terms of motives having nothing to do with the present group; the overpersonals explain all in terms of acceptance and rejection in the present group.

Subphase 5 belongs to the counterpersonals as subphase 4 belonged to the overpersonals. Subphase 4 might be caricatured as hiding in the womb of the group; subphase 5 as hiding out of sight of the group. It seems probable that both of these modalities serve to ward off anxieties associated with intimate interpersonal relations. A theme that links them together can be verbalized as follows: "If others really knew me, they would reject me." The overpersonal's formula for avoiding this rejection seems to be accepting all others so as to be protected by the others' guilt; the counterpersonal's way is by rejecting all others before they have a chance to reject him. Another way of characterizing the counterpersonal orientation is in the phrase, "I would lose my identity as a member of the group." The corresponding overpersonal orientation reads, "I have nothing to lose by identifying with the group." We can now look back on the past two subphases as countermeasures against loss of self-esteem; what Sullivan once referred to as the greatest inhibition to the understanding of what is distinctly human, "the overwhelming conviction of self-hood—

this amounts to a delusion of unique individuality". The sharp swings and fluctuations that occurred between the enchantment and euphoria of subphase 4 and the disenchantment of subphase 5 can be seen as a struggle between the "institutionalization of complacency" on the one hand and anxiety associated with fantasy speculations about intimacy and involvement on the other. This dissociative behavior serves a purpose of its own: a generalized denial of the group and its meaning for individuals. For if the group is important and valid then it has to be taken seriously. If it can wallow in the enchantment of subphase 4, it is safe; if it can continually vilify the goals and objectives of the group, it is also safe. The disenchantment theme in subphase 5 is perhaps a less skilful and more desperate security provision with its elaborate wall of defenses than the "group mind" theme of subphase 4. What should be stressed is that both subphase defenses were created almost entirely on fantastic expectations about the consequences of group involvement. These defenses are homologous to anxiety as it is experienced by the individual; i.e. the state of "anxiety arises as a response to a situation of danger and which will be reproduced thenceforward whenever such a situation recurs" (7, p. 72). In sum, the past two subphases were marked by a conviction that further group involvement would be injurious to members' self-esteem.

Subphase 6: Consensual validation. In the groups of which we write, two forces combine to press the group toward a resolution of the interdependency problem. These are the approaching end of the training course, and the need to establish a method of evaluation (including course grades).

There are, of course, ways of denying or avoiding these realities. The group can agree to continue to meet after the course ends. It can extricate itself from evaluation activities by asking the trainer to perform the task, or by awarding a blanket grade. But turning this job over to the trainer is a regression to dependence; and refusal to discriminate and reward is a failure to resolve the problems of interdependence. If the group has developed in general as we have described, the reality of termination and evaluation cannot be denied, and these regressive modes of adaptation cannot be tolerated.

The characteristic defenses of the two subgroups at first fuse to prevent any movement toward the accomplishment of the evaluation and grading task. The counterpersonals resist evaluation as an invasion of privacy: they foresee catastrophe if members begin to say what they think of one another. The overpersonals resist grading since it involves discriminating among the group members. At the same time, all members have a stake in the outcome of evaluation and grading. In avoiding the task, members of each subgroup are perceived by members of the other as "rationalizing", and the group becomes involved in a vicious circle of mutual disparagement. In this process, the fear of loss of self-esteem through group involvement is near to being realized. As in subphase 5, it is the independents —in this case those whose self-esteem is not threatened by the prospect of intimacy—who restore members' confidence in the group. Sometimes all that is required to reverse the vicious circle quite dramatically is a request by an independent for assessment of his own role. Or it may be an expression of confidence in the group's ability to accomplish the task.

The activity that follows group commitment to the evaluation task does not conform to the expectations of the overpersonal or counterpersonal members. Its chief characteristic is the willingness and ability of group members to validate their self-concepts with other members. The fear of rejection fades when tested against reality. The tensions that developed as a result of these fears diminish in the light of actual discussion of member roles. At the same time, there is revulsion against "capsule evaluations" and "curbstone psychoanalysis." Instead, what ensues is a serious attempt by each group member to verbalize his private conceptual scheme for understanding human behavior—his own and that of others. Bringing these assumptions into explicit communication is the main work of subphase 6. This activity demands a high level of work and of communicative skill. Some of the values that appear to underlie the group's work during this subphase are as follows: 1. Members can accept one another's differences without associating "good" and "bad" with the differences. 2. Conflict exists but is over substantive issues rather than emotional issues. 3. Consensus is reached as a result of rational discussion rather than through a compulsive attempt at unanimity. 4. Members are aware of their own involvement, and of other aspects of group process, without being overwhelmed or alarmed. 5. Through the evaluation process, members take on greater personal meaning to each other. This facilitates communication and creates a deeper understanding of how the other person thinks, feels, behaves; it creates a series of personal expectations, as distinguished from the previous, more stereotyped, role expectations.

The above values, and some concomitant values, are of course very close to the authors' conception of a "good group". In actuality they are not always achieved by the end of the group life. The prospect of the death of the group, after much procrastination in the secret hope that it will be over before anything can be done, is likely to force the group into strenuous last-minute efforts to overcome the obstacles that have blocked its progress. As a result, the sixth subphase is too often hurried and incomplete. If the hurdles are not overcome in time, grading is likely to be an exercise that confirms members' worst suspicions about the group. And if role evaluation is attempted, either the initial evaluations contain so much hostile material as to block further efforts, or evaluations are so flowery and vacuous that no one, least of all the recipient, believes them.

In the resolution of interdependence problems, member-personalities count for even more than they do in the resolution of dependence problems. The trainer's behavior is crucial in determining the group's ability to resolve the dependence issue, but in the interdependence issue the group is, so to speak, only as strong as its weakest link. The exceedingly dependent group member can ride through Phase I with a fixed belief in the existence of a private relationship between himself and the trainer; but the person whose anxieties are intense under the threats associated with intimacy can immobilize the group. (*Table II* summarizes the major events of Phase II.)

Conclusions

Dependence and interdependence—power and love, authority and intimacy —are regarded as the central problems of group life. In most organizations and societies, the rules governing the distribution of authority and the degree of intimacy among members are prescribed. In the human relations training group, they are major areas of uncertainty. While the choice of these matters as the focus of group attention and experience rests to some extent with the trainer, his choice is predicated on the belief that they are the core of interpersonal experience. As such, the principal obstacles to valid interpersonal communication lie in rigidities of interpretation and response carried over from the anxious experiences with particular love or power figures into new situations in which they are inappropriate. The existence of such autisms complicates all discussion unduly and in some instances makes an exchange of meanings impossible.

Stating the training goal as the establishment of valid communication means that the relevance of the autistic response to authority and intimacy on the part of any member can be explicitly examined, and at least a provisional alternative formulated by him. Whether this makes a lasting change in the member's flexibility, or whether he will return to his more restricted formula when confronted with a new situation, we do not know, but we expect that it varies with the success of his group experience—particularly his success in understanding it.

We have attempted to portray what we believe to be the typical pattern of group development, and to show the relationship of member orientations and changes in member orientations to the major movements of the group. In this connection, we have emphasized the catalytic role of persons uncon-

TABLE II   PHASE II. INTERDEPENDENCE—PERSONAL RELATIONS

	SUBPHASE 4—ENCHANTMENT	SUBPHASE 5—DISENCHANTMENT	SUBPHASE 6—CONSENSUAL VALIDATION
Emotional Modality	Pairing-Flight. Group becomes a respected icon beyond further analysis.	Fight-Flight. Anxiety reactions. Distrust and suspicion of various group members.	Pairing, understanding, acceptance.
Content Themes	Discussion of "group history", and generally salutary aspects of course, group, and membership.	Revival of content themes used in Subphase 1: What is a group? What are we doing here? What are the goals of the group? What do I have to give up—personally—to belong to this group? (How much intimacy and affection is required?) Invasion of privacy vs. "group giving". Setting up proper codes of social behavior.	Course grading system. Discussion and assessment of member roles.
Dominant Roles (Central Persons)	General distribution of participation for first time. Overpersonals have salience.	Most assertive counterpersonal and overpersonal individuals, with counterpersonals especially salient.	Assertive independents.
Group Structure	Solidarity, fusion. High degree of camaraderie and suggestibility. Le Bon's description of "group mind" would apply here.	Restructuring of membership into two competing predominant subgroups made up of individuals who share similar attitudes concerning degree of intimacy required in social interaction, i.e. the counterpersonal and overpersonal groups. The personal individuals remain uncommitted but act according to needs of situation.	Diminishing of ties based on personal orientation. Group structure now presumably appropriate to needs of situation based on predominantly substantive rather than emotional orientations. Consensus significantly easier on important issues.
Group Activity	Laughter, joking, humor. Planning out-of-class activities such as parties. The institutionalization of happiness to be accomplished by "fun" activities. High rate of interaction and participation.	Disparagement of group in a variety of ways: high rate of absenteeism, tardiness, balkiness in initiating total group interaction, frequent statements concerning worthlessness of group, denial of importance of group. Occasional member asking for individual help finally rejected by the group.	Communication to others of self-system of interpersonal relations; i.e. making conscious to self, and others aware of, conceptual system one uses to predict consequences of personal behavior. Acceptance of group on reality terms.
Group movement facilitated by:	Independence and achievement attained by trainer-rejection and its concomitant, consensually some effective means for authority and control. (Subphase 3 rebellion bridges gap between Subphases 2 and 4.)	Disenchantment of group as a result of *fantasied expectations of group life*. The perceived threat to self-esteem that further group involvment signifies creates schism of group according to amount of affection and intimacy desired. The counterpersonal and overpersonal assertive individuals alleviate source of anxiety by disparaging or abnegating further group involvement. Subgroups form to ward off anxiety.	The external realities, group termination and the prescribed need for a course grading system, comprise the barometric event. Led by the personal individuals, the group tests reality and reduces autistic convictions concerning group involvement.
Main Defences	Denial, isolation, intellectualization, and alienation.		

flicted with respect to one or the other of the dependence and interdependence areas. This power to move the group lies mainly in his freedom from anxiety-based reactions to problems of authority (or intimacy): he has the freedom to be creative in searching for a way to reduce tension.

We have also emphasized the "barometric event" or event capable of moving the group from one phase to the next. The major events of this kind are the removal of the trainer as part of the resolution of the dependence problem; and the evaluation-grading requirements at the termination of the course. Both these barometric events require a catalytic agent in the group to bring them about. That is to say, the trainer-exit can take place only at the moment when it is capable of symbolizing the attainment of group autonomy, and it requires a catalytic agent in the group to give it this meaning. And the grading assignment can move the group forward only if the catalytic agent can reverse the vicious circle of disparagement that precedes it.

Whether the incorporation of these barometric events into the training design merely makes our picture of group development a self-fulfilling prophecy, or whether, as we wish to believe, these elements make dramatically clear the major forward movements of the group, and open the gate for a flood of new understanding and communication, can only be decided on the basis of more, and more varied, experience.

The evolution from Phase I to Phase II represents not only a change in emphasis from power to affection, but also from role to personality. Phase I activity generally centers on broad role distinctions such as class, ethnic background, professional interests, etc.;

Phase II activity involves a deeper concern with personality modalities, such as reaction to failure, warmth, retaliation, anxiety, etc. This development presents an interesting paradox. For the group in Phase I emerged out of a heterogeneous collectivity of individuals; the individual in Phase II emerged out of the group. This suggests that group therapy, where attention is focused on individual movement, begins at the least enabling time. It is possible that, before group members are able to help each other, the barriers to communication must be partially understood.

References

1. BION, W. R. "Experiences in Groups: I." *Hum. Relat.*, Vol. I, No. 3, pp. 314–320, 1948.
2. BION, W. R. "Experiences in Groups: II." *Hum. Relat.*, Vol. I, No. 4, pp. 487–496, 1948.
5. FRENKEL-BRUNSWIK, E. "Intolerance of Ambiguity as an Emotional and Perceptual Personality Variable." In Bruner, J. S., and Krech, D. (eds.), *Perception and Personality*. Durham, N. C.: Duke Univ. Press, 1949 and 1950, p. 115.
6. FREUD, SIGMUND. *Group Psychology and the Analysis of the Ego*. Translated by J. Strachey. London: International Psycho-Analytical Press, 1922; New York: Liveright, 1949.
7. FREUD, SIGMUND. *The Problem of Anxiety*. Translated by H. A. Bunker. New York: Psychoanalytic Quarterly Press and W. W. Norton, 1936.
8. FREUD, SIGMUND. *Moses and Monotheism*. London: Hogarth Press, 1939; New York: Vintage Books, 1955.
10. GOULDNER, ALVIN. *Wildcat Strike.*

Yellow Springs, Ohio: Antioch Press, 1954; London: Routledge & Kegan Paul, 1955.

12. LEIGHTON, A. H. *The Governing of Men*. Princeton: Princeton Univ. Press, 1946.

14. PARK, ROBERT E. "The Strike." *Society*. New York: Free Press of Glencoe, 1955.

16. SCHUTZ, W. C. "Group Behavior Studies, I–III." Cambridge, Mass.: Harvard Univ., 1954 (mimeo).

17. SCHUTZ, W. C. "What Makes Groups Productive?" *Hum. Relat.*, Vol. VIII, No. 4, p. 429, 1955.

19. SULLIVAN, H. S. "Tensions, Interpersonal and International." In Cantril, Hadley (ed.), *Tensions that Cause Wars*. Urbana, Ill.: Univ. of Illinois Press, 1950.

20. SULLIVAN, H. S. *Conceptions of Modern Psychiatry*. Washington, D.C.: William Alanson White Psychiatric Foundation, 1940, 1945; London: Tavistock Publications, 1955.

22. WHYTE, W. F., Jr. *Patterns for Industrial Peace*. New York: Harper, 1951.

❖❖❖❖❖❖❖❖❖❖❖❖❖❖❖❖❖❖ THE GROWTH OF A GROUP

Herbert Thelen and Watson Dickerman

Wʜᴀᴛ are these [the common] stereotypes about the operation of groups and how are they related to the stages by which a group grows in productivity? Groups which were in operation for three weeks at the 1948 session of the National Training Laboratory on Group Development [1] serve to illustrate stereotypes at various stages of group growth. We shall try to describe both the phases in the development of these groups and the stereotypes about policies of operation which accompanied these phases. Our data are the sound recordings of the discussions of the eight groups at different stages in their development and the daily written records of the observer in each group.

In the light of what happened in these eight groups at the NTL, a group may perhaps be seen as going through four phases as it grows in ability to operate efficiently. *In the first phase various members of the group quickly attempt to establish their customary places in the leadership hierarchy.* In effect, this may be thought of as an attempt to establish the "peck order" of the group. *Next comes a period of frustration and conflict brought about by the leader's steadfast rejection of the concept of peck order and the authoritarian atmosphere in which the concept of peck order is rooted. The third phase sees the development of cohesiveness among the members of the group, accompanied by a certain amount of complacency and smugness.* This third

[1] Report of the Second Summer Session, National Training Laboratory in Group Development, Division of Adult Education Services, NEA, $1.25.

From Herbert Thelen and Watson Dickerman, "Stereotypes and the Growth of Groups," *Educational Leadership, Vol. 6, No. 5, February 1949, pp. 309–316. Used by permission.*

phase seems to be characterized by a determination to achieve and maintain harmony at all costs. Insofar as this effort is successful, it results in an atmosphere of deceptive "sweetness and light," which, nevertheless, is sufficiently permissive to enable the members to assess their own positions, modes of interaction, and attitudes in the group. This phase is unstable because it is unrealistic, and it gives way to a fourth phase. *In the fourth phase the members retain the group-centeredness and sensitivities which characterized the third phase, but they develop also a sense of purpose and urgency which makes the group potentially an affective social instrument.*

We turn now to an effort to identify some of the stereotypes about policies of operation which seem to characterize these four phases of the growth of our groups.

Phase One
Individually Centered

Every group needs a strong, expert leader.

Good group membership consists of active, oral participation; those who do not talk are not good group members.

The group is wasting its time unless it is absorbing information or doing something active—listening to lectures, receiving bibliographies, making long lists on the blackboard, role playing, working in sub-committees, passing resolutions.

The group cannot become cohesive or efficient until each member has certain "necessary" information about the other members—occupation, title, job responsibilities, age, education, family, hobbies.

The group's observer makes his assessment of the group's process by using his intuition. He gives the members interesting information about themselves.

Any expression of feeling, particularly of aggression or hostility, is bad. It upsets the group and should be squelched.

The chief function of the leader is to manipulate the group toward the goals which he knows are appropriate for it because of his competence and authority.

Each member sees the other members primarily as individuals rather than as parts of a group. Each must be dealt with individually through the kinds of appeals which are persuasive for him.

Phase Two
Frustration and Conflict Among Stereotypes

The stereotypic conflicts which characterize this phase are perceived quite differently by the members of the group at the beginning of the phase and at its end. At the beginning the leader is seen as a frustrating figure because he has refused to fit the stereotypes which characterized Phase One. This results in the direction of a good deal of hostility against him, which may be expressed quite overtly. By the end of Phase Two, this and other stereotypic conflicts are seen as simply the verbalization of the ambivalences of members of the group. In other words, they are seen as representing unsolved problems which plague all of us but which we manage to repress if our group has a strong leader who is willing to act as such. These conflicts seem to the writers to pose some of the most fundamental problems that individuals have to solve before they can become secure as members of a group. Typical stereotypic conflicts which characterize Phase Two follow:

We must have a leader who is strong to the point of being dominating and autocratic *versus* We must have a leader who is permissive to the point of being laissez faire.

Our troubles of operation would disappear if only the leader would tell us the theory of group dynamics *versus* Our troubles can disappear only when we have acquired skill in formulating a theory about and assessing the operations of our group.

Democratic group process requires a strong leader who is subject to criticism and recall by the group at any time *versus* Democratic group process requires a chairman whose primary job is to conciliate interpersonal conflicts among the active members of the group.

Efforts to assess our own group processes are an invasion of the sacredness of individual personalities *versus* Assessment of group process is a sounder starting point for intelligent group action than is attention to motivations and attitudes of individual members of the group.

Our basic problem is that members do not take enough initiative and responsibility *versus* Members who exhibit initiative and willingness to assume responsibility are competing with the leader.

A decision by majority vote is binding on all members of the group *versus* No individual should be coerced into going along with what he thinks is wrong.

Leadership is a role vested in a single competent member of the group *versus* Leadership is a complex function which should be distributed among all members of a group.

The first problem, which runs through most of these conflicts, appears to be the notion that the answer must be either A or B. Such thinking is most fruitless when neither A nor B is satisfactory. Members of a group must learn to ask, "Under what conditions is this policy wise?" rather than, "What policy is wise under all conditions?" The latter alternative is, of course, a legitimate question. But its answer would require appraisal of each of the alternative policies, followed by identification of the essential criteria for answering the first question. The answer to the second would probably be: any policy is wise if it satisfies this list of criteria: and the list of criteria would then have to be given.

It seems likely that the members of a group must reorient their ideas about how knowledge should be formulated. The notion that a set of generalizations about psychological phenomena can be given is less tenable than the notion that the legitimate content of psychological knowledge is only description and rationale for a set of procedures by which appropriate policy can be determined in a given situation. We are asserting, in effect, that content knowledge in the area of group dynamics consists not of generalizations about psychological phenomena *per se*. Rather, it consists of generalizations about how to proceed in determining right conduct. Generalizations of the first kind enter into generalizations of the second kind only insofar as they help us to speculate about whether or not a suggested method of procedure will have the consequences required by the criteria.

A second major problem which a group faces, in the light of the conflicts which have been described, is how to ask the right kind of questions—those which will lead to fruitful answers.

For example, an important question is: What is the relationship between an individual's rights and his duties to society? An unfruitful way to get at this relationship is to ask: What are the rights of individuals? The question might better be phrased: What are the characteristics of individual participation which most facilitate those types of interaction through which both the individual and his society can develop in desirable directions? The change in wording makes a *sine qua non* of neither the inalienable rights of individuals nor the demands of society. Instead, it focuses attention on the kinds of individual action which can contribute most both to his own individual growth and to a healthy society.

A third problem is partly one of insight of the group's goal and the steps necessary to reach it, and partly one of skill in communicating such insight to one another. Many of the conflicts arose because members of the group felt forced to take untenable positions—for example, on the nature of good leadership or the characteristics of democratic group process. When one has taken an untenable position, he is vulnerable to attack and is likely to become defensive because even he can see that his position is weak.

By the development of insight about goals and of skill in their communication, could each member's responses have contributed to the sequential solution of the problems the group was trying to solve rather than frittering away the group's time and strength on inconsequential flank skirmishes? For example, it may be that these destructive side battles could have been avoided if the members had seen the group's goal in terms of a series of sub-goals, each of which was to be reached through group action. One such sub-goal might be the existence of enough permissiveness so that members could alleviate their anxieties rather than project them into stereotypic conflicts. Another might be orientation in the methodology of action research so that members would acquire more know-how about solving problems. Another might be the acquisition of skill in making group decisions. Surmounting each of these sub-goals would carry the group forward progressively toward the final goal instead of encouraging endless and fruitless stereotypic conflicts.

Phase Three
Attempted Consolidation of Group Harmony

During this phase, the group's major purpose appears to be to avoid conflict of the sort that was so debilitating during the second period. This requires the development of skill in playing supportive roles, conciliating roles, integrating roles. It also requires the members to become more responsive to subtle cues and to take more responsibility for indicating agreement or disagreement with tentative notions, rather than flat rejections or acceptances of proposed solutions. Perhaps the major pitfall to be avoided at this point is that of glossing over significant differences for the sake of apparent harmony.

During the third period, then, we

find the following stereotypes dominant:

The goal of the group is cohesiveness not productivity.

Group-centered behavior is essentially a kind of polite behavior which avoids upsetting the group. Each individual must curb his impulses in such a way that conflict does not become open.

The leader is essentially a laissez faire chairman.

Planning or steering committees should be used to make concrete proposals for the group's consideration.

A person who is silent must be brought into the discussion so we can tell if he is unhappy.

Our most important goal is satisfaction for each individual in the group. We must work at this objectively and with considerable self-assessment. The self-assessment, however, must not reveal apparent individual weaknesses but rather the difficulties of a normal individual who is struggling with difficult problems.

Our leader may be seen as a fairly worthy person to have brought us to this pleasant position but, nevertheless, we will divide the job of chairmanship among ourselves.

During this third phase there is a marked increase in the sense of individual responsibility for satisfying group needs. One might see the preceding period of frustration as one in which every individual became highly involved emotionally in the group's process; in it, it is no longer possible to sit back to judge or to be amused. On the other hand, the desire to avoid further bitterness and conflict acts as

a strong disciplining influence and stimulates the development of skill which the members did not previously possess—those skills which allow a person to participate and yet avoid conflict. The former leader is now reinstated, not as a leader but as a resource person; and the group discussion shows fairly clearly that it is rejecting the concept of leadership as a personal role in favor of the concept of leadership as one aspect of good group membership—a function which is shared by all.

In a very real sense, the test of whether the preceding experiences of the members of the group have resulted in understanding may well be whether they move out of this stage in which "we all love each other with qualifications" but in which also significant skills are developing, to a later stage in which the group becomes a social instrument geared for action, directed outward toward the improvement of its environment rather than inward toward the adjustment of members to the present environment. Until this moving on to a later state takes place, it is as if the group were operating with some elements of phantasy, primarily in regard to its own goals. This phantasy is perilously close to the institutionalization of complacency on the one hand and to fear of ideational and other conflicts associated with solving action problems on the other.

It is probable that the only way in which this socially reinforced complacency can be broken down is through each individual's objective self-assessment. This will enable him to realize that if this period is too prolonged it will become an obstacle to any further growth on his part. It is necessary, then, for skills to be de-

veloped in a new functional area—
skills which will enable each individual
to realize his own needs for action in
the group as distinguished from skills
required for the individual to realize
his needs for position and security.
Along with this, at the conceptual
level, must come the understanding
that security is not a sufficient goal in
itself, but is the necessary condition
for effective action.

Phase Four
Individual Self-Assessment, Flexibility of Group Processes, and Emphasis Upon Productivity in Problem Solving

We present the apparent stereotypes
of this fourth phase with somewhat
less confidence than those of the other
phases because most of our groups did
not go on into the social action stage.
They did not actually tackle problems
of adjusting their own environment.
One had the feeling that the Laboratory ended with the groups in the middle of a phase, with things yet to happen. It is quite possible, also, that even
if there had been time for this fourth
phase to completely develop, other still
more mature phases may lie beyond it.
There are, however, a number of impressions that most of the observers
seemed to concur in, which suggest directions such as those described in the
preceding paragraph and which require the development of skills beyond
those required in the third phase.

The two most obvious characteristics
of this fourth phase are the attainment
by the members of much greater objectivity with regard to individual roles
in the group, and the attainment of
much greater ease in making decisions
and much more flexibility in controlling group processes. For a third characteristic of the fourth phase, namely,
participation as a group in problem-solving activities designed to change
or modify the social scene through direct impact on it rather than merely
through the changed attitudes and
skills of individuals, we have less evidence than expectation. But there is
some reason to believe that readiness
for this kind of activity is developing.

Another difficulty encountered in
trying to describe the stereotypes which
govern this fourth phase is that stereotypic thinking was much less frequent,
and in many of the group members
there was a definite feeling of revulsion
whenever anyone attempted to produce a capsule evaluation as to whether
the chairman was behaving in a
"democratic" manner or not. It is as
if the conceptualization had been
driven down into a much deeper level,
whose complexity made verbalization
difficult. Permissiveness had developed
at the level of individual thinking;
that is, individuals are now free to
theorize about these processes in their
own way.

It is the introduction of this element
which takes the method of control out
of the laissez faire area in which there
is considerable permissiveness of specific
behaviors but very little permissiveness of conceptualization and thinking
about behaviors. It is because of the
deeper, more personalized conceptualizations that frustration and impasse
due to conflict can be avoided in a
climate having this second sort of permissiveness.

The stereotypes that we can identify,
then, in the fourth phase, should probably be thought of not as verbalizations whose relation to operation is
vague and conflicting in the minds of
members, but rather as principles of
operation which have developed in-

ductively and more or less consciously as by-products of the individual's attempt to meet his own needs in the group. Among these notions are:

Each individual has a personality of his own which is different from that of other group members and is not to be judged as either good or bad.

The nature of this personality determines the efficiency and ease with which individuals will be able to play different roles in the group.

If a member of a group is to grow in ability to participate in the group, other members must help him by demonstrating their expectation that he will grow and their approval of his growing ability to formulate perceptions about group process.

This, in turn, means that all individual perceptions and differences among them have to be treated as realities. It also means that we cannot assume that any one individual's perceptions are the "right" ones.

Contributions of each individual must be assumed to be relevant to the problem under consideration. It is up to the group to find out what the relevance is. Only thus can the goal directions of each individual be continually woven into the goal direction of the group as a whole.

Although the deeper meanings of each individual's contribution cannot be taken for granted, enough rapport has developed that the members know about what to expect from each individual. It is only when these expectations are violated by the introduction of novel and threatening elements into the situation that a serious problem arises.

The question of "What is our purpose at this point? What is the problem we are trying to solve?" is recognized as one of the most helpful questions that can be asked instead of one of the most obstructing questions which should, at all costs, be avoided and resented.

In a sense, every member is expected to play all roles at appropriate times. The question of which roles should be formally structured by the group and assigned to particular individuals and for what periods of time remains unanswered. The members seem to feel that the answer lies in analysis of what roles are needed by the group for the solution of the problems at hand and of the interests and needs of individuals for playing these roles.

The place of ethics, as a source of guidance for the group, lies in making the formulation of criteria for success in particular situations easier. It does not, in itself, provide the policies for running the group.

A Hypothesis Proposed

The identification of the four phases of group growth which have been discussed amounts to stating a hypothesis about the course of group growth:

Beginning with individual needs for finding security and activity in a social environment, we proceed first to emotional involvement of the individuals with each other, and second to the development of a group as a rather limited universe of interaction among individuals and as the source of individual security. We then find that security of position in the group loses its significance except that as the group attempts to solve problems it structures its activities in such a way that each individual can play a role which may be described as successful or not in terms of whether the group successfully solved the problem it had set itself.

It is not our contention that these four phases develop in sequential order. We have attempted to identify some of the stereotypes which seem to us to represent the perceptions of the members of these groups at different stages in the development into groups. We do not claim that this particular course of development of stereotypes about policies of operation would be found in all groups under all conditions. We do feel that identification of the members' stereotypes about policies of operation would help many groups in their growth as individually satisfying social milieux and as effective social action instruments.

✧✧✧✧✧✧✧✧✧✧✧✧✧✧✧✧✧✧✧✧ SOME DIMENSIONS OF GROUP GROWTH

National Training Laboratories

1. Intercommunication between members of group
   a. Mechanics of communication—vocabulary, rules of procedure, semantic sensitivity, *et cetera.*
   b. Permissiveness for all members in expressing fears, needs, concerns, ideas, *et cetera,* to the group.

2. Group objectivity towards its own functioning
   a. Ability by all members to make and accept interpretation about members and group functioning.
   b. Ability to collect and use appropriate process information about itself.

3. Interdependent responsibility by all members for
   a. Sharing leadership functions—direction setting, being a resource for the group, *et cetera.*
   b. Achieving skill in flexible adjustment to member and leader when required by the group at various stages of group production.

   c. Achieving mutual sensitivity to the needs and styles of participation of the members.
   d. Distinguishing between member role contributions and personality characteristics.

4. Group cohesion adequate to permit
   a. Assimilation of new ideas without group disintegration.
   b. Assimilation of new members in a way to strengthen rather than to disrupt the group.
   c. Holding to long-range goals.
   d. Profiting from success experiences.
   e. Learning from failure experiences and setting of realistic goals.
   f. Making constructive use of internal conflicts.

5. Group ability to inform itself and to think straight and decide creatively about its problems
   a. Utilizing contribution potential of all members.
   b. Discovering and utilizing ap-

Excerpted from the National Training Laboratories, "Some Dimensions of Group Growth," Dynamics of Group Life, *National Training Laboratories Trainers' Workbook, No. 7, National Training Laboratories, Washington, D.C., 1958, pp. 97-98. Abridged and used by permission.*

propriate resource materials and persons.

c. Detecting and correcting fallacies in group thinking.

6. Group ability to detect and control rhythms of group metabolism

a. Fatigue, tension, tempo, pace, emotional atmosphere, *et cetera*.

7. Skill in recognizing and achieving control of significant sociometric factors in its own group structure.

8. Satisfactory integrations of member ideologies, needs, and goals with common group traditions, ideology, and goals.

9. Group ability to create new functions and groups as needed and to terminate its existence if and as appropriate.

CHAPTER 7

Characteristics of
Other Client-Systems

In preparing this chapter the authors faced the almost impossible task of selecting from a vast range of social science literature representative statements (of relevance to change-agents) about social systems other than small groups. Our selections have been unavoidably drastic. But a rationale did guide our processes of selection.

First, we wished to present the basic notions of "self," "role," "organization," and "community," because these concepts are important tools in the diagnosis and analysis of behavior at various social levels. The concept of "self" has been singled out from the field of personality theory and research since it represents a "part" of personality that is relatively accessible for scrutiny, analysis, and change by change-agents who are not psychotherapists. Furthermore, "the self" is involved both in the dynamics of personality and in the dynamics of the social settings in which persons function.

"Role" is one of the most useful concepts for change-agents, since even more explicitly than "self" it links the person to his society. "Role," the behavioral patterns expected and enacted in a social interaction, combines aspects of personality—especially the self—with the social settings in which people operate and with the organized structures and larger systems of which particular social settings are a part. The term "role" is thus a major bridging term for interrelating the ideas derived from the psychology of the individual and from the sociology of groups. The fact that the major conceptual formulations of "role" and the bulk of the empirical studies of it have pivoted around role conflict and role difficulties further indicates its strategic importance for a change-agent in diagnosing the difficulties of a client-system. "Self" and "role" are portrayed in interpersonal relations, in small groups, in organizations, in communities, and in cultures. Chapter 6 has emphasized the small group, while concepts about "organization" are more heavily represented, though all too briefly, in this chapter.

Harry Stack Sullivan occupies a prominent place in recent efforts to tie together the psychodynamic notions of Freud with ideas and concepts of social interaction. His paper on *Multidisciplined Coordination of Interpersonal Data* traces the place of anxiety in both the processes of personality development and the dynamics of interactive interpersonal relations.

Sullivan uses a system model basically, although he also utilizes stages or "modes" of socialization as applied to personality. His interpersonal theory can be seen to be utilizing an intersystem model.

In contrast, Rogers, an avowed proponent of the view that personality can be approached through studying changes in self-conceptions, presents an intriguing developmental model in his paper *A Process Conception of Psychotherapy*.

The concept of "role" is represented by three papers in this chapter, each of which employs a system model. Baumgartel, in *The Concept of Role,* summarizes in nontechnical fashion, and from the viewpoint of a change-agent, selected aspects of current theory about role and role conflict.

"Role" is used as the key term in a paper by Getzels, *Administration as a Social Process*. He analyzes the process of administration in terms of social or interpersonal relationships between subordinates and superordinates.

The Resolution of Role Conflict within the Family, by Spiegel, draws a closed boundary around family members to show how equilibration, disequilibration, and re-equilibration occur when role conflict is present. In tracing through how such processes happen, he illustrates very well the "mechanisms" of the role system of the family in the behaviors of family members as they affect each other.

Organizational Analysis, by Gouldner, clarifies two modes of analysis used by sociologists in analyzing large-scale organizations—the rational model and the natural system model.

Moe, in *The Nature of a Community,* applies system-thinking to a community, in viewing it as a system of systems.

Sanders, in *Approaches to Social Change,* describes the major current sociological and anthropological approaches to the study of social change.

In brief, Chapter 7 exemplifies the extension of thinking in terms of "system" and "developmental" models to concepts of "self," "role," "organization," and "community."

◇◇◇◇◇◇◇◇◇◇◇◇◇◇◇◇◇◇◇◇ MULTIDISCIPLINED COORDINATION
OF INTERPERSONAL DATA

Harry Stack Sullivan

IN any discussion about personality considered as an entity, we must use the term, *experience*. Whatever else may be said about experience, it is in final analysis experience of *tensions* and experience of *energy transformations*. I use these two terms in exactly the same sense as I would in talking about physics; there is no need to add adjectives such as "mental"—however "mental" experience itself may be conceived to be.[1]

In the realm of personality and culture, tensions may be considered to have two important aspects: that of tension as a potentiality for action, for the transformation of energy; and that of a *felt* or wittingly noted state of being. The former is intrinsic; the latter is not. In other words, tension *is* potentiality for action, and tension *may* have a felt or representational component. There is no reason for doubting that this contingent rather than intrinsic factor is a function of experience rather than of tension *per se*, for it applies in the same way to energy transformations. They, too, *may* have felt or representational components, or transpire without any witting awareness.

[1] For a discussion of the philosophical aspects of the concept of *tension*, see Dunham, Albert. PSYCHIATRY 1:119–179, 1938.

Yet the undergoing of tensions and of energy transformations, however free the events may have been from any representative component, is never exterior to the sum total of *living* and in many instances not beyond the possibility of some kind of *recall*—indication as of the dynamically surviving, actual past, with detectable influence on the character of the foreseen and dynamically significant neighboring future.

These observations have required the hypothesis that *experience occurs in three modes:* the *prototaxic*, the *parataxic*, and the *syntaxic*—of which the last mentioned is by far the easiest to discuss, though the least frequently encountered. All the experience of the first months of postnatal life is in the prototaxic mode; much of anyone's life experience is in the parataxic mode; and some widely varied part of one's experience from say around age three years is in the syntaxic mode.

A person's experience in the prototaxic mode is quite probably a discrete series of significantly different momentary states of the psychophysical organism extending from an indeterminately early time to the present. It cannot be a continuum. The factor of significant difference in momentary states is doubtless both a function of

Excerpted from Harry Stack Sullivan, "Multidisciplined Coordination of Interpersonal Data," Culture and Personality, edited by S. Stansfeld Sargent and Marian W. Smith, Wenner Gren Foundation for Anthropological Research, Inc., 1949, pp. 175–190. Abridged and by permission of the William Alanson White Psychiatric Foundation, Inc.

TABLE I [2]

EXPERIENCE is of	{ tensions energy transformations		
occurs in 3 modes	{ prototaxic parataxic syntaxic		
TENSIONS are those of	{ needs anxiety	{ general zonal	
ENERGY TRANSFORMATIONS are	{ overt covert		

[2] The Tables and Figures are reproduced by courtesy of PSYCHIATRY: Journal for the Operational Statement of Interpersonal Relations, published by the William Alanson White Psychiatric Foundation, Washington, D.C.

biological developmental emergents and a function of past experience. Prototaxic experience of the most elaborated kind may be the wholly unformulable—and, therefore, wholly uncommunicable—part of some mystical experiences of "cosmic identification" and the like, and of some dreams. The one *relationship* which certainly exists between items of experience in the prototaxic mode is succession, place in organismic or biological time.

As one's capacity to adduce relations among the events of one's experience grows, many of these experiences come to show an increasingly *general* character; they "take on personal meaning" —are organized into one or another of the *personifications* of "myself" which centers around increasing acquaintance with *"my body,"* and into personifications of sundry other people in the case of the more signficant of whom the personifications grow to be and function as *eidetic* people.

To the extent that observation, analysis, and the eduction of relations is subjected to *consensual validation* "with" others, it ensues in experience

in the syntaxic mode. All the rest is experience in the parataxic mode.

Needless to say consensual validation does not mean the establishment of correctness in some absolute sense; it means only that degree of approximate agreement with a significant other person or persons which permits fairly exact communication by speech or otherwise, and the drawing of generally useful inferences about the action and thought of the other. A great deal of most people's syntaxic experience is bound by the prescriptions and limitations of the culture; the exceptions to this being the results of rigorous "thinking" from actually adequate premises, and testing by crucial experiments.

I trust that this condensed statement has not obscured to you the fact that most of the experience which enters into our living occurs in and remains in the parataxic mode. Some of it occurs in, or is subsequently elaborated into, the syntaxic mode. I have put *thinking,* above, in quotation marks because, so far as I can discover, *known* thought—referential processes within awareness—is but a perhaps small part of the covert processes that are concerned in any thinking. For all I know, experience in the prototaxic and parataxic mode is always or very frequently involved in the unknown processes which underlie or culminate in known reveries and logically formulated ideas in the "contents of consciousness."

Referring back to Table I, it is to be noted that tensions are subdivided into those of *needs*—with two subdivisions, general and zonal—and those of anxiety. The tensions of *general* needs have, one might say, physiological basis; they reflect, for example, the biological requirements of the human animal, for metabolic activities, for other factors in survival, and for reproduction. The *zonal* needs are additional to these general needs, however closely the totality of zonal needs may be related to that of general needs. They arise from, or as a specific manifestation of, what we conceptualize as the *zones of interaction* with the environment; the specifically characterized organizations of *experience and* biological factors which constitute the discriminable loci of other events with events of "my body" at the conscious or witting level, and with the totality of the human being. Let me hint at the meaning of this by mentioning some of these zones: the oral zone, the manual zone, the anal zone, the genital zone; and, in a somewhat different category, the general tactile zone, the temperature zone, the aural zone, and visual zone.

Tensions of anxiety are of a quite different nature. Let me quote here from a study in the course of preparation for another purpose: [3] "Like any

[3] Since published as "The Meaning of Anxiety in Psychiatry and in Life", PSYCHIATRY, 1948, 11:1–13.

mammalian creature, man is endowed with the potentialities for undergoing *fear,* but in almost complete contradistinction to infrahuman creatures, man in the process of becoming a person always develops a great variety of processes directly related to the undergoing of *anxiety.*

"As felt experience, marked fear and uncomplicated anxiety are identical; that is, there is nothing in one's awareness of the discomfort which distinguishes the one from the other. Fear, as a significant factor in any situation, is often unequivocal. Anxiety, on the other hand, in anything like the accustomed circumstances of one's life is seldom clearly represented as such in awareness. Instances of fear in the course of accustomed peacetime living are not numerous while instances of—generally unrecognized—anxiety are very frequent in the waking life of a great many people.

"The significant pattern of situations characterized by the tension of fear is not recondite and is roughly the same for all people, excepting for the effects of habituation. The significant pattern of situations which arouse anxiety is generally obscure; can be almost infinitely varied among people; and shows much less, and very much less obvious, effects of habituation.

". . . Anxiety from its mildest to its most extreme manifestation interferes with effective alertness to the factors in the current situation that are immediately relevant to its occurrence, and thus with the refinement and precision of action related to its relief or reduction.

". . . Anxiety as a factor in behavior is first manifested in early infancy . . . Very young infants show grossly identical patterns of behavior when they are subjected to 'frightening' situations and when they are in contact with the person who mothers them *and that person is anxious, angry, or otherwise disquieted.* Something which develops without a break into the tension state which we have discriminated on the basis of its specific differences from fear can be *induced* in the infant by *interpersonal influence,* in contrast to the evocation of primitive fear by sundry violent influences from 'outside' or 'inside' the infant's body.

"This *interpersonal induction* of anxiety, and the exclusively interpersonal origin of every instance of its manifestations, is the unique characteristic of anxiety and of the congeries of more complex tensions in later life to which it contributes . . .'"

Table I finally contrasts the energy transformations which are "objectively" manifest with those the occurrence of which may only be inferred—"introspective accounts" notwithstanding, for these accounts are overt energy transformations often by no means sim-

ply related to the covert processes to which they are presumed to be related.

"The next Table carries us somewhat further. The term, *euphoria*, refers to a polar construct, an abstract ideal, in which there is *no* tension, therefore no action—tantamount in fact perhaps to something like an empty state of bliss. The level of euphoria and the level of tension are inversely related. There is no zero or utter degree of either. Terror is perhaps the most extreme degree of tension ordinarily observable; the deepest levels of sleep, perhaps the nearest approach to euphoria."

By the device of this Table, I hope to suggest that no experience of tension or action in the prototaxic mode is witting. It is all, in the jargon of some years since, "unconscious." On the other hand fully consensually validated action and "thought" may also be wholly unwitting, as we see in instances of what are called the manifestations of *dissociated* motivation. Tensions, to repeat myself, may be felt

TABLE II

EXPERIENCE					
	mode of			character of	
ACTION	syntaxic		witting		unwitting
	parataxic				
	prototaxic				
[EUPHORIA]					
TENSION	prototaxic				
	parataxic				
	syntaxic		felt		otherwise manifest

tensions; but, particularly for those experienced in the parataxic and the prototaxic mode, may have no representation in focal awareness but are otherwise manifested—as in the case of a person whose skeletal musculature shows a high oppositional postural tone, without his being aware that he is "tense."

You may have noticed a certain clumsiness in the expression "human being considered as a substantive unit" used earlier, and wonder if this is equivalent to the term "person" and to the term "personality."

Person is a relatively non-specific general reference to unquestionably extant, "purely imaginary," or—the usual—blend of demonstrable biological reality and imposed personification to which many people refer as human individuals. Table III reflects the precise meaning of the term "personality." At first glance, this may seem to be a great come-down from the conviction of unique individuality which each of you entertains about yourself.

forms it can make a number of mistakes; and any but the most remarkable of oboists, truly disconcerting noises; yet these differences do not obscure the pattern of the Quartet. It can even be "swung," by a dance orchestra and still, if one's irritation is not too great, be recognized as a systematic distortion of the wonderfully complex pattern of sounds and relations which is the Quartet.

The study of personality cannot, then, deal with individual transient phenomena or with unique episodes, but only with delineable patterns of recurrent processes in interpersonal fields, except when a transient phenomenon or unique episode is recognized as a significant difference from a delineated pattern—and, as such, either *a chance occurrence* or an item in some other pattern of presumptively recurrent interpersonal field.

The determination of the probability that an observed significant difference in the shape of a transient phenomenon or incongruous episode *is* a

TABLE III

PERSONALITY: the relatively enduring pattern of recurring interpersonal situations which characterize a human life.

PATTERN: the envelope of all insignificant differences.

Much depends on grasping the particular denotation of the term, "pattern." Insignificant differences are included in any particular pattern. As soon as a difference becomes significant, the pattern is not the same but a different one. The realm of perceived articulated sound—whether speech, music, or another—is, so to say, nothing but patterns. Take, for example, Mozart's Quartet in F Major (K. 370). Any member of a quartet which per-

(mathematically) chance occurrence or the sign of a usefully meaningful change of pattern is a recurrent task in the earlier phases of any adequate intensive study of personality. The difficulty of this task is somewhat reduced by the use of heuristic frame of reference, the stages of development of potentialities for interpersonal relatedness, and the history of corresponding patterns of relations which the subject-person can be led to reveal.

TABLE IV [4]

Stages in the development of potentialities which may be manifested in interpersonal fields [from mostly West European data]

---

1. INFANCY to the maturation of the capacity for language behavior

2. CHILDHOOD to the maturation of the capacity for living with compeers

3. JUVENILE ERA to the maturation of the capacity for isophilic intimacy

4. PREADOLESCENCE to the maturation of the genital lust dynamism

5. EARLY ADOLESCENCE to the patterning of lustful behavior

6. LATE ADOLESCENCE to maturity

---

[4] Since the occasion of this Conference, I have changed the statement of criteria of Stages 4 and 5—the above statements of which had survived unchecked from an earlier formulation. I now consider that Preadolescence ends and Early Adolescence is ushered in by maturation of capacity for intimacy with a member of the other sex—which, so far as I know always occurs, if at all, after the physiological puberty change. Late Adolescence occurs upon the patterning of lustful, heterosexual behavior. These revised criteria take better account of the many deviations which are lumped under "sexual peculiarities."

A rigorous analysis of lustful integrations (1943) shows that three factors are concerned: the intimacy need and precautions concerned; the preference as to partner or substitute therefor; and the form of genital participation or substitution. There are 54 meaningfully possible patterns arising from combinations of these factors; overt manifestation by the male of 6 of which is improbable; of 3 others, certainly infrequent. Forty-five different pattern of *sexual behavior* and 54 patterns of sexual *revery processes* have to be recognized in characterizing a person's dynamic participation in such a field. Twenty-three of the 54 are confused in "homosexual behavior or tendencies;" 25 of the 54, in "heterosexual behavior or tendencies." It is not strange, therefore, that many previous discussions of sex have been rather unhelpful.

However infrequently the fact may have been noticed, nothing is clearer than that personality undergoes rather striking changes at comparatively well-marked times in the progression from birth towards maturity, as well as in certain critical circumstances, such as those of the eruption of acute mental disorder, or recovery therefrom, or when one has had an exceedingly fortunate or unfortunate experience. From the more biologically timed of these changes, it is evident that the maturation of the more significant capabilities of the underlying human animal takes from 10 to 17 or more years of lifetime. Obviously, infantile experience, and the experience of childhood, as here defined, is far from an adequate explanation of the potentialities for and characteristics of interpersonal relations at later stages, although I can go with Freudian and related approaches to human development to the extent of saying that sufficiently unfortunate experience at stage one or two can make a desirable progression through subsequent stages less probable. Whenever great warp has been incorporated in personality, it takes very fortunate experience in a later stage to eliminate serious deviation as a permanent result. But, in complete contradistinction to the ordinarily accepted Freudian and related views I will assert that it is adequate experience in stage 4 that determines one's automatic ease or unvarying stress in dealing with any significant member of one's own sex; as adequate experience in stage 5 determines one's ease or discomfort in dealing with significant members of the other sex—regardless of anything that has gone before.

Let me now pass on to the most dubious part of this talk, a discussion of interpersonal fields with the aid of some merely suggestive diagrams.[5] Fig. 1 shows a way of depicting "a personality," the hypothetical entity which we posit to account for interpersonal fields.

"Looking first at the upper figure, note that there is a complete central disc—representing the serially matured inborn capabilities; half of which have been developed by experience as shown in the sectors; half of which, in this instance, have not been realized because no related experience has occurred— this being indicated by the semicircle of dashes.

"Each of these sectors in itself indicates a major motivational system. Please do not think that there are but six major motivational systems; it is convenient to draw six sectors. In each of these sectors, you will note that in

[5] The following several paragraphs are mostly quoted from the paper cited in reference footnote 3, which used the herewith black-and-white reproductions instead of the colored diagrams actually utilized in the course of this presentation.

their periphery, there are three types of shading. The dotted shading is that part of experience organized in the particular motivational system which is in the *self-system*—which ordinarily means that it is readily accessible to awareness, recall, and so on. The cross-hatched section next to it represents the experience which is fraught with anxiety. The single-hatched area beyond represents the part of experience related to that particular motivational system which is not in the self-system and, under all ordinary circumstances, is quite difficult or impossible of access to awareness.

"The drawing below this represents an extension in time of the more recent phases of the personality under discus-

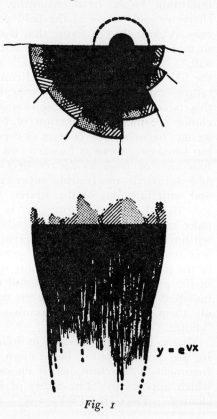

$$y = e^{vx}$$

Fig. 1

sion up to the immediate present. The formula indicates that the boundaries of each of the sectors will be instances of the so-called snowball law, the law of growth—$y = e^x$—the v in the formula represents a complex variable about which I will content myself by observing that it increases rapidly in the immediate neighborhood of each of the developmental thresholds indicated in Table IV, and diminishes thereafter to the proximity of the next threshold."

The near future is just as real an element in interpersonal relations as is the near past. The dynamic importance of both may be low, as in the case of a so-called *psychopathic personality*. On the other hand, foresight may be a very important factor in determining the character and course of the field processes. A great deal of living that is said to manifest "good judgment," "strong will," "steadfast determination," and the like—all with a rosy ethical connotation—can be explained by appeal to this factor of foresight. Decision and choice are mostly a function of foreseeing "hypothetical" courses of events, but foreseeing them as forward-looking functions of both easily recollectable and ordinarily inaccessible experience, and with full play of the anxiety factor. In other words, foresight is no more entirely a witting process wholly within awareness than is observation and analysis of the momentary present or the past. In some people, many steps in the process can be recalled and formulated; in others; few or even none of them but the end result—the "choice."

Figure 2 and the discussion following are quoted from or based upon the treatment of "a schizophrenic episode" which appears in "The Study of Psychiatry" (PSYCHIATRY, 1947, 10:-355–371), which may well be read as a supplement to this lecture. Be warned that the same devices of shading are used in depicting durable personality organizations and in indicating shifting field forces.

"In Fig. 2 we are no longer concerned with the representation of a hypothetical personality but with depicting an instance of an interpersonal situation, the sort of thing that can be studied by a psychiatrist. I attempt to show a simplification of the early stage in a relatively durable relationship of two people, one of whom you will observe is more nearly a 'well-rounded' or more developed personality than the other. Let me for brevity call the six-sectored representation, Johnnie Jones, and the other, Richard Roe.

"You will note that the uppermost line representing a field force is cross-hatched. This is intended to represent force which tends to keep these two people from growing more intimate, what may be called disjunctive force, and *the* great disjunctive force in interpersonal relations is anxiety. Below that there are shown two dotted lines of force which represent conjunctive forces, forces tending to improve the relationship, or in ordinary discourse, to draw the two people closer together.

"Let us notice that the uppermost sector of the left-hand figure, Mr. Jones, is very much smaller in area than is the corresponding sector in Mr. Roe to which it is linked by 'Jones' anxiety.' At the risk of adding confounding to confusion, let us make these sectors 'heterosexual motivation.' The disjunctive force arises from the anxiety-laden part of Mr. Jones' very limited development of heterosexual motivation. This means that Johnnie Jones cannot discuss comfortably with his friend, Mr. Roe, matters pertaining to this phase

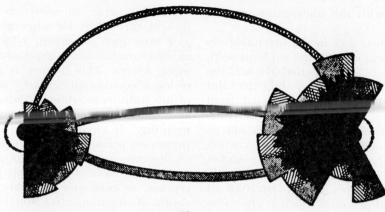

Fig. 2

of living. Mr. Roe readily becomes aware of the embarrassment and avoidances that ensue after any remarks which touch upon Jones' deficiencies in this area."

Other diagrams can be used to depict both disjunctive and conjunctive forces representing later stages of the relationship.[6] For example, a dotted line drawn between the non-self areas of two other sectors reflects a situation often observed in interpersonal relationship; namely, that powerful conjunctive force can arise from congruent motivational systems and exert influence in the interpersonal field wholly exterior to the awareness of the persons concerned.

Further elaboration and modification of Fig. 2 may be used to depict onset of the schizophrenic episode in the relationship of Jones with his friend. One can see how contact becomes relatively fixed through an eidetic personification forcibly shutting off further acquaintance with Mr. Roe. A new disjunctive force may appear, *uncanny* emotion, reflecting an impor-

[6] The reference cited in footnote 3 contains three additional diagrams not included here because of space limitations.

tant aspect of personality development; namely, the interlocking connection of past experience not only in, as it were, the sub-sections of personality currently manifested, but also throughout the historic past of personality.

A "surface" pattern modification of Figs. 1 and 2 may be used to show all Mr. Jones' experience from his initial meaningful contact with Mr. Roe to the point where actual contact with Mr. Roe has yielded to a relative equilibrium with an eidetic Mr. Roe after the onset of the psychotic relationship.

"In the study of any anxiety-fraught experience one discovers that the particular pattern of the situation which provokes anxiety can be traced to a past relationship with particular significant people in the course of which one experienced anxiety that was more or less clearly observed to relate to particular interaction with them.

"The complement of eidetic people which each of us carries with us and lives with reaches back in every instance to the first pair of our personifications: the *good mother* associated with the relaxation of the tensions of recurrent needs, and the bad or *evil mother* associated with the undergoing of anxiety.

"The next link in the inevitable developmental chain is the triple personifications of Good Me, Bad Me, and the always rather shadowy but dreadful Not-me. Bad Me is constructed from experience with anxiety-fraught situations *in which the anxiety was not severe enough to preclude observation and analysis.* Not-me grows out of mostly retrospective analysis of observed precursors to the paralysis of referential processes which is always associated with sudden severe anxiety.

"Anxiety as a functionally effective element in interpersonal relations has to be mild in degree or gradual in its increasing severity. Sudden severe anxiety, or anxiety which increases very swiftly in severity is undergone in later life as what I call *uncanny emotion,* chilly crawling sensations, and the like, often meant by the words 'awe,' 'dread,' 'loathing,' and 'horror.' Uncanny emotion is an all but functionally ineffective element in interpersonal relations; it arrests useful transformations of energy other than (1) certain obscure covert processes which, if they occur, may be called "adjustment to the uncanny" with escape into more refined and less paralyzing anxious states, (2) those which make up the schizophrenic disturbance of awareness with its varying influence of the Not-me components, or (3) apathy—which I shall not here discuss."

In case my comments on eidetic people are not clearly communicative, let me attack the problem from another standpoint. All of you must occasionally be afflicted by the necessity of writing "papers" or books, as well as by the necessity of giving "talks." I have far more trouble with the former than with the latter. While I talk to you, I vocalize a series of sentences which present themselves for utterance; but, as I utter each statement, a "part" of me, a characterizable subpersonality of mine, *listens*. This listener is a more or less adequate representation of those of my auditors to whom I "hope to be able to communicate something of my meaning." If a particular sentence impresses my private listener as equivocal, ambiguous, subject to misinterpretation on the basis of a probable preconception, or otherwise probably unsuccessful of communicative function, supplementary sentences are produced for utterance in that connection, before the particular topic is left. This private listener has grown as a complex function of information I have picked up over the years, of experience I have undergone and more or less formulated, in the activity of vocal exchange of ideas. The way "he" intervenes on a particular occasion is more or less adjusted to presumed characteristics of the particular "real" audience to whom I am speaking—or rather to the part of it above specified, made up of those I can foresee as learning something of my views if "he" does a good job of running correction.

This may seem to be a tedious process but it is as nothing to the trouble I have with my private "reader." My "listener" can use my eyes and ears, and adjust "himself" to signs from the "real" audience *in medias res*. Not so, my "reader," who has to represent a mediate public. "He" is so troublesome that I have had to make a study of the patterns characterizing "his" activity. I conclude that "he" is a queer combination of a high-grade imbecile and a bitterly paranoid critic. Every sentence has to be tortured into such shape that it cannot be misunderstood by the stupid or savagely misconstrued by an intelligent but bitterly hostile critic. My dealings with "him" are simply exhausting, and my writings reflect this—and a perhaps erratic recourse to his "alternate" whom I built up by borrowing from the late W. I. Thomas the idea that one writes books for a very small audience of respected colleagues, any and all other readers being "gravy."

This is the more difficult element in the field theory of interpersonal relations. It requires attention to the surviving influence and foresightful impact of unembodied but none the less characterizable personified existents, these eidetic [7] people historically related to "real" people of one's past experience, but related to them in a dynamic rather than a mere static survival way. I mean here that eidetic people, these potent personifications, change, however slowly; they too are altered by experience subsequent to the occasions on which their particular prototypes exerted their effect on one. Under effective psychotherapy, some of them may change very greatly, quite

[7] This word, I have borrowed from Jaensch, but without any of the context of meaning in which he used it as a term.

swiftly, and particularly fortunate experience unrelated to intentional therapeutic interventions may be equally effective.

Personality, then, is to be observed in interpersonal relations, in field processes including two or more loci. It is the abstract of relatively durable patterns of such fields, considered from the standpoint of *one* of these loci. These patterns, however, on scrutiny show the coincidence and dynamic interaction of other fields, all but one of the loci of which are of the eidetic kind. These latter, unrealistic loci are in equilibrium with the "real" personal locus; which, however, does not mean that they are inert. Quite the contrary, they and their equilibrium relations constitute a large part of the personality system which is the "real" person under consideration. This accounts for much of the inadequacy and inappropriateness of the field processes in which the particular person gets himself involved, for the eidetic personalities which are also involved limit or restrict the freedom of the situation through *self-esteem effects* and the disjunctive force experienced as anxiety.

✦✦✦✦✦✦✦✦✦✦✦✦✦✦✦✦✦✦✦ A PROCESS CONCEPTION
OF PSYCHOTHERAPY   *Carl R. Rogers*

I WOULD like to take you with me on a journey of exploration. The object of the trip, the goal of the search, is to try to learn something of the *process* of psychotherapy, or the *process* by which personality change takes place.

I would warn you that the goal has not yet been achieved and that it seems as though the expedition has advanced only a few short miles into the jungle. Yet perhaps if I can take you with me, you will be tempted to discover new

From Carl R. Rogers, "A Process Conception of Psychotherapy," The American Psychologist, *Vol. 13, No. 4, April 1958, pp. 142–149. Used by permission.*

and profitable avenues of further advance.

The Puzzle of Process

My own reason for engaging in such a search seems simple to me. Just as many psychologists have been interested in the invariant aspects of personality—the unchanging aspects of intelligence, temperament, personality structure—so I have long been interested in the invariant aspects of *change* in personality. Do personality and behavior change? What commonalities exist in such changes? What commonalities exist in the conditions which precede change? Most important of all, what is the process by which such change occurs?

Puzzling over this problem of getting at the process has led me to realize how little objective research deals with process in any field. Objective research slices through the frozen moment to provide us with an exact picture of the interrelationships which exist at that moment. But our understanding of the ongoing movement—whether it be the process of fermentation, or the circulation of the blood, or the process of atomic fission—is generally provided by a theoretical formulation, often supplemented, where feasible, with a clinical observation of the process. I have thus come to realize that perhaps I am hoping for too much to expect that research procedures can shed light directly upon the process of personality change. Perhaps only theory can do that.

A REJECTED METHOD

When I determined, more than a year ago, to make a fresh attempt to understand the manner in which such change takes place, I first considered various ways in which the experience of therapy might be described in terms of some other theoretical framework. There was much that was appealing in the field of communication theory, with its concepts of feedback, input and output signals, and the like. There was the possibility of describing the process of therapy in terms of learning theory or in terms of general systems theory. As I studied these avenues of understanding, I became convinced that it would be possible to translate the process of psychotherapy into any one of these theoretical frameworks. It would, I believe, have certain advantages to do so. But I also became convinced that, in a field so new, this is not what is most needed.

I came to a conclusion which others have reached before: in a new field perhaps what is needed first is to steep oneself in the *events,* to approach the phenomena with as few preconceptions as possible, to take a naturalist's observational, descriptive approach to these events, and to draw forth those low-level inferences which seem most native to the material itself.

THE MODE OF APPROACH

So, for the past year, I have used the method which so many of us use for generating hypotheses, a method which psychologists in this country seem so reluctant to expose or comment on. I used myself as a tool. I have spent many hours listening to recorded therapeutic interviews—trying to listen as naively as possible. I have endeavored to soak up all the clues I could capture as to the process, as to what elements are significant in change. Then I have tried to abstract from that sensing the simplest abstractions which would describe them. Here I have been much stimulated and helped by the thinking of many of my colleagues, but I would like to mention my special indebtedness to Eugene Gendlin, William Kirtner, and Fred Zimring, whose demonstrated ability to think in new ways about these matters has been particularly helpful and from whom I have borrowed heavily.

The next step has been to take these observations and low-level abstractions and formulate them in such a way that testable hypotheses can readily be drawn from them. This is the point I have reached. I make no apology for the fact that I am reporting no empirical investigations of these formulations. If past experience is any guide, then I may rest assured that, if the formulations I am about to present check in any way with the subjective experience of other therapists, then a great deal of research will be stimulated, and in a few years there will be ample evidence of the degree of truth and falsity in the statements which follow.

A BASIC CONDITION

If we were studying the process of growth in plants, we would assume certain constant conditions of temperature, moisture, and sunlight in forming our conceptualizations of the process. Likewise in conceptualizing the process of personality change in psychotherapy, I shall assume a constant and optimal set of conditions for facilitating this change. I have recently tried to spell out these conditions in some detail (7). For our present purpose, I believe I can state this assumed condition in one word. Throughout the discussion which follows, I shall assume that the client experiences himself as being fully *received*. By this I mean that, whatever his feelings—fear, despair, insecurity, anger; whatever his mode of expression—silence, gestures, tears, or words; whatever he finds himself being in this moment, he senses that he is psychologically *received*, just as he is, by the therapist. There is implied in this term the concept of being understood, emphatically, and the concept of acceptance. It is also well to point out that it is the client's experience of this condition which makes it optimal, not merely the fact of its existence in the therapist.

In all that I shall say, then, about the process of change, I shall assume as a constant an optimal and maximum condition of being received.

THE EMERGING CONTINUUM

In trying to grasp and conceptualize the process of change, I was initially looking for elements which would mark or characterize change itself. I was thinking of change as an entity and searching for its specific attributes. What gradually emerged in my understanding as I exposed myself to the raw material of change was a continuum of a different sort than I had conceptualized before.

Individuals move, I began to see, not from a fixity or homeostasis through change to a new fixity, though such a process is indeed possible. But much the more significant continuum is from fixity to changingness, from rigid structure to flow, from stasis to process. I formed the tentative hypothesis that perhaps the qualities of the client's expression at any one point might indicate his position on this continuum, might indicate where he stood in the process of change.

Seven Stages of Process

I gradually developed this concept of a continuum of process, discriminating seven stages in it, with examples from recorded therapeutic interviews illustrating the qualities of the process at each stage. It would be quite impossible to give all of this crude scale here, but I shall try to suggest something of its nature by describing very briefly Stages 1 and 2, to illustrate the lower end of the continuum, and describing more fully Stages 5, 6, and 7, to fill in the upper end of the scale.[1]

FIRST STAGE

The individual in this stage of fixity and remoteness of experiencing is not likely to come voluntarily for therapy. However, I can to some degree describe the characteristics of this stage:

There is an unwillingness to communicate self. Communication is only about externals.

Feelings and personal meanings are neither recognized as such nor owned.

Personal constructs (to use Kelly's helpful term, 4) *are extremely rigid.*

Close and communicative relationships are construed as dangerous.

No problems are recognized or perceived at this stage.

There is no desire to change.

There is much blockage of internal communication.

Perhaps these brief statements will convey something of the psychological

[1] An amplification of this paper, giving the whole scale with more extended illustrations, may be obtained from the author by those who are interested in using it for research purposes.

fixity of this end of the continuum. The individual has little or no recognition of the ebb and flow of the feeling life within him. He construes his experience rigidly in terms of the past. He is (to borrow the term of Gendlin and Zimring) structure-bound in his manner of experiencing, reacting to now "by finding it to be like a past experience and then reacting to that past, feeling *it*" (3). The individual at this stage represents stasis, fixity, the opposite of flow or change.

SECOND STAGE OF PROCESS

When the person in the first stage can experience himself as fully received, then the second stage follows. We seem to know very little about how to provide the experience of being received for the person in the first stage, but it is occasionally achieved in play or group therapy where the person can be exposed to a receiving climate, without himself having to take any initiative, for a long enough time to experience himself *as received*. In any event where he does experience this, then a slight loosening and flowing of symbolic expression occurs, which tends to be characterized by the following:

Expression begins to flow in regard to nonself topics.

Ex. "I guess that I suspect my father has often felt very insecure in his business relations." [2]

Problems are perceived as external to self.

[2] The many examples used as illustrations are taken from recorded interviews, unless otherwise noted. For the most part, they are taken from interviews which have never been published, but a number of them are taken from the report of two cases in a chapter of a forthcoming book (6).

Ex. "Disorganization keeps cropping up in my life."

There is no sense of personal responsibility in problems.

Ex. This is illustrated in the above excerpt.

Feelings are described as unowned, or sometimes as past objects.

Ex. Counselor: "If you want to tell me something of what brought you here. . . ." Client: "The symptom was—it was—just being very depressed." This is an excellent example of the way in which internal problems can be perceived and communicated about as entirely external. She is not saying "I am depressed" or even "I was depressed." Her feeling is handled as a remote, unowned object, entirely external to self.

Feelings may be exhibited, but are not recognized as such or owned.
Experiencing is bound by the structure of the past.

Ex. "I suppose the compensation I always make is, rather than trying to communicate with people or have the right relationship with them, to compensate by, well, shall we say, being on an intellectual level." Here the client is beginning to recognize the way in which her experiencing is bound by the past. Her statement also illustrates the remoteness of experiencing at this level. It is as though she were holding her experience at arm's length.

Personal constructs are rigid, and unrecognized as being constructs, but are thought of as facts.

Ex. "I can't ever do anything right—can't ever finish it."

Differentiation of personal meanings and feelings is very limited and global.

The preceding example is a good illustration. "I can't *ever*" is one instance of a black and white differentiation, as is also the use of "right" in this absolute sense.

Contradictions may be expressed, but with little recognition of them as contradictions.

Ex. "I want to know things, but I look at the same page for an hour."

As a comment on this second stage of the process of change, it might be said that a number of clients who voluntarily come for help are in this stage, but we (and probably therapists in general) have a very minimal degree of success in working with them. This seems, at least, to be a reasonable conclusion from Kirtner's study (5), though his conceptual framework was somewhat different. We seem to know too little about the ways in which a person at this stage may come to experience himself as "received."

THE FIFTH STAGE

I shall omit any description of Stages 3 and 4. Each involves a further loosening of symbolic expression in regard to feelings, constructs, and self. These stages constitute much of psychotherapy. But going beyond these stages, we can again mark a point on the continuum and call it Stage 5. If the client feels himself received in his expressions, behaviors, and experiences at the third and fourth stage, then this sets in motion still further loosenings, and the freedom of organismic flow is increased. Here I believe we can again delineate crudely the qualities of this phase of the process:

Feelings are expressed freely as in the present.

Ex. "I expected kinda to get a severe rejection—this I expect all the time . . . somehow I guess I even feel it with you.

. . . It's hard to talk about because I want to be the best I can possibly be with you." Here feelings regarding the therapist and the client in relationship to the therapist, emotions often most difficult to reveal, are expressed openly.

Feelings are very close to being fully experienced. They "bubble up," "seep through," in spite of the fear and distrust which the client feels at experiencing them with fullness and immediacy.

Ex. Client is talking about an external event. Suddenly she gets a pained, stricken look. Therapist: "What—what's hitting you now?" Client: "I don't know. (She cries) . . . I must have been getting a little too close to something I didn't want to talk about." The feeling has almost seeped through into awareness, in spite of her.

There is a beginning tendency to realize that experiencing a feeling involves a direct referent.

The example just cited illustrates this in part. The client knows she has experienced something, knows she is not clear as to what she has experienced. But there is also the dawning realization that the referent of these vague cognitions lies within her, in an organismic event against which she can check her symbolization and her cognitive formulations. This is often shown by expressions that indicate the closeness or distance the individual feels from this referent. Ex. "I really don't have my finger on it. I'm just kinda describing it."

There is surprise and fright, rarely pleasure, at the feelings which "bubble through."

Ex. Client, talking about past home relationships, "That's not important any more. Hmm. [Pause] That was somehow very meaningful—but I don't have the slightest idea why. . . . Yes, that's it! I can forget about it now and—why, it *isn't* that important. Wow! All that miserableness and stuff!"

There is an increasing ownership of self feelings, and a desire to be these, to be the "real me."

Ex. "The real truth of the matter is that I'm not the sweet, forbearing guy that I try to make out that I am. I get irritated at things. I feel like snapping at people, and I feel like being selfish at times; and I don't know why I should pretend I'm *not* that way." This is a clear instance of the greater degree of acceptance of all feelings.

Experiencing is loosened, no longer remote, and frequently occurs with little postponement.

There is little delay between the organismic event and the full subjective living of it. A beautifully precise account of this is given by a client. Ex. "I'm still having a little trouble trying to figure out what this sadness—and the weepiness— means. I just know I feel it when I get close to a certain kind of feeling—and usually when I do get weepy, it helps me to kinda break through a wall I've set up because of things that have happened. I feel hurt about something and then automatically this kind of shields things up and then I feel like I can't really touch or feel *anything* very much . . . and if I'd be *able* to feel, or could *let* myself feel the instantaneous feeling when I'm hurt, I'd immediately start being weepy right then, but I can't."

Here we see him regarding his feeling as an inner referent to which he can turn for greater clarity. As he senses his weepiness, he realizes that it is a delayed and partial experiencing of being hurt. He also recognizes that his defenses are such that he can not, at this point, experience the event of hurt when it occurs.

The ways in which experience is construed are much loosened. There are many fresh discoveries of personal constructs as constructs, and a critical examination and questioning of these.

Ex. A man says: "This idea of needing to please people—of *having* to do it—that's really been kind of a basic assumption of my life (he weeps quietly). It's kind of, you know, just one of the very unquestioned axioms that I *have* to please. I have no choice. I just *have* to." Here he is clear that this assumption has been a construct, and it is evident that its unquestioned status is at an end.

There is a strong and evident tendency toward exactness in differentiation of feelings and meanings.

A client speaks of "Some tension that grows in me, or some hopelessness, or some kind of incompleteness—and my life actually is very incomplete right now. . . . I just don't know. Seems to be, the closest thing it gets to, is *hopelessness*." Obviously he is trying to capture the exact term which for him symbolizes his experience.

There is an increasingly clear facing of contradictions and incongruences in experience.

Ex. "My conscious mind tells me I'm worthy. But someplace inside I don't believe it. I think I'm a rat—a no-good. I've no faith in my ability to do anything."

There is an increasing quality of acceptance of self-responsibility for the problems being faced, and a concern as to how he has contributed. There are increasingly freer dialogues within the self—an improvement in, and reduced blockage of, internal communication.

Sometimes these dialogues are verbalized. Ex. "Something in me is saying: 'What more do I have to give up? You've taken so much from me already.' This is *me* talking to *me*—the *me* way back in there who talks to the *me* who runs the show. It's complaining now, saying, 'You're getting too close! Go away!' "

I trust that the examples I have given of this fifth phase of the process continuum will make several points clear. In the first place, this phase is several hundred psychological miles from the first stage described. Here many aspects of the client are in flow, as against the rigidity of the first stage. He is very much closer to his organic being, which is always in process. He is much closer to being in the flow of his feelings. His constructions of experience are decidedly loosened and repeatedly being tested against referents and evidence within and without. Experience is much more highly differentiated, and thus internal communication, already flowing, can be much more exact.

As a general comment on the description thus far, it would be my observation that a person is never wholly at one or another stage of the process. There is, however, a general consistency in his manner of experiencing and expressing. Thus, a client who is generally at Stage 2 or 3 seems unlikely to exhibit any behaviors characteristic of Stage 5. This is especially true if we limit observations to a single defined area of related personal meanings in the client. Then I would hypothesize that there will be considerable regularity, that Stage 3 would rarely be found before Stage 2, that Stage 4 would rarely follow Stage 2 without Stage 3 intervening. Such tentative hypotheses can, of course, be put to empirical test.

THE SIXTH STAGE

If I have been able to communicate some feeling for the scope and quality of the increased loosening, at each stage, of feeling, experiencing, and construing, then we are ready to look at the next stage, which appears, from observation, to be a very crucial one. Let me see if I can convey what I perceive to be its characteristic qualities.

Assuming that the client continues to be fully received in the therapeutic relationship, then the characteristics of Stage 5 tend to be followed by a very distinctive and often dramatic phase. It is characterized as follows:

A feeling which has previously been "stuck," has been inhibited in its process quality, is experienced with immediacy now.
A feeling flows to its full result.
A present feeling is directly experienced with immediacy and richness.
This immediacy of experiencing, and the feeling which constitutes its content, are accepted. This is something which is, *not something to be denied, feared, struggled against.*

All the preceding sentences attempt to describe slightly different facets of what is, when it occurs, a clear and definite phenomenon. It would take recorded examples to communicate its full quality, but I shall try to give an illustration without benefit of recording. A somewhat extended excerpt from the eightieth interview with a young man may communicate the way in which a client comes into Stage 6.

Client: "I could even conceive of it as a possibility that I could have a kind of tender concern for me. . . . Still, how could *I* be tender, be concerned for *myself*, when they're one and the same thing? But yet I can *feel* it so clearly. . . . You know, like taking care of a child. You want to give it this and give it that. . . . I can kind of clearly see the purposes for somebody else . . . but I can never see them for . . . myself, that I could do this for me, you know. Is it possible that I can really want to take care of myself, and make that a major purpose of my life? That means I'd have to deal with the whole world as if I were guardian of the most cherished and most wanted possession, that this *I* was between this precious *me* that I wanted to take care of and the whole world. . . . It's almost as if I *loved*

myself—you know—that's strange—but it's true." Therapist: "It seems such a strange concept to realize. Why, it would mean I would face the world as though a part of my primary responsibility was taking care of this precious individual who is me—whom I love." Client: "Whom I care for—whom I feel so *close* to. Woof!! That's another *strange* one." Therapist: "It just seems *weird*." Client: "Yeah. It hits rather close somehow. The idea of my loving me and the taking care of me. [His eyes grow moist.] That's a very, very nice one—very nice."

The recording would help to convey the fact that here is a feeling which had never been able to flow in him, which is experienced with immediacy, in this moment. It is a feeling which flows to its full result, without inhibition. It is experienced acceptantly, with no attempt to push it to one side or to deny it.

There is a quality of living subjectively in the experience, not feeling about it.

The client, in his *words*, may withdraw enough from the experience to feel about it, as in the above example, yet the recording makes it clear that his words are peripheral to the experiencing which is going on within him and in which he is living. The best communication of this in his words is "Woof!! That's another *strange* one."

Self as an object tends to disappear.

The self, at this moment, *is* this feeling. This is a being in the moment, with little self-conscious awareness, but with primarily a reflective awareness, as Sartre terms it. The self *is*, subjectively, in the existential moment. It is not something one perceives.

Experiencing, at this stage, takes on a real process quality.

One client, a man who is approaching this stage, says that he has a frightened feeling about the source of a lot of secret thoughts in himself. He goes on: "The butterflies are the thoughts closest to the surface. Underneath there's a deeper flow. I feel very removed from it all. The deeper flow is like a great school of fish moving under the surface. I see the ones that break through the surface of the water—sitting with my fishing line in one hand, with a bent pin on the end of it—trying to find a better tackle—or better yet, a way of diving in That's the scary thing. The image I get is that *I* want to be one of the fish myself." Therapist: "You want to be down there flowing along, too."

Though this client is not yet fully experiencing in a process manner, and hence does not fully exemplify this sixth point on the continuum, he foresees it so clearly that his description gives a real sense of its meaning.

Another characteristic of this stage of process is the physiological loosening which accompanies it.

Moistness in the eyes, tears, sighs, muscular relaxation are frequently evident. Often there are other physiological concomitants. I would hypothesize that in these moments, had we the measures for it, we would discover improved circulation, improved conductivity of nervous impulses. An example of the "primitive" nature of some of these sensations may be indicated in the following excerpt:

The client, a young man, has expressed the wish his parents would die or disappear. "It's kind of like wanting to wish them away, and wishing they had never been. . . . And I'm so ashamed of myself because then they call me, and off I go— swish! They're somehow still so strong. I don't know. There's some umbilical—I can almost feel it inside me—swish" [and he gestures, plucking himself away by grasping at his navel]. Therapist: "They really do have a hold on your umbilical cord." Client: "It's funny how real it feels . . . like a burning sensation, kind of, and when they say something which makes me anxious I can feel it right here [pointing]. I never thought of it quite that way." Therapist: "As though, if there's a disturbance in the relationship between

you, then you do just feel it as though it was a strain on your umbilicus." Client: "Yeah, kind of like in my gut here. It's so hard to define the feeling that I feel there."

Here he is living subjectively in the feeling of dependence on his parents. Yet it would be inaccurate to say that he is perceiving it. He is *in* it, experiencing it as a strain on his umbilical cord.

In this stage, internal communication is free and relatively unblocked.

I believe this is quite adequately illustrated in the examples given. Indeed the phrase "internal communication" is no longer quite correct; for, as each of these examples illustrates, the crucial moment is a moment of integration, in which communication between different internal foci is no longer necessary, because they become *one.*

The incongruence between experience and awareness is vividly experienced as it disappears into congruence.
The relevant personal construct is dissolved in this experiencing moment, and the client feels cut loose from his previously stabilized framework.

I trust these two characteristics may acquire more meaning from the following example. A young man has been having difficulty getting close to a certain unknown feeling. "That's almost exactly what the feeling is, too—it was that I was living so much of my life, and seeing so much of my life, in terms of being *scared* of something." He tells how his professional activities are just to give him a little safety and "a little world where I'll be secure, you know. And for the same reason. [Pause] I was kind of letting it seep through. But I also tied it in with you and with my relationship with you, and one thing I feel about it is fear of its going away. [His tone changes to role-play more accurately his feeling.] Won't you let me have this? I kind of *need* it. I can be so lonely and scared without it." Therapist: "M-hmm, m-hmm. 'Let me hang on to it because I'd be terribly scared if I didn't!' . . . It's a kind of pleading thing too, isn't it?" Client: "I get a sense of—it's this kind of pleading little boy. It's this gesture of begging" [putting his hands up as if in prayer]. Therapist: "You put your hands in kind of a supplication." Client: "Yeah, that's right. '*Won't* you do this for me?' kind of. Oh, that's terrible! Who, *me? Beg?* . . . That's an emotion I've never felt clearly at all— something I've never been. . . . [Pause] . . . I've got such a confusing feeling. One is, it's such a wondrous feeling to have these new things come out of me. It amazes me so much each time, and there's that same feeling, being scared that I've so much of this. [Tears] . . . I just don't know myself. Here's suddenly something I never realized, hadn't any inkling of—that it was some *thing* or some *way* I wanted to be."

Here we see a complete experiencing of his pleadingness, and a vivid recognition of the discrepancy between this experiencing and his concept of himself. Yet this experiencing of discrepancy exists in the moment of its disappearance. From now on he *is* a person who feels *pleading,* as well as many other feelings. As this moment dissolves the way he has construed himself, he feels cut loose from his previous world— a sensation which is both wondrous and frightening.

The moment of full experiencing becomes a clear and definite referent.

The examples given should indicate that the client is often not too clearly aware of what has "hit him" in these moments. Yet this does not seem too important because the event is an entity, a referent, which can be returned to, again and again if necessary, to discover more about it. The pleadingness, the feeling of "loving myself" which are present in these examples, may not prove to be exactly as described. They are, however, solid points of reference to which the client can return until he has satisfied himself as to what they are. It is, perhaps, that they constitute a clear-cut

physiological event, a substratum of the conscious life, which the client can return to for investigatory purposes. Gendlin has called my attention to this significant quality of experiencing as a referent. He is endeavoring to build an extension of psychological theory on this basis (2, especially Chap. 7).

Differentiation of experiencing is sharp and basic.

Because each of these moments is a referent, a specific entity, it does not become confused with anything else. The process of sharp differentiation builds on it and about it.

In this stage there are no longer "problems," external or internal. The client is living, subjectively, a phase of his problem. It is not an object.

I trust it is evident that in any of these examples it would be grossly inaccurate to say that the client perceives his problem as internal or is dealing with it as an internal problem. We need some way of indicating that he is further than this and, of course, enormously far in the process sense from perceiving his problem as external. The best description seems to be that he neither perceives his problem nor deals with it. He is simply living some portion of it knowingly and acceptingly.

I have dwelt so long on this sixth definable point on the process continuum because I see it as a highly crucial one. My observation is that these moments of immediate, full, accepted experiencing are in some sense almost irreversible. To put this in terms of the examples, it is my observation and hypothesis that with these clients, whenever a future experiencing of the same quality and characteristics occurs, it will necessarily be recognized in awareness for what it is: a tender caring for self, an umbilical bond which makes him a part of his parents, or a pleading small-boy dependence, as the case may be. And, it might be remarked in passing, once an experience is fully in awareness, fully accepted, then it can be coped with effectively, like any other clear reality.

THE SEVENTH STAGE

In those areas in which the sixth stage has been reached, it is no longer so necessary that the client be fully received by the therapist, though this still seems helpful. However, because of the tendency for the sixth stage to be irreversible, the client often seems to go on into the seventh and final stage without much need of the therapist's help. This stage occurs as much outside of the therapeutic relationship as in it and is often reported, rather than experienced, in the therapeutic hour. I shall try to describe some of its characteristics as I feel I have observed them:

New feelings are experienced with immediacy and richness of detail, both in the therapeutic relationship and outside.
The experiencing of such feelings is consciously used as a clear referent.
There is a growing and continuing sense of acceptant ownership of these changing feelings, a basic trust in his own process.

This trust is not primarily in the conscious processes which go on, but rather in the total organismic process. One client puts it: "I seem to work best when my conscious mind is only concerned with facts and letting the analysis of them go on by itself without paying any attention to it."

Experiencing has lost almost completely its structure-bound aspects and becomes process experiencing —that is, the situation is experienced and interpreted in its newness, not as the past.

An example in a very specific area is given by a client in a follow-up interview as he explains the different quality that has come about in his creative work. It used to be that he tried to be orderly. "You begin at the beginning and you progress regularly through to the end." Now he is aware that the process in himself is different. "When I'm working on an idea, the whole idea develops like the latent image coming out when you develop a photograph. It doesn't start at one edge and fill in over to the other. It comes in *all over*. At first all you see is the hazy outline, and you wonder what it's going to be; and then gradually something fits here and something fits there, and pretty soon it all comes clear—all at once." It is obvious that he has not only come to trust this process, but that he is experiencing it as it *is*, not in terms of some past.

The self becomes increasingly simply the subjective and reflexive awareness of experiencing. The self is much less frequently a perceived object and much more frequently something confidently felt in process.

An example may be taken from the same follow-up interview with the client quoted above. In this interview, because he is reporting his experience since therapy, he again becomes aware of himself as an object; but it is clear that this has not been the quality of his day-by-day experience. After reporting many changes, he says: "I hadn't really thought of any of these things in connection with therapy until tonight. . . . [Jokingly] Gee! maybe something *did* happen. Because my life since *has* been different. My productivity has gone up. My confidence has gone up. I've become brash in situations I would have avoided before. And also, I've become less brash in situations where I would have become very obnoxious before." It is clear that only afterward does he realize what his self as an object has been.

Personal constructs are tentatively re-formulated, to be validated against further experience, but even then to be held loosely.

A client describes the way in which such a construct changed, between interviews, toward the end of therapy: "I don't know what [changed], but I definitely feel different about looking back at my chilhood, and some of the hostility about my mother and father has evaporated. I substituted for a feeling of resentment about them a sort of acceptance of the fact that they did a number of things that were undesirable with me. But I substituted a sort of feeling of interested excitement that—gee—now that I'm finding out what was wrong, *I* can do something about it—correct their mistakes." Here the way in which he construes his experience with his parents has been sharply altered.

Internal communication is clear, with feelings and symbols well matched, and fresh terms for new feelings.
There is the experiencing of effective choice of new ways of being.

Because all the elements of experience are available to awareness, choice becomes real and affective. Here a client is just coming to this realization: "I'm trying to encompass a way of talking that is a way out of being scared of talking. Perhaps just kind of thinking out loud is the way to do that. But I've got so *many* thoughts I could only do it a little bit. But maybe I could let my talk be an expression of my thoughts, instead of just trying to make the proper noises in each situation." Here he is sensing the possibility of effective choice, perhaps approaching this seventh stage rather than being in it.

By no means all clients move this far on the continuum; but when this seventh stage is reached, it involves us in another dimension. For it will be evident that the client has now incorporated the quality of motion, of flow, of changingness into every aspect of his psychological life. He will therefore continue to be a continually changing person, experiencing with freshness and immediacy in each new situation, responding to its newness with real and accepted feelings, and construing its meaning in terms of what it *is*, not in terms of some past experience.

Recapitulation

I have tried to sketch, in a crude and preliminary manner, the flow of a process of change which occurs when a client experiences himself as being received, welcomed, understood as he is. This process involves several threads, separable at first, becoming more of a unity as the process continues.

This process involves a loosening of feelings. From feelings which are unrecognized, unowned, unexpressed, the client moves toward a flow in which ever-changing feelings are experienced in the moment, knowingly and acceptingly, and may be accurately expressed.

The process involves a change in the manner of experiencing. From experiencing which is remote in time from the organic event, which is bound by the structure of experience in the past, the client moves toward a manner of experiencing which is immediate, which interprets meaning in terms of what is, not what was.

The process involves a loosening of the cognitive maps of experience. From construing experience in rigid ways which are perceived as external facts, the client moves toward developing changing, loosely held construings of meaning in experience, constructions which are modifiable by each new experience.

The process involves a change in the self. From being a self which is not congruent with experience, the client moves through the phase of perceiving self as an object, to a self which is synonymous with experience, being the subjective awareness of that experience.

There are other elements, too, involved in the process: movement from ineffective to effective choice, from fear of relationships to freely living in relationship, from inadequate differentiation of feelings and meanings to sharp differentiation.

In general, the process moves from a point of fixity, where all these elements and threads are separately discernible and separately understandable, to the flowing peak moments of therapy in which all these threads become inseparably woven together. In the new experiencing with immediacy which occurs at such moments, feeling and cognition interpenetrate, self is subjectively present in the experience, volition is simply the subjective following of a harmonious balance of organismic direction. Thus, as the process reaches this point, the person becomes a unity of flow, of motion. He has changed; but, what seems most significant, he has become an integrated process of changingness.

References

1. BERGMAN, D. V. Counseling method and client responses. *J. consult. Psychol.*, 1951, 15, 216–224.
2. GENDLIN, E. The function of experiencing in symbolization. Unpublished doctoral dissertation, Univer. of Chicago, 1958.
3. GENDLIN, E., & ZIMRING, F. The qualities or dimensions of experiencing and their change. *Counseling Center Discussion Papers*, 1955, 1, No. 3. (Univer. of Chicago Counseling Center)
4. KELLY, G. A. *The psychology of personal constructs*. Vol. I. A theory of personality. New York: Norton, 1955.
5. KIRTNER, W. L. Success and failure in client-centered therapy as a function of personality variables. Unpublished master's thesis, Univer. of Chicago, 1955.
6. LEWIS, M. K., ROGERS, C. R., & SHLIEN, J. M. Two cases of time-limited client-centered psychotherapy. In A. Burton (ed.), *Case studies of counseling and psychotherapy*. New York: Prentice-Hall, 1959.
7. ROGERS, C. R. The necessary and sufficient conditions of therapeutic personality change. *J. consult. Psychol.*, 1957, 21, 95–103.

✦✦✦✦✦✦✦✦✦✦✦✦✦✦✦✦✦✦✦ THE CONCEPT OF ROLE

Howard Baumgartel

WE can think of society as a social system, a network of patterned relationships among people, much as we can think of the organization chart

From Howard Baumgartel, Some Notes on the Human Relations Approach and the Concept of Role, *unpublished manuscript, pp. 3–5. Used by permission.*

for a company or a military unit. These patterned relationships involve roles. As sociologists have pointed out, there are many cleavages in society. People are involved in different occupations; people differ with regard to age and sex; people belong to different social classes and ethnic groups; people exist at different levels in the hierarchies of wealth, power, and prestige. Each of these points, so to speak, in the social system or the network of interpersonal relations is a role. The role concept is abstracted from the concrete behavior of the people in particular points in the social system, and can be thought of in two ways. On the one hand we can think of the regularities in the behavior of, say, factory foremen and abstract out of the behavior of many foremen the particular manner of acting in this role. These regularities in behavior are also accompanied by regularities in the ways of thinking and feeling about other people as referring to the expectations other people have about the way a particular kind of person should behave, how students think a professor should behave, for example.

The anthropologists have drawn our attention to the wide variety of ways in which roles and role systems may be arranged. Sociologists have done much to map or describe the complex role system in our own society, the behavior patterns, shared attitudes, shared expectations associated with particular roles. Psychologists have been interested in understanding the relationship between "personality" and the social system through the concept of role, using the "role" as the meeting point of the person as psychological system and the society as the social system of which he is a part.

The concept of role can be useful in diagnosing human problems for a number of reasons. Primarily, with it we can identify some of the sources of conflict and dissatisfaction in human relationships. Some of these sources of difficulty are as follows:

1. A person may want to do something contrary to the shared expectations about what is "proper" for a person in his role. (A Negro may want to go swimming in the local swimming pool. A young person may want to build a life pattern different from what his friends and parents expect of him.)

2. People may disagree about what a person in a particular role should do. (Parents may disagree about what is an appropriate amount of freedom for a teen-age daughter. Citizens may disagree about what the public school personnel should include in curriculum content.)

3. A person may find himself in two roles that make conflicting demands on his time, energy, and attitudes. (Family and work associates may expect different uses of leisure time.)

4. A person may be in inner conflict over the roles he wishes to take. (Problems of career choice are difficult in an "open" social system that provides wide choice of role and career.)

5. Well-established and fully shared role systems may no longer be appropriate. (The deferential and authoritarian roles of a feudal society may be inappropriate for the rationality of an industrial society. Discrimination in advancement based on race, class, or ethnic group may not serve the needs of a society requiring the maximum use of human resources.)

6. The differences in attitude and values associated with different roles may lead to conflict. (Managers and union officials often find it difficult to understand each other. Middle-class managers cannot see the point of view of working-class employees. Psychologists may be unhappy with the subordinate role assigned them by psychiatrists. Older people and younger people may find great difficulty in communicating with each other.)

7. The role system may not provide adequate "room" for the variety of personalities in a society. (Perhaps in a different society, people now in prisons or mental institutions would have places to exist on their own.)

8. Difficulties are experienced in changing roles. (A young man who has been a P.O.W. may have great difficulty relearning how to exist in civilian society. Attitudes toward authority learned while being a subordinate may be difficult to unlearn when advancement comes.)

9. There may be a lack of clarity in the definition of a role—little consensus in the expectations of people about how to behave in a given role. (Some people have observed that the role of the women in contemporary American society is very unclear. Few guides are available for indicating how to behave as a woman—or as a husband, for that matter.)

10. A person may experience confusion about his own role—who he is, what it is to be a worker, a man, a supervisor. (Many lonely people devoid of significant human association experience acute discomfort and disorientation—people without a role or niche in society or people with neurotic problems.)

11. Individuals may be over-rigid in taking roles in a changing society. (A downward mobile person may continue to behave in ways no longer appropriate—the stereotype of the last of old Southern families clinging desperately to old ways of acting and thinking.)

12. The shared expectations regarding a role or the role definition may be more or less functional. (Supervisory practices desired by higher management may impair group effectiveness and create problems for the foreman in getting the job done.)

Perhaps the two most important considerations in thinking about the role concept are: (1) the realization that roles and role systems are not inherent but are the creations of man, and (2) the realization that roles become part of the very fabric of personality. The nature of the role system may be experienced as stable and permanent. Many people seem to change little after acquiring an adult role. However, role systems and individuals can and do change continuously with the push and pull of forces for change both within personality and within society. From an awareness of the nature of roles we can see that there is an element of choice in the particular ways roles are defined. We know little about how roles may be changed. The interlocking nature of roles makes a change in one part of a role system difficult without other concurrent changes. A change in the "role of wife" implies a change in the role of husbands. However, it is now possible to think constructively about what are appropriate and inappropriate ways of playing certain roles as well as about what new roles are desirable.

Parents seek to become more adequate parents by modifying the role in a way that leads to more desirable results. Management groups seek to identify the patterns of supervision that get results. The role system has, in a word, become itself an object of analysis and change. Most social change can be viewed in terms of changing role relations. The resources of society, wealth, power, and prestige are differentially distributed. High rewards go with certain roles. Political and social reform often aim at a redistribution of these values, most particularly with respect to who and how the role system itself shall be controlled.

As a final word, we might say that the science of human relations is a social movement aimed at obtaining changes in the general role of being a person. Most typically, we say we have a human relations problem when some people do not do what other people think they ought to do. A college student behaves "irresponsibly," that is, he does not play his role. A wife does

not do what her husband thinks she ought to do—she does not fulfill her role. Factory workers protest the promotion of a new foreman, and managers become upset because they feel the role of worker includes obedience and deference. What the human relations approach asks of the person with the problem is that he include in his role definition behavior that has diagnostic value: Why is this person deviating from what I think he ought to be doing? What concepts and ideas are useful in this instance? What new alternatives of action are opened up by this diagnostic understanding of the problem?

◆◆◆◆◆◆◆◆◆◆◆◆◆◆◆◆◆◆◆◆◆ ADMINISTRATION AS A SOCIAL
PROCESS   *Jacob W. Getzels*

[Getzels, in the preceding sections here omitted, shows the place that theory should play in the analysis of any phenomena.]

PERHAPS it might be well to say something first about our intention in constructing the model. The model was constructed with three specific criteria in mind: (1) the model must provide a set of integrated concepts and relations capable not only of answering questions already asked in administration but of posing questions that still need to be asked; (2) the concepts and relations must be operational in that they not only give direction to our understanding but simultaneously provide blueprints for investigation; (3)

the model must be able to handle as many of the commonplaces or familiar issues in administration as possible within a single set of concepts and relations. In short, we sought a model that was at once heuristic, operational, and that had the elegance and power of parsimony. It goes without saying that we did not altogether succeed in our intention. But I cannot help adding that the very attempt may be of interest and perhaps even of some value.

Just one more introductory word, if I may: I would like to take this opportunity to make two acknowledgments —first to Talcott Parsons, whose influence will be apparent throughout the paper, although he may want to disown what I say specifically, and second to Egon Guba, who collaborated

Excerpted from Jacob W. Getzels, "Administration as a Social Process," Administrative Theory in Education, edited by Andrew W. Halpin, Chicago: Midwest Administration Center, 1958, pp. 150–162. Abridged and used by permission.

with me on many of these formulations.[1]

The Model

Let us begin with a general conception, if not a definition, of administration. Not that I think we are able to
provide an entirely satisfactory conception, but at least a statement of a
conception in explicit terms will give
us something to agree with or depart
from meaningfully.

Let me say then that we may conceive of administration *structurally* as
the hierarchy of subordinate-super-
ordinate relationships within a social
system. *Functionally,* this hierarchy of
relationships is the locus for allocating
and integrating roles and facilities in
order to achieve the goals of the social
system. It is here, in these relationships,
that the assignment of statuses, the provision of facilities, the organization of
procedures, the regulation of activity,
and the evaluation of performance
takes place.

Of course, these functions are the responsibility of the superordinate member of the hierarchy, but each function
becomes effective only insofar as it
"takes" with the subordinate member.
It is this circumstance, that is, that administration always operates in an interpersonal—or, if you will, *social* relationship—that makes the nature of this
relationship the crucial factor in the
administrative process.

We may begin the description of our
model with a consideration of the most
general context of interpersonal or social behavior, i.e., a given social system.
The term "social system" is of course

conceptual rather than descriptive and
must not be confused with society or
state, or as somehow applicable only
to *large* aggregates of human interaction. So within this framework, for
one purpose a given community may
be considered a social system with the
school a particular organization within
the more general social system. For
another purpose, the school itself or
even a single class within the school
may be considered a social system in its
own right. The model proposed here is
applicable regardless of the level or
size of the unit under consideration.

We conceive of the social system as
involving two classes of phenomena
which are at once conceptually independent and phenomenally interactive.
There are first the institutions with
certain roles and expectations that will
fulfil the goals of the system. And there
are second the individuals with certain
personalities and need-dispositions inhabiting the system, whose observed interactions comprise what we generally
call "social behavior." We shall assert
that this social behavior may be understood as a function of these major elements: institution, role, and expectation, which together constitute what
we shall call the *nomothetic* or normative dimension of activity in a social
system; and individual, personality,
and need-disposition, which together
constitute the *idiographic* or personal
dimension of activity in a social system.

To understand the nature of observed behavior—and to be able to predict and control it—we must understand the nature and relationship of
these elements. We shall briefly make
four points of definition in this connection:

1. The term "institution" has received a variety of definitions, and
nothing will be gained from a review

[1] See Jacob W. Getzels and Egon G. Guba,
"Social Behavior and the Administrative
Process," *School Review,* LXV (Winter, 1957),
423–41.

of all possible meanings. For our purposes it is sufficient to point out that all social systems have certain imperative functions that come in time to be carried out in certain routinized ways. These functions—say, governing, educating, policing within a state—may be said to have become "institutionalized," and the agencies established to carry out these institutionalized functions for the social system as a whole may be termed "institutions."

2. The most important analytic subunit of the institution is the role. Roles are, to use Linton's terminology, the "dynamic aspects" of the positions, offices, and statuses within an institution, and they define the behavior of the role incumbents or actors.[2]

3. Roles are defined in terms of role expectations. A role has certain normative obligations and responsibilities, which may be termed "role expectations," and when the role incumbent puts these obligations and responsibilities into effect, he is said to be performing his role. The expectations define for the actor, whoever he may be, what he should or should not do as long as he is the incumbent of the particular role.

4. Roles are complementary. Roles are interdependent in that each role derives its meaning from other related roles in the institution. In a sense, a role is a prescription not only for the given role incumbent but also for the incumbents of other roles within the organization, so that in a hierarchial setting the expectations of one role may to some extent also form the sanctions for a second interlocking role. Thus, for example, the role of sergeant and the role of private in the army

[2] Ralph Linton, *The Study of Man* (New York: Appleton-Century-Crofts, Inc., 1936), p. 14.

cannot really be defined or implemented except in relation to each other. It is this quality of complementarity which fuses two or more roles into a coherent, interactive unit and which makes it possible for us to conceive of an institution as having a characteristic structure.

So far we have examined the elements constituting the nomothetic or normative aspects of social behavior. At this level of analysis, it was sufficient to conceive of the role incumbents as only "actors," devoid of personalistic or other individualizing characteristics—as if all incumbents were exactly alike and as if they implemented a given role in exactly the same way. This is not, incidentally, by any means to derogate the power of this typical sociological level of analysis. Indeed, for certain gross understanding and prediction of behavior this is exactly the right level of abstraction. For example, if I know the roles in a given military or educational institution, I can make some rather accurate predictions of what the people in these institutions do without ever observing the actual people involved.

But roles are of course occupied by real individuals, and no two individuals are alike. Each individual stamps the particular role he occupies with the unique style of his own characteristic pattern of expressive behavior. Even in the case of the relatively inflexible roles of sergeant and private, no two individual sergeants and no two individual privates fulfil their roles in exactly the same way. To understand the observed behavior of *specific* sergeants and *specific* privates, it is not enough to know the nature of the roles and expectations—although, to be sure, their behavior cannot be understood apart from these—but we must also know the nature of the individuals inhabiting the roles and reacting to the expectations. That is, in addition to the nomothetic or normative aspects, we must consider also the idiographic or individualizing aspects of social behavior. We must, in addition to the sociological level of analysis, include the psychological level of analysis.

Now just as we were able to analyze the institutional dimension into the component elements of role and expectation, so we may, in a parallel manner, analyze the individual dimension into the component elements of personality and need-disposition. We may turn to a brief consideration of these two terms.

The concept "personality," like the role or institution, has been given a variety of meanings. For our purposes, personality may be defined as the dynamic organization within the individual of those need-dispositions that govern his *unique* reactions to the environment (and we might add, in the present model, to the expectations in the environment). The central analytic elements of personality are the need-dispositions, which we can define with Parsons and Shils as "individual tendencies to orient and act with respect to objects in certain manners and to expect certain consequences from these actions." [3]

Returning to the example of the sergeant and the private, we can now make an essential distinction between two sergeants, one of whom has a high need-disposition for "submission" and the other, a high need-disposition for "ascendance," and a similar distinction between two privates, one with a high need-disposition for "submission" and

[3] Talcott Parsons and Edward A. Shils, *Toward a General Theory of Action* (Cambridge, Mass.: Harvard University Press, 1951), p. 114.

the other for "ascendance," in the fulfilment of their respective roles, and for the sergeant-private interaction.

In short, as we have remarked before, to understand the behavior of specific role-incumbents in an institution, we must know both the role-expectations and the need-dispositions. Indeed, needs and expectations may both be thought of as motives for behavior, the one deriving from personalistic sets and propensities, the other from institutional obligations and requirements.

One troublesome facet of the model to which it seems to me insufficient attention has been given—and which I should like to take this occasion to remedy to some extent if I can—is the problem of the dynamics of the interaction between these externally defined expectations and the internally determined needs. To put the problem concretely, we may ask: How is it, for example, that some sergeants and privates—or to generalize the case, some complementary role incumbents—understand and agree at once on their mutual obligations and responsibilities, while others take a long time in reaching such agreement and quite frequently do not come to terms either with their roles or with each other at all?

The essential relevant concept I should like to propose here is *selective interpersonal perception*. In a sense, we may conceive of the publicly prescribed normative relationship of two complementary role incumbents—the prescribed interaction as set forth in, say, a table of organization—as being enacted in two separate private situations, one imbedded in the other. On the one hand, there is the prescribed relationship as perceived idiosyncratically and organized by the one role incumbent in terms of his own needs, dispositions, and goals; on the other hand, there is the same prescribed relationship as perceived idiosyncratically and organized by the other role incumbent in terms of *his* needs, disposition, and goals. These private situations are related through those aspects of the existential public objects, symbols, values, and expectations, which have to some extent a counterpart in the perceptions of both individuals.[4]

When we say that two role incumbents—e.g., a subordinate and a superordinate—understand each other, we mean that their perceptions and private organization of the prescribed complementary expectations are congruent; when we say that they misunderstand each other, we mean that their perceptions and private organization of the prescribed complementary

by the specific role incumbents. Indeed, the relevant research suggests that congruence in the perception of expectations often takes priority over actual observed behavior or even accomplishment in determining which outcomes of administrative interaction will be reported favorably by the participants in the interaction, and which unfavorably.

By way of summarizing the argument so far, we may represent the general model pictorially as indicated in Figure 5. The nomothetic axis is shown at the top of the diagram and consists of institution, role, and expectation, each term being the analytic unit for the term preceding it. Thus, the social system is defined by its institutions, each institution by its constituent roles, each role by the expectations attaching to it. Similarly, the idiographic axis is

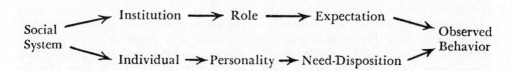

Nomothetic Dimension

Idiographic Dimension

Fig. 5   General model showing the nomothetic and idiographic dimensions of social behavior

expectations are incongruent. As we shall show in the first of our derivations from the model, the functioning of the administrative process depends not only on a clear statement of the public expectations but on the degree of overlap in the perception and private organization of the expectations

[4] See Jacob W. Getzels, "A Psycho-sociological Framework for the Study of Educational Administration," *Harvard Educational Review*, XXII (Fall, 1952), 235–46.

shown at the lower portion of the diagram and consists of individual, personality, and need-disposition, each term again serving as the analytic unit for the term preceding it.

A given act is conceived as deriving simultaneously from both the nomothetic and idiographic dimensions. That is to say, social behavior results as the individual attempts to cope with an environment composed of patterns of expectations for his behavior in ways consistent with his own independent pattern of needs. Thus we may write the general equation: $B=f(R \times P)$, where B is observed behavior, R is a given institutional role defined by the expectations attaching to it, and P is the personality of the particular role incumbent defined by his need-dispositions.

There is a crucial difference between this formulation and the famous equation given by Lewin,[5] i.e., $B=f(P \times E)$, where P is personality and E is environment, which highlights better than anything I know the specific character for good or ill—of the model we are presenting. In Lewin's formula, P and E are not independent, since one defines the other; i.e., environment is defined by the perception of the person. In the formula we are presenting, R and P *are* independent, since P is defined by the internal determinants within the role incumbent, and R is defined not by the role incumbent but by external standards set by others. Thus, in Lewin's formula E represents a personal life space that cannot be specified apart from the personality of the specific perceiver; in the present formula R, which is of course E defined in terms of expectations, must be specified apart from the personality of the specific perceiver. The role expectations are the "givens" in the situation prior to any idiosyncratic role-perceptions or role-behaviors of the actual role incumbents. Although the expectations may be misperceived or may serve only as points of departure for the actual role incumbents, the crucial significance of the expectations as "blueprints" for what should be done is not thereby nullified. Indeed,

we could not recognize the misperception or misbehavior if there were not these prior "givens." To cite but one example, the fact that people assume that judges take graft, or for that matter the fact that many judges do indeed take graft, does not alter the expectation for the role of judge that he will not take graft.

The proportion of role and personality factors determining behavior will of course vary with the specific act, the specific role, and the specific personality involved. The nature of the interaction can be understood from another graphic representation, as indicated in Figure 6.

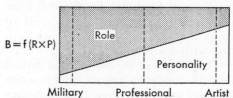

$$B=f(R \times P)$$

Military   Professional   Artist

Fig. 6   The interplay between role and personality in a behavioral act

A given behavioral act may be conceived as occurring at a line cutting through the role and personality possibilities represented by the rectangle. At the left, the proportion of the act dictated by considerations of role-expectations is relatively large, while the proportion of the act dictated by considerations of personality is relatively small. At the right, the proportions are reversed, and considerations of personality become greater than consideration of role-expectation. In these terms, we may, for example, have on the one hand the behavior of an army private conforming almost entirely to role demands and on the other the behavior of a free-lance artist deriving almost entirely from personality dispositions.

[5] See, for example, Kurt Lewin, *A Dynamic Theory of Personality* (New York: McGraw-Hill Book Co., 1935), chap. iii.

In a given milieu, administration always deals with proportions of both these components. It would incidentally be interesting to see where this line would be drawn for university professors in various institutions.

In any case, however, whether the proportion tends toward one end or the other, behavior insofar as it is *social* remains a function of both role and personality, although in different degree. When role is maximized, behavior still retains some personal aspect because no role is ever so closely defined as to eliminate all individual latitude. When personality is maximized, social behavior still cannot be free from some role prescription. Indeed, the individual who divorces himself from such prescription is said to be autistic, and he ceases to communicate with his fellows.

The relevance of the general model for administrative theory and practice becomes apparent when it is seen that the administrative process inevitably deals with the fulfilment of both nomothetic and idiographic requirements within the context of a particular social system.

Some Derivations and Relevant Research Studies

There is little point in general models if they do not give rise to specific conceptual derivations and empirical applications. I think we had better stop spinning out these models unless we can show some results, however modest, either in illuminating day-to-day practices or in raising significant issues for research investigations. Accordingly, I should like to turn now to a number of specific derivations and applications.

1. *Interpersonal perception and su-perordinate-subordinate consensus.* We may mention first a very simple derivation, that is, that the administrative relationship always functions at two levels of interaction. The first level derives from the particular offices or statuses in the social system and is determined by the nature of the roles involved in the interaction. This is, of course, the nomothetic dimension of our model. The second level of interaction derives from the particular people or individuals in the social system and is determined by the personalities involved in the interaction. This is, of course, the idiographic dimension of our model. You will recall that we said that the publicly prescribed nomothetic relationship is enacted in two separate private idiographic situations—one by the subordinate and one by the superordinate. The functioning of the administrative process will, we said, depend on the nature of the overlap— i.e., on the relative congruence or discrepancy—between the separate perceptions of the expectations in the two situations.

I should like to mention very briefly here some empirical work bearing on this formulation. Stated in extreme terms, the basic hypothesis underlying the investigations was that when the perceptions of the expectations of participants in an administrative interaction overlap, the participants feel satisfied with the work accomplished no matter what the actual behavior or accomplishment; when the perception of the expectations does not overlap, the participants feel dissatisfied.

Ferneau studied the interaction of consultants and administrators in a school setting.[6] A problem-situation

[6] Elmer Ferneau, "Role-Expectations in Consultations" (unpublished Ph.D. dissertation, University of Chicago, 1954).

instrument was constructed in which varying expectations for the consultant role could be expressed. The instrument was given to 180 administrators who were known to have had consultant service and to 46 consultants who were known to have provided this service. Each administrator and each consultant was also asked to evaluate the outcome of the consultation. It was then possible to compare the expectations for the consultant role held by the consultant himself and by the consultee and to analyze the effect of the congruence or discrepancy of these perceptions on the evaluation of the actual interaction.

The results were clear-cut. When an administrator and a consultant agreed on the expectations, they tended to rate the actual consultation favorably; when they disagreed, unfavorably. Here, then, is one explanation of the success or failure of a typical administrative interaction. And note that the success or failure was apparently independent of the specific character either of the expectations or of the manifest behavior—provided that the participants' perception of the expectations, whatever their character, overlapped.

Moyer, in a second study along similar lines, investigated by Q-sort the relationship between the expectations of teachers and administrators for leadership in the educational setting and the effect of congruence or discrepancy in this relationship upon teacher satisfaction.[7] Again, the results were consistent with the derivation from the model: the greater the agreement between teacher and principal on the expectations for leadership, the more fa-

[7] Donald C. Moyer, "Teachers' Attitudes toward Leadership as They Relate to Teacher Satisfaction" (unpublished Ph.D. dissertation, University of Chicago, 1954).

vorable the attitudes toward the work situation.

2. *The genesis and nature of institutional and individual conflict.* Conflict may be defined simply as the "mutual interference of reactions." The model points to three primary sources of conflict in the administrative setting: role-personality conflict, role conflict, and personality conflict. *Role-personality conflicts* occur as a function of discrepancies between the pattern of expectations attaching to a given role and the pattern of need-dispositions characteristic of the incumbent of the role. Recall our example of the army private with a high need for "ascendance" and the army sergeant with a high need for "submission." There is a mutual interference between nomothetic expectations and idiographic dispositions, and the individual must choose whether he will fulfil individual needs or institutional requirements. If he chooses to fulfil the requirements, he is in a sense shortchanging himself; if he chooses to fulfil his needs, he is shortchanging his role. In either case, there is conflict. In practice, of course, we most often find compromise, but in any event, the nature of the forthcoming behavior is quite different when the expectations and the dispositions are discrepant than when they are congruent.

Role conflicts occur whenever a role incumbent is required to conform simultaneously to a number of expectations which are mutually exclusive, contradictory, or inconsistent, so that adjustment to one set of requirements makes adjustment to the other impossible or at least difficult. Role conflicts in this sense are situational givens and independent of the personality of the role incumbent. They are evidence of disorganization in the nomothetic dimension and may arise in several ways:

(a) from disagreement within the referent group defining the role; e.g., the principal of the school may be expected by some teachers to visit them regularly for constructive help and by others to trust them as professional personnel not in need of such supervision; (b) from disagreement among several referent groups, each having a right to define expectations for the same role; e.g., the university faculty member may be expected by his department head to emphasize teaching and service to students but by his academic dean to emphasize research and publication; (c) from contradiction in the expectations of two or more roles which an individual is occupying at the same time; e.g., an individual may attempt at once to be a devoted mother and a successful career woman.

Personality conflicts occur as a function of opposing needs and dispositions within the personality of the role incumbent himself. The effect of such personal disequilibrium is to keep the individual at odds with the institution either because he cannot maintain a stable relationship to a given role or

because his autistic tendencies cause him to misperceive the expectations placed upon him. Existential objects and events have minimal representation in his private world, and there is little correspondence between his private world and the private worlds of other role incumbents with whom he must interact. In a sense, no matter what the situation, the objective role is detached by the individual from its institutional context and function and used by him to work out personal and private needs and dispositions, however inappropriate these may be to the social system as a whole.

In the terms of our model, these three types of conflict represent incongruence in the nomothetic dimension, in the idiographic dimension, or in the interaction between the two dimensions. Such incongruence is symptomatic of administrative failure and leads to loss in individual and institutional productivity.

[Getzels proceeds to derive an empirical test of some of the ideas discussed above.]

❖❖❖❖❖❖❖❖❖❖❖❖❖❖❖❖❖❖❖ THE RESOLUTION OF ROLE
CONFLICT WITHIN THE FAMILY *

John P. Spiegel

Iɴ an investigation of the relations among cultural value conflict, family

* This study is supported by research grants from the National Institute of Mental Health, and the Pauline and Louis G. Cowan Foundation.

conflict, and the emotional adjustment of the individual, in which I am participating with Florence R. Kluckhohn and a number of co-workers, the concept of social role is being used to observe and analyze the details of be-

Excerpted from John P. Spiegel, "The Resolution of Role Conflict Within the Family," in The Patient and the Mental Hospital, *Milton Greenblatt, Daniel Levinson, and Richard H. Williams (eds.), 1957. Abridged and used by permission of The Free Press of Glencoe, Inc., New York.*

havior which is functional or dysfunctional for the family as a whole. The social role concept is useful for this purpose because it facilitates observation of the way the individual members of the family become involved in the family as a superordinate system of behavior. (See, for example, Ackerman, 1951; Ackerman and Sobel, 1950; Parsons and Bales, 1955; Pollak, 1952; Spiegel, 1954.) It helps to describe not only the interaction of two members as they adjust to each other, but also the transactions of a plurality of members as they interweave in the special type of compulsiveness or control which a going system always imposes on its members. (See: Bentley, 1950; Dewey and Bentley, 1949; Kluckhohn and Spiegel, 1954; Spiegel, 1956.) Since the uniquely compulsive elements of the family system leave a characteristic stamp upon the personality development of the child, it is important to have a way of tearing apart the rather subtle elements of which it is composed.

In studying a group of families of emotionally disturbed children and comparing them with families in which the children are free of clinically manifest disturbance, we have found evidence of what promises to be a consistent difference between the two groups. In the first group, the children inevitably become involved in a conflict or disequilibrium situation which exists between the parents. Most frequently neither the child nor the parents are aware of this fact, nor are they aware of the ways in which it comes about. In the second group of families, although there may be sources of tension between the parents, the children are minimally involved in it. In order to avoid excessive variability in our two sets of families, we have kept them similar with respect to size, ethnic, regional, and class variables. Nevertheless, the sources of tension can be related in every case to differences and incompatibilities in cultural value orientations and, as a corollary, in definitions of social role expectations. These incompatibilities have a pronounced bearing upon the object relations and unconscious psychodynamics of the transacting members of the family. However, this is not the place to deal with the origin of the cultural value conflict or its direct relation to the intrapsychic process. These connections will be reported in subsequent communications. In this paper they will be assumed to underlie the role conflict in the family, and our attention will be centered rather on the ways in which the role conflict [1] is handled.

The Equilibrium-Disequilibrium Balance

I hope these all too brief examples of contrasting husband-wife role patterns illustrate how complementarity can be maintained in spite of variation in goals, values, and concrete sequences of acts within the role systems. The principle of complementarity is of the greatest significance because it is chiefly

[1] The expression, "role conflict," has been used in two different ways. In the first, and perhaps more common, usage it refers to a situation in which ego is involved in a difficult or impossible choice between two different roles toward two different alters. No matter what decision he makes, he is in trouble with one or the other of his role partners in the situation. In the second usage, ego and alter have conflicting or incompatible notions of how to play their reciprocal role. The conflict is not over which of several possible roles to take, but rather how to enact the role they have both decided to take. It is the second definition which is used in this paper. Settlement of the terminology problem should not prove too difficult, but will have to be postponed for the present.

responsible for that degree of harmony and stability which occurs in interpersonal relations. Because so many of the roles in which any of us are involved are triggered off by cultural cues in a completely complementary fashion, we tend not to be aware of them. We enact them automatically, and all goes well. This automatic function of role systems has significance for psychological economy of effort. We are spared the necessity of coming to decisions about most of the acts we perform because we know our parts so well. This saves our efforts for those acts which occur in less stabilized role systems. In this way role reciprocity confers spontaneity upon human behavior. Self-consciousness and self-guarding enter the scene along with role conflict which sharply raises the number of decisions which have to be made with respect to any sequence of acts. As long as complementarity is maintained at high levels of equilibrium,[2] decisions are decentralized, so to speak. They are taken care of by the system of role relations rather than by the individual acting in a self-conscious manner.

However, it is a part of the human condition that high levels of equilibrium figured by precise complementarity of roles are seldom maintained for long. Sooner or later disharmony enters the picture. Complementarity fails; the role systems characterizing the interpersonal relations move toward disequilibrium. The role partners disappoint each others' expectations. The failure of complementarity feeds back into the awareness of the participants

in the form of tension, anxiety or hostility, and self-consciousness. If the process continues without change, it will end in the disruption of the system. This process is so familiar and inevitable that it seems to merit no further comment. Yet, it has appeared to us that it may contain some general elements which can throw light on family behavior, if it were to be subjected to critical scrutiny. The key to its analysis would consist of a study of the conditions leading to the breakdown of complementarity and to its subsequent restoration. Although this study has not been carried as far as I would like, our current experience indicates that there are at least five causes for failure of complementarity in role systems within the family. Because of limitations of time and space, I will review them here very briefly, without the extended discussion and illustration which they deserve.

Cognitive discrepancy. One or both individuals involved in the role system may not know or have sufficient familiarity with the required roles. This is especially likely to occur with respect to age roles, and therefore frequently characterizes sources of disequilibrium between parents and children. When the pattern of acts constituting the role is not clearly mastered or not cognitively mapped or internalized, complementarity can be maintained only with difficulty. Cues are misinterpreted, and misunderstanding reduces complementarity of expectations. Both participants must have a relatively high tolerance of frustration and failure, and both must alternatively assume informally the roles of teacher and learner alternately. This alternation and reversal of roles will be discussed later in connection with the mechanisms of restoration of comple-

[2] In this context "equilibrium" does not denote a rigid, static state, but rather a balancing of process in a moving or changing state. The phrase "moving equilibrium" might, perhaps, be a better name.

mentarity. In our culture cognitive discrepancy is a characteristic problem between adolescents and the adult world. It also occurs between husband and wife at various developmental crises, or with respect to any sudden, new situation. For example, the wedding and immediate post-nuptial situation requires much new learning of roles. So does the birth of the first child, the first severe illness, and so forth.

Discrepancy of goals. Roles are patterns of acts directed toward immediate or ultimate goals. The goal of ego, interlocking with the goal of alter, determines the motivational principle behind the individual's taking of the role. Some goals serve the purpose of gratification, while others are chosen for the sake of defense. The same goal may serve either purpose, but if there is a shift in motivation, there is usually a shift in the definition of the role. For example, in one of our "sick" Italian families an eleven-year-old daughter, the middle one of three girls, repeatedly made demands upon her father for gifts of all sorts. Her motive was originally desire for gratification, but it was mixed with a defensive need to test whether she were being rejected or not. At first the father gratified her demands intermittently and inconsistently. He gave when he felt like and at other times refused. Both giving and refusing represented satisfactions for him, and he included rewarding and withholding as legitimate goals in his conception of the father's role. However, the daughter gradually defined his withholding as confirmation of her fear of rejection and tested more intensively by increasing her demands. The father defined this as "pestering" and responded with increased withholding and disapproval while claiming that he was trying his best to satisfy her. This claim was not true since he consistently rewarded the older sister more than this middle girl. But now the goal of withholding had become defensive against the implied meaning of her demands—that he actually preferred the older sister. In this complicated transaction, the defense was accomplished on the father's side through defining the daughter's motivation as coercive and pinning this down in the informal role, "pest," while giving himself the informal role of "victim." Although a tenuous complementarity was maintained by the defensive establishment of the informal "pest-victim" relation, actually their goals became more and more discrepant. This discrepancy of goals was one of the chief reasons why the family brought the girl into the psychiatric clinic for treatment. The parents verbalized the failure of complementarity by characterizing the girl to our interviewers as a bad and disobedient daughter. They had tried their best to teach her "right" from "wrong" but she was unable to "learn." It is significant of the defensive problem in this family that her behavior was ascribed to a cognitive and value discrepancy—that she couldn't "learn" the correct behavior—when actually it was due to a motivational problem concerning unavowed goals.

Another source of discrepancy in goals is biologically determined, rather than of motivational origin. Fatigue, illness, and lack of maturation are accompanied by a *restricted capacity for goal attainment.* Other biological limitations such as deficiency of intelligence have the same effect. Such limitations produce disequilibrium when one of the role partners is unable to accommodate through a change in level of expectancy of goals as rewards, for example, the parent who can't accept the limited intelligence of his child.

Allocative discrepancy. In any particular social situation there is a question of the individual's right to the role he wishes to occupy. There are four principal ways in which roles are sorted out among those who contend for them.

(1) Some roles, such as age and sex roles, are *ascribed,* (Linton, 1936). This means that they are universally expected and the individual has practically no leeway: He is not free to decide to change his sex or age role. If a man tries to change his sex role, as in transvestism, he is likely to invoke intense criticism. The same is true, though to a lesser extent, of age roles. The child who tries to act like an adult usually produces a critical response, and the same thing holds for the reverse situation.

(2) Some roles, such as occupational and some domestic roles, have to be *achieved,* (Linton, 1936). As an allocative principle, achievement involves effort, the satisfaction of prerequisites, and some form of ceremonial recognition such as licensure, contract, conferring of a diploma, appointment, and so forth. There is more leeway than in the case of ascribed roles, but strong sanctions will be invoked if an achieved role is simply taken without observing the required formalities.

(3) Some roles, in the main of an informal character, can be taken simply through *adoption.* No one has to ask permission to take an adopted role, although there may not always be approval for it. For example, the father in the Italian family just discussed adopted the role of "victim." He could have responded to his daughter's demands with some other role activity. He could have treated them as childish antics and laughed them off in the role of amused "spectator." This was ac-

tually a tack he frequently took when his feelings were not so intensely involved. By adopting the role of "victim," however, he *assigned* her the complementary role of "pest." The assignment was implicit rather than explicit. This is to say that it was concealed or masked, and that on the whole he treated her as if she had spontaneously adopted the role of pest toward him. Thus adoption-assignment describes for role transactions what is denoted for the individual by the concepts of introjection-projection. If he had been able to laugh off her demands, he would have treated her behavior as essentially playful.

(4) Playfulness is the sign of the last allocative principle, which is based on *assumption.* Assumed roles are not serious. They are taken in games or play, and are held to be at some distance from "reality." The child who plays "mother" is not really confusing herself with her mother. Thus there are no sanctions invoked for assumed roles, provided the individual has emitted the culturally appropriate cue indicating the assumption of a role. The facial configuration referred to in the expression—"smile when you say that"—is such a cue. It is obvious that assumed roles are of the greatest importance to the development and socialization of the child. But they are of equal importance to adults, not only for the sake of recreation and informality, but also to escape from a disequilibrium situation. The formula— "I was only kidding"—changes an adopted or achieved role into an assumed one, and thus establishes a new type of complementarity when the old one was threatened with failure. In this connection, withholding a cue indicating whether a role is adopted or assumed is frequently used to conceal or

mask motivation. Alter is left in the dark or misinterprets whether ego was serious or not.

The most common sources of allocative discrepancy leading to a failure of complementarity are: (a) use of a culturally invalid or inappropriate allocative principles (b) withholding of a cue indicating the allocative principle being used; and (c) emission of a misleading cue which gives alter the impression that one allocative principle is in use when in fact another one is actually present. For example, in the Italian family that I have been discussing, the mother was angry about the favoritism and excessive attention which the father showed toward their oldest daughter. In her eyes his behavior was largely seductive. At the same time she was ambivalent about his behavior, and unable to express the full range of her feelings. She preferred to attack him on the grounds that he was not a typical American Daddy. She reproached him for showing favoritism, for being unfair to the other children, saying nothing about the competitive feelings toward her daughter which his behavior stimulated in her. His response was to deny anything inappropriate in his behavior toward his daughter, and to accuse his wife of being irritable and unduly apprehensive in this situation. Actually neither of them wanted to push the situation to the full extent of their feelings. There was an implicit agreement to avoid it and to substitute in its place their cooperative concern with the excessive demands and "disobedience" of the middle daughter.

An analysis of the allocative principles involved in this source of disequilibrium between the parents reveals that (a) the mother defines the father's role as invalid. In her eyes he acts like a lover to his daughter and this is doubly inappropriate. It is not a part of his ascribed role as a father, nor of his achieved role as a husband. He has no right to this role. (b) The father agrees with the mother's view of the allocative principles but denies that he has taken a lover's role. But since both the accusation and the denial are implicit—that is, they are only hinted at, not directly verbalized —we have to look for the operations through which the potentially explosive aspects of this situation are avoided. This occurs by a mutually unconscious shift of the dispute to the ground of a cultural value discrepancy—the father's failure to be a typical American rather than a misguided Italian Daddy. At the same time, according to the observations of the interviewers who are studying the family, there is an ill-defined but quite intense intimacy between the father and daughter. It is hard to decide whether it is merely a playful aspect of filial attention and devotion, or whether it is something more than this. At times the daughter seems actually to take the mother's role toward the father. The cue distinguishing this as an assumed, adopted, achieved, or ascribed role is missing. But the father's direct description of his activity (how he perceives his behavior) on being questioned is that it is merely a part of his generally ascribed role as father. He even goes so far as to deny to the interviewer that he shows any favoritism, claiming that he treats all his children alike.

Withholding allocative cues or emitting misleading cues are in part attempts to avert the full denouement of failure of complementarity with its accompanying intense disequilibrium. Insofar as they have this function they will be discussed below in connection with that step in the restoration of equilibrium for which I will propose the term *masking*. It is probably obvious that these are general processes occurring in transactions at all levels of the social system. Withholding allocative cues universally produces a masked or ambiguous situation favorable for the "reading in" or projection of intentions. Emitting misleading cues is also a familiar device, whether in the hands of spies, at the international level, or confidence men on home territory. Be that as it may, their connection with failure of complementarity is this: That at the point at which the situation becomes unmasked, the allocative discrepancy is revealed in all its starkness. The disequilibrium is characterized by disillusionment ("You deceived me!"), protest ("You have no right to do what you did!"), alarm ("I've been robbed!"), and various similar phrasings in the vocabulary of victimization.

Instrumental discrepancy. A review of the origins of failure to maintain complementarity in role relations can not neglect the fact that nonhuman events and objects form part of the context of all behavior. Insofar as role activities require technical instruments, equipment, furniture, props, costumes, climate and other appropriate physical facilities (including money!), a deprivation or insufficiency of these instrumental prerequisites interferes with role transactions. The point is so obvious that it is represented in various traditional and contemporary maxims, of somewhat dubious accuracy. When equestrian skills were at a premium, instrumental discrepancy was pictured as "For want of a nail, the shoe was lost. For want of a shoe, the horse was lost. For want of a horse, the battle was lost. . . ." Today, in a less heroic cultural climate, one frequently hears, "There's nothing wrong with him that money won't cure!"

Despite the therapeutic oversimplification, such sentiments underscore the potential for severe frustration inherent in instrumental discrepancy. In addition to legitimate and actual deprivation, instrumental discrepancy easily assumes displaced or symbolic functions. For example, in our Italian family, the father complained that he did not have the money to buy the things that his family demanded. Actually he tried desperately to earn more money by taking extra jobs in addition to his main employment. These frenzied efforts defined him as a failure in the dominant American cultural pattern of occupational and economic success because he was unable to plan, budget, or save any money. On the other hand, this strenuous activity relieved him of the potential accusation of neglect—of not caring for his family's welfare. Yet the need to neglect underlay much of his over-compensatory striving. Unconsciously he resented having to take the role of the father, the provider, and would have preferred to compete with his children as the recipient of parental care and concern. This source of role discrepancy, however, had to be hidden from his conscious awareness and its energy had to be partly displaced into other types of activity or passive avoidance of activity.

Unconsciously contrived instrumental deficiency admirably served this purpose. The family suffered from protean forms of equipment failure. The screens had holes, the cellar frequently flooded, the car broke down, the ice box was constantly in need of repair, fuses blew, pipes broke, paint peeled. In the midst of this chaos, the father gave the impression of much activity, rushing about to attend to the latest crisis, accompanied by strident advice from his wife. Actually, he neglected repairing obvious defects until it was too late. The result of the neglect was painful to the wife who had high standards of housekeeping. He met all criticism from her with the attitude, "What can I do? I'm doing my best!"

From this description, it is apparent that instrumental discrepancy can be consciously or unconsciously motivated. To the extent that this is true, it is closely related to goal discrepancy. It must be kept in mind, however, that it can occur quite fortuitously, as in the case of accidental loss or deprivation by fire, robbery, or some other external agent.

Discrepancy in cultural value orientations. As was said before, roles are patterned in accordance with the value orientations of a culture or subculture. In mixed marriages, in families that have moved suddenly from one culture to another as in emigration, and in families that are moving up or down the social class ladder, the possibilities of confusion or outright conflict in cultural values are very great. However, even in families not involved in such dramatic transitions, there is a possibility of discrepancy of cultural value orientations. This is especially true in the United States, because of the extreme mixture of values beneath the surface layers of apparent uniformity of the social system. In this country, cultural traditions are so various and so frequently at odds with each other that almost any individual will have internalized some degree of cultural conflict.

In our project we are using the scheme of variation in cultural value orientations proposed by Florence Kluckhohn (1953; 1957) to keep track of the cultural attitudes which can give rise to conflict. This has proved very useful, but it is too detailed and involved to set forth here. However, the way in which cultural value discrepancies can give rise to disequilibrium can be illustrated again in the case of the Italian family discussed above. The mother was born in this country of native Italian parents. The father was born in Italy and did not come to the United States until he was eight years old. Consequently, the mother considers herself, correctly, to be more Americanized than the father. In both of them there is a great deal of conflict and confusion over the transition to the American patterns, but on any specific issue between them, she is always closer to the American middle-class cultural orientation. She would like to cook only American food, but he insists on Italian dishes. She would like to get away from the home, visit with friends and ultimately obtain a job, but he insists that she stay home and care for the children constantly. She would like her husband to show more initiative and independence though she has the capacity for making decisions and solving problems. He backs away from responsibility and is unable to discipline the children. She would like to plan for their future and the future of the children, but he is occupied with present concerns and he can't get his eyes on the future as a good American would.

These discrepancies in cultural values are associated with incompatible definitions of their roles as husband and wife, mother and father. Thus the complementarity of their role relations is always somewhat strained. The strain would be reduced if the father were moving, culturally, in the direction the mother wants to go. But her activity toward him makes it impossible for him to utilize what potentials for movement he possesses, since he is continuously defined as a failure in terms of the American patterns. He defends himself by pleading incapacity, by claiming that he is "trying" as hard as he can, and by asking that she accept as culturally adequate substitutes other informal roles. One of these is the role of comedian which he plays with great skill, offering entertainment in the place of successful performance. However, his position *vis-à-vis* the value of discrepancy is essentially destructive to his self-esteem. He takes his revenge on his wife through his seductive relations with his oldest daughter. In this way a value discrepancy, in which he is the loser, is compensated by an allocative and goal discrepancy in which he is the victor. Since these complicated transactions represent attempts to stabilize or restore equilibrium through *masking* and *compromise,* their further discussion will be postponed until we take up the discussion of these processes.

It is apparent that in discussing the varieties of failure of complementarity in any concrete empirical focus it is virtually impossible to avoid discussing simultaneously the efforts occurring in the system of transactions to compensate or re-establish equilibrium. Failure of complementarity is so disruptive that it is almost always accompanied by processes of restoration for which I would like to use the term, *re-equilibration.* In any ongoing system of relations such as a family, then, one can observe re-equilibration occurring whenever the balance of equilibrium to disequilibrium in the state of the system moves too close to the disequilibrium pole. It seems to me that it is the empirical admixture of these three processes—that is, of equilibrium (high complementarity), disequilibrium (low complementarity), and re-equilibration—that has made the processes involved in the stabilization or healthy internal adjustment of the system so difficult to recognize.

References

ACKERMAN, N. W., and SOBEL, R. "Family diagnosis: an approach to the pre-school child." *American Journal of Orthopsychiatry,* 1950, 20, 744–753.

ACKERMAN, N. W. " 'Social role' and total personality." *American Journal of Orthopsychiatry,* 1951, 21, 1–17.

BENTLEY, A. F. "Kennetic inquiry." *Science,* 1950, 112, 775–783.

BURKE, K. *A rhetoric of motives.* New York: Prentice-Hall, 1950.

DEWEY, J. and BENTLEY, A. F. *Knowing and the known.* Boston: Beacon Press, 1949.

JOHNSON, ADELAIDE M., and SZUREK, S. A. "The genesis of antisocial acting out in children and adults." *Psychoanalytic Quarterly,* 1952, 22, 323–343.

JOHNSON, ADELAIDE M. "Factors in the etiology of fixations and symptom choice." *Psychoanalytic Quarterly,* 1953, 22, 475–496.

KLUCKHOHN, FLORENCE R. "Dominant and variant value orientations." In: Kluckhohn, C., Murray, H. A., and Schneider, D. M., (eds.). *Personality in nature, society, and culture.* New York: Knopf, 1953.

KLUCKHOHN, FLORENCE R. *Variants in value orientations.* Evanston, Ill.: Row, Peterson, 1957.

KLUCKHOHN, FLORENCE R., and SPIEGEL, J. P. *Integration and Conflict in family behavior* (Report N. 27). Topeka, Kansas: Group for the Advancement of Psychiatry, 1954.

LINTON, R. *The study of man*. New York: Appleton-Century, 1936.

MEADE, G. H. *Mind, self, and society*. Chicago: Univ. Chicago Press, 1936.

MILLS, T. M. "Power relations in three-person groups." In: Cartwright, D., and Zander, A., (eds.). *Group Dynamics*. Evanston, Ill.: Row, Peterson, 1953.

MILLS, T. M. "The coalition pattern in three person groups." *American Sociological Review*, 1954, 19, 657–667.

MORENO, J. L. "The discovery of the spontaneous man—with special emphasis on the technique of role reversal." *Group Psychotherapy*, 1955, 8, 103–129.

PARSONS, T., BALES, R. F., and SHILS, E. A. *Working papers in the theory of action*. New York: Free Press of Glencoe, 1953.

PARSONS, T., BALES, R. F. *Family, socialization, and interaction process*. New York: Free Press of Glencoe, 1955.

POLLAK, O. *Social science and psychotherapy for children*. New York: Russell Sage Foundation, 1952.

SIMMEL, G. "Quantitative aspects of groups." In: Wolff, K. J., (trans. & ed.). *The sociology of Georg Simmel*. New York: Free Press of Glencoe, 1950.

SPIEGEL, J. P. "The social roles of doctor and patient in psychoanalysis and psychotherapy." Psychiatry, 1954, 17, 369–376.

SPIEGEL, J. P. "A model for relationships among systems." In: GRINKER, R. R., (ed.). *Toward a unified theory of human behavior*. New York: Basic Books, 1956.

SULLIVAN, H. S. *The interpersonal theory of psychiatry*. New York: Norton, 1953.

✦✦✦✦✦✦✦✦✦✦✦✦✦✦✦✦✦✦ ORGANIZATIONAL ANALYSIS

Alvin W. Gouldner

DURING the historical development of organizational analysis, two distinct approaches to the study of complex organizations have emerged in the work of sociologists. One of these, best exemplified by the work of Max Weber, is a conception of the organization in terms of a "rational" model. The other, which can be termed the "natural system" model, ultimately derives from Comte, was later reinforced by Robert Michels, and is now best exemplified in the work of Philip Selznick and Talcott Parsons.

One of the central problems of organizational analysis is to reconcile the divergent implications of these two models and to synthesize a new and

Excerpted from Alvin W. Gouldner, "Organizational Analysis," Sociology Today: Problems and Prospects, edited by Robert K. Merton, Leonard Broom, and Leonard S. Cottrell, Jr., © 1959 by Basic Books, Inc., publishers, pp. 404–412. Used by permission.

more powerful model. In the following pages, I shall attempt to clarify some of the advantages and limitations of each of these models.

The Rational Model of Organizational Analysis

In the rational model, the organization is conceived as an "instrument"— that is, as a rationally conceived means to the realization of expressly announced group goals. Its structures are understood as tools deliberately established for the efficient realization of these group purposes. Organizational behavior is thus viewed as consciously and rationally administered, and changes in organizational patterns are viewed as planned devices to improve the level of efficiency. The rational model assumes that decisions are made on the basis of a rational survey of the situation, utilizing certified knowledge, with a deliberate orientation to an expressly codified legal apparatus. The focus is, therefore, on the legally prescribed structures—*i.e.,* the formally "blueprinted" patterns—since these are more largely subject to deliberate inspection and rational manipulation.

This model takes account of departures from rationality but often tends to assume that these departures derive from random mistakes, due to ignorance or error in calculation. Fundamentally, the rational model implies a "mechanical" model, in that it views the organization as a structure of manipulable parts, each of which is separately modifiable with a view to enhancing the efficiency of the whole. Individual organizational elements are seen as subject to successful and planned modification, enactable by deliberate decision. The long-range development of the organization as a

whole is also regarded as subject to planned control and as capable of being brought into increasing conformity with explicitly held plans and goals.

The Natural-System Model of Organizational Analysis

The natural-system model regards the organization as a "natural whole," or system. The realization of the goals of the system as a whole is but one of several important needs to which the organization is oriented. Its component structures are seen as emergent institutions, which can be understood only in relation to the diverse needs of the total system. The organization, according to this model, strives to survive and to maintain its equilibrium, and this striving may persist even after its explicitly held goals have been successfully attained. This strain toward survival may even on occasion lead to the neglect or distortion of the organization's goals. Whatever the plans of their creators, organizations, say the natural-system theorists, become ends in themselves and possess their own distinctive needs which have to be satisfied. Once established, organizations tend to generate new ends which constrain subsequent decisions and limit the manner in which the nominal group goals can be pursued.

Organizational structures are viewed as spontaneously and homeostatically maintained. Changes in organizational patterns are considered the results of cumulative, unplanned, adaptive responses to threats to the equilibrium of the system as a whole. Responses to problems are thought of as taking the form of crescively developed defense mechanisms and as being importantly shaped by shared values which are deeply internalized in the members.

The empirical focus is thus directed to the spontaneously emergent and normatively sanctioned structures in the organization.

The focus is not on deviations from rationality but, rather, on disruptions of organizational equilibrium, and particularly on the mechanisms by which equilibrium is homeostatically maintained. When deviations from planned purposes are considered, they are viewed not so much as due to ignorance or error but as arising from constraints imposed by the existent social structure. In given situations, the ignorance of certain participants may not be considered injurious but functional to the maintenance of the system's equilibrium.

The natural-system model is typically based upon an underlying "organismic" model which stresses the interdependence of the component parts. Planned changes are therefore expected to have ramifying consequences for the whole organizational system. When, as frequently happens, these consequences are unanticipated, they are usually seen as divergent from, and not as supportive of, the planner's intentions. Natural-system theorists tend to regard the organization as a whole as organically "growing," with a "natural history" of its own which is planfully modifiable only at great peril, if at all. Long-range organizational development is thus regarded as an evolution, conforming to "natural laws" rather than to the planner's designs.

The Two Models Compared

Needless to say, these two models are ideal types in the sense that few modern sociologists studying organizations adopt one to the complete exclusion of the other. Nevertheless, as we have mentioned previously, some sociologists tend to stress one model more than the other.

Each of these models has certain characteristic strengths and weaknesses. The rational model, for example, has the indisputable merit of focusing attention on some of the very patterns which distinguish the modern organization, particularly its rationality. At the same time, however, it tends to neglect the manner in which those patterns which the modern organization shares with "natural" groups may also effect behavior within them. The fact is, of course, that the distinguishing characteristics of a bureaucratic organization are not its only characteristics; systematic attention must also be directed to those features of modern organizations, such as the need for loyalty, which they have in common with other types of groups.

The natural-system model, on the other hand, has the merit of focusing attention on the spontaneous and unplanned (that is, "informal") patterns of belief and interaction that arise even within the rationally planned organization. Often, however, the natural-system model tends to neglect the distinctively rational features of the modern organization.

Sometimes both of these models are used in organizational analysis in an eclectic manner; one part of the organization is analyzed in terms of the rational model and another part in terms of the natural-system model. Studies using this approach tend to present the organization as two distinctive parts, running eternally on parallel tracks; many of them fail to work out the manner in which the rational and informal patterns merge into and influence each other. For example, in the Western Electric studies, Roethlisberger and Dickson distinguished between the logics of cost and efficiency, on the one hand, and the logic of sentiment, on the other. They maintain that the former characterizes managerial elites, whereas the latter is distinctive of employee or worker echelons.[1] Warner and Low's study of industrial conflict in Yankee City [2] makes a similar point. These authors regard the managerial group as dominated by the aim of producing "at the lowest possible cost and highest profit," and maintain that advancement is given primarily to those who contribute more to the "efficiency of production." As a result of this dichotomy between the rational and the natural-system models, the non-rational, traditionalistic orientations of management personnel have been obscured and informal organization tends to be examined primarily among lower ranking personnel. Conversely, the rationalistic orientations of lower echelons, at least with respect to their own ends, tends to be treated as a façade for their own underlying non-rational needs.

Applied Social Science and Organizational Analysis

The statement that the natural-system model neglects the distinctive features of the modern organization means, above all, that it tends to minimize the significance of rationally organized structures and patterns of planned adaptation. It tends, for example, to overlook the full implications of the fact that the modern organization

[1] F. J. Roethlisberger and W. J. Dickson, with the assistance of H. A. Wright, *Management and the Worker*, Harvard University Press, 1939, p. 565.

[2] W. L. Warner and J. O. Low, *The Social System of the Modern Factory*, Yale University Press, 1947, pp. 172–73.

meets its own peculiar needs, as well as those which it shares with all groups, in certain distinctive ways. To illustrate: modern organizations systematically evaluate the degree to which their policies are effective; they rationally appraise the relative effectiveness of the various departments within the organization; they conduct market researches and public-opinion studies which keep them in touch with their suppliers and outlets; they select new recruits and evaluate group members through various kinds of psychological tests; they defend policies with the use of research; they wage war against competitors with facts and figures and rationally documented argumentation; and they prepare for unforeseeable contingencies by briefing their administrators with digests of scientifically accumulated "background information." Indeed, these administrators may stake their very authority on what they know or on what knowledge they can purchase. All this is too well known to require further elaboration. There is a question, however, whether its full significance has been appreciated and theoretically assimilated by those using the natural-system model.

One pattern of particular interest to sociologists deserves to be stressed in this connection. In the modern organization, behavioral science has become a kind of working equivalent for, or supplement to, the profit and loss statement; various types of social research have supplanted the bookkeeper's ledgers as bases of rational decision in cases in which pecuniary consequences cannot be calculated. The very rationality of the modern organization has made it increasingly dependent upon the kinds of information that can be supplied by operations or market researchers, opinion pollsters, industrial sociologists, morale surveyors, and group dynamicists.

Although these newer patterns require only a small part of the organization's budget, they have substantial theoretical implications for organizational analysis. For applied social science has, in effect, become one of the planned functional substitutes for the spontaneous adaptive mechanisms by means of which the rational organization responds to external threats, reduces internal disruptions, and controls various forms of social deviance. As such, it merits a place in the theoretical models and the empirical researches of organizational analysts. So far, however, organizational analysts have neglected to include in their researches a systematic study of the uses made of applied social science in the modern organization.

The neglect of applied social science within the organization, as an object of analysis and research, is, however, simply a special instance of a larger lacuna in organizational analysis. Modern organizational analysis by sociologists is overpreoccupied with the spontaneous and unplanned responses which organizations make to stress, and too little concerned with patterns of planned and rational administration. Only a few sociologists, notably Peter Blau, whose study of the use of statistical techniques of personnel rating is a trail-blazing research,[3] have investigated the latter area. Nonetheless, many of the current studies guided by the natural-system model are still fixated on the Comteian level.

In general, the natural-system model tends to induce neglect of the rational structures characterizing the modern organization, of the forces contributing

[3] Peter Blau, *The Dynamics of Bureaucracy*, University of Chicago Press, 1955, Chapter 3.

to their growth, as well as of the distinctive ways in which they are maintained. It tends to take as given rather than as problematic such distinctive features of the modern organization as its complex division of labor, its legally formalized codes, its reliance upon professional and technical experts, its utilization of systematic bodies of knowledge, and its rationalistic orientation.

Use of the natural-system model tends to focus the analyst's concern on the forces that undermine the organization's impersonal principles and subvert its formal ends to "narrower" interests, rather than on those that sustain these and bolster the distinctively bureaucratic structures. It tends to lead to a focus on the characteristics that all occupations share, rather than on the distinctive features of the modern professional expert, who utilizes a body of systematized information. Nonetheless, the very rationality of the modern organization, as well as its other typical characteristics, varies in degree, and this very variation is itself in need of explanation.

The natural-system model, which developed in the course of polemics against the rational model, tends to minimize the role of rationality in human affairs and to counterstress the way in which organizational behavior is affected by nonrational norms. Theorists who use this model have typically emphasized the inherent vulnerability of rationally planned action, particularly action directed toward what might be termed "liberal" goals. From its Comteian inceptions, the natural-system model has been infused with a conservative and antiliberal metaphysical pathos. In Michels' work this was expressed by an emphasis on the organizational constraints that inherently thwart democratic aspirations. But, characteristically, the natural-system theorists have tended to neglect study of the organizational constraints that conduce to the *realization* of democratic values. It is only recently that this line of analysis has been systematically developed by such organizational analysts as Lipset, Trow, and Coleman.[4]

Manifest and Latent Patterns

There is no doubt, however, that the focus of the natural-system model on the spontaneous mechanisms common to all groups has enabled it to make its most important contribution to the study of organizations. This focus has facilitated the discovery and analysis of the so-called informal organization, which tends to be obscured by the rational model. Yet there is a noteworthy ambiguity in the natural-system model concerning the meaning of "informal organization." In other words, although it is clear that the natural-system model directs attention beyond and away from the formally constituted organizational system, there remains a question concerning what it is that the model directs attention toward.

The notion of informal organization is a residual or cafeteria concept of diverse and sprawling contents. Some informal patterns are organizationally unprescribed culture structures—that is, patterns of belief and sentiment; for example, the belief that one should not be a "rate buster." Other informal patterns are organizationally unprescribed

[4] S. M. Lipset, M. Trow, and J. Coleman, *Union Democracy*, Free Press, 1956. For an early statement of my own thinking on this problem, see A. W. Gouldner, "Attitudes of 'Progressive' Trade Union Leaders," *Amer. J. Sociol.*, 52 (1947), 389–92.

social structures; *e.g.*, the cliques that develop among those working near one another. Further, although the term "informal group" is sometimes used to refer to a primary relation, not all informal patterns involve friendly intimacy and closeness. Some may entail personal enmities, feuds, and conflicts.

Informal patterns vary in other significant ways. Some are patterns prescribed by the traditional values in the larger society which are recognized as relevant within the organization; for example, the "no squealing" rules or the special deference which a supervisor may give to an elderly worker. Other informal patterns are prescribed only by the values traditional to a particular organization; for example, the tendency of professors on some campuses to address or refer to one another as "Mr."

Still other informal patterns are not prescribed by any traditional values, either in the larger society or in the particular organization, but largely derive from the competition or conflict for scarce information or goods; for example, the salesman's "personal following," or the congregation of males around their employer's private secretary. It is precisely this last type of informal pattern, which is not normatively prescribed, that characteristically tends to be neglected in the work of the natural-system theorists. Neglect of this pattern accounts in part for the fact that little systematic research has been done on the effects of machinery and office equipment, so characteristic of the modern organization, on social relations within it.

Some of the distinctive characteristics of the modern organization generate peculiar hazards for organizational analysis. In particular, the specialized roles within the organization, having such a high visibility, tend to become a focus of research, and analysis thus tends to become confined to these prescribed and institutionalized roles. This is a hazard to which both the rational and the natural-system models are susceptible, although not equally so. The natural-system theorists, somewhat more astute about this danger, have been concerned about the ways in which the "social" characteristics of personnel may shape organizational policy and behavior. Selznick's study of the TVA is an excellent example of this. Other studies have analyzed the manner in which the ethnic or religious origins of personnel affect their chances of mobility and the allocation of power within the organization.[5] As yet, however, organizational analysts have not incorporated in their theoretical models a systematic concern with the way in which the diverse social identities that people bring into the organization affect organizational behavior.

It is obvious that all people in organizations have a variety of "latent social identities"[6]—that is, identities which are not culturally prescribed as relevant to or within rational organizations—and that these do intrude upon and influence organizational behavior in interesting ways. For example, there is usually something occurring between people of opposite sexes,

even though this is prescribed neither by the organization's official rules nor by the societal values deemed appropriate for that setting.[7] Yet many sociologists who study factories, offices, schools, or mental hospitals take little note of the fact that the organizational role-players invariably have a gender around which is built a latent social identity. One does not have to be a Freudian to insist that sex makes a difference, even for organizational behavior. (It should be noted that there is no analytic distinction between giving attention to the ways in which latent ethnic or religious identities affect organizational behavior and examining the implications of latent sexual identities for organizational patterns.)

The point, then, is that there is a need to distinguish systematically between those social identities of organization members which are consensually regarded as relevant or legitimate in that setting, and those identities which are defined as irrelevant or inappropriate to consider in that context. The manner in which both the manifest and the *latent* social identities shape organizational behavior requires more attention. Study of latent identities and roles within organizations promises to be fruitful because, among other reasons, it provides a lever for approaching problems of organizational tension. For the pressure of the latent roles on the manifest or formal roles within organizations is a persistent source of strain on the equilibrium of every organization.

---

[5] See, for example, Orvis Collins, "Ethnic Behavior in Industry," *Amer. J. Sociol., 51* (1946), 293–98; Melville Dalton, "Informal Factors in Career Achievement," *Amer. J. Sociol., 56* (1951), 407–15; and E. C. Hughes, "Queries Concerning Industry and Society Growing Out of the Study of Ethnic Relations in Industry," *Amer. sociol. Rev., 14* (1949), 211–20.

[6] The concepts of latent and manifest organizational identities and roles is discussed in A. W. Gouldner, "Cosmopolitans and Locals: Toward an Analysis of Latent Social Roles— I," *Admin. Sci. Quart., 2* (1957), 281–306.

[7] Among the perhaps esoteric but still theoretically interesting patterns partly structured by latent sexual identities is the "touch system," which regulates interpersonal bodily contacts. See Erving Goffman, "The Nature of Deference and Demeanor," *Amer. Anthrop., 58* (1956), 486–88.

✧✧✧✧✧✧✧✧✧✧✧✧✧✧✧✧✧✧ THE NATURE OF A COMMUNITY

Edward O. Moe

A COMMUNITY is viewed, after Loomis and others, as a social system or as "patterned interaction" in which certain elements such as goals, norms, roles, and authority-power are observable, and in which certain basic processes such as communication, decision-making, systemic linkage, and boundary maintenance are operating. The same systemic concept is applied to groups and organizations. A community is thought to come into existence in the acceptance of common or similar definitions in situations that confront people in the daily routines of living, working, and playing. The particular content of the elements and the nature of the processes in turn give a certain uniqueness of character to the community. The distinctive content and configuration of the various elements and processes in the social system of the community may be, and in most cases will be, different from those of particular groups and organizations in the community.

Some significant differences are observable between the social systems of organization and community. Perhaps the most important are these:

The community is a system of systems. A community, even a small one, includes a great many different institutions and organizations and the formal and informal sub-groups that grow up within them. These organizations and groups are social systems and they are part of the social system of the community.

The community is not structurally and functionally centralized in the same sense as a formal organization. The great range and diversity of the needs, interests, goals and activities of people of the community are met through a variety of separate institutions and groups—no one of which holds a completely dominant position in relation to the others.

The community as a social system is implicit in nature as compared with the explicitness of a formal organization. This is true both of the community system as a totality, as well as of the various elements such as the goals of the people who live in the community, the prescribed means of achieving goals, and the underlying values.

Excerpted from Edward O. Moe, "Consulting with a Community System: A Case Study," Journal of Social Issues, *Vol. 15, No. 2, 1960, pp. 29–35. Used by permission.*

✧✧✧✧✧✧✧✧✧✧✧✧✧✧✧✧✧✧✧✧ APPROACHES TO SOCIAL CHANGE

Irwin T. Sanders

Five General Approaches to Social Change

EACH of us has some sort of approach to social change. It may not be fully formulated, nor even systematic, but it does influence the way we react to changes to us and about us. There are at least five general approaches used by scholars today, and I am sure that all five of these will have their enthusiasts and exponents among you. The differences among these approaches stem largely from the definition one gives to the term "social" and the way each theory tries to answer the question "What changes?" when social change occurs.

The grand theories. Some theories are broad, encyclopaedic, and would define as *social* everything affecting man. Some of the "grand" theorists have been Herbert Spencer and his evolutionary emphasis; Karl Marx and his concentration upon modes of production and the class struggle; Pitirim Sorokin and his analysis of ideational, idealistic, and sensate cultures; and Arnold Toynbee and his theory of challenge and response. This list of grand theorists could be considerably expanded, but the common thread running through the grand theories is

their stress upon the why's of history. The units with which they deal are civilizations, total societies, socio-cultural systems on a comparative basis geographically and from earliest times down to the present. There is a majesty to the intellectual sweep of such theories, an evident erudition, and a tantalizing quality to the questions which they pose. For example, ancient Athens, shortly after its flowering into its golden age, was overcome by Sparta, a garrison state. So, such a theorist might ask, is the United States, where political and economic freedom have reached such heights, to be overcome shortly by another garrison state, this one from Eastern Europe? Many of the grand theorists are wedded almost entirely to the historical method, although some of them, like Sorokin, also construct many kinds of indices of change based on the tabulation of information about leadership, art forms, religious participation, and the like for the periods they study.

I find such theories intriguing and stimulating. They jolt me out of all complacency, but unfortunately they seldom give me any guide to action or any useful suggestions about the kinds of concrete studies of social change in which I become involved from time to

Excerpted from Irwin T. Sanders, "Approaches to Social Change," Education for Social Work, 1960 Proceedings, Eighth Annual Program Meeting, Council on Social Work Education, New York, New York, pp. 3-23. Address delivered in Oklahoma City, Oklahoma, January 20, 1960. Article is reprinted with permission from the Council on Social Work Education.

time, whether it be the analysis of changes in social work as a profession or a community development program in Indonesia. Interestingly enough, I find on my visits to Eastern Europe that there the social scientists, most of whom think that they have in the encyclopaedic theory of Marx an explanation for most social phenomena, are baffled when it comes to studying many of their pressing problems. Their grand theory gives them little guidance as to how they can change a land-oriented peasant into a factory worker, how they can motivate members of a collective farm to work hard once they have gotten rid of all private property in land (to which Marx ascribed so many ills), or how they can deal with a generation of youth for whom the old standards have little validity and who have not accepted the new standards which the Communist regimes seek to impose. Is it not strange, therefore, that the Eastern European regimes are turning once more to sociology, formerly utterly condemned as a bourgeois discipline, since they realize that their most pressing need is not more social philosophy but some empirical studies which tell them where they are going and why they are not getting there any faster. One of these days they will be discovering social work, too, and you will be asked how your approach fits in with the Marxian dialectic.

Cultural change. In a search for another approach to social change we may turn to the voluminous literature on *acculturation,* prepared chiefly by anthropologists. Although these writers differ in their definitions of *cultural* change, much of what they say has a direct bearing upon *social* change. They have proved beyond any doubt that sociological variables (those connected with social interaction) exist in a cul-

tural envelope and that they must be understood, in part at least, in terms of these cultural factors. It is perhaps misleading to try to characterize in a sentence or two such a wide array of acculturation studies as exist, but their common emphasis seems to be upon culture traits (artifacts such as a plow, social traits such as a kinship system, or mental traits such as beliefs and values). They tell us much about the origin of these traits, how they spread through cultural diffusion or borrowing, and how they become integrated into a particular culture. You will notice that in presenting my limited approach to social change, I shall draw heavily upon some of the cultural features. Since so many studies of cultural change concentrate on traits, they are not in position to give sufficient insight into the connection between social change and social interaction, which happens to be the topic of most interest to me as a sociologist. I admit that this is a personal preference and in no sense a refutation or minimizing of the cultural change approach.

Technological change. Although the studies of technological change are closely tied in with cultural change, so much work has been done on technology that we can consider it a respectable approach in its own right. The focus is on the development of tools and techniques, but this approach usually examines social effects of technological innovation as well. Some writers, such as Leslie White of the University of Michigan, have tied man's social achievements concretely to his discovery and mastery of new forms of energy. Fred Cottrell, of Miami University, has also concerned himself with the same problem. And it was out of the study of technological change that William Ogburn, of the University of

Chicago, developed his cultural lag theory, to which you all were exposed in your undergraduate social science courses. Today, the students of technological change are telling us that the automation stage, which we are just entering, can be a truly revolutionary period in many social patterns as well as in the industrial process itself. This approach, more than any other, calls our attention to the significance of the tempo of change; it reminds us that technological development can outstrip social adjustment, that men who are politically and socially in the horse-and-buggy era have the capabilities of the hydrogen bomb in the push-buttons beneath their finger tips. The very questions which this approach poses drive us of necessity into a consideration of man's social arrangements through which he can put to rational use these godlike powers, powers so great that they make Zeus on Mount Olympus seem like a schoolboy prankster. We cannot, therefore, consider technological change equivalent to social change, though we recognize its direct relationship.

Selected change processes. The social sciences in the Western world have developed to the point that they can now deal in sophisticated fashion with specific change processes such as industrialization, urbanization and political centralization. It is in this approach that economists, demographers, and some political scientists join with others in their studies of social change. Here we find some of the most elaborate statistical models in use and an effort to treat comprehensively all data dealing with a given change process. Sometimes in an interest in using that which can be statistically manipulated most easily, we fail to take into account some of the sociological variables for which

there are no easily-available figures. For example, I prefer to see the march of industrialization not just in terms of the factories, railroads, and consumer goods it leaves in its wake, but rather in terms of the changing relationships which are antecedent as well as subsequent to its manifestation. The coming of the first factories into a developing country calls for the creation of many new kinds of relationships before the factories are ever built. The first planning for industry involves a number of intricate relationships within the economy or the governmental bureaucracy and with educational leaders concerned with the production of needed worker skills. A complex bureaucratic network comes into existence, often a rearranging of these in already existing networks, before any great labor force is recruited. Then, new management relationships must be introduced, along with the creation of new employer-employee relationships. Eventually, the bonds among the workers themselves have to be fashioned, tentatively at first, as production gets under way. At the same time, regulations (or norms) are being worked out; an older value system is being challenged, and many people are being taught new roles for statuses (lathe operators, truck drivers) which they have never occupied before.

Urbanization, like industrialization, can be viewed chiefly as changed social relationships. Some of these changes precede and others follow urbanization but this general process itself is the name we give to the movement of change pertaining to one facet of life —the growth of cities in size and importance. In one sense, in the urbanization of a developing country people break off relationships with their fellow villagers and move to a nearby town or city to form new relationships, to fill new statuses. Or, if they stay in their village and take up "city ways," this is the same as saying that they accept the urban value system which affects their view of the status hierarchies in which they are involved, causing them to discard old roles and to learn new ones, and even to subscribe to different rules of the game. All of this can happen while those who stay at home remain in the same statuses (farmer, peasant, father, mother) which they have had before.

It would be foolish to claim that these mighty change processes moving so fast around the world (secularization, mechanization, democratization, and the like) should be viewed only in terms of social relationships. They have their economic, their motivational, their political and technological sides; but, if they are to be studied as evidences of social change, the analysis of their connection with social relationships is crucial. For example, no theory of industrialization is adequate if it does not tell what social relationships are modified prior to the outset of industry, accompany its development, and result from it.

Systemic change. We now come to the last general approach to be considered: that of systemic change. If the ramifications of these various approaches seem to overwhelm you, then you will be more conscious of and charitable toward the task I faced in trying to delineate these approaches and decide on which I think will be of considerable use. If we had had several hours together I probably would have tried to deal fully with this systemic approach which views groups, institutional complexes (such as government or the economy), or even whole societies as social systems. We would have gone into the components of such systems, as well as the operations which must be carried out if they are to persist; once we had done this we could then define social change as any change which becomes incorporated in the system to such an extent that it modifies the structure of the system (the arrangements among its components) or the operations of the system (communication, allocation of power, social mobility, and the like). In developing such a theory of change we would have drawn heavily from the findings of these following the other approaches mentioned, but with this approach we would have had a conceptual scheme into which to fit what otherwise might seem unrelated data.

CHAPTER 8 ❖ *Some Strategic Leverage Points*

What are the criteria for a general diagnostic framework useful to a change-agent? Two questions may be asked over and beyond the diagnosis and analysis of a situation that might be performed after a detailed and scientific observation of events. These questions represent the special requirements of diagnosis by a change-agent who is concerned with action and intervention: (1) what can the change-agent or client-system or both do or not do now? (2) what is the most important things to do or not do now?

The question of what can or cannot be done, the question of feasibility, requires selective attention to those parts of the client-system that can be affected, altered, or in some way influenced. Feasibility, then raises questions about the *accessibility* and *manipulability* of variables or factors in the situation of the change-agent and client system. It may also be used to question the value of including in the diagnostic schema factors that do not lend themselves readily to joint diagnosis and action. For example, diagnoses that emphasize the basic personality make-up of an individual client-system ordinarily are not very useful to change-agents, except in programs of change where deep personality therapy is the goal. The change-agent and client-system may not be able to affect or wish to delve into certain factors. In brief, part of the diagnosis may well be in terms of the limits of reconstruction of the client-system, as of the present time. A point to be remembered is that feasibility or nonfeasibility is not an absolute criterion but must be assessed against present situational realities and against the type of change envisioned. The change-agent faces both realistic issues and value problems in deciding upon what is feasible or not feasible, and in saving his diagnosis from a priori assumptions about what can and cannot be done. If feasibility is his only criterion he may fall into the trap of working to produce adjustment and conformity to existing conditions, rather than envisioning and supporting revolutionary—or evolutionary—changes that may take a long time in working out.

In considering what is important to do or not to do, the change-agent faces both conceptual and prudential questions. In selecting from among possible actions, how does one assess their relative importance? The social scientist has given us his analyses of the centrality of certain factors and their causal interdependencies, which—we may hope—can be used to predict and produce probable chain reactions. That is, the change-agent's diagnostic orientation about interventions may include an assessment of how much of a desirable or undesirable chain reaction one intervention may unleash as compared to another. In addition, prudential questions arise in assessing importance. For example, what is the diagnosis for an intervention where a precarious and tense equilibrium exists? How near or remote from the point of greatest tension in the system should an intervention be made?

The selection of variables to serve as part of the change-agent's diagnostic orientation depends upon his purposes and values, as well as upon the answers to the questions raised above. Our selections for this chapter present some of the key variables as these have been studied by social scientists. We are suggesting, therefore, that a change-agent might find here a sample of themes which recur in situational diagnosis. "Motivation," "communication," and "power" are themes explored in several articles. (Lippitt's article on consultation in Chapter 4 should be compared for a statement about strategic variables in the diagnostic frameworks of change-agents.)

Bennis' analysis of distortions in *Interpersonal Communication* suggests what is often one of the most direct and fundamental intervention points in a client-system. If some degree of valid communication can be established among parts of a client-system, many consequences in power, role, leadership, and conflict relationships may follow. Communication as a variable for the diagnostic framework of a change-agent meets the criteria both of feasibility and of importance in many situations.

Another point of leverage is the system of power relationships. Cartwright, in *Power: A Neglected Variable in Social Psychology,* summarizes recent social-psychological research about "power" and, in showing neglect of this variable by many psychologists, demonstrates the substantial basis for using "power" as a part of the change-agent's diagnostic framework.

McGregor's article, *The Human Side of Enterprise,* breaks new ground in management theory. In bold strokes, he reexamines assumptions about people's motivations. For him, a strategic leverage point can be obtained by adding self fulfillment needs to traditional lists of social and ego needs in our thinking about motivation. In so doing, new orientations to the task of management emerge from what he calls Theory Y, with far-reaching consequences. McGregor provides us with a theoretical and psychological underpinning for managers, and, we suggest, by extension, for all change-agents. His Theory Y, based on Maslow's theory of self-fulfillment needs, is a major contribution to a theory of changing an organization, a small group, or a community.

"Leadership" represents another aspect of a social system that may be used as a point of intervention. Gordon Lippitt describes various conceptions in his paper, *What Do We Know about Leadership?* Bennis, in his *Leadership Theory and Administrative Behavior,* reminds us of the fact that the variables of power, authority, and influence take different shapes, according to the goals of the organization toward which they operate. Implicit in his analysis is the possibility that different segments of an organization may make different "definitions of the situation" and of the goals, and that these may lead in turn to struggles over appropriate criteria for judging the effectiveness of an organization. Clarification of the evaluational criteria and the related determinants of organizational functioning can be a point of leverage in intervention.

Conflict, of course, needs no justification as marking an aspect of a client in which intervention may be urgent. The study of conflict is an area where behavioral science researches are providing change-agents with the techniques and viewpoints for a theory of changing in terms of conflict resolution.

Dahrendorf, in *Two Models of Society,* contrasts structural-functional or integration models of society with conflict models. For him, the explanation of social change lies in social conflict theory, with special attention to the authority structures of social organizations.

Thompson, in *Organizational Management of Conflict,* shows how some types of conflict arise from the structural arrangements of the organization as a system, but, in contrast to Dahrendorf, points to the role of the administrator in managing the conflicts.

Conflict between the social groups within a community and across the lines of nations are discussed in the next two papers. Benne, in *An Approach to Problems of Interreligious Conflict,* points to the fact that there are realistic as well as unrealistic (or irrational) elements in interreligious conflicts. The former are often overlooked and underplayed. His suggestion is that realistic factors in conflict, and not merely nonrational factors such as prejudices and misperceptions, need direct attention in resolving interreligious conflicts.

Blake, in *Psychology and the Crisis of Statesmanship,* also acknowledges the existence of "fundamental value conflicts not based on distortions," but devotes major attention to delineating approaches to the reduction of intergroup tension and to summarizing the available research evidence for the different approaches to this problem.

In these papers no pat formulas are offered and no strident claims for the primacy of one leverage point over another are defended. Our criteria of selection precluded such huckstering. Diagnosing a situation demands a large measure of personal judgment by the change-agent. Social science knowledge can help him in making such judgments if strategically applied. But judgments and chance-taking are still inescapable. Here again is an area of creative tension for the change-agent in his relations to the social sciences.

✧✧✧✧✧✧✧✧✧✧✧✧✧✧✧✧✧✧ INTERPERSONAL COMMUNICATION

Warren G. Bennis

The human being is distinguished from lower forms of animals by his ability to communicate and to develop systems of communication about communication. Mathematics is perhaps the most elegant and unambiguous form of symbols about communication. Unfortunately, there are many aspects of communication that are not easily rendered in formal symbols—particularly those matters dealing with interpersonal relations. We have only the crudest of tools and the vaguest of concepts to communicate to each other about the human conditions. The ambiguity and complexity of human behavior probably explains to some extent one of the reasons why the science of human behavior is the youngest offspring of the physical and natural sciences. The very object of study, the human being, is also the individual conducting the study; which is another way of explaining the difficulty of interpreting group behavior.

The purpose of this presentation is to offer some notions about communication, most particularly *listening* and *talking;* notions that might be helpful in formulating a wide range of communication behavior. I will focus especially on communications between two persons, independent of any organization setting, status, or personality factors. The decision to focus on only two people was made primarily because the complexities of looking at group communication confound the analysis to be presented. It is hoped, however, that the analysis of the two-person relationship can be generalized to more complicated settings.

Communication—Verbal and Nonverbal

Communication plays a large part in our total personality make-up. It is communication that "presents our self" to others; it is communication that we use to negotiate and exchange interpersonally; it is communication that we utilize to expose our innermost feelings and that provides the data by which inferences about our innermost feelings are made. Figure 1 presents an oversimplified way of viewing com-

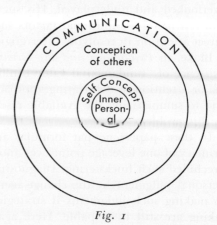

Fig. 1

From the unpublished manuscript of a lecture given at Arden House, Harriman, New York, January 1959. Used by permission.

munication as the mediator between our personality and the outside world of reality.

Now, not all our communication is verbal; in fact, at times the most persuasive and important part of our communication apparatus is nonverbal; a gesture, dress, accent, manner of speech, posture, even our home furnishings, cars, and so on. While I said earlier that communication is what saves us from being savages, the communication tangles, which also characterize humans, seem at times to make us savages. What are some of these blocks and barriers toward greater understanding between people?

Selective Inattention

One of the problems in communication is that we very often communicate to others elements that we do not intend to, and that in fact may be at some variance with what we intended to communicate. This element of communication is directly related to the "not-self" and contains aspects of ourselves that have not been entirely integrated with our self-concept. The trouble is they are transmitted with ease to the listener. Sometimes these hidden elements are communicated in surprising ways. The best example that comes to mind is a woman who denied herself any gratification of her own impulses. She abhorred marriage and refused to have anything to do with men. At the same time she was "victimized" by a facial habit, a tic, which seemed to offset her puritanical notions quite directly. Every so often, and quite involuntarily she would wink with her right eye. To the listener, her unequivocal and stern values would be contradicted by the flirtatious wink. Examples, more subtle, of this kind

could be multiplied. The point is that A communicates to B certain aspects of A's personality which are blocked off from A for whatever reasons but which are communicated to B. This "selective inattention" on the part of A creates what I will call an "arc of distortion between A and his listener B.

Figure 2 below illustrates this.

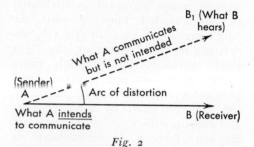

Fig. 2

In this diagram we see that A is really communicating at least two things to B, the intended as well as that which is selectively unattended to by A. This puts B in quite a bind as to how he should respond. Usually, as adults, we attempt to discover at which level the talker would like us to communicate, and then reciprocate at A's expected level.

The "arc of distortion" may be further confounded by B's "selective inattention." It may well be that B "hears" A saying something which A not only did not intend, but which he in fact *did not* communicate. The following example, while an extreme and pathological one, best illustrates this. The paranoic typically complains that others are rejecting him and persecuting him; he tends only to hear hostility and aggression, whether or not it is present.

One realistic way to reduce the "arcs of distortion," on the part both of the listener and of the talker, is to have an opportunity to check what the other is saying by feeding back to A what you, B, think he was saying, perhaps checking with other group members, and then to see how closely this matches A's intentions.

Multiple Meanings

The richness of language is tied up with the range of meanings attributed to a given symbol. Thus one word, like "dig," may mean excavating earth, understanding jazz music at the "gut level," probing, and probably other things. Our sentence structure and phraseology further muddy the meaning. One can start by a compliment and end up with a whip-lash criticism. Stephen Potter's Gamesmanship is filled with examples such as these. "My, George, you're looking well today," somehow implying that this is rather an unusual event for poor George.

Double meanings in everyday language provide an expression for our basic "ambivalence" toward other human beings. Thus, the mother who is sick and tired of her 10-year-old child, but who cannot directly tolerate negative feelings toward him, may ask her child if he would like to go to camp this summer. On the one hand the child is delighted with the idea of enriching his experience with a "sleep-away camp"; on the other hand, he may also wonder if his mother does not want to get rid of him for a while. Sometimes these interpersonal communications are implicit in the content of the discussion: Grandfather talks incessantly about the lack of energy and initiative of modern youth in order to impress others with the fact that he is a successful self-made man. Grandmother talks incessantly about sickness, calamity, and death, to remind others

that the time may be short to repay her for the sacrifices she has made for her children. Grandmother never says, "You should feel guilty and devoted to me." She may only be quoting from the obituary column of the evening paper. Grandfather's remark may be concerned with the 40-hour work week.

Principle of Training

The meanings of our communication—as they are interpreted by the listener—often have a narrow and restricted range. Without our necessarily being aware of it, we tend in many situations to train others to respond to us in ways that we find comfortable to us; ways that help maintain our self-image. That is, we typically "train" others to respond to us in definite ways. This training is an involuntary reflex action that tends to pull from the other the behavior we want. Thus the passive, meek, and dependent subordinate typically finds himself in a situation where he is working for a dominant and aggressive boss. This seems to satisfy both subordinate and supervisor; they have found each other compatible because they have successfully trained each other to reciprocate their behavior with preferred behavior.

So often the trainer does not realize he is training at all. I have talked to many individuals who desire very much to change their interpersonal situations. The passive and meek person mentioned above may resent finding himself continually in a subordinate position; he finds that he is not fulfilling all his needs in this situation. He complains bitterly that he always finds himself working for the same kind of boss. What he does not realize is that he evokes and *directly pulls* from other people in his working situation dominant behavior toward him because he transmits to the others cues which can only be responded to by "taking care of him." What I am trying to communicate here is that there is a degree of self-determination in the way the other relates to you; that we often elicit from others behavior which is at extreme variance with what we basically want, that by becoming aware of this training behavior—or by increasing our repertory of communication reflexes—a new set of interpersonal relations can develop.

Reality Testing

One path to better understanding of others is through some mechanism for testing the communication. "Feedback" is introduced as one mechanism for communicating about communication. Ways have to be developed to increase the range of valid communication by developing methods whereby individuals can develop ways of communicating about their communication.

✧✧✧✧✧✧✧✧✧✧✧✧✧✧✧✧✧✧✧✧✧ POWER: A NEGLECTED VARIABLE IN SOCIAL PSYCHOLOGY

Dorwin Cartwright

Bотн early social psychology and modern society recognize the importance of power. If, however, we examine social psychology since the beginning of its scientific epoch, we search in vain for any concentrated attack on the problem. Surely this constitutes a weakness of modern social psychology. We can only conclude that twentieth century social psychologists have been "soft" on power. Direct investigation has been evaded in many ways. One mode of evasion has been to study power in safe or weak populations— witness the classical stature of research on pecking order among chickens and on dominance among children. Another has been to convert the problem of power into one of attitudes, expectations, and perceptions. Thus, there is

more interest in authoritarianism than authority; expectations are made the critical element in the notion of role rather than behavioral restrictions or compulsions; prestige is studied because it can be investigated apart from any specific situation of interpersonal interaction and influence.

It is not here suggested that social psychologists have been cowardly; the fact is that the softer aspects of power have been more accessible to investigation. Nor is it implied that these softer aspects are irrelevant or psychologically uninteresting. The complaint is, rather, that power is often seen as essentially not a psychological problem. When asked about power the social psychologist has typically referred the question to the political scientist, sociologist,

Excerpted from Dorwin Cartwright, "Power: A Neglected Variable in Social Psychology," Studies in Social Power, *University of Michigan, Research Center for Group Dynamics, 1959, pp. 2–14. Used by permission.*

or economist; or, worse, he has given answers based upon purely personal values. In any case, the social psychologist has not seen how the central body of his knowledge could be brought to bear on such problems. But surely inability to deal with power within traditional theories does not mean that the problem should be ignored in the future.

The point may be stated differently: it simply is not possible to deal adequately with data which are clearly social psychological without getting involved with matters of power.

Some Illustrative Problems Involving Power

To document the point it is necessary to show how power is inevitably a part of the accepted phenomena of social psychology. This task is made difficult by the fact that there is considerable ambiguity concerning the boundaries of the field. Nevertheless, it is possible to identify certain phenomena (problem areas) as essentially social psychological in nature. Allport (2) has provided a list of these, not intended to be exhaustive, which contains the following: leadership, public opinion, rumor, propaganda, prejudice, attitude change, morale, communications, race relations, and conflicts of value. We shall attempt to show that phenomena of this sort cannot be adequately understood without the concept of power.

LEADERSHIP AND SOCIAL ROLES

Empirical research has progressively forced a restatement of the problem of leadership from that of identifying personal traits of the leader to one of determining the causes and consequences of leadership behavior. In this analysis concepts like "social situation," "position," "function," and "role" have come to the fore. As long as leadership was viewed only as a particular combination of personality traits, properties of the social system could easily be ignored. A major advance in the study of leadership therefore came with the abandonment of this narrow point of view, mistakenly labeled "psychological."

Some of the features of the new approach may be illustrated by brief reference to a study of the relation between supervisory practices and employee satisfaction. In this investigation, carried out by the University of Michigan Survey Research Center, Pelz (28) analyzed data from a large manufacturing company to determine whether employee satisfactions were related to certain supervisory practices which could be classified along a continuum from employee goal facilitation to hindrance. His results proved to be inconclusive until he separated the supervisors into two classes: those with high influence in their department at large and those with little influence. The results then formed a consistent pattern. Considering only high-influence supervisors and their subordinates, 19 of 28 correlations between supervisory practices and employee attitudes were positive (goal facilitative behavior of the supervisor being associated with employee satisfaction). For the low-influence supervisors, 20 out of the 28 correlations were zero or negative. The significance of these results is clear: a supervisor who is helpful in form only is not appreciated or even resented, and a spiteful supervisor who cannot carry out his malevolent designs offers no real threat.

The implications of such findings as

these have been explored with regard to leadership training in an excellent study by Fleishman, Harris, and Burtt (12). Their careful evaluation of a foreman training program operated by a large industrial concern revealed that there is often a discrepancy between the behavior taught in the program and that expected by the foreman's supervisor. They conclude that "when what is taught in the School is at variance with what is practiced in the plant, the latter is generally the more powerful influence." (p. 58) They show, moreover, that trained foremen who are returned to a setting whose leadership climate is at odds with the style of leadership advocated by the School display signs of conflict.

The gradually accumulating evidence from studies such as these fosters a dim view of supervisory training schemes which ignore the power structure of the organization; any theory of leadership which ignores power cannot be viewed more favorably.

If we turn our attention to the general theory of role, we are forced to conclude that here too power is inevitably involved. Since recent work on role, especially that of Newcomb (26), has broadened the scope of social psychology and increased its ability to deal with important phenomena in an integrated fashion, the significance of this conclusion is far-reaching.

Perhaps the best way to communicate the qualitative flavor of the phenomena of role is to quote some anthropological reports made by Campbell (8) from his participant-observing among the tribe Social-Researcher. Here is his account of the role of research administrator.

"The researcher who assumes the position of administrator is likely to be slower in recognizing his new role than are the people whom he directs. . . . The people who now report to him know immediately that he has become the 'gatekeeper' on a variety of critical decisions. They see him almost at once in his new role and they quickly develop expectations for appropriate administrative behaviors for him.

"This change of roles may be difficult for the new executive to accept. He has to learn to modify his behavior in many subtle ways. He has to guard against casual thoughtless remarks that might be interpreted as criticism and to be wary of hopeful observations that may be recalled later as promises. He must not indicate undue uncertainty about future appropriations or appointments for fear of setting disquieting rumors spreading through his staff. He learns not to make light of salary levels in his organization or of other perquisites which his staff may feel they deserve.

". . . He cannot escape the basic fact that as the director he has the ultimate word on many questions of great personal importance to his associates, and that he is universally seen by these people as having this power." (p. 225)

Certain features of this description deserve emphasis. (a) The occupant of the position of research administrator (and this may be generalized to other positions in society) can determine whether or not certain other people are able to satisfy their important needs. The occupant of this position also has a decisive voice in group action, so that when others engage in behavior relevant to the group they must relate their behavior to his. (b) The occupant of even a powerful position is not personally free to do certain things and not to do others. (c) If we consider the same person when he is located inside and outside a given position, we find that others behave toward him in drastically different ways under the two conditions. (d) Any communications originating from the occupant of a powerful position are likely to be highly authoritative, that is, have pronounced effects on others.

Strodtbeck (31, 32) has devised an ingenious experimental method for determining the relative influence of roles. He has used this method to study the roles of husband, wife, and son in different cultures. The procedure is to place members of a family in a situation where they will have a difference of opinion and then to record the ensuing events. He finds, for example, that among Navahos the wife wins 46 arguments to the husband's 34. But among Mormons it is husband 42 to 29! The son seldom wins except by forming coalitions. This research of Strodtbeck and that of others makes it clear that even in groups having no formal table of organization the power of one person to influence another depends upon the role he occupies.

The program of investigations by Shartle, Stogdill, Hemphill and others in the Ohio State Leadership Studies (30) is providing important documentation for our theories of role. In their work the concept of responsibility is assuming fundamental importance; each member of an organization is responsible for the performance of certain activities and is responsible to certain other individuals. Positions in an organization can be described in terms of these two aspects of responsibility. What people in the organization do, with whom they interact, whom they like, from whom they receive recognition, and so forth—all these factors depend to a high degree upon the nature of the responsibility structure. Members of the organization may vary in the extent to which they accept this structure, but if a member does accept it, his behavior is then guided by certain other people and organizational requirements. Stated differently, the whole organizational structure acquires power over the member and consequently certain other people have power over him, the specific persons depending upon his position in the organization.

This raises the ancient sociological problem which Jaques (20) has analyzed in some detail and has referred to as the "sanctioning of authority." It seems that a group member cannot simply proclaim a new position of power with himself as the occupant. The authority of a position must be sanctioned by others if it is to possess power. In one of the earliest experiments upon the process of interpersonal influence, Frank (13) found that when students agreed to be subjects they automatically gave such authority to the role of experimenter that he could not get them to resist his efforts to have them perform very disagreeable tasks. He finally had to instruct them to resist before he could measure the relative effectiveness of his different techniques of pressure! In a study on changing mothers' behavior toward their children, Brim (7) found that mothers were more likely to try out advice given by a doctor the more they attributed high prestige to the role of doctor. Much of the research on the effects of prestige and credibility, it would seem, can best be interpreted in terms of the sanctioning of the authority of certain roles.

This line of theorizing raises an important question: what determines whether a person accepts the authority of a position occupied by others (or even by himself)? Although there is no research which answers this question directly, the work relating group cohesiveness to strength of group standards (discussed below) suggests that if the authority structure of a group is functionally equivalent to the standards of a group, then the more strongly members are attracted to the group the more will they accept its authority structure. This hypothesis could readily be tested.

The personality characteristics of individuals may also be expected to influence their readiness to sanction the authority of a role. Much of the work on authoritarianism can be interpreted as dealing with this problem. Another provocative approach is represented by the research of Jeanne and Jack Block (6) who, though not investigating directly the sanctioning of authority of a role, do show how the amount of influence exerted by a role on a person is related to certain of his personality characteristics. In this experiment they asked subjects to do a monotonous and repetitive task until satiated. When the subjects stopped, the experimenter (assumed to be an authority figure) asked, "Don't you want to do some more?" Subjects either continued or not. Certain personality variables of all subjects had previously been evaluated, and relations between these variables and compliance with the experimenter's request were examined. The results show compliance to be related to (a) a trichotomy on "ego control" into over-controllers, appropriate controllers, and under-controllers; (b) scores on the California test of ethnocentrism; and (c) speed of establishing norms in an experiment on autokinetic movement. The Blocks propose that conforming

to a suggestion from an authority is the expression of a more general "structuring" approach to an unpredictable environment. This predisposition, in turn, may be viewed as part of a larger syndrome of ego control which they term "over-control." The results of this one study do not, of course, tell us whether these over-controllers tend to accept the authority of all roles which might claim authority or whether they are inclined to give sanction only to certain sorts of potentially authoritative roles.

An experiment by Hoffman (15) should also be mentioned in this connection. He, too, related behavior in an experimental setting to personality variables. In his study, subjects were dichotomized into conformers and nonconformers on the basis of conformity to an announced group average of judgments of perceived distance. His results show that the conformers scored significantly higher on such measures as parental dominance, inability to tolerate impulses, overconcern for the well-being of parents, and strict moralism. Whether submitting to an authority figure is psychodynamically the same as conforming to the norms of a group and how "ego control" relates to Hoffman's personality measures need to be known before the results of these two studies can be put together. In any case it appears that we may soon be able to isolate relatively enduring attributes which predispose people to give sanction to certain roles and to the norms of certain groups.

This brief overview of research on role raises doubt that such soft properties as expectations and perceptions adequately characterize the actual phenomena of role. The harder properties of power are inextricably a part of the phenomena referred to by the concept of role.

COMMUNICATION

If we turn to research on communication, we find that power must be recognized here, too. In fact, it is the power aspect of communication which gives the concept such a central place in current social psychological theory. Communication is the mechanism by which interpersonal influence is exerted. Without communication there would be no group norms, group goals, or organized group action. Let us examine the evidence for these conclusions.

First, it is perfectly obvious as soon as one bothers to raise the question that all communications are not equally influential. This, of course, has been known for a long time, and there is a respectable literature on the effectiveness of different kinds of content in communications. We are not so well supplied, however, with findings concerning the way in which the relations between communicator and recipient influence the effectiveness of communication. The work of Hovland and Weiss (16) and Kelman and Hovland (23) on source credibility dramatizes the importance of treating separately the content of a communication and its source. They have shown that the so-called "sleeper effect" depends upon the more rapid decay over time of the effects of the source than of the content. Future work in this productive program might well examine sources of communication more integrally related to the groups to which people belong to see whether the effectiveness of source decays over time when source and recipient maintain a concrete relationship.

A program of research conducted at the Research Center for Group Dynamics adds further insight into the nature of communication. First, Festinger, Schachter, and Back (11) and Back (4) show that a communication between people in a group to which they are strongly attracted is more effective than a similar communication between people in a less attractive group. To account for such findings, Festinger has developed the concept of the "internal power of a group." The upshot of this work supports the view outlined by Barnard (5) that all communications carry some degree of authoritativeness and that a person, role, or group capable of giving authority to communications possesses power. Thus, we start out to study communication but are soon asking questions about the determinants of power.

Second, the direction and content of the flow of communication in an organized group or community are not indifferent to the social position of the people involved. Orders, for example, seldom flow up a power hierarchy, but certain other types of communication are quite likely to do so. The studies by Hurwitz, Zander, and Hymovitch (18), Jackson (19), Kelley (22), and others are beginning to reveal how upward communication may serve an individual as a substitute for upward locomotion in a power hierarchy, how a person may use communication as a device for minimizing the dangers of hostile actions by those in higher positions, and how a person of superior power may tailor the content and direction of his communications to maintain the belief among others that his superior behavior justifies his position. Thus, we must specify the power relations among people to understand either the frequency and content of communications passing among them or the authority of such communications.

Third, even the study of rumor cannot safely ignore the power situation. This conclusion dramatically arose from the experience of an action-research project in a community where the project leaders unexpectedly became the target of a hostile rumor (10). As a result of the project's stimulation of several new community activities, such as a cooperative nursery school and a softball league, new leaders began to emerge to replace the old ones. Suddenly, when everything seemed to be moving along well, the new activities came to a halt. A rumor was sweeping the community that the project leaders and the new local leaders were taking orders from Moscow. If we try to understand what happened, it seems especially significant that the content of the rumor was about power (namely, who was controlling people's behavior), that it was initiated and spread by those losing power, and that it was credible to those who believed it because they did not in fact know why these new activities were being undertaken in their community. (In a desire not to contaminate the experiment the community had not been given this information.) A general hypothesis is suggested that rumors are especially likely to flourish among people who see that their fates are in other people's hands.

If communication is to be a basic concept of social psychology, so too is power.

INTERPERSONAL AND INTERGROUP RELATIONS

Let us turn now from abstract concepts like role and communication to more concrete social problems. One such problem which has long interested social psychologists deals with the kinds of things referred to by the phrase "human relations." What are the causes of harmony and conflict among people? Although systematic theories have been slow to emerge from efforts to answer this question, a sizable body of empirical data has accumulated. From this wealth of material we cite only a few specific findings to illustrate the critical place of power in shaping human relations.

A few years ago the Research Center for Group Dynamics was asked by a group of junior high school teachers to help them understand better the sources of conflict and irritation in the relations among teachers, parents, and students. A project was organized by Jenkins and Lippitt (21) which included interviews with a sample of each of these populations. Respondents were asked to indicate what they believed were the things that each group did that each other group liked (for example, "What are the things that parents do that teachers like?"). They were also asked parallel questions to indicate disliked behavior.

Consider, first, the teacher-student relationship. Of all categories of teacher behavior, the one having most significance for students is that the teacher be fair. This seems to imply that the teacher is a sort of judge who hands down decisions of importance, thus making fairness a matter of real concern. When we examine the other side of the relationship and consider the responses of teachers, we get further confirmation of the teacher's power over students. Seventy-three per cent of the teachers mention as important student behavior "being respectful" and "accepting the teacher as authority." Forty-two per cent mention "obedience."

The relations between parents and students turn out to be much the same, but with different realms of behavior coming under the control of parents. Complaints about parents consist of a long list of things "they won't let us do" and of other things "they make us do." Though parents tend not to mention the importance of obedience and respect as much as teachers, the students nonetheless report that parents do place major emphasis upon compliance to parental authority.

More subtle is the finding concerning teacher-parent relations. Here it is clear that teachers have strong needs for friendship with adults and for acceptance as members of the community. Parents chiefly control the fate of teachers in this respect; they can give or withhold gratification of these needs. This relation is, moreover, one way; there is no indication that parents would feel deprived without the friendship, recognition, or acceptance of teachers. Knowledge of this asymmetrical power relation is essential for understanding the behavior, attitudes, and feelings of teachers and parents.

Experience with intergroup discrimination and prejudice points the same lesson. Can we really hope to explain these phenomena or to build programs of social action solely with such variables as authoritarianism, ethnocentrism, displaced aggression, and attitude? How do these concepts help to understand the substantial improvement of conditions for Negroes in the automobile industry following certain union policy-decisions or the presence of a nonsegregated dining room at Montgomery, Alabama—on the Air Force Base? Kurt Lewin (24) recognized the importance of power in intergroup

relations when he asserted that "discrimination against minorities will not be changed as long as forces are not changed which determine the decisions of the gatekeepers." (p. 186) With such a perspective social psychologists will take more than passing notice of such findings as that of Hunter (17) in his study of the power structure of Regional City—a medium sized city with a Negro population of nearly one-third the total. Through various devices he was able to construct a list of 40 people who could safely be called the city's most powerful; the approval of these people is required for the success of any community project. Those who wish to better intergroup relations in this city might be well advised to work with this group. They should know, however, that not a single Negro is on this list of influential people. (Only 3 could be considered even nominees on a list of 175.)

Whether one's objective is social action or understanding human behavior, one should examine the possibilities of reducing discrimination and prejudice through the *fait accompli,* legal action, and administrative order. It is interesting in this connection to note the conclusion reached by Deutsch and Collins (9) from their study of the effects upon interracial attitudes of different patterns of interracial public housing.

"We are, in effect, rejecting the notion that has characterized much of sociological thinking in the field of race relations: the notion, originating with William S. Summer, that 'stateways cannot change folkways.' The evidence of our study is that official policy, executed without equivocation, can result in large changes in beliefs and feelings despite initial resistance to the policy. Thus, it is clear from our data that although most of the white housewives in the integrated projects we studied did not, upon moving into the projects, like the idea of living in the same buildings with Negro families (and certainly the community as a whole did not favor it), a considerable change in attitudes and 'folkways' has taken place as a consequence of their experiences resulting from a 'stateway.'" (p. 127)

Unfortunately there is as yet insufficient systematic knowledge about the social psychology of power for us to specify with much conviction the conditions under which administrative orders and legal action will carry along attitudinal changes or will stimulate heightened resistance.

SOCIAL DETERMINANTS OF EMOTIONAL ADJUSTMENT

The importance of the concept of power for social psychology may be illustrated with respect to one other social problem. What determines the mental health or illness of individuals? While it is clear that physiological determinants are important, it is now known that social situations differ significantly in their impact upon the emotional adjustment of all those involved in them. Perhaps one of the clearest demonstrations of such influences was provided by the experiment of Lewin, Lippitt, and White (25) on different styles of leadership. Here it was found that the aggressiveness of a given child depended upon the style of leadership provided by the adult in charge of the group. Although the different styles of leadership studied in this experiment differed from one another in a number of ways, it appears that the most critical aspects of leadership were the size of the space of free

movement allowed the children and whether the leader's power was used to support or obstruct the behavior of the children. The leader's use of power basically affected the emotional climate of the group.

In any social situation, and especially in hierarchical ones, certain people have power to help or hinder the goal-directed behavior of others. Emotional security depends rather directly upon the magnitude of this power and upon the benevolence of its use.

Experiments by Arsenian (3) and Wright (33) have examined this conception in greater detail. They propose that a person's feeling of security is determined by the relative magnitude of two sets of factors which may be expressed as a ratio. The numerator is the person's perception of the magnitude of his own power plus all friendly or supportive power he can count upon from other sources; the denominator is the person's perception of the magnitude of all hostile power that may be mobilized against him. In the Arsenian experiment the emotionality of young children was measured when they were left alone in a strange room and when put there in the presence of a friendly (but passive) adult. Consistent with the formulation of the determinants of security proposed, Arsenian found less emotional disturbance when the supportive power of the adult was present. The experiment by Wright may be interpreted in similar terms. He compared the reactions to frustration of pairs of children varying in the strength of their friendship and found that strong friends displayed less reduction in constructiveness of play, less negative emotionality, more cooperation between themselves, and more aggression against the experimenter than did weak friends. The power of each of the strong friends was supportive to the other.

Consistent with this general conception of the relation between security and power are the findings of a rather different sort of experiment conducted by Pepitone (29). He placed boys in a situation where the achievement of an attractive object was under the control of a panel of three judges. After a standardized interaction between the boy and the panel, each boy was asked to rate the relative power and relative benevolence of each member of the panel. In this setting Pepitone found perceptual distortions designed, as it were, to minimize the threatening power of the panel members—if a member was rated as powerful, his benevolence was rated higher; and if he was rated as malevolent, his power was rated lower.

From the findings of research of the sort reported here it seems clear that the impact of social situations upon emotional adjustment will be adequately understood only if power is explicitly recognized.

Summary

This brief overview of the field of social psychology leads to four conclusions:

1. A major deficiency of the theories of social psychology is that they have been soft on power.

2. The important social problems which demand our attention raise questions about power—questions which our systematic knowledge cannot answer.

3. Quite apart from any practical considerations, a social psychological theory without the concept of power (or its equivalent) is incomplete. Such concepts as communication, role, at-

titude, expectation, and norm cannot by themselves account realistically for the processes of influence to which they refer, nor can they deal effectively with social change and resistance to change.

4. A concerted attack on the problem of power should produce a major advance in the field of social psychology. Such an advance will consist of an improved understanding of the proper subject-matter of social psychology and a reorganization of its conceptual systems.

References

1. ADLER, A. "A study of organ inferiority and its psychic compensations." *Trans. Nerv. ment. Dis. Monogr. Ser.,* 1917, 24.
2. ALLPORT, G. W. "The historical background of modern social psychology." In G. Lindzey (ed.), *Handbook of social psychology.* Cambridge: Addison-Wesley, 1954, 3–56.
3. ARSENIAN, J. M. "Young children in an insecure situation." *J. abnorm. soc. Psychol.,* 1943, 38, 225–249.
4. BACK, K. W. "Influence through social communication." *J. abnorm. soc. Psychol.,* 1951, 46, 9–23.
5. BARNARD, C. I. *The functions of the executive.* Cambridge: Harvard Univ. Press, 1938.
6. BLOCK, J., & BLOCK, J. "An interpersonal experiment on reactions to authority." *Hum. Relat.,* 1952, 5, 91–98.
7. BRIM, O. G., JR. "The acceptance of new behavior in child-rearing." *Hum. Relat.,* 1954, 7, 473–491.
8. CAMPBELL, A. "Administering research organizations." *Amer. Psychol.,* 1953, 8, 225–230.
9. DEUTSCH, M., & COLLINS, M. E. *Interracial housing: A psychological*

evaluation of a social experiment. Minneapolis: Univ. Minnesota Press, 1951.

10. FESTINGER, L., CARTWRIGHT, D., et al. "A study of a rumor: Its origin and spread." *Hum Relat.*, 1948, 1, 464–486.

11. FESTINGER, L., SCHACHTER, S., & BACK, K. W. *Social pressures in informal groups.* New York: Harper, 1950.

12. FLEISHMAN, E. A., HARRIS, E. F., & BURTT, H. E. *Leadership and supervision in industry: An evaluation of a supervisory training program.* Columbus: Ohio State University Bureau of Educational Research, 1955.

13. FRANK, J. D. "Experimental study of personal pressures and resistance: I. Experimental production of resistance." *J. gen. Psychol.*, 1944, 30, 23–41.

14. HOBBES, T. *Leviathan.* Reprint of 1st (1651) ed., Cambridge: Univ. Press, 1904.

15. HOFFMAN, M. L. "Some psychodynamic factors in compulsive conformity." *J. abnorm. soc. Psychol.*, 1953, 48, 383–393.

16. HOVLAND, C. I., & WEISS, W. "The influence of source credibility on communication effectiveness." *Pub. Opin. Quart.*, 1952, 15, 635–650.

17. HUNTER, F. *Community power structure.* Chapel Hill: Univ. North Carolina Press, 1953.

18. HURWITZ, J. I., ZANDER, A. F., & HYMOVITCH, B. "Some effects of power on the relations among group members." In D. Cartwright & A. Zander (eds.), *Group Dynamics: Research and theory.* Evanston: Row, Peterson, 1953, pp. 483–492.

19. JACKSON, J. M. "Analysis of interpersonal relations in a formal organization." Unpublished doctor's dissertation, Univ. Michigan, 1952.

20. JAQUES, E. *The changing culture of a factory.* London: Tavistock, 1951.

21. JENKINS, D., & LIPPITT, R. *Interpersonal perceptions of teachers, students and parents.* Washington: Nat. Train. Labor. Group Devel., 1951.

22. KELLEY, H. H. "Communication in experimentally created hierarchies." *Hum. Relat.*, 1951, 4, 39–56.

23. KELMAN, H. C., & HOVLAND, C. I. " 'Reinstatement' of the communicator in delayed measurement of opinion change." *J. abnorm. soc. Psychol.*, 1953, 48, 327–335.

24. LEWIN, K. *Field theory in social science.* New York: Harper, 1951.

25. LEWIN, K., LIPPITT, R., & WHITE, R. K. "Patterns of aggressive behavior in experimentally created 'social climates.' " *J. soc. Psychol.*, 1939, 10, 271–299.

26. NEWCOMB, T. *Social psychology.* New York: Holt, Rinehart and Winston, 1950.

27. NIETZSCHE, F. *Der Wille zur Macht.* Book 3, sec. 702. In Nietsche's complete *Werke*, vol. 16. Leipzig: Alfred Kröner, 1912.

28. PELZ, D. C. "Influence: A key to effective leadership in the first line supervisor." *Personnel*, 1952, 3, 3–11.

29. PEPITONE, A. "Motivational effects in social perception." *Hum. Relat.*, 1950, 3, 57–76.

30. STOGDILL, R. M. "Leadership, membership and organization." *Psychol. Bull.*, 1950, 47, 1–14.

31. STRODTBECK, F. L. "Husband-wife interaction over revealed differences." *Amer. sociol. Rev.*, 1951, 16, 468–473.

32. STRODTBECK, F. L. "The family as a three-person group." *Amer. sociol. Rev.*, 1954, 19, 23–29.

33. WRIGHT, M. E. "The influence of frustration on the social relations of young children." *Charact. Pers.,* 1943, 12, 111–122.

❖❖❖❖❖❖❖❖❖❖❖❖❖❖❖❖❖ THE HUMAN SIDE OF ENTERPRISE

Douglas M. McGregor

Iᴛ has become trite to say that the most significant developments of the next quarter century will take place not in the physical but in the social sciences, that industry—the economic organ of society—has the fundamental know-how to utilize physical science and technology for the material benefit of mankind, and that we must now learn how to utilize the social sciences to make our human organizations truly effective.

Many people agree in principle with such statements; but so far they represent a pious hope—and little else. Consider with me, if you will, something of what may be involved when we attempt to transform the hope into reality.

Let me begin with an analogy. A quarter century ago basic conceptions of the nature of matter and energy had changed profoundly from what they had been since Newton's time. The physical scientists were persuaded that under proper conditions new and hitherto unimagined sources of energy could be made available to mankind.

We know what has happened since then. First came the bomb. Then, during the past decade, have come many other attempts to exploit these scientific discoveries—some successful, some not.

The point of my analogy, however, is that the application of theory in this field is a slow and costly matter. We expect it always to be thus. No one is impatient with the scientist because he cannot tell industry how to build a simple, cheap, all-purpose source of atomic energy today. That it will take at least another decade and the investment of billions of dollars to achieve results which are economically competitive with present sources of power is understood and accepted.

It is transparently pretentious to suggest any *direct* similarity between the developments in the physical sciences leading to the harnessing of atomic energy and potential developments in the social sciences. Nevertheless, the analogy is not as absurd as it might appear to be at first glance.

To a lesser degree, and in a much more tentative fashion, we are in a position in the social sciences today like that of the physical sciences with respect to atomic energy in the thirties. We know that past conceptions of the nature of man are inadequate and in many ways incorrect. We are becoming quite certain that, under proper conditions, unimagined resources of

From Douglas McGregor, "Adventures in Thought and Action," Proceedings of the Fifth Anniversary Convocation of the School of Industrial Management, Massachusetts Institute of Technology, Cambridge, Mass., April 9, 1957. Used by permission.

creative human energy could become available within the organizational setting.

We cannot tell industrial management how to apply this new knowledge, in simple, economic ways. We know it will require years of exploration, much costly development research, and a substantial amount of creative imagination on the part of management to discover how to apply this growing knowledge to the organization of human effort in industry.

May I ask that you keep this analogy in mind—overdrawn and pretentious though it may be—as a framework for what I have to say this morning.

Management's Task: Conventional View

The conventional conception of management's task in harnessing human energy to organizational requirements can be stated broadly in terms of three propositions. In order to avoid the complications introduced by a label, I shall call this set of propositions "Theory X":

1. Management is responsible for organizing the elements of productive enterprise—money, materials, equipment, people—in the interest of economic ends.

2. With respect to people, this is a process of directing their efforts, motivating them, controlling their actions, modifying their behavior to fit the needs of the organization.

3. Without this active intervention by management, people would be passive—even resistant—to organizational needs. They must therefore be persuaded, rewarded, punished, controlled —their activities must be directed. This is management's task—in manag-

ing subordinate managers or workers. We often sum it up by saying that management consists of getting things done through other people.

Behind this conventional theory there are several additional beliefs— less explicit, but widespread:

4. The average man is by nature indolent—he works as little as possible.

5. He lacks ambition, dislikes responsibility, prefers to be led.

6. He is inherently self-centered, indifferent to organizational needs.

7. He is by nature resistant to change.

8. He is gullible, not very bright, the ready dupe of the charlatan and the demagogue.

The human side of economic enterprise today is fashioned from propositions and beliefs such as these. Conventional organization structures, managerial policies, practices, and programs reflect these assumptions.

In accomplishing its task—with these assumptions as guides—management has conceived of a range of possibilities between two extremes.

The Hard or the Soft Approach?

At one extreme, management can be "hard" or "strong." The methods for directing behavior involve coercion and threat (usually disguised), close supervision, tight controls over behavior. At the other extreme, management can be "soft" or "weak." The methods for directing behavior involve being permissive, satisfying people's demands, achieving harmony. Then they will be tractable, accept direction.

This range has been fairly completely explored during the past half century, and management has learned some things from the exploration. There are difficulties in the "hard" approach. Force breeds counterforces: restriction of output, antagonism, militant union-ism, subtle but effective sabotage of management objectives. This approach is especially difficult during times of full employment.

There are also difficulties in the "soft" approach. It leads frequently to the abdication of management—to harmony, perhaps, but to indifferent performance. People take advantage of the soft approach. They continually expect more, but they give less and less.

Currently, the popular theme is "firm but fair." This is an attempt to gain the advantages of both the hard and the soft approaches. It is reminiscent of Teddy Roosevelt's "speak softly and carry a big stick."

Is the Conventional View Correct?

The findings which are beginning to emerge from the social sciences challenge this whole set of beliefs about man and human nature and about the task of management. The evidence is far from conclusive, certainly, but it is suggestive. It comes from the laboratory, the clinic, the schoolroom, the home, and even to a limited extent from industry itself.

The social scientist does not deny that human behavior in industrial organization today is approximately what management perceives it to be. He has, in fact, observed it and studied it fairly extensively. But he is pretty sure that this behavior is *not* a consequence of man's inherent nature. It is a consequence rather of the nature of industrial organizations, of management philosophy, policy, and practice. The conventional approach of Theory X is based on mistaken notions of what is cause and what is effect.

"Well," you ask, "what then is the *true* nature of man? What evidence leads the social scientist to deny what is obvious?" And, if I am not mistaken, you are also thinking, "Tell me—simply, and without a lot of scientific verbiage—what you think you know that is so unusual. Give me—without a lot of intellectual claptrap and theoretical nonsense—some practical ideas which will enable me to improve the situation in my organization. And remember, I'm faced with increasing costs and narrowing profit margins. I want proof that such ideas won't result simply in new and costly human relations frills. I want practical results, and I want them now."

If these are your wishes, you are going to be disappointed. Such requests can no more be met by the social scientist today than could comparable ones with respect to atomic energy be met by the physicist fifteen years ago. I can, however, indicate a few of the reasons for asserting that conventional assumptions about the human side of enterprise are inadequate. And I can suggest—tentatively—some of the propositions that will comprise a more adequate theory of the management of people. The magnitude of the task that confronts us will then, I think, be apparent.

Perhaps the best way to indicate why the conventional approach of management is inadequate is to consider the subject of motivation. In discussing this subject I will draw heavily on the work of my colleague, Abraham Maslow of Brandeis University. His is the most fruitful approach I know. Naturally, what I have to say will be over-generalized and will ignore important qualifications. In the time at our disposal, this is inevitable.

Physiological and Safety Needs

Man is a wanting animal—as soon as one of his needs is satisfied, another appears in its place. This process is unending. It continues from birth to death.

Man's needs are organized in a series of levels—a hierarchy of importance. At the lowest level, but preeminent in importance when they are thwarted, are his physiological needs. Man lives by bread alone, when there is no bread. Unless the circumstances are unusual, his needs for love, for status, for recognition are inoperative when his stomach has been empty for a while. But when he eats regularly and adequately, hunger ceases to be an important need. The sated man has hunger only in the sense that a full bottle has emptiness. The same is true of the other physiological needs of man—for rest, exercise, shelter, protection from the elements.

A satisfied need is not a motivator of behavior! This is a fact of profound significance. It is a fact which is regularly ignored in the conventional approach to the management of people. I shall return to it later. For the moment, one example will make my point. Consider your own need for air. Except as you are deprived of it, it has no appreciable motivating effect upon your behavior.

When the physiological needs are reasonably satisfied, needs at the next higher level begin to dominate man's behavior—to motivate him. These are called safety needs. They are needs for protection against danger, threat, deprivation. Some people mistakenly refer to these as needs for security. However, unless man is in a dependent relationship where he fears arbitrary depriva-

tion, he does not demand security. The need is for the "fairest possible break." When he is confident of this, he is more than willing to take risks. But when he feels threatened or dependent, his greatest need is for guarantees, for protection, for security.

The fact needs little emphasis that since every industrial employee is in a dependent relationship, safety needs may assume considerable importance. Arbitrary management actions, behavior which arouses uncertainty with respect to continued employment or which reflects favoritism or discrimination, unpredictable administration of policy—these can be powerful motivators of the safety needs in the employment relationship *at every level* from worker to vice president.

Social Needs

When man's physiological needs are satisfied and he is no longer fearful about his physical welfare, his social needs become important motivators of his behavior—for belonging, for association, for acceptance by his fellows, for giving and receiving friendship and love.

Management knows today of the existence of these needs, but it often assumes quite wrongly that they represent a threat to the organization. Many studies have demonstrated that the tightly knit, cohesive work group may, under proper conditions, be far more effective than an equal number of separate individuals in achieving organizational goals.

Yet management, fearing group hostility to its own objectives, often goes to considerable lengths to control and direct human efforts in ways that are inimical to the natural "groupiness" of human beings. When man's social needs—and perhaps his safety needs, too—are thus thwarted, he behaves in ways which tend to defeat organizational objectives. He becomes resistant, antagonistic, uncooperative. But this behavior is a consequence, not a cause.

Ego Needs

Above the social needs—in the sense that they do not become motivators until lower needs are reasonably satisfied —are the needs of greatest significance to management and to man himself. They are the egoistic needs, and they are of two kinds:

1. Those needs that relate to one's self-esteem—needs for self-confidence, for independence, for achievement, for competence, for knowledge.

2. Those needs that relate to one's reputation—needs for status, for recognition, for appreciation, for the deserved respect of one's fellows.

Unlike the lower needs, these are rarely satisfied; man seeks indefinitely for more satisfaction of these needs once they have become important to him. But they do not appear in any significant way until physiological, safety, and social needs are all reasonably satisfied.

The typical industrial organization offers few opportunities for the satisfaction of these egoistic needs to people at lower levels in the hierarchy. The conventional methods of organizing work, particularly in mass production industries, give little heed to these aspects of human motivation. If the practices of scientific management were deliberately calculated to thwart these needs—which, of course, they are not —they could hardly accomplish this purpose better than they do.

Self-fulfillment Needs

Finally—a capstone, as it were, on the hierarchy of man's needs—there are what we may call the needs for self-fulfillment. These are the needs for realizing one's own potentialities, for continued self-development, for being creative in the broadest sense of that term.

It is clear that the conditions of modern life give only limited opportunity for these relatively weak needs to obtain expression. The deprivation most people experience with respect to other lower-level needs diverts their energies into the struggle to satisfy *those* needs, and the needs for self-fulfillment remain dormant.

Now, briefly, a few general comments about motivation:

We recognize readily enough that a man suffering from a severe dietary deficiency is sick. The deprivation of physiological needs has behavioral consequences. The same is true—although less well recognized—of deprivation of higher-level needs. The man whose needs for safety, association, independence, or status are thwarted is sick just as surely as is he who has rickets. And his sickness will have behavioral consequences. We will be mistaken if we attribute his resultant passivity, his hostility, his refusal to accept responsibility to his inherent "human nature." These forms of behavior are *symptoms* of illness—of deprivation of his social and egoistic needs.

The man whose lower-level needs are satisfied is not motivated to satisfy those needs any longer. For practical purposes they exist no longer. (Remember my point about your need for air.) Management often asks, "Why aren't people more productive? We pay good wages, provide good working conditions, have excellent fringe benefits and steady employment. Yet people do not seem to be willing to put forth more than minimum effort."

The fact that management has provided for these physiological and safety needs has shifted the motivational emphasis to the social and perhaps to the egoistic needs. Unless there are opportunities *at work* to satisfy these higher-level needs, people will be deprived; and their behavior will reflect this deprivation. Under such conditions, if management continues to focus its attention on physiological needs, its efforts are bound to be ineffective.

People *will* make insistent demands for more money under these conditions. It becomes more important than ever to buy the material goods and services which can provide limited satisfaction of the thwarted needs. Although money has only limited value in satisfying many higher-level needs, it can become the focus of interest if it is the *only* means available.

The Carrot and Stick Approach

The carrot and stick theory of motivation (like Newtonian physical theory) works reasonably well under certain circumstances. The *means* for satisfying man's physiological and (within limits) his safety needs can be provided or withheld by management. Employment itself is such a means, and so are wages, working conditions, and benefits. By these means the individual can be controlled so long as he is struggling for subsistence. Man lives for bread alone when there is no bread.

But the carrot and stick theory does not work at all once man has reached an adequate subsistence level and is motivated primarily by higher needs. Management cannot provide a man with self-respect, or with the respect of his fellows, or with the satisfaction of needs for self-fulfillment. It can create conditions such that he is encouraged and enabled to seek such satisfactions *for himself,* or it can thwart him by failing to create those conditions.

But this creation of conditions is not "control." It is not a good device for directing behavior. And so management finds itself in an odd position. The high standard of living created by our modern technological know-how provides quite adequately for the satisfaction of physiological and safety needs. The only significant exception is where management practices have not created confidence in a "fair break" —and thus where safety needs are thwarted. But by making possible the satisfaction of low-level needs, management has deprived itself of the ability to use as motivators the devices on which conventional theory has taught it to rely—rewards, promises, incentives, or threats and other coercive devices.

Neither Hard nor Soft

The philosophy of management by direction and control—*regardless of whether it is hard or soft*—is inadequate to motivate because the human needs on which this approach relies are today unimportant motivators of behavior. Direction and control are essentially useless in motivating people whose important needs are social and egoistic. Both the hard and the soft approach fail today because they are simply irrelevant to the situation.

People, deprived of opportunities to

satisfy at work the needs which are now important to them, behave exactly as we might predict—with indolence, passivity, resistance to change, lack of responsibility, willingness to follow the demagogue, unreasonable demands for economic benefits. It would seem that we are caught in a web of our own weaving.

In summary, then, of these comments about motivation:

Management by direction and control—whether implemented with the hard, the soft, or the firm but fair approach—fails under today's conditions to provide effective motivation of human effort toward organizational objectives. It fails because direction and control are useless methods of motivating people whose physiological and safety needs are reasonably satisfied and whose social, egoistic, and self-fulfillment needs are predominant.

For these and many other reasons, we require a different theory of the task of managing people based on more adequate assumptions about human nature and human motivation. I am going to be so bold as to suggest the broad dimensions of such a theory. Call it "Theory Y," if you will.

1. Management is responsible for organizing the elements of productive enterprise—money, materials, equipment, people—in the interest of economic ends.

2. People are *not* by nature passive or resistant to organizational needs. They have become so as a result of experience in organizations.

3. The motivation, the potential for development, the capacity for assuming responsibility, the readiness to direct behavior toward organizational goals are all present in people. Management does not put them there. It is a responsibility of management to make it possible for people to recognize and develop these human characteristics for themselves.

4. The essential task of management is to arrange organizational conditions and methods of operation so that people can achieve their own goals *best* by directing *their own* efforts toward organizational objectives.

This is a process primarily of creating opportunities, releasing potential, removing obstacles, encouraging growth, providing guidance. It is what Peter Drucker has called "management by objectives" in contrast to "management by control."

And I hasten to add that it does *not* involve the abdication of management, the absence of leadership, the lowering of standards, or the other characteristics usually associated with the "soft" approach under Theory X. Much on the contrary. It is no more possible to create an organization today which will be a fully effective application of this theory than it was to build an atomic power plant in 1945. There are many formidable obstacles to overcome.

Some Difficulties

The conditions imposed by conventional organization theory and by the approach of scientific management for the past half century have tied men to limited jobs which do not utilize their capabilities, have discouraged the acceptance of responsibility, have encouraged passivity, have eliminated meaning from work. Man's habits, attitudes, expectations—his whole conception of membership in an industrial organization—have been conditioned by his experience under these circumstances. Change in the direction of Theory Y will be slow, and it will require extensive modification of the attitudes of management and workers alike.

People today are accustomed to being directed, manipulated, controlled in industrial organizations and to finding satisfaction for their social, egoistic, and self-fulfillment needs away from the job. This is true of much of management as well as of workers. Genuine "industrial citizenship"—to borrow again a term from Drucker—is a remote and unrealistic idea, the meaning of which has not even been considered by most members of industrial organizations.

Another way of saying this is that Theory X places exclusive reliance upon external control of human behavior, while Theory Y relies heavily on self-control and self-direction. It is worth noting that this difference is the difference between treating people as children and treating them as mature adults. After generations of the former, we cannot expect to shift to the latter overnight.

Before we are overwhelmed by the obstacles, let us remember that the application of theory is always slow. Progress is usually achieved in small steps.

Consider with me a few innovative ideas which are entirely consistent with Theory Y and which are today being applied with some success:

Decentralization and Delegation

These are ways of freeing people from the too-close control of conventional organization, giving them a degree of freedom to direct their own activities, to assume responsibility, and, importantly, to satisfy their egoistic needs. In this connection, the flat organization of Sears, Roebuck and Company provides an interesting example. It forces "management by objectives" since it enlarges the number of people reporting to a manager until he cannot direct and control them in the conventional manner.

Job Enlargement

This concept, pioneered by I.B.M. and Detroit Edison, is quite consistent with Theory Y. It encourages the acceptance of responsibility at the bottom of the organization; it provides opportunities for satisfying social and egoistic needs. In fact, the reorganization of work at the factory level offers one of the more challenging opportunities for innovation consistent with Theory Y. The studies by A. T. M. Wilson and his associates of British coal mining and Indian textile manufacture have added appreciably to our understanding of work organization. Moreover, the economic and psychological results achieved by this work have been substantial.

Participation and Consultative Management

Under proper conditions these results provide encouragement to people to direct their creative energies toward organizational objectives, give them some voice in decisions that affect them, provide significant opportunities for the satisfaction of social and egoistic needs. I need only mention the Scanlon Plan as the outstanding embodiment of these ideas in practice.

The not infrequent failure of such ideas as these to work as well as expected is often attributable to the fact that a management has "bought the idea" but applied it within the framework of Theory X and its assumptions.

Delegation is not an effective way of exercising management by control. Participation becomes a farce when it is applied as a sales gimmick or a device for kidding people into thinking they are important. Only the management that has confidence in human capacities and is itself directed toward organizational objectives rather than toward the preservation of personal power can grasp the implications of this emerging theory. Such management will find and apply successfully other innovative ideas as we move slowly toward the full implementation of a theory like Y.

Performance Appraisal

Before I stop, let me mention one other practical application of Theory Y which—while still highly tentative—may well have important consequences. This has to do with performance appraisal within the ranks of management. Even a cursory examination of conventional programs of performance appraisal will reveal how completely consistent they are with Theory X. In fact, most such programs tend to treat the individual as though he were a product under inspection on the assembly line.

Take the typical plan: substitute "product" for "subordinate being appraised," substitute "inspector" for "superior making the appraisal," substitute "rework" for "training or development," and, except for the attributes being judged, the human appraisal process will be virtually indistinguishable from the product inspection process.

A few companies—among them General Mills, Ansul Chemical, and General Electric—have been experimenting with approaches which involve the individual in setting "targets" or objectives *for himself* and in a *self*-evaluation of performance semi-annually or annually. Of course, the superior plays an important leadership role in this process—one, in fact, which demands substantially more competence than the conventional approach. The role is, however, considerably more congenial to many managers than the role of "judge" or "inspector" which is forced upon them by conventional performance. Above all, the individual is encouraged to take a greater responsibility for planning and appraising his own contribution to organizational objectives; and the accompanying effects on egoistic and self-fulfillment needs are substantial. This approach to performance appraisal represents one more innovative idea being explored by a few managements who are moving toward the implementation of Theory Y.

And now I am back where I began. I share the belief that we could realize substantial improvements in the effectiveness of industrial organizations during the next decade or two. Moreover, I believe the social sciences can contribute much to such developments. We are only beginning to grasp the implications of the growing body of knowledge in these fields. But if this conviction is to become a reality instead of a pious hope, we will need to view the process much as we view the process of releasing the energy of the atom for constructive human ends—as a slow, costly, sometimes discouraging approach toward a goal which would seem to many to be quite unrealistic.

The ingenuity and the perseverance of industrial management in the pursuit of economic ends have changed many scientific and technological dreams into commonplace realities. It is now becoming clear that the application of these same talents to the human side of enterprise will not only enhance substantially these materialistic achieve- ments but will bring us one step closer to "the good society." Shall we get on with the job?

♦♦♦♦♦♦♦♦♦♦♦♦♦♦♦♦♦♦♦ WHAT DO WE KNOW ABOUT LEADERSHIP?   *Gordon L. Lippitt*

Whether we are administrators, teachers, or supervisors, we constantly find ourselves functioning in leadership capacities. We are interested in the development of the leadership of the youth in our schools and in the leadership development of the adults who are working with us.

Frequently, the various fields of psychology or education have advanced different theories of what makes for good leadership. A look at some of these varying points of view may improve our understanding of leadership.

I. The Trait Approach

Over the past 50 years, there have been hundreds of studies made comparing the physical, intellectual, or personality traits of leaders and followers. Frequently, these studies come up with a list of traits that make for "good" leadership. On the whole, this approach to leadership has been disappointing. Only 5% of the traits in over 106 such studies appeared in four or more studies.

Inasmuch as these results indicate that a variety of persons with different personality, environmental, and hereditary backgrounds can make successful leaders, the trait approach seems to be inadequate.

II. Situational Approach

The situational approach is based upon the hypothesis that a leader's behavior may vary from one setting to another. The different situations require different leadership behavior. Many variables enter into producing leaders. However, there are only two types of forces which influence how a leader arrives at a leadership position:

Sometimes people are motivated by personal drives to become leaders; sometimes they find themselves in leadership positions as the result of external forces, of which they may or may not be aware. Usually both factors are at work. (See Diagram 1.)

III. Behavior Approach

Another approach has been to analyze the kinds of functions which people carry out when they are in positions of leadership. The kind of leadership position a person holds will determine the degree to which he carries out certain functions.

In these studies it has been found that most leaders perform, to one extent or another, four major functions:

1. A leader may perform a symbolic function, such as the queen of England performs at present. 2. Or a leader may

From Gordon L. Lippitt, *"What Do We Know About Leadership?"* National Education Association Journal, *December 1955, pp. 556–557. Used by permission.*

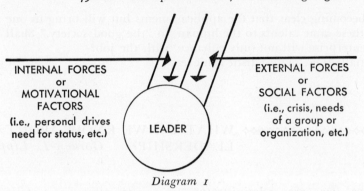

| INTERNAL FORCES or MOTIVATIONAL FACTORS (i.e., personal drives need for status, etc.) | LEADER | EXTERNAL FORCES or SOCIAL FACTORS (i.e., crisis, needs of a group or organization, etc.) |

Diagram 1

perform primarily a decision-making function. This could be exemplified by the political "boss," who makes decisions behind the scenes to be carried out by other individuals. 3. Another function that most leaders perform in one degree or another is giving information or advice. 4. A function that is common to most positions of leadership is the one of initiating plans.

Of course, all four of these functions are indispensable to people who are in positions of leadership. Studies indicate, however, that some jobs will make certain behavior more of a requirement than do other jobs. (See Diagram 3.)

IV. Styles-of-Leadership Approach

In the past 15 years a great deal of attention has been given to investigat-ing what kind of group climate is created by different styles of leadership behavior. Studies done at the University of Iowa in 1938 and 1940 included a thoro investigation of the effects of different styles of adult leadership behavior on groups of young people.

These studies identified the three styles of leadership as autocratic, laissez-faire, and democratic. The basic difference in these three styles is the location of the decision-making function. It resides in the *leader* in the autocratic group, in the *individual* in the laissez-faire group, and in the *group* in the democratic situation.

Studies of styles of leadership with adult groups in the fields of industry, government, and large organizations indicated that a benevolent-autocratic leadership prevailed that was different

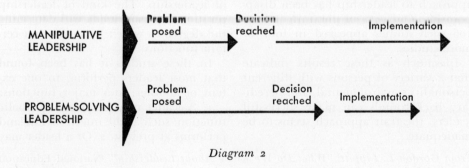

| MANIPULATIVE LEADERSHIP | Problem posed | Decision reached | Implementation |
| PROBLEM-SOLVING LEADERSHIP | Problem posed | Decision reached | Implementation |

Diagram 2

from the democratic, laissez-faire, and autocratic styles of behavior. Apparently most of such leadership has the same intent as democratic leadership, but the benevolent-autocratic leader does not possess the basic skill in human relations which permits the problem-solving approach in his work with others.

Research and experience subsequent to these studies appear to indicate that it is incorrect to sterotype a leader as being one type or another. Leaders tend to vary their behavior according to the situation.

V. Functional-Leadership Approach

This concept of leadership seeks to discover what actions are required by groups under various conditions if they are to achieve their objectives and how different members take part in these actions. Leadership is viewed as the performance of those acts which are required by the group.

The group-functions approach to leadership incorporates the other approaches discussed, except for the trait concept. Groups differ in a variety of ways. Actions vary from one group to another. The nature of leadership acts will accordingly vary from group to group. Situational aspects will determine what functions are needed and who will perform them (e.g., nature of the group's goals, structure of group, attitudes of members).

There appear to be two main classifications of leadership needs in groups: the achievement of the group goal and the maintenance or strengthening of the group itself. Any specific behavior may be helpful for both or favor one at the expense of the other.

For example, a group may be so in-

tent upon maintaining good relations that it avoids friction at all costs, thereby retarding its problem-solving process. On the other hand, wise solution of a problem may help the solidarity of the group.

The distribution of leadership functions in a group occurs in several ways. Usually, in a mature group, members will assume responsibility for group roles necessary for effective group functioning. Studies and experiments indicate that groups which distribute leadership functions get "better" results (e.g. greater productivity, higher morale).

Studies of the roles of group members show that there tend to be group-centered, task-centered, and self-centered member functions. Studies of the effects of these roles indicate that certain functions are required for a group to make a decision, come to a conclusion, or resolve a conflict.

Some of the group-building and maintenance functions are: encourager, feeling-expresser, harmonizer, compromiser, gate-keeper, standard-setter, consensus-tester, follower.

Some of the work-doing functions are: initiator, information-seeker, information-giver, opinion-seeker, clarifier, elaborator, summarizer.

Functional leadership means that group members have a shared responsibility to carry out the various tasks of leadership. The designated leader, however, has a responsibility for being sensitive to those functional needs and for seeing that they are taken care of.

Problems of leadership cannot be separated from problems of group functioning. To understand leadership, we must understand groups.

One observation frequently made by leaders is: "Democratic or problem-solving leadership is all right, but it is

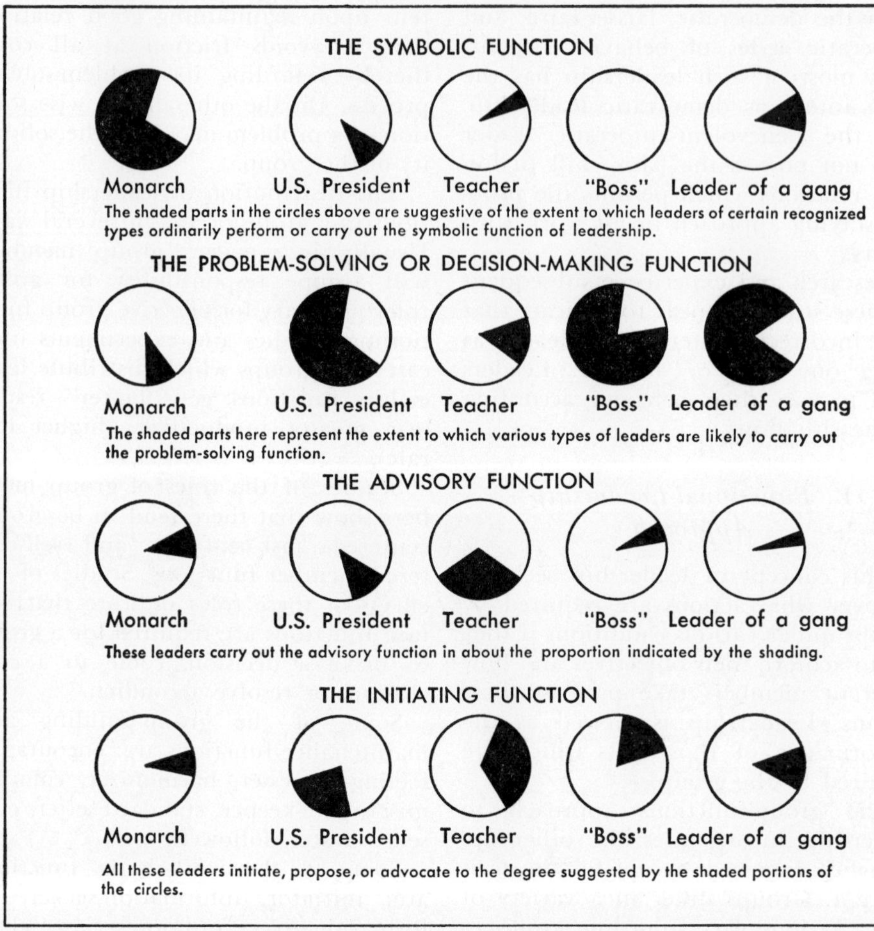

THE SYMBOLIC FUNCTION

Monarch   U.S. President   Teacher   "Boss"   Leader of a gang

The shaded parts in the circles above are suggestive of the extent to which leaders of certain recognized types ordinarily perform or carry out the symbolic function of leadership.

THE PROBLEM-SOLVING OR DECISION-MAKING FUNCTION

Monarch   U.S. President   Teacher   "Boss"   Leader of a gang

The shaded parts here represent the extent to which various types of leaders are likely to carry out the problem-solving function.

THE ADVISORY FUNCTION

Monarch   U.S. President   Teacher   "Boss"   Leader of a gang

These leaders carry out the advisory function in about the proportion indicated by the shading.

THE INITIATING FUNCTION

Monarch   U.S. President   Teacher   "Boss"   Leader of a gang

All these leaders initiate, propose, or advocate to the degree suggested by the shaded portions of the circles.

Diagram 3   Functions of leadership

too time-consuming, and I have a job to get done."

It is true that when reaching a decision is the sole objective, problem-solving leadership usually takes longer than manipulative or autocratic leadership. However, studies show that problem-solving leadership can be more effective even from the time point of view if we consider the total time elapsed from the emergence of a problem to its implementation.

Diagram 2 shows that altho problem-solving leadership takes longer to reach a decision, implementation is much more rapid than in the case of manipulative leadership. This is because members of a group that participates in making the decision feel more responsible for carrying it out.

Practice of Democratic Leadership

The implications of these different approaches to leadership seem important if we realize that the strength of any democracy is directly proportional to the practice of it by its citizen leaders. If democratic leadership is to be practiced, it needs to be understood in its operational terms so that as leaders and trainers of leaders we can make real our understanding of the democratic processes.

◆◆◆◆◆◆◆◆◆◆◆◆◆◆◆◆◆◆◆◆ LEADERSHIP THEORY AND
ADMINISTRATIVE BEHAVIOR

Warren G. Bennis

W<small>E</small> can place the organizational theories and ideologies concerning the concept of authority into a loose historical framework. In general, two important models emerge: the classical rational theory and the subsequent human relations model. This latter model was spurred by a number of economic and cultural conditions, and especially by some early seminal social science research. Gouldner, in his recent article on organizations, calls these approaches the "rational" model and the "natural system" model,[1] terms which seem to be compatible with this historical survey. The major difference between these two systems of thought with relevance to the problem of authority can be diagrammed as in Table 1. This diagram is a gross oversimplification of the differences between the two approaches, but in the next section we hope to sharpen the issues involved.

The Questions Reformulated and a Partial Answer

If we recall the welter of confusion in leadership theory, it is no surprise that organizational leadership philosophies and attitudes have mirrored, or reinforced, these confusions. Reversals and contradictions have reflected the conditional nature of the research and writing on leadership. What we will now attempt is another examination of some of the basic questions raised throughout this paper and then a fitting of some of the possible answers into a typology of organizations.

It is believed that questions of organizational leadership can be reduced to five major issues:

1. *Basis and functions of authority.* We see on the one hand that authority is arrogated by those who simply maintain role incumbency and, on the other hand, by the role occupant with technical competence and expertise. Weber, as Gouldner points out, felt that bureaucracy rests on both of these factors: "Obedience is due a superior, not merely because of his technical knowledge, but also because of the office he occupies." [2] Yet Weber did not work out the theoretical consequences of this split role of authority, and it is on this

[1] Gouldner, "Complex Organizations."

[2] *Ibid.*, p. 402.

Excerpted from Warren G. Bennis, "Leadership Theory and Administrative Behavior: The Problem of Authority," Administrative Science Quarterly, Vol. 4, No. 3, December 1959, pp. 259–301. Used by permission.

TABLE 1.

	Classical theory	Human relations approach
Assumptions about "human nature"	a. Weber: Man's passion must be controlled b. Taylor: Man's energy can be harnessed toward productive goals c. Administrative management: Man is inert and passive	For man to work effectively, he must be motivated through social and psychological gratifications, most particularly through anchoring his sentiments in a friendly and cohesive work group
Sources of power	Role incumbency and technical competence of superior extend incentives	Group norms Self-control Superior's ability to reduce status elevation and be a trainer to subordinate
Types of rewards	Economic and physiological need satisfaction	Social and psychological need fulfillment: self-esteem, group approval
Manipulator of rewards	Superior	Reference groups
Type of knowledge necessary for superior role incumbency	Task Technical expertise	Maintenance Human relations skills

issue that so much of the authority question founders.

The issue gets increasingly complicated when we assert that technical knowledge or expertise must be differentiated into at least two elements: knowledge of performance criteria (such as production, marketing, and so on) and knowledge of the human aspects of administration (such as coordination, communication, and so on). Kerr and Fisher identified these apparently mutually exclusive requirements (reminiscent of Barnard's famous "effectiveness" and "efficiency") when they discussed the economist's and sociologist's view of organization. For the economist, the task of the manager is efficient management of productive resources; for the sociologist, the obligation is the management of social systems to produce coherence, stability, and a sense of community.[3]

A political scientist writing in a recent issue of *The Reporter* focuses on the same issue:

One of the paradoxes of an increasingly specialized, bureaucratized society is that the qualities rewarded in the rise to eminence are less and less the qualities required once eminence is reached. Specialization encourages administrative and technical skills, which are not necessarily related to the vision and creativity needed for leadership. The essence of good ad-

[3] Kerr and Fisher, *op. cit.*

ministration is co-ordination among the specialized functions of a bureaucracy. The task of the executive is to infuse and occasionally to transcend routine with purpose.[4]

There is no essential paradox, as Kissinger believes, but simply the fact that as organizations grow and develop into large, interdependent units *both* types of knowledge are required: knowledge of purpose and knowledge of administration. Too often we seem to get impaled on false dichotomies, as Kerr and Fisher do, and do not recognize the fact that contemporary organization leadership sets up two kinds of requirements, the technical expertise and the administrative knowledge, and both have to be balanced by the executive.

2. *The sources of power.* The generation of power can be both subtle, as through identification processes, or crude, as in terms of rewards and punishments. Throughout the literature on leadership four primary loci of leadership are most frequently implied: (a) rewards and punishments, instrumentally supplied by some exogenous agent; (b) self-control, typically generated through internalization of professional norms or other standards of excellence; (c) the institutions of authority and contract as filtered through universalistic rules;[5] and (d) group norms. As we shall see below, each of these systems of power may be appropriate under certain conditions. Self-control, for example, would probably be appropriate only in those organizations (and only for those work-

ers) where there are certain external standards for performance, such as professional associations.

3. *Objectives versus relationships.* A significant reversal was made when McGregor re-emphasized management by objectives. One would think it almost absurd that the fundamental *raison d'être* of organizations should have to be re-emphasized, yet the trend in education, industry, and other organizational settings has tended to move from *task* to relationship requirements.[6]

Even in the distantly related field of psychotherapy we see a similar reversal. Psychoanalysis, starting off as a method whereby the analyst imparted certain information via interpretations concerning the patient's unconscious, moved to an ego psychology where the relationship between the analyst and the patient became the dominant focus of psychotherapy. The raw content ("id psychology") of unconscious processes was eclipsed by and subjugated to the "relationship." Nowadays we witness a reversal that parallels the return of management to objectives. Leslie Farber, in an article entitled "The Therapeutic Despair," puts it this way:

Despite the modern tendency to regard all teaching relationships as primarily interpersonal in character, it is obvious that a teacher's primary dedication must be not to his students but to his subject matter. Were this not so, teaching would consist only of this romantic relation, based on vanity or power, which the psychotherapist has learned to call "transference" situations. . . .

Obviously any student who spent his time in class thinking only about the teacher's personal life, or imagining his private thoughts and feelings, would not

[4] Henry A. Kissinger, "The Policy Maker and the Intellectual," *The Reporter*, 20 (March 1959), 30.

[5] T. Parsons, "Suggestions for a Sociological Approach to the Theory of Organizations," II, *Administrative Science Quarterly*, 1 (1956), 227.

[6] The influence of Harry Stack Sullivan can be felt in this emphasis. For an excellent theoretical discussion of his theory applied to organizational behavior, see Presthus, *op. cit.*

be learning much. And the same is true of a reader, for it is only after a prolonged acquaintance with an author that the man himself will begin to emerge somewhat from his work. Any premature effort to detach him—to imagine what he himself is wishing, feeling, perceiving, thinking—would be as self-defeating in the arts as it would be destructive of any other educational process. Although teacher and student may both confirm and be confirmed in their mutual endeavor, this process must remain both indirect and secondary to the goal of learning. True dialogue here, as with all collective efforts, would be concerned not with the other person but with a mutual dedication to the same end.[7]

4. *Distance versus closeness.* A recent cartoon in the *New Yorker* poses the issue very neatly. Two executives are standing at a bar, and the older one says (looking determined), "Forget that 'Mr. Meredith' business. My name is Freddie. We're not boss and employee here; we're just a couple of guys having a friendly drink together. Now then, in all sincerity, what's your honest opinion of me?"[8] Specifications as to the appropriate distance between leaders and followers in terms of social sensitivity, friendliness, helping relations, and so on, clearly distinguish the classical theorists from the human relations specialists. The latter have been typically associated with a philosophy of participatory, consultative, or group-centered leadership with all the accouterments of diagnostic sensitivity. The revisionists, also, except for McMurray, assert a closer, more collaborative relationship. But is this possible? Or stated differently, under what conditions is it possible? The empirical evidence does not support the "closeness" position. Steiner, writing in the *Psychological Review*, asserts on an analysis of the pertinent data that interpersonal acuity may be functional only under certain conditions:

if: (a) the group members are motivated to cooperate; (b) the accurately perceived qualities are relevant to the activities of the group; (c) members are free to alter their own behaviors in response to their perceptions of other members; and (d) the behavioral changes which are a consequence of accurate social perception are the kinds which produce a more thoroughly integrated dyadic system. Whenever any *one* or more of these conditions is not met, accurate social perception should fail to have the effect predicted.[9]

Most formal organizations would abrogate at least one of these conditions.

Two other complications should be mentioned briefly. First there is a prevailing notion in some of the vulgarized human relations literature that the leader should be "liked" by his men, "be one of the boys," and other variations on this theme. Bales's findings cast some doubt on this notion, since it appears that the person who exerts the most influence also receives strong negative reactions. The psychoanalytic position, about which no firm evidence exists, follows along these same lines, that productive work is partially a function of the expression of hostility to the leader.[10] The fact is that there is no solid systematic theory or research on the effects of negative

---

[7] *Psychiatry,* 21 (February 1958), 19.
[8] March 21, 1959.

[9] I. Steiner, "Interpersonal Behavior and Accurate Social Perception," *Psychological Review,* 62 (1955), 268–274. Steiner includes a bibliography of contradictory results on this issue.
[10] Nietzsche suggested this in his *Genealogy of Morals,* Essay III, "What is the meaning of ascetic ideals?" "Getting rid of the blasting stuff in such a way that it does not blow up the herd and the herdsmen that is his [priest's] real feat, his supreme utility." T. M. Mills at Harvard is presently working on the hypothesis mentioned in the test.

and positive feelings toward the superior with respect to effectiveness, satisfaction, or group formation.[11]

Second, there is a tendency to regard subordinates as desiring close relationships with the superior,[12] whereas the latter is thought to erect restrictive barriers against this. In addition to the work of Fiedler, which brings this seriously into question, some other factors also must be considered. It can be asserted that the satisfaction gained through colleague and peer relationships would be reduced by a close relationship with a superior.[13] These may be "secondary gains," according to the psychoanalysts, who claim that subordinates universally desire a close relationship to authority in preference to peer relationships and accept the latter chiefly because a close relationship with authority is impossible. Nevertheless, this "reaction-formation" is observed frequently enough to cause speculation.

Again the research is spotty in this area. There is some research on how certain leadership styles affect group behavior and a good deal of research on group members' attitudes toward leaders. There is practically no data on how specific leadership styles affect group members' relationships.[14]

5. *Consensual validation and decision making.* Group decision making and its variations appear to be one of the basic pillars of the human relations approach in contradistinction to more traditional theory where all responsibility is channeled into one office. The basic issue here is not whether groups are more effective than isolated individuals in problem solving and creative thinking—and the evidence is far from conclusive on this score [15] —but stems from more fundamental psychological and philosophical issues.

One of the most significant contributions to social psychology was made by Leon Festinger and his associates in a series of experiments on informal social communication. The major postulate of this theoretical framework concerned the question of social reality.[16] Festinger postulated that establishing validity on ambiguous items of an interpersonal or social nature could only come about through some system of group consensus; that is, a social reality was only possible when individuals anchored their judgments in a strong reference group. This assumption has gained support through the work of Sherif,[17] Asch,[18] and others

[11] One important exception to this is the recent, splendid work of M. Horwitz, "The Veridicality of Liking and Disliking," in *Person, Perception and Interpersonal Behavior,* ed. by R. Taguiri and L. Petrullo (Stanford, Calif., 1958), chap. xiii.

[12] For example, the "substitute locomotion" hypothesis: H. Kelley, "Communication in Experimentally Created Hierarchies," *Human Relations,* 4 (February 1951), 39–56.

[13] E. Jaques, "Social Systems as a Defense against Persecutory and Depressive Anxiety," in *New Direction in Psychoanalysis,* ed. by M. Klein *et al.* (New York, 1955), chap. xx.

[14] To my knowledge only one theoretical and one empirical paper deals with this problem in any detail with respect to the emotional and intermember relationships which evolve as a consequence of certain types of leaders: F. Redl, "Group Emotion and Leadership," *Psychiatry,* 5 (1942), 573–596; R. Lippitt, "An Experimental Study of the Effect of Democratic and Authoritarian Group Atmospheres," *University of Iowa Studies in Child Welfare,* 16 (1940), 43–195.

[15] I. Lorge *et al.,* "A Survey of Studies Contrasting the Quality of Group Performance and Individual Performance, 1920–1957," *Psych. Bull.,* 55 (1958), 337–372; W. G. Bennis, "Decision-Making in Groups," *Group Psychotherapy,* 10 (December 1957), 287–299.

[16] Festinger, *op. cit.*

[17] M. Sherif, "A Study of Some Social Factors in Perception," *Arch. Psychol.,* 23, no. 187 (1953).

[18] S. E. Asch, *Social Psychology* (New York, 1958).

working in the area of interpersonal influence.[19]

The decision maker, then, faced with no operable means for evaluating a decision—as is often the case—and with limited data, has no other recourse than to utilize a group, both as a security operation and as a validity tester. This is not to say that this method is the most effective; quite the opposite. It may be the most expensive, invalid, and tedious. Nevertheless, psychologically, it is functional.

From the philosophical point of view Kissinger puts it this way in the previously cited article:

Most Americans are convinced that no one is ever entirely "right," or, as the saying goes, that if there is disagreement, each party is probably a little in error. The fear of dogmatism pervades the American scene. But the corollary of the tentativeness of most views is an incurable inward insecurity. Even very eminent people are reluctant to stand alone, and they see in concurrence one of their chief tests of validity.[20]

It would seem then that philosophical conviction and psychological needs in combination create a situation where the group-versus-individual dilemma cannot be reduced to an "effectiveness" issue, but to the problem of the insecurity and validity testing of the decision maker. And in today's organizations—scientific, military, government, and education—the consequences of decisions may have such far-reaching effects that no one individual, even if all the knowledge were available on which to make a decision, would feel sufficiently courageous to make it.

This is not to say that there is a

failure of courage at the top levels of American enterprise today; there would be no way to prove or disprove such a statement. However, this does point to a basic antagonism between the new and the old, rather simplified model of organization, in which the effects of a decision may not have been so consequential as in the complicated and interdependent leviathans of today.

Now we come to the final step, an attempt to sketch out a typology for an analysis of leadership. Generalizations about organizational leadership, as has been hinted throughout this paper, frequently founder because of the diversity of situations where influence occurs: from formal professional organizations to formally organized assembly lines; from tightly organized gangs with stable leadership to newly formed and emerging friendship groups. The conditions of leadership, in terms of the nature of the task, history, and formation of organization, similarity of goals, types of rewards available, have to be specified. Before the typology is presented, let us explain the concept of leadership in order to determine its logical properties.

For our purposes leadership can be defined as *the process by which an agent induces a subordinate to behave in a desired manner.* From this preliminary definition we can extract five elements involved in the concept of leadership: (1) There is an *agent,* which can be a person, a designated status (role incumbent), or a group. (2) The *process by which an agent induces* depends upon the agent's ability to control the appropriate means to satisfy the needs of subordinates.[21] Induction,

[19] E. Schein, "The Chinese Indoctrination Program for Prisoners of War," *Psychiatry,* 19 (1956), 149–172.

[20] Page 31.

[21] This is derived from the fundamental postulate of need reduction theories. See D. McGregor for an elaboration of this as applied to an organization setting: "The Staff

then depends upon two elements, the types of rewards manipulable and the sources or (legitimation) of these rewards by the agent. (3) *Subordinates* represent the objects of induction, i.e., those who act in the desired manner. In order for the subordinates to accept induction two conditions must be met by the agent: the agent must accurately perceive what will be genuinely need satisfying to the subordinates, and the agent must be capable of controlling these means. In addition, the subordinate must perceive the agent as being capable of controlling the appropriate rewards. (4) The induced *behavior* has to do with the process of influence by which the subordinate consents to act in certain ways. This consists of two elements: the psychological processes by which he internalizes the induction and the type of satisfaction he gains from the process. (5) *In a desired manner* deals with some operable goal or path by which goal attainment is achieved.

We can now reformulate a definition of leadership which involves three major components: (a) an agent who is typically called a *leader;* (b) a process of induction or the ability to manipulate rewards that here will be termed *power;* and (c) the induced behavior, which will be referred to here as *influence.*

Power is thus the perceived ability to control appropriate rewards; a leader is an agent who in fact wields these rewards (or implied punishments); and influence results from an agent exercising control over the subordinates' need satisfaction. Leadership, then, is viewed as a tripartite concept involving means control over rewards (power), an agent who manipulates

these rewards, and an influence process. Power residing in an agent leads to influence. Thus influence is viewed as a consequent variable dependent on the ability of the agent to manipulate the appropriate rewards.[22]

From this vantage point we can now proceed with our paradigmatic approach. First, a rough typology of organizations will be presented (Table 2). This typology is derived from the part in the logical breakdown of the leadership concept designated as "in a desired manner." That is, when a leader attempts to exert influence, he presumably is oriented toward some definite *goal* or criterion variable. As Parsons points out: "As a formal analytical point of reference, *primacy of orientation to the attainment of a specific goal is used as the defining characteristic of an organization* which distinguishes it from other types of social systems."[23] Table 2 presents a framework for characterizing four different types of organizations based on a specific criterion or effectiveness variable (goal).

Obviously, these "pure" types are rarely observed empirically—for one thing, effectiveness criteria are rarely this simple and monolithic—but they serve to sharpen the differences among formally organized activities. One of the major purposes of this paper is to clarify the conditional nature of leadership propositions; thus the first step is to outline the conditions of organizations, which Table 2 attempts to do.

[22] This is based on the "law of effect" that behaviors that seem to lead to rewards tend to be repeated, whereas behaviors that do not seem to lead to rewards tend not to be repeated. See M. Haire, *Psychology in Management* (New York, 1956), chap. ii.

[23] T. Parsons, "Suggestions for a Sociological Approach to the Theory of Organizations," I, *Administrative Science Quarterly,* 1 (1956), 64.

Function in Human Relations," *Journal of Social Issues,* 4 (Summer 1948), 6–23.

TABLE 2.

TYPOLOGY OF ORGANIZATION

Type of organization	*Major function*	*Examples*	*Effectiveness criterion* *
Habit	Replicating standard and uniform products	Highly mechanized factories, etc.	No. of products
Problem-solving	Creating new ideas	Research organizations; design and engineering divisions; consulting organizations, etc.	No. of ideas
Indoctrination	Changing peoples' habits, attitudes, intellect, behavior (physical and mental)	Universities, prisons, hospitals, etc.	No. of "clients" leaving
Service	Distributing services either directly to consumer or to above types	Military, government, advertising, taxi companies, etc.	Extent of services performed

* These effectiveness criteria are oversimplified. Obviously, organizations set up multiple criteria and have to co-ordinate them. The criteria specified here were selected for their accessibility to quantitative terms and their formal significance.

For further purposes of this analysis, let us take only two of these categories, the habit and problem-solving organizations. (This is done for two reasons: for heuristic simplicity and because the habit and problem-solving organizations are seen empirically as paired opposites.) Furthermore, let us add to their descriptions.

The problem-solving organization can be characterized, in addition to the specifications mentioned in Table 2, as having a high degree of similarity of goals between superior and subordinate, high degree of professionalization, important outside reference groups (such as professional associations), high degree of autonomy for workers, high usage of abstract and inferential thinking, difficulty in evaluating effectiveness, and long-term and intangible goals. For simplicity, let us characterize the habit organization as having the opposite characteristics and let us add a third category, the informal group. This is done primarily to include another aspect of organizational reality that occurs in both the aforementioned types of organizations.

Table 3 presents these three categories of organization in the vertical columns and the major leadership variables as explained above in the horizontal rows. Before reference to the table in detail, a few qualifications must be made.

First of all, for purposes of analysis it was decided to place in one cell a characterization that could actually apply in others. Obviously, for example, "identification" occurs in the influence process in organizational conditions other than informal groups; affective relations are not dominant in the more formalized contexts. Yet it is seen as more *likely* to occur in an informal group than in a habit organization. Thus a choice was made primarily on the basis of an assumed frequency distribution. (Another criterion affecting the choice will be discussed below.) Second, no specification is made of the *level* of organizational structure at which the superior-subordinate nexus occurs; this still remains ambiguous. However, the paradigm is particularly appropriate to any superior-subordinate interpersonal relationship. Third, no distinction is made between staff and line. Naturally, habit organizations contain units that could be labeled problem-solving; this distinction is obscured by the paradigm.

Finally, it should be stressed that the types presented are "ideal types" in the sense that they represent an imagined world, but still an empirically possible state. This brings us to the usage of the other criterion mentioned above. The "ideal type" methodology has been criticized, among other reasons, for representing a value prescription of what ought to be rather than of what is.[24] It has also been criticized on the ground that it is not a fair approximation of reality because of its abstract, prescriptive qualities. The paradigm presented in Table 3 can be criticized on both accounts. But what should

[24] D. Martindale, "Sociological Theory and the Ideal Type," *Symposium on Sociological Theory*, ed. by L. Gross (Evanston, Ill., 1959), chap. ii.

be made explicit here is that the normative prescription for the choices was based primarily on the criterion variable of the organization. That is, where problem-solving organizations are found, those factors that will lead to realization of the criteria of effectiveness will be the ones to be inserted in the cells appropriate to the problem-solving organization; the same holds true, of course, for the informal group and the habit organization. Thus the strength of the paradigmatic approach utilized here rests on its potential for setting up a series of hypotheses for testing leadership propositions under a variety of organizational conditions with respect to particular effectiveness or pay-off variables.

In general it can be said that the habit organization and informal organization characterized in Table 3 refer to classical theory and the human relations approach respectively. The problem-solving organization is probably most compatible with management by objective approach. Thus some derivations bearing on the tension between these approaches are possible with this typology. For example, self-control as a modality of power is attainable only in an organizational setting where problem solving is the dominant focus. If empirically true, this raises serious questions about the utility of self-control in situations where there can be no internalization of professional norms; as, for example, by an unskilled employee. Also we see that technical competence is the main basis of power in a problem-solving organization in contrast to role incumbency and administrative ability in the habit organization. Another derivation from the chart bears on the role of the supervisor. In the problem-solving organization his ability to control the

TABLE 3.*

Leadership variable	Power		Influence			Leader	
Type of organization	Basis	Type of reward given	Process*	Type of satisfaction gained	Function	Distance	Agent
Problem-solving	Knowledge, expertise	Information	Internalization (self-control)	Self-esteem	To promote conditions for congruence of individual and organization goals	Double reference	Role and person
Habit	Role incumbency (status)	Exogenous physiological and economic rewards	Compliance (obedience to leader)	Economic and lower-order need fulfillment	To set up and enforce performance criteria to meet organization goals	Distant	Role incumbent
Informal	Norms	Affective relations	Identification (own acceptance)	Group approval	To bring about acceptance of group norms	Close	Person or group personification

* These formulations of social influence are suggested by H. C. Kelman, "Compliance, Identification and Internalization," MS, 1956.

"When an individual complies, he adapts induced behavior not because he *believes* in the content of that behavior, but because he expects to gain specific rewards . . . and avoid punishments by conformity.

"Internalization occurs when an individual adopts behavior derived from another person or a group because he finds the content of that behavior satisfying . . . where as an influencing agent's power to induce compliance depends on his means-control, his power to induce internalization depends on his credibility. . . .

"Identification occurs when an individual adopts behavior derived from another person or a group because their behavior is associated with a satisfying, self-defining relationship to this person or group . . . ; it depends on the ability to provide satisfying relationships for the individual."

rewards and punishments of the subordinate is drastically restricted in comparison to the superior in the habit organization. He can only indirectly control the rewards and punishments by promoting conditions whereby the subordinate can realize his own goals.[25] The difficulty of controlling self-esteem (when this comes from an external professional body) in contrast to controlling economic and physiological aspects of satisfaction can be readily seen. This may account, furthermore, for the split

[25] In a recent study conducted in a hospital setting we found that none of the satisfactions most desired by nurses were manipulable by the supervisors. Obviously, then, the sources of powers (in terms of rewards) must stem from other than the formal authority system. Our data suggest that these satisfactions are derived mainly from the intrinsic value of the work and colleague relations. Only indirectly can these be controlled by the superiors. We suspect that this may be rather general in professional organizations. See W. Bennis, N. Berkowitz, M. Affinito, and M. Malone, "Authority, Power, and the Ability to Influence," *Human Relations,* 11 (May 1958), 143–155.

in organizational roles which Gouldner and others have commented on regarding "locals and cosmopolitans"; [26] the latter are not considered to be good organization men while the "locals" are more loyal. Upon analysis we can see why. The cosmopolitan derives his rewards from inward standards of excellence, internalized and reinforced through professional identification. His rewards, even those that are exogenous to him, such as a government research contract, cannot usually be controlled by formal organizational leadership.

The paradigmatic approach suggested here in no way solves all the issues involved in a theory of organizational leadership. But it is hoped that it does serve to sharpen some of the issues and provide an over-all framework for the testing of hypotheses.

[26] A. W. Gouldner, "Locals and Cosmopolitans: Toward an Analysis of Latent Social Roles," I, *Administrative Science Quarterly,* 2 (1957), 281–306.

✧✧✧✧✧✧✧✧✧✧✧✧✧✧✧✧✧✧✧✧ TOWARD A THEORY OF SOCIAL CONFLICT   *Ralf Dahrendorf*

Two Models of Society

IF we extrapolate the analytical approaches of the structural-functional theory somewhat beyond their boundaries and investigate their implicit postulates, we can construct a model of society which lies at the base of this theory and determines its perspectives. The essential elements of this societal model are these:

1. Every society is a relatively persisting configuration of elements.[1]

[1] There is much controversy over this implication of the structural-functional approach. Most functionalists deny that they make such an assumption. Indeed, assertions to the contrary are found in the works of Parsons, Merton, and others. Nevertheless, it can be shown that these assertions are, from the point of view of structural-functional theory, mere declarations. The notion of equilibrium and the concept of a system would have little sense if they did not make the assumption of stabil-

Excerpted from Ralf Dahrendorf, "Toward a Theory of Social Conflict," Journal of Conflict Resolution, *Vol. 11, No. 2, 1958, pp. 174–179. Abridged and used by permission.*

2. Every society is a well-integrated configuration of elements.

3. Every element in a society contributes to its functioning.

4. Every society rests on the consensus of its members.

It should be clear that a theory based on this model does not lend itself to the explanation, not even the description, of the phenomena of social conflict and change. For this purpose, one needs a model which takes the diametrically opposite position on all the four points above:

1. Every society is subjected at every moment to change: social change is ubiquitous.

2. Every society experiences at every moment social conflict: social conflict is ubiquitous.

3. Every element in a society contributes to its change.

4. Every society rests on constraint of some of its members by others.

The remarkable nature of our vantage point becomes evident when we examine the two groups of postulates with respect to their truth content, that is, if we ask ourselves which of the two models promises greater utility for cognition of reality. It appears that the juxtaposed pairs of postulates are in no way mutually exclusive with respect to social reality. It is impossible to decide by an empirical investigation which of the two models is more nearly correct; the postulates are not hypotheses. Moreover, it seems meaningful to say that both models are in a certain

sense valid and analytically fruitful. Stability and change, integration and conflict, function and "dysfunction," consensus and constraint are, it would seem, two equally valid aspects of every imaginable society. They are dialectically separated and are exhaustive only in combination as a description of the social problems. Possibly a more general theory of society may be thought of which lifts the equivalidity of both models, the coexistence of the uncombinable, onto a higher level of generality. As long as we do not have such a theory, we must content ourselves with the finding that society presents a double aspect to the sociological understanding, each no better, no more valid, than the other. It follows that the criticism of the unapplicability of the structural-functional theory for the analysis of conflict is directed only against a claim of generality of this theory but leaves untouched its competence with respect to the problem of integration. It follows, on the other hand, also that the theory of conflict and change is not a general theory. Comparisons between natural and social sciences always carry the danger of misunderstanding. However, it may be maintained, without attributing to this analogy more than a logical meaning, that the situation of the sociologists is not unlike that of the physicists with respect to the theory of light. Just as the physicists can solve certain problems only by assuming the wave character of light and others, on the contrary, only by assuming a corpuscular or quantum theory, so there are problems of sociology which can be adequately attacked only with an integration theory and others which require a conflict theory for a meaningful analysis. Both theories can work extensively with the same categories, but they emphasize different aspects.

---

ity of societies. However, two limitations are to be observed: (1) we have to do here (also in the implications which follow) not with a metaphysical postulate but rather with an assumption made for the purpose of analysis; and (2) stability does not mean statics in the sense of complete absence of processes within the "system."

While the integration theory likens a society to an ellipse, a rounded entity which incloses all of its elements, conflict theory sees society rather as a hyperbola which, it is true, has the same foci but is open in many directions and appears as a tension field of the determining forces.

The Tasks of a Theory of Social Conflict

The double aspect of society and the dialectics of the two types of sociological theory are in themselves a most fruitful object of reflection. Nevertheless, another problem seems to be more urgent. The theory of social integration has recently developed to a flourishing state as the structural-functional approach in ethnology and sociology. Our theory of conflict, however, is still in a very rudimentary state. It is an approach based on postulating ubiquitous social change and social conflict, the "dysfunctionality" of all the elements of social structure, and the constraining character of social unity. Our considerations put us in a position to formulate some requirements of such a theory:

1. It should be a scientific theory (as is the theory of social integration), that is, it should be formulated with reference to a plausible and demonstrable explanation of empirical phenomena.

2. The elements of the theory should not contradict the conflict model of society.

3. The categories employed should, whenever possible, agree with those of the integration theory or at least correspond to them.

4. A conflict theory should enable us to derive social conflicts from structural arrangements and thus show these conflicts systematically generated.

5. It should account both for the multiplicity of forms of conflict and for their degrees of intensity.

The last goal of a social theory is the explanation of social change. The integration theory gives us a tool for determining the point of departure of the process. To find the locus of the forces which drive the process and social change is the task of a theory of conflict. It must develop a model which makes understandable the structural origin of social conflict. This seems possible only if we understand conflicts as struggles among social groups, that is, if we make our task precise to the extent that it reduces to the structural analysis of conflicting groups. Under this supposition three questions come especially to the forefront, which conflict theory must answer:

1. How do conflicting groups arise from the structure of society?

2. What forms can the struggles among such groups assume?

3. How does the conflict among such groups effect a change in the social structures?

Wherever men live together and lay foundations of forms of social organization, there are positions whose occupants have powers of command in certain contexts and over certain positions, and there are other positions whose occupants are subjected to such commands. The distinction between "up" and "down"—or, as the English say, "Them" and "Us"—is one of the fundamental experiences of most men in society,[2] and, moreover, it appears

[2] Empirical corroborations for these generalizations are found in two significant publications of last year: Heinrich Popitz *et al.*, *Das Gesellschaftsbild des Arbeiters* ("The Worker's Image of Society") (Tübingen, 1957); Richard Hoggart, *The Uses of Literacy* (London, 1957).

that this distinction is intimately connected with unequal distribution of power. The main thesis of the following attempt to construct a model for the structural analysis of conflict is that we should seek the structural origin of social conflict in the dominance relations which prevail within certain units of social organization. For these units I will use Max Weber's concept of "imperatively co-ordinated group." The thesis is not new; it is found (however often with important modifications) in the formulation of many social scientists before and after Marx. But we shall make no attempt to trace the history of this thesis.

Authority and Authority Structures

The concepts of power and authority are very complex ones. Whoever uses them is likely to be accused of lack of precision and of clarity to the extent that he tries to define them "exhaustively." Is the influence of a father on his children, the influence of an industrial combine on the government, or the influence of a demagogue on his followers an instance of an authority relation? Here, as in most other cases, it is basically not a question of a definition but rather a question of an "operational definition," as it is often called today: a method of determination which allows us to identify as such the state of affairs when we are actually confronted with it. However, for the purpose of analysis and identification, Weber's determination of authority is sufficient: "The likelihood that a command of a certain content will be obeyed by given persons."[3] This de-

[3] Max Weber, "Wirtschaft und Gesellschaft," in *Grundriss der Sozialökonomik,* III (3d ed.; Tübingen, 1947), 28.

termination contains the following elements:

1. Authority denotes a relation of supra- and subordination.

2. The supra-ordinated side prescribes to the subordinated one certain behavior in the form of a command or a prohibition.

3. The supra-ordinated side has the right to make such prescriptions; authority is a legitimate relation of supra- and subordination; authority is not based on personal or situational chance effects but rather on an expectation associated with social position.

4. The right of authority is limited to certain contents and to specific persons.

5. Failure to obey the prescriptions is sanctioned; a legal system (or a system of quasi-legal customs) guards the effectiveness of authority.

This determination of authority makes possible the identification of a cabinet minister, an employer, and a party secretary as occupants of authority positions—in contrast to an industrial syndicate or a demagogue, neither of which satisfies condition 3 above.[4]

It is not the intention of our "definition" of authority to solve all analytical and empirical problems of this category.[5] In fact, the very first step of our

[4] This third condition, that of legitimacy, denotes the distinction between power (as an actual command relationship) and authority (cf. Weber's "Definitionen," *op. cit.*).

[5] Thus it is clear that the phenomenon of authority is here deliberately treated unilaterally. The double aspect of society may be illustrated in this category, as in practically any other. Integration theory, too, treats of authority. However, this theory emphasizes not the polemical, conflict-generating aspect of this social relation but, on the contrary, the integrative, unifying aspect. Parsons is doubtless right when he says that authority "is the capacity to mobilize the resources of the society for the attainment of goals for

model leads us deep into these problems: in each imperatively co-ordinated group, two aggregates can be distinguished: those which have only general ("civil") basic rights and those which have authority rights over the former. In contrast to prestige and income, a continuum of gradual transition cannot be constructed for the distribution of authority. Rather, there is a clear dichotomy. Every position in an imperatively co-ordinated group can be recognized as belonging to one who dominates or one who is dominated. Sometimes, in view of the bureaucratic large-scale organization of modern societies—under the influence of the state—this assumption may at first sight seem problematic. However, a sharper analysis leaves no doubt that here also the split into the dominating and dominated is valid, even though in reality a considerable measure of differentiation is discernable among those in the dominating group.[6]

---

which a general 'public' commitment has been made, or may be made. It is mobilization, above all, of the action of persons and groups, which is *binding* on them by virtue of their position in society" ("The Distribution of Power in American Society," *World Politics*, X, No. 1 [October 1957], 140). However, in a way C. Wright Mills, who is criticized by Parsons, is also right when he emphasizes, as we do, the "presumptive illegitimacy" and "dysfunctionality" of all authority.

[6] The position of authority of the bureaucrat was already of concern to Max Weber and to many sociologists since. Here there seems to be indeed a differentiation of authority. However, it is a differentiation of a special kind. In modern bureaucratic administration, the exercise of authority has undergone to a certain degree a division of labor; hence the multiplicity of positions, distinguishable by the number of "assignable persons" and the scope of "specific content" to which authority privileges are attached. In the sense of our analysis, there can be no doubt that the entire bureaucracy belongs (at times!) to the ruling side.

The Conflict-Theory Model

The dichotomy of social roles within imperatively co-ordinated groups,[7] the division into positive and negative dominance roles, is a fact of social structure. If and insofar as social conflicts can be referred to this factual situation, they are structurally explained. The model of analysis of social conflict which is developed against a background of an assumption of such a dichotomy involves the following steps:

1. In every imperatively co-ordinated group, the carriers of positive and negative dominance roles determine two quasi-groups with opposite latent interests. We call them "quasi-groups" because we have to do here with mere aggregates, not organized units; we speak of "latent interests," because the opposition of outlook need not be conscious on this level; it may exist only in the form of expectations associated with certain positions. The opposition of interests has here a quite formal meaning, namely, the expectation that an interest in the preservation of the status quo is associated with the positive dominance roles and an interest in the change of the status quo is associated with the negative dominance roles.

2. The bearers of positive and negative dominance roles, that is, the members of the opposing quasi-groups, organize themselves into groups with manifest interests, unless certain empirically variable conditions (the condition of organization) intervene. In-

[7] In what follows, I shall designate the roles to which the expectation of the exercise of authority is attached as "positive dominance roles" and, conversely, the roles without authority privileges as "negative dominance roles."

terest groups, in contrast to quasi-groups, are organized entities, such as parties, trade unions; the manifest interests are formulated programs and ideologies.

3. Interest groups which originate in this manner are in constant conflict concerned with the preservation or change in the status quo. The form and the intensity of the conflict are determined by empirically variable conditions (the conditions of conflict).

4. The conflict among interest groups in the sense of this model leads to changes in the structure of the social relations in question through changes in the dominance relations. The kind, the speed, and the depth of this development depend on empirically variable conditions (the conditions of structural change).

The intent of such a model is to delimit a problem area, to identify the factors pertinent to it, to put them into order—that is, to propose fruitful questions—and at the same time to fix precisely their analytical focus. We have delimited our problem area by viewing social conflict as a conflict among groups which emerge from the authority structure of social organizations. We have identified pertinent factors in the conditions of organization, of conflict, and of change. Their order, however, can be expressed on the basis of the model in three functions: interest groups (for example, parties) are a function of conditions of organization if an imperatively co-ordinated group is given; specific forms of conflict (e.g., parliamentary debates) are a function of the conditions of conflict if the interest groups are given; specific forms of change (e.g., revolutions) are a function of the conditions of change if the conflict among interest groups is given. Thus the task of the theory of conflict

turns out to be to identify the three sets of conditions and to determine as sharply as possible their respective weight—ideally, by quantitative measure.[8] The following remarks are hardly more than a tentative indication of the sorts of variables in question.

Empirical Conditions of Social Conflict

As far as the conditions of organization are concerned, three groups of factors come to mind. First, we have certain effective social conditions: for example, the possibility of communication among the members of the quasi-group and a certain method of recruitment into the quasi-groups. Next there are certain political conditions which must be fulfilled if interest groups are to emerge. Here, above all, a guaranty of freedom of coalition is important. Finally, certain technical conditions must be fulfilled: an organization must have material means, a founder, a leader, and an ideology.

Under conditions of conflict, two kinds are immediately conspicuous: the degree of social mobility of individuals (or of families) and the presence of effective mechanisms for regulating social conflicts. If we imagine a continuum of intensity of social conflict among interest groups, ranging from democratic debate to civil war, we may conjecture that the presence or absence of social mobility and of regulating mechanisms has considerable influence on the position of specific given conflicts on this continuum. Here, as with the other conditions, the determination

[8] By this remark is meant (1) a mathematical formulation of the functions, (2) a development of measurement scales for each of the conditions, and (3) the adjustment of the combined scales to groups of conditions.

of the exact weights of the factors is a task of empirical investigation.

Finally, a third group of conditions or variables determines the form and the extent of social structural changes which arise from the conflict of interest groups. Probably a relatively intimate connection exists between the intensity of the conflict and the change, that is, also between the conditions of conflict and of the structural changes. However, additional factors come into play, such as the capacity of the rulers to stay in power and the pressure potential of the dominated interest group. The sociology of revolutions and especially the unwritten sociology of uncompleted revolutions should contribute considerably to making these factors precise.

It need hardly be re-emphasized that these unsystematic observations can, as such, hardly lay a foundation of a theory of conflict. Nevertheless, we put ourselves in a position to ask meaningful questions both on the theoretical level and with respect to empirical problems. Each of the conditions mentioned offers a fruitful object of theoretically oriented investigations. And in the empirical sphere, the systematic association of factors in such an investigation redirects our questions from a haphazard search for *ad hoc* relations in the world of coincidences to a meaningful study of specific interdependencies, whose locus and meaning are fixed by a general perspective. By the nature of the subject, our exposition up to this point had to remain somewhat abstract in form.

In spite of the tentative nature of the above-mentioned frame of reference, it is nevertheless possible to test its resolving power on some empirical problems.

✧✧✧✧✧✧✧✧✧✧✧✧✧✧✧✧✧✧✧✧ ORGANIZATIONAL MANAGEMENT
OF CONFLICT   *James D. Thompson*

THERE are important questions to be raised about organization-wide management of conflict, as distinct from the local settlement of conflict. The purpose of this paper is to add to our understanding of (1) the sources of conflict within organizations, (2) the vulnerabilities of different organizations to conflict, and (3) the devices employed by organizations to control conflict.

Attention will not be confined to devices deliberately employed by administrators to control conflict, but will include patterns that may have been developed for very different purposes. In specific cases they may even have evolved without formal, conscious consideration; they may have been borrowed, unwittingly, from other organizations. Whether organizations employ control mechanisms out of habit, tradition, or design is not an important question here. If planned processes are to be understood, they must first be seen as part of the larger context.

Excerpted from James D. Thompson, "Organizational Management of Conflict," Administrative Science Quarterly, *Vol. 4, No. 4, March 1960, pp. 389-409. Some footnotes omitted. Abridged and used by permission.*

Conflict is identified here simply as *that behavior by organization members which is expended in opposition to other members.*

Sources and Forms of Organizational Conflict

TECHNOLOGY AND ADMINISTRATIVE ALLOCATION

It has long been known that specialization of activity and responsibility in complex organizations is accompanied by questions about the division of rewards and of resources for achieving rewards.

Some standards for equating inducements and contributions arise in every organization to handle problems associated with division of labor and resources, but official standards do not always prevent feelings of relative deprivation,[1] which may, in turn, lead to conflict. Soldiers, for example, may feel that the "top kick" runs the army but that the "shavetail" gets the privileges. Foremen may feel that they keep the company going, although the boss participates in a stock bonus plan. Professors may believe that *they* are the university but that fund-raising officers get the high salaries.

The more complex the division of labor, the more difficult the formulation and application of standards for equating inducements and contributions. Even when organization members accept abstract standards as fair and legitimate, they may complain about their interpretation and application in specific instances. When

organization members compare themselves to other members, to the extent that they believe they contribute more in proportion to their awards, to that degree will they have feelings of deprivation.

A particular technology may set minimum requirements, not only for differentiation but also for communication or interaction between those performing differentiated activities. While differentiation per se may not lead to conflict, interaction of members of different categories makes comparisons likely and may lead to conflict. But while differentiation and interaction are intrinsic to modern technologies, organizations usually have alternatives in assigning specific activities and responsibilities to specific members, and also in dividing inducements. These matters are largely subject to administrative discretion, to be settled by habit, precedent, or deliberate decision. We may therefore refer to conflict based on feelings of relative deprivation as *conflict generated by administrative allocations.*

That alternatives are available within the framework of a given technology is easily illustrated. In industrial circles, the relative merits of functional versus product division for the same kind of work are often debated. In governmental circles, similar debates occur over areal and functional divisions.

Chester I. Barnard has pointed out that specialization may be based on (*a*) the place where work is done; (*b*) the time at which work is done; (*c*) the persons with whom work is done; (*d*) the things upon which work is done; and (*e*) the method or process by which work is done.[2] But it must be empha-

[1] This concept is taken from S. A. Stouffer et al., *The American Soldier* (Princeton, 1949), I. For a more formal analysis of the concept and its utility, see Robert K. Merton and Paul Lazarsfeld, eds., *Continuities in Social Research* (Glencoe, Ill., 1950).

[2] Chester I. Barnard, *The Functions of the Executive* (Cambridge, Mass., 1938), pp. 128–129.

sized that the choice of one criterion for specialization does not necessarily exclude the others; it simply specifies which has priority. The manufacturing firm which organizes along product-division lines, for example, often finds that the geography of its market requires sales staffs and warehousing and delivery systems which cut across and blur product lines. Whatever the form of organization, the differences in the aggregate of activities is probably far less significant than the differences of grouping and hence of interaction required of members.[3]

The systems by which inducements are allocated are also subject to administrative discretion within rather wide limits established by organizational technologies. Hierarchical differentiation is an indispensable feature of organizations containing two or more primary groups, but the number of categories and their pervasiveness are not fixed. The number of ranks in the military organization, for example, has not been constant through even modern history. The military organization also affords a good example of categorization which in the official ideology is all pervasive: officer and enlisted distinctions are to be maintained in every type of relationship.

In addition to hierarchical differentiation, most organizations also categorize their members in other ways to facilitate the distribution of rewards and penalties. The American military system classifies its members as regular, reservist, or National Guard; the Air Force distinguishes rated (qualified to

fly) from nonrated (or ground duty only) personnel. Rewards or penalties are distributed partly on the basis of the member's category.

While categorizations of these types seem indispensable for modern complex organizations, their number and nature are not necessarily fixed, administrators have choices in these matters.

In summary we are saying that technologies require differentiation and interaction, but that organizations have some control over (1) the number of categories and (2) the patterns of interaction among members of different categories. *Hence within limits administrative allocations determine the relative deprivations experienced by organization members, and thereby control potential conflict inherent in modern technologies.*

LABOR FORCE AND LATENT ROLES

In the complex cultures in which formal organizations exist, there is a wide variety of distinctions between categories of persons. Many of these social and cultural distinctions are irrelevant to the official roles and technologies of a particular organization, but they may "spill over" into it. Each individual recruited into an organization brings to it not only the particular skills, beliefs, dispositions, and the like that are appropriate but also talents, beliefs, or attitudes that are irrelevant to the technology. Individuals may distinguish among themselves on a great many criteria, separating old from young, Yankees from rebels, Republicans from Democrats, friendly drinkers from abstainers. Racial and ethnic origins, family lineage, socioeconomic class, and religious beliefs are frequently applied.

---

[3] Despite the fact that these are age-old questions of concern to many organizations on a recurring basis, there have been few objective, empirical investigations of the impact of various organizational forms on organizational behavior.

In the "ideal type" conception of formal organization or bureaucracy the roles associated with such distinctions are usually irrelevant to the purposes and technology of the organization, and thus *remain latent* whenever members are acting on behalf of the organization.[4] We know, however, that empirically these nonorganizational roles of members can become active in organizational contexts. Nepotism, patronage, and favoritism are some examples.

The vulnerability of an organization to conflict based on latent roles depends largely on the composition of that portion of society from which the organization recruits.[5] The more heterogeneous the labor force, the greater the likelihood that members will possess differentiated latent roles as well as skills. The occupational needs of the organization thus place both imperatives and limitations on the types of individuals who can be considered potential members. To the extent that occupational qualifications are associated with particular latent roles, the organization seeking those qualifications must also accept the related latent roles. But the organization retains some discretion in the matter. *To the extent that recruitment and selection procedures limit diversity or maintain it within manageable patterns, the organization can manage the potential conflict in latent role diversity.*[6]

COMPETING PRESSURES AND ORGANIZATIONAL POSTURE

Organizations and their environments are interdependent, and actions by elements of the environment can create dilemmas for the organization. Whether dilemmas are handled by "minimax" methods, hunch, or other means, dissension often occurs among members who feel handicapped in their spheres of operation, and conflict between winning and losing factions may result. Debate over dilemma decisions may be as heated among those lacking power to make such choices as among the decision makers, and the debates may continue long after a commitment is made.

"The environment," of course is a residual term, and it seems useful to restrict our consideration to *task environments.*[7] We are not referring,

---

[4] For a penetrating analysis of latent roles and their impact on organizations, see Alvin W. Gouldner, "Cosmopolitans and Locals: Toward an Analysis of Latent Social Roles—I and II," *Administrative Science Quarterly*, 2 (1957–1958), 281–306 and 444–480.

[5] Diversity of latent roles does not necessarily result in organizational conflict, because such roles may remain latent. The problem, from the standpoint of the organization, is that it is difficult to foresee or prevent the triggering that activates such roles. If latent role differences create a potential for conflict, and if the organization lacks control over that potential, the safest procedure is to eliminate the potential.

[6] In reviewing knowledge of voluntary associations, C. Wayne Gordon and Nicholas Babchuk use the concept "degree of accessibility," or the exclusiveness of membership criteria. See their "A Typology of Voluntary Associations," *American Sociological Review*, 24 (1959), 22–29.

[7] The concept of task environment, defined somewhat differently, is taken from William R. Dill, "Environment as an Influence on Managerial Autonomy," *Administrative Science Quarterly*, 2 (1958), 409–443. There have been few attempts to describe and differentiate environments *from the point of view of an organization.* Economic characterizations of markets (competitive, monopolistically competitive, oligopolistic, etc.) might serve to describe environments for economic organizations just as characteristics of international relationships might serve as a basis for describing the environments of nation states. For a recent suggestive work in the latter category, see Morton

therefore, to the total community or society, but to those parts of it that are not indifferent to the organization. The more heterogeneous the task environment, the more likely is the organization to be caught up in conflicting demands, expectations, or pressures. The extent of differentiation in the task environment may be beyond the control of the organization (although it may have some choice even here), but to the extent that the organization can choose between various *postures* relative to the task environment, it can manage conflict stemming from competing pressures.

The concept of "organizational posture" requires elaboration. We are referring to the *relationship* between an organization and its task environment, not to characteristics of either the organization or the environment per se. Since it is the relationship which is at issue, the organization does not have full discretion over its posture, but it can, by changing its structure, affect the relationship. Hence the management of organizational posture seems to have elements of gamesmanship, and game theory might be appropriately applied to its analysis.

One important aspect of organization posture is the degree of distinctiveness or eliteness possessed by the organization in relation to the task environment. The organization with a prestigefully unique, unusual, esoteric, or important competence is likely to enjoy appreciation, respect, or awe of the task environment, and thereby have members' identification and loyalty reinforced through interaction with the environment.[8]

Another important aspect of posture is the nature of exposure to the environment.[9] Under some conditions, at least, constant exposure of members tends to erode their identification with the organization. Apparently this is especially true when organization members are regularly in interaction with the same elements of the task environment, and less true when members interact with clients or customers on a one-visit basis.

The proportion of members exposed may vary from organization to organization and also make a difference in the kinds and numbers of problems faced. Where many members are exposed and their loyalties pull in different directions, the problems of maintaining membership identification undoubtedly are different from where conflicting demands and interests are focused on a few central offices and

---

Kaplan, *System and Process in International Politics* (New York, 1957). James Coleman, focusing on controversies in communities, suggests four variations in the social organization of the community: (*a*) variation in member identification with the community, (*b*) density of organizations and associations in the community, (*c*) distribution of participation among citizens, and (*d*) interlocking of organizational memberships. See Coleman, *Community Conflict* (Glencoe, Ill., 1957). Frank A. Pinner, studying high schools in relation to the value structure of the environing community, writes in terms of "degrees of 'looseness' and 'tightness' of a community structure." See Robert K. Merton, *Social Theory and Social Structure* (rev. ed.; Glencoe, Ill., 1957), p. 404, note 13a.

[8] Gordon and Babchuk, *op. cit.*, refer to "status conferring capacity," or the ability of an organization to bestow prestige or to be associated with prestige, which accrues to its members. They suggest that this is associated with the degree of accessibility referred to earlier.

[9] In a study of sect development, Bryan Wilson finds two principal types of mechanisms by which sects govern their own and members' relationships to the external world: isolation and insulation. See his "An Analysis of Sect Development," *American Sociological Review*, 24 (1959), 3–14. It seems probable that distinctiveness is one means of insulation.

are resolved before being translated into programs for the organization at large.

Thus by varying the distinctiveness of the organization, the proportion of members exposed, and the frequency and regularity of their exposure, the organization gains a measure of control over conflict stemming from potential reactions to competing pressures.

We have hypothesized that organizations face three types of potential conflict, that each rests on a different set of conditions, and that for each there is an appropriate defense:

Type of conflict	Source of conflict	Defense device
Administrative allocation	Technology	Organizational structure
Latent roles	Labor force	Recruitment and selection
Competing pressures	Task environment	Organizational posture

<><><><><><><><><><><><><><> AN APPROACH TO PROBLEMS
OF INTERRELIGIOUS CONFLICT

Kenneth D. Benne

W E will discuss here problems that are difficult to discuss—problems of interreligious conflicts. We need to examine these problems dispassionately, yet we know how difficult it is for ourselves and for others to be dispassionate in exploring our religious differences.

This difficulty arises from several sources. And it is well to be aware of these at the start. Religious phenomena deeply involve human passions, human faiths and commitments that go beyond the counsels of reason and common sense. It is not easy for people with differing life-commitments to discuss the bases or the effects of their differences with objectivity.

Another reason it is hard to be disinterested in examining problems of interreligious conflicts is the relative lack of social research on these problems. We cannot refer our differences

to any sizeable body of rationally and empirically tested research results and theories that we all accept as valid so far as they have gone. We are more fortunate, though far from blessed, in the related areas of interracial and interethnic tensions. Whatever the reasons for this lack, it is probably true that the long-range attainment of greater objectivity in discussions of religious affairs depends on the extension of research efforts into their careful study. Perhaps one of the most desirable effects of such discussions is to clear the way for the development of required research efforts. Certainly discussions are no substitute for research but they may be a stimulus to developing it.

Another reason for the difficulty of our discussion is that objective analyses of interreligious conflicts are so in-

From the unpublished manuscript of a speech delivered at the National Association of Intergroup Relations Officials, Boston, Mass., November 17, 1954. Used by permission.

frequent in the nonscientific as well as the scientific community. No neutral laymen's language for analysis exists. Perhaps we can make some headway in developing such a language here. I have taken quite seriously the general title of our commission—"nature, theory, and scope —in what I am to say. I am attempting a diagnosis, not prescribing a treatment, in my remarks, though implications for treatment are not, I hope, absent from my diagnostic statements.

Yet, remembering the difficulty in what we are doing, we should also remember its importance and its urgency. Put positively first, the threat to religious freedom from totalitarian tendencies in modern experience, whether they stem from political left or right, is no merely academic threat. The collaboration of religious bodies and religious people is, most of us feel, essential in maintaining and extending the conditions of effective, genuine, and meaningful freedom in which the appeal of totalitarianisms is reduced to a minimum. Yet, blocking the path toward such collaboration, are various interreligious tensions and conflicts.

Or take the negative side of the urgency of our problem. We do not have to go back to the religious wars of the sixteenth and seventeenth centuries in Europe to find examples of the self-righteous horror of violent religious conflict. We can remember the Ku Klux Klan in our recent American history and remember further that the Klan mentality is by no means dead today. In our own lifetime, Hitler's anti-Semitism mounted to a ghastly crescendo that can hardly be matched in previous interreligious conflict (I say interreligious here advisedly). And we know when we are being honest that anti-Semitism runs widely and

deeply just below the surface of American life. We know how we divide politically along religious lines, Catholic vs. non-Catholic, on issues such as public education and planned parenthood. And we know how hard it is to get reason into our deliberations about such issues. The problem of interreligious tension is an urgent one, practically and morally, for us. It remains for us to resolve that the very moral urgency of the problem requires us to be as dispassionate as possible in our probing and examination of its roots.

I propose first to summarize, selectively of necessity, a point of view that does rest in part on research knowledge about the character of intergroup conflicts in general. For, whatever else it is, interreligious conflict is a species of intergroup conflict. Valid knowledge about intergroup conflict in general should, therefore, apply to the diagnosis of interreligious conflict. Against this general background, we can then try to discover some of the special features and difficulties in interreligious conflict as such.

Realistic Competition among Groups

I begin with the fact of realistic competition among groups, rather than with the distortions of reality that frequently characterize the attitudes of members of different groups toward one another or the official postures of groups or organizations in their relations to each other. There are certain values in any society that are at any one time "scarce and distributable values." As one group gets these values, others are denied them. The values of wealth, power, prestige, and control of communication channels and processes are examples. Groups do struggle for a larger share of these values and this conflict of interests is realistic, in the sense that disinterested students of their relationship would affirm the discrepancy and conflict of interests.

This is not to deny that there are other cultural values which can be shared without loss to any person or group involved. Philosophers of value speak of health and knowledge as such values and in a sense they are right. The health of any group, far from being diminished by better health in other groups, may actually be enhanced by a wider distribution of the values of health. And so also with the values of knowledge. When it comes to the expenditures of money required for extending health benefits, conflicting attitudes toward a scarce value important in our culture come into play and programs to extend health benefits are caught up in intergroup competition. Similarly, a differential access to knowledge may be a factor in group power, and programs to extend knowledge to certain groups, through expansion of educational opportunities, may become objects of realistic conflict, even though ideally knowledge is a sharable value.

The assertion of the fact of realistic conflict among groups does not deny the possibility of groups settling their conflict of interests by orderly means. The fact that a conflict is realistic, in the sense that it is rooted in a state of affairs that can be empirically studied, actually maximizes the possibility of its rational settlement. And in processes of rational settlement, creative bargaining, which may extend the supply of scarce values, or discover or create new common values, may actually enhance the lives of all parties to the conflict. When groups can together face the realities of their situa-

tion, including their discrepant interests, the possibility and probability of resolution of conflict by rational and orderly means are enhanced, not reduced.

Realistic intergroup conflict can become communal conflict, as some sociologists name it, in the sense just suggested. But it need not be so. Commonly accepted "rules of the game" for settling conflicts may not be available. Or some parties to the conflict may refuse to abide by the accepted "rules of the game." Or effective mechanisms for joint settlement of differences may not be available to the conflicting parties. Under the stress of tension, however realistically grounded, conflict may become noncommunal and disruptive of the values and interests of people and groups not directly involved in the conflict and prejudicial to the long-range interests of the direct parties to the conflict as well. Conflict can be destructive if it cannot be socially controlled and channeled.

I have stressed the fact of realistic intergroup conflict and its potentially benign character for two reasons. The first is that those of us engaged in intergroup work sometimes recoil from conflict as such. We seem to aim, however unrealistically, toward the elimination of intergroup conflict, rather than toward a realistic facing of conflict and the invention of effective ways by which such conflict may be channeled into common benefit. Actually, American society places a strong stress upon competition for distributive values as a measure of success. Striving for success is so emphasized in our reward system that it becomes almost an obligatory demand upon group as well as individual behavior. Similarly, American society has developed a smaller core of shared, nondivisible values, than have most more stable and homogeneous societies. We individually may prefer more emphasis upon group and individual motivation in terms of the pursuit of shared and nondivisible values. But, realistically, we must accept the depth of the alternative system of motivation in American culture, whether we are finally to accept it or attempt to change it. Meanwhile, the fact of intergroup competition is a fact and an honored fact as well within our system of social rewards.

My second reason for stressing "realistic" intergroup conflict is due to what I consider a recent overstress upon irrational motivations and processes within intergroup life. "Irrational" factors, as I understood the term, refer to mechanisms, forces, influences that distort reality, that inhibit a group from facing and exploring the realities of its situation, including its interests in that situation and the similar and discrepant interests of other groups in the same situation. Certainly, we cannot deny the generation and operation of "irrational" factors in intergroup tension and conflict or the importance of understanding these. But the measure of the "irrational," as well as the goal of its treatment, as I see it, is some ideal and practice of rationality. We need the concept of realistic conflict amenable to rational resolution as a tool for delimiting the irrational elements of conflict, whether our goal is just to understand or to change these.

Irrational Factors in Intergroup Conflict

I will outline one among several approaches to the explanation of distortions of reality as they occur in conflict situations. A number of recent studies of human motivation and behavior have rightly emphasized the presence in all individuals reared in human society—and that is all of us—of hostility toward other individuals and/or social groups. The amount as well as the manifestations of hostility vary widely from person to person, from group to group, and from social system to social system, as well as from time to time in each of these.

Hostility is related to the frustration of important drives. It is realistically channeled when it is directed against the correctly determined source of the frustration. But there are forces which operate at times to keep hostility from being directed against the actual source. The source of frustration may be hard to define and locate. Take the case of an economic depression that depletes one's pocketbook, threatens and takes one's job. Even economists disagree as to the causes of an economic depression, though they would probably agree that the causes are rooted more in impersonal conditions than in the decisions and the behavior of one or more persons or groups. In the midst of this uncertainty it is not surprising that the man on the street should project his hostility on some persons or groups thought, however wrongly, to be responsible for the frustrating depression—Wall Street, perhaps the Jews on Wall Street, that man in the White House, the Communists, or what not. There are two factors intertwined here in explaining the deflection of hostility—one is a lack of knowledge of the source of frustration, another is a habit of mind that looks for *persons* to blame, rather than for many factors, personal or impersonal, in responding to a frustrating event.

There are other factors that operate to deflect hostility from the realistic source of frustration, as we all know. The source of the frustration may be too powerful to attack—we may deflect our hostility into conflict with a weaker or more vulnerable opponent. The frustrated person may also be morally inhibited from finding fault in, from being hostile or aggressive toward, the actual source of his frustrations. The older child may be inhibited from becoming consciously angry with a new baby in the family who is frustrating him in countless ways, forcing him to change his normal expectations with respect to his parents' behavior toward him, by the moral admonition, which he accepts, to love and be nice to his little brother or sister. He may channel his hostility in many off-target ways.

Because deflected hostility is not realistic with respect to its object as source and cause of the frustrations underlying the hostility it cannot easily be corrected by facts about the object or the situation. The hostility generates its own "facts," selecting, distorting, rationalizing the situation in which life for both hostile agent and object of hostility must go on. In some such way, prejudices that are at least in part rationally and empirically groundless are generated and sustained among men.

So far we have not hooked up the phenomenon of deflected hostility directly to the group and intergroup setting. This is not difficult to do, in a general way at least. The fact of membership in groups is a basic fact within the life and the security system of each of us. Our way of life is learned basically in the family group in which at first our membership is total and unitary. And independence from the family as one grows up means not grouplessness but a multiplication of new group memberships, more or less closely related to the different functions of our lives. In each group to which we belong and to which we are loyal, there is an obligation thrust upon us as a condition of membership to repress in some degree our hostilities toward fellow members. In such groups, hostilities, those pointed both within the group and within the social environment of the group, cannot easily, without guilt, be channeled toward other members of our group, even though realistically they should be channeled there. Hostilities tend to be directed outside our in-groups toward other groups and members of other groups.

In most areas of realistic competition for scarce and distributable values, where social categorization of groups exists in the situation, there will be some distortions of reality along group lines. Most intergroup conflicts, therefore, present a mixture of realistic and unrealistic perceptions and explanations of the conflict and of its possible resolution. Where lack of interaction and communication have led to discrepant and confused definitions of the situation on the part of each party to the conflict, where each feels morally justified in its demands and expectations, where there are no acceptable common rules of the game to guide personal and official contact and interaction between the groups, a condition of noncommunal conflict, with strong probability of violence of various sorts, is most likely.

There are three general strategies for handling intergroup conflicts. They are not stated here in order to evaluate them carefully—complete evaluation of them is not possible apart from a diagnosis of the concrete situation in which some strategy is to be applied. They are reviewed here, rather, in order to clarify further the relations between realistic and unrealistic conflict. One strategy is to find more or less harmless channels in which groups and members of groups may channel their hostilities—games, drama, art, fulminations against a common enemy or impersonal condition, and so on. Another strategy is to build up strong sanctions, legal and moral, against certain ways of expressing intergroup conflict. This does not of itself reduce the underlying conflicts and under some conditions may intensify them. A third strategy is to find ways of reducing the distortions of reality in the conflict situation, of helping groups or group members to face the realistic conflicts among them and, through communication, mediation, and deliberation, to reduce discrepancies in interest or to compromise them. It seems to me that, whenever the third strategy is possible, it offers the greatest long-range promise of social good. And I am writing on this assumption in the rest of this paper.

On the basis of what we have already said, we may expect to find both opposition and help in reducing unrealistic intergroup hostilities and in defining accurately the realistic bases of conflict and causes of frustration in three sources—within the internal organization of the groups, within the situation between the groups, and within the larger cultural situation in which both groups operate. These cannot be spelled out fully here. But perhaps each kind of barrier and support can be illustrated briefly before we apply our general analysis of intergroup conflict to interreligious competitions and conflicts.

The more strongly a group inhibits its members from expressing and consciously feeling hostility and aggression against other members of the group, the more need there will be to deflect hostilities generated within the group to outside targets and so to distort perceptions of the reality both of the situation within the group and the situation outside. The inhibitions are perhaps most productive of such channeling of hostility when they are built into the persons of the members as moral demands, when the assumption is that our group is good, beyond criticism and that evidence of lack of appreciation for our group, its officials, its ways of working is an occasion for guilt, is evidence of subversion and disloyalty. When members of a group are permitted and encouraged to recognize frustrations arising from their life within the group, to explore these, to work them through deliberately, the need for deflection of hostility unrealistically to outside groups and persons is reduced.

The intergroup situation may inhibit public recognition and admission of realistic intergroup competition and conflict or it may not provide commonly accepted methods for reconciling conflicts as they are recognized and faced. Sometimes in American middle-class communities there are strong taboos against open admission of conflicting interests. It is considered inappropriate to admit and discuss conflicts in interest, however realistic these may be. We are enjoined not to knock but to boost. Under the veneer of politeness and the boosting spirit, of course, actual conflicts fester and sometimes intensify. Mutual correction of distorted perceptions, group to group, can hardly thrive in this atmosphere.

Even where discrepant and conflicting interests are recognized and admitted, mechanisms for constructive mediation and reconciliation of these interests may not be available. Or mechanisms may be available which do not command the trust of all parties to a conflict.

The larger cultural situation may present complications in the efforts of groups to face and deal with their conflicts realistically. For example, social change is an ever-present fact in modern American culture. Old balances of interest and power are broken down, normal expectations, group to group, are violated. Old hierarchies are challenged. No group quite seems to know its place in the scheme of things and the traditional answers no longer satisfy. Intergroup hostility and conflict are almost certain to be enhanced in a changing society unless the fact of change is accepted and unless the anticipation of and foresight into needed adjustments appear on the agenda of every group and organization. Such a planful and scientific approach to change is far from uniform within contemporary American culture.

A Look at the Sociology of Religion

Before identifying some of the special features of interreligious conflict, a look at the sociology and social psychology of religious groups is needed. This must necessarily be brief and oversimplified. An important hold of religious groups upon their members arises from the fundamental character of the problems that religion helps people to meet. The religious problems are basic problems of human existence. Moreover, they are problems where solutions go beyond the common-sense ways by which a culture group meets its everyday problems of living. Such a problem is the problem of premature death. It does not make

sense in terms of common-sense knowledge. It cannot be handled by common-sense techniques. Each religious group offers a rationale to its members to face both the prospect of such untoward and shocking events and the restrospect for those who continue to live after death has struck. Such events are not limited to the fact of premature death. The important point here is that religious groups have traditionally supplied their members with ways of adjusting meaningfully to such events.

The help of a religious group is thus most relevant to members at points of maximum strain and tension in human experience. In the face of such strain and tension, when frustration is deepest, they help their members to affirm their faith in themselves, in others, in the universe. Such affirmation of faith necessarily goes beyond the common sense of a culture group and its experience, since, by definition, the resources of common sense are inadequate to make sense of the events with which religion is most basically concerned. There must be a transcendence of common sense within the cultus of every religion. Moreover, to be effective with its members, a religious group must tap deep levels of emotional contentment as well as intellectual levels of conscious belief.

In fulfilling its functions, each religious body develops the following resources, in some degree, and in one form or another:

a. A set of beliefs, more or less integrated, about sacred, often supernatural, objects.

b. A system of symbols, acts, objects, and persons, that express emotional states relevant to the religious sphere of life.

c. A set of prescribed and obligatory activities—rituals—related to the major turning points and crises in human life.

d. Some sense of constituting with others of like devotions and commitments a moral community.

e. Some sense of relationship between religious beliefs and practices and the moral values that govern the nonreligious activities of life.

f. Some form of social organization and some working relationships with other associations in which members live out their lives: families, schools, economic systems, and governments.

Here, all too badly put, is some indication of the depth of hold of religious organizations upon the lives of their members, as well as of the complexity of religious claims and organization.

We need to remember one other fact about religious experience in America pertinent to our concern of this afternoon. This is our variety and multiplicity of religious organizations. Each makes claims, at least for its members, of some special way of defining the bases of moral conduct. Each demands the central loyalty and devotion of its members to the special faith and way of life for which it stands. Common elements there are no doubt and these are perhaps too easily forgotten in the presence of conflict. But it is the special character of each religious claim that is most pertinent to the problems of interreligious conflict.

Realistic Competition among Religious Groups

In this context, conflict among religious organizations is inescapable. Their interests do differ. And these interests do lead to conflict when they are projected beyond the area of strictly intragroup concerns, such as affairs of worship. It is no reasonable counsel to say that religious organizations should confine themselves merely to matters of intragroup concern and so avoid conflict with other religious bodies. In the first place, they are social organizations. They must survive within a context of other social organizations, religious and secular. They must compete for economic support against the demands of other associations. They must compete for prestige and power in our kind of society where the hold of any association upon its members depends in part upon its success in the struggle for power and prestige.

Moreover, religious organizations are drawn into competition as they seek to control the extrareligious activities of their members in conformity to their favored scheme of morality. They cannot be indifferent to the mores and practices of the surrounding society or the conflicting influences of other religious bodies upon these mores and practices. Their moral concerns lead religious bodies inescapably into politics where they see their moral concerns involved in the settlement of public issues—issues of war and peace, economic justice, planned parenthood, education, health, rights of minorities, and so forth. No, interreligious conflict is inescapable in American life—and in world life today. It is not alone inaccurate to deny these conflicts. A failure to face these conflicts is to delay whatever constructive resolution is possible.

It is in interreligious conflicts that the distinction between realistic and nonrealistic conflict is perhaps most needed. If our greatest hope of rational resolution of intergroup conflict is for parties to the conflict to correct the distortions of group motives and characters and to face the realistic discrepancies of interest, we must ask, why is this particularly difficult in inter-religious affairs?

Irrational Factors in Inter-religious Conflict

We must look, as we have noted, for peculiar barriers to facing the realistic bases of conflict in three sources—in the internal organization of religious bodies, in the intergroup situation between religious organizations, and in the relations of organized religions to the wider cultural situation. I suspect that religious bodies tend to repress the hostility of members toward their religious organizations more than do most secular groups. I suspect this is true because the religious organization is considered more or less sacrosanct by its members and leaders, the bearer and conveyor of sacred beliefs and rituals. To feel hostile toward other members of the moral community of the church or temple, to feel critical toward his religious organization as the source of his frustration, is to create guilt in the member threatened by these feelings. Deflected hostility toward persons and groups outside the in-group is increased where such repression of hostile feeling within the group prevails.

Perhaps, paradoxically, the very high ideals of the brotherhood of man which all major religions teach, get in the way of realistic facing of the frustration and conflict within the church organization and membership. Church and temple members and officials, believing strongly in their ideals of brotherhood, may cultivate the moralistic atmosphere in their religious organizations described by one of the once popular textbook poetesses, the Carey sisters: "Little birds in their nest agree and tis a shameful sight / When children

of one family fall out and chide and fight." Yet if people are ashamed and guilty about facing their hostile feelings toward members of their religious family and working these through, these feelings are likely to be deflected toward members of other competing religious families and toward these other families themselves. Meanwhile, the sources of frustration in the religious organization—and these are present in every organization of people—are not cleared up. The best service to our ideals is not to confuse them with the actualities of our relationships. Ideals can distort reality if men forget that their ideals are ideals and not descriptions of empirical reality.

One fruitful focus of inquiry in the area of interreligious conflicts might well be studies of the relationship between the religious prejudices of members and the freedom of members to face, express, and channel hostility toward other members and officials of the religious organization. Certainly, inquiry is needed. If I am right in my guesses, one constructive way of coming better to face the realistic bases of interreligious conflict is to modify the internal atmosphere of religious organizations. This will probably mean more than internal democratization of relationships, though this might help where it is lacking. It will probably mean also finding ways of removing repressions of realistic hostility among members and officials of religious bodies. Mental hygiene, like charity, may well begin at home.

When we look closely at the *intergroup* situation between religious bodies in America, we will probably find a general lack of opportunities for the close communication and deliberation between members and representatives of religious organizations which the accurate delineation of realistic conflicts requires. When different groups perceive their joint situation in widely discrepant ways, when they have no common agreement as to the appropriate behavior of parties to a conflict one to another, usually only sustained group deliberation in a spirit of inquiry can attain a common perception and commonly acceptable procedures. Opportunities for such communication among religious bodies are hard to create. Because their basic premises on matters of ultimate concern do differ, discussion of immediate and proximate differences is frequently prejudged to be fruitless. In many interfaith gatherings, conflicts are carefully avoided. Secular differences in interest which can be compromised, if not resolved, by rational-empirical means are all too seldom faced. By definition, differences in ultimate faith cannot be settled by rational-empirical means. When these are kept at the forefront, where those discussing are not properly equipped philosophically, the chances for fruitful sorting out of realistic from nonrealistic conflicts are reduced.

American secular society has established many mechanisms for settling realistic conflicts among groups of people. And the invention and testing of new means to meet new kinds of conflict are continually in process. Labor-management mediation, town meetings, joint boards, interracial committees, planning councils, and conferences are examples of these. Many of these operate with governmental sanction and participation. Perhaps the separation of religious bodies from government in America has operated to keep religious organizations from joining in the process of inventing commonly acceptable means and mecha-

nisms of mediation and collaboration. Of course, it was in part the prejudgment of interreligious conflicts as inherently divisive and unresolvable that led to the secularization of our political processes in the first place. Perhaps the increased interdependence of all parts of society and recognition of the painful effects of persistent interreligious conflicts upon religion generally in an industrial secularized society will change the picture. Recognition of these effects may operate as a force toward experimentation by religious bodies in search for commonly acceptable mechanisms and methods of mediation and collaboration with respect to issues of proximate if not of ultimate religious concern. Certainly my observations and hypotheses about the intergroup situation with respect to religion require careful inquiry and examination. Whether I am right or not in my hypotheses, the inquiry is urgently needed.

Finally, what of the larger cultural situation in which interreligious affairs are set? We have noted that one of the prominent features of this larger situation is the fact of continuous and accelerating change. This very fact of change, I have claimed, accents the tensions and conflicts among groups. What of interreligious tensions in this setting? In their efforts to conserve the essential values of their traditions in the midst of a radically changing environment, religious bodies have often resisted the fact of change. Recognizing correctly that science and invention are major dynamic elements in modern change, religious organizations have not infrequently pitted their truths *against* the truths of science and technology. While the earlier conflicts between "science" and "religion" have been eased or moderated—at least in intellectual circles—I suspect religious bodies have not generally come to see social science and social technology as resources in the better diagnosis and treatment either of their intraorganizational conflicts or of interreligious conflicts. If the human sciences and their applications are indispensable resources in the intelligent management of human relationships and organizations in a changing society, as I believe, then religious organizations, no more than industrial, educational, or governmental organizations, can afford to neglect this resource in the management of their organizational lives. On this line of reasoning, the problems of collaboration between religious leaders and organizations and social scientists become important areas of inquiry and experimentation. Perhaps that suggests the larger significance of our session this afternoon. Certainly it is my faith that collaboration between social scientists and lay and professional leaders of religion in the study of religious conflicts will not only promote the advancement of social science in a better understanding of religious affairs. I believe that it will help also to extend the influence of essential religious values in helping to meet the basic needs of men in a changing and conflict-ridden society.

◇◇◇◇◇◇◇◇◇◇◇◇◇◇◇◇◇◇◇ PSYCHOLOGY AND THE CRISIS OF
STATESMANSHIP [1]   *Robert R. Blake*

Resolution of conflict between groups of people—whether between nations, between management and labor, the departments of a business or university, or between social agencies within a community setting—requires the exercise of statesmanship. Permanent resolutions may be brought about through a realistic approach to the source of conflict. Whatever the circumstances, however, attempts at resolution involve people—people who talk, make judgments, and give commitments, usually under face-to-face conditions. In a word, solutions and resolutions involve psychological aspects. Statesmen are confronted with designing psychological structures that can contribute to the handling of differences. Occasionally statesmen are successful. Too frequently they fail.

Fundamental divisions between groupings of peoples confront us today. They affirm that the problem of statesmanship is crucial. On the international scene there rages a full blown cold war. The first satellite appears in the sky and is described here as a "hunk of iron." Two weeks later the sputnik cocktail is available: one part of vodka and two of sour grape juice. Within social groupings segregation and integration constitute burning issues of the hour. Troops, not statesmanship, prevent the eruption of conflict. On the

[1] Presidential Address, Southwestern Psychological Association, 1958. Appreciation is expressed to Muzafer Sherif and Jane Srygley Mouton for suggestions regarding this manuscript.

From Robert R. Blake, *"Psychology and the Crisis of Statesmanship,"* The American Psychologist, *Vol. 14, 1959, pp. 87–94. Used by permission.*

economic front, a fundamental breach separates labor and management on basic issues regarding the organization of work, even on ways toward bringing an end to the current recession. Bickering among military services goes on unabated. Religious differences split groups and generate the very rivalry and discord the precepts of religion are intended to diminish or obliterate. There seems no end. Some divisions produce constructive competitiveness and are healthy. Many are not. The result is unwanted and unnecessary friction that blocks more basic pursuits.

Secret negotiations in smoke-filled rooms, in palaces or on yachts; slick operators pulling strings and making deals; and blind resistance with bland refusal to examine issues have not served too well in managing or relieving differences between groupings of peoples. Statesmanship in all fields is faltering. Without theory statesmen lack clear-cut guides for planning and action. Yet principles of behavior are involved. Some have been identified through psychological research. The resurgence of statesmanship is contingent on the effective use of such knowledge. My purpose is to examine approaches for resolving differences between groups against the background of psychological theory and research. Research in this area is only in the early stages of development, but it does provide guidelines for clarifying the nature and the scope of the problems and for identifying solutions that may bring permanent reduction in intergroup conflicts.

Approaches to the Management of Intergroup Disputes

When groups stand opposed, four ways of terminating the conflict are possible: (*a*) isolate the groups and eliminate contact between them; (*b*) unite them into one group, even if it means "cracking their heads together"; (*c*) join the contest, let the more powerful annihilate the weaker: "Right will prevail"; and (*d*) maintain the identity of each group and through functional relations seek resolution by interaction, discussion, and decision. Except for rare instances the first three: isolationism, enforced unification, and extinction all contain significant negative components more repugnant than the conflict they seek to relieve. They will not be commented upon further. The fourth way holds genuine promise. It seems so obvious. "When you have a difference, sit down and talk it through. If not that, tell it to a neutral person and let him decide." Yet the path that seeks resolution through interaction, discussion, and decision itself is permeated with subtle difficulties. Here is where true statesmanship enters, for to take cognizance of the psychological characteristics of various approaches is to increase the probability of successful resolution of intergroup conflict.

Resolution of Differences Through Interaction, Discussion and Decision

Six fundamental approaches to the reduction of intergroup tensions through interaction are: negotiations by group members, use of the "good offices" as an intermediary, exchange of persons, handing the conflict to judges, the use of special decision-making panels to plot solutions that involve specific common goals, and intergroup therapy. Each is examined below from the standpoint of research evidence when available and, where not, from the point of view of field experience and logical analysis. The goal is to provide a general orientation to problems of intergroup relations.

NEGOTIATIONS BY GROUP MEMBERS

Negotiations by representatives. Solutions are sought most commonly through negotiations carried on by representatives, either the leaders themselves or persons specifically designated to negotiate. The United Nations is an example on the international level. Within universities and companies, members of departments are called together as committees where each participant is expected to represent his department in the resolution of matters that affect it. Bargaining teams in labor-management negotiations also are composed in this way. A key for evaluating this approach is found in the fact that the representative is a *member* of the group he represents. He knows the problem from an ingroup point of view.

As background for evaluating the representational approach, consider the following. Two or more groups stand opposed on a critical issue. Each has a preferred solution which its members support. Both solutions are publicly known in advance of negotiations. Representatives meet. Frequently the interaction develops into a win-lose contest, with each representative maintaining his group's position while attempting to provoke the other representative to capitulate. The representative who exerts influence on the opposing representative and in doing so obtains their acceptance of his group's position may be accorded a "hero" reaction within his group for bringing it victory (Blake & Mouton, 1958). On the other hand, the representative who relinquishes his group's position, thus giving victory to the opposition, often is treated as dis-

loyal or as "traitorous" by members of his own group. The representative who wins stands to enjoy increased status within his group, and he senses it. The representative who capitulates loses prestige and is confronted with possible ostracism. He knows that too (Roethlisberger, 1945). It is probable that the more cohesive the group and the more basic the issue in the life of the group, the more the "hero" or "traitor" reaction is magnified, since the hero has supported the group's position and the traitor has deviated from it in a significant manner (Schachter, 1951).

"Deadlock" is one result of the traitor threat. If a representative cannot win, through deadlocking the issue he can avoid losing. Through deadlocking, a traitor reaction can be avoided, but representatives of both sides stand to suffer reduction in membership status relative to the increased power accompanying victory. Another alternative to defeat is "compromise": give as little as possible and get as much, or create the appearance that both sides have yielded some, but with neither suffering defeat. Unfortunately such compromises often may be mechanical and brittle, constituting artificial solutions rather than real resolutions.

When negotiations take a win-lose turn, as they often do if preferred positions constitute public standards announced in advance, then quest for resolution by representatives may be replete with obstacles. The core of the difficulty seems to be that representatives are "committed" people. From the standpoint of their own group membership they are not entirely "free" to act in accord with "fact," or even to engage in compromise, if to do so would be interpreted by group members as "defeat." To a degree the limitations noted here may be reduced when representatives are freed to negotiate without prior instructions. Even then, however, they may be "expected" to act in certain ways even though formal instructions have not been placed on them.

The critical limitation in seeking resolutions through representatives seems to be in the "conflict of interest" aspect. For the representative to suffer defeat may be for him to place his membership status in jeopardy while by gaining victory he may enhance his membership position. In the negotiation situation though, logical considerations may require that the representative renounce his group's prior position in order to gain a valid resolution of the intergroup problem. Where there is conflict of interest, the situation in such that in-group loyalty can overwhelm logic.

Negotiations through Summit Conference. When negotiations by representatives fail, the plea is heard: "If only the *leaders* would get together, that would do more good than any other one step that could be taken." Let us examine this one. It is tricky. On first glance it appears to be a most practical and concrete approach. If leaders cannot agree, who can?

Modern history shows that Summit Conferences on the international scene have resulted in something less than complete success to either side. One has only to recall Yalta, Potsdam, and Geneva within the recent past for examples. White House Conferences on education, social welfare, and so on have fared little better. Repeated parleys by the Joint Chiefs of Staff have not resulted in satisfactory unification of military activity.

Leaders face the inherent limitations of any representative in negotiating. A further consideration in this approach is related to the source from which the leader's power is derived. To the degree he is an autocratic leader, with power to regulate followers through control of their physical, economic, or political systems, he also has power to negotiate and to commit. Why? The logic is that he can go against existing standards and norms within his group, still retain his power, and enforce the changes to which he has committed himself. Not so when leadership power is derived through an elective system. Evidence suggests that under elective conditions the leader may be even *less* free to negotiate than are other group members. It may be that the norms for leadership are more exacting and require greater responsibility than for others within the group (O. J. Harvey, 1953; Whyte, 1943). Then too, Kelley and Volkart (1952) have demonstrated an inverse correlation between evaluation by a person of his membership in a group and his susceptibility to communication on topics opposed to group norms. Also, O. J. Harvey (1952) has shown that middle and lower status group members have higher expectations for leaders than for other members and that the leader shares their expectations for his own performance. A leader, in other words, seems to be more subject to regulation by his own group than other members are. Efforts to change leaders, and other members as well, which would make them deviate from these norms will encounter strong resistances (Cartwright, 1951).

When prevailing leadership has failed to bring about resolution or when it has made no attempt in this direction, according to Pelz (1951) the result may be increased frustration of the group expectations and consequent loss of influence by the leader. Under these conditions the suggestion to "get new leaders" frequently is heard. Leaders do come and go, and often a new leader will try, by traditional means, to accomplish what predecessors have failed to attain. No less frequently does a new leader fail. He stands in the same or a similar relationship to accepted standards and norms within his group as did the old one. The Merei study (1949) suggests his difficulty. Strong leaders were brought into groups whose traditions and standards already had been formed. To exert leadership influence within the group, they had first to *accept* the very positions they sought to change. In other words the "fresh" approach soon dies under the impact of prevailing conditions. The rule seems to be that, rather than "a new broom sweeping clean," the "new look" is rapidly transformed into an old wheeze.

THE USE OF INTERMEDIARIES

An approach in some respects comparable with the use of representatives or with the search for resolution of intergroup conflict through formal leaders involves the intermediary. Intermediaries usually hold membership in neither of the contending groups, but are from an outside organization or a level in an organization higher than the groups which are in conflict. The intermediary is expected to pass between the groups and to aid in the reduction of conflict through identifying areas of agreement, clarifying areas of disagreement, and developing proposals designed to ease tensions which are acceptable to both sides in a controversy. The intermediary, in other words, supplies a critical link of communication. He can pierce the boundaries which otherwise constitute barriers to communication. Usually he acts

without formal authority. His success is based primarily on the goodwill and confidence that his reputation and his status as one who belongs to neither group creates.

The intermediary role needs experimental evaluation before a critical appraisal of its advantages and limitations can be given. History contains examples of conspicuous successes and outstanding failures of this approach. From a logical point of view it does appear, however, to have the advantage of increasing communication between contending groups. It has the further advantage that final responsibility for resolution rests, not on the judgment of the intermediary, but on attitudes within the competing groups themselves. A major limitation is in the fact that many situations of intergroup conflict are such that there is no organization outside or above the groups which are in disagreement which can arrange the appointment and acceptance from both sides of an intermediary.

A further disadvantage is possibly of greater importance. Basic communication between groups is not necessarily improved through actions of an intermediary since arrangements for intergroup communication are likely to remain the same after his departure or as they were before his services were employed. The result in that *conditions* similar to those responsible for the initial eruption of conflict may remain unchanged. In a sense the intermediary role is better suited to the relief of symptoms than to the correction of basic causes.

EXCHANGE OF PERSONS

An approach said to have implications for resolving intergroup differences in the long-term view involves exchange of persons across the boundaries of the competing groups. The idea is that exposure on a people-to-people basis for the purpose of getting to know others, their institutions and cultural products can serve to increase understanding as a background for future cooperation. The appeal is that if people will but look and see with their own eyes they will penetrate their prejudices and stereotypes. Educational exchanges from student activities to the Fulbright fellowship program are examples in the academic field. Examples from business and industry include exchanges of industrial productivity teams between the United States and Europe as well as the pattern in business of rotating personnel from one position to another in the effort to develop managers who have a company orientation rather than a provincial, departmental point of view. There may be other advantages to this approach aside from its contribution to the resolution of intergroup differences, but that is the aspect being considered here.

Findings from a half-dozen experiments involving exchanges between political and racial groupings point to two general conclusions (Ram & Murphy, 1952; Saenger, 1953). One is that people-to-people interaction across groups may serve to make those whose attitudes initially are pro, more pro, and those who initially are anti, more anti. Rather than being subject to fundamental alteration it appears that attitudes and convictions which already are established undergo intensification, though there is some evidence that changes related to the specific conditions of interaction may appear.

A second generalization is based on the observation that social, political, and economic attitudes, rather than being determined solely on an individual personality basis, are significantly anchored in reference groups. If, through an exchange experience, an individual's attitudes shift in a direction away from those formerly held, on return to his group he is subject to confrontation from his peers for expressing attitudes contrary to those accepted by them. The Bennington study (Newcomb, 1943) is an outstanding early example of the extent to which individuals express attitudes which maintain congruency with attitudes anchored in their group memberships. French and Zajonc (1957) have carried the analysis of the problem further, presenting evidence which suggests that when an individual is faced with an intergroup norm conflict the attitudes expressed are those which are most congruent with situational factors. That is to say, an individual who is under exchange of persons conditions and moves from one group to another is more prone to express attitudes consistent with the views of the group in which he is located. Another consideration is that contact between groups does not always lead to a lessening of conflict. A study in the Near East shows that ingroups may be most hostile to those groups with which they come in closest contact (Dodd, 1935).

While exchange programs as approaches for resolving intergroup conflict leave much to be desired, two implications can be drawn. One is that those who initially are neutral are most susceptible to influence. Without preformed attitudes there is a real possibility that the increased exposure provided can result in a more objective appraisal of experiences. It is from an awareness of this consideration that the most intensive efforts by both sides in the cold war are concentrated on the so-called "uncommitted" people. The effort is to move them away from a neutral position on the argument of the "immortality of neutrality."

The other implication is that plans involving the exchanges of *groups* may create a favorable background for future intergroup resolution, where person-to-person programs fail. The reason is that, when individuals undergo new experiences *as a group,* attitudes anchored at the group level may themselves be subject to modification. Refusal by an individual to maintain altered attitudes then constitutes deviation from the group norms with consequent rejection confronting the individual who refuses to change (Schachter, 1951). Thus reinforcement of changed attitudes comes about through group membership.

THE USE OF "JUDGES"

Resolution of differences is sought through judges, persons trained to evaluate materials relevant to the issue under examination. Since judges hold membership in neither of the competing groups, they are not subject to the conflict of interest situation described above; therefore, they can be "fair." The Supreme Court and federal and state legal systems all are based on gaining resolution through the use of judges. Because of the judge's "outside" position, contestants are expected to accept the outcome as an impartial one.

Do they? the answer depends on where you sit. It is likely to be "Yes," if the decision favors your group; "No," if it goes against the position your group embraces. Listen to the following remarks from exploratory studies (J. Harvey, 1957; Human Relations Training Laboratory, 1958). They are

reactions toward "neutral" judges from those defeated by his decision.

The judge is biased, unfair and incompetent . . . he has no grasp of the problem . . . he does not possess the intelligence prerequisite to be fair and unbiased . . . he doesn't seem to know too much about the subject . . . he didn't take enough time.

In other words, when group members are committed to their position and a judge decides against it, either the group is wrong or the judge is wrong. In their initial reactions group members have *little* doubt as to which: it is the judge. Results from several sources suggest that the stronger the commitment of a group to its solution, the more relevant the problem to the life of the group, and the more cohesive the group, the greater the negative reactions to a judge whose decision defeats them. Even though obligated to accept the verdict, attitudes remain more or less consistent with convictions held prior to the rendering of the judgment.

When intergroup competition has been generated for study purposes under laboratory training conditions with resolution of the conflict placed in the hands of a judge, a delayed reaction of considerable importance has been noted among members within some defeated groups (Human Relations Training Laboratory, 1958). Though the initial reaction in the defeated group toward the judge is as noted above, "it's the judge who is at fault," a delayed reaction among some members is, "it's our group which is at fault." Such a reaction seems to arise among the members who were the least committed to the group's position before the issue was submitted. Rather than venting their frustrations from defeat on the judge, they discharge it by aggressive attacks on other group members. A consequence is that the group tends to "splinter," to lose its former degree of cohesion and to disrupt.

When the judge renders a verdict favoring a group's position, two things are evident. The judge is experienced as being fair and unbiased all right, because the judgment he proclaims "only proves that we were right in the first place." He is experienced as being a *good* judge because he sees the situation as members themselves see it. "If there was any doubt in our minds before, his ruling eliminated it. Now we know we're right." Resolutions thus attained may have administrative consequences, particularly if the judge's decision is reinforced by sanctions. To those who lose, the resolution retains an arbitrary, mechanical quality. Losers comply because the ground rules require it, but they remain unconvinced.

By comparison with a representative or a leader a judge is not gripped in the vise of a conflict of interest situation. Yet the judge is as suspect by those whose position he defeats as is the representative who goes against his group. The inherent difficulty is that the judge's decision may carry little force in comparison with the strength of the group's commitment to its position. The defeated frequently are not moved to alter their position.

COMMON GOALS WITH CRISSCROSS PANELS

A situation favoring resolution is present when both of the opposing sides are confronted with a common goal which can only be reached through interdependent effort. This set of circumstances has confronted social agencies in raising operating budgets.

Competing with one another was found to be less than successful; but, when agencies came together and agreed on a superordinate goal which could only be reached through joint effort, greater success was achieved. Each group maintained its identity, and yet through embracing a common goal the area of conflict was eliminated and one of cooperation was created. Another example of a new grouping designed to achieve a common goal is the proposed single agency to take the place of competing individual services in the development and coordination of approaches to outer space. Control of military uses of atomic energy and programs for world reduction of arms constitute goals at the international level which have been dreamt about but not yet realized. Companies that have introduced cost concern programs on a common goal basis have found this approach quite successful (Hood, 1957). Only recently, however, has experimental work been oriented toward a more systematic assessment of the approach.

In three highly ingenious studies Sherif, who originally formulated the problem discussed here, has explored a variety of ways of relieving differences between contending groups (Sherif, 1958; Sherif & Sherif: 1953, 1956). Groups were placed in competition on a win-lose basis. Unsuccessful in relieving the tensions thus produced were contacts between members, contacts between leaders, and preaching and coercion. More fruitful was the solution of competing groups joining together in order to defeat a third, outside group, but in this way the arena of conflict was widened. The most appropriate way found was that of confronting contending groups with a common problem which could be resolved only through their joint efforts. Once a superordinate goal was accepted as a challenge by high status members of both sides then mutual efforts by individuals, with less regard for primary group affiliations, became more common. Contending groups started to pull together, and contacts between members turned to positive purposes instead of serving as occasions for accusations and mutual irritations.

Several conditions are necessary for employing the superordinate goal approach. Both sides must *desire* a genuine solution, and the mere presence of friction is not by any means indicative that they do. The absence of such requisite problem-solving motivation precludes the success of any approach. In addition there is a need for a single definition of the problem developed by both sides without a prior statement of preferred solutions. This way avoids commitments which are prone to become irreversible when one side appears to be losing, and strategies for dealing with the "loss of face" problem become unnecessary. Fundamental conditions for successful resolution are present when both of these considerations have been met.

A limitation in employing the superordinate goal approach is in the fact that all members of competing groups rarely are able to combine efforts toward attaining superordinate goals. There is need of a way for representatives to interact toward the attainment of superordinate goals which can provide freedom of action without the status reduction that occurs with going against one's own group's position.

There is a possibility which avoids difficulties encountered by other methods. Each side develops a list of nominees whom they consider qualified to represent them with respect to one particular source of friction. Next, from the list of nominees, members of both groups elect a decision-making panel through voting on representatives from *both* sides. The final panel contains members who represent their own group and yet who simultaneously represent the other group as well.

By the conditions of their selection, being jointly elected, representatives are more free to confront the problem, without facing the hero-traitor dynamic that arises from the usual unilateral group orientation. Why? The reason is that group members from both sides experience such representatives as oriented toward a "fair" solution. Even when they go against a prevailing standard of their group the action is experienced as more "legitimate" than when they do so as unilateral representatives. Furthermore, representatives themselves are motivated to examine issues from the frames of reference of both groups, rather than from that of their own group alone.

The crisscross panel is a way of approaching the resolution of intergroup disputes that is currently under experimental evaluation. The procedure constitutes but an extension of democratic methods to the solution of problems. Even now a modification of it is employed to settle labor-management disputes which have gone into deadlock. The method provides the possibility of progress toward reduction of intergroup conflict, whether the point of application involves disputes between nations, labor-management, government agencies, departments of a company organization, or between social agencies within a community.

INTERGROUP THERAPY

A final possibility remains when other approaches fail. It is based on therapeutic conceptions that deal with problems of relationship. The *unit* of therapy, rather than being focused on the individual, the interpersonal level, or the group, is comprised of competing groups *in relationship* with one another. The rationale is that groups may hold perceptions and stereotypes of one another which are distorted, negative, or so hidden that they prevent functional relationships from arising between them. Only *after* basic problems of relationship have been eliminated is effective interaction possible. If the contending groups are so large as to eliminate the possibility of interchange among all members simultaneously, segments of groups may be employed, with the procedure repeated until fundamental sources of intergroup animosity have been neutralized.

One procedure of intergroup therapy is to bring contending groups together as *groups*. In private each discusses and seeks to agree on its perception and attitudes toward the other and its perceptions of itself as well. Then *representatives* of both groups talk together in the presence of other group members from both sides who are obligated to remain silent. During this phase representatives are responsible for accurate communication of the picture that each group has constructed of the other and of itself. They are free to ask questions for clarification of the other group's point of view, but ground rules prevent them from giving rationalizations, justifications, etc. The reason for using representatives is that communication remains more orderly and responsibility is increased for them to provide an accurate version of the situation. Members of both groups then discuss *in private* the way they are perceived by each other in order to develop understanding of the discrepancies between their own view of themselves and the

description of them by the other side. Finally, again working through representatives, each helps the other to appreciate bases of differences, to correct *invalid* perceptions, and to consider alternative explanations of past behavior. Fundamental value conflicts not based on distortions also can be identified and examined, then suggestions can be developed for ways of working on problems which can result in solutions apart from basic value conflicts.

Intergroup therapy is relatively unexplored, although it has been tried with success in industrial settings on several occasions. Many problems, themselves subject to solution through the superordinate goal approach, cannot even be faced until deeper animosities *between* groups have been resolved or at least explored and neutralized. If emotion-laden negative attitudes and stereotypes are dealt with first, it becomes increasingly possible in a second phase to formulate and work toward the attainment of superordinate goals as described above.

Now to return to my thesis. Statesmanship is faltering. Many problems of tremendous import continue to be handled by statesmen on an intuitive basis—a paradox in a world where scientific method has advanced understanding so far. Approaches frequently are used which fail to recognize the psychological characteristics of people and the dilemmas confronting them when engaging in discussion intended to resolve intergroup disputes. What are some of the psychological characteristics of people that must be considered?

Take, for example, the situation of a typical representative. In negotiation he is faced with a fundamental conflict of interest. Stephen Decatur in 1816 said: "Our country! In her intercourse with foreign nations, may she always be in the right; but our country, right or wrong!" In this remark he was identifying the dilemma facing all representatives of groups which are in competition, whether leaders or other members. If to yield or to compromise means defeat, it exposes the responsible person to rejection and ostracism by his peers. To resist and gain victory can lead to his acclamation as a hero. The consequence is that representatives are motivated to win, or at least to avoid defeat, even though a realistic solution of an intergroup problem may be sacrificed in the process. An intermediary who holds membership in neither group may be employed to develop solutions acceptable to both groups. This approach, which has some positive merits, when it is possible to appoint an intermediary from some outside group may be successful in resolving a specific problem, but is likely to do little to effect resolution of basic cleavages between groups since lines of communication supplied by the action of this intermediary are likely to be eliminated after his departure.

Resolution of conflict through the action of judges also suffers a critical limitation. Rendering a judgment which defeats a side does not convince the vanquished protagonists of the error of their ways. Further, the force to implement the verdict is not within the group, but must be added from the outside. Neither understanding, nor acceptance, nor commitment, but coercion is likely to be the force which prevents the extension of conflict. The limitations of this procedure frequently outweigh its possible merits for the simple reason that punitive action, or the threat of it, is basic to enforcement.

There is another way which seems more constructive. Acting with respect to common goals, representatives can be selected through a crisscross election method in such a way as to free them to confront the problem more squarely, rather than trying to "win" from a partisan point of view. When this is done, subscribing to the outcome is an obligation within *both* groups. It can occur through acceptance and commitment, without coercion. Concrete application should begin with problems of lesser significance at low levels in order to permit an assessment of the method and the development of skill in using it in specific situations. Then, with success, the procedure can be applied to more important problems at higher levels until issues of substance and significance are being dealt with in a constructive manner.

When an approach to resolution of intergroup problems through superordinate goals cannot be made because of negative, emotionally saturated perceptions, attitudes and stereotypes, a possibility of solution still remains. Through insertion of a preliminary phase involving the concepts of intergroup therapy, conditions favoring problem-solving may be created. If the approach "unblocks" intergroup relationships, then the actions required by superordinate goal considerations can be introduced.

Theory of behavior relating to individuals in group situations and relations between groups is basic to the enlightened practice of statesmanship. It provides guidelines for planning and action. The outcome of the crisis of our times may well rest on whether or not statesmen can design situations for the resolution of intergroup disputes which are sound. Introduction of a psychological point of view may constitute a condition for survival.

References

BLAKE, R. R., & MOUTON, JANE S. "Heroes and traitors: Two patterns of representing groups in a competitive situation." *Int. J. Sociometry*, 1958.

CARTWRIGHT, D. "Achieving change in people: Some applications of group dynamics theory." *Hum. Relat.*, 1951, 4, 381–392.

DODD, S. C. "A social distance test in the near east." *Amer. J. Sociol.*, 1935, 41, 194–204.

FRENCH, J. R. P., JR., & ZAJONC, R. B. "An experimental study of cross-cultural norm conflict." *J. abnorm. soc. Psychol.*, 1957, 54, 218–224.

HARVEY, J. "Subjective reactions to a judge as a function of his verdict." Unpublished manuscript, University of Texas, 1957.

HARVEY, O. J. "Status relations and expectations in informal groups." Unpublished manuscript, University of Oklahoma, 1952.

HARVEY, O. J. "An experimental approach to the study of status relations in informal groups." *Amer. sociol. Rev.*, 1953, 18, 357–367.

HOOD, R. *Concern for costs.* Ann Arbor: Survey Research Center, Univer. Michigan, 1957.

Human Relations Training Laboratory. *Proceedings.* Taos, New Mexico: Human Relations Training Laboratory, 1958.

KELLEY, H. H., & VOLKART, E. H. "The resistance to change of group-anchored attitudes." *Amer. sociol. Rev.*, 1952, 17, 453–465.

MEREI, F. "Group leadership and institutionalization." *Hum. Relat.*, 1949, 2, 23–39.

NEWCOMB, T. M. *Personality and social change.* New York: Holt, Rinehart and Winston, 1943.

PELZ, D. C. "Leadership within a hierarchical organization." *J. soc. Issues*, 1951, 7, 49–55.

RAM, P., & MURPHY, G. C. "Recent investigations of Hindu-Muslim relations in India." *Hum. Organization*, 1952, 11, 13–16.

ROETHLISBERGER, F. J. "The foreman: Master and victim of double talk." *Harvard bus. Rev.*, 1945, 23, 283–298.

SAENGER, G. *The social psychology of prejudice.* New York: Harper, 1953.

SCHACHTER, S. "Deviation, rejection, and communication." *J. abnorm. soc. Psychol.*, 1951, 46, 190–207.

SHERIF, M. "Reduction of intergroup conflict." *Amer. J. Sociol.*, 1958, 53, 349–356.

SHERIF, M., & SHERIF, CAROLYN W. *Groups in harmony and tension.* New York: Harper, 1953.

SHERIF, M., & SHERIF, CAROLYN W. *An outline of social psychology.* (2d ed.) New York: Harper, 1956.

WHYTE, W. F. *Street corner society.* Chicago: Univ. Chicago Press, 1943.

PART THREE

Dynamics of the Influence Process

"**S**i: But I would like to know, first of all, why you think individuality is declining in America. What do you think, Dy?

"Dy: Declining because David Riesman says so. The killers of individuality have already been convicted. They have made *Time, Life,* and *Fortune.* Do you want the textbook inventory? Urbanization, mechanization, structuralization, bureaucratization, departmentalization, specialization, system . . ."

Henry Murray [1]

Influence processes are active in every style of interpersonal and organizational existence. Our own society appears to be particularly preoccupied with the nuances and consequences of influence. The national argot reflects this. We have "influence men" and a magazine for "Influentials"; hidden persuaders and lobbyists; influence games and the "softsell"; power elites, "sincere" ties, payola, conformity, opinion-leaders, and pressure groups. And, in addition to these verbal images, everyday influence includes the positive function of education and psychotherapy, forms of friendship, and relationships in bureaucracies, in marriage,

[1] Henry Murray, "Individuality: The Meaning and Content of Individuality in Contemporary America," *Daedalus, 87:*25–47, 1958.

479

and in international affairs. Part III attempts to capture some of the theoretical and practical significance of the influence process for the study of human change.

In Part I we attempted to provide an historical backdrop, a prolegomenon to the concept of planned change. We are now ready to plunge headlong into one of the key dimensions of planned change (or, for that matter, of any of the changes explicated in Bennis' typology in Part I), *the influence process*. We simply assume that if planned change is to take place some influences have to occur, and accordingly we are interested in the vicissitudes and complexities of the processes of influence.[2]

This overarching concept escapes any precise or all-inclusive definition. However, in a general way we say that it implies a relationship between persons or groups where one or the other party (or both) utilize some form of interpersonal (or intersystem) operation to induce the other to do, or feel, or think that which the influencer believes is desirable. The clumsiness of this initial definition is only partly a syntactical problem. The fact is that only such a general and elusive statement can possibly embrace the variegated forms of the influence process.

For example: The teacher instructing students in French; the tennis coach demonstrating a proper lob; the "con man" setting up his mark as well as "cooling him out"; the editor helping the author; the psychiatrist interpreting to the patient; Henry Higgins correcting Eliza's cockney "oh"; Iago hinting to Othello of Desdemona's "infidelity"; the political candidate reviewing his qualifications to a TV audience; the applicant at the job interview; the interviewer at the job interview; the boy 'phoning a girl for a date; the boss issuing an order; the father coaxing his son to play the trumpet for friends; the staff man "selling" the line on a course of action; the "gamesman" outwitting his opponent at a cocktail party. These are all examples of the influence process. In fact, it is hard to imagine any event in the social relations of everyday lfe untinctured by the elements of social influence.

In the next two chapters material on the influence process will be presented primarily as the backdrop for Part IV, which deals centrally with planned change.[3] Thus, Chapter 9 reviews learning, social and interpersonal, and socialization models for inducing influence. Chapter 10, on the other hand, provides concrete examples of the influence process as enacted on the four levels of system analysis; self, role, group, and larger social systems.[4]

---

[2] Although we are focusing on influence per se in this section of the book, we were guided in our selections by our interest in planned change.

[3] Influence is, of course, a necessary feature in planned change. However, it is only one element in the total process of planned change. In Part I, we attempted to distinguish several kinds of change and influence processes associated with them. The reader may find it profitable to review Chapter 4 at this point.

[4] We have had to restrict the readings in this volume to face-to-face interaction influence models. This stricture, due to space needs, omits a substantial amount of significant research on audience and mass influence. The work of such students as B. Berelson, D. Katz, P. Lazarsfeld, M. Janowitz, and Carl Hovland and his associates deserve attention we could not possibly provide here. See *Reader in Public Opinion and Communication*, edited by B. Berelson and M. Janowitz (New York: The Free Press of Glencoe, Inc., 1953).

Before we proceed to a detailed introduction of the selections in Chapter 9, let us take a general look at "influence." Its complications and diffuseness have already been pointed out. The remainder of this essay will try to sort out and clarify some of the basic issues this concept raises. In doing this we will draw on the ideas of contributors to Part III, for the most part, and secondarily upon other authors whom we would have liked to have included in the volume, but for space considerations could not. For a first approximation we can propose the following issues: (1) Institutional arrangements in the influence process: (2) Purposes of influence; (3) Kinds of influence processes; (4) Dialectics in the influence process; and (5) Responses to influence.

1. INSTITUTIONAL ARRANGEMENTS

The institutional environments examined in Part III run the gamut from prison camps and mental hospitals to industry and schools. Obviously, the kind of institution determines to a large extent the dynamics of influence; for example, prisoners of war live in fear of their lives under conditions of great deprivation, and in a "total institution." [5] There can be no planned change in this sort of situation because there is no attempt to create a collaborative relationship (notwithstanding the fact that change may indeed be "planned" by those in power).[6] Or, as another example, an outpatient receiving psychotherapeutic help twice a week from a local hospital is in a position very different from that of the hospitalized patient who receives constant care and surveillance. The degree to which the institution is *total* dictates the amount of control the institution wields over the life-space of the "clients."

Another institutional parameter of importance is the primacy of the goal orientation. Is indoctrination the organization's *raison d'être* or is it only a peripheral and latent function? Hospitals, prisons, schools come to mind as centers for creating changes, for indoctrination. Whether or not the relationship is voluntary, both parties have some inkling as to the nature and purpose of the relationship. The degree to which the institutional arrangements provide cognitive clarity as to the nature of the relationship is an important factor in the influence process. (It is interesting to note in this regard that mental hospitals try

[5] "When we review the different institutions in our Western society we find a class of them which seems to be encompassing to a degree discontinuously greater than the ones next in line. Their encompassing or total character is symbolized by the barrier to social intercourse with the outside that is often built right into the physical plant, locked doors, high walls, barbed wire, cliffs and water, open terrain, and so forth. These I am calling total institutions. . . ." Erving Goffman, "Characteristics of Total Institutions," in *Symposium on Preventive and Social Psychiatry,* Walter Reed Army Institute of Research, April 15–17, 1957, pp. 43–44.

[6] We do not wish to imply here that *planned change* cannot take place in a total institution. It is very possible that developing collaborative methods which will lead to planned change can be undertaken in total institutions. In fact, many mental hospitals are taking steps in this direction.

very hard to establish the point with new patients that they *are* patients, i.e., sick, and need help.)

Unfortunately, we have no wealth of data on the institutional arrangements that facilitate or hobble influence attempts. Much more needs to be known. The three variables that appear important at this point are the degree to which the institution is total; the degree to which the relationship is voluntary; and the degree to which the institution's main goal orientation is indoctrination or change.

2. PURPOSES OF INFLUENCE

George Price, a cartoonist who manages to hit psychological targets regularly, once had one of his tough unregenerates sitting by the TV set wearing hair-curlers and applying woman's hair spray. His response to his querulous wife who had just returned from work was that he "just had the urge to rush right out and buy them." In this age of "hidden persuaders" and "brainwashing," questions regarding manipulation and ulterior forms of persuasion naturally becloud the collective mind. But we must ask *what* kinds of influence? [7] Buying popcorn or cokes? Voting for a particular candidate? Hypnosis to prepare for painless surgery? Learning to ride a bike? Emotional reconstruction? Aid in breaking a harmful addiction?

Lewin and Grabbe in their article (Chapter 9) attempt to categorize the purposes of influence into three classes: cognitive, emotional, and motoric. These categories seem adequate and exhaustive, although not mutually exclusive. It would be hard to imagine certain motoric skills not affecting the cognitive structure or even, though not so obviously, affective states. Where value changes come into the picture is somewhat moot; obviously values and value-change enter into and encompass all three areas. Cora Du Bois, in her article on the public health worker as an agent of sociocultural change (Chapter 9), stresses the idea that regardless of the influence goal, important cultural dimensions must be taken into account. Using Du Bois' terminology we can say that technical changes (possibly equivalent to cognitive and motoric goals) have to be filtered through and ultimately sanctioned at the formal and informal levels of a cultural system.

Another way to look at the purposes of influence is to ask whether the goal is to impart learnings or induce change along *methodological* or *content* lines. Perhaps an example or two will help explain what we mean here by methodological and content. If in a history course the teacher provides lectures and readings on salient aspects of America's past, this is *content;* the teacher who attempts to acquaint the students with historical methods is providing an example of in-

[7] Marie Jahoda's article "Conformity and Independence: A Psychological Analysis" (*Human Relations* 12:99–120, 1959) illuminates this question elegantly. Unfortunately, space limitations preclude its inclusion here.

fluence with a methodological goal. Similarly, the statistics instructor who imparts information on various tests to use under special circumstances can be contrasted with the statistics instructor who stresses probability theory and asks the students to use this method for solving statistical problems. Content goals emphasize various forms of problem-solving while methodological learning entails learning methods of problem-solving. Or, put differently again, content influence deals with goal attainment, while methodological influence is concerned with the paths to the goal.

This is a consequential distinction. In one case influence focuses on acquaintances with certain stimuli (content) and in the other case influence is concerned with methods by which stimuli of value can be received. Psychoanalysis, for example, is commonly misunderstood to employ content influence, whereas, for the most part, treatment fails or succeeds according to how well the client has mastered the method of psychoanalysis; i.e., "the fundamental rule," free association. Similarly, Schein's article on "brainwashing" (Chapter 9) underlines the content aspirations of the Chinese thought-reform apparatus. Even though various methods were employed, such as confessionals, the major goal was to restructure attitudes toward certain stimuli, not to provide a method whereby stimuli could be evaluated more accurately.[8] We would guess that methodological influence is more radical, durable, and difficult to exert than content influence. (The insidious correlation between values and method should once again be apparent. They are intertwined so finely that separation—in practice—is impossible. A particular teaching or influence method always implies some value-orientation.) [9]

As a paradigm for examining influence goals we can arrange cognitive, affective or emotional, and motoric dimensions on one axis and then arrange methodological and content categories on the other. This taxonomy should account for the majority of influence goals.

3. KINDS OF INFLUENCE PROCESSES

We have been suggesting that the influence process is not a monolithic, unidimensional property. And perhaps more important than the institutional condi-

[8] Schein would probably not altogether agree with this. According to him methodological ground rules would be a very important emphasis in "brainwashing" attempts. The real difference here appears to lie in the idea that the Chinese methodology could lead to only one acceptable solution.

[9] A simple footnote and statement cannot do justice to the value question touched on here. Our own value position favors, in the final analysis, a methodological approach. Heavily involved in this is a rationalistic bias—that it is a good thing to know what you are doing. This "scientific temper"—not a rigid "scientism"—pervades our value-stance. This attitude or stance consists, as we see it, of a tentativeness and respect for probable error as well as a willingness to expose ideas to procedures and operations. For a full discussion of these issues—and one that reflects our own positions—see "Values and the Social Scientist," edited by Kenneth D. Benne and G. Swanson, *Journal of Social Issues*, Vol. 6, No. 4, 1950, particularly the papers by Geiger and the editors.

tions and goals of influence we have discussed is the question: what *type* of influence and under what conditions and with what effects? Kelman's article (Chapter 9) provides the most systematic and useful framework available for answering these questions. It might be timely to summarize his framework at this point. Kelman identified three processes as they relate to the formation of and change in attitude and opinions: (*a*) *Compliance,* which refers to cases in which a person adopts an attitude another individual or group wants him to adopt without actually accepting the attitude. (The community in Kansas that votes dry and drinks wet. Or the Morrano Jews in Spain, who for five centuries subscribed publicly to Catholicism and privately continued their Hebrew worship.) (*b*) *Identification,* which refers to cases in which a person accepts the role of another individual and in so doing adopts the attitudes that are held by this other person. ("Identification with the aggressor" would be one example of this.) (*c*) *Internalization,* which refers to cases in which a person adopts the content of an attitude because it solves a problem for him.

The important factor here is that there appear to be not one kind of influence, but several; and of these, some are strongly internalized, others not; some unconscious, some not; some are adopted out of fear and intimidation, others out of reality considerations. Du Bois, particularly—and to some extent Schein—utilize Kelman's formulations to great advantage in their papers. In fact, Kelman's work helps to relieve some of the ambiguity surrounding the types, as well as antecedents and consequences, of the influence process.

4. DIALECTICS IN THE INFLUENCE PROCESS

The dialectic between cognition and experience   Balancing the cognitive and experiential skills is directly dramatized in the Lewin and Grabbe article *Principles of Re-education* (Chapter 9). Principle three, for example, emphasizes the limitation of experience, while principles five and seven undermine confidence in a solely cognitive approach to change. This subtle, constantly shifting emphasis between "facts" and "experience," between goal attainment and relationships, dominates a good share of the readings included in this volume and has caused too many individuals to be precariously perched on one side or another of an essentially false dichotomy. Dichotomies are proliferated and understanding is corrupted by over exaggeration of one or another point of view.

The literature abounds, however, in articles emphasizing the cognitive orientation *over* value or emotional orientation or vice versa; problem-solving *over* process activities or vice versa; maintenance *over* task orientation; etc., etc. The point here, which our authors continually make, is that for any enduring influence to occur, cognitive components (theory and constructs) and affective components have to be delicately woven into one fabric.

For these inner contradictions to be resolved, time, energy, patience, suspension of judgment, research output, and historical trends all have to be relied on. For example, psychoanalytic practice started out as "id psychology" wherein the patient would discuss his dreams and associations and the analyst would interpret the "truth." One could just as well mail one's dreams to the analyst to interpret for the amount of attention paid to the process or relationship. Marked mainly by Anna Freud's monograph, *Ego and the Mechanism of Defense*,[10] id psychology gave way to emphasis on the relationship betweeen therapist and patient and the "analysis of the resistance" to the therapist's inductions.

Similarly, in the study of groups and organizations attention has focused alternately on the two parts of Barnard's important distinction between "efficiency" (internal working relationships and organizational dynamics) and "effectiveness" (goal attainment): between "task" and "maintenance"; between "socialization" and "achievement"; between "content" and "process"; etc. Olmsted,[11] who conducted an experiment setting up, in effect, task groups and maintenance groups, discovered that neither fulfilled the task requirements as well as groups that attempted to work on both prerequisites. His task groups were preoccupied with "getting things done" to the detriment of maintenance problems, while the maintenance groups had such "anxiety over process" that they could not successfully accomplish the task.

It is undoubtedly true that the bulk of the human relations literature tends to give lopsided attention to the relationship, affective, maintenance side of things, unduly neglecting the cognitive, theoretical, construct approach. But even this imbalance is being redressed. Leslie Farber has said recently: "Despite the modern tendency to regard all teaching relationships as primarily interpersonal in character, it is obvious that a teacher's primary dedication must be not to his students but to his subject matter. Were this not so, teaching would consist only of this romantic relation based on vanity or power, which the psychotherapist has learned to call 'transference' situations. . . ."[12]

This balance has to be evened up so as always to include both of these elements as an integrated—if at times dissonant—whole. To study one sort of phenomenon without attention to the other is very much like a music student paying attention only to the high notes.

Our authors are in almost all cases painfully aware of this dialectic and attempt in various ways to cope with it. Schein and Kelman, the latter in an extraordinarily systematic way, attempt to sort out the cognitive and emotional elements in influence attempts. Kelman's systematizing suffers only one slight defect, which Schein's analysis of the Chinese Communists' brainwashing process overcomes: neglect of the insidious interpenetration and interaction of the emotional and cognitive antecedents and effects of influence. Cora Du Bois, using Kelman's

[10] New York: International University Press, 1946.
[11] M. Olmsted, "Orientation and Role in the Small Group," *American Sociological Review*, 19:741–751, 1954.
[12] "On Therapeutic Despair," *Psychiatry*, 21:19, 1950.

paradigm as a guide for public health education workers, suggests a sequential pattern of influence types.

Bradford, who stresses a transactional model reminiscent of the philosophy of Dewey-Bentley, emphasizes the transactional-interpersonal dimension of the teaching process.

The dialectic between necessity and desirability   Benne *et al.*, in their paper, "The questions which practical deliberations must answer," [13] have chosen to focus on those practical situations which contain definite clashes in value perspectives and which demand a common policy. Throughout this paper, the authors dart back and forth between testing the necessary and desirable state of affairs, in terms both of the existing state of affairs and of outcomes. In a standard Hegelian analysis, they plot a three phase sequence from a diagnosis of the existing state, on to an ideal state, and finally arriving at a synthesis of the ideal and existent in a program of action. These processes, they claim, "do not go on separately or in any regular chronological order. Rather, they interact with one another, in mutual correction, as the total judgment shapes up in a common course of action, and a common acceptance of the actions as possible, necessary, desirable, and efficient."

The dialectic between the self and the other   Lewin's major contribution to the study of man was his continual insistence that change and influence occur most powerfully and economically through the medium of the group. Man generates sentiments and feelings in conjunction with salient membership and reference [14] groups; he also anchors these beliefs and attitudes in his group membership. To attempt to change an individual's attitudes without taking into account his strong group loyalties and attachments would be useless. The very fabric of attitude formation and reinforcement is the social group. To this extent Lewin, a psychologist, was strongly influenced by sociological thought. Never such a radical realist as Durkheim—he did not, for example, believe as Durkheim did that psychology is irrelevant to the facts of society and historical change—he did insist on the social—the "human-group"—basis of facts that arise in accordance with autonomous principles that cannot be reduced to the level of individual facts.[15]

Not one author in Chapter 9 has failed to accentuate the salience of the primary group: not one author has substantially departed from the doctrine that the development of "self-hood" stems directly from group and "other" influences. Thus we see here a convergence of the transactional psychology and epistemology

[13] Kenneth D. Benne, G. E. Axtelle, B. O. Smith, R. B. Raup, "The Questions Which Practical Deliberation Must Answer," in *Human Relations in Curriculum Change*, edited by Kenneth D. Benne and Bozidar Muntyan, New York: Holt, Rinehart and Winston, 1951, pp. 342–352.

[14] H. H. Kelley distinguishes two meanings of reference groups: (1) a group that is in a position to award or withhold recognition; (2) a group that serves as a checkpoint which the person uses in making judgments. In *Readings in Social Psychology*, New York: Holt, Rinehart and Winston, 1952, p. 412. We are using this term loosely to include both types.

[15] We are indebted to S. Asch's discussion of this point in his *Social Psychology*, New York: Prentice-Hall, Inc., 1952, Chapter 1.

of Dewey, the self-other circularity of G. H. Mead; the self-other dialogue of Baldwin and James, the "looking-glass self" of Cooley, and the striking importance of the primary group stated by such seminal thinkers as Lewin, Mayo, and Durkheim.

Each article testifies to the conviction that change-induction requires, at the very least, understanding the matrix of group forces operating on the individual. Du Bois' paper implies group forces on every level of her analysis, Bradford and Lewin emphasize the classroom group dynamics as an essential element in the teaching process. Kelman's attitude-change model is substantially an interpersonal model. Schein's work on "brainwashing" is distinguished by his attention to group factors; collaboration was influenced primarily by a subtle array of manipulative devices emerging out of group acceptance and rejection.[16]

Of course, there are psychological assumptions behind this social orientation. And for the most part, writers such as Schein and Kelman have advanced Lewin's earlier formulations by invoking these psychological principles. Primarily they have probed more deeply into the question of why group affiliation becomes so important. Their answer, on the whole, has been considerably influenced by the work of H. S. Sullivan; namely—to oversimplify—that man's definition of himself arises from group identification, that without this surefooted identity, anxiety ensues; that his self-esteem is inextricably linked to his acceptance and support from significant groups and others. Thus, one important derivative from the sociological orientation of these writers has been the *social* origin of anxiety.

Accordingly, when we think *practically* about change, we perforce have to shift back and forth in precarious equilibrium between the individual and the group, for without one or the other we are distorting the universe. It is perhaps more obvious to observe that individuals are in groups than it is to observe that groups are "in" and influence individuals. It is this latter, often neglected, insight that our authors concern themselves with.

The dialectic between knowledge and action [17]   Possibly the most insidious polarization is that between science or knowledge and action. It is clearly the most dangerous, particularly at this moment in history, when reasonable and rational action becomes a literal matter of life and death. Parsons' analysis of the German debacle between the two World Wars turns on the increasing dichotomy, the schismogenesis, between the German intellectual and policy maker.[18] The United States as well—McCarthyism is only one recent example—is not immune from the polarization of thought and action.

The fact is that knowledge is explosive and radical; it continually threatens

[16] Possibly the most outstanding evidence of the "other's" influence is seen in the work of Erving Goffman. Here the individual is seen as emerging and being defined by his "presentation of self" where life is the stage and the "play's the thing." See particularly the introduction to his *The Presentation of Self in Everyday Life,* New York: Anchor Doubleday, 1959.

[17] This theme permeates the entire volume. It cannot be reiterated too often. See Part I for further elaboration.

[18] T. Parsons, *Essays in Sociological Theory* (rev. ed.), New York: The Free Press of Glencoe, Inc., 1954.

"received notions" and the *status quo*. This particularly applies to knowledge about social phenomena. Wirth illustrates this with the dramatic example of Japan, where technological methods and products were eagerly accepted but social, economic, and political influences from the outside were regarded with suspicion and tenaciously resisted.[19] The latter were subsumed under what the Japanese called *kikenshiso* or "dangerous thoughts." Along these lines, Freud once remarked that science has dealt three mortal blows to man's narcissism: the Copernican revolution whereby the geocentric theory was reversed—man was not at the center of the universe; the Darwinian revolution whereby man's heritage and genealogy was divorced from the grand design of divinity; and the psychoanalytic revolution that exposed some of man's "baser" motives and passions.

To live dangerously, then, is to live with dangerous thoughts; and new knowledge perennially threatens our cherished habits, values, and organized patterns of action. Ambivalence toward knowledge permeates the human condition, and, given the change-basis of knowledge, the ambivalence is almost completely based on fear.

In the readings that follow, Du Bois, Lewin and Grabbe, and Bradford particularly urge a thoughtful infusion of science and action. Their work takes Lewin's famous dictum that "there is nothing so practical as a good theory" seriously. But, for them, it is not enough that administrators and policy holders hire social scientists and consultants and even use the results of their findings in some way or other. They believe that policy and action are threaded with intelligence and vice versa; there is basically no discontinuity between science and action, as one is the arm of the other. For example, Lippitt argues for the superimposition of the norms of science upon policy action (Chapter 11). This point is not so bizarre as it first sounds: Anatole Rapaport points out that the ethical systems of other professions, such as business and the military, have become models for whole societies. Rapaport wonders why the practice of science cannot also provide such a model.[20]

"It may be argued," says Leighton, "that administration cannot afford to be scientific because of the pressure it is usually under from the urgings or attacks of well-meaning enthusiasts, vested interests, and political forces. Granting this to be a serious problem because of the emotions and conflicting, often hidden, motives that suffuse social issues, one may still insist that narrow expediency and secretiveness do not seem to be very effective means for solution, even temporarily."[21]

---

[19] L. Wirth, in preface to Karl Mannheim's *Ideology and Utopia*, New York: Harcourt, Brace & World, Inc., p. xiv.

[20] Cited in Nevitt Sanford, "Social Science and Social Reform," Address of the President, SPSSI, given at the American Psychological Association annual meeting, August 28, 1958, Washington, D.C.

[21] From Alexander Leighton, *The Governing of Men*, Princeton, N.J.: Princeton University Press, 1946. This book is rich in insights on social change and the problems of applying the findings of social science to human predicaments. His first chapter distills a number of principles for administrators of organizations faced with problems of rapid change.

Science and action require synthesis as no other dichotomy requires it. Our existence relies on it.

5. RESPONSES TO INFLUENCE

So far, we have laid major emphasis on the process of influence. Now we want to turn to some of the major responses to it, a problem that preoccupies a great number of intellectuals and scientists. There seem to be at least two major responses to influence, that of conformity (which contemporary society abhors to the point of a new orthodoxy) and that of revolution (which worries others either for its absence or its presence). An insidious split-vision then transpires, when with one breath we abjure our current trends in "affectlessness" (the Beat Generation representing one variation on this theme) and with the other recall a precious nostalgia for the "old days" when, to quote Melville, we said "No in thunder."

Conformity is undoubtedly the new "godhead" term that replaces "individuality," whose death we collectively mourn as we struggle to be independent together. Yet, gibes aside, an issue so focal deserves judicious consideration and our authors represented in this book do just this: they take Spinoza's words seriously, for they have labored hard not to mock, lament, or execrate. They have tried to understand.

Let us consider three positions, two from papers represented in the book and the other in an essay by Henry Murray.[22] Zander, in Chapter 9, concerns himself with resistance to change and influence within organizational settings. In effect, he is *assuming* strong resistance to change and prescribes methods by which this resistance can be overcome. His recommendations include participation and involvement in the planning and implementing of change (the Strauss article in Chapter 10 is particularly apposite), cognitive clarity as to the purposes of change, as well as to change itself, and self-diagnosis by the groups involved in the change.

Cartwright and Lippitt (in Chapter 6), on the other hand, worked the opposite side of the street: the lack of resistance to change, i.e., conformity, particularly that which is levered by group pressures. Theirs is a tightly reasoned, data-based argument, difficult to refute and salted with researchable ideas. They prefer a technique of asking questions in pairs to one that tends to undermine preconceived biases. They start out by asking: under what conditions does conformity arise? And what kinds of conformity? After all, they reason (with no casuistry), could there not be a rigid norm (conformity) for free expression (nonconformity). They then try to account for those conditions that lead to heterogeneous responses. Their answers take them as far as the data permit: Groups are "real" and they have effects. These effects may be harmful (in terms of constricting responses and

[22] *Op. cit.*, reference 1.

creativity) and they may be positively liberating. There is little question that groups provide enormous emotional support for the individuals who comprise them. They also imply that—given our pluralistic society, with its jurisdictional disputes over the "life-space" of the individual and marginal memberships—the possibility of monolithic control by one group—à la *Brave New World*—appears as fictional as any other disutopia.

Murray's paper, "Individuality," is an elfin dialogue. Refusing to be trapped by readers who desire to compartmentalize the world into neat categories, he peoples his stage with three characters who waspishly take extreme positions on contemporary America, circa 1984. If we read him correctly (and who can tell?), Si is the author's mouthpiece. And Si seems to be saying that individuality and its obverse, conformity, are no greater a problem now than they were in yesteryear, and if so, who can prove it? The forms of creativity and conformity undergo generational metamorphoses and the wise observer will catalogue these rather than mourn the death of what never was.

We are not attempting to minimize the anxiety and anguish connected with certain trends toward conformity and compliance that we notice all around us. We have seen too many examples of the deleterious effects of "group think," from the ingenious study of S. Asch, in which subjects reported incorrect responses under group pressure, to authoritarian societies.[23]

Rather more to the point is the underlying premise that behind every influence attempt is an "appropriate response," a realistic one that makes sense under the particular conditions. We cannot define this appropriate response as precisely as we would like. But certainly, there are times to conform and times to deviate and even revolt. Erich Fromm distinguishes the rebel from the revolutionary; the former being a compulsive type who cannot yield to any form of influence no matter how rational, from learning mathematics to putting on a coat warm enough to confront the wintry air.

In addition to this "appropriate" response, one other aspect of influence should be mentioned. We live in a tightly interdependent society. Like it or not, we have to work in and collaborate with other individuals or groups, whether it be the family or the work group. Certain unique needs are satisfied in this way. But this interdependence extracts its pound of flesh, that partial giving up of autonomy required by any form of genuine collaboration. Ultimately, we cannot have it both ways. We must either insulate ourselves from influence and die or learn to work with others (give and receive influence) without total surrender of the self. This is the challenge.

These five aspects of the influence process highlight the main features of Chapters 9 and 10. They embrace the promise as well as the problematics in the proc-

[23] "Effects of Group Pressure Upon the Modification and Distortion of Judgments," in *Readings in Social Psychology*, E. E. Maccoby, T. M. Newcomb, and E. L. Hartley, eds. (ed. 3), New York: Holt, Rinehart and Winston, 1958.

esses of influence as an important aspect of planned change. However, we should now like to turn briefly to some of the unsolved problems in this area. There are at least four that come to mind and that merit considerably more attention than we can provide here.

1. The first of these is the conspicuous lack of knowledge extant on intergroup change and influence. We seem to have a surfeit of knowledge about the dynamics of the small group and change adduced to the individual as a resultant of group forces, but no strong research literature on intergroup change.[24] This is particularly glaring insofar as the primary conflict areas today are *between* nations, *between* institutions (such as labor and management), and *between* various groups within organizations and communities.

2. The ethical-value issues embedded in the influence process have to be continually examined without the bias of the pamphleteer or apologists. Ends do not justify means, particularly in our culture, and the means and methodologies of change induction have to be located in some philosophical and empirical frame of reference.

3. There is the danger that the authors who work within an "interpersonal theory" and small group framework may tend to eclipse the unique and concrete individual. This is nowhere better portrayed than in Erving Goffman's brilliant work, where the individual is determined and defined by "projecting a definition of the situation." [25] Here in this Pirandello-esque world, complete with stage, wings, audience, and other dramaturgical devices, appearance and reality become fused because the appearance is the reality and vice versa. In this "as if" world it would seem that there are no internal nutriments, no internal guides, no biological self, no ontological structure, no ego-strength, no person—except that which is defined by interpersonal cues. This "interpersonal" tradition, forged by Mead, Sullivan, *et al.* (and developed elegantly by Goffman and Strauss) represents an indispensable antidote to the instinctualists, who represent man as being harried solely by a cruel set of inner forces. However, as we see it, the play cannot be the *whole* thing, as it ultimately leads to a solipsistic view of man playing an interpersonal shell game with himself and others. The fact is that certain aspects of "ego-psychology" have to fuse with the interpersonal man in order to determine man's complete social self.[26]

[24] The recent work of R. R. Blake is the most forceful contribution to this problem. See his "Psychology and the Crisis of Statesmanship" (Chapter 8 in this volume). Also, see his "Typical Laboratory Procedures and Experiments," in *An Action Research Program for Organization Improvement* (in Esso Standard Oil Company), Foundation for Research on Human Behavior, Ann Arbor, Michigan, 1960, pp. 7–30. Blake's ingenious experiments are an elaboration of M. Sherif and C. W. Sherif, *Groups in Harmony and Tension: An Integration of Studies of Intergroup Relations,* New York: Harper & Brothers, 1953.

[25] The reader is directed to the following: "Alienation from Interaction," *Human Relations, 10:*47–60, 1957. *The Presentation of Self in Everyday Life,* New York: Doubleday Anchor Company, 1959. "The Moral Career of the Mental Patient," *Psychiatry,* 22:123–143, 1959. "On Fore Work: An Analysis of Ritual Elements in Social Interaction," *Psychiatry, 18:*213–231, 1955.

[26] See David Rapaport, "The Theory of Ego-autonomy: A Generalization," *Bulletin of the Menninger Clinic,* 22:13–25, 1958.

4. Finally, more attention needs to be given to the *transactional* basis of influence. While we have amassed significant data about the effects on the influenced we have few accounts—except those that fiction provides—of the effects on the influencer. In short, all change attempts manage to produce ironic feedbacks: subtle, even imperceptible, effects on the influencer. We are not here speaking only of counter-transference or the unconscious reaction of the influencer; rather of the effects *on* the influencer—the change-agent—in creating change.[27]

[27] T. M. Mills, for example, is working on the concept, "Identification with the Victim," a reciprocal counterpart of "Identification with the Aggressor." Rather than focusing on the effects on the client, Mills is interested in determining the effects on the "changer," in this case the aggressor.

CHAPTER 9

Models of Influence

THE TEACHING-LEARNING
TRANSACTION   *Leland P. Bradford*

A RE-EXAMINATION of the teaching-learning process is long overdue. Explorations into the many complex motivational, perceptual and emotional forces in learning are needed even more than studies of procedures for presenting knowledge or methods of measuring recall. Analysis of the conditions which must be present before the individual can learn and change need also to be made.

An effective teaching-learning process should include two basic assumptions based on present research and experience with processes of learning and changing.

1. That the teaching-learning process is a human transaction involving the teacher, learner and learning group in a set of dynamic interrelationships. Teaching is a human relational problem. Teachers and learners engage together in a complex process of exploration and diagnosis of needs for and resist-

ances to learning and change; of experimentation and fact-finding; of testing and planning for utilization of learning and change in the life of the individual. The relationships among learners and between teacher and learners have a great deal to do with the ultimate learning.

2. That the target of education is change and growth in the individual and his behavior; and thus in his worlds. This is a deeper and broader goal than cognitive learning only.

While cognitive and attitudinal learnings are basic aspects of individual growth and behaviorial change, they do not guarantee that growth and change will occur. Each individual faces the task of continuously reorganizing, remaking and relating his internal and external worlds. His learning should be directed toward this task. Learning which remains merely cognitive and doesn't become part of his internal sys-

From Leland P. Bradford, "The Teaching-Learning Transaction," from Adult Education, Vol. 8, No. 3, Spring 1958, pp. 135-145, published by the Adult Education Association of the U.S.A., 743 North Wabash Avenue, Chicago 11, Illinois. Used by permission.

tems and external behavior, becomes compartmentalized and doesn't successfully affect his problems of living.

Creating Learning Conditions

These two assumptions lay a basis for a re-examination of a teaching-learning theory. They indicate the need to combine teaching procedures and understandings of the motivational, emotional and cognitive characteristics of the teacher and learners, with skills of working with learners and learning group in creating conditions for learning and change.

The following seven areas are some of those which must be examined in developing an effective teaching-learning theory.

1. What the learner brings to the transaction (in addition to ignorance and abilities).

2. What the teacher (helper) brings to the transaction (in addition to subject knowledge).

3. The setting in which learning and change takes place.

4. The interaction process.

5. The conditions necessary for learning and change.

6. The maintenance of change and utilization of learning in the life of the learner.

7. The establishment of the processes of continued learning.

What the Learner Brings

What, for example, are the learner's perceptions about the need for learning and change? How deep is his dissatisfaction with his present situation? How acutely, to use an analogy, does he feel pain? Are external pressures to learn and change reacted to but not really accepted internally? Where is the balance between desire for and resistance to learning and change?

What implicit theory about learning drawn from a variety of past experiences does the learner bring? If his concept is built around hearing lectures, reading, being quizzed, he will feel uneasy with and resist a learning process which more deeply involves him. If his concept of learning keeps him a passive recipient he will fail to enter into an effective learning transaction. Perhaps the first major task of the teaching-learning transaction is to help the learner learn different ways of learning.

What are the learner's perceptions about the potentials for learning in himself, the teacher and the learning situation? Does he perceive the learning as abstract and irrelevant to his needs? Does he perceive the teacher as capable of understanding and helping him? To what extent does he even recognize the kinds of help he would most appreciate as well as most need? Does he feel acceptance or rejection from the teacher and the group? Does he have security in the learning situation and the learning group?

Inevitably each person enters a change situation with actual or latent concerns and anxieties. To learn poses unknown possibilities. To change raises images of potential failure, discomfort, pain. What threats to self-image are present as the individual opens himself up to consideration of present inadequacies in knowledge or behavior? We all recall what fears and anxieties we can have in learning a new language or a different course in mathematics.

A Perceptual Screen

Each person has a perceptual screen filtering out or distorting communication to him. Information too threatening for him to accept because it attacks his self-image is blocked out or interpreted in such a way as to pose less of a threat. Adults, particularly, have self-images more resistant to the subordinating role of accepting knowledge from others. What information about personal performance does the learner accept or reject?

How much does he pigeon-hole knowledge, or turn it into abstractions, thus removing or modifying its threat to his self-image? To what extent does he maintain the ability of verbal recall but reject internalization into being and behaving? Does he have sufficient acceptance of himself as he is to accept need for improvement?

Motivation, perceptions, anxieties, all influence and affect the teaching-learning transaction. Self-perceived threats to the learner as a person become real blocks to learning.

Passive Learning

Venturing into the unknown means leaving the tried and sure and safe, unsatisfactory as it may be. Resistance to leaving the safe, but at the same time wanting the new, frequently causes the learner to prefer the kind of presentation of knowledge which can be copied and recalled but never internalized, rather than a deeper process of learning involved in a program of change. Students frequently encourage more passive but less effective methods of learning and, by their satisfaction in being protected from important learning, reward teachers for ineffective teaching and thus perpetuate poor teaching.

Each learner brings to the learning situation his skills, or lack of skills, in group membership. If he lacks the ability to work effectively with others in a group situation, it is difficult for

him to enter into the human transaction of learning.

Inadequate ability to listen or interact with others makes it less possible for him to learn from the learning group, thus increasing his tensions and anxieties about himself, decreasing his satisfaction with the learning transaction and very likely increasing his resistance to learning.

Approach to Learning

Because the learner is one part of the human transaction of teaching-learning, his motivational, perceptual, emotional and attitudinal systems are very important factors in how he approaches learning and change and how open he is to them. It is the total individual, not just his mind, that comes to the learning experience. When only part of him is understood and approached, all of him is not reached, and learning does not get very deeply into him and his actions.

The emerging field of social science is beginning to contribute much to our total understanding of the process of learning and changing. From psychiatry and clinical psychology come knowledge of individual anxieties and concerns. From social psychology and sociology come knowledge about resistance to change and the process of changing. From psychology comes knowledge of motivation and perception. Educators need to utilize such knowledge in broadening and improving understanding of the teaching-learning transaction.

What the Teacher Brings

The teacher, like the learner, brings far more to the teaching-learning situation than a knowledge of the subject, skill in organizing and presenting material, or ability to test for recall.

First, he brings a certain degree of awareness or lack of awareness that the teacher-learning process is basically a delicate human transaction requiring skill and sensitivity in human relations.

The effective teacher's role is that of engaging in a relationship with the learner and the learning group in which the learners and the teacher go through the process of diagnosis of change needs and blocks together, of seeking and analyzing relevant information from outside sources and from the interaction of the learning group, of experimenting in new pathways of thought and behavior, and of planning for use of new behavior.

The teacher's role of helping in the complex process of learning and change, however, is based upon a set of human relationships precariously established with the learner and the learning group. These relationships are always precarious because of the anxieties of the learner, the threat of the teacher as a judge and expert, and the mixed feeling held by the learner about his dependency on the teacher. The teacher needs to be aware of the importance of these human relationships, sensitive to changes in them, and adept at repairing them.

Awareness of Needs

Second, the teacher as a partner in the transaction of learning needs to be aware of his own needs and motivations and of their consequences to the learning process. To what extent do his needs to control people, to maintain dependency upon himself, or to seek love and affection, distort and disturb his helper function and the learning transaction? To what extent does his fear of hostility

develop repression in the learner so that healthy conflict as a basis of learning is lacking?

To what extent does his fear of relationship with people keep the learner at arm's length and thus reduce the possibility of an effective teaching-learning transaction? (This does not mean the other extreme of having to make himself love the learner. Rather it means the ability to enter planfully into a human transaction without need for either rejection or over acceptance.) Knowing one's own motivations and their possible consequences on others better enables one to keep motivations under direction and control.

Acceptance as a Person

Third, the teacher brings an ability, or lack of ability, to accept the learner as a person. Acceptance means ability to respect and listen to the other and to separate the person from unliked parts of his behavior. The physician who, hating disease, also hates and rejects the person who has the disease, is not an effective doctor. Yet teachers frequently are not aware that they reject learners because of lack of knowledge, abilities or effectiveness in relating to them. Acceptance does not mean approval of the present status of being and behaving of the learner. It rather marks the basic point from which the teacher tries to enter into a helping relationship.

The teacher works with a learning group. Good teacher-group relations are certainly as important as good teacher-student relations. The degree of ability in group leadership and membership skills on the part of the teacher has much to do with learning of the individuals in the class group.

The teacher is a second part of the

teaching-learning transaction. His emotional, motivational, perceptual and attitudinal systems, and his awareness of them and their consequences for learning and change are important forces in effective teaching-learning. Social science again has much to contribute to understanding the teacher.

Most education takes place in group situations. Thus the teaching-learning transaction includes teacher, learner and learning group. Each has its forces and impact on the learning outcome for the individuals. The class group is not merely an economical way of teaching. It should be at the heart of the learning process. Group impact and influence on its members can be a powerful force toward learning or toward supporting the learning process.

The Teacher-Learner Transaction

Recent research into the dynamics of group behavior indicates how powerful group forces are in group and individual productivity. Some groups have the task of making machine parts, others of reaching decisions, and still others of increasing the learning of their members. In all instances, for the group to be successful, attention must be given to helping the group form, organize, grow and keep in good repair. Just as the leaders in work groups should assume responsibility for encouraging the growth and maintenance of the work group, so should the teacher of the learning group.

As teachers recognize emotional aspects of group behavior, individual anxieties and hidden motives, interpersonal threats and competition, problems of relations to leadership and authority, factors of individual involvement in groups, they will be better able to help classes become groups where the

group task is individual learning and where group forces of cohesion are exerted on the learning of each individual.

As it is, group forces, inevitably present in all group situations, often work against the teacher and against learning. The class group bands against the teacher to reduce learning because the teacher did not know how to develop an effective learning group where members helped members and where morale was high.

How many teachers fail to encourage, or even allow, learners to help educate each other? If teachers were able to create learning groups in which member influenced and helped member, learning results would be far greater.

The learning group is the third part of the teaching-learning transaction. Educators are just beginning to realize the powerful forces present in groups which could measurably increase individual learning and change. Research in group dynamics in many university centers and experimentation with applied group dynamics carried out by the National Training Laboratories has much to offer an expanding teaching-learning theory.

The Interaction Process

The interaction process is basically a network of interactions taking place in a group setting. Teacher interaction with one student may be heard in many different ways and with different consequences by others. Praise or reward to one student may be heard as punishment to another because he was not selected for reward. To the learner, interactions of support and reaction from the group may be more valuable or more readily acceptable than from the teacher.

The teacher needs to be aware of the consequences of any interaction on all members of the learning group and on the group itself. Does an interaction designed to give needed knowledge to one learner create greater unhealthy dependency on the teacher by other group members?

The interaction process has two basic purposes: first, to establish and maintain relationships which reduce anxieties and defensiveness in the learner and help him open up for learning, and second, to bring about learning and change.

A Supportive Climate

It is a false assumption, more common in secondary and higher than in elementary education, that the mature person doesn't need sensitive teacher-student relationships or group support. Fortunately many adult educators have discovered the fallacies in this assumption and have come to realize the importance of developing a supportive climate that reduces resistance to learning.

With the interaction process basic in learning, the actual interventions of teachers and learners, and the response to them, are of critical importance.

What are the consequences, for example, of action or lack of action by the teacher on shifting the balances of motivation of the learner? What are the consequences in increasing or decreasing a feeling of support or of changing the perceptions of the learner? What are the consequences for the helping relationship between teacher and learner? Does any particular action create over-dependency on the teacher?

It is unfortunate that there is a dearth of studies dealing with the effect of teacher intervention on the learning process. In the fields of consultation and therapy, much more has been done

to train for sensitivity to the interaction process. In these fields, as well as in the field of medicine, the interaction process is recognized as basic in diagnosis and treatment.

If the interaction process is basic to learning, then experience in the area of consultation and therapy, and research in the social science fields of social and clinical psychology are important to a full development of a learning theory. Recent work on human relations training carried on by the various group development laboratories has been exploring the area of teacher intervention in the interaction process. Experience in clinical psychology is highly relevant to this area. Finally, recent studies in social psychology on the process of change and the function of helping with change have importance.

Learning and Change

Learning and change take place most effectively only when certain conditions are present, making it possible for the learner to enter into a process of diagnosis, experimentation, information finding, generalization, practice and application leading toward learning, growth and change. These conditions, discussed by the author in a previous issue of this journal, will be merely outlined here.

1. *Revealing thoughts, feelings, behavior.* Until the thoughts, feelings and behavior needing change are brought to the surface for the individual and made public to those helping him (in formal learning situations, the teacher and other members of the learning group), there is little likelihood of learning or change. Buried, they are blurred and indistinct for the learner, covered by misperceptions of adequacy, anxieties, defensiveness. Surfaced, they can be ex-

amined by learner, teacher and learning group in the light of greater reality.

Until thoughts and behavior are revealed and exposed, there is little that the learner or his helpers can take hold of to bring about improvement or change.

Not to Fill a Void

Learning is not a matter of filling a void with information. It is a process of internal organization of a complex of thought patterns, perceptions, assumptions, attitudes, feelings and skills, and of successfully testing this reorganization in relation to problems of living.

The basis for reorganization, and thus for learning, is diagnosis of inadequacy. Such diagnosis should be made collaboratively by the learner and those helping him. It is ineffectual for someone else to make the diagnosis for the learner —a frequent fault in education.

The diagnosis is never simply that of general inadequacy. It should include motivations, desires, anxieties, defensiveness, insecurities, perceptions. In combination they create the normal ambivalences found in learning and change.

Diagnosis depends on having adequate data. Surfacing or revealing the thought, feeling and behavior patterns of the learner provides a common experience for learner, teacher, and learning group to make possible a collaborative diagnosis.

Group Reactions

2. *Seeking reactions to revealed ideas and behavior.* Revealing inner thoughts, attitudes, behavior without securing accurate and acceptable reactions from the teacher and learning group, from additional sources of information, or from self would be without much value. *We do not learn by doing only.* We learn by doing under conditions in which relevant, accurate and acceptable reactions which we are able to use get through to us.

Increasingly, it is clear that the concept of feedback has important meaning for the educational process. Information following exposure which recognizes the individual's perceptual system and which has for its purpose development rather than destruction is the heart of learning. Feedback must be clearly and completely heard. Here is where the human relationship aspect of teaching-learning perhaps has greatest importance.

In an executive development program recently, one member told the group in various ways that he saw himself as a warm-hearted person who liked people and who was a democratic executive. His recital of his problems of apathy, irresponsibility and lack of creativity in his immediate subordinates revealed him as fearful and hostile toward people and certainly autocratic in his management.

Lectures or discussions about good executive behavior would have been heard by this man as referring to himself. Only as his behavior was revealed to himself and to other members of the learning group, and as he gradually received helpful feedback reactions enabling him to correct his perceptions of himself and ultimately some of his behavior, did real learning and change take place.

A Climate for Learning

3. *Climate.* Revealing thoughts and behavior and accepting reactions about

them takes place effectively only when the atmosphere or climate in the learning group and the teaching-learning transaction is one which reduces threat and defensiveness and which also provides emotional support while the learner is undergoing the difficult process of changing patterns of thought and behavior.

The teacher has the important responsibility of helping to create a climate conducive to learning. It is crucial that the teacher *help the group* create this climate. The temptation to the teacher is to attempt to supply, himself, all the understanding and support necessary for each learner. This keeps the learner in the bondage of emotional dependency on the teacher.

If the climate is built by the group, with encouragement and assistance from the teacher, the individual learner can accept emotional support interdependently, rather than dependently, because he is contributing to the group support given to other members.

4. *Information seeking and receiving.* Knowledge from a variety of sources is vital to the learning process. Some comes from the analysis of the learning situation, some from immediate reactions of teacher and peers, some from experimentation and research results, some from past experiences of the individual and others, and some from the wide wisdom and vast experience of the past.

Knowledge-giving as a factor of learning, however, has attributes and consequences, all of which need much further exploration. The first is timing. Like a road map which is useless to the person who has made no decision to take a trip, information is often presented in teaching situations before the individual has made any personal decision about learning and change. Teachers need constantly to realize that attendance in a learning group does not necessarily mean commitment to the process of learning and change.

New Ways of Thinking

5. *Experimentation and practice with new ways of thinking and doing.* Knowledge which remains basically outside the being and doing of the individual is likely to become compartmentalized. Learning tends not to become a basic part of the being and doing of the individual until he has had opportunity to try out in practice situations new possibilities for thinking and doing. Experimentation and practice are important conditions in the total process of teaching-learning.

6. *Application of change into the learning situation of the individual.* Application of learning and change in the life of the individual is a far more difficult task than initial learning and change in a protected learning situation. Unless the teacher and the learning group give time and attention to individual problems of internalizing and using learning, regression and loss of the learning is likely.

These conditions need much further exploration and research in terms of completeness, relative importance and integration. In various sections of the social sciences, some exploration is present. New research on feedback, or information theory, has immediate value for an enlarged concept of teaching-learning. The various approaches to counseling and therapy have developed experience in the area of establishing receptive climates. Research in human relations training has stressed the integration of these conditions and methods of training for application. Social psychology and sociology has worked on the problem of helping to apply and maintain change.

Overcoming Resistance to Change

Education has long recognized the importance of transfer of learning. Too frequently such transfer has meant only the application of principles to new situations. This has ignored many of the problems of resistance to putting change into practice in the individual and in his worlds.

The problem of maintenance of change and utilization of learning have both emotional and cognitive aspects. The learner's motivations to maintain change in thought and behavior must be sufficiently strong to overcome his own hesitations and the forces in his environment pushing against change. Many a summer school program has inspired teachers to want to improve teaching practices, only to find resistance among colleagues, students and parents back in the school system. Change, to be maintained, must be well rooted in the individual and well supported by forces in his external worlds.

If maintenance of change and utilization of learning is a necessary part of a theory of teaching-learning, then efforts must be made during the process of formal teaching-learning to prepare for the problem of maintenance. A number of helping steps can be taken at that time.

Steps Toward Change

1. Help needs to be given to the learner in diagnosing forces of resistance to change, and support for change likely to be found in himself and his environment. Basically he needs help in locating and building supports in his internal and external worlds to maintain new learning and change.

2. Help needs to be given to the learner in assessing his own potential strengths and weaknesses in terms of support for change.

3. Help should be given the learner in planning how to re-establish himself in his outside worlds (after leaving the teaching-learning situation).

A few years ago the author helped a team from Europe to develop skills in human relations training. It became clear, as the three-month training program came to an end, that their first and most crucial task back home was to gain reacceptance as Europeans. If they were seen as "Americanized," any efforts to maintain changes in themselves and introduce changes in their situations would meet with strong resistances from those around them. Each person needs a foundation from which to encourage change in himself and his situations. Learning which totally removes such a foundation will not lead to continuing change.

4. Help needs to be given in planning how to create supports away from the learning situation. Supports for change in the situation must be matched by supports in the back-home situation.

5. Help needs to be given the individual to develop a continuing system of learning. Methods of experimentation and analysis can be taught which will encourage the person to continue to learn from a variety of experiences.

Only recently has systematic thought been given in the social sciences to the problem of maintenance of change. Lewin's earlier concept of the unfreezing-freezing-unfreezing-freezing cycle of change has had important implications in recent research. The National Training Laboratories efforts to develop methods for training change agents and of planning for back-home application of learning represents another area of experience and research.

Work in sociology as well as in social psychology has analyzed problems of change in relation to social system.

The teaching-learning process should endeavor to help the learner learn how to learn more effectively so that more of his experiences can lead toward learning and change.

As individuals learn to use scientific methods of experimentation, observation, and analysis in daily decision-making and problem-solving, instead of stereotypes, perceptual distortions, and closed eyes and ears, learning and changing from experiences can more likely become a continual process.

As individual learners become more aware, through an effective teacher-learner transaction, of their own anxieties and resistance to learning, they may be able to reduce them more frequently and thus enhance learning and change.

As individual learners become more accepting of themselves and gain more internal security, they will become less defensive and more able to perceive accurately and to use reactions to their thought and behavior patterns.

In brief, a basic purpose of education in all teaching-learning situations is first to help the individual learner open himself up for learning by being able to bring his problems and needs for learning to the surface, and to listen and accept relevant reactions about his problems and behavior. The second purpose is to help the learner gain methods of experimenting, analyzing and utilizing experiences and knowledge resulting from daily problem-solving.

Conclusion

An effective teaching-learning transactional process should include, in addition to the seven areas discussed above, pedagogical methods of presenting knowledge and developing experiences and methods of testing with the learners their learning and change.

As this broadened picture of teaching-learning is developed, it is obvious it has major implications for the entire field of teacher training. It will not be enough merely to add social science subject knowledge to what the prospective teacher is expected to "learn." Engaging in the complex human transaction of teaching-learning requires more than knowing about human behavior. It calls for sensitivity and awareness to on-going relationships and for skills of interacting with the learner and the learning group. These sensitivities and skills are not gained from traditional methods of teacher training. They will require a process of experiential learning in which the prospective teacher is helped to gain self awareness, understanding of how others perceive his behavior (the consequences of his behavior on others), practice in diagnosing human relations and group problems, experience in sharpening sensitivity to what others are feeling and trying to communicate. These awarenesses and sensitivities are primary and teaching procedure secondary.

A healthy expansion of our knowledge of the teaching-learning process thus needs to be followed by an equally long overdue re-examination of methods of teacher training.

❖❖❖❖❖❖❖❖❖❖❖❖❖❖❖❖❖❖❖ PRINCIPLES OF RE-EDUCATION

Kurt Lewin and Paul Grabbe

THE re-educative process affects the individual in three ways. It changes his *cognitive* structure, the way he sees the physical and social worlds, including all his facts, concepts, beliefs, and expectations. It modifies his *valences and values,* and these embrace both his attractions and aversions to groups and group standards, his feelings in regard to status differences, and his reactions to sources of approval or disapproval. And it affects *motoric action,* involving the degree of the individual's control over his physical and social movements.

If all three of these effects (and the processes which give rise to them) were governed by the same laws, the practical task of re-education would be much simpler. Unfortunately they are not, and the re-educator, in consequence, is confronted with certain contradictions. For instance, treatment involving the training of a thumb-sucking child in certain roundabout hand movements, designed to make the child aware of his thumb-sucking and thereby giving him more control over these movements, may set the child apart from other children and undermine his emotional security, the possession of which is a prerequisite for successful re-education.

How these inner contradictions may be avoided is one of the basic problems of re-education. A correct sequence of steps, correct timing, and a correct combination of individual and group treatments are presumably essential. Most important, however, is a thorough understanding by the re-educator of the way in which each of these psychological components—the cognitive structure, valences and values, and motoric action —are affected by any specific step in re-education.

The discussion that follows touches but two of the main problems here involved, one related to a change in cognition, the other, to the acceptance of new values.

Change in the Cognitive Structure

The difficulties encountered in efforts to reduce prejudices or otherwise to change the social outlook of the individual have led to a realization that re-education cannot merely be a rational process. . . . We know that lectures or other similarly abstract methods of transmitting knowledge are of little avail in changing his subsequent outlook and conduct. We might be tempted, therefore, to think that what

Excerpted from Kurt Lewin and Paul Grabbe, "Conduct, Knowledge, and Acceptance of New Values," The Journal of Social Issues, Vol. 1, No. 3, August 1945, pp. 56–64. Used by permission. The first two principles developed by Lewin and Grabbe and not reprinted in full here are: (1) The processes governing the acquisition of the normal and abnormal are fundamentally alike. (2) The re-educative process has to fulfill a task which is essentially equivalent to a change in culture.

is lacking in these methods is first-hand experience. The sad truth is that even first-hand experience will not necessarily produce the desired result. To understand the reasons, we must examine a number of premises which bear directly on the problem.

3. EVEN EXTENSIVE FIRST-HAND EXPERIENCE DOES NOT AUTOMATICALLY CREATE CORRECT CONCEPTS (KNOWLEDGE)

For thousands of years man's everyday experience with falling objects did not suffice to bring him to a correct theory of gravity. A sequence of very unusual, man-made experiences, so-called experiments, which grew out of the systematic search for the truth were necessary to bring about a change from less adequate to more adequate concepts. To assume that first-hand experience in the social world would automatically lead to the formation of correct concepts or to the creation of adequate stereotypes seems therefore unjustifiable.

4. SOCIAL ACTION NO LESS THAN PHYSICAL ACTION IS STEERED BY PERCEPTION

In any situation we cannot help but act according to the field we perceive; and our perception extends to two different aspects of this field. One has to do with facts, the other with values.

If we grasp an object, the movement of our hand is steered by its perceived position in the perceived surroundings. Likewise, our social actions are steered by the position in which we perceive ourselves and others within the total social setting. The basic task of re-edu-

cation can thus be viewed as one of changing the individual's social perception. Only by this change in social perception can change in the individual's social action be realized.

Let us assume that inadequate information (knowledge) has somehow been replaced by more adequate knowledge. Does this suffice to change our perception? In answering this question, let us again take a lead from the field of physical perception by asking: How can false physical perception, for instance, visual illusions, be rectified?

5. AS A RULE THE POSSESSION OF CORRECT KNOWLEDGE DOES NOT SUFFICE TO RECTIFY FALSE PERCEPTION

Our insight into the conditions which determine the correctness or incorrectness of perception is still very limited. It is known that some relation exists between visual perception and knowledge. However, the lines which appear curved in an optical illusion do not straighten out as soon as we "know" that they are straight. Even first-hand experience, the measuring of the distances in question, usually does not eliminate the illusion. As a rule, other types of change, such as the enlarging or the shrinking of the area perceived or a change in the visual frames of references are needed to straighten out the lines.

When we consider resistances to re-education we usually think in terms of emotional obstacles. It is important, however, not to underestimate the difficulties inherent in changing cognition. If we keep in mind that even extensive experience with physical facts does not necessarily lead to correct physical perception, we will be less surprised at the resistances encountered when we attempt to modify inadequate social stereotypes. . . .

[French and Marrow tell the story of a forelady's attitude toward older workers. She clings to the conviction that older workers are no good, although she has older workers on her floor whom she considers very efficient. Her prejudices stand in direct opposition to all her personal experience.]

This example from industry is well in line with studies on Negro-White relations dealing with the effect of common schooling and with observations on the effect of mingling. They indicate that favorable experiences with members of another group, even if they are frequent, do not necessarily diminish prejudices toward that group.

Only if a psychological linkage is made between the image of specific individuals and the stereotype of a certain group, only when the individuals can be perceived as "typical representatives" of that group, is the experience with individuals likely to affect the stereotype.

6. INCORRECT STEREOTYPES (PREJUDICES) ARE FUNCTIONALLY EQUIVALENT TO WRONG CONCEPTS (THEORIES)

We can infer, for instance, that the social experiences which are needed to change improper stereotypes have to be equivalent to those rare and specific physical experiences which cause a change in our theories and concepts about the physical world. Such experiences cannot be depended on to happen accidentally.

To understand the difficulties in the way of changing conduct, an additional point has to be considered:

7. CHANGES IN SENTIMENTS DO NOT NECESSARILY FOLLOW CHANGES IN COGNITIVE STRUCTURE

Even if the cognitive structure in regard to a group is modified in an individual, his sentiments toward this group may remain unchanged. The analysis of an opinion survey on the Negro problem, involving white respondents with varying educational backgrounds, . . . shows that knowledge and sentiment are independent to a marked degree. The sentiments of the individual toward a group are determined less by his knowledge about that group than by the sentiments prevalent in the social atmosphere which surrounds him. Just as the alcoholic knows that he should not drink—and doesn't want to drink; so the white American soldier who observes a Negro dating a white girl in England may feel that he should not mind—and he might consciously condemn himself for his prejudices. Still he may frequently be helpless in the face of this prejudice since his perception and emotional reaction remain contrary to what he knows they ought to be.

Re-education is frequently in danger of reaching only the official system of values, the level of verbal expression and not of conduct; it may result in merely heightening the discrepancy between the super-ego (the way I ought to feel) and the ego (the way I really feel), and thus give the individual a bad conscience. Such a discrepancy leads to a state of high emotional tension but seldom to correct conduct. It may postpone transgressions but is likely to make transgressions more violent when they occur. . . .

A factor of great importance in

bringing about a change in sentiment is the degree to which the individual becomes actively involved in the problem. . . . Lacking this involvement, no objective fact is likely to reach the status of a fact for the individual concerned and therefore influence his social conduct.

The nature of this interdependence becomes somewhat more understandable if one considers the relation between change in perception, acceptance, and group belongingness.

Acceptance of New Values and Group Belongingness

Since action is ruled by perception, a change in conduct presupposes that new facts and values are perceived. These have to be accepted not merely verbally as an official ideology, but as an action-ideology, involving that particular, frequently nonconscious system of values which guides conduct. In other words,

8. A CHANGE IN ACTION-IDEOLOGY, A REAL ACCEPTANCE OF A CHANGED SET OF FACTS AND VALUES, A CHANGE IN THE PERCEIVED SOCIAL WORLD—ALL THREE ARE BUT DIFFERENT EXPRESSIONS OF THE SAME PROCESS

By some, this process may be called a change in the culture of the individual; by others, a change of his super-ego.

It is important to note that re-education will be successful, i.e., lead to permanent change, only if this change in culture is sufficiently complete. If re-education succeeds only to the degree that the individual becomes a marginal man between the old and new system of values nothing worth while is accomplished. . . .

One of the factors which has been shown to have a very important bearing on the success or failure of the re-educative process is the manner in which the new super-ego is introduced. The simplest solution seems to lie in outright enforcement of the new set of values and beliefs. In this case a new god is introduced who has to fight with the old god, now regarded as a devil. Two points may be made in this connection, illustrating the dilemma facing re-education in regard to the introduction of a new set of values.

a. Loyalty to the old and hostility to the new values. An individual who is forcibly moved from his own to another country, with a different culture, is likely to meet the new set of values with hostility. So it is with an individual who is made a subject of re-education against his will. Feeling threatened, he reacts with hostility. This threat is felt all the more keenly if the individual is not voluntarily exposing himself to re-education. . . . A comparison of voluntary and involuntary migration from one culture to another seems to bear out this observation.

One would expect this hostility to be the more pronounced the greater the loyalty of the individual to the old system of values. Accordingly, persons who are more socially inclined, therefore less self-centered, can be expected to offer stronger resistances to re-education, for the very reason that they are more firmly anchored in the old system.

In any event, the re-educative process will normally encounter hostility. The task of breaking down this hostility becomes a paradox if one considers the relation between acceptance of new values and freedom of choice.

b. Re-education and freedom of acceptance. . . . Much stress is laid on the creation, as part of the re-educative process, of an atmosphere of freedom and spontaneity. Voluntary attendance, informality of meetings, freedom of expression in voicing grievances, emotional security, and avoidance of pressure, all include this element. Carl Rogers' emphasis on self-decision by the patient stresses the same point for the psychotherapy of the individual.

There seems to be a paradox implied in this insistence on freedom of acceptance, and probably no other aspect of re-education brings more clearly into the open a basic difficulty of the process. Since re-education aims to change the system of values and beliefs of an individual or a group, to change it so as to bring it in line with society at large or with reality, it seems illogical to expect that this change will be made by the subjects themselves. The fact that this change has to be enforced on the individual from outside seems so obvious a necessity that it is often taken for granted. Many people assume that the creation, as part of the re-educative process, of an atmosphere of informality and freedom of choice cannot possibly mean anything else but that the re-educator must be clever enough in manipulating the subjects to have them think that they are running the show. According to such people, an approach of this kind is merely a deception and smoke-screen for what to them is the more honorable, straight-forward method of using force.

It may be pointed out, however, that if re-education means the establishment of a new super-ego, it necessarily follows that the objective sought will not be reached so long as the new set of values is not experienced by the individual as something freely chosen. If the individual complies merely from fear of punishment rather than through the dictates of his free will and conscience,

the new set of values he is expected to accept does not assume in him the position of super-ego, and his re-education therefore remains unrealized.

From this we may conclude that social perception and freedom of choice are interrelated. Following one's conscience is identical with following the perceived intrinsic requirements of the situation. Only if and when the new set of values is freely accepted, only if it corresponds to one's super-ego, do those changes in social perception occur which, as we have seen, are a prerequisite for a change in conduct and therefore for a lasting effect of re-education.

We can now formulate the dilemma which re-education has to face in this way: How can free acceptance of a new system of values be brought about if the person who is to be educated is, in the nature of things, likely to be hostile to the new values and loyal to the old?

9. ACCEPTANCE OF THE NEW SET OF VALUES AND BELIEFS CANNOT USUALLY BE BROUGHT ABOUT ITEM BY ITEM

Methods and procedures which seek to change convictions item by item are of little avail in bringing about the desired change of heart. This is found to be one of the most important experiences for those engaged in the field of re-education. Arguments proceeding logically from one point to another may drive the individual into a corner. But as a rule he will find some way—if necessary a very illogical way—to retain his beliefs. . . . No change of conviction on any specific point can be established in more than an ephemeral way so long as the individual has not given up his hostility to the new set of values as a whole, to the extent of having changed from hostility at least to open-mindedness.

Step-by-step methods *are* very important in re-education. These steps, however, have to be conceived as steps in a gradual change from hostility to friendliness in regard to the new system as a whole, rather than as a conversion of the individual one point at a time. Of course, convictions in regard to certain points in the total system may play an important role in the process of conversion. It is, however, important for the over-all planning of re-education not to lose sight of the fact that efforts directed toward bringing about a change from hostility to open-mindedness and to friendliness to the new culture as a whole be given priority over conversion in regard to any single item or series of items of the re-educative program.

How, then, can acceptance of the new values be established if not by an item-by-item change in conviction?

Creation of an In-group and the Acceptance of a New Value System

One of the outstanding means used today for bringing about acceptance in re-education, as discussed above, is the establishment of what is called an "in-group," i.e., a group in which the members feel belongingness. Under these circumstances,

10. THE INDIVIDUAL ACCEPTS THE NEW SYSTEM OF VALUES AND BE-LIEFS BY ACCEPTING BELONGING-NESS TO A GROUP

. . . Allport formulates this point as a general principle of teaching people when he says, "It is an axiom that people cannot be taught who feel that

they are at the same time being attacked."

. . . In other words, in spite of whatever status differences there might be between them, the teacher and the student have to feel as members of one group in matters involving their sense of values . . . the normal gap between teacher and student, doctor and patient, social worker and public, can be a real obstacle to acceptance of the advocated conduct.

The chances for re-education seem to be increased whenever a strong we-feeling is created. The establishment of this feeling that everybody is in the same boat, has gone through the same difficulties, and speaks the same language is stressed as one of the main conditions facilitating the re-education of the alcoholic and the delinquent. . . .

When re-education involves the relinquishment of standards which are contrary to the standards of society at large (as in the case of delinquency, minority prejudices, alcoholism), the feeling of group belongingness seems to be greatly heightened if the members feel free to express openly the very sentiments which are to be dislodged through re-education. This might be viewed as another example of the seeming contradictions inherent in the process of re-education: Expression of prejudices against minorities or the breaking of rules of parliamentary procedures may in themselves be contrary to the desired goal. Yet a feeling of complete freedom and a heightened group identification are frequently more important at a particular stage of re-education than learning not to break specific rules.

This principle of in-grouping makes understandable why complete acceptance of previously rejected facts can be achieved best through the discovery of these facts by the group members themselves. . . . Then, and frequently only then, do the facts become really *their* facts (as against other people's facts). An individual will believe facts he himself has discovered in the same way that he believes in himself or in his group. The importance of this fact-finding process for the group by the group itself has been recently emphasized with reference to re-education in several fields. . . . It can be surmised that the extent to which social research is translated into social action depends on the degree to which those who carry out this action are made a part of the fact-finding on which the action is to be based.

Re-education influences conduct only when the new system of values and beliefs dominates the individual's perception. The acceptance of the new system is linked with the acceptance of a specific group, a particular role, a definite source of authority as new points of reference. It is basic for re-education that this linkage between acceptance of new facts or values and acceptance of certain groups or roles is very intimate and that the second frequently is a prerequisite for the first. This explains the great difficulty of changing beliefs and values in a piecemeal fashion. This linkage is a main factor behind resistance to re-education, but can also be made a powerful means for successful re-education.

❖❖❖❖❖❖❖❖❖❖❖❖❖❖❖❖❖ PROCESSES OF OPINION CHANGE *

Herbert C. Kelman

The Study of Social Influence

SOCIAL influence has been a central area of concern for experimental social psychology almost since its beginnings. Three general research traditions in this area can be distinguished: (1) The study of social influences on judgments, stemming out of the earlier work on prestige suggestion; [1] (2) the study of social influences arising from small group interaction; [2] and (3) the study of social influences arising from persuasive communications.[3] In recent years, there has been a considerable convergence between these three traditions, going hand in hand with an increased interest in developing general principles of social influence and socially induced behavior change.

One result of these developments has been that many investigators found it necessary to make qualitative distinctions between different types of influence. In some cases, these distinctions

---

* This paper is based on a research program on social influence and behavior change, supported by grant M-2516 from the National Institute of Mental Health.

[1] See, for example, S. E. Asch, *Social Psychology*, New York, Prentice-Hall, 1952.

[2] See, for example, D. Cartwright and A. Zander, editors, *Group Dynamics*, Evanston, Ill., Row, Peterson, 1953.

[3] See, for example, C. I. Hovland, I. L. Janis, and H. H. Kelley, *Communication and Persuasion*, New Haven, Yale University Press, 1953.

Excerpted from Herbert C. Kelman, "Processes of Opinion Change," Public Opinion Quarterly, Spring 1961. © Princeton University Press, 1961. Footnotes renumbered. Abridged and used by permission.

arose primarily out of the observation that social influence may have qualitatively different effects, that it may produce different kinds of change. For example, under some conditions it may result in mere public conformity—in superficial changes on a verbal or overt level without accompanying changes in belief; in other situations it may result in private acceptance—in a change that is more general, more durable, more integrated with the person's own values.[4] Other investigators found it necessary to make distinctions because they observed that influence may occur for different reasons, that it may arise out of different motivations and orientations. For example, under some conditions influence may be primarily informational—the subject may conform to the influencing person or group because he views him as a source of valid information; in other situations influence may be primarily normative—the subject may conform in order to meet the positive expectations of the influencing person or group.[5]

[4] See, for example, L. Festinger, "An Analysis of Compliant Behavior," in M. Sherif and M. O. Wilson, editors, *Group Relations at the Crossroads*, New York, Harper, 1953, pp. 232–256; H. C. Kelman, "Attitude Change as a Function of Response Restriction," *Human Relations*, Vol. 6, 1953, pp. 185–214; J. R. P. French, Jr. and B. Raven, "The Bases of Social Power," in D. Cartwright, editor, *Studies in Social Power*, Ann Arbor, Mich., Institute for Social Research, 1959, pp. 150–167; and Marie Jahoda, "Conformity and Independence," *Human Relations*, Vol. 12, 1959, pp. 99–120.

[5] See, for example, M. Deutsch and H. B. Gerard, "A Study of Normative and Informational Social Influence upon Individual Judgment," *Journal of Abnormal and Social Psychology*, Vol. 51, 1955, pp. 629–636; J. W. Thibaut and L. Strickland, "Psychological Set and Social Conformity," *Journal of Personality*, Vol. 25, 1956, pp. 115–129; and J. M. Jackson and H. D. Saltzstein, "The Effect of Person-Group Relationships on Conformity Processes,"

My own work can be viewed in the general context that I have outlined here. I started out with the distinction between public conformity and private acceptance, and tried to establish some of the distinct determinants of each. I became dissatisfied with this dichotomy as I began to look at important examples of social influence that could not be encompassed by it. I was especially impressed with the accounts of ideological conversion of the "true believer" variety, and with the recent accounts of "brain-washing," particularly the Chinese Communist methods of "thought reform."[6] It is apparent that these experiences do not simply involve public conformity, but that indeed they produce a change in underlying beliefs. But it is equally apparent that they do not produce what we would usually consider private acceptance—changes that are in some sense integrated with the person's own value system and that have become independent of the external source. Rather, they seem to produce new beliefs that are isolated from the rest of the person's values and that are highly dependent on external support.

These considerations eventually led me to distinguish three processes of social influence, each characterized by a distinct set of antecedent and a distinct set of consequent conditions. I have called these processes *compliance, identification,* and *internalization.*[7]

Journal of Abnormal and Social Psychology, Vol. 57, 1958, pp. 17–24.

[6] For instance, R. J. Lifton, " 'Thought Reform' of Western Civilians in Chinese Communist Prisons," *Psychiatry*, Vol. 19, 1956, pp. 173–195.

[7] A detailed description of these processes and the experimental work based on them will be contained in a forthcoming book, *Social Influence and Personal Belief: A Theoretical and Experimental Approach to the Study*

Three Processes of Social Influence

Compliance can be said to occur when an individual accepts influence from another person or from a group because he hopes to achieve a favorable reaction from the other. He may be interested in attaining certain specific rewards or in avoiding certain specific punishments that the influencing agent controls. For example, an individual may make a special effort to express only "correct" opinions in order to gain admission into a particular group or social set; or in order to avoid being fired from his government job. Or, the individual may be concerned with gaining approval or avoiding disapproval from the influencing agent in a more general way. For example, some individuals may compulsively try to say the expected thing in all situations and please everyone with whom they come in contact, out of a disproportionate need for favorable responses from others of a direct and immediate kind. In any event, when the individual complies, he does what the agent wants him to do—or what he thinks the agent wants him to do—because he sees this as a way of achieving a desired response from him. He does not adopt the induced behavior—for example, a particular opinion response—because he believes in its content, but because it is instrumental in the production of a satisfying social effect. What the individual learns, essentially, is to say or do the expected thing in special situations, regardless of what his private beliefs may be. Opinions adopted through compliance should be expressed only when

the person's behavior is observable by the influencing agent.

Identification can be said to occur when an individual adopts behavior derived from another person or a group because this behavior is associated with a satisfying self-defining relationship to this person or group. By a self-defining relationship I mean a role relationship that forms a part of the person's self-image. Accepting influence through identification, then, is a way of establishing or maintaining the desired relationship to the other, and the self-definition that is anchored in this relationship.

The relationship that an individual tries to establish or maintain through identification may take different forms. It may take the form of classical identification, that is, of a relationship in which the individual takes over all or part of the role of the influencing agent. To the extent to which such a relationship exists, the individual defines his own role in terms of the role of the other. He attempts to be like or actually to *be* the other person. By saying what the other says, doing what he does, believing what he believes, the individual maintains this relationship and the satisfying self-definition that it provides him. An influencing agent who is likely to be an attractive object for such a relationship is one who occupies a role desired by the individual—who possesses those characteristics that the individual himself lacks—such as control in a situation in which the individual is helpless, direction in a situation in which he is disoriented, or belongingness in a situation in which he is isolated.

The behavior of the brain-washed prisoner in Communist China provides one example of this type of identification. By adopting the attitudes and

of Behavior Change, to be published by John Wiley and Sons.

beliefs of the prison authorities—including *their* evaluation of *him*—he attempts to regain his identity, which has been subjected to severe threats. But, this kind of identification does not only occur in such severe crisis situations. It can also be observed, for example, in the context of socialization of children, where the taking over of parental attitudes and actions is a normal, and probably essential part of personality development. The more or less conscious efforts involved when an individual learns to play a desired occupational role and imitates an appropriate role model would also exemplify this process. Here, of course, the individual is much more selective in the attitudes and actions he takes over from the other person. What is at stake is not his basic sense of identity or the stability of his self-concept, but rather his more limited "professional identity."

The self-defining relationship that an individual tries to establish or maintain through identification may also take the form of a reciprocal role relationship—that is, of a relationship in which the roles of the two parties are defined with reference to one another. An individual may be involved in a reciprocal relationship with another specific individual, as in a friendship relationship between two people. Or, he may occupy a social role which is defined with reference to another, reciprocal role, as in the relationship between patient and doctor. A reciprocal role relationship can only be maintained if the participants have mutually shared expectations of one another's behavior. Thus, if an individual finds a particular relationship satisfying, he will tend to behave in such a way as to meet the expectations of the other. In other words, he will tend to behave in line with the requirements of this particular relationship. This should be true regardless of whether the other is watching or not: quite apart from the reactions of the other, it is important to the individual's own self-concept to meet the expectations of his friendship role, for example, or those of his occupational role.

Thus, the acceptance of influence through identification should take place when the person sees the induced behavior as relevant to and required by a reciprocal role relationship in which he is a participant. Acceptance of influence based on a reciprocal role relationship is similar to that involved in classical identification in that it is a way of establishing or maintaining a satisfying self-defining relationship to another. The nature of the relationship differs, of course. In one case it is a relationship of identity; in the other one of reciprocity. In the case of reciprocal role relationships, the individual is not identifying with the other in the sense of taking over *his* identity, but in the sense of empathically reacting in terms of the other person's expectations, feelings or needs.

Identification may also serve to maintain an individual's relationship to a group in which his self-definition is anchored. Such a relationship may have elements of classical identification as well as of reciprocal roles: to maintain his self-definition as a group member an individual, typically, has to model his behavior along particular lines and has to meet the expectations of his fellow members. An example of identification with a group would be the member of the Communist Party who derives strength and a sense of identity from his self-definition as part of the vanguard of the proletarian revolution and as an agent of historical destiny. A similar process, but at a low degree of intensity, is probably involved in many of the conventions that people acquire as part of their socialization into a particular group.

Identification is similar to compliance in that the individual does not adopt the induced behavior because its content per se is intrinsically satisfying. Identification differs from compliance, however, in that the individual actually believes in the opinions and actions that he adopts. The behavior is accepted both publicly and privately, and its manifestation does not depend on observability by the influencing agent. It does depend, however, on the role that an individual takes at any given moment in time. Only when the appropriate role is activated—only when the individual is acting within the relationship upon which the identification is based—will the induced opinions be expressed. The individual is not primarily concerned with pleasing the other, with giving him what he wants (as in compliance), but he is concerned with meeting the other's expectations for his own role performance. Thus, opinions adopted through identification do remain tied to the external source and dependent on social support. They are not integrated with the individual's value system, but rather tend to be isolated from the rest of his values—to remain encapsulated.

Finally, *internalization* can be said to occur when an individual accepts influence because the induced behavior is congruent with his value system. It is the content of the induced behavior that is intrinsically rewarding here. The individual adopts it because he finds it useful for the solution of a problem, or because it is congenial to his own orientation, or because it is demanded by his own values—in short, because he perceives it as inherently

conducive to the maximization of his values. The characteristics of the influencing agent do play an important role in internalization, but the crucial dimension here—as we shall see below—is the agent's credibility, that is, his relation to the content.

The most obvious examples of internalization are those that involve the evaluation and acceptance of induced behavior on rational grounds. A person may adopt the recommendations of an expert, for example, because he finds them relevant to his own problems and congruent with his own values. Typically, when internalization is involved, he will not accept these recommendations *in toto,* but modify them to some degree so that they will fit his own unique situation. Or, a visitor to a foreign country may be challenged by the different patterns of behavior to which he is exposed, and he may decide to adopt them (again, selectively and in modified form) because he finds them more in keeping with his own values than the patterns in his home country. I am not implying, of course, that internalization is always involved in the situations mentioned. One would speak of internalization only if acceptance of influence took the particular form that I described.

Internalization, however, does not necessarily involve the adoption of induced behavior on rational grounds. I would not want to equate internalization with rationality, even though the description of the process has decidedly rationalist overtones. For example, I would characterize as internalization the adoption of beliefs because of their congruence with a value system that is basically *irrational.* Thus, an authoritarian individual may adopt certain racist attitudes because they fit into his paranoid, irrational view of the world.

Presumably, what is involved here is internalization, since it is the content of the induced behavior and its relation to the person's value-system that is satisfying. Similarly, it should be noted that congruence with a person's value-system does not necessarily imply logical consistency. Behavior would be congruent if, in some way or other, it fit into the person's value-system, if it seemed to belong there and be demanded by it.

It follows from this conception that behavior adopted through internalization is, in some way—rational or otherwise—integrated with the individual's existing values. It becomes part of a personal system, as distinguished from a system of social role expectations. Such behavior gradually becomes independent of the external source. Its manifestation depends neither on observability by the influencing agent, nor on the activation of the relevant role, but on the extent to which the underlying values have been made relevant by the issues under consideration. This does not mean that the individual will invariably express internalized opinions, regardless of the social situation. In any specific situation, he has to choose among competing values in the face of a variety of situational requirements. It does mean, however, that these opinions will at least enter into competition with other alternatives whenever they are relevant in content.

It should be stressed that the three processes are not mutually exclusive. While they have been defined in terms of pure cases, they do not generally occur in pure form in real-life situations. The examples that have been given are, at best, situations in which a particular process predominates and determines the central features of the interaction.

Antecedents and Consequents of the Three Processes

For each of the three processes, a distinct set of antecedents and a distinct set of consequents have been proposed. These are summarized in Table 1. First, with respect to the antecedents of the three processes, it should be noted that no systematic quantitative differences between them are hypothesized. The probability of each process is presented as a function of the same three determinants: the importance of the induction for the individual's goal achievement, the power of the influencing agent, and the prepotency of the induced response. For each process, the magnitude of these determinants may vary over the entire range: each may be based on an induction with varying degrees of importance, on an influencing agent with varying degrees of power, and so on. The processes differ only in terms of the *qualitative* form that these determinants take. They differ, as can be seen in the table, in terms of the *basis* for the importance of the induction, the *source* of the influencing agent's power, and the *manner* of achieving prepotency of the induced response.

1. The processes can be distinguished in terms of the basis of the importance of the induction, that is, in terms of the nature of the motivational system that is activated in the influence situation. What is it about the influence situation that makes it important, that makes it relevant to the individual's goals? What are the primary concerns that the individual brings to the situation or that are aroused by it? The differences between the three processes in this respect are implicit in the descriptions of the processes given above: (a)

TABLE I

SUMMARY OF THE DISTINCTIONS BETWEEN THE THREE PROCESSES

	Compliance	*Identification*	*Internalization*
ANTECEDENTS:			
1. Basis for the importance of the induction	Concern with social effect of behavior	Concern with social anchorage of behavior	Concern with value congruence of behavior
2. Source of power of the influencing agent	Means-control	Attractiveness	Credibility
3. Manner of achieving prepotency of the induced response	Limitation of choice behavior	Delineation of role requirements	Reorganization of means-ends framework
CONSEQUENTS:			
1. Conditions of performance of induced response	Surveillance by influencing agent	Salience of relationship to agent	Relevance of values to issue
2. Conditions of change and extinction of induced response	Changed perception of conditions for social rewards	Changed perception of conditions for satisfying self-defining relationships	Changed perceptions of conditions for value maximization
3. Type of behavior system in which induced response is embedded	External demands of a specific setting	Expectations defining a specific role	Person's value-system

To the extent that the individual is concerned—for whatever reason—with the *social effect* of his behavior, influence will tend to take the form of compliance. (b) To the extent that he is concerned with the *social anchorage* of his behavior, influence will tend to take the form of identification. (c) To the extent to which he is concerned with the *value congruence* of his behavior (rational or otherwise), influence will tend to take the form of internalization.

2. A difference between the three processes in terms of the source of the

influencing agent's power is hypothesized. (a) To the extent to which the agent's power is based on his *means-control,* influence will tend to take the form of compliance. An agent possesses means-control if he is in a position to supply or withhold means needed by the individual for the achievement of his goals. The perception of means-control may depend on the agent's *actual* control over specific rewards and punishments, or on his *potential* control, which would be related to his position in the social structure (his status, authority, or general prestige). (b) To the extent to which the agent's power is based on his *attractiveness,* influence will tend to take the form of identification. An agent is attractive if he occupies a role which the individual himself desires [8] or if he occupies a role reciprocal to one the individual wants to establish or maintain. The term "attractiveness," as used here, does not refer to the possession of qualities that make a person likeable, but rather to the possession of qualities on the part of the agent that make a continued relationship to him particularly desirable. In other words, an agent is attractive when the individual is able to derive satisfaction from a self-definition with reference to him. (c) To the extent to which the agent's power is based on his *credibility,* influence will tend to take the form of internalization. An agent possesses credibility if his statements are considered truthful and valid, and hence worthy of serious consideration. Hovland, Janis and Kelley [9] distinguish two

bases for credibility: expertness and trustworthiness. In other words, an agent may be perceived as possessing credibility because he is likely to *know* the truth, or because he is likely to *tell* the truth. Trustworthiness, in turn, may be related to over-all respect, likemindedness, and lack of vested interest.

3. It is proposed that the three processes differ in terms of the way in which prepotency is achieved. (a) To the extent to which the induced response becomes prepotent—that is, becomes a "distinguished path" relative to alternative response possibilities—because the individual's choice behavior is limited, influence will tend to take the form of compliance. This may happen if the individual is pressured into the induced response, or if alternative responses are blocked. The induced response thus becomes prepotent because it is, essentially, the only response permitted: the individual sees himself as having no choice and as being restricted to this particular alternative. (b) To the extent to which the induced response becomes prepotent because the requirements of a particular role are delineated, influence will tend to take the form of identification. This may happen if the situation is defined in terms of a particular role relationship and the demands of that role are, more or less, clearly, specified: for instance, this role is made especially salient and the expectations deriving from it dominate the field. Or, it may happen if alternative roles are made ineffective because the situation is ambiguous and consensual validation is lacking. The induced response thus becomes prepotent because it is one of the few alternatives available to the individual: his choice behavior may be unrestricted, but his opportunity for selecting alternative responses is limited by the fact that he is operating exclusively

[8] This is similar to John Whiting's conception of "Status Envy" as a basis for identification. See J. W. M. Whiting, "Sorcery, Sin, and the Superego," in M. R. Jones, editor, *Nebraska Symposium on Motivation,* Lincoln, University of Nebraska Press, 1959, pp. 174–195.

[9] *Op. cit.,* p. 21.

from the point of view of a particular role system. (c) Finally, to the extent to which the induced response becomes prepotent because there has been a reorganization in the individual's conception of means-ends relationships, influence will tend to take the form of internalization. This may happen if the implications of the induced response for certain important values—implications of which the individual had been unaware heretofore—are brought out, or if the advantages of the induced response as a path to the individual's goals, compared to the various alternatives that are available, are made apparent. The induced response thus becomes prepotent because it has taken on a new meaning: as the relationships between various means and ends become restruc-

tured, it emerges as the preferred course of action in terms of the person's own values.

Depending, then, on the nature of these three antecedents, the influence process will take the form of compliance, identification, or internalization. Each of them corresponds to a characteristic pattern of internal responses—thoughts and feelings—in which the individual engages as he accepts influence. The resulting changes will, in turn, be different for the three processes, as indicated in the second half of the table. Here, again, it is assumed that there are no systematic quantitative differences between the processes, but rather qualitative variations in the subsequent histories of behaviors adopted through each process.

◆◆◆◆◆◆◆◆◆◆◆◆◆◆◆◆◆◆◆◆◆ INTERPERSONAL COMMUNICATION, GROUP SOLIDARITY, AND SOCIAL INFLUENCE   *Edgar H. Schein*

THE purpose of this paper is to examine some relationships between communication, group solidarity, and influenceability. Few topics in psychology have received as much attention as communication. We have looked at the nature of communication systems, at the flow of information within them, at the structural properties of languages, and at the function which communication plays in organized systems, be they groups, individuals, or neural networks. Only more recently, however, have we begun to consider some of the more subtle semantic and communication

problems which, I believe, lie at the root of social relationships. In particular, except in the study of psycho-therapy, we have not given enough attention to that aspect of communication which relates to the *maintenance* of social relationships, roles, and self-images. It is this maintenance of social relationships, roles, and self-images which, I believe, accounts in large measure for the stability both of groups and of individual personalities, and which represents, therefore, one of the greatest forces against change or influenceability. When we see behavior change and

From Edgar H. Schein, "Interpersonal Communication, Group Solidarity, and Social Influence," Sociometry, Vol. 23, No. 2, June 1960, pp. 148-161. Abridged and used by permission.

social influence occurring, or when we think it should be occurring, yet it is not, we might well focus our analysis on the interpersonal communication processes which are occurring and consider their implication for the social situation and the individuals within it.

The conceptual model which I will attempt to spell out below grew out of my studies of Chinese Communist techniques of controlling civilian and military prisoners during and after the Korean conflict. Most of my examples will be drawn, therefore, from the experiences of the prisoners. These experiences highlight the role which interpersonal communication plays in the destruction of the subject's social and personal integration and in his subsequent increase in influenceability. My aim in presenting these examples is not limited, however, to providing a sociopsychological explanation of what has popularly come to be termed as "brainwashing." An additional and perhaps more fundamental purpose is to provide some bases for a more general theory of influence which could encompass the kinds of attitude and value changes which we can witness in our own society.

A Conceptual Model: Creating Influenceability through Social Alienation [1]

In any ongoing situation the things that people *say* to each other, and nonverbally *do* with respect to each other carry two kinds of information: one, information directly relevant to the task that they are engaged in, and two, information about their feelings toward each other and toward the task,

[1] For many of the ideas in this formulation, I am indebted to the sociologist Erving Goffman.

reflecting in particular the value they attach to each other and to the task. In order for people to accomplish any kind of task together they must have a certain level of regard for each other, which is usually reflected in the degree of attention they give to each other, and they must have a certain level of involvement in the situation. If such regard or involvement is improperly low or high, it is a signal that the person cannot be trusted to fulfill his proper function, or worse, cannot be trusted not to take advantage of the other participants in the situation.

Such information is usually communicated through a host of gestures and non-verbal cues as well as through the content of what is said. For example, the way we dress, our social manners, the degree of deference we pay to the high status people, and the degree of energy with which we approach a task all serve to communicate to others whether we are properly involved or motivated, and therefore, whether we can be counted on to fulfill our role, be it in an office, on a combat mission, or at a party.

The importance of this type of interpersonal communication is twofold: *First,* the flow of cues which indicate that we have proper regard for each other and are properly involved in situations is critical for the maintenance of organized activity and group solidarity. *Second,* it is also critical for the maintenance of personal identity and security. Much of our personality is learned in and supported by a social context through the information which our significant others communicate to us concerning their evaluation of us. Because of this fact, we become susceptible to change when our social supports are destroyed or removed. Such potential influenceability can be hypothesized at the following levels of psychological functioning:

1. We become more influenceable at the level of *opinions and beliefs,* particularly in regard to those beliefs which are socially shared and operate as norms or standards of conduct. If we cease to have the kinds of relationships which imply mutual trust and regard, we cease to have access to each others' opinions and beliefs which, in turn, makes it virtually impossible for us to establish, check, or enforce social norms or standards.

2. Our *image of ourselves,* both its conscious and unconscious components, depends to a great extent on the confirmation provided to us by others through interpersonal communication. A good example is given by Goffman: In order for a girl to perceive herself as "beautiful" she must obtain from others a whole range of communication cues such as compliments, invitations to dates, "passes" made at her, etc., because beauty has no absolute standard against which it can be judged. The same sort of cues are, of course, required for us to see ourselves as intelligent, witty, manly, or what have you. In most of our daily life we operate in situations and groups which are fairly well integrated, hence we are largely unaware of the constant flow of such interpersonal communication and the confirmation of our selves which it provides. Only when such cues are absent or are manipulated in a destructive manner, as they were by the Chinese Communists, do we realize their importance.

3. Our *fundamental values,* whether we think of them in terms of super-ego, or moral conscience, or some other concept, probably depend to a great extent on the social support of individuals or institutions which operate as surrogates for the parents or the significant others from whom they were learned. One would at least suspect this conclusion from the frequent statements by psychotherapists that change can be produced in the patient only when such surrogate relationships are exposed and re-evaluated. Again, it is difficult to see this process in ordinary social life; only when marked social disorganization occurs do we see the manner in which morals are supported by social relationships.

In summary, the ongoing integrity of the individual is at several levels of his functioning dependent on adequate social integration which, in turn, is based on adequate interpersonal communication. When interpersonal cues cease to confirm the social relationships upon which the individual depends, he becomes socially alienated and susceptible to change at the level of opinion, belief, self-image, or basic value; the degree and depth of influenceability depend on the degree of alienation, the degree of pressure to change, and the availability of new opinions, beliefs, self-images, or values.

Social relationships here are not meant to be limited to face-to-face relationships. This term applies as well to the symbolic relationships which are implied by identifications with others who are absent or identifications with groups and organizations.

Interpersonal cues which cease to confirm social relationships can be of two kinds: (a) cues which tend to be destructive—that is, cues which tell us that we are held in contempt by others, that our social value is very low; and (b) cues which tend to be neutral—that is, cues which tell us that we are not regarded highly enough to be allowed to participate in intimate relationships or share confidences, but which do not devaluate us except as potential friends or confidants. Both kinds of cues tend to destroy the kind of social integration which is required to sustain high personal integration, but there is a difference in degree, if not in kind, between the destructive effect of being held in contempt and the destructive effect of being merely mistrusted.

Thus far I have tried to argue that the reduction of confirming interpersonal cues makes a person more influenceable because it removes some of the forces which ordinarily operate to make him resist being influenced; in effect, such reduction "unfreezes" him by removing some of the "restraining forces," to use Lewin's terminology. If such unfreezing occurs, what is the probability that it will be followed by influence or change? The probability is high for two reasons: First, social alienation is an unsatisfying psychological state which induces strong motives toward regaining old or finding new social relationships. Such social reintegration can probably not occur without some personal change. Second, social alienation, by cutting off the individual from accustomed sources of information on which to base his judgment, heightens his susceptibility to cognitive re-definition. By cognitive re-definition I mean a process of accepting new definitions for existing concepts, placing concepts into new scales of evaluation, or shifting the anchors or neutral points on such scales. Whichever of these processes occurs, the individual's judgments and consequently his behavior will change, as a result. The adoption of new definitions, scales, or anchors occurs through the process of learning to pay attention to how others in the environment view the alienated individual and the total situation, and by identifying with them. If

no alternative models are available and the situation is ambiguous, the individual probably redefines it in a direction which maximizes his immediate chances of social reintegration and also minimizes other stresses to which he is exposed.

Creating Social Alienation in POWs

In the case of the Chinese Communist treatment of United Nations prisoners of war, we have excellent examples of undermining without completely destroying the bonds which hold groups together, thus reducing the flow of confirming interpersonal cues, and thereby heightening social alienation and the individual prisoner's susceptibility to being influenced to collaborate with his captor. This result was accomplished by manipulating the overall situation, the communication channels and the communication content.

One basic device was to destroy the authority structure of the group by systematically segregating leaders and other key personnel from the remainder of the group, or systematically undermining their own authority. As examples of the latter may be cited the rather frequent choice of low ranking enlisted men as squad leaders in prison camp, on the grounds that under Communism rank no longer had any significance and that it was the workingman who should get all the breaks. A further device was to threaten the higher ranking officers with punishment of their group if they failed to cooperate with the Chinese by providing slanted radio broadcasts or other kinds of propaganda. Attempts by the higher ranking officers to work out compromises which would satisfy the Chinese, yet which would provide increased chances of survival for their men, would often appear to the lower ranking officers like collaboration. They would then either covertly or overtly fail to obey orders, thus destroying the chain of command.

This process of social decay was aided by the fact that the first months of captivity had been marked by extreme physical privation and a high prisoner death rate which stimulated some competition for the very scarce supplies of food, medicine, and other means of survival. From the very beginning, the Chinese indicated to the prisoners that, if they were cooperative in re-educating themselves and learning the "truth" about the Korean war, they could expect better treatment. Of course, being cooperative meant being willing to give radio broadcasts and other propaganda to the effect that being a prisoner of war in Chinese hands was a pleasant affair, and so on.

In any *large* group of men such as an army, there will be a few opportunists, psychopaths, and psychotics who will take advantage of any situation for personal gain. The willingness of these men to compete and to collaborate, and the rewarding of such behavior by the Chinese began to create a general atmosphere of mutual mistrust which was heightened by several additional techniques of manipulating the POWs. For example, a sizeable group of men would be told that, if they cooperated by giving propaganda broadcasts, they would be repatriated; then the group would be split up into smaller groups some of which would be marched off in the direction of the front lines and then taken to another collection point for prisoners, leaving the impression that they had cooperated, given broadcasts, and been repatriated or rewarded in some other fashion. Also, Chinese guards would spy intensively on conversations of the most trivial and intimate nature, look for infractions of camp rules, pull in the culprit and accuse him, force him to confess, then leave him in a state of wondering how they could have known of his words or deeds unless there were more informers in camp than he had previously suspected. During interrogations a man would often be asked a question and after continued refusal to answer would be shown that the Chinese already had the answer. Then he would be asked if he would copy the answer out of the Chinese document. If he did so to get the Chinese "off his back" for a little while, his copy would be shown to another man who was being interrogated with the statement: "Why do you continue to hold out; look, your friend so-and-so has already given us the answer." These and many other devices were used to create the image that almost everyone else was collaborating, so why not you?

The Communists also prohibited any organized activity not specifically sanctioned by them. For example, religious services, social gatherings, athletic events, and so on were prohibited for most of the first two years of captivity. Thus, not even by shared rituals could prisoners reaffirm their solidarity. Any attempt at organized resistance or escape was severely punished and the group responsible split up.

The most striking examples of actual interference in the communication process were the uses of what might be called testimonials. I have already cited the example of tricking an individual into writing out material in interrogation and presenting this to another prisoner as if it had been spontaneously given. In the same category fell the utilization of a small number of men who had made germ-warfare confessions and who were then sent to various camps to give lectures and answer questions. The sincerity of their answers and the small details of their confessions were very convincing to many a prisoner. Still another device was to offer prizes like fruit or cigarettes for essays or articles in the camp newspaper. Of course, the winning essay was usually the one which most agreed with the Communist line. Once obtained by the Chinese, such an essay would be circulated widely among the other prisoners. Those few men who found themselves in a position of cooperating regularly with the Chinese would be used to try to get other prisoners to be more cooperative as well.

Identifications with groups and individuals outside of prison camp also became the targets of Chinese Communist manipulation. The best example was the selective delivery of mail. In some cases, the Chinese did not give a man any of his mail, at the same time solicitously pointing out that there had been no mail for him, which could only mean that his loved ones at home no longer cared about him. In other cases, they only delivered mail which contained bad news or was completely devoid of anything meaningful, and withheld mail which was either directly reassuring or contained news which could be reassuring. At the same time, the mass media of communication were completely saturated by Communist propaganda. Most prisoners did not see a Western non-Communist newspaper or hear a non-Communist radio broadcast during their entire captivity, unless, of course, such a medium contained news which played into Communist hands. Our manifest lack of concern about the Korean war would be a good example of the kind of news which the prisoners were surely given.

Of course the most obvious example of cutting communication channels was solitary confinement which was used for varying lengths of time up to two years or more in the case of some prisoners. However, the effects of solitary confinement were by no means clearcut. In many men it led to a tremendous need to communicate with someone, a need which interrogators have played upon for centuries; in such men it sometimes also led to real loss of assurance about their personal identity and self-image, particularly if they were deprived of the means of living in a civilized fashion, for example if they were deprived of any means of keeping clean. For other men, however, the total lack of interpersonal cues was less threatening to their integrity and sense of integration with reference groups than being systematically given cues that they were not trusted by others or were not worthy of any regard. In particular, men whose reference group identifications were very strong and whose self-images were in part organized around solitude and meditation, for example highly religious individuals, welcomed solitary confinement as a relief from pressure. This fact, by the way, highlights the superiority of actively manipulating interpersonal communication over a mere cutting of the communication channels for the production of social alienation. A man can be most alienated in the very midst of many others, as the examples below will show

The systematic manipulation of communication and social relationships among prisoners of war produced a degree of social alienation which was characterized in most men by a systematic withdrawal of involvement from *all* social situations. They lived increasingly in a shell, going through certain of the motions of cooperating with the Chinese without getting overinvolved, or so they believed, at the same time giving up attempts to establish relationships with other prisoners whom they did not really trust or regard highly. However, the social alienation was not sufficient in most instances to disconfirm the prisoners' self-image or destroy his basic values. At most, the process made a man doubtful and insecure.

Creating Social Alienation in Civilians in Chinese Communist Prisons

To find examples of a more intensive destruction of identification with family and reference groups, and the destruction of social role and self-image we must turn to the experiences of civilian political prisoners interned within Chinese Communist prisons. In such prisons the total regimen, consisting of physical privation, prolonged interrogation, total isolation from former relationships and sources of information, detailed regimentation of all daily activities, and deliberate humiliation and degradation, was geared to producing a complete confession of alleged crimes, and the assumption of a penitent role depicting the adoption of a Communist frame of reference. The prisoner was not informed what his crimes were, nor was it permissible to evade the issue by making up a false confession. Instead, what the prisoner learned he must do was re-evaluate his past from the point of view of the Communists and recognize that most of his former attitudes and behavior were actually criminal from this point of view. For example, a priest who had dispensed food to needy peasants in his mission church had to recognize that he was actually a tool of imperialism and was using his missionary activities as a cover for exploitation of the peasants. Even worse, he may have had to recognize that he was using food as blackmail to accomplish his aims.

The key technique used by the Communists to produce social alienation to a degree sufficient to allow such redefinition and re-evaluation to occur was to put the prisoner into a cell with four or more other prisoners who were somewhat more advanced in their "thought reform" than he. Such a cell usually had one leader who was responsible to the prison authorities, and the progress of the whole cell was made contingent upon the progress of the least "reformed" member. This condition meant in practice that four or more cell members devoted all their energies to getting their least "reformed" member to recognize the truth about himself and to confess. To accomplish this they typically swore at, harangued, beat, denounced, humiliated, reviled, and brutalized their victim twenty-four hours a day, sometimes for weeks or months on end. If the authorities felt that the prisoner was basically uncooperative they manacled his hands behind his back and chained his ankles, which made him completely dependent on his cell mates for the fulfillment of his basic needs. It was this reduction to an animal-like existence in front of other humans which, I believe, constituted the ultimate humiliation and led most reliably to the destruction of the prisoner's image of himself. Even in his own eyes he became something which was not worthy of the regard of his fellow man.

If, to avoid complete physical and personal destruction, the prisoner began to confess in the manner desired of him, he was usually forced to prove his sincerity by making irrevocable behavioral commitments, such as denouncing and implicating his friends and relatives in his own newly recognized crimes. Once he had done this he became further alienated from his former self, even in his own eyes, and could seek security only in a new identity and new social relationships. Aiding this process of confessing was the fact that the crimes gave the prisoner something concrete to which to attach the free-floating guilt which the accusing environment and his own humiliation usually stimulated.[2]

Influence through Identification and Social Reintegration

As I indicated previously, I am assuming that adult humans are powerfully motivated to know themselves, to have some kind of positive viable self-image and a set of social roles which are confirmed in interaction with others. A state of social alienation, therefore, implies powerful motives toward personal and social integration, and initiates searching behavior on the part of the alienated individual for some meaningful relationship, role, and self-image. The usual case, both in the prisoner of war camps and in the political prisons, was that the only relationships which were permitted to grow were with the Communists or with prisoners who were cooperating with them. Such relationships were strongly encouraged and facilitated by a variety of means. A good example was the plight of the sick and wounded prisoners of war who, because of their physical con-

finement, were unable to escape from continual contact with their interrogator or instructor, and who therefore often ended up forming a close relationship with him. Chinese Communist instructors often encouraged prisoners to take long walks or have informal talks with them and offered as incentives cigarettes, tea, and other rewards. If the prisoner was willing to cooperate and become a "progressive," he could join with other "progressives" in an active group life.

Within the political prison, the group cell provided not only the forces toward alienation but also offered the road to a "new self." Not only were there available among the fellow prisoners individuals with whom the prisoner could identify because of their shared plight, but, once he showed any tendency to seek a new identity by truly trying to re-evaluate his past, he received again a whole range of rewards of which perhaps the most important was the interpersonal information that he was again a person worthy of respect and regard. The force of the motivation to have some identity can be deduced from the fact that positive relationships typically formed in the group cell in spite of the ever present atmosphere of mutual hostility.

Influence through Cognitive Re-definition

When groups become disorganized through the kinds of manipulation cited above for POW groups, not only does it become impossible to communicate and enforce existing norms, but it becomes impossible to share in the formation of new norms for situational contingencies not previously encountered. Being a prisoner of war, in the first place, and being handled in the

---

[2] The number of cases in which such a process occurred is extremely small. The description presented here is included to illustrate the model of influence, not as a typical account of how prisoners fared in Chinese Communist prisons. In many such prisons the thought reform program was ineffective and could be successfully resisted by the prisoner.

pseudo-benevolent manner which characterized the Chinese Communist approach, in the second place, were for most men highly novel and highly ambiguous situations to which our cultural norms and standards of conduct did not readily apply. The problem, then, was not that a man became unsure of his moral principles, such as the wrongness of collaborating with the enemy. Rather, the new and ambiguous situation made it difficult to determine what sort of behavior would actually be a violation of such moral principles.[3] The Chinese put considerable effort into providing the prisoner with suitable rationales for collaborative behavior, which would allow him to re-define his situation in a manner that would absolve him. Such re-definition might take the form of not recognizing that his behavior was in fact helping the enemy, or might take the form of re-evaluating relative priorities where conflicting values were involved. An officer might see less harm in giving the Chinese propaganda than in risking having his men shot; a prisoner might see greater importance in letting his loved ones at home know that he was alive by making a radio broadcast than in preventing the Chinese from getting a bit of propaganda out of him; or to put the matter more extremely, a man might see less harm in collaborating than in letting a friend die because the Chinese would not give him medicine unless he collaborated.

The important point about these examples is that they all involve some

cognitive evaluations and some judgments concerning the consequences of a given course of action. The ambiguity of the situation, the Chinese saturation of the informational environment with their concept of the "truth," and the physical pressures on the men made it quite likely that some shifts in scales of judgment would occur, and that errors in assessing the consequences of collaborative behavior would also occur. However, it was also quite likely that in the whole prisoner population there were many who, because of previous experience or specialized knowledge, could have made more accurate assessments which could have become the basis for shared norms and standards of conduct. However, in a situation in which men were prevented from communicating with each other, did not trust each other, or had low regard for each other, there was no opportunity to share such knowledge. This statement is confirmed by the accounts of many men that successful resistance was usually organized around a few key individuals, often non-commissioned officers with broad experience, who were able to maintain clandestine relationships with other prisoners of war, and who would advise them how far they could co-operate with the Chinese without giving them anything of real propaganda value or getting involved with them in an ir-revocable fashion. These instances of failure to produce alienation highlight the importance of effective communication channels as prerequisites to resistance.

In the political prison the pressure toward cognitive re-definition was, of course, present to an even more intense degree. Not only was there unremitting pressure on the prisoner to shift his frame of reference and to re-evaluate his own self-image and past behavior, but

[3] This ambiguity is actually still present after the fact, as evidenced by the difficulty in our own country of enunciating a clear policy toward POW behavior. Accounts in the press and popularized analyses have shifted markedly in the last few years from blaming collaboration on Communist mistreatment to blaming it on POW misconduct.

there were available ever present models of how to do this, combined with complete isolation from all contacts which could in any manner affirm the old self-image or social norms. Through identifying with cell mates, the prisoner came to pay attention to their point of view which led to a re-defining of his own. Behavior previously seen as innocent could then be judged as criminal, and a past life based on capitalist premises could be seen as evil.[4]

Recapitulation and Conclusions

Social and personal integration depend on interpersonal cues which confirm social norms and the individual's beliefs, self-image, basic values, and social role. When such cues are absent or disconfirming, the individual becomes socially alienated, which makes him susceptible to influence for three reasons: First, forces against change are reduced or removed; second, motives toward re-integration are induced; and third, cognitive redefinitions are facilitated.

My reasons for emphasizing this kind of influence model are twofold. First, we need a better understanding of the technique employed by the Communists in attempting to influence captives and their potential or actual effects.

[4] The degree of permanence of the change which was produced in a few individuals by a process such as that described depended, of course, on the kinds of interpersonal cues they were exposed to following their repatriation. If their newly acquired identity and set of attitudes were not acceptable to their "significant others" back home, a new and comparable influence process was set into motion. In the few cases where such changes have persisted, there is good evidence that the individuals sought out and attached themselves emotionally to others who would support the new identity and attitude structure. These observations are based on a recent follow-up study of some of the civilian repatriates.

Certainly we need to go beyond some of the thinking often expressed in our mass media—that the behavior of prisoners of the Communists is either the result of mysterious occult devices or is the result of personal weakness reflecting social pathology in our society. Second: we need conceptual tools with which to explore further those institutions within our own society which are presumably geared to producing profound and lasting changes in their adult inmates, students, or patients.

When one examines institutions such as prisons, mental hospitals, basic training centers, intensive educational workshops, and so on, one is struck by the need to conceptualize what goes on in them at a level somewhat broader than is reflected in most experimental studies of social influence. In particular, one is struck by the number of similarities in such institutions with respect to the manipulation of social relationships. For example, a frequent practice in prisons, mental hospitals, educational workshops, reformatories, religious retreats, basic training centers, monasteries, nunneries, academies, and so on, is to isolate the inmates from their former social relationships, either by physically confining them or by regimenting their daily routine to such an extent that they do not have time to maintain such relationships.

In authoritarian institutions, like prisons, to which inmates are sent involuntarily, there also tend to be systematic efforts on the part of the staff to destroy the internal organization of the inmate group. This fact has been noted in the prison situation and is embodied in the admonition to prisoners to "serve their *own* time." Evidences of internal organization among prisoners result in punishment for some men, removal to another cell block for others. At the same time, social alienation is fostered by the bestowing of special favors, rewards, or privileges for cooperation with the authorities. In reformatories in which there is a reasonably high rate of success of reform, one finds the key to this success in the identification of the inmates with one or more members of the staff through whom they learn new norms, self-images, and values. Such identifications can only occur when old social bonds have been undermined.

In the mental hospital we have recognized that therapy operates through the medium of forming a relationship with a psychiatrist or some other member of the staff. What we have recognized less often is that sometimes the hospital staff will, in a number of subtle ways, destroy the internal organization of the patient group, usually by moving patients from one ward to another, thus preventing stable friendships. Whether the alienation of the patient from other patients is an aid or hindrance to therapy I am not prepared to say, but it would seem to be a problem worthy of investigation. In many of these institutions, a major function of reducing inmate organization is to maintain better control over the inmate population, but perhaps such practices have other functions as well.

By focusing on social alienation, I do not wish to bypass the fact that in many change-producing institutions social organization among inmates is encouraged and is considered to heighten rather than weaken influenceability. This emphasis would certainly be true of educational workshops, religious revivals, voluntarily entered group therapy, and so on. The fact that these institutions are voluntary would appear to be one common feature which differentiates them from prisons and mental hospitals. They also differ in that the participants presumably are motivated to change or be influenced, and that the staff does not feel it necessary to impose its own authority coercively over the inmates. Instead, participants themselves are expected to assume a certain amount of responsibility and authority. An interesting middle ground is found in institutions which are entered voluntarily and with motivation to change, but which involve total submission to authority—for example, monasteries and academies. The fact that such institutions initially tend to destroy the internal organization of inmates would suggest that such destruction is more closely related to the nature of authority in the institution than to the degree of voluntariness of entry or motivation to change.

THE PUBLIC HEALTH WORKER AS AN AGENT OF SOCIO-CULTURAL CHANGE   *Cora Du Bois* *

I NEED not underscore my pleasure at being asked to join you in honoring Dorothy Nyswander. Most of us here this evening have honored her for many years, but it is pleasant to have annually a public and formal opportunity that serves to punctuate our continuing esteem. But the very purpose of this occasion places serious responsibility on a speaker. The title selected nonchalantly last fall is a further challenge. Fortunately, the intervening months have been spent at the Center for Advanced Study in the Behavioral Sciences where many ideas are in ferment and there are many intellectual resources. To those intervening months and the Fellows at the Center, I am deeply indebted.†

Both analysts and practitioners in the contemporary world have an almost compulsive interest in change—and small wonder! The Western World has undergone in the first half of the Twentieth Century changes so momentous and so often stressed that they need no comment. Similarly, at least the leadership of the non-Western World holds aspirations for their societies that promise changes there even more dramatic than those experienced in the West.

It is not so much what these changes are, in a descriptive sense, that need concern us here, as the question of understanding how they occur. More particularly, as public health workers you are concerned with change that is both induced and planned. Neither revolutionary processes of change nor accidental ones (if there be any) need preoccupy us tonight.

The Intrapsychic Approach to Change

The approaches to change are as varied as the discipline concerned with the question. Psychologists are likely to see change from inside the individual looking out. They perceive change as alterations in people's perceptions, cognitions, affects, and attitudes, and on through the armamentarium of concepts used by psychologists. For example, last year Dr. Gordon Allport of Harvard, who delivered the second Dorothy B. Nyswander Lecture, spoke

---

* Zemurray Professor (anthropology), Harvard University and Radcliffe College, Cambridge, Massachusetts.

† I am also greatly indebted to Dr. Melford E. Spiro for a careful reading of this paper. Dr. Jerome Frank was also kind enough to give me the benefit of his advice. It is a pleasure to acknowledge my debt to both.

From Cora Du Bois, "The Public Health Worker as an Agent of Socio-Cultural Change," Health Education Monographs, No. 5, 1959, pp. 3–19, published by the Society of Public Health Educators, Inc., Oakland, Calif. Used by permission. Originally, this was the third Dorothy B. Nyswander Lecture. It was delivered in Berkeley, April 24, 1959. The lectureship was established in honor of Dr. Nyswander upon her retirement as Professor of Health Education at the University of California.

of "Perception and Public Health," (1) and gave wise and learned counsel on personal and cultural proceptual differences, and the role they may play in public health work. Or, for example, Dr. Leon Festinger in his recent book on "A Theory of Cognitive Dissonance" (?) gives us a more important lead into the dynamics of the strain for consistency and its bearing on attitude changes. He points out that cognitive dissonance arises when new events, new information, or decisions face an individual. Through the process of rationalization the individual attempts to reestablish consonance, i.e., consistency, by changes of cognition, or changes of behavior, or changes of values. However, if the discrepancy between established and new information is too great, one way of maintaining consonance is to reject the new. While it is important for the public health worker to realize that the strain for consistency may work for him in inducing change, it is equally important to realize that it may work against him, if the gap between the old and the new is too disturbing. People will avoid individuals and situations that are likely to increase dissonance to the point of discomfort. In sum we can say: The higher the involvement the greater the dissonance, and the more vigorous the rejection of the new. Since cognition is primarily determined by reality (or at least reality as it is proceived—to use Dr. Allport's term) relevance becomes an important issue. If two facts are opposites in a logical sense, that is, if two facts cannot be put into one category; if they are mutually exclusive and exhaustive, that means they are likely to arouse dissonance on a cognitive level. But if two facts are simply irrelevant, if they appear to bear no relation to each other, then cognitive dissonance

is presumably in abeyance. For example, a thing cannot be both red and green. To insist that they are is to arouse dissonance. But to know that roses are red and sugar is sweet is to know two irrelevant facts.

In arguments of this kind examples are often helpful. For example, if a health educator enters a community where it is commonly held that fever is caused by a grandfather's punitive ghost and if the health worker proclaims that this belief is false and that the truth is that fever is caused by mosquitoes, he will precipitate dissonance. But it will be a dissonance difficult to test. The health worker will be hard put to prove that grandfather's ghost does *not* cause fever and equally hard pressed within the proceptive framework of the community to prove that mosquitoes *do* cause fever. On the other hand, if the health worker merely says that mosquitoes breed in water and produce fever, he will be engaging in irrelevances within the proceptive framework of that community. In the first instance, the health worker may be avoided as a person who precipitates unpleasant dissonances. In the second instance, even though the health worker may succeed in having all the standing water drained, he has made no headway precisely because no cognitive dissonance has been aroused. When the health worker leaves, the ameliorative measures will be abandoned. No more than irrelevant activity has taken place. The resources for change inherent in cognitive dissonance have not been tapped.

But now let us suppose that a health worker claims that injections cure yaws whereas the common belief in the society is that poultices cure yaws. Here is dissonance, but dissonance subject to the reality testing of cognitive powers. The strain for consistency will be enlisted to change beliefs and behaviors. Injections and the cure of yaws can be cognitively brought into consonance. A *technical* change has been successfully introduced. When preventive and curative medicine are isolated from each other, the possibility of reality testing in the technical dimension of culture is diminished. In my opinion, this separation of preventive from curative medicine was an important element in reducing the success of the Rockefeller health demonstration units in India during the 1920's and 1930's. Speaking theoretically, exclusive emphasis on preventive medicine minimizes the possibility of reality testing and fails to exploit cognitive dissonance and the strain for consistency in the human personality.

We must return to this subject later in a different context—particularly in the context of designating the change described as a technical one.

The Interpersonal Approach to Change

Although many other intrapsychic sources for change could undoubtedly be found, my intention is not to survey systematically but only to illustrate. So, let us shift from the intrapsychic to the interpersonal level in the appraisal of change. Osgood and Tannenbaum, in an article discussing congruity and attitude changes, conclude that if a highly regarded person holds views different from one's own, the change may be either toward a lower regard for the person or a modification of one's opinion. The higher the esteem in which the person is held, the more likely it is that the opinion will change.(3) Merton reaches analogous conclusions. Speaking of value-homophily between friends

he says, "In the give-and-take of the friendship, initial divergences of value tend to be reduced. If the friends have an approximately equal emotional stake in the relationship, this is likely to occur through mutual accommodation of their values. If one is more deeply involved in the relationship than the other, his values are more likely to be modified to accord with the values of the less deeply involved."(4)

Kelman(5) working at a comparable level of analysis adds further dimensions to Merton's and Osgood's proposals. Kelman charts the antecedents and consequences of three different processes of attitude change which he labels compliance, identification, and internalization. It is difficult to do justice to Dr. Kelman's argument in so brief a condensation. However, let us select some diagnostic features of these three processes and assume for our present purposes that the agent is the public health worker and that the actor is the person he hopes to persuade.

In compliance, the agent of change possesses means of control or surveillance. The actor adopts the induced behavior because he expects to gain specific rewards or approval and avoid specific punishment or disapproval by conforming. The response of the actor, however, does not become part of his framework of values.

Any health worker who has done field work will readily recognize this type of change, particularly if he has worked in underdeveloped countries where he has entered a community, or served in a newly established Ministry of Public Health, backed by the prestige of a powerful government or of an international agency. Where change depends on compliance, permanence of change is unlikely. As soon as the foreign worker leaves, the innovations that were initiated are likely to be abandoned.

Now let us turn to the process of attitude change called identification by Kelman. In identification the agent of change is an attractive figure. The actor accepts influence because he wants to establish or maintain a satisfying, self defining relationship to the agent. This is congruent with what Merton has to say about value-homophily in friendship. The actor believes in the responses which he adopts, but their specific content is more or less irrelevant. The new response is accepted as a value, but it is isolated from other values held by the actor.

Again any experienced health worker can recall example after example of this kind of experience. One that comes to mind is of a Minister of Health, recently returned from training abroad, who called out the army to administer mass inoculations in the capital city on market day, when people streamed in from the countryside. In this case, the Minister of Health had identified with Western medicine and wanted to define himself as related to it. The people inoculated obviously only complied.

Kelman's third process of attitude change, internalization, represents the kind of change all serious health workers wish to achieve. In internalization, the agent of change is credible rather than just attractive. The actor's cognitive field is reorganized. (To use Festinger's language the force of cognitive dissonance is utilized to establish consistency.) The actor sees the nature and utility of the new behavior and perceives its relevance to issues. The new is not only valued; it is also integrated with other values.

I should like to suggest that Kelman's three processes of attitude change, seen from the viewpoint of an anthropologist studying acculturation, may have diachronic (i.e. sequential) implications. This also is a point to which I shall return later.

In any event, Osgood, Merton, and Kelman, all see change as a function not only of intrapsychic forces but also of interpersonal relations. The implications for the public health worker are legion. The credibility and/or the affection in which he is held in any community, the kinds of interpersonal relations he is capable of establishing, are crucial factors in effecting change. But equally crucial are the persons in the community who are prepared to establish a relationship with the health worker. Induced or planned change can be viewed as a relationship between agent and actor. Readiness must exist in both. Such formulations remove from the field worker's shoulders exclusive responsibility for the success of a program. They should place in more realistic context the goals that planners may legitimately formulate for practitioners.

The importance of such interpersonal relationships are stressed because they have been insufficiently emphasized by technically minded planners. Personal relationships and the sociology of small groups make up a relatively new field of investigation in the social discipline. Important as that field is, it remains still largely unassimilated into other less interstitial fields of social inquiry.

But please understand me, while stressing the importance for change, of interpersonal and small group relations, I am not claiming that all elements of change reside in such interactions, but only that it is a significant area and one too often ignored by those who plan and carry out health programs.

No one would claim, for example, that the introduction of cattle, disease, and western artifacts into the Hawaiian Islands toward the end of the 18th century and the beginning of the 19th were insignificant in producing changes. But it could be argued that the long and faithful service rendered by a British seaman to King Kamehameha I was equally formative. Also it could be argued that the early missionaries were potent influences leading, after the death of Kamehameha I, to the repudiation by his queen of the whole tabu system on which Hawaiian social relations and subsistence rested.

In the same vein, the defeat of Japan in World War II and the policy of democratization pursued by SCAP (Supreme Commander for the Allied Powers) were certainly not negligible. But the results were not always in the direction foreseen. Nor had they always the hoped-for permanence. What was perhaps *not* foreseen was the very great influence of the G.I. in his interpersonal relations and particularly in contracting legal or illegal relationships with Japanese women. In fact, so little was the potential for change foreseen in these informal personal ties that every effort was made to restrict them.

In any society that tends to view life technically, to persuade by mass media, to fragment people into congeries of traits appropriate for statistical analysis, to see change in terms of goals that must be achieved in one to five years— in any such society it becomes necessary to plead the importance of interpersonal relationships and of small groups if this significant dynamic for change is not to be overlooked. Trusted counselors and friends, wives and mistresses, parents and children, esteemed colleagues, can often make or break the best laid programs of planners.

Modes of Adaptive Behavior

Let us now turn from these intimate, though dynamic, forces bearing on socio-cultural change to another work of Robert Merton. In *Social Theory and Social Structure*(6) Merton discusses deviant behavior. He suggests five categories of role behavior that describe *modes of adaptation,* not personalities. The five proposed modes of adaptive behavior are: conformity, innovation, ritualism, retreatism, and rebellion. Although Merton discusses these categories in terms of role behavior within the American cultural scene, I believe they may have cross-cultural implications, since Vogt, working on acculturation processes among Navaho veterans, independently emerged with some analogous categories.(7) I also believe that Merton's categories of adaptation may provide the public health worker with at least some preliminary guides for identifying groups or individuals who may be crucial allies, or deadly opponents, in effecting social changes.

Conformity, as a mode of adaptation, means that cultural goals are closely meshed with institutional means for their achievement. Groups or individuals possessing this mode of adaptation are not likely to be easily changed. They represent the stable and conservative elements in a society although this does not necessarily mean that they are its most powerful or successful members. The French peasantry of the early Twentieth Century or the upper middle class of small urban communities in the United States might possibly be considered examples of groups for whom goals and the available institutions mesh. There is no gap or at least a minimum gap between aspirations on the one hand and means for their realization on the other hand. If their goals do not already coincide with those of the public health worker, they will not be easily persuaded to change. They would at most react in the manner proposed by Kelman in his compliance category. If on the other hand, their goals do coincide with those of the health worker, Merton's conformist mode of adaptation would coincide with Kelman's proposed internalization category.

Innovation, as a mode of adaptation, means by Merton's definition that there are no, or inadequate, institutional means for the achievement of cultural goals. In other words, there is a gap between aspirations and ways of implementing them. Groups or individuals in this position are probably the most receptive to institutional innovations. Psychologically they may be considered to fit Kelman's identification category. I suspect that the leaders of many of the new nations belong to this mode of adaptation. They have accepted Western goals and wish to create the institutions necessary to support them. With such groups the role of the public health worker is relatively, but only relatively, easy. The task is the creation of cadres of trained personnel and the institutional framework within which they can work. The task, with such groups, is not to persuade, nor even to achieve the goal of improved health, but rather to provide such innovators with ways and means for them to build their own appropriate, supporting institutions for goals the health worker and innovators share. I see this task as the primary and most feasible one facing the World Health Organization or our own overseas health assistance program. Since these agencies can operate in countries only on the invitation of governments, they are assured of a group already sharing somewhat the goals of Western medicine. The international or foreign agency's task is then to assist such groups in establishing effectively organized and staffed departments of public health.

Merton's third mode of adaptation is ritualism. In ritualistic groups or individuals the cultural goals are muted compared to a compulsive insistence on institutional means. Groups and individuals to whom this mode of adaptation is congenial are not hard to identify. Bureaucracies and professions are frequently, and the world over, prone to ritualistic adaptation. Here the role of the public health worker is fraught with a double danger. Our own medical and health traditions frequently encourage ritualistic behavior at the expense of ultimate goals. Vaihinger's law of "the preponderance of the means over the end" has in my observation often led medical and health workers to insist on forms at the expense of content. Ritualism as a mode of adaptation is a professional hazard. When it runs head on against another group's ritualism, deadlock, rather than change, too often results.

The fourth mode of adaptation suggested by Merton is retreatism. Here both goals and institutional means are rejected. As Merton says, "people who adapt (or mal-adapt) in this fashion are, strictly speaking, *in* the society but not *of* it."(8) Like those who resort to ritualism, retreatists are not hard to identify. They may be objects of concern for the public health worker but they are not fulcrums for induced socio-cultural change. We need not linger over this mode of adaptation.

Merton's last and fifth mode of adaptation is rebellion. He states, "When the institutional system is regarded as the barrier to the satisfaction of legitimized goals, the stage is set for rebellion as an adaptive response."(9) There is no doubt that the rebellious mode of adaptation can be the source of massive socio-cultural change. It is also true that in certain communities the public health worker may inadvertently foster the rebellious adaptation or be a focus for those individuals and groups who find such an adaptation congenial. Nevertheless, since most health workers do, and must, work within institutional boundaries, to use these potentially powerful groups and individuals to effect change can be hazardous and should not be done without full cognizance of the risks involved.

Merton's five modes of adaptation serve to underline the importance of knowing the social orientations of those with whom the health worker must deal and the potential assets and liabilities of such orientations for the practitioner's tasks. It is clear, if one agrees with the validity of such categories, that the innovative type of adaptation provides the obvious and easiest channel to change; that the retreatist is practically useless; that the rebellious is hazardous. There remain the ritualistic and conformist modes of adaptation. These are both difficult, but I would suggest not impossible, channels through which to work. Groups and individuals with a ritualistic adaptation may be fired to initiate change if they can be persuaded of new and more potent goals than the old ones which, for them, have lost primacy. Identification, in Kelman's sense, may fire ritualists to new goals and transform their ritualistic to innovative modes of adaptation. Similarly, groups and individuals with a conformist adaptation may be subject to persuasion precisely in those areas

where they sense cognitive dissonance in their own culture, i.e., incongruities between values, incongruities between institutions, and incongruities between values and institutions. These areas of cognitive dissonance may be crucial leverage points for change in the conformist mode of adaptation.

I have reviewed Merton's modes of adaptation at some length because they provide the practitioner one kind of rough and ready way of analyzing in any society the groups or individuals who are most likely to want, and to be able, to effect change.

Goals, Roles and Induced Change

However, in every society, goals have different valences. It is analytically useless to say that in one society wealth is more prized than piety, or that in another society equity is more valued than justice. For the practitioner more trenchant formulations are needed. Again Merton(10) has a useful set of preliminary distinctions. In discussing social controls he distinguishes between prescribed and proscribed behavior, and adds two intermediate types that he calls preferred and permitted. In our society, for example, parental care of offspring is prescribed; murder and espionage are proscribed. Marriage with non-kin is preferred but permitted within bounds of cousinship. The point once made and labelled is obvious; this, however, does not mean that it is unimportant. Among the groups and individuals designated earlier as innovators there will be prescribed and proscribed goals. Should innovators disregard such goals they risk suffering social disapproval that would make such persons poor mediators of social change in the larger society. Therefore it is in the realm of permissible and preferred behaviors and goals that the public health practitioner should look for ways of inducing change.

Spiro(11) gives this idea of kinds of social control a somewhat different and useful elaboration in respect to social roles. Like Merton he points out that goals are either sanctioned or prescribed. The prescribed goals are mandatory, the sanctioned ones approved. To use his example, the goal of becoming a physician is sanctioned, i.e., it is permitted and even approved, but to retain the status associated with the goal, the role required of the physician is prescribed or mandatory. That is, once a sanctioned goal is sought, the social role associated with it becomes mandatory. Why this should be so need not delay us here. The point of interest to us is the idea that roles can be as binding as goals; that social controls can arise from participating in institutions (which are simply congeries of roles) as much as from subscribing to or rejecting social goals. Again the implications for those who are charged with introducing change are clear. In any society groups or individuals whose roles prescribe behavior, and for whom deviation from their roles would entail social penalties or the abandonment of goals, are frequently limited agents of change. In our own society this is nicely illustrated in the relative flexibility of the politician compared to the civil servant. The politician's social role is far less subject to social control, is less prescribed, than that of the civil servant (although I am by no means sure that this is the case in every nation).

So far we have sought congruencies between the concepts and findings of investigators from different disciplines.

The creation for this search is that the concepts and congruities should provide analytic guides to public health workers who are concerned with induced socio-cultural change.

We have said that within the proceptive field of individuals, the strain for cognitive consistency may be, if properly used, a dynamism for change. But changes in behavior, attitudes, and values are often mediated by interpersonal relations and are of varying depth and permanence. Further, in any society the relationship between goals on the one hand, and institutional resources for achieving them on the other hand may be differently perceived by groups and by individuals. Varying modes of adaptation may result from the differences in perception. These modes of adaptation have varying potentialities for change. However, we must also recognize that goals have different valences. Similarly, the congeries of roles which constitute institutions vary in the extent to which they are prescribed.

Class and Socio-cultural Change

In developing this argument, two areas frequently included in any discussion of change have not been touched upon. The first is social class and the other is culture-trait inventories. Reasons for giving them short shrift will now be discussed.

The relationship between social class and social change has been a subject of considerable research. Sorokin, for example, in a study of the class provenience of some 3,000 saints over 20 centuries reaches the conclusion "that as a rule the upper classes are the first innovators and importers of the new cultural values in a given society and its culture, and especially the first molders of its highest ideals and values. The lower classes ordinarily lag behind and follow or imitate when the values cease to live and function within the upper classes. In other words, the stream of innovations in a given society flows from the top to the bottom."(12) On the other hand, Barnett, working within the framework of cultural comparisons, says, "It is a transparent fact that the members of privileged classes have a vested interest in the system on which they thrive and that they resist changes in it which will deprive them of their advantages. Changes which threaten the social, political and economic prerogatives which they cherish are understandably not welcome by them. . . . When cultures meet, the majority of those who switch their allegiances are individuals with the least opportunity for full participation in the most valued activities in their own society."(13) Dr. Barnett would have difficulty reconciling this generalization with Dr. Sorokin's and neither, I believe, could make their generalizations stick. It is not that social class is irrelevant to social change, or to the problems facing a public health worker. Simmons' excellent article on the *Implications of Social Class for Public Health*(14) is ample testimony that it is important. But its importance lies not in class *per se* but in class as an index to cultural goals and institutional roles. For our purposes here social class is a dependent and not an independent variable. The public health worker responsible for analyzing a society must go beneath the surface of class groupings. As Karl Polanyi persuasively argues in *The Great Transformation*, "Mere class interests cannot offer . . . a satisfactory explanation for any long-run social process."(15)

Acculturation and Induced Change

Turning now to culture-trait inventories:—the older literature of acculturation in anthropology is replete with *obiter dicta* concerning those aspects of a society that are most subject to change. For example, Malinowski stated that "the vanguard of change is often found in 'works of leisure' and supererogation."(16) By contrast it is often claimed that material culture and technology are the first aspect of culture to change in the contact situation and religion the last. But it is not in these external and relatively easily observable aspects of society that we find the most useful clues to where and how socio-cultural change occurs. Rather we must look to the socio-psychological factors that underlie these external manifestations.

And here, in the socio-psychological sub-strata of change recent research by anthropologists has possibly most to contribute to practitioners of induced change. Perhaps the best way to illustrate this area of research is to summarize very briefly Hallowell's classic study of acculturation.(17) Hallowell set up four levels of acculturation from the least to the most westernized of Ojibwa Indians. These levels are based on easily observable culture traits like clothing, language, food, etc. The least acculturated level cannot be studied directly but is known from seventeenth and eighteenth century travelers. The most acculturated are the Lac du Flambeau Ojibwa of Northern Wisconsin, practically all of whom speak English, 80 percent of whom have white blood, and whose children attend government schools. The signal finding is the "persistent core of psychological characteristics sufficient to identify the Ojibwa personality constellation, aboriginal in origin, that is clearly discernible. . . . All the evidence points to far more complicated psychological processes than those which have led to the acquisition of the culture traits which were used as empirical guides to the different levels of acculturation. Consequently, descriptive facts of this order are no direct index to facts pertaining to personality adjustment and personality organization."(18) In other words, it is not to culture traits but to psychological factors that one must look if the intimate and immediate dynamics of socio-cultural change concern us.

Hallowell's "principle of psychic persistence" has been confirmed by many other investigators working in different areas and with different techniques. "Anthony Wallace in a recent study of Iroquois acculturation, states a now perhaps widely held view that 'no cultural form can be successfully introduced, within the space of one generation' which 'requires behavior which is uncongenial to personality structure.' Hallowell himself goes further in saying that it is 'hard to imagine' how basic sets of personality structure could be changed fundamentally in 'less than three generations.' Keesing, however, has suggested that if the crucial cultural surrogates (e.g., the mother or foster parents in an entirely outside setting) are sufficiently in the new tradition, the essentials of such a shift might be made in two generations—though this is quite exceptional."(19) Vogt(20) in a study of Navaho veterans suggests that value change occurs first through imitation and then internalization of white norms and that this process is facilitated (among other factors) by a lack of satisfying affective ties and by personal conflict and insecurity with respect to fellow Navaho. And that in general the

acculturated Navaho is a second generation phenomenon—that such a man is the son of parents already deviant to Navaho culture.

We seem now to have come full circuit. We have been looking for congruence between various levels and fields of inquiry as to the nature of socio-cultural change. We have been particularly interested in those concepts that might assist practitioners of induced change. From anthropological research in acculturation we find that Kelman's three processes of attitude change—compliance, identification, and internalization—may have diachronic (i.e., sequential) significance. One might suggest that compliance, identification, and internalization are equivalent to three stages of socio-cultural change and conceivably (although this is pure speculation) that they may entail as many generations. Also, in the course of such slow changes over generations, many groups and individuals will evince modes of adaptation that Merton suggests, namely: conformity, innovation, ritualism, retreatism, and rebellion.

But how are we to explain such slow changes when we know that human beings, as opposed to other social animals, have all the plasticity that learning as an adaptive mechanism provides? Bruner suggests the hypothesis of early learning to account for the principle of psychic persistence. He claims that what is transmitted early in a child's training is most resistant to change. (21) Although Bruner's hypothesis of early learning is persuasive and warrants wider investigation, and although it has the virtue of simplicity, I suspect that it is not adequate to the complexity of the situations facing agents of induced change. It may be useful therefore to review still another way of conceptualizing socio-cultural phenomena that may yield some explanation for the principle of psychic persistence, or, if you wish, for cultural stability.

Cultural Levels and Induced Change

Dr. Hall, long a collaborator of George Trager, has recently published a book called *The Silent Language*. (22) In it he follows the lead of distinguished predecessors, like Gregory Bateson, in treating culture as a communication system. We need not follow Hall's full argument but consider only the distinction he makes between formal, informal, and technical levels on which all dimensions of culture operate.

At the core of every cultural dimension whether it be temporality or territoriality, learning or play, subsistence or association, there is a formal level of culture. This is learned through precept and admonition. "Men never do such and such." "Don't say goed, say went." It is what we generally mean by "child rearing." People are fully aware of the formal aspects of their culture, but they do not question them. It is the "perfectly natural," "just common sense," the "human nature," "what everyone knows" kind of approach that is accepted without challenge. Patent violations of such formal aspects of culture arouse a flood of explicit emotions. Change in the formal aspects of culture come slowly.

Surrounding this core of the formal level of culture is the informal. The informal level of culture, like the formal one, is learned. However, it is not learned through precept and admonition, but rather through the imitation of a model and by observation. Informal levels of culture are customarily out-of-awareness and automatic. But if

breached, anxiety usually follows. Resistance to change at the informal level will be characterized by the defense mechanisms congenial to particular individuals or groups.

The third level of culture is the technical. It is transmitted explicitly from teacher to student, either orally or in writing, often accompanied by logical analysis and according to a coherent procedure. It is what we generally mean when we speak of education at the institutional level. The technical level of culture operates at the highest level of consciousness. Here change can be effected with far greater ease than in the formal and informal levels.

You will recall that I suggested earlier this evening, in connection with Festinger's work on cognitive dissonance, that it would be relatively easy to convince a community that an injection was a more effective way of curing yaws than a poultice because the change was in the *technical* realm. On the other hand, substituting a mosquito for grandfather's punitive ghost as the cause of fevers would be difficult because the cognitive dissonance would be too great. Now phrasing the issue in Hall's language, we can say it is because a formal aspect of culture is challenged; —one of those beliefs everyone shares, that is "just common sense."

Again, you will recall that I suggested using Kelman's concepts of compliance, identification, and internalization that one might through surveillance and/or attractiveness persuade a community to fill in mosquito breeding puddles, but that such behavior would have little chance of entering permanently into community practice. Now we may further argue that puddle-fillers were not models that people had learned, informally and through observation, to imitate when they were learning their culture; nor were they formally admonished to fill puddles. While technically to learn the relationship between puddles, mosquitoes, and malaria requires grounding in a whole system of thought not easily conveyed and one that might well test the credulity of people accustomed to trust their "common sense."

Dr. Hall's thesis, needless to say, is far more complex than this hasty and partial reference indicates. But if one considers only his three levels of culture and if one considers that these three levels tend to reinforce each other over time through the operation of the strain for consistency, then it becomes much clearer why socio-cultural change is a slow process, why it is often attended by personal dislocation, and why the public health worker whose professional orientation is "putatively" purely technical is frequently bewildered by the resistance he meets in attempting to introduce changes.

Before leaving Dr. Hall's thesis, I should like to quote one of his summary sentences. "Change is a complex circular process. It proceeds from formal to informal to technical to new formal."(28) In other words, Dr. Hall seems to see socio-cultural change in terms of a feedback system in which cause and effect are not seen as linear but circular. And as Bateson says, drawing on cybernetic theories, "Such circular causal systems must in the nature of the case either seek a steady state or undergo progressive exponential change; and this change will be limited either by the energy resources of the system, or by some external restraint, or by a breakdown of the system as such."(24) We all know from history that societies can seek a steady state, may be limited by their energy resources, have been restrained by external forces, or have broken down.

We may assume that the public health worker aims to limit socio-cultural change to the resources of a society without producing a breakdown of the system and without making it endlessly dependent on external resources. If this be a fair assumption, then we may turn to the final issue of this paper.

The field worker is on the firing line of any public health program. He bears the burden of trying to induce change. His skills, insights and sensitivity are rightly considered crucial to the successful implementation of any plan. It is therefore customary on occasions such as these to issue them encouragement or warnings, particularly if the program is an intercultural one. It is customary to remind them of "culture shock"; or to urge them to recognize and use their privileged position as strangers; or to insist that their work rest on surveys (which are usually far too superficially descriptive to be useful on any dynamic level of analysis); or to warn them that they too bring with them a series of valuational prejudgments as well as technical skills, or to provide them with illustrations of difficulties ingeniously analyzed and surmounted elsewhere (but which are unfortunately usually so specific that they hardly serve as guides to other situations).

None of these is my intention. There is no need to focus again on the long-suffering, much-harangued field worker or to give him more gratuitous advice than he already has had. Rather my intention is to focus on the planner of programs in public health.

Much that has been said bears directly on what should be properly planned, what are the legitimate expectations from such planning and what may be realistically expected of the field technician.

Planning for Induced Change

First of all, planning is rationalizing. It is not only theoretically at the technical level of culture; it is also often an attempt to impose a technical approach (in Hall's sense of the word) on the formal and informal aspects of culture. However, if we see change as a complex circular process in which activity at the technical level feeds back into the formal and itself becomes a formal aspect of culture, then planning itself must beware of becoming as unquestioned, as "perfectly natural," as any moral precept in the formal aspect of culture. Its rational and secular quality thereby risks being vitiated. I suspect this is particularly true in societies where planning is prescribed rather than preferred.

Ideally, the objective of any plan should be unambiguous, internally consistent, and quantifiable. But as Dr. Eckstein has so well demonstrated in his interesting study of the English Health Service, this is rarely possible. (25) It therefore behooves planners, while striving to keep their objectives clearly in mind and to cope technically with their problems, to remember that there is usually considerable "slippage" for precisely the reasons here discussed. As Eckstein so well puts it, "We need only realize that the engineering reason [for which, in Hall's terminology, we may read technical reason] is rigidly circumscribed and liable to falter altogether . . . and that the fully rational direction of social activities is possible only under one condition: if the norms we impose on conduct, whether relating to ends or means, are precisely those highly delimiting norms that make rational action possible."(26)

Competent planning must in the first place recognize what level or levels of culture are likely to be most immediately affected. As we have said earlier, and as Eckstein clearly indicates, planning is a technical process. If it deals with a technical level of culture, planning is relatively easy and may be reasonably precise. For example, there are difficulties, but no insurmountable ones, in campaigns of mass inoculation or vaccination where one competes only with a different pharmacopia in the indigenous society. As Festinger might say it, the dynamics of cognitive dissonance can be constructively employed. Under such circumstances, given sufficient resources and assistance, disease may be eradicated if specifics for the diseases are known. In such situations, it is relatively simple to achieve compliance through surveillance, to use Kelman's language, and eradicate smallpox or yaws. Such enterprises are the traditionally cited success stories of public health. The formal two-year, five-year, or ten-year time spans for such undertakings may still be within the compass of rational, engineering, or technical programs (depending on the language that is congenial).

If, however, the program entails alterations in the informal aspects of culture, that is, in the models people learn through imitation and that are largely out-of-awareness, if, for example, alterations deal with habitual cultural orientations in time and space the task becomes of necessity a long and subtle one. Change at this level must be reckoned not in two-, five-, or ten-year programs, but on a generational basis. The same holds true for alterations that deal with the formal level of culture. Persistence and persuasion will be necessary. Here Kelman's process of identification must occur in the first generation before the second generation may, at best, actually internalize the alterations. But, even this suggestion may be too optimistic. If we use Hall's concept of informal and formal levels of culture; if we combine this suggestion with the principle of psychic persistence in which a minimum of two generations is essential to effect changes in personality structure; and if we add Kelman's suggestions of identification and internalization in a diachronic sense, and assume that the first generation adopts a new response as a value but isolates it from other values, whereas the second generation integrates the new response with other values—if we make all these assumptions, the model is still far too simple. For it implies that the interpersonal relations essential for such transformations of informal and formal aspects of culture to the technical level have operated with maximal effectiveness. In any population aggregate, nothing is more improbable. Rather, there will be the types of "wastage" that Merton has categorized in his modes of adaptation as ritualism, retreatism, and rebellion.

Planners of public health programs who ignore such psycho-social and socio-cultural processes are 1) misleading themselves, their organization, or their governments; 2) are wasting their material resources; 3) are disheartening their field technicians, and 4) may be unwittingly encouraging unconstructive modes of adaptation. Planners and trainers of public health workers, alert to such considerations, would never insert in a manual for rural community health workers (I quote), "To more or less complete a program in a community will probably take at least two years, especially if adequate educational results are to be obtained along with such physical improvement as privies."(27)

This sanguine suggestion flies in the face of both experience and theory. It illustrates better than anything said in academic language the fallacies of assuming that socio-cultural change can be usefully planned on *only* the technical level and of assuming that psycho-social learning is *solely* a matter of rational indoctrination. It ignores that goals must be identified with; that the innovative elements of society must have opportunities to develop institutions that support such goals; that the learning of much of cultural behavior requires identification through models and precepts before it can be internalized; and that the integration of new goals and behaviors with the rest of experience requires shifts in the consciously held formal levels of culture, as well as in the informal levels of culture that are out-of-awareness.

Needless to say, I have not spoken tonight of socio-cultural change achieved by force and the liquidation of resistive elements of a population. Such changes I have assumed are not techniques appropriate to a public health program in a democratic society.

References

1. ALLPORT, GORDON W. "Perception and Public Health." *Health Education Monograph.* No. 2, pp. 2–15, 1958.
2. FESTINGER, LEON. *A Theory of Cognitive Dissonance.* Evanston, Ill. Row, Peterson and Co., 1957. I should also like to thank DR. KIM ROMNEY for his advice on these points.
3. OSGOOD, C. E. and TANNENBAUM, P. "The Principle of Congruity and the Prediction of Attitude Change," *Psycho. Rev.,* v. 62:42–55, 1955.
4. LAZARSFELD, PAUL F. and MERTON, ROBERT K. "Friendship as Social Process: a Substantive and Methodo-

logical Analysis," in Berger, Morroe et al. *Freedom and Control in Modern Society.* N.Y. Van Nostrand Co., 1954, p. 33.

5. KELMAN, HERBERT C. "Compliance, Identification and Internalization: Three Processes of Attitude Change," *Journal of Conflict Resolution,* v. 2; no. 1:51–60, March 1958. In addition, charts from a draft manuscript dated 1956 were consulted.

6. MERTON, ROBERT K. *Social Theory and Social Structure.* Glencoe, Ill. The Free Press, 1957. Rev. enl. ed., p. 140 ff.

7. VOGT, EVON Z. "Navaho Veterans: A Study of Changing Values." *Papers of Peabody Museum of American Archeology and Ethnology,* Harvard University, v. 41, no. 1, 1951.

8. MERTON. *Social Theory,* p. 153.

9. MERTON. *Social Theory,* p. 156.

10. MERTON. *Social Theory,* p. 133.

11. SPIRO, MELFORD E. *Social Systems, Personality and Functional Analysis,* mimeo. 1959.

12. SOROKIN, PITIRIM A. *Altruistic Love.* Boston, Beacon Press, 1950, p. 134.

13. BARNETT, HOMER G. *Innovation: The Basis of Cultural Change.* N.Y. McGraw-Hill Book Co., 1953, p. 404.

14. SIMMONS, OZZIE G. "Implications of Social Class for Public Health." *Human Organization,* v. 16, no. 3:7–10, Fall, 1957.

15. POLANYI, KARL. *The Great Transformation . . .* Boston, Beacon Press, 1957 (paper back ed.), pp. 150–159.

16. Quoted in KEESING, FELIX M. "Culture Change . . ." *Stanford Anthropological Series,* no. 1, p. 29, 1953.

17. HALLOWELL, A. IRVING. "Ojibwa Personality and Acculturation." *International Congress of Americanists, Proceedings 29th,* 105–112, 1952.

18. Quoted from SIEGEL, BERNARD J. "Acculturation: Critical Abstracts, North America." *Stanford Anthropological Series,* no. 2, p. 186, 1955.

19. Quoted from KEESING, FELIX M. "Culture Change . . ." *Stanford Anthropological Series,* no. 1, p. 90, 1953.

20. VOGT, EVAN Z. "Navaho Veterans: A Study of Changing Values," *Papers of Peabody Museum of American Archeology and Ethnology,* Harvard University, v. 41, no. 1, 1951.

21. BRUNER, EDWARD M. "Cultural Transmission and Cultural Change." *Southwestern J. of Anthropology,* v. 12; no. 2:191–199, 1956.

22. HALL, EDWARD T. *The Silent Language.* New York, Doubleday and Co., 1959.

23. HALL. *op. cit.,* p. 116.

24. BATESON, GREGORY. *Naven . . .* Stanford, Calif., Stanford University Press, 1958, 2nd ed., p. 288.

25. ECKSTEIN, HARRY. *The English Health Service: Its Origin, Structure and Achievement.* Cambridge, Mass., Harvard University Press, 1958. See particularly Chapter IX.

26. ECKSTEIN. *op. cit.,* p. 282.

27. TEXTOR, ROBERT B., McCULLOUGH, J. C. and OTHERS. *Manual for the Rural Community Health Worker in Thailand.* Published for the Ministry of Public Health by the Thai-American Audiovisual Service. Bangkok, 1958, p. 60.

RESISTANCE TO CHANGE— ITS ANALYSIS AND PREVENTION

Alvin Zander

IN order to derive the benefit from research in industrial relations, someone must plan a program of action to apply them. When one begins implementing, he must change the social system in some way. The creation of this change can cause the development of resistance in those influenced by the change.

First, we shall look at what resistance is; second, the conditions that appear to be associated with its development; and third, some means whereby resistance may be prevented or decreased.

Nature of Resistance

Let us look at some examples of resistance growing out of administrative changes.

A large number of foremen in a company were given training in how to treat their men like human beings. They liked the course and were eager to apply their learnings on the job. The company found, however, that relatively few of the foremen are really behaving any differently on the job. They know their stuff but do not use it.

In one of the paper-shuffling government agencies a new data form was developed which all admitted was briefer, more logical, and easier to use. Yet, this department found that the employees often omitted much of the data needed on this form, their speed of work decreased, and they objected to it on many insignificant grounds.

Our favorite example of resistance was furnished by a farmer in the TVA area. He assured us that he knew all about contour plowing, the rotation of crops, and the use of what he called "phosaphate" for improving the soil. He allowed as how these were good ideas, "But," he said, "I don't do it that way."

These examples have one common denominator which might serve here as a definition of resistance. They describe behavior which is intended to protect an individual from the effects of real or imagined change. This reaction might be to either real or imagined change since the resister might be reacting to things that were really not changed but he thinks were, or fears that they might be. If a person believes a change has been made, or fears potential change, it makes no difference whether or not it is true in fact. He will act as though there has been a change.

How can one recognize when resistance is working? Unfortunately, there is no list of typical behavior which can be described as the symptoms of resistance, which, if present, indicate that one is dealing with this phenomenon. It is the protective function which the behavior is providing which determines whether or not a person is resisting,

From Alvin Zander, "Resistance to Change: Its Analysis and Prevention," Advanced Management, Vols. 15–16, January 1950, pp. 9–11. Used by permission.

rather than the kind of thing he does. By the same token, all behavior which opposes change is not necessarily resistance. Some opposition to change may be perfectly logical and grounded on well supported reasons. The behavior must be attempting to protect the person against the consequences of the change in order for it to be resistance. This may be clearer if we look at the origin of the concept.

The Hostility Pattern

The term and the concept we are using here has been borrowed from psychotherapy. When a therapist is attempting to change the behavior of the patient, he expects resistance from him. The therapist takes the position that the pattern of behavior used by the patient (which makes him a "sick" person) is a means to some satisfaction for him even though it also may make him ineffective or unhappy. Resistance occurs in the patient when the process of change (therapy here) comes close to being successful. When faced with the unpleasant necessity of giving up the behavior he does not like, but somehow needs, he begins to balk. He becomes silent, blushes, changes the subject, tells fibs, comes late to appointments, becomes angry with the therapist, or any of a number of similar things. The therapist watches for the context in which these signs of resistance occur since these indicate the crucial problems in the way the patient sees and deals with his world.

For the administrator, resistance may occur under fairly similar conditions. When he attempts to create a change the administrator may develop, unintentionally, many threats to the person or groups with whom he works. The behavior used by the resister may take many forms.

It may take the form of hostility either openly expressed or obliquely implied. The aggression may be directed against the change itself or against the administrator. What is done depends on how the person can safely resist without further endangering himself in that situation. Other symptoms of resistance may be sloppy effort after the change has been made, or fawning submissiveness which is a hybrid of applepolishing and apathy. It can occur by lowering the level of aspiration to an inefficient degree, discouragement, or the development of unhappy cliques and outspoken factions. It is important, however, to remind ourselves, that it is the function which such actions are performing for the person that makes them resistance rather than what they look like.

Where Resistance Starts

It will be helpful if we look at a few conditions conducive to resistance.

1. Resistance can be expected if the nature of the change is not made clear to the people who are going to be influenced by the change. In one of the largest government agencies, a change required one department which originally had the responsibility of processing papers involved in contacts with certain industries to share this task with another office. Announcement of the change was issued in a brief statement. The immediate reaction was violent objection, even though some of the workers privately admitted that it was a wise and necessary move. They were reacting to incomplete information. Many people fear incomplete information about changes which influence them. It is

more comfortable to know exactly where one stands.

There is some evidence to support the hypothesis that those persons who dislike their jobs, will most dislike ambiguity in a proposed change. They want to know exactly what they must do in order to be sure to avoid the unpleasant aspects of their jobs. Some administrators may attach too much importance to the value of information itself. Apparently they reason that people "ought not" to resist the way they do because the administrator has told them everything he thinks is important for them to know about the impending change.

2. Different people will see different meanings in the proposed change. Some of the resistant reaction described above came about because some workers saw the change as an indication that they had been doing a poor job, others assumed it meant their office would soon be abolished, still others were troubled since they were losing some of the power they had formerly controlled. We tend to see in our world the things that we expect to see. Complete information can just as readily be distorted as incomplete information, especially so if the workers have found discomfort and threats in their past work situation.

3. Resistance can be expected when those influenced are caught in a jam between strong forces pushing them to make the change and strong forces deterring them against making the change.

4. Resistance may be expected to the degree that the persons influenced by the change have pressure put upon them to make it, and will be decreased to the degree that these same persons are able to have some "say" in the nature or direction of the change. In a garment factory a change was required. The switch meant that workers would be asked to change their jobs and in many cases, to develop working relationships with new people. An experiment was made in which three different styles of introducing this change were tried out. One group of workers were simply informed about the change and were allowed to ask questions. They developed the most resistance as measured by turnover, absenteeism, and slowness in learning the job. Resistance was *less* in those groups who sent representatives to a meeting in which the nature of the change was discussed and all persons present made plans to carry out the change.

Resistance was *least* in the groups in which those to be affected discussed the nature of the change, laid plans for making it, and as a total group made decisions which were satisfactory to the entire group. In this latter group everyone participated. They had an opportunity to develop their own motivation instead of making the change only on the basis of orders from the boss. The fact that they were able to develop their own understanding of the need for the change and their own decisions about how to do it, reduced resistance most effectively.

5. Resistance may be expected if the change is made on personal grounds rather than impersonal requirements or sanctions. A supervisor posted the following notice:

I have always felt that promptness is an important indicator of an employee's interest in his job. I will feel much better if you are at your desk at the proper time.

Employees responded to this notice by appointing a committee to get information which would justify their late arrival at the office. Many administrators can expect trouble in establishing a change if it is requested in terms of what "I think is necessary"; rather than making the request in the light of "our objectives," the rules, the present state of affairs, or some other impersonal requirement.

6. Resistance may be expected if the change ignores the already established institutions in the group. Every work situation develops certain customs in doing the work or in the relations among the workers. The administrator who ignores institutionalized patterns of work and abruptly attempts to create a new state of affairs which demands that these customs be abolished without further consideration will surely run into resistance.

These are a few of the conditions in which resistance might be expected to occur. There probably are many others.

Decreasing Resistance

Some procedures on the part of the administrator might be useful in preventing or decreasing the resistance which arises in a changed situation. Let us look at a major principle in preventing resistance and some of its basic implications:

Resistance will be prevented to the degree that the changer helps the changees to develop their own understanding of the need for the change, and an explicit awareness of how they feel about it, and what can be done about those feelings.

This principle implies that the administrator can use resistance as an important symptom. Specifically, he can use the nature of the resistance as an indicator of the cause of resistance. It will be most helpful to him as a symptom, if he diagnoses the causes for it

when it occurs rather than inhibiting it at once. The same resistant behavior, for example, may indicate that one person feels that he has lost prestige by the change, to another it may mean that he has lost power over an area of influence which he formerly controlled, and to still another it may mean that he fears that his friends will think less well of him. An administrator must know what the resistance means in order that he may effectively lessen it by working on the causes instead of the symptom.

There has been a good deal of experience in recent years in staff meetings and in work conferences like the National Training Laboratory for Group Development with the use of a group observer. This observer gives to the group, and the leaders, information about the group and the nature of any resistance. In these cases, the data about itself is made common group property for all members to discuss and to use in planning better work relations.

This communication must go in both directions. If two-way communication is not maintained, negative attitudes created during resistance will tend to persist.

Restoring Understanding

In a utility company a new office was formed with a new set of supervisors. The entire staff of supervisors called the workers together and scolded them for shortcomings in their performance. The tone used by the supervisors was so aggressive that the employees found it difficult thereafter to discuss anything with them except those topics directly related to the effectiveness of production. The workers kept themselves at a distance from the supervisors and the supervisors made no move to close the gap. The result was that distance between these two groups made it impossible for them to come to any new understanding of each other. This mounting hostility was lessened only when the personnel department advised a number of "gripe-sessions" with small groups of workers in which the two levels developed a new understanding of each other.

Another implication in the above principle is that there is value in blowing off steam. The psychologists call this a "catharsis." There is good evidence that new attitudes can be accepted by a person only if he has a chance to thoroughly air his original attitude. Resistance to accepting the rigid, and often apparently meaningless, rules of military life, showed itself in flagrant violation of the rules, often in a most aggressive manner. Punishment only increased the resistance. Relief was provided by group sessions in which men were able to thoroughly gripe. After this relief of tension, they were able to turn to a reasonable discussion about what they could do to learn to live in terms of these requirements. It is as though new air can be put in the tire only after the old air is released.

A third implication of the earlier expressed principle is that resistance may be less likely to occur if the group participates in making the decisions about how the change should be implemented, what the change should be like, how people might perform in the changed situation, or any other problems that are within their area of freedom to decide. The experiment in which three ways of introducing a change were tried out showed that the workers, who had a chance to make a group decision about the ways in which the change should be made, developed much less resistance than did those who were simply called together to be told about the change and have all of their questions answered. What is important here is that the workers feel that they have a chance to discuss the major factors involved in the change, a chance to understand the nature of the fears they have in facing this change, and a chance to plan what they will do to calm their fears.

Self-Diagnosis Gets Action

Still another implication is that resistance will be less likely to develop if facts which point to the need for change are gathered by the persons who must make the change. A number of high level supervisors in a utility industry came to feel that the workers had many negative attitudes about their jobs which were due to poor supervisory practices. Each supervisor, quite naturally, felt that other supervisors were at fault. Top management set up a number of study groups in which the supervisors first learned how they could diagnose the causes of these negative attitudes. Each supervisor then returned to his own work place and gathered facts that would be necessary for him to analyse the causes of negative attitudes he could spot among his workers. Later the supervisors came together to report their findings. At this meeting their enthusiasm for change in their own practices was high because they had participated in gathering the facts which best described their problems. People will be more likely to act in terms of information they gather themselves than in terms of information gathered by others and delivered to them. If it is clear that a change is indicated in a given state of affairs, but the people who must abide by the change are resisting the shift, they can come to see it themselves by obtaining the facts which properly "case" the situation.

To summarize, we have said that resistance is a problem which any person who is responsible for social change must face. Even though it is strange and unexpected behavior, there are causes for the development of this phenomenon. These causes may be understood, and resistance may be prevented, if the administrator will help the changees develop their own understanding of the need for change and explicit awareness of how they feel about it, and what can be done about those feelings.

◆◆◆◆◆◆◆◆◆◆◆◆◆◆◆◆◆◆◆◆◆ TRANSFORMATIONS OF IDENTITY

Anselm L. Strauss

Regularized Status-Passage

MEMBERSHIP in any enduring group or social structure inevitably involves passage from status to status. In order that a group persist and flourish, each status must be filled, jobs must be done. The incumbents of positions die, retire, leave, fail, and sometimes betray the organization. New kinds of goals develop and so new positions are created. Other positions get sloughed off, and persons who previously filled them must shift or be shifted elsewhere. Lengthy retention in a given status may hide a genuine shift of social position, as old duties and prerogatives are dropped and new ones accrue. Unless a group were to be wholly undifferentiated, its members necessarily have to move up, down, and sideways.

Many passages of status are highly institutionalized, so that individuals move through them in orderly sequence. Professorial ranks in colleges and universities are an instance of such a step-by-step progression; but so is the normal movement from bride to wife to pregnant mother to rearer of children. When movement is thus regularized, this means that there are predecessors and successors: people have been there before and will follow you. This gives continuity not only to the group or organization, but also to personal experience. In a host of ways, you are prepared for what is to come, are made aware of the immediacy of the next transition, are reminded that you have just now made a passage. The attainment of status may require that you have certain experience, and meet certain standards of conduct and performance; these, myth and story, example and direct instruction, are indispensable. The more subtle aspects of preparation include forewarning you that certain things will soon happen, that you will experience certain experiences, and feel certain feelings; and when you do, certain predecessors will stand ready with interpretations of such predicted events. Their interpretations embody the special language of the group. *Post facto* explanations are also at hand, so that when a person en-

From Anselm L. Strauss, Mirrors and Masks, *New York: The Free Press of Glencoe, Inc., 1959, pp. 100–118. Footnotes omitted. Abridged and used by permission.*

counters situations for which he has no definitions, he will be offered ready-made ones. "We all went through this." "At your age, that happened to me too. It means that. . . ."

Providing that the definitions offered are not too many and too divergent, you are thereby moved along an orderly line of development. By organizing your action in terms of preferred rationale, you thereby confirm their usefulness and validity. I say validity because your action then can be easily named by other people, and familiarly, even comfortably, responded to. Merton in another connection has called this the "self-fulfilling prophecy"—although I am emphasizing here primarily the continuity that an acceptance of rationale affords. Thus, advice given within an occupation to incoming personnel about clients serves to perpetuate certain relationships and experiences with the clients.

If conflicting rationales leave a person in definitional confusion, or if for other reasons he reaches novel interpretations of his experience, the regulated chain of status-progression is threatened. However, alternative explanations of given events may traditionally exist within a single institution, so that the acceptance by a novice of one or another explanation sets immediate conditions for the pursuit of alternative career routes. This, indeed, is true not merely at the inception of a career but at any point along it, providing that unexpected situations and experiences are traditionally rationalized. Thus a young professor who discovers that he has neither the ability nor the incentive for genuinely excellent research, can find institutional sanction and rationale for devoting himself to building a reputation as an outstanding teacher of undergraduates.

When positional mobility follows known sequences, different motivations frequently become appropriate at each successive status. Passage from one to another involves not only changes of action and demeanor, but of the verbalized reasons that are associated with them. Indeed, the stability of a given social structure rests largely upon a proper preparation for these sequential steps. Motivations appropriate to earlier —and usually lower—status must be sloughed off or transmuted, and new ones added or substituted. This necessity is marvelously illustrated in a description by Arensberg and Kimball of family transition in Irish peasant families. At the time of the son's marriage, a series of cognate changes in status, act, and motivation are intended to occur simultaneously. The father must yield control of family policy and cease active work; the son must assume responsibility and ardently wish to do so; the mother must become a household guide and teacher to her son's wife; and the latter must remain temporarily subservient. But the younger woman must also be properly motivated to leave her own family, physically and psychologically, and to become a mother as quickly as possible. When her child is born, the young mother must enthusiastically assume full household responsibility. Simultaneous with this momentous event, the old couple pass to a status of old age. This latter change carries with it an organization of perspective and activity that can be called "making ready for death," the next—and last—status. At any step of this complicated drama of progression, things will go awry if the actors lag behind or speed up unduly in their action or rationale. And, in fact, the strains in family and community life fall exactly at those points where the speed of transition gets out of alignment.

Even in relatively stable structures, where career paths are regular and well regulated, there always arise problems of pacing and timing. Ideally speaking, successors and predecessors should move in and out of offices at equal speeds, but they do not and cannot. Persons who are asked to move may be willing to do so, but must make actual and symbolic preparation to leave. Meanwhile, a successor may be waiting impatiently to take over. In status-passage, transition periods are a necessity, for people often invest heavily of themselves in a position, come to possess it as it possesses them, and it is no easy matter for them to sever themselves from it. If the full ritual of leave-taking is not allowed, a person may be for some time only partially in his new status. On the other hand the institution stands ready with devices to make him forget, to plunge him into the new office, to point out and allow him to experience the gratifications accruing to it, as well as to force him to abandon the old. Where statuses pyramid so that each is conceived as the logical and temporal extension of the last, severance is not such a disturbing experience. But even here if a person must face his old associates in unaccustomed roles, problems of loyalty become knotty. For this reason, a period of tolerance immediately after formal admission to the new status is almost a necessity. This tolerance is rationalized with phrases like "it takes time," "he is not quite yet in it," "we all make mistakes when starting, until we learn that. . . ."

But people not only drag their heels, they may be too zealous, too eager. Those who are new to a position often commit the indelicate error of taking formal promotion or certification much too literally, when actually there exist intervening informal stages that must be traversed before the full prerogatives of position are attained. This passage may involve tests of loyalty as well as the simple accumulation of information and skill. These informal status grades are referred to in the special language of rankings: "he's a *new* lieutenant" or "that board member is one of the oldtimers." An overeager person may be kept in line by all kinds of controlling devices; for instance, a new sales manager discovers that it will take "just a little while" before things can be arranged so that he can institute the changes he envisages in his department. Even a newly appointed superior has to face the resentments or cautiousness of personnel who have preceded him in the organization; and he may, if sensitive, pace his "moving in on them" until he has passed unspoken tests.

When a man is raised to the rank of his former superiors, an especially delicate situation is created. Officially he is now equal to, or like, his former teachers and elders. But equality is neither created by that official act nor, even if it were, could it come about without a certain awkwardness. Imagery and patterns of responses must be rearranged on both sides, and strong self-control must be exerted in order that acts be kept appropriate—even to the self-conscious use of first names, often violating an outmoded but still strongly operative sense of propriety. Slips are inevitable, for although the new status may be fully granted proper situational identities may be temporarily forgotten to everyone's embarrassment. The former subordinate may come eventually to command, or take precedence over, someone toward whom he previously looked for guidance. At the very least, the colleagues may have to oppose each other over some crucial issue which arises and divides people of the same rank. When former sponsors and sponsored now find it necessary to array themselves differently on such issues, recrimination becomes overt and betrayal explicit. It is understandable why men who have been promoted often prefer to take office, or are advised to do so, in another agency or organization or branch office, however great their desire for remaining at home.

The problems attending the speed of status-passage are merely part of the larger organizational problem of recruiting members for various posts. Recruitment is generally thought of only in connection with bringing newcomers into the structure; but insofar as replacements must be found for each position, on every level, personnel either must be brought in from the outside or trained in other internal positions. In both cases, persons must be induced to give up current endeavors and commitments in order to move onward and, usually, upward. Within the organization, certain persons must be deterred from aiming too high, but others must be induced to cease practicing prized skills and to give up clear satisfactions in exchange for the presumed rewards of the next position. If the latter rewards seem great enough, candidates for each position will be found; but if they are improperly motivated to move to the new position, they will experience considerable strain in transit. Until engineers became used to the idea that their careers frequently involved beginning as engineers and ending as administrators, they experienced severe shocks to personal identity when as administrators they ceased

practicing their engineering skills. E. C. Hughes has recounted the story of one engineer who dreamed a nightmare, in which he had lost the capacity to operate a slide rule. In social science research nowadays, it has become necessary for some research professors to spend time and energy finding research money for their junior colleagues. "I spend my time on this. I'm always working on it, I spend my evenings writing letters, seeing people, telephoning. I have to make sacrifices in my own research, of course." The Harvard professor from whom this quote is taken must be ready and willing to append "of course" to his sacrifice of research and its satisfactions—otherwise his personal dissatisfactions will outweigh the benefits, accruing to his juniors and to the department, of his contribution toward the common organizational task of raising necessary funds.

Indeed, at every level of an organization, personal stress can arise if motivations are inappropriate for further passages. Self-conceptions may mesh with or grate against institutional arrangements for sequential movements. At Harvard University, few assistant professors can expect to attain the tenure ranks; most anticipate going to other colleges and universities after a maximum of five years. If an assistant professor regards his years at Harvard as stimulating and prestigeful preparation for a better post elsewhere, he is relieved of many strains of competition. But he must guard himself—and some do so insufficiently—against putting down roots into the community and prevent himself from hoping, however vaguely, that he will be extended tenure. Harvard is able to recruit its assistant professors so effectively—from its own graduate schools as well as from other universities—only because this rank is an early step of career that is completed elsewhere.

When occupancy of a status is accompanied by acute strain, there is an enhanced possibility that the regular or institutionalized sequence of steps will be abandoned. At these points, people break away in desperation or with defiance, and leave occupations, families, social classes and other such organizing frameworks of commitment and loyalty. If recruits are plentiful and not too much time, effort, and money have been expended upon them, their loss may be regarded as minimal. Otherwise, steps must be taken to prevent such defection. The conditions that are causing personal stress must be examined, greater rewards offered, in order that stress can better be endured; and alternative career paths must be opened up, or at least seem to aspirants to have opened up. However, the occurrence of stressful situations may not force a man entirely out but merely lead him to aim at a different career within the organization or establishment; causing him to abandon the greater effort necessary to reach the top ranks or to shift his aspirations to other channels. Some choices of specialty and vocation involve this kind of shifting as when one abandons a line of occupational endeavor but uses it or its skills to make the shift. Hence in certain specialties, until the routes of entry become institutionalized, recruits are drawn from many fields, often from their failures or their rebellious members. This means that these men are embarked upon an uncertain though not necessarily hazardous future, since the sequences of status-passage have not yet been precisely laid down and sanctified by tradition.

When organizations and institutions are expanding, forming, disintegrating, or in any way changing radically, the personal lives of their members are rendered more tortuous and uncertain and at the same time more dangerous and more exciting. The opportunities for power and personal advance in expanding social structures are obvious, but even when the latter are disintegrating, some clever or fortunate people forge new career opportunities. The dangers of rapid organizational change—whether of expansion or contraction—can be illustrated by what happens to oldtimers who reach high positions only to find these no longer carry distinctive prerogatives and honors. Danger also dogs the novice who blindly follows old career models, for a model always is in some significant regard out of date, unless the times and the institutions are relatively stable. During such periods of great institutional change, the complexities of career are further compounded by what is happening to the careers of those others with whom one is significantly involved. The ordinary ties of sponsorship weaken and break because those in positions to sponsor are focused upon matters more immediately germane to their own careers. The lower ranks feel the consequences of unusual pressures generated among the ranks above. People become peculiarly vulnerable to unaccustomed demands for loyalty and alliance which spring from unforeseen organizational changes.

Insofar as careers can be visualized and implemented because of the relative stabilities of those social structures within which one has membership, the continuity and maintenance of identity is safeguarded and maximized, and methods of maintenance and restoration are more readily utilized and evolved. However, the movement from status to status, as well as the frustration of having to remain unwillingly in a status, sets conditions for the change and development of identities. Although my examples have been chosen mainly from work organizations, this way of looking at adult development is not at all restricted to occupational life. The lives of men and women can—theoretically at least—be traced as a series of passages of status. Insofar as this is so, we most heartily agree with Erikson's striking statement that a sense of identity "is never gained nor maintained once and for all. Like a good conscience, it is constantly lost and regained. . . ."

Coaching

When passages of status are more or less well regulated, those who have gone through the recognized steps stand ready, as I have said, to guide and advise their successors. This guidance is essential, for even regulated passage is perhaps more hazardous than my account has indicated.

In the well known novel, *The Late George Apley,* J. P. Marquand portrays the well ordered life of George as it follows the traditional Bostonian upper class pattern of growing up and growing old. As a young man, George is in danger of being drawn off the track, when he becomes fond of an Irish girl far below him in social position. He is brought to heel through family pressure and by being shown how this incident "really" fits into his entire expected life cycle. Natural as it is for him to dally with such a girl, the "escapade" is not to be treated as a serious venture. The great danger of such an escapade is that through it some George Apley—if not this one—will be drawn off expected paths and lost to family and social class. However,

the counsel of elders is requisite to status passages for reasons other than hazard, since all the future steps are clear only to those who have traversed them. Certain aspects of what lies over the horizon are blurred to the candidate, no matter how clear may be his general path. This forces his predecessors not only to counsel and guide him, but to prepare and coach him beforehand. Coaching is an integral part of teaching the inexperienced—of any age.

Once we see this function of "the coach," we are prepared to discuss coaching quite apart from regularized status steps, and within wider contexts than athletics or professional drama. A coaching relationship exists if someone seeks to move someone else along a series of steps, when those steps are not entirely institutionalized and invariant, and when the learner is not entirely clear about their sequences (although the coach is). The football coach attempting to turn out a good half-back, Iago seeking to induce Othello along the path of jealousy, the piano teacher trying to make a concert pianist out of a young man, the revivalist trying to work his audience into a frenzy of conversion, the psychiatrist carefully maneuvering his patient back to better psychological integration, and the confidence man manipulating his victim through sequential steps of involvement in an illicit deal: all are instances of coaching relationships, albeit each has different aspects. In each instance there is a man who has yielded himself (whether he knows it or not) to a teacher who guides him along at least partly obscure channels. Since every field in which such teaching goes on has its own prescriptions and rules of thumb, my discussion of coaching quite obviously must be very general, and will be pointed particularly toward those changes of identity that take place during coaching.

The general features of the coaching relationship flow from the learner's need for guidance as he moves along, step by step. He needs guidance not merely because in the conventional sense he needs someone to teach him skills, but because some very surprising things are happening to him that require explanation. The coach stands ready to interpret his responses, which may otherwise only have the status of ambiguous signs. If you look at something as nonpsychological as learning a physical skill, perhaps you can see the point more easily. The learner leans upon the coach's expert advice, for instance, whether a given muscular movement is going to lead forward, or down a false path; and without the coach he may not even notice his own movement. The coach literally calls attention to new responses: "Look, this is the first time you have managed to do this." Likewise, the coach explains away responses, saying "pay no attention" for what is happening either should be regarded as of no importance or as something that happens only "at this stage." The next steps are pointed out ("Don't worry, wait, this will happen"). In sum: because the sequences of steps are in some measure obscure, and because one's own responses become something out of the ordinary, someone must stand prepared to predict, indicate, and explain the signs.

But the tutor generally assigns himself a far more active role than I have suggested. He does not merely wait for the student to develop new responses; he throws him into situations so as to elicit certain responses from him. This provides an opportunity to indicate, interpret, and predict. Understandably, this involves the coach in a certain kind of duplicity upon occasion (as when a fencing teacher allows his pupil to hit him for the first time); the coach's position also requires that he may have to function like a playwright, arranging episodes, setting scenes, getting supporting characters to act in a certain way. Of course the pupil, by virtue of his acquisition of new skills or new perspectives, can be counted upon to engage other persons in new interactions. Like the infant who upon learning his first words encounters his parents differently, the learner's recently gained skills will throw him into novel situations. Some outcomes will be gratifying, but of course others can be terrifying or at least frightening. The coach utilizes both kinds of outcomes to retain control, occasionally even allowing him his head so as to be able to say—"I told you so, now then you see. . . ." The point is that the untutored cannot see until he has tried for himself, just as generally he cannot visualize much of the proper path beforehand.

In malevolent kinds of coaching—as in seduction, or in conning by confidence men—the relationship is one of trapper and victim. However, in almost all coaching there appears to be a strong element of inducement, temptation, and behind-the-scenes action. The con man baits, tempts, induces; but so does, although in less obvious ways, the art teacher, the basketball coach, or the psychiatrist. Abstractly stated, the coach not only works on current desires to get action directed along given paths, but seeks to create new desires and aims. He seeks to create a new identity for the pupil—or the victim—and to do this involves him in a variety of canny maneuvers.

In general, we should be struck by the importance of timing in all coaching. Because the pupil is being guided in his moves—muscularly, psychologically, socially—the coach is preoccupied with teaching him certain things at correct places and times. To begin with, the coach may be rejected if he forces too fast a pace, especially at the outset. The pupil may lose face or become frightened or otherwise distressed. In psychiatric coaching the patient may go elsewhere for help or, if the relationship is involuntary as when he is committed to a mental hospital, simply withdraw psychologically. On the other hand, the pupil (whether a patient, victim, or convert) may be lost to his mentor if the latter moves too slowly —lost through boredom, shattering of faith, or other reasons. Of course, the teacher may call attention to his superior experience and wisdom, as well as draw upon the resources of trust placed in him by the other, in order to set the pace; but he does so always at some risk. This risk is unavoidable and can only be minimized by shrewd tactics. The coach has to know when to force his man over a hurdle, and when to let him sidle up to it; when to schedule definite moves, and when to allow a period of relatively free play. The coach must skillfully balance between two poles: he must not pressure the student by his own impatience; yet he must force movement at those junctures when the fellow appears ready but reluctant to move, is in fact really "there" but does not realize it.

Crucial tactics in this delicately balanced process are the prescription, the schedule, the challenge, the trial, and the accusation. Prescriptions for action are sometimes called "routines" or "exercises" or "lessons"; they are traditional step-by-step progressions that prepare the way for further movement. When the coaching relationship is well-institutionalized, such routine practices become a very visible and sometimes hampering part of the coaching profession. The schedule is also an integral aspect of the coaching process; notions arise of how fast or how slowly the pupil should move, and at what points he should move slower or faster. There is at least an implicit set of norms governing how quickly he should progress through certain stages. Recently, a psychologist has suggested to a group of psychiatrists how a standardized set of norms might be used to measure the progress of their patients. In the coaching relationship, a considerable potential strain exists because the coach must control his own impulses to standardize schedules too greatly.

Challenges or dares are also an invariant aspect of coaching. Since a person is being asked to relinquish old modes of doing and seeing, he is in effect being asked to do and say and even think things that look risky or dangerous. I recently heard a psychiatrist say to a patient, "It is now time to do. . . . You may fail but you are likely not to; it is a risk worth taking." Of course, there are clever and institutionalized ways of cushioning failure, but the important thing is that the person by meeting the challenge receives an indication of how far he has progressed. His overcoming of a challenge provides a marker, a milestone of his development.

Essential also to coaching is the accusation, hurled or insinuated. The coach will conceive of his pupil on occasion as backsliding, as giving in to old habits, old temptations, and therefore must be frankly reprimanded. The pupil will also be accused of loss of faith or trust: "How can you benefit from what I have to teach you if you do not trust me now." From the learner's perspective, the coach may be neglecting his job, ruining one's talents, breaking faith, even engaging in betrayal. Accusations both block the process of learning and are vitally important for those reconciliations that mark turning points on the road forward.

I have mentioned the elements of risk and trust involved in the coaching relationship, although they loom as more obvious in some kinds of relationships than in others. The novice airplane pilot literally puts his life at the disposal of his instructor. In seduction or in confidence games the secret motivations that are involved highlight the risk and danger. Even in such mundane pursuits as piano and voice teaching or training for track meets, the pupil's potential level of performance may be greatly endangered by improper counsel. Insofar as the coaching process also leads to great changes of identity —as in G. B. Shaw's apocryphal drama *Pygmalion*—you, as a pupil, are in large measure ceding an unknown destiny to a mentor who presumably knows where he is taking you. A special danger is that the relationship may be broken off midstream, before "the treatment" is completed, with potential danger to both but particularly to the learner. One of the great, and inevitable risks of coaching is precisely that the coach may die, or move away, leaving the student vulnerable in various ways: because he is in a stage of self-imputed personal helplessness, or standing upon the brink of a learning crisis, or not yet properly out of love with the coach ("transference"), or in the midst of meeting a great challenge. But a comparable risk is that the student has the final responsibility of judging when the coaching relationship is genuinely harmful to himself or to his "potential." There is a point beyond which he must

not, like Cinderella, stay. The coach may have poor judgment. It is not impossible even that he evinces faulty judgment because he loves or hates his pupil too much; although he may be actually malevolent or merely indifferent. The learner always has an obligation to himself of assessing when he is being harmed and when he is being helped, even in those very traditional situations where the coach is supposed supremely knowledgeable.

The reverse side of great risk and danger is trust and faith. To this should be added what the psychoanalysts call "identification"; that is, a very close modeling of self after the other, or after certain of his aspects. The coach is not only a partial model ("do as I do"), but in certain stages may become almost a total model ("be as I am" or "wish to be what I am"). The tutor, of course, may consciously utilize this desire or propensity. On the other hand, in many types of coaching, particularly after the earlier stages of learning, mere imitation is not sufficient for progress.

Let us now consider more explicitly the shifts of identity brought about through coaching, as against the mere acquisition of skill. One cannot, of course, discuss risk, trust, identification, duplicity, challenge, and merely talk of the acquisition of skill. In some coaching, the person may be taken as a *tabula rasa,* as if he had no previous commitments of the kind the coach is now about to build; the task is simply to build upon unimpeded ground. More often this is not a realistic stance for the coach to take. The learner has something to unlearn, to cope with, and this will enter the trajectory of his learning early and often stay with him until very late. This is perhaps another way of saying that the coach must challenge old modes of doing, seeing, and thinking, as well as point out new modes. When the learning and re-learning is extreme—and I shall consider a variety of this in the next section— there must be massive and frontal attack upon identities. In less drastic kinds of change, through the agency of coaches, a man is requested also to turn his back upon his past, to discount previous accomplishments, to divest himself of earlier prides, to disidentify himself with old practices, old allies, and even old loves.

One may sometimes observe during the initial sessions of a new coaching relationship how the participants gingerly hold back from much involvement until they are "sure." This is especially true of the student, but the teacher also may have provisos. Traditionally, the early phases may be coached in terms of "make-believe" or "not for keeps"; and institutionally they may take the form of not yet counting the score or recording the performance. All this, in a sense, represents a trial period; one is involved, but without much commitment to his own performance, and can retreat with honor and dignity. It is as if there were a kind of moratorium, during which effort is great but during which both sides ceremonially ignore negative performances. Of course, such a moratorium and such make-believe run all through the coaching process, perhaps particularly during the new phases in cycles of learning, when the person is particularly sensitive to criticism and must be encouraged and must encourage himself to chance certain endeavors. You can see this procedure operating in reverse when young art students are so jealous of their paintings, so serious about their performances, that they bridle when the teacher lays a brush upon their work.

In his fondest moments, the coach may believe that he has total control over the progress of his pupil. But the very character of coaching is likely to set into motion unpredictable changes of identity. The best model for visualizing this learning is not as a steady progression through a series of stages, mostly known to the coach, but rather to imagine a tree with many branches and twigs. The pupil moves along certain branches until he reaches alternatives, and the coach stands ready to guide or channel his movement until the next set of alternatives arises. But the best pupils, like the best children, get out from under the control and the vision of the best teachers, and the best teachers are pleased that this is so. At the outer limits of learning, the stages can no longer be as standardized as at the beginning; and the pupil discovers his own style, whether we are talking of religious conversion, musical composition, or anything else. For the coach, too, the process may be open-ended; he too may end with a different identity. This mutual change may be, as Nelson Foote has suggested, "a winning pattern for each," but unfortunately it may also be mutually destructive or end happily for one but not for the other.

Something should now be added to counteract the notion that coaching is merely a two-way relationship between a coach and a coached person, for many if not most coaching processes occur in organization or institutional context. Thus the teacher hands on pupils to higher or more famous teachers, saying "I can teach you no more, you are now beyond me—or at least it is said that you are beyond me." Although I shall not develop the point, you ought to recognize that the organizational framework within which the coaching goes on vitally affects the process and outcome of coaching. In some organizational contexts the coach may move his students too quickly (for his own fame, or to get them sponsored jobs), or his coaching may become standardized (because of great numbers of pupils, or because of the excessively strict requirements of the organization), or he may handle his pupils far too impersonally (because of personal tensions engendered by his position, or because of rewards placed upon other activities associated with his position). He may bind his students too closely to himself for their rapid or maximum develop-

ment (because of his own anxieties created again by his position); or he may fail to sustain proper trust of himself (because close relationships among age ranks are frowned upon in the organization). Since coaching is thus linked with social structure and with the positions and careers of both the coaches and the coached, one can scarcely speak of process as divorced from structure. My discussion of process has been exceedingly general and its details must be spelled out in relation to particular structures and worlds. This is a task for meticulous and thoughtful research.

CHAPTER 10

Selected Examples of the Influence Process

Morison, in his article in this chapter, reminds us of Ecclesiastes, who glumly pointed out, "men persist in disordering their settled ways and beliefs by seeking out many inventions." Why men persist in disordering their settled ways is a moot and paradoxical question. For as trite as it is to say that the only constant of existence is change, it is equally trite to remark that men actively and with great strength resist changes they are perpetually inflicting on themselves. In fact, a recent book on organizational theory [1] propounds a new law, Gresham's Law, arrogated from economics, which in its new form states that structured (or programmed) activity drives out unstructured activity. It is undoubtedly true that man's greatest follies and triumphs emanate from his responses to a changing environment.

This chapter attempts to illuminate the processes of influence by presenting concrete examples of influence attempts cutting across the four levels of systems that occupy our interest. The reader should be warned that no clear-cut boundaries separate the four levels. The Schwartz and Will paper, however, is mainly concerned with influence as it is exerted on *persons*. (Although it could be argued that the nurse's *role* is the significant feature.) The target of change in the Marrow and French paper comprises various levels of an industrial organization; the content of the change is attitudes toward a *role*, that of the older worker. Strauss' article, based on an anecdote by Bavelas, recounts how a *group* of workers managed to activate significant changes—changes that had such strong repercussions throughout the rest of the organization that the energy developed by the group had to be dissipated. It is both a success and a failure story. In the final section, on *larger social systems*, Morison presents a detailed observation of a change in the Navy and some of the social consequences linked to it. Finally, Mann suggests a procedure for using survey research results to effect organizational change.

[1] J. March and H. Simon, *Organizations*, New York: John Wiley and Sons, Inc., 1958.

559

Let us attempt to summarize briefly some of the major themes running through these papers.

Failure and Loss Always Involved in Change   In his brilliant paper, "On Cooling the Mark," Erving Goffman dwells on a theme most of us seem to— or would like to—forget, the loss (of face, status, position, skills, etc.) that appears to be inevitably linked to change processes.[2] Taking off from the con-man operation of "cooling out the mark" or sucker, wherein an accomplice of the con-man tries to readjust the self-picture of the mark to some acceptable form (so that he won't squeal to the authorities), he goes on to raise some penetrating questions about adjustment to failure in our society. What means do we have in social life to adjust individuals to failure? In what ways can the mark cool himself out? What institutional mechanisms can be created to facilitate promotions and degradations? In what areas of social life does it become necessary to cool out a mark? What are some common ways in which individuals are cooled out? What happens if the mark refuses to be cooled out? The point underlying Goffman's analysis, and evident in all the writing on change, is the tragic vision of loss that accompanies change. If our society is predominantly a "rapidly changing" one, as most social observers seem to acknowledge, then attention must be directed to the loss as well as to the gain, to the face lost as much as to the face saved.[3]

Morison's paper illustrates this. By showing how change was resisted in the Navy because of the status disequilibration wrought by the anticipated elevation (and degradation) of certain officers, he depicts the fear and anxiety the specter of change brings about. In the Marrow and French article, the change brought about forced a new orientation to older workers and a concomitant loss of a functional stereotype.

The Need for Interpersonal Support During Change   Considering the stressful aspects of change with its attendant uncertainties about the future and fearful fantasies about loss, successful change can only be realized, it would seem, by providing the actors in the situation with sufficient emotional nutriments for them to cope with the anxiety-producing situation. Schwartz and Will, in their case study of a nurse undergoing an accelerated withdrawal pattern from patients and staff, present a method of intervention whereby the process of inter-

[2] Erving Goffman, "On Cooling the Mark Out: Some Adaptations to Failure," *Psychiatry,* 8:451–463, 1952. See also H. Garfinkel, "Conditions of Successful Degradation Ceremonies," *American Journal of Sociology,* 61:420–424, 1956.

[3] "During all human history until this century, the rate of social change has been very slow. So slow, that it would pass unnoticed in one person's lifetime. That is no longer so. The rate of change has increased so much that our imagination can't keep up. There is *bound* to be more social change, affecting more people, in the next decade than ever before. There is bound to be more change again in the 1970's. In the poor countries, people have caught on to this simple concept. Men there are no longer prepared to wait for periods longer than one person's lifetime." C. P. Snow, *The Two Cultures and The Scientific Revolution,* New York: Cambridge University Press, 1959, p. 45.

vention itself helped defer and redirect the withdrawal pattern. The very fact of intervention—which she experienced as "someone being interested in her" —began to revise her feeling that nobody cared and started her on a reality-testing program that modified the well-developed pattern of low morale and withdrawal.

The intervention discussed by Schwartz and Will has a certain kinship to Goffman's "cooling out" process. For in this instance, by insisting on a participant-observer orientation for the nurse—which ultimately snapped the inexorable chain of events—the change-agents re-equilibrated the nurse's image of herself and uplifted her failing self-esteem. One might conceptualize many varieties of change-agent intervention as methodologies dealing with the cooling-out process. At any rate, the need for interpersonal support during the critical period of change is seen as necessary in order to provide the necessary props until new skills or certainty or order has been attained.

The Limitation of "Facts" in Change Events   If man behaved as a wholly rational being, the friction generated by creating change would substantially abate. This is not the case, as the Strauss, Mann, Morison, and Marrow and French papers testify. In the latter two cases, data were shown which conclusively supported a specific policy action: in one case continuous-aim firing (3000 percent improvement); in the other, the slightly greater productivity of the older worker compared to the younger (which cut across the grain of a widely held negative attitude toward older workers). In both cases there was severe resistance to the data, the conclusions drawn from them, and the possible action alternatives derived from them. The resistance ranged from a simple rationalization of the results to massive retaliation against the individuals suggesting the change. It was not until President Theodore Roosevelt personally intervened that Admiral Sims' position on continuous-aim firing was upheld. In the Marrow-French report, data was blocked by a stubbornly held stereotype. It was only when Marrow and French involved various levels of the hierarchy in their own research efforts that the stereotype faded.

Fact, rationality, reasoned arguments appear to have little appeal given the forces arrayed against change. This is particularly true if the anticipated change has important and uncertain consequences that might entail loss to the interested groups.[4]

The Unanticipated Consequences of Change   When we assume interdependence and *system* [5] to be essential aspects of organized life, we must also assume that any change may have consequences for elements not considered as central in the change inductions. This is as true of planned change as of unplanned

[4] But ultimately we must rely on "fact" again in order to reduce and understand the resistance to change. Irrationality exists, which can be dispelled only through some form of rationally *understanding* the irrationality. Certain "facts" can make sense only when they have been preceded by "experience," but we must come to grips with rationality and fact.

[5] See Chapter 5 for elaboration of the "system" concept.

change. Given this we have to be aware of the unanticipated changes originating with the very best of plans; there is no way we presently know of whereby all changes and all effects of changes can be predetermined. Naturally, the more we know, the better we can predict, but the intricate interplay of forces and our own "bounded rationality" make it necessary for us to recognize the "chancy" nature of change, particularly in complicated social systems.

A number of articles included in this chapter attest to this view. In a way that the authors can only vaguely account for, the "breakthrough" achieved with one nurse seemed to bring an entire ward to a new equilibrium. Morison recounts the difficulty of accepting a change, one validly proven, because of unanticipated effects on other parts of the Navy social system. An undoubtedly successful plan had to be given up, according to Strauss, because of its effects on other parts of the organization.

Lewin once said that if we want to understand how a system works we should try to change it. The only problem is that we have to wait until the change is made before we can approach the whole truth.

So far we have delineated some of the problems in creating change: the failure or loss involved, the need for interpersonal support during the disorder and *anomie* created by change, the limitations of rationality, and the unanticipated consequences. Finally, there is left to discuss some of the conditions that promote innovation or change, ideas that were culled primarily from Morison's paper.

Conditions for Facilitating Innovative Climates   Morison's suggestive piece makes a number of interesting hypotheses concerning the conditions under which innovation may develop; conditions which range from the personalities of the innovator and entrepreneur to the fertility of the social system. He noticed, for example, that the innovator's or entrepreneur's goals differed qualitatively from those of the actual originator of the idea, the latter being less revolutionary than the former. Implied in this formulation is another truth: that practice many times precedes theory,[6] that the innovator shrewdly exploits what every innocent inventor knows.[7] What seems impossible to the top echelon administrator is adaptation to new circumstances, not the appropriateness or the feasibility of the innovation.

Along these lines Morison suggests that for innovation to be accepted, some exogenous force (in this particular case, a President of the United States) has to intervene. We suggest that this is true to the extent that the system is static and rigid.[8] Given changing environmental demands where consequential change can be evoked *only* by some force outside the system—a *deus ex machina*—the system will degenerate. This amendment to Morison's hypothesis is, at any rate, capable of empirical testing.

[6] See Gouldner in this volume, Chapter 2.

[7] Reminiscent of Whitehead's aphorism that every idea was discovered before its founder.

[8] See Chapter 5 for more precise definition of these system terms. What we mean here simply is a system highly impervious to change.

One final point should be made concerning Morison's prescription for organizational flexibility. He recommends that organizations should somehow communicate the grand purpose of the organization and build loyalties toward the grand objective which "might serve as a unifying agent against the disruptive local allegiances of the inevitable smaller elements that compose any group." Organizations as well as persons have to develop an adaptive orientation wherein greater attention is paid to an adaptive *process* than to the product.[9]

But now we have come full circle, for loyalty breeds attachments and attachments beget rigidities. Morison would probably argue that the loyalties must be directed toward an adaptive organizational *ethos,* not toward particular ends or products. Yet it appears that just at this juncture we come head on against one of the most difficult problems in social change. How can we develop loyalties —which are after all more than transient feelings—and maintain an adaptive orientation? How can organizations transmit certain learnings that the faithful learn (and learn too well!) and then expect these faithful to change their faith at certain unexpected times? We remarked at the beginning of this introduction that change involves a loss of one kind or another. But it also involves a folly, a tragic folly that now falls into focus: Organizations require men to learn certain skills and techniques. These are reinforced through the variegated "socialization" procedures the organization uses to gain compliance. The good student learns his lesson well; the best student overlearns his lesson so well that his responses become rote (developing what Veblen called "trained incapacity"). Then circumstances change, more and more rapidly, and our good students of yesterday become the misfits of tomorrow—the tragedy being that their punishment is caused by their folly of attempting to superimpose their hard-earned knowledge on an essentially new set of conditions.[10]

Cooling out the mark would appear to be our only refuge—unless we find salvation in Morison's hope that we "identify ourselves with the adaptive process and thus share . . . some of the joy, exuberance, satisfaction, and security . . . to meet the changing time." [11]

[9] This is identical to the methodological-content distinction we proposed in the introduction to Part III. It is also reminiscent of John Dewey's remark that the mature self (or group or organization) finds its central identification in the *method* of its own remaking.

[10] The British colonel in the *Bridge on the River Kwai* is an excellent example of this folly. So was Pontius Pilate. Read K. D. Benne, "Education for Tragedy," *Educational Theory,* Vol. I, Nos. 3 and 4, 1951, for elaboration of this point.

[11] In Alvin Gouldner's article, "Cosmopolitans and Locals: Toward an Analysis of Latent Social Roles, II" (*Administrative Science Quarterly*, Vol. 2, No. 4, 1958), there is a brilliant discussion of the conflict between loyalty and professionalization that bears directly on this entire argument.

❖❖❖❖❖❖❖❖❖❖❖❖❖❖❖❖❖❖❖❖ INTERVENTION AND CHANGE
ON A MENTAL HOSPITAL WARD

Morris S. Schwartz and Gwen Tudor Will

IN this study we attempt to demonstrate one way in which a situation of low morale on a mental hospital ward was analyzed and intervened in. The study was part of a larger project investigating the types of nursing and administrative intervention and of social structure that facilitate or deter the movement of patients in the direction of mental health.[1] In this larger project the investigators not only observed, evaluated, and recorded intrastaff and patient-staff activity, but also participated with the ward staff in the formulation of modes of intervention which would maximize the patients' opportunities for improvement.

The data were gathered on the disturbed ward of a mental hospital in which psychoanalytically oriented intensive psychotherapy is the principal form of medical treatment. The ward ordinarily has 15 patients and is staffed with one charge nurse, two to four staff nurses or aides, and one to three student nurses on the day shift, with ap-

proximately one less person on the evening shift. In the course of the larger investigation we noted that certain social situations became obvious problems for ward staff members. Among these was the problem of maintaining their own morale at an optimum level. Not quite so conspicuous to the ward staff was the problem of mutual withdrawal,[2] the continuation of which had serious adverse effects on patients. Even less conspicuous to the ward staff was the relation between the morale of any one nurse and the process of mutual withdrawal and the relation of both of these to the ward context. The investigators attempted to study the relation between these processes by selecting out one nurse for intensive study during a period when the ward as a whole was undergoing low morale.

Continuum of Morale and Participation

In evaluating the morale of the ward personnel we defined morale not as a *state* which the nurse *has* but as a mode

[1] For the purpose of our discussion, facilitating the movement of patients in the direction of mental health means: facilitating the patients' realistic communication and participation, fulfilling the patients' needs, increasing the patients' self-esteem, and, in general, facilitating interpersonal relations with patients that will increase their satisfaction and security.

[2] We are using the term mutual withdrawal here to represent a process of reciprocal avoidance in which the patient and staff member minimize or eliminate face-to-face contact as well as communicative opportunities. The integration of mutual withdrawal will be elaborated in the body of the paper.

Excerpted from Morris S. Schwartz and Gwen Tudor Will, "Low Morale and Mutual Withdrawal on a Mental Hospital Ward," Psychiatry, *Vol. 16, No. 4, November 1953, pp. 337–353. Some footnotes omitted. Abridged and used by permission.*

of participation in the social process on a continuum. Thus we have viewed the low morale end of the continuum as a process of ineffective participation with patients and the high morale end of the continuum as a process of effective functioning with patients. In a parallel fashion, we have viewed as a continuum the integrations maintained by patients and staff. At one extreme are those integrations which maintain and reinforce the patients' illness, of which mutual withdrawal is one example. At the other extreme are the integrations of optimum participation that facilitate the movement of patients in the direction of mental health, of which mutual enjoyment and increased security and self-esteem in the participation are aspects.

The Problem

In this paper, we have restricted our focus to the therapeutic effects on patients stemming from the interaction between and among nursing personnel, especially as this interaction was participated in by a particular nurse. Because patients are in continuous, inescapable, and emotionally important relationships with nurses, the activities of the nurses on the ward merit close investigation. Such a restriction in focus, however, has both advantages and disadvantages. On the one hand, by limiting our field we can analyze it more intensively. On the other hand, by omitting from consideration the roles played by the therapists, the administrator of the ward, and the institution as a whole, we exclude from our investigation other important influences in the patients' lives.

We shall be concerned with three approaches to the social field and their interrelations: (1) the pattern of processes constituting a particular nurse's low morale, (2) the integrations of mutual withdrawal she maintains with patients, and (3) the ward equilibrium. Since similar overt processes were being manifested by most of the staff during this period of low ward morale, we assumed that the intensive study of one nurse would give us data about her covert processes and also some indication of the covert processes being experienced by the rest of the ward personnel. Thus by focusing on one nurse we shall try to elaborate the nature of the processes involved in the development of low morale, viewing this nurse's participation in the social field as a series of successive and simultaneous transactions having both covert and overt aspects. We shall then attempt to analyze the contribution of these interpersonal processes of low morale to a type of integration which maintains the patient's illness—mutual withdrawal. Further, we shall analyze the ward equilibrium as being constituted in part by the pattern of processes of low morale and the integrations of mutual withdrawal. Thus we shall attempt to show how these three aspects of the social field mold and shape each other and how a patterned feedback system is formed in which each aspect reinforces the other. Finally we shall demonstrate how the processes of low morale and mutual withdrawal of a particular nurse were interrupted.

Setting

Early in the course of our investigation we noted that the ward, which functioned effectively most of the time with a difficult group of patients, was operating much below its ordinary level of performance. At the same time we observed that Miss Jones, a nurse who was ordinarily useful and constructive on the ward (seriously interested in patients, effective in participation with them, and cooperative in her relations with ward personnel), was also functioning in a markedly ineffective fashion. Her ineffective functioning had begun during her first week back after a brief absence from the ward (designated as *first week* for purposes of this paper). We thought that Miss Jones' low morale might be investigated by careful observations of her on the ward and by discussions with her regarding her feelings, thoughts, and actions in this situation, without attempting to determine her unconscious motivations or to evaluate her difficulties in psychiatric diagnostic terms. During the *second week* the senior investigator approached Miss Jones and attempted to initiate these discussions. Because Miss Jones was hesitant at first to talk about her difficulties, discussions did not begin until the *third week*. During the *third, fourth, and fifth weeks* the senior investigator obtained data from her about the first and second weeks in retrospect and also current data on the situation at the time of the interviews. During these discussions it was noted that her mode of participation gradually changed—that is, her morale improved. Thus the processes of data gathering and intervention occurred simultaneously. During the *fifth week*, there was a period of discussion on how the intervention came about and how it affected her mode of participation. In addition, during these five weeks the junior investigator was observing Miss Jones' activities on the ward.

Before we describe the situation of Miss Jones' low morale, it is useful to indicate what it means to live and work on this disturbed ward as the in-

vestigators have experienced it and as they understand the staff's experience. Many of the patients have been mentally ill a long time (over 10 years); many of them suffer from intense feelings of loneliness and anxiety. Because of the nature of their illness these patients experience much misery which is unrelieved for long periods of time. In this condition, near panic and despair are common; feelings of helplessness about altering their situation are firmly rooted in their attitudes toward themselves; fear, distrust, and dread of others are prevalent. It is these defeated and hopeless persons that the ward personnel experience day after day for eight hours at a time—experience not in a casual and aloof manner but with interest, concern, and planning for their needs, with compassion for their plight and hopefulness for their eventual movement in the direction of health. Personnel throughout the hospital attempt to provide a therapeutic milieu by maintaining enthusiasm and interest in their work despite very great difficulties. Favorable changes in patients are slow, and when these changes take place, they are often only barely perceptible. It is inevitable in the course of working with patients that ward personnel will become discouraged at times and that the burden of caring for these patients will sometimes be too heavy to bear. At such times personnel become tired and less effective in their functioning. It is one of these situations of low morale that we have selected for study. We have focused upon an extreme situation in order to highlight certain aspects of morale which are ordinarily not easily observable and which are conspicuous when they appear in an extreme form.

Miss Jones' low morale on the ward had a clear beginning. After her absence from the ward, she returned to her regular duties with enthusiasm, eager to resume her work. When she came on the ward, she discovered that the regular charge nurse was absent and that the ward was being run by a substitute. There was a shortage of personnel; plans which had previously been made for patients were not being carried out; patients were upset; patients' needs were being met with less than usual adequacy; and in general the ward staff was tired, discouraged, and much less effective both in their coordination with each other and in dealing with patients. Thus a context of low morale was already structured on the ward within which Miss Jones had to work.

The nurse thought that in a few days things would settle down and the staff would be able to proceed more effectively. However, they did not. Within this context Miss Jones gradually became more discouraged, so that by the end of the first week she was sharing the feelings and attitudes of the other staff members and functioning in the same ineffective way.

Low Morale

In looking at the social field from the point of view of the nurse's low morale, we are considering her morale as an aspect of the current social situation on the ward. We have assumed that her total personality configuration, which is left outside the scope of this inquiry, is incorporated in the nurse's mode of participation on the ward.

THE INTERPERSONAL PROCESSES

The particular pattern of Miss Jones' low morale consisted of a number of interpersonal processes which occurred

consecutively and simultaneously: failure, anger and resentment, guilt and blame, discouragement and indifference, constriction of perspective, and isolation and withdrawal.

Failure. Miss Jones initially thought that by offering suggestions for the improvement of the ward routine and patient care, she might help to bring about some alteration in the effectiveness of the ward personnel. Some of her suggestions were met with little enthusiasm; others were met with opposition and resistance, because of the low morale prevailing in the group. When she was unable to alter the attitude or functioning of ward personnel, she decided to concentrate on working with the patients on a one-to-one basis. However, at the end of the first week she was failing more than usual in face-to-face relationships with patients: she was not participating with them so appropriately; she was not so effective in communicating with them; and she was not responding to their needs so adequately. The patients themselves contributed to the nurse's ineffectiveness in two ways: (1) they became more difficult because their needs were not being met on the ward at that time, and this in turn made it more difficult for Miss Jones to succeed in meeting their needs; and (2) they were made so anxious by the general ward disorganization that the tendencies to defeat others (and thus themselves), which are a conspicuous part of their armor, were readily called into action. Miss Jones came more and more to experience the patients as being very difficult to deal with. Withdrawn patients seemed to withdraw more from her; aggressive patients became more aggressive; some patients became more demanding; other patients became panicky; and many were resistant and negativistic when Miss Jones approached them. She indicated this in the following statement.

I began to be more and more unsuccessful in my relationships with patients. My hostility toward them was most disturbing. I actually began to visualize them as irritating, demanding people. This was sensed by them as they seemed to withdraw from me. Aggressive patients began to snarl at me. Miss F's remarks about my being ineffectual were more frequent and my anger was personal and intense. Disparaging remarks from other patients would upset me, and I would keep away from them.

As Miss Jones had more difficulty with patients, she began to conceive of herself as a failure. Her self-esteem as a nurse was related in part to having satisfactory and constructive relationships with patients. Not only did she think that she ought to perform adequately with patients, but this expectation was implicit in the structure of the institution. When she did not fulfill both her own and the institution's expectation, she came to think that there must be some defect in her as a nurse and as a person. Her feelings of being unworthy and a failure reflected her lowered self-esteem and contributed to an increased inability to function effectively; as she became more discouraged with herself she continued to fail with patients; as she continued to fail with patients, she became more discouraged. In this condition she came to perceive even those situations in which she had participated in a fairly effective way as ones in which she had failed.

Anger and resentment. Because of the resistance of the staff to her suggestions and because she felt the others were responsible in some way for her low morale, Miss Jones became angry and resentful toward the ward staff. She

could not openly ventilate her anger; it continued, and her covert resentment interfered with her relations with the ward staff.

In order to avoid facing her anger at personnel and her frustration with them, Miss Jones turned toward the patients for her job satisfaction. As she also failed with patients she became angry and resentful toward them:

The more I found out about patients from their histories, the more chronic I thought the patients were. And when I went on the ward I found out that I was furious with them.

The nurse began to feel that the patients, too, were frustrating and anxiety-provoking to her. The more "difficult" and "resistant" patients were, the more irritating and demanding she saw them to be. When she approached these patients with resentment and with her attitude-feeling that they were irritating or demanding, some of them attacked her verbally. These attacks only "proved" to her that she was correct in her appraisal of patients. She experienced these attacks so intensely that she tended to withdraw from patients in order to prevent experiencing further discomfort with them. Her personal discomfort and withdrawal encouraged some patients to withdraw from her. Other patients became very resistant to her efforts, and she became resentful and irritated with this resistance. As her irritation increased, so did the resistance of the patients.

Guilt and blame. Miss Jones felt that the ward staff contributed to her discouragement and failure with patients by communicating their own discouragement to her and by their minimum participation with patients. At first she blamed the temporary charge nurse for the disorganization on the ward; then she developed guilt feelings about having such strong negative feelings toward persons with whom she worked closely and whom she liked. In order to alleviate this guilt toward the ward staff, she blamed the hospital as a whole for the low morale of the ward as well as for her own difficulties:

The charge nurse just couldn't do anything because the nursing office wouldn't give her any help. So I began to feel very hostile toward the hospital. Nobody cared what was going on on the ward.

Her attitudes toward the hospital became stabilized at: "The hospital doesn't understand nursing problems; the nursing service is inadequate; nobody in the hospital is really concerned about the patients."

Most important in contributing to her guilt were her attitudes toward and feelings about patients. The more uncomfortable she became with them and the more she saw herself as a failure, the more hostile she felt toward patients. This hostility reached the point where she felt she couldn't *stand* patients. She then developed strong guilt feelings about this hostility. These only served to make her withdraw more from the source of guilt. She attempted to get out of this failure-hostility-guilt-withdrawal cycle by rationalizing her failure with: "It's difficult to help patients because they are so sick and nothing will help them." In this way she explained to herself that her lack of success was not due to something wrong with her, but to something intrinsic in the patients. The more her relationships with patients deteriorated, the more guilty she felt and the more hopeless she became about being able to do anything constructive with them. The more hopeless she became about herself, the more she saw the patients as

hopeless. Seeing the patients as chronic alleviated her guilt slightly and excused her for not attempting very much with them: "If patients are hopeless, why should I feel guilty if I can't work with them?" At the same time she felt that there was something wrong with this attitude, especially since she was not convinced that the patients were chronic and hopeless.

Discouragement and indifference. The configuration of failure-anger-resentment-guilt-blame preceded and contributed to a process of discouragement and indifference. With the development of this interpersonal process, Miss Jones reached the point of lowest morale. It was overtly manifested by extreme fatigue and disinterest on the ward.

One aspect of her discouragement and indifference was her attitude-feeling that *"nobody cares—*either about nurses or patients." She felt that other personnel were not concerned about patients, and she rationalized her own lack of concern with:

What do I care if A soils—nobody else does. . . . I'd go into C's room and she would snarl at me. It was something I'm sure that she felt in me; she had never done that before. I had no contact with B, and I just couldn't talk to her. I was short-tempered with A. And I looked at all the patients very differently than I had before, as if they were hopeless, mean, and nasty—not sick. I felt that I couldn't make any decent relationships with them. So I thought I would stay away for a few days, and I stayed away.

She also felt that the hospital was neglecting her and the ward: no efforts were made to provide the additional personnel who were badly needed; the nursing service seemed to be indifferent to how poorly the ward was operating and the difficulties the personnel were having. The lack of support from the hospital and from other ward personnel only increased the nurse's helpless feelings about herself and patients.

As she experienced the indifference of the institution toward her, she continued her indifference toward patients, even toward those with whom she had previously had a good relationship. Her attitude crystallized specifically into: "Nobody cares about *me,* so I won't care about anyone either."

The loss of interest in the patient as an aspect of the nurse's discouragement and indifference is illustrated in the following situations:

1. Miss B had been secluded all day and nobody had attended to her bath or gotten her dressed. When I discovered this, I noticed I felt indifferent about it. I said to myself, "I think I'll go in and try to talk with her." When I did this I found I couldn't talk with her and I left immediately. I thought, "I'll come back a little later," but I never got back to her that day. In thinking about the situation I felt the reason I left was because the patient was so unresponsive to me. I thought maybe I could do something for another patient, instead of staying with her. But when I look back upon it, I didn't make any attempts with any other patients either at that time.

2. I couldn't function on the ward. I had no semblance of relationship with patients. So I'd sit in the office or I'd sit in the hall moping. I'd try something with a patient and it usually failed—at least I thought it did.

The development of discouragement and indifference served a dual purpose for the nurse: it reduced the amount of felt anxiety she experienced in the situation, and it permitted her to continue on the ward. In this ward situation, three possibilities appeared to be open to her: (1) she could continue to be

covertly angry and hostile and thus continue with her failure and frustration; or (2) she could resign from the institution; or (3) she could fit herself into the ward situation. By accepting the third possibility, she identified more with ward personnel, thus reducing her conflict, her guilt, and her anxiety.

Related to the nurse's discouragement and indifference and contributory to the configuration of low morale were two other interpersonal processes: constriction of her perspective, and isolation and withdrawal.

Constriction of perspective. In this condition of low morale, the nurse *selectively focused on the negative.* Her repeated failure and her discouragement contributed to circumscribing her attention to limited aspects of the ward situation. With reference to the institution as a whole, she restricted herself to looking upon those aspects which were directly related to the maintenance of her low morale, and thus she blocked out the positive aspects. Similarly, on the ward, her feelings were in an all or nothing fashion: "There isn't *any* useful nursing on the ward and *nothing* of benefit is being done for the patient." This confinement to negative aspects of the situation was especially distressing to her when applied to patients. Her selective attention to certain aspects of patient behavior is illustrated by the following:

I began to feel a marked change in my perception of patients. I began to see only the negative. This patient had been ill for 13 years; another had five hospitalizations; another had presented much less disturbed behavior when she was admitted than she was doing right now. I suddenly became aware that the difficulty was not with me, but with patients; these were chronic patients of long standing. Repeated efforts in therapy had met with failure. These patients were overwhelmingly difficult. There seemed to be little reason to try different ways of approaching them, and I couldn't see how I might approach them differently.

This selective focus on the negative made it difficult for Miss Jones to see any success she had with patients or to see any favorable change in the ward situation. Whatever actual, or potential, warmth and responsiveness there was in both patients and staff even in the low-morale situation could not be experienced by her. Thus even if the ward situation had begun to change toward a more favorable direction, Miss Jones might not have been able to recognize it at this time. Because patients were so difficult to deal with, because she felt they were hopeless, and because of her limited vision and restriction in seeing the range of alternatives in any situation with the patients, her responses to patients became more and more stereotyped and thus less successful and satisfying to both her and the patients. This confirmed her feelings of being a failure and increased her need to keep away from patients.

This selective attention to the negative produced sufficient discomfort for Miss Jones so that she had to defend herself against it. She developed a detached view of the ward situation and of patients. Her attitude was expressed as follows: "If I make no effort to move toward patients, I won't fail. If I don't get involved with them, I won't be uncomfortable." She tried to keep herself detached—that is, affectively withdrawn from patients—and through this detachment became less interested in the patients' welfare. She depersonalized patients and began to see them as objects with whom she had little relatedness and toward whom she felt little warmth.

Associated with her detachment and subsequent to it appeared a great deal of self-preoccupation and self-involvement. She became preoccupied with her own welfare and her own unmet needs in the ward situation and could not focus on patients' needs. She avoided situations which might occasion anxiety and discomfort. She felt helpless and ineffective but was unable to see either the content or the form of her low morale very clearly, experiencing only vague feelings of dissatisfaction and recognizing that these were related to her total condition of low morale. When the investigator questioned her, she said she was unable to think of any ways in which she might solve or alter the situation of her low morale.

Because of her selective focus on the negative, her circumscribed imagination, her detachment, her self-preoccupation, and her despair, the sick aspects of patients were experienced as *overwhelming*. Since she could not cope with these overwhelming feelings, she avoided them by withdrawing from patients.

Isolation and withdrawal. In conjunction with the interpersonal processes described above, the nurse experienced a lack of relatedness to others. Her feelings of isolation were manifested by affective withdrawal, communicative withdrawal, and physical withdrawal. She withdrew her emotional investment in the ward. She felt that there "wasn't anything to say" to others; if she did not talk about her failures and inadequacy, she would avoid having others develop a low opinion of her; in some vague, magical way, not talking about her failures would mean that she would not have to repeat them. Her physical withdrawal took the form of staying away from the ward sporadically because of illness. On the ward itself, her work became meaningless to her. She derived little satisfaction from continuing to nurse patients, and saw little value in it. She felt that she had no real contribution to make, that she was not really *in* the situation but on the outside looking in. And this in turn made it even more difficult for her to function with consistency and persistence.

THE PATTERN OF PROCESSES OF LOW MORALE

In focusing our attention on the nurse's low morale as one aspect of the social field, we have concentrated on her interpersonal processes from her perspective and have considered only tangentially the relation of these to the integrations of mutual withdrawal and the maintenance of the ward equilibrium. These interpersonal processes comprising her low morale are, of course, a complex pattern. In describing them we need to emphasize not only their sequential development but also the concurrence of their emergence and the circularity of the relations between them. Thus the pattern of low morale can be seen as an interacting system in which the processes constituting it are interdependent. On the one hand, the interpersonal processes themselves are constituted by various transactions which are patterned; on the other hand, these processes mutually reinforce each other to form the pattern of low morale. Each of these processes is not a separate entity but combines with, influences, and is influenced by every other process either directly or indirectly. *The pattern of low morale is constituted by an interweaving and interpenetration of the interpersonal processes, and it is difficult to assess the relative importance of each process in contributing to*

the maintenance of the total pattern. The pattern is a self-confirming, self-perpetuating, and self-reinforcing system. The system remains relatively closed as long as: (1) it is maintained in a context of ward low morale, (2) the patients and nurse maintain integrations of mutual withdrawal, and (3) there are no significant interventions into the pattern from other parts of the social field.

Integrations of Mutual Withdrawal

Looking at the social field from the point of view of the types of integrations this particular nurse maintained with certain patients on the ward while she was functioning with low morale, we noticed that a predominant integration was mutual withdrawal. We noted that she withdrew from patients, including those with whom she had previously had a good relationship and with whom she had functioned effectively most of the time. At the same time, these same patients withdrew from her. The withdrawal of each from the other appeared to be stabilized, with the withdrawal of the nurse perpetuating the withdrawal of the patient, and the withdrawal of the patient reinforcing the nurse's withdrawal. This integration was maintained in a ward context where the withdrawal of staff from patients was much more frequent than usual.

To illustrate the integration of mutual withdrawal the following observations of Miss Jones' contacts with one patient have been abstracted from our data. These observations were made by the investigators prior to and during the time Miss Jones was functioning with extremely low morale.

The patient, Miss Q, had previously been very successful in creating distance between herself and the staff by her unusually "messy" behavior, often drooling and carrying saliva around in her hand or a handkerchief. She had much difficulty communicating with the staff, speaking only in one- or two-word phrases and often in an explosive, stuttering manner. She stayed by herself a great deal, curled up in the bed or in a corner. At mealtime she smeared her food on her face, hands, and clothing, and clung to her tray and dishes. She often became upset and threw food across the room when personnel attempted to remove her tray. Many staff members developed successful ways of dealing with the problem she presented at mealtime.

Ordinarily, Miss Jones was interested, persistent, and often original in her approaches to this patient and was usually successful in her experiences with her. Before mealtime Miss Jones washed the patient's face and hands and got her ready for the meal. She then sat with her, fixed her food, and spoon-fed her to start her eating. Miss Jones stayed with Miss Q immediately after taking her tray as well as at other times. The patient's difficulties had been frequently discussed in ward meetings. There was agreement that there had been a gradual change in the patient's eating and withdrawal pattern as a result of the staff's efforts.

We made the following observations of Miss Jones and this patient during the period of low morale:

Breakfast trays were served. Miss Jones brought in Miss Q's tray: "Ready to eat breakfast?" Miss Q did not reply. The tray was placed beside her. Miss Jones started fixing the egg, but did not sit down.

She soon left and went to the office, returning about five minutes later. "You haven't started to eat. Don't you want your breakfast?" No reply. Miss Jones picked up a spoonful of egg and started to feed the patient. Miss Q scooped the egg off the spoon and smeared it on her bathrobe. "Really, Miss Q, you can do better than

that." Miss Q started muttering and holding on to her dish of eggs. "Damn it, damn it." The next several spoonfuls she refused. Miss Jones walked away, saying, "I'll be back in thirty minutes for your tray." However, in about five minutes she returned with some hot coffee. "I brought you some more coffee." Miss Q was still sputtering and as Miss Jones approached her, Miss Q threw the tray of food on the floor.

Miss Jones was asked in retrospect about the episode and expressed her feelings as follows:

It had a lot to do with how I was feeling, I think. I certainly didn't approach her as I had before. I got sort of tired of her messing around, I guess. As I cleaned up the food, I was not really angry. I felt I didn't care if she ate her food or threw it at me, and I didn't speak to her or offer to get her more breakfast.

I didn't report this incident or put it in the patient's record, partly because I felt I had failed and partly because I felt no one else would care, or read the notes. Also I felt rather isolated from the rest of the personnel and didn't want to discuss the problem with them or seek their advice.

These examples illustrate how a nurse with temporary low morale and a patient with chronic low morale interacted with each other to maintain integrations of mutual withdrawal.

The same behavior which we examined from the point of view of the nurse's self-interactions will now be examined as it relates to her *withdrawal* from patients.

1. Her continuing failure with patients made the maintenance of relationships with them uncomfortable. In order to avoid failure, with its reduction in self-esteem and accompanying anxiety, the nurse *minimized her participation with patients, confining it to the briefest essential contacts.*

2. In a context of ward low morale,

patient needs were fulfilled much less than usual, and patients became resistant to the nurse's efforts. She, in turn, became angry and resentful toward them, and to avoid her guilt about this, she *avoided the source of guilt*—the patients.

3. In order to rationalize her failure with patients she *saw them as chronic patients incapable of being helped*. This made any relationship *appear to be useless*.

4. Indifference on the part of the nurse evoked indifference on the part of the patient. The nurse *could not persist* in her relations with patients because of her own and their indifference.

5. Discouragement about herself and hopelessness about patients led to repeated *stereotyped responses* in her relations with patients.

6. Her selective focus on the negative aspects of patients' behavior made their sick behavior appear overwhelming. *Minimizing communicative opportunities* permitted the nurse to avoid feeling overwhelmed.

7. The nurse became detached from the ward situation and *withdrew her affective investment* in it; this resulted in her *losing interest in patients*. Her loss of relatedness with others fostered a preoccupation with her own needs, which facilitated her *looking upon patients as objects and ignoring their needs*.

8. The more hopeless she became about herself, the more she envisioned patients as hopeless—*"Nothing will help them."*

It might be well to examine both partners in these integrations of mutual withdrawal in a more general way. The withdrawn schizophrenic patient on the ward as a partner in this integration characteristically participates in the following manner: She is a shy person whose approaches to others are tentative and hesitant, hemmed in with much precaution and anticipation of rebuff. She is fearful of maintaining an interpersonal relationship with another; at the same time she has an intense longing to do so. Her tendency is to withdraw, to wait, and to see whether the other is really interested in her. She can only maintain a little initiative in relating to another, and this initiative must be constantly supported and encouraged by the other. She is extremely sensitive to rejection on the part of others, especially when they constitute her daily social context. When such rejection is experienced, she withdraws into herself. Because of her repeated experiences of disappointment, she maintains an expectation that others will not provide her with satisfaction and security. It takes repeated contrary experiences to dislodge this expectation. With this configuration of processes she is ordinarily ever-ready to remain distant and guarded.

The patient will continue to function with this pattern of withdrawal as long as the partner in the social situation does not act in a way appropriate to interrupting and altering the pattern in the direction of increased communication and participation. If the partner withdraws herself, this inevitably contributes to, reinforces, and increases the patient's withdrawal. The patient's withdrawing from the nurse increases and reinforces the nurse's withdrawal, so that a stable integration of mutual withdrawal, circular and feeding back into itself, is formed, in which each is perpetuating the withdrawal of the other. This integration can only serve to maintain and reinforce the patient's schizophrenic mode of participation: her isolation and loneliness, her fear of contact with others, her distrust of others, her feelings of unworthiness, and the conviction that others cannot contribute to an increase in her satisfaction and security. It follows from this that the interruption of the integration of mutual withdrawal is one way in which the patient's mental health can be facilitated, since this integration is one means through which the patient's mental illness is maintained.

On the basis of our data we have formulated the following hypothesis: *Withdrawal of patients on the ward is in part a function of the nurse's withdrawal, and the nurse's withdrawal is an aspect of her low morale. The withdrawn behavior on the part of the patient is not only a function of his past development, but is part of and takes into account the current social situation—that is, the withdrawing behavior of the nurse. The patient's withdrawal becomes part of a stable equilibrium of mutual withdrawal, in which the withdrawal of each reinforces that of the other, as long as the nurse continues to function with low morale.*

Ward Equilibrium

Looking at the social field from the point of view of the ward equilibrium, we noted that the nurse's low morale and the integrations of mutual withdrawal were initiated, developed, and maintained in a context in which the general level of effectiveness was much lower than usual, and in which personnel were withdrawing from patients with greater frequency and regularity.

At the initiation of Miss Jones' low morale, a general mood of discouragement was conveyed to her by the other personnel. They seemed fatigued, and had difficulty in approaching patients

and in getting through the routine care of the day. The nursing staff spent more time than usual away from patients, and there was a marked reduction in the fulfillment of patients' needs. Personnel were more often occupied with tasks in the nursing office or with cleaning up on the ward. In talking with each other, personnel frequently mentioned that "the ward is out of hand," "the ward is overcrowded," "we are too short of help."

The ward as seen by Miss Jones when she first returned from her brief vacation (first week) is described below:

When I came back on the ward, only the negative factors were presented in the morning report. Many of the patients had regressed from their previous behavior. Miss J was tearing her clothes and was incontinent again; S was not eating; H was in bed all day; B was very demanding and very critical of personnel; A was vomiting and spitting again, and T was so assaultive that people were afraid to go near her.

Some attempts were made by Miss Jones to bring about better organization on the ward, but these attempts did not succeed. At the end of the first week, she too became discouraged and began to share the views and attitudes of the other personnel and to function like them.

The withdrawal of staff from patients and from staff relations with each other appeared to the investigators to proceed in a circular fashion: Each of the staff members was expecting some kind of support from the others which was not forthcoming. The acting charge nurse felt discouraged and wanted some support from her nursing staff. But the ward nursing staff also expected some support from her; at this time neither was able to give it to the other. Thus the absence of expected support and mounting difficulties from patients served to reinforce the mood of discouragement. Instead of this shared mood bringing them together, it only served to keep them further apart, because it was partially colored by anxiety and resentment toward each other. The ward staff expected support from the rest of the institution, since the ward was overcrowded with patients and there was a shortage of personnel. The central nursing office of the hospital, however, did not respond to their request for help. The ward personnel felt let down by the institution and blamed it for their difficulties. There was much talk of quitting and of the great strain in working under the conditions created by the hospital. Thus the lack of internal support among and between ward members themselves and the lack of support from the rest of the institution maintained their low morale.

We also noted two parallel attitudes prevailing at different levels in the institution which facilitated ward staff members' perception of the situation as one in which nobody cared about them and facilitated their not caring about patients. The first attitude was one of *indifference*. The institution as a whole appeared to be indifferent to the ward's needs; the ward as a whole was indifferent to the needs of its individual staff members; the individual staff member (Miss Jones, for example) was indifferent to the needs of the patient. In this situation some patients responded by becoming withdrawn; others became excited, upset, or incontinent. The other attitude was one of *feeling isolated*. The ward staff felt isolated from the rest of the institution; there was little cohesiveness on the ward as a whole, and individual staff members were isolated from each other. Miss Jones experienced this isolation

from other staff members, and she felt unrelated to patients.

The interrelations between Miss Jones' low morale, the integrations of mutual withdrawal, and the ward equilibrium may be briefly stated:

Although the nurse returned to the ward with high morale her effective functioning could not be maintained in a context of widespread low morale. Instead, an interpersonal process of low morale emerged and functioned in such a way as to form a self-confirming and self-perpetuating pattern. With her low morale the nurse integrated situations of mutual withdrawal with patients, which integrations contributed to the stabilization of her low morale. This pattern of low morale was in addition shaped by, sustained by, and fitted into the context of ward low morale. At this time, the ward context was constituted in significant part by the patterned processes of low morale and withdrawal from patients on the part of one staff member integrating with and reinforcing the patterned processes of low morale and withdrawal of every other staff member. Thus the ward equilibrium was a pattern of a multiplicity of patterns in which the pattern of low morale and integrations of mutual withdrawal predominated. There was a constant feedback between the whole and the parts in which each modified, constituted, and continued the other, and the pattern formed by this reciprocity constituted the ineffective functioning of the ward.

The ward equilibrium can be evaluated in terms of the extent to which it provides a therapeutic milieu for patients. If one thinks of the ward equilibrium as a continuum, the concept "therapeutic milieu" can be defined more precisely. At one extreme of this continuum a pattern of patterns predominates which stabilizes the patient's mental illness. At the other extreme, a pattern of patterns predominates which facilitates the movement of patients in the direction of mental health. Over any period of time, this ward equilibrium shifts. When the equilibrium is closer to one end of the continuum, the milieu is nontherapeutic; low morale and the integrations of mutual withdrawal are patterned at this end of the continuum. When the equilibrium is closer to the other end, a therapeutic milieu prevails; conspicuous constituents of this end of the continuum are patient-staff satisfaction and security in participation, facilitation of the patient's realistic communication, and fulfillment of the patient's needs.

The Intervention

We can view the intervention in Miss Jones' pattern of low morale as a process of social change. This process of social change consisted of a number of interpersonal processes which brought about an alteration in the nurse's mode of participation.

As previously indicated, Miss Jones started her discussions with one of the investigators during the third week. After the first few discussions some alteration in the nurse's mode of participation was noticed. Thus we discovered the value of the discussions in altering the nurse's low morale. As these discussions continued, the nurse gradually revealed her feelings, attitudes, and thoughts and related her experiences on the ward; she continued to alter her mode of participation so that during the fifth week she came to function as effectively as she had previously. At that time, the investigator and the nurse looked back on this process and reached a consensus as to those aspects

which were significant in bringing about an alteration in her mode of participation.

The investigator's general approach to the nurse during these discussions was: "If you're able to find out something about the content of your low morale, how it developed and what it's related to, you might be able to help yourself, as well as other nurses, prevent it in the future." Initially, the nurse had some difficulty in expressing herself, but after the first few discussions she began to reveal some of the details of her experiences on the ward, especially her feelings in and about the ward situation. During the expression of these feelings and thoughts it was noted that she derived some relief from the *opportunity to ventilate her feelings.* Up to this point she had maintained her angry and resentful feelings covertly and had been afraid to reveal them to anyone else. Since the investigator had *no formal authority in the social structure,* she felt freer to express herself. Also, in the course of expressing herself she found that the other person was not critical of her and that her feelings were not so terrible as she had thought. This made it less difficult to reveal how much of a failure she felt she had been. In these initial discussions, the content of her talk revolved primarily around her impulses to flee the ward situation—how impossible it was to work on the ward and how difficult it was to put up with her own low morale. At this time she could not attempt very much evaluation or understanding of what had occasioned her low morale or how it had developed over time.

As the nurse became more comfortable in the discussions, the recital of facts about the nurse's functioning on the ward expanded, and the investigator introduced the idea that the nurse might be able to investigate her own low morale by looking upon it as a process which could be examined in an objective way: "Instead of focusing only on your failures, your difficulty in functioning, your poor relations with patients and staff, and your discomfort on the ward, you might be able to take a little different approach. In addition to participating on the ward with low morale, you might also become an observer of this low morale and see how it works." It was suggested that she might be able to develop an *attitude of inquiry* toward herself and her relations with other people on the ward. In addition, an hypothesis was presented that if she could develop such an attitude-approach toward her low morale, both her feelings and her mode of functioning with patients and other staff members would be altered indirectly, and she would become more effective in her participation.

Large portions of the discussions were devoted to the nurse's attempts to develop a new perspective toward her interpersonal processes on the ward. In the discussions, the investigator and the nurse focused upon the details of the nurse's interaction on the ward and probed for alternative possibilities in any particular situation. She was also encouraged to express her feelings about ward situations and the emotional responses she had in them.

The nurse originally had difficulty in becoming a participant observer of her own activities. As the investigator continued to raise detailed questions about the experiences she related, she gradually came to have less intense feelings about her low morale and started to reflect upon, examine, and see the connections between her low morale, the ward situation, and her relations with patients.

As the nurse became more successful as a participant observer of her own interactions, a number of processes occurred concurrently:

1. The nurse developed the impression that the investigator was not only trying to find out about the course and development of her low morale but was also interested in discovering what might be useful in helping her alter her low morale. She experienced this as *someone being interested in her*. She began to revise her feeling that nobody cared, as well as to abandon the rationalizations that went along with it.

2. As she focused on and discussed the details of her functioning on the ward, she broadened her perspective and developed a greater awareness of her own covert and overt transactions. As she made these discoveries, her morale began to alter. As her morale altered, she became more aware of the implications and significance of the interpersonal processes in which she was engaged. Her greater awareness then encouraged her to talk more about it. *Thus each of these processes facilitated in turn the expansion of the others: the discussion of her transactions, the growing awareness of the nature of her low morale, and an alteration in her low morale.*

3. *A redefinition of goals took place.* She had been preoccupied, on the one hand, with escaping from the situation of low morale and, on the other hand, with altering it by pulling herself up by her bootstraps. Failing to do either, she continued to feel she was a failure. In the discussion, she changed her goal to that of learning about the ways in which her low morale developed and of understanding the interpersonal proc-

esses constituting it. With this new perspective she focused less of her attention on her failure in the ward situation and more on the possibilities of success in understanding how the low morale process worked. She saw the possibility of deriving something positive from a situation which up to this point had appeared to her as exclusively negative.

4. *Taking the role of participant observer increased her effectiveness as a nurse on the ward.* She noticed that the change of perspective facilitated her effective functioning with patients. Functioning more effectively encouraged her to develop greater facility in taking this different perspective toward her own activities.

5. *The hypothesis was verified.* The nurse had originally been skeptical that a change in her attitude and perspective would also be accompanied by a change in her morale. The fact that she was able to function with increased effectiveness while she was developing this new perspective dissipated her discouragement about herself and made her increasingly aware of the usefulness of this approach.

6. As her curiosity was stimulated by investigating her transactions in a detailed way, she developed increasing alertness to herself and the events in which she participated. In this way her *indifference diminished.*

7. As the nurse became more proficient at taking a more detached approach to her own low morale and the ward as a whole, she was able to see the interrelations and self-reinforcing nature of the pattern of her low morale. She saw how this pattern facilitated her withdrawal from patients and theirs from her, and how she was a product of and contributed to the ward disorganization. With this awareness her *guilt and blame decreased,* and she developed the conception that she did not have to assume total responsibility for her ineffective functioning—that it was part of the total ward low morale, initiated and maintained by it. At the same time, however, she realized that her behavior contributed to the maintenance of her own and the ward's low morale.

8. As Miss Jones extended her observations of her interactions with others, she *relinquished her self-preoccupation.*

The pattern of interpersonal processes constituting the intervention also operated in the manner of a feedback. Each of the processes reinforced the others so as to form a chain of reciprocal effects through which the temporary closed pattern of the nurse's low morale was interrupted and from which a new pattern of morale emerged. At the same time the intervention served as a transition stage in interrupting the integrations of mutual withdrawal. This alteration in the integrations of mutual withdrawal was illustrated in the reports Miss Jones made to the investigator during the fifth week. These reports indicated a marked shift in the type of participation she had with patients and personnel. Four examples follow:

Patients seem to respond so differently now, or maybe I am more in tune with their responses. You catch a flicker of interest in B's eyes. X smiles—real warm and spontaneously—not that old vacant grin. R actually seemed to be enjoying her lunch today and not protesting at all. They all seem to respond so much more—I feel differently—like I was doing something real —well, something useful and worth-while. It isn't really anything so outstanding— it's just little things. But I feel eager to get to work in the morning—anxious to know how so and so slept the night before, what has gone on while I was away and things like that.

You look at it in a different light. Even when E won't move from the bed day after day, at least you can spend some time with her, and as you do you notice a change. Like today—I sat with her for a long time—she didn't say anything, move, or respond much in any way, but she was more relaxed. Her hands weren't tight fists. She kept looking at me; we both seemed at ease. I thought that today there were 15 or 20 minutes that she was a little more comfortable. My expectations of her and myself were different. I felt it was a useful thing for both of us.

I feel very differently toward the personnel than I did before. Sort of a wanting to share things and help each other. Things happen that are just as difficult as before and the ward is still having a tough time, but the feeling is different. I don't seem to be discouraged by it. We talk more freely about what happened and what we might do. It seems if I have a suggestion someone else has one too. Then together we usually figure out something pretty useful. Like yesterday when H got so upset. She usually gets real combative and everyone is quite afraid. She was yelling about "killing" us. I took her arm and said something like, "We won't let you hurt us, H, we won't let you get hurt either." She became quiet very soon. Several people were right there to help, so no one was really afraid. After the upset, we were all so pleased that H was more comfortable. Usually before, she has had to be packed when she becomes upset like that.

I got group singing going on the ward today. About six or seven patients joined in. There was a lot of laughing and making suggestions for songs. The rest of the personnel seemed more receptive—actually getting a bang out of it. I had a feeling of real enjoyment and satisfaction. The ward seemed to come alive. There are a lot more activities going on now.

Two questions must be considered with reference to the interruption of the nurse's low morale: (1) What is the difference between the situation after the nurse's return to the ward and the situation after the intervention? In the former situation she returned with high morale and was unable to maintain it; how was it possible then for her improved morale to emerge from her pattern of low morale? (2) What is the relation between the interruption of the nurse's low morale and the alteration in the morale of the ward as a whole?

On the basis of our data the first question is easier to answer than the second. Initially the nurse had no insight into the processes whereby she developed and maintained her low morale and came to share the attitudes and feelings prevailing on the ward. In the course of the intervention she developed such insight into the characteristics of her low morale. Thus the intervention served as a vehicle for improving her low morale by increasing her awareness of the processes constituting it. Unfortunately our data are insufficient to show a clear connection between the improvement of the nurse's morale and the improvement in the morale of the ward as a whole. Our impression is that Miss Jones' improved morale preceded that of the ward and that she in effect contributed to the reestablishment of more effective ward functioning. It appears to us that the above sequence of events occurred rather than an improvement in ward morale contributing initially to an improvement in her morale. We believe that this sequence of events was made possible by the intervention occurring from outside the formally constituted social system in the form of the investigator's discussions with the nurse.

Of course, once the process of improved morale, both for the nurse in particular and the ward as a whole, had been initiated, they contributed reciprocally to the maintenance and increase of each other's effective functioning.

Summary and Conclusions

We have studied the structure of social relations on a mental hospital ward from the perspective of morale by investigating in detail one situation of extreme low morale. This situation was selected in order to: (1) examine the ways in which the pattern of low morale was initiated, developed, and maintained for a particular nurse; (2) determine the contribution of low morale to integrations of mutual withdrawal with patients and suggest the significance of these integrations for the clinical course of patients; (3) discover the connection between low morale and the ward equilibrium; and (4) learn how low morale could be interrupted. The tentative conclusions we have reached have both practical and theoretical implications.

PRACTICAL IMPLICATIONS

1. The pattern of low morale of a staff member has serious adverse effects on patients because it contributes to integrations of mutual withdrawal, which maintain the patients' schizophrenic mode of participation. Thus it becomes imperative to devise some means of either (a) preventing or minimizing low morale on a ward or (b) automatically bringing it to the attention of those persons in the institution who can help alter it before it has proceeded to an extreme stage where intervention is more difficult and time-consuming. The informal means that the institution uses for intervention may be too slow in identifying the low morale and in times of crises are apt to break down. One way of handling the problem of low morale of nurses might be to institutionalize a formal role of consultant on staff problems, in which the person is without authority in the institution.

2. By specifying and describing the extreme end of the morale continuum, a rough construct is provided with which the morale of any particular nurse on the ward may be compared; with this construct, we may be able to identify the incipient stages of low morale before it crystallizes into a self-reinforcing pattern.

3. The pattern of low morale was self-reinforcing; it was part of, and was shaped by, both the ward context and the institution as a whole. From this we conclude that the morale of a nurse and the integrations she maintains with patients will be, in significant part, a function of the way in which she is treated by the institution. The attitude-approaches that the institution takes toward its individual staff members determine to a significant degree the attitude-approaches these staff members take toward patients. Interest in patients, concern and respect for them, and the facilitation of their satisfaction and security by the nurse is a function of the institution's interest in nurses, concern and respect for them, and facilitation of their job-connected satisfaction. If the institution considers the needs of its personnel in an individualized manner, this will encourage personnel to consider the patients' needs in a similar manner, and this will facilitate the movement of patients in the direction of mental health.

4. One way of interrupting the self-reinforcing nature of the pattern of low morale is by detailed inquiry into

the nurse's current activities on the ward in an attempt to develop an understanding with her of the ramifications and significance of these activities. In the case we have studied, the alteration occurred as a result of discussing the day-to-day experiences of the nurse. In other cases, it might be necessary to discuss more intensively the unconscious dynamics of the nurse before the pattern of low morale could be interrupted.

THEORETICAL IMPLICATIONS

This investigation has been a study of process. We have tried to delineate the constituents and operations of the psycho-dynamic process and the social process, and we have attempted to trace the connections between these processes.

From our point of view there need be no hiatus between the individual and the group or between the psychodynamic and the social process. When we look at the social field from the point of view of the pattern of interpersonal processes with which any particular individual functions, we are concerned with the psychodynamic process. When we focus our attention upon the pattern of patterns formed by a number of individuals integrating with each other into larger and more complex units, we are concerned with the social process. In our analysis, the social process has been seen as a pattern of patterns integrated by the ward participants into a stable equilibrium. In a similar fashion, the institution can be seen as the stabilization of a more complex patterning of patterns. At any level, social structure may be viewed as the equilibrium of these patterns maintained at any point in time. Social change is an emerging set of patterned processes interrupting an equilibrium and constituting a new equilibrium.

Areas for Future Research

Because of our restricted focus, our inquiry into the process and products of a pattern of low morale of a particular nurse has raised more questions than have been answered. Some of the areas that would profit from further study are the following:

1. *Including the personality dimension in the problem of low morale.* What is the relation of the personality dynamics of personnel to the rapidity with which they enter into a condition of low morale and emerge from it? What connections can be drawn between a nurse's unconscious motivations and the ways in which she maintains her ineffective functioning on the ward? What role do different "personalities" play in maintaining or interrupting the low morale of the ward as a whole?

2. *Investigating situations other than mutual withdrawal that a nurse integrates with patients while functioning with low morale.* In what way do these integrations affect the therapeutic course of patients?

3. *Including in the investigation other persons in the patients' social field, such as therapists and the administrator of the ward.* In what ways are the morale situation and the integrations of mutual withdrawal altered and maintained by them?

4. *Investigating other types of intervention into a pattern of low morale, both on the individual and the group level.*

5. *Exploring intensively the relation between a nurse's patterns of morale and the group's patterns of morale.* How do the nurse's and the ward's mo-

rale affect each other? What are the sequences of events in the alteration of morale for the nurse and the ward? Is there a cause and effect relationship or do such alterations occur concomitantly? What are the conditions under which a nurse's morale remains high while the group morale is low and vice-versa?

6. *Investigating the conditions under which high morale is maintained on a ward, both for a particular nurse and for the ward as a whole.* What are the consequences of such high morale for staff participation with patients? How can the persistence of high morale be facilitated?

❖❖❖❖❖❖❖❖❖❖❖❖❖❖❖❖❖❖❖ CHANGING A STEREOTYPE IN INDUSTRY

Alfred J. Marrow and John R. P. French, Jr.

A MEMBER of the management group in industry, whether executive or first-line supervisor, is trained to be fact-minded. It is expected that his decisions will be based on factual evidence objectively appraised. Actually many of his judgments derive not from facts but from attitudes of which he may not be at all aware. Stereotypes such as "only men who look you in the eye are honest" or "all Negroes are lazy" are examples of these emotionally toned reactions. Such biased judgments in industry, whether in the employment office or at the management level, create problems for both company and worker. They may, for instance, be the basis on which some otherwise qualified persons are rejected for employment. Usually these fixed beliefs are held on the unconscious level, and it is this hidden aspect of the stereotype which makes it the more difficult to change.

In most of the mass production industries it has been accepted that for skilled jobs older women workers are inferior to younger ones. As a result, many large companies consistently refuse to employ women over thirty. This policy remained unquestioned until the growing labor scarcity, caused by the war-time expansion, became acute. In the particular garment factory here under discussion, this tightening of the labor supply forced a reconsideration of the policy affecting the hiring of older women. To modify the policy, however, proved to be no simple matter.

The impulse for change originated when a psychologist joined the staff. From a general acquaintance with psychological findings about the relation between age and ability, he did not think that a great decrement in learning ability in women over thirty years of age was likely to exist. He therefore advocated a change in policy, but opposition to such a change evidenced itself in all quarters, from the top management of the organization down to the lowest levels of supervision. Until a

From *Alfred J. Marrow and John R. P. French, Jr., "Changing a Stereotype in Industry,"* Journal of Social Issues, *Vol. 2, No. 1, 1945, pp. 33–37. Used by permission.*

series of re-education steps was taken which introduced the new idea directly, no headway could be made in altering the group stereotype.

The first step had to be taken with the top management group. A method had to be found for changing their rigid ideology concerning age, for it soon became evident to the plant psychologist that every argument cited in favor of hiring women over thirty met with a stiff counterargument. Older workers, it was said, never attained adequate speed in production. They were frequently absent. They had a shorter working life. They were almost impossible to teach. When high production figures for workers who had exceeded the thirty-year age limit in the company's employ were brought to the attention of management, they were looked on as exceptions. The high figures were attributed to years of experience.

As arguments proved to be of no avail, the plant psychologist turned to a different approach. Involvement of the top management group in research was sought. A modest research project was suggested to determine how much money the company was losing through the employment of older women and management's cooperation in this project was sought. This suggestion was promptly accepted, so the next step was to get management's criteria for the value of a worker to the company. These criteria included all the factors advanced in the previous arguments, namely, rate of production, rate of turnover, absenteeism, and speed of learning. The group was fully questioned to make certain that no important criteria were omitted. Now it was possible to gather data; and here again all the methods of collecting facts about these criteria came from the management. They were the ones to decide whether the daily production record or the payroll record provided a better measure of production speed. They were the ones to suggest that an analysis be made of all stitching operators in the factory. By now the members of the top management group were thoroughly involved in the project and their interest showed itself in daily inquiries.

The scene was set for the actual study —a comparison of the company's 700 employees on four essential criteria: production per man-hour, speed of learning a new skill, days lost through illness, and rate of turnover. In order to compare the various age groups, workers were subdivided as follows: Sixteen to twenty; twenty-one to twenty-five; twenty-six to thirty; thirty-one to thirty-five; and those above thirty-five years of age.

Man-hour production per worker per day was tabulated. Analysis of this data revealed the surprising fact that older women not only equaled but surpassed the younger women in production. Using 100 per cent as the standard production for skilled workers, the average production level of workers above thirty was 112 per cent (the level of the thirty-one to thirty-five group was 111 per cent; those over thirty-five, 113 per cent); whereas, the sixteen to twenty group, however, were found to be 95 per cent of standard; twenty-one to twenty-five group, 93 per cent. Analysis of speed in acquiring specialized skills showed a similar trend. The older workers were able to learn new skills slightly more rapidly.[1] They also

[1] In regard to velocity of learning, it was found that after 96 hours of training the younger groups had reached the level of about 40 per cent, whereas the groups above 30 years

showed a slight superiority in their attendance record. Their superiority was even more striking in the annual rate of turnover. Thus, in all four criteria which the management itself had specified as essential, the findings showed that women workers over thirty are as good if not better than younger ones. Even more interesting than the figures themselves was the reaction to this experiment of the top management group. They were both excited and pleased at having participated in this important discovery which had become their own. They wanted the findings published so that other war industries could profit by them. What is more, they moved to have the employment agencies notified of a change in the company's hiring policy. From now on women over thirty were to be given the same opportunity as younger women. Finally, the position of the psychologist had changed; management was now willing to leave to his judgment what the top age limit should be. The battle, however, was only half won. The task still remained not only of informing but—as it turned out—of convincing all supervisory employees in the plant. As yet, practically the entire staff remained rigidly set against the employment of older women. A method of group re-education had to be worked out for them.

of age reached 50 per cent of standard. Comparing the attendance, we found an average absenteeism of 7.62 per cent for the 30 to 35 year group and 8.35 per cent for the group over 35 as compared with 13.36 per cent in the 16 to 20 year group and 9.51 per cent in the 21 to 25 year group. The percentage of annual turnover for the 30 to 35 year age group was 29.3 per cent, and for the groups of 36 and above 18.9 per cent. Percentages for the 16 to 20 year age group were 64.2 per cent, and for the 21 to 25 year age group, 37 per cent.

A Forelady Is Exposed to the Facts

Before the findings were discussed with the staff, a sample reaction was elicited. For this purpose one of the most representative foreladies was selected. In the course of a general discussion of production problems, she was asked how one of the older workers in her unit was getting along. The reply came that this woman was one of the mainstays of her assembly line. Similar inquiries about each of the eight older workers in her department of seventy workers elicited similar comments.

When it had become established that all of the older workers in this unit were highly satisfactory, the forelady was told that the employment office had a number of applicants over thirty who might fill existing gaps in her unit. She was shocked at this suggestion and rejected it on the ground that older people are not strong enough to stand the pace. At this point she was shown the findings of the research project, and it was pointed out to her that they tallied with her own satisfactory experience with older women workers. The forelady did not challenge these figures, but immediately countered with various objections, for instance, that older people learned more slowly, were absent more frequently, quit the job after a short tenure. All evidence left her adamant.

It is obvious that the forelady's individual experience failed to offer any challenge to her stereotype. She could express great satisfaction with individuals in her department who were over thirty years old without relinquishing her fixed belief that older women were inadequate as workers. She had no insight into the inconsistency of her position. Apparently she could be unprejudiced in a discussion of specific individuals, but when a generalization was made, the preconceived notion asserted itself and rejection followed automatically.

From the vigor of this sample reaction it was apparent that the supervisory employees could not be convinced individually and that re-education would be necessary throughout the plant. Therefore the findings were presented to groups of subleaders. Discussions followed, centering around the origin of the stereotype and the possible motivations for believing in it. In the course of these meetings, insights into the original bias gradually developed. What is more, group decisions were reached recommending that an experiment be made in the training of older workers. In this way the idea of hiring older women workers was gradually established. Only with this group shift in attitude did the new policy become a reality.

The Dynamics of Change

The ideology at the plant had changed, and the reasons for this change became more apparent a year later when a new engineer joined the staff. He soon manifested the same old stereotype. As he put it, production was hindered by "too many old women around the plant." The plant superintendent explained to him how the value of older workers had been proved. But the new engineer remained as unconvinced by the facts and figures as the others had been initially by mere theories and arguments until the time they had become involved as a group.

And why did group involvement and decision succeed in overcoming resistance where other methods failed? Apparently it is the manner in which the experience is introduced which seems to be the decisive factor in producing a change in attitude. The stereotype withstands prestige suggestions by an experienced psychologist, by the personnel manager, by the plant manager, by the president of the company, and by a combination of these. It is impervious to all facts, be they specific examples drawn from the individual's own experience, or general arguments and theories, or the results of scientific research. It should be noted that the resistance to change existed despite the fact that all individuals concerned had a strong need for more workers. Facts are useful only when the stereotype bearer himself is reoriented in his search for a new solution.

Our experiment at the Harwood Manufacturing Corporation demonstrated that whereas arguments and persuasion had failed to uproot a strong institutional stereotype crystallized into company policy, other methods succeeded. Chief among them were participation of management in research and participation of supervisors in group discussion and decision. Thus, through a process of guided experiences which are equally his own, a person may be reoriented so that he gradually takes on within himself the attitudes which he would not accept from others.

◇◇◇◇◇◇◇◇◇◇◇◇◇◇◇◇◇◇◇◇ GROUP DYNAMICS AND INTERGROUP
RELATIONS

Alex Bavelas and George Strauss [1]

THIS is the story of an experiment that failed because it succeeded too well.

The Hovey and Beard Company manufactured wooden toys of various kinds: wooden animals, pull toys, and the like. One part of the manufacturing process involved spraying paint on the partially assembled toys and hanging them on moving hooks which carried them through a drying oven. This operation, staffed entirely by girls, was plagued by absenteeism, turnover, and low morale.

A consultant, working with the foreman in charge, "solved" the problem. But the changes that were made in order to solve it had such repercussions in other parts of the plant that the company abandoned the new procedures, despite their obvious benefits to production in that local area.

The Problem

Let us look briefly at the painting operation in which the problem occurred.

The toys were cut, sanded, and partially assembled in the wood room.

[1] This chapter was written by George Strauss, based upon information furnished him by the consultant in the story, Alex Bavelas. The consultant also reviewed and revised the chapter.

Then they were dipped into shellac, following which they were painted. The toys were predominantly two-colored; a few were made in more than two colors. Each color required an additional trip through the paint room.

Shortly before the troubles began, the painting operation had been re-engineered so that the eight girls who did the painting sat in a line by an endless chain of hooks. These hooks were in continuous motion, past the line of girls and into a long horizontal oven. Each girl sat at her own painting booth so designed as to carry away fumes and to backstop excess paint. The girl would take a toy from the tray beside her, position it in a jig inside the painting cubicle, spray on the color according to a pattern, then release the toy and hang it on the hook passing by. The rate at which the hooks moved had been calculated by the engineers so that each girl, when fully trained, would be able to hang a painted toy on each hook before it passed beyond her reach.

The girls working in the paint room were on a group bonus plan. Since the operation was new to them, they were receiving a learning bonus which decreased by regular amounts each month. The learning bonus was scheduled to vanish in six months, by which

From Alex Bavelas and George Strauss, "Group Dynamics and Intergroup Relations," in W. F. Whyte, Melville Dalton, et al., Money and Motivation, New York: Harper & Brothers, 1955, pp. 90–96. Used by permission.

time it was expected that they would be on their own—that is, able to meet the standard and to earn a group bonus when they exceeded it.

By the second month of the training period trouble had developed. The girls learned more slowly than had been anticipated, and it began to look as though their production would stabilize far below what was planned for. Many of the hooks were going by empty. The girls complained that they were going by too fast, and that the time-study man had set the rates wrong. A few girls quit and had to be replaced with new girls, which further aggravated the learning problem. The team spirit that the management had expected to develop automatically through the group bonus was not in evidence except as an expression of what the engineers called "resistance." One girl whom the group regarded as its leader (and the management regarded as the ringleader) was outspoken in making the various complaints of the group to the foreman. The complaints had all the variety customary in such instances of generalized frustration: the job was a messy one, the hooks moved too fast, the incentive pay was not being correctly calculated, and anyway it was too hot working so close to the drying oven.

Introducing the New Approach

The consultant who was brought into this picture worked entirely with and through the foreman. After many conversations with him, the foreman felt that the first step should be to get the girls together for a general discussion of the working conditions—something, incidentally, which was far from his mind originally and which in his own words would only have been "begging for trouble." He took this step

with some hesitation, but he took it on his own volition.

The first meeting, held immediately after the shift was over at four o'clock in the afternoon, was attended by all eight girls. They voiced the same complaints again: the hooks went by too fast, the job was too dirty, the room was hot and poorly ventilated. For some reason it was this last item that they complained of most. The foreman promised to discuss the problem of ventilation and temperature with the engineers, and he scheduled a second meeting to report back to the girls. In the next few days the foreman had several talks with the engineers, and it seemed that the girls' cynical predictions about what the engineers would say were going to be borne out. They and the superintendent felt that this was really a trumped-up complaint, and that the expense of any effective corrective measure would be prohibitively high. (They were thinking of some form of air conditioning.)

The foreman came to the second meeting with some apprehensions. The girls, however, did not seem to be much put out, perhaps because they had a proposal of their own to make. They felt that if several large fans were set up so as to circulate the air around their feet, they would be much more comfortable. After some discussion the foreman agreed that the idea might be tried out. (Immediately after the meeting, he confided to the consultant that he probably shouldn't have committed himself to this expense on his own initiative; also, he felt that the fans wouldn't help much anyway.) The foreman and the consultant discussed the question of the fans with the superintendent, and three large propeller-type fans were purchased. The decision was reached without much difficulty, since it seemed that the fans could be used elsewhere after their expected failure to provide relief in the paint room.

The fans were brought in. The girls were jubilant. For several days the fans were moved about in various positions until they were placed to the satisfaction of the group. Whatever the actual efficiency of these fans, one thing was clear: the girls were completely satisfied with the results, and relations between them and the foreman improved visibly.

The foreman, after this encouraging episode, decided that further meetings might also be profitable. He asked the girls if they would like to meet and discuss other aspects of the work situation. The girls were eager to do this.[2] The meeting was held, and the discussion quickly centered on the speed of the hooks. The girls maintained that the time-study men had set them at an unreasonably fast speed and that they would never be able to reach the goal of filling enough of them to make a bonus.

The turning point of the discussion came when the group's leader frankly explained that the point wasn't that they couldn't work fast enough to keep up with the hooks, but that they couldn't work at that pace all day long. The foreman explored the point. The girls were unanimous in their opinion that they could keep up with the belt for short periods if they wanted to. But they didn't want to because if they showed that they could do this for short periods they would be expected to do it all day long. The meeting ended with an unprecedented request: "Let us adjust the speed of the belt faster or

[2] These subsequent meetings were effective largely because of the reduced tension and the good will engendered by the original discussions.

slower depending on how we feel." The foreman, understandably startled, agreed to discuss this with the superintendent and the engineers.

The engineers' reaction naturally was that the girls' suggestion was heresy. Only after several meetings was it granted grudgingly that there was in reality some latitude within which variations in the speed of the hooks would not affect the finished product. After considerable argument and many dire prophecies by the engineers, it was agreed to try out the girls' idea.

With great misgivings, the foreman had a control with a dial marked "low, medium, fast" installed at the booth of the group leader; she could now adjust the speed of the belt anywhere between the lower and upper limits that the engineers had set. The girls were delighted, and spent many lunch hours deciding how the speed of the belt should be varied from hour to hour throughout the day.

Within a week the pattern had settled down to one in which the first half hour of the shift was run on what the girls called medium speed (a dial setting slightly above the point marked "medium"). The next two and one-half hours were run at high speed; the half hour before lunch and the half hour after lunch were run at low speed. The rest of the afternoon was run at high speed with the exception of the last forty-five minutes of the shift, which was run at medium.

In view of the girls' reports of satisfaction and ease in their work, it is interesting to note that the constant speed at which the engineers had originally set the belt was slightly below medium on the dial of the control that had been given the girls. The average speed at which the girls were running the belt was on the high side of the dial. Few if any empty hooks entered the oven, and inspection showed no increase of rejects from the paint room.

Production increased, and within three weeks (some two months before the scheduled ending of the learning bonus) the girls were operating at 30 to 50 per cent above the level that had been expected under the original arrangement. Naturally the girls' earnings were correspondingly higher than anticipated. They were collecting their base pay, a considerable piece-rate bonus, and the learning bonus which, it will be remembered, had been set to decrease with time and not as a function of current productivity. (This arrangement, which had been selected by the management in order to prevent being taken advantage of by the girls during the learning period, now became a real embarrassment.)

The girls were earning more now than many skilled workers in other parts of the plant. Management was besieged by demands that this inequity be taken care of. With growing irritation between superintendent and foreman, engineers and foreman, superintendent and engineers, the situation came to a head when the superintendent without consultation arbitrarily revoked the learning bonus and returned the painting operation to its original status: the hooks moved again at their constant, time-studied designated speed, production dropped again, and within a month all but two of the eight girls had quit. The foreman himself stayed on for several months, but, feeling aggrieved, then left for another job.

Analysis of Success and Failure

It is not difficult to understand why installing the fans and permitting the speed of the hooks to be controlled by them should have affected the girls the way it did. No normal person is happy in a situation which he cannot control to some extent. The fans may not have actually changed the heat or the humidity, but they were a visible and daily reminder that worker ideas were given consideration.

About the speed of the hooks an additional observation may be made. The idea that efficient work results from proceeding at a constant rate derives certainly from the operations of machines and not from the characteristic operation of human beings. If anything is clear about human performance it is that it is characterized by changes of pace. Some production operations by their nature permit little variation in this respect, but even when the possibility exists it is not readily perceived by many engineers as a source of increased efficiency. From the operator's point of view, to be paced unvaryingly by a machine which he may not even shut down with impunity may be psychologically uncomfortable. In such a situation the only avenue left for the expression of any independence is that of complaint: the machine or its master, the engineer, must be shown to be wrong. Also, there appear to be inherent and unconscious defensive mechanisms which operate against the threat of being "stretched out."

Control over the speed of the hooks in this situation not only allowed changes of pace which were in themselves restful and refreshing, but also allowed the operator the natural enjoyment of operating at top speed without fear that he might be compelled to stay there. Of course, the manner in which the change was instituted was significant. The opportunity to exercise initiative, the gratification of being listened to seriously, helped to bring about changes in the emotional overtones of the situation which were in themselves favorable to increased effort.

In the light of all this it is not surprising that the situation fell apart so completely when the management retrogressed. And the management's action, while it may not have been wise, was certainly an understandable response to what had become an uncomfortable situation. Along with improved production in the paint room had come a host of embarrassments. The extra production in the paint room had created a pile-up in front and a vacuum behind, and both results were unwelcome to the adjoining departments. The wage structure of the plant had been shaken. The prestige of the engineers had suffered, and some of the prerogatives of management were apparently being taken over by employees.

It is clear from this instance that *local* improvements can often be obtained by the methods described here; but it is also clear that they may not lead to benefits for the enterprise as a whole. Changes in one part of an integrated organization may require widespread changes elsewhere, and the cost of such readjustments may far outbalance the benefits received in the local situation.

The changes made in the paint room implied over-all managerial attitude and philosophy that were not in fact present. This being the case, there was no conceptual or philosophic resource for dealing with the eventual implications of what had been done in the paint room. The management neither expected nor was ready to make the kind of changes that seemed necessary. It would have been far better if the consultant had done with the relevant management group what he had done with the foreman in the initial discussions, so that there would have been some shared understanding of the long-range implications of the moves. In a real sense, the superintendent was justified in feeling that the foreman and the consultant between them had put him on the spot. True, his assent to the changes had been secured, but the consultant had not been sufficiently concerned with his genuine understanding of the possible consequences.

The factory is a social system, made up of mutually dependent parts. A drastic change in one part of the system—even a change that is viewed as highly successful within that part—may give rise to conflict reactions from other parts of the system. It may then be dangerous for management to try a new approach in one small part of the system unless it is prepared to extend this approach to the whole organization.

Can the group methods that have been so successfully applied in small groups and single departments be applied on a factory-wide scale? We shall seek to answer that question in subsequent chapters.

❖❖❖❖❖❖❖❖❖❖❖❖❖❖❖❖❖❖ A CASE STUDY OF INNOVATION

Elting E. Morison

IN the early days of the last war, when armaments of all kinds were in short supply, the British, I am told, made use of a venerable field piece that had come down to them from previous generations. The honorable past of this light artillery stretched back, in fact, to the Boer War. In the days of uncertainty after the fall of France, these guns, hitched to trucks, served as useful mobile units in the coast defense. But it was felt that the rapidity of fire could be increased. A time-motion expert was, therefore, called in to suggest ways to simplify the firing procedures. He watched one of the gun crews of five men at practice in the field for some time. Puzzled by certain aspects of the procedures, he took some slow-motion pictures of the soldiers performing the loading, aiming, and firing routines.

When he ran these pictures over once or twice, he noticed something that appeared odd to him. A moment before the firing two members of the gun crew ceased all activity and came to attention for a three-second interval, extending throughout the discharge of the gun. He summoned an old colonel of artillery, showed him the pictures, and pointed out this strange behavior. What, he asked the colonel, did it mean? The colonel, too, was puzzled. He asked to see the pictures again.

"Ah," he said when the performance was over, "I have it. They are holding the horses."

This story, true or not, and I am told it is true, suggests nicely the pain with which the human being accommodates himself to changing conditions. The tendency is apparently involuntary and immediate to protect oneself against the shock of change by continuing in the presence of altered situations the familiar habits, however incongruous, of the past.

Yet, if human beings are attached to the known, to the realm of things as they are, they also, regrettably for their peace of mind, are incessantly attracted to the unknown and to things as they might be. As Ecclesiastes glumly pointed out, men persist in disordering their settled ways and beliefs by seeking out many inventions.

The point is obvious. Change has always been a constant in human affairs; today, indeed, it is one of the determining characteristics of our civilization. In our relatively shapeless social organization, the shifts from station to station are fast and easy. More important for our immediate purpose, America is fundamentally an industrial society in a time of tremendous technological development. We are thus constantly presented with new devices or new forms of power that, in their

From *Elting E. Morison, "A Case Study of Innovation," reprinted from* Engineering and Science Magazine, *published at the California Institute of Technology, Pasadena, California, April 1950. Used by permission.*

refinement and extension, continually bombard the fixed structure of our habits of mind and behavior. Under such conditions, our salvation, or at least our peace of mind, appears to depend upon how successfully we can in the future become what has been called in an excellent phrase a completely "adaptive society."

It is interesting, in view of all this, that so little investigation, relatively, has been made of the process of change and human responses to it. Recently psychologists, sociologists and cultural anthropologists have addressed themselves to the subject with suggestive results. But we are still far from a full understanding of the process, and still farther from knowing how we can set about simplifying and assisting an individual's or a group's accommodation to new machines or new ideas.

With these things in mind, I thought it might be interesting and perhaps useful to examine historically a changing situation within a society; to see if from this examination we can discover how the new machines or ideas that introduced the changing situation developed; to see who introduces them, who resists them, what points of friction or tension in the social structure are produced by the innovation, and perhaps why they are produced and what, if anything, may be done about it. For this case study, the introduction of continuous-aim firing in the United States Navy has been selected. The system, first devised by an English officer in 1898, was introduced into our Navy in the years 1900–1902.

I have chosen to study this episode for two reasons. First, a navy is not unlike a society that has been placed under laboratory conditions. Its dimensions are severely limited; it is beautifully ordered and articulated; it is

relatively isolated from random influences. For these reasons the impact of change can be clearly discerned, the resulting dislocations in the structure easily discovered and marked out. In the second place, the development of continuous-aim firing rests upon mechanical devices. It, therefore, presents for study a concrete, durable situation. It is not like many other innovating reagents—a Manichean heresy, or Marxism, or the views of Sigmund Freud—that can be shoved and hauled out of shape by contending forces or conflicting prejudices. At all times we know exactly what continuous-aim firing really is. It will be well now to describe, as briefly as possible, *what* it is.

The governing fact in gunfire at sea is that the gun is mounted on an unstable platform—a rolling ship. This constant motion obviously complicates the problem of holding a steady aim. Before 1898 this problem was solved in the following elementary fashion. A gun pointer estimated the range of the target—ordinarily about 2800 yards. He then raised the gun barrel to give the gun the elevation to carry the shell to the target at the estimated range. This was accomplished by turning a small wheel on the gun mount that operated the elevating gears. With the gun thus fixed for range, the gun pointer peered through open sights, not unlike those on a small rifle, and waited until the roll of the ship brought the sights on the target. He then pressed the firing button that discharged the gun. There were, by 1898, on some naval guns, telescope sights which naturally enlarged the image of the target for the gun pointer. But these sights were rarely used by gun pointers. They were lashed securely to the gun barrel and, recoiling with the barrel, jammed back against the unwary pointer's eye.

Therefore, when used at all, they were used only to take an initial sight for purposes of estimating the range before the gun was fired.

Notice now two things about the process. First of all, the rapidity of fire was controlled by the rolling period of the ship. Pointers had to wait for the one moment in the roll when the sights were brought on the target. Notice also this: There is in every pointer what is called a "firing interval"—the time lag between his impulse to fire the gun and the translation of this impulse into the act of pressing the firing button. A pointer, because of this reaction time, could not wait to fire the gun until the exact moment when the roll of the ship brought the sights onto the target; he had to will to fire a little before, while the sights were off the target. Since the firing interval was an individual matter, varying obviously from man to man, each pointer had to estimate, from long practice, his own interval and compensate for it accordingly.

These things, together with others we need not here investigate, conspired to make gunfire at sea relatively uncertain and ineffective. The pointer, on a moving platform, estimating range and firing interval, shooting while his sight was off the target, became in a sense an individual artist.

In 1898, many of the uncertainties were removed from the process, and the position of the gun pointer radically altered, by the introduction of continuous-aim firing. The major change was that which enabled the gun pointer to keep his sight and gun barrel on the target throughout the roll of the ship. This was accomplished by altering the gear ratio in the elevating gear to permit a pointer to compensate for the roll of the vessel by rapidly elevating and depressing the gun. From this change

another followed. With the possibility of maintaining the gun always on the target, the desirability of improved sights became immediately apparent. The advantages of the telescope sight, as opposed to the open sight, were for the first time fully realized. But the existing telescope sight, it will be recalled, moved with the recoil of the gun and jammed back against the eye of the gunner. To correct this, the sight was mounted on a sleeve that permitted the gun barrel to recoil through it without moving the telescope.

These two improvements—in elevating gear and sighting—eliminated the major uncertainties in gunfire at sea and greatly increased the possibilities of both accurate and rapid fire.

You must take my word for it that this changed naval gunnery from an art to a science, and that gunnery accuracy in the British and our Navy increased about 3000 per cent in six years. This doesn't mean much except to suggest a great increase in accuracy. The following comparative figures may mean a little more. In 1899 five ships of the North Atlantic Squadron fired five minutes each at a lightship hulk at the conventional range of 1600 yards. After twenty-five minutes of banging away two hits had been made on the sails of the elderly vessel. Six years later one naval gunner made 15 hits in one minute at a target 75 x 25 feet at the same range; half of them hit in a bull's eye 50 inches square.

Now with the instruments (the gun, elevating gear, and telescope), the method, and the results of continuous-aim firing in mind, let us turn to the subject of major interest: how was the idea, obviously so simple an idea, of continuous-aim firing developed; who introduced it; and what was its reception?

Introduction of an Idea

The idea was the product of the fertile mind of the English officer, Admiral Sir Percy Scott. He arrived at it in this way, while, in 1898, he was the captain of H M S *Scylla.* For the previous two or three years he had given much thought, independently and almost alone in the British Navy, to means of improving gunnery. One rough day, when the ship, at target practice, was pitching and rolling violently, he walked up and down the gun deck watching his gun crews. Because of the heavy weather they were making very bad scores. Scott noticed, however, that one pointer was appreciably more accurate than the rest. He watched this man with care and saw, after a time, that he was unconsciously working his elevating gear back and forth in a partially successful effort to compensate for the roll of the vessel. It flashed through Scott's mind at that moment that here was the sovereign remedy for the problems of inaccurate fire. What one man could do partially and unconsciously, perhaps all men could be trained to do consciously and completely.

Acting on this assumption, he did three things. First, in all the guns of the *Scylla,* he changed the gear ratio in the elevating gear, previously used only to set the gun in fixed position for range, so that a gunner could easily elevate and depress the gun to follow a target throughout the roll. Second, he rerigged his telescopes so that they would not be influenced by the recoil of the gun. Third, he rigged a small target at the mouth of the gun, which was moved up and down by a crank to simulate a moving target. By following this target as it moved, and firing at it with a sub-calibre rifle rigged in the breech of the gun, the pointer could practice every day. Thus equipped, the ship became a training ground for gunners. Where before the good pointer was an individual artist, pointers now became trained technicians, fairly uniform in their capacity to shoot. The effect was immediately felt. Within a year the *Scylla* established records that were remarkable.

At this point I should like to stop a minute to notice several things directly related to, and involved in, the process of innovation. First, the personality of the innovator. I wish there were space to say a good deal about Admiral Sir Percy Scott. He was a wonderful man. Three small bits of evidence must suffice, however. First, he had a certain mechanical ingenuity. Second, his personal life was shot through with frustration and bitterness. There was a divorce, and a quarrel with the ambitious Lord Charles Beresford—the sounds of which, Scott liked to recall, penetrated to the last outposts of empire. Finally, he possessed, like Swift, a savage indignation directed ordinarily at the inelastic intelligence of all constituted authority—especially the British Admiralty.

There are other points worth mention here. Notice first that Scott was not responsible for the invention of the basic instruments that made the reform in gunnery possible. This reform rested upon the gun itself, which as a rifle had been in existence on ships for at least forty years; the elevating gear, which had been, in the form Scott found it, a part of the rifled gun from the beginning; and the telescope sight, which had been on shipboard at least eight years. Scott's contribution was to bring these three elements, appropriately modified, into a combination that made continuous-aim firing possible for the first time. Notice also that he was allowed to bring these elements into combination by accident, by watching the unconscious action of a gun pointer endeavoring through the operation of his elevating gear to correct partially for the roll of his vessel.

The Prepared Mind Is Not Enough

Scott, as we have seen, had been interested in gunnery; he had thought about ways to increase accuracy by practice and improvement of existing machinery; but able as he was, he had not been able to produce on his own initiative and by his own thinking the essential idea and modify instruments to fit his purpose. Notice here finally, the intricate interaction of chance, the intellectual climate, and Scott's mind. Fortune (in this case the unaware gun pointer) indeed favors the prepared mind, but even fortune and the prepared mind need a favorable environment before they can conspire to produce sudden change. No intelligence can proceed very far above the threshold of existing data or the binding combinations of existing data.

All these elements that enter into what may be called "original thinking" interest me as a teacher. Deeply rooted in the pedagogical mind often enough is a sterile infatuation with "inert ideas", there is thus always present in the profession the tendency to be diverted from the *process* by which these ideas, or indeed any ideas, are really produced. I well remember with what contempt a class of mine, which was reading Leonardo da Vinci's *Notebooks,* dismissed the author because he appeared to know no more mechanics than, as one wit in the class observed, a Vermont Republican farmer of the present day. This is perhaps the result to be expected from a method of instruction that too frequently implies that the great generalizations were the result, on the one hand, of chance—an apple falling in an orchard or a teapot boiling on the hearth—or, on the other hand, of some towering intelligence proceeding in isolation inexorably toward some prefigured idea, like evolution, for example.

This process by which new concepts appear, the interaction of fortune, intellectual climate, and the prepared imaginative mind, is an interesting subject for examination offered by any case study of innovation. It was a subject that momentarily engaged the attention of Horace Walpole, whose lissome intelligence glided over the surface of so many ideas. In reflecting upon the part played by chance in the development of new concepts, he recalled the story of the three princes of Serendip who set out to find some interesting object on a journey through their realm. They did not find the particular object of their search, but along the way they discovered many new things simply because they were looking for *something*. Walpole believed this intellectual method ought to be given a name—in honor of the founders—Serendipity; and Serendipity certainly exerts a considerable influence in what we call original thinking. There is an element of Serendipity, for example, in Scott's chance discovery of continuous aim firing in that he was, and had been, looking for some means to improve his target practice and stumbled upon a solution, by observation, that had never entered his head.

Educating the Navy

It was in 1900 that Percy Scott went out to the China Station as commanding officer of H.M.S. *Terrible.* In that ship he continued his training methods and his spectacular successes in naval gunnery. On the China Station he met up with an American junior officer, William S. Sims. Sims had little of the mechanical ingenuity of Percy Scott, but the two were drawn together by temperamental similarities that are worth noticing here. Sims had the same intolerance for what is called spit-and-polish and the same contempt for bureaucratic inertia as his British brother officer. He had for some years been concerned, as had Scott, with what he took to be the inefficiency of his own Navy. Just before he met Scott, for example, he had shipped out to China in the brand new pride of the fleet, the battleship *Kentucky*. After careful investigation and reflection he had informed his superiors in Washington she was not a battleship at all—"but a crime against the white race."

The spirit with which he pushed forward his efforts to reform the naval service can best be stated in his own words to a brother officer: "I am perfectly willing that those holding views different from mine should continue to live, but with every fibre of my being I loathe indirection and shiftiness, and where it occurs in high place, and is used to save face at the expense of the vital interests of our great service (in which silly people place such a child-like trust), I want that man's blood and I will have it no matter what it costs me personally."

From Scott in 1900 Sims learned all there was to know about continuous-aim firing. He modified, with the Englishman's active assistance, the gear on his own ship and tried out the new system. After a few months' training, his experimental batteries began making remarkable records at target practice. Sure of the usefulness of his gunnery methods, Sims then turned to the task

of educating the Navy at large. In 13 great official reports he documented the case for continuous-aim firing, supporting his arguments at every turn with a mass of factual data. Over a period of two years, he reiterated three principal points: First, he continually cited the records established by Scott's ships, the *Scylla* and the *Terrible* and supported these with the accumulating data from his own tests on an American ship; second, he described the mechanisms used and the training procedures instituted by Scott and himself to obtain these records; third, he explained that our own mechanisms were not generally adequate without modification to meet the demands placed on them by continuous-aim firing. Our elevating gear, useful to raise or lower a gun slowly to fix it in position for the proper range, did not always work easily and rapidly enough to enable a gunner to follow a target with his gun throughout the roll of the ship. Sims also explained that such few telescope sights as there were on board our ships were useless. Their cross wires were so thick or coarse that they obscured the target, and the sights had been attached to the gun in such a way that the recoil system of the gun plunged the eyepiece against the eye of the gun pointer.

This was the substance not only of the first but of all the succeeding reports written on the subject of gunnery from the China Station. It will be interesting to see what response these met with in Washington. The response falls roughly into three easily identifiable stages.

First stage: no response. Sims had directed his comments to the Bureau of Ordnance and the Bureau of Navigation; in both bureaus there was dead silence. The thing—claims and records of continuous-aim firing—was not credible. The reports were simply filed away and forgotten. Some indeed, it was later discovered to Sims' delight, were half eaten away by cockroaches.

Second stage: rebuttal. It is never pleasant for any man to have his best work left unnoticed by superiors, and it was an unpleasantness that Sims suffered extremely ill. In his later reports, beside the accumulating data he used to clinch his argument, he changed his tone. He used deliberately shocking language because, as he said, "They were furious at my first papers and stowed them away. I therefore made up my mind I would give these later papers such a form that they would be dangerous documents to leave neglected in the files." To another friend he added, "I want scalps or nothing and if I can't have 'em I won't play."

Sims Gets Attention

Besides altering his tone, he took another step to be sure his views would receive attention. He sent copies of his reports to other officers in the fleet. Aware, as a result, that Sims' gunnery claims were being circulated and talked about, the men in Washington were then stirred to action. They responded —notably through the Chief of the Bureau of Ordnance, who had general charge of the equipment used in gunnery practice—as follows: (1) Our equipment was in general as good as the British; (2) since our equipment was as good, the trouble must be with the men, but the gun pointer and the training of gun pointers were the responsibility of the officers on the ships; (3) the most significant—continuous-aim firing was impossible. Experiments had revealed that five men at work on the elevating gear of a six-inch gun could not produce the power necessary

to compensate for a roll of five degrees in ten seconds. These experiments and calculations demonstrated beyond peradventure or doubt that Scott's system of gunfire was not possible.

Only one difficulty is discoverable in these arguments; they were wrong at important points. To begin with, while there was little difference between the standard British equipment and the standard U.S. equipment, the instruments on Scott's two ships, the *Scylla,* and the *Terrible,* were far better than the standard equipment on our ships. Second, all the men could not be trained in continuous-aim firing until equipment was improved throughout the fleet. Third, the experiments with the elevating gear had been ingeniously contrived at the Washington Navy Yard—on solid ground. It had, therefore, been possible in the Bureau of Ordnance calculation, to dispense with Newton's first law of motion, which naturally operated at sea to assist the gunner in elevating or depressing a gun mounted on a moving ship. Another difficulty was of course that continuous-aim firing was in use on Scott's and some of our own ships at the time the Chief of the Bureau of Ordnance was writing that it was a mathematical impossibility. In every way I find this second stage, the apparent resort to reason, the most entertaining and instructive in our investigation of the responses to innovation.

Third stage: name calling. Sims, of course, by the high temperature he was running and by his calculated overstatement, invited this. He was told in official endorsements on his reports that there were others quite as sincere and loyal as he and far less difficult; he was dismissed as a crack-brain egotist; he was called a deliberate falsifier of evidence.

Sims Gets Action

The rising opposition and the character of the opposition was not calculated to discourage further efforts by Sims. It convinced him that he was being attacked by shifty, dishonest men who were the victims, as he said, of insufferable conceit and ignorance. He made up his mind, therefore, that he was prepared to go to any extent to obtain the "scalps" and the "blood" he was after. Accordingly he, a lieutenant, took the extraordinary step of writing the President of the United States, Theodore Roosevelt, to inform him of the remarkable records of Scott's ships, of the inadequacy of our own gunnery routines and records, and of the refusal of the Navy Department to act. Roosevelt, who always liked to respond to such appeals when he conveniently could, brought Sims back from China late in 1902 and installed him as Inspector of Target Practice, a post the naval officer held throughout the remaining six years of the Administration.

With this sequence of events (the chronological account of the innovation of continuous-aim firing) in mind, it is possible now to examine the evidence to see what light it may throw on our present interest—the origins of and responses to change in a society.

First, the origins. We have already analyzed briefly the origins of the idea. We have seen how Scott arrived at his notion. We must now ask ourselves, I think, why Sims so actively sought, almost alone among his brother officers, to introduce the idea into his service. It is particularly interesting here to notice again that neither Scott nor Sims invented the instruments on which the innovation rested. They did not urge their proposal because of pride in the instruments of their own design.

The Engineer and the Entrepreneur

The telescope sight had first been placed on shipboard in 1892 by Bradley Fiske, an officer of great inventive capacity. In that year Fiske had even sketched out on paper the vague possibility of continuous-aim firing, but his sight was condemned by his commanding officer, Robley D. Evans, as of no use. Instead of fighting for his telescope Fiske turned his attention to a range finder. But six years later Sims took over and became the engineer of the revolution.

I would suggest, with some reservations, this explanation: Fiske, as an inventor, took his pleasure in great part from the design of the device. He lacked, not so much the energy as the overriding sense of social necessity, that would have enabled him to *force* revolutionary ideas on the service. Sims possessed this sense. In Fiske we may here find the familiar plight of the engineer who often enough must watch the products of his ingenuity being organized and promoted by other men. These other promotional men, when they appear in the world of commerce, are called entrepreneurs. In the world of ideas they are still entrepreneurs.

Sims was one, a middle-aged man caught in the periphery (as a lieutenant) of the intricate webbing of a precisely organized society. Rank, the exact definition and limitation of a man's capacity at any given moment in his own career, prevented Sims from discharging all his exploding energies into the purely routine channels of the peacetime Navy. At the height of his powers he was a junior officer standing watches on a ship cruising aimlessly in friendly foreign waters. The remarkable changes in systems of gunfire to which Scott introduced him gave him the opportunity to expend his energies quite legitimately against the encrusted hierarchy of his society. He was moved, it seems to me, in part by his genuine desire to improve his own profession but also in part by rebellion against tedium, against inefficiency from on high, and against the artificial limitations placed on his actions by the social structure, in his case junior rank.

Responding to Change

Now having briefly investigated the origins of the change, let us examine the reasons for what must be considered the weird response we have observed to this proposed change. Here was a reform that greatly and demonstrably increased the fighting effectiveness of a service that maintains itself almost exclusively to fight. Why then this refusal to accept so carefully documented a case; a case proved incontestably by records and experience? Why should virtually all the rulers of a society so resolutely seek to reject a change that so markedly improved its chances for survival in any contest with competing societies?

There are the obvious reasons that will occur to everyone—the source of the proposed reform was an obscure junior officer 8000 miles away, he was, and this is a significant factor, criticizing gear and machinery designed by the very men in the bureaus to whom he was sending his criticisms. And furthermore, Sims was seeking to introduce what he claimed were improvements in a field where improvements appeared unnecessary. Superiority in war, as in other things, is a relative matter, and the Spanish-American War had been won by the old system of gunnery. Therefore, it was superior even though of the 9500 shots fired, at varying but close ranges, only 121 had found their mark.

A less obvious cause appears by far the most important one. It has to do with the fact that the Navy is not only an armed force; it is a society. In the forty years following the Civil War, this society had been forced to accommodate itself to a series of technological changes—the steam turbine, the electric motor, the rifled shell of great explosive power, case-hardened steel armor, and all the rest of it. These changes wrought extraordinary changes in ship design, and, therefore, in the concepts of how ships were to be used; that is, in fleet tactics, and even in naval strategy. The Navy of this period is a paradise for the historian or sociologist in search of evidence of a society's responses to change.

To these numerous innovations, producing as they did a spreading disorder throughout a service with heavy commitments to formal organization, the Navy responded with grudging pain. It is wrong to assume, as civilians frequently do, that this blind reaction to technological change springs exclusively from some causeless Bourbon distemper that invades the military mind. There is a sounder and more attractive base. The opposition, where it occurs, of the soldier and the sailor to such change springs from the normal human instinct to protect oneself and more especially one's way of life. Military organizations are societies built around and upon the prevailing weapon systems. Intuitively and quite correctly the military man feels that a change in weapon portends a change in the arrangements of his society.

Think of it this way. Since the time that the memory of man runneth not to the contrary, the naval society has been built upon the surface vessel. Daily routines, habits of mind, social organization, physical accommodations, convictions, rituals, spiritual allegiances have been conditioned by the essential fact of the ship. What then happens to your society if the ship is displaced as the principal element by such a radically different weapon as the plane? The mores and structure of the society are immediately placed in jeopardy. They may, in fact, be wholly destroyed. It was the witty cliché of the 20's that those naval officers who persisted in defending the battleship against the apparently superior claims of the carrier did so because the battleship was a more comfortable home. What, from one point of view, is a better argument?

This sentiment would appear to account in large part for the opposition to Sims; it was the product of an instinctive protective feeling, even if the reasons for this feeling were not overt or recognized. The years after 1902 proved how right, in their terms, the opposition was. From changes in gunnery flowed an extraordinary complex of changes: in shipboard routines, ship design, and fleet tactics. There was, too, a social change. In the days when gunnery was taken lightly, the gunnery officer was taken lightly. After 1903, he became one of the most significant and powerful members of a ship's company, and this shift of emphasis naturally was shortly reflected in promotion lists. Each one of these changes provoked a dislocation in the naval society, and with man's troubled foresight and natural indisposition to break up classic forms, the men in Washington withstood the Sims onslaught as long as they could. It is very significant that

they withstood it until an agent from outside—outside and above—who was not clearly identified with the naval society, entered to force change.

This agent, the President of the United States, might reasonably and legitimately claim the credit for restoring our gunnery efficiency. But this restoration by *force majeure* was brought about at great cost to the service and men involved. Bitternesses, suspicions, wounds were caused that it was impossible to conceal or heal.

Now this entire episode may be summed up in five separate points:

(1) The essential idea for change occurred in part by chance, but in an environment that contained all the essential elements for change, and to a mind prepared to recognize the possibility of change.

(2) The basic elements—the gun, gear, and sight—were put in the environment by other men; men interested in designing machinery to serve different purposes, or simply interested in the instruments themselves.

(3) These elements were brought into successful combination by minds not interested in the instruments for themselves, but in what they could do with them. These minds were, to be sure, interested in good gunnery, overtly and consciously. They may also, not so consciously, have been interested in the implied revolt that is present in the support of all change. Their temperaments and careers indeed support this view. From gunnery, Sims went on to attack ship designs, existing fleet tactics, and methods of promotion. He lived and died, as the service said, a stormy petrel, a man always on the attack against higher authority, a rebellious spirit.

(4) He and his colleagues were opposed on this occasion by men who

were apparently moved by three considerations: honest disbelief in the dramatic but substantiated claims of the new process; protection of the existing devices and instruments with which they identified themselves; and maintenance of the existing society with which they were identified.

(5) The deadlock between those who sought change and those who sought to retain things as they were was broken only by an appeal to superior force; a force removed from and unidentified with the mores, conventions, devices of the society. This seems to me a very important point. The naval society in 1900 broke down in its effort to accommodate itself to a new situation. The appeal to Roosevelt is documentation for Mahan's great generalization that no military service should or can undertake to reform itself. It must seek assistance from outside.

Now with these five summary points in mind, it may be possible to seek, as suggested at the outset, a few larger implications from this story. What, if anything, may it suggest about the general process by which any society attempts to meet changing conditions?

No Society Can Reform Itself?

There is, to begin with, a disturbing inference half concealed in Mahan's statement that no military organization can reform itself. Certainly civilians would agree with this. We all know now that war and the preparation of war is too important, as Clemenceau said, to be left to the generals. But military organizations are really societies—more rigidly structured, more highly integrated than most communities, but still societies. What then if we make this phrase to read, "No society can reform itself"?

Is the process of adaptation to change, for example, too important to be left to human beings? This is a discouraging thought, and historically there is some cause to be discouraged.

This is a subject to which we may well address ourselves. Our society, especially, is built, as I have said, just as surely upon a changing technology as the Navy of the 90's was built upon changing weapon systems. How then can we find the means to accept with less pain to ourselves and less damage to our social organization the dislocations in our society that are produced by innovation? I cannot, of course, give any satisfying answer to these difficult questions. But in thinking about the case study before us, an idea occurred to me that at least might warrant further investigation by men far more qualified than I.

A primary source of conflict and tension in our case study appears to lie in this great word I have used so often in the summary—the word, *identification*. It cannot have escaped notice that some men identified themselves with their creations—sights, guns, gear, and so forth—and thus obtained a presumed satisfaction from the thing itself, a satisfaction that prevented them from thinking too closely on either the use or the defects of the thing; that others identified themselves with a settled way of life they had inherited or accepted with minor modification and thus found their satisfaction in attempting to maintain that way of life unchanged; and that still others identified themselves as rebellious spirits, men of the insurgent cast of mind, and thus obtained a satisfaction from the act of revolt itself.

This purely personal identification with a concept, a convention, or an attitude would appear to be a powerful barrier in the way of easily acceptable change. Here is an interesting primitive example. In the years from 1864–1871 ten steel companies in the country began making steel by the new Bessemer process. All but one of them at the outset imported from Great Britain English workmen familiar with the process. One, the Cambria Company, did not. In the first few years those companies with British labor established an initial superiority. But by the end of the 70's, Cambria had obtained a commanding lead over all competitors.

The Bessemer process, like any new technique, had been constantly improved and refined in this period from 1864–1871. The British laborers of Cambria's competitors, secure in the performance of their own original techniques, resisted and resented all change. The Pennsylvania farm boys, untrammeled by the rituals and traditions of their craft, happily and rapidly adapted themselves to the constantly changing process. They ended by creating an unassailable competitive position for their company.

How then can we modify the dangerous effects of this word *identification?* And how much can we tamper with this identifying process? Our security, much of it, after all, comes from giving our allegiance to something greater than ourselves. These are difficult questions to which only the most tentative and provisional answers may here be proposed for consideration.

The Danger of Limited Identifications

If one looks closely at this little case history, one discovers that the men involved were the victims of *severely limited* identifications. They were pre-sumably all part of a society dedicated to the process of national defense, yet they persisted in aligning themselves with separate parts of that process—with the existing instruments of defense, with the existing customs of the society, or with the act of rebellion against the customs of the society. Of them all, the insurgents had the best of it. They could, and did, say that the process of defense was improved by a gun that shot straighter and faster, and since they wanted such guns, they were unique among their fellows—patriots who sought only the larger object of improved defense. But this beguiling statement—even when coupled with the recognition that these men were right, and extremely valuable and deserving of respect and admiration—cannot conceal the fact that they were interested too in scalps and blood. They were so interested, in fact, that they made their case a militant one and thus created an atmosphere in which self-respecting men could not capitulate without appearing either weak or wrong or both. So these limited identifications brought men into conflict with each other, and the conflict prevented them from arriving at a common acceptance of a change that presumably, as men interested in our total national defense, they would all find desirable.

It appears, therefore, if I am correct in my assessment, that we might spend some time and thought on the possibility of enlarging the sphere of our identifications from the part to the whole. For example, those Pennsylvania farm boys at the Cambria Steel Company were, apparently, much more interested in the manufacture of steel than in the preservation of any particular way of making steel. So I would suggest that in studying innovation we look further into this possibility: the possibility that any group that exists for any purpose—the family, the factory, the educational institution— might begin by defining for itself its grand object, and see to it that that grand object is communicated to every member of the group. Thus defined and communicated, it might serve as a unifying agent against the disruptive local allegiances of the inevitable smaller elements that compose any group. It may also serve as a means to increase the acceptability of any change that would assist in the more efficient achievement of the grand object.

There appears also a second possible way to combat the untoward influence of limited identifications. We are, I may repeat, a society based on technology in a time of prodigious technological advance, and a civilization committed irrevocably to the theory of evolution. These things mean that we believe in change; they suggest that if we are to survive in good health we must become an "adaptive society." By the word "adaptive" is meant the ability to extract the fullest possible returns from the opportunities at hand: the ability of Sir Percy Scott to select judiciously from the ideas and material presented both by the past and present and to throw them into a new combination. "Adaptive," as here used, also means the kind of resilience that will enable us to accept fully and easily the best promise of changing circum stances without losing our sense of continuity or our essential integrity.

We are not yet emotionally an adaptive society, though we try systematically to develop forces that tend to make us one. We encourage the search for new inventions; we keep the mind stimulated, bright, and free to seek out fresh means of transport, communica tion, and energy; yet we remain, in part, appalled by the consequences of our ingenuity and, too frequently, try to find security through the shoring up of ancient and irrelevant conventions, the extension of purely physical safeguards, or the delivery of decisions we ourselves should make into the keeping of superior authority like the state. These solutions are not necessarily unnatural or wrong, but historically they have not been enough, and I suspect they never will be enough to give us the serenity and competence we seek.

A New View of Ourselves

If the preceding statements are correct, they suggest that we might give some attention to the construction of a new view of ourselves as a society which in time of great change identified itself with and obtained security and satisfaction from the wise and creative accommodation to change itself. Such a view rests, I think, upon a relatively greater reverence for the mere *process* of living in a society than we possess today, and a relatively smaller respect for and attachment to any special *product* of a society—a product either as finite as a bathroom fixture or as conceptual as a fixed and final definition of our Constitution or our democracy.

Historically such an identification with *process* as opposed to *product,* with adventurous selection and adapta tion as opposed to simple retention and possessiveness, has been difficult to achieve collectively. The Roman of the early republic, the Italian of the late fifteenth and early sixteenth century, or the Englishman of Elizabeth's time appear to have been most successful in seizing the new opportunities while conserving as much of the heritage of the past as they found relevant and useful to their purpose.

We seem to have fallen on times similar to theirs, when many of the existing forms and schemes have lost meaning in the face of dramatically altering circumstances. Like them we may find at least part of our salvation in identifying ourselves with the adaptive process and thus share with them some of the joy, exuberance, satisfaction, and security with which they went out to meet their changing times.

✧✧✧✧✧✧✧✧✧✧✧✧✧✧✧✧✧✧✧✧✧ STUDYING AND CREATING CHANGE

*Floyd C. Mann * *

SOCIAL organizations are functioning entities with interdependent structures and processes. They are not fixed, static structures, but rather continuously moving patterns of relationships in a much larger field of social activity. To understand what their essential elements and dimensions are, what it is that gives an organization its unity, it is necessary to study and create social change within organizational settings.

Relatively little is known about organizational change. Social scientists stress the study of the dynamic in social systems, but few [1] accept the risks involved to gain the knowledge and skills needed to create and measure changes in functioning organizations. This is not surprising, for research within large-scale organizations is at such an early stage that the social scientist knows little about how (1) to gain access to these research sites, (2) to initiate and sustain organizational change, and (3) to measure such changes. We have only begun the systematic codification of the working knowledge and skills necessary for the researcher to get into, and maintain himself within, the social science laboratories of functioning organizations.[2] Systematic, quantitative measurement of change processes in complex organizational settings is in its infancy. Longitudinal studies are rare—social scientists seldom attempt to obtain more than a single "before" and "after" measurement and are often content to try and decipher findings from *ex post facto* study designs. The actual steps and skills necessary to initiate and sustain changes within an organization are not only relatively unknown, but there is even some suspicion that knowledge of social ac-

* Drs. Rensis Likert, Daniel Katz, Robert Kahn, and Norman R. F. Maier have made especially helpful suggestions concerning the organization and presentation of this material. They can, of course, in no way be held responsible for the shortcomings which remain.

[1] For an account of a conspicuous exception to this, see N. C. Mare and E. Reimer, "The Experimental Manipulation of a Major Organizational Variable," *Journal of Abnormal and Social Psychology* (1956).

[2] F. Mann and R. Lippitt, eds., "Social Relations Skills in Field Research," *Journal of Social Issues*, VIII, No. 3 (1952).

Excerpted from Floyd C. Mann, "Studying and Creating Change: A Means to Understanding Social Organization," Research in Industrial Human Relations, *Industrial Relations Research Association, Publication No. 17, 1957, pp. 146–167. Abridged and used by permission.*

tion and an ability to engineer change are not appropriate for the social scientist.

While social scientists are not spending any sizable proportion of their time in learning how to change interpersonal and intergroup relations in functioning organizations, a wide variety of practitioners are. These include at the one extreme the consultants or the "operators" who take over organizations which are failing and rebuild them, and at the other extreme, the "human relations" trainers. Most of these men know very little theoretically about processes of organizational, attitudinal, and behavioral change, but they do know a great deal intuitively about the problems of changing people in an organization. This is especially true of the training men.

This suggests that there should and can be a closer working relationship between those concerned with actually *changing* organizational structure and processes and those researchers concerned with *understanding* organizational change. Social scientists have not begun to take advantage of their opportunities for learning about organizations from those in the "practicing professions"—those who are *doing*.[3] Observations and systematic measurements around the practitioner's efforts to alter systems of relationships in organizations can provide the researcher with valuable insights into the dynamics of organization. Gaps in knowledge become excruciatingly apparent; new sources of data and problems for research emerge. In turn, social scientists can contribute to practitioners by helping them assess what effect their actions as change agents have. Most practitioners—and

especially those trainers who are concerned with changing the human relations skills of supervisors—have very little systematic, and no quantitative, evidence on the success of their efforts to create changes in individuals or organizations. It seems clear that there is a broad basis for cooperation here. Systematic studies of the work of those attempting to change the way things are done in an organization may contribute to our understanding of social organizations. And developments in measurement and the procedures used by researchers to understand organizations better may contribute to the working knowledge of trainers and others in the "practicing professions."

In this chapter we will focus on the description and evaluation of several different types of procedures designed to change interpersonal and intergroup relations in complex organizations. We will first look at two human relations training programs whose effects have been systematically and quantitatively studied. Then we will describe briefly the development and evaluation of a change procedure with which we are experimenting to increase the understanding, acceptance, and utilization of survey research findings. At the close of the chapter these two specific types of procedures for creating change in organizational settings are contrasted as a first step in identifying facets of change processes which merit greater experimentation and in providing insights into the structure and functioning of organizations.

Changing Interpersonal Relations Through Training Supervisors

Recurrent opportunities for social scientists to study a change process

---

[3] Donald Young, "Sociology and the Practicing Professions," *American Sociological Review*, XX (December 1955), pp. 641–648.

within an organizational setting are provided by human relations training programs for supervisors. As change procedures, these programs are formal, rational, purposeful efforts to alter institutional behavior. In contrast to the day-to-day attempts of management to bring about change, they are bounded in time and organizational space, and are thus easily studied intensively.

Because of several historical developments, management by the late forties began to be convinced that training might be useful for their supervisors, and there has since been a wholesale adoption of human relations training programs. While there was and still is a remarkable range in the content, methods, and settings of these programs, nearly all of them have centered around improving supervisory skills in dealing with people—either as individuals or in face-to-face groups. They are frequently directed at teaching the supervisor how to work with an employee as an individual, occasionally at working with employees as members of a small group, but only rarely at understanding and working within the complex social system of the large corporation or factory. Another way of saying this is that the courses have drawn heavily from psychology, to a lesser extent from social psychology, and usually not at all from sociology.

There are no commonly agreed-upon ways by which these programs can be described. The following headings are, however, useful: objectives, content, methods, setting, training leader, and training unit. For example, the objectives of these programs are usually very general and quite ambitious: "to assist supervisors in developing the skills, knowledge, and attitudes needed to carry out their supervisory responsibilities," or "to improve morale, increase production, and reduce turnover." Their contents usually include human nature, personality, motivation, attitudes, and leadership, and other information about relevant psychological principles and research findings may also be included. More often than not the methods of training are some variant of the "lecture-discussion method." The settings are frequently in a classroom away from the job. The trainers are generally staff men whom the trainee did not know before the training; the trainees, first-line supervisors or foremen meeting with other supervisors from other parts of the organization.

Few systematic, quantitative studies have been made to investigate the effectiveness of these programs.[4] This is not to say that there has been no interest in evaluation. Any review of the literature will indicate many such attempts and many testimonials about the relative advantages of different procedures of training. Mahler and Monroe[5] reported a number of "evaluative studies" after reviewing the literature and conducting a survey of 150 companies known to have training programs. While these studies almost without fail acclaim the many benefits of such training, few of them meet more than a frac-

---

[4] A nonquantitative, but extraordinarily thorough and insightful study of foreman training was made by A. Zalenznik, *Foreman Training in a Growing Enterprise* (Boston: Graduate School of Business Administration, Harvard University, 1951).

[5] W. R. Mahler and W. H. Monroe, *How Industry Determines the Need for and Effectiveness of Training*, Personnel Research Section Report 929 (Washington: Department of the Army, 1952). See also R. R. Canter, "A Human Relations Training Program," *Journal of Applied Psychology*, XXXV (February 1951), pp. 38–45; E. A. Fleishman, E. F. Harris, and H. E. Buntt, *Leadership and Supervision in Industry* (Columbus: Personnel Research Board, Ohio State University, 1955).

tion of the requirements necessary for a rigorous test of the basic underlying assumptions.

What are these assumptions? In general, they are that training supervisors in human relations will result in changes in the supervisors' attitudes and philosophy, that these changes will be reflected in their behavior toward employees on the job, that this changed behavior will be seen by the employees, and that they will in turn become more satisfied with their work situation, then more highly motivated, and, ultimately, more productive workers.

While there is a good deal of evidence that human relations training programs do meet part of these assumptions—e.g., they do appear to change the verbal veneer of supervisors—there are few scientifically rigorous, quantitative studies which have demonstrated that these changes in what supervisors *know* affect their attitudes and behavior as seen or experienced by their subordinates. Few studies show that human relations training of supervisors is related to changes in the attitudes or productivity of employees under those supervisors. . . .

At best, these studies suggest that this type of training has little or no general effect on the behavior of foremen in the plant. At worst, they suggest that the unanticipated consequences of separating foremen from their work groups and making them keenly aware of their role in management more than offset the anticipated consequences of making the foremen more considerate of employees as human beings. Fleishman's finding that *leadership climate* appeared to be a better predictor than *training* of foremen's plant attitudes and behavior underscores the importance of considering the constellation of expectation pat-

terns in which the trainee is embedded. Training which does not take the trainee's regular social environment into account will probably have little chance of modifying behavior. It may very well be that human relations training—as a procedure for initiating social change—is most successful when it is designed to *remold the whole system of role relationships of the supervisor.*

The findings from these four studies suggest that trainers, researchers, and others interested in social change need to rethink what forces are necessary to create and sustain changes in the orientation and behaviors of people in complex systems of relationships. There is a good deal of evidence that management and trainees are enthusiastic about these training courses in general. Management's enthusiasm may be an index of whether the training will continue, but it does not indicate whether training is achieving changes in behavior. And while trainee satisfaction and acceptance may be important as an antecedent to learning, these factors do not indicate whether the training will produce attitudinal and, more significantly, on-the-job behavioral changes.

It should be stressed that the criterion which has been used here for measuring the effects of human relations training is not easily met. There is ample quantitative evidence in the preceding studies that supervisors' information about, and verbal understanding of, human relations principles can be increased. There is much less evidence that these courses have an effect on the trainee's on-the-job behavior as seen by those working under him. And the hard fact remains that there are no quantitative studies which indicate that these courses in leadership affect workers' job satisfactions or motivations.

Feedback: Changing Patterns of Relationships Between Superiors and Subordinates by Using Survey Findings

Long-range interest in the actual varying of significant variables in organizations has necessitated that members of the Human Relations Program of the Institute for Social Research, University of Michigan, not only study existing programs for training and changing people in organizations, but that we *develop* new techniques for changing relationships, and that we learn how to *measure* the effects of such changes within organizations. As a result, we have invested a good deal of professional effort in exploring the effectiveness of different procedures for changing attitudes, perceptions, and relationships among individuals in complex hierarchies without changing the personnel of the units. The latter is an important qualification, for we have found that the changes in subordinates' perceptions and attitudes which follow a change in supervisory personnel are frequently of a much larger order than those generated by training or other procedures for changing the attitudes or behavior of incumbents.

EXPLORATORY AND DEVELOPMENTAL
PHASE

One procedure which we developed and subsequently found to be effective in changing perceptions and relationships within organizations has been called "feedback." This change process evolved over a period of years as we tried to learn how to report findings from human relations research into organizations so that they would be understood and used in day-to-day operations. Work began on this process in 1948 following a company-wide study of employee and management attitudes and opinions. Over a period of two years, three different sets of data were fed back: (1) information on the attitudes and perceptions of 8000 nonsupervisory employees toward their work, promotion opportunities, supervision, fellow employees, etc.; (2) first- and second-line supervisor's feelings about the various aspects of their jobs and supervisory beliefs; and (3) information from intermediate and top levels of management about their supervisory philosophies, roles in policy formation, problems of organizational integration, etc. We had several aims in this exploratory phase: (1) to develop through first-hand experience an understanding of the problems of producing change; (2) to improve relationships; (3) to identify factors which affected the extent of the change; and (4) to develop working hypotheses for later, more directed research.

The process which finally appeared to maximize the acceptance and utilization of survey and research findings can be described structurally as an interlocking chain of conferences. It began with a report of the major findings of the survey to the president and his senior officers, and then progressed slowly down through the hierarchical levels along functional lines to where supervisors and their employees were discussing the data. These meetings were structured in terms of organizational "families" [6] or units—each superior and his immediate subordinates considering

[6] F. Mann and J. Dent, "The Supervisor: Member of Two Organizational Families," *Harvard Business Review*, XXXII (November–December 1954), pp. 103–112.

the survey data together. The data presented to each group were those pertaining to their own group or for those subunits for which members of the organizational unit were responsible.

Members of each group were asked to help interpret the data and then decide what further analyses of the data should be made to aid them in formulating plans for constructive administrative actions. They also planned the introduction of the findings to the next level. The meetings were typically led by the line officer responsible for the coordination of the subunits at a particular level. Usually, a member of the Survey Research Center and the company's personnel staff assisted the line officer in preparing for these meetings, but attended the meetings only as resource people who could be called upon for information about the feasibility of additional analyses.

These meetings took place in the office of the line supervisor whose organizational unit was meeting, or in the department's own small conference room. All of the survey findings relative to each group were given to the leader and the members of his organizational unit; they decided what to consider first, how fast to work through each topic, and when they had gone as far as they could and needed to involve the next echelon in the process.

This feedback change procedure was developed in an organization where a great amount of effort had already been invested in the training of management and supervisors. During the war the company had participated in the various J-programs sponsored by the War Manpower Commission, and more important, during the several years we were experimentally developing the feedback process, Dr. Norman R. F. Maier was working with all levels of management

to improve their understanding of human relations and supervision.[7] The supervisors with whom we were working to increase their understanding of their own organizational units therefore had a great deal of training in the application of psychological principles to management.

Our observations of the feedback procedure as it developed suggested that it was a powerful process for creating and supporting changes within an organization.[8] However, there was no quantitative proof of this, for our work up to this point had been exploratory and developmental.

A FIELD EXPERIMENT IN
ACCOUNTING DEPARTMENTS

In 1950, when eight accounting departments in this same company asked for a second attitude and opinion survey of their seventy-eight supervisors and eight hundred employees, we had an opportunity to initiate the steps necessary to measure the effects of this organizational change process. The questionnaires used in this resurvey were similar to those used in 1948 and provided the basis for a new cycle of feedback conferences. The general plan for the handling of these new resurvey data was to let everyone in the departments—employees and department heads—see the over-all findings for eight accounting departments combined as soon as they were available, and then to work intensively on their use in *some* departments, but not in others until there had been a third survey.

[7] For a thorough description of this training, see N. R. F. Maier, *Principles of Human Relations* (New York: Wiley, 1952).

[8] F. Mann and R. Likert, "The Need for Research on Communicating Research Results," *Human Organization*, XI (Winter 1952), pp. 15–19.

While our objective was to test the effectiveness of the basic pattern of feedback developed during the preceding two years, we encouraged department heads and their supervisors to develop their own variations for reporting data to their units and maximizing their use in the solution of problems. After the all-department meetings had been concluded, the chief executive of the accounting departments held a meeting with each department head in the experimental group. At this meeting, the findings for the department head's unit were thoroughly reviewed. The findings included comparisons of (1) changes in employee attitudes from 1948 to 1950, (2) attitudes in that department with those in all other departments combined, and (3) employees' perceptions of supervisory behavior with supervisory statements about their behavior. Department heads were encouraged to go ahead with feedback meetings as soon as they felt ready, tentative next steps were discussed, and assistance from the researchers and the company personnel staffs was assured. Four departments launched feedback activities which were similar to each other in purpose but somewhat different in method. The programs varied in duration (13-33 weeks), in intensity (9-65 meetings), and in the extent to which nonsupervisory employees were involved in the process. During the eighteen months that these differences were unfolding, nothing was done in two of the remaining four departments after the first all-departments meetings. This was done so they might be available as "controls." Changes in key personnel eliminated the remaining two departments from any experimental design.

A third survey of attitudes was conducted in these departments in 1952

after the natural variations in the feedback programs had run their courses. In 1950 and 1952 surveys were then used as "before" and "after" measurements, the four departmental programs as "experimental variations," with the two inactive departments as "controls."

Our findings indicate that more significant positive changes occurred in employee attitudes and perceptions in the four experimental departments than in the two control departments. This was based on two measures of change: (1) a comparison of answers to sixty-one identical questions which were asked in 1950 and 1952, and (2) of a comparison of answers to seventeen "perceived change" questions in which employees had an opportunity to indicate what types of changes had occurred since the 1950 survey. In the experimental group, a fourth of the sixty-one items showed relative mean positive changes, significant at the .05 level or better; the change for another 57 per cent of the items was also positive in direction, but not statistically significant. Major positive changes occurred in the experimental groups in how employees felt about (1) the kind of work they do (job interest, importance, and level of responsibility); (2) their supervisor (his ability to handle people, give recognition, direct their work, and represent them in handling complaints); (3) their progress in the company; and (4) their group's ability to get the job done. The seventeen perceived-change items were designed specifically to measure changes in the areas where we expected the greatest shift in perceptions. Fifteen of these showed that a significantly higher proportion of employees in the experimental than in the control departments felt that change had occurred. More employees in the experimental departments saw changes in (1) how well the supervisors in their department got along together; (2) how often their supervisors held meetings; (3) how effective these meetings were; (4) how much their supervisor understood the way employees looked at and felt about things, etc. These indicate the extent to which the feedback's effectiveness lay in increasing understanding and communication as well as changing supervisory behavior.

Comparisons of the changes among the four experimental departments showed that the three departments which had the two feedback sessions with their employees all showed positive change relative to the control departments. The change which occurred in the fourth was directionally positive, but it was not significantly different from the control departments. In general, the greatest change occurred where the survey results were discussed in both the departmental organizational units *and* the first-line organizational units. The greater the involvement of all members of the organization through their organizational families—the department heads, the first-line supervisors, *and* the employees—the greater the change.

IMPLICATIONS OF THESE FINDINGS

The basic elements of this feedback process described above are not new. They involve (1) the orderly collection of information about the functioning of a system, and (2) the reporting of this information into the system for (3) its use in making further adjustments.

Work by Hall [9] and others who have had considerable practical experience

⁹ Milton Hall, "Supervising People—Closing the Gap Between What We Think and What We Do," *Advanced Management,* XII (September 1947), pp. 129–135.

with the use of information about a system for creating change show a similarity in both action steps and basic approach. This suggests there are certain psychological and sociological facts which must be taken into consideration in attempting to change the attitudes and behavior of an *individual* or a *group of individuals* in an *organizational setting.*

1. Attitudes and behavior of an individual are functions of both basic personality and social role. *Change processes need to be concerned with altering both the forces within an individual and the forces in the organizational situation surrounding the individual.*

2. Organizations, as systems of hierarchically ordered, interlocking roles with rights and privileges, reciprocal expectations, and shared frames of reference, contain tremendous forces for stability or change in the behavior of individuals or subgroups. Change processes need to be designed to harness these forces for creating and supporting change. *As forces already in existence, they must first be made pliable, then altered or shifted, and finally made stable again to support the change.*

3. Essentially, unilateral power and authority structures underlie the hierarchical ordering of organizational roles. *Expectations of the superior are therefore more important forces for creating change in an individual than the expectations of his subordinates.* Also, those with a direct authority relationship—line superiors—have more influence than those without direct authority—staff trainers.

4. The attitudes, beliefs, and values of an individual are more firmly grounded in the groups which have continuing psychological meaning to him than in those where he has only temporary membership. The supervisor's role of interlocking the activities of two organizational units requires that he have continuing membership in two groups: (a) the organizational unit directed by his superior in which he is a subordinate along with his immediate peers; and (b) the organizational unit for

which he is responsible. *Change processes designed to work with individual supervisors off the job in temporarily created training groups contain less force for initiating and reinforcing change than those which work with an individual in situ.*

5. Information about the functioning of a system may introduce a need for change. This is especially true when the new data are seen as objective and at variance with common perceptions and expectations. Change processes organized around objective, new social facts about one's own organizational situation have more force for change than those organized around general principles about human behavior. *The more meaningful and relevant the material, the greater the likelihood of change.*

6. Involvement and participation in the planning, collection, analysis, and interpretation of information initiate powerful forces for change. Own facts are better understood, more emotionally acceptable, and more likely to be utilized than those of some "outside expert." *Participation in analysis and interpretation helps by-pass those resistances which arise from proceeding too rapidly or too slowly.*

7. Objective information on direction and magnitude of change—knowledge of results—facilitates further improvement. *Change processes which furnish adequate knowledge on progress and specify criteria against which to measure improvement are apt to be more successful in creating and maintaining change than those which do not.*

Comparison of "Classroom" Human Relations Training and Organizational Feedback

This is only a partial listing of the points with which a scientifically based technology of social change in organizational settings will have to be concerned. Our conceptualization and the identification of the relevant individual and organizational variables and their interrelationship is at a primitive stage.

The systematic quantitative investigation of the effectiveness of different change procedures has scarcely begun. Even at this early date, however, a comparison between the structure and process of feedback and "classroom" human relations training as two different types of change procedures may be a useful exercise. It may help identify variables or facets of change processes which merit greater experimentation and investigation both by the practitioners and by those researchers interested in organizational change. By a "classroom" human relations program we mean a training which would consist of a series of classroom-like meetings in which supervisors from many different points of the organization meet to listen to a presentation of psychological principles which a trainer from the personnel department thinks they ought to know about and be ready to use on the job after a brief discussion following the training. This kind of training experience differs from the feedback process in a number of respects. These differences are stated to keep the comparisons reasonably brief and to sharpen the contrasts.

1. What are the objectives?

"Classroom" Training—Improve supervisor-subordinate relations through changing the supervisors' understanding of human behavior, attitudes, and skills.

Organizational Feedback—Improve organizational functioning through changing understanding, attitudes, and behavior among all members of the organization.

2. What is the setting in which change is being attempted?

"Classroom" Training—Trainees are taken off the job and out of the network of interpersonal relationships in which they normally function for training in an "encapsulated" [10] classroom-like situation.

Organizational Feedback—Change is at-

[10] M. Haire, "Some Problems of Industrial Training," *Journal of Social Issues,* IV, No. 3 (1948), pp. 41-47.

tempted as a regular part of the day's work in established organizational relationships.

3. What is the informational content?

"Classroom" Training—General psychological principles of human behavior, case materials, or data from outside the training group and often the organization, only occasionally using problems from the group's own experience.

Organizational Feedback—Objective quantitative information about attitudes, beliefs, and expectations of the trainees themselves, or the subordinates in their own organization.

4. What is the method?

"Classroom" Training—Lectures, presentations, films, skits, and occasionally role-playing followed by discussion on how to apply what has been learned back on the job.

Organizational Feedback—The progressive introduction of new information about the problems within the groups for which the trainees are responsible. Group discussions of the meaning and action implications of the findings, followed by group decisions on next steps for changing or handling the situation.

5. Who are the trainees?

"Classroom" Training—First-line supervisors and foremen whose superiors may have, but more often have not, had the course.

Organizational Feedback—Everyone in the organization from the top down [11]— the president, top management, intermediate and first-line supervision, *and* employees.

6. What is the training unit?

"Classroom" Training—An aggregate or collection of individual supervisors from different departments throughout the organization. A functional conglomerate without continuing psychological meaning for the individuals. Frequently seen as a "group" simply because the individuals are in close spatial proximity to one another.

[11] N. R. F. Maier, "A Human Relations Program for Supervision," *Industrial and Labor Relations Review,* I (April 1948), pp. 443-464.

Organizational Feedback—An organizational unit whose members have an organizational function to perform and whose members (a superior and his immediate subordinates) have continuing psychological meaning perceptually and behaviorally to one another as a team or family.

7. Who is the change agent?

"Classroom" Training—An outsider— an expert, a staff man—who has no direct, continuing authority or power over the trainee and few recurrent opportunities to reinforce the training.

Organizational Feedback—The organizational unit's line supervisor, who is given some help through pre- and post-meeting coaching by the expert outsider.

8. How is the pace or rate of change set?

"Classroom" Training—The trainer sets the pace, attempting to gear the training to average trainee's ability to comprehend and assimilate the material.

Organizational Feedback—The members of the group move from one topic to another as they are ready for the next step.

9. How long does the change process continue?

"Classroom" Training—A fixed number of days or weeks, seldom less than 16 or more than 80 hours.

Organizational Feedback—No fixed length of time, the change procedure usually continues over a period of months—6 to 24 months.

10. How much tension is there?

"Classroom" Training—Usually relatively little, most trainees feel they already know a good deal about human behavior and how others feel.

Organizational Feedback—Frequently considerable, as objective information and particularly the differences between supervisory beliefs and practices come into a focus so sharp that complacency is shattered and the security about what is social reality is shaken.

11. What assumptions are made about attitudes and how they are changed? [12]

"Classroom" Training—The primary assumption is that the trainee does not know

[12] I. Sarnoff and D. Katz, "The Motivational Bases of Attitude Change," *Journal of Ab-*

certain facts, that his previous organization of relevant information will be altered when he understands the new facts. Attitudes are seen as a function of the range of information available to the trainee; they are changed by altering cognitive structure.

Organizational Feedback—Here the assumptions are that the trainee already has satisfying ways of seeing things and relating to others, that attitudes and behavior can be changed only by altering their motivational bases. Norms of psychologically relevant groups are seen as more important determinants of attitudes than cognitive processes.

12. How is effectiveness of the change measured?

"Classroom" Training—Usually by informal comments of trainees, occasionally by interviews or questionnaires with the trainees after the training.

Organizational Feedback—By changes in employees' perception of their supervisor's behavior.

The differences drawn between these two types of procedures for creating change in an organizational setting may not be as marked as presented here. Human relations training programs do vary tremendously from company to company and from time to time. There is no single pattern. Since we know little about the frequency of different species of human relations training programs, the specific mix of content, method, setting, etc., which we used as the basis of our contrast may no longer be found

normal and Social Psychology, XLIX (January 1954), pp. 115–124.

in organizations. Our comparison aimed to emphasize the extent to which various characteristics of change processes vary on the basic dimension of *motivation for change.*

Different contents, different methods, different settings, different training units, and different change agents contain different motivational impacts for change. What constitutes the most effective combination for changing behavior in organizations is not known. Few practitioners have really done any bold experimenting; almost none have combined measurement and experimenting to search for the most significant dimensions and variables in change processes. This is an area in which there is a great need for social experimentation and social invention.

In the social sciences, as in the physical sciences, invention plays a crucial role. Inventions in social technology—skills and processes for creating change—and innovations in measurement both contribute speedily to progress in understanding social phenomena. The responsibility of experimenting with different methods of measuring change and with new procedures for investigating the interrelationship of functioning organizational processes rests heavily with the students of social organization. The rate at which knowledge about organization is developed will probably be closely correlated to the rate at which we try new approaches to the study of problems in this area.

PART FOUR

Programs and Technologies of Planned Change

Part IV can be regarded as the "practical" part of this volume, dealing concretely with specific programs and technologies of planned change. Looking back over the organization of the book, we can regard Parts I–III as evolving toward implementation and action. Part I provided the historical, philosophical, and social basis of planned change. In Part II we attempted to present critical concepts from the social sciences—revolving around the idea of *system* and development—which have solid application to change and changing. Finally, in Part III, the concept of influence was analyzed as a focal element in all types of changes.

Now in Part IV we are ready to explore some specific planned change programs; programs that are based on many of the concepts covered in the preceding section. Chapter 11 outlines three pivotal functions in planned change: *training*, *consulting*, and *applied research*. Under each of these major strategies, readings are provided that discuss the essential ingredients of the process as well as the collaborative relationships involved between the change-agent and the client-system.

Chapter 12 can, in some ways, be viewed as an elaboration of Chapter 6, for it focuses on the use of the small group in planned change. The distinction between Chapters 6 and 12 is, however, important and explains the rationale for the inclusion of the latter in Part IV. For the most part, the papers on the small group in Chapter 6 emphasize the structural and conceptual properties of small groups. Chapter 12, on the other hand, treats the small group as a medium of change, as a tool in altering various levels of systems, from selfs to larger social systems. Thus, this chapter can be seen, for the most part, as an extension of the first two papers in Chapter 11, a catalogue of specific training devices using group methods.

Chapter 11 focuses primarily on conscious and deliberate programs that aim specifically at certain action goals, and on the *strategies* that underlie them. We have selected three types of programs, not because they are inclusive, but rather because of their proven efficacy and common employment. They are training, consulting, and research.[1]

Why these three? Consulting is usually defined as an interpersonal relationship between a client-system and change-agent (consultant), in which the latter tries to help the former solve a problem. Training is typically viewed as the action-enabling step; teaching the skills and knowledge necessary to carry out the prescribed action. Finally, (applied) research is the tool for evaluating the results of the action taken, a feedback about the validity of the initial consulting and skills attained. Thus, consulting leads to adequate *diagnosis,* training to *internalization of prerequisite skills,* and research to *evaluation* of the two prior steps.

But admittedly this is a rather oversimplified and compartmentalized view; a view implying a neat sequential relationship that never occurs in reality. In the first place, as the papers below point out, there are many different types and styles of training, consulting, and research. Their proliferation and differentiation attest to the vitality of these strategies. In training we have the case-study method and the incident-process method, role playing, and "training" (or T) groups, to mention only a few. Similarly, consulting roles are almost as numerous as the kinds of problems clients bring to the consultant. In the research area, Chin specifies six different kinds of research, five of which would fall under the category of "applied."

There is therefore no neat demarcation within this trinity of functions. Training usually involves problem-solving as well as internalization; research may involve some training as well as consulting; consulting may involve research and training. A number of authors in this section, in fact, merge two of the three categories (see particularly Seashore and Van Egmond) and we have consultant-trainers, and so on. In fact, only arbitrarily can we separate these three functions. Accordingly, we view change programs as a subtle mixture of training, consulting, and research, with each providing diagnostic, action, and evaluation support to the others.[2]

---

[1] Obviously, a complete Baedeker of change programs would include education, various forms of coercion and persuasion, various systems of governments, and many other control mechanisms. (See Chapter 4 for the change explication.)

[2] An example of this interplay is the applied research project conducted by one of the authors in the hospital organization. Starting out as an applied research project, the research staff used some of the data for "feedback" training exercises. These sessions opened the way

What we have said so far is that training, consulting, and research make up the basis for planned-change programs; that they vary to some degree in terms of specific intent, but that in fact they overlap—and indeed, need to overlap. And finally, what we did not mention here but have emphasized throughout is that all require an interpersonal relationship with fairly standard—that is, collaborative—conditions.

The readings in Chapter 11 are organized in identical manner, according to the *dimensions* of the change program and the *relationship* matters between client-systems and change-agent: in short, according to the content of the program, its strategies, and its relationship imperatives. Let us now examine briefly these three programs of planned change, referring when appropriate to sources other than those included in the readings.

TRAINING

Benne's paper, *Case Methods in the Training of Administrators*, initially develops a microcosm of the manager's multifaceted role. In a nutshell, it consists of balancing task (goal attainment) and maintenance (interpersonal relationships) requirements. The manager's effectiveness hinges on this subtle interplay of forces. In order to cope with complexity the manager has to develop diagnostic skills and intervention skills, awareness and action abilities. In short, to use Shepard's term, he has to become an "observant participant." Benne believes that traditional training (standardized classroom procedures) has failed because it has emphasized either one or the other—diagnosis *or* action—without considering the necessary connection between the two. In understressing diagnosis, the courses have become sterile "how-to-do" exercises, not unlike an etiquette book, which presents, for example, ten ways to make a subordinate feel comfortable. Overstressing diagnosis results in abstractions derived from some basic discipline (such as economics or psychology), with compartmentalization of subjects grossly inadequate to deal with complex and concrete situations. Moreover, these courses do not convert the basic knowledge into operable action alternatives. It may be edifying for a group of executives to spend a six-week course reading Plato, Joyce, and Proust—and the humanistic orientation this course implies is commendable—but its relationship to social change is at best ambiguous.

Benne goes on to enumerate different methods of case study as an instrument in human relations training, starting with the original conception of the Harvard Business School and moving to the Pigors' Incident Process method, to

for further data which led to various consultative sessions with the hospital staff. See *The Role of the Nurse in the Outpatient Department*, W. Bennis, N. Berkowitz, M. Malone, and M. Klein, in press, American Nurses Foundation, 1961. See F. Mann, pp. 605–610.

role playing and to the training group.[3] This sequence is related to the degree to which the training method utilizes the "here and now" (experienced) behavior and the extent to which it emphasizes *both* diagnosis and action.

Interestingly enough, all the training methods rely heavily on group processes. Why this emphasis? Obviously, one answer is convenience and economy. It is cheaper and less trouble to bring a dozen or twenty people together than to deal with each individual separately. But this is only part of the answer, and a minor part at that. Bradford provides a richer explanation on the basis of solid empirical evidence—touched on in Chapter 6—which indicates that learning, particularly of an emotional and attitudinal nature, is facilitated by group membership.[4] Group membership is more of a necessity than a convenience.[5] Furthermore, group conditions can be set up that represent in a realistic sense the underlying dynamics of the actual organizational setting in which change is to be made. *"Change processes,"* as Mann points out, *"need to be concerned with altering both the forces within* an individual and the forces in the *organizational situation* surrounding the individual"* (see Chapter 10; author's italics). Thus, isolating the individual from the organizational context, his normative structure which rewards him and represents a significant reference group, makes no sense. In fact, if it sets up countervailing norms and expectations, it may be deleterious, both to the organization and to the individual.[6]

But this raises an interesting issue. What about group composition? At Bethel, Maine, using the case of the National Training Laboratories, groups are composed on the basis of heterogeneity; they come from different backgrounds, from different institutional settings, etc. Heterogeneity is a major objective in training group composition. Over time these training groups develop and elaborate their own unique "culture" and decision-making apparatus. It is striking to observe how insulated, potent, and involving the subgroups within the total "training

---

[3] Constant reference is made in this section and throughout the rest of the book to the training or "T-group." This method was developed by the National Training Laboratories at Bethel, Maine, in 1947. Since then it has undergone various elaborations and improvements and has been used with visible success in a number of institutional settings. Essentially it is a way of learning about groups and change process, self-other operations, etc., whereby group members, with the help of a trainer, utilize their own experienced group experience in a diagnostic fashion. The "case" is the group; the crucible, the group member's own social experience. See M. Miles, pp. 716–725 for further elaboration. See also *Explorations in Human Relations Training* (mimeo., 1958), NTL, available through NEA, 1201 16th Street, N.W., Washington 6, D.C.

[4] See also Hugh Coffey *et al.*, "The Conditions of Good Training," in *Training Group Leaders*, Adult Education Association, 1956, pp. 9–16.

[5] It is interesting to note in this regard that group psychotherapy was started because of the disproportion between the number of individuals who required help and the number of psychotherapists available. Necessity seems to be the mother of invention, for out of this developed the established practice of group psychotherapy, which is presently regarded *sui generis*—not as a substitute for individual therapy.

[6] This is not a trivial problem. Fleishman *et al.* show how supervisors attending a human relations training course regressed—although they had demonstrated improvement at the training course—when they got back on the job; see *Leadership and Supervision in Industry*, Columbus Personnel Research Board, OSU, 1955.

lab" become.[7] Then we have to ask: how transferable are the learnings from Bethel—or, for that matter, from any training "island" (isolated from the organization, both physically and emotionally)—to the "back-home" situation where presumably the improvements effected by the training have to be reflected? This is not an argument for or against group training; rather it is a question about the conditions and member-composition of the group training and the transferability of training to where it should be directed—organizational improvement.

This is an important question and not an easy one to resolve without raising other equally important problems. But the fact is, as far as we can tell from evaluation studies of off the job training in human relations laboratories, that, as Shepard remarks:

> . . . laboratory experience was seen by participants as more helpful to them *as individuals* than *to the organization*. Thus it was obvious to the action researchers that if there was to be an impact on the organization as a whole, something beyond the laboratory was required.[8]

Several alternatives have been tried and seem promising. The National Training Laboratories have, for example, set up laboratories for specific institutional groups such as industry, national organizations, education, community organization, youth groups, religion. Judging by the increased enrollment and general popularity—as well as by the staff judgments—these laboratories have narrowed the gap between training and institutional needs. Another approach has been tried by the Esso Company. In an exciting series of activities they have attempted to introduce change-programs into the organizational structure. At several of their largest refineries they have established a two-week laboratory experience —off the job—composed of management personnel taken from a "diagonal slice" of the refinery, that is, from different levels of the hierarchy across several departmental lines. These laboratories have proven to be effective primarily, we suspect, because they have been able to reap the advantages of a cultural island (with the potentiality it provides for "unfreezing") while at the same time preserving a continuity with the actual organizational problems.[9]

The main question here is this: how can a training program provide an opportunity in which individuals can learn new behaviors, new perceptions, new

[7] One rather common manifestation of this cloistered uniqueness is the typical training group's reactions to visitors, observers, and guests, and even to other training groups. The veneer put on and defenses elaborated against "the outsider" are pervasive.

[8] See Herbert Shepard, "An Action Research Model," in *An Action Research Program for Organizational Improvement* (in Esso Standard Oil Company) Foundation for Research on Human Behavior, Ann Arbor, Mich., 1960, pp. 31–32.

[9] Douglas McGregor has informed us that Tavistock Institute has been tackling their problem in a rather different and creative way. Before the actual training begins a member of the training staff spends some time with the trainee *at the work place* and tries to diagnose work-relevant problems that ultimately are used as a basis for the training design. The Human Relations Center at Boston University has used a similar method.

orientations—which may require some isolation from the everyday pressures of the organization—and still have the learnings feed back into the organization? Put another way: If change can come about only by "unfreezing" certain normative structures—which requires a training ground apart from the organization—how can the *new* normative structures be applicable to the "old" organization? The same question applies to consulting, so let us now turn our attention to that.

CONSULTING

The key word here is "attachment"; how does the attachment of a new person (the consultant) to an existing social system (client) come about? How does this "stranger," drenched in the charism of the "expert," help bring about change?

Glidewell's paper, *The Entry Problem in Consultation,* is a basic introduction to this problem. The consultant, typically brought in from the "outside," has a peculiar relationship to the client system, a relationship characterized by its temporary character and its predictable termination. It is also a relationship that makes extreme demands on both parties (insofar as it requires an emotional involvement and closeness), and yet specifies a natural conclusion. Unlike consulting on an "engineering" or a mathematics problem, consulting in the human relations area involves personal relationships. The very core of the problem is inextricably linked to the way the client views, diagnoses, and attempts to solve the problem. The consultant-client interaction, then, provides a miniature prototype of the system to which help must ultimately be supplied. In order for this model to acquire greater validity, more and more verisimilitude to the actual life-space of the client must be derived from the "here and now" relationship between the client and consultant. In other words, the consultant-client relationship becomes the learning microcosm from which learnings about the "problem" may be derived. The extent to which the consultant (whether psychoanalyst or industrial consultant) can make the transfer from the here-and-now relationship to the other locations in the client's life depends on the emotional involvement of the two actors with each other. And the nature of this relationship seems to be the concern of our authors.

Gouldner, in *Engineering and Clinical Approaches to Consulting,* differentiates two types of consulting models: the "engineering" and the "clinical." The former borders on technocracy. Truth is imported, grafted on to the *status quo,* and assimilated somehow or other. Gouldner's major point here is that truth is not as transportable as we academicians would like to think it is. Gouldner suggests another model, a model more viable insofar as it takes into account the client's needs, resistances, defenses, hypotheses; and which does not confuse an ethical imperative (rationality) with a description of the learning process:

When the applied sociologist recognizes that he has the problem of helping his client learn something, and when he recognizes that learning is not accomplished by fact-finding or communication techniques alone, then he is on his way to becoming a clinician. Unlike the engineer, the clinician seeks to identify the specific sources of the client's resistance to his findings and he attempts to develop and learn new skills enabling him to cope with his resistance.

So again we come back to "attachment." For if Gouldner is correct (and we believe he is), the involvement between a consultant (and for that matter any change-agent) and a client is not a neutral, affectless one; rather it is infused with some of the same elements present in the client's "back-home" location. But how can this "outsider" [10] attach himself to an already existing social system, invest energy and gain commitment, and still remain neutral enough to observe and help objectively? How can he provide actual help, given the neutrality of his role and his emphasis on only indirect intervention? How can he switch hats and go from a problem-solving phase to an action phase? (Or should he?) And finally, how can he *leave* such a social system once he has developed the necessary emotional involvements?

Bindman, in an interesting paper, attempts to provide answers to some of these problems.[11] He enumerates some key differencess between consultation and the educational and psychotherapeutic processes. Consultation, he comments, is based on an "authority of ideas" and not authority inherent in administrative relationships; the consultant "plays an advisory role and does not have to implement a plan to solve the problem"; the consultant does not get trapped by attempting to answer "how-to-do" questions; he does not go too deeply into the intrapsychic functioning of the client and attempts to deal with only those interpersonal areas that have direct relevance for the way the client deals with his work-world; he focuses on the *problem* of the client, rather than on the client.

Glidewell stresses the mutual "construing" and convergences of interpersonal cognitions in the relationship. While deeply aware of the strong emotional investments of both actors in the relationship, he believes that the consultant has some responsibility in setting-up the conditions so that clarification of role-expectations can occur. He also makes an interesting distinction between the

[10] Again, it is not always that the consultant emanates from "outside"; he may be "staff" or an administrator. It is interesting to note in this respect that one of the authors (an outsider) works in concert with an internal staff man as a change-agent. The internal and outside men are —as far as can be judged—perceived by the organization as twins, no differentiation either in their work or how they are perceived having been made except superficially. It is also interesting to notice in the good-natured jibes made to them—"headshrinkers," "N.Y. headquarters men," "spies," etc.—a present-day version of attitudes toward "the stranger."

[11] Arthur J. Bindman, "Mental Health Consultation: Theory and Practice," *Journal of Consulting Psychology,* 23:473–482, 1959.

consultant and consultant-trainer. The latter role includes prescription (or medi-cation, to use the medical analogy) as well as responsibility for the client's acquir-ing those skills necessary to perform the treatment; the consultant, according to Glidewell, "requires the application of objects, skills, ideas, or feelings which the client need never possess or control (like prescribing medication or greasing an auto)." This latter definition of the consultant's role has an equivalence to Gould-ner's "engineering" model. The consultant, in effect, "solves" the problem for the client and goes away. The consultant-trainer, on the other hand, utilizes a modified clinical style. He tries to equip the client with the methodologies and skills necessary to solve his own problems. This is reminiscent of the distinction we have made before between content and methodological learnings.

Seashore and Van Egmond, in *The Consultant-Trainer Role,* elaborate and pro-vide a rationale for the fusion of the consultant and trainer roles. Without this confluence, *training* takes place in a matrix foreign to the actual problems of the client; *consulting* (or problem-solving) has no contextual relationship to ac-tion or providing the skills necessary for action. Seashore and Van Egmond also argue strongly for the exogenous role of the consultant-trainer. He must come from outside the system in order to effect significant change: only the outsider can free personnel in the organization to participate in the change process, can serve as a stimulus for redefining the situation, can provide initiative in explor-ing difficult or unknown problem areas, can provide continuous support as the change process is started, can aid in continuous diagnosis of problems, and can aid in providing information in effecting change.

The concept of the trainer-consultant role appears to reduce the gap between diagnosis and action and provides what appears to be a reasonable answer to the questions raised in the training section concerning the transferability to the ac-tion setting. It still leaves unsolved the problem of the uneasy relationship be-tween the "neutrality" of the change-agent's role and the action imperatives in-herent in the Seashore and Van Egmond model.

So we have come full circle. Starting out with a general concern with how the change-agent can be related adequately to the client's life space—the prob-lem of entry—we moved to the problems of attachment. But attachment and pro-viding effective help extract their pound of flesh: overdependence on the change-agent, relegation of the important problems to the consultant, fear of separation. In fact, we now see the reverse of Gouldner's concern. Gouldner is generally fearful of a technocratic-engineering applied social science; "advice" that can be of no help because it neglects the basic dynamics between client and change-agent. Glidewell, and Seashore and Van Egmond, provide models that deal with getting "in," and approaches that lead to clear linkages between the client's real problems and certain action steps. Somehow, though, consulting has to avoid the Scylla of a detached, olympian technocracy and the Charybdis of consultants *qua* administrators. There are no ready guides for these treacherous waters.

RESEARCH

We have remarked earlier that we have separated training, consulting, and research only for heuristic purposes. It should be obvious by now that the research function, at least applied research, is knit into the very fabric of consulting and training functions. It would be as difficult in practice to conduct research without consulting (and, to a lesser degree, without training) as it would be to consult without a model for research.

But an applied research has its peculiar problems. For one thing it has no clear role-model as training has with educational processes and consulting with clinical practice. Research stems from a rather anachronistic model of the experimental sciences and the value systems of the academic community. Both the experimental and the value systems are part mythology, part tradition, and almost wholly anomalous with respect to the new requirements and demands for an applied social science.[12]

Chin, in *Problems and Prospects of Applied Research,* directs his attention to this problem by enumerating six varieties of research, only one of which—the use of knowledge for science building—falls into the traditional usage of the term. All the other types can be generally called applied research. One sense of applied research is the adaptation ("development") of basic findings to specific settings. One meaning of action research is the institutionalizing of research functions as a continuing part of an action program. Both are different from research that is limited to evaluation of a given program or institution. Chin makes these distinctions and others. His paper (Chapter 11) helps to dispel the rather common mistake that research can be of only two kinds, outcome or evaluation research and "pure" research.

Benne, in *Operational Research in Health Education,* discusses the application of research for use in building and testing a "practitioner's theory of changing." He first indicates that practitioners, whether they know it or not, operate in terms of a theoretical orientation. They are equipped with hypotheses, assumptions, postulates, and techniques for checking on data. Too often, though, even with the most successful and "intuitive" practitioner, the theories are not explicit. Occasionally, a gifted practitioner, seasoned with years of experience, can articulate principles and theory. A Chester Barnard, a Mary Follett, are examples. But all too often a practitioner's work is dumb art; effective as it can be, it is difficult to transmit to others and impossible to explore scientifically.

For their part, according to Benne, scientists, who pride themselves for their

[12] See Herbert Shepard, "Basic Research and the Social System of Pure Science," *Philosophy of Science,* 23:48–57, 1956.

reliance on the noble theories and scientific method and detachment from practitioners, are also practitioners; practitioners vis-à-vis subjects, equipment, measurement devices. etc. The question Benne directs himself to is the polarity between common sense and science, between theory and practice. Or in his words:

> Is "common sense" (an amalgam of traditions, lore, wisdom, principles abstracted from practical experience, and the advices and preferences of reigning elites) more dependable, reliable, and valid as a basis for policy and program construction and reconstruction than knowledge drawn from basic research in the behavioral sciences or knowledge derived from the application of scientific methodologies to the study of policy problems in the setting of practice?

Launched by this question, he presents a paradigm whereby the distinguishing and common features of practitioner theory and scientific theory are propounded.

Paul, in an interesting paper,[13] deals with another point mentioned by Chin: that constant peril of applied research, the search for the appropriate *criterion variable*. As do our authors, Paul expands and re-angles the old, outworn categories. What variables are selected for gauging the success of a program is, of course, a critical problem. The variables have to reflect what the program administrators believe should (and do) happen; they have to be measurable; they have to be empirically possible to obtain without damaging the goals of the program. Riecken, in his excellent book on evaluation research, points to the conflict of interests here between the program administrator and the applied researcher:

> The [program director] has a particular immediate interest in each participant as a unique individual. He wants to maximize the changes that the program will be successful in every individual instance. At the same time, he is necessarily concerned with pleasing the voluntary participants. The social scientist, on the other hand, tends to regard each participant as a case, an instance in a series; and he is primarily concerned with achieving some order in his sample of instances. To put the case extremely, the social scientist is willing to singe a few subjects in order to determine the heat of the flame—the program director is not.[14]

But Paul adds two other types of criterion variables that do not directly concern the participants. One he refers to as amount of *effort* put into the activity, such as miles traveled, lectures given, movies shown, or communities visited. The

---

[13] B. Paul, "Social Science in Public Health," *American Journal of Public Health,* 46:1390–1393, 1956.

[14] H. Riecken, *The Volunteer Work Camp: A Psychological Evaluation,* Cambridge, Mass.: Addison-Wesley Publishing Co., 1952, p. 18. This study remains one of the superb examples of evaluation research.

other is far more consequential; the *process* by which the activity has been executed, what was going on during the course of the evaluation. The assessment of process, by no means easy, may in fact provide the explanatory cues for a particular program's success or failure. It would appear also, although Paul does not say this, that the assessment of process underlying a particular program is the most appropriate evaluative research line for a social scientist. It enables him to capitalize on his diagnostic abilities for the understanding of the basic dynamics of change.

Speaking of change once again reminds us that we should reiterate a fundamental point that Gouldner makes in his paper in Chapter 2: that what distinguishes applied research from pure research is the former's presumption of change. Floyd Mann's paper (Chapter 10) is an exemplar of this. Starting out with a survey method for collecting data and a promise to report and interpret the data to the subjects, he and his associates (among them Howard Baumgartel [15]) have developed a scheme for using the results of a survey for training methods.

We suspect that once again necessity has been the mother of invention. Research subjects today desire "feedback" for their effort, as well as for their curiosity and their interest in improvement. Turning this necessity into a research training tool is but another "happy accident" of a new applied science. The pragmatic virtues of this feedback may not have been so apparent at first, but as Argyris points out in "Creating Effective Relationships in Organization," "It [feedback] can also serve as an opportunity for the extension and deepening of the research." [16]

Riesman, in *The Researcher and His Audience,* makes a good deal of this new type of relationship between subjects and researchers. No longer are subjects inert and passive instruments. Subjects are verbal, intelligent, and are researched in their native habitats. Subjects are *us.*

To dramatize this problem let us quote from a recent editorial in a social science journal.

> A small upstate New York village has now been immortalized in anthropological literature under the name of "Springdale." The local newspaper reports that the experience has not been entirely a pleasing one. We pass on this account:
> "The people of the Village waited quite a while to get even with [the author], who wrote a *Peyton Place* type book about their town recently.
> "The featured float of the annual Fourth of July parade followed an authentic copy of the jacket of the

---

[15] Floyd Mann and Howard Baumgartel, "The Survey Feedback Experiment: An Evaluation of a Program for the Utilization of Survey Findings," November 1954 (mimeo.), University of Michigan, Ann Arbor, Mich.

[16] Chris Argyris, "Creating Effective Research Relationships in Organization," *Human Organization,* 17:34–40, 1958.

> book, *Small Town in Mass Society,* done large scale by
> Mrs. Beverly Robinson. Following the book cover came
> residents of Springdale riding masked in cars labeled
> with the fictitious names given them in the book.
> "But the pay-off was the final scene, a manure-spreader
> filled with very rich barnyard fertilizer, over which was
> bending an effigy of The Author." [17]

The account suggests that a good time was had by all—on this particular occasion. Nevertheless, local observers report that the disturbance caused by the book in the village has not been entirely compensated for by even such a ceremony of exorcism carried out in the best anthropological traditions.

This editorial, which goes on to raise a number of important issues, indicates some of the present dilemmas of the applied social scientist. For one thing, he is no longer dealing with docile subjects such as white rats, college sophomores, or preliterate people who cannot talk back. It should be clear that the applied social scientist has some responsibility to his subjects, but he also has responsibility to report to his scientific colleagues the substantive findings of his research. The ethical balance between responsibility to the users of research—the subjects turned clients—and to fellow-producers of research is not an easy equilibrium to reach. And now that social scientists are studying more and more modern and powerful organizations, this ethical problem has become more prominent.

The underlying issue here is: what is the nature of the contract between the researcher and the organization under study? Karl Menninger, in his recent book, diagrammed contractual relationships between a number of bargaining relationships: customer-vendor, barber-client, doctor-patient, psychoanalyst-patient.[18] In all these cases, something was given for something obtained. Now what is the applied researcher giving in return for the opportunity to collect scientific data? Primarily, we can say he is giving information that may be valuable to the client-organization. But this raises two other problems. First, can he give information away? After all, who really *owns* the information, the subjects who responded, the organization who cooperated with the research effort and made the subjects available, the researchers? Second, if the issue of ownership were settled, an even stickier problem emerges. Let us suppose that the data are important and useful. If this is so, then undoubtedly in many cases the nature of the information will be unpalatable and even noxious to the recipient. Psychotherapy has developed a rich literature on the "analysis of the resistance" to interpretations. Data can be accepted as "valid" by the recipients only when, we believe, there is a feeling of mutual trust and confidence between the researcher and the subject population. To develop this relationship, a good deal of time and effort must be invested. And even then, it appears to some that the goal of research—which is to understand—is antithetical to the goal of organization, which is to produce.

We cannot overemphasize the importance of this problem concerning the

---

[17] "Editorial," *Human Organization, 17:*1, 1958.
[18] *Theory of Psychoanalytic Technique,* New York: Basic Books, Inc., 1958, pp. 15–42.

nature of the contract and mutual responsibilities of the researchers and their clients. A recent example may provide an illustration. A hospital in a study conducted in seven out-patient departments [19] decided to withdraw from the study after almost three years of cooperation. The reasons given for this termination— that there was no explicit contract in the files which legitimized the research activity—are not even at this point clear. This withdrawal came as a surprise to the researchers, as they had enjoyed a long tenure and apparently satisfactory relationships with the hospital. It may be no accident that this action followed immediately after asking the physicians in the various clinics to fill out a short questionnaire. Nurses may indeed be more docile than physicians; but our hunch is that when research activity touches on sensitive organizational nerves, resistances and balkiness become apparent. And if the applied researcher is doing his job properly, he cannot avoid symptoms that the organizations at times sacrifice considerable energy to ignore. And someday undoubtedly we will see various organizations riffling through a number of researchers until they find the one who will tell them what they want to hear.

The whole point of this discussion is that until some explicit contractual arrangement is developed, the applied researcher has no basis of power or authority to maintain the relationship. And unlike the analyst or even the general practitioner, he does not have available the legitimacy or leverage of the transference.

So far we have been discussing, in a general sense, applied research in terms of a complex of relationships: between the applied science and scientific method, between the applied scientist and his subjects, organization, and subjects turned clients. Finally, let us turn to the role of the applied social scientist, his values and conflicts.

Frank Miller writes elegantly of the inelegance of the applied researcher's role:

> We [applied researchers] are often forced into accepting roles as marginal men among behavioral sciences— "half-breeds" who possess the less desirable traits of a practitioner father and Alma Mater. Even the veteran researcher may be a bit defensive or apologetic about how he measures up to the canons of "scientific procedure" compared to his brethren whose activities are confined to the laboratory or the classroom.[20]

Miller goes on to discuss the "innate cussedness of things" in applied research reminiscent of annoying troublesome irritations such as the "elusive collar button, the bloodthirsty razor blade, the banana peel lying in wait—these are examined, and made to give evidence that the (so-called) inanimate world stands always ready to humiliate, confuse, and discomfit the unwary human being."

This innate cussedness, we assume, has to do with the newness of research on

[19] W. G. Bennis, N. Berkowitz, M. Malone, and M. Klein, *The Role of the Nurse in the Out-patient Department: A Preliminary Report,* in press, American Nurses Foundation, 1961.

[20] "Resistentialism in Applied Social Research," *Human Organization,* 12:5–8, 1954.

the human object. J. W. N. Sullivan, in his book *The Limitations of Science*, wrote (in 1933) about the social irrelevance of scientific work:

> But the matters with which science has hitherto been concerned are comparatively indifferent to us. For that reason, science has been so successful. . . . The splendid moral integrity manifested in scientific work, therefore, is due very largely to the nature of scientific material. . . . Science is truthful because it has practically no temptation to be anything else.[21]

Now the scientific material which Sullivan had in mind in no way resembles the scientific material on which applied research is based. For here we are dealing with human subjects manifesting behavior—which again is not controlled by the researcher in many cases—sometimes of a primitive nature and always complex and not easily defined. In short, the scientific material that has to be analyzed is not the cellophane-wrapped, sanitary material Sullivan writes about so glowingly.[22] Today's applied social research is fraught with value dilemmas we pretend to ignore, but that plague us at every turn. Ronald Lippitt, in *Value Judgment Problems of the Social Scientist in Action Research*, attempts to articulate these ethical value dilemmas by pointing to the significant choice-points during the course of an applied research project.[23]

Out of this welter of difficult transformations and connections—particularly between the methods of applied research and more traditional methods—a new research technology must be forged. However, as is no doubt true of all the methodologies of planned change—training, consulting, and research—the innate cussedness of things will be with us for a long time, possibly forever.

[21] New York: The Viking Press, Inc., 1933, pp. 174–175.

[22] "A critique of group therapy research," *International Journal of Group Psychotherapy, 10*:63–77, 1960. Bennis feels that some techniques have to be developed whereby the social scientist can "work through" his resistances to the material. This is obviously impossible to do by himself, for it has been said that the only trouble with self-analysis is counter-transference. See also Lawrence Kubie, "Some Unresolved Problems of the Scientific Career," *American Science*, 4:596–613, and S. E. Perry, "Observations on Social Processes in Psychiatric Research," *Behavioral Science*, 1:290–302, 1956.

[23] See also Benne and Swanson (eds.) "Values and the Social Scientist," *Journal of Social Issues*, 1950, Vol. 6, No. 4, and Andie L. Knutson, "The Influence of Values on Evaluation," *Health Education Monographs*, No. 3, 1959, 25–31.

CHAPTER 11

Three Pivotal Functions in Planned Change: Training, Consulting, and Research

CASE METHODS IN THE TRAINING OF ADMINISTRATORS

Kenneth D. Benne

SOME image of the social role of the administrator is required in order to assess the uses and limitations of case methods in the training of persons to perform the role. My delineation of the role must be brief.

The administrator in any organization with work to perform must simultaneously meet two sets of organizational requirements in any decision he is called upon to make. One set of requirements may be called system *task* requirements. The other set may be named system *building* and *maintenance* requirements.[1] The *task* requirements look to the effective organization of interdependent effort in and around the system in order to meet its production goals and, in an industrial establishment, its sales and distribution goals as well. The *building* and *maintenance* requirements have to do with keeping the interpersonal, interdepartmental, and public relations of the social system in good repair and in improving these where they need improvement.

Task and building-maintenance requirements in an organization do not always jibe, though both are important. The technically soundest change in a method of production, fully justified from the point of view of task effectiveness, may, if introduced by an administrator without adequate attention to the maintenance requirements of the organization, result in deepened and irrational tensions within the internal and external relationships of the organization, and in increased suspicion and distrust among personnel that may disrupt both the communication and power-authority systems in the plant.

[1] See Kenneth D. Benne, and Paul Sheats, "Functional Roles of Group Members," *Journal of Social Issues*, 4:42–47, 1948, for a fuller development of the distinction between task and maintenance requirements in the organization of the social system of a group.

From Boston University Human Relations Center, Research Papers and Technical Notes, No. 28. Used by permission.

On the other hand, an administrator, seeking only to create a "happy" crew within and a "happy" public outside the organization, may jeopardize the task effectiveness previously achieved by the organization and thwart further improvements in task effectiveness. Both sets of requirements must be served and reconciled simultaneously in adequate administrative judgments and actions.

Actually, the human situation in which the role of the administrator is embedded is more complex than this analysis suggests. The requirements of the confronting situation upon the administrator in his role are communicated to him through the expectations of people—persons and groups—whom he perceives to be significant in his environment—"significant others" as the social philosopher George Mead called them. And his perceptions, both of which others are significantly to be taken into account in his judgments and of what their expectations with respect to his conduct are, are subject to all the distortions, conscious and unconscious, to which human perception generally is subject. The expectations, as he perceives these, stemming from his board, from his subordinate managers, from employees, from customers, from unions, from his own ideal image of an administrator, from other administrators in his professional group, these and others—varied, often conflicting—play upon him in the actual definition of his administrative role judgments and behaviors.

This view of the human situation of the administrator in its determination of his judgments and conduct raises a whole series of questions about the training he needs, in addition to the more familiar questions concerning the knowledges and skills required with respect to technical processes of production, sales, and distribution. How sensitive is the administrator to the complex of interrelated human forces and factors in his working situations? How accurate are his perceptions of the actual demands and expectations of the various reference groups and persons that he must take into account in making his practical judgments? How able is he to gather relevant and accurate information from observing, talking with, and listening to the people with and through whom he must work? How well can he set priorities in stepwise planning for conflict resolution, reconciling factors of urgency and importance in his judgments? How flexible is he in adapting his strategy of intervention in the processes of his organization to changing demands and conditions without impairing the integrity of his own value system and role image? How aware is he of his own motivations —which, if unknown to him, may cloud his judgments, often deluding himself more than others around him? How well can he translate his judgments of what he needs to do into actual behavior consistent with these judgments? Do his skills of timing and intervention square with his diagnostic judgments of the changing requirements of his situation? Can he hold multiple and conflicting factors, forces, and requirements in mind as he judges, acts, and evaluates the effects of his judgments and actions?

It is training questions such as these that have led many of those responsible for administrative training and development to turn to case methods of instruction to supplement or to supplant more traditional methods of educating administrative leaders. This shift has been due both to dissatisfactions of practicing administrators with the effectiveness of their traditional training in equipping them to answer affirmatively such questions as above, and to the fact that traditional methods were not designed primarily to answer the kinds of training questions indicated.

The questions fall logically into two general classes. The first class of questions has to do with the arts of *diagnosing* administrative situations (including the self of the administrator), arts involving observation, listening, analysis and assessment of forces and factors, and prediction of trends, potentialities, and valid directions. The second class has to do with the arts of *intervention* and *participation* in the situation as diagnosed, arts involving strategic planning, manipulation of forces and factors, behavior and action. In brief, administrators require training in the combined and interrelated arts of *observation* and *participation* in the setting of the organizational systems they administer.

Traditional methods of administrator training have erred in two principal ways. First, they have understressed the arts of diagnosing action situations in terms of their manageability and changeability. Second, they have tended to separate diagnostic training from prescriptive training on how to act in particular practical situations. Some of the important conceptual tools for use in diagnosis have been taught traditionally in departmentalized courses in the humanities, particularly history, and, more recently, in the behavioral sciences —psychology, sociology, economics (often not taught as a behavioral science), and anthropology. But the learning of these conceptual tools has not typically been hooked up in the educational process to concrete decision situations where

historical, psychological, sociological, economic, and anthropological variables are complexly intertwined and need to be seen and weighed in their interrelations for purposes of adequate situational diagnosis. Nor, typically, have administrators been taught to see the operational meanings of these concepts in terms of directly observable clusters of symptomatic behaviors and patterns of immediate experience.

Training in strategies of action, participation, and intervention, where formalized, has tended to take the form of rules of conduct and principles of method, taught apart from the diagnosis of actual situations in and to which rules and methods must be adapted and applied. Some "average" situation is assumed in the prescriptions proffered by the trainer, though the administrator always must act in a unique, never in an "average," situation. This assumption of an "average" or "normal" situation has prevailed in much "practical" training in how to do this or that— how to delegate, how to discipline a subordinate, and so on. Prescriptive training has typically been undertaken apart from the diagnosis of concrete and unique situations, however necessary such diagnosis is for any intelligent determination of what rules of action or strategy are appropriate and applicable and of what adaptations of general rules needs to be made. Where action training has been undertaken exclusively through apprenticeship in actual work situations, it has been difficult for the trainee to get the degree of detachment and freedom necessary for achieving generalizable learnings through making "mistakes" and analyzing and evaluating these, in terms of both their "diagnostic" and their "action" adequacies and inadequacies. The actual work situation sets more or less drastic limits to "experimental" and potentially "mistaken" behavior, however necessary such behavior may be for adequate learning.

In its most general sense, what do "case methods" involve? Case methods involve the confrontation of people in training with concrete human situations, situations with some temporal and developmental span, in which a whole complex of determinants of behavior are at work. Trainees are asked to diagnose these situations, to analyze them in terms of why events happen as they do, why the people involved act as they do. If the trainees are asked to prescribe and test verbally alternative behaviors for managing the situation confronted, they are asked to do so in terms of the diagnosis made, of the evidence available as to the dynamics of the situation, including the dynamics of the "manager" in it. Diagnosis and prescription are thus tied together in any adequate case analysis.

What typical forms has "case method," in this general sense, taken in its American development? And what are the virtues and limitations of these various forms in relation to the requirements upon administrator training outlined above?

1. One form of case is a printed description of some actual organizational behavior in which an administrator takes part.[2] When a trainee analyzes such a case in a group setting—as it

should always be analyzed for full training effect—he discovers the variety and complexity of factors that function in an actual situation to determine what happens in it. He discovers also the differences between his viewpoint, which assumes some implicit or explicit schema of human motivation and social determination, and the viewpoints of others in the group. He may thus discover gaps and inconsistencies in his own diagnostic apparatus, blindspots to certain kinds of factors and forces, overweightings of some kinds of variables as compared with others, projections of subjective interpretations which he finds it difficult to distinguish from the "objective" evidence presented, etc. And, if the case discussions are well conducted, he may, over time, broaden his repertoire of diagnostic schemes and acquire some of the attitudes required for dependable and accurate diagnosis—suspension of judgment, acceptance of variety in people and situations, and humility before the complexities of organizational, group, and individual behavior. These are goods in training for the administrative skills of participant-observation.

2. But cases studied in this way are still "out there" so far as the trainee is concerned—away from his own responsibility for moving from diagnostic judgments to action as part of a changing and developing situation. One adaptation of case method designed to open up a trainee's own processes of practical judgment to self-examination (and, hopefully, improvement) has been called the incident-process method.[3] This method was devised by Paul Pigors as a tool for training industrial managers. It involves the confrontation of

[2] Kenneth Andrews, *Case Methods of Teaching Human Relations and Administration,* Cambridge, Mass.: Harvard University Press, 1951. Roethlisberger, Fritz, "Training for Human Relations: An Interim Report of a Program for Advanced Training and Research in Human Relations," Harvard University, Division of Research, Graduate School of Business Administration, Boston, 1954.

[3] P. & F. Pigors, "Case Methods on the Spot," *Adult Leadership, 3:* No. 6, 1954, pp. 7–8, 28–29.

trainees with a critical incident in the human relations of an organization—an incident requiring adjudication and decision. Originally, Pigors used actual arbitration cases as subject matter. The situation is briefly presented. The training group must decide what further information it needs in order to make a decision. Further information is available but the trainer who has it will furnish any part of it only if asked specifically by the group for that part. Individual decisions are written after the group has gathered information seen as needed and has discussed it. These decisions are presented publicly and debated with pressure toward a common decision. The group then hears the official decision and analyzes where and why its fact-finding and fact interpretation processes fell short.

This method moves the trainees closer to self-examination of actual decision-making processes and may, therefore, be used to diagnose and improve processes of practical administrative judgment. But again, the behavior, the action, of the trainee based upon such judgments is not brought to the point of behavioral testing and of subsequent analysis of behavioral consequences. The behavior analyzed is the behavior of someone else, the situation judged is a situation of which the trainee, strictly speaking, is not a part, though his own thinking about this situation is pressed toward closure, made public, and analyzed. Diagnosis and judgment are still separated, from the point of view of training, from the shape and testing of one's own actual behavior in a situation based on one's own accompanying diagnosis and judgment of that situation.

3. A case method designed for action-training by J. L. Moreno has sought to bridge this gap. This method,

originally named sociodrama, has been elaborated by others under the different names of reality-practice, role-playing, and participative case method.[4] A problematic situation is presented to or invented by the trainees, and some trainees are asked, not to talk about the situation, but to assume parts (roles) of people in it and to enact the developing situation toward some sort of resolution. Other trainees as well as the trainer observe the actual behavior as dramatically developed. Observations are made public along with inner feelings and thoughts of the actors. Faults in diagnosis, faults in action on diagnosis, discrepancies between diagnoses and actions are located and clarified through analysis and discussion. The same or analogous situations may be re-practiced to test the analysis and to retrain both the diagnoses and actions of the participants. This method brings processes of diagnosis and action into close relationship within the training process. It brings the trainee's own behavior and actions into the open for analysis and guided practice. It thus moves toward the ideal of training of the administrator as actor-judger or participant-observer. But the situation is still not completely "real"—the players are acting but they are enacting a character which is at least in part some one else in a situation which is in a measure projected beyond or outside the actual training situation. Many of their own personal projections into the role played are revealed in the action and analyzed in the analysis of the action. But the situation is still a make-believe one.

4. A further refinement of case

[4] J. L. Moreno, *Psychodrama*, Vol. 1, New York: Beacon House, 1946, and J. L. Moreno, *Who Shall Survive?*, New York: Beacon House, 1953.

method requires members of a group of trainees to analyze their own actual behavior in a group situation as a living example of an organization in process of development.[5] The task of the group must be sufficiently undefined, its procedures sufficiently unprescribed and unroutinized, to permit and require members to reveal their own behavior as participant-observers and actor-judgers for public observation and analysis as they struggle to organize the life and production of the group. The case in this form is not "out there" as it happened or is happening to some one else. The self of the trainee is in it, a part of it, revealing its characteristic patterns of relating to and dealing with itself, with superiors, peers, and subordinates for analysis by the trainee, with the reactions of others to his own behavior and his reactions to the behavior of others as part of the data for testing and analysis. Such training has been shown to lead in many instances to effective transfer to a variety of practical administrative situations outside the protected environment of the "laboratory" group. What is transferred seems to be not alone the particular substantive skills of diagnosis-action actually practiced and learned

[5] Kenneth D. Benne, "Comments on Training Groups," and Warren G. Bennis, "Patterns and Vicissitudes in Training Groups." These papers are obtainable on request from the Boston University Human Relations Center and are to appear later in a book on training groups which the National Training Laboratories, National Education Association, Washington 6, D.C. plan to have published. Also, National Training Laboratories, *Explorations in Human Relations Training; An Assessment of Experience, 1947–1953*, NEA, Washington, D.C.

in the training group. A method of learning through participant-observation is also transferred to the work situation so that on-the-job growth by the administrator can continue with some measure of commitment and discipline achieved to support this continuation of growth.

In summary, an analysis of the role of the administrator has emphasized his responsibility for helping the people in and around the social system of an enterprise to meet more adequately and collaboratively the task and building-maintenance requirements of that enterprise. This role image emphasizes the understandings, values, and skills of participant-observer, of judger-actor, as essential to its effective performance. But the skills of observation and of participation, of diagnostic judgment and of action must be learned in relation to each other if role behavior is to be effectively trained. Traditional methods of administrator training have understressed the development of diagnostic judgment and have tended to separate diagnostic from action training. Case methods that involve the confrontation of trainees with a concrete, complex behavioral situation for analysis (diagnosis, judgment, and prescription) have been developed to meet these faults in traditional training. A spectrum of case methods, all with demonstrated usefulness in administrator training, has been reviewed, with the degree of the trainee's own personal involvement and participation in the case to be analyzed as the chief dimension of difference.

◇◇◇◇◇◇◇◇◇◇◇◇◇◇◇◇◇◇◇◇◇ THE T-GROUP AS TRAINING
IN OBSERVANT PARTICIPATION

Herbert A. Shepard

Value Premises and Training Goals

THE trainer's primary responsibilities are to facilitate the development of valid communication in the group and to help members make explicit the processes of that development. The purpose of the former is to provide to members the experience of working in a group with a high potential for member satisfaction and problem solving; the purpose of the latter is to ensure that members profit from the experience by gaining skill in observant participation so that they can improve the productive potential of other groups in which they participate.

Thus development of the group towards valid communication is not an end in itself: it is part of the training method for improving skills in observant participation. By skills in observant participation are meant the abilities not only to act but also to monitor the action and accurately assess its consequences for the actor in relation to the others, and for the group in relation to its goals. The skills are easier to describe than to learn. Barriers to learning are produced by the process of socialization. Maturation in any society entails learning to ignore certain matters just as it entails learning to notice certain things. Such analyses as Riesman's [1]

[1] David Riesman, *The Lonely Crowd*, New Haven: Yale University Press, 1950.

point to preoccupation with the consequences of action in terms of individual goals—popularity or power— and inattention to consequences in terms of collaborative achievement. Cultural emphasis on individualism, that is, on the dangers of risking one's reputation on another's judgment, reduces potential for cooperating and sharing responsibility. In a culture that makes personal isolation synonymous with personal autonomy, T-group training means the reawakening of painful processes which gave rise to present patterns of interpersonal adaptation.

The ultimate value premise underlying the T-group is one which also underlies scientific work, namely, that it is a good thing to know what you are doing. The trainee should come to have a better understanding of what takes place between himself and others; he should be able better to assess the consequences for himself and others of actions that he is moved to take; and with this enhanced alertness a wider range of action alternatives should become available to him. In short, he should gain greater control over his external and internal communication.

Knowledge of what one is doing is never complete, but there are plateaus of understanding coordinate with degrees of self-acceptance. The T-group has a limited potency. More modestly, then, its purpose is to increase understanding, possibly at the risk of certain

From Herbert A. Shepard, "The T-Group as Training in Observant Participation," Theory of Training, *Massachusetts Institute of Technology Series. Used by permission.*

defenses of the self; while providing a richer basis for self-esteem coupled with apperceptive habits for understanding more fully. The T-group training should enable the member to see more, and to use what he sees constructively for himself and others.

Valid Communication as a Training Objective

The term "valid communication" can be understood by identifying two organic properties of individuals and groups: their components are living and in communication. If a person is to "know what he is doing," the "components" of the person must come to be in non-distorting communicative relations with one another and with the environment. A person's communication with self and others is often characterized by what Sullivan [2] called "selective inattention," whereby he quite consistently overlooks certain aspects of what transpires. For example, he may by gesture or tonal quality, or modal behavior patterns, tell others more than he intends, or something more than or other than, he tells himself.

Groups are also capable of selective inattention. For example, member involvement in what is apparently a mutually enlightening discussion of leadership theory may be motivated by a need to influence the trainer, or may constitute a fight for dominance among some of the members. In other words, the activity of the group tells the observer something more than or other than, it tells the members. Like a person, the group has cause for such oversights. Recognition of these other aspects of

group activity would destroy some operating assumptions about the character of mutual relations in the group, assumptions that are needed for the maintenance of a reasonable degree of comfort.

Valid communication in a group is associated with the absence of such phenomena as selective inattention. More positively, valid communication refers to such states as the following: the member's perception of his relation to the group and of the effects of his action on the group are in accord with other members' perceptions of these things; the announced purpose of an activity corresponds with the efforts being made by members. Conditions necessary for valid communication appear to be the existence of sufficient mutual acceptance and identification among members that feelings about any issue arising in the group can be expressed and accepted.

Characterization of valid communication by the statement that the announced purpose of an activity corresponds with the efforts being made by members matches Sullivan's [3] description of mental health for the person, namely, that the self becomes co-extensive with the personality. In this sense, one might speak of T-group training as therapy of the group as a human entity, to be distinguished from "group therapy" for the individuals in the group.

The Trainer's Role

The trainer's major responsibility is to help the group identify and overcome obstacles to valid communication. For this task, his own skills of observant participation are his principal resource. Any set of rules for trainer behavior

[2] Harry Stack Sullivan, *Conceptions of Modern Psychiatry*, Wash., D.C.: William Alanson White Psychiatric Foundation, 1947.

[3] *Ibid.*

would have to be bound by many conditional statements. Moreover, experience has not progressed far enough to validate any system. Hence, adherence to a doctrine is likely to prove as unserviceable to trainer and group as does adherence by a trainee to the imperatives of social relations that he brings to the group.

However, certain features of the training situation should be borne in mind by the trainer as guides to action. The first is his role as a projective figure for the group. During the early meetings he appears to be the group's *raison d'être:* most members see no other cause for meeting and no other force restraining them from leaving. Members' conscious and unconscious fantasies about the trainer are the major determinants of group activity. Most members feel that the trainer is observing them keenly; they may describe themselves as guinea pigs. In fact, however, it is the behavior of the trainer that receives careful scrutiny. His face is studied for obscure messages, his place in the seating arrangement noted, his cigarette consumption watched. His remarks are carefully attended to and judged unintelligible. He is an object of love and hate, of oppression and protection, of desertion and impotence, and his importance to the group is vigorously denied and affirmed.

From this it follows that the trainer can be quite sure of being misunderstood in a variety of ways. But the knowledge that he will be misunderstood gives him no license: what he does and how he does it are important. Misunderstanding one's situation is a most reliable means of avoiding learning. Assuming that there are a number of things the trainees would have learned before now had it been safe to do so, some protective misunderstanding

is to be expected. A large part of the trainee's task is to sort those of his reactions which are based on misunderstanding from those which are based on accurate perception. For that task, the trainer's behavior is of considerable importance. If the trainee tends to project certain kinds of unacceptable motivations and activities on a certain class of other persons, and if the trainer is in that class, it will simplify the trainee's task if the trainer's behavior does not provide objective confirmation of the trainee's misgivings. Projection of undesirable features on the trainer is one thing; production of undesirable features by the trainer is another. This does not mean that the trainer should be a paragon of virtue; only that he should be free to choose whether to act in accordance with his impulses, and that he make his choice with the group's welfare in mind.

In particular, the trainer should avoid exploiting or being victimized by the dependency and counterdependency needs of members. This rule places severe restrictions on the trainer's freedom of action. For example, even reflecting an individual's statement in a group setting may be an unfortunate act. It singles out the individual for response by the trainer, legitimizes his fantasy of uniqueness, and assures him that a special bond exists between himself and the trainer. Similarly, a supportive statement by the trainer may confirm the member's worst suspicions about himself—namely, that his survival depends on the support of more powerful persons.

The existence of dependency phenomena implies that, in general, the trainer should not treat the group members as "individuals." It implies that his contributions should be largely restricted to comments directed to the group about the group. How then can the trainer respond to individual appeals? He may ask whether the question is a matter of concern to the whole group. If he receives an affirmative response, it becomes a group appeal, and can be responded to. If he receives a negative response, other members will relieve him of the necessity for carrying the matter further. Or he may explicitly assume that the member's statement is representative of, or on behalf of, an effective segment of the group. These may not be the only, or the most appropriate alternatives. The point is that he should be aware of the disservice he can do the group member by responding inappropriately. It is difficult to avoid either the dependency seduction or the counterdependency trap, and the counterdependent's charge that the trainer "won't tell us anything" or "won't give a straight answer" often contains a grain of truth because of the trainer's difficulties in finding an appropriate way of responding to individual appeals and challenges.

Through the portion of group life when the trainer is the focus of dependency and counterdependency needs of members, he has a certain range of choice regarding the extent to which these needs are to be highlighted and made the subject of special experiential and theoretical consideration. The personality and training philosophy of the trainer, as well as the professional needs of the group members, determine his interest in introducing or avoiding explicit consideration of dependency, and this in turn has much to do with his method of opening a T-group. Trainers who do not wish dependency and authority problems to be given special emphasis provide the protection usually given by authority figures without demanding the usual price of that protection, namely, control over member behavior. Trainers who would emphasize dependency neither provide protection nor seek to control.

The trainer who provides protection without demanding control may arouse feelings of guilt so that the group tries to outguess him and carry out his desires, but as the group gains in cohesiveness, the trainer can drop any paternalistic elements in his role and reduce the guilt and concern with pleasing him.

The trainer who violates expectations of protection, however, arouses hostility which can be readily turned against himself. He gives the group no reward for efforts to please him. Moreover, he withholds protection when the group is confronted with a situation full of uncertainties, and thus is responsible for creating an anxious situation. Rather than being a permissive leader, he is a leader who fails. Needless to say, the authority-dependency-counterdependency problem comes into sharp focus.

Both of these training modes produce a power gap, so that a leadership struggle usually ensues among the group members. It is possible that members who seek to control the group receive more punishment from the other members if the trainer has been a permissive leader. Although hostility aroused by the leader who fails may be expressed in intermember combat, there is, so to speak, a natural tendency for it to be directed against the trainer himself, and he can, with the exercise of a little skill, assist nature.

Trainer dependency and power struggle die away together, since they are aspects of the same problem. The end of this phase is usually symbolized by some ritual of acceptance of the trainer as member. After this point, power consideration are less frequently sources of distortion in communication, and the central issues become those of intimacy, trust, and sharing responsibility.

The keynote of the T-group is interpersonal uncertainty, and training is learning to reduce uncertainty by consensual validation of experience. The ambiguity of the trainee's relationship to the trainer accounts for only part of the interpersonal uncertainty, and attention is focussed on this relationship only as long as the trainer is seen as the major source of reward or punishment. The logic appears to be that if a particular kind of relationship can be established with the trainer, the trainee need not be concerned about the rest of the group. When this possibility evaporates, the trainee is likely to become alarmed. The intensity with which dangers of being engulfed by the group, of losing his personal identity, of enforced conformity are felt by the trainee is in a way a measure of his self-acceptance, or lack of it. Thus, when the central issues are interdependence and responsibility sharing, members may feel their self-esteem and "integrity" threatened by the group.

Neither in his relations with the trainer nor in his relations with other members, however, is the trainee likely to consider consensual validation a feasible method of reducing interpersonal uncertainty. The reasons for this are twofold; first, the trainee may fear that his real feelings and view of the situation would not be shared by other members, especially if his real feelings are already threatening to his self-esteem. Hence, to communicate them might make his situation worse. Second, the group culture is both a consequence and cause of this reticence

on the part of members. It is, typically, a denial of members' real feelings. Instead of consensual validation, a number of other methods for reducing uncertainty are adopted by the group, and the adoption of these methods by the group implies to each member that his feelings are not shared by the others. The alternative methods of reducing uncertainty are, broadly speaking, efforts to transform perceptions or efforts to transform the situation, or both. Perceptual transformations involve classifying the experience as something familiar and either irrelevant to or supportive of self-esteem: such descriptive terms as "boring," "unreal," "fascinating" or "bull session" represent efforts at reclassification. Attempts to transform the situation include adopting Robert's rules of order, efforts to make the trainer take an "instructor" role, inviting in experts, and undertaking to split or fragment the group (by adjournment, scapegoating of members, coffee breaks, fighting, voting, buzz-grouping, etc.)

Obviously the trainer will not be of service to the group by actively contributing to the construction of these transformations. But since they are necessary collaborative moves to avoid anxiety, he can only complicate the situation by confronting the group with a threatening interpretation. In other words, neither rewarding behavior nor punishing behavior is appropriate. All that the trainer seeks is that group members have a better understanding of why certain events took place, of what made the events necessary. Moreover, the trainer should avoid being caught up in individualistic delusions in his own understanding of the group movement; that is, he should avoid scapegoating any members, which is one of the group's favorite methods of avoiding responsibility.

Given these considerations, there are a number of constructive roles that the trainer may take. One of these is clarification of the group's problem. Another is an estimate of possible consequences of present activity. A third is summarizing what appear to be different orientations expressed by various segments of the group. A fourth is uncovering group-shared hidden agenda —but this requires the most painstaking examination of possible consequences, since it is the most powerful method available to the trainer.

It should be borne in mind that whatever the trainer does during the dependency phase is likely to be misapprehended—his statements will appear weak and ineffectual to dependent members, obstructive and confusing to counterdependent members. They are likely to be treated as incomprehensible, or apparently ignored. When this happens, it is tempting to think that they were just poorly timed, or poorly phrased, or that they were wrong, or "too far ahead" of the group. Quite often, however, they have considerable private significance to some group members, but the terms on which these members are integrated with one another at the moment preclude shared consideration of the trainer's statement —not necessarily in the sense that *any* statement of the trainer's must be ignored, but that consideration of this particular statement would alter the terms under which they are collaborating.

The problems of the trainer's role are only the problems of any group membership role, with certain added complications. One of these derives from the trainer's prior commitment to the group: he retains a strong sense of responsibility for what happens throughout all phases of the training. The fact that he has, realistically, relatively little control over some of the things that may happen, simply means that he is more like other group members than he or they sometimes think. The other special complications of the trainer's role are the expectations and projections of group members, which are strongly focussed on him during at least part of the group life. These expectations and projections are the major distinctive features of the trainer's role. In some ways they make the trainer exceptionally powerful; in other ways they greatly restrict his effectiveness.

These characteristics of the trainer role must also be taken into account in his contacts with group members outside the group meetings. As might be expected, one of the commonest out-of-meeting situations confronting the trainer is the dependent member seeking a private, exploitative relationship. However, forces other than dependency may cause a trainee to seek a private relationship with the trainer. The important principles for the trainer to bear in mind are that all private relationships involving segments of the group create communicative confusion in the group, and that the centrality of the trainer's role means that his concealed involvements are especially disconcerting. This consideration has led some trainers to establish a rule of no communication with members outside the meeting. In the usual laboratory environment, the objection to this rule is that it is impossible to obey. An amendment to the effect that the trainer will not discuss the T-group outside meetings is a false remedy, since the relationship rather than the subject matter—the process rather than the content—is what concerns the trainee.

A more workable rule is that significant trainer-member or member-member relationships outside the meetings be discussed in the group as soon as it becomes feasible to do so, since they are likely to be crucial elements of process and a basis for generalization about group relations. For example, if the process of communicating back-home status and presenting other credentials is not done at the meeting, it will inevitably be done outside the meeting as a way of discovering subgroups into which to escape, and it is important to make the existence of this process explicit at the group meeting.

The rule that significant outside relationships should be discussed in the meetings does not provide an answer to all questions that can be raised about trainer-member relations. The trainer's desire to examine such relationships in the meetings should be made explicit to members, but the initiative, as well as the timing, should rest with them. A member may have been unable to form any attachments in the group to relieve intense anxiety, and sought out the trainer as a last resort. The trainer would only increase the member's distress by exposing the relationship before the latter is ready. It is possible, but unlikely, that the member will be unable to bring up the matter in the group at any time. Similarly, the trainer may sometimes take the initiative in seeking out a member where the group's development or the member's integrity has been seriously threatened by events in the meeting. This is a matter of the trainer's judgment in predicting events that will probably occur if he does not intervene privately to prevent the immobilization of the group or member. In the sadder cases, where his judgment was not adequate to the situation, the trainer may have to seek out members privately to begin the process of restoring working relationships in the group after an unfortunate event.

✧✧✧✧✧✧✧✧✧✧✧✧✧✧✧✧✧✧✧ ENGINEERING AND CLINICAL
APPROACHES TO CONSULTING

Alvin W. Gouldner

Engineering and Clinical Sociology

THERE is a second key assumption which seems to shape the growth of the applied social sciences. While it is never explicitly stated, it is nonetheless of considerable influence. This assumption seems to be that there is but one type of, or one model for, applied social science. In the pages that follow the suggestion will be made that there are at least two significantly different models available for applied social science, the "engineering" and the "clinical," and an attempt will be made to clarify a few of their underlying differences.

The distinction between an engi-

Excerpts from Alvin W. Gouldner, "Explorations in Applied Social Science," Social Problems, Vol. 3, No. 3, January 1956, pp. 173–181. Abridged and used by permission.

neering and a clinical approach can be considered initially by inspecting a typical case, derived from my own experience, of an engineering research in the social sciences. An industrial concern contracts with a "management consulting" firm to conduct an employee attitude survey among its own employees. The stated aims of this research are to determine whether employees are satisfied with their working conditions, hours, wages, or supervisors. By and large, the consulting firm consents to do this on the terms specified by the hiring company. In the end, the consultant conveys a report to the company which indicates the percentage of employees who are satisfied with their wages, their supervision, or the chances for promotion. Not uncommonly, this report may also incude some recommendations for changes in the company's labor relations policies. Usually, the company management invites the consultant to a discussion concerning the implications of these findings. Then, after a decent interval, the report may be quietly interred in that great graveyard of creativity, the filing room. Although crudely outlined, this is probably a representative history of the engineering type of applied social research. It is often with such a case in mind that people discuss the "gap between research and policy-making."

Notice that in the above example the consulting "engineer" has conceived and completed his assignment largely in terms formulated by his client. The consultant has failed to ask himself just why it was that the company management requested this survey in the first place; what kinds of problems produced a felt need for such a research among the company people; and will these problems persist even after the proposed survey is successfully completed according to management's prescriptions?

Many industrial sociologists would concur in believing that, underlying a request for an employee attitude survey, there usually exist a number of vaguely sensed tensions. For example, there has probably been some attenuation of informal communication between management and the worker. In short, the employer attitude survey may well serve as a functional equivalent for informal networks of communication which have deteriorated.

Such a survey, however, usually does little to alert the client to the existence of this underlying problem. Still less does the survey mend the ruptured informal channels, however much it supplies reliable data about employee attitudes. Indeed, the survey now makes it easier to continue operation *despite* the breakdown in informal organization. To that extent, then, the survey paradoxically preserves the very tensions which brought it into existence.

Again, an employee survey may also be used as a way of outflanking the union, by making it seem that management is better (because "scientifically") informed than the union leaders about the workers' feelings. In this case, one of the tensions promoting the research was a cleavage between management and the union. Here, once again, the tension is in no way mitigated by the use of the survey. If anything, the union feels increasingly threatened as a result of the research, and labor-management tensions are heightened rather than curtailed.

In contrast with these procedures, we may take a recent study in applied anthropology as a case which approximates, if it does not fully conform to, the clinical model. This is a project reported by Alan Holmberg which involved an Indian community in Peru, Hacienda Vicos. "When we first began to work at Vicos," writes Holmberg, "we soon discovered that one of the principal causes of in-group strife among the Indians was disagreements and fights over the ownership of cattle. . . . In view of this, it occurred to us—as it had apparently not occurred to the Indians—that one of the best ways in which to solve this problem would be to initiate a program of branding. This was suggested to the Indian leaders who heartily agreed, as did the people themselves with whom we discussed this matter in a general assembly." (4)

Branding irons were then made and offers of assistance were advanced. At first few takers were found, whereupon the matter was again discussed with the Indian leaders. Only after the wealthier leaders themselves consented to have their own cattle branded did others follow suit. Finally, through this means, community disputes concerning ownership of cattle were eliminated.

Even from this brief account certain contrasts between the clinical and engineering models are already evident. Most importantly, the "clinicians" at Hacienda Vicos did not assume, as had the "engineers" in the management consulting firm, that their clients' own formulation of their problem could be taken at face value. Instead the clinicians took their clients' complaints and self-formulations as only one among a number of "symptoms" useful in helping them to arrive at their own diagnosis of the clients' problems. In the employee attitude study, the engineers studied what they were

told to; at Hacienda Vicos, the clinicians made their own independent identification of the group's problems.

The "Value-Free" Assumption

Although this is only one difference between the engineers and clinicians, it is an extremely significant one. It is significant, above all, because it makes us re-examine one of the most cherished assumptions guiding work in the applied social sciences. This is the assumption that social science, pure or applied, cannot formulate and specify ends for its client group. Legitimated by references to the conceptions of a "value-free" social science, which were advanced by Max Weber and John Stuart Mill, many applied social scientists have claimed that all they can properly do is to study the diverse consequences of different policies, or to suggest efficient means for the realization of ends already specified by their client. (12)

The important questions concerning this assumption are pragmatic ones: To what extent does it truly describe the work of applied social scientists? To what extent does it provide clear and unambiguous directives for their actual operations? Is this assumption likely to be as congenial to engineers as to clinicians? There are many problems which the applied social scientist confronts for which this assumption, treated as a directive, provides no solutions. And there are many operations in which the applied social scientist engages which this assumption, treated as a description, does not accurately portray.

For example, in the event of employment by a client whose values differ from those of the group whom the applied scientist is asked to change, with whose values and to whose ends shall the scientist conform? If the work of industrial sociologists exhibits little uncertainty in this matter, the work of applied anthropologists employed by colonial governments evidences considerable uneasiness and perplexity. (3) Furthermore, suppose the client does not know what his values are, or suppose he does not know in what priority to order his values? As sociologists very well know, this is a cultural condition which is very likely to give rise to all manner of tensions for the client. Is the applied scientist to deny assistance in these matters, to refuse to help his client formulate his values and goals, under the justification that his is a value-free science? And if he does aid his client in specifying his ends—as evidenced for example by the work at Hacienda Vicos—then is the scientist giving more than "lip service" to the postulate that he should not specify ends for his client?

Again, what of the client who pursues values which may be somewhat incompatible—e.g., desegregation vs. political stability? (14) Should not the applied social scientist somehow indicate that the client's own values may be somewhat incompatible and that this incompatibility may be generating tensions for him? And if the applied scientist does these things, is he not then influencing the values of his client group? If the postulate of a value-free social science is not an accurate description of what applied social scientists do, and, above all, if this postulate is not translatable into clear-cut, unambiguous, operational directives, facilitating the applied scientist's solution of his professional problems, then the postulate itself—if not operationally meaningless—would seem to be in need

of consideration respecification. This is not to imply that the postulate, as presently formulated, is totally useless. For the postulate of a value-free social science may be most useful as an ideological mechanism. That is, it may successfully serve the social scientist as an instrument of status defense, deflecting the suspicions of client groups who fear that the social scientist wishes to impose his own values upon them and is a silent competitor for administrative power. (6)

In any event, engineers and clinicians among applied social scientists seem to differ with respect to their interpretation of the value-free postulate. The clinician is less likely to take his client's own values as given, and he establishes a relation with the client in which they may legitimately come up for reexamination in the light of their connection with the client's problems.

There are many other respects in which clinician and engineer apparently differ and, in the remaining space, only a few of these can be examined. It will have been noted that the "clinicians" at Hacienda Vicos carefully consulted with all who would be affected by their diagnosis and proposed remedy of that community's problems. In contrast, the management "engineers" conferred with only one segment of the group, namely, the top echelon; they did not consult with the workers.

One reason for this difference is the differing anticipations which clinicians and engineers have concerning client resistance to their findings, and their differing interpretations of the sources of this resistance. The engineer fatalistically assumes that resistance to his findings is not his legitimate problem and, at worst, is due to the present deficiencies of his own research methods. He expects that inevitable improvements in research methods will sooner or later dissipate this resistance. (8) The clinician, however, assumes that findings produced by even the most perfect research technologies will continue to meet with resistance. He assumes that this resistance is his problem and that he has a responsibility for coping with it.

Assumptions Concerning Resistance

Without doubt inadequate research impairs the relations between applied social scientists and their clients, leading to many failures in the practical use of social science. But the client's resistance to social science findings is undoubtedly motivated by many considerations. Today no one is able to weight the various factors contributing to breakdowns in the scientist-client relationship. It is well known, however, that there are important cases where this breakdown cannot be attributed to the dereliction of the researcher or to the inadequacies of his research technology. This becomes evident when a research technology is employed in two comparable settings. In one case it is given successful application, and its findings are used by the client. In another very similar setting, however, this same research method will be employed but its findings are ignored and go unused. This seems to have been the case with personnel research which was successfully conducted and fully utilized by the Army Air Force during World War II, while the Navy made very little application of the personnel research which had been conducted for it. (10)

The experience of other applied disciplines also suggests, unfortunately, that the utilization of their findings is by no means entirely dependent upon their validity. It is noteworthy that physicians have sometimes been quite successful in securing acceptance of certain of their recommendations which were far from well validated and which, in fact, they themselves later rejected. For example, American doctors persuaded many parents to feed their infants on a rigorous and regular time schedule, say once every three hours, and even succeeded in diffusing this practice to certain parts of Latin America. Yet, later, the medical profession maintained that infants should be placed on a "demand schedule" and be fed as they wished. It seems evident that, in the case of personnel research, its scientific adequacy was not sufficient to secure its equal utilization in all cases, while the inadequacy of earlier infant feeding research was not sufficient to prevent its utilization.

Pure and applied scientists alike may be relied upon to improve their research technologies and, with this, the scope and reliability of their findings. By itself, however, this will not solve the utilization problem and will not automatically guarantee that these findings are successfully put to use. Applied social science does have to contend with a kind of client resistance which has nothing to do with the deficiencies of scientific research. As suggested by the situation at Hacienda Vicos, clinicians, unlike engineers, fully anticipate and systematically prepare to cope with such client resistance.

They never suppose that client resistance is solely, or even mainly, reinforced by the researcher's ignorance or incompetence. It is clear, for example, that we do know a great deal about certain fields, for example, about criminology and penology, not to speak of ethnic discrimination and prejudice. Nonetheless, it is also painfully clear that this knowledge is grudgingly put to use, if at all. Indeed, it may well be true, as some psychiatric clinicians avow, that the *nearer* the social scientist approaches to the nerve centers of his client's problems, the more resistant the client becomes.

There are many reasons for resistance to the findings of social research, other than those residing in the defects of the research itself. One reason may be, as the Freudians and others have insisted, that the client actually derives certain satisfactions or gains from his disturbances. As a result, he is not entirely and singlemindedly ready to accept knowledge which exerts pressure to remedy these problems. Another reason may be that the research itself may serve as one or another form of defense mechanism. In brief, the client sometimes undertakes a research so that he does *not* have to solve certain problems, and so that he need *not* change. In this case, the very conduct of research provides participation in a problem-solving ceremonial. It is a ritual particularly pleasing to the consciences of men reared in a rational tradition. Moreover, it provides a publicly evident token of the client's good faith and of his sincere interest in resolving the problem. But it does not inevitably entail the client's commitment to the conclusions of the research, or to the recommendations for change which may be proposed.

Kenneth Burke, a gifted sociologist who obstinately calls himself a literary critic, has termed this pattern of resistance the "Hamletic strategy." Named after the Great Procrastinator, this pattern of resistance is one in which the very preparations for action are transmuted into devices for postponing action. Nor is this always a matter of *unconscious* resistance. As Burke reminds us, "we may note how legislatures regularly adopt the 'Hamletic' strategy as a way to avoid embarrassing decisions. For if you would forestall a final vote on a measure, and would do so in the best 'scientific' spirit, you need but appoint a committee empowered to find more facts on the subject." (1)

In attempting to account for the resistance to social science findings and the failure to utilize them fully for practical purposes, some emphasis has recently been placed on the status of the social scientist, which is often lower than his client's. The point has been well made that "other things being equal, the amount of utilization is likely to increase with esteem for a science and its practitioners." (10) While this is undoubtedly correct, nonetheless it must be understood that the social scientist has a complex social role which involves much more than hierarchical qualities such as prestige, power, or class. This role consists of a culturally standardized complex of expectations and definitions of function, which leads the social scientist to develop his relationships with clients in specific ways. To understand properly the failure to use social science findings, it would seem useful to examine not only the social scientist's prestige but the other aspects of his role as well, his role conceptions, and the resultant patterns of interaction with his client. It may be useful, therefore, to examine some of the differences beween the clinical and engineering models, in terms of the varying role definitions which they entail.

The Engineering Model

Up to the present, the dominant role definitions of researcher and policy-maker, adopted by most sociologists, have been cast in the classic utilitarian mold. That is, the policy-maker defines his difficulties as deriving from inadequate knowledge. He formally operates on the assumption that, if he only had greater knowledge, his problems would capitulate. It is with this in mind, presumably, that he calls upon the applied sociologist. The policy-maker also tends to assume that the inadequacy of his knowledge is somehow accidental or a matter of neglect. He rarely entertains the dismaying thought that his very ignorance may be functional to him.

The applied sociologist who accepts such a definition of his client's role is more likely to conform to the engineering model and to define himself, in turn, as the bearer of facts and figures. He assumes that the client really wants to solve the problems of which he complains. The engineering sociologist recognizes, of course, that he has a job of "communication" to do. But the engineering sociologist is prone to regard this communication as well done if he reduces his report to fourteen-word sentences and mimeographs it neatly on multi-colored paper. As Wilbur Schramm puts it, "Utilization is sometimes thought of as a process of 'telling people'—writing better pamphlets, drawing better charts, making more and better teaching films, cranking up the transmitters of the mass media. This is clearly an inadequate picture." (10) Inadequate though it is, this is very much the way

in which the engineers among the applied social scientists approach the problem of the utilization of social science. It is a fascinating anomaly that, while utilitarianism has been expunged from the *theories* of most sociologists, utilitarian assumptions such as those above still remain deeply embedded in their own role relations with clients. Their heads protrude into the twentieth century, but they shall remain among the half-born so long as their feet are still rooted in the nineteenth century.

The role conceptions of applied social scientists are, of course, still very much in flux and are taking new shapes as they are subjected to new client pressures and temptations. Unaware that the utilization process is, as Schramm calls it, a two-way hookup, the engineers are particularly vulnerable to an unwitting redefinition of their roles in ways which obliterate their professional distinctiveness and identity.

Thus one finds the "policy scientists" taking over whole the military language of their clients, or would-be clients, and talking, for example, about the need for "intelligence" rather than for information or data. (7) The general tone of their writing has the atmosphere of a military staff issuing urgent directives, mobilizing resources, and preparing for battle. Their rediscovery that ours is "one world" takes on the flavor of geopolitics; their insistence upon "time factors" is devoid of the humanism of the historian and has, instead, the perspective of the tactician. Their new self-images apparently emphasize tough-mindedness, worldliness, and realism, which are well oriented to the military crisis of our time and well adapted for interaction with a military elite. It is another and more doubtful matter, however, whether these new self-images of the engineering sociologists are equally valuable for the development of an independent and self-conscious social science, pure or applied.

The Clinical Model

A point has now been reached where some of the characteristics of the clinical model can be brought into sharper focus. There are a great variety of such characteristics which need to be clarified; here, however, the clinical model will only be considered as a social system, particularly as it is expressed in its distinctive role relations with clients. (5, 13)

a. From an engineering standpoint, the problems as formulated by the client are usually taken at face value; the engineer tends to assume that his client is willing to reveal the problems which actually beset him. The clinical sociologist, however, makes his own independent diagnosis of the client's problems. He assumes that the problems as formulated by the client may often have a defensive significance and may obscure, rather than reveal, the client's tensions. Not only does the clinician assume that the client may have some difficulty in formulating his own problems but he assumes, further, that such an inability may in some sense be motivated, and that the client is not entirely willing to have these problems explored or remedied. The clinician, therefore, does not take his client's formulations at their face value, any more than he does comments made by an ordinary interviewee; but he does use them as points of departure in locating the client's latent problems. As Emile

Durkheim who more than any other classical sociologist used a clinical model) remarked: ". . . a sick man faultily interprets the feelings that he experiences and most often attributes them to a cause which is not the true one. But these feelings, such as they are, have their interest, and the clinician notes them with great care and takes them seriously. They are an element in the diagnosis, and an important one . . . he is not indifferent as to where they are felt, when they began." (2)

b. The engineer focusses largely on his relations with those from whom he secures the information necessary to fill his order. He is concerned, for example, about problems of sampling, questionnaire design, or interviewing technology largely as these affect his data collection from respondents. In contrast, the clinical sociologist takes his relationship with his *client* as seriously as he does his relations with interviewees. The clinician does not allow his relationship with his client to be governed by the all-too-common "come back and see me when you've done something" approach. He attempts to arrange his relationship with a client so as to secure the latter's consent to examine the underlying problems of his group.

c. The engineering sociologist expects his findings to be accepted by his client, and particularly so if they have been acquired in conformity with the best canons of scientific research. The clinical sociologist, however, expects his clients to resist his findings, perhaps because "he that increaseth knowledge increaseth sorrow." The engineering sociologist assumes that his relationship with his client is regulated by the postulate that ignorance is evil, and knowledge power, and that men unequivocally prefer enlightenment to ignorance. Writing in what may be regarded as an engineering vein, E. A. Shils comments, "Truth is always useful to those who exercise power, regardless of whether they wish to share that truth with those over whom their power is exercised. . . ." (11) This is very dubious. Men in power are not merely technicians, concerned solely about the use of effective means to their ends; they are also politicians, committed to morally tinged precepts and symbols, and striving like all other men to maintain a decent self-image. (9) Truths which are inconsistent with their own self-images are demoralizing and thus, in this very real sense, by no means "useful" to them. By assuming that his client wishes to learn the truth, the engineering sociologist has confused an ethical imperative with a description of the learning process. When the applied sociologist recognizes that he has the problem of helping his client *learn* something, and when he recognizes that learning is not accomplished by fact-finding or "communication" techniques alone, then he is on his way to becoming a clinician. Unlike the engineer, the clinician seeks to identify the specific sources of the client's resistance to his findings and he attempts to develop and learn new skills enabling him to cope with his resistance.

It needs to be underscored that these are only a few of the differences between an engineering and clinical sociology. It should also be remembered that there has been a focus on their differences, and a resultant neglect of the similarities which they both share as applied sociologies. What has been attempted were approximate models of the clinical and engineering approaches; any given piece of applied sociology may therefore possess some characteristics of both models. Furthermore, despite this writer's interest in the clinical model, it should not be supposed that he sees no value in the engineering model and no difficulties in the clinical. If the engineer lacks a sophisticated conception of the client relation and an adequate appreciation of the depth and meaning of client resistance, the clinician typically lacks a sophisticated conception of research design and technology. Moreover, one may well be concerned about the practical possibilities of securing client acceptance of the clinical model in relations with groups—as distinct from individuals—and particularly with large scale organizations. Undoubtedly there are important difficulties here, but as the work proceeding at the Tavistock Institute suggests, not insurmountable ones.

An applied sociology has much to learn from the clinical disciplines. It should not be assumed, however, as is so often done these days, that the only clinical discipline which can usefully serve as a concrete model is psychoanalysis. There is much to be learned from it, particularly if it is constantly borne in mind that psychoanalysis is an applied *psychology*. As sociologists we are interested only in borrowing elements which are properly applicable to the analysis of *groups,* or for the development of change-inducing relations with them.

Physical medicine itself, or bacteriology, to name only two other clinical disciplines, may be just as valuable as psychoanalysis for the development of a clinical sociology. What we happen to know best is not necessarily what we can best use. Nor should it be supposed that a clinical sociology is characterized primarily by the use of one or another therapeutic device, such as "consultative" or "nondirective" methods. Such devices are probably better suited to a clinical than an engineering sociology. The clinicians' basic commitment, however, is not to a particular therapeutic technique, but, rather, to a distinctive role definition. In short, a clinical discipline is not as such a psychological discipline, nor is it distinguished by a cultish commitment to any specific change-agent.

In fine, then, it has been proposed that applied sociology can profit by deliberately modeling itself, particularly its strategy of client relations, on the *several* clinical disciplines and by adapting them to its own needs. To do so effectively, however, it will have to examine reflectively and to codify systematically the elements of clinical activity in the variety of disciplines where they are presently employed. In this way, we may yet fashion a new branch of applied sociology, a clinical sociology, which can aid in mending the rift between the policy maker and the social scientist and in helping groups in their time of trouble.

References *

1. KENNETH BURKE, *Grammar of Rhetoric,* New York: Prentice-Hall, 1952, p. 247.
2. Translated by the author from the French of Emile Durkheim, *Le Socialism,* Paris: Librairie Felix Alcan, 1928, Ch. 1 (page reference not available at time of writing).
3. RAYMOND FIRTH, *Human Types,* London: Thomas Nelson and Sons, Ltd., 1950.
4. ALAN R. HOLMBERG, "Participant Observation in the Field," unpub-

* The references not pertinent to this excerpt have been omitted.

lished dittoed paper, May 5th, 1955, p. 6. May be obtained by writing Alan R. Holmberg, Cornell University.
5. For another perspective on the clinical model cf. ALFRED McCLUNG LEE, "The Clinical Study of Society," *American Sociological Review,* 20 (December 1955), 648–653.
6. Cf. ALEXANDER H. LEIGHTON, *Human Relations in a Changing World: Observations on the Use of The Social Sciences,* New York: E. P. Dutton and Co., 1949, esp. pp. 138, 153, 176.
7. E.g., DANIEL LERNER and HAROLD D. LASSWELL, *The Policy Sciences,* Stanford: Stanford University Press, 1951, esp. Ch. 1.
8. See ROBERT K. MERTON, "The Role of Applied Social Science in the Formation of Policy," *Philosophy of Science,* 16 (1949), 161–181. There is a full discussion of the whole problem in this article, which accents factors somewhat different from those we discuss here.
9. For a generalized discussion of this problem see WILBERT E. MOORE and MELVIN M. TUMIN, "Some Social Functions of Ignorance," *American Sociological Review,* 14 (December 1949), 787–795.
10. WILBUR SCHRAMM, *Utilization of the Behavioral Sciences,* Report of a Planning Review for the Behavioral Sciences Division, Ford Foundation, mimeographed, September 1, 1954.
11. E. A. SHILS, "Social Science and Social Policy," *Philosophy of Sciences,* 16 (1949), pp. 222–223.
12. Cf. SOL TAX, "Anthropology and Administration," *America Indigena,* 5 (1945), pp. 21–33.
13. For another perspective on the clinical model cf. DAVID N. ULRICH, "A Clinical Method in Applied So-

cial Science," *Philosophy of Science,*
16 (1949), esp. pp. 246–247.
14. Cf. Robin M. Williams, *The Re-*

duction of Intergroup Tensions, New
York: Social Science Research Council, 1947, esp. p. 5.

◆◆◆◆◆◆◆◆◆◆◆◆◆◆◆◆◆◆◆◆◆◆ THE ENTRY PROBLEM IN
CONSULTATION   *John C. Glidewell*

THE aim of this paper is to contribute
to the definition of a complex problem
—the problem faced by a consultant
and a client when they first try to enter
into a working relationship. It would
be presumptuous to propose a solution
to such a knotty problem. It seems more
appropriate and realistic to limit this
paper to defining the problem.

The paper is based upon the assumption that the entry of the consultant
is a special case of a more general
problem: the attachment of a new person to an existing social system.

Examples are legion. They might
include the introduction into a family
of a tutor for a child temporarily unable to attend school, the attachment
of a social work consultant to an existing nursing staff, the assignment of a
nursing consultant to a teaching staff,
or the introduction of a human relations consultant to a corporation
board. In each case the members of a
functioning social system find that some
operations are being initiated and performed by a new person. In this case,
the new person, being a consultant, is
presumably authoritative, and also, being new, he is relatively unpredictable.
The problem is that some relationship
to this new person must be developed.
Some relationship must be developed

so that his performance, and the responses of others to it, can be better
predicted. Better prediction will make
his performance more amenable to control in the interests of the goals of the
system—both substantive achievement
goals and affiliative human relations
goals.

Limitations on the Problem

For the purposes at hand, a special
and limited meaning will be given to
the phrase, "attachment to a social
system." It will be used to refer to the
process of development of relationships
with a person who is to be only temporarily a member of the system. It will
not be used to refer to the process of
development of relationships with a
person who is to be a permanent member of the system.[1] It is clearly true
that the consultant role is often being

[1] The term "attachment to a social system"
was borrowed from Jules Henry (1959) who
uses it to refer to the state of being an integral part of a social system—in no way
limited to temporary membership. For present
purposes, however, "attachment" seems to carry
the implication of a temporary arrangement
as intended here. Perhaps the appropriate
analogy is the military arrangement by which
a person who is "attached" to an organization
is only temporarily associated and entitled to
only limited support from the organization.

From John C. Glidewell, "The Entry Problem in Consultation," Journal of Social Issues,
Vol. 15, No. 2, 1959, pp. 51–59. Used by permission.

established these days as a permanent one, but this permanence involves either the development of a new role and, therefore, a basic structural change, or it involves the socialization of a new person into an existing role. Both are more fundamental processes than can be explored here.

Accordingly, this paper is limited to the exploration of the process of initiating a relationship between a client system and a temporary consultant. The consultation functions are to be performed temporarily either because the need is temporary or because the functions can be taken over—after a time —by existing roles.

Consultant versus Consultant-Trainer

It is important to differentiate those functions which are expected to terminate at the expiration of a short term need from those which are expected to be taken over and continued by existing roles. The first requires the application of objects, skills, ideas, or feelings which the client need never possess or control (like prescribing medication, or greasing an auto). The second requires that the client acquire possession and control of the objects, skills, ideas, or feelings, and it, therefore, implies learning (like the improvement of a golf swing, or the recognition of the proper consistency of a pancake batter). The first relationship involves a consultant role; the second, a consultant-trainer role. This paper will be concerned with both roles. The distinction should be kept in mind, however, because the role of the consultant provokes less concern about demands for change in the system than does the consultant-trainer role.

Organizational Attachment and Predictability

It is proposed that a basic criterion of attachment to a social system is predictability. This is a special case of the general proposition that a basic criterion of the existence and nature of relationships is predictability. The statement of lawful relationships takes the form of predicting some aspect of one object or force from a knowledge of other objects or forces.

Any application of this proposition to social relations must take account of the notion that social systems develop ultimate values and immediate goals. For the members of the system, the significant predictability for social roles is the forecast of performance in relation to ultimate values and immediate goals. The kinds of relationships to be developed in the process of attachment to a social system are those which insure, not that one knows just what a member will do in a given situation, but that, whatever he does, it will contribute to ultimate values and immediate goals. If the people in the system set a great store by creativity and invention, it may be important that the exact nature of the performance be *unpredictable*—so long as its goal-orientation is assured. To illustrate, it is not too important to predict just what sort of medicine a doctor will give you when you are sick. You may, in fact, feel that if he is a really good doctor, his treatment will be so clearly unique to the time, to you and your illness, that it would be impossible to predict from facts previously known to you. It is quite important, however, to insure that the physician contributes to the ultimate value of survival (that he doesn't kill you) and to the immediate goal of relief from distress and disability.

A Redefinition of the Problem

From the foregoing conceptions, limitations, and distinctions, the entry problem can be redefined as that of initiating the development of relationships to provide a basis for predicting the contribution to ultimate values and immediate goals of a set of functions having certain characteristics, namely:

They are now needed by the system, although probably to a different degree by different members.

They either are needed only temporarily or can be taken over by existing roles.

They are not now available in the system.

They can be performed expertly by the prospective consultant.

In summary the entry problem becomes more or less difficult, depending upon the goodness of fit between the consultant and the client system with respect to stabilities and change tendencies in terms of perception of need, assignment of values, role expectation, resource and reward allocation, and feelings about the control of dependency. Goodness of fit is intended to imply both congruence (as with values) and complementation (as with roles). The significant dimensions to be fitted can be outlined as follows:

1. Perception of need, in terms of the
   a. extent of consensus in the total system that an immediate need exists, and
   b. importance of the need as measured against the ultimate values of the total system.
2. Perception of appropriateness of role allocation by those empowered to allo-

cate roles, in terms of the criteria that
   a. the needed resources are not available in appropriate persons within the system, and
   b. the needed resources are available in the prospective consultant.
3. Perception of the appropriateness of resource distribution by those empowered to distribute resources, in terms of the criteria
   a. the consultant will be available to the different members on an equitable basis, and
   b. any new objects, ideas, skills, or feelings developed by the consultation process will be equitably distributed.
4. Perception of the appropriateness of reward distribution by those empowered to distribute rewards, in terms of the criteria that
   a. the consultant's fee is appropriate to the need (relative to other needs), and of the quality and quantity of service proposed, and
   b. any rewards (income to the system) accruing from the prospective need reduction will be equitably distributed among the members.
5. Perception of the appropriateness of the probable emotional interchange between the consultant and the members of the system, in terms of the criteria that
   a. the members do not become so dependent that they will not be able to work without consultative support, and
   b. the members do not become so hostile toward or frightened by the dependency involved in the consultation that the consultant cannot be constructively employed.

Each of the five dimensions carries its own dynamic for change. Need perceptions are never entirely satisfactory, and the search for the "real" needs is perpetual. Role allocation can never truly fit the individual differences among people and the ever-changing requirements of the tasks of the system. Both formal and informal role reallocation is continuous, although sometimes painfully slow. Resource distribution can never keep pace with changing needs nor reward distribution with the balance between needs and changing contributions (Parsons & Shils, 1952; Parsons, 1954). Finally, the exchange of feeling can never be all-supportive. Interdependencies always yield fears of dependency. Deprivation —even relative deprivation—yields apathy or rebellion. Evaluation yields fight and flight. Even support can yield jealousy. Any situation into which the consultant intervenes has its own dynamic for constructive changes and restraints (Lewin, 1947). The task is to find and reduce the restraining forces —liberating the growth potential of the system.

Variations in Optimal Conditions for Entry

The foregoing outline of the significant conditions for entry were cast in terms of perceptions. It might be construed to mean that the optimal conditions for entry are those in which the perceptions of the consultant and those of the power centers of the system are in substantial agreement. Such a construction was not intended—and it seems unlikely that such a situation can ever be found. The entry of the consultant into the system implies more or less change in the system— due in part to success or failure in substantive problem solving and in part to the impact of the attachment of a new role to the old system of role, resource, and reward allocation. The

question of optimal entry conditions involves estimates of the extent to which the consultant and the client system may hold congruent, complementary, or conflicting perceptions and change tendencies. Congruence implies almost no change; complementation, slow change; and conflict implies fast change or fast termination of the attachment. The possible combinations of conditions are tremendously large, but it seems likely that most of them have been met somewhere or other in the practice of the helping professions.

Consultation in conflict. Sometimes a consultant finds himself motivated to attach himself to a social system which disagrees with him in all significant respects: about the existence of the need, about the internal availability of resources, about the consultant's resources, about the basis for role, resource, and reward allocation, and about the feelings appropriate in reaction to the consultant's efforts.

The great tradition of the reformer carries with it the theme of consultation in conflict. The theme has had many variations, but more often than not the reforming consultant and his client system have differed most sharply in their perception of the proper locus of power. For example, Poston's work has been stimulated by a gnawing dissatisfaction with power vested in central control of material resources.

Human values were lost in a maze of punch cards and number systems which were devoid of flesh and blood. Neighborhood life in any meaningful sense, the environment which had nurtured initiatives, civic integrity, and social responsibility, began to grow sterile. The control which men had once exercised over their own lives gradually slipped away into distant offices of a centralized and impersonal society. (Poston, 1953, p. 6.)

It was the intent of the consultant to alter the locus of power in the system, and consequently the distribution of roles, resources, and rewards. The success of the first foray of such a reform movement would appear to depend in part upon the direction of changes already under way in the system and in part upon the availability of a sub-system ready to promote the reform. Taylor's dream of a "third force" of efficiency experts independent of both labor and management lacked a power point of entry—until it sold its independence to either management or labor (Taylor, 1911). Poston (1953) seeks his power point of entry in community organization of dormant leadership. His goal is to transfer power from existing "non-democratic" organizations to the new democratic community organization.

Where resistance to consultation is involved, some consultants have been successful as methodologists who suggest and assist in the conduct of self-surveys or other interpretative appraisals by the client system. Attempts to provide interpretive consultation in conflict have produced some remarkable successes, as with the work of Jacques (1952) and the Tavistock Institute, and Lindemann (1957), Kline (1958), and their associates at Wellesley.

One can ask, quite justifiably, whether such change agents as Poston or especially Alinsky (1946) were acting in the consultant's role. There is a broad and vague area which separates the consultant group from the assault force, but, differentiated or not, both must select carefully the point in the power structure at which they enter.

Entry in the dark. As often as not a consultant is called upon to enter the system without any information about the state of affairs within the system with respect to the dimensions significant to entry. He must gather data as he enters, and he must face the possibility that the need is not seen by the most powerful member (e.g. Poston in Montana); that there is no place for the consultant role in the correct perception of role, resource, and reward allocation; and that the typical emotional reaction to the prospect of the consultant role is one of hostility or fear or both. The entering consultant can assume that, in spite of manifest pleas for help, within the informal channels of communication in the client system, many members are committed—each to a different diagnosis, doctor, and treatment plan. Considering the amount of resistance that consultants regularly encounter, the fact that a consultant will enter in the dark is either a compliment to his courage, a comment on his conceit, or a manifestation of his masochism—or all three.

The observation phase. Is there a properly humble posture a prospective consultant can take? Perhaps. He can propose that a provisional relationship be established, enabling him to study the client system and enabling the system to study him. His "entry" is thus confined to the observer role. Observation is threatening to the system, to be sure, but less potent than the active consultant role. And the system is invited to make the observation a two way activity, so that the consultant withholds no information from any members who could be affected by the problem (so far as he knows). If such a temporary arrangement can be made, data can be collected to provide an estimate of whether any active entry can be made at all, and, if so, at what time and place in the system. Where negative indications are found, a constructive withdrawal is presumably possible.

Congruent need perception. A consultant or a client may feel that a minimum requirement for entry is the mutual recognition of the need and its importance. Working on the congruence alone as a base for entry, he will undertake—after an observation phase—a trial period of active consultation. He will propose that the trial period will reveal, first, whether the needed resources are available within the system. If they are found, the relationship can be curtailed and gradually terminated. If they are not found, his own skills can be tested for quality. The distribution of his services among the members of the system can be evaluated from time to time and modified to meet agreed upon requirements for equity. In a like manner the equity of the distribution of other resources and rewards can be insured, with particular attention to the separation of the consultant's and the executive's roles. Finally, the feelings of the members about the consultant's activities can be assessed and, when interpretation seems appropriate, interpreted to the members of the system.

This experimental period is much like the "pilot run" proposed by the Tavistock group (Jacques, 1947), but it differs in that it is seen as a more extensive period of experimentation. It runs through a series of phases but never really ceases to maintain its experimental orientation, particularly where the consultant-trainer role is required (Thelen, 1954).

The crux of the experimental approach is the initial agreement between the consultant and the power figures of the system on the criteria and the rules of evidence by which the experimental results are to be evaluated. Such an agreement may or may not entail a congruence of ultimate values; it must entail agreement on methods and immediate goals.

In developing mental health consultant-trainer roles in public schools, the St. Louis County group began with observation, used a series of conferences to explore perceptions of needs and definition of roles, and to develop a provisional action plan, with a "built-in" evaluation technique. The results were a program with steady growth but a wide variation in need perception, consultant role definition, and action plans, including, in a few cases, the withdrawal of the consultant, (Buchmueller and Domke, 1956; Gildea, et al., 1958; and Glidewell, 1955).

Congruent need and role perceptions. A less adventurous consultant will want not only an agreed upon need, but also an authoritative establishment of the need for and acceptability of his role as consultant and the client's role as consultee. Resistance to consultation is often due to the feeling of the executive that he "ought to" be able to solve the problem without consultation. A successful solution by consultation is feared because, in the eyes of the executive, it would discredit his competence. The establishment and acceptance of the complementary consultation roles can neutralize such a source of resistance.

Given the agreement upon need and role allocation as a basis for entry (this assures the rate of the fee if not its cumulative amount), the consultant and the client system will try to agree upon a series of experiments with resources and reward distribution. Again, the necessary time investment must be made to reach initial agreement on experimental methods and evaluative criteria.

Bases and experimentation. A consultant may seek more and more congruence and leave less and less to experimentation, but at least two limits appear.

The consultant who expects fully to insure appropriate and realistic interchange of feelings between himself and the members is asking for some rather unusual advantages. He is asking for valid and reliable data about the feelings of persons, and this is hard to come by. He is also asking that both he and the client system resolve their conflicts about authority and dependency before he enters. Ten years of human relations training and research and experience by the National Training Laboratories has reaffirmed the significance of dependency conflicts, but it has also established the difficulty of resolving them (e.g., Stock and Thelen, 1958).

A second limit is set by the strength of the value set upon progress and change. At least in western civilization (and certainly in modern India and China) the value set on progress is as strong as the resistance to change. The more the congruence of perception needed by the consultant as a basis for entry, the fewer are the opportunities for change. Most consultants seem to try to strike a balance between an assaultive consultation in conflict and a pedestrian consultation in comfort.

There are, of course, all sorts of possible combinations of agreement and experimentation. Role, resource, and reward distributions often get established before there is an agreement about the nature of the problem. Data collection follows. Sometimes constructive feeling interchanges emerge first and substantive experimentation follows. The situations are as varied as life.

The consultation is often admonished to enter "at the top" of the power structure, but, as has been pointed out (e.g., by Demerath, 1952), in complex organizations there may be many "tops" which will provide points of entry. The combinations and permutations of wholes and parts of a social system present infinite variety.

Experimentation is uncertain, costly in time and work and provisional even in its outcome. Judgment about entry is a matter of calculated risk. Knowledge of the dimensions of the problem aid in the calculation.

Summary

In summary, it has been suggested that the entry problem can be defined in terms of the goodness of fit (in congruence, complementation, or conflict) between the consultant and the client social system with respect to three principal variables:

1. Perception of need.
2. Perception of prospective equity of role, resource, and reward distribution.
3. Perception of prospective appropriateness of feeling interchange, with special concern about dependency and counter-dependency.

References

ALINSKY, SAUL D. *Reveille for Radicals.* Chicago: Univ. of Chicago, 1946.

BUCHMUELLER, A. D. & DOMKE, H. R. "The role of the public health department in preventive mental health services." *Children,* 1956, *3,* 225–231.

DEMERATH, NICHOLAS J. "Initiating and maintaining research relations in a military organization." *Journal of Social Issues,* 1952, *8,* 11–23.

FESTINGER, LEON & KELLEY, HAROLD, H. *Changing Attitudes through Social Contact.* Ann Arbor: Research Center for Group Dynamics, University of Michigan, 1951.

GILDEA, MARGARET C. L. "Community mental health research: findings after three years." *American Journal of Psychiatry,* 1958, *114* (11), 970–976.

GLIDEWELL, JOHN C. "An experimental mental health program in Webster Groves." In *Third Yearbook, American Association Public Schools.* New York: Columbia, 1955.

HENRY, JULES. "Concepts of Social Structure and Personalization." Unpublished manuscript, Washington University, St. Louis, Mo., 1959.

JAQUES, ELLIOTT (ed.) "Social therapy." *Journal of Social Issues,* 1947, *3,* (2), 1–66.

JAQUES, ELLIOTT. *The Changing Culture of a Factory.* New York: Holt, Rinehart and Winston, 1952.

KLEIN, DONALD C., & ROSS, ANN. "Kindergarten entry: a study of the role transition." In Morris Krugman (ed.) *Orthopsychiatry and the School.* New York: American Orthopsychiatric Association, 1958.

LEWIN, KURT, "Frontiers in group dynamics." *Human Relations,* 1947, *1,* 5–41.

LINDEMANN, ELIZABETH. "Mental health in the classroom: The Wellesley experience." A paper presented at the annual meeting of the American Psychological Association, New York, 1957.

LIPPITT, RONALD, WATSON, JEANNE, & WESTLEY, BRUCE. *The Dynamics of Planned Change.* New York: Harcourt, 1958.

MANN, FLOYD C., & LIPPITT, RONALD (eds.) "Social skills in field research." *Journal of Social Issues,* 1952, *8,* (3) 1–58.

PARSONS, TALCOTT, & SHILS, EDWARD A. (eds.) *Toward a General Theory of Action.* Cambridge: Harvard, 1952.

PARSONS, TALCOTT (ed.) *Essays in Sociological Theory.* New York: Free Press of Glencoe, 1954.

POSTON, RICHARD W. *Small Town Renaissance.* New York: Harper, 1950.

POSTON, RICHARD W. *Democracy is You.* New York: Harper, 1953.

STOCK, DOROTHY, & THELEN, HERBERT A. *Emotional Dynamics and Group Culture.* Washington, D.C.: National Training Laboratories, 1958.

TAYLOR, FREDERICK W. *The Principles of Scientific Management.* New York: Harper, 1911.

THELEN, HERBERT A. *The Dynamics of Groups at Work.* Chicago: Univ. of Chicago, 1954.

◇◇◇◇◇◇◇◇◇◇◇◇◇◇◇◇◇◇ THE CONSULTANT-TRAINER ROLE

Charles Seashore and Elmer Van Egmond

THE problem of interpersonal relations among staff members is one of the most difficult areas in which to accomplish planned change in an organi-

From Charles Seashore and Elmer Van Egmond, "The Consultant-Trainer Role in Working Directly with a Total Staff," Journal of Social Issues, *Vol. 15, No. 2, 1959, pp. 36–42. Used by permission.*

zation. Both the nature of the problems and the ways in which resource persons have been utilized have frequently made change attempts fruitless.

Two approaches to the use of outside consultants can be distinguished. One of these centers around consultation and the other around training. Many organizations make use of consultants who have two major functions, diagnosing problems and making recommendations for changes to be carried out by the staff. This approach often fails to achieve changes because initiative, skills, and resources of the staff are not sufficient to implement the change.

A second approach to human relations training involves selecting individuals from an organization and providing them with a learning experience away from the job setting. Here, both the trainer and the trainees are far removed from the locus of specific organizational problems, and the major targets of change are the individual's attitudes and skills, without reference to the other persons in his particular organization. More often than not the individual change is not supported after return to the staff situation and previous patterns of behavior are soon in evidence. The assumption that individual change can lead to organizational change is rarely warranted for this type of training. This is primarily because the training centers on the action of an individual rather than on the interaction of several persons who may be involved in the problem situation.

This paper presents an alternative approach designed to overcome some of these resistances to planned change. In brief, it consists of providing assistance in both diagnosing problems and

carrying out change by involving all members of the organization who are directly related to the problem situation in the development of the skills and resources needed to overcome the difficulty.

Situationally Relevant Training in Effecting Organizational Changes

The orientation of resource persons can be thought of in three terms: the definition of their role, the kinds of problems which serve as the content of the training, and the composition of the groups which serve as the units for training at different stages in the program.

In this approach the role of the resource person combines the functions of the consultant and trainer. As consultants, aid can be given in the diagnosis of problems and the formulation of workable solutions. The trainer function involves helping members of the organization acquire the knowledge and skills necessary to implement changes and establish effective methods for reaching their goals.

The content of the training is derived directly from the kinds of problems which members of the organization are facing. Thus, rather than casting a broad net and utilizing resource materials of a very general nature, the focus is upon handling the immediate problems which confront staff members. An attempt is made to derive generalizations from work on specific situations relevant to the organization as the basis for transfer of training to the work setting rather than depending on deductions from general principles.

The composition of the group involved in training includes staff members most closely connected with the problem being considered. In most cases this group will include members of different status levels so that the training is focused on a "vertical" cross-section of the organizational structure. This is done on the assumption that transfer will be greatly increased if all of the specific problems contributing to interpersonal misunderstanding can be dealt with in the training situation. For example, a subordinate feels insecure in the presence of a superior and is unable to communicate freely to him, with the result that minor irritations on the subordinate's part often become major blocks to the accomplishment of that person's work. This, then, would be taken as a problem for both the individuals involved and the training focus becomes these two persons in interaction rather than either person alone. This method permits a continuous assessment of the problem while directing the energies of both persons toward seeking solutions to the problem. Skill practice can be given to the subordinate in communicating with his specific supervisor rather than in the more abstract skill of communicating to supervisors generally.

Characteristics of the Consultant-Trainer Approach

One of the important implications of this approach is that all staff persons involved in a given problem become aware of how others perceive the situation and participate in the formulation of solutions. Everyone has an opportunity to share both the attempts and the progress of others in bringing about necessary changes in skills and attitudes. This is in contrast to the kind of training where individuals receive assistance outside of the problem situation and thus are unaware of the attempts and intentions of others involved to bring about changes. Awareness of the diagnoses, attitudes, skills, and attempts to change both oneself and others is seen as a critical factor in integrating efforts of individuals in an organization toward a more effective level of functioning.

It must be emphasized, however, that the consultant-training program is not seen by the individuals involved as a part of the everyday functioning of the organization. By virtue of the presence of resource persons, participants defined the situation so that they felt "Now we are doing something different." Different standards of what is appropriate and not appropriate as a focus for attention are applied than is the case in normal daily work situations. Thus, it might better be called "at the elbow" training for an organization rather than "on the job" training.

This is a rather simple and direct answer to the often voiced and often justified complaint of individuals who have been involved in human relations training programs, "This was a wonderful experience, and it's too bad my boss couldn't have been here because he's really the one who needs this." To be sure, this answer carries with it several disadvantages not found in the more traditional approach, especially the unwillingness of persons to expose themselves to criticism or to criticize others who are higher in status structure. We have found that the advantages of a group effort at change and direct application to the everyday work in an organization outweigh the impact of the inhibitions mentioned above.

This approach to training is, so far as we know, somewhat distinctive in that more than one status level in an organization is involved in a training program oriented toward specific interpersonal tensions which exist between persons on different levels. Changes which reduce tensions involve changes in attitudes, behavior patterns, and skills in interpersonal relations. In the next section we would like to illustrate three ways in which these changes were brought about by describing this image of the consultant trainer in a concrete consulting situation.

The Application of this Approach to Three Kinds of Problems

The consultant-trainer approach was applied to work in a school system where the program focused on staff relationships. The training group involved the superintendent, principal, assistant principal, and twenty teachers. Meetings of the group were held bi-monthly on after-school time. Participation in the program was on a voluntary basis. Approximately half of the teaching staff elected to participate. The program was initiated by the school's request for consultant help.

Communication within the staff was the problem area selected for training by the members of the group. This included many kinds of specific problems ranging from the sending of messages to the attitudes and feelings of individuals which were blocking or facilitating communication. We have selected three problems which are closely interrelated in their effect upon the organization but distinct in the sense that a different training design was appropriate for each of them.

1. THE BLOCKING OF COMMUNICATION DUE TO UNWARRANTED ATTITUDES AND FEELINGS OF STAFF MEMBERS TOWARD ONE ANOTHER

Where there is infrequent contact between members of an organization who are dependent upon one another for efficient work, it is quite likely that unwarranted opinions and feelings will develop since all the facts are neither available nor freely communicated. These opinions and feelings can then serve as a screen through which behavior of the other person is interpreted, causing distortion of the communication which does take place.

We were aware of this kind of problem in listening to various persons talk about the factors which helped or hindered them in their jobs. It became clear that both the intentions and the behavior of co-workers were being misunderstood and distorted. This generated attitudes which further inhibited communication.

Utilization of a group setting which included all of the relevant persons enabled three activities to take place: catharsis, reality testing, and problem solving. Frustrations had grown up over a period of time and we found that it was necessary for these to be expressed before good channels of communication could be set up. In the process of catharsis, it was also possible to do some reality testing to see if the attitudes and feelings were warranted or whether they had arisen out of lack of communication and resulting frustrations. Following reality testing of attitudes and opinions, those which did seem to be warranted were examined in terms of whether or not they were functional to the achievement of the goals of the individuals and organization and, if not, what conditions needed to be changed to make them functional.

Our attempt here was to first "unfreeze" the old attitudes and feelings and move toward a more realistic and functional set of beliefs on the part of individuals. Our next concern was to "freeze," at least temporarily, these new perceptions. Thus, our link to the future operation of the organization was the immediate establishment and maintenance of new attitudes which would allow us to move ahead on other facets of the communication problem.

2. THE LACK OF CORRECTIVE METHODS FOR ALTERING MALADAPTIVE PATTERNS OF BEHAVIOR

New information is constantly generated in an organization and this requires further alterations in feelings, attitudes, and behavior. As new things are tried, evaluation is needed to assess the helpfulness of changes. There is also the possibility that misunderstandings and misconceptions may develop since perfect communication does not exist at all times. This is particularly true of high status persons in the organization who do not ordinarily receive information from lower status members without the occurrence of some screening process. For a superior to desire feedback on how his behavior affects others is not enough; those who are able to give the information must see his willingness to listen and feel that the transmission of information can result in a desirable change in the superior's attitudes and behavior.

Following a request by the superintendent for feedback from the staff, a meeting which included representatives from different staff levels was planned. In this small group setting, staff members were able to express to the superintendent how they felt his behavior related to specific problem situations. As consultant-trainers, our function included setting the standards of the meeting, acting as initiators, and either probing, remaining passive, or providing emotional support to indi-

viduals as it seemed appropriate. The attempt here was to provide an opportunity for the status person to discover how specific behaviors on his part affected others, and to relate these feelings to his intentions. Discrepancies between one's intentions and the reactions one evokes in others can then be used as the basis for change. A summary of this meeting was given to the entire training group at their next meeting.

This served as a learning method which might continuously be used by the staff in assessing discrepancies between their intentions and the way their behavior is seen by those with whom they are interacting. The link between our activity as consultant-trainers and future change in the organization was to provide a model of a corrective mechanism which could be used for continuous evaluation and change *after* we terminated our relationship with them.

3. LACK OF DIRECT COMMUNICATION CHANNELS BETWEEN DIFFERENT PARTS OF THE ORGANIZATION

One of the major problems of the top men in organizations concerns the demands that are made upon their time by others. Everybody wants to talk to the top management, but this usually is an impossibility. Although much of the responsibility and authority had been delegated to assistants in this organization, there still remained a real need for those on the staff to have direct communication on matters about which only the superintendent was fully informed. The problem was to devise a method which would meet the needs but not put undue demands upon his time.

When this problem became apparent

to members of the group, it was decided to try out some different approaches to solving the difficulty by taking actual areas where staff members felt the need for communication. A meeting was designed to meet this need while keeping within the realistic limits of the amount of available time the superintendent would actually have. Training involved setting up a model which could be evaluated and revised on the basis of some trial runs.

Many of the factors which were present in the real situations were built into the training model so that it could be easily adapted and transferred to the existing structure of the organization. So a third link between consultant-trainer activity and organizational change is setting up a model which involves as many of the real elements of the normal daily operation as possible with the group members then having responsibility for transferring the model into the routine operation of the institution either during or after the consultant-trainer activity.

The Consultant-Trainer as an Agent of Organizational Change

From this experience we see several different ways in which consultant-trainers can contribute to the change process.

1. FREEING PERSONNEL IN THE ORGANIZATION TO PARTICIPATE IN THE TRAINING PROCESS

It is very difficult for persons within an organization to act as consultant-trainers in dealing with interpersonal situations in which they may be involved. As outside persons we could take a neutral stand, that is, a problem-solving rather than an evaluative at-

titude, toward the situation. We were able to free persons at all levels of the organization to be active in both diagnosing and working out solutions to problems, and to open up the possibility of examining how each person in the organization related to the situation in question.

2. SERVING AS THE STIMULUS FOR REDEFINING THE SITUATION

By our very presence, it was possible for individuals to see this as a different situation from the normal daily operation of the school. The meetings were seen by most participants as a situation in which they could be secure in the expression of attitudes and feelings which would have been very threatening had they been expressed in the job situation. This security was derived at least in part, from the perception of common commitment and purpose by those who elected to be in the change program, with the consultant-trainer roles seen as instrumental in this process. It is interesting to note that even where we took a very passive role we were still seen as necessary members in enabling the group to work on the problem.

3. PROVIDING INITIATIVE IN EXPLORING DIFFICULT OR UNKNOWN PROBLEM AREAS

In this organization, as in most, there had developed norms and standards against certain types of behavior such as evaluation of the performance of those higher than oneself in the status structure, exposure of areas of weakness in one's own abilities, or even communicating with persons on status levels other than one's own. Even though these were recognized and defined as problem areas by the members of the group, there was still considerable hesitation in violating the old standards. By providing a model and by sanctioning as legitimate those behaviors necessary to explore the problem, the consultant-trainers were able to help the group move forward in areas seen by the staff as involving difficult interpersonal relationships.

It is also possible for a neutral person to see when there is readiness to move ahead on a problem although neither party in a conflict may be sure in his own mind that the other is ready. For example, even though the superintendent had expressed a desire to receive some feedback, and members of the staff wanted to communicate their feelings to him, neither was able to initiate this type of discussion without some impetus from the consultant-trainers. Once started, it was possible for the staff to continue working on the problem by themselves.

4. PROVIDING CONTINUOUS SUPPORT AS THE CHANGE PROCESS IS STARTED

Most changes in the interpersonal relations in an organization will involve negative as well as positive experiences for the individuals concerned. By having a continuing responsibility over a period of time during which change is occurring, the consultant-trainer can help to provide support which aids the group in getting over the negative and sometimes very painful experiences which lie along the path toward a more effective level of functioning.

5. AID IN CONTINUOUS DIAGNOSIS OF PROBLEMS

Many of the implications of the process of change cannot be foreseen, and in fact the change process may bring about or reveal other problems as serious as those which it is designed to alleviate. The consultant-trainer can help in the diagnosis and treatment of these secondary problems by working with the group in the process of change rather than merely providing a prescription for changes based on his initial diagnosis.

6. PROVIDING HELPFUL INFORMATION, PROCEDURES, AND RESOURCES

One of the major contributions of the consultant-trainer is the knowledge he brings to the situation of kinds of learning situations and skills that might be helpful in dealing with specific kinds of problems. Thus, through both conceptual ability and skill in structuring learning situations the consultant-trainer can provide a path toward the solutions of problems. This skill may vary from providing relevant reading material or setting up a role-playing situation to leading a discussion in a particularly difficult area or giving a lecture. As such he is bringing resources and skills to the organization which generally are not available among members of its staff.

◇◇◇◇◇◇◇◇◇◇◇◇◇◇◇◇◇◇◇◇◇◇ PROBLEMS AND PROSPECTS
OF APPLIED RESEARCH *Robert Chin*

Loosening up of the positions of researcher and practitioner in areas which do not affect the core goals of each role will make for better working relations. The present chapter attempts to explore the flexibility of research activities, justify some of these research choices in terms of the educational practitioners' requirement and, in this sense, move the researcher closer to the practitioner. The purpose of this chapter, then, is to examine policy choices in conducting research on educational programs. First, this examination will be undertaken in terms of type of research to be done; then within types, choices of variables and their bases will be examined. Thus the first section deals with the different uses of research. Next, we list some dimensions which need to be taken into account in choosing the dependent or criterion variables. The statements throughout the chapter are offered in the form of positive assertion rather than in a spirit of inquiry. Repeated qualifications and disclaimers would tend to obscure the presentation.

This chapter violates a canon presented later, namely, the principle of reasonableness of achievement. Admittedly, no research project can fulfill all of the conditions raised in this presentation. They are presented in the spirit of illuminating the more general field of research, setting forth policy choices, and providing some of the bench marks or guidelines with which studies of citizenship education might proceed. We have not canvassed systematically or catalogued all of the relevant applied and evaluation research studies, but we will use some of these as illustrations of our points. Our general position might be made explicit: we assume that social practice needs a specialized approach to research, which can contribute to the practitioner's science and provide some hunches for his art. Thus, we have kept an eye on a wide spectrum of evaluation and applied research, assuming that all such fields face some problems in common.

Uses of Research on Programs of Education, Action, Training, or Treatment

Underlying all research is the use of the scientific method as a spirit or mode of approach and as an assumption in a philosophy of science. Throughout this chapter, we assume that the canons of scientific method are not violated. We *are* concerned with the various forms which scientific inquiry may take. We suggest that there are distinguishably different purposes in conducting research on programs of action and that the purposes affect our design, the factors studied, the kinds of conclu-

Excerpts from Robert Chin, "Problems and Prospects of Research: Research Approaches to the Problem of Civic Training," in The Adolescent Citizen, *by Franklin Patterson and others. New York: The Free Press of Glencoe, Inc., 1960, pp. 247–268. Abridged and used by permission.*

sions we may draw, and the contribution we make. Our efforts will be more feasible and, in turn, more useful, when we are cognizant of our primary goals, or combination of goals, in conducting research on programs of action designed to improve training. Chein, Cook, and Harding decry arguments over "pure" and "applied" science and state that

scientific techniques may be adapted to nonscientific practical purposes, but if the sole concern is with the practical purposes and not at all with exploring the unknown or contributing to the systematization of knowledge, then the adapter may be a high grade technologist, but he is not a scientist, "pure" or "applied." A physician, for example, does not become a scientist merely by doing urine analyses.[1]

As we shall see, an orientation to the development of systematic knowledge underlies many of the positions to be stated.

Our approach uses the language of independent, dependent, and criterion variables, since we are concerned with the determining conditions of events. Independent variables are those variables that are altered from their usual state in order to see what happens to the event. A program of action, education, or training is created or altered to see what improvements occur. The term *criterion variable* is used here to refer to the selected dependent variables which are considered to be at the "criterion," the "pay off," or success-failure level. That is, criterion variables are deliberately selected from the gamut of dependent variables, on the basis of some practical interest other than scientific requirements.

[1] I. Chein, S. Cook and J. Harding, "The Field of Action Research." *American Psychologist*, 3:43–50, 1948.

The six uses of research we distinguish below are not always separable in a project. More frequently than not, however, we can determine the primary aim, or usable result, of a study. A chart is presented as a concise statement of our judgments about the variables, design and control, and the kinds of utility they may have to practitioners.

RESEARCH USED FOR DETERMINING EFFECTIVENESS OF A PROGRAM OF ACTION OR TRAINING

The usual distinction separating evaluation research from basic research is that evaluation research in social practice is centered around determining the effects of a specific program of action or training, for instance, a therapy program, an educational experiment, a workshop, or an institute. Increasingly, practitioners in education, social work, therapy, re-education, and group training are willing and eager to conduct evaluation research on their programs. Practitioners have been concerned with estimating the effectiveness of their programs or educational designs or justifying to an administration the policy and budget of an experimental program, and, at times, with reassuring themselves in order to quell their own gnawing doubts. In general, the research emphasis is on determining whether any other "changes" occurred. Two studies of youth groups in summer nonschool programs may be cited as illustrations. Riecken studied the Quaker Work Camps[2] for college students by using pre- and postmeasures

[2] H. W. Riecken, Jr., *Volunteer Work Camp: A Psychological Evaluation*. Cambridge, Massachusetts: Addison-Wesley Press, Inc., 1952.

of variables that were representative of the sponsoring organization's goals. The Hyman and Wright study[3] of the Encampment for Citizenship (ages 17–24) is a very sophisticated and ingenious analysis of pre- and postquestionnaire data on citizenship. Hyman and Wright designed questionnaire instruments for assessing six areas. (1) campers' basic values—free response to questions about worthy ambition, ingredients of an ideal society, personal sacrifice, criteria for ranking occupations, and personal career goals; (2) action orientation—check lists, scales, free response procedures on local, national, and international problems; (3) cognition of social problems—batteries and indices on optimism, time perspective perceived, individual and group potency; (4) salient social attitudes and opinions —15 scales; (5) perceived relationship with rest of society—three scales; (6) conduct—free responses and sociometric friendship.

Methodologically, in such studies dependent variables, also called the criterion variables, were chosen on the basis of the sponsor's goals, and various aspects of the program as a whole were used as independent variables. The design has varied from simple postprogram subjective reactions of clients-trainees or the practitioner, to *post hoc* quasi-experimental designs, to sophisticated pre- and posttests with control groups. The researcher's role has been to provide technical competence for handling problems of measurement and design. There have usually been a great number of uncontrolled factors

[3] H. H. Hyman and C. R. Wright, *Youth in Transition: An Evaluation of the Contribution of the Encampment for Citizenship to the Education of Youth.* New York Bureau of Applied Social Research, Columbia University, 1956. (Mimeographed)

in such studies, some of which it has been possible to separate out by ingenious analytic procedures. For instance, Hyman and Wright separate out some of the "background" factors which might be producing change with the Encampment program.

However helpful to the sponsors such studies may be, such evaluation, in our opinion, produces few guides for the improvement of programs, for practical decisions, or for general knowledge relevant to other practitioners. In other words, we do not have any more understanding of the process of action and of action implications for use by practitioners. We can only say, "Go and do likewise," but we do not specify what is the thing to do. For the sponsor, any change in the program becomes tampering and tinkering, since such efforts represent a blind stab at a jumble of swirling factors, any one of which could have produced the obtained degree of effectiveness. Some values, however, are derivable indirectly from such research. The practitioner knows what general kind of program produces some results. He has demonstrated that the criterion variable can be altered toward the desired direction. Further, evaluated demonstration projects, or pilot projects, provide practioners with clues for their technologies and methods. The conditions for spread of the influence of a demonstration or pilot project need to be conceptualized in a theory of long-range changing if we are to avoid the dying out of consequences soon after the pilot project is stopped. The social historian, with his tools of retrospective analysis, has an important role in helping to analyze and test a theory of influence of pilot projects.

RESEARCH USED FOR SOME DECISION, POLICY, OR FUTURE SITUATION

Research may be conducted for prediction of how people will fare in the future. In the field of psychometrics, for example, we are beginning to realize that generalized measurement of people's attitudes, aptitudes, and so on, is not so valuable (nor in one sense possible) as evaluation research done in the light of the requirements of a decision, policy alternative, or future situation.

The kinds of questions involved typically are: What would happen if we decided to do this rather than that? What consequences are involved in one policy as against another policy? The field called policy science or strategy analysis (theory of games), for example, uses relatively fixed alternatives (criterion variables) and studies the conditions and consequences of one kind as over against another kind of decision. The second type of research, which uses future situations as criterion variables, is included in this section because of the preselection of future states. Ideally, a long time span is needed in a research project of this kind to check whether the predictions hold. A difficulty in design of the research, namely, the self-fulfilling prophecy, needs to be attended to in studying the effects of a decision based on predictions in social affairs.

Such procedures of evaluation are essentially correlative in design, with minimum attention paid to the explanation of how or why the events occur. One advantage of such applied research, in addition to its practicality, is the notion of "levels." We can more realistically estimate the potential of a program in the light of "costs," including the social costs, and the balance of other educational program needs. While practical in this sense, such evaluation research is limited in the amount of understanding it provides.

RESEARCH USED FOR STUDYING AND IMPROVING SPECIFIC PROCEDURES, TECHNIQUES, OR INTERVENTIONS

Research on action programs may be used for studying, examining, and, hopefully, improving a specific procedure, technique, treatment, or intervention. The physical sciences have developed their practical engineering knowledge along this line. The medical sciences have undertaken extensive empirical studies, basic and applied, to evaluate drugs, therapies, and treatments.

Such uses differ from the use of research for general effectiveness in that the research on effectiveness (first category above) is global and not differentiated in isolating its techniques or treatments, while this use is designed specifically to tell how a treatment or technique works. The criterion variable is usually some preselected desired outcome with known validity and reliability. Studies as these, as well as the first type, are apt to be questioned in terms of their "Hawthorne effect," where the very fact of doing something produces self-reported changes. Colds get better with or without antihistamines; workers improve their productivity in the Western Electric Hawthorne plant; workshoppers feel they change; and so forth. Further, theories and conceptual formulations face a major issue, "the notion of unanticipated consequences." Sociologists such as Merton, among others, point out that the actor cannot anticipate all the consequences in a deterministic explanation of his social action, a notion forcefully applicable to present-day social practitioners, due partly to limitations of available knowledge and also to the nature of persons, groups, and social institutions and their processes. A well-designed and controlled attempt, which failed for other reasons, is a study where a specific hypothesis about how a group leader might act in interracial situations was tested. The hypothesis was: "Where friendly feelings characterize the relationships between members of a group of mixed ethnic composition and individual differences from the stereotypes become apparent, the 'isolation' process can be appreciably lessened, and the generalization of the newly developed feelings of friendship to the entire ethnic group promoted if the group leaders frequently call attention to the ethnic affiliations of the group members."

Another issue is whether the description of the intentions and actions of the program as given by the staff are sufficient, or whether we need to assess by direct observation, or even by obtaining from the students their perceptions of the stimulus value of the program or treatment. We need to know the student's "definition of the situation," namely, the program or treatment, before we have an adequate statement of the program under evaluation.

Evaluation to Affect the Conductors of a Program

Much research on programs of action has been conducted under the heading of action research, or "participant action research," or cooperative inquiry. In education, we find a deep concern with involving teachers in a program of action in order to in-

duce learning and change. The Detroit Study and Teachers College Studies are examples of community action studies; action research is closely associated with the programs of Kurt Lewin, Stuart Cook, and Ronald Lippitt. The assumption is that people who are to take action must also be involved in the research process from the very beginning. Not only will they more keenly realize the need for the particular action program finally decided upon, but their ego investments, to use Lippitt's phrase, are brought in on the side of the action program. Without this collaboration, research, diagnosis, and recommendations for change tend to stimulate insecurity, aggression, and rationalization rather than motivated efforts to make changes.

In the evaluation studies called action research, evaluators report, mostly by anecdote, the involvement, good will, increased sensitization, and so forth, of the conductor-teachers-leaders. Such an approach or use of evaluation research has much theoretical and empirical justification in terms of installing, maintaining, and expanding change. If this is the primary use of the evaluation or action research, then the degree of precision of data gathered on the students may be irrelevant, so long as action is steered into the desired channels. However, our position is that both the students' learnings and the teacher's new way of behaving and teaching must be assessed and measured independently. The action-research studies in the community face the same difficulty.

I suggest that, due to the institutional networks in which the learning process is conducted, and to the suggestions emerging from the theoretical emphases on the interdependency of forces involved in change and resistance to change, we need to take into account the involvement of the whole system, especially the teachers and administrators and pupils. Engaging such people in evaluation research jointly with the researchers has been proposed as a procedure to unfreeze the situation, establish direction, and move to a new level of performance on the part of all, with some sacrifice of the quality of data.

RESEARCH USED FOR BUILDING AND TESTING THE PRACTITIONER'S THEORY OF CHANGING

Social practitioners need to develop a systematic body of principles and tested theory relevant to their practices. They need to arrive at a general theory of changing others—the client system—and get beyond seeing only specific and concrete programs of action or treatment. Research used for building and testing the practitioner's theory of changing differs in orientation from the other uses described in this section. This orientation involves a more conceptual and explicit subsumption of the specific practices in each situation or even discipline, deliberate choice of independent and criterion variables according to some dimensions (outlined later in this chapter), explicit recognition of and "philosophizing" about inherent value questions, analysis of the practical judgments called for in relating theory and confronting cases, and subjecting all of this to as much empirical research as possible. Such research is not interested in a practice by a person with one kind of clients-students, as such, but uses such situations to test general propositions about a theory of changing or action.

Lippitt, Watson, and Westley in their study of the dynamics of planned change present a conceptual orientation for the analysis of the role of the consultant-change agent. The work by Hovland, *et al.*, on attitude change takes on some of the properties of a general theory of changing. The National Training Laboratory's theorization and empirical studies of "training groups" represent the formulation and testing of propositions relevant to groups designed for the specific purposes of learning and re-education, with attention paid to the role and style of the trainer and its effects.[12] The anthropologists' analyses of propositions about deliberate interventions into cultural systems are also instances of using research for building and testing the practitioner's theory of changing persons, situations, and cultures.

This chapter as a whole, in fact, has been analyzing the problems and prospects of research from the point of view of one who feels that the building and testing of the practitioner's theory of changing is the most useful approach for our purposes.

USE OF RESEARCH FOR SCIENCE BUILDING

At times, research on programs of action may be used for purposes of basic science building. In such cases, since the problems of investigation are dictated by the conceptual schema, or a difficulty in the schema, a gap of knowledge, a conflict of theory, or an unknown factor, the research uses the program of action as a convenient place to observe and test phenomena. It is often agreed that basic social science will contribute more to the field of practice than applied research. There are enough historical examples to justify this statement. It is our thesis that two of the categories above—Research Used for Studying and Improving Specific Procedures, Techniques, or Interventions, and Research Used for Building and Testing the Practitioner's Theory of Changing—*can be* basic research and *are* science building. Our present category is a residual category of basic science and is included in this chapter as a proper and justifiable activity in research on programs of action.

In problems of citizenship education, gaps of information about adolescents, educational and learning processes, social organization of schools, peer culture, personality development, group membership roles, and development of attitudes toward the operation of power in our society are more numerous than solid theory and knowledge. Other chapters in this volume survey the state of theory and knowledge in these areas.

Selection of Criterion Variables

The selection of the criterion variables depends upon the uses to which a study is put, of course. We are using the term criterion variable to refer to the selected dependent variable which is accepted as the "pay-off." In all of the following points, it is assumed that there are options and choices open to the investigator and that these choices do not violate any of the requirements of the scientific method. We attempt to spell out one set of values which determines the choices; we assume one guiding set of values to be that research on programs of action should be of relevance to a practitioner.

1. Do not assume unitary and highly correlated variables for such criteria as "group movement," "improvement

in therapy," "increased effectiveness," "better mental health." The same point holds for "citizenship." It should not be assumed that the multitude of psychological, sociological, and behavioral events involved are correlated. The problem is one open to empirical investigation.

2. Value judgments about the criterion variables have to be made, and should be made, explicitly. Some sources of validation for such judgments come from the goals and concepts of the profession, sociocultural ethos, the acknowledged requirements of the situation of action, and inferences drawn from available technical knowledge. One dimension of such value judgments is the question of whether we define citizenship as the absence of known "bad," pathological, or undesirable characteristics, or the presence of some desirable state or gestalt of factors. It is easier, given present knowledge, to define and study the concept in terms of the absence of undesirable traits, such as the lack of authoritarian characteristics.

3. Try to gather information from the subjective ratings of the client-trainee and the program-conductors, as well as the "objective" tests and ratings. Many of the attributes of citizenship are probably subjective.

4. Choose criterion variables on the basis of centrality to other related concepts and avoid trivial criteria whenever possible. For instance, a central criterion not usually listed is learning how to learn.

5. Make sure that the criterion chosen is accessible to observation and measurement.

6. Do not load the dice against the program of training by choosing ultimate and "perfect state" criterion variables. Be realistic about the "rea-

CHART FOR LOCATING DESIGN AND UTILITY FACTORS ACCORDING TO RESEARCH USE

	1 EVALUATIVE RESEARCH	*2* PREDICTIVE RESEARCH	*3* TECHNIQUE RESEARCH	*4* ACTION RESEARCH	*5* PRACTITIONER THEORY RESEARCH	*6* SCIENCE BUILDING RESEARCH
	Assessing effectiveness of a program	*For making decision*	*Testing a method*	*Affecting conduct*	*Building practitioner basic science*	*Building, testing general basic social science*
A. DESIGN AND RESEARCH						
1. Criterion or Dependent Variables	Program sponsors' goals	Predictive value	Preselected pay-off variable	Actions, reactions of conductor	Based on theory, hypotheses, options	Based on theory, hypotheses, options
2. Independent Variables	Descriptive program	Not relevant, correlates	Method Treatment	Unknown	Theory and levers of action	Theory
3. a. Design Model	Post reactions, prepost	Statistical, correlational	Experimental manipulation	Unknown	Full range of models	Full range of models
3. b. Uncontrolled Factors Inherent	Great	Great	Slight	Great	Varies according to design	Slight
3. c. Attention to Characteristics of Persons in Programs	Slight	Great	Slight	Great	Great	Moderate
B. UTILITY TO PRACTITIONER						
1. Explanation and Understanding	None	None	Slight	None	Great	Moderate
2. Generality	None	Slight	Moderate	Slight	Great	Great
3. Action Levers Exposed	Slight	Moderate	Great	Slight	Great	Slight to moderate

sonableness of achievement" of the criterion for such a program. Is it reasonable that a one-semester course should change authoritarians into democratic citizens? Or that emotional adjustment should be attained by a social studies curriculum? Or that a fifteen-hour citizenship indoctrination program in the armed forces should protect the men from their enemies' "brainwashing"? We need to set up as the level of the criterion variables reasonable small steps or stages *toward* the ultimate (and unattainable) perfect states.

7. We need to do more examination of the negative or side effects of a program of action. Do people in learning membership roles also develop intolerance toward group decision as well as appreciation? Do citizenship education programs also develop a sentimental sense of sacredness about our social institutions and values which acts as a block against social change and healthy social criticism? Are we also teaching conformity, albeit to our approach or values?

8. We need to choose our variables for maximum significance, generality, and utility for practitioners. Our criteria should be potentially reachable under other leadership, staff persons, or school situations. We should maximize the available levers of action that are accessible most reasonably in terms of minimum costs and energy required. Pilot studies in citizenship education with large and important goals might seem to say to the schools not included in the original study: "If you want to do what we have accomplished, go get yourself the same size grant from a foundation!" or "hire some of our skilled staff," or "get someone with the personality pattern of our director."

9. Choose on the basis of giving more attention to the more manipulable factors that bring about the desired outcome. For instance, if we suspect both social class and role are involved, choose role as your independent variable, since it can be more readily manipulated. Or choose attitudes as compared to intelligence for your independent variable.

10. Include some laymen's hypotheses and variables. Ask for and test the ideas, notions, hypotheses of teachers and students on "what brings about good citizenship?"

11. Plan for unanticipated consequences in outcome. Use some open-minded questions about outcomes to catch the consequences not originally planned for either by the program or by the evaluators.

12. In interpretation, and possibly in design, minimize the effects of the "placebo effect," or "Hawthorne effect." In your questionnaire or interview, disguise or use indirect tappings of increases of manifestation of citizenship. Or use in questions alternatives which are perceived as equally legitimate and desirable so as to avoid the respondent's giving back what he thinks you want.

Measurement Problems

The first and central issue is the question of defining the variables under study in such a way that some operational coordinates may be found. The Detroit Study laid out three levels to cope with this question: goals, criteria, and manifestations. The manifestations can then be looked for by whatever techniques seem appropriate.

The technical questions of empirical research of reliability and validity are paramount. We shall pass over the issues of reliability of the measuring instrument, since the technical issues need not concern us at this time except to reiterate the necessity of assessing and reporting the reliability of the measuring instrument being used. The issue of validity (is the instrument measuring what it is purporting to measure?), however, is of more concern. A recent statement by Cronback and Meehl provides some clues for study of aspects of citizenship education. They distinguish four kinds of validity in measurement: predictive, concurrent, content, and construct. It is the last which is of interest to us. They say "construct validation is involved whenever a test is to be interpreted as a measure of some attribute or quality which is not 'operationally defined.' " It is used when the tester has no definite measure of the quality with which he is concerned and must use indirect measures. They point significantly to personality tests and some tests of ability as instances where con-

struct validity needs to be employed. They make these points:
1. A construct is defined implicitly by a network of associations or propositions in which it occurs. Constructs employed at different stages of research vary in definitions.
2. Construct validation is possible only when some of the statements in the network lead to predicted relations among observables.
3. The network defining the construct, and the derivation leading to the predicted observation, must be reasonably explicit so that validating evidence may be properly interpreted.

Difficult as this process of theory-building and hypothesis-deriving may be, it seems the most fruitful, if not the only possible, way to engage in research on citizenship education. Measurement then becomes a matter of establishing the reliability of the procedure to tap the attitudes and values or actions and conduct of the youth.

❖❖❖❖❖❖❖❖❖❖❖❖❖❖❖❖❖❖ OPERATIONAL RESEARCH

Kenneth D. Benne

I WOULD like to start with some of the possible treatments of "operational research" which I am *not* attempting here. (1) I am not *selling* "operational research" as the answer for: (a) the upgrading of the profession of health educators; (b) the filling of all gaps in the professional knowledge needed by contemporary health educators; or

(c) the major tool for transforming health education programs toward greater effectiveness and efficiency. I sincerely believe that "operational research" can contribute to all of these desirable outcomes. But I also believe that critical evaluation *by* professional leaders of what is called variously "action," "operational," and "applied"

From Kenneth D. Benne, "Operational Research in Health Education," Health Educa-tion Monographs, No. 5, 1959, pp. 20–28. Originally the keynote address made at the annual conference of the Society of Public Health Educators, St. Louis, Missouri, October 25, 1958. Used by permission.

research is better calculated at the present time to advance these contributions than *selling* to professional leaders. (2) I am not trying to demonstrate verbally that operational research, stimulated, led, and carried through by social practitioners in the interest of more adequate professional policies and programs, is possible. This may well have been useful when John Collier and other pioneers began to urge the feasibility and desirability of "operational research" a quarter of a century ago, but we now have numerous examples of operational research to point to in many professions. Its possibility has been demonstrated in fact. What is needed now is critical appraisal. (3) I am not trying to explicate the many technical problems of problem selection and delimitation, experimental design, construction and adaptation of instruments for data collection, sampling, etc., which dog "operational researchers," as they also dog "basic researchers," though with added complications for the former. Dealing with such technical problems is important but more appropriate to an extended seminar than to a brief professional conference.

A Context for Critical Appraisal

What, therefore, I propose to do is to take the stance of the sympathetic but critical appraiser of "operational research" in the professional activities of health educators. The critic needs to place what he is appraising in a context which permits him to relate it to other alternatives and to a test in terms of its wider consequences, its feasibility, and its desirability. In what context should we place "operational research" in appraising it, particularly from the standpoint of professional health educators?

We are now living in the midst of a dangerous and widening gap between "common sense" and "science" as arbiters of choices and decisions in human affairs. (I prefer this polarity to the all too familiar dichotomy of "theory" and "practice." For "common sense" has its theoretical aspects, often sweeping ones, though frequently unacknowledged and unsystematized, as well as its practices and techniques. And "science" has its practices and techniques, implicit and explicit, as well as its "theories.") Do health educators, along with associated lay boards, councils, and committees, decide what programs to undertake, what program goals to emphasize or de-emphasize, what methods and organization to employ on the basis of "common sense" or on the basis of "science"? Is "common sense" (an amalgam of traditions, lore, wisdom, principles abstracted from practical experience, the advices and preferences of reigning elites) more dependable, reliable, and valid as a basis for policy and program construction and reconstruction than knowledge drawn from basic research in the behavioral sciences or knowledge derived from the application of scientific methodologies to the study of policy problems in the setting of practice?

The gap continually widens between the two methods as scientific research is pursued in physics, chemistry, and biology, and as related engineering or applied science disciplines use scientific methods to translate these findings into technologies in the practices of health, industrial production, war and defense. In human affairs, a vocal and influential part of our culture counsels dependence upon *common sense,* and its rationalizations in traditional humanities and religions, and opposes the extension of science into the solution of human problems. Other parts of our culture promote the extension of *science,* basic and applied, in the management of human affairs. So the split becomes a social and cultural, as well as an intellectual, split.

And the split extends also into the persons who must negotiate this divided culture in their life and work. This split is nowhere more poignant than in professionals in the fields of social practice. Health educators are taught scientific approaches to health and disease, diagnosis, treatment and prevention. Their task is to communicate this knowledge to people in a way to affect their conduct with respect to the maintenance and restoration of health and the prevention of disease. But how are their policies and programs for communicating with people, influencing their learning and conduct, organizing them both to learn and to act in health matters, determined? Partly no doubt on the basis of scientific research into the behavior of people as persons, groups, and communities or into the processes of their learning, communication, and motivation. But much more fully, I venture to say, on the basis of "common sense" notions of human conduct, human learning, of distribution of power and prestige in situations, of conventional assumptions with respect to what can go and what can't go in a group, an organization, or a community. And counsels to practice from the two bases don't always jibe. The result is conflict within the person of the professional.

How does "operational research" fit into this gap? It is an effort to bridge the gap—to bring the methods and approaches of the behavioral scientist into the processes by which program priorities are determined, by which programs are defined, by which program effects are evaluated. It goes one step further than drawing upon the "products" of behavioral research and translating these into program meanings and implications. It involves the practitioner and his associates in using the methodologies of the behavioral scientist in extending and validating their operating knowledges and techniques, in assessing and evaluating program success and failure, and in correcting and reconstructing relevant "common sense," both in themselves and in their associates.

Criticisms of "Operational Research" From Fore and Aft

It is not surprising that efforts in "operational research" have met with criticisms from both "anti-scientific" and "scientific" sides of the current split. An extreme case of the former is Whittaker Chambers who in *Witness* equates scientific method in human affairs with communism, his word for the devil. In making our judgments of what should be done he believes we must rely on our traditions, upon God, not upon human intelligence or experimentation. Other anti-scientists urge, more temperately, that human values are lost in any scientific or engineering approach to human problems, that science is amoral if not immoral, that wisdom comes from sources other than scientific study—in my terms, from "common sense."

Raymond Cattell(1), psychologist, speaks for many on the "scientific" side:

"I should . . . point out . . . a bastard philosophy, very prevalent in some social sciences under the name of 'action research,' which mingles 'revealed' religious ethics, i.e., non-scientific, ready-made ethics, with the experimental principles of social science and attempts to call the offspring 'scientific' and to claim for it the prestige and character of science.

"Every recommendation in 'action research' argues first from a chain of truly scientific mechanisms—if A is done, then B and ultimately, Z will follow—and secondly from a value system—because Z is good, A is good. It is my conviction that confusion of thought and damage to scientific prestige will result if we permit these callow enthusiasts to apply such labels as 'research' or 'science' to their recommendations unless they first demonstrate that their statement, 'Z is good,' can also be made from a scientific basis. This has not been done; indeed, naive 'high school' moral values have been combined with 'college' science without the glimmer of a realization that this great new possibility of a totally scientific ethic exists or that action research is 50 percent unscientific."

What can we learn from these fore and aft criticisms of "operational research," pertinent to our present purpose of appraisal? Allowing for the rhetoric, the slogans, posturings and polemics, which mark the language of partisans in any emotionalized split in a society or culture, one clear issue seems to emerge. This is the unavoidable confrontation with value judgments, judgments of what should and should not be, in the program and policy decisions which practitioners must make one way or another. Setting the goals of a program, allotting priorities among specific goals, require value judgments and, in our divided communities, these mean unavoidably some choice with respect to value-issues and value-conflicts.

How competent are the methods of science in making such choices? How far can research methods solve problems which involve decision upon issues

of value? Is science as a human pursuit devoid of values? Must the practitioner, as he chooses and decides, operate on extra-scientific values? If so, how are these validated? Can the values of science be integrated with such extra-scientific values inherent in the "common sense" of the situation confronted? If they clash, which must yield? It is in relation to questions such as these that we must undertake a critical appraisal, must assess the virtues and limitations of "operational research" in the processes of professional functioning and development.

The Common Meeting Ground of "Common Sense" and "Science"

The common meeting ground for "common sense" and "science" is in processes of problem-solving. Most theorists appeal to the similar form of problem-solving in situations of practical judgment and of basic research in urging the extension of operational research in professional and practical affairs.

Stephen M. Corey(2), for example, identifies five stages common to both processes and problem-solving: defining the problem; hypothesizing actions and predicting effects; designing a way of testing the hypotheses; collecting evidence; generalizing the results. We may agree, I believe, that processes of practical judgment and scientific research involve these subprocesses. And, in a fundamental sense, the goal of operational research is to bring the methods and disciplines of the scientist into the informing and rendering more valid of processes of "common sense" judgment in any or all of its phases.

But in what ways do the values of the basic researcher and of the social

The Role of Behavioral Scientist and the Role of Social Practitioner
(Health Educator)

BEHAVIORAL SCIENTIST	HEALTH EDUCATOR
1. Both make choices in their work and so must be guided by some system of values as well as by professional knowledge and skills.	
2. On top of his hierarchy of values is valid knowledge-building about the behavior of people—values of *improving* the functioning and intelligence of people he studies is secondary.	2. On top of his hierarchy of values is *improving* the functioning and intelligence of people with whom he works—extending basic knowledge of their behavior is instrumental to this aim.
3. People with whom he works are subjects who serve his purposes of extending generalizable and valid knowledge—he is not interested in particular cases except as instances to confirm or invalidate generalizations.	3. People with whom he works professionally are clients—he is concerned centrally with particularized cases and situations in order to apply knowledge in improving these.
4. Both are influenced in their choices and work by persons and associations significant to them in evaluating, rewarding, punishing their efforts and contributions.	
5. The scientist is particularly influenced by persons and associations in his field of scientific specialization—he is shielded from direct influences from men of action and social power as determinants of his choices.	5. Professional associations are one reference group for the health educator—but he and the profession by the nature of their work are more directly influenced by social need, by men of action, and men and groups in power positions, as coaches of their decisions.
6. Time in the form of pressing decisions does not influence his judgments and choices so directly as it does those of practitioners—he can reserve judgment, waiting for the accumulating weight of evidence—a longer time perspective operates in his judgments of what needs to be done now and later.	6. Time presses the practitioner to decide and act—judgments can not wait—he must judge in order to meet deadlines, whether the evidential basis for judgment is "complete" or not.

practitioner enter differently into their processes of problem-solving? In the answer to this question, we may find some clearer view of the difficulties of extending operational research in the life and work of professional practitioners. The following analysis suggests both similarities and differences in the value orientations of the two social roles.

What Then Are the Key Problems in Extending Operational Research in Health Education Settings?

a. *Effective operational research will require some integration, preferably conscious and deliberate, of the role of behavioral scientist with the role of so-*

cial practitioner in the persons of the health educator and of those with whom he works. This is true from the other direction for the behavioral scientist who cooperates and consults in such researches. This means not alone an integration of skills and techniques but of values and role-prescriptions as well. There are certain to be tensions and compromises in such processes of integration. These should be accepted without guilt or denial. The resulting problems chosen and research designs effected will not be equivalent to either basic research designs or "common sense" patterns, unless the health educator tries to deny his social practitioner role, "makes like" a basic researcher, and tries surreptitiously to slip "basic" research designs into his work, unknown to his lay associates. This is not desirable ethically nor, in the long run, is it prudent.

We can predict from this role analysis some of the charactistics of research problems and designs consonant with practitioners' values. They will serve educational purposes for those who take part as well as knowledge-building purposes. They will involve greater degrees of cooperation in planning and decision on the part of "clients," become for the time "subjects" as well, for study by self and others. Problems for study will be chosen for the promise of practical pay-off in the results of study. Tensions in practice will provide a way of locating problems to be studied (the practitioner's way) along with gaps in existing professional knowledge (the scientist's way). Both criteria should be used simultaneously. Variables selected for study will be chosen in terms of their accessibility to manipulation by practitioners and clients and of their strategic importance as well as their probable relationship, theoreti-

cally, to the more adequate explanation of phenomena studied. There will be greater interest in the processes of interaction among many variables in particular concrete cases or situations than in the isolation of single variables for study in a wide variety of situations. Values and goals will be studied along with non-normative facts and factors. Yet the two should be distinguished— the operational researcher must become in some measure philosopher as well as scientist-practitioner.

This is as it should be. Operational research is not better or worse than basic research; it is different, because it serves somewhat different purposes. Yet both can be "scientific."

b. *Inquiry Rather Than Justification.* But the results of operational research will not be scientific if the value system of the scientist as well as his methods and techniques are not taken over into the integration. For science has inherent values, an inherent ethic, however much some scientists and anti-scientists may deny it. It may be summed up as the spirit of inquiry. This clashes with the spirit of justification which pervades much "common sense" evaluation and diagnosis. How can the spirit of justification be validly replaced by, or strongly tinctured with, the spirit of inquiry? Many health educators work for agencies and organizations, public and private, which must justify their existence, their way of working, to the persons who are sources of funds and of moral support and who apply over-simplified and emotionalized criteria in judging success or failure. What if evaluation research applied to our program gives evidence that we are not living up to our public relations and fund-raising appeals? What if admitting the need for research on what we are doing is taken as evidence that our agency doesn't already know what it is doing? Studies undertaken in this atmosphere are likely to be distorted in the image of justification, and the spirit of inquiry will be a casualty in the process. It is better not to go through the forms of inquiry, if the conditions necessary to support valid inquiry are not in some measure present.

This is no easy problem. The answer seems to lie in two directions. First, choose problems where some readiness to inquire and to abide by the results of inquiry already exists. This may mean tackling less crucial problems first. Second, use participation of key people in the inquiry to widen their inquiry span, to extend the areas in which they are willing to inquire rather than to justify and reenforce what they already "know" on the grounds of "common sense."

c. This latter discussion suggests what has long been recognized—that *operational research is a methodology for training and change as well as for gaining new knowledge*. The latter goal must not be lost sight of, lest the spirit of inquiry be lost and "scientistic" manipulation of attitudes and values take its place. But the former goal needs to be kept in mind too in selecting problems and designing studies. Specific learnings about communities, programming, prevention, epidemiology, etc., will result from participation in particular operational researches. These learnings are important, but they are not the basic learnings. The basic learnings have already been suggested—skill, confidence, and commitment to the use of the values, methods, and resources of the behavioral sciences, along with those of "common sense," in analyzing and solving practical problems that confront us now and in the future.

This means helping to heal the cultural and personal split between "science" and "common sense" in human affairs.

d. *Using Scientific Expertise Wisely*. Expertise from the behavioral sciences will often be needed by practitioners in meeting the technical problems which operational research present. The main goal is to develop a cooperative, nondefensive relationship between expert and practitioner. Health educators must work to overcome whatever inferiority feelings they may have as "mere" practitioners in the presence of "scientific" expertise. They must accept and discount the hesitations of many behavioral scientists who naturally fear losing caste with their pure peers by risking the impurity of contact with practice and action. Understanding of the differences in roles, mutual respect for the different values and value-hierarchies involved in these roles, agreement on plans which invalidate neither set of values—these are the substantive goals of research expert-practitioner relationships that must be sought and built.

e. *Strategies of Installing Operational Research*. Some general points of strategy have been suggested in the previous discussion. These may be pulled out in summary fashion at this point.

1. Health educators are in the first instance social practitioners. If they are to do whole-hearted "operational research," they must recognize the differences of value orientation and emphasis in the roles of "social practitioner" and of "scientific researcher" and must work to integrate these two roles without denying either. Wisdom in effective operational research, as elsewhere, begins at home.

2. People accustomed to functioning as *clients* vis-à-vis health educators must

in operational researches function as *subjects* of study, furnishing data, having their behavior analyzed and interpreted. There must be sufficient cooperation by clients in deciding to do research on a policy problem and in determining what problem to study to insure that they are willing to become *subjects as well as clients and to accept* the pains and tribulations of the former estate. This means that erstwhile *clients* must understand and accept the differences between the roles and relationships of *clients* and *subjects* and accept the latter role in the interest of eventual program and policy improvement. Reeducation along this line should in some degree precede the installation of an operational research project as it most certainly will follow if the results of the research study are taken seriously in subsequent policy and program decisions.

3. Initial problems should be selected in a way to meet the criteria of both practical importance and "researchability." This means that an initial problem should be one which those concerned, including the power persons and groups related to the program, can approach in a spirit of inquiry, ready to change ideas and practices if the study indicates the need for change, rather than a spirit of justification, in which results are selected, twisted or rejected in order to maintain and justify established ideas and practices.

4. The help of research expertise will often be needed by practitioners in dealing with the technical problems they are certain to encounter in installing researches. A relationship of equal status cooperation needs to be developed if such consultation and collaboration are to work well. This reemphasizes point 1 above which applies not alone to practitioners but to behavioral scientists as well, though in reverse direction.

The Special Opportunity for Health Educators in Operational Research

1. Health educators work in a field with an overall value—improved public health—that is less riddled by controversy in current American culture than are the fields of welfare, economic policy, international relations, etc. True enough, health policy verges at times on all of these—as controversies about socialized medicine, fluoridation, etc., indicate. But a core value, common to the American public, is the central concern of their profession. This is a position of strength in efforts to bridge the gap between "science" and "common sense" as determinants of public policy and program.

2. The health education profession is probably less encrusted with its own "common sense" traditions than any other health profession. It is, therefore, probably freer than any other to adapt its traditions to new currents of thought from the behavioral sciences.

3. It is oriented to "education," and operational research in its installation requires an educational approach, just as its processes are inherently educational in effect for those taking part, if validly carried through.

4. Its relative lack of prestige among health professions may be a disvalue as well as a value in getting things started. But, in the long run, it may have more value, if the profession itself does not translate lack of prestige into an unjustified feeling of inferiority. For changes in the practices of less prestigeful professions are sometimes less ominous and so less subject to irrational resistance from other collabora-

ting professions than are changes in the more prestigeful collaborators.

I, therefore, commend your past efforts and look forward to your future efforts in operational research designed to advance the improvement of your profession. You can by these efforts, I feel sure, contribute not only to putting your own professional activities on a firmer basis of tested knowledge and value but also contribute to the will of other professions to heal, in their own spheres of professional activity, the dangerous split between "science" and "common sense" in our divided culture.

References

1. CATTELL, RAYMOND B. "The Ethics of Beyond," contribution to Symposium on "Values and the Social Scientist," BENNE, K. D. and SWANSON, G. E. (eds.). *Journal of Social Issues*, Vol. VI, No. 4, 1950.
2. COREY, STEPHEN M. *Action Research to Improve School Practices.* New York: Teachers College, Columbia, Bureau of Publications, 1953.

◆◆◆◆◆◆◆◆◆◆◆◆◆◆◆◆◆◆◆ THE RESEARCHER AND HIS AUDIENCES   *David Riesman*

Introduction to *Crestwood Heights*

When I was in the middle of the manuscript of *Crestwood Heights,* I had the good luck to attend a meeting in Park Forest, a new-model suburb which is comparable to Crestwood Heights in the intensity with which it has been studied. The meeting was addressed by William H. Whyte, Jr. of *Fortune,* its imaginative, incisive, and not unsympathetic main surveyor. En route to the meeting Whyte observed that, when he had been interviewing in Park Forest, he had had the strange feeling of being virtually the only male in the place during the daytime; the men were all at work downtown or at various plants around Chicago, and there were some joking references to his being loose in a harem. Moreover, the problems to which he had addressed himself in his justly famous series of articles on Park Forest had frequently been those felt most keenly by the homebound wives: problems of sociability and privacy in the rental courts; of the limits of idiosyncracy in décor; of how to put down roots while remaining, on behalf of their husbands' careers, potential transients. At the meeting where he was asked to speak, however, Whyte was surrounded—and kept at a distance from the mixed audience—by a panel composed entirely of men; these, and their friends in the first several rows of the audience, asked him questions largely of a technical "male" sort, e.g.,

Excerpt from Crestwood Heights, *A study of the Culture of Suburban Life, edited by John R. Seeley, R. Alexander Sim, and Elizabeth W. Loosley,* © *1956, New York: Basic Books, Inc., Publishers, pp. 5–10. Used by permission.*

concerning social science methodology or zoning regulations; only one woman managed to get in a word during the entire evening. Many of the questions were hostile, and appeared to spring from resentment of the possibility or claim that an outsider could learn anything that was not obvious to the local experts and founding fathers of 1947–1948, the date of first settlement.

This volume by Seeley, Sim, and Loosley makes several important contributions to understanding such encounters. A brilliant chapter is devoted to the "triangle" between male experts and researchers, their female clients, and the latter's husbands. The husbands work all day in the city; they pride themselves on being practical, no-nonsense men—a pride partly maintained by polarizing themselves from their allegedly emotional, starry-eyed wives; they are willing to buy (and bury) social science in personnel and marketing departments (as one appurtenance, thanks in part to the corporation tax, of their being up-to-date), but not in affairs pertaining to their suburb and its schools. The wives have the leisure and education and energy to make a career out of suburbia—and to be anxious about themselves and their children. The social science experts, often marginal members of new professions, require lay co-operation in order to have subjects, financing, and the prestige sometimes denied them in the scholarly world. These experts, much like artists, appear male vis-à-vis their female clients, counsellees, and devotees, but not quite manly to the latter's spouses. The experts also have the advantage of being in the community in the daytime, and of having prestige in the eyes of subsidiary experts such as school teachers, social workers, and other semi-professionals of limited theoretical pretensions. It is understandable that the husbands, uneasy in any case because they are wedded to their work and only peripherally to their families, resent the experts with their psychological know-how, their intimate knowledge of the community, and their permissive notions of child-rearing (Whyte's notions were quite different, but this did not save him from triangulation).

The concern that Seeley, Sim, and Loosley have with this triangle and its dangers for all parties concerned—not least the expert, whose success with a lay public will divorce him still further from his academic colleagues—is part of a wider concern which runs through the book for the consequences of social research upon the communities (and other "objects") studied. Anthropologists have developed an ethical program to protect the tribes they visit from being unduly influenced by their presence, or that of other Westernized people; cultural relativism is part of this program, with its now much qualified mandate of equal detachment from all cultures, a mandate as it were of attachment to the principle of culture as such. In their efforts to combat the parochialism and ethnocentrism of missionaries and administrators, they have until recently been able to aim their research reports entirely at their audience at home; by definition, "their" tribe would not read what was written about them, and would presumably be disturbed as little as possible by having an anthropologist living unassumingly among them, seeking to learn their language and sympathetically to understand their values. But today it gets harder and harder to find "uncontaminated" tribes and to assume one can leave them that way (Mrs. Bowen's *Return to Laughter* beautifully indicates the complexities and moral ambiguities involved), and anthropologists have become much more sensitive to their subjects as the world has shrunk. When the Lynds published their first *Middletown* book and when W. Lloyd Warner came back from an Australian tribe and started work on the "Yankee City Series," social science was directly plunged into the problem of reporting on its subjects to its subjects. Witness *Point of No Return*.

Seeley and his collaborators, like their predecessors in American community studies, have—unlike the *Fortune* articles—granted a kind of courtesy anonymity to their suburb, more as a sign of goodwill than in any hope that one can hide so distinctive a feature of the landscape as Crestwood Heights. But the authors collide, like Whyte, with a problem their predecessors only brushed against, for they are writing about *us,* about the professional upper middle class and its business man allies, not about a New England museum for the upper class, such as Yankee City, or a small and rather parochial town in the South or Midwest, such as Jonesville or Elmtown. They are writing, as they are almost too aware, about themselves, their friends, their "type" (I "type" the authors, of course, no doubt unjustly, by treating the trio as if they were one person). Moreover, the enterprise on which they report involved much more than simply a one-shot data-gathering expedition; this was "action research," with teams of clinicians for the school children, discussion leaders for the school teachers and parents (as implied above, only the mothers, by and large, took part), and leaders of Human Relations classes in the schools—classes in which the young people were encouraged, quite bravely, to bring up any problems of concern to them. In the High School, many of the suburban teen problems of parents, cars, sex, cliques arose, along with Crestwood Heights' exceptional sensitivity to inter-ethnic (mainly, Jewish-Gentile) amity; there also arose some very probing questions concerning the search for personal identity and integrity. So intertwined, in fact, is the research with the community that this book gives the impression that its authors are still stuck in the tar-baby; their moral intensity about their task and their responsibilities both as researchers and as reporters is, in all its humorlessness and intensity, rare and admirable.

I have occasionally asked novelists how they feel about using their friends and families, barely disguised, in an autobiographical book. Usually, if they have thought about the question at all, the immensely powerful ideology of *l'art pour l'art,* developed for use against the Philistines, suffices to dismiss any scruples. Moreover, partly because of this ideology, writers have a vanity that researchers repress or seldom gain; as one, whose whole family garnishes a lurid novel, told me, "My book will be alive when all my family is dead"; his implication was they should be grateful for this immortality. To be sure, Randall Jarrell's *Pictures at an Institution* bursts with its tirade against a lady novelist who "heartlessly" cases a college community (the book in turn cruelly cases the lady). But Jarrell, as befits the author of *The Age of Criticism,* is unusually self-conscious about reflexivity for a literary man; most novelists so far as I can make out (Thomas Wolfe is a notable exception) take exploitation of their "material" for granted.

As I have implied, the consciences of the authors of *Crestwood Heights* are so involved with their research experience that I wish at times they had had the novelist's insouciance as well as the novelist's sensitivity to anxiety and other forms of mental suffering among the well-to-do. I myself often prefer, for reasons which I'm sure won't stand full examination, to suppose that social scientists exaggerate their power for weal or woe—hence in such cases as this their feelings of responsibility. Most social scientists, however, duck such moral issues by believing only in their subjects' subjectivity and not in their own, or by seeking to couch their findings in an opaque language which their subjects can presumably not decipher or which in any case is believed to be free from bias. Whatever discomfort is associated with the path chosen by Seeley, Sim, and Loosely, I will take it any day over the self-deceptions and ethical insensitivities of the majority. The authors of *Crestwood Heights* are not purse-proud about their professional training (and they lack the innocence of supposing that technical terms can long conceal one's values); one result is that there is not a line in this book with which I would suppose an educated non-professional reader will have any serious difficulty. In some measure, I rather regret this, for it means that the writing, for my taste, is not sufficiently dense and allusive; everything is painstakingly spelled out. And in one respect this prolixity is perplexing, for if one assumes that readers and subjects are, apart from accidents of residence, the same people, then one would not need all the ethnographic detail which overburdens this book. Though the authors have a keener eye for moral impasse and

arabesque than for the material culture or for the merely sociable, they insist on telling us what the houses are like, or the orbits of time and season, and there is a long chapter on summer camps which seems to assume that the reader will neither have seen such a camp nor sent his children there.

This chapter, incidentally, has a waspishness of tone—though not a penetration of idea—reminiscent of Mary McCarthy. And camps of course, with their pseudo-Indian lore, their parents who seek surrogates to toughen and discipline their children, their counsellors who "goof off," are easy targets for satire. Elsewhere in the book, one feels that the authors are trying not to be too severe on their own kind, not to join the current intellectual critique of liberal middle-class professional people, such as make up a considerable part of the population, as well as the leadership, of Crestwood Heights. But it is hard for description not to become parody when we are reading, not about strata or tribes remote from us, but about our own suburban (or in the case of the camps, in Spectorsky's phrase, "exurban") life. Compare the following, from the description of a presumably typical family:

Despite these separate rounds of activity, which intersect only occasionally (the husband states: "I am home so little, I only see the kids for an hour in the evening, that is if I'm not going off to a meeting"), the affection on the part of the children towards each other and their parents is demonstrative and this behavior is given high approval. . . . The giving of presents in this family is a highly regarded token of love and esteem. An equally strong norm, on the other hand, insists upon separate activities for each member of the family, with less frequent events in the nature of holiday or anniversary celebrations involving the whole group (the summer holiday together must be planned for a year or more in advance). Only a high degree of efficiency (faintly reminiscent of that of a well-run club or office) in operating the household makes this individualistic pattern of outside activities workable at all. The actual help given by the children can be symbolic only; more helpful, and unusual, is the presence of the same maid with this family over a six-year period.

Veblen knew that the apparently deadpan could be devastating, and part of Mary McCarthy's genius is to be able to say, for instance, that "the professor came into the room carrying his briefcase" so that the descriptive remark appears to undress him, to show him as he really ridiculously is, without pretence or illusion. But when I read such a passage as the one quoted above, and many like it, I wonder whether it is I who bring to the material a sardonic reaction or whether I find it there, in the use of the term "efficiency," in the comparison with the club or office, and in the awkwardness—neither quite jargon nor quite literature—of such phrases as "highly regarded token of love and esteem."

Readers will have to answer such questions for themselves, but it is part of the context that it is the very niceness of the Crestwood Heights people that lays them open to scrutiny either by the researchers or by the readers. The suburbanites (or at least the women and experts) invited the research team in; they welcomed long and probing interviews and tests, in a way that less agreeable and perhaps less vulnerable people would not have done. (It is perhaps an aspect of this ethos which leads Crestwood Heights, if not always to welcome the influx of Jews, at least not to tolerate any restrictions or quotas.) The same defencelessness of Crestwood Heights appears in its devoutness, the women's that is, towards each passing fad in child-rearing, and in the social and psychological professions generally. The authors could not help but be struck by the way in which mothers rejected their own experience in favor of some formula—and if the researchers criticized the formula they were themselves in danger of becoming the new priests, only to be overthrown in turn. The anthropologist who goes into a culture that has successfully hardened against white contact does not face this danger, nor does the industrial sociologist, whom the workers in a factory regard as a tool or fool of management or of themselves. But every perceptive teacher does have the experience of fearing a discipleship which robs the student of independence, and might even prefer students' disdain to their passivity. As I have already indicated, it is the researchers' own niceness and defencelessness that makes them aware of the ethical ambiguities of their invasion of Crestwood Heights; under the circumstances, they could hardly be expected to possess the serene confidence in science, in evidence, that a Martin Arrowsmith struggled for. Moreover, Arrowsmith wanted to cure something obvious and concrete, something "outside," while the problems of Crestwood Heights are on another level. Possibly the very existence of the suburb itself (and the researchers studying themselves studying it) marks something of a retreat from the intractable problems of society, though it would seem fairer to say only that there is some loss of traditional forms of venturesomeness as the echoing internal frontier replaces the vanishing external one.

✦✦✦✦✦✦✦✦✦✦✦✦✦✦✦✦✦✦ VALUE-JUDGMENT PROBLEMS
OF THE SOCIAL SCIENTIST IN
ACTION-RESEARCH   *Ronald Lippitt*

Our discussion will consider the question: What guiding principles can a social scientist use in making the many value judgments he does make when he takes an active role in action-research projects?

The question that arises from this is whether there is or can be any consensus among social scientists as to professional standards for behavior as scientists in these value-judgment situations. The APA Committee on Ethical Standards for Psychology has been working on these problems with collaboration from the membership for two years and has formulated a series of suggested guidelines for the adequate conduct of psychological research. I believe that these already represent a very important bit of progress. As yet they do not seem to me to touch on some of the crucial decision issues that have come up for me during participation in various action-research projects.

Let me mention a few examples of action-research situations and decision problems to give the context of the experiences I am talking about:

1. A member of management of an industrial organization requests help on a study to improve productivity of work groups. From initial discussion it is clear that this person is only representing one department of top management in his definition of the problem and the desire for the study. Representatives of organized labor in the plant have not been consulted. Should I consider working in this situation? On what condition?

2. A classroom teacher asks for consultation on what to do about a disruptive clique of children in her room. She says she knows what the trouble is but she doesn't know any techniques for dealing with it. Is this an important problem to work on? I feel she is a rather punitive type of person. Should this make any difference in my decision? Should the children be involved or can I make the decision without consulting them? Is a social scientist needed here, or just a "wise person," or what is the difference in such a case?

3. A representative of a local political party asks for help in determining the reasons for the apathy of the local party membership and in formulating a remedy for this situation. This is not a political party in which I have membership. Should this make any difference to me as a social scientist? Who will "own" the data? Should this make a difference?

4. The chief of a government bureau proves himself quite research-minded.

From Ronald Lippitt, "Value-Judgment Problems of the Social Scientist Participating in Action-Research." Paper presented September 1950, American Psychological Association meetings. Symposium sponsored by SPSSI and Division of Personality and Social Psychology. Unpublished manuscript. Used by permission.

He requests help in setting up an experiment in trying out two different supervisory procedures in different parts of the bureau. This means making changes in the life situation of quite a number of persons and keeping it secret so as not to spoil the design. Is it ethical to do this sort of thing without the permission of the subjects?

The first question which arises for me is: Why should I be interested in any of these requests? What scientific contribution will I make by getting hooked up in this obligation to be of some service to the "subjects" of my research? Cannot I spend my time more productively on more sharply focused laboratory research where the scientific problem to be solved is more clearly delineated?

As I try to clarify this decision point for myself I think I find the following values operating:

Value 1. As a social scientist I have an obligation to contribute to a stockpile of basic knowledge integrated by a network of basic concepts.

Value 2. But as a social scientist I also feel an obligation to see the scientific attitude and methodology applied to the solution of more and more of the disruptive problems of society. I believe this is possible and is necessary for the survival and beneficial reconstruction of the culture which will permit and nourish scientific activity.

Value 3. Also, as a social scientist I am in a professional communication network so that I receive and possess information about research results elsewhere which have *application relevance* in this particular social situation—and I feel an obligation to communicate my perceptions of relevance and to test

their validity in a variety of real-life situations similar to the one from which this request for help is coming.

When I try to relate these three values to the decision situation of whether or not to participate in field research with a service obligation, two additional questions come up:

1. Are there some or even many of the phenomena on which basic research is necessary that we can only discover the existence of and gain access to for study by this type of field-research relationship?

2. Might it be possible in such field settings to get enough identification of the organization (subjects) with the value of making a general scientific contribution over and above the solution of the immediate problem, so that a worthwhile basic research contribution can be made as a complementary product to the scientific solving of the problem disturbing this group (assuming it is unlikely that the two designs would be identical)?

At this general level of decision I have concluded that it is desirable for me as a social scientist to spend at least part of my time participating in appropriate action-research projects. From this analysis I have also arrived at the tentative conclusion that there are at least three roles in which I can perceive myself as functioning as a social scientist:

1. One role is that of attempting to formulate and solve a "scientific problem" derived from previous theoretical development and empirical research. The "problem tension" comes from perception of "a gap in our understanding of phenomena."

2. The second and third roles focus on contributing to the scientific solving of specific social problems, where the "problem tension" comes from feelings of pain or disequilibrium in some part of our social structure, and where I as a social scientist can make a particular contribution.

a. (Role 2) By applying scientific methodology to the diagnosis and/or experimental solution of the problem.

b. (Role 3) By applying general principles from the stockpile of research knowledge to the action-decisions called for in this concrete problem situation.

At some points these roles seem clearly to overlap and be in harmony with each other. At other points they seem to pull in different directions so far as goals for my behavior are concerned.

Let us return now to my further decision problems, once I have personally decided I can and should function as a social scientist in action-research projects. By what criteria shall I define "an appropriate action-research project" for me to participate in? As I review the decisions made in the four illustrative situations mentioned above, it seems to me the following values served as guiding ones. Let me formulate each one and try to indicate some of the implications for direction of decision.

Value 4. It is desirable to spend one's energy working on problems that are widespread and/or crucially disruptive, or in which the solution is likely to be widely applicable to other problems of this widespread or crucial sort; or with a group whose influence is widespread, and so on.

On the basis of this criterion it seemed to me that preference should be given to the problems of apathy in

political behavior and productivity in work groups working on monotonous tasks (in the examples above) rather than to the specific classroom problem and the comparison of two specific methods of supervision. To arrive at such preferences, using this criterion (which it is assumed would be weighted along with others) demands asking questions about the degree to which this problem is typical, the seriousness of the social disruption or disorganization caused by the continuation of the problem, and its dynamic similarity to other problems. For example, the problems of a community council might not seem at first sight to be particularly significant, but the conflicting loyalties of the instructed organizational delegates might cast a great deal of light on international committee problems and labor-management negotiation situations that are less accessible for research.

Value 5. It is desirable that helping a group or organization to apply a scientific outlook and methodology to one of its problems should result in the "internalization" of this outlook and method so that they will be applied to the open-minded discovery and solution of other problems.

This is, as I see it, one of the crucial guiding values. I suggested that one might choose to work with an important organization even though the particular problem was not of great significance. This might be because of a favorable prognosis of the group's ability to learn how to diagnose and solve its own problems, and therefore of its readiness to apply scientific procedures to the broader evaluation of its objectives and operations once it had learned how. In one case, after considerable soul-searching, I accepted the invitation to work on a relatively superficial problem with a significant group with whose program objectives I did not agree. This was on the basis of the hunch that if this group became identified with a research-oriented outlook in tackling its problems it might very well launch into a program evaluation that might affect its basic objectives. The hunch proved correct in this particular case. Obviously it is necessary to attempt to do a lot of hard-headed thinking about the application of this value criterion, and also to use skills of relationship beyond those of merely doing good sound research. In order to test, and to avoid, some of the traps, another standard for appropriate behavior as an action-researcher seems to me implied.

Value 6. It is desirable that all parties, or representatives of all parties, involved in the problem should recognize the problem, should desire its solution, and agree on seeking help from the social scientist or research organization. In many cases it may be necessary to specify a trial period during which the scientist does not have such representative collaboration but is attempting to get it established.

First of all, it seems like quite a trap scientifically to move into a situation where many of the relevant data are going to be inaccessible because of the attitudes of the persons toward voluntary collaboration in the project. If, as in the case of the government bureau example, experimental manipulation is called for, there is the additional need for some level of discussion and acceptance of the project and—usually —commitment to share the discoveries that have been made possible by the cooperation. Third, the probability of

acceptance of the findings is much lower if there has not been an initial acceptance of the problem and help toward solving it. A closely related point constitutes my seventh value criterion.

Value 7. It is also desirable that the organization or conflicting parties be ready to participate in whatever way is appropriate in the process of scientific analysis and experimentation, (*a*) to help guarantee receptivity to the findings; (*b*) to develop skill and motivation to use the same process in the location and solution of other problems.

Several self-survey projects, in communities, industry, and school systems, have indicated that with guidance and training by a social scientist many citizens, workers, and even children within the projects can be trained to do a competent job of interviewing, observing, and analysis. This is not just a matter of research economy. The major result is greater acceptance, understanding, and use of the findings and greater readiness and ability to solve other problems by the same methodology. Usually a continuing relationship to technical methodologists is needed. Sometimes the result is the setting up of a permanent research department within the organization.

These last two criteria have been very helpful in testing the potential working relationship with many groups in making the decision whether it seemed to me possible—ethical if you will—to work as a social scientist with the particular group. As I think of the political party example, and the industrial example, another important criterion stands out.

Value 8. It is necessary that there be a readiness to understand, accept, and explicitly define the role of the social scientist as that of a methodologist in scientific problem-solving, or as a resource person on relevant research done elsewhere; as one who is highly motivated to help solve this particular problem, but who has an open, experimental attitude toward what the data will or should reveal, or what will turn out to be the best method in an experimental project.

I believe every scientist who works in action-research projects must carefully plan the interpretation of his role in this regard and must vigorously demonstrate this position, particularly when working with conflicting groups. Standing by itself as a single guiding principle this value is of course vulnerable to the question, "Is the social scientist, then, only the hired technical servant of any group, no matter what its objectives?" I have already stressed other values to be weighted in the judgment, such as the crucial nature of the social problem, the readiness of the group to learn and apply scientific method to other problems, and so on. I believe, however, that the role of scientific methodologist, or interpreter of data from elsewhere with high standards of interpretation, must be vigorously defined and maintained if we are to make our maximum contribution to the rational solution of social issues.

I have stated the opinion that in most adequate action-research projects the findings will have some general scientific value as well as the value of helping the particular group to solve a particular problem. For this reason I believe it is frequently desirable to apply another value standard in guiding decisions about who to work with and how to work with them.

Value 9. It is desirable that the group or organization be ready to permit and support the communication of relevant discoveries to other groups and to the public as well as using the data to resolve its own problem.

This does not mean that I think the data should belong to the consulting scientist, or that he can demand unilateral rights to publication in an action-research project. In many cases I think this is a quite unreasonable request that denies the whole notion of partnership in the project. I have implied all through these remarks that the scientist should spend his energies in those action-research projects where his relationship to the project seems to promise adequate power to guide the methods used in data collection and analysis, and adequate power to secure activity involvement in the research process, but I do not believe this can or should be the asymmetrical power relationship many of us try to make it to avoid traps to our scientific integrity and reputations. Every such venture involves an opportunity for much learning on both sides and for many decisions to be made jointly on a step-by-step basis, rather than a single pre-project contract in which the scientist tries to get commitments on all the problems he thinks might come up that might embarrass him. I think the more adequate procedure usually is to define a tentative or try-out phase of the working relationship.

Let me try now to summarize as best I can the main notions of this approach to the role of the social scientist in the action-research situation.

First, it has been accepted as a starting point for this paper that values are the products of decision-situations where competing interests are concerned. Some values then become more general guiding principles (Benne calls them "validating preferences") in other decision situations.

Second, it has been suggested that a social scientist, in his membership role as a social scientist, has accepted a number of validating preferences concerning "scientific methodology and attitude" as guidelines for his behavior in decision situations. Geiger has summarized these in his paper in the *Journal of Social Issues* [1] to include such notions as "the hypothetical attitude," the feeling of tentativeness, respect for probable error, experimentalism in examining ideas, certain standards of methodology, etc. These represent a constellation of validating preferences for guiding decision where one's membership character as a social scientist is concerned.

Third, I have stated the belief that, in the action-research social problem-solving situation, conflicts arise between the scientist role and other membership roles such as political party membership, civic associations, etc. I have maintained that in these situations it is possible to maintain one's scientist role and still work vigorously on the solution of these problems if cer-

[1] K. Benne, and G. E. Swanson (eds.). Values and the social scientist. *Journal of Social Issues*, 6, No. 4, 1950.

tain conditions of working relationship can be achieved and maintained.

Fourth, I have suggested that one value of the scientist is that certain values of the scientific community concerning the use of scientific method should become common values of the total community as the basic approach to the continuous assessment of action and reconstruction of values. It seems to me this is probably the meeting point of the scientist's value system and the general ideology of democracy. This needs much more intensive philosophical examination.

Fifth, I have suggested that the scientist should not take an absolute value position about the conditions of his collaboration as a scientist in action-research projects. The reconstruction of values is a complex psychological process that can be stimulated by adequate collaborative relationships. This educational responsibility to teach the scientific method should be part of the value system of the social scientist as social scientist.

I am sure there is a high probability of error in many of the notions I have expressed here. I *am* fairly certain that this problem of defining the appropriate professional role of the social scientist in working relations with the great population of action groups, organizations, and agencies is a critical issue at the present time and will continue to grow as a problem for all of us here.

CHAPTER 12 ⟨⟨⟨ *The Small Group in Processes of Planned Change*

In the glance at the history of small group study presented in Chapter 6, the concurrent development of research and theorizing on group behavior and of experimentation in the application of knowledge of groups was discussed. The readings in that chapter sampled the results of research and theorizing with an eye on those results which seem most useful to change-agents generally. The present chapter presents a sampling from the literature on application.

It has been suggested previously that the small group occupies a strategic place in the instrumentation of planned change. Linking as it necessarily does persons and larger social systems, changes in a small group can be utilized to induce changes both in the persons of its members and in the larger social structures in which the group is set. The group can be utilized as a medium for changing the persons who seek and find membership within it. In such utilization, the group operates as a learning or training or therapy group. The group can also be used as an instrument in planning and effecting changes in the social structures in which it is set. In this use, the group functions as an action or policy- and program-building group.

In either form of utilization, attention to the social organization of the group in terms of its appropriateness and aptness to the goals it is designed to serve is frequently necessary. If the group organization is found to be inept or inappropriate, the social system of the group becomes the *target* of change effort so that its more adequate functioning as a *medium of planned change* or *instrument of social change* can be assured.

In the first reading of this chapter, *Achieving Change in People*, Cartwright stresses the importance of the small group in the armamentarium of the change-agent. This argument emphasizes the importance of valid concepts about groups as part of the required conceptual equipment of the change-agent, whether his primary concern is social action or individual re-education or some combination of the two.

695

In the next reading, discussions of various training methods that employ the small group as a medium of planned change are presented. Benne's *Case Methods in the Training of Administrators* is included in Chapter 11 of this book. It may be reread as an introduction to the training methods presented in this chapter and its argument need not be repeated here.

One caution against imputation of superiority to one group training method over the others is perhaps appropriate here. A temptation for practitioners is to adopt one method as the right one and to defend it against all others. Schools of practice then grow up around the defense and propagation of this method. One of the authors was called upon recently to consult with a conference of practitioners, all of whom were devoted to restoring blinded people to ambulatory status. He found in this conference a tragicomic division and conflict between practitioners who were committed to the cane technique and those devoted to the seeing-eye–dog technique. The problem all were committed to solve was lost in vigorous debates over the merits and demerits of the two procedures. It was only after the blinded people in the conference found their voices and were listened to by the practitioners that the problem to be solved took precedence over the battle of techniques, which could then be subjected to evaluation and critical scrutiny.

Practitioners devoted to organizational or community improvement and utilizing re-education as a part of the process of changing frequently find themselves in similar controversies over which of several group-training methods is best. Selection of a training method ideally is influenced by the character of the changes sought. Any comprehensive change program in an organization or a community will ordinarily require different methods at different times, for different populations, and for different specific change-objectives. The problem is properly one of design in which various combinations of techniques are employed. This problem is likely to be lost sight of if partisan identification with one technique or method obscures the superior values of other techniques or methods in specific circumstances.[1]

To illustrate this point, let us briefly review the group training methods included in the next five readings. To begin with, all the training approaches appear to have one common denominator: the utilization of group members' *experienced* behavior. Rather than relying on material external and unfamiliar to the participants, these training methods exploit the group members' own behavior. To this extent, these approaches employ a "laboratory" technique.

For example, in role-playing, a problem situation is constructed—it might have arisen from the group itself or have been selected by other criteria—and is "acted out" by the role-players. The role-players, with the help of observers, then evalu-

---

[1] It would be worth while to remark on the possibility of hidden normative or value elements in techniques. We are not referring to "vested interest" devotion to a technique, but to the "unphilosophical" assumptions behind them, which may be factors in devotion or antagonism lying below the level of consciousness. It is, we think, either dangerous or impossible (or both) to assume that practitioners can always pick over the armamentarium of available techniques as if they were all neutral objects like wrenches.

ate their own performances. The full significance of the training is only in a minor way related to the elegance of the problem-solution. Rather, what is focused upon is the relationships and interpersonal impacts of the actors in the process of solving the problem.

This emphasis on the experienced behavior—in the "here and now" situation —is true of all the other training approaches. It does vary somewhat, however. For example, in role-playing, the Incident Process, and Slater's modification of the Case Approach, certain stimuli, external to the group, are imported; a case an incident, a problem. These stimuli, provided by the trainer, are merely devices that provide an entry into the difficult process of analyzing group members' *own* behavior—a process that meets with substantial resistance on the part of group members unaccustomed to and/or defensive of personal inquiry.

The training group and therapy group, because they do not provide "conversation pieces," are usually more stark and anxiety-producing, for the trainer as well as for the participants. In fact, Slater points out that the fear of "breakage" in the training-group situation led to the innovation he and his associates developed. Consequently, all these training programs vary to the extent the trainer structures the situation and can comfortably program the behavioral outcomes.

One further consequence is this. Where the trainer provides minimal structure and few cues of expectations, anxiety increases that typically leads to defensive behavior on the part of participants. This being so, the kinds of behavior expressed in training and therapy groups may be wider in range, more idiosyncratic, and, frequently, unconscious. Accordingly, we would expect more personal, intimate, and threatening material under those conditions than in variations of the case study and role-playing variety. In the latter cases, however, the expressed behavior may be far more germane and transferable to everyday situations.

Two other factors that should be taken into account in considering the merits of these training programs are: (*a*) experience of the trainer, and (*b*) length of training period. In comparison with the training and therapy group, role-playing and the Incident Process are easy to learn. Pigors has informed one of the authors that after several exposures to the Incident Process, foremen could adequately employ this method for training their own men. This is probably true of role-playing as well, though in both cases there necessarily are intangible variations in sophistication and skill. The training and therapy group, as well as Slater's displacement approach, require considerable background and experience. While no clear-cut credential demands exist, the trainer is expected to have a doctorate in the social sciences or a medical degree, in addition to some knowledge about his own needs and anxieties (having, for example, gone through psychoanalysis) and having passed through a demanding apprenticeship. The background, skill, and experience required by the trainer are important factors to consider in selecting a training device. Length of training period is critical as well. Semrad conducts his training groups for an hour and a half each week over a fifty-week period. Training groups, in order to be effective, are believed to require at least twelve two-hour sessions over a fairly short span of time, say a week to ten days.

(Some trainers, however, have conducted training groups in the course of a regular academic term. Three-day institutes are not uncommon.)

The point in all this discussion should be clear. Training techniques differ in terms of goals, prerequisite trainers' skills, and expected participant reactions. They should be viewed and used, not as a grab-bag of techniques, but as a menu of training activities appropriate under specific conditions.

One limitation in the readings of this section should be noted. The group methods reviewed are concerned with the use of groups in the re-education of members, not with the utilization of groups for social action. It is true that any of these group methods may be used to train persons for social action, for policy-making, or for social planning as well as for greater self-understanding or for more effective interpersonal skills. The fact remains, however, that the methods presented emphasize only the utilization of small groups as a medium for the re-education of members. The literature on the building and management of groups designed for social action is not sampled here. This very conscious omission has been necessitated by lack of space for readings. It is no indication of the authors' devaluation of the use of groups for social action.

The final section of this chapter presents readings on methods of changing a group as a social system, whatever the ultimate uses the group is designed to serve. The methods suggested fit into the over-all methodology of "action research." ("Action research" methodology is reviewed in Chapter 11 in this volume.) In its present usage, it refers to efforts by group members to identify difficulties in the function of their group, to collect information relevant to these difficulties, to utilize this information in diagnosing needed changes in the group, to plan and undertake changes in the light of the diagnosis, and to evaluate the results of change undertaken. This cycle of self-study leading to planned changes with further self-study leading to further planned changes epitomizes in the miniature social system of the group the process of planned change that change-agents seek to normalize at various levels of human organization in our complex society.

◆◆◆◆◆◆◆◆◆◆◆◆◆◆◆◆◆◆◆◆◆ ACHIEVING CHANGE IN PEOPLE

Dorwin Cartwright

THE word "change" produces emotional reactions. It is not a neutral word. To many people it is threatening. It conjures up visions of a revolu-

Excerpted from Dorwin Cartwright, "Achieving Change in People," Human Relations, Vol. 14, No. 4, 1951, pp. 381–392. Original paper based on a lecture delivered in 1950 as part of the Leo M. Franklin Lecture Series at Wayne University. Abridged and used by permission.

tionary, a dissatisfied idealist, a trouble-maker, a malcontent. Nicer words referring to the process of changing people are education, training, orientation, guidance, indoctrination, therapy. We are more ready to have others "educate" us than to have them "change" us. We, ourselves, feel less guilty in "training" others than in "changing" them. Why this emotional response? What makes the two kinds of words have such different meanings? I believe that a large part of the difference lies in the fact that the safer words (like education or therapy) carry the implicit assurance that the only changes produced will be good ones, acceptable within a currently held value system. The cold, unmodified word "change", on the contrary, promises no respect for values; it might even tamper with values themselves. Perhaps for this very reason it will foster straight thinking if we use the word "change" and thus force ourselves to struggle directly and self-consciously with the problems of value that are involved. Words like education, training, or therapy, by the very fact that they are not so disturbing, may close our eyes to the fact that they too inevitably involve values.

Another advantage of using the word "change" rather than other related words is that it does not restrict our thinking to a limited set of aspects of people that are legitimate targets of change. Anyone familiar with the history of education knows that there has been endless controversy over what it is about people that "education" properly attempts to modify. Some educators have viewed education simply as imparting knowledge, others mainly as providing skills for doing things, still others as producing healthy "attitudes", and some have aspired to instil a way of life. Or if we choose to use a word like "therapy", we can hardly claim that we refer to a more clearly defined realm of change. Furthermore, one can become inextricably entangled in distinctions and vested interests by attempting to distinguish sharply between, let us say, the domain of education and that of therapy. If we are to try to take a broader view and to develop some basic principles that promise to apply to all types of modifications in people, we had better use a word like "change" to keep our thinking general enough.

The proposal that social technology may be employed to solve the problems of society suggests that social science may be applied in ways not different from those used in the physical sciences. Does social science, in fact, have any practically useful knowledge which may be brought to bear significantly on society's most urgent problems? What scientifically based principles are there for guiding programs of social change: In this paper we shall restrict our considerations to certain parts of a relatively new branch of social science known as "group dynamics". We shall examine some of the implications for social action which stem from research in this field of scientific investigation.

For various reasons we have found that much of our work has been devoted to an attempt to gain a better understanding of the ways in which people change their behavior or resist efforts by others to have them do so. Whether we set for ourselves the practical goal of improving behavior or whether we take on the intellectual task of understanding why people do what they do, we have to investigate processes of communication, influence, social pressure—in short, problems of change.

In this work we have encountered great frustration. The problems have been most difficult to solve. Looking back over our experience, I have become convinced that no small part of the trouble has resulted from an irresistible tendency to conceive of our problems in terms of the individual. We live in an individualistic culture. We value the individual highly, and rightly so. But I am inclined to believe that our political and social concern for the individual has narrowed our thinking as social scientists so much that we have not been able to state our research problems properly. Perhaps we have taken the individual as the unit of observation and study when some larger unit would have been more appropriate. Let us look at a few examples.

Consider first some matters having to do with the mental health of an individual. We can all agree, I believe, that an important mark of a healthy personality is that the individual's self-esteem has not been undermined. But on what does self-esteem depend? From research on this problem we have discovered that, among other things, repeated experiences of failure or traumatic failures on matters of central importance serve to undermine one's self-esteem. We also know that whether a person experiences success or failure as a result of some undertaking depends upon the level of aspiration which he has set for himself. Now, if we try to discover how the level of aspiration gets set, we are immediately involved in the person's relationships to groups. The groups to which he belongs set standards for his behavior which he must accept if he is to remain in the group. If his capacities do not allow him to reach these standards, he experiences failure, he withdraws or is rejected by the group and his self-esteem suffers a shock.

Suppose, then, that we accept a task of therapy, of rebuilding his self-esteem. It would appear plausible from our analysis of the problem that we should attempt to work with variables of the same sort that produced the difficulty, that is to work with him either in the groups to which he now belongs or to introduce him into new groups which are selected for the purpose and to work upon his relationships to groups as such. From the point of view of preventive mental health, we might even attempt to train the group in our communities—classes in schools, work groups in business, families, unions, religious and cultural groups—to make use of practices better designed to protect the self-esteem of their members.

Consider a second example. A teacher finds that in her class she has a number of trouble-makers, full of aggression. She wants to know why these children are so aggressive and what can be done about it. A foreman in a factory has the same kind of problem with some of his workers. He wants the same kind of help. The solution most tempting to both the teacher and the foreman often is to transfer the worst trouble-makers to someone else, or if facilities are available, to refer them for counselling. But is the problem really of such a nature that it can be solved by removing the trouble-maker from the situation or by working on his individual motivations and emotional life? What leads does research give us? The evidence indicates, of course, that there are many causes of aggressiveness in people, but one aspect of the problem has become increasingly clear in recent years. If we observe carefully the amount of aggressive behavior and the number of trouble-makers to be found in a large collection of groups, we find that these characteristics can vary tremendously from group to group even when the different groups are composed essentially of the same kinds of people. In the now classic experiments of Lewin, Lippitt, and White on the effects of different styles of leadership, it was found that the same group of children displayed markedly different levels of aggressive behavior when under different styles of leadership. Moreover, when individual children were transferred from one group to another, their levels of aggressiveness shifted to conform to the atmosphere of the new group. Efforts to account for one child's aggressiveness under one style of leadership merely in terms of his personality traits could hardly succeed under these conditions. This is not to say that a person's behavior is entirely to be accounted for by the atmosphere and structure of the immediate group, but it is remarkable to what an extent a strong, cohesive group can control aspects of a member's behavior traditionally thought to be expressive of enduring personality traits. Recognition of this fact rephrases the problem of how to change such behavior. It directs us to a study of the sources of the influence of the group on its members.

Let us take an example from a different field. What can we learn from efforts to change people by mass media and mass persuasion? In those rare instances when educators, propagandists, advertisers, and others who want to influence large numbers of people, have bothered to make an objective evaluation of the enduring changes produced by their efforts, they have been able to demonstrate only the most negligible effects. The inefficiency of attempts to influence the public by mass media would be scandalous if there were

agreement that it was important or even desirable to have such influences strongly exerted. In fact, it is no exaggeration to say that all of the research and experience of generations has not improved the efficiency of lectures or other means of mass influence to any noticeable degree. Something must be wrong with our theories of learning, motivation, and social psychology.

Within very recent years some research data have been accumulating which may give us a clue to the solution of our problem. In one series of experiments directed by Lewin, it was found that a method of group decision, in which the group as a whole made a decision to have its members change their behavior, was from two to ten times as effective in producing actual change as was a lecture presenting exhortation to change. We have yet to learn precisely what produces these differences of effectiveness, but it is clear that by introducing group forces into the situation a whole new level of influence has been achieved.

What conclusions may we draw from these examples? What principles of achieving change in people can we see emerging? To begin with the most general proposition, we may state that the behavior, attitudes, beliefs, and values of the individual are all firmly grounded in the groups to which he belongs. How aggressive or cooperative a person is, how much self-respect and self-confidence he has, how energetic and productive his work is, what he aspires to, what he believes to be true and good, whom he loves or hates, and what beliefs and prejudices he holds—all these characteristics are highly determined by the individual's group memberships. In a real sense, they are properties of groups and of the relationships between people. Whether they change or resist change will, therefore, be greatly influenced by the nature of these groups. Attempts to change them must be concerned with the dynamics of groups.

In examining more specifically how groups enter into the process of change, we find it useful to view groups in at least three different ways. In the first view, the group is seen as a source of influence over its members. Efforts to change behavior can be supported or blocked by pressures on members stemming from the group. To make constructive use of these pressures the group must be used *as a medium of change.* In the second view, the group itself becomes the *target of change.* To change the behavior of individuals it may be necessary to change the standards of the group, its style of leadership, its emotional atmosphere, or its stratification into cliques and hierarchies. Even though the goal may be to change the behavior of *individuals,* the target of change becomes the group. In the third view, it is recognized that many changes of behavior can be brought about only by the organized efforts of groups *as agents of change.* A committee to combat intolerance, a labor union, an employers' association, a citizens' group to increase the pay of teachers—any action group will be more or less effective depending upon the way it is organized, the satisfactions it provides to its members, the degree to which its goals are clear, and a host of other properties of the group.

An adequate social technology of change, then, requires at the very least a scientific understanding of groups viewed in each of these ways. We shall consider here only the first two aspects of the problem: the group as a medium of change and as a target of change.

The Group as a Medium of Change

Principle No. 1. If the group is to be used effectively as a medium of change, those people who are to be changed and those who are to exert influence for change must have a strong sense of belonging to the same group.

Kurt Lewin described this principle well: "The normal gap between teacher and student, doctor and patient, social worker and public, can . . . be a real obstacle to acceptance of the advocated conduct. In other words, in spite of whatever status differences there might be between them, the teacher and the student have to feel as members of one group in matters involving their sense of values. The chances for re-education seem to be increased whenever a strong we-feeling is created." [1] Recent experiments by Preston and Heintz have demonstrated greater changes of opinions among members of discussion groups operating with participatory leadership than among those with supervisory leadership. The implications of this principle for classroom teaching are far-reaching. The same may be said of supervision in the factory, army, or hospital.

Principle No. 2. The more attractive the group is to its members the greater is the influence that the group can exert on its members.

This principle has been extensively documented by Festinger and his co-workers. They have been able to show in a variety of settings that in more cohesive groups there is a greater readiness of members to attempt to influence others, a greater readiness to be influenced by others, and stronger pressures toward conformity when conformity is

[1] Kurt Lewin, *Resolving Social Conflicts,* p. 67.

a relevant matter for the group. Important for the practitioner wanting to make use of this principle is, of course, the question of how to increase the attractiveness of groups. This is a question with many answers. Suffice it to say that a group is more attractive the more it satisfies the needs of its members. We have been able to demonstrate experimentally an increase in group cohesiveness by increasing the liking of members for each other as persons, by increasing the perceived importance of the group goal, and by increasing the prestige of the group among other groups. Experienced group workers could add many other ways to this list.

Principle No. 3. In attempts to change attitudes, values, or behavior the more relevant they are to the basis of attraction to the group, the greater will be the influence that the group can exert upon them.

I believe this principle gives a clue to some otherwise puzzling phenomena. How does it happen that a group, like a labor union, seems to be able to exert such strong discipline over its members in some matters (let us say in dealings with management), while it seems unable to exert nearly the same influence in other matters (let us say in political action)? If we examine why it is that members are attracted to the group, I believe we will find that a particular reason for belonging seems more related to some of the group's activities than to others. If a man joins a union mainly to keep his job and to improve his working conditions, he may be largely uninfluenced by the union's attempt to modify his attitudes toward national and international affairs. Groups differ tremendously in the range of matters that are relevant to them and hence over which they have influence. Much of the inefficiency of adult education could be reduced if more attention were paid to the need that influence attempts be appropriate to the groups in which they are made.

Principle No. 4. The greater the prestige of a group member in the eyes of the other members, the greater the influence he can exert.

Polansky, Lippitt, and Redl have demonstrated this principle with great care and methodological ingenuity in a series of studies in children's summer camps. From a practical point of view it must be emphasized that the things giving prestige to a member may not be those characteristics most prized by the official management of the group. The most prestige-carrying member of a Sunday School class may not possess the characteristics most similar to the minister of the church. The teacher's pet may be a poor source of influence within a class. This principle is the basis for the common observation that the official leader and the actual leader of a group are often not the same individual.

Principle No. 5. Efforts to change individuals or subparts of a group which, if successful, would have the result of making them deviate from the norms of the group will encounter strong resistance.

During the past few years a great deal of evidence has been accumulated showing the tremendous pressures which groups can exert upon members to conform to the group's norms. The price of deviation in most groups is rejection or even expulsion. If the member really wants to belong and be accepted, he cannot withstand this type of pressure. It is for this reason that efforts to change people by taking them from the group and giving them special training so often have disappointing results.

This principle also accounts for the finding that people thus trained sometimes display increased tension, aggressiveness toward the group, or a tendency to form cults or cliques with others who have shared their training.

These five principles concerning the group as a medium of change would appear to have readiest application to groups created for the purpose of producing changes in people. They provide certain specifications for building effective training or therapy groups. They also point, however, to a difficulty in producing change in people in that they show how resistant an individual is to changing in any way contrary to group pressures and expectations. In order to achieve many kinds of changes in people, therefore, it is necessary to deal with the group as a target of change.

The Group as a Target of Change

Principle No. 6. Strong pressure for changes in the group can be established by creating a shared perception by members of the need for change, thus making the source of pressure for change lie within the group.

Marrow and French report a dramatic case-study which illustrates this principle quite well. A manufacturing concern had a policy against hiring women over thirty because it was believed that they were slower, more difficult to train, and more likely to be absent. The staff psychologist was able to present to management evidence that this belief was clearly unwarranted at least within their own company. The psychologist's facts, however, were rejected and ignored as a basis for action because they violated accepted beliefs. It was claimed that they went against the direct experience of the foremen.

Then the psychologist hit upon a plan for achieving change which differed drastically from the usual one of argument, persuasion, and pressure. He proposed that management conduct its own analysis of the situation. With his help management collected all the facts which they believed were relevant to the problem. When the results were in they were now their own facts rather than those of some "outside" expert. Policy was immediately changed without further resistance. The important point here is that facts are not enough. The facts must be the accepted property of the group if they are to become an effective basis for change. There seems to be all the difference in the world in changes actually carried out between those cases in which a consulting firm is hired to do a study and present a report and those in which technical experts are asked to collaborate with the group in doing its own study.

Principle No. 7. Information relating to the need for change, plans for change, and consequences of change must be shared by all relevant people in the group.

Another way of stating this principle is to say that change of a group ordinarily requires the opening of communication channels. Newcomb has shown how one of the first consequences of mistrust and hostility is the avoidance of communicating openly and freely about the things producing the tension. If you look closely at a pathological group (that is, one that has trouble making decisions or effecting coordinated efforts of its members), you will certainly find strong restraints in that group against communicating vital information among its members. Until these restraints are removed there can be little hope for any real and lasting changes in the group's functioning. In passing it should be pointed out that the removal of barriers to communication will ordinarily be accompanied by a sudden increase in the communication of hostility. The group may appear to be falling apart, and it will certainly be a painful experience to many of the members. This pain and the fear that things are getting out of hand often stop the process of change once begun.

Principle No. 8. Changes in one part of a group produce strain in other related parts which can be reduced only by eliminating the change or by bringing about readjustments in the related parts.

It is a common practice to undertake improvements in group functioning by providing training programs for certain classes of people in the organization. A training program for foremen, for nurses, for teachers, or for group workers is established. If the content of the training is relevant for organizational change, it must of necessity deal with the relationships these people have with other subgroups. If nurses in a hospital change their behavior significantly, it will affect their relations both with the patients and with the doctors. It is unrealistic to assume that both these groups will remain indifferent to any significant changes in this respect. In hierarchical structures this process is most clear. Lippitt has proposed on the basis of research and experience that in such organizations attempts at change should always involve three levels, one being the major target of change and the other two being the one above and the one below.

These eight principles represent a few of the basic propositions emerging from research in group dynamics. Since research is constantly going on and since it is the very nature of research to revise and reformulate our conceptions, we may be sure that these principles will have to be modified and improved as time goes by. In the meantime they may serve as guides in our endeavors to develop a scientifically based technology of social management.

In social technology, just as in physical technology, invention plays a crucial role. In both fields progress consists of the creation of new mechanisms for the accomplishment of certain goals. In both fields inventions arise in response to practical needs and are to be evaluated by how effectively they satisfy these needs. The relation of invention to scientific development is indirect but important. Inventions cannot proceed too far ahead of basic scientific development, nor should they be allowed to fall too far behind. They will be more effective the more they make good use of known principles of science, and they often make new developments in science possible. On the other hand, they are in no sense logical derivations from scientific principles.

I have taken this brief excursion into the theory of invention in order to make a final point. To many people "group dynamics" is known only for the social inventions which have developed in recent years in work with groups. Group dynamics is often thought of as certain techniques to be used with groups. Role playing, buzz groups, process observers, post-meeting reaction sheets, and feedback of group observations are devices popularly associated with the phrase "group dynamics". I trust that I have been able to show that group dynamics is more than a collection of gadgets. It certainly aspires to be a science as well as a technology.

This is not to underplay the importance of these inventions nor of the function of inventing. As inventions they are all mechanisms designed to help accomplish important goals. How effective they are will depend upon how skilfully they are used and how appropriate they are to the purposes to which they are put. Careful evaluative research must be the ultimate judge of their usefulness in comparison with alternative inventions. I believe that the principles enumerated in this paper indicate some of the specifications that social inventions in this field must meet.

◆◆◆◆◆◆◆◆◆◆◆◆◆◆◆◆◆◆◆◆ LEARNING THROUGH ROLE PLAYING

Grace Levit and Helen H. Jennings

MORE and more people are talking about role playing. And for almost every person who talks about how he saw role playing used in an industrial training session, a discussion group, a classroom or a conference, there is someone else who says, "I've heard of it, but just exactly what is it?"

Role playing is a relatively new educational technique in which people spontaneously act out problems of human relations and analyze the enactment with the help of other role players and observers. Role playing, sociodrama, and psychodrama are closely related, and the terms sociodrama and role playing are sometimes used interchangeably.* People who have run across all three of them are often understandably confused about the distinctions between them. Role playing is a general term referring to the spon-

taneous acting out of roles in the context of human relations situations. It is part of the two broad methods devised by Dr. J. L. Moreno—sociodrama and psychodrama. Both sociodrama and psychodrama require not only players, but an audience who help the players interpret their roles. Sociodrama deals with the interactions of people with other individuals or groups as carriers of some specified *cultural role,* such as supervisor, leader, mother, father, employee, etc. Sociodramatic situations always involve more than one person and deal with problems a majority of the members of the group face in executing their roles.

While psychodrama may also be practiced in a group setting, it is mainly concerned with the unique problems of a particular individual. A crucial difference between psychodrama and sociodrama is the greater emphasis upon the private or personalized world of some individual in the former, and the greater emphasis on what is common in the social roles of many individuals

* We have chosen to use the term role playing rather than sociodrama simply because it is more common. This pamphlet is concerned with the sociodramatic, and not the psychodramatic uses of role playing.

From Grace Levit and Helen H. Jennings, "Learning through Role Playing," Adult Leadership *Pamphlet No. 6, 1960, pp. 5–10. Used by permission.*

in the latter. For example, a son or daughter has much in common with all sons or daughters in a particular culture. But at the same time every son or daughter has a personal and interpersonal world which is uniquely his. With the latter, sociodrama has least, and psychodrama, most concern. Because psychodrama is concerned with unique individual needs and problems it should not be attempted except under the guidance of a trained therapist.

Why Use Role Playing?

The growing interest of all kinds of groups in role playing makes it the more important that we answer this question clearly. Part of the answer is that role playing is novel; it is an absorbing group activity; and it provides opportunities for much more active participation by group members than do many other educational methods. These are good reasons, as many groups still suffer from a rigidly narrow range of methods, or from methods which do not highly involve the members. But they are by no means the most important reasons for using role playing.

A major advantage of role playing as an educational method is that it can bring out data about human behavior and human relations which are not made available by more traditional methods. Written records or lectures may give a group useful data and may stretch the boundaries of the group's previous experience, but the data they bring is limited by the fact that it must always be presented to the group through the medium of words. They cannot provide the group with direct common experience of what is being talked about. Role playing, so to speak, caters to the whole person of the learner. He not only hears about a problem or tells about it; he *lives through it* by acting it out—he experiences it emotionally and then uses this experience to produce and test insights into the problem and generalizations about ways of dealing with it. He may also practice what he has learned until it becomes a part of himself. Thus, through role playing individuals may develop new skills for dealing with problems in human relations. Furthermore, role-playing allows groups to get case material which, unlike the written or even the filmed record, can be tailored readily to fit the specific needs and situation of the particular group that is going to use it. For example, worker's education groups can do role playing on handling grievances, discussion groups on handling overtalkative members, etc.

Because role playing helps people to get insight into their own and others' feelings, it has been widely recognized as a method of helping people to broaden their understanding of and to empathize with other people; to see things from the point of view of the person on the other side of the table (or tracks, or globe).

Another value of role playing is that it allows many attitudes and feelings that fundamentally affect group process, but are usually left unexpressed and subjective, to be brought before the group for review. Thus role playing can serve as a method for illustrating and objectifying many of the causal and dynamic factors in group process and human relations that are frequently ignored. Role playing can also serve as a method of presenting information about what particular individuals in a group have been doing, for example, when a subgroup wishes to *show* its parent group what it has been doing, rather than just to *tell about* the results.

But perhaps the most important value of role playing is that, because it is a way of presenting human relations problems in the context of a classroom, training group, or social laboratory, group members can experiment with their behavior, make mistakes and try new skills without chancing the hurts that experimentation in real-life situations may involve. In this artificial environment the learner can try out new behavior in the presence not of judges, but of co-learners.

The Role Playing Process

How does a group go about using role playing as a learning device? Like most dramatic presentations, role playing needs a director who is responsible for all the procedural aspects involved in the process and who helps the actors and other group members (observers) become emotionally involved with the situation to be acted out. The director may be the leader of the group or some other member who is familiar with the role playing process. Unlike a director in a legitimate theatre, however, whose main function is to help actors interpret already written lines and characterizations, a director of role playing is mainly concerned with helping the actors to be *spontaneous* in presenting the characters they are portraying, and in helping the audience observers to analyze the situation and behaviors presented in the role playing in order to increase their insights into problems and their effective knowledge of how to deal with them.

As an educational technique, role playing involves more than the simple acting out of roles. It is made up of a series of steps, of which the actual act-

ing is only one, and it is the director's job to see that all these steps are taken care of in every role playing situation and that the function of each step is understood by everyone in the group. In practice, these steps usually flow into one another quite naturally, and the different steps have greater or less importance in different role playing situations. But the director needs to recognize the steps and help the group understand the significance of each of them. In brief, the steps in the role playing process are: Defining the problem; establishing a situation; casting characters; briefing and warming up actors and observers; acting; cutting; discussing and analyzing the situation and behavior by actors and observers; and making plans for further testing of the insights gained or for practicing the new behavior implied.

Most groups will welcome a suggestion to try role playing in their meetings, as most people like opportunities for dramatic expression and like to try new ways of bringing content into their group meetings. Some groups, however, may be more hesitant about role playing, or even frightened because they do not see themselves as "actors" or because they are afraid such spontaneous expression and exploration of problems may get too close to personal anxieties and problems.

Groups which appear hesitant about role playing will quickly learn to feel at ease with it by starting with some very simple situation which can be initiated out of some problem the group is presently dealing with. One member of a discussion group, for example, might be having a heated argument with another over the right of farmers to receive production subsidies. The first member insists that the second member cannot look at the problem objectively because he is from a farm background and will always be in favor of anything that helps the farmers, whether or not it hurts the rest of the country. A third member of the group, or the group leader, could easily introduce role playing as a way of helping each party to this argument get a better understanding of the other's point of view. He might suggest that each of the contenders stop the argument and portray the other person, seeing how accurately each can represent the other's point of view. After a few minutes of this attempt to reverse roles, each person could be asked to describe how he felt in the role of the other, or if he though he might have been oversimplifying or stereotyping the other's position. This simple, but effective, way of using role playing has the advantage of needing almost no preparation. It automatically briefs and warms up the participants. After such an experience, some other uses of role playing could be described to the group.

Generally when role playing is used for the first time, the situation selected should be simple enough to allow group members to discuss it profitably. It is important that group members have the experience of discovering that they can, with the leader or director's guidance, explore a problem, break it down into factors which may be causing it, and construct ways of meeting the problem through changing the situation or their behavior. Generally, it is also true that while an experienced group leader can take on the job of directing role playing readily, an inexperienced group leader may feel too burdened to charge himself with sole responsibility as a director and may want to involve group members in this task with him.

Avoiding overpersonalization of problems. The role playing director can do much to help a group steer clear of psychodramatic situations and analyses by being on the alert to avoid situations and roles which lead to personal exposures or are so closely related to personal and private feelings that psychodramatic expression can hardly be helped. The director sets the tone for portrayals and analyses in introducing briefing and discussion, by pointing out that the job of the observers is to look at the actors in terms of their *roles*. It should be made clear that each actor is playing a specified role in a specific situation, and is merely giving his spontaneous interpretation of how such a character would be likely to respond in such a situation.

Avoiding overuse of role playing. Groups which are new to role playing as an educational technique sometimes get very interested in it and begin to use it as a cure-all or a gadget. Such inappropriate over-use may lessen its effectiveness when it should be used. If role playing is to be an effective training tool it must assume its proper place among other educational methods in the group's repertoire. It is wise to remember that role playing is useful in dealing with a very distinct group of problems only—that is, problems involving human relations. There are many other procedures which are sufficient to meet the educational requirements of many group situations, and sometimes it is wise to reserve role playing only for those situations where it is crucially required.

Finally, when role playing *is* used, it can be enriched and varied by adapting variations and new forms to the basic structure. Groups that have gained some experience with the basic technique will want to build new or more complex structures for getting at specific problems. Some such ideas, such as the use of alter-ego techniques, consultants to the actors, etc., are described in the literature on role playing, but many groups will be able to invent these adaptations in relation to their own specific needs. In fact, the basic role playing technique offers one of the best opportunities for exploiting the inventive abilities of any group.

◆◆◆◆◆◆◆◆◆◆◆◆◆◆◆◆◆◆◆◆ THE INCIDENT PROCESS—LEARNING BY DOING * *Paul and Faith Pigors*

Wʜᴀᴛ the Dodo said of the Caucus race fits the Incident Process, too: "The best way to explain it is to do it." The nearest we can get to that, here, is to imagine that you have enrolled in a course to analyze cases by this method. So, here we are, sitting around a conference table, ready to begin.

At this first meeting, the members of this writing team will take two of the leading roles—serving as the Director (who is responsible for the whole series of meetings) and also as the Team Leader (who is presenting a case and leading a discussion on it). As yet, no other member of the group has had time to prepare himself for leading, in either role. And, for this trial run, we shall do without our third leader, the Observer-Reporter. (His job is to notice and record the facts of performance and

to bring key facts to our attention in his report.)

Before we start work on a case, let's make sure that we all have the same idea as to what our analytical method is. To analyze a case is to explore a given territory, hunting for meaning. At every step of the way we are inquiring. And each step covers a distinctive kind of question. By outlining the whole series of decisive questions, now, we can give a bird's-eye view of the Incident Process.

A Process of Questioning

1. As each member *studies the Incident,* he asks himself: What seems to be going on here? How can I get my bearings in this new situation? What do I need to find out, in order to clarify facts and get down to the issues?

2. In the *fact-finding phase,* these questions are put into words. All members of the discussion group work together on the decisive and inclusive question: What are the facts, and which are key facts? This gets us to the still more decisive question—

3. *What needs to be decided now?* Having thus defined the immediate is-

* In an earlier article the authors discussed their belief that: (1) The long-term aim in studying cases of social relations is to promote improvement in social relations. (2) We are not making satisfactory headway toward this aim until (3) we can show that by studying cases we are developing the kind of understanding that is needed to prevent and to reduce difficulties between people. (4) In order to do this, our method of work must be such that we test and apply in our own behavior what we learn in theory from cases—we must learn by doing.

From Paul and Faith Pigors, "The Incident Process—Learning by Doing," *Massachusetts Institute of Technology Series 2, No. 46. Used by permission.*

sue, we are ready to set about deciding it.

4. First, each member writes his own answer to the question: What is my *decision* on this issue, and what are my *supporting reasons?* By a quick count of these decisions, we find out: How does the group, as a whole, stand on this issue? If there is some difference of opinion (as there usually is): What is the strongest line of reasoning in support of each position? We then test all this reasoning by turning to the question: What actually was decided, not in this group, but in the case situation itself?

Having got the immediate issue out of the way, we can ask the kind of question which, more than all others, contributes to learning.

5. As we look back, *to evaluate* a whole series of actions, decisions and consequences, what seems useful and constructive? If we now focus on preventing difficulties, what possibilities are there for doing better? What *general propositions* can we see and take with us, as working hypotheses, for the future?

Now let's get going on a case. That's what we would be doing in the first meeting, after a brief explanation. We'll now hand around a written statement of an Incident. Here it is:

Incident

(From a case concerning the proper activity of a firstline supervisor)

"On Saturday, January 27, 1951, Assistant Foreman Feldman was observed working on various production jobs. Later that day, Liebig (a tool inspector and chairman of the Union Grievance Committee) said to Bauer (shop steward): 'That s-o-b Feldman is at it again.

It's about time we hit him with another grievance!' "

1. STUDYING THE INCIDENT

When you examine such a sketchy statement as this, you will see at once that the next step is to get facts. Some of your first mental questions might be these: Who "observed" Feldman? What evidence is there that he actually "worked on various production jobs?" What did Liebig mean by "at it again?" Does the existing labor agreement have any bearing on this matter? In thinking of such questions, you will already be beginning your work as a case analyst in a specific role. This role assignment is appended, in writing, to each Incident. For example, in this case, you will find one of the two following instructions:

"You are the general foreman, to whom this case has come in the regular course of the Grievance Procedure. What action might you take?" Or,

"You are the impartial arbitrator to whom this case has been referred after failure of the parties to settle it themselves. You will be expected to render your award (which is binding) and to outline your discussion (your reasoning)."

In undertaking either of these assignments you will be helping yourself, in several ways, to work on this case efficiently. (1) You will know at once what *kind of decision* you are expected to make; an administrative decision or an arbitrator's award. (2) You will immediately feel a *sense of involvement* because it is obvious that your decision will become an important factor in this developing situation. (3) You will be all set to work cooperatively with other members of your discussion group because this assignment is *collective.* (4)

By putting yourself into any such *specific role,* you will get a more realistic understanding of the opportunities and restrictions that go with that particular position and function.

Your work on this first sub-operation will take from two to five minutes; depending on whether you just glance at the statement of the Incident, or actually study it. When everyone is ready, we'll take the next step.

2. FACT-FINDING

Now you will do your share in conducting a group interview with the leader who has the facts of this case. And you will get your facts systematically, starting from the *scene of action* as sketched in the Incident. You may find it hard to stick to the scene of action long enough to get a clear picture of what was going on. This is because most of the questions which need to be asked about the Incident also lead away from it, if followed up. And, of course, once you have an accurate picture of the facts of behavior during the Incident, you will need to follow these leads into *the larger context,* so that you can see the Incident in its setting. Otherwise you could not understand what the facts mean, or appreciate why those people behaved as they did.

Someone is bound to ask: Was there some trouble like this before? Did any previous dispute provide a reliable precedent for deciding this case? Sooner or later, questions about what Feldman was doing will lead naturally to the history of difficulties that induced him to work on production jobs. (By this time you will have established the fact that he actually did some such work.) Also, if you are analyzing this case as an arbitrator, you will have a chance to

learn something from interim developments. What were the consequences of Feldman's work on production jobs? Was any worker displaced, or did anyone lose any pay? Was there any reason to fear that any such consequences might come later?

At this stage, too, your question about applicable contract clauses will need to be answered. This will be one of the questions that can best be answered in writing. And it is part of a discussion leader's job to be prepared for this. Among other duplicated material for distribution, we have copies of the two contract clauses that are relevant.

After half an hour or so of such questions and answers, the mass of information will look more like a "mess" than like an orderly case report. Getting this material together has been fun. Since everyone pitches in, the work goes easily and quickly. It's more like the old-fashioned custom of barn-raising, than like the solitary homework that so many people dislike.

But now comes the hard part, sorting and condensing. Can you do this for us? If you jotted down key points as they were brought out, or made mental notes, you can probably lift them out for us, clearly and concisely, in an effective summary. Particularly at this first meeting, you will be doing us a service by volunteering for this difficult task, even if you are not sure of being able to do a perfect job. Other members can easily correct, amplify or condense your summary, if necessary, once you have done the rough sorting. Everyone knows how much easier it is to edit a statement than to make the first draft. Having now reduced "the whole story" (or full-length case report) to manageable proportions, we are ready to tackle the issue.

3. WHAT NEEDS TO BE DECIDED?

This brings us to the decisive question: What is the immediate issue, and how can we state it most effectively? The way in which one sees and formulates an issue (or problem) largely predetermines the decision (or solution). Therefore, in the Incident Process, we'll make a point of working hard on this question. But we're not going to expect to make a home run the first shot out of the box.

For instance, in the Feldman case the first statement of the issue may be this: "Was Feldman wrong in doing production work?" But is this formulation good enough? Isn't there more at issue here than Feldman's personal behavior? And isn't the word "wrong" too moralistic? Can't we get a statement that will (1) pinpoint the crux of this misunderstanding but also (2) indicate the referents for impartial decision and (3) emphasize some typical features of this case? Working according to these specifications, you might suggest the following formulation: "In such circumstances, and under the existing contract, is an assistant foreman carrying out his proper functions by doing the kind and amount of work on production jobs that Feldman did on the day in question?"

Such a statement will be equally useful whether you are working on this case as the general foreman or as an impartial arbitrator. Another advantage is that when we have decided this issue, we shall have learned something that we can use in other cases, too. But at this first meeting, unless your discussion group is exceptional, we may not do an outstanding job on the issue. Your group is probably impatient to hurry ahead to decision, so let's go. But

whatever you agree upon, as the issue, we wind up this phase by having your whole group write it down. This means that when members write their individual answers, everyone is at least starting from the same question.

4. MAKING AND TESTING DECISIONS

You will now spend five or ten minutes in thinking and writing. This may seem peculiar in a discussion meeting. But there's a reason for it: to test and develop your decisiveness and ability to reason. Your written paper will give not only your decision but also your supporting reasons. Now that you're right up against it, you may be surprised to find that you still lack some facts that you need to work with. For instance, perhaps no one asked whether Feldman checked with his immediate supervisor or talked the matter over with the shop steward before taking action that invited misunderstanding by union officers. Similarly, you may wish that there had been more discussion as to the relative importance of various items that were established as facts. As it happened, in this case, the two contract clauses that are relevant were not wholly consistent. When that is a fact, how is a first-line supervisor supposed to make up his mind what to do? If there are technical difficulties that are holding up production (as in this case), is he entitled to tackle them, even when this means working production jobs himself?

In this case it makes little difference whether your immediate decision is made as the general foreman or as an impartial arbitrator. Here, as so often, what is valid reasoning for an arbitrator is no less valid for a management representative or a union official. One general proposition that does not need to be stated tentatively is this: If management representatives and union officers could learn to think more nearly like arbitrators, there would be far less work for outside arbitrators to do.

By the time members of your group have turned in their signed decisions, you will probably welcome a five-minute break. During this interval, the writing team (doubling now as Observer-Reporter) will sort the papers. In this case, so far, every group has divided on the issue. Let's assume that it has happened here too. The next step is for each subgroup of likeminded members to go into a huddle, consolidate their position, and elect a spokesman. The stage is now set for a sharp debate, and this form of verbal combat can go on for a few minutes, just long enough to demonstrate its futility for our purpose. But soon your group will shut off the debate by answering a question from the leader. For instance: "Does anyone think we're getting anywhere this way?" The chorus of "noes" that greets this question may be the first expression of unanimity so far.

The writing team now apply another kind of test by giving you the facts on what actually was decided in the case situation. And since this case went to arbitration, you can know not only what the management decision was, but also how this line of reasoning (and the union's position) looked to the arbitrator, and what his award and discussion were.

But that's not the end of our work on this case. In fact, when we reach the final phase of case analysis, we are just getting going on the most important part, distilling a residue of learning.

5. EVALUATING AND GENERALIZING

Now that we are ready to go to the heart of this case, as a whole, we must broaden and lengthen our thinking. This situation is far more than a dispute. And more is at stake here than the behavior of one foreman on any one day. More fundamental issues concern the continuing relations between a management and a union. These people have been engaged in doing technical work in the same place. But they have developed little efficiency in working *together*. Perhaps they have not thought this important or even desirable. But that's no reason why case analysts should not explore the possibilities. In thinking about such issues, we can't afford to be restricted by the existing labor agreement, or even by company policies, procedures, and rules *as now written*. Therefore, if you have been working on this case so far as an arbitrator, why don't you now take on the role of personnel administrator? From that angle, you will need to decide questions like this: What might have been done better, especially by our management group, as leaders? What might be done, now, to improve our relations with the union?

This line of inquiry leads naturally to generalizing. Your decisions will still need to be grounded in facts. But they must also extend toward the future and reach up to the level of general ideas. As you look around at other cases and connect them with your own experience, you cannot help seeing some of the main threads in "the evertangled skein of human affairs." For instance, this is not the only case in which a dispute might have been avoided if a foreman had felt like talking things over with a shop steward before hand. So, what about it? How might we work toward this in the future?

Probably at this first session our time will have run out before we get far with the step where analyzing the past can build toward the future. But as a regular member of this group, you will have more time to work at this later.

You Will Learn by Leading

Also, you will learn more about social relations by doing more of the leading. As a Team Leader, you will select a case, write up an Incident, and prepare for discussion by making a detailed teaching plan. If you are a leader who can follow spontaneous leads from group members, the discussion will not wholly conform to your plan. But your work in planning won't be wasted. It has given you an intensive, special experience in case analysis. And it will give you something to fall back on if, at any stage of discussion, no one else has relevant ideas.

You will also take a turn at the job of Observer-Reporter. And you will probably be surprised at how much you can see and learn from that angle. As the silent partner (during discussion), you will be freed from all responsibility both for "getting out production" on the case, and for supervising this work. Therefore, you can give your whole attention to observing and recording the facts that we need for evaluating our own performance as case analysts, and for learning how to do better. In gathering this material: (1) You will start by paying attention to a scene of action. (2) You will get facts, summarize and interpret them, and then weigh their relative importance in this case (our work situation). (3) In preparing your report you will probably highlight one or two difficulties (or issues) because you think it will pay us to tackle them now. (4) You will make up your mind as to how we might do better, and also as to how you can most effectively present your opinion to us in writing. (5) You will be giving us a good lead for joint evaluation when you stress what we have done well, show where we have made progress, and measure our current performance by the aims and standards on which we have agreed, in theory.

What about the Director?

As Observer, you will probably notice that the Director is contributing something, too. And when you think about his share in the work, you will realize that this kind of leadership is needed. He did all the preliminary planning, briefed the group on the method, and presented the first case. Later, he starts from scratch on each case with other discussion members. But he is more than just another member. If necessary, he will provide items of general information that are needed in order to interpret specific facts of a case. And his cumulative experience enables him to reenforce a Team Leader in helping members to get going on the last and most difficult phase of case analysis. In such ways he is always on tap. The greater his success as a teacher, the *less* he will need to do as other members *learn to do more* for themselves and by helping each other. But he is not absolved from any of his executive responsibilities for standards of work and behavior merely because he has delegated some of these to a succession of subleaders.

Where Do We Go from Cases?

As we work on cases by the Incident Process, in all these roles, we do more than just talk. By thinking out loud together about a variety of experiences, we keep on making connections. And a valuable by-product of this way of working is that we soon start making some changes in our own attitudes and behavior. As we look at the record (supplied by our own members as Reporters), we can see signs that we are developing more of the special blend of understanding that is so greatly needed in human relations. For example, a gain that is both intellectual and practical, is to find that we are learning something from the experience of other people, as reported in cases. Socially speaking, perhaps we make the most headway by experiencing the opportunities and responsibilities of working, as members, in a variety of roles. In this way we see clearly that there is no absolute separation between being a responsible worker and doing a share of the leading. We also develop more practical judgment. After working on a few cases, members agree that however "elegant" a solution may be in theory, it won't help us now if it won't work.

In all these ways, we are learning by doing, as members. In thus breaking down the artificial barrier between education and living, we begin to meet the full challenge of case study in human relations.

❖❖❖❖❖❖❖❖❖❖❖❖❖❖❖❖❖❖❖ THE TRAINING GROUP

Matthew B. Miles

For a variety of reasons, which will be discussed later, training for better group behavior takes place best in a *training group*. Such groups differ in certain respects from work groups, from classroom groups, and from psychotherapy groups. A description of these differences may help to clarify the nature of training further.

FOCUS ON MEMBER CHANGE

A training group differs most centrally from a *work group* on the job in placing less emphasis on the accomplishment of a specific external task and more emphasis on improvement of its members' skills. For example, a work group that had great difficulty in reaching decisions would be a flop on the job. When a training group has decision-making difficulties, however, they are grist for the mill. The members can analyze the difficulties, try again, and learn from the experience. This is the essential nature of the laboratory approach.

Since a training group's objective is *change* in its members' ways of doing things, their procedures, their practices, most training groups do not also try to accomplish "work" tasks. Their work, in effect, is to cause themselves to learn to be better group participants. Since a training group does *not* have to make up new curriculum guides, agree on playground policy, or clarify bond issue proposals, the members are freer to experiment and learn about group behavior. This idea is often puzzling to

From Matthew B. Miles, Learning How to Work in Groups, *N.Y.: Bureau of Publications, Teachers College, Columbia University, 1959, pp. 35–45. Footnotes omitted. Abridged and used by permission.*

people who have not attended training groups. "What on earth do you talk about?" The answer—it is perhaps a maddeningly vague one—is that a training group talks about any and all group process problems that appear in the course of its work.

Most training groups, then, have a limited life span. They remain together for a specified period of time. It is assumed that their members, as they move back to their work groups, will keep on behaving in the new, more effective ways they have learned in the training group.

FOCUS ON THE HERE-AND-NOW

How does a training group differ from the usual *classroom group?* Both are concerned with changes in their members' behavior, yet these changes are of somewhat different sorts.

In a classroom, the content discussed and the skills learned are ordinarily drawn from the surrounding culture. Thus children are to learn to read, to write, to handle numbers, to be familiar with certain facts and generalizations essential to adequate functioning in the adult world. Most of this content is externally given, originating outside the classroom in time and space. The teacher's task, in a sense, is to help the child relate his here-and-now experience to this body of content.

In a training group, on the other hand, the here-and-now is the major source of content. What is discussed originates almost completely within the group. The members of a training group are actively motivated to discuss group process difficulties of a sort which a teacher may well choose to ignore, handle without mentioning, punish, or only analyze wearily in the teachers' room with friends. In some classrooms

(for example, core classes, homerooms), a large fraction of time may be spent in discussing here-and-now behavior and nearly all teachers encourage such discussion occasionally (as in evaluation of committee work). But it is unusual to see a class situation where almost exclusive attention is paid to the analysis of what is happening between people, right now, as a means to learning. This is as it should be. The classroom group is not primarily a training group.

FOCUS ON THE SOCIAL SELF

It may be asked, finally, what the difference is between a training group and a *group for psychotherapy*. Both groups are concerned with changes in their members' behavior, and both use here-and-now content.

Although all positive change in people has therapeutic aspects, there are some important differences between training and therapy. In a therapy group, the participants are patients. They are ill. Illness implies that something in the person has gone wrong, that the person is troubled or suffering and needs cure.

In a training group, on the other hand, the members are healthy, are not suffering, but do have dissatisfactions about their own *skills.* They would like to be able to do something better, to cope with everyday problems in an improved manner.

Finally, in a training group, as the distinctions above imply, there is less emphasis on a person's inner workings and much more emphasis on his "outer workings"—the way he relates to people. A training group is usually less concerned with the inner reasons for *why* someone does something, and more concerned with *how* he does it, what the impact is on others, and how he can improve what he does to become more skillful.

A member of a training group may discover for himself how his inner problems are hindering his effectiveness with other people, but the training group is not the place for him to work out all the intricacies of these problems. It is the place for him to gain more insight into his social self—to see how his behaviors impinge on others. This distinction cannot, of course, be sharply made, but the emphasis is as stated.

In summary, then, a training group is a group designed to help its members make constructive changes in their social selves, by means of analysis of here-and-now experiences. The remainder of this book (Miles, 1959) is devoted to explaining specifically how training works, and what must be done if it is to be successful.

It might be added here, incidentally, that the relatively impersonal account above probably communicates little of the specific sense of excitement and involvement that is a part of most training group sessions.

How People Learn through Training

Given the background comments above on the nature of training, it may be helpful to present here a description of the process of learning better group behavior. What is the experience of a person like, as he grows and learns during one or several training activities? The following is a general outline of the psychological steps in the training process, expressed in graphic form.

The process of learning is here shown as cyclical. After going from step A_1

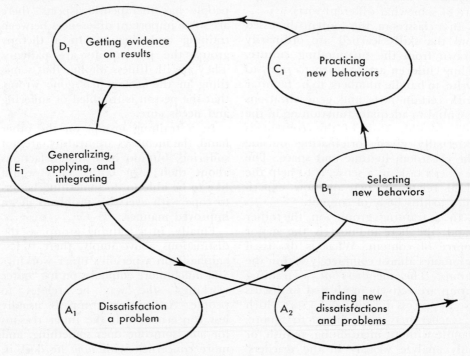

Steps in the training process

through step E_1, the learner returns to step A_2, which is then followed by B_2, C_2, and so on. Over a period of time, the learning cycle would be repeated many times:

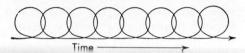

Time ──────────────►

If training is effective, this spiral moves, over time, in the direction of better and better behavior in groups.

It should immediately be said that learning is more than a rational process. At each of the stages above, the person faces emotional problems and stresses, since what is involved is change —*change in me.* For this reason, learning during training is not the neat, stepwise progression implied; but it is useful to look at a simplified model as a means of understanding the living, exciting process of learning more clearly. Here again the reader is invited to turn to his own model of learning for comparison. The ideas presented below have roots in more general conceptions of learning (compare John Dewey's treatment in *How we think,* for example), but are focused on the special case of learning to work more effectively in groups.

Below, each of several stages in learning is discussed in turn, and the basic feelings involved are explored. The problem of training, in effect, is to provide conditions to help this learning process go forward effectively.

Why *would* a person want to change and learn? Before there is likely to be much significant improvement in a person's group behavior, the person himself must first, believe that effective group work is an important matter for him; and second, be dissatisfied to some extent with his own attitudes, un-

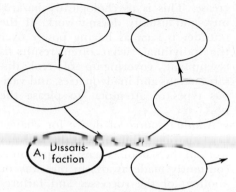

Dissatisfaction, a problem

derstandings, and behaviors as a participant in working groups. Initially, this may be a vague, unfocused feeling of discomfort, but as learning proceeds, it becomes more defined ("How can I explain my ideas more clearly to others?"). The learner must, in effect, come to feel some more or less specific *inadequacy* in relation to his own role in groups, or learning cannot go forward. This inadequacy is a relative matter; even a very capable group participant may wish to improve what he does, even though he feels his behavior is fairly effective already.

Immediately, emotional problems are involved; frequently the natural desire is to protect the self by believing that all human relations problems are somehow due to the inadequacies of others. And old fears of punishment and failure are at work; so it is hard for the individual to feel—let alone openly express—inadequacy. If all this is so, how do feelings of dissatisfaction and perceived inadequacy come to increase before and during a training program?

If an "outsider," such as a consultant, a supervisor, or a status leader, points out some of the person's limitations to him, the person's dissatisfaction with his own group behavior may in-

crease. This is psychologically hazardous—and usually doesn't work. If the
outsider is seen as having power over
the individual, what often results is
resentment, covering-up of real dissatisfactions and inadequacies, and various types of attempts "to please the
boss."

Another source of desire for change
is a situational difficulty in the person's
work in the school. A sensitive person is
constantly made aware, in one way or
another, of the successes and failures
of his work. ("Why are the committee
members so apathetic?" "Did I handle
the situation all right when Mary kept
going off on a tangent?" "Why don't
the principals carry through on decisions they seemed to agree to?")
Most school people want strongly to do
better what they are already doing,
and this is a basic source of creative
dissatisfaction.

Finally, if the person has become dissatisfied enough with his own behavior
to enter a training activity (which he
hopes will reduce the dissatisfaction),
additional desires for change may appear. In a supportive training group,
he may learn that "I'm not the hot-
shot I thought I was," as one principal
ruefully remarked. He may be able to
shift from blaming others to looking
at what he himself is contributing to
make group work ineffective. Until
such a shift can be made—and it is
difficult—he may feel frustrated or angry that he is not getting the answers
he had hoped for.

Practical experience in training programs suggests this generalization:
When the primary motivation for improvement comes from an individual's
concern about what "outsiders" want
him to do, the changes in his behavior
are apt to be confused, transitory, unintegrated, and irrelevant to the real

demands of the job. When the primary
motivation for improvement comes
from the strong desires of the person—
aided by "insiders" who are members
of the same training group—to improve
his own ways of working with others,
then the changes in his behavior can
become increasingly systematic, permanent, integrated, and job-related.

Even when there is intrinsic motivation for changing, however, there are
still emotional problems of resistance,
loss of status, and fear of failure. An
atmosphere must be developed in which
people can safely talk about the tensions, dissatisfactions, and difficulties
they personally are experiencing. Such
expressions serve as a basis for training.
But dissatisfaction with one's effectiveness in work is not likely to be voiced
in an atmosphere that involves hazards
of threat, punishment, or criticism. It
is important to use off-the-job meetings,
role playing, and other methods to increase psychological safety.

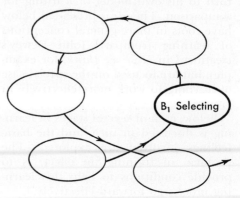

Selecting new behaviors

Given dissatisfaction and the willingness to attend a training activity to reduce that dissatisfaction, there is a next
important step.

The person in training must become
aware of, and consider trying out, new

actions which promise to help him solve the problem(s) he faces in his work with groups. That is, the learner needs to think creatively of different practices that might reduce his dissatisfactions with his present behavior. ("Maybe I don't have to hold the reins so tightly when I am the chairman," or "Perhaps I should try to listen more carefully instead of thinking of what I'm going to say next.")

These pictures in the mind, or models of better behavior in groups, stem from many different sources. They may come from books or materials on group work, from the observed behavior of other members of the group (including, quite frequently, the trainer), and from the comments and suggestions of other associates.

In effect, the learner is now framing an action hypothesis which might read: "*If* I try this new behavior (for example, 'Shut up in meetings for a change'), *then* some desirable consequences will result ('Other people will take more responsibility and be less apathetic')."

At first, people do not usually consider a very wide range of different behavioral possibilities. In early meetings of training groups, members may not think of ideas much more challenging than "talking more" and "talking less." This restriction on possibilities for changed behavior is not just happenstance. Most people have specialized in certain ways of behaving for so long (being the aggressive deflater, the smooth harmonizer, the non-listener) that freely and frankly considering the idea that one could behave differently is quite difficult. And the idea that problems in groups are really *someone else's* fault is a very durable one. For these reasons, the creative non-judging atmosphere of the good training group is important. It can help to widen the

range of new possible behaviors from which to select. Too, if the group members hold the expectation that everyone is in the process of changing and learning—and that this is to be desired —then visualizing new and improved behaviors is really aided.

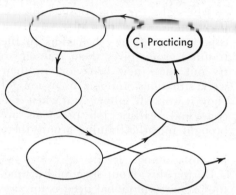

Practicing new behaviors

Given the felt need to learn, and some new ideas about what might work, the person must have numerous opportunities to practice, with reasonable safety, some of the behaviors that he and others consider to be promising. This practice can be thought of as a provisional try, taking place under circumstances that involve a minimum of threat and risk. In effective training programs, considerable energy usually goes into the planning of methods that permit behavioral experimentation with little risk. Role playing, for example, can be used to practice skills and behaviors under semi-real conditions before they are tried out in job situations.

Role playing is not the only way to practice new behavior. In a training group where people have supported each other through initial phases of frustration and hesitancy in admitting inadequacy, a person who has been extremely vigorous and articulate, even interruptive, may decide to keep quiet for a meeting to "see how the other half feels." Or someone who wants chairmanship skills may volunteer to serve as chairman while the next agenda item is discussed.

In a good training program, group members also carry on considerable experimentation on the job. Successful experience with new behaviors in the training group gives them courage to try out these new behaviors in their work situations. Intense discussions of "how it worked" follow. And when concrete and realistic job problems are brought into the training group, there is considerable promise for improved job functioning.

During this tryout stage of learning, the primary emotional need is for *support*. The individual has, in effect, unfrozen some of his old ideas about the way to work with people, wants to try out some new ones, but is unsure what the consequences of The New Departure are likely to be. He is defenseless and awkward at this point. If others in the training group accept and admit their own uncertainty as they try out changes, this can supply much support to all.

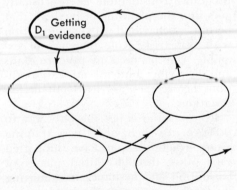

Getting evidence on results

The person who is experimenting with his behavior in a training situation must be able to get *evidence* as to the effectiveness of what he does. Learning by doing is not enough. The learner must, in addition, see the actual effect of his new behavior on others. What happened when, ever so gently, he invited non-participant Jane to comment? If in spite of all his attempted tact Jane says she felt put on the spot, then this information is important evidence for the learner to have as a basis for generalizing and applying his learnings further.

One of the limitations most of us struggle under on the job is our inability to get honest appraisals of our impact on others. We have to rely on fleeting facial expressions and official protestations, and we do not learn how we're doing in groups very often, or very accurately.

In the language of training, the term for a report to the learner of how his behavior is affecting others is "feedback." This technical term comes originally from the field of automation (ex: thermostat gives feedback to a furnace on how well the furnace is doing at heating the house), but seems clearly applicable to training as well. To be most helpful for learning, feedback must: (1) be clear and undistorted; (2) come from a trusted, non-threatening source; (3) follow as closely as possible the behavior to which it is a reaction. With quick, accurate, trusted evidence, the learner can proceed to correct his behavior effectively.

Much of the power of human relations training seems to stem from building in regular feedback procedures as a part of the training setup. Evaluation at the end of meetings, analysis of role playing, use of a process observer who reports what he sees to the group, playback of tape recordings—all these can serve as a mirror, and give the learner more and better information about "what behavior leads to what" than he has ever had before. And it's exciting.

accept, deep down. Otherwise the learnings stay at the "talk" level and never really become a part of his normal ways of behaving.

Finally, the learner almost inevitably

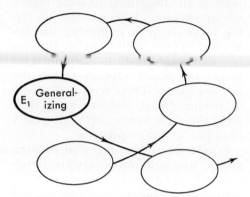

Generalizing, applying, and integrating

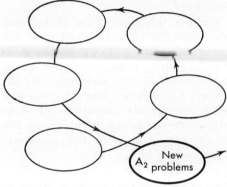

Finding new dissatisfactions and problems

Now that the learner knows what works (or perhaps more frequently, what doesn't work), he must tie this new knowledge into his picture of himself, relate it to his job situation, and in general make it part of the way he sees group life. Concrete action implications need to be drawn ("Do not call on anyone unless he clearly wants to get into the discussion and can't"). The learner needs to see links between the training experience and his job situation. ("Here in the training group, we found we had all these hidden feelings about the decision to meet Thursday night, and that's why we didn't carry it out. I think that same kind of thing may account for the poor attendance at my grade level meetings. What can I do about that?")

During this stage, careful, sober thinking is needed—but even here the person needs support and positive emotional reinforcement from other learners in the group, as he considers new learnings that are hard for him to

emerges from a process like that described above with *new* dissatisfactions and problems, in addition to new insights and ways of behaving. ("All right, apathy may mean that the goal of the group is not clear to some people, but what can you do to make it clear, then?" or "Bringing out the gripes did seem to clear the air in this group, but I'm not sure I'd know how to encourage it —or whether I would want to—in the principals' meeting.")

New ways of behaving lead to new problems (which might never have occurred under the old ways of behaving), and the training cycle continues. In other words, after the feedback of evidence which helps him see the consequences of his own group behavior, the individual realizes that his behavior is still inadequate, or is inadequate in some new respect. He then repeats the process of getting creative ideas regarding further change, trying them out in both contrived and real situations, seeing what works, and generalizing about the results. It is through steady repetitions of this experimental learning process that he becomes more sensitive to what is going on in groups, has clearer diagnostic ideas as to what is needed and why, and can act more effectively.

Getting this conception of learning built into the person is even more important than his learning specific skills of "handling conflict," "stimulating participation," or whatever. If the learner has *learned how to grow and learn,* how to take an experimental approach to the problems of group life he encounters, then he will grow and learn on the job.

The Training Group As a Place to Learn

It may serve as a useful review of the process of learning better group behavior if the special usefulness of the training group, as such, is discussed. The training group has been repeatedly mentioned above, and the question might be raised: "Why can't an interested person improve his behavior in groups independently?"

Clearly, much individual reflection, analysis, and experimentation may be necessary before a person comes to the realization, as did one teacher, that *"I am really the only person whose behavior I can do much of anything about."* Experience with many different training programs, however, suggests that individual growth and learning about group behavior takes place best in a group setting. There seem to be reasons for this.

SHARED SUPPORT

In the first place, change in one's own group-relevant behavior, like any change, inevitably involves risk. If behavior changes are attempted by members of a group, the support they can give each other is extremely helpful. The training group is a collection of persons all dissatisfied to some degree with their group behavior. All are trying to get help in improving this behavior, and are willing to be vulnerable, in a sense—open to learning. This makes for shared support within the training group. There is often the sense of having "lived together a lot in a short time," as one person said, with a resultant feeling of warmth.

Furthermore, in a successful training group, standards or norms are developed which encourage and support experimental change.

After the training group has disbanded and members are attempting innovations on the job, each individual also receives support—and sometimes concrete help—from the fact that colleagues are trying similar things as they go about their work. Often recollection of what went on in the training group seems to serve as a kind of "conscience" for the member, continuing to encourage him at difficult points. Attitudes or values learned in the training group often have considerable carry-over, for this reason.

ADDED RESOURCES

Training goes well in a group setting because different individuals can provide widely varied resources for intelligent behavior change by any particular learner. Many different ideas about job innovations can emerge. Ingenious procedures for learning can be devised more quickly. There is a greater possibility of penetrating, mistake-correcting analysis. In addition, because of group support, each person can hear and respond to group suggestions about his behavior which he might ignore if they were the suggestions of an outside expert or status figure.

THE GROUP AS LABORATORY

A third reason for the effectiveness of the group situation is that it provides a learning laboratory which helps the individual observe himself in relation to others. Not only can he see the effect that his behavior has on other people, but he can get frank, objective statements from them—their reports of the effects of his behavior. The group provides the individual with a testing ground where he can experiment with promising new behaviors. In a real sense, trying to study and improve one's own group functioning without being in a group is something like trying to learn to swim without going into the water.

IMMEDIACY

Another advantage of the group situation is its immediacy. New behaviors are practiced *where* they are needed (in the group) and *when* they are needed (just following feelings of difficulty or dissatisfaction). Learnings are not postponed to another place or time, but are worked on here and now.

REALISTIC SUCCESS

Finally, the group situation helps insure that learning goes on within realistic limits. (This, of course, assumes that the group makes its own decisions instead of having them made for it by the trainer.) Group members are not likely to attempt new behaviors that look extremely difficult. But the group can and does support innovations that are both challenging and feasible. During training, positive success experiences with new behaviors are essential —otherwise they will never be tried out on the job.

◇◇◇◇◇◇◇◇◇◇◇◇◇◇◇◇◇◇◇ DISPLACEMENT IN GROUPS

Philip E. Slater

DEFENSIVE processes have not traditionally been viewed as assisting in any way the development of insight. We tend to regard them simply as static obstacles, an attitude due in part to the often constricting analogy on which the term "defense" is based. This is unfortunate, since although a straight line may be the shortest distance between two points in space, it is often the longest in time, as every driver knows. The path to self-understanding is full of obstructions, and one must often choose between a detour and a total halt. If we are dealing with a group of persons seeking insight into their own group process, the problem is more complicated, since the obstructions will be overpowering to some and easily surmounted by others. In such a situation a defensive detour may keep the group from shattering.

Prepared especially for this volume. Used by permission.

I should like to describe a procedure in which such a defense has been "built in." The defense is that of displacement, while the procedure centers around an imposed task—clinical discussion and analysis of case material. The context in which the method is imbedded is an academic course in the study of individual and group behavior.[1] In this course a body of psychological, sociological, and anthropological material is transmitted to the student through readings. All classroom time, however, is spent in group discussion, and examinations attempt to evaluate the student's ability not only to understand and manipulate concepts, but also to observe the operation of psychological and sociological processes in concrete cases—particularly in his own group. During the first term of the course (which runs through a full academic year, meeting three hours each week) about one-half of the discussion is devoted to case analyses, about one-third to analysis of group process in the immediate situation, and the remainder to conceptual issues in the assigned reading. During the second term, less time is devoted to cases and more to the immediate situation, but in addition there is a far less rigid separation between the three areas, so that it becomes rare for one to be discussed without reference to the other two.

During the spring term, for example, the biblical story of Joseph is assigned as a case. Discussions of this case are marked by frequent references to Freud's *Totem and Taboo* and to examples of sibling rivalry and favoritism within the group. It is, in fact, precisely this fusion of (*a*) the abstract principle, (*b*) the concrete but objective instance, and (*c*) the subjectively and emotionally experienced instance, which the course seeks to achieve.

Training groups that combine the first and third of these aspects are not uncommon. The only special feature of this situation is the introduction of case materials as a discussion topic, and it is the uses and effects of these cases with which this paper is primarily concerned.[2]

---

[1] The title of this course in the Harvard College catalogue is "Social Relations 120: Case Analysis." Prior to the year 1959–1960 it was called "Social Sciences 112: Human Relations." No change in content or personnel was involved in this transition. The present teaching staff consists of Robert F. Bales, Theodore M. Mills, Charles P. Whitlock, and the author. Also associated with the course in recent years were Warren G. Bennis and Kiyo Morimoto. I am grateful to all five for the many suggestions they have contributed to this paper. The examples included in the text were drawn from the tape recordings of our class meetings.

[2] It should be noted, however, that although the discussion following tends to point up the contrasts between this course and the open-agenda training group, the historical development of the case-discussion course has been one of movement toward the training group rather than away from it. It began as a practical course in industrial sociology and business administration, with cases used primarily to suggest alternative courses of action. Most of the cases concerned administrative problems in industrial situations, and little attention was given to the underlying theoretical issues. During a long period of transition, the action emphasis disappeared, the industrial cases were gradually eliminated and replaced by cases dealing with family, college, and dating situations of more immediate concern to students, while the reading material came to deal more with standard social science classics and to emphasize the understanding of processes rather than problems of practical action. In the beginning there was no group self-analysis, all class time being devoted to assigned cases. Such analysis would not have been particularly meaningful, since all interaction was channelled through the instructor. The result was that once a proficiency in case analysis was achieved, students quickly lost interest in the situation, since the al-

The cases themselves are drawn largely from students. During the spring term each student is asked to write and to analyze a case report of an interpersonal situation in which he has been involved. Some of these cases are subsequently released to us for discussion purposes. As a result of this procedure and our criteria for selection, the cases deal with situations that would be considered "normal" (the individuals appearing in them do not manifest any marked psychopathology), but that involve some of the fundamental emotional issues of human experience.

In addition to these "everyday life" cases, the case pool is supplemented by "classic" case studies (such as those of Freud), literary "cases" (such as the plays of Ibsen, Williams, Miller, and O'Neill), and stories from myth and folklore.

It should be clear that to a considerable extent an effective case discussion is an end in itself, and in addition to making the usual observations of group process, the instructor is concerned with the intellectual quality and insightfulness of the group product. But more important, perhaps, than either of these, the instructor is always listening to what the student is saying about the group and the student's own feelings through his remarks about the case. In each case discussion the instructor assumes, to some degree, an analogue between the case and the group, and the interpretations he verbalizes to the group are often based on these parallels.[3]

A few examples may serve to illustrate the kinds of parallels drawn:

1. Early in the year a group discussed a case of a young married woman spending her first summer with her in-laws. A considerable length of time was devoted to an evaluation of the mother-in-law's wisdom in attempting to make the young woman "one of the family." This was interpreted as a reflection of the group's concern over how close to one another the members wished to become.

2. On another occasion a group attributed some of the conflicts and difficulties in communication experienced by a young couple in a case to the intervals they spent away from each other, during which time they were continually changing. The instructor interpreted this as a reflection of the students' own difficulties in relating to one another on a three-hours-a-week basis.

3. On a third occasion a change in behavior by the instructor appeared to elicit some unusual perceptions of the case material. The instructor had made a momentary departure from the permissive group-leader role to announce that under no conditions would extensions be granted on a paper due a week hence. During the ensuing four sessions there was considerable argument as to whether the central male characters in the two cases discussed were really "human," or whether they were "cold" and "unfeeling."

4. In one group, an analysis of a

---

ternative of an expansion in depth was closed to them. To remedy this defect, more attention was focused on the group itself, and the role of the instructor was modified to permit free interaction among group members.

[3] Symbolic equations of this kind are in no way a new development. The notion that every topic has relevance to the immediate transference relationship is basic—e.g., to psychoanalytic thinking regarding both individual and group psychotherapy. The peculiar fertility of case discussions in this regard, however, and the facility with which they lend themselves to this kind of "understanding-through-analogue," was first pointed out to me by Robert F. Bales during the observation of an experimental group in 1952.

family case, occurring during the fourth week of the course, seemed to deal with three interrelated themes at once. The first was a concern over whether the instructor was aggressive, sadistic, and omnipotent or passive, vacillating, and incompetent. The second was a concern over whether the males in the group were sufficiently virile to overthrow him and take his place, or whether they were too inhibited, passive, and dependent. The third was whether the group members could ever become open enough, and intimate enough, to provide emotional support for each other.

The following quotation is from a male student who expresses the first and third of these themes.

This case, it impresses me. I don't know how much we gain by discussing it further. For two reasons: it's indistinct what the relationships are, except that they're indistinct. All the materials mostly give you some sort of picture of the father, of the way he acts, and perhaps the son—but the son only in relation to the father. We don't know anything about the people, their backgrounds. We can't really try to explain why they are the way they are. Everything that we could find—I mean you could build up so many explanations of why the father is the way he is. There are so many types of personality that fit the action. I wonder if it really pays to go any further. It's . . . it's . . . it's too unclear. The father is . . . I mean . . . I mean, all right, they . . . the family doesn't have good . . . doesn't seem to communicate among themselves. We know that there seems to be a lack of intuition on the part of anyone in the family. But I don't think there's any point in trying to go on.

Neither the group nor the instructor seems to offer any security to this member. But a little later a female student suggests, "Why then, can't this family come out and say, 'Well, Daddy, look, this is what I want to do. Now how are you going to react to it?' " To which a male student replies, "But they're afraid he's just going to pound the table again." A few minutes later another male student likens the family "to a benevolent dictatorship, like one of those islands around South America where the people are very happy with their dictator, who tries as much as he can to do what they want. Does anyone want to tear that to pieces?" And again, "He's not too steady in his dictatorship and knows that they could put him out at any time, but right now they're happy with him." It should be noted that this remark anticipated a revolt against the instructor a month later, in which this student took an active role. At this point, however, the role of revolutionist is consistently declined by the males. Another member now suggests that the family reminds him of "musical chairs, where everyone gets up and moves to the next chair" (this member sat nearest to the instructor's chair), but objects to the "dictator" analogy. When challenged on this point he remarks, "Well, any family revolves somewhat around its leader." The use of "leader" instead of "father" in this statement indicates how thin the disguise is getting. Slips of this kind (never infrequent in case discussions) begin to bring smiles as the meeting progresses.

One of the girls now attacks the lack of ambition and aggression on the part of the son in the case (the mother and daughter of the family were scarcely mentioned during this hour). She suggests that the son is seeking an "easy way out" of having to compete, "and come up, and be a strong man."

This challenge is still ignored, however, as a male student makes a plea that the father "as head of the family . . . *should* assert a great deal of authority," and closes with the diagnosis that "this whole situation has developed, perhaps, because the members of the family don't really understand each other, and hence there's a great deal of insecurity. And it's like, their actions toward each other are similar to those of people who have just met, and are continually trying to please one another, whereas they should understand each other by now. . . ."

5. In another group, a discussion of Freud's analysis of the case of "Little Hans," led to the following oblique references to the instructor's role: "It seems to me that a person in Hans' position would look to his father as a . . . symbol of strength and authority, so that when he got frightened or something, why he could run to his father and expect protection. But when Hans runs to his father and only gets a series of questions as to what's going on, almost as if his dad was trying to reason with him man-to-man, with a five-year-old kid, why Hans isn't going to have the protective shield. . . ." Later the group became concerned with the "positive side of Hans' ambivalent attitude toward his father," wondering where love for the father began. One student asked, "But why should [Hans] love his father in the first place? His father's just a doctor." When the instructor offered the notion that one usually loves a source of gratification, the student replied that "in this case the father is a source of frustration," and asked if this father love were "completely homosexual." A few minutes later another student remarked, "Somehow I have the feeling that as a result of this analysis Hans has some mild degree of homosexual tendencies." When the instructor asked "from what?" the student said "I don't know, I just get the feeling. If he continues to grow up in this type of atmosphere this is what will happen."

Here we have a rather succinct description, in displaced form, of the process through which homosexual anxiety develops in groups. The passive and unhelpful role played by the instructor activates dependency needs in the student. A more permanent reservoir of yearning for paternal protection and love is tapped by this feeling, and the entire combined affect transferred to the person of the instructor. It now seems inappropriate, and, for the males, carries the frightening suggestion of homosexuality. It should be noted that this discussion followed an intensely hostile attack on the instructor, wherein the counterbalancing negative feelings were discharged, throwing the positive ones into relief. This process is echoed in the language of the group's concern over the "positive side of the ambivalence."

6. One of the ways in which this anxiety is resolved is through a successful effort to convert the females in the group from sisterly competitors to motherly rewarders. In one group, toward the end of the year, one of the girls began to play this latter role. Its first manifestation occurred in the following excerpt from a discussion of Tennessee Williams' *Cat on a Hot Tin Roof*. The excerpt illustrates the way in which the displacement situation can be used by group members to communicate difficult thoughts to one another. The entire conversation, which begins with an insight about the play, was carried on in an extremely sub-

dued, depressed atmosphere. The issue under discussion was the origin of Brick's homosexual relationship with his friend Skipper.

Mr. W: Does Skipper . . . uh . . . could Skipper represent any member of . . . of Brick's family, whom he would have had a similar relationship with if he could?

Miss G: Quite possible.

Mr. W: Who?

Miss G: Big Daddy, perhaps?

Mr. W: I thought perhaps . . . ?

Instructor: What do the servants call Big Daddy?

Mr. A (apathetically): "Captain."

Mr. W: Wha . . . what is it?

Mr. E (resignedly): "Captain."

Pause.

Mr. J: Well, what about that?

Mr. F: Was Skipper a captain?

Mr. W: *Skipper!*

Laughter.

Mr. M: Yeah, *Skipper.*

Pause.

Mr. I: Ummm.

Long pause. Even background noise is absent.

Mr. L: Kind of a weak connection.

Quiet laughter. Pause.

Miss G (softly): Maybe so, maybe not.

Pause.

Mr. K: Maybe it shows the kind of relationship he would have liked to have had with his father.

Miss G (gently): If you can accept that, then you're very good.

Miss G thus rewards insight and suggests that a frank recognition of these needs is not cowardice but courage. This remark seemed important in enabling the males in the group finally to accept the insight, not only as it applied to the case but as it applied to themselves.

Several weeks later the issue of the role that females should play in the group became explicit. When the males accused the females of "unfair competition," of being both intellectually agile and seductive toward the instructor, Miss G said that the boys were "more brilliant in discussion." A little later the following exchange took place.

Mrs. Y: . . . I don't think the girls in this class are sidling up to Dr. S.

Mr. A: Why aren't they sliding . . . sidling up to other members of the class?

Mr. E: What would they gain by it?

Mr. A: Approval, on a nonintellectual basis. For example, we all asked to see Angela's (Miss G's) sweater when she got it finished.

This was a reference to a conversation at the beginning of the hour when Miss G had begun knitting a sweater. It was not coincidental that the next assigned case, which most of them had read by this time, included a fairy tale by Grimm in which a girl saves her brothers from enchantment by remaining silent for several years and knitting them sweaters. The analysis of this case was one of the high points of the year, and Miss G continued to play the role desired for her by the males.

These examples may be summarized by saying that in the analysis of a case, group members identify with characters in the case, and project many of their own feelings onto them. Some of these feelings pertain to the group situation, and just as the group can serve as an arena for the working out of interpersonal problems transferred from early family experiences, so can the case serve as an arena for the discussion of group problems in displaced form. Feelings toward parents will be displaced not only upon the leader, but also upon parental figures in cases, while feelings toward siblings will be reflected not only in attitudes toward fellow group members but toward sibling figures in cases. Furthermore, if a case topic develops enough interest to be discussed by several persons, and at length, one can feel some confidence that its primary resonance is for the immediate group situation.

We may now raise the question as to what function this displaced area serves in bringing a group more swiftly to an understanding of itself. It might be argued that the presence of this "external" task is merely a distraction from the more important group task of self-analysis. From this viewpoint the achievement of clinical skill in interpreting the behavior of others would be bought at the price of diminished attention to the interpreting of one's own behavior.

In most training groups, however, it is unusual for any more time to be devoted directly to self-analysis. Instead, the members embark on a variety of topical discussions, which the trainer utilizes for interpretive purposes in much the same manner as we use case discussion. Cases have the advantage over such topical discussions of having more detailed relevance to the immediate situation. They also provide a fund of common factual knowledge to which all can refer, instead of each being dependent upon the subjective reports of others ("in *my* family," or "I read somewhere"). The difference is somewhat analogous to the greater ease of interpreting a series of TAT protocols as compared with a series of dreams.[4]

But there are other arguments that might be advanced in favor of the case method. As in all situations in which

[4] This analogy was suggested by Theodore Mills.

learning of any importance takes place, there is a high degree of "breakage" in the typical training-group situation. By this I mean that there are a number of individuals who are unable to tolerate either the freedom or the insights which the situation provides, and that these individuals become alienated and flee the group, nursing fierce and undying grudges against every aspect of this approach to learning. A certain amount of this "breakage" is unavoidable, but any technique that might serve to minimize it bears close examination. The training group creates considerable stress in the individual. At times it demands more ego-strength and insight than he can muster. The defenses he usually adopts are being challenged, and the best defense left to him often is to reject the entire situation as meaningless, stupid, and unproductive, or indecent, improper, and unfair. Some individuals are chronically unable to move as quickly as the rest of the group, while at any given moment, others, normally "in the swim," may fall behind when some particularly sensitive issue is touched upon. It is difficult to meet the needs of everyone at the same moment.

Yet this is not all the story. At times the group as a whole may "fall behind." This happens when the group runs head on into a problem which no one is able or willing to talk about. The discussion grinds to a halt. The group backs off. The trainer interprets. The group makes another onslaught on the problem but is still unable to face the issue. Since there is no sanctioned means of escape the group undergoes a strong failure experience. Unfortunately, if this occurs early in the group's experience, the entire group may adopt the same defensive rejection of the training experience that the "failing" individual adopts, particularly if the group lacks psychologically sophisticated individuals who can understand what is taking place.

What we are saying then, is that "breakage" in the training group results in part from a kind of rigidity or massive inertia in the training group situation. There is no sanctioned way to approach a problem obliquely. There are no breathing spells, no accepted ways for an individual to pause by the wayside and catch up later. Rest is indissolubly linked with defeat.

It is possible that during the early stages, the use of cases tends to minimize breakage by introducing flexibility into the situation, so that the individual (or the group as a whole) can move more at his own pace. It would, of course, be legitimate to argue at this point that we are trying to promote defensiveness and permit escape from the pressures of the training situation—that we are trying to dilute the impact of this type of experience. In a sense this is true. But since we would favor the maintenance of a constant pressure toward insight and self-understanding, it would be more accurate to say that we wish to permit greater elasticity in the response to such pressure, believing that in the long run, the impact will be greater and more universal.

A recent study by Murray and Berkun [5] illustrates this position. Using both clinical examples from psychotherapy sessions and experimental studies of maze behavior in rats, they argue that displacement is not merely a means of escaping a conflict-laden field, but a device for re-approaching this field with diminished anxiety. Both their con-

flicted rats and their conflicted patients were able to move farther toward a conflict-laden goal in a displaced situation and seemed to feel more free to return to the original situation following "successful" experimentation in the displaced situation.

We feel that this is precisely what takes place in our groups. Problems too disturbing to attack directly in the group are attacked in effigy in the case material. When this has occurred without disaster, it may be turned back into the group and discussed directly. Such a direct discussion uncovers deeper issues which will again be displaced upon the case, and so forth.

This process is particularly appropriate to the development of insight, which often seems to proceed in a kind of cyclical fashion. By this we mean that awareness, knowing, or understanding vary in depth and breadth in extremely subtle ways. The distinction, for example, between "intellectual" and "emotional" awareness or insight has often been drawn. But there are many more levels than this. The same insight may recur many times and appear each time to be newly felt, either because more of the affect pertaining to a thought has been drawn into it, or because the implications of the thought are more fully understood, or because the thought has been more completely embedded in the context of other thoughts, reversing, as it were, the process of dissociation. The weaving back and forth of case and self discussions facilitates and stabilizes this process of deepening and broadening an initial insight.

The use of cases, then, provides a means by which the group may move constantly forward, however irregular the course, much as a sailboat does when tacking into the wind. When

[5] H. J. Murray and M. M. Berkun, "Displacement as a function of conflict." *J. abnorm. soc. Psychol.*, 51:47–56, 1955.

flight occurs it may be utilized as a regulated mechanism for moving the group forward. Murray and Berkun's rats moved all the way to the goal in the "displaced" corridor: their patient revealed full-blown his hostility toward his mother when discussing his aunt.[6] Our students will in the same manner discuss in full their unexpressed and at the moment inexpressible feelings, when talking about a case.

The analogy must not be exaggerated, however. It would be pleasant if we could argue that while escaping from a problem within the group, the class skillfully attacked its analogue in the case, made a cogent clinical analysis from which everyone derived intellectual benefit, and returned from their flight period refreshed from a success experience and ready to attack the group issue head-on. Unfortunately, however, progress is more halting, due to the fact that blocks tend to generalize, so that a group will frequently be unable to understand or work through an issue in the case which has not been faced up to in the group. It may be approached, talked around, value judgments may be made about it, a cautious feeling-out of one another's attitudes may occur, but a success experience is unlikely until the problem has been at least in part resolved in the group. In other words, while progress may be considerably greater in the "displaced corridor," it is not necessarily experienced subjectively as a triumph. There will be many transitions back and forth between case and self discussions before the issue is worked through. At this point not only does understanding occur in both areas, but the relationship between the two becomes clear, as well as the way in which the displacement process took place.

[6] *Ibid.*

This raises two further questions. The first concerns the interpretive role of the instructor. When and how does he draw interpretive parallels between the case and the group? Second, if group members become aware of the displacement process—if the instructor is continually pointing out the parallels, will displacement still take place? Will not all the flexibility which has been posited now be lost?

It should be obvious that displacement interpretations must be sparing during the early stages of the group. Too frequent interpretations of relationships between case discussion and class process will tend to paralyze the former. In order for a discussion to be pursued it must be perceived as having intrinsic importance, and continually pointing out its unconscious determinants will tend to undermine this perception, which is, after all, shared by the instructor. When the group achieves some facility in rapidly switching frames of reference in the midst of discussion, the instructor can draw parallels with more freedom.

But how does one know when a case-to-group translation is appropriate? Does one always read "group" for "family" and "instructor" for "father"? Are not some remarks completely determined by the nature of the case material? As usual, experience is of great value. Having heard a case discussed many times, the instructor becomes very sensitive to differences in emphasis, or preoccupation with some specific aspect of the case. In general, the length of time spent on a given topic is the best indicator of its relevance for the group's own process. If the group members discuss the father in the case to the relative exclusion of all other characters, they generally prove preoccupied with their relation to the instructor. If they focus upon communication, intimacy between members is likely to be the major problem in the group, and so forth.

Sometimes, however, it is not the length of time spent on an issue, but its inappropriateness in terms of case data that suggests its relevance to group problems. An interpretation of the material that contradicts the data, or is unsupported by the data, is more likely to be determined by group issues than one that is well grounded empirically.

An example may serve to illustrate this point. Our groups move through phases which approximate roughly those outlined by Bennis and Shepard.[7] In one of our groups, the angry revolt which the authors describe under "subphase 3" was predicted solely by certain remarks made during a case discussion. The case in question concerns a conflict between a young girl and her mother, and is rich in oedipal symbolism. The discussion was lively, productive, and insightful, and the group seemed to have achieved a state of balance and integration. The members were task-oriented, cooperative, and friendly. A recurrent preoccupation, however, isolated from other interpretations and unsupported by evidence, was the notion that the girl in the case felt guilty over her father's death because she had at times desired it. Although he did not verbalize it to the class, the instructor interpreted this idea as evidence of rapidly mounting hostility toward himself which the group felt difficulty in controlling. At the same time an increase in dependence expressed itself in the form of an outburst of hand-raising—a regression to the first hours of the course when students expected the instructor to take a traditional academic role.[8] On the day following the discussion of this case the anticipated revolt suddenly occurred, with no other warning.

The use of validity as an index, however, raises the problem so vexing in intellectual arguments between psychologically sophisticated persons: to what extent is it appropriate to interpret the motivation behind an intellectually adequate inference? One of the reasons for avoiding overinterpretation during early case discussions is that it seems to insult the intellect of the students. But Freud once pointed out the essential independence between emotional determination and intellectual adequacy, suggesting that the motive behind a given theory may be clearly visible, but the theory must stand or fall on its own ground. It is possible for strong inner feelings either to (*a*) increase an individual's sensitivity to the underlying causes of a situation, or to (*b*) distort and bias his perception of them. For interpretive purposes one notes the intensity of and degree of preoccupation with the argument. For intellectual purposes one subjects it to the usual criteria of inductive logic.

In one instance, for example, an ex

---

[7] W. G. Bennis and H. A. Shepard, "A theory of group development." *Human Relations*, 9:415–437, 1956. It should be added that our students, who read this paper during the spring term, do not regard the approximation as rough at all, but rather as one of terrifying exactness. The emotional reaction to this would constitute an interesting study in itself, since the fear of being shown to be predictable is one of the stronger sources of resistance to psychology.

[8] It would be difficult to find a more instructive symptomatic act than this one—so inappropriate, so contagious, so visible to all, so unconscious for the one who does it. It occurs sporadically throughout the year, sometimes after intervals of several months. Often it is directed toward other group members rather than toward the instructor.

tremely cogent analysis of a mother playing the role of mediator between father and son, in a case under discussion, was made by a highly intelligent female student in the class. Although the argument in this instance was flawless, it nevertheless called the intructor's attention to the hitherto unobserved fact that this student was beginning to play an analogous role in the class—voicing the group's feelings to the leader and helping the group develop the techniques of analysis that the leader seemed implicitly to be demanding. It might be added that it was not only her role in the group that sensitized her to the dynamics of the case, since she tended to adopt this role in most of her interactions in her everyday life.

Let us now turn to the second question, regarding the effect of continued interpretation on displacement. The reader is quite correct if he assumes that the use of cases as objects on which to displace feelings about the group is greatly impaired by revealing the relationship between the two domains, but this process takes more time than one might expect. The group's life is typically more than half over before a full appreciation of the displacement function is internalized by the majority of group members. Partial understanding, however, occurs quite early, as in the following remarks by a student in the sixth meeting of one group. "Carl" refers to a character in a case study who is typically viewed as somewhat passive and dependent, and who, in middle age, moves back into the household of his aging and rather dominating mother.

Last class at the beginning we avoided Carl, possibly because we associated ourselves with him. And I think a possible reason for that is that . . . uh . . . we're all college students and that question is in the back of our minds . . . we're still dependent on our parents. Are we going to be . . . ah . . . shiftless Carl (laughter), supported by his parents for the rest of his life?

Here we have an awareness of identification, but not of the identifications and displacements that occur in response to the "here and now" group situation. In contrast to this, note the two examples that follow, both drawn from meetings held in the second half of the course.

1. The first example involves the same group and the same case as the previous one. Toward the end of the year the group decided to re-analyze the case and then listen to a tape recording of their earlier analysis. On the third day they compared the two analyses, and one student remarked on how preoccupied they had been, during the re-analysis, with the theme of the "loss of power" incurred by Carl upon moving back into his parents' home. The student suggested that this reflected the loss of power they themselves felt in "moving back" to listen to their old tape, drawn from what they described as the "childhood of the group," and which "embarrassed" them when they heard it. This incident also points up the fragility of the group's solution of the dependency problem.

2. The second example is a quotation from a student in another group, during an analysis of the biblical tale of Joseph and his brothers.

I think one of the most threatening things, at least to me, about this case is that Joseph *did* distinguish himself from his brothers, and every time I open my mouth I feel as if, well, I'm breaking a silence here, and I don't particularly like to have people think that I'm identifying with

Joseph. Because I don't, I identify with Reuben. So I think that's why I don't initiate discussion although sometimes I follow up.

Here, although the insight is incomplete, the analogues in the group situations are clearly delineated. When this ability becomes general, the instructor no longer controls the interpretive process. Once group members have taken over this function, parallels may be drawn before the group is fully ready to deal with them. Thus, although displacement occurs, it tends to be quickly revealed as such, and the "flexibility" previously present is largely lost. Paralyzing resistances may now occur, and failure experiences may be undergone.

But by now the group is relatively hardy. They have faced and in part resolved many of their more basic problems. They have experienced many successes and many insights. They "know the ropes," and the stress produced by current crises is relatively uncontaminated by the early bewilderment and panic of wondering what is going on.

At this point in the group's development, a strange reversal takes place. Whereas earlier in the year group members tend to prefer case discussions, and are somewhat nervous about discussing themselves, now it is the other way around and self-analysis is used defensively, to avoid talking about cases.[9]

A case discussion begins, encounters a snag, and bogs down. Someone offers an interpretation of the difficulty in terms of some group problem. There follows a visible relaxation of tension and the group is soon engrossed in self-analysis. Now these discussions are superficially insightful and productive, but tend largely to cover ground which has already been explored. No major new insights seem to emerge.

The reason for this is that the displacement process is never entirely circumvented. As one student put it, "if we keep talking about old problems we won't have to face new ones, but if we talk about cases we may reveal unresolved problems." In other words, it is almost impossible to participate actively in a case analysis and still keep a constant eye on what one may be revealing about one's own feelings. The danger posed by case discussions is that they may seduce the student into a lapse of self-consciousness—a spontaneous projection or displacement, the meaning of which would be apparent to the rest of the group and to the instructor, before it was apparent to him. And what applies to the individual applies to the group as a whole. To paraphrase Hamlet, the group would rather discuss those ills they now have, then run the risk of revealing others they know not of. This suggests that when this feeling is worked through the task of the group is at an end.

---

[9] All the above generalizations regarding time sequences involve considerate oversimplification. Isolated instances of both the defensive use of self-analysis and the failure of displacement occur throughout the year, around specific issues. The frequency nonetheless increases rapidly after the middle of the year. This may be largely due, as Theodore Mills has suggested, to anxieties about separation. Avoiding the case becomes an avoidance of life outside the group, beyond its protection.

◇◇◇◇◇◇◇◇◇◇◇◇◇◇◇◇◇◇◇ THE USE OF GROUP PROCESSES IN
TEACHING GROUP DYNAMICS

Elvin V. Semrad and John Arsenian

Introduction

THIS paper presents some observations on the use of group processes in teaching group dynamics. In efforts to conduct group psychotherapy with psychotics we faced the problems: (1) of learning more about group dynamics and (2) of teaching our therapists how to conduct groups. We started discussion seminars to pool our knowledge and experience. We observed the dynamics of these seminars to have much in common with the dynamics observed in our group therapy groups. We therefore examined and utilized the material from seminar groups to give members the opportunity to learn from experience what a group is like, how it functions, and what problems it presents.

Freud noted that emotional ties and currents are the essence of most groups and remarked on the conflicts and difficulties of group members in handling jealousy, rivalry, and tender feelings. Jaques, Lewin, and McNassor have written on the use of groups in teaching group dynamics. Although our formulations on the psychology of individuals in groups are not new, the particular use made of them seems worth communication to those who are trying to teach group dynamics.

Method of Study

This discussion is based on observations and records of teaching groups widely varied in composition and size, mixed hospital staff groups of psychiatrists, social workers, nurses, psychologists, and occupational therapists; psychiatrists in training at a veterans' hospital; groups of trained social workers; graduate students in social work; and graduate students in clinical psychology. The groups studied consist of group therapists and/or group observers engaged in discussion of group dynamics in order to improve their technique as group observers and/or therapists.

Verbatim records were made. The generalizations we formulate are verified by repetition of experiences rather than statistical procedures. A creditable measure of validity is postulated because others who used the tactics of group management outlined here described similar findings.

Organization of a Teaching Group

The first step is a brief orientation followed by the making of a working agreement (a contract). Matters of time, setting, number of meetings, purpose

From Elvin V. Semrad and John Arsenian, "The Uses of Group Processes in Teaching Group Dynamics," American Journal of Psychiatry, Vol. 108, November 1951, pp. 358–363. Footnotes omitted. Abridged and used by permission.

of meetings are contracted for. An attempt is made to assess how much the potential members are ready to invest in the work.

The number of persons in the groups varied from 10 to 30 and the number of meetings from 6 to 80. The leader structured his role from the beginning by asking members about their expectations. He outlined alternative ways in which such a group might function: by reading books about groups and discussing them, by discussing other groups in which they have had experience, or by participating in the group formation. No matter what the choice, so long as the leader (here referred to as "central figure") plays a certain role, a group will emerge.

Observations

Group interaction seems to follow something of a pattern although the pattern is not fixed in sequence.

When a group of persons agrees to meet over a period of time around a central figure, they early set about sizing up and testing the central figure and each other. Each member tests the situation to see what he can expect in feelings of anxiety and demands for his attention or for work. Simultaneously each member closely watches the fate of his associates' ventures at interaction with each other and the central figure. If the members knew each other beforehand, they may have already formed emotional ties and a dominance order that they repeat in the group. Unless the leader is an outsider who does not accept the current distribution of affection and deference, this phase of functioning may not show itself as clearly as when a group of strangers meets.

The various roles played by group members depend on their habitual ways of getting along with other people, their defense mechanisms, modes of handling anxiety and anxiety tolerance. Other relevant factors are their ambitiousness; type of response to authority and their peers; also, to a lesser extent, their knowledge about the material being considered.

From the outset the central figure is interested in how each member thinks and reacts to whatever issue happens to be before the group and tries to accept all reactions uncritically—except those that threaten to dissolve the group. He acts as a catalyst to expand and explore ideas and to get all persons involved. His nonauthoritarian manner gives the situation an openness in which people feel free to participate. Under these circumstances a variety of integrated responses to the situation and central figure emerges.

Members will become active rivals for position of central figure and contend with other members. They may play the role of pretender, manifesting an aloof silence in the central figure's presence, quietly awaiting his deposition and confidently expecting to succeed him. Some members will protect the central figure; self-dedicated and self-appointed they will counter all expressions of criticism and hostility. Others revolt against the central figure and scorn other members who accept the situation. Some remain spectators; from among them may emerge a *spokesman*. Some passively object, maintain silence, and may be discerned by expressive gestures such as frowning, scowling, sleeping, etc. Others object actively and attack with intellectual weapons and incisive words. Some curry the central figure's favor and have a keen eye for his pleasures, preferences, and wishes and devote themselves to anticipating these. Some effectively collaborate; in fact, they work better in groups than alone. Certain members are tuned to what the leader is saying as well as the group's resistance and can bridge this gap, often doing more than translating by supplying relevant examples or elaborations that help to clarify the points at issue. Sometimes one undertakes to be the chronicler of the group. He tells members precisely what was said and felt by whom, when, and in what context. In addition, many groups will find persons who will fill parts as the wit, the pet, the pacificer, the loyal lieutenant, the reasoner, or the sorrier part of the scapegoat.

Note that all groups do not present consistently the same patterns of response and that the emergence of some seems dependent on the composition of the group—that is, the personalities entering into it, and their interplay. The advantage of the group method of teaching resides in the display of reactions and interactions in a setting where one is alternately a participant and an observer. When members begin to examine their own patterns of response and those of others and to compare their efficiency and acceptability on criteria of how well they work in the group, they are then in a position to learn either by conscious imitation or unconscious copying.

As the group progresses there are strongly charged emotional experiences. Participants get to know what it is like to be drawn by the central figure, to wish to have all his attention, to feel the sting of his apparent preference for someone else, to feel anxiety about not knowing where one stands, with whom and against whom; to feel strong ambivalence, covert and overt hostility. Also one sees others repeat these experiences in varying order and

becomes aware that others may momentarily become so distressed by intense feelings that they can't hear truly, say anything, or think logically. One may feel the self attracted to others, themselves in the stage of openly expressing one's own inner anger or ambivalence, and feel pleased or anxious by such vicarious expressions of feeling.

These experiences shared in the group result in a bond between members that may carry its own anxieties and defenses. While one may have such experiences in natural groups, the value of this type of learning situation stems from the interpretative comments of the central figure. He tries to be sensitive to the range of feelings in a group and tries to clarify feelings. He helps members by working over their understanding of group processes as they appear.

To formulate the experience at the level of group process is more difficult than to describe typical patterns of response. Yet there is roughly a sequence of phases of group activity that is seen along with the varied responses and is characteristic even where the responses vary widely.

Closely following the orientation phase, there appears a general feeling out or testing of the situation, which members engage in actively or passively. This testing seems to have the aim of establishing how comfortable or uncomfortable they are going to feel in the group setting.

Then no matter how democratically or reasonably the central figure defines the work load or contract, there is usually resistance to it. If the issue is not who is going to do the work, it may be the tacit questions: What right has he to ask anything of me? What right has he to be the contral figure? This phase, the most persistent and insidious, is termed resistance. At this stage, much energy of the members is consciously or unconsciously devoted to defeating and disrupting the group by a variety of tactics such as delaying, digressing, devaluating, and so on. Such resistance may be explained by considering that to be a group member is to sacrifice individuality and be exposed to pressure to accommodate to others.

A phase of struggle seems characteristically to follow the testing phase often commencing with it. The principal combatants are readily identifiable attempting to take over the role of the central figure or, less ambitiously, to compete strenuously for the position of favorite. This phase of struggle may persist throughout the life of a group and may be utilized by the leader to encourage people to work. Yet it may split the group into embattled cliques whose members are opposed on principle to anything said by the opposition, and lasting dissatisfaction or ambivalences negatively weighted may ensue. Some of this combativeness may stem from hostility toward the central figure displaced onto another group member, and is thus an acting out of resistance.

If aggregates are not shattered by resistance and combat and hence prevented from becoming a group, the ensuing phase is a working through of resistance. Most group processes may be thought of as a playing or working out of one resistance after another where resistances are both recurrent, recharging, and reverberating as from one member to another. Once the resistance of a member is expressed and reduced by acceptance or understanding, he may become a contributor only

later to find his willingness to cooperate again in need of analysis.

Concomitant with resistance are processes of group cohesion. The first cohesive process may well take place in the service of resistance. Members may be united in their will or desire to be disbanded. Not uncommonly a group may be united by a common bond of hostility to the central figure. If he is not able to tolerate this hostility or if group members have too much anxiety about hostility to authority, the group may focus on a weak or errant person and banish him. The central figure must direct to himself the hostility, analyze the resistance, and thus preclude the need for a scapegoat.

As the experience of being and sharing with others continues, members may develop a common bond of affection for each other and for the central figure. Sometimes, as Freud described the process, the positive feelings of each individual for the central figure make possible the derivative of positive feelings each for all. On the other hand in some groups the central figure may always be viewed as a highly ambivalent figure, especially if there is work to be done or painful anxiety involved in analyzing resistance. He is then seen as a hard taskmaster who spoils the fun and fellowship of the group. These ambivalent attitudes can readily be seen when on the central figure's tardy entry to a group, animated conversation gives way to respectful but more or less tense silence.

Ambivalence for the group itself is observed among those made anxious by the combative phase. Rugged individuals, by being part of any group, may suffer a narcissistic injury by the closeness and the tender feelings of the members. These may cause anxieties perhaps because of the absence of any way in which to express one's love for a group. Thus there may be anxiety about the possible dissolution of the group, as a pleasant experience, and about its continuation as producing feelings that provoke anxiety. Out of this ambivalence often come testimonials. The testimonials usually come when a group has a wish to leave or break off, or paradoxically, in response to some external threat to the group. In both cases testimonials may serve to keep the group together. They consist of expressions of mutual admiration as between members and for the central figure. Admiration typically involves positive feelings toward the self; pleasure in being admired introduces another resistance to change. Members may resist change lest their alteration come at the expense of losing the regard of their associates. Some reaction patterns are, then, stabilized by virtue of the emotional ties of members and at this point the group may cease to be of help unless this situation is analyzed.

Ambivalence toward the central figure may exist through the life of a group. In positive peak phases there is excessive admiration for the central figure with ascription to him of great powers of mind, insight, and judgment. The view that the central figure is omniscient seems in part to stem from anxiety over the manner in which discussions are conducted. Such idealization serves as insurance against the insecurity of not knowing where or to what or whom the discussion will turn next. Adoration of the leader may also stem from the narcissistic wound that would follow if any ordinary person saw through one's defense systems. It is more consoling to suppose that it

takes a mastermind to see through the self, and consequently the group gives itself balm for its wounds and exposures by exalting the leader.

An ending phase of a teaching group would come about when members understood both their reaction patterns and the needs they fulfilled and the role they ascribed to the central figure. The central figure must encourage members to explore his "bag of tricks" and experiment with them, taking into themselves those that seem fitting and useful. After members have made some progress in modifying attitudes and traits, whether by borrowing, identification, or discarding and softening, conditions are best for productive collaboration, in the direction of better understanding group dynamics.

Difficulties with teaching groups center about 3 related problems: anxiety, hostility, and acting out. They seem to stem from the intensity of feelings generated and the tendencies to act out on strong feelings rather than verbalize them within the group.

Specific manifestations of acting out vary: permanent withdrawal from the group with refusal to reenter, chronic lateness or absence, and a sullen presence with refusal to participate are common. As already mentioned, more active members may initiate efforts to disorganize the group. These efforts are sometimes cloaked under the guise of being helpful. At other times there is a more or less frank attempt to induce dissatisfaction in others. Some participants may find their affects governable inside the group, but act out outside, creating trouble with their associates in business, agency, or university.

The acting out appears connected with strong feelings of love or hating, often with the same modes of defense regardless of whether hate or tender feelings are the core. Some people are unable to express with finesse tender feelings and/or anger and thus constitute a problem both to themselves and their associates. Often the issues can be clarified only after the emotional tension is reduced. Through encouragement of verbalization rather than through acting out at lower integrative levels, the central figure urges the group to face, consider, and reconsider issues with a more objective, mature viewpoint.

The role of the central figure also creates problems. His permissive role almost inevitably results in the exposure of child-like or emotionally determined patterns of behavior in group members, especially in vying for his favor. The central figure who responds warmly and approvingly to all reactivates dependent needs and creates the condition for a sibling struggle, which he later analyzes. Because an equal distribution of favor is pleasing neither to ambitious nor compulsively good people, nor passive characters, rivalrous patterns are set off with resulting hostility. The central figure should occupy his position only by virtue of experience and relative maturity in this type of situation. Growth is fostered if members are encouraged to see that their feelings are understandable and that the role of central figure is one that can be studied in the group process.

Concerning the management of anxiety in groups, its level is a matter for experienced judgment. If there is too much anxiety members are pressed to modes of defense that disrupt the group or reduce its level of functioning. On the other hand, if the anxiety level sinks too low, everyone feels comfortable and there is no incentive to growth or change. At the disposal of the leader are devices for evoking anxiety. For example, the leader's friendliness to one individual shown by calling him by first name, or referring to an approved idea as one member's idea evokes anxiety in those worried about others getting ahead of them. Also inviting a sullen rebel to speak freely evokes anxiety in those who are suppressing their hostility and resistance. They might be called upon next. A statement critical of the group's functioning usually produces an effect, either by precipitating covered resistances or by producing more work. Similarly anxiety is increased if any member is singled out for special comment either directly or by implication.

Finally it seems appropriate to say a few words about the difference between teaching group dynamics by the group method and group therapy. Because of its potentialities for yielding an experience of growth or change, one may ask how is this different from group therapy. The actual experience is about the same; the aim, emphasis, and focus of interpretive comments differ more or less. Depending upon the amount to which people invest themselves, it may come close to an experience of self- and others' revelation with repetition of older patterns and an opportunity for some insight. The central figure must use judgment as to how far to let personal problems come into focus. His role in analyzing emotional difficulties should be limited to dealing with those that prevent maximum devotion to the task at hand.

This process of teaching differs also from conventional teaching mostly in focus. Educators of adults tend to devote themselves to the presentation of subject matter, while the group process described is more concerned with the total growth of the persons. Subject matter—the cognitive issues—is here used more as material for clarifying emotional issues, whereas conventional education has the opposite focus.

In assumptions about students there is a difference too. Educators generally assume a will to learn whereas the central figure is soon impressed with people's resistance to change, and their uncontrolled tendencies to repeat patterns. Similarly, teachers of adults tend to ignore problems of transference (positive and negative feelings) but the central figure, trying to communicate something of group dynamics via the experiment of creating a group, cannot afford to ignore overdetermined emotional responses.

A statistical study of 80 sentence-completion questionnaires filled out by members of these teaching groups revealed that 70% liked the experience, 14% disliked it, and the rest seemed ambivalent. Eighty-four percent felt they learned something either about themselves or about group technique. Social workers and clinical psychologists placed emphasis on self-insight while physicians placed a somewhat greater emphasis on useful didactic knowledge. The chief objections centered around the central figure's refusal to supply information didacticly and the lack of time to work through the details of issues. To some, especially those desiring a therapeutic experience rather than a teaching one, the pursuit of issues to the point of illustrating dynamic principles, rather than pursuing issues to full personal working through, was a complaint against the method.

Conclusions

A method of teaching group dynamics by forming groups is described and some of our experience with it detailed. In evaluating the experience, the opinions of participants vary widely but most report that they have learned something and may have carried over their newly formulated experience into other groups. The bridge between theory and practice is readily crossed by this method of teaching and many people come away with new insights into how to observe and/or conduct both themselves and group meetings more effectively.

✧✧✧✧✧✧✧✧✧✧✧✧✧✧✧✧✧✧ GROUP OBSERVATION

Warren G. Bennis and Herbert A. Shepard

THIS paper is an introduction to the subtle art of observing group process. Perhaps "subtle" is the wrong word: the major subtleties lie in making one's already shrewd observations explicit to oneself, and in deciding which of them to communicate to others. For we are all great process observers at heart.

From Warren G. Bennis and Herbert A. Shepard, "Group Observation," Boston University Human Relations Center, Research Papers and Technical Notes, No. 7. Abridged and used by permission.

When Arthur Godfrey is playing his ukelele on TV and glowers at his pianist, we forget the song he's playing long enough to wonder about Mr. Godfrey's relations with his staff. And when a teacher is asked a perceptibly hostile question by an aggressive student, we lose interest in what the question was about and observe how the professor handles the situation and the student.

When any ordinary mortal enters a strange group he tries to size up the situation, perhaps cautiously by quiet scrutinization, perhaps aggressively by sticking his neck out to see how far he can go. He learns who the leaders are, how the other members are lined up, what the rules of the game are. His methods of learning these things and of getting into the group are peculiarly his own; they are part of his personality. He has his characteristic means of getting his own way, of keeping out of trouble—or of getting into trouble—of competing, and of gaining approval. He usually does not talk about them or think about them; most of the time he is hardly aware of the enormous skill he demonstrates in using them.

"I don't know what I've said until I've heard the response to it" is one of Professor Norbert Wiener's aphorisms. This is especially true in an unfamiliar social setting, where communication is strange and strained. Every statement is a sort of trial balloon in which the speaker ascends only a little way—in order not to be badly hurt by the fall should the balloon fail. The little "feelers" people put out in such a situation are extraordinarily delicate and sensitive antennae—superbly constructed for detecting the signs of approval and disapproval, of warmth and hostility, of submission and domination. Everybody has a pretty good set of instruments for group observation.

In fact, the ordinary mortal's instruments of group observation are so well constructed that they are taken for granted. He is usually content to use them at about 10 percent of capacity, and he neglects their maintenance and repair. He may not even recalibrate them as his experience widens and his values change. But since they were mostly developed in early youth, in a family group quite different from groups he encounters later in life, he may well be missing something.

Renovating the antennae is not an easy job. The principal method recommended in this book is first, making a rigorous effort to observe what is going on, and second, comparing one's observations with observations made by other members of the group. Easier said than done! Before a person can share his interpretations of what is going on, of how he feels, he has to be in a situation where he is not likely to get hurt for his courage. He has to be anchored in a group that shares his sentiments, beliefs, and feelings about many important matters; a group in which he is received with warmth and understanding. Yet process observations are themselves means to greater understanding. So he is in a dilemma: should he demand understanding as a condition for making process observations, or should he demand process observations as a means for better understanding?

Observations based on systematic collection and analysis of obvious data are easy to communicate, easy to understand. Hence, one way out of the dilemma is to start with observations which are based on straightforward methods of data collection. The rest of this chapter describes four such methods.

The following excerpt from a group

discussion will be useful in illustrating the four methods of observation.

BILL: I'm beginning to gather that the subjects we speak on are relatively unimportant. The trend of the group is sort of beginning to fascinate me. In other words, what we have, if anyone follows me, but what we have is a group-centered sort of deal. I believe that at the first meeting that we needed leadership, which Jim and other people still both admire. I believe now though that the group is becoming sufficiently adjusted so that we want to have a diffused leadership. In other words, we all want to share in leadership and that is what Gordon, for instance, thinks is the most efficient way that a group can act. In other words, it's real unanimous approval rather than an authoritarian mind. It seems to me that we have been destroying leadership that we needed in the past, that is for the last three or four meetings we have been doing that. And I wonder if that is really what is happening, if we are trying to accomplish this diffused leadership.

JIM: This diffused leadership, I don't think it's a question of efficiency. I think it's a question of satisfaction. As far as efficiency, if someone says "You do this, that, and the other thing," that gets things done faster, and it gets more things done, but as far as people in the group feeling that they are part of a decision . . .

BILL: If something doesn't last, it's not efficient, that's the only way I look at it. In other words, unless it's a real approval . . .

JIM: In other words, efficiency . . .

BILL: or participation. I don't consider it to be efficient.

JIM: You mean efficiency doesn't mean getting things done and the quantity . . .

BILL: Yeah, well, I didn't mean that, that's a good point.

JIM: You had the idea of satisfaction.

BILL: Right. That's probably a better way of putting that.

VIC: Are the same people bored week in and week out?

BILL: Hmm?

VIC: Are the same . . . ?

JOE: I think we've exhibited something in the last three weeks which is very characteristic of a so-called group of leaders, and that's the selfishness on the part of every individual. I think the initiator of the topic, Jim last week and Vic this week, and Ed this week, has, I think, felt this a little subconsciously or maybe consciously when they've asked for group approval of their subject because they realized that they couldn't get it done or that they couldn't get the topic of conversation without everybody in the group approving it wholeheartedly and this selfishness has manifested itself in quite . . . well I thought, three different ways to the point where everybody wants to be a part of the original idea.

Carrying on with Vic's point, I have tried to observe since the "boredom" discussion came up a few weeks ago, just which people are bored and how frequently, and I've found that the same people are bored every week and only to the point where they will talk or be excited about a topic if they themselves are the initiator of this topic. Otherwise they have sat back and looked bored. Another way of not approving of a topic or not having felt that it was theirs was the extreme pessimism expressed as to the outcome of any discussion. The third way, people avoid topics completely. That's what happened with Jim last week. Until the point where, until, back to last week again, we ended up discussing the topic. Only it was this time instead of Jim's idea it was everybody's idea. Everybody came in on the discussion. I think it's very characteristic of a group like this, because everybody wants to be . . . it's the same thing, going back to fighting, what we talked about at the beginning, when we talked about this leadership discussion: whether we should have a formal leader appointed or would one grow out of the group. The people that didn't want to appoint a formal leader I think were afraid to. Because they felt they had their chance to be leader, why shouldn't I be able to fight for it?

ART: Is that true of you, Joe, because you were one of the great fighters?

JOE: I think it's partly true, yes. I can see it, I can see it very easily now. I think that it's happened continuously from one leader to the next—if we want to modify our definition of leader a little bit, each initiator . . . has been thought of as a leader. And everybody else has knocked them down. And I think it's all part of our own selfishness in something like this.

BERT: I agree in a large percentage with what Bill has had to say. It's something that you, at least in my case, you don't confirm too easily with evidence but you sort of sense it when you're speaking. You're not speaking with ideas, but you're speaking with weapons more or less. It's your status which is involved in everything you have to say. You're either saying something to make yourself stand out or knocking someone else down. It's a very difficult atmosphere in which to express yourself. It makes you very insecure. If you wanted evidence, about the only thing I could dig up I guess would be the fact that, first, it's terrible difficult to enter any conversation, and second, it's very difficult for the group to reach a decision on anything, and third, probably is that subgroups have been marked by a tremendous amount of disregard for the rest of the group and the conversation has been carried on among themselves.

I'm not sure whether any group ever achieves a state where everyone's status is accepted to a certain extent and what they say isn't a reflection on themselves personally, but I should think it would be something which the group would like to strive for possibly if you were trying to get something done. And it's one of the things I would like to learn out of a group of this sort—how something like that could be accomplished. Maybe it can be and maybe it can't, I don't know.

The above excerpt might be summarized in the minutes of the meeting as follows, "Leadership problems were discussed." Perhaps if one were describing the meeting to an absent member, a little more might be said: "Bill and Joe and Bert talked about how people have been acting in the group, and pointed out that people who try to get the group to do something never succeed. Joe showed his usual tendency to monopolize the conversation but the group was interested in what he was saying, though some of them may have resented it."

In this case the observer said a little bit about the participants' feelings, their roles in the group, and how the interaction among them proceeded. There were undoubtedly some more process factors that the observer either did not see or refrained from reporting. But the observer cannot watch everything. There is a lot of activity going on in most groups, and what the observer perceives depends on what he attends to, as well as on the acuity of his perception. If he tries to attend to everything at once, he will be so distracted that he is likely to report a simple handshake as an utterly chaotic social situation. (Sometimes it is, of course.) Hence, the observer has to start by being sensitive only to certain aspects of the situation, and peacefully oblivious to others.

This adjustment may sometimes make the observer sound blind rather than perceptive when he reports his observations, since he may seem to have missed the whole point of the meeting, while watching very carefully some aspect that was of little consequence. However, the seeming blindness lasts only through a period of experimenting with different ways of looking at the situation, or frames of reference for observing it. After that, he can decide which one is appropriate for a particular meeting, or use several at once.

The Interactionists

The observer might begin by concentrating on one aspect of the situation that is basic to any kind of group activity: who interacts with whom. The interactionists say: "Group life is the outcome of interaction among organisms."[1] The most extreme interactionists undertake to observe *only* the patterns of interaction, without reference to the content of communication. From the interaction patterns, whether of a two-person relationship, a small group, a large organization, or a whole society, it is possible to make predictions about other aspects of the group —its power structure, for example. There are some areas of disagreement among the various authors who use interaction analysis. For example, Whyte and Homans introduce "sentiments" as important items to observe.[2] However, all interactionists share the view that much can be inferred from habitual patterns and changes in patterns in the interaction of members of a group.

When we chart the interaction of a group we are not interested in who hates whom and who loves whom, we are interested primarily in who interacts with whom. An interactionist observing a group is not concerned with what people are saying or how they are saying it. He is concerned only with the frequency of interaction, the participants in interaction, the initiation of interaction, the ordering of interaction, the duration of actions, and the interruption of actions.

Studies using interaction-analysis methods range from studies of decision-making in small groups to studies of the communication systems of large industrial organizations.[3] Strodtbeck, in his study of the family as a three-person group, found that "the most-speaking person wins the largest share of decisions and in all cases the least-speaking person wins least."[4] In his study of clerical workers engaged in repetitive work, Homans showed that high interaction was closely correlated with personal popularity and productivity.[5]

There are several ways of mapping interaction patterns. One method of showing the pattern for the excerpt quoted on pages 745–746 is shown in Figure 3.

Interaction Process Analysis

As a social scientist, the interactionist is interested in predicting behavior and in correlating interaction patterns with other aspects of the situation. As an observer, however, he is interested only in systematically recording an aspect of the situation that is obvious and unambiguous.

Some of the interactionists are interested in observing more than interaction patterns, however, and place

[1] C. Arensberg, "Behavior and Organization: Industrial Studies," in *Social Psychology at the Crossroads* (Rohrer and Sherif, eds.), New York: Harper & Brothers, 1951.

[2] William F. Whyte, *Patterns for Industrial Peace*, New York: Harper & Brothers, 1951, pp. 162–163; George Homans, *The Human Group*, New York: Harcourt, Brace & Co., 1951.

[3] F. L. W. Richardson and C. R. Walker, *Human Relations in an Expanding Company*. New Haven, Yale University Labor and Management Center, 1948. See also E. D. Chapple (with the collaboration of C. M. Arensberg), "Measuring Human Relations: An Introduction to the Study of the Interaction of Individuals," *Genetic Psychology Monograph*, 22:3–147, 1940.

[4] F. L. Strodtbeck, "The Family as a Three-Person Group," *American Sociological Review*, 19:23–29, 1954.

[5] George Homans, "The Cash Posters: A Study of a Group of Working Girls," *American Sociological Review*, 19: No. 6, pp. 724–733, 1954.

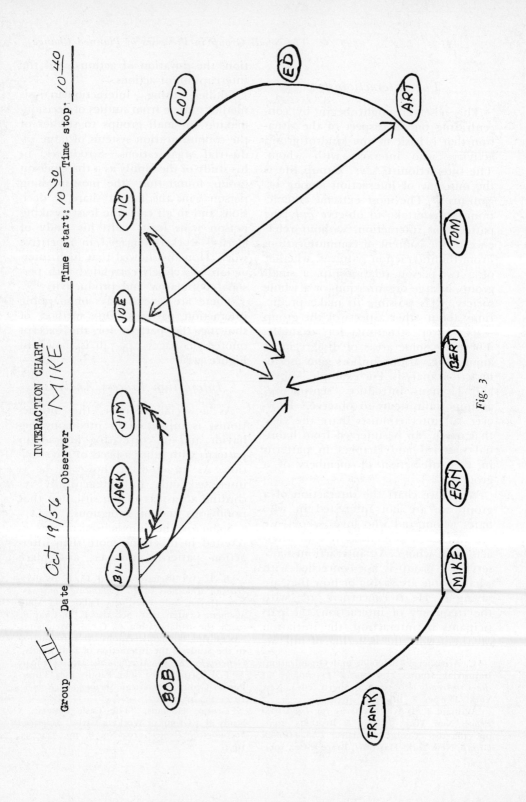

INTERACTION CHART

Group ___III___ Date ___Oct 19/56___ Observer ___MIKE___ Time start: 10 30 Time stop: 10 40

Fig. 3

enough emphasis on feelings, intentions, and meanings for them to earn consideration as a separate group. R. F. Bales has developed a system for categorizing behavior known as interaction process analysis. This is an ingenious method for analysing not only the interactions among group members, but also the sentiments accompanying interaction. It is "a way of classifying direct, face-to-face interaction as it takes place, act-by-act, and a series of ways of summarizing and analysing the result data so that they yield useful information." [6]

The complete outfit for applying Bales' method includes a one-way mirror, intercommunication equipment, and an Interaction Process Recorder machine with slow moving tape so that notations can be preserved in the same order that they occur in the group being observed. Without going to all this expense, however, a good deal of educative pleasure can be obtained with pencil and paper only, if the paper be drawn up as shown in Figure 4. As Bales points out, his selection of the set of categories shown in Figure 4 is a practical compromise among demands of theoretical adequacy, ability of observers to categorize, and simplicity. In the first three and last three categories are recorded "social-emotional" units of interaction— positive and negative reactions of the group members to one another and to the group's task. The middle six categories are "task-oriented"—they cover exchanges of information among the group members related to the job of solving some problem under discussion.

Profile No. 1 on the chart of Figure

5 shows the pattern of interaction of a children's play group. Profile No. 2 is the average profile of interaction for five married couples. Profile No. 3 is the average profile of some 23,000 scores derived from a variety of discussion groups. Note the difference between the children's profile and Profile No. 3 in the social-emotional categories. Note also the relatively high degree of antagonistic social-emotional interaction in the husband-wife profiles. How would you account for these variations?

The completed interaction graph can tell us a good deal about group process. In it we can see the fluctuations of the group as it moves from hostile to friendly reactions, from problems of communication to problems of evaluation. Bales' studies indicate that in small discussion groups, where the group has a problem to solve, the process typically tends to follow a sequence of four phases. First, there is the "adaptive" phase of pooling information and other resources, and seeing how they can be used to accomplish the task. Second is the "goal-attainment" phase of actually working out the decisions and taking the action that completes the task. Third, there is an "integrative" phase of re-establishing group solidarity, which may have been disturbed in the second phase. The fourth phase, which overlaps the third, is a period of "tension-release," which consists of joking, laughter, and other expressions of relief that the job has been accomplished.

But how can acts, gestures, statements, and looks by a group be reliably deposited into twelve compartments by several different observers? How can one decide what constitutes a "unit" of interaction? Applying Bales' observation system requires more skill than that of merely count-

[6] R. F. Bales, *Interaction Process Analysis*, Cambridge, Mass.: Addison-Wesley Publishing Co., 1950, pp. 5–6.

#	Category											
1	SHOWS SOLIDARITY, raises other's status, gives help, reward:											1-2
2	SHOWS TENSION RELEASE, jokes, laughs, shows satisfaction:											
3	AGREES, shows passive acceptance, understands, concurs, complies:								1-2			
4	GIVES SUGGESTIONS, direction, implying autonomy for other:											
5	GIVES OPINION, evaluation, analysis, expresses feeling, wish:	1-0			2-1	2-1	2-1					
6	GIVES ORIENTATION, information, repeats, clarifies, confirms:	1-0 1-0	2-1					1-2 2-1	2-1	1-2	2-1	
7	ASKS FOR ORIENTATION, information, repetition, confirmation:	1-0										
8	ASKS FOR OPINION, evaluation, analysis, expression of feeling:											
9	ASKS FOR SUGGESTION, direction, possible ways of action:											
10	DISAGREES, shows passive rejection, formality, withholds help:		2-1				1-2					
11	SHOWS TENSION, asks for help, withdraws "Out of Field":							1-2				
12	SHOWS ANTAGONISM, deflates other's status, defends or asserts self:											

Fig. 4

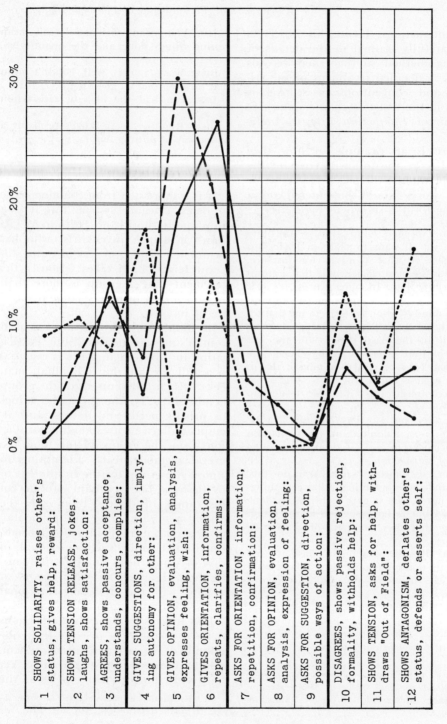

Fig. 5

Profile 1 ·······   Profile 2 ———   Profile 3 ———

ing interactions. Hence his observers are carefully trained in the details of scoring method so that their records agree. A detailed treatment of the criteria and conventions of scoring is given in the first two chapters and Appendix of *Interaction Process Analysis*.[7]

Here is an example of how they would score the following part of the excerpt quoted on pages 745–6. (How these scores would be entered on a scoring form is shown in Figure 4.)

BILL (*Speaker 1, to group*): In other words, we all want to share in leadership and that is what Gordon, for instance, thinks is the most efficient way that a group can act (*6, 1–0*). In other words, it's real unanimous approval rather than an authoritarian mind (*6, 1–0*). It seems to me that we have been destroying leadership that we needed in the past, that is for the last three or four meetings we have been doing that (*5, 1–0*). And I wonder if that is really what is happening, if we are trying to accomplish this diffused leadership (*7, 1–0*).

JIM (*Speaker 2*): This diffused leadership (*6, 2–1*), I don't think it's a question of efficiency (*10, 2–1*). I think it's a question of satisfaction (*5, 2–1*). As far as efficiency, if someone says, "You do this, that, and the other thing," that gets things done faster, and it gets more things done (*5, 2–1*), but as far as people in the group feeling that they are part of a decision (*5, 2–1*) . . .

BILL: If something doesn't last, it's not efficient, that's the only way I look at it (*10, 1–2*). In other words, unless it's a real approval (*6, 1–2*) . . .

JIM: In other words, efficiency (*6, 2–1*) . . .

BILL: . . . or participation, I don't consider it to be efficient (*10, 1–2*).

JIM: You mean efficiency doesn't mean getting things done and the quantity (*6, 2–1*) . . .

BILL: Yeah (*3, 1–2*), well, I didn't mean that (*6, 1–2*), that's a good point (*1, 1–2*).

JIM: You had the idea of satisfaction (*6, 2–1*).

BILL: Right (*3, 1–2*). That's probably a better way of putting that (*1, 1–2*).

Analysis of Group Mentality

It is a short step from common sense to Bales' category system. But it is a transatlantic hop from Bales to W. R. Bion,[8] a British psychiatrist who has formulated group process in quite different terms. Bion takes seriously the statement that a group is more than the sum of its members—that it has a life of its own.

In Bion's view groups are essential to man's mental-emotional life. Participating in group mental life is essential to a full life for the individual; man seeks his fulfillment through group membership. To the group he brings his private needs and desires, and attempts to derive corresponding satisfactions from the group. Picture now the several members, each attempting to exploit the group for the fulfillment of his desires. The resultant product of this tangle of desires Bion calls the *group mentality*. The group mentality is a potpourri of individual needs, contributed to by each individual in ways of which he is unaware, influencing him disagreeably when he is at variance with the prevailing emotional forces within the group.

The process is somewhat analogous to the working of a price system: one individual, in a competitive system, cannot autonomously set the price. Yet the eventual equilibrium price is the

[7] R. F. Bales, *Interaction Process Analysis: A Method for the Study of Small Groups*, Cambridge, Mass.: Addison-Wesley Publishing Co., 1951.

[8] W. R. Bion, "Experiences in Groups: I–VII," *Human Relations*, 5, Nos. 1–4, 1948.

result of the activities of all the individuals, each of whom contributes to this result. As in an economic system, there is a disparity between what the individual wants from the group, and how much of the emotional pie the group is going to accord him. The group's method of organization for settling this dispute Bion calls the *group culture:* "I employ the phrase 'culture of the group' in an extremely loose manner: I include in it the structure which the group achieves at any given moment, the occupations it pursues, and the organization it adopts." [9]

Herbert A. Thelen and his associates have formalized Bion's ideas into a set of categories for recording group behavior.[10] In their version, the group mentality is differentiated into three emotional modalities, or recurring patterns of expressive behavior. These are "fight-flight," "pairing," and "dependency." *Fight-flight* represents the desires of the group to escape the task that faces the group, either by fighting it (or one another) or by running away from the task. *Pairing* represents the desire of the group to seek security by establishing pair relationships between members of the group. This is manifested in a number of ways: friendly smiles and winks, mutually supportive statements, and so on. *Dependency* represents the group's need to remain dependent on the leader, to retain him as protector, judge, and commander.

A fourth category of the group mentality, called, of all things, *work,* represents the desire of the group to engage in problem-solving activity. The work needs are frequently in conflict with

the other needs of the group, and every member is caught in this struggle. A person who tends to support one of the other modalities is said to have a high *valency* for the modality. Persons who lead the group from one modality to another are called *barometric.* For purposes of categorizing, the work modality can be differentiated into four classes. *One-level work* is personally need-oriented. One-level statements may be triggered off by what is happening in the group, but they are expressions of personal need, and are not group-oriented. An observer watching one-level work feels that it interrupts the flow of the group, and is an expression of purely personal need. *Two-level work* involves maintaining or following through on the task the group is working on. An observer watching two-level work feels that it is group-oriented and necessary, but routine. *Three-level work* is group-focused work that usually has some new ingredient. It includes suggestions of new methods of attack on a problem, the visualization of goals, reality-testing of ideas. An observer watching three-level work feels that it is group-oriented, focused, and energetic, and that it has direction and meaning for the group. *Four-level work* is creative, insightful, and integrative. It usually involves an appropriate and insightful interpretation that brings together for the group a whole series of experiences and infuses meaning into them, and at the same time has immediate relevance to present problems. An observer watching four-level work feels that it is creative and exciting.

The relations between work achievement and activity in the other modalities of group mentality is an important matter for students of group dynamics. The definition of work levels helps in

[9] W. R. Bion, "Experiences in Groups: II," *Human Relations,* 5, No. 1, 1948.

[10] H. Thelen *et al., Methods for Studying Work and Emotionality in Group Operation,* University of Chicago Press, 1954.

reaching an assessment of the achievement of discussion groups. Examples of statements representing the various categories of emotionality and work are given below.[11] Content is, of course, important in determining how to classify any statement made in a group, but the examples given below are more or less self-explanatory.

I. *Ratings of Emotionality*

A. FIGHT STATEMENTS (*f*)

1. Attacking, deprecating the group; aggressive impatience with the group.
    ex. "You say you're satisfied and yet people feel withdrawn. I question the effectiveness of a group in which people don't feel involved."
    ex. "Aren't we ready to go? We've wasted enough time."

2. Attacking specific members.
    ex. "I question his motives."
    ex. "You feel you're just an average person, don't you?"

3. Blocking the group.
    ex. "Do you ever get any expression in role-playing that means anything? I wonder about the validity of the whole idea."
    ex. "I have not understood any of this."

4. Self-aggrandizement at the expense of others.
    ex. "I feel a responsibility to the group. I just can't sit back and let the group flounder."
    ex. "I resisted that idea every time it came up."

5. Projected hostility.
    ex. "I will volunteer to be the scape-goat."
    ex. "I don't mind being used by the group this way."

B. FLIGHT STATEMENTS (*fl*)

1. Withdrawal or lessened involvement.
    ex. Silence
    ex. Doodling

2. Humor, fantasy, facetiousness, tension-releasing laughter.

[11] Adapted from Thelen *et al., op. cit.,* pp. 23–30.

ex. (The dog barks, in response to a general tension in the group.) "He's our alter-ego." (Group laughs.) "He wants coffee." "He's smarter than we are." (Group leaves room.)

3. Inappropriate, overintellectualized, overgeneralized statements.
    ex. "Any correlation between emotional tension and productivity is inverse . . ." (etc. etc.)

4. Total irrelevancy.
    ex. "I suggest coffee."
    ex. "We went to the best restaurant in Quebec."

C. PAIRING (*p*)

1. Expressions of intimacy, warmth, and supportiveness.
    ex. "We all missed you yesterday."
    ex. "I felt a lot better when you said that."

2. Support of another person's idea.
    ex. "I believe we missed Bob's idea —that observation or process is a good starting-point."
    ex. "I agree very much with what Bill has been saying."

3. Expressions of commitment and warmth directed toward the whole group.
    ex. "We've come a long way since the first few days."
    ex. "We were really on the ball to-day."

D. DEPENDENCY (*d*)

1. Appeals for support or direction.
    ex. "I'd feel better if the instructor would tell us just what he expects of the group."
    ex. "I don't know—what is the correct way?"

2. Reliance on a definite structure, procedure, or tradition.
    ex. "Why don't we appoint a chairman?"
    ex. "I think we should have some way of starting off each day. Maybe the observer should read his report from the previous meeting."

3. Reliance on outside authority.
    ex. "Is this the sort of thing that happens in other groups?"

ex. "Why don't we get a speaker to talk about personality?"

4. Expressions of weakness or inadequacy.

ex. "I'm all confused. Where do we go from here?"

ex. "We *are* disorganized. Can't someone tell us what to do next?"

II. *Ratings of Work*

ONE-LEVEL WORK

ex. "I was amazed when the group laughed at what I said. I didn't think it was funny."

ex. "I'm used to dealing with people who express things more directly."

TWO-LEVEL WORK

ex. "When should the observer start?"

ex. "What will we get out of having an observer?"

ex. "Does Joe really want to be the observer?"

ex. "Let's ask him."

THREE-LEVEL WORK

ex. "So far we've covered three parts of this plan, is there anything left to do?"

"Well, we ought to get into the question of what we're going to do with this information after we get it."

FOUR-LEVEL WORK

ex. "Permissiveness can be a trap. When you have something to fight, you might get a lot more involvement. And then there are hazards along with that—things may get destructive. The question is how to get involvement along with permissiveness."

Role Analysis

In formally organized clubs and associations, some of the members hold special "offices"—chairman, secretary, etc. In connection with their offices, the chairman and secretary have certain duties—they have special roles in the organization. For example, the chairman chairs the meeting; the secretary reads the minutes.

In any group, whether formally organized or not, there are a number of roles played that are not dignified by a title, but that affect the way the group as a whole operates. If there is one member who habitually opposes all suggestions made by other group members, one cannot assume that he has recently been elected to the office of Group Opposer—it is simply the role that he characteristically takes in the group. Some persons are skilled in playing a number of group roles, but most of us have only a few at our disposal and can be pigeonholed more easily.

The role that a person plays in a group sometimes surprises those who know him well apart from the group. The way a friend of yours behaves when he is a member of a group of several people may be quite different from the way he behaves in the two-person group consisting of him and you. In the larger group you see only one side of his personality—his group or membership role.

Membership roles have received a good deal of study. There are four main questions that can be asked about a membership role. First, what are its consequences for the person playing the role—what needs of his does it satisfy and what problems does it create for him? Second, what are its consequences for the other members of the group—what needs of theirs does it satisfy, what needs does it arouse? Third, what are its consequences for the integration of the group—does it increase or decrease cohesiveness, solidarity, mutual respect, etc.? Fourth, what are its consequences for the performance of the group's task—does it contribute towards the solution of the group's problem, or does it interfere with solving the problem?

A number of systems have been worked out to describe the variety of roles that occur in a group. Any one of these systems may be useful for assessing the potentialities of a group or understanding some of the difficulties the group has in working together. Two systems are presented below. Both of these, one developed by Benne and Sheats and one other by the Gibbs,[12] have been arrived at by asking the four questions listed above. Thus both systems have a set of roles—the Group Task roles—which are primarily useful for contributing towards problem solution (Question 4). The second set, Group Building and Maintenance Roles, are primarily useful for satisfying the needs of other members and contributing to group integration (Questions 2 and 3). The third set, Individual Roles, are expressions of personal, as opposed to group, needs. They are antithetical or irrelevant to achievement of the Group Task or

Group Building and Maintenance. The Gibbs distinguish a fourth set of roles which are simultaneously task- and group-oriented.

Gibbs' System

I. *Task Roles*
Initiating activity; Seeking information; Seeking opinion; Giving information; Giving opinion; Elaborating; Coordinating; Summarizing; Testing feasibility.

II. *Group Maintenance Roles*
Encouraging; Gate keeping; Standard setting; Following; Expressing group feeling.

III. *Task and Group Roles*
Evaluating; Diagnosing; Testing for consensus; Mediating; Relieving tension.

IV. *Individual Roles*
Being aggressive; Blocking; Self-confessing; Competing; Seeking sympathy; Special pleading; Horsing around; Seeking recognition; Withdrawing.

[12] K. D. Benne and P. Sheats, "Functional Roles of Group Members," *Journal of Social Issues*, 2:42–47, 1948. J. R. Gibb and L. M. Gibb, *Applied Group Dynamics*, University of Colorado Press.

◇◇◇◇◇◇◇◇◇◇◇◇◇◇◇◇◇◇◇◇ GROUP SELF-EVALUATION

David H. Jenkins

A GROUP discussion is an ongoing process. It is the group mechanism by which the raw materials of subject matter, stated problem, information, and suggestion are integrated, sorted, and refined so as to produce an end product of solution, decision, or learning. As was brought out in the Basic Skill Training Groups, the efficiency of

the mechanism has a direct effect on the time that is required to produce the result and also upon the quality of the result. We wish to interest ourselves here in the mechanism, or process of discussion which for purposes of clear analysis needs to be kept separate from the content, or subject matter of the discussion; *what* is being discussed is

From David H. Jenkins, "Feedback and Group Self-Evaluation," The Journal of Social Issues, Vol. 4, No. 2, Spring 1948, pp. 50–60. Used by permission.

different from the *how* it is discussed. An efficient mechanism is usable for a wide range of subject matters.

As an ongoing process the group discussion has three qualities: it has a direction toward a goal, rate of progress, and at a given moment, a position or location on the path toward its goal. It is obvious, of course, in our common experiences with groups, that one or more of these qualities may be neither clearly stated, nor even implicit in the group behavior. Each of us has undoubtedly participated in groups where either the direction of the group was undefined or where, during a discussion, the group attempted to go in several directions simultaneously. But in a productive discussion group there is a clear direction and a goal, and knowledge of both the rate of progress and of the present position of the group.

Frequently members of a group are not aware of the nature of the difficulties in the mechanism of discussion. They may become aggressive toward each other or escape from the topic through apathy and boredom. They may have a vague feeling that "we aren't getting anywhere", or a concern over "what *are* we talking about, anyway?", but they are unable to put their finger on the difficulties at hand. There is the feeling of inefficiency and frustration, but the group lacks the proper information, perspective, and diagnostic skill which is necessary in order to identify the reasons for the inefficiency and to determine some methods for reducing it.

Several different kinds of information about itself are required by a group before changes in its own behavior are possible.

1. Do we have a direction toward a goal? How successful have we been in keeping oriented in that direction, staying on the subject, not "wandering off course"?

2. Where are we now located in our discussion? Are we in the stage of diagnosing the problem, in the stage of suggesting solutions, or are we ready for final decisions?

3. What has been our rate of progress? Are we actually moving ahead in our discussion at a reasonable or efficient rate, or have we "bogged down"?

4. Are we applying our total group potential, the creative and analytic abilities of *all* our members, to our problem or are we operating with "half of our furnaces banked"?

5. Are we making any improvement in our ability to work together more efficiently?

Only when the group secures information about itself in answer to these questions does it have a basis on which to make the necessary adjustments to improve its efficiency. Until then it cannot recognize clearly the need to act, nor the nature of the change which is demanded.

Most groups, however, have not set up for themselves any mechanism for the "feedback" of this kind of information into the discussion process—no procedure by which the group can become aware of its own difficulties, the reasons for those difficulties, and the corrections which are necessary. In these groups we have an ongoing process which, by its lack of self-correcting (or self-improving) devices, continues at an unnecessarily low level of productivity. Much of the criticism directed at the "committee method" seems based on the assumption that low productivity is inherent in the group method.

The groups at Bethel, feeling that they had not yet tapped the creative resources in the group approach to problems, were concerned with the improvement of their own efficiency. They had in their groups a mechanism for the "feedback" of information to the members about their own method of operation. This mechanism was the group training observer, or group productivity observer. He served as the feedback and self-correcting device for the group along with the group self-evaluation, the general discussion about the meaning of the observer's comments.

By using the productivity observer, the group increases rather than reduces its own responsibility for analyzing itself and planning for changes and improvements. From the information and stimulation supplied by the comments of the observer, the group spends time examining *how* it has performed as a group. Let us look briefly at a portion of a feedback and evaluation session before we describe the nature of the observer's job and the group self-evaluation process.

The meeting, which is the third one for this group, has been in session for about two hours. It is now about fifteen minutes before the adjournment.

Leader: Well, let's stop and take a few minutes to look at our meeting today. Let's hear from our observer first and then we will all share our ideas. Remember that we will want to see whether we felt as our observer did about what happened here, but we will also want to analyze for ourselves why we did what we did and perhaps spend time on suggesting changes which we may want to make in our procedure. Go ahead, Joe.

Observer: I felt our meeting was pretty fair today. According to my tabulations I find that all of us took some

part in the discussion for the first time since we started these meetings. One of the things which seemed important today happened when the leader tried to get the group to pull out some conclusions from the discussion we had been having. He suggested, about three times I think, that perhaps we should summarize our ideas. Each time, however, the group continued talking about the specific problems. I felt that we needed to move ahead at that point, but for some reason we didn't seem ready. How did the rest of you feel about it? (*Note the use of objective data at the beginning and with approving comments. Then come the more critical comments, given as a leader problem, augmented by the observer's own feelings, and then referred to the group.*)

Member A: It seemed to me that we were not quite ready to draw conclusions, there were so many details to clear up. (*Compulsion for details of content causes rejection of the point about process.*)

Member B: There were a lot of details, but perhaps we needed to stop and look where we were going once in a while, and see where we'd been. We were so busy looking at the trees today, I'm wondering if we didn't forget which part of the forest we were supposed to be in. (*Goal-oriented member supports and amplifies observer's suggestion.*)

Member C: Frankly, I think now that I was so interested in the things we were talking about I just forget that we needed to reach some conclusions. I just didn't realize what the leader was trying to do. (*Member shares his own feelings with the group and accepts personal responsibility.*)

Leader: At the time, I know, I felt a little lost, I was wondering to myself,

"What can I do to get us to move ahead. We are not making the progress we should because we have bogged down in details". Is there something we could have done differently to avoid this? (*Leader shares his feelings of difficulty with group—doesn't assume omnipotence.*)

Member B: Perhaps it would have been better if we had decided before we started our discussion what we were going to do. Then, if one of our aims was to come out with some conclusions by the end of the meeting, we would have wanted the leader, or anyone for that matter, to point it out to us when we were bogging down. We could do something about it that way. (*Members can be creative, make positive suggestions.*)

Other suggestions were made with the group deciding that they needed to plan an agenda for each meeting so they would know what they were to accomplish during that session. The evaluation continues:

Observer: One other point which might be worth mentioning: it seemed that during the time we were trying to suggest some solutions to the problems two or three of us seemed to want to criticize the idea immediately. We seemed impatient to tear a new idea apart. I made a little record of how many times new ideas were followed by critical comments. Out of seven suggestions that were made, six of them were criticized immediately. B.J. criticized four of them and J.R. criticized the remaining two. Right after that the group seemed to run out of suggestions for solutions. I was wondering at the time if we might not have gotten more ideas, or perhaps better ones, if we had held our critical comments until after most of our ideas about solutions were on the blackboard. (*Criticism*

of individuals by using objective data with suggestions for alternative methods.)

J.R.: I guess you're right. I have been so in the habit of reacting to a new idea critically I fail to recognize that it may not be the most helpful procedure. I never was really conscious, until now you mention it, of what effect the criticism could have on the discussion. (*Member insight through being made aware of his own behavior.*)

B.J.: It sounds to me, though, that your idea would waste lots of time. Why not dispose of the ideas as they come? (*Member needs further analysis of problems.*)

The entire group then spends several minutes analyzing the effects of improperly timed criticism on their own contribution to the group, with the other members helping the resistant member to see the implications of the problem.

The Productivity Observer

With this description as a background, let us turn to the analysis of the role of the productivity observer.

The productivity observer is a member of the group who is assigned a special responsibility in the same manner as the recording secretary or the leader is given a special task. His function is to watch the group during their discussion and then feed back to the group his ideas about what happened during their discussion. In order to give his full attention to the behavior of the group the observer does not participate in the general discussion. The assumption is, of course, that even though the group is deprived of the contributions of one of its members during the problem-centered discussion, the total productivity of the group can be profitably increased through utilizing this member as an observer. Sometimes groups bring in a specially trained person to serve as their observer, especially to get the observer role started and adequately identified. This permits the total group to participate in the problem discussion. Frequently the observer job is rotated among the members of the group to give each a chance for the experience and to keep no one from contributing to the general subject matter which is discussed from meeting to meeting.

Non-participation of the observer is necessary to keep him from thinking about the subject matter rather than about the behavior of the group. To become involved in *what* is being said prevents focusing on the questions of *how* it is being said, its relation to the direction of the discussion, etc. The observer needs to maintain his vantage point of objectivity at almost any cost, yet without losing his feeling of membership in the group.

The attention of the observer may be directed at a variety of behavior in the group. He notes the general level of motivation, the general work atmosphere of the group, the orientation of the group, leadership techniques, and other factors which affect productivity. Here is an example of the kind of observation sheet used in several recent discussion groups with some sample notes of the kind an observer makes.

Group Discussion Observation

A. Direction and Orientation
1. How far did we get? *Covered only half of agenda. Spent too much time on details.*
2. To what extent did we understand what we are trying to do?

Several members not clear on goals. Some continual disagreements on purposes.
3. To what extent did we understand how we are trying to do it? *Almost no discussion about procedure, resulting in confusion at times.*
4. To what extent were we stymied by lack of information? *None. Relevant information at hand in group.*

B. Motivation and Unity
1. Were all of us equally interested in what we are trying to do? *No. Two or three not sure problem is worth the time.*
2. Was interest maintained or did it lag? *Slowed down during time leader made lengthy contribution.*
3. To what extent did the group feel united by a common purpose? *Rather low feelings of any unity. Two or three not feeling united with group at all.*
4. To what extent were we able to subordinate individual interests to the common goal? *Antagonisms between R.K. and L.M. outside of group tended to show up here.*

C. Atmosphere
1. What was the general atmosphere of the group?
   a. Formal or informal? *Fairly formal, although some first names used.*
   b. Permissive or inhibited? *Fairly permissive except for period after leader lectured.*
   c. Cooperative or competitive? *Little competition, some positive evidence of cooperative feelings.*
   d. Friendly or hostile? *Lukewarm friendly.*

Observations on the contributions of individual members of the group:

A. Contributions of members

1. Was participation general or lopsided? *All participated at least to some extent. Some monopolization by B.C. and W.U.*

2. Were contributions on the beam or off at a tangent? *Hard to determine as goals not clear.*

3. Did contributions indicate that those who made them were listening carefully to what others in the group had to say? *At points of higher interest in the discussion some were not listening to others.*

4. Were contributions factual and problem-centered or were the contributors unable to rise above their preconceived notions and emotionally held points of view? *Some tendency toward bias, especially during first hour.*

B. Contributions of Special Members of the Group

1. How well did special members serve the group?

a. Leader: *A little tendency to dominate, but catches himself before group reacts negatively. Tried unsuccessfully to get group to draw conclusions.*

b. Recorder: *Asked for clarification occasionally. This seemed to help group to clarify for itself.*

c. Resource person: *None in group today.*

Other observations:

J.R. and B.J. criticized solutions while they were being suggested. Is that why so few suggestions came out?

Although an alert, untrained observer can sometimes be sensitive to many of the obvious difficulties in the group, training can greatly increase the value of the observer. Especially is this true in the ability of the observer to detect the causes or relationships which produce the symptoms which he notices. For example, there may be no apparent reason for the sharp remark one member passed to another unless one recalls that earlier in the meeting the second member had criticized unnecessarily one of the contributions of the first member. There may have been some antipathy that developed which had not yet been resolved. With improved sensitivity the observer becomes increasingly valuable to the group in helping them go behind the symptoms and recognize the causes of the difficulty.

A group need not assume that lack of a trained observer prohibits use of this technique for improvement, for the tactful, objective member who is alert to problems of interpersonal relations can function satisfactorily in this role. Increased sensitivity will undoubtedly come with continued experience. The responsibility for self-analysis to which the group commits itself by establishing the role of group productivity observer extends to include assistance to the untrained observer to help him do the best job possible for the group . . .

The observer is a resource which is available to the group at any time. Sometimes groups set aside ten to fifteen minutes at the end of each meeting to discuss their progress and skill with the observer. Sometimes effective use is made of the observer by calling for his help at a crucial or difficult point in the discussion, using his analysis to assist in untangling the difficulty in which the group finds itself. Only infrequently does the group spend any large amount of time on this kind of discussion, and then only as it is felt to be profitable.

Not only does the observer serve a useful role for the group as a whole, he also becomes a "teammate" working closely with the leader of the group. The leader-observer team often spends considerable time together outside of the group session sharing reactions about the meetings and planning together the procedures and techniques for the future. A special value of this relationship is that the observer can serve as the "eyes" for the leader who, because of his own responsibility for the discussion, is unable to attend as closely to the difficulties in the group process and to be as objective in his own feelings.

Feedback

The first experience of the group with "feedback" of information from the observer is relatively crucial and requires skill by the observer in presenting his comments. As they are not generally accustomed to put themselves voluntarily into a situation where they might be criticized, the members tend to be a little defensive in their feelings even though no points are actually made about them as persons. With experience they find that the observer's comments are valuable information and need not cause self-consciousness.

To reduce the resistance of the group, the observer can use several techniques. If he and the leader have developed the desired "team" relationship the observer's first comments, and perhaps the majority of his comments in the first session or so, will be about the techniques of the leader. Because of his experience and understanding the leader will be able to accept these comments objectively and easily and to serve as an example for the group to copy in their own reactions to the observer. "If these comments don't upset the leader, who is in a more crucial

position than I, I guess my feelings of insecurity are unnecessary." Later comments about the behavior of the members may be more comfortably received.

The observer frequently phrases his comments about data which he has tabulated or observations he has made in the form of tentative hypotheses or expressions of his feelings and then asks the group if they were feeling the same way. In our description we saw how the observer used this technique. Presenting his observations and especially his interpretations in this tentative manner permits the group to reject them without difficulty if the members are not yet emotionally ready to accept them. The observer can just be "in error" and he can "admit it" at this point with a minimum of damage being done to the relationship.

The skilled observer is alert to the maturity of the group. He is aware of the symptoms of change and the increased capacity to handle conflicts. It may be necessary for the observer to "forget" to mention a serious conflict in the group for several meetings because the group will not have had, in the early meetings, opportunity to develop sufficient cohesiveness to absorb the shock of a discussion likely to arouse strong emotions. By the later meetings they will have gained sufficient experience in group self-evaluation so that they can approach such a problem more objectively.

An untrained observer sometimes feels that he must spend a major part of his time commenting on the "nice" things he observed in the group, and give only casual notice to difficulties and conflicts. Although comments about the effective things that occurred in the group should not be overlooked, the members usually feel that the observer "lets them down" if he doesn't talk about the difficulties. Sometimes the group members wonder if he has enough courage to tell them about something of which they are all quite conscious in the group, but which they, as participating members, feel unable to verbalize. Once the observer suggests such an item, he is usually greeted with nods of agreement and perhaps little sighs of relief "the problem material is now something we can talk about."

The principal advantage of the use of an observer rests in the comparative ease with which comments about behavior which is not usually talked about can be brought into the group discussion. A participating member would find it extremely difficult to offer such comments because of his own involvement and his role in the group. But the observer, although he, too, is an accepted member of the group, can make the comments "as a part of his job." The group is then able to orient their remarks toward "what the observer said" rather than toward "what is wrong with our group." This slightly different direction in the orientation presents major differences in the amount of emotional blocking in the discussion of the same problem, even though the same contributions are made.

Group Self-evaluation

We have talked at length about the role of the observer and the feedback process. Let us now look at the direction the group discussion takes during the evaluation session. The leader in our example suggested three things the group needed to do: (1) get a common agreement on what actually happened, (2) analyze the reasons behind the

event, and (3) suggest some ways of improving the procedure in the future.

The leader of the evaluation in the basic skill training groups encouraged expressions of recognition about the description that was reported by the observer by asking, "Is that the way the rest of you felt it happened?" There may be disagreement among the group members about the actual event, but a common understanding needs to be sought before the discussion continues to the other phases. Sometimes the individual who is most concerned in the situation may be the only one unaware of the event. Often "problem behavior" of group members is something they do of which they are totally unaware until the observer and the group mention it.

Once the event itself is agreed on, the group turns to the discussion of "why did it happen?" Everyone can express his feelings here as feelings are the facts which are often most relevant in group interaction. In our illustration we found members indicating quite different reactions to the same situation. Recognition of these differences may lead to a relatively quick understanding of the causes of the difficulty.

The leader needs to help the group in its self-evaluation to move from analyzing their difficulties to the discussion of desirable changes in group procedure. To become acutely aware of a problem, and no more, may sow the seeds for group disruption. A consideration of the possible solutions to the problem and a decision to try out a tentative solution allows the discussion to terminate on a positive note. In future meetings attention may be given to evaluating the success of the solution as it has worked out in practice. Satisfactory experiences in changing its procedures encourage the group to become more experimental in instituting new techniques.

Not only, however, does the self-evaluation result in specific changes in techniques or behaviors by the group but it frequently builds improved feelings of group cohesiveness. When one of us, as a group member, becomes able to share his feelings of happiness or frustration with members in our group, others are stimulated to participate in a similar vein. Shared feelings become common property. It is this common property which heightens the identity with the group and feelings of belongingness to the group. Increased cohesiveness makes the group more able to handle constructively larger amounts of overt conflict.

Self-evaluation by the group trains the members to become more sensitive to the difficulties in interaction and discussion which exist in the group, their causes, and some techniques for avoiding them. In truth, this increased awareness is a learning which can be generalized, a new or improved skill which the individual person can utilize when he enters new group situations. As he gains this skill he begins to mature as a productive group member.

Summary

If it is to be an effective producing unit a discussion group must give attention to its mechanics of operation. Awareness of its direction and goal, its rate of progress, present location on its path to the goal, use of the member's potential ability and its ability to improve itself, are important factors which lead to increased efficiency. The use of the group productivity observer as a feedback mechanism and the self-evaluation of its process by the group are techniques which have been worthwhile in improving the functioning of groups.

Index

acculturation, 536–538
acting out, in development of teaching group, 741–742
Adams, Henry, 14
adaptation, modes of, 532–534
adjustment, automatic, 29–31, 32–34
administration
    analysis of, as social process, 376–384
    definition of, 377
administrator
    case method training of, 634–636
    research, 413
    training of, 632–634
    work of, 631–632
adolescence, 274, 356
    and identity, 42, 43
affection
    as interpersonal need, 298
    and phases of group development, 304
aggression, in groups, 266, 700–701
aggressiveness, and adult leadership, 419
alienation, see social alienation
Alinsky, Saul D., 657
allocation, administrative, as source of organizational conflict, 452–453, 456
Allport, G. W., 237–238, 412, 508, 528–529
ambiguity, and influenceability, 524–526
ambivalence, 246
    in group development, 740, 741
    in social therapy, 167
"Americanization," and subcultural values, 38
anomie, 268
    in suburbs, 41
anthropology, 53, 114, 685–686
anti-Semitism, 457
anxiety, 321
    and fear, 353–354
    and group cohesion, 266

anxiety (continued)
    and group development, 741
    of nurse, on mental hospital ward, 570, 571
    social origin of, 487
    in suburbs, 42
    in teaching group, 742
    and tension, 351, 352, 353–354, 357, 360, 361
    as uncanny emotion, 360
Apley, George, 553
applied social science, see social science, applied
"approach," 244
Arensberg, C., 549
Argyris, Chris, 627
Arsenian, J. M., 419, 737–743
Asch, S. E., 269, 490
aspiration-level, groups and, 700
    see also goals
attitude formation, and reference groups, 471–472
attitudes, change of, 484
    in organizations, 612–613
    principles of, 702–705
authoritarianism, modern, rise of, 32–34
authority
    acceptance of, 414–415
    basis and functions of, 435–437
    in case analysis, 728, 729
    conflicts in, 105–106
    dichotomous nature of, 449
    elements of, 448
    as interpersonal problem, 295–296
    in modern world, 30–31
    and phases of group development, 303
authority relations, in group, 322–323
automatic adjustment, 29–31
    collapse of, 32–34
automation, 403
"avoidance," 244
Ayres, C. E., 191